THE EXCAVATIONS AT DURA-EUROPOS

THE

Excavations at Dura-Europos

CONDUCTED BY

YALE UNIVERSITY AND THE FRENCH ACADEMY

OF INSCRIPTIONS AND LETTERS

FINAL REPORT VIII, PART I

EDITED BY

A. R. Bellinger, F. E. Brown, A. Perkins, and C. B. Welles

AUGMENTED EDITION

FOREWORD

by Jaroslav Pelikan

PROLEGOMENON

by Harald Ingholt;

INDEX

by Betty Ellis and Harald Ingholt

ADDENDUM

by Stanley Insler

KTAV PUBLISHING HOUSE, INC.

1979

It is intended to issue eight Final Reports, as follows:

I. HISTORY; II. ARCHITECTURE AND TOWN PLANNING; III. SCULPTURE, FIGURINES, AND PAINTING; IV. MINOR FINDS; V. INSCRIPTIONS, PARCHMENTS AND PAPYRI; VI. COINS; VII. ARMS AND ARMOR; VIII. THE SYNAGOGUE, MITHRAEUM, AND CHRISTIAN CHAPEL. These will be issued in parts as they are completed and, within the separate Reports, the parts will be numbered in order of appearance.

Already issued:

FINAL REPORT IV, PART I, FASCICLE 1. N. P. TOLL, THE GREEN GLAZED POTTERY.
FINAL REPORT IV, PART I, FASCICLE 2. D. H. COX, THE GREEK AND ROMAN POTTERY.
FINAL REPORT IV, PART II. R. Pfister and Louisa Bellinger, THE TEXTILES.
FINAL REPORT IV, PART III. P. V. C. Baur, THE LAMPS.
FINAL REPORT IV, PART IV, FASCICLE 1. Teresa G. Frisch and N. P. Toll, THE PIERCED BRONZES; the ENAMELED BRONZES; the FIBULAE.
FINAL REPORT VI. A. R. Bellinger, THE COINS.

Library of Congress Cataloging in Publication Data

Kraeling, Carl Hermann, 1897-1966.
  The synagogue.

  Reprint (with new foreword and indices) of final report 8, pt. 1 in the series: Excavations at Dura-Europos originally published in 1956 by Yale University Press, New Haven.
  Includes bibliographies and indexes.
  1. Dura, Syria. Synagogue. I. Title. II. Series: The Excavations at Dura-Europos ; final report 8, pt. 1.
DS99.D8E92 vol. 8, pt. 1 [BM389.D8] 935s   78-27871
ISBN 0-87068-331-4 [296'.0935]

The Synagogue

By CARL H. KRAELING

with contributions by

C. C. TORREY, C. B. WELLES, AND B. GEIGER

PUBLISHED THROUGH THE GENEROSITY OF

LOUIS M. RABINOWITZ

CONTENTS

CONTENTS

LIST OF PLANS

LIST OF PLATES

LIST OF FIGURES IN THE TEXT

LIST OF ABBREVIATIONS

Cabrol, *Dictionnaire*: F. Cabrol, *Dictionnaire d'archéologie chrétienne et de liturgie*, 1907–1932.

CRAI: Académie des inscriptions et belles-lettres, Paris, *Comptes rendus des séances*, 1857–

Cumont, *Fouilles*: F. Cumont, *Fouilles de Doura-Europos 1922–1923*, 1926.

Daremberg-Saglio: *Dictionnaire des antiquités grecques et romaines, d'après les textes et les monuments*, edd. Ch. Daremberg, Edm. Saglio, E. Pottier, 1877–1919.

Du Mesnil du Buisson, "Les Deux synagogues": Comte Du Mesnil du Buisson, "Les Deux synagogues successives à Doura-Europos," *Revue biblique*, XLV, 1936, pp. 72–90.

Du Mesnil du Buisson, "Une Peinture": Comte Du Mesnil de Buisson, "Une Peinture de la synagogue de Doura-Europos," *Gazette des beaux-arts*, XIV, 1935, pp. 193–203.

Du Mesnil du Buisson, "Les Peintures": Comte Du Mesnil du Buisson, "Les Peintures de la synagogue de Doura-Europos," *Revue biblique*, XLIII, 1934, pp. 105–119.

Du Mesnil de Buisson, *Peintures*: Comte Du Mesnil de Buisson, *Les Peintures de la synagogue de Doura-Europos, 245–256 après J.-C.*, 1939.

Du Mesnil de Buisson, "Nouvelles découvertes": Comte Du Mesnil de Buisson, "Les Nouvelles découvertes de la synagogue de Doura-Europos," *Revue biblique*, XLIII, 1934, pp. 546–563.

Du Mesnil du Buisson, "Nouvelles observations": Comte Du Mesnil de Buisson, "Nouvelles observations sur une peinture de Doura-Europos," *Gazette des beaux-arts*, XV, 1936, pp. 305f.

Final Report IV, I, 1, etc.: *The Excavations at Dura-Europos, conducted by Yale University and the French Academy of Inscriptions and Letters. Final Report* IV, I, 1. N. Toll, *The Green Glazed Pottery*, 1943. *Final Report* IV, II. R. Pfister and L. Bellinger, *The Textiles*, 1945. *Final Report* IV, III. P. V. C. Baur, *The Lamps*, 1947. *Final Report* VI. A. R. Bellinger, *The Coins*, 1949.

Grabar, "Le Thème": A. Grabar, "Le Thème religieux des fresques de la synagogue de Doura (245–256 après J.-C.)," *Revue de l'histoire des religions*, CXXIII, 1941, pp. 143–192; CXXIV, 1941, pp. 5–35.

Hopkins and Du Mesnil du Buisson, "La Synagogue": C. Hopkins and Du Mesnil de Buisson, "La Synagogue de Doura-Europos," *CRAI*, 1933, pp. 243–254.

E. G. Kraeling, "Meaning of the Ezekiel Panel": E. G. Kraeling, "The Meaning of the Ezekiel Panel in the Synagogue of Dura," *Bulletin of the American Schools of Oriental Research*, 78, 1940, pp. 12–18.

Pearson, *Guide:* H. Pearson, *Guide de la synagogue de Doura-Europos*, Beyrouth, 1940.

RE: *Real-encyclopädie der classischen Altertumswissenschaft*, edd. A. F. von Pauly and others, 1894–

Rep. I, etc.: *The Excavations at Dura-Europos, conducted by Yale University and the French Academy of Inscriptions and Letters, Preliminary Report of the First Season of Work*, etc.

Röm. Mitt.: *Mitteilungen des (kaiserlichen) deutschen archäologischen Instituts, Römische Abteilung*, 1876–

Roscher, *Lexikon*: W. H. Roscher, *Ausführliches Lexikon der griechischen und römischen Mythologie*, 1884–1937.

Rostovtzeff, "Die Synagoge": M. Rostovtzeff, "Die Synagoge von Dura," *Römische Quartalschrift*, XLII, 1934, pp. 203–218.

Schneid, *The Paintings*: N. Schneid, *The Paintings of the Synagogue of Dura-Europos*, 1946 (in Hebrew).

Sonne, "The Paintings": I. Sonne, "The Paintings of the Dura Synagogue," *Hebrew Union College Annual*, XX, 1947, pp. 255–362.

Sukenik, *The Synagogue*: E. L. Sukenik, *The Synagogue of Dura-Europos and its Paintings*, 1947 (in Hebrew).

Trans.: *The Babylonian Talmud, translated into English with notes, glossary and indices under the editorship of I. Epstein*, Soncino Press, 1935–1952.

de Vaux, "Un Détail": R. de Vaux, "Un Détail de la synagogue de Doura," *Revue biblique*, XLVII, 1938, pp. 383–387.

Wischnitzer, *Messianic Theme*: R. Wischnitzer, *The Messianic Theme in the Paintings of the Dura Synagogue*, 1948.

Wischnitzer-Bernstein, "Conception of the Resurrection": R. Wischnitzer-Bernstein, "The Conception of the Resurrection in the Ezekiel Panel of the Dura Synagogue," *Journal of Biblical Literature*, LX, 1941, pp. 43–55.

Wischnitzer-Bernstein, "The Samuel Cycle": R. Wischnitzer-Bernstein, "The Samuel Cycle in the Wall Decorations of the Synagogue at Dura-Europos," *Proceedings of the American Academy for Jewish Research*, XI, 1941, pp. 85–103.

Wodtke, "Malereien": G. Wodtke, "Malereien der Synagoge in Dura und ihre Parallelen in der christlichen Kunst," *Zeitschrift für die neutestamentliche Wissenschaft und die Kunde der älteren Kirche*, XXXIV, 1935, pp. 51–62.

YCS: Yale Classical Studies

FOREWORD

The reissue, after twenty years, of Carl H. Kraeling's *The Synagogue* is an event for which scholars have been waiting eagerly, for it makes available again a monograph whose influence on its field has been far more significant than the relatively small number of copies of the first edition would suggest. Even in scholarly publishing, where we sometimes seem to glory in limited circulation, such an impact seems to require explanation.

One factor that helps to explain why Kraeling's *Synagogue* is a work cited throughout the scholarly literature on the history of Judaism during the early centuries of the Common Era is certainly the intrinsic interest of its subject matter. The excavations at Dura-Europos opened up to twentieth-century readers a world of religious experience and artistic expression of whose existence they had been only dimly aware before. Not even the discovery of the Coptic texts of the Gnostics hidden at Nag Hammadi or the appearance of the Essene scrolls stored away in the caves of the Dead Sea, important as they were for the history of religious ideas, provided as complete a documentation of the concrete life of several religious communities as did this archeological find. For here was palpable evidence of how Judaism, Mithraism, and Christianity had existed side by side in one place, and, more specifically, of how Judaism maintained its own particularity within such a setting. Even scholars like myself, who have concentrated their historical attention on the development of ideas rather than of either institutions or practices, must acknowledge the special importance of the materials collected here; for the ideas whose evolution interests us most had a communal matrix, and in the understanding of that matrix within the Judaism of the Diaspora there is still no match for the insights that come from the study of the synagogue at Dura.

Clearly the most important of these insights is still the recognition that the Judaism of the Dispersion lived in a Gentile setting that helped to shape its basic thought and life, in short,

that at least in some centers of Jewish activity there was a significant interaction with the non-Jewish environment. Professor Kraeling was cautious—perhaps excessively cautious—in extrapolating from the evidence of Dura to what he called over-hasty generalizations (p. 346b) about the situation of Diaspora Judaism generally; for even one important exception to the claim that Judaism was consistently exclusivistic serves to undermine that claim. Even within the confines of his caution, however, it did prove possible for him to speak, near the beginning of the work, of "the religious and iconographic syncretism of the later centuries of ancient history [and] the importance attaching to the personification of abstract ideas" (p. 42) in the Judaism of Dura, and, near the end of the work, of an "intermingling of different cultural forms and of their respective forms of expression" (p. 323a). As he notes in the later place, "this is nowhere more clearly illustrated than in the sphere of art," for which Dura continues to be our most articulate monument.

Not only are the graphic arts the most telling indices of the relation between one culture or one religion and another; but in the case of Judaism, especially the Judaism of the Diaspora, the problem of representational art was the most telling indication of its relation to its Gentile milieu. The reason was, of course, the commandment of Exodus 20:4: "Thou shalt not make unto thee any graven image, or any likeness of any thing that is in heaven above, or that is in the earth beneath, or that is in the water under the earth." Even a cursory perusal of the magnificent plates included in this volume will show that a literal and legal application of this prohibition was flagrantly violated in the very decor of the Dura synagogue. All sorts of "graven images" and representations of such creatures were part of that decor—not of a private home, nor of a public bath, but of a building dedicated to the exposition of the Torah and to the worship of the one true God. Kraeling urges (p. 343) that the attitude of Palestinian Judaism toward artistic representation is a problem to which scholars in art history and in religious history will have to return; and the late Professor Erwin Goodenough's multi-volume collection, whatever may be one's judgment about its hypotheses, did assemble a vast amount of documentation on the subject. As the archeological work currently being carried on in Israel proceeds—and we are told that practically every tourist there carries a copy of the Hebrew Bible and an archeologist's pick—we may hope that there will be further corroboration, as there has already been, of Kraeling's sense that Judaism, even in the Holy Land itself, did find it possible to portray the creation, if not the Creator, in pictures.

As one whose most recent book is a history of Christian thought in the Byzantine era, I may perhaps be forgiven for giving some special attention to the implication of Carl Kraeling's research for the historical problem of the icons. At several points in his account, Professor Kraeling draws lines of connection between the art of Dura and the art of the Christian Church. For example, in his analysis (p. 194b) of the treatment of Ezekiel, he invokes the "analogy" of the figure of the apostle Paul in Christian art to explain how the Jewish artists had introduced the prophet at the center of a narrative composition in which he was prominent. Later (p. 231a) a study of the way Joshua appears in one of the Dura panels prompts him to contrast this Joshua with the figure in the mosaics at Santa Maria Maggiore. (I must add, however, that in view of the Christian use of the name "Joshua" as a type of the name "Jesus," this particular contrast might conceivably have been carried even further.) These and other references to Christian parallels with Jewish iconography, interesting and important though they are, scarcely prepare the reader for the bold hypothesis that appears near the end of the book (p. 384b): "The paintings of Dura can properly be called forerunners of Byzantine art." In view of the elaborate efforts by John of Damascus and other defenders of iconodule orthodoxy to validate the Byzantine reverence for images on the basis of early usage, the evidence provided by Dura may at least in part make up for the absence of more artistic remains from the early centuries of Christian history.

The reference to the writings of John of Damascus does, however, raise an interesting question about the kind of Judaism represented in the Dura Synagogue: Was there any literary counterpart to the artistic works found in these excavations? For Christian art, the literary defenses of the pictures are older than most of the surviving pictures, but the situation within Judaism must have been quite different. Kraeling does cite (p. 395b) the intriguing idea "that in the days before the Dura Synagogue and the synagogues of northern Mesopotamia there already existed manuscripts with illustrations of Biblical narratives," but he warns that "the suggestion must be received with great caution." The Jewish attitude toward the Torah was not consistent with the notion that such manuscripts were produced. Moreover, as John of Damascus and his colleagues pointed out at great length, the Christian dogma of the incarnation of the Logos in the person of Jesus Christ made a decisive difference in the doctrine of God and therefore in the attitude toward representations of divine subjects in pictures. At the same time, the role of the written word in Jewish thought must make one wonder, after examining the materials assembled here, whether there did not exist somewhere both illustrations and discussions of the propriety of illustrations, evidence that would be of inestimable value in continuing and deepening the insights that the author was forced to develop on the basis of what was available to him.

Let me close this brief foreword on a more personal note. Carl H. Kraeling was a product of, and a participant in, three scholarly communities: the Lutheran seminary, Yale University, and The University of Chicago. So was I, though at a later time and in a slightly different order. We became friends during the years that I was his junior colleague at The University of Chicago, although he was in the Oriental Institute and I was in the Divinity School. And fifteen years ago, when I had accepted the invitation to come to Yale, we spoke of how these three traditions had interacted. From those conversations I learned to know Professor Kraeling as one who managed to combine rigorous critical judgment about biblical and historical questions with a continuing sensitivity to the meanings that these texts and ideas have had in the development of Judaism and Christianity. That combination was, and is, a rare phenomenon, even (or especially) among scholars. As an attribute of person, it set him apart from most. As an attribute of mind, it gave his scholarly work a special quality, of which *The*

Synagogue (next only perhaps to *John the Baptist*, my favorite among his works) is an outstanding illustration. I am gratified to be able to pay this tribute to the book and to the memory of its author.

JAROSLAV PELIKAN
Sterling Professor of History and Religious Studies

Dean of the Graduate School Yale University

PREFACE

It was our revered master, Michael Rostovtzeff, who assigned to me the preparation of the Final Report on the Synagogue of Dura. If his health and life had been spared, the publication might have been ready at an earlier date and would certainly have benefited greatly from his advice and criticism and from his mastery of both the myriad facets and the great sweep of ancient history. As it is, the completion of the work has been long delayed — in part by the vicissitudes of the war, in part by the additional duties I assumed at Yale after the war, and in part by my removal to the Oriental Institute at Chicago in 1950. It has suffered somewhat both from the lapse of time between the preparation of the earlier and the later chapters, and by reason of the distance separating me from my colleagues at Yale, all of whom are much more continuously involved and more expert than I in the affairs of the Dura excavation.

Many factors have contributed to the prosecution of the enterprise. While serving as Annual Professor at the American School of Oriental Research at Jerusalem under William F. Albright in 1934–1935, I had the opportunity to visit Dura with him. The excavation of the Synagogue was at that time virtually completed, but I had ample occasion to see and to discuss with Henry Pearson the exposed remains of the "earlier building" and to learn what the work in the field had revealed. Subsequently, in 1946, I spent the entire summer at Damascus, where the "later building" of the Synagogue with its paintings had meanwhile been re-erected by Pearson as one wing of the National Museum. With the assistance of Frank E. Brown, then Director of the Department of Antiquities of Syria, I was able to study in great detail, and with the use of movable scaffolding especially erected for me, every part of the large body of paintings. Without this long and careful examination many difficult questions of fact posed by the material could not have been answered. That I was able to discuss my findings on the spot with Brown was of no small value in leading to an understanding, for instance, of the development of the Central Area on the west wall of the Synagogue.

Meanwhile, my comprehension of the material was advanced by the invitation extended to me by Albert M. Friend, Jr. of Princeton University to participate with Kurt Weitzmann, also of Princeton University, in a three-day Symposium on the Dura Synagogue. The Symposium was held at the Dumbarton Oaks Research Library and Collection of Harvard University in Washington D. C. in the spring of 1945. Here I learned to relate the material to the problems of early Christian art and manuscript illustration. During the academic year 1946–1947, which I spent at Dumbarton Oaks as Henri Focillon Scholar in Charge of Research upon the invitation of Paul Sachs of Harvard University, I was able to devote myself largely to the description of the individual compositions that make up the decorations of the building. The interpretative chapters of the Report have been written since my removal to Chicago, partly, however, in the course of visits to New Haven.

It will be obvious from the above that I am deeply indebted to many persons in connection with my work on this Report. The first to be mentioned in this connection are, of course, Michael Rostovtzeff and Sophie Rostovtzeff, of whom the former set the horizon for the undertaking, while the latter has never ceased to provide encouragement and to act as counsellor and friend to me as an individual and as a member of her beloved *gens Durana*. Next to be mentioned surely are those who have participated with me in the undertaking by providing each a part of the section on the inscriptions of the Synagogue; namely, Charles C. Torrey, C. Bradford Welles, and Bernhard Geiger. To them I owe a special debt of gratitude. Among my colleagues at New Haven, the Editors of the Dura Volumes, Alfred R. Bellinger, Frank E. Brown, Ann Perkins, and C. Bradford Welles, have been unstinting in the help they have given, particularly in the criticism of my presentation and interpretation. Herbert J. Gute of the Department of Design has made a major contribution with his meticulous copies of the Synagogue paintings, several of which are reproduced in this volume, and has in addition drawn or corrected numerous text figures and rendered valuable assistance during the printing of the color plates. Among the former members of the New Haven circle, now like myself a part of the dispersion, I owe much to Nicholas Toll, who guided patiently my earliest efforts, was always ready to discuss and answer questions, and provided access to the records; to Henry Pearson, who remembered clearly the relevant facts about the construction and excavation of the buildings; and to Clark Hopkins, whose detailed field notes on the paintings while they were first being uncovered yielded important information on details that became obscure after they had been exposed to daylight. At Princeton, I am indebted to the sage council and friendship of Albert M. Friend, Jr. and to the learning and kindness of Kurt Weitzmann. At Dumbarton Oaks, Ernst Kitzinger and Glanville Downey were always available for discussion and assistance. At Harvard, Arthur Darby Nock and Harry A. Wolfson have been most helpful, and at the University of Chicago, Ralph Marcus.

The present detailed study of the Synagogue naturally supersedes that of the Preliminary Report (*Rep. VI*). To the latter I contributed only the section dealing with the decorations of the Synagogue. Here I have had to assume responsibility for the description of the buildings, the decorations, the furnishings, and the pictorial graffiti and dipinti, as well as for the interpretation of all of the material. In preparing for this Final Report the section describing the "later building," I have leaned upon Pearson's account of the structure published in *Rep. VI*; but all details have been verified or corrected by direct check upon the field records, plans, and photographs, and points at issue have been discussed with Pearson himself. In describing the "earlier building" I was able to supplement the information provided by Pearson and the records from my own inspection of the remains.

For the factual record of the Dura Synagogue all of us are indebted especially to three individuals; namely, Henry Pearson, Comte Du Mesnil du Buisson, and Nicholas Toll. Pearson produced all the basic field drawings of the block and the buildings (Plans II–VI, VIII), some of which were eventu-

ally rendered with slight changes at New Haven by Norris C. Andrews (Plans II, V, VI). In addition we owe to Pearson a series of drawings of architectural and other details, serving here as Figs. 2 to 10, 72, 123–124, and the basic designs used in Pls. XVII and XXXIII. To Du Mesnil du Buisson, whose important separate publications on the Synagogue are given constant and grateful consideration in the body of our text, we owe above all the hand copies of some of the inscriptions (Figs. 88–98, 102–108, 120, 122) and the tracings of details reproduced in his *Peintures*, some of which we have borrowed (Figs. 11, 12, 29, 32). Nicholas Toll compiled virtually the entire photographic record of the structures, their paintings and dipinti, especially the color-separation negatives from which the color plates were made. He also prepared the diagrams of Plans IX–XII in correspondence to a similar set incorporated in Pearson's *Guide*. Herbert Gute produced the drawings reproducing the wall and ceiling decorations of the earlier building (Pls. XLIX, L) and made from his color copies the outline drawings used here as Figs. 43, 45, 54, 57–58, 60, 75 and on Pls. XXX and XXXII. To this body of material I was able to add a collection of tracings representing details of the decorations and a few photographs of inscriptions. The tracings used to make text figures were rendered in ink by various individuals, including Nicholas Toll, Herbert Gute, Charles Torrey, and my Assistant at Chicago, Margaret F. Bell.

To have contributed to the Final Reports on the excavations at Dura-Europos this volume on the Synagogue has been a high privilege, and that in the main for two reasons. The first is the importance of the structure as the most revealing archaeological monument of the history of ancient Judaism known to date. The second is the delightful and profitable association which the work itself has afforded with colleagues in so many institutions of learning. I cherish deeply and shall always have reason to be grateful for that privilege.

CARL H. KRAELING

August 1, 1955.

BUILDINGS

I. LOCATION AND LOCALITY

The Dura Synagogue is not a free-standing edifice, but one of a group of contiguous buildings that together make up a typical city block, the block designated L7 on the key map of the excavations (see Plan I). Belonging to the west-central section of Dura, the block lies in the shadow of the great wall that encloses and defends the city at the west. From the wall it is separated only by the width of the north-south thoroughfare known as Wall Street. During the Hellenistic period of the city's history the area to which the block belongs was for the most part unoccupied, the struggling Macedonian settlement having its natural center at this time in the more easterly portion of the plateau upon which Dura was built.[1] But the plan of regularly intersecting streets that the Greek settlers used in laying out the site, following the so-called Hippodamian pattern, permitted of extension to the limits set by the fortifications, and by the middle of the third century of our era the area in which the Synagogue stood had been entirely built up and was evidently quite densely populated.

In Block L7 the first traces of construction seem to go back to late Hellenistic or early Parthian days, but the buildings that stood here in the third century belong in the main to the late Parthian and the Roman period, that is, to the first two centuries of our era. Some of them, including the Synagogue, were rebuilt as late as the middle of the third century. For the structural development of the area, the growing importance of the city as a commercial center, the consequent increase in the number of its new inhabitants, the large additions made to its military garrison for the control of the frontier and for the protection of travelers, the expropriation of almost a fourth of the city's area by the military for its own purposes, and the resettlement of the dispossessed civilians in the non-military zone were of outstanding importance.

Though closely associated with the commercial life of the city and with the connections between it and the outside world, the quarter to which the Synagogue belonged was none the less basically residential in character. Block L7, like its neighbor L5, was originally devoted in its entirety to private dwellings and contained at one time ten separate domestic establishments. In size and appointments these houses seem less luxurious than the dwellings of Blocks C7 and D5 in the southeastern part of the city.[2] Yet they were more regular in plan and more elaborate in arrangement than those in Block B2, in the immediate shadow of the Citadel, and may thus be said to represent typical dwellings of Dura's middle class. Here, then, the Jewish community of Dura created for itself and for its kinsmen who were transients from other cities a center of religious and social life.

1. For a pictorial reconstruction of Seleucid Dura, see M. Rostovtzeff, *Dura-Europos and its Art* (1938), p. 35, Fig. 5.

2. *Rep. IV*, Pls. IV–V.

II. EXCAVATION AND STATE OF PRESERVATION

The remains of Dura's Synagogue lay buried in the deep deposit of earth and sand that sloped upward from the level of the city's streets to the top of the defensive wall forming its western boundary. Elements of house walls were occasionally noted by members of the expedition staff in the slope of the deposit, especially after a rain, and eventually the course of some of these walls was traced by means of shallow trenches, one set of trenches revealing the presence near Tower 19 of an unusually large rectangular chamber (Pl. I, 1). On November 22, 1932, excavation was begun in the area contained within the rectangle, and the first indications of the presence of the Synagogue were discovered. So significant were the discoveries that ultimately the entire block, in fact the entire region covered by the deposit along the wall, was completely excavated.

The preservation of the Synagogue and of the other buildings buried in this region we owe to the peculiar circumstances that produced the great sloping deposit along the wall in the first place. When the site of ancient Dura was first examined in modern times, it was quite naturally supposed that the deposit along its western defenses was an accumulation of sand created by the natural action of the wind blowing in from the desert over a period of many centuries. Excavation revealed that this was not the case and that the deposit was in fact, except for a light coating of sand, an earthen embankment purposely erected to cope with special conditions prevailing in the very last days of the city's history. The conditions in question were a military campaign in upper Mesopotamia and Syria by the Sassanians and the threat of a siege, the very siege which *ca.* A.D. 256 actually brought Dura's history to a violent end. Faced with this threat from without, the commander of the Roman garrison of the city undertook a series of defensive measures, the most important of which, so far as we can know them from archaeological evidence, was the defense of the city's walls against Persian siege operations. The procedure employed by the enemy engineers in such operations was to under-

mine the foundations of the city wall at one or more points, to support it temporarily by heavy timbers, and after a sufficiently large section had been undermined to set fire to the timbers, causing the wall to sink and to disintegrate in the process.[3] In anticipation of such operations the commander of the garrison ordered the construction of heavy earthen embankments against the inner and outer faces of the entire length of Dura's most readily accessible western wall. These could not prevent the enemy's mining operations but could reduce their threat by preventing the walls from disintegrating and leaving an open breach when they sank.[4]

In the area of the Synagogue the construction of the inner embankment was a process involving at least three steps. These steps permit us to reconstruct with full confidence the condition of the buried buildings and the stratification of the superimposed layers of earth. As the first step in the process (cf. Plan IV, 2) the entire length of Wall Street was filled in almost to the level of the housetops.[5] This gave support to the city's defenses and created an easier means of access to the *chemin de ronde* from which the wall was defended. In constructing their fill the army engineers naturally subjected the walls of the houses on the eastern side of the street to a tremendous strain. This they counteracted immediately, or after a brief interval, by buttresses introduced into the interior of the chambers to which the walls belonged. The but-

3. On the procedure see *Rep. VII–VIII*, pp. 43–48, especially p. 41, Fig. 18, as well as the interesting, well-illustrated article of R. Du Mesnil du Buisson, *Mémoires de la Société Nationale des Antiquaires de France*, LXXXI (1944), pp. 5–60. Procopius, *Historia* II, 17, lines 23–24, describes the procedure.

4. Tower 19 near the northwest corner of the Synagogue was actually the scene of such an operation and of one of the most dramatic struggles of the siege. Cf. *Rep. VI*, pp. 188–199.

5. The fill was superimposed upon an earlier natural deposit which in the course of time had already raised the level of the street above its original plane (Plan IV, 1). On the stratification of the earlier deposits in Wall Street and their importance for the history of the successive phases in the development of the Synagogue, see below pp. 27, 327.

tresses consisted of embankments of earth and carefully packed mud, which in the case of the Synagogue extended upward toward the ceiling at a sharp angle from a line halfway across the width of its most important chamber, the House of Assembly (Plan IV, 2; Pl. I, 2). Apparently the weight of this buttress, which naturally interfered seriously with the use of the room, was not enough to counteract the thrust from the fill in the street, for the west wall of the House of Assembly was severely cracked and pushed inward at the middle and at the top. The movement of the western wall transmitted itself to its northern and southern neighbors, whose upper elements were also moved slightly eastward. Here, on the surfaces not covered by the buttressing embankment, dislocations of several centimeters in the once continuous lines of the painted figures occurred, revealing the damage done to the structure of the room and to its buried west wall.[6] Then, perhaps to prevent additional damage, a second element was added to the buttressing embankment. The new addition filled the floor of the entire House of Assembly and ran from a line between two and three meters high on its east wall upward to the level of the line of windows near the very top of the west wall (Plan IV, 3). Its weight and scope were certainly enough to keep the structure from suffering further irreparable damage.

In character and function these steps in the construction of the embankment were relatively conservative and belong no doubt to the earlier preparations for the siege. Finally, however, under circumstances that are unknown but must have seen the defenders in more desperate straits, conservatism was abandoned and the embankment was extended by extremely drastic procedures. The walls and roofs of the buildings that projected from the buttressing embankments along Wall Street were demolished and the debris permitted to fall upon the earlier accumulations of earth and sand. Much additional material was brought in, with which the embankment was somewhat heightened and greatly extended (Plan IV, 4). To obtain this additional material and to create behind the embankment an open defensive zone, all the structures in the blocks adjacent to the city wall were

6. The displacements are still noticeable today. Cf. below pp. 70, 95, 135, 138, 181; Pl. V, 1.

sacrificed. Houses were razed, earth was excavated from floor level down to bed rock, and even the foundations of walls were removed on occasion in the process. Thus the garrison prepared the scene for hand-to-hand combat inside the city should the defense of the walls fail, as eventually it did.

Since it extended through the whole width of Block L7, the Synagogue complex suffered grievously from these drastic measures taken in behalf of a city preparing to fight for its very existence. The parts farthest toward the east were razed to the very foundations and are sometimes definable only in their general outlines (Pl. II, 2). Fortunately for us, however, the most important part of the complex, its House of Assembly, stood on the Wall Street side of the block. Extensive portions of the walls of this chamber were buried deep in the earlier phases of the embankment, and remains of its ceiling were left scattered about where they fell when the projecting parts of the building were destroyed. All these remains together with their precious decorations were protected from the ravages of the city's capture and from centuries of rain and sunlight by earth heaped about and above them, and thus preserved intact to our day. Having them, we can forego closer acquaintance with the easterly part of the complex, as well as with the furnishings of the several chambers, which the owners naturally removed from the premises when they were called upon to sacrifice the Synagogue to the welfare of the city.

The Dura Synagogue of the mid-third century, whose demolition and miraculous preservation are thus part and parcel of the city's own history, consisted of three elements; namely, a dwelling (House H), a Forecourt accessible only from House H, and a House of Assembly accessible only from the Forecourt. All three were structures of some elegance, testifying to the wealth of the community that reared them. That they could be arranged in a continuous series running through the heart of Block L7 from Street A to Wall Street was made possible by the union of two parcels of land that were originally quite separate and may well have been acquired in successive stages of the Jewish community's development. The community had not always been as large or as wealthy as the property holdings and the spacious, well-decorated buildings of its last years suggest. At a time whose remoteness from the period of relative affluence has still to be determined, it was much more modest in size and in means. This fact was revealed when the western part of the Synagogue complex was excavated to bedrock, bringing to light the remains of a much smaller structure that had also at one time served the purposes of worship after the Jewish faith. This occupied only the parcel of land covered by the later Forecourt and House of Assembly, being in fact but one of a row of houses in the western half of the block remodeled to suit and provided with access only from Wall Street.

In the treatment of the Dura Synagogue we have to deal, then, with two successive structures: an earlier building with its entrance on Wall Street, covering only the area between House B and House C (Plan II); and a later building running through the center of the block, comprising House H, a Forecourt, and a House of Assembly, and entered only from Street A.[7] The description of the structures must begin naturally with the later and uppermost of the two buildings, the inner elements of which, according to the dedicatory inscription, were erected in the year 244/245 of our era.[8]

7. The term "House of Assembly" is used throughout to denote the innermost of the several rooms of the Synagogue. Being in fact the room in which the religious services of the Jewish community were conducted, it may be properly so called in translation of the Hebrew term *bet hakenneset*.

8. Inscr. no. **1**, below, p. 263.

III. THE LATER BUILDING

A. House H

House H, the most easterly element of the later building, is known to us almost entirely from such elements of its foundations and substructure as remained by chance or by reason of their solidity when the superstructure above them, the earth about them, and the rubble of their less resistant elements were removed in the last phase of the construction of the embankment (Plan IV, 4). That it can none the less be described with some degree of accuracy is due to a combination of three factors. The first is the fortunate preservation of certain remains of crucial value for the reconstruction. The second is the basic similarity of House H to its less rudely handled neighbor, House I (cf. Plan II), from which it is distinguished mainly in features it acquired when being adapted to Synagogue use. The third is the relative homogeneity of domestic architecture at Dura as known from large numbers of private houses situated in other, better preserved portions of the city.

The private houses of Dura, like so many dwellings in the Orient even today, were unimposing structures seen from the outside. They presented to the beholder large wall surfaces plastered with a heavy coating of mud or plaster, surfaces unbroken save by a single doorway and a few small windows near the ceiling of the largest room, and unadorned save for the trim of the door frame. From the door a narrow passageway that normally made a right-angle turn led to the open central courtyard, around which the rooms of the house were grouped and upon which they opened. In the large establishments of the wealthy there was often a plurality of such courtyards, some of which were paved and set out with peristyles or porticoes. In the simpler dwellings there was but one and this, like the several chambers about it, had a floor of earth beaten hard by usage. Rooms were naturally of various types and served a variety of purposes depending upon the size and the excellence of the establishment, but two at least were standard even in the most modest dwellings. The first is the diwan,

entered from the courtyard by a formal doorway, where the life of the family and especially of the master of the house had its center. The second is an inner chamber, possibly a storeroom or bedroom, normally accessible only from the diwan. Standard appointments for the diwan were low, wide rubble-work or wooden benches that ran around three sides of the room, and a small plaster block just inside the doorway where the brazier stood that provided heat in cold weather. Cooking was done usually in the courtyard, from which a staircase led up to the housetop, and where a cesspool provided the sole instrument of sanitation that the house afforded.[9]

Of the better dwellings of the middle-class type, at least five of the ten houses that formed Block L7 are typical. House H, forming part of the expanded Synagogue complex, was the largest of these, covering an area approximately 26 m. × 18 m.[10] It was entered not directly from Street A, but from an alley that ran westward from the street into the heart of the block and led also to House C (area 71 on Plans II and VI). The alley opened at the street end with a doorway only slightly larger than the entrance to a normal house.[11] The doorway, if fitted with a door, naturally gave an extra measure of control over the alley to those whom it

9. Typical details of the private houses of Dura are set forth in preliminary fashion in *Rep. V*, pp. 31–34 and Pl. VI. As indicated there, the houses of Dura are fundamentally Oriental in character. Analogies will be found in the Parthian adaptation of the traditional pattern known from the excavations at Assur; see W. Andrae and H. Lenzen, *Die Partherstadt-Assur (Wissenschaftliche Veröffentlichungen der deutschen Orient-Gesellschaft*, LVII, 1933), e.g., Pls. 10, 12.

10. Actually the lot is somewhat irregular, ranging from 17.75 m. to 18.50 m. in width, and from 25.70 m. to 27 m. in length.

11. Remains of the doorway found in place include a stone sill 1.6 m. long between jamb lines, a stone step leading up from the street, and a section of a terracotta drain running under the sill. For this and all similar details of extant remains of House H, see the field drawing, Plan V, and the description in the Preliminary Report, *Rep. VI*, pp. 220–223, 312.

7

served.[12] At the left side of the alley, just inside the alley door, lay the actual entrance to House H, the sole means of access to the entire Synagogue complex. The doorway here gave on a flight of two steps leading down to the level of an entrance corridor, now largely obliterated, that ran southward along the inner face of the house's eastern outside wall. Elsewhere at Dura such entrance corridors in private dwellings either make a right-angle turn before terminating in the central courtyard or else continue in a straight line to a dead end and give access to the court through a doorway let into the appropriate side wall.[13] In this instance the passage ran a straight course and was therefore probably connected with the courtyard H9 by a door near the end of its western wall.[14] The unusual length of the passageway and the existence of remains of a second doorsill halfway along its course suggest that in this instance the corridor was divided by an archway into two sections, each *ca.* 5 m. long and slightly more than 2 m. wide (rooms H1 and H2).[15] The natural corollary of this conclusion is that each of the two sections of the passageway had a door in its western wall giving upon different portions of the establishment. Since passageways normally provide access to courtyards, the two sections of passageway and the two doors leading from them would suggest the existence of two courtyards in the interior of House H. To this suggestion the nature and disposition of the two contiguous areas of the house (namely, H3 and H9) give ready support. H9 is necessarily a courtyard by reason of its size and its position, and of the analogous character of H3 there are several clear indications.[16]

The fact that it had two contiguous courtyards is without doubt the most unusual architectural feature of House H. In all likelihood the house acquired this feature when it was adapted to serve the needs of the Jewish community and of the House of Assembly to which it gave access.[17] Certainly the effect of the change was to create under one roof two distinct suites of rooms, each complete in itself. The outer suite, entered from H1, consisted of the rooms H1, H3 (courtyard), H4, and H5; while the inner suite comprised the remainder of the house; namely, rooms H2, H9 (courtyard), H8, H7, and H6. The two suites were connected by the entrance passageway and by doors between the courtyards (H3 and H9) and between the terminal rooms (H5 and H6). The outer suite, giving access to the House of Assembly, was of necessity semi-public in character, while the inner suite preserved at least something of its privacy.

Of H3, the courtyard of the outer suite, little is known save that it was of fair size (7.75–8.00 m. long and 6.50–7.20 m. wide), that it was connected by a doorway with the adjacent courtyard to the south, and that it must have had a doorway into room H4 to the west.[18] Its cesspool, already mentioned, lay before but slightly to the south of where the door to H4 must have been (Pl. II, 2).

H4, the third room of the suite, occupied in its relation to the courtyard the position of diwan. With its length of 9.15 m. and its width of 4.60 m., it had the proper size for a chamber of this character and along the southern end of its eastern wall were found remains of a bench such as frequently appears in diwans throughout the city. Yet the

---

12. Alleys and streets closed by doorways are found elsewhere at Dura; for instance, in Block D5 (*Rep. IV*, p. 29 and Pl. IV, entrance T, room 36) and in Blocks H2 and H4 (*Rep. III*, p. 4 and Pl. IV).

13. For an example of the former in Block L7, see the entry to House A (rooms A38 and A34 on Plan II), and for an example of the latter, the entry to House G (room G88 on Plan II).

14. Of this western wall and the door nothing remains. The course of the wall can, however, be plotted by continuing to their intersection the spurs running out from the east and north walls of the house.

15. Cf. Plan VI. The dimensions of the two sections are actually irregular — H1 being 5 m. long and 2.25–2.40 m. wide; and H2, 4.70 m. long and 2.15–2.25 m. wide.

16. The first is the size of the area H3 (more than 7 m. × 6 m.), the second is the fact that the trim of the doorway between H3 and H9 faces H3, and the third is

the presence of a cesspool in the western part of H3. The awkward position of the cesspool may derive from its relation to an earlier structure, see *Rep. VI*, p. 221.

17. Originally perhaps the northern part of the court H3 was occupied by a chamber corresponding to room 76 in House I (Plan II). The entrance corridor, after passing this room, would have turned sharply to the right before entering the somewhat larger predecessor of the courtyard H9. This would account for the archway that in the days of the Synagogue divided the straight passage into two sections. Such archways are usually associated with corridors that turn at an angle, and serve the very necessary purpose of providing support for the roof at the angle of the turn.

18. All traces of the door to H4 have disappeared, together with much of the party wall between the two courtyards. At the end of what remains of the party wall is a portion of the bedding of the sill of the doorway that pierced it.

room provided the only means of approach to the Synagogue's Forecourt and House of Assembly, and cannot therefore have had the privacy usually associated with the diwan. Entrance to the Forecourt of the Synagogue was effected from H4 through a doorway cut into the west wall of the room near its southern end at a height of 0.60 m. above the level of the floor.[19] The height of the doorsill above the floor of the room marks the difference between the level of House H and of the Forecourt and House of Assembly, and implies the existence in H4 of a flight of steps leading to the higher level.[20] Only two other features of the room require comment. The first is an irregularity in the course of the western wall and a pier or pedestal associated with it (Pl. II, 2). The pier projects into the chamber a distance of 0.33 m., across the way from the probable location of the door from the courtyard.[21] The second is a lesser doorway leading from H4 into H5.

H5 was a somewhat smaller chamber, 4.90–5.00 m. long and 4.40 m. wide. At their junction its north and west walls jutted out into the Forecourt of the House of Assembly at an awkward angle, thereby testifying to an element of irregularity in the original construction of the house or of its neighbor to the west. The room apparently had no direct access to the inner courtyard along which it lay, but was connected by a narrow doorway with a cupboard-like room to the south (H6).[22] In its dependence upon H4 and its relative isolation, it reveals the characteristic traits of the chamber off the diwan sometimes used for storage or sleeping purposes.

The inner suite, entered through H1 and H2, was of a more private character. Its courtyard, irregular in shape, had a width of 8.85–9.30 m. and, including the alcove to the east, a length of about 10.65 m. Whether it was at one time paved or had merely the more usual floor of hard-packed earth can no longer be determined. In the alcove along the eastern wall of the house stood a plaster platform or counter ca. 3.30 m. long and over a meter wide, raised several centimeters above the probable level of the courtyard. Similar plastered areas are sometimes found at Dura in cupboards installed under stairways mounting from the courtyard to the roof,[23] and are usually an adjunct of the normal open-air kitchen. If the analogy holds, the alcove was the place where the cooking for the household was done. The difficulties are that there is better evidence for the location of the stairway along the western side of the court, that the plaster platform is unusually large, and that the supposed location of the kitchen in the alcove makes rather more elaborate provision for it than is usually the case in other establishments.[24] Conceivably the platform supported a wicker granary, of the type still seen in Oriental courtyards mounted on plaster bases, or a wooden crib containing food supplies of various types.

To the south of the courtyard lay the diwan of the suite (H8), a large room 5.70–6.30 m. wide and 10.00–10.30 m. long. It was entered through a formal doorway with a raised sill, from which steps at one time led down into the interior of the chamber.[25] An offset in its rear wall, occasioned by arrangements made to give the adjacent House G a wider entry, introduced an element of irregularity into the room that can scarcely have been very noticeable in view of its size. Presumably, as

19. The trim of the doorway has disappeared completely; only a stone set into the rubble bedding of the sill at the right and marking the spot where the flange of the door jamb projected over the sill is preserved. A difference in the construction of the rubble wall where the sill was bedded shows that the doorway was let into the wall at a date later than that of its original construction, when House H became part of the Synagogue complex.

20. All trace of the flight of steps has disappeared.

21. The projecting mass as found consisted of a gypsum block surrounded by rubble. Its function is obscure, but scarcely architectural.

22. The east wall of the room has completely disappeared, as Pl. III, 1 shows; but if, as seems probable, the stairway running from the court to the roof mounted along its outer face (cf. Plans III and VI), a door from H5 to the court would have been impossible. On the staircase see below, p. 10.

23. *Rep. IX, 1*, p. 89 and *passim*.

24. Du Mesnil du Buisson has suggested that the alcove provided the "kosher kitchen" for the Jewish merchants visiting Dura (*Syria*, XX, 1939, pp. 23–34). It is probably true that the Synagogue provided for the welfare of the itinerant Jewish merchants, as we shall see below (pp. 10 f.), but this should not be permitted to settle in advance, by a possible explanation of the extent of its provisions, the issue of the use of the alcove. Certainly the lintel with the Hebrew proper names and the dubious Greek texts, which he connects with the supposed restaurant, is not appropriate to the size of the alcove.

25. The entire northern wall of the diwan has disappeared save for the plaster bedding of the raised doorsill (Plan V; Pl. III, 1). From the rectangular insets of the wall ends in this bedding, it is probable that the doorway was 1.90 m. wide and proportionately high.

in other similar chambers, low plaster or wooden benches skirted the walls and a low plaster pedestal supporting a brazier stood at one side of the doorway, but of these appointments no traces remain.[26]

Toward the west the inner suite continued with H7, the typical adjunct of the diwan, a room between 5.15 m. and 5.65 m. wide and 6.30 m. long. It may have served as a storeroom or bedroom. Usually such rooms are accessible only from the diwan. In this instance, however, a doorway was apparently provided connecting it with room H6, and through H6 with the courtyard and the outer suite.[27] The departure from the usual practice in this particular suggests that in the establishment safeguards were not deemed as necessary as the accessibility of materials and the means of free intercommunication.

H6, the last room of the inner suite, is at the same time the smallest of the entire establishment, 2.50 m. wide and between 4.10 m. and 4.15 m. long. Its size, its position between the two suites, and its relation to the courtyard imply that it provided servants' quarters. From the courtyard H6 was separated, not by a wall but by a thin plaster partition possibly containing a narrow window. This window looked out upon an area paved with gypsum slabs and covered in all probability with a low archway deeper than the thickness of the adjacent house wall.[28] This archway, if such there was, would have served to carry to the roof of the house the open stairway mounting from the courtyard along the east wall of rooms H5 and H6 (Plan III).[29] If, therefore, the alcove at the east end of the courtyard was not the kitchen, it was in the area before the entry to room H6 that the cooking for the household was conceivably done.

In House H, as elsewhere throughout the city, the roofs of the several chambers were doubtless

constructed of layers of wattle covered with a thick coating of mud above and with a layer of plaster below. The height of the rooms varied in proportion to their size and importance (Plan III), but the trim of the doorways was probably relatively uniform, consisting of jambs, capitals, and architraves made of stone and carved with a pattern of moldings that was standard at Dura (cf. Plan VI and Pl. VI, 3).[30]

SYNAGOGUE HOSTEL AND RESIDENCE

The association of such residential quarters with a synagogue raises an interesting question and makes a significant contribution to our knowledge of ancient synagogue architecture and organization. The question is: what purpose did the dwelling serve in the over-all life of the Jewish community at Dura? The contribution is suggested by the most reasonable answer to the question; namely, that at least a part of the duplex house, House H — probably the outer suite comprising rooms H1, 3–5 — served as a guest-house for transient fellow-Jews. In a caravan city such as Dura, and particularly in a city located on the highroad between the large Jewish communities of southern Mesopotamia and those of Syria and Palestine, such a guest-house for travelers was distinctly in order. In non-Jewish circles the hospice is an institution known to have existed at much earlier times in many parts of the ancient world, whether to provide lodgings for visitors from allied civic communities, to house pilgrims visiting national shrines, or to care for out-of-town members of widely diffused cult associations.[31] The ritual and dietary requirements of the faithful Jews made the adoption of this institution highly desirable once peaceful conditions and the growth of the Diaspora raised the number of transients above that which could conveniently be accommodated in local households.

It has long been evident from rabbinical writings that accommodations for travelers were actually provided in synagogues of the Dispersion.[32] The

26. The only indication of such appointments is the recess near the base of the west wall (Plan V), which marks the location of the usual small cupboard intended perhaps for valuables.

27. Remains of an earlier wall under the floor of room H7 (Plan V) indicate that room H8 was eventually reduced in length.

28. Fragments of the plaster partition, approximately one third the thickness of the foundations upon which they stood, and of the gypsum slabs covering and paving the other two thirds were found in position (cf. Plan V).

29. All that remains of the stairway is a buttress projecting from the face of H6 into the courtyard a distance of 0.70 m. (cf. Pl. III, 1, and Plan V).

30. Lucy T. Shoe, *Berytus*, IX, 1 (1948), pp. 1–40.

31. See now E. Ziebarth in Ἐις Μνήμην Σπυρίδωνος Λάμπρου (Athens, 1935), pp. 339–348, using material that bears upon Delphi, Delos, Alexandria, and Edessa.

32. See especially the familiar statement of Samuel, a contemporary of the Dura Synagogue, who speaks from a knowledge of conditions in lower Mesopotamia and refers

Vettenos inscription with its references to a synagogue provided with guest-chambers that served as an inn for those abroad who might need it, has given tangible proof of the existence of such establishments for Jews from the Dispersion even at Jerusalem itself.[33] More recently additional inscriptions have been interpreted as referring to such hospices, and certain chambers of Palestinian synagogues whose purpose is not otherwise definable have been pointed to as providing guest accommodations.[34] In none of these instances is the evidence conclusive. At Dura, however, the residential character of House H is so clear from comparison with other private houses of the city as to leave no doubt that here for the first time

we have a guest-house of the type that must have been a familiar feature of the synagogues of the Dispersion, particularly of those in the Near East.

While part of House H may thus be said to have served to accommodate transients, this cannot have exhausted the function of the establishment. House H, it will be recalled, contained two complete suites of rooms of which the inner (rooms H2, 7–9) was of a more private character. The privacy it afforded and the size of the rooms suggest that it was the residence of a synagogue official. For the *hazzan* or "superintendent," of whom rabbinical texts speak as living in ancient synagogues, the quarters are probably too luxurious.[35] It seems preferable, therefore, to associate them with some more prominent person, a dignitary comparable to Tiberius Polycharmos, the "father of the synagogue at Stobi," who, having built the entire synagogue complex of the Macedonian city with his own money, reserved for himself and his heirs for life authority over and property rights in all of its "upper chambers."[36] At Dura the comparable person would have been the "archon" and "elder" Samuel, who played a prominent part in the building of the edifice, as the dedicatory inscriptions here also tell us.[37] Conceivably, what happened was that, as the owner of House H, he placed his property at the disposal of the community, thus enabling it to develop the larger synagogue complex running through the entire block and to make provision also for transients, while reserving for himself the right to inhabit the inner suite of rooms in the remodeled dwelling.[38]

33. Dated before A.D. 70, the Greek inscription honors a certain Theodotos, apparently a freedman of the Vetii, who built the synagogue and its hospice. Discovered in 1914, it was first published by T. Reinach, *Revue des études juives*, LXXI (1920), pp. 46–56. Text and photograph readily accessible in L. H. Vincent, *Revue biblique*, XXX (1921), pp. 247–277.

34. See the inscription from Al-Rama which Ben-Zevi interprets as honoring a rabbi who "built this house as a guesthouse" (I. Ben-Zevi, *Journal of the Palestine Oriental Society*, XIII, 1933, pp. 94–96). S. Klein supports (*op. cit.*, pp. 553f.) and E. Sukenik violently disputes the reading (*Journal of the Palestine Oriental Society*, XV, 1935, p. 167, n. 2). The rooms of the fifth-century synagogue of Hamath-Gadara regarded by Sukenik as guest-rooms are those along the eastern side of the building; see E. L. Sukenik, *The Ancient Synagogue of el-Hammeh* (Jerusalem, 1935), p. 77 and Pl. VII. On the supposed guest-room in the synagogue at Beth She'arim, see *Jewish Palestine Exploration Society, Bulletin* IX, 1 (1941), Pl. 2, 2.

to travelers eating, drinking, and sleeping in a synagogue (Pesachim 101a). The material has now been gathered and is conveniently accessible in S. Klein, *Mitteilungen der Gesellschaft für die Wissenschaft des Judentums*, LXXVI (1932), pp. 545–557, 603f. Klein argues properly with the Tosaphoth (*ad loc.*) that the eating, drinking, and sleeping was done, not in the rooms set aside for worship, but in special quarters connected with them. He believes he can show from Genesis Rabbah XCII, 6 (Soncino Translation, pp. 852f.) that the door of a synagogue equipped with such quarters was at the same time the door to the hospice. The argument is not convincing, but the arrangement suggested is analogous to that of the Dura Synagogue, where the House of Assembly is entered through the hospice. N. B. For the benefit of those who cannot use the rabbinical material in its original language, references to translations are provided whenever possible. Unless otherwise specified, references to the translations of the several parts of the Babylonian Talmud and the Midrash Rabbah are to those prepared by the Soncino Press in England. For these the standard form of reference is: (Trans., p. —).

35. On the *hazzan*, see S. Krauss, *Synagogale Altertümer* (1922), pp. 121–131. Yoma 11a (Trans., p. 47) indicates that a synagogue which contains a dwelling-place for a *hazzan* must have a *mezuzah*.

36. First published by N. Vulić in the *Spomenik of the Royal Serbian Society*, LXXI (1931), p. 238, the text of the inscription is conveniently accessible in S. Klein, *Mitteilungen der Gesellschaft für die Wissenschaft des Judentums*, LXXVII (1933), pp. 81–83. Actually the inscription has no bearing upon the hospice as an institution, and the building in which it was found is a private palace transformed into a church, rather than a synagogue. On the whole subject see E. Kitzinger, *Dumbarton Oaks Papers*, 3 (1946), esp. pp. 129–146.

37. Cf. Inscrs. nos. **1, 23,** below pp. 263, 277.

38. This would explain the change from the earlier building located on Wall Street to the larger complex under discussion here, and the importance attached to Samuel in the inscriptions.

B. The Forecourt

The second element of Dura's Synagogue complex is the Forecourt interposed between House H and the House of Assembly (Plans V–VI; Pls. II, 2–III). Here the modest proportions of domestic architecture were exceeded, and a structure was reared whose monumental character provided a fitting transition to, and setting for, the magnificence of the innermost chamber. Lying in the very heart of the city block and of the Synagogue complex, the Forecourt was enclosed on all four sides by walls, and was set out on three of them; namely, to the west, the north, and the south, by porticoes with tall, massive columns. The area it embraced was 13.30 m. wide and 10.25–10.40 m. deep. To reach it the worshipers had of necessity to pass through House H, proceeding from the entrance passageway (H1) through the courtyard (H3) and the westerly chamber (H4) of the outer suite. From H4 a set of steps led through a doorway in the southwest corner of the room into the Forecourt itself. Though the level of the Forecourt was half a meter above that of House H, its remains are better preserved, for its floor was covered by the outer reaches of the embankment, which the material from the demolished House H was used to construct.

Of the four walls enclosing the Forecourt, the one to the west, forming the entrance wall of the House of Assembly, is the best preserved. It stands to a height of between two and three meters and has a smoothly plastered surface which, however, was marred by scratchings of various sorts and even smudged by fire.[39] Of the other three walls, that to the north was relatively thin compared to the others, especially to that forming part of the House of Assembly. Since it is actually a party wall with House C to the north and the northern end of the west stylobate of the court does not abut it, the chances are that the construction of the wall was undertaken by the owner of the adjacent premises in connection with the Synagogue's building enterprise.[40]

To receive the columns of the peristyle that embellished the Forecourt, the builders prepared a heavy stylobate built in three sections. One section ran across the entire court from north to south. It extended along the front of the House of Assembly. The other two sections were spurs running out from the first in the direction of House H. In construction all three reveal the characteristics of the more economical among the building methods used in Dura.[41] The peristyle itself consisted of six columns, four set in a line across the face of the House of Assembly, the other two, aligned with the terminal members of the group of four, carrying the colonnade and its architrave eastward toward House H (Plans V–VI). The columns, each about 0.96 m. in lower diameter, were constructed of rubble covered with plaster, and this was marked to give it the appearance of stone and had incisions to simulate drum joints. Gypsum, covered with a layer of fine plaster, was used to fashion bases and capitals. The bases took the form of a low plinth and the capitals that of a quarter-round set against an abacus identical in size and shape with the base. One of the capitals, found in the courtyard (Pl. III, 2), still shows traces of red paint. In general the order reflects the Doric tradition established in the city in the Seleucid period of its history and commonly followed there to the end.

The colonnade probably supported a flat roof constructed of poles overlaid with mats or bundles of reeds and covered with layers of plaster and stamped mud. There is no direct way of ascertaining its height and the height of the columns supporting it, but it is certain that it joined the enclosing walls on a line above that of the lintel of the main door of the House of Assembly. As computed below, this doorway is 4.35 m. high from the top of the raised threshold to the bottom of the lintel.[42] The columns of the peristyle, if restored on the analogy of the proportions of height and thickness commonly found throughout the city, will have stood between 5.50 m. and 6.00 m. high.

39. Loose plaster fragments, probably remains of the destroyed walls, were found in the excavation of the Forecourt, some of them incised with graffiti. Cf. Inscrs. nos. **12–14, 35, 70,** below pp. 272f., 280f., 320.

40. On the ownership of House C, cf. below p. 330.

41. Two types of binder were used in this more economical form of masonry construction. Only the stones that formed the faces of the stylobate wall were laid in gypsum mortar. For the core of the wall a mud binder was used instead. At intervals a layer of gypsum mortar was spread through the thickness of the wall, producing the effect of courses and bonding the facings and wall together.

42. Cf. below, p. 18.

Near the northwest corner of the open courtyard enclosed by the peristyle a few fragments of paving tiles were found *in situ*, set against the western section of the stylobate. Between the line on which the tiles were set and the northern section of the stylobate a tile drain pipe came to light, constructed in the form of an *L* and set with its mouth in a vertical position. The drain apparently led through the stylobate to a cesspool located farther to the west.[43] Analogy to the earlier Synagogue building suggests that the drain carried off the water from a laver basin set into the northwest corner of the open court.[44] The paving tiles found in place here may merely be a part of a frame enclosing it. More probably, however, they are part of the tiling with which the entire open court was at one time paved.[45]

SYNAGOGUE FORECOURTS, THEIR FUNCTION AND ORIGIN

Courtyards with porticoes such as that described here are by no means unusual at Dura or in the construction of ancient synagogues generally. The most familiar examples in the field of synagogue architecture are those associated with the basilical structures erected by the Jewish communities of Galilee in the Antonine and Severan periods.[46] There a peristyle normally lies at the side of the basilica and, being constructed of cut stones, shows a careful attention to the proper use of the Greek architectural orders. In later synagogues of the same type the tendency is to transfer the colonnaded courtyard to the front of the building.[47]

That such enclosed courts should be common features of ancient synagogue construction is not difficult to understand. Synagogues in antiquity did more than provide places of worship for pious Jews. They were the centers of all phases of later Jewish communal life, and for the less formal aspects of the assembly of the faithful the courtyards attached to synagogues were admirably suited. Here questions of common importance were discussed, here public announcements were made, here scholars studied and debated the interpretation of the Law, and here, no doubt, children were instructed.[48] The presence of the laver basin in the court of the Dura Synagogue calls attention to one additional function of such courtyards. They provided the means and the opportunity for the washing of hands that was a prerequisite of prayer and thus of attendance upon the worship in the House of Assembly.[49]

The question of the immediate architectural ancestor of the synagogue with attached court is somewhat more difficult to answer. For such courtyards with peristyles the likeliest antecedents are in the sphere of domestic architecture. At Dura the courtyards of the better private houses were occasionally set out with porticoes on one or more sides. This was true, not only in the House of the Large Atrium (Block D5), but also in such comparatively modest establishments as the Christian House (Block M8) and the earlier building of the Synagogue.[50] In features such as these the domestic architecture of Dura, though fundamentally Oriental in character, shows clearly the influence of Hellenistic models, representing a union of eastern and western elements.[51] Whatever be true about Galilee, the Dura Synagogue's Forecourt derives from this modification of local domestic architecture.

43. The position of the cesspool partly under the northeast column of the peristyle (Plan V) is explained by the fact that it belonged to the private house which became the earlier synagogue. Cf. below, p. 28.

44. Cf. below, p. 28.

45. Remains of an ash bedding, such as is usually employed with tiles, came to light at various points in the courtyard. Against the north side of the base of the column at the northwest corner of the peristyle a small half-basin of plaster was attached (cf. Plan V). Its function is obscure.

46. Cf. H. Kohl and C. Watzinger, *Antike Synagogen in Galilaea* (*Wissenschaftliche Veröffentlichungen der deutschen Orient-Gesellschaft*, XXIX, 1916), Pls. II, VII–VIII, X, XII, XV. In all but the first the existence of such courts is inferred from the presence of side entrances to the House of Assembly.

47. So, for instance, at Gerasa (see C. H. Kraeling, *Gerasa, City of the Decapolis*, 1938, Plan XXXVI); at Beth She'arim (see B. Maisler, *Beth She'arim*, 1944, p. 17,

Fig. 3 [in Hebrew]); and at Beth Alpha (see E. L. Sukenik, *The Ancient Synagogue of Beth Alpha*, Jerusalem, 1932, Pl. VI).

48. See in general, Krauss, *Synagogale Altertümer*, pp. 182–198.

49. On the washing of hands before prayer, see the Letter of Aristeas, 305, and in general E. Schürer, *Geschichte des jüdischen Volkes im Zeitalter Jesu Christi*, 4th ed. (1907), II, p. 519.

50. For the House of the Large Atrium, see *Rep. IV*, Pl. IV; for the Christian House, *Rep. V*, Pl. XXXIX; and for the earlier building of the Synagogue, Plan VIII.

51. The relevant material for Hellenistic private houses is now conveniently accessible in the article by D. M. Robinson in *RE*, Supplementband VII (1940), cols. 262–278, *s. v.* "Haus (hellenistisch)."

C. The House of Assembly

To the west of the Forecourt stood the third and last element of Dura's Synagogue complex, its magnificent House of Assembly (Plans V–VI, Pl. XXV). The structure occupied the entire width of the plot of land between the Forecourt and Wall Street, covered an area 15.47 m. × 9.76 m. on the exterior, and 13.65 m. × 7.68 m. on the interior,[52] and formed one of the largest single rooms of which we have knowledge at Dura. It had two doors of unequal size, both set into its long eastern side. The larger of the two lay behind but slightly to the north of the axis of the central intercolumniation in the Forecourt's western portico.[53] The smaller was entered from the extreme southwest corner of the peristyle (Plan VI). Broken only by these doors and by the line of the portico's roof, the walls of the House rose unadorned to a height of almost 7 m. The high walls and flat roof gave it a boxlike appearance, quite in keeping with that of other structural units at Dura, both private dwellings and temples, but quite in contrast to that of the synagogues of Palestine. The impressiveness of the Dura Synagogue's House of Assembly lay primarily in the spaciousness and height of the chamber as seen from within, and eventually too in the nature and extent of its mural decorations.

I. FOUNDATIONS

The walls forming the shell of the House were built after the pattern commonly followed in the city, of mud bricks set upon rubble foundations. Those to the east and the west, carrying most of the weight of the roof, were 1.04 m. thick, while those to the north and south were thinner by 0.12 m. The rubble foundations of the wall, constructed in the same economical fashion as the stylobate of the Forecourt and laid in courses approximately 0.50 m. high, were carried up to different levels at different points (Fig. 1). To the west, along the entire Wall Street side they rose to a height of *ca.* 3 m. above floor level, chiefly

because of the higher street level and of the necessity of guarding the mud brick superstructure against street wear and water seepage.[54] To the north and south they were regularly only two courses; i.e., approximately 1 m. high, and on

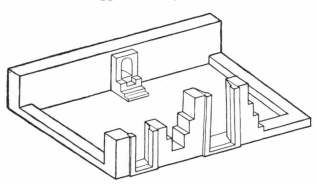

FIG. 1. House of Assembly, Varying Foundation Heights

either side of the doorways in the east wall they were stepped up probably to the height of the door lintel.[55] This served to strengthen the entire structure materially.

As a part of this foundation work there was constructed near the center of the long west wall[56] a heavy block of rubble masonry containing a semi-circular recess. It was 2.80 m. high and 1.56 m. wide, projecting a distance of 0.41 m. into the room (Fig. 1). The recess was rounded above to form a niche 0.83 m. wide, 1.51 m. high, and 0.91 m. deep. On a line 0.71 m. above floor level and 0.43 m. below the floor of the niche a step framed by pedestals was set against the block, approached by two lower steps.[57] The steps and the block together provided the basic structural core of an aedicula

---

52. The length given is that of the west wall. The east wall is shorter.

53. The axis of the door lay 0.24 m. to the north of the center of the intercolumniation. The intercolumniations were quite irregular, it should be noted.

54. For the level of Wall Street in its relation to the floor level of the House see Plan IV. On the importance of the rising level of Wall Street, see below p. 169. Unless otherwise indicated, measurements involving height above floor level are calculated from the latest floor level.

55. Embedded in the rubble of the foundations were found pieces of plaster belonging to the earlier building and fragments of jars, some of them painted, others bearing inscriptions (cf. Inscrs. nos. **18, 19, 37, 38**, below pp. 274, 281).

56. Actually the axis of the block is 0.10 m. north of the center of the west wall.

57. Beginning at the bottom the steps were 0.26 m., 0.20 m., and 0.25 m. high respectively, and 0.26 m., 0.33 m., and 0.33 m. deep.

that formed the sole architectural embellishment and the focus of attention in the chamber, for it served, no doubt, as a Torah Shrine to house the *aron* or Scroll Chest.[58]

2. WALLS

Upon the rubble foundations thus prepared were set the mud bricks that carried the walls up to their full height of *ca.* 7.00 m.[59] Just below ceiling level, three narrow rectangular windows with reveals widely splayed toward the interior must have been let into the east and the west walls after the manner commonly followed at Dura.[60] These were subsequently sealed at the outside end with glass or gypsum crystal and provided the only light for the chamber save that admitted through the doorways. Toward Wall Street the outside of the wall was finished with a coating of mortar made of clay and finely chopped straw, while the interior of all four walls and the exterior of the east wall (facing the Forecourt) were covered with a coat of plaster.[61]

3. CEILING

The fact that the flat roof which the walls supported can be described with complete accuracy we owe to the preservation of certain of its elements on top of the second phase of the interior embankment, and to the existence of remains of similar ceilings in other parts of the city. Structurally the basic elements of this roof were two wooden beams

laid across the top of the room from east to west, dividing the area crosswise into three equal sections (Pl. VII). The beams in turn supported rows of joists running north and south from beam to beam and from beam to wall. These were laid at intervals of *ca.* 0.55 m. on centers. Upon the joists were ranged rows of baked clay tiles each *ca.* 0.41 m. square and *ca.* 0.045 thick (Fig. 2).[62] All the wood

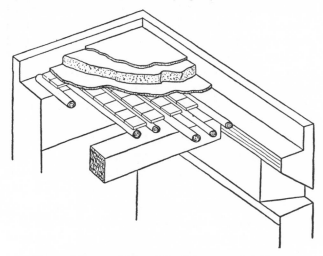

FIG. 2. House of Assembly, Diagram of Ceiling Construction

and many of the tiles were removed when the ceiling was torn down and must have been used in the defense of the city, but the tiles that were left in the embankment provide all the information needed to reconstruct the arrangement as here described.[63] After the tiles had been put in place, the ceiling was given solidity and coherence by an outer covering of plaster, upon which was spread a thick coating of a poorer binder resembling clay

58. The thrust exercised by the Wall Street fill upon the west wall of the Synagogue can be seen from the fact that the block forming the core of the aedicula was tipped forward, breaking off the projecting rubble mass that composed the lower steps. The second step was therefore found in a completely ruined condition (cf. Pl. V, 1).

59. The bricks were of two kinds, a harder red brick and a softer gray variety. A mortar made of the mud used in the gray bricks, and reeds set into the mortar at about every fifth course bound the materials together. The thick walls were laid two and a half bricks deep.

60. The number can be inferred safely from what is known about the construction of the ceiling. For examples of such windows at Dura in the same block, see *Rep. VI*, Pl. XVII, 1 (House of the Scribes, room A31).

61. Such an outer coating of the walls is still in use in the Orient today and has to be replaced about every eight years. On the west wall of the Synagogue it was found in a badly worn condition.

62. These are proper inferences from the remains of analogous ceilings and roofs elsewhere at Dura; see *Rep. IV*, pp. 42–52 (House of the Cistern in Block D5), and *Rep. VI*, pp. 274, 283–299 (House of the Scribes in Block L7). On the Synagogue ceiling tiles and their decorations see below, pp. 41–54.

63. Most of the information came from a close study of the remains of the plaster binding that at one time held the tiles in place. Sections of this binding still adhering to the tiles showed that they had been ranged in rows upon wooden joists. The curvature of the plaster binding gave diameters for the joists up to 0.18 m. It was easy to infer from the diameters that the joists could not have spanned the entire room but must have been set upon beams, and two is the logical number of the beams, considering the arrangement of the doors in the west wall. Traces of color appearing on the edges of the tiles even showed that the joists upon which they rested had been painted red.

rolled sufficiently hard to shed the rain. Rain water in all probability channeled through a coping and away from the walls in short wooden troughs or pipes.[64]

4. AEDICULA

The interior of the House of Assembly had as its sole architectural embellishment the aedicula near the center of the western wall. This formed the core of the Torah Shrine that housed the *aron* with its sacred scrolls (Pls. V, XXV, LI; Figs. 1, 3)

FIG. 3. House of Assembly, Aedicula, Section

and because of its sacred function was set out in such elegance as the community could provide, both architectural and decorative. Architectural elegance was imparted by applying to the rubble core already described an ornamental façade. It consisted of a pair of rubblework columns set to flank the central niche and supporting a heavy rubblework arch whose face was extended upward above the core of the aedicula.[65] To fashion this

arch and to provide the columns with bases and capitals the builders used rectangular floor tiles of the same dimensions as those found in the court-yard of the earlier building.[66] To give the interior of the aedicula its measure of decorative distinction, the niche-head was decorated in plaster with the flutings of a conch, and the entire surface of the structure was decorated in rich colors and appropriate designs.

5. BENCHES

The one item of furniture with which the House of Assembly was equipped by its builders was the masonry benches set against its four walls. These were interrupted only by the two doors in the east wall, and by the aedicula near the center of the west wall (Plan VI; Pls. V–VI). They consisted of rubble masses coated with plaster and so arranged as to form two steps rising from the floor to the wall.[67] Among the benches forming the upper step two types can be distinguished, the one with, the other without a raised footrest (cf. Plan VI; Pl. XXV).[68] The benches without footrests were those most directly accessible from the smaller of the two doors in the eastern wall. What we know about the nature of the wall decorations in this area, and what we can infer from the existence of the smaller door, makes it clear that the benches in question were those normally used by the women and that here the raised footrests were omitted lest modesty and propriety be offended.[69] Along the south wall in the benches used by the women two additional provisions were made to safeguard modesty and simultaneously to provide easier access. One was a rectangular recess in the lower bench where it abutted on the reveal floor of the smaller door, the

64. Cf., e.g., *Rep. VII–VIII*, pp. 184 (Temple of Zeus Theos) and 238 (Temple of the Gaddé).

65. The columns were 0.26 m. in diameter and 1.13 m. high, while the superimposed block, of equal thickness with the columns along its lower edge, was 1.06 m. high and 1.47 m. wide. At the top the block projected 0.40 m. above the rubble core of the aedicula and thinned down to 0.05 m. The columns stood upon pedestals 0.30 m. high, 0.40 m. wide, and 0.31 m. deep that had been constructed as terminal elements of the step in the rubble core as described above.

66. The tiles are 0.26 m. square and 0.04–0.06 m. thick.

67. The rubble of which the benches were made contained fragments of pottery, two of them inscribed (cf. Inscrs. nos. **40** and **41**, below, p. 282), and portions of fifteen column drums whose diameter ranged from 0.37 m. to 0.42 m. and whose average length was 0.65 m. The drums seem to have belonged to five columns 1.95–2.00 m. high, tapering 0.05 m. toward the top. They probably formed part of the earlier building. Cf. below, p. 28.

68. The footrest, set upon the rear part of the next lower bench, was constructed of lines of tiles *ca.* 0.23 m. square and 0.05 m. thick, possibly also re-used from the earlier building.

69. On the decorations of the south wall and on the asymmetrically placed southern door, see below, pp. 20, 147.

other a rectangular platform set into the southwest corner of the chamber floor before the lower bench.[70] Both afforded intermediate steps to the upper bench. To the north next to the main doorway, in the section used by the men, a pillow-like rise at the very end of the upper bench prevented anyone from sitting so close to the door as to be hit by it when it was opened.

In the course of their circuit of the walls the benches varied noticeably in their dimensions. The height of the lower step fluctuated between 0.29 m. and 0.47 m. and that of the upper step between 0.29 m. and 0.38 m. Where the lower bench included provision for a footrest, its depth varied from 0.51 m. to 0.57 m., while elsewhere it remained fairly constant at 0.40 m., which was also the average depth of the upper bench.

6. ELDER'S SEAT

Where the benches along the west wall abutted against the north side of the aedicula they were overlaid after their initial surfacing with a mass of plaster-covered rubble ca. 0.76 m. long, forming a series of five steps (Plan VI; Pls. V, XXV).[71] The uppermost of these steps provided a seat that lay ca. 0.28 m. above the level of the upper bench. The next to the last, serving as its footrest, was deeply worn. Clearly the seat was a place of especial dignity and of importance for the conduct of worship.

7. FLOORS

Two floor levels of successive date were found. In its later phase the area enclosed by the benches was covered with a carefully prepared floor, consisting of a layer of pebbles mixed with plaster, having an average depth of 0.10 m. Obviously poured on and tamped down or puddled when still wet, the floor varied in texture and level from place to place, yet it was clearly of one piece and the surface upon which it was poured had been carefully prepared by a bedding of sand. This served

to keep the floor both warmer and drier. There were many indications of wear on the floor, but these were confined to a zone ending ca. 1.40 m. from the edge of the surrounding benches.[72] Inside the zone of wear along the east, north, and south walls the floor contained groups of smaller and larger holes, most of them shaped and molded, and therefore apparently made when the floor was laid. From them and from the degree of wear inferences can be drawn about the chamber's furnishings.[73]

The complete excavation of the area showed that the floor already described was added at a later time to a base prepared when the building was erected. This base lay at a depth of between 0.24 m. and 0.30 m. below the final covering. In the main doorway a well-worn step led down to the earlier level, showing that the final covering was added after an interval of time.[74] Of the same general type as the final covering, it did not reveal the same care of construction but this difference is to be expected if the earlier covering was only the base for the later. With the addition of the final covering, the extraordinary rise of the lower bench (0.60–0.70 m.) was reduced to a more normal height for sitting, thus doubling the effective seating capacity of the benches.

8. MAIN DOOR

Of the two doors giving access to the House of Assembly from the Forecourt, the larger lay near the center of the east wall (Plan VI; Pl. IV, 1–3; Figs. 4–6).[75] As elsewhere at Dura, the trim was set

70. Cf. Plan VI and Fig. 7. The raised platform, constructed of re-used tiles, was 0.99 m. long, 0.44 m. wide, and 0.15 m. high.

71. The rise of the five steps was 0.12 m., 0.18 m., 0.18 m., 0.23 m., and 0.36 m. beginning at the bottom, and the tread 0.16 m., 0.20 m., 0.23 m., 0.30 m., and 0.43 m.

72. At various places on the benches and on the floor, particularly beyond the floor's zone of wear, paint spots were still in evidence.

73. Cf. below, pp. 255 f.

74. The two floor levels here mentioned should not be confused with the floor, still more deeply buried, which belonged to the earlier building. Pl. V, 1 shows the three levels clearly: at the lower right the floor of the earlier building, at the lower left the base of the later floor, and by the lines along the lower part of the first bench the final level of the later floor. This last had already been removed when the picture was taken. On the earlier building see below, p. 30.

75. Actually it stood ca. 0.51 m. north of the middle of the wall. Because of the fact that the niche block stood ca. 0.10 m. north of the center of the west wall, it is impossible to speak of an actual axial alignment of the two most important architectural features of the chamber. Yet it does seem that the center of the door leading from House H to the Forecourt and the center of the door to the House of Assembly are set on a line parallel to the south wall of the inner sections of the complex.

in place and the doorway finished only after the walls had been completed and the chamber had been roofed. This was possible because foundation courses were stepped up at either side of doorways to a level higher than that of the lintel, a row of timbers being built into the wall at this level to span the aperture and to carry the superstructure. In the case of the Synagogue the House of Assembly was not only roofed but apparently also given a first decoration and put into temporary use before the trim was added, as remains of a coat of red paint on the face of the foundation courses later covered by the door reveals indicate.[76] In type and general appearance the door frames of the House of Assembly correspond to those found elsewhere in the city and in House H, consisting of a gypsum sill, stone jambs set in such a way as to make the doorway taper slightly toward the top, molded jamb capitals, and a lintel cut with the same moldings as the capitals.[77] Of the frame itself only the stones that formed the sill and two unequal sections of the jambs were found in place (Pl. IV, 1, 2), but these sufficed to give the essential

this height to a width of *ca.* 1.70 m.[78] The missing jamb capitals and the lintel were probably carved with the Greek (Ionic) moldings commonly used in the city.[79]

The fact that the door frame was built up in sections, that the sections of the sill are of unequal width, and that the jambs were widened across the face by the addition of plaster strips gives the impression of shabby workmanship and suggests the possibility that here again building material from some other structure has been re-used. It should be said, however, that such methods of construction were common in the later phases of Dura's history and that the structural deficiencies were obliterated by a fine coat of plaster covering the entire door frame.

Attached to the rubble wall with a heavy filling of plaster, each jamb of the main door had a rebated extension on the interior projecting beyond the line of the sill (Pl. IV, 2–3; Fig. 5). The rebate on each side determined the angle for the splay of the door

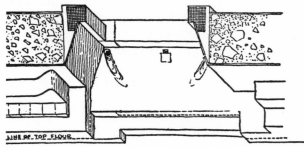

FIG. 5. House of Assembly, Main Doorway

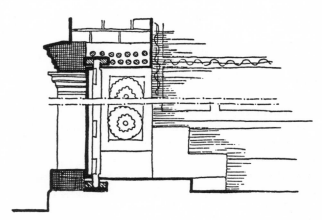

FIG. 4. House of Assembly, Main Doorway, Section

details (Figs. 4–6) and to show that the doorway was 2.02 m. wide at the bottom and therefore approximately 4.35 m. high, probably tapering at

78. The sill was composed of three blocks each 0.47 m. long, but the central block was 0.09 m. wider than its neighbors. The blocks were bedded upon a section of rubble foundation and projected 0.32 m. from the face of the building. The jamb sections were of unequal height, were so set as to project from the wall of the House a distance of 0.18 m., and were widened on the face which they presented to the Forecourt by the addition of strips of plaster 0.05 m. wide. Upon a section of the plaster strip applied to the right jamb an Iranian graffito was inscribed (See below pp. 283f.). The door frames at Dura are usually slightly more than twice as high as they are wide. In the case of the Synagogue it is probable that the line of the reveal soffit coincides with the top of the lowest of the three registers of pictorial decorations on the interior of the House (Register C). The figure 4.35 m. suggested as the height of the doorway is arrived at by subtracting from that of the height of Register C above the level of the reveal floor (*ca.* 4.50 m.) the necessary projections of sill and lintel. The degree of tapering is constant in the domestic architecture of the city and can be calculated once the height has been determined.

76. A thin layer of dirt between the rubble bedding and the mortar used to set the sill in place is a further indication that the doorway was used before the trim was put in place.

77. For the type see *Rep. VI*, Pl. X. For the reconstruction of the doorway according to the type, see below, Pl. VI, 3.

79. See in general Shoe, *Berytus*, IX, 1 (1948), pp. 1–40.

reveals, which continued in plaster beyond the projecting line of the jamb, and so secured for the trim a firm hold on the masonry.

In the trapezoidal area bounded by the sill and the reveals there was introduced as the last element in the construction of the doorway the reveal floor.[80] This was extended into the chamber beyond the inner face of the wall as far as the edge of the upper tier of benches, except to the south where a projection *ca.* 0.47 m. wide carried it out to the edge of the lower tier, to provide easier access to the benches used by the women (Pl. IV, 2). From the reveal floor a step with an analogous projection at the north end led down to the level of the construction floor of the chamber.[81] In the construction of the later floor the step was covered to a depth of 0.06 m., but its projecting northern element was built up to the height of the reveal floor to balance that at the southern end (cf. Pl. IV, 3). As discovered, the reveal floor showed the effects of much wear, for its central area was overlaid with a heavy patch of concrete (Pl. IV, 3).

Directly behind the line of the sill the reveal floor contained three holes, one circular hole in each corner for the doorposts and one rectangular hole 0.25 m. to the south of center for a vertical lock bar (Fig. 5; Pl. IV, 3).[82] The doorpost holes had been broken out toward the inside of the chamber when the building was dismantled and the doors were removed, but the cavity remaining in the reveal floor indicated clearly the nature of the door socket, which consisted of a wooden block hollowed out and mounted on an iron plate (Fig. 6).[83] The doorpost pivoted in the hollowed

block and rested on the iron plate. Toward the east the cavity housing the socket had a noticeable extension (point *F* in Fig. 6). This lay under the

FIG. 6. House of Assembly, Main Doorway

door sill itself, being gouged out of the rubble bedding upon which the sill was set. In the pocket of the cavity was found a collection of bones that are reported to have been parts of two human fingers.[84] Their presence at this point cannot have been the result of an accident, because of the genuine inaccessibility of the pocket and because of the discovery of analogous remains in the socket of the south doorway. The bones, whatever their character, must therefore represent a foundation deposit of the kind known to us also at Dura from pagan structures.[85] That the practice of making foundation deposits survived in Mesopotamia at so late a date is by no means surprising; what does surprise is that it should have been followed in the construction of a synagogue.[86]

80. Since the doors were hung in sockets and the sockets were themselves set into the reveal floor, the latter could naturally not be fashioned until the doors had been hung, unless some makeshift such as the south door shows was used. Cf. below, p. 20.

81. The rise from the level of the construction floor to the doorsill was 0.50 m., of which 0.20 m. constitutes the rise from the floor to the step, 0.20 m. the rise from the step to the reveal floor, and 0.10 m. the rise from the reveal floor to the top of the sill.

82. The lock bar hole, 0.11 m. long, 0.07 m. wide, and 0.09 m. deep, was faced toward the interior with a small tile to give the bar stronger support. Being set to the south of center, the hole shows that the southern flange of the door normally remained closed; being set 0.05 m. in from the sill, it provides an indication of the thickness of the lower rail of the door.

83. The block in this instance was 0.24 m. long, 0.19 m. wide, and 0.15 m. thick.

84. *Rep. VI*, p. 316. It has not been possible to verify the report. The bones apparently were among the materials left in the expedition house at Dura, which was destroyed in the fighting during the course of the last war.

85. See, e.g., *Rep. VI*, p. 399 (Temple of Artemis); *Rep. VII–VIII*, p. 240 (Temple of the Gaddé).

86. For foundation deposits in the ancient Near East, see, e.g., E. D. van Buren, *Foundation Figurines and Offerings* (1931); for the survival of the custom in the first Christian century see the discoveries at Seleucia (L. Waterman, *Second Preliminary Report upon the Excavations at Tel Umar, Iraq*, 1933, pp. 21, 54). As applied to synagogues the custom has apparently left no traces either in later Jewish literature or in synagogue buildings discovered hitherto. Indeed in Palestine the presence of human remains would have been presumed to render impure both the site and the persons approaching it. What the use of such foundation deposits in a synagogue implies for our understanding of the nature of the community that

9. SOUTH DOOR

The second of the two doors giving access to the House of Assembly lay near the extreme southern end of its eastern wall. Though its location at this point flaunts all the established canons of architectural symmetry, it is perfectly clear both from the adjustment in the height of the benches at either side and from the undisturbed condition of the foundations in its immediate vicinity that the door was planned and built as an integral part of the structure. What is known about the nature of the adjacent benches and about the adjacent decorations shows that the door was intended to provide a separate entrance for the women. Its location corresponds to that of a similar doorway in the earlier building.

Structurally analogous to the main door, the south door was appreciably smaller in its proportions and provided a passageway not more than 1.35 m. wide and approximately 2.75 m. high (Fig. 7; Pl. IV, 4).[87] In addition to the sill and

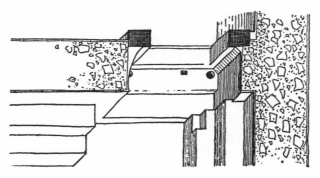

FIG. 7. House of Assembly, South Doorway

portions of the jambs, a piece of the lintel was found in the debris, the stone in this instance giving clear indication of its having been borrowed from some other structure.[88] Because of its unusual position in the corner of a room, the south doorway departed from the norm in the development of the reveals. The south jamb had only a narrow triangular filling of plaster behind it to hold it in position against the short offset that formed the southern end of the east wall of the room (Fig. 7). The northern jamb was backed by a heavier plaster mass, here given a concave form, probably to keep the north door flange from reducing the width of the passageway needlessly. In this instance the builders laid the reveal floor before the doors were hung, placing it some 0.24 m. below the level of the sill and extending it only to the inner face of the House wall. When the doors were ready to be put in place, a rough plaster step was contrived on top of the reveal floor directly behind the sill, and into this the two door sockets and the hole for the lock bar were set. Though these sockets too had been broken out, apparently with less effort, they still contained materials that apparently belonged to a foundation deposit, namely three teeth.[89] As originally laid, the floor of the chamber was a step down from the reveal floor of the south door, but when the second, higher floor was introduced, the difference in level all but disappeared. As seen on the plan (Plan VI), the end of the benches along the south wall seems to obstruct the doorway awkwardly in spite of the rectangular recess cut in the lower step. It should be recalled, however, that the south flange of the door was normally kept closed and that the obstruction was therefore less disturbing.

10. SYNAGOGUE TYPES AND STRUCTURAL PRINCIPLES

With all its inelegancies and irregularities, the later building of the Dura Synagogue is none the less a significant structure, judged by local standards. The organization of its several component elements into a single complex serving the several

sanctioned them can be discussed only in connection with the evidence for additional liberties exercised by the Jews of Dura; for instance, in the nature and use of the decorations applied to their House of Assembly. Cf. further below, pp. 340–363, especially p. 361.

87. The estimated height is determined by the proportions known to exist at Dura between width and height of doorways. In this instance the trim projected only *ca.* 0.04 m. from the face of the house wall. Strips of plaster were applied here also to widen the outer face of the trim, a similar strip being attached also to the sill to make it project beyond the face of the jambs.

88. For the profile of the lintel see Shoe, *Berytus*, IX, 1 (1948), Pl. VI, no. 126. The lintel was longer than necessary and had been notched at the back to fit the size of the smaller doorway.

89. Two were found in the north socket hole and one in the south. The teeth are said to have been human, but again no verification is possible because of the loss of the objects.

needs of the local Jewish community, and the spaciousness of its Forecourt and particularly of its House of Assembly, characterize it as the work of an ambitious group that sought to create for itself a center of corporate and religious life suited to the dignity of its faith.

As a structure, the later building of the Dura Synagogue contrasts sharply with the synagogues known to us from Palestine and the region immediately east of the Jordan. In these areas, at least from the Antonine period to the days of Justinian, most synagogues, so far as we know them today, were of the basilical type.[90] Characteristic of buildings of this type are their character as freestanding structures, their construction of welldressed stones, their use of architectural ornament, their doors symmetrically placed in one of the short sides, and the fact that their interior was set out with a double row of columns running parallel to the long sides of the building and helping to carry the gabled roof. They were commonly provided with stone benches ranged against the side walls, and from at least the Constantinian period on acquired an apse to house the *aron* or Scroll Chest, thus bringing to adequate organic and architectural expression the importance of the Law for the worshiping community.[91]

As glaring as are the contrasts between the structural elegancies of these Palestinian synagogues, where in an Oriental variation at least the themes of Imperial architecture are preserved, and the inelegancy of Dura's House of Assembly, a simple mud-plastered cube, so vivid are also the contrasts in general organization and disposition. In the basilical synagogues the axis of the building runs parallel to the long sides of the rectangular structure, access being provided through doorways symmetrically distributed in one of the short sides. At Dura the House of Assembly is a *Breithausbau*, whose entrances are unsymmetrically distributed in one of the long sides and whose axis runs parallel to the short sides.[92] To this type of construction analogies are now available in the synagogues at Hamam-Lif (ancient Naro) in North Africa, at Priene, and at Eshtemo'a in Palestine, suggesting that the variation is by no means uncommon.[93] It is not clear at the present time, however, whether the four structures in question actually represent a distinct *Breithausbau* type. Rather it would seem that they are a group of comparable departures from what, in Palestine at least, was a standard since the middle of the second century of our era, and that if a second "type" of ancient eastern synagogues is ever to be determined, it will be because further excavation, particularly in southern Mesopotamia, will meanwhile have given us a fuller knowledge of the kind of building in use there.[94] For the time being, therefore, the *Breithausbau* of the Dura Synagogue has to be judged by itself, which means naturally in the light of its own architectural context.

It is important in this connection to recognize at least certain elements of similarity between the Synagogue and the pagan temples of Dura, whose

90. For Palestine see especially Kohl and Watzinger, *Antike Synagogen*; Sukenik, *Ancient Synagogue of Beth Alpha*; and Maisler, *Beth She'arim*. For the area east of the Jordan see Kraeling, *Gerasa*, Plan XXXVI; and Sukenik, *Ancient Synagogue of el-Hammeh*. In general E. L. Sukenik, *Ancient Synagogues in Palestine and Greece* (1934).

91. On the development of the Christian basilica with apse, see now the important publications of A. Grabar, *Martyrium. Recherches sur le culte des reliques et l'art chrétien antique*, 2 vols. (1946); and J. Lassus, *Sanctuaires chrétiens de Syrie* (1947). The two developments are analogous but not apparently directly interrelated any more than the removal of the peristyle court from the side of the basilical synagogues and its emplacement before the entrance (see above, p. 13), which has the effect of creating in synagogue architecture a counterpart to the atrium of the Christian basilica. The change may be the result merely of economic factors in the life of the Jewish communities, for it provided a way of escape from the expensive architectural and decorative embellishment of the basilical façade.

92. On this type of construction see H. Glueck, *Der Breit- und Langhausbau in Syrien* (*Zeitschrift für Geschichte der Architektur*, Beiheft 14, 1916).

93. For the plan of the synagogue at Hamam-Lif see E. Renan, *Revue archéologique*, Ser. 3, III (1884), p. 274. For Priene see T. Wiegand and H. Schrader, *Priene* (1904), p. 480 (mistaken for a church); the structure is now correctly interpreted as a synagogue in the light of certain of its sculptured decorations, e.g., by Sukenik, *Ancient Synagogues in Palestine and Greece*, pp. 42 f. For Eshtemo'a see L. A. Mayer and A. Reifenberg, *Journal of the Palestine Oriental Society*, XIX (1939), pp. 314–326.

94. It will be noted that of the four structures in question here, those at Hamam-Lif and Eshtemo'a have their doorways in the short sides of the building. This fact and the presence in both of a vestibule set out with columns brings them closer to each other and separates them from the structures at Dura and at Priene. The synagogue at Priene, moreover, has been so pulled about, even to the extent of being given basilical traits, that it can hardly be compared structurally with any of the other three.

sanctuary units normally have simple rectangular pronaoi or naoi or both so arranged that their axes cut across their long sides as in the Synagogue.[95] The ultimately Oriental origin of Dura's pagan sanctuary units and the survival in them of old Babylonian temple forms has often been noted and need not be discussed here.[96] In view of the strong element of traditionalism in the architecture of Dura generally and in view of the presence of foundation deposits in the Synagogue, it is entirely reasonable to look for at least a measure of relationship between the architectural form of the Synagogue and that of other contemporary religious structures of the city and the region. Yet it would seem unwise to exaggerate the extent of this relationship, partly because of the traditional attitude of Judaism to pagan worship and idolatry, and partly because of the fact that there are distinct differences between the pagan sanctuaries of Dura and the Synagogue both in outward form and in function.[97] In view of these facts it may be better to regard the relations that undoubtedly exist between pagan and Jewish religious edifices at Dura as incidental and indirect rather than as definitive and normative. This is the more logical because in its outer form the House of Assembly of the Dura Synagogue is in effect, like the pronaoi of the Dura temples, but an oversize version of a room of a private house.[98]

While in its general form and axial organization the Synagogue's House of Assembly can be explained as a derivative of the domestic architecture of Mesopotamia (which in turn shares certain traits with temple architecture), there are two specific points at which it seems to depend directly upon contemporary religious edifices. The first is the size of the room itself, a monumental hall for which parallels exist at Dura only in the pagan temples, and the second is its aedicula, set against the center of its west wall. In the synagogues of Hamam-Lif, Priene, and Eshtemoʿa mentioned above, provision was also made in the center of one of the long sides of the buildings to house the sacred scrolls of the Law. But what these synagogues provide are simple niches and recesses, whereas in the Dura Synagogue the Scroll Chest was kept in a separate structural element, an aedicula. For such aediculae there are analogies in several of the Dura temples, both in a central position in the naos and in the courtyards of temple complexes.[99] These aediculae have an importance in the religious architecture of the Roman Orient far in excess of their appearance in rudimentary forms in the Dura temples. We find their monumental counterpart in many of the largest temples of the Near East in the adyta set into the Greek temple cellae.[100] Deriving, perhaps, from the

95. For the Temple of Bel, see Cumont, *Fouilles*, Pl. XXV; the Temples of Artemis and Atargatis, see *Rep. III*, Pl. IV; the Temples of Adonis and Zeus Theos, see *Rep. VII–VIII*, Fig. 42, opp. p. 150 and Fig. 48, opp. p. 194. For a statement about the type see *ibid.*, p. 183.

96. So first J. H. Breasted, *Oriental Forerunners of Byzantine Painting* (Oriental Institute Publications, I, 1924), p. 68; Cumont, *Fouilles*, p. 34; *Rep. III*, pp. 18–24; Rostovtzeff, *Dura-Europos and its Art*, pp. 41–46; A. R. Bellinger, *Seminarium Kondakovianum*, IV (1931), pp. 173–177.

97. In the pagan sanctuaries of Dura three elements are normally present: the outer court, the pronaos, and the naos. It is the pronaos that bears the closest structural similarity to the form of the Synagogue. The court normally has a quite different arrangement in the temples, and in the Synagogue, naturally, a true naos is lacking. Moreover, the communal purposes served by the Synagogue's House of Assembly are usually served in the pagan shrines by rooms other than the naoi or the pronaoi, save where the latter are arranged as *salles aux gradins*, as for instance in the Temple of Atargatis (*Rep. III*, Pl. IV). Instructive in this connection is the story reported by Josephus that Jewish mercenaries in Alexander's army refused to participate in the building of the Temple of Bel at Babylon (*Contra Apionem* I, 22 = § 192).

98. This analogy becomes cogent for the interpretation of the chamber by reason of the relation between it and the corresponding chamber of the earlier building. Cf. below, pp. 29, 32 f.

99. So, e.g., in the Temple of Bel (Cumont, *Fouilles*, Pl. XXV) to which Du Mesnil du Buisson has called attention in this connection (*Peintures*, p. 11); in the Temple of the Gaddé (*Rep. VII–VIII*, p. 249, Fig. 64, and Fig. 67 opp. p. 254); and in the Temple of Adonis (*ibid.*, pp. 148 f. with Fig. 40). J. B. Ward Perkins, *Papers of the British School at Rome*, XX (1952), pp. 111–121, would recognize as a synagogue the fifth-century South Chapel of the Severan Basilica at Lepcis Major, because of the presence of an apse with a raised seat beside it. My own position is negative, cf. *ibid.*, p. 116, n. 11.

100. So, e.g., in the Temple of Bel at Palmyra, Th. Wiegand, *Palmyra* (1932), pp. 134–138, Pl. 75; in the small temple at Baalbek, Th. Wiegand, *Baalbek*, I (1921), Pl. 14; and in the Kasr Firaun at Petra, H. Kohl, *Kasr Firaun in Petra* (Wissenschaftliche Veröffentlichungen der deutschen Orient-Gesellschaft, XIII, 1910), p. 2, Fig. 2. See in general D. Krencker and W. Zschietzschmann, *Römische Tempel in Syrien*, 2 vols. (1938). See now also R. Amy, *Syria*, XXVII (1950), pp. 82–136.

palace architecture of the Near East, more particularly from the dais and the baldachin that set off the royal throne, and transferred to religious architecture because of the intimate relation of monarch and deity, the aediculae in the later temples of the Orient served primarily to house the cult image of the deity. But eventually their function was extended and they became a device of religious architecture generally, serving in the Dura Mithraeum to frame the cult niche with its reliefs and in the Christian Chapel to house the baptismal font.[101] Under the circumstances it is difficult to escape the impression that the aedicula of the Dura Synagogue is related structurally at least to the religious architecture of the later Orient generally speaking. But what particular connotation the aedicula assumed in connection with its use as a Torah Shrine is a different question, and one that can be answered only on the basis of a study of the decorations applied to its façade by its builders.[102]

Its is of great interest and no small importance historically to compare what is known about the later building of the Dura Synagogue with information about synagogues and their appointments supplied directly or by implication in later Jewish literature.[103] Much will eventually be gained from such a comparison, especially in proportion as it passes into the hands of those who are in full command of the material. Here only a few details can be considered. In the case of a city built as Dura is upon a relatively flat terrain, it would be difficult to apply the traditional criterion that a synagogue should be located at the highest point of the city, nor is it clear that this principle could

always be followed.[104] Similarly, it is difficult to know whether the Talmudic dictum about the roof of the synagogue being higher than that of other structures in the city may be said to have applied.[105]

To those familiar only with the basilical synagogues of Galilee the location of Dura's House of Assembly in the innermost part of a group of buildings may seem unusual; but for its location, its flat roof, its tiled ceiling, and its splayed windows there were direct analogies in other synagogues of antiquity, particularly in Babylonia.[106] Still more unusual, perhaps, are the arrangements made at Dura for the participation of women in the worship of the synagogue. In Galilee, it will be recalled, the women probably occupied a gallery above the main floor of the synagogue, to which access was provided by a staircase on the outside of the building.[107] At Dura the women shared equally with the men in the use of the House of Assembly, though they entered by a special doorway and sat on benches reserved especially for them.[108] The arrangement is no doubt more primitive than that of the Galilean structures, for galleries of the type they provided were made possible only by the basilical nature of the construction, which comes in at a relatively late date. At the

101. For the arrangement of the Middle Mithraeum see *Rep. VII–VIII*, p. 103, Fig. 36; for the Christian Chapel see *Rep. V*, Pls. XL–XLIII.

102. See below p. 61. The decoration of the niche head of the aedicula with a conch done in plaster, a feature not common in the aediculae of the pagan shrines at Dura, illustrates the sense of freedom with which the builders of the Synagogue handled the decoration of the structure. The conch is, of course, a familiar element of the decorative tradition in the architecture of the Roman Orient and often represents a baldachin. See in general M. Bratschkova, *Bulletin de l'institut archéologique bulgare*, XII (1938).

103. We reserve for a later context the consideration of the Elder's Seat, and the arrangements for the veil and the canopy over the Torah Shrine, both of which will be treated in connection with furnishings (see below, pp. 256–260).

104. Tosephta to Megillah, IV, 23 (ed. Zuckermandel, p. 227).

105. Shabbath 10b (Trans., p. 39). The relevant statement attributed to Rab reads: "Every city whose roofs are higher than the synagogue will ultimately be destroyed." This apropos of Ezra 9.9.

106. The existence of outer chambers is implied in the statement of Deut. Rabbah VII, 2 (Trans., p. 133) where Prov. 8.34 is applied as follows: "When you come to the synagogue to pray do not remain standing at the entrance and pray there, but see to it that you enter within the inner door." Flat roofs are presupposed in the statement of the Mishnah, Megillah, III, 3 (Trans. H. Danby, *The Mishnah*, 1933, p. 205, hereinafter quoted merely as "Danby" with the appropriate page number), where it is forbidden to spread out produce upon the roof of a synagogue even if the building is in disuse and disrepair; and in the passage of the Talmud, Nidda 13a (Trans., p. 86), where we hear of Rab Judah and Samuel standing on the roof of a synagogue. On the form of the windows known at Dura and inferred for the Synagogue, see the statement Num. Rabbah XV, 2 (Trans., VI, p. 642): "When a man builds a house he makes in it windows that are narrow on the outside and broad within, so that the light may enter from the outside and illumine the interior."

107. Cf. Kohl and Watzinger, *Antike Synagogen*, p. 35 and Pl. II.

108. See above, pp. 16f.

same time, the arrangement is more liberal than that known from the synagogues of Palestine and more liberal also than that of the earlier building at Dura itself.[109] Whether in admitting the women to the same room as the men the elders provided some means of physical separation beyond that of the assignment of special benches is not evident. What we learn about the means for the separation of sexes in Babylonia, presumably at weddings and when there was occasion to hear sermonic discourse, suggests that any such means were portable and makeshift.[110]

Of particular interest, finally, is the bearing of the evidence supplied by Dura's Synagogue upon the question of orientation in synagogue construction. The basilical structures investigated by Kohl and Watzinger revealed that in Palestine one of the short sides of the buildings; namely, that containing the three monumental doorways, normally faced Jerusalem.[111] From this was deduced the principle that synagogue orientation was toward Jerusalem. The principle is fundamentally sound, but requires clarification in the light of more recent discoveries. In the past decades several basilical synagogues of later date, the entrance walls of which face away from Jerusalem, have come to light in Palestine and Jordan.[112] These also may properly be said to be oriented upon Jerusalem, but in quite another fashion, for orientation is expressed in these instances by the placement not of the entrance façade, but of an apse attached at the opposite end of the building. To understand how both the earlier and the later basilical synagogues of Palestine can be said to be oriented upon Jerusalem it is necessary only to realize that the fundamental determinant in the whole procedure was the orientation of the wor-

shiper himself.[113] It is amply attested in rabbinical literature that the worshiper in prayer is to face Jerusalem, or more particularly the Holy of Holies of the Temple with its Ark of the Covenant.[114] In the basilical synagogues of the earlier type we must assume that the worshiper in prayer faced the entrance wall of the building. This must have proved awkward. When, therefore, it became possible to add apses to such basilical structures, the principle of orientation was so applied as to have the worshiper face the interior and the apse while at the same time facing Jerusalem. Henceforth the synagogues were erected in such a way that the entrance façade was turned away from Jerusalem, which explains why these façades were no longer so ornately set out. The fact that the change occurred in connection with the addition of an apse indicates the presence of one additional factor in the principle of orientation; namely, that in praying with his face turned toward Jerusalem, the worshiper faced also the Torah Shrine, for naturally the apse was added only to provide a monumental repository for the Scroll Chest. In the earlier non-apsidal basilicas of Galilee, we must therefore assume that the Scroll Chest, having no architectural repository, was portable, and having been brought in, must have been placed between the congregation and the entrance façade.[115]

At Dura, these observations teach us, the principle of congregational orientation was fundamentally the same as in Palestine, for the worshiper facing the Torah Shrine simultaneously

109. See below, p. 31.

110. The important passage in this connection is Kiddushin 81a (Trans., p. 417), where it is said that Abaye made a partition of jugs and Raba one of canes when men and women were gathered together, to avoid contact between them. It is Rashi who explains this as applying to occasions such as sermons or weddings.

111. Kohl and Watzinger, *Antike Synagogen*, p. 139.

112. E.g., the synagogue at Naʿaran and Beth Alpha (Sukenik, *Ancient Synagogue of Beth Alpha*, p. 51, Fig. 46, and Pl. XXVII), at Jerash (Kraeling, *Gerasa*, Pl. XXXVI), and at el-Hammeh (Sukenik, *Ancient Synagogue of el-Hammeh*, Pl. VII). At el-Hammeh the doors are not actually in the short wall that would normally afford entrance to the building.

113. So properly Krauss, *Synagogale Altertümer*, pp. 317–334.

114. See especially in the Mishnah, Berakoth IV, 5 (Danby, p. 5) the statement: "If he was riding on an ass he should dismount [to say the *Tefillah*]. If he cannot dismount he should turn his face [toward Jerusalem]; and if he cannot turn his face, he should direct his heart toward the Holy of Holies." See also the statement in the Talmudic tractate Berakoth 30a (Trans., pp. 182 f.): "If one is standing outside of Palestine he should turn mentally towards Eretz Israel.... If he stands in Eretz Israel he should turn mentally towards Jerusalem, etc." The statement refers to blind people and those who cannot tell the cardinal points of the compass, and applies literally to all the rest.

115. The materials identified by Kohl and Watzinger (*Antike Synagogen*, pp. 35–38) as the remains of a monumental repository for the Torah Shrine at Capernaum have more recently been assigned by Sukenik to the façade of the building (*Kedem*, II, Jerusalem, 1945, pp. 121 f.).

faced westward toward Jerusalem. In one particular, however, the structural arrangements exemplified at Dura were superior to those of the strictly contemporary buildings in Palestine; namely, that in facing the Torah Shrine and Jerusalem, the worshiper also faced the interior of the building, the line of orientation being marked by the aedicula housing the Scroll Chest. Whoever first conceived of preparing a structural repository for the portable Scroll Chest and of setting it against the inner wall of a building on a line that was simultaneously axial for the construction and proper for the worshiper at prayer, can in effect be said to have discovered what was for the ancient world, and in some measure is still today, the formal principle of synagogue construction. The importance of the Dura Synagogue as a building is not merely that it clarifies the nature of this discovery and shows us how early it was made, but also that it permits us to see the circumstances under which it was first applied. This the analysis of the earlier building will demonstrate.

IV. THE EARLIER BUILDING

The structure described in the preceding pages was not the first utilized by the Jewish community of Dura as its house of worship. At a time whose distance from the period of the later building we can only calculate from incidental evidence, one part of the site was occupied by an earlier structure.[116] This fact was already suggested by the difference between the level of House H and that of the Forecourt and the House of Assembly in the later building, a difference of approximately 0.60 m.[117] It was further documented when fragments of an earlier building, especially pieces of painted plaster and sections of columns, came to light in the walls and in the benches of the House of Assembly.[118] It was finally demonstrated when excavation was continued below bench and floor level to bedrock itself. Here, under an earth fill between 0.45 m. and 0.65 m. deep, there came to light the remains of what was in effect a modified private house. The nature of its modifications and the epigraphical material discovered among its ruins showed beyond doubt that it represented the Dura Synagogue in an earlier phase of its architectural history. It will be referred to here as the "earlier building" of the Synagogue.

The earlier building of the Dura Synagogue (Plans VII, 2–VIII) occupied a plot of land 21.50 m. long and 15.50 m. wide, identical to all intents and purposes with that occupied by the Forecourt and House of Assembly of the later structure. It lay in the western half of Block L7, and was accessible only from Wall Street, upon which its entrance door opened. Planned as a private dwelling, it was more modest in its proportions than even House H of the later complex. With all the changes it had

undergone in being adapted to Synagogue use, it still showed close affinities in plan to the adjacent dwelling, House B (Fig. 8), the two having been erected simultaneously as part of a single develop-

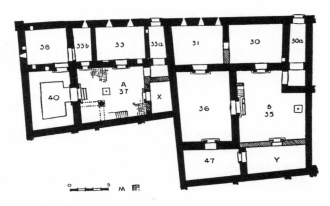

FIG. 8. L7, Probable Original Plan of Houses A and B

ment.[119] This is a fact of outstanding importance for the interpretation of its extant remains and for our knowledge of the way in which it was adapted to Synagogue usage.

From the extant remains it is clear that, like the other houses of the city and the neighboring House B, the earlier building of the Synagogue consisted of a series of chambers grouped about a central courtyard, the only possible approach to which lay in the northwest corner of the lot (Plan VIII, locus 15). When the later edifice was erected upon the premises, the north and west walls of its predecessor were removed down to their very foundations, perhaps because they were not deemed of sufficient strength to carry the superstructure. This has affected seriously our knowledge of the entryway, but sufficient traces of its southern wall remain (Plan VIII, loci 14 and 20) to show that it took the usual form of a passage, and was ca. 5.50 m.

---

116. On the circumstances under which the rabbis considered it legitimate or illegitimate to tear down one synagogue and build another in its place, see the statements in Baba Bathra 3b (Trans., pp. 9f.).

117. Cf. Plan VII, 1.

118. On the fragments see above, p. 14 n. 55 and p. 16 n. 57. The walls and benches were torn down to permit the removal of the paintings to Damascus and the reconstruction of the chamber at Damascus as a part of the National Museum of Syria.

119. This is revealed by the fact that the north side of the doorway giving upon House B formed an integral part of the south wall of the earlier Synagogue building.

long and *ca.* 1.75 m. wide.[120] At the east end of the passageway remains of a plastered sill came to light (Plan VIII, 19) that seems at one time to have marked the end of the passage and later to have been covered by a rising step. This suggests that the floor of the passage was raised at some point in its history from a level identical with that of the central courtyard to one appreciably higher, involving the interposition of a flight of steps. This is known to have happened in the other houses along Wall Street in Block L7 in consequence of the extensive rise in the level of the street.[121] Instead of being filled in to the new level, the floor of the raised passageway was probably supported on poles set into the walls across its width (Fig. 9), providing underneath it a cellar that could be used for storage purposes. That such a cellar ex-

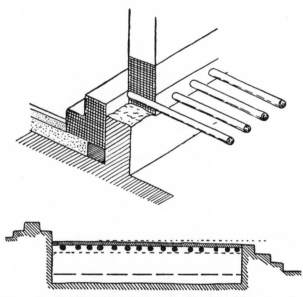

FIG. 9. Earlier Building, Passage 3, Details of Construction

120. The traces of the south wall consisted not only of its rubble corner made square by a frame of boards (Plan VIII, 20) and of elements of its foundations (Plan VIII, 14 being the most extensive of these), but also of an unplastered area, rectangular in shape, at the foot of the new intrusive west wall, directly above these foundations. The area remained unplastered because the lower courses of the south wall of the passageway were still standing at the time, preventing the masons from applying plaster to the new construction directly behind them.

121. Cf. *Rep. VI*, p. 226 (House B) and p. 274 (House A, the House of the Roman Scribes). In the latter instance because of the rising street level the western entrance was ultimately given up and a new entrance constructed, giving to the south (*ibid.*, Pls. VII and XI).

isted under the passageway is suggested by a break in the plastered bench near the northeast corner of room 2 (Plan VIII, 16), and by the continuance of the plastered floor under the bench west of this break to the edge of the wall behind it. This apparently represents the location of the opening through which persons could crawl into the cellar.[122] The matter would not be of sufficient importance to present in such detail did it not affect at certain crucial points our knowledge of the history of the Synagogue.[123]

The courtyard to which the passageway led was an open area 6.55 m. long and 6.05 m. wide. When the house was adapted to Synagogue use, it was paved with tiles laid over a bed of ashes and analogous in size with those found re-used in the House of Assembly of the later building.[124] To the west the paving came to an end against a plastered bench 0.40 m. wide that ran along the exterior of the east wall of room 2.[125] To the south, so a break

122. Because the floor continued to the edge of the wall, the part of the bench running from the break eastward was a later addition, made when the use of the cellar was given up. In House B the cellar was entered in analogous fashion, from the corresponding room (cf. *Rep. VI*, p. 225).

123. Cf. below, p. 328. In House B the raised entrance passage lay in a plane 1.73 m. above the floor of the courtyard, as we know from the holes made by its supporting poles in the south wall of the Synagogue (Fig. 9). In the original entrance to House A the difference was even greater, as much as 2 m., the earlier sill, itself 0.80 m. above courtyard level, having been raised 1.20 m. before the doorway was entirely closed up (*Rep. VI*, Pl. XI). It is a fair assumption that the rise of the street level in front of the earlier building of the Synagogue was analogous to that before the other houses. The two flights of steps on Plan VII, 1, from the street to the passage and from the passage to the courtyard, have been supplied on the basis of this assumption.

124. A section of the paving came to light at locus 21 on Plan VIII; remains of the ash bedding were found at several points (e.g., Plan VIII, 23). The tiles were *ca.* 0.22 m. square and *ca.* 0.04 m. thick.

125. The existence of the bench can be inferred from the plaster facing of the terminal tiles of the court along the line of Plan VIII, 24. This line in turn was identical with that of the squared eastern end of the passageway wall (Plan VIII, 20), showing that this is to be construed as a pilaster projecting from the east wall of room 2 and carrying the end of the portico's architrave (cf. Plan VIII). Near the edge of the bench *below* the level of the tile paving a shallow plaster basin lined with sherds came to light (Plan VIII, 22), which belonged to the simple domestic equipment of the house (water basin for fowl?). This shows that the tile paving was a secondary feature in the development of the house, probably part of its adaptation to Synagogue purposes.

in the ash deposit tells us, it was bounded by the line either of a wall or a sill (Plan VIII, 34). To the north and apparently also to the east it abutted against stylobates which intersected at right angles.[126] Upon the stylobates there had been mounted at points marked by perimetric and cross lines columns *ca.* 0.42 m. in lower diameter and originally probably five in number. The drums found re-used in the core of the benches belonging to the later building fitted the markings exactly (Pl. VI, 2).[127] *Ca.* 2 m. high, the columns to which these drums belonged provided the court with porticoes to the east and the north *ca.* 1.40 m. and 1.70 m. wide respectively. Into the floor of the peristyle at its northeast corner was set a shallow stone laver basin, a fragment of which came to light in the excavation (Pl. VI, 4; Fig. 10; and Plan VIII, 40).[128] From the plastered bedding underneath the basin a drainage channel led through the stylobate toward a cesspool (Plan VIII, 36).[129] From the awk-

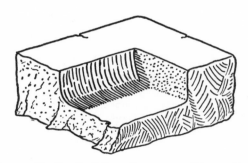

FIG. 10. Earlier Building, Fragment of Laver Basin

wardness of its position in relation to the stylobates of both Synagogue buildings and from the excellence of its construction, it can be inferred that it lay at first in an open courtyard like that of House B to the south, and that the porticoes are therefore, like the pavement, a part of the later embellishment of the house occasioned by its adaptation to Synagogue use.

Around the courtyard to the east, the south, and the west lay the several chambers of the building. The chambers to the east are shown by remains of the west wall (Plan VIII, 42) and by the party wall of House H (Plan VIII, 47) with its twin westward projections (Plan VIII, 48 and 49) to have been two in number.[130] The first of these, room 4, took the normal form of a diwan, with its doorway to the west and benches ranged about its walls.[131] In the center of the room a rectangular plaster block projected from the floor of the room.[132] It was not in the proper position to serve as a stand for the braziers used to heat such rooms in winter,[133] yet its top contained in a shallow depression marks of fire. It may have served as the stand for a lamp. Room 5 to the south is entirely unknown, but its dimensions can be inferred from what is known about room 4 and about the size of the house. It has been reconstructed on Plan VIII as the storeroom or bedroom usually associated with the diwan in the houses of Dura and entered only from the diwan. To the west of room 5 there must have existed originally at least one additional chamber. The only traces of it still extant are a section of

126. Plan VIII, 35 and 38. The stylobates were 0.525 m. wide and extended 0.265 m. above the pavement of the court.

127. Cf. above, p. 16 n. 67. The extension of the colonnade along the west side of the courtyard is indicated by the intersection of the stylobates and by the number of column drums found. These were sufficient for five columns, precisely the number required by the arrangement that is to be inferred from the remains found and the extension suggested (cf. Plan VIII).

128. The basin was only 0.08 m. deep and had a flat rim 0.06 m. wide. It was set between the intersecting stylobates (Plan VIII, 38) and the adjacent house walls, fragments of which (Plan VIII, 39) still held traces of the plaster bedding of the basin. The relation of these wall fragments to the end of the stylobate of the later Forecourt (Plan VIII, 37) shows that the north wall of the earlier building was still standing when the later stylobate was constructed and was only subsequently torn down and replaced (cf. above, p. 12).

129. The cesspool had a circular aperture 0.704 m. in diameter and a neck 0.40 m. long. Below the neck it bellied

out in the shape of a lemon, achieving a maximum diameter of 2.25 m., and ended with a sump 3.10 m. below the level of the courtyard.

130. The dimensions of room 4 can be determined accurately. It was 6.85 m. long and 4.15 m. wide. Room 5 was therefore 5.15 m. long, and if its west wall continued in the direction of the fragment Plan VIII, 42, as seems likely, about 3.95 m. wide.

131. Plan VIII, 43 represents one section of the doorsill 0.37 m. wide found still in place and marked with a scratch for the location of the jamb on a line 0.42 m. from the end of the wall fragment. Plan VIII, 44 represents the remains of the plaster benches *ca.* 0.49 m. wide and 0.22 m. high ranged against the east and west walls.

132. Plan VIII, 45. The block was 0.67 m. long and 0.62 m. wide and projected 0.27 m. from the floor, the level of which was indicated by the fragment still attached to the bench at locus 46 on Plan VIII.

133. Similar blocks supporting braziers usually stood just inside and to the left of the diwan doorway in the houses of Dura.

the foundation of its north wall, incorporated into the stylobate of the later Forecourt (Plan VIII, 41) and some indication of the point where the southern face of its west wall projected from the outer wall of the house (Plan VIII, 33). Reconstructed on Plan VIII as room 6, it is necessarily somewhat irregular in shape and opens directly upon the courtyard.[134]

The differences between the earlier building of the Synagogue and its neighbor and contemporary, House B, so far as we have described them, are recognizable as elementary modifications of the simple private house, because they occur elsewhere at Dura. The remaining differences, while not so readily intelligible on this score, are nonetheless fundamentally of the same general type.

To the west, south of the entrance passageway, a section of the lot that would normally have afforded space for two chambers was devoted to one large room, room 2 (Plan VIII), the Assembly Room of the earlier structure. Except at the south only occasional fragments of its walls remain, but these are sufficient to indicate its irregular yet generally rectangular shape, 10.65–10.85 m. on the long sides and 4.60–5.30 m. on the short sides.[135] Like its counterpart in the later building, room 2 was entered by two doorways, one set slightly to the north of the middle of its west wall, the other at the southern extremity of the same wall. Save for a single fragment of a gypsum door socket found lying loose in the debris, all the elements of the main door opening from the courtyard were missing. But its position was fixed by a narrow strip of rubble bedding originally set against the foun-

dations of the wall to support the projecting part of the sill (Plan VIII, 1), and its width by the ends of the benches flanking the doorway in the interior of the room. The width suggested by these remains is 1.50 m., and if proportions and procedures standard for the rest of the city were followed here, the doorway was probably *ca.* 3.02 m. high (Plan VIII). So far as the smaller south door is concerned, its position was indicated by the termination of the benches on either side of the wall into which it was let (Plan VIII, 7 and 27), by a step leading up to it from the floor of room 7 (Plan VIII, 32), and by a section of the bedding of the trim which at its southern end rose high enough above the floor of the room to preserve the doorpost hole (Plan VIII, 10). The plaster bedding at this point in both its horizontal and vertical elements preserved the imprint of graining and thereby showed that the door trim was of wood rather than of stone and plaster. The door itself cannot have been more than a meter wide and 2 m. high. The analogy of the later building suggests that it was associated with the women's attendance upon the services of worship.

Following standard proportions it can readily be estimated that room 2 was *ca.* 4.90 m. high. Of the upper elements of its walls, pierced as they doubtless were by windows set just below ceiling level to the east and the west, nothing is known; but of the ceiling, elements have survived in the debris. These are enough to show that, like all but the largest and most formal chambers of Dura's structures, it was roofed with mats of wattles supported by concealed beams and finished above and below with a layer of plaster.[136] Like its successor on the higher level, room 2 contained benches set against the base of its four walls and made in this instance of mud bricks covered with a heavy layer of plaster. To the west (Plan VIII, 12) they had been cut away at the back to provide enough room for the thicker west wall of the later building, and to the north the upper surface of the bench was preserved only at the extreme west (Plan VIII, 13),

---

134. Its proposed length varies from 4.25 m. to 4.30 m. and its width from 3.97 m. to 4.10 m.

135. The south wall (Plan VIII, 8) was preserved to its western corner at a height of 1.73 m. above floor level and used as a basis for the superstructure of the later building. This was necessary because it was a party wall with House B and because at the height mentioned it carried the beams supporting the raised floor of House B's entrance passageway. The west wall was destroyed entirely save for the turn of the angle that gave its width at locus 11. Of the east and north walls remains of the lowest foundation courses at loci 14 and 25 were all that remained. Since the removal of the west and north walls, obviously to supply material for the foundations of the later building, took the form of a trenching operation, the benches set against them were preserved, giving their course accurately.

136. Numerous fragments of the interior plaster coating found on the premises still showed on the one side the marks of the wattles and on the other remains of the design with which it was painted. The finds included not only elements of a painted design but also remains of gilt rosettes mounted in its panels. On the decorations of the chamber see below, pp. 34–38.

but elsewhere they remained quite undamaged (Pl. VI, 4). From the relation of floor and benches and from differences in the material used, we can infer that some sections of the benches were built later than others. Along the north wall, for instance, the bench originally stopped short at locus 16 on Plan VIII. It was subsequently extended, covering a section of the floor as originally laid.[137] The most northerly section of the east bench (Plan VIII, 17) was of a piece with the flooring of the chamber, but its adjacent element (Plan VIII, 18), with a footrest made largely of stone and plaster, was either an extension or, more probably, a repair. As in the case of the later building, some of the benches have footrests and others have none. Judging by their distribution, however, the distinction is not determined in this instance by the sex of the persons for whose use they were intended. Rather it would seem that the footrests serve to make up for inequalities in the height of the benches.[138]

The area surrounded by the benches was paved with a floor composed of plaster mixed with pebbles. This mixture had been spread thinly over a layer of red earth 0.03–0.05 m. thick, which in turn covered a fill of rammed earth 0.43 m. deep (Plan VIII, 5). In the middle of the room, directly west of the main doorway, the floor contained a patch 0.82 m. × 0.86 m. composed of a finer white plaster unmixed with pebbles (Plan VIII, 2). It covered a rectangular hole in the floor as originally laid and doubtless marks the position of some projecting object or contrivance which was ultimately removed from the room.[139]

In the area immediately behind the patch a number of significant details came to light. The first was the fact that at two points directly north and south of the patch, the footrest of the bench

along the west wall showed an unusual degree of wear (Plan VIII, 4). This seems to imply that the places in question were invariably occupied and that they flanked immediately some object or structure set between them. The second was the fact that in the area between these two worn spots the bench itself projected slightly, showed faint traces of paint, and was constructed of stone rather than mud brick (Plan VIII, 3).[140] This indicates that in the area in question the bench was developed more formally or was expected to bear something of a load. The third and last detail bearing upon the matter in hand was the discovery of fragments of stone colonnettes in the debris directly before the bench in this vicinity (Pl. VI, 4).[141] They may well have belonged to a superstructure set upon the bench, which, after the analogy of the later building, can scarcely have been anything other than an aedicula intended to house a Scroll Chest. At two points in the excavation pieces of plaster came to light inscribed with pictorial graffiti that may be said to reproduce in design the structure in question.[142] An aedicula is therefore incorporated in the restoration of the room on Plan VIII, but whether the aperture it enclosed extended into the wall itself, as in the case of the later building, can no longer be said.

Like the ceiling, the carefully plastered walls of the chamber were painted to at least part of their height. On the south wall, of which a section 1.73 m. high was preserved, the lower elements of the painted design were still clearly visible. Some of its upper elements are illustrated by fragments of plaster found in the debris, but the discussion of the material and of the design as a whole belongs to the next chapter.[143]

Beyond the south door of room 2 lay another unusual chamber set against the southern wall of

137. The section of the floor covered here originally gave access to the cellar under the entrance passageway (Plan VIII, area 3).

138. At the south and along the southern end of the west wall, where the benches were 0.34 m. high and 0.45 m. wide (Plan VIII, 12 and 6), and between the doors where they measured 0.25 m. × 0.39 m. (Plan VIII, 7), footrests were obviously quite unnecessary. Toward the north of the room, however, the floor level seems to have dropped a good deal, raising the benches to a height of approximately 0.45 m. Here the introduction of a footrest 0.14 m. high and 0.30 m. wide was natural.

139. Pl. V, 1 shows the hole in the floor excavated below floor level.

140. One of the stones, shown on Pl. VI, 4, was carved with a molding, being a re-used architectural fragment from some other structure.

141. One of the colonnettes was *ca.* 0.48 m. high and tapered in diameter from 0.15 m. at the base to 0.12 m. at the top of the shaft. It was cut in a single piece, with a capital consisting of an abacus 0.14 m. square and 0.08 m. high, and a crude echinus 0.035 m. high. They were made of gypsum and probably originally coated with plaster.

142. One *in situ* on the face of the bench along the south side of a room, the other on a fragment of loose plaster re-used in the foundations of the later building. Cf. Inscrs. nos. **71, 72,** below p. 320.

143. Cf. below, pp. 34 f.

the house (room 7, Plan VIII). Its limits were fixed to the west by the course of the wall of room 2, and to the east by the turn of the plaster that marked the line of the wall separating room 7 from room 6 farther to the east (Plan VIII, 33). To the north the remains of a rubble pier projecting from the east wall of room 2 (Plan VIII, 26) and the line where the ash bedding of the tiled courtyard ended (Plan VIII, 34) served the same purpose. The chamber was thus approximately 3.85–3.97 m. long and 3.75 m. wide. On its floor of pebbles mixed with plaster (Plan VIII, 29) the remains of a painted plaster archway came to light, one of the elements of which bore Aramaic graffiti.[144] The archway had a span of *ca.* 2.70 m. and must have extended from the pier at the northwest corner of the room (Plan VIII, 26) eastward toward a corresponding pier at the northeast corner (along the line indicated on Plan VIII, 28), creating an arched opening from the courtyard (Plan VII, 2). Inside, at least along its southern and western walls, and probably also against its eastern wall, the chamber was equipped with low benches, one of them even supplied with a footrest.[145] A low plaster step interposed between the two benches in the southwest corner of the room and leading to room 2 (Plan VIII, 32) showed signs of heavy usage. Standing elements of the south wall and plaster fragments found on the floor of the chamber indicated that wall and ceiling had been carefully decorated, and that room 7 belonged therefore with room 2 to the more formal part of the house.[146] If, after the analogy of the later building, the south door of room 2 was associated with the women's attendance upon the services, room 7, constituting the only means of access to this door, must have been at their disposal also. One fact will be evident in this connection; namely, that room 7 with its benches and its decorations was more than a mere passageway to room 2. We must assume, therefore,

that the earlier builders provided more lavishly for the women than those of the later period were able to do, or we may suggest that room 7 was itself the area from which the women participated in the worship conducted in room 2, or finally we may imagine that room 7 served other purposes besides those involving the women.

What the western and southwestern portions of the house were like before they were adapted to Synagogue usage by the arrangements that have been described, we can only conjecture. Since the house was built at one and the same time with its neighbor, House B, the safest conjecture is that they were at the outset much alike. This would mean that the area occupied by room 2 was originally divided between two chambers (like rooms 30 and 31 on Fig. 8) and that the area occupied by rooms 6 and 7 was at the outset contained within one chamber (like room 36 on Plan II), constituting the diwan of the house. That such was in fact the case can no longer be demonstrated. There are actually but three indications of earlier construction in the western and southwestern parts of the lot, marked A, B, and C respectively on Plan VIII, and of these only B associates itself readily with the suggested arrangement.[147] But whatever the arrangement of the rooms in the western and southern part of the house may originally have been, its reconstruction in that area is inherently probable. Witness to this is supplied by House B, whose entrance on Wall Street was at one time, like that of House A, on a level with its courtyard. Eventually, because of the rise of the street level, its doorsill was raised almost two meters, and a raised passageway, carried on poles, was run into the interior. The ends of these poles, it will be recalled, were bedded in the south wall of the Synagogue's earlier Assembly Chamber. For them to be installed there in this way it was necessary that either the south wall of the Assembly Chamber or the north wall of room 30a in House B be torn down and rebuilt; and since the entire history of House B is one of growing depreciation and spoliation, while the adjacent properties on either side

144. The pieces of the archway are shown laid out on the floor of room 2 in Pl. VI, 4. For the graffiti see Inscrs. nos. **20–22,** below, pp. 274 f.

145. Plan VIII, 27, 30, and 31. The bench to the west was 0.25 m. high and 0.40 m. wide, that to the south a centimeter higher. The footrest was only 0.06 m. high, but all of 0.36 m. wide. Benches and footrest were constructed of mud bricks covered with plaster. The south bench was plastered at the same time as the wall behind it and at the same time that the floor of the chamber was laid.

146. On the decorations of room 7 see below, pp. 35 f.

147. Like A it represents no more than a fragment of mud brick construction. C is a section of a rubble foundation. Its position is analogous to that of the wall against which the entrance passageway of House B (area 30a) comes to an end.

were continually being improved, the probability is that House B benefited by the adaptation of its northern neighbor to Synagogue purposes, rather than vice versa. Other elements of this adaptation, as we have already seen, were the raising of the entrance to the rebuilt house, the probable installation of the cellar under its entrance passageway, the removal of the terminal wall of the passageway, the introduction of the colonnaded porticoes, the installation of the laver basin, and the paving of the courtyard. That more of the earliest form of the structure was not preserved will be readily intelligible if the extent to which the earlier Synagogue building was pillaged to supply materials for the later be kept in mind.

THE HOUSE-SYNAGOGUE

What is known about the earlier building of the Dura Synagogue has been presented in such detail because only a full knowledge of this detail will demonstrate the validity of the reconstruction in plan and elevation, and because the building as reconstructed is of such great importance for our knowledge of the development of the synagogue generally, both as an institution and as a structure. Though the earlier building is apparently as much as seventy-five years older than the later, even a casual comparison of the two reveals certain distinct analogies between them.[148] In both cases the essential elements are a courtyard and an assembly room, the two elements following each other in regular succession from east to west. Moreover, the assembly room in both cases is a *Breithausbau*, its axis running parallel to the short side of the chamber; it has two doors asymmetrically placed and an aedicula set against its western wall opposite the main doorway. This means that we are dealing with the same type of synagogue building in both levels. Since the type is a simple adaptation of domestic architecture,[149] it is more primitive fundamentally than the type of the Galilee synagogues, in which a formal structure, the basilica, has been adapted to religious use.

While in the order and arrangement of their basic elements the earlier and the later buildings

of the Dura Synagogue are thus analogous, there are also differences between them. Apart from size and proportion, the most noticeable differences are in the nature of the provision made for the attendance of women, for the housing of transients, and for the residence of a synagogue official. As regards the provision for the women in the earlier building, it will be noted that they were apparently not admitted to the Assembly Room (room 2), but sat outside (in room 7) attending upon such parts of the worship services as they could hear through the door between the two chambers. This may reflect a more conservative attitude in the matter, determined perhaps by the persistence of Babylonian usage in the community at this time, or again it may be merely that the Assembly Room proper was not of sufficient size to accommodate both the men and the women.[150] The fact that the building was directly accessible from Wall Street implies that it was continuously inhabited, if only to guard the premises. Rooms 4, 5, and 6 provide properly for habitation, and of these rooms the first two supply the minimum of residential requirement for a *hazzan*, perhaps even for the elder of the community. This would leave only room 6 for the accommodation of the transients, who in this period would certainly have been fewer than in later years. The marked contrast between the residential facilities of the two buildings is a measure of the growth in the community's prosperity, but the range of the activities for which provision was made is apparently almost the same.

If the comparison of the earlier and the later building of the Dura Synagogue shows how much the two are alike and how the later continues in the tradition of the earlier, it shows also and still more importantly what is the essential nucleus from which the earlier developed, and in so doing provides an important insight into the growth of the synagogue as an institution. The archaeological evidence makes it entirely clear that the earlier building is nothing more or less than an adapted private dwelling. Most of the alterations made in the original structure are innocuous in themselves,

148. On the date of the earlier building and of its adaptation to synagogue use, see below, pp. 326 f.

149. See immediately below.

150. It can be argued that the period beginning with the Roman occupation of Dura (A.D. 165) gradually brought about a change in the attitudes of the local Jewish community, being the occasion of much closer contacts with, and an influx of new members from, the Dispersion of the Syrian area. See below, pp. 330, 335.

and add nothing alien to the basic pattern. That the courtyard should have been paved and set out with porticoes merely accommodates the area to more extensive and more formal usage, having its counterpart in other private and semi-private establishments in the city.[151] That two chambers at the west end of the premises should have been thrown together to make one large room, room 2, is not in itself strange, especially since the room preserved even in its new form the essential characteristics of the diwan, the standard central feature of the social and architectural organization of all private houses in the city.[152] What really made the difference was in effect the introduction of the aedicula and its emplacement against the middle of the west wall of room 2. While this again underlines the importance of the aedicula properly placed as the fundamental element in the development of a synagogue architecture, its significance in the present context is to show how little it actually took to transform a private house into a synagogue. Throughout its history, then, we are actually confronted at Dura with a house-synagogue that grows and develops, but in the course of its development from the earlier to the later building never belies entirely its roots and origin.[153] This corroborates what has been said above about the improbability of a direct relation between the later building and the pagan shrines of Dura, and at the same time indicates that at Dura in the earlier of the two buildings we have before us the most primitive type of synagogue structure that we can ever expect to find. It represents the private house, the natural locus for the development of a congregational group, adapted by a minimum of changes to meet the needs of the group in worship. Naturally, Jewish homes that were also meeting places of synagogue groups existed at a much earlier time than the latter half of the second century, and their distribution was by no means limited to the Babylonian area. Yet this does not change the verdict to which the archaeological evidence necessarily leads, it being evident that a private house in which no formal provision had been made for the housing of the Scrolls would not be identifiable certainly as a synagogue. At Dura we happen to have a structure in which the union of the formal principle and domestic setting is so lucidly presented that what we see there is the synagogue building, in type at least, at the very point of its creation.[154]

What has been said above is not meant to imply that the synagogue as a structure originated in the middle of the second century, but only that from the second century there has been preserved for us a synagogue building in which the most primitive type is still clearly reflected. The fact that this building came to light in an area under Babylonian influence, and that in Palestine, in the magnificent synagogues then being erected, the formal principle was not yet being employed suggests one further inference. It is this: that Babylonia rather than Palestine should be regarded as the pioneer in, and the most significant contributor to, the development of the synagogue as a formal structure.[155]

---

151. Cf. e.g., the House of the Large Atrium, *Rep. IV*, Pl. IV, and the Christian Building, *Rep. V*, Pl. XXXIX.

152. Cf. above, p. 7 n. 9.

153. The formal principle here established within the confines of the house-synagogue; namely, the introduction and the axial emplacement of the monumental repository for the Torah Shrine, was of course transferable to other types of structures and did, as we have seen, go over into the basilical synagogue when the latter developed its apse.

154. For a preliminary statement see C. H. Kraeling, *Bulletin of the American Schools of Oriental Research*, LIV (April, 1934), pp. 18–20. The Christian Chapel of Dura, which is also an element of a private house, shows the Christian community of Dura following the same pattern in its early efforts to create a sanctuary appropriate to its cultus. For the Chapel see *Rep. V*, Pls. XXXIX–LI. In Christianity the development leading from these earlier efforts to the fullgrown Christian church is not rectilinear as in Judaism.

155. On the moot question of the Babylonian and the Palestinian origin of the synagogue as an institution, a question which is here seen in a new light, see G. F. Moore, *Judaism in the First Centuries of the Christian Era. The Age of the Tannaim*, I (1927), pp. 284–289; W. Bousset and H. Gressmann, *Die Religion des Judentums im späthellenistischen Zeitalter*, 3rd ed. (1926), pp. 171 f.; and Schürer, *Geschichte des jüdischen Volkes*, II, pp. 499–506.

DECORATIONS

When the city's defenders buried the Dura Synagogue complex in the depths of their embankment, they unknowingly preserved for a distant future far more than its walls, however important these may be in themselves. With the walls, they covered up and protected from the ravages of the siege and from the destructive forces of sunshine and rain large portions of the painted decorations that adorned them. By far the most important part of these decorations are the scenes depicting episodes of Biblical story that were portrayed upon the walls of the House of Assembly in the later of the two Synagogue buildings. By these scenes the reputation of the Dura Synagogue was first established, and upon them it will in large measure continue to rest. Yet in themselves they by no means exhaust the contribution that Dura has made to our knowledge of the history of synagogue decoration. In part this is because the decoration of the later House of Assembly developed in two stages, and in part it is because enough remains of the earlier building erected on the same site to provide a fair estimate of its adornment also. As in the sphere of synagogue architecture, so in that of synagogue decoration, we are therefore in a position to follow a process of development at Dura which adds not a little to the importance of the material preserved. In discussing the architecture we had of necessity to proceed from a description of the later to a description of the earlier remains. Here the process can be reversed and the decorations of the earlier building can be treated first and thus find their proper place in the sequence of development.

I. THE DECORATIONS OF THE EARLIER BUILDING

A. The Elements

How the earlier building was decorated is known from sections of its wall left standing, from elements of the superstructure scattered about in the debris at floor level, and from pieces of its plaster re-used as binder in the walls of the later structure. The evidence indicates that only two of the rooms were ornamented; namely, the Assembly Room and the one beside it, which was probably reserved for the women (rooms 2 and 7 on Plan VIII), and that the decorations included both walls and ceilings.

For purposes of decoration the walls of room 2 were divided horizontally into three zones (Pl. XLIX). The lowest of these was developed in imitation of an unbroken marble plinth 0.87 m. high, whose basic color was probably originally yellow, and whose diagonal veins in yellow ochre and green were still clearly visible when the surface was first exposed. The highest zone was apparently left blank, as quantities of plain white plaster fragments found on the floor seem to testify, while the second zone just above the plinth was developed as an ornamental dado well over a meter high. Of the dado enough was still preserved *in situ* and in the form of scattered plaster fragments to give a picture of its organization.

Following the fashions of the time and the locality, the dado was developed as a painted imitation of marble incrustation work. It was bordered at the bottom and presumably also at the top with a wide reddish-purple band, suggestive of porphyry, which in turn was set off at the lower edge by narrow yellow and black stripes. The field between the borders was laid out in a series of rectangular panels arranged in orthostate fashion, each appropriately framed. Certain terminal panels (perhaps those adjacent to the doorways) extended the full height of the field from border to border, but the rest were contained within a framework separating them from the borders and from each other, and thus slightly reducing their height. The inner framework was rendered in imitation of moldings as yellow bands subdivided by black lines into narrow strips whose color was varied by yellow ochre overlay. At the bottom (and presumably also at the top) of the framework the strips are two in number; between panels and at the end of the field they are three. The panels enclosed by this elaborate design the artist developed alternately in solid and composite fashion. Reddish purple turned the solid panels into representations of porphyry slabs set in a separate light yellow frame. The remaining panels were alternately divided by black diagonals or inscribed with diamonds inset with discs at their centers. For the panels divided diagonally the lighter colors were used, opposing pairs of triangles being light yellow and possibly yellow ochre — in imitation, perhaps, of Numidian marble. The panels inscribed with diamonds provided an opportunity for the combination of darker and lighter shades. The diamonds themselves continued the emphasis upon the richer porphyry, but the discs at their centers were either green or (probably) yellow, depending upon the colors used in the four right-angle triangles that filled the remainder of the rectangle. In these right-angle triangles two different color schemes were employed, both involving the use of meandering lines to show quarter-sawn veining. One scheme superimposes brown veins upon a yellow background, the other gray veins upon a green background.

The builder's desire to give room 2 a formal development by the use of color, as in the dado just described, comes to clearest expression in the decoration of the ceiling (Pl. L). Here, it will be recalled, the decorators had only a flat plastered surface with which to work. This surface they transformed into an imitation of a coffered ceiling by a design painted in colors of the brightest hues, particularly the reds and blues that are absent from the dado. The design they developed consisted of rows of panels set upon a gridiron of beams intersecting at right angles and at equal intervals. At their intersections the beams enclosed discs, and therefore cut arcs upon the panels ranged between them. Plaster rosettes were mount-

ed in the panels, and perhaps also on the discs at the intersections of the beams.[1] The framework of the design as a whole the decorators rendered in white, outlining it in black and breaking the white surface with a narrow red stripe. For the discs introduced at the intersections of the beams they chose red, while for the sunken panels they used a brilliant blue. The moldings framing the individual panels, also outlined in black, were painted in two different colors, red being applied to two of the straight sides and their adjacent segmental surfaces, and pink to the others. This imitated the effect of shadows thrown by a strong sidelight and created the illusion of depth in the design. The rosettes, done in gold, added a measure of brilliance to the decorations. Black and red bands, separated by a white line and running around the entire room, framed the design as a whole.

In room 7, from which the south door of the Assembly Chamber was approached, the decorations were of a more modest and a somewhat different character. They are less fully known, for here the fragments of plaster found in the debris were less numerous and less revealing. So far as the walls are concerned, only two facts can still be established. The first is that the south wall (Plan VIII, locus 9) was divided horizontally into two unequal sections by a red band 1.05 m. from the floor of the room. The second is that, while the lower section forming a wainscot remained white and unpainted, the upper section was given an over-all coat of yellow upon which foliage, fruit, and flowers were represented in green, red, and black. The several elements of this floral design were apparently not scattered about in random fashion, but were combined in a continuous design. The ceiling of room 7 (Pl. L) was divided by red bands into a large number of small square fields outlined in black on two sides to give depth to the design. Each field contained a separate fruit or floral motif painted in bright colors upon a white background. Pomegranates and citrus fruits have been identified upon remains of the ceiling, each with its appropriate foliage; four-petaled roses

1. Fragments of these plaster rosettes were found in goodly quantity in the earth fill covering the floor. They were built about a small wooden peg by which the rosettes were attached to a similar peg let into the center of the panel.

seem also to have been used.[2] The entire design was framed by a border of red, blue, and black stripes developed upon a cove molding introduced between the walls and the ceiling. From the combination of the floral and fruit motifs in the fields and of the latticework of the bands enclosing them, it is clear that the fundamental conception underlying the design as a whole is that of a garden trellis.

The decorations of the earlier building, as we have described them, contrast sharply with those of the later edifice. They are much simpler and contain no representations of animate beings.[3] Whether this reflects merely the limited financial and artistic resources of the local Jewish community in its earlier days, or whether it reflects also a point of view hostile to the use of such representations, is unknown. What is evident is that the decorations do not rise above the conventional, and restrict themselves to designs that had become commonplace by the second century of our era. In itself, this does not make them any the less significant for our knowledge of the history of decorative wall painting.

B. The Decorative Traditions

So far as the walls of the two chambers are concerned, they exhibit two different decorative traditions, both of them quite well known. Those of room 7, though imperfectly preserved, seem to represent a late form of what Rostovtzeff has called the "floral style" of wall decoration.[4] Originating perhaps in the tents of nomadic tribes hung with carpets that were woven with flower designs, the floral style appears in the eastern part of the Mediterranean in Hellenistic times, particularly in tombs, where it is applied to ceilings and to the upper zones of wall surfaces, but also on mosaic pavements and painted ceramic ware. It depicts against a monochrome background a floral ornament, usually in the form of scattered sprigs, leaves, and flowers. Occasionally this pattern is varied as time goes on by the introduction of garlands, of the figures of animals, and of scenes representing the hunt, armed combat, and the personified forces of nature, as in the tombs of Marissa, of Kertch, and of Jel el-'Amad.[5] In room 7 the position of the floral design on the wall, more particularly its location above a high, plain wainscot, still reflects clearly the tradition of its usage developed in the Hellenistic period. But the design itself, remote as its appearance at Dura is from the centers of the naturalistic trend in later Hellenistic and Roman art, has been stylized into a coherent over-all pattern.[6]

In room 2, whose decorations are more fully known, we have an example of another style of decorative painting that developed in the Hellenistic period and came to flower in the early centuries of our era — the incrustation style.[7] This is apparently associated in its origin or development with the earlier "structural style," in which the several architectural elements of simple stone buildings were imitated in design by dividing wall surfaces into zones, developing each zone as a tier of large blocks, and painting each tier in a different color.[8] In Hellenistic tombs of Alexandria be-

2. R. Du Mesnil du Buisson, "Les Deux synagogues," p. 78. The designs were analogous to those on the ceiling tiles of the later building, as described below, pp. 45 f.

3. What is known about the nature of these decorations makes it highly improbable that the missing sections contained figures of animals or of human beings.

4. Cf. his article, *Journal of Hellenic Studies*, XXXIX (1919), pp. 144–163, esp. pp. 151 f.; and his fundamental works, *Ancient Decorative Painting in South Russia* (in Russian) (1913–14), and *Correspondence of the Imperial Russian Archaeological Commission* (in Russian), IX, 3–4 (1897), see esp. pp. 294 and 298.

5. For Marissa, see J. P. Peters and H. Thiersch, *Painted Tombs in the Necropolis of Marissa* (1905), Frontispiece and Pls. VI–XV; for Kertch see in addition to the works of Rostovtzeff listed in the previous note, also W. Stassoff, *Compte rendu de la commission impériale*

archéologique pour l'année 1872 (1875), esp. Pls. IV–XIII; for Jel al-'Amad see D. le Lasseur, *Syria*, III (1922), pp. 1–26, especially Pls. II–III. On the later development of the floral style in general, see M. Swindler, *Ancient Painting* (1929), esp. p. 352.

6. Examples of the more naturalistic treatment and of the over-all pattern are found side by side in western monuments of the fourth century; for instance, in the ring vaults of Santa Costanza. Cf. *ibid.*, Figs. 616–617.

7. On incrustation in general see O. Deubner, *RE*, Supplementband VII (1940), cols. 285–293, *s.v.* "Inkrustation."

8. On the incrustation style and its origin, see the works of Rostovtzeff listed above, and for a full discussion of the terminology and the development, A. Adriani, *Municipalité d'Alexandrie: Annuaire du musée gréco-romain (1933–34, 1934–35)* (1936), pp. 113–132.

longing to the second century before our era, we already find imitations of marble appearing in decorations of the structural style, and shortly thereafter these imitations also come to light in the three lowest zones of the decorations of private houses at Delos.[9] In the Roman period the imitation of stonework, and particularly of marble, in painted wall decoration reaches a stage to which the term "incrustation style" is truly applicable, for the nature of the designs portrayed now shows beyond the shadow of a doubt that wall sheathing, not wall construction, is being represented. Monuments of the so-called First Pompeian Style, dependent as it was upon an older architectural style of the West and upon the later phases of the structural style of the East, contain so many examples of such incrustation work that there is no need to list any of them separately. But painted incrustation work was not limited in its later usage to the context of the First Pompeian Style; it existed also apart from that context as a part of the decorative *koine* of Roman imperial art, both in combination with the floral style — as at Kertch in the tomb on the property of the notary Feldstein — and in combination with pictorial decorations — as at Rome in the villa under San Sebastiano, or at Palmyra in the Tomb of the Three Brothers.[10]

At Dura itself late survivals of the incrustation style are by no means found only in the earlier building of the Synagogue. The same type of decoration appears also in room 33 of House E4, in room 1 of the structure in Block F3, and in rooms 12, 18, 19, and 20 of the Palace of the Dux.[11] In the first of these instances the chamber

in question was decorated with an incrustation dado when transformed into a bath by members of the Roman garrison, while in the second instance the chamber was from the outset part of a large bathing establishment. To the evidence supplied by these buildings must be added that provided by religious edifices at Dura, for instance by the Temple of the Gaddé and the Christian Chapel.[12] Taking into account what is known about the distribution of incrustation work among temples, baths, tombs, and private houses, it is clear that we are dealing with a kind of embellishment applicable in Roman times to any formal structure, or to such parts of private establishments as might seem to call for more or less formal treatment. To a structure of the type represented by the earlier building of the Dura Synagogue, it is entirely appropriate. As regards the specific design used in this building, three observations are in order. The first is that the position of the incrustation dado in the second zone of the wall's decoration is in line with the tradition followed elsewhere: in Egypt (Sidi Gaber), in south Russia (Vassiurin), and in Greece (Delos). The second is that the panels into which the band is divided are set upright, with their short sides parallel with the floor, as in so many of the examples from the First Pompeian Style, recalling their relation to the orthostates of ancient buildings and to the structural style. The third and most important is the fact that the design of diamonds containing discs and inscribed in rectangles, familiar as it is from many parts of the ancient world, actually appears again in combination with panels divided diagonally in room 33 of House E4 at Dura.[13] This is important in showing how thoroughly conventional the design was. So far as the ceilings of rooms 2 and 7 are concerned, they also represent two different decorative traditions, each harmonizing with the system of wall decoration with which it is used. Room 7, whose walls reflect the floral style, continues on the ceiling with floral motifs; but instead of being scattered about at random as elsewhere — for instance at

9. For imitations of marble in the tombs of Sidi Gaber and Mustapha Pasha, *ibid.*, p. 123, Fig. 55, 6; p. 131, Fig. 56; p. 117, Fig. 50. On the Anfoushy tomb see E. Breccia, *Alexandrea ad Aegyptum* (*Guide de la ville ancienne et moderne*, 1914), esp. p. 119, Fig. 31. On Delos see M. Bulard, *Peintures murales et mosaïques de Délos*, (*Monuments Piot*, XIV, 1908), esp. pp. 127–132 and Figs. 46–48.

10. For the tomb at Kertch see Rostovtzeff, *Ancient Decorative Painting*, e.g., Pl. LXXIV. For the Roman villa see F. Wirth, *Römische Wandmalerei vom Untergang Pompejis bis ans Ende des dritten Jahrhunderts* (1934), Pls. 19–20. For the Palmyrene tomb see B. V. Farmakovski, *Proceedings of the Russian Archaeological Institute, Constantinople*, VIII (1903), pp. 172–198, esp. Pls. XXIV–XXV (in Russian).

11. Cf. *Rep. VI*, pp. 25f. and Pl. XLI, 2; p. 51. For the Palace of the Dux see *Rep. IX, 3*, pp. 22–25; cf. p. 94,

where it is erroneously stated that flat painted ceilings are not known elsewhere at Dura, and where the tiles of the later Synagogue are attributed to the early building.

12. For the Temple of the Gaddé see *Rep. VII–VIII*, p. 253, and for the Christian Chapel see *Rep. V*, esp. Pl. XLVIII.

13. See *Rep. VI*, Pl. XLI, 2.

Kertch and in the tomb at Jel el-'Amad — the motifs are contained within a structural frame, that of the trellis. The trellis itself is by no means as common as other forms of ceiling decoration, but it is not entirely unknown.[14] Whatever be true about the relative frequency of its use as a design on painted ceilings, the object itself was a common feature of the ancient garden and of landscape painting, from either of which it could have passed over into decorative design directly without the help of Egyptian funerary usage.[15] Indeed the presence of fruits in the squares of the lattice of the Dura ceiling suggests that in this instance it probably did.

The same propriety of relationship that exists between the wall and the ceiling decorations of room 7 is to be found also in room 2. Here, where the dado is more formal, a descendant ultimately of the structural style of decorative art, the ceiling design is correspondingly structural, calling to mind the wood and stone coffering that had for many centuries graced the ceilings of Greek temples, and had in Hellenistic and Roman times been adapted also to use in other types of public buildings and in the private homes of the wealthy.[16] Such wood and stone construction was eventually imitated on floors in mosaics and on ceilings in stucco and in painting as here.[17] In the palaces, villas, and tombs of the West, the search for variety of form and the license given by the use of stucco broke up the regularity of the patterns with which coffering began, leading over in this way to the fanciful linear compositions familiar from the

paintings of the catacombs. In the East, so far as the evidence now available permits us to judge, regularity of pattern tended to preserve itself more effectively, whether because of the impression created by the stone coffering of the great temples erected here in Roman times, or because local forms of ceiling construction encouraged decorators to look elsewhere than to structural form for the variation of their product.[18] Hence in the earlier building of the Dura Synagogue we find a painted imitation of a coffered ceiling still adhering faithfully to regularity of architectural design in a period in which western ceiling decoration had already become largely fanciful. The particular design used in the Synagogue is also found at Dura in the Palace of the Dux[19] and reappears at Rome in the catacomb of the Villa Torlonia, which happens also to be associated with a Jewish community, though this is, of course, of no significance for the appearance of the parallel.[20]

The decorations of the Dura Synagogue's earlier building are therefore entirely conventional and traditional. Certainly there is nothing in these decorations that could be called specifically Jewish, or that would suggest they were eventually to be followed by the pictorial compositions that covered the walls of the later structure. All they reveal is that by their use the Jewish community of Dura sought to adorn certain rooms of its Synagogue building in a manner becoming to the significance of their religious usage, and that in seeking to accomplish this purpose they chose their designs tastefully and well from the limited repertoire of the local artists.

14. Cf. the example from Anfoushy reproduced in Rostovtzeff, *Ancient Decorative Painting*, p. 63, Fig. 12. For earlier examples from Egypt see M. Meurer, *Vergleichende Formenlehre des Ornamentes* (1909), pp. 208, 330–332.

15. On the trellis in gardens, see now P. Grimal, *Les Jardins romains* (*Bibliothèque des écoles françaises d'Athènes et de Rome*, 155, 1943), esp. p. 276. Examples of trellises in landscape paintings are numerous; for example, in the Villa of Fannius Sinister at Boscoreale (now in the Metropolitan Museum at New York) and in the Casa dei Vettii at Pompeii.

16. On the coffered ceiling in general, see Ebert in *RE*, XXVII (1924), cols. 369–375, *s.v.* "lacunar."

17. For a reproduction of a coffered ceiling in a floor mosaic, see that at Teramo, F. Winter and E. Pernice, *Die hellenistische Kunst in Pompeji*, VI (1938), Pl. 6, 1; coffered ceilings in stucco are common and will be found alongside of painted reproductions of coffering in Wirth, *Römische Wandmalerei*, Pls. 8, 16, 28, etc.; for the painted imitation from the Villa of Hadrian see *ibid.*, p. 70, Fig. 31.

18. The coffered ceilings of the great Roman temples of the Near East are nowhere better illustrated than at Palmyra and Baalbek. Cf. R. Wood, *Palmyra* (1753), esp. Pls. VIII, X, XIII, XXXVII, XLI, XLII, LV; Wiegand, *Palmyra*, Pls. 30, 44, 76; *idem, Baalbek*, I, (1921), Pls. 61, 133–134. In the lands at the eastern end of the Mediterranean vaults and the use of stucco for outlining ceiling designs seem to have been rare compared with the West. Flat ceilings predominated and in larger chambers required the use of beams which could not be concealed, thereby making structural reticulation of ceilings an accepted feature of decorative ceiling design. Cf. the ceiling of the later Synagogue building described below and its analogies elsewhere at Dura.

19. *Rep. IX, 3*, Pl. VIII, 1.

20. Cf. H. W. Beyer and H. Lietzmann, *Die jüdische Katakombe der Villa Torlonia in Rom* (1930), Pl. 9. The analogy was pointed out by Du Mesnil du Buisson in "Les Deux synagogues," p. 81 and Fig. 6.

II. THE DECORATIONS OF THE LATER BUILDING

While the decorations of the earlier building have painstakingly to be reconstructed from a few scattered remains, those of the later complex are directly accessible and comparatively well preserved. House H at the eastern end of the complex has, of course, disappeared almost entirely, and with it any decorations of which it may once have boasted. Of the Forecourt only this is known, that the echini of the Doric capitals belonging to the columns of its peristyle (and perhaps also, after the analogy of the House of Assembly, the beams supporting the roof of the peristyle) were once painted red. But the chances that much has been lost here are very meager. In all probability it was the House of Assembly at the western end of the complex that was most lavishly decorated, and it is precisely this room of which the protecting embankment has preserved intact the most considerable remains.

As those who gathered there for worship saw it in its best days just before the Sassanian danger became acute, the House of Assembly was a veritable treasure-chamber of mural decoration. Practically the entire interior from the benches upward was at that time covered with pictorial compositions and ornamental designs. This was in keeping with the tradition current at Dura for the embellishment of sanctuaries and of the most important rooms of public and private buildings.[21] But since the Synagogue's House of Assembly was actually a meeting place for a large community of worshipers and not merely either the naos of a temple or the audience room of an individual, its size and the extent of its decorations exceeded that of any comparable structure in the entire city. The

21. For the painted sanctuaries of Dura, see especially Cumont, *Fouilles*, pp. 41–164, Pls. XXXI–LX (Temple of Bel); *Rep. V*, pp. 102 f. (Temple of Aphlad), pp. 254–283 (Christian Chapel); *Rep. VII–VIII*, pp. 104–116 (Mithraeum), pp. 158–163 (Temple of Adonis), pp. 196–210 (Temple of Zeus Theos), pp. 268–274 (Temple of the Gaddé). For decorations in private houses see especially House B in Block D5 (House of the Large Atrium), *Rep. IV*, p. 31, Pls. VI–VII; House F in Block C7, *Rep. IV*, pp. 182–199, Pls. XVII–XVIII; and House A in Block L7 (House of the Scribes) *Rep. VI*, pp. 275–299, Pls. XLIII–XLV.

siege of Dura by the Sassanians brought about the loss of almost half of its paintings; but even with what remains the room is highly impressive, as those will testify who have seen it at Damascus in Syria, where it has been reconstructed to form the eastern wing of the National Museum (Pls. XVIII–XXV). For, in spite of all that has been lost, the Dura Synagogue's House of Assembly is actually the largest and most elaborate monument of decorative wall painting of the entire Roman Near East.

Excavation has shown that in the final stage of their development the decorations of the Synagogue's House of Assembly covered all three of the main structural elements of the room: its ceiling, its walls, and the Torah Shrine set against the west wall. The decorations of the ceiling consisted mainly of the designs applied to the lower faces of the tiles that carried the roof. Those of the Torah Shrine included a pictorial composition on its arch and the imitation of marble incrustation work on its base, its columns, and the niche it enclosed. Those of the walls were both the most extensive and the most elaborate, being arranged in five zones (cf. Plans IX–XII). The decorations of the uppermost zone are lost, but must originally have been entirely formal, presenting in all probability a painted architrave that gave the fiction of architectural support to the beams and joists of the ceiling, and was itself supported by the painted pilasters that were represented in the corners of the room. The second, third, and fourth zones, counting from the top, were developed as registers containing panels of varying length in which were portrayed the all-important scenes and figures of Biblical story. To them the designations Registers A, B, and C are here applied, beginning at the top. On the west wall in Registers A and B directly above the Torah Shrine, the artist arranged his panels in symmetrical fashion, in each instance framing a wide center panel with two narrow side panels, the six panels together constituting what can properly be called the Central Group. As for the fifth zone, which brought the decorations down into immediate proximity to the benches, this was developed as an elaborate dado imitating marble incrustation work of the finest type.

Even the first complete inspection of the decorations gave reason to suspect that they had not all been executed at one and the same time. In the area of the Center Panels in particular, the presence of several superimposed layers of paint, each imperfectly preserved, provided evidence of a succession of efforts. At first it seemed that here, as in one scene on the north wall, only certain minor changes in a specific composition were involved.[22] A careful analysis of the construction of the edifice, an examination of the entire painted surface, and the study of the style of the paintings themselves has made it clear, however, that the changes in the area of the Center Panels were incidental to a change in the plan for the decoration of the entire room, and that fundamentally two stages in the development of the plan have to be distinguished. In its first stage the plan was comparatively simple, and contained no provision for the register divisions and the narrative compositions that are the outstanding·feature of its later development. Actually it was a combination of four elements that fitted well together and would have left the greater part of the wall space bare but suitably framed. The four elements were:

1. The ceiling decorations.
2. The decorations of the Torah Shrine.
3. A design in the middle of the west wall above the Torah Shrine, reaching almost to the top of the space later occupied by Register A.
4. A high ornamental dado just above the level of the benches, and (probably) pilasters in the corners of the room and a painted architrave directly under the ceiling.

Of these elements, the first was executed in the course of the construction of the building, and the second and third before the room was put into service, as the minimum appropriate to its dignity.[23] The fourth was never rendered as originally projected, and is known to us only from the preparations made for its rendering and by inference from the adapted form in which its several parts were later executed as elements of the second stage in the decorative process.[24]

Eventually a second, more ambitious, plan for the decoration of the walls was developed, making room particularly for the three registers of narrative compositions. In this second plan the fourth element of the original plan was incorporated, albeit with some modification, and actually executed. At first the attempt was made to incorporate also the third element of the earlier plan by making certain slight additions; but in this instance the combination proved unsatisfactory, and the area involved was recomposed and repainted, the new composition preserving only those features that had recently been added to the earlier design. Thus the entire body of wall decoration was unified in terms of the principle of zonal organization, with the emphasis upon the use of the decorations for narrative purposes, and with a corresponding subordination of purely ornamental elements.

Before they were finally engulfed in the embankment, the paintings that were accessible were subject also to defacement and even abuse. Testimony to this fact is contained in the dipinti and graffiti scattered about on the lower portions of the wall surfaces and in the efforts that were made to gouge out the eyes of the figures represented in the narrative compositions. In the last part of this report it will be possible to use what is known about the development of the decorations and their abuse as a source for the history of the Jewish community at Dura and of the building. Here attention must be focused upon the description of the decorations themselves, beginning with those that belong to the first stage in the decorative process.

22. Cf. *Rep. VI*, pp. 367–371.
23. The evidence for these statements is given in connection with the description of the elements themselves.

24. The evidence for the projected dado is the scratch lines that defined its upper and lower borders and that are still to be seen running through the field of Register C. Cf. below, pp. 65 f. In the Preliminary Report (*Rep. VI*, p. 329) the lines were incorrectly interpreted as suggesting a plan for four registers of pictorial compositions.

A. Elements of the First Stage in the Decoration of the House of Assembly

I. THE CEILING (PL. VII)

The construction of the ceiling of the House of Assembly, with its baked clay tiles, each *ca.* 0.42 m. square and 0.045 m. thick, arranged in rows upon joists that were borne in turn by heavy beams, has been described above.[25] From the traces of red paint found in the curved masses of gypsum mortar still adhering to the edges of certain of the tiles where they had been bedded upon their supports, it is evident that at least the joists (and therefore probably also the beams) were painted before the tiles were mounted upon them. The tiles themselves were also decorated before being put in place. This follows from the fact that in certain instances the designs were covered by elements of the mortar bedding that once held them in place, as well as from the designs themselves, which were drawn with a fluidity of line hard to develop in working from a scaffold.

The tiles that once belonged to the ceiling of the House of Assembly were found on top of the deposit of earth forming the second phase in the development of the embankment. Altogether parts of no less than 234 came to light, many of them fragmentary and some with their painted surfaces less well preserved than others.[26] The number found constitutes slightly more than one half that originally used, for in the restoration of the chamber in the Damascus Museum a total of 450 was required.[27] Though much has thus been lost, it is probable that the tiles preserved give a good cross-section of the decorative materials used in the embellishment of the ceiling, for the total number of recurrent designs (eighteen) multiplied by the largest number of tiles with the same type of design (twenty-four) yields a figure approximately that of the total number of tiles required to roof the chamber.

Broadly speaking the tiles fall into two unequal groups; namely, those with regularly recurrent pictorial designs, and those with inscriptions or with apotropaic devices. Among the recurrent designs six different classes can be distinguished; namely, personifications, astrological symbols, animals, flowers, fruit, and grain. The inscriptions are six in number and the apotropaic devices two. The arrangement is not certain. The reconstruction of the ceiling in Damascus is based on the plausible assumption that the recurrent designs were spaced at regular intervals, and that the inscribed tiles were given prominence in the middle of the room. It seems likely, however, that the apotropaic devices located near the center in the reconstruction were assigned to places near the doorways.[28]

a. Personifications

(1) Personifications of Vegetation: twenty-three examples, three types (Pl. VIII).[29]

Type A. Somber oval face; heavy mat of reddish-brown hair outlined in black, arranged to follow very closely the contour of the head and ending at the side of the face; light red face with white highlights and brown outlines, and with eyebrows, eyelashes, and irises in black; green leaves and pink flowers project from the hair at irregular intervals.

Type B. Florid angular face; large mass of curly red hair outlined in brown, arranged in a loose two-lobed pompadour at the top with a few tresses falling along the curve of the neck and shoulders; light red face with red outlines, and with eyebrows, eyelashes, and irises in black; green leaves and pink flowers project from the hair at irregular intervals.[30]

Type C. Small pear-shaped face with disproportionately large features; scant wavy hair, black or

---

25. Cf. above pp. 15 f.

26. The designs on many of the tiles are disturbed by unevennesses in their surface, most commonly by shallow pairs of troughs cutting across the surface either diagonally or, in one instance, in wavy lines (see e.g., Pl. IX, 3–4). The troughs were made by workmen running two fingers across the surface of the clay before it was baked.

27. The missing tiles were undoubtedly removed for use in bolstering the defenses of the city.

28. The apotropaic device is that of the eye. Its use in connection with doorways is well illustrated at Palmyra in the Tomb of the Three Brothers (Farmakovski, *Proceedings of the Russian Archaeological Institute, Constantinople*, VIII, 1903, Pl. XXVII) and at Dura in room W6 of the private house in M7, where the eye appears immediately opposite the doorway (*Rep. VI*, pp. 155–157, Pl. XLII, 3).

29. Two examples are preserved in the Yale University Art Gallery (1933.266; 1933.267). Examples of all types are preserved also in the National Museum at Damascus.

30. In one example a ribbon hanging loosely about the neck is knotted below the chin.

brown with black outlines, arranged in a small topknot above and ending in long loose curls on the shoulder; dark red face outlined in brown, with eyebrows, eyelashes, and irises in black; green leaves and reddish-brown flowers project from the hair at irregular intervals.[31]

That we are dealing here not with a mask, but with a face should be evident from the features portrayed as well as from the context in which the face appears.[32] It has been suggested that the face represents the "goddess" Flora.[33] But since Flora is really an Italic figure and one whose iconography has not yet been fixed,[34] it would be better to suppose that we are dealing here with a late rendering of the ubiquitous Demeter-Persephone of the eastern Mediterranean.[35] Demeter and Kore heads analogous to Types A and B of our tiles appear in the B. Bliznetsy and the Zaitsev tombs at Panticapaeum (Kertch), the former with the characteristic sprays of leaves and flowers in the hair.[36] Without the help of such parallels we today cannot explain the iconography and establish the identity of the faces in question. Whether those who painted and those who saw them on the ceiling of the House of Assembly would have identified them forthwith as Demeter-Persephone may be questioned. The religious and iconographic syncretism of the later centuries of ancient history, the importance attaching to the personification of abstract ideas, and the numerous apparently unidentifiable and quite innocuous female heads represented, for instance, on the mosaics of Antioch, suggest that in the period and the area with which we are dealing, the precise identity of such faces as those on the ceiling tiles was no longer entirely obvious, and that they were beginning to represent the vegetative powers of nature generally, in traditional form.[37]

b. Astrological Symbols

(2) *Pisces*: two examples (Pl. IX, 1).[38]

The fish are turned in opposite directions. Their bodies are outlined and hatched in black; gills outlined in red; fins indicated by series of short red and black lines. There is no sign of a string connecting the fish.

(3) *Capricorn*: seventeen examples (Pl. IX, 2).[39]

Forward part of the animal rendered in yellow, outlined in black, and shaded in red; rear part of animal rendered in blue above and white below, with black hatching; tail and upper part of body outlined in black; lower part of body outlined in red; red fins.

(4) *Centaur*: twenty-one examples (Pl. IX, 3).[40]

The lower, equine part of the body is seen in profile, the upper, human part in a frontal pose. Its forelegs lifted from the ground, the creature advances toward the right, its left arm extended forward holding a fish, its right hand raised to the side of the head. The entire body is rendered in reddish brown and outlined in black. In the curly black

---

31. A similar motif is known from a house in D5; see *Rep. IV*, Pl. VI, 4.

32. Against Du Mesnil du Buisson, *Peintures*, p. 136.

33. So, e.g., *Rep. VI*, pp. 290, 385, and 387.

34. Cf. Steuding in Roscher, *Lexikon*, I (1884–1890), cols. 1483–1487, *s.v.* "Flora."

35. Of the many different renderings of Demeter and Persephone-Kore see F. Bräuninger in *RE*, XXXVII (1937), cols. 944–972, *s.v.* "Persephone"; Kern in *RE*, IV (1901), cols. 2713–2764, *s.v.* "Demeter"; and L. Bloch in Roscher, *Lexikon*, II, 1 (1890–1897), cols. 1284–1379, *s.v.* "Kora und Demeter." In contrast to deities like Athena and Hera, Demeter normally has the more feminine appearance of the face on our tiles. The ears of grain originally associated with Demeter as her proper symbol later find their counterpart in the fruits and flowers borne by Persephone-Kore. Standing or seated figures of the goddesses, characteristic of the classic period of Greek art, are later replaced on the one hand with representations of entire scenes from the Demeter and Persephone myths (especially on sarcophagi), or on the other hand by busts and faces. It is the latter development that is reflected in the Synagogue tiles.

36. Cf. Rostovtzeff, *Ancient Decorative Painting*, Pls. VII, 2; VIII; LVII.

37. On the personifications of abstract ideas see L. Deubner in Roscher, *Lexikon*, III, 2 (1897–1909), cols. 2068–2169, *s.v.* "Personifikationen," and F. Stössl, *RE*, XXXVII (1937), cols. 1042–1058, *s.v.* "Personifikationen." On personifications of abstracts in the Antioch mosaics, see *Antioch on the Orontes*, III (1941), e.g., Pls. 57, 58, 59, 64; for the seemingly purely decorative female heads see *Antioch*, II (1938), e.g., Pls. 28, 35, 44, 61, 76; and Rostovtzeff, *YCS*, V (1935), Pl. 32 A (Pompeii).

38. An analogy to this design is provided by a tile from Block D5 now in the Yale University Art Gallery (1931.403); see *Rep. IV*, Pl. VII, 2.

39. Two examples in the Yale University Art Gallery (1933.271; 1933.272). An example from D5 is published in *Rep. IV*, Pl. VII, 1. A further example in the Louvre is reproduced in *Encyclopédie photographique de l'art*, II (1936), p. 127.

40. Two examples at the Damascus Museum, one in the Yale University Art Gallery (1933.268).

hair red flowers appear. Red fillets project at either side from the nape of the neck. From the shoulders a white cloak outlined in black and dotted, it seems, with black spots billows out to the right and the left. The fish in the left hand is outlined in black above and brown below, with black hatching to indicate the scales.[41] Below the belly the background against which the figure is painted is yellow.

Of the three astrological symbols depicted on the tiles, two; namely, Pisces and Capricorn, are readily identifiable as being zodiacal in character. It is tempting to suppose that the third is also zodiacal and represents Sagittarius. But the characteristic bow is missing, and the fish which he holds in his hand would on this interpretation be troublesome. In all probability it is better, therefore, to associate the third figure with the non-zodiacal Centaur who belongs to the southern celestial hemisphere.[42] This Centaur appears for the first time on the globe of the Farnese Atlas and later in manuscripts such as *Vaticanus Graecus 1087*, invariably with a Θηρίον, which he normally holds in his outstretched right hand.[43]

c. Animals

(5) Dolphin: fifteen examples (Pl. IX, 4).[44]

The animal is set against a yellow background, black being used for the outline of the back and the tail as well as for the hatching of the body, red appearing in its place to outline the belly, the eyes,

the large beaklike snout, and the dorsal fin. In all important respects the representation follows the pattern in vogue in the later Roman period, the contortion of the body, its tail raised high above the back, reflecting the efforts of Hellenistic artists to intensify the expression of motion at the expense of the simpler, more graceful styling of earlier models.[45]

(6) Serpent: three examples (Pl. X, 1).[46]

The serpent is a hybrid monster with the body of a snake, a tail of the type usually associated with fish, and a duck-like bill or snout. The head and the body are white, the latter spotted above with black marks. The tail, the undulating bends of the body, and the head are outlined in black. The bill is red, but with black contours.

Hybrid animals of this type have a long history in the glyptic art of the Orient, and one of the ancient Babylonian animal lists actually mentions a snake in the form of a duck.[47] Landsberger associates the creature with one mentioned in mythological texts that deal with astral powers, and finds that it was depicted in later times for apotropaic purposes.[48] It is tempting therefore to regard our hybrid as an astrological symbol.[49] The difficulty is that the serpent of the tiles is invariably represented against a conventional, but none the less real, background of vegetation which takes the form of a highly schematized tree with red trunk and branches, and black and green leaves. Since in Hellenistic art the fish-tailed hybrid developed a great variety of forms, appearing as sea-centaur, -bull, -stag, -lion, -panther, -goat, -bird, and -dog, there is no reason why a comparable combination with serpent and duck cannot have been invented independently in that

---

41. In one example the creature advances toward the left rather than the right and holds the fish in his right hand.

42. Cf. Boll-Gundel in Roscher, *Lexikon*, VI (1924–1937), cols. 1012–1014. On the distinction between the Centaur and Sagittarius, see F. Boll, *Sphaera* (1903), pp. 130f. and 143–148.

43. Cf. Boll-Gundel, *op. cit.*, cols. 897–898, Figs. 4–5; and col. 1013, Fig. 19. The general analogy in the representations is very close, extending to the details of the billowing cloak and the flowers in the hair. But the non-zodiacal Centaur in these later western representations is a hunter, and the Θηρίον in his hand therefore a hare or a panther. In what context he might have been conceived of also as a fisherman is unknown. The non-zodiacal Centaur does not appear in Babylonian astronomy, nor on the Denderah disc. The section of the Qusayr 'Amra fresco on which he may have been depicted has been destroyed. Cf. F. Saxl, in K. A. C. Creswell, *Early Muslim Architecture*, I (1932), pp. 289–294 and Pls. 50–51.

44. One example in the Yale University Art Gallery (1933.273).

45. For late analogies in the same tradition, see *Antioch*, II, Pl. 38; and *Antioch*, III, Pls. 61, 66, 69.

46. Two examples in the Yale University Art Gallery (1933.274; 1933.275).

47. B. Landsberger, *Die Fauna des alten Mesopotamien* (*Abhandlungen der sächsischen Akademie der Wissenschaften zu Leipzig*, XLII, 1934), p. 54, quoting the words of a fragmentary text which reads: "[Gestalt der Schlange: wie (?)] eine En[te (?) ......].. diese Schlange heißt Seeschla]nge (?)."

48. *Ibid.*, p. 55.

49. On the dolphin and the various serpentine figures of the astrological symbolism (Hydra, the snake of Anguitenens, and even Ceteus), see Boll-Gundel in Roscher, *Lexikon*, VI, s.v. "Sternbilder," *passim*.

context.[50] Certainly the conventions used in the rendering recall those of the Hellenistic age and environment. Quite a different artistic tradition comes to expression in the tiles depicting quadrupeds.

(7) Gazelles: two examples (Pl. X, 2–3).[51]

Clearly members of the *antilopina* family, the animals, probably gazelles, appear in pairs, one slightly behind and above the other. They are shown at the moment of a graceful leap, their forelegs raised from the ground. The bodies are painted a dark yellow outlined in black. Long pointed ears and still longer straight horns suggest the desert gazelle (*gazella leptoceros leptoceros* Cuvier) common in the plains of the Near East. Curving trees with heavy red trunks and red branches ending in circular masses of green foliage outlined in black, together with green and black scrolls arising from the base of the trees, provide the suggestion of a silvan background.[52]

(8) Deer: five examples, two types (Pls. X, 4; XI, 1).[53]

The animal is in each instance shown singly, but otherwise in the same general pose and with the same background as the gazelles. The two types are distinguished from each other by the fact that in the one instance (Type A) the animal faces forward in the direction of its line of movement, while in the other instance (Type B) it looks back in the direction from which it flees. In the best examples of Type B, what remains of the base of the horns suggests that these branch outward in the manner of the deer of the hunting scene of the Dura Mithraeum. No example of Type A is sufficiently well preserved to show the horns, but the upper edge of the body is marked here, as in examples of Type B, with a row of heavy dots, a detail which also distinguishes the deer from the gazelles in the

Mithraic hunting scene.[54] Their graceful lines made the deer and the gazelle favorite subjects in the art of the ancient Orient throughout its entire history.[55] The pose in which they appear on the Synagogue tiles; namely, that of flight, and the direct connection between the conventions used on the tiles and those employed by the artists of the Dura Mithraeum indicate that their prototypes are to be found in this instance in the Parthian and Sassanian hunting scenes, whose realism and style they so clearly reflect.[56]

(9) Birds in wreath, pecking at fruit: fourteen examples, four types(?).

The wreath is the same in all instances. Its ground color is a light pink, save for two insets at opposite sides, to the right and the left, which are green. The floral part of the wreath is marked with red lobes to represent the several blossoms and give a wide red outline. The insets, probably intended to represent the leaves and stems of the flowers, are similarly lobed but outlined in black. Inside the wreath the background is yellow, and against this the birds and fruits are set. The latter include blue grapes outlined in black, pomegranates, and a round yellow fruit outlined in brown. If any real difference of type exists between the several examples of the design, it is to be found in

50. Cf. K. Shepard, *The Fish-Tailed Monster in Greek and Etruscan Art* (1940), esp. p. 78.

51. One example in the Yale University Art Gallery (1938.4882).

52. The same animals and the same trees, the former less graceful in execution, are found in the hunting scenes on the north and south walls of the Dura Mithraeum (last phase, A.D. 240–256). Cf. *Rep. VII–VIII*, Pls. XIV–XV.

53. Two examples (Type A) in the Yale University Art Gallery (1933.269; 1933.270).

54. On the hunting scene, see n. 52 above. In the preliminary report (*Rep. VI*, pp. 384, 387), made without the benefit of the comparative material from the Mithraeum, the gazelles were interpreted as antelopes, and the deer either left unidentified or interpreted as gazelles.

55. For representations of the earlier period, see O. Weber, *Altorientalische Siegelbilder* (1920), Figs. 521, 538 (deer), 487, 490, 547, etc. (antelopes). For the Hellenistic and the Roman periods, see the antelopes of the Marissa tomb (Peters and Thiersch, *Painted Tombs in the Necropolis of Marissa*, Pl. IX), and the deer and antelope of the ceiling of the tomb near Ascalon (J. Ory, *Quarterly of the Department of Antiquities in Palestine*, VIII, 1939, pp. 38–44, Pls. XXV–XXIX). See also for the later period *Antioch*, II, Pl. 73; and *Antioch*, III, Pl. 91.

56. On the relation of the hunting scenes of the Mithraeum to the Iranian art tradition see *Rep. VII–VIII*, pp. 112–115. On the wider aspects of the problem see Rostovtzeff, *YCS*, V, esp. pp. 262–272. For specific examples of deer and gazelles in the Iranian tradition, see Rostovtzeff, *Ancient Decorative Painting*, Pl. LIX A, 1; LXXVIII, 2; LXXXIX, 1 (note that in LXXVIII, 2, the deer is associated with the identical convention for trees used on the tiles); and A. U. Pope, *Survey of Persian Art*, IV (1938), Pls. 163B, 168B, 206, 214 (period of Shapur II and Chosroes II).

the association of several varieties of birds each with a different type of fruit.

Type A: eight examples (Pl. XI, 2).[57]

A stubby gray bird outlined in black, with thick neck, short heavy beak, short depressed tail (possibly a crow) pecking at pomegranates. One tile (1933.260) seems to show two birds; another (1933.259) has only two pomegranates.

Type B: one example.

A small bird, its outlines only faintly visible, holding its tail erect.

Type C: two examples (Pl. XI, 3).[58]

A large gray bird outlined in black with red beak, legs, and claws. It has a long thin beak, a long gracefully curved neck, and a heavy full-feathered tail, and is in all probability a peacock. The fruit at which it pecks is yellow, but not a pomegranate.

Type D: three examples (Pl. XI, 4).[59]

A large bird with a dark red body outlined in black, bright red comb and wattles. Its wings droop slightly, making the individual feathers visible. The long tail is raised halfway. Except for the longish neck, the bird resembles closely a cock.[60]

The conventions employed by the Synagogue artists in these tiles have their own long history, going back ultimately to the representations of birds in the realistic, if stylized, garden scenes and landscapes of the ancient Orient.[61] Such garden scenes and landscapes, popularized by Hellenistic art, eventually provided the inspiration for Roman decorative designs involving the combination of animals, particularly birds, and plants or fruits,[62] and at the same time became a quarry for motifs used to fill the interstices between the scrolls of rinceaux, and to adorn geometric borders and

fields.[63] From the motif of birds pecking at fruit in a grapevine rinceau, the transition to the wreath with birds and fruit is by no means difficult and entirely understandable.

d. Flowers

(10) Four-petaled flower in wreath: twelve examples (Pl. XII, 1).[64]

The wreath is pink outlined in red and has green insets outlined in black. Continuous wavy lines cutting across the wreath replace the lobes in no. 9 used to indicate the separate blooms and leaves of which the wreath is composed. The four heart-shaped petals of the flowers enclosed by the wreaths are pinkish at the extremities. They are outlined in red and radiate from a red calyx. Leaf sprays in green and black project from between the petals.

(11) Four-petaled flower: twenty-nine examples, two types.

Type A: twenty-four examples (Pl. XII, 2).[65]

The flower is identical in every respect with the one in the preceding design except that in the absence of the wreath the flower is rendered in much larger form to fill the entire central position of the tile.

Type B: five examples, all fragmentary.

Three flowers identical in all particulars with those of the preceding designs, only smaller, are arranged in a pyramid upon the tiles.

Commonly spoken of as a rose, the flower enjoyed great favor as a decorative design in Egypt and Syria and reappears at Dura in the Fresco of the Tribune from the Temple of Bel, in the banquet scenes of room 6 of House W in Block M7, and in

---

57. Three examples in the Yale University Art Gallery (1933.259; 1933.260; 1933.261).

58. Two examples in the Yale University Art Gallery (1933.263; 1933.264).

59. One example in the Yale University Art Gallery (1933.262).

60. Cf. *Antioch*, II, Pl. 41, mosaic 55, section 2, bird at extreme right end, done in exactly the same manner.

61. For birds in trees in Assyrian garden scenes, see C. J. Gadd, *The Stones of Assyria* (1936), Pls. 40–42. For Egypt see E. A. W. Budge, *Wall Decorations of Egyptian Tombs* (1914), Pl. VII.

62. The over-all vine trellis design of the mosaics, with birds and other animals dispersed among the curling branches, is perhaps the most common of these designs. Cf. e.g., the mosaic of the second century of our era in the Roman villa at Uthina in Tunis (P. Gauckler, *Monuments Piot*, III, 1896, pp. 177–229 and especially Pl. XXI).

63. Birds and fruit in rinceau borders are extremely common; see J. M. C. Toynbee and J. B. Ward Perkins, *Papers of the British School at Rome*, XVIII (n.s., V) (1950). See also the border of Room 1 of a house at Daphne (*Antioch*, II, Pl. 41) and from an earlier period Winter and Pernice, *Die hellenistische Kunst in Pompeji*, VI, p. 150, Pls. 24, no. 1, and 52.

64. One example in the Yale University Art Gallery (1933.258).

65. Two examples in the Yale University Art Gallery (1933.276; 1933.277); 1933.276 contains graffiti made when the clay was still wet. Cf. below, Inscrs. nos. **26–28**, p. 279. One example at the Princeton Museum of Historic Art (33.32).

a decorated textile.[66] In the Fresco of the Tribune the flower serves as the emblem of the city of Dura; in the Synagogue, however, it should probably be understood to have only ornamental significance, as in the banquet scene of the house in M7.[67]

(12) Floral wreath with disc: three examples (Pl. XII, 3).[68]

The wreath is identical with that in no. 9 above. The disc is painted a plain ochre yellow and is surrounded by a heavy red rim. The wreaths of the type used here and in designs 9, 10, and 20 are thoroughly familiar as objects and as symbols in the Hellenistic and the Roman periods in pagan, Jewish, and Christian circles, and appear upon the monuments in a variety of forms and under various circumstances.[69] Where in the Jewish use of art they are given especial prominence, they probably have a particular symbolic significance. Here, where they are interspersed with designs representing fruits, flowers, and animals, they seem to serve no higher purpose than to show vegetation in its brightest and most pleasing aspects, providing the festive air that is associated also with the use of floral garlands in the banquet rooms and temples of Dura.[70] The discs contained in the wreaths have been interpreted as solar symbols, but could also represent fruits, or may be merely appropriate geometrical designs.[71] If the discs represent the sun, their association with a wreath of the flowers that thrive on its light would be entirely natural.

e. Fruit

(13) Cluster of pomegranates: twenty examples, two types.

Type A. Three in a cluster: four examples (Pl. XII, 4).[72]

Type B. Four in a cluster: sixteen examples (Pl. XIII, 1).

Set in a random mass of green foliage outlined in black, the fruit with its characteristic calyx-lobe is rendered in pink and outlined in red. The twig from which the cluster hangs is not evident in the design or has faded out. The background is yellow.

(14) Three bunches of grapes: fourteen examples (Pl. XIII, 2).[73]

The three bunches are grouped in a compact cluster, as though hanging from a single stem. Above the cluster sprays of large green leaves are outlined in black, and between the bunches curling green tendrils hang down similarly outlined. Variety is introduced into the design by giving the terminal bunches a different color from that of the one in the middle. In twelve of the fourteen examples the bunches at the right and the left are blue grapes, outlined in black,[74] and the bunch at the center pink grapes outlined in red. In the remaining examples the color scheme is reversed.

66. For the Fresco of the Tribune see Cumont, *Fouilles*, Pl. L; for the house in Block M7 see *Rep. VI*, Pl. XLII; and for the textile see *Final Report* IV, 2, Frontispiece. The literature concerning the origin and use of the design will be found in *Rep. IV*, p. 51, n. 41; and in *Final Report* IV, 2, p. 8.

67. There is no reason to suppose that the flower had in the Synagogue the astral significance ascribed to it by Du Mesnil du Buisson, *Peintures*, p. 134.

68. Two examples in the Yale University Art Gallery (1933.265; 1938.4881). The paint flaked off the latter in transit, revealing a graffito and dipinto (Inscrs. nos. **1b** and **1c**, below pp. 266–268).

69. On the wreath or crown see now the important article by E. R. Goodenough, *Art Bulletin*, XXVIII, 3 (1946), pp. 139–159, where the older literature is cited (p. 150, n. 81); and K. Baus, *Der Kranz in Antike und Christentum, Theophaneia*, II (Bonn, 1940).

70. Cf. *Rep. VI*, Pl. XLII; and Cumont, *Fouilles*, p. 134, and Pl. LV. On analogous floral wreaths and filleted garlands in literary texts and on wall decorations, see M. I. Rostovtzeff, *The Social and Economic History of the Hellenistic World*, III (1941), pp. 1490f., n. 119. Note the presence of interwoven floral garlands on the door reveals of the Synagogue. Wreaths surrounding the text on tiles bearing inscriptions (design 20 below) are probably honorific.

71. Cf. *Rep. VI*, p. 385; and Du Mesnil du Buisson, *Peintures*, pp. 133–135. For flowers and fruits in wreaths, see designs 9 and 10. Similar discs appear in the intertwined garlands that decorate the door reveals (below, p. 253 and Fig. 71) and in lozenges in the imitation of marble incrustation work in the Torah Shrine of the chamber (see below, p. 55). In the latter instance they are certainly, and in the former instance quite probably, only geometrical designs.

72. One example in the Yale University Art Gallery (1933.278). Another example in the Princeton Museum of Historic Art (33.31).

73. Two examples in the Yale University Art Gallery (1933.280; 1933.281).

74. The blue color appears here, as elsewhere in the paintings, as a gray.

(15) Cluster of three oranges: four examples (Pl. XIII, 3).[75]

Grouped closely together, the three carefully rounded fruits of this cluster have a yellow hue, are outlined with thin black lines, and are highlighted with light yellow and white. A black dot occasionally appears near the edge of the fruit at a point opposite to the stem. About the cluster there are random indications of foliage in green and black, representing thin branches with small tender leaves. That the fruit is actually an orange and not a citron,[76] is made likely by recent investigations into the history of citrus fruits and by a Pompeian mosaic in which a similar fruit, probably an orange, is depicted.[77]

(16) Cluster of three cones: twenty-two examples (Pl. XIII, 4).[78]

The cones are sometimes white, sometimes yellow or green, but always cross-hatched and outlined in black. At least two are normally joined to a single red branch or stock by shorter or longer stems. Red spirals project from the sides of the stock and fill the intervals between the cones. The foliage suggested recalls anything but the needles of a conifer, but the probability is that the fruit represented is a cedar cone, nonetheless. Long associated with religious usage in ritual and monuments, the cedar cone appears elsewhere alongside other fruits in the vocabulary of Roman decorative art in Syria.[79]

With the exception of the orange, all of these fruits are so common in Hellenistic and Roman art that no special discussion of the provenience of the designs is necessary. That the four designs in question form a group is indicated by the fact that they reappear on the intrados of the arch on the façade of the Synagogue's Torah Shrine.[80] There their association with the cult makes them particularly appropriate, giving them a symbolic significance.

f. Grain

(17) Three ears of grain: sixteen examples (Pl. XIV. 1).[81]

The design shows three yellow spikes, dotted with black to represent the kernels and overlaid with opposing rows of diagonal black lines to indicate the beard. The yellow or black stems rise from a common root set in a heavy ground-line. Pairs of lanceolate green leaves outlined in black are interposed between the ears and provide terminal elements for the entire design. The grain has been spoken of as wheat, but may rather be taken to be barley, which was not only more common but is also more frequently represented.[82]

75. One example in the Yale University Art Gallery (1933.279).

76. On the façade of the Synagogue's Torah Shrine there is depicted a circular fruit which can only represent the citron, or ethrog. The artificial stylization to which it owes its form is absent from the tiles, and this makes the argument from analogy impossible.

77. On the introduction of the more common fruits into the Hellenistic and Roman world, see Rostovtzeff, *Social and Economic History of the Hellenistic World*, II, p. 1166, and III, pp. 1610f., n. 103. On the history of the orange in particular, which the author argues was brought into Hellenistic Egypt and used in Roman gardens for decorative purposes, see S. Tolkowsky, *Hesperides. A History of the Culture and Use of Citrus Fruits* (1938), esp. pp. 95–103. His color plate (Pl. XXVIII) shows the Pompeian mosaic that depicts a fruit like that of the tiles (Museo Nazionale, Naples, no. 9992).

78. Four examples in the Yale University Art Gallery (1933.283; 1933.284; 1938.4883 and 1938.4884).

79. Cones are common in Assyrian bas-reliefs of ceremonial functions (see E. Bonavia, *The Flora of the Assyrian Monuments*, 1894, pp. 65–71). They are now interpreted as

cedar cones rather than as citrons (see H. Frankfort, *Cylinder Seals*, 1939, p. 204). Normally, it would seem, the irregular protuberances of citrons are represented by a scale pattern of lobes, rather than by cross-hatching. Cf. e.g., the ethrog on a glass vessel from Rome (P. R. Garrucci, *Storia della arte cristiana nei primi otto secoli della chiesa*, VI, 1880, Pl. 490, no. 2) and a citron on a marble slab from the Tomb of the Haterii (Tolkowsky, *op. cit.*, Pl. XVII, opp. p. 88). For the representation of cones alongside other fruits in Roman Syria, see the sarcophagus in G. Perrot and C. Chipiez, *History of Art in Sardinia, Judaea, Syria and Asia Minor*, I (1890), p. 247, Fig. 159; and the bas-relief of the cult scene from the Temple of Bel at Palmyra, *Syria*, XV (1934), Pl. XXII, opp. p. 172. Mishnaic legislation endeavored to prevent Jews from selling pine cones to pagans at the occasion of religious festivals, lest they be used for idolatrous purposes (Abodah Zarah, I, 5).

80. Cf. below, p. 55. Grapes and pomegranates are similarly represented on the aedicula of the Christian Chapel at Dura (see *Rep. V*, p. 255, and Pl. XLI).

81. Three examples in the Yale University Art Gallery (1933.285; 1933.286; 1933.287).

82. Interpreted as wheat in *Rep. VI*, p. 384, and by Du Mesnil du Buisson, *Peintures*, p. 134. For cereals identified as barley see the Pergamene frieze (*Altertümer von Pergamon*, VII, 2, 1908, pp. 325 f., Fig. 408 a, c) and the coins of Herod Agrippa (A. Reifenberg, *Ancient Jewish Coins*, 1940, p. 79 and Pl. VIII, no. 59).

(18) Three sesame pods or blooms: five examples (Pl. XIV, 2).[83]

The design depicts three cone-shaped pods or blooms done in pink or in yellowish-green, and cross-hatched and outlined in black, rising from separate red or black stems out of a common node. Long thin leaves, curled at the top and rendered in green, black, or red fill the intervals between the large pods and complete the design at the ends. So far as the pod itself is concerned, the closest analogy is the spathe containing the flowers and fruits of the palm tree.[84] But the analogy to the design used to represent barley suggests that the blooms or seed pods of the sesame plant are what is being portrayed.[85] In both cases the stems of the plant are shortened to make a compact design. The greater degree of stylization suggests that the vocabulary of design is being extended in these instances beyond the range of the older, more common and more realistic fruit and flower motifs.

g. Apotropaic and commemorative

To complete the roster of tile designs it is necessary to add to these eighteen, each repeated originally in excess of twenty times, a smaller group that was not repetitive to the same degree. Here two different designs have to be distinguished. The one has an apotropaic, the other a commemorative, significance.

(19) The eye: two examples, two types.

It has been suggested that these two tiles were mounted in the vicinity of the doors giving access to the chamber, where apotropaic symbols were traditional.[86] Unfortunately in both instances the

83. One example in the Yale University Art Gallery (1933.282).

84. For a representation of the "Palmkohl," see B. Meissner, *Babylonien und Assyrien*, I (1920), p. 414, Fig. 130.

85. Other representations of the sesame plant are apparently not available for purposes of comparison. Cf. Steier in *RE*, II, 4 (1923), cols. 1849–1853, *s.v.* "sesamon." On the cultivation of the plant see Rostovtzeff, *Social and Economic History of the Hellenistic World*, III, p. 1610, n. 100.

86. In addition to what was said on this subject above, p. 41, n. 28, it should be noted that the evil eye in the Antioch mosaic (*Antioch*, III, Pl. 56) appears in the vestibule of a room.

designs on the tiles are so badly faded as to make many of the details quite uncertain. The colors are faint and often indistinguishable.

Type A: one example (Pl. XIV, 3; Fig. 11).

The central feature of this eye is the black iris set in a white eyeball. A curved black line with

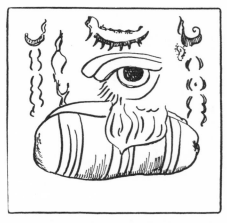

FIG. 11. Design of Ceiling Tiles: Apotropaic Eye

projecting black strokes marks the lower lid and the eyelashes. The upper eyelid is outlined in red and surmounted by a wide band with black lines projecting upward, intended no doubt to indicate the eyebrow. The space about the eye is enclosed in all four directions. Above the eyebrow there is an elongated, slightly curved mass with wavy outlines and simple cross lines that may once have been pink framed in red.[87] At either side, knobby yellow lampstands, each surmounted by a lamp with a curved handle, flank the central motif. Between the lampstands and the eye itself cone-shaped masses, perhaps originally pink, are introduced. Below the eye there is a heavy green bolster ornamented with three pink stripes cut by red lines. Overlapping the eye and the bolster an elliptical mass with perpendicular red lines and dots is to be noted. Du Mesnil du Buisson has interpreted it as a flame kindled in the cushion and ready to destroy the eye.[88] It might with equal justice be interpreted as something issuing from the eye.

87. Du Mesnil du Buisson has interpreted this mass as a caterpillar (*Peintures*, p. 136). It might with equal accuracy be interpreted as a garland.

88. *Ibid.*, p. 136.

Type B: one example (Fig. 12).

So indistinct to begin with that it defied efforts to photograph it, the design has since faded still more and is therefore known only from the sketch

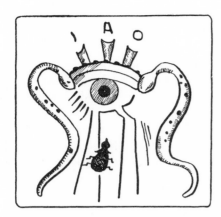

FIG. 12. Design of Ceiling Tiles: Apotropraic Eye

of Du Mesnil du Buisson and the copy contrived by Pearson for the reconstruction of the ceiling in the Damascus Museum (Pl. VII). In general its elements are more familiar. The eye is attacked from the left and the right by snakes and from below by an insect or, more probably, a scorpion. Above, three nails or daggers are portrayed, imbedded in the eyebrow.[89]

Comparative material is available at Dura, in Syria generally (more especially Palmyra, the Jebel Druze, and Antioch), and in many other parts of the ancient world.[90] This provides a full explanation of the details incorporated in the design Type B, but throws no light upon the unusual iconography of the Type A. In the latter instance,

far from being attacked by noxious creatures, the eye is surrounded with amenities and safeguards: the bolster, the lampstands, the garland (if such it be), and the pinkish cone-shaped masses between it and the lampstands, conceivably sesame blooms or pods.[91] If the indistinct elliptical mass between the eye and the bolster could be regarded as representing the light issuing from the eye, the design might more properly be interpreted as portraying the Good Eye as distinct from the Evil Eye.[92] In any event the presence of such apotropaic designs on the ceiling of a Synagogue is by no means surprising in view of what is known about the importance of the powers of the Evil Eye in ancient Judaism generally and in Babylonia in particular.[93]

(20) Inscriptions enclosed in wreaths: 3 examples (Pl. XLIII, 1–3).

Altogether six tiles were found bearing inscriptions, three in Aramaic and three in Greek. The tiles with the Aramaic inscriptions had no decorations, but the Greek inscriptions were enclosed in wreaths.[94] The wreaths are identical in every respect with the second of the two types listed above, so that the design itself needs no further description. It should be noted, however, that the association of a wreath with an inscription is a common feature of pagan, Jewish, and Christian monuments.[95] That in this connection the wreath

89. Projections from the shafts of these imbedded objects are interpreted by Du Mesnil du Buisson's sketch as the letters *I A O* (the familiar Gnostic name of the deity) and in Pearson's copy as the shafts of the daggers. Du Mesnil du Buisson himself leaves their identity open (*Peintures*, p. 136).

90. Cf. for Dura, Cumont, *Fouilles*, pp. 137–139; *Rep. VI*, pp. 156f. and Pl. XLII, 3; and Du Mesnil du Buisson, *Peintures*, p. 137, Fig. 97; for Palmyra, Farmakovski, *Proceedings of the Russian Archaeological Institute, Constantinople*, VIII (1903), Pl. XXVII; for the Jebel Druze (Kafer) *Syria*, VII (1926), Pl. LXVIII; for Antioch, *Antioch*, III, Pl. 56. The general literature on the subject beginning with O. Jahn, *Berichte über die Verhandlungen der königlich sächsischen Gesellschaft der Wissenschaften, phil.-hist. Klasse*, VII (1855), pp. 28–110, is conveniently summarized again in Doro Levi, *Antioch*, III, pp. 220–232.

91. On the use of sesame as a prophylactic against eye disease, see Steier in *RE*, II, 4 (1923), cols. 1849–1853, *s.v.* "sesamon."

92. The ὀφθαλμὸς ἁπλοῦς as contrasted to the ὀφθαλμὸς πονηρός in Matt. 6.22–23. The distinction between the עין רעה and the עין טובה is typical of Jewish thought. Cf. H. L. Strack and P. Billerbeck, *Kommentar zum Neuen Testament aus Talmud und Midrasch*, I (1922), pp. 431f. *ad* Matt. 6.22–23. There is to my knowledge no other example of a representation of the Good Eye.

93. Rabbinical references to the Evil Eye are gathered *ibid.*, pp. 833–835. On the suggestion that the Jews of Babylonia, including Rab, a contemporary of the Dura Synagogue, regarded the Evil Eye as particularly dangerous, and that the Jews of Palestine thought its occurrence to be particularly common in Babylonia, see Lev. Rabbah XVI, 8 (Trans., IV, p. 208).

94. Cf. Inscrs. nos. **23, 24, 25**, below, pp. 277f. One example in the Yale University Art Gallery (1933.257).

95. In addition to the article of Goodenough, *Art Bulletin*, XXVIII, 3, see F. Cumont, *Recherches sur le symbolisme funéraire des romains* (1942), pp. 481–484. In the Jewish sphere examples occur on coins (P. Romanoff, *Jewish Symbols on Ancient Jewish Coins*, 1944, pp. 57–68

has more than purely decorative significance should be clear. In all probability, since the texts it encloses concern themselves with living persons, the significance is honorific in the same sense in which the crown voted to persons of distinction by cities and "corporations" in antiquity was honorific.[96]

h. Comparative materials

The description of the designs that appear upon the tiles of the House of Assembly gives some idea of the wealth of color which the ceiling added to the room, and of the extent of the decorative repertoire available to the artists. The richness of the repertoire, combining designs of long standing in the Mediterranean basin and of equally ancient Oriental vintage with others typical of the Hellenistic Near East and of the Parthian or Sassanian tradition, is characteristic of the artistic syncretism of the later Roman Orient and perhaps one of the best examples of that syncretism; for here the component elements appear side by side instead of having to be disentangled carefully from a single composition.

Among the designs portrayed, a relatively large number employs motifs found elsewhere on the monuments of Jewish art. Those with the longest history in Jewish usage are the flowers and fruits, some of which appear upon Jewish coins and funeral monuments as early as the Maccabean and Herodian periods.[97]

Birds and four-footed animals, possibly including a centaur, are added to the fruit and flower

motifs in the medallions formed by the rinceaux on the pulvinated friezes and the lintels of the Galilean synagogues in Antonine days; and in the Catacomb of the Villa Torlonia analogies to the dolphin can be seen.[98] Zodiacal symbols, common on the mosaics of later synagogues such as Beth Alpha and Na'aran, can be traced back to a much earlier period in the bas-reliefs from the synagogues at er-Rafîd, Kefr Birim, and Capernaum.[99]

The fact that of the designs of the Dura Synagogue ceiling, a goodly number reappears elsewhere on Jewish monuments is not sufficient in itself to explain their occurrence here. As a matter of fact, certain of those listed above, particularly the personifications of vegetation, are not otherwise attested in ancient Jewish art; and some of the most typical of Jewish symbols, such as the palm-tree, the lyre, the cup, the basket, do not appear on the Dura Synagogue tiles. Furthermore, there is still so much that is obscure about the reason for the use in Jewish art of even the most commonly attested symbols — for instance, those of zodiacal character — that merely to refer to earlier examples is to leave the basic problem of the principle of selection and of the significance of the symbolism quite unresolved. That part of the larger problem which concerns us here; namely, the part that would make the origin and the nature of the Dura Synagogue ceiling with its decorations clear, can best be approached from at least a brief recapitulation of what is known about similar ceilings and decorations at Dura itself.

It is important to realize in this connection that the type of ceiling construction used in the Dura Synagogue, far from being unique, is rather common at Dura in larger chambers, and that ceiling blocks — whether of baked clay, plaster, or gyp-

and Pl. 4), and on funerary and commemorative monuments, as for instance the tomb at Beit Jibrin (F. J. Bliss and R. A. S. Macalister, *Excavations in Palestine during the Years 1898–1900*, 1902, p. 201 and Pl. 91) and the el-Hammeh synagogue (Sukenik, *Ancient Synagogue of el-Hammeh*, p. 40, Fig. 13).

96. Cf. Saglio in Daremberg-Saglio, I, 2 (1887), pp. 1520–1537, *s.v.* "corona;" and Fiebiger, *RE*, IV (1901), cols. 1636–1643, *s.v.* "corona."

97. The pomegranate appears singly on coins of Herod the Great and in groups of three on the shekel and half-shekel of the First Revolt, the grape in single bunches on coins of Herod Archaelaus, the wreath on coins of John Hyrcanus, and three ears of barley on a coin of Herod Agrippa I (see on the coins in general, Reifenberg, *Ancient Jewish Coins*, and Romanoff, *Jewish Symbols on Ancient Jewish Coins*). For flowers, flowers in wreaths, and grapes on the pediments and friezes of rock-cut tombs in the vicinity of Jerusalem from the period before the First Revolt, see C. Watzinger, *Denkmäler Palästinas*, II (1935), Pls. 26–29.

98. Cf. Kohl and Watzinger, *Antike Synagogen*, esp. Figs. 17, 18, 65, 66, 99c and e; and Beyer and Lietzmann, *Jüdische Katakombe der Villa Torlonia*, Pl. 7b.

99. For er-Rafîd, see Sukenik, *Ancient Synagogue of el-Hammeh*, p. 91, Fig. 32 (Pisces); for Kefr Birim, S. Yeivin, *Jewish Palestine Exploration Society, Bulletin* III (1936), pp. 117–121 (in Hebrew); and for Capernaum, Kohl and Watzinger, *Antike Synagogen*, Figs. 65–66 (Capricorn). The door-lintel of a Jewish house in the Hauran reproduced by A. Reifenberg (*Denkmäler der jüdischen Antike*, 1937, Pl. 33, 1) is carved with a design analogous to that of the Kefr Birim synagogue. In this instance the original zodiacal signs have been excised, but the design may include a representation of an eye (upper row, to the left of the central device).

DESIGNS	SYNAGOGUE	HOUSE OF SCRIBES	HOUSE B BLOCK L7	HOUSE OR BATH, C3	TOWER 15	HOUSE OF THE LARGE ATRIUM IN BLOCK D5
Persons and Personifications						
Historical		11	4		I	×
Persephone (?)	23	2				×
Pan (?)		2				
Silenus (?)		I				
Astral Symbols						
Capricorn	17			×		×
Pisces	2				I	×
Centaur	21					
Animals						
Dolphin	15					
Serpent	3					
Gazelle	4	I	I			
Deer	3					
Birds	14					
Flowers						
Rose	36	18		×		×
Wreath	3			×		×
Garland		19				
Fruit						
Grapes	14 (threes)	11 (singles)	I (singles)			×
Pomegranates	30 (threes & fours)	7 (fours)	I	×		×
Oranges	4 (threes)	18 (fours)				
Apples (?)						×
Cones	22 (threes)	17 (fours)				×
Grain						
Barley	21					
Sesame	5					
Other Designs						
Peltae				×		×
Eye	2					
Inscribed Wreath	3					

(× indicates that the design is reported but not the number of tiles bearing it)

4*

sum — analogous and even identical with those of the Synagogue in their decorations, have actually been found in at least five other structures. The largest number of tiles — 115 — came to light in the House of the Scribes, located in the same block as the Synagogue (L7) and known to be virtually contemporary in its latest form with the Synagogue. Twenty were discovered in the bath in Block C3, coming apparently from the house next door; enough fragments to identify eleven designs in a house in D5; seven in a room of House B in Block L7; and two each in Tower 15 and section W12 of Wall Street west of Block M7.[100] A table will show the distribution of designs among the tiles from the several structures, with the exception of those from M7W12, for which there is no information (see p. 51).

The table is helpful in a number of ways. It brings to light in the first place certain differences between the ceiling decorations of the Synagogue's House of Assembly and those of other structures. One difference is that the range of the designs used in the Synagogue is larger. This is because the room was larger, and because the artists sought to avoid an excessive repetition of the same design. A second difference is the absence of the portraits of historical persons actually associated with the use or the construction of the premises. At this point a fundamental contrast between the Jewish point of view and that expressed, for instance, in the Konon frescoes of the Temple of Bel comes to light. The Jewish conception of the place of the contemporary individual in the religious and historical order was such as to make Jews doubt the propriety of such representations in a house of worship.[101] For the portraits of historical persons such as Heliodorus, the Actuarius, in the House of the Scribes, and for the votive scenes with historical individuals that are a common feature of the mural

decorations of pagan sanctuaries at Dura, the Synagogue apparently substituted the commemorative inscriptions enclosed in honorific wreaths, as described above.

More important than these differences is the general homogeneity of the Dura ceiling decorations both in the range and type of design and in the style of rendering.[102] The relationship of the art of the Dura Synagogue to that of the city as a whole is nowhere more clearly visible.

Of more direct significance for our immediate purposes is the fact that within the general range of this homogeneity there is apparently the same predilection for floral and vegetal designs. Since all the patterns were simplified and stereotyped, this cannot be the result merely of the artists' desire to use as often as possible the easiest designs. Rather it suggests that the decorations of the Dura ceilings by and large had a floral and vegetal scheme as a core and an ultimate source. Actually it is not difficult to understand how, on this assumption, at least the major categories of non-vegetal motifs were added to the repertoire. Given a basic nucleus of floral and fruit designs and the necessity of expanding it to decorate with sufficient variety relatively large ceilings, the inclusion of a figure personifying the powers of vegetation (Demeter-Persephone) and of Pan and Silenus is quite natural. The addition of grains poses no problem once the Demeter-Persephone design has been admitted, even though grains grow on the ground; and once the limitations of realism had been surmounted in this way, the presence of birds in fruit design could lead on to the representation of four-footed animals, reptiles, and even aquatic animals and hybrids. The zodiacal signs too, since they were associated with the seasons of the year, had a natural place in such an expanding repertoire.[103]

100. Cf. *Rep. IV*, pp. 42–47; *Rep. VI*, pp. 97, n. 9; 283–299. The ceiling blocks of the house in D5 were identical in size with those of the Synagogue (0.41 m. square × 0.05 m.), while those of C3 were smaller (0.25–0.29 m. square × 0.04 m.), and those of the House of the Scribes were larger (0.47–0.48 m. × 0.26–0.27 m. × 0.05–0.06 m.).

101. The same general restraint comes to light in the formula "whose name the Lord knows" used in early Christian dedicatory inscriptions (cf. e.g., *Gerasa*, Inscr. 309, p. 481). Later, of course, donor portraits are common in the decorations of Christian churches, as they had long been in pagan temples.

102. A comparison of the Synagogue tiles with the blocks of the House of the Large Atrium reproduced in *Rep. IV*, Pls. VI–VII will make this evident.

103. The fact that the range of the astral and zodiacal signs is so limited, both in the Dura Synagogue and in other buildings of the city, is undoubtedly important, but precisely what the import of the selection was, it is difficult to determine. The choice may have been dictated by the association of the signs with important phases of the agricultural year, as in the *menologia rustica*, or again with the season of the year in which certain events in the history of the building or the community occurred. For analogies in these areas, see F. Cumont in Daremberg-Saglio, V (n.d.), pp. 1046–1062, *s.v.* "Zodiacus."

The full import of the comparison with the remains of similar ceilings can be understood only when the inference about the essential nucleus of the decorations is associated with what is known about the form and structure of the ceiling. The basic element of the Synagogue ceiling is, as we have seen, the square tile. As a structural unit it has its counterpart, no doubt, in the square slab of stone or wood that closed the aperture between intersecting beams in the paneled ceilings of Greek temples and Hellenistic private houses.[104] Yet as we find them in the buildings of Dura, these units are normally not set in separate frames, but ranged in rows of ten or more upon the parallel joists that divide the ceiling actually into long rectangular strips.[105] Clearly the classical system of square ceiling units is here being combined with one traditional in Babylonia, where the normal ceiling unit is the long rectangular strip bounded by the beams spanning the width of the room. The strips originally consisted of mats covered with wattles and stamped clay.[106] It is not clear that in Babylonia these ceiling strips were ever decorated; but in Greece, of course, the application of decorative elements to the coffers of paneled ceilings, whether in the form of gilded rosettes or in the form of painted representations of acanthus leaves or masks, was a matter of long standing.[107]

From the decorated paneled ceilings that once existed in the houses of Hellenistic Greece and Egypt (Vitruvius, *De architectura* VI, 3, 9), those of the structures at Dura are separated by more than merely the modifications deriving from traditional Babylonian structural form. A third element has still to be added to explain the lighter, less formal manner of these eastern products and to provide the latitude for the introduction of a wider repertoire of decorative design. This third element is none other than the garden trellis covered with fruits and flowers, which existed both as a reality and as a decorative ceiling design in the ancient Near East and has already been used to explain the ceiling decorations of room 7 of the earlier Synagogue building.[108] The significance of this element in the composition will be evident when it is recalled that eventually the walls of the Dura Synagogue were decorated at the corners with painted pilasters along which vines climb upward. The pilasters in turn probably carried painted architraves that provided the fiction of support for the beams and joists of the ceiling.[109] Though actually executed some years after the ceiling, for reasons that need not concern us here, these corner pilasters and the architraves they carried were probably part of the original decorative scheme of the Synagogue. Taken together with the beams and joists of the ceiling, they provide the structural elements necessary for the representation of a trellis seen from within. In so doing they reveal that, tectonic modifications to the contrary notwithstanding, the underlying principle of the ceiling decorations was to the Synagogue artists that of a garden trellis. Hence the predominant interest in fruit and flower designs noted above.

What has been said about the unity and the basic significance of the Synagogue's ceiling decorations is not without a bearing upon our knowledge of the life and outlook of the Jewish community that authorized their execution. It is clear from the analogies available that what was being authorized was a ceiling of a type familiar to the members of the community from other structures in the city and from the cultural environment of which the city was a part, only larger and more ambitious than any other of which we have knowledge at Dura itself. The fact that the ceiling was fundamentally conventional is no doubt one reason why female heads recognizable to us as deriving ultimately from representations of Demeter-Persephone appear in it. Allowance will, of course, need to be made in this connection also for a Jewish

104. Cf. in general Ebert, *RE*, XXVII (XIV, 1, 1928), cols. 369–375, *s.v.* "lacunar."

105. In one case — the House of the Scribes (see above p. 52, n. 100) — the tiles themselves are rectangular, but only in the Temple of the Gaddé were masses of plaster introduced between the individual slabs of the several rows to complete the pattern of recessed squares. Cf. *Rep. VII–VIII*, pp. 253 f. and Fig. 66.

106. Cf. J. Jordan, *Beiträge zur Bauwissenschaft*, XVIII (1910), pp. 32–36; Meissner, *Babylonien und Assyrien*, I, pp. 278 f.

107. On the introduction of "painted ceilings" see Pliny, *Hist. Nat.* XXXV, 124; W. Helbig interprets this passage to mean that pictures were painted on the flat surfaces enclosed by the beams of paneled ceilings (*Untersuchungen über die campanische Wandmalerei*, 1873, pp. 132–134).

108. Cf. above, pp. 37 f. The Hellenistic design appears as far east as the Ajanta Caves. Cf. V. Goloubew, *Ars Asiatica*, X (1927), Pls. LX–LXXI.

109. For these corner pilasters see below, p. 252, Fig. 70, Pls. XVIII–XIX.

attitude toward pagan art forms differing strongly from that of the Palestinian purists of the first century of our era.[110] Yet due consideration of the extent to which convention and abstraction enter into the artistic tradition of the late Roman period will reveal how dangerous it would be to infer from the presence of these heads that the Jews of Dura had abandoned the basic premises and allegiances common to Judaism as a whole. The restraint reflected in the absence of heads of contemporary persons provides one element of assurance at this point. The basic fact, so far as what was represented is concerned, is that the decoration of the Synagogue's ceiling was in large measure a "commercial" job.[111]

2. THE TORAH SHRINE

The second element of the first phase in the decoration of the House of Assembly is the Torah Shrine set against its western wall.[112] Serving as a repository for the Scroll Chest and as a point of orientation for the worshipers at prayer, the Torah Shrine was decorated with particular care, its decorations being composed of two different elements (Pls. XV–XVI, LI). The first is entirely conventional and consists of the ornament applied to the niche, the uppermost step of the niche-block, the columns of the façade, and the intrados of the archivolt. The second element is pictorial and consists of objects and scenes developed on the face of the arch, each fraught with significance for the religious life and observance of the Jewish worshiper. It seems proper to begin by describing the conventional element of the decorations and to proceed from this to the treatment of the pictorial material. From a discussion of the material, the style, and the iconography of the decorations, their place in the history of the chamber's embellishment will become evident.

The interior of the niche the artists developed in three parts. The uppermost is the exquisite conch that fills the niche-head. This was tinted a light blue which faded out almost at once after excavation.[113] The outer surface of the shell where it projects from the curving niche-head is painted a rich green. Below the conch the surface of the niche has a dark blue coloring. This second zone of blue comes to an end *ca.* 0.60 m. above the floor of the niche against a band that is now white but still contains traces of the original yellow. The area below this band is developed in imitation of incrustation work to represent a marble wainscot with five rectangular panels that are separated from each other by vertical red bands and framed above and below by pink bands (Pl. XV, 1; Fig.13). Each of the several bands is set off from the neighboring designs by narrow black stripes. Of the five panels the first and the fifth, and the second and the fourth are treated as pairs and executed in identical fashion. The terminal pairs the artists divided by

110. On the general question of the Jewish attitude toward art, see below, pp. 340–346.

111. In view of the elaborate hypothesis about the inscriptions on the tiles advanced by J. Obermann (*Berytus*, VII, 1942, especially pp. 128–134), it may not be amiss to add here certain further observations about the tiles and their decoration, especially those decorated with inscriptions. It is highly improbable that any of the tiles used in the ceiling of the later House of Assembly came from the earlier building: (a) because the earlier building was not roofed with tiles; and (b) because the tiles used in other parts of the earlier building were uniformly of a much smaller size. It is probable, as explained above, that the ceiling tiles for the later House of Assembly were decorated on the ground before being put in place, and it is evident that the painters were competent to render in good form and with the proper honoring wreaths the Greek commemorative texts supplied by the Elders. There is a clear distinction between the professionalism in the execution of the Greek texts and the amateurism of the Aramaic texts. The Aramaic texts were therefore probably done by the members of the Jewish community themselves, upon blanks supplied by the builders. That the amateurism visible in the finished product should have led the responsible members of the community to arrive at the full form of their Aramaic text only after tentative beginnings recorded on another tile is quite natural under the circumstances. So also is the fact that the builders should have salvaged a blank spoiled by the amateurs, and should have covered the first attempts at an Aramaic text with a decorative design, as indicated above. As to the contrast between the first and the second versions of the Aramaic inscription in the procedure of rendering (Inscrs. nos **1b** [graffito] and **1c** [dipinto]), see the inscription on the façade of the Torah Shrine (Inscr. no. **2**) which was first incised and was probably to be rendered later in paint, as the blank space where it stands suggests.

112. For the construction of the aedicula, see above, p. 16. Its significance as an element of synagogue architecture is discussed above, pp. 22 f., 33, and below, p. 60.

113. For all such details we are fortunate to have available the detailed field notes of Professor Clark Hopkins, the director of the expedition, made on the spot during the excavation of the building and the uncovering of the decorations. Of the value of his notes, which have been drawn upon throughout, particularly in color descriptions, acknowledgement is made herewith.

FIG. 13. Torah Shrine, Design at Base of Niche

diagonal black lines into triangles. Opposing pairs of triangles having the top and the bottom of the panels as their bases are stippled in red and inscribed with peltae; opposing pairs of triangles having the sides of the panels as their bases are inscribed with irregular concentric shapes of brown lines forming "eyes," each with a green dot at the middle. The intermediate panels are set off from the red and pink bands of the over-all frame by special frames of their own in which red dots and strokes alternate against the white background in imitation of the bead-and-reel design save at the corners, where groups of three petal-like strokes are introduced. Inside this special frame wavy green and dark green lines of varying thickness, running diagonally downward from the sides of the panels, are drawn to meet at the center, forming a succession of V's and reproducing the effect of matching pieces of marble cut from the same slab and set alongside each other. The central panel of the series, at the rear of the niche, is inscribed with a veined black diamond that contains at its center a yellow disc. The diamond is enclosed by the same narrow frame with the bead-and-reel design that surrounds the intermediate panels of the series. The four triangles filling the corners of the rectangular field are decorated with a scale pattern of brown.

To complete the description of the conventional decorations applied to the Torah Shrine, three further items have still to be listed. The first is the design painted upon the riser of the uppermost step of the niche-block between the pedestals. This is a rectangle inscribed with a diamond, the several elements of which are each outlined with black lines. The diamond, lying in a horizontal position and having at its center a disc now brown, but perhaps originally purple, imitates green marble slabs with dark green veins, the slabs being cut in such a manner that the veins form horizontal V's. To frame the diamond the artists introduced a continuous red band set off from the diamond by a narrow white strip. The corner triangles of the rectangle they finished in imitation of a white marble with pink, red, and brown veins. The second item to be listed is the green and dark green veining applied to the columns of the façade to produce V's, quite in the manner of the intermediate panels of the wainscot and the design on the step. The third and last is the design developed on the intrados of the arch surmounting the columns. (Pl. XV, 2–3). This consists of a continuous fruit garland outlined with double rows of diagonal brush strokes — the outer in green, the inner in red — and crossed diagonally with pairs of yellow ribbons that divide the garland into seven fields. The fields are decorated with clusters of pomegranates, grapes, oranges, and cedar-cones, in red, black, yellow, and green respectively.[114]

Concerning these conventional elements of the decorations of the Torah Shrine, two things are to be noted. The first is that the treatment of the columns and the intrados is virtually identical with that of the corresponding elements of the aedicula housing the font in the baptistery of the Christian Chapel at Dura and executed some fifteen

114. From left to right the order of the fruit designs is as follows: three pomegranates; a bunch of grapes; three oranges; a bunch of grapes; three cedar-cones; three oranges; one pomegranate.

years earlier.[115] This merely underlines what was said above about the conventional nature of such decorations, particularly the fruit designs. The second thing to be noted is that in the painted incrustation work of the niche there appears the same alternation of vertical panels divided diagonally and inscribed with diamonds that has already been noted in the dado of the earlier Synagogue building.[116] There is a continuity of design here, not unusual in itself, but marked in its contrast to the type of dado used to adorn the rest of the House of Assembly (Pls. XVIII–XXIV, XXXVII–XXXIX). It is difficult to escape the impression that while the dado around the four walls of the room followed the style of the pictorial panels, the wainscot of the Torah Shrine followed merely the decorative tradition employed in the earlier Synagogue. This is one reason for assigning the decorations of the Torah Shrine to the first phase in the inner embellishment of the chamber.

Leaving these conventional designs, we come now to the most important among the decorations of the Torah Shrine, those developed upon the face of its arch (Pl. XVI). The spandrels and the high panel above were treated as a single rectangular field 1.47 m. wide and 1.06 m. high framed by a pink border that is 0.04–0.05 m. wide and set off by a black line. The field itself is painted a clear blue, and upon it are represented objects and scenes significant for the worship and the religious life of the Jewish community and particularly appropriate, we must imagine, to this spot. At the center, directly above the head of the niche, a rectangular architectural object is portrayed, the identity of which is not absolutely clear. To the right is a representation of the Sacrifice of Isaac, and to the left the great Menorah (the seven-branched lampstand) with an ethrog (citron) and a lulab (palm-branch) beside it.[117] Each of the three main elements of this combination will require some discussion.

115. Cf. *Rep. V*, pp. 254 f., and Pls. XLIII and XLVIII. One of the designs of the garland in the Christian Chapel represents ears of grain, which reappear on the Synagogue ceiling instead of on its Torah Shrine.

116. Cf. above, pp. 34 f.

117. The lower left corner of the field, which would have provided ample room for such objects as the shofar (ram's horn), is left bare. Upon its surface there appears a graffito of two lines commemorating the donor of the Torah Shrine. Cf. Inscr. no **2**, below, p. 269.

To illustrate the familiar story of Gen. 22.1–19, the space available on the right half of the field was ill adapted. What the artist could produce under the circumstances was in large measure only a vertical combination of the major elements necessary to the pictorial rendering of the story. In the center of the space available, he portrayed at the right the figure of Abraham, tall of stature compared with the other figures in the picture, and clad in a white himation and a long-sleeved white chiton ornamented with two pink clavi. Ankle-high brown boots cover the feet of his reddish legs. In his outstretched right hand he holds upright a large, sharp-pointed, white knife. Of his head only a mass of black hair is visible, for Abraham is seen from the rear.[118] For a figure of paramount importance this pose is highly unusual and requires explanation. Apparently the explanation is not poor craftsmanship, but the set purpose of the artist; namely, to associate Abraham with, and to dissociate him from, certain elements of the scene.

At the left, slightly above Abraham, the scene presents the first element with which he is associated, a large white altar outlined in black. The altar consists of several superimposed blocks, some rectangular with cut fasciae, others cylindrical with projecting fillets and bulging tori.[119] In shape it differs from all other altars of the Synagogue. Upon the top of the altar, draped over a pink mass that must represent the fagots, lies the small limp figure of Isaac, crudely drawn, his legs red, his chiton white, his head represented by a mass of black.[120] The second element of the scene with which Abraham is correctly associated by

118. This position conceals the left arm that normally is seen to hold the ends of the himation wrapped tightly about the right side of the body above the hips, while at the same time it reveals the presence on the rear of the chiton of the clavi usually visible only on the front of this garment. Though this is not visible on the photographs, the clavi actually reappear above the area covered by the himation, extending to the top of the shoulder.

119. For altars combining rectangular and cylindrical elements, and cylindrical altars with architectural moldings, see G. Perrot and C. Chipiez, *History of Art in Phoenicia and its Dependencies*, I (1885), p. 261, Fig. 191; and E. Unger in Ebert, *Reallexikon der Vorgeschichte*, I (1924), p. 111.

120. There is no indication that Isaac is bound. The use of red in the representation of the fagots may imply that they are already ablaze. The red covers also a triangular area atop the altar, perhaps a horn or a projection intended to hold the sacrifice in place.

his unusual position is the Hand of God that is seen above the altar. This Hand, which appears here for the first time among the many instances of its usage in the Synagogue, is apparently already an established convention of Jewish pictorial art in the middle of the third century, and represents the intervention of God in world affairs — particularly, if not exclusively, when a "miracle" is involved.[121] Its appearance in this context is motivated, not so much by the divine command to Abraham, as by the miraculous appearance of the ram in the thicket. In form it differs from all other examples preserved in the Synagogue in that at the wrist the red of the Hand is set off against a white mass doubly bordered in black and red, which could represent either the light of the divine presence, a sleeve, or a cloud (Fig. 14).

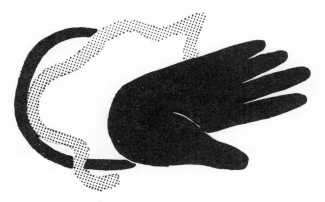

FIG. 14. Torah Shrine Façade. Hand of God

While facing the altar as he should, Abraham by his unusual position is at the same time correctly dissociated from the details of the scene presented

at the bottom of the vertical arrangement. These details are the ram which the divine intervention supplies unknown to him and which he sees "behind (him)" (Gen. 22.13), and the tree which the artist has substituted for the "thicket" of the Biblical text, following the rendering of the story familiar also from the Targumim.[122] The tree with its trunk outlined in red and brown curves sharply to the left, bringing the semicircular black and green crown into position below the altar. This leaves room in the lower right corner for the large ram whose head almost touches the lowest branches of the tree. Its well-proportioned gray body is outlined in brown.[123]

In the upper right corner of the field the artist has added a further detail that has caused some discussion, but is probably to be interpreted as a tent. It is conical in shape and light green in color. A widely curved opening in its side gives a view into the interior, which is done in pink. The reappearance of a curved pink band at the top of the tent suggests that it has a flap which can be rolled back.[124] Inside the tent stands a small figure dressed simply in a white chiton with pink clavi. Of the head only a mass of black hair is visible, indicating that the figure is seen from the rear, like the others in the scene.[125] In recent discussion the tent has

---

121. The Hand first appears in Christian art in the fourth century; e.g., in certain frescoes of the catacombs of Callixtus and Domitilla (see J. Wilpert, *Die Malereien der Katakomben Roms*, 1903, Pls. 139, 201, 237). On the general subject see H. Leclercq in Cabrol, *Dictionnaire d'archéologie chrétienne et de liturgie*, X (1931), cols. 1205–1219, *s.v.* "Main"; and R. Romanoff, *Bodn*, I (1934), pp. 61–72. Analogies to representations of the hand in bas-reliefs of the Near East (see especially F. Cumont, *Syria*, XIV, 1933, pp. 381–395, where the examples are reproduced and a full list of material is given) and in the bronze votive offerings of the Sabazios cult (see Eisele in Roscher, *Lexikon*, IV, 1909–1915, esp. cols. 245 f., Figs. 245–246, *s.v.* "Sabazios") illustrate the wider background of the convention in ancient metaphor and gesture, some elements of which as they appear in classical tradition have been treated by O. Weinreich, Θεοῦ Χείρ, Diss. Heidelberg (1908).

122. *Targum Onkelos* here uses אילנא to translate Hebrew סבך.
123. In shape the tree differs sharply from those depicted on Panel NC 1. The ram, however, is not unlike that in Panel WB 2.
124. Du Mesnil du Buisson has suggested that the structure is to be interpreted as a house (*Peintures*, pp. 24 f.), referring in this connection to the beehive-shaped houses of the villages east of Aleppo and northwest of Palmyra (*ibid.*, Pl. XIV, 1) and to details on the mosaics of Santa Maria Maggiore. The structure is admittedly different from the tents portrayed in the narrative panels of the Synagogue (e.g., WB 1, NC 1), but so are most of the other details of the iconography of the scene. Tents of conical form are, however, to be found on Assyrian bas-reliefs (see Meissner, *Babylonien und Assyrien*, I, Fig. 63) and a reed hut of similar form (*seriph*) is mentioned in Sukkah 19b (Trans., p. 82). The Hebrew conception that the heavens are a "tent" seems to presuppose an analogous tent form. Of course Abraham's tent would be his dwelling. The pink interior is also an unusual feature, representations of interiors in the Synagogue being normally black.
125. The flesh color used for the legs is a dark red as elsewhere in this scene. The arms are not indicated, whether because they are assumed to be held in front of the body or because in a figure of this size (0.11 m.) such details could not be indicated.

been interpreted as a temple or the Temple, and the small figure on its threshold as either Abraham (which is unlikely because of the dress) or as Isaac himself.[126] The choice between these and other alternatives involves a decision regarding principles of interpretation that are of basic importance for the understanding of the entire body of pictorial materials presented in the Dura Synagogue. The discussion of these principles has naturally to be presented in another context.[127] Here it can only be said that in our judgment where Biblical scenes are portrayed, the artist intended the meaning to be conveyed primarily by the picture as a whole. The corollary of this judgment would seem to be that the primary function of detail is descriptive rather than interpretative. In this instance the interpretations suggested seem inadmissable because they attach to details intelligible without them, elements of meaning properly reserved for the scene as a whole in its relation to the context in which it stands. Hence it would appear preferable to regard the tent as one of the type in which the artist, following the Biblical story itself, thought of Abraham as living — in this case the tent which he took with him on the three-days' journey to the land of Moriah — and of the small figure in the tent as one of the two "young men" left behind a short distance before proceeding to the sacrifice.[128] The fact that the "young man" faces the interior of the tent means no more than that, as the story itself implies by virtue of Abraham's act, the servants were not to be participants in the sacrifice.[129]

126. Cf. Du Mesnil du Buisson, *Peintures*, pp. 23–27; and Grabar, "Le Thème," pp. 144–146.

127. Cf. below, pp. 354 f.

128. For the tent as Abraham's normal habitation, see Gen. 12.8; 18.1, 6, 9. The expression "yonder" (עד־כה) in Abraham's words to his servants, "Abide ye here with the ass, and I and the lad will go yonder" (Gen. 22.5), is explicitly interpreted by Rashi as meaning "a short distance; to the place just ahead of us."

129. The tradition recorded by Tabari that Isaac was placed on the altar on his right side (Du Mesnil du Buisson, *Peintures*, p. 24) I take to be a reflection of such pictures as that of the Dura Synagogue rather than their inspiration. To make the prone figure identifiable the artist had of necessity to show both its legs, hence place it on its side. In a figure of such small proportions (0.17 m.) he naturally chose to show it from the rear. There would seem to be eminently sound practical reasons why all three figures in the Sacrifice of Isaac should have been seen from the rear. It seems doubtful, therefore, that religious scruples had anything to do with the matter.

The Sacrifice of Isaac, familiar as an important element of the repertoire of early Christian artists from the period of the catacombs on, is one of the few incidents of Biblical story of which there is now more than one representation also in ancient Jewish art.[130] Together they give visible expression to the importance which the episode had in Jewish piety and religious thought. Among the various directions in which rabbinical thought moved in trying to express for the benefit of the pious the significance of the episode, two that stem no doubt from the homiletic tradition and have been recorded in the literature of popular piety are of interest in the present context. The first is predicated upon the identification of the mountain in the "land of Moriah" (Gen. 22.2) with the hill (Mt. Moriah) upon which the Temple was later built,[131] and involves an interesting association of the site of the *Akedah* and the Ark of the Covenant (i.e. the *aron*) — the one as the source of reverence, the other as the source of "spiritual" illumination.[132] The second suggests, without the help of popular etymologies, that the binding and deliverance of Isaac and the promise made to Abraham as the reward for his obedience are in some sense a guarantee of God's forgiveness to Israel.[133] Early Jewish prayers prescribed for fast days, and the benedic-

130. On the Sacrifice of Isaac in early Christian art, see A. M. Smith, *American Journal of Archaeology*, XXVI (1922), pp. 159–173. In ancient Jewish art the scene occurs first in the Dura Synagogue, then on a gem with a (much later) Hebrew inscription on the reverse (See Pl. XL, 4), and next in the Beth Alpha mosaic; see Sukenik, *Ancient Synagogue of Beth Alpha*, Pl. XIX. The scene is frequently represented, of course, on Jewish silverware and in illuminated manuscripts of the Renaissance. For examples see *Encyclopaedia Judaica*, VIII (1931), frontispiece and pp. 481 f.; and R. Wischnitzer-Bernstein, *Gestalten und Symbole der jüdischen Kunst* (1935), pp. 22 f., Figs. 16–17.

131. This identification is as old as the Chronicler (II Chron. 3.1), reappears naturally in Josephus (*Antiquitates* I, 224–226), and pervades the Midrashim (e.g., Gen. Rabbah LV; Trans., pp. 482–487). Cf. also the Targum to II Chron. 3.1, which is most explicit.

132. So in the section of Gen. Rabbah already referred to and more fully in Song of Songs Rabbah IV, 4 (Trans., IX, p. 197), where we hear that Mt. Moriah was so called because reverence (*morah*) issued forth from there, while the Ark is called *aron* because light (*'orah*) issued from there to the world.

133. E.g., Lev. Rabbah XXIX, 9 (Trans., IV, p. 376), the Fragment-Targum on Gen. 22.14 (ed. Moses Ginzburger, *Das Fragmententhargum*, 1899, p. 13), and Rashi (on Gen. 22.14).

tion *Zikronoth* added to the *Musaf* prayer for New Year's, make special mention of the episode with this in mind,[134] and Gen. 22 became the lesson for the second day of the New Year Festival. These associations of the story it is important to keep in mind, not as an explanation of the iconography, but in connection with the position assigned to the scene on the Torah Shrine as a part of a composition embodying also other elements that have still to be described.

At the extreme left side of the field, balancing the scene of the Sacrifice of Isaac, three familiar Jewish symbols are depicted. The most prominent of these is the great yellow (that is, golden) Menorah or lampstand. Its shape differs radically from the representation found on the narrative panels of the Synagogue, for the seven arms rise in straight lines from a solid, narrow-waisted base which in turn is supported on ball-shaped legs. The three feet, each two balls high, are joined at the bottom by lunette-shaped bands for support. On the narrow waist of the heavily molded base an eight-pointed rosette or star is represented.[135] The seven arms of the lampstand, fashioned to represent the "knops" of the Biblical description (Exod. 25.31–36), are shown as rods on which lines of hollow balls are mounted by means of nails or pins. At the top each arm bears a lamp similar in shape to those of earthenware in common use in the later Roman Orient, with a curved handle at one end and a projecting nozzle at the other.[136] A flame appears from each nozzle at the right; that is, to the north. Alongside the Menorah two additional objects of symbolic importance are depicted: the ethrog (citron), which appears merely as a yellow ball, and the yellow lulab, whose care-

fully spined palm leaf is apparently wound about at the base with other materials in the traditional fashion. The Menorah and the symbols associated with the Feast of Booths according to the ordinance of Lev. 23.40 have each their own religious significance — the former undoubtedly the more fully developed and many sided, as its popularity on monuments of Jewish art and archaeology indicates. To fix this significance in the context of the Dura Synagogue precisely would be quite impossible, save to the extent that it was a reminder of the Temple and of the cult which the Lord himself ordained as the instrument of man's forgiveness before Him. In this sense it may be associated properly with the ethrog and lulab, about which we hear in the Midrash that when God sees the people appearing before his presence with ethrog and lulab He forgives their sins.[137] The most obvious meaning of the designs at the extreme left side of the façade of the Torah Shrine is thus not far removed from that of the scene at the extreme right, the Sacrifice of Isaac. Whether this is significant depends upon the central element of the composition.

The central element of the composition is a temple-like structure, the identity of which has become the subject of some discussion. Its architectural décor is done in yellow, to represent gold, and contrasts with a pink background which, if the analogy to the temple in Panel WB 4 (Pl. LVI) holds, can only represent the masonry of a cella. The framework of the structure comprises a crepidoma; at either side, a pair of long, slender columns, fluted to approximately one third of their height; and a molded entablature. The columns have plinths and bases and end in schematized Egyptianizing capitals. The entablature consists of a simple architrave surmounted by a row of semicircular antefixes. There is no pediment. Contained within this outer framework is a further architectural element rendered in yellow. It is framed by two smaller, wreathed or spirally fluted columns that support a rounded, rather than molded, architrave surmounted by a conch or a fan enclosed in an arch. The capitals of the columns are dissimilar, but probably again Egyptianizing, and the shafts have knobs set in the intervals be-

134. Reference to the *Akedah* in prayers for fast days is documented as early as the Mishnah (Ta'anith II, 4; Danby, p. 196). The text of the second benediction of the *Musaf* prayer reads in part as follows: "Remember in our favor, O Lord our God, the oath which Thou hast sworn to our father Abraham on Mount Moriah; consider the binding of his son Isaac upon the altar when he suppressed his love in order to do Thy will with a whole heart. Thus may Thy great love suppress Thy wrath against us.... etc."

135. Perhaps the rosette is the result of the artist's desire to introduce a *perah* (blossom) somewhere in his design, since *perahim* were a part of the decorations of the Menorah according to Exod. 37.17.

136. E.g., *Final Rep*. IV, Part III, Pl. XIV, 424.

137. Lev. Rabbah XXX, 2 (Trans., IV, pp. 383 f.).

tween the diagonal flutings.[138] The columns apparently enclose a door whose leaves are ornamented with bosses at the appropriate height and supplied with an overlapping flange studded with smaller bosses or nails.

For the interpretation of this central element of the composition on the facade of the Torah Shrine, the salient point is the existence of a similar design on the Jewish coins of the Second Revolt issued in Palestine in the reign of Hadrian.[139] The design has the same architectural framework, consisting of crepidoma, terminal pairs of columns, and entablature, and shows within this framework a rectangular device, rounded at the top and supplied with two boss-like projections on its face. The difference is that on the coins the central feature of the design, instead of being a part of the architectural construction, is contained within it and seems to stand on legs. That the design on the coin and the design on the façade of the Torah Shrine are related seems unquestionable. The difficulty is that in the past the one on the coin has itself been interpreted in various ways: as the Temple, the Holy of Holies, the Mercy Seat, a gate, etc.[140] Meanwhile, however, the relevant material has been augmented by archaeological discovery, it being clear from the Torah Shrine of the Dura Synagogue as a whole, and from a bas-relief of the Jewish catacomb at Beth She'arim representing a Torah Shrine with a Scroll Chest in it,[141] that the design on the coin and the design under discussion here are not without bearing upon the architectural form of structures built in synagogues to house Scroll Chests. In the same way it has become evident that the form of ancient Scroll Chests themselves, including those depicted on ancient monuments and one reported to have existed in

Abyssinia, is related on the one hand to the aediculae constructed to house them, and on the other to the Ark of the Covenant as portrayed in the Dura Synagogue — for instance, in Panels NB 1, WB 4, and WB 2 — and on the synagogue at Capernaum.[142]

The interrelation of these several types of objects indicates that we are confronted at this point with an important nexus in the origin and meaning of structural forms associated with the development of the ancient Jewish synagogue, its appointments, and its art. Only a genuinely significant point of departure can explain the multiple relationship. We suggest that the basis of the relationship is the conscious effort of later Judaism to model significant elements of synagogue construction and equipment after the supposed or schematized forms of more ancient Jewish *sacra*, particularly those of the Temple. In this case the design on the coins should be a schematic representation of the Temple, showing the Ark of the Covenant within, and the design on the Dura Synagogue's Torah Shrine should show the Temple itself with the Ark become the door of the Temple.[143]

138. Partially fluted and spirally fluted columns are common in Roman decorative art, particularly on the lead sarcophagi of the second and third century from Palestine and Syria (see M. Avi-Yonah, *Quarterly of the Department of Antiquities in Palestine*, IV, 1935, pp. 87–99 and 138–153 for a convenient summary of the material, and p. 145, Fig. 3, for the types of columns represented), and appear also on representations of Torah Shrines (for an example from Peki'in in Galilee see Sukenik, *Ancient Synagogue of Beth Alpha*, p. 25, Fig. 26).

139. Cf. G. F. Hill, *British Museum: Catalogue of the Greek Coins of Palestine* (1914), pp. CV–CVI, Pls. 32–33.

140. For a bibliography and resumé of the discussion, see Reifenberg, *Ancient Jewish Coins*, pp. 294 f.

141. Cf. Maisler, *Beth She'arim*, Pls. XXXII–XXXIII.

142. Ancient Scroll Chests are depicted on stone, in painting, and on gold glass in two ways: first, as simple chests with or without legs; and second, with flanking columns and entablature, whether as part of the chest itself or as part of its setting. For the former see those depicted at Capernaum (Kohl and Watzinger, *Antike Synagogen*, p. 40, Fig. 76), Na'aran (Sukenik, *Ancient Synagogue of Beth Alpha*, p. 26, Fig. 27), on the bronze plate from Na'ana (R. Dussaud, *Les Monuments palestiniens et judaïques, Musée du Louvre*, 1912, no. 97), at Beth She'arim (see preceding note), and on gold glass from Rome (Garrucci, *Storia della arte cristiana*, VI, Pl. 490, nos. 1, 2, 6). For the latter see *ibid.*, Pl. 490, no. 3; Beyer and Lietzmann, *Jüdische Katakombe der Villa Torlonia*, Pl. 12; Sukenik, *op. cit.*, p. 25, Fig. 26. For the portable Scroll Chest that is said once to have existed at Axum, where it was believed to be the original Ark of the Covenant, see J. Zwarts, *XIVe Congrès international d'histoire de l'art, Actes* I (1936), pp. 36–38. The suggestion of Zwarts is engaging but based upon multiple inferences. All that is visible at Axum is the large reliquary in which the supposed Ark of the Covenant is said to have been kept. Photographs of the reliquary, kindly supplied by Mr. A. Davico of Rome through the courtesy of Prof. Frank E. Brown, show that the reliquary had a round-headed aperture and nothing more.

143. Analogous doorways giving access to the Temple courtyard are to be found in Panel WB 2 of the wall decorations of the Synagogue. What has been said above about the central feature of the decorations of the Torah Shrine façade is a departure from the view expressed in the Preliminary Report (*Rep. VI*, p. 343), where the

The description and identification of the several scenes and objects portrayed there make it possible now to draw certain conclusions regarding the decorations on the façade of the Dura Torah Shrine in their entirety. The first conclusion concerns the relation of the various elements to each other. All three — the Temple in the center, the Sacrifice of Isaac at the right, and the ceremonial objects at the left — are associated by locality, because they represent objects and events connected with the holy hill of Jerusalem. They are associated also in meaning because they concern the basic problem of man's reconciliation with God, dealing on the one hand with institutions divinely ordained as the instruments of that reconciliation, and on the other hand with the essential response of man to the divine ordinances — above all, with obedience and devotion to the divine will, no matter what sacrifice it may entail. If in the period after the destruction of the Temple, the Jews of Syrian Dura brought these thoughts to pictorial expression on the façade of the Torah Shrine of their Synagogue, where during worship its holy scrolls were housed, it was to testify that they acknowledged in its nature and scope the entire range of the divine revelation (including the parts which a divine judgment prevented them from fulfilling), and that they understood and accepted the nature of the response required on their part. Simultaneously, by decorating with these scenes and objects the structure that served, not only as the focus of attention in worship, but also as the point of orientation as they faced toward Jerusalem in prayer, they kept clearly before the eyes of the pious what it was that made their relation to the homeland so precious.

The second conclusion concerns the connotation of the Torah Shrine seen in the light of the decorations applied to its façade. Here the important point is that the relation between the Torah Shrine and the Scroll Chest it contained is analogous to that between the schematized Temple and the Ark of the Covenant on the coins of the Second Revolt.

The analogy is indicated, not only by the columnar nature of the two structures, but also by the close similarity in form between the Ark of the Covenant as represented in the Synagogue's pictorial panels and that of a portable Scroll Chest shaped to fit the conch-headed recess of the Torah Shrine.[144] It is a fair inference that in using a columnar structure as a Torah Shrine the Jewish community of Dura meant it to symbolize the traditional Hebrew Sanctuary, of which one form was the Temple at Jerusalem. That in representing this Sanctuary it copied a simple architectural form current, as we have seen, in contemporary pagan architecture, proves merely that the community was not a society of antiquarians.[145]

The third conclusion to be drawn concerns the relation between the decorations of the Torah Shrine, seen from the technical and iconographic angle, and those of the remainder of the Synagogue. In what was said above, it has been pointed out that at many salient points the repertory of iconographic forms used on the façade of the Torah Shrine differs radically from that employed in the narrative panels. To these differences of form noticeable in the rendering of Temple, Menorah, lulab, altar, tree, and Hand of God, must be added those of technique and style. The artist who decorated the Torah Shrine used for his background a color — blue — not employed in similar fashion elsewhere in the building. Moreover, he painted with a much finer brush; and his work, save in the case of the ram, lacks the assurance of line and dexterity in the handling of clichés noticeable in the narrative panels. True, he seems to stand in a tradition, as the relation of his Temple to the device on the coins of the Second Revolt indicates, but the tradition is another than that used in the narrative panels; namely, one that is symbolic in character. His solution of the problem of how to arrange the Sacrifice of Isaac, while ingenious in view of the limitations of space, is scarcely on a par with the solutions of analogous problems in the narrative panels. These facts, together with what

design was interpreted as itself a Torah Shrine. This view a closer study of the original, providing the first intimation of the pink background representing the cella wall, made impossible. It is doubtful whether the capitals described above owe their form to any attempt to reproduce the lily and pomegranate designs of the capitals in the original Temple of Solomon (I Kings 7.19–20) as Du Mesnil du Buisson suggested (*Peintures*, p. 20), but the suggestion is apposite none the less.

144. For representations of the Ark of the Covenant in the Synagogue paintings, see below, Pls. LIV, LVI, LX.

145. See above, pp. 22 f. The same type of relationship with the contemporary scene appears in all parts of the pictorial decorations: in the rendering of dress, of objects, and of architectural form. The artists naturally use the forms current in their day.

has already been said about the conventional decorations on the lower parts of the Torah Shrine, indicate that the work was done by other artists than those who painted the narrative panels on the walls of the building. Together with the initial design on the wall directly above, the decorations of the Torah Shrine, therefore, belong to the first stage in the community's efforts to enrich artistically the interior of the House of Assembly.

3. THE DESIGN ABOVE THE TORAH SHRINE

So far as the history of its decoration is concerned, the section of the west wall just above the Torah Shrine (Pl. XXIV) is by all odds the most difficult part of the Synagogue to interpret. This is because the area, later developed to form the two Center Panels, was repeatedly repainted in antiquity. Under normal circumstances we might have remained ignorant of all but the very last phase of its development; but fading, on the one hand, and the flaking of the several superimposed layers of paint, on the other, have brought into view also elements of the earlier phases. These now appear in continuous confusion with the elements of the later composition. The problem is to disentangle the evidence of the several strata, each of which is imperfectly known, in such a way as to produce a coherent account of the successive treatments of the area. The essential facts, established by a careful analysis of the surface, are as follows.

The area later devoted to the two Center Panels was at first a single field decorated by a design painted without the use of a solid background color, and apparently not enclosed in a frame. This design was subsequently amended by the introduction of certain figures, and in this amended form was incorporated in the scheme of register decorations, being enclosed by a frame that made the area upon which it was developed a single panel running through Registers A and B. Save for the figures added in the second stage of the development, the design was next expunged by a red cover-coat that for the first time gave a solid background to the field. The field was then divided horizontally into two parts by the extension of the band separating Registers A and B, and in it were portrayed the two compositions that form the two Center Panels. In these compositions the figures

from the intermediate stage were incorporated.[146] The original design can safely be attributed to the first stage in the decoration of the chamber as a whole because certain of its elements can be seen running into the area subsequently assigned to the Wing Panels of the Central Group.[147]

The design originally painted above the Torah Shrine, traced directly from the wall itself shortly after the completion of the excavation by the technical expert who handled and preserved the paintings, is reproduced on Pl. XVII.[148] It contained at least three elements, of which the central and most important is a large tree. The tree has a heavy trunk that tapers rapidly, however, and gives place to thin vine-like branches running out horizontally and vertically to form a well-balanced, almost quadratic design. While the trunk is brown, the branches, like the irregular leaves and tendrils, are a bright green.

It is tempting, in view of the form of the leaves and of the presence of the tendrils, to identify the object forthwith as a schematized vine.[149] A vine

146. For a more detailed account of the process see below, pp. 215–227. The process is complicated by the fact that after the first and again after the final painting a canopy adorning the Torah Shrine was anchored to the wall in the area of the Lower Center Panel, partly obscuring its imagery and causing additional changes in the rendering.

147. Cf. especially in Pl. LXXVII, the left side of Panel III (lower right Wing Panel of the Central Group), where the tips of the green branches of the tree can be seen projecting into the field above and below the level of the hip of the standing figure, having been brought into view by the disintegration of the background color of the panel.

148. The tracing, made on cellophane, is the work of Henry Pearson. Among the several attempts made by members of the expedition staff to recapture the original design, it has revealed itself as the most reliable. Sketches of parts of the design, held in confusion with elements of the overpainting, will be found in Du Mesnil du Buisson, *Peintures*, p. 28, Fig. 23, and Pl. XXIII. It should be noted in this connection that the rendering offered by Grabar, "Le Thème," p. 162, Fig. 4, is clearly described as a secondary derivative from Du Mesnil du Buisson's drawings, being intended only to show the iconographic scheme, and therefore lacks independent value. The photomontage attempted by Wischnitzer, *Messianic Theme*, is a similar derivative and in details entirely misleading.

149. Erect vines occur on Assyrian bas-reliefs; e.g., Gadd, *Stones of Assyria*, Pl. 16; and in mosaics of at least the late Roman period heavy trunk-like stocks appear, but these are borrowed largely, it would seem, from the "acanthus-head." Cf. F. Biebel in *Gerasa*, pp. 302 f. and Pl. LIXb; and the Sabratha mosaic, H. Peirce and R. Tyler, *L'Art byzantin*, II (1934), Pl. 115. The trunk in this instance seems unrelated to the "acanthus-head."

would indeed be fitting in a synagogue; for the vine, having long been a favorite metaphor in Biblical literature and Jewish speech, had frequently been represented in Jewish art; for instance, on Jewish coins, on the great portal giving access to the Temple at Jerusalem, and on the friezes of the Galilean type of synagogue.[150] In the Bible and the Midrash it is a standard, if not the most common, metaphor for the Chosen People itself, and in this sense would be entirely appropriate in Dura's House of Assembly. In other parts of Jewish literature, however, it serves as a figure of the Torah, a sense in which it would also be apposite in the area just above the Torah Shrine.[151] Yet, apart from the heavy trunk, there is one feature of the design which calls its identification as a vine into question. This is the fact that painted grape clusters are absent and that the tree seems at one time to have been studded with blossoms in the form of applied plaster rosettes. Fragments of such rosettes were found on the floor of the chamber, and the holes that held the wooden pegs by which they were affixed are visible at irregular intervals in the area covered by the design.[152] Aside from the vine the only object in the form of a tree that might have merited representation in a Jewish Synagogue is the familiar Tree of Life (Gen. 2.9). This tree has a long history in Oriental art and in the Jewish art, both of the Roman period and of the Renaissance.[153] In the literary tradition — apocryphal, syncretistic, Jewish, and Christian — it is described in many different ways or said to beggar all description. Apart from its size, the one point upon which most ancient authors are inclined to agree is that of the pleasant odors proceeding

from it, especially from its blossoms.[154] While the Tree of Life can also serve as a symbol of the Torah, and in this sense would be appropriate as a design surmounting the Torah Shrine, it is evident from the literature that its primary associations are with Jewish eschatological hopes, more particularly with the paradise of the blessed.[155] Taking the position that the further development of the area in the second phase of the decoration of the House of Assembly emphasized the national hope, we are inclined to regard the tree in the original design as the Tree of Life.[156] But due consideration must be given in this connection also to the other parts of the design, for which a concordant interpretation must be provided.

Beneath the tree two objects were represented in the original design, one at either side of the trunk. Both are quite indistinct and only dimly visible through the overpainting.[157] This makes them difficult to describe accurately and doubly difficult to interpret. At the left of the tree stood a piece of furniture with turned legs and a flat top. The object seems to have been yellow in color, hence of gold or sheathed in gold. Upon it lay something of which we can know only the oval shape.[158]

150. For the vine as a metaphor in Biblical usage, see e.g., Isa. 5.1; Jer. 2.21; Ezek. 19.10; Hos. 10.1. For the vine on coins see Romanoff, *Jewish Symbols on Ancient Jewish Coins*, pp. 43–45, 75. For the vine on Herod's Temple see Josephus, *Bellum* V, 5,4 = § 211. For vines in synagogue decoration see Kohl and Watzinger, *Antike Synagogen*, e.g., p. 50, Fig. 99b, c; p. 104, Fig. 199.

151. So e.g., Hullin 92a (Trans., p. 515).

152. The overlay of Pl. XXXIV shows the location of the holes in the area. Some of them, particularly along the bottom, anchored the canopy that covered the Torah Shrine, but the larger proportion of them must have served a different purpose. On the canopy see below, p. 258.

153. For details and for the earlier literature on the subject, see now Z. Ameisenowa, *Journal of the Warburg Institute*, II (1938–39), pp. 326–345.

154. So in both the earlier literature (see especially *Ethiopic Enoch* 24, 4; *Slavonic Enoch* 8, 3) and in the later literature. For the latter, see, e.g., *Midrash Gan Eden* (ed. Jellinek, *Beth ha-Midrasch*, III, pp. 52 f.; trans. A. Wünsche, *Aus Israels Lehrhallen*, III, 1909, p. 22) and *Seder Gan Eden* (Jellinek, *op. cit.*, III, p. 138, trans. Wünsche, *op. cit.*, p. 62) and in general, L. Ginzberg, *The Legends of the Jews*, V (1925), p. 119, n. 113.

155. On the former see comments of Rabbi Banna'ah and Rabbi Naḥman ben Isaac in Ta'anith 7a (Trans., pp. 25 f.) referred to also by Sukenik (*The Synagogue*, p. 58). On the latter see IV Ezra 8.52, texts like the *Midrash Konen* (ed. Jellinek, *Beth ha-Midrasch*, V, p. 47, trans. Wünsche, *Aus Israels Lehrhallen*, III, pp. 180f.), and Rev. 22.2. In view of the further development of the area originally devoted to the picture of the tree in the Synagogue, it should be noted that Abraham, Isaac, Jacob, David, and all the generations of Israel are said to dwell in the shade of the Tree of Life in the hereafter.

156. See below, pp. 215–227.

157. At some points actual elements of the original design are available, at others we have only indirect evidence of their shape and character. The latter is supplied by the areas where the existence of an underpainting caused the later layers to pull the entire accumulation of paint away from the wall, leaving the plaster bare, but in so doing revealing at least the shape of the object originally represented.

158. It was represented by an area devoid of all traces of paint when first discovered. The light film of red now covering it was acquired when loose red pigment from the

It was probably a cushion or bolster. If the cushion appears today in a crescent form, this is because it supported another object, the character of which is even more indeterminable. It seems to have been circular in form, possibly with a knob or projection at the very top.[159] Below the piece of furniture early observation indicated the possible presence of still another object, rendered in our drawing as a duplicate of the one on the cushion or pillow above. The duplication suggested seems unlikely, for the dignity assigned to the object above by its position on a pillow should preclude its reappearance under the piece of furniture. What normally appears under similar pieces of furniture in the paintings of the Synagogue is a footstool (Pls. LXIII, LXV, LXVIII, LXXIV).

At the right of the tree there are visible as parts of the object originally portrayed here elements of two yellow — that is, golden — lions. The lions are in the erect, rampant pose and face each other, their tails describing graceful arcs, their bodies sleek and devoid of indications of a mane. It is evident that their extended paws cannot be supposed to have touched, which suggests that they held something between them, but all attempts to give it substance and outline must be regarded as fanciful.[160] Whatever it was that filled the space between the lions, it did not extend far above their heads, for the design is terminated at this level by a horizontal yellow band representing a bar or the edge of a plane. Extensive traces of this are still clearly visible.

A variety of interpretations has been suggested for the two symbols, each using one or more superficial indications of their character. But general allusions to the table of the shew-bread or to the Lion of Judah are of little help for the understanding of the composition of which these symbols were a part. Beginning with matters of iconography and with the more unusual object at the

right of the tree, it appears that its prototype can readily be found in the glyptic art of Mesopotamia and Syria, where tables whose tops are supported by confronted rampant lions are occasionally depicted. They stand in the presence of a seated god or king when he receives suppliants.[161] If the object at the right of the tree should properly be regarded as an ornate table, that at the left of the tree cannot possibly be a table also, for such variation of iconographic pattern would be unlikely in the period with which we are dealing. Instead it should be a backless throne, perhaps with footstool, of the type familiar in Oriental and western iconography.[162] The object represented upon the cushion should in this case be one of the insignia of royalty, conceivably a mitre or filleted crown, such as is worn by Ahasuerus in Panel WC 2 (Pl. LXV) and by the lyre-player in the Lower Center Panel (Pl. LXXIV).

If table and throne may thus be said to appear together in appropriate fashion, the question is what they represent and what their association with the tree may be thought to imply. The objects are, of course, of gold, hence particularly important, rivaling in the later decorations of the Synagogue the throne of Solomon (Panel WA 2, Pl. XXVIII) and contrasting with that of Pharaoh (Panel WC 4, Pl. LXVIII). Since throne and table are bare — the one of the person to occupy it, the other of the food

upper parts of the overpainting was carried along by the protecting coat of varnish recently applied to the entire surface of the panel.

159. The remains of yellow color in the area of the object on the cushion belong to the garment of Jacob in the overpainting, for the yellow is on top of the red wash used to expunge the original design.

160. There are traces of yellow pigment at the right and left of the right lion (near the head and under the belly) underneath the red cover coat that preceded the overpainting.

161. See e.g., G. Contenau, *La Glyptique syro-hittite* (1922), p. 115, Pl. XLI (no. 309b) and XLII (no. 310); and Frankfort, *Cylinder Seals*, pp. 285f., Fig. 92, and Pl. XLIII, o. The type is continued in Hellenistic furniture, where griffins usually replace the lions and where the animals are usually addorsed instead of being affronted; see Winter and Pernice, *Die hellenistische Kunst in Pompeji*, V (1932), p. 2, Fig. 1.

162. On the backless throne see the article by Hug in *RE*, 2nd ed., IV, 1 (VII, 1931), cols. 398–422, *s.v.* "Stuhl," and the representations of Sassanian monarchs on silver dishes such as that in the Hermitage showing Chosroes I (K. Erdmann, *Die Kunst Irans*, 1943, Pl. 67). The difficulties of interpreting the object as a shew-bread table are manifold and arise not only from what is known about the number and the shape of the shew-bread (twelve loaves according to Lev. 24.5–6, and square according to the Mishnah, Menahoth 11b), but also from the form of the table in actual fact (see H. Holzinger, *Zeitschrift für die alttestamentliche Wissenschaft*, XXI, 1901, pp. 341f.) and in iconographic tradition, both Jewish (Codex Hebr. 7 of the Bibliothèque Nationale at Paris, conveniently accessible in Wischnitzer-Bernstein, *Gestalten und Symbole der jüdischen Kunst*, p. 26, Fig. 19) and Christian (Cod. Vat. 747, fol. 146).

that should be displayed upon it — the allusion can only be to some future ruler and future occasion. The ruler would in this instance most naturally be the Messianic king, perhaps David himself, and the occasion, that of the banquet prepared by God at the end of time as described, for instance, in the *Midrash Gan Eden we Gehinnom*, in which the table and throne of David both play a part.[163] The fact that the Messianic banquet occurs at the final consummation and can be described as taking place in *Gan Eden*, the Garden of Eden, gives a possible basis for the association of the Synagogue's symbols with the Tree of Life; for the tree, standing in the midst of the paradise of the blessed, provides the setting for the gathering of all the generations of Israel and for their leaders, who live henceforth in its shade.[164] So interpreted, the original design above the Torah Shrine may be said to be unified in itself, and may be thought to provide the basis both for the inclusion of its elements in the later scheme of decorations, and for the train of thought that governs the modification of these elements in the further development of the area.

4. DADO AND OTHER DECORATIVE ELEMENTS

The original scheme for the embellishment of the Synagogue's House of Assembly embraced still other elements than those already considered. This conclusion is based on inference, for the elements in question were never actually executed as planned. Apparently the Synagogue building was put into service at the earliest possible moment, even before the trim of the doorways had been put in place. It was in consequence of this fact that the decorators were required to apply a coat of red paint to the foundation courses of the doorway against

which the door reveal was eventually built.[165] Why any additional embellishment planned for the interior of the House of Assembly should not have been executed at once — whether because the community had momentarily overextended itself financially in the building operation, or because the artists had other commitments to prevent them from carrying on at the time — we do not know. Probably there was an interval of six years between the construction of the Synagogue and the first phase of its decorations, on the one hand, and the inauguration of the second, more ambitious decorative program, on the other. When that period had elapsed, the community had clearly developed, not only in financial competence, but also in numbers; and the incomplete portions of the first plan of decoration were executed in modified form as parts of the second.

The basic fact upon which inferences about additional elements of the original scheme of the Synagogue decorations rest, is the existence of scratch-lines on the face of the west wall of the House of Assembly. Such scratch-lines are, of course, used by artists to lay out areas of a wall in advance of the application of color. Strangely enough, the artists who later executed the narrative panels did not incise their scratch-lines, which often makes the registers develop unevennesses in their course about the room. It is doubly strange therefore to find incised scratch-lines running horizontally through the fields occupied by the panels of Register C and marring the compositions. In the Preliminary Report it was suggested that originally the artists had projected four rather than three registers of narrative scenes;[166] but this suggestion has been rendered valueless by the fact that no similar lines were used to lay out the registers actually executed, and by the further observation that on this assumption respective heights of the registers would have been disproportionate to their location on the walls. Hence it follows that the scratch-lines are part of the first scheme in the decoration of the House of Assembly.

One of the two scratch-lines can actually be traced along the entire length of the west wall,

163. See Jellinek, *Beth ha-Midrasch*, V (1938), pp. 45 f.; and Ginzberg, *Legends of the Jews*, IV (1913), pp. 115 f., and VI (1928), pp. 272 f., nn. 128–130. The story tells how David seated on his throne is asked by God to say the blessing over the cup on the table. David in this account is himself acting in a Messianic capacity.

164. So, e.g., the *Midrash Konen* (Jellinek, *Beth ha-Midrasch*, II, pp. 28 f., trans. Wünsche, *Aus Israels Lehrhallen*, III, pp. 180 f.). The interpretation here proposed has been approximated also by Wischnitzer-Bernstein, *Messianic Theme*, pp. 91–93, but on the basis of materials and with implications for the interpretation of the narrative panels which I cannot accept.

165. See above, p. 18. Corroborative evidence was supplied by the indications of wear on the foundations under the reveal floor.

166. *Rep. VI*, p. 374.

running at a height of approximately 1.15 m. above the top of the benches and on a level 0.15 m. above the painted base line of the narrative panels of Register C (Pls. LXIII–LXVIII). The second can be followed only on the north half of the west wall, to the right of the Torah Shrine and runs at a level 0.60 m. above the first (Pls. LXVI–LXVIII). To interpret their meaning we must revert momentarily to the earlier building of the Synagogue and its decorations, where, it will be recalled, the walls were developed with an imitation of a solid marble plinth at the bottom, surmounted by a dado imitating marble incrustation work approximately 0.50 m. high, the upper part of the wall being left bare. Given the fact that the decorative patterns followed in the earlier building carried over into the first phase of the decorative work on the later House of Assembly — as, for instance, in the embellishment of the niche of the Torah Shrine — it seems safe to suggest that the scratch-lines were intended to lay out for development an imitation marble plinth and dado, comparable to those in the earlier building.[167] Such a development of the walls carried about the room would have lessened the barrenness of the large surfaces they presented to the worshiper.

The question may at least be raised in this connection, whether the original scheme of wall decoration did not include also other elements of a formal nature. What raises the question is the existence in the later scheme of certain elements not apparently treated as seriously by the artists as one would expect. These are the pilasters represented at the ends of each of the four walls, whose function it is to lend the fiction of support to the painted architrave that apparently ran along the top of each wall, undergirding the ceiling beams. The peculiar feature of these corner pilasters is that they hang in the air, so to speak, coming to an end at the bottom of Register B, instead of being carried down to the level of the benches. Apparently the later artists found themselves so pressed for space in executing the narrative panels of Register C that they merely discontinued the pilasters and used the space these would have occupied for pictorial purposes. Such a step would be the more intelligible if the demand for the representation of pilasters was something they had inherited from the Synagogue officials as part of the original scheme of decoration, rather than something they themselves had formulated.

Should this line of speculation have any value, we might need to visualize as the original plan for the embellishment of the House of Assembly a scheme calling for an ornate ceiling, a fully decorated Torah Shrine, and an architectural element framing, but not filling, each of the four walls. This last element would have consisted of plinth, dado, corner pilasters, and architrave, and would have been enriched on the west wall by the addition of the design over the Torah Shrine, which it served ultimately to frame. So interpreted, the original scheme would be a late derivative of the structural style of decoration used in the earlier building.[168]

B. Elements of the Second Stage in the Decoration of the House of Assembly

1. ORGANIZATION OF THE DECORATIONS

In contrast to those that had preceded them, the decorations of the House of Assembly in the second stage of their development were most elaborate, the product of a program that called for the embellishment of all four walls of the room from the benches to the ceiling. Dura provides analogies in such elaborate over-all decorations as the painted cellas of the temples of Bel, of Zeus Theos, of Adonis, and of Mithras, but the rooms in question are all of relatively modest proportions.[169] In a chamber 13.72 m. long and 7.68 m. wide, whose walls rose to a height of almost 7 m., the inauguration of a program intended to achieve the same result was no mean undertaking. Of the devotion of those who authorized and executed this undertaking, the pictures themselves and the importance

167. In the revised scheme executed some years later the plinth was omitted and the dado given a position lower down on the wall to provide sufficient space for three registers of narrative panels.

168. See above, p. 37.

169. On the paintings of the Temple of Bel (Palmyrene Gods) see Cumont, *Fouilles*, pp. 41–145. For those of the temples of Mithras, Adonis, and Zeus Theos, see *Rep. VII–VIII*, pp. 104–116, 158–163, 196–210.

they have acquired in the study of ancient decorative art — pagan, Jewish, and Christian — are a fitting memorial.

For the organization of the decorations the artists adopted the old familiar system of dividing the walls horizontally into zones, in this instance five zones of unequal height (Plans IX–XII). The uppermost of these, directly under the ceiling, is not preserved, but it was probably something less than a meter high, matching in this particular the lowest, to which a height of 0.70 m. was assigned.[170] The three intermediate zones, which we here designate Registers A, B, and C respectively, beginning at the top, were each well over a meter high, and by that token important decorative areas. Of the three, Register B was the highest, *ca.* 1.50 m.; A the lowest, *ca.* 1.10 m.; and C intermediate in height, *ca.* 1.30 m. The actual dimensions fluctuate by as much as 0.10 m. from wall to wall and from one end of a wall to the other.[171] These discrepancies undoubtedly arise in part at least from the fact that each wall was decorated separately, and do not in the least nullify the artists' intention that the several zones should be understood as continuing on the same plane about the entire chamber. The failure of the zones to meet at precisely the same level is masked by the fact that at the ends of each wall vertical strips 0.36–0.50 m. wide have been set aside, running through Registers A and B. These may be thought of as extensions of the decorations in the uppermost zone.

The decorations of the two narrow zones, along the bottom and the top of the walls respectively, were no doubt equally conventional in character, the former consisting of a continuous dado in imitation of marble incrustation work, the latter in all probability a painted imitation of molded architraves, giving imaginary support to the beams of

the ceiling and being themselves supported by the painted pilasters that filled the vertical strips at the ends of the walls in the corners of the room. The decorations of the three intermediate zones consisted of narrative compositions portraying incidents, persons, and institutions that had served to reveal and to mediate the divine favor shown toward Israel in the past, and prophetic pronouncements that gave assurance of the culmination of that favor in the future. They are therefore fundamentally Biblical and historical.

The subject matter of the decorations of Registers A, B, and C — chosen, combined, and divided in accordance with certain principles clear to the artists but not always equally clear to us — was presented upon the walls in compact scenes framed by ornamental bands. These bands are here spoken of as "register bands" where they frame the top and the bottom of the panels, for here they form continuous lines dividing the zones from each other. They are spoken of as "panel bands" where they divide the several scenes of a single register from each other.

In arranging the narrative compositions, the artists were apparently not normally constrained by the principles of symmetrical space distribution. On the north wall, for instance, a single large composition occupies a space in Register C that on the south wall is divided into four separate panels. Within the area of a given wall, moreover, symmetry of panel arrangement is also absent save in one particular instance; namely, at the center of the west wall. Here, in the area directly above the Torah Shrine, Registers A and B have each a Center Panel of equal length, flanked at either side by unusually narrow Wing Panels containing single standing figures (Pl. XXIV). The arrangement of these six panels, here designated the "Central Group," is clearly the result of planning. It was undoubtedly intended to give the decorative scheme a focal element analogous to that of the Torah Shrine in the architectural organization of the chamber. This unifies the work in the two media and gives the Central Group a special significance among the narrative scenes.

As regards the organization of the narrative compositions, two further matters must be mentioned in passing. The first concerns the principle determining the relative height of Registers A, B,

170. To take up the unevenness in the rise of the benches from the level of the floor and to reduce wear on the decorations of the lowest zone, a strip along the bottom of the walls was left bare. Its height varies from 0.13 m. to 0.27 m.

171. On the west wall Register B varies between 1.435 m. at its southern end and 1.56 m. at its northern end, while Register C fluctuates between 1.31 m. at either side of the Torah Shrine to 1.29 m. at the ends of the wall. On the north wall Register A is *ca.* 1.20 m. high, and on the south wall Register C begins at the left with a height of only 1.26 m.

5*

and C. What happened here apparently was that the top of the smaller doorway at the south end of the east wall fixed the upper limit of Register C, and that of the large central doorway the upper limit of Register B, leaving for the topmost register, A, only the modest space between B and the painted architrave undergirding the beams of the ceiling.[172] The second matter concerns the placement of the Central Group in its relation to the Torah Shrine. It will be evident from Plan IX and Pl. XXIV that, as actually developed upon the west wall, the axis of this group of panels is 0.18 m. off and to the south of the axis of the Torah Shrine.[173] This is very noticeable from the main doorway and destroys for our tastes much of the symmetry which the artists clearly endeavored to create. In part the inaccuracy in the placement of the Central Group may be but a further reflection of that same Oriental lack of concern for the niceties of execution that has already come to our attention at many other points. Fundamentally, however, the displacement may be said to result from the unequal development of the design originally executed in the area covered by the center panels.[174] The fact that the artists who painted the Tree of Life in this area did not align its trunk with the axis of the Torah Shrine and extended its branches farther to the right than to the left — which in an unframed composition is quite understandable — apparently caused the artists of the later period, when they decided to incorporate it in their decorations, to arrange the vertical lines delimiting its field without due consideration of the precise position of the Torah Shrine. If they began their work at the top of the wall, this could readily have happened.[175]

As an example of the survival and combination of older types, the arrangement of the decorations in the Dura Synagogue is by no means uninteresting. Far removed from the elaborate systems familiar from the murals of Campania, and only slightly more reminiscent of the "linear" framework used in the West in the third century of our era by virtue of the relative simplicity common to both,[176] it is in effect a synthesis of earlier eastern and the western elements. Five are worthy of mention in this connection.

Basic to the entire arrangement is the tradition of a zonal division of interior wall space such as is exhibited in the tombs of Mustapha Pasha and Sidi Gaber in Egyptian Alexandria, of Pydna in Macedonia, and of Panticapaeum in South Russia, as well as in at least one house of Delos.[177] This Hellenistic, and ultimately structural, method of dividing wall space, the forebear apparently of the so-called First Pompeian Style, is reflected in the Synagogue, not only in the existence of multiple zones, but also in the treatment of the lowest zone as an imitation of marble incrustation work.[178] Instead of being rendered in plain, solid colors, the upper zones of the Synagogue become the medium for the representation of rows of narrative compositions, recalling in this connection as a probable second contribution to the decorative synthesis the "strip" arrangement of historical and mythical scenes that is so constant a feature of the bas-relief sculpture of the ancient Near East. In its latest phases, as reflected in the bas-reliefs of Sassanian times, for instance, at Shapur, these frieze-like representations break down into smaller panels arranged in registers quite as in the painted decorations of the Synagogue.[179]

A third factor in the synthesis is the architectural framework represented by the corner pilasters and the painted architraves which they support. This is in all probability not a late echo of the complicated architectural ornament of Pompeian

172. The height of the two doorways, inferred from proportions (see above pp. 18, 20) corresponds quite accurately to the height of the two registers above floor level if the elevation of the door sills above the floor of the chamber is added.

173. The center panel of Register B extends *ca.* 0.40 m. beyond the aedicula to the south and only *ca.* 0.04 m. beyond the aedicula to the north.

174. Cf. above p. 62, n. 147.

175. The effect of imbalance is heightened by the fact that the Torah Shrine itself is off-axis in relation to the main door of the chamber. Actually the main door is 0.51 m. north of the center of the east wall, and the aedicula is 0.11 m. north of the center of the west wall. This puts the aedicula some 0.41 m. to the south of the axis of the doorway.

176. On the later, more simplified forms of wall decoration in the West, see Wirth, *Römische Wandmalerei*, p. 138, Fig. 68; p. 179, Fig. 93; Pl. 32, etc.

177. Cf. A. Adriani, *Municipalité d'Alexandrie: Annuaire du musée gréco-romain* (1933–34, 1934–35), pp. 113–132; and Rostovtzeff, *Journal of Hellenic Studies*, XXXIX (1919), pp. 147–150.

178. Cf. Adriani, *op. cit.*, e.g., p. 123, Fig. 55.

179. Cf. F. Sarre and E. Herzfeld, *Iranische Felsreliefs* (1910), e.g., Pl. XLV.

wall decoration, but rather a reminiscence of the more fundamental association of zonal wall decoration and actual architectural form such as can now be seen in the graves of Mustapha Pasha and may underlie the "architectural style."[180] More important than this architectural framework is, in the fourth place, the division of the registers and their several panels into separate entities by the introduction of register and panel bands. The development of this particular feature of the decorations can be followed at Dura over a period of more than a century and a half. It begins with the elaborate architectural framework that encloses the several scenes and persons of the naos of the Temple of Bel, where it forms an integral part of the composition, yet also makes a division between registers.[181] This apparently was reduced in the next stage to bands representing moldings, as in the Temple of Zeus Theos and the Temple of Adonis, and eventually degenerated into a series of parallel lines such as we find dividing the registers in the Christian Chapel.[182] Finally in the third century a single wide band is used as a means of register and panel division and as a frame for isolated scenes, as on the north wall of the pronaos of the Temple of Bel, in the Roman bath in Block E3, and in the last form of the Mithraeum.[183] In the Synagogue, belonging as it does to the very last years of Dura's history, the monochrome panel and register band is enlivened by a twisted ribbon pattern, a fact which marks the completion of its transition from the architectural into the decorative sphere.

One additional feature of the organization of the decorative material in the second stage of the embellishment of the House of Assembly still has to be noted. It is the accentuation of the focal area

directly over the aedicula by a specially balanced Central Group of panels. The full significance of this feature cannot be developed except in connection with an interpretation of the nature and meaning of the decorations which the well-organized framework contains. This, however, should be noted in the present context; namely, that there is in the decorations of the painted temples of Dura, as well as in the Christian Chapel, a tendency so to organize the pictorial material as to make a distinction between the focal rear wall of the chamber and the side walls. In the Temple of Bel, as in that of Zeus Theos, the rear cella wall received an oversize representation of the deity to whom the temple was sacred, and the side walls, representations of his worshipers performing acts of devotion before him.[184] Such representations were not feasible for the religious communities of Jews or Christians by reason of the nature of their religious belief, and by reason of a different understanding of the nature of the religious relationship. Yet apparently the principle of organization carried over from the one sphere of religious art to the other for very definite practical reasons, and the recognition of the principle is a matter of outstanding importance for the interpretation of the decorations of the Synagogue, as well as for the interpretation of the systems of decoration employed in later Christian churches.[185]

In discussing here the material belonging to the second stage of the decorations of the House of Assembly, we shall begin with the scenes developed in the registers that run the circuit of the walls, and proceed from these to the conventional materials represented by the dado of the lowest zone, the corner pilasters, the decorations of the door reveals, and the register and panel bands. The pictorial compositions will naturally receive the fuller treatment, in keeping with their greater importance. In dealing with these narrative scenes we shall presuppose what has already been said about their arrangement, and shall separate out from the larger body those comprising the Central Group. These will be discussed last. As for the sequence in which the rest of the scenes are examined, this is largely pragmatic and should not be taken to pre-

180. Cf. Adriani, *op. cit.*, esp. Pls. III, 2; VIII, 1; and A.

181. Cf. Cumont, *Fouilles*, Pls. XXXI–XXXII. The paintings are of the late first century of our era.

182. For the moldings dividing the registers of the Temple of Zeus Theos and framing the decorations of the Temple of Adonis, see *Rep. VII–VIII*, p. 197, Fig. 50, and p. 159, Fig. 44. The structures are dated *ca.* A.D. 114–116 and A.D. 150–160 respectively. For the Chapel see *Rep. V*, pp. 255f. and Pl. XLVIII. Date prior to A.D. 232.

183. For the late paintings from the Temple of Bel see Cumont, *Fouilles*, Pls. LIV, XLIX (*ca.* A.D. 230); for the baths in E3 see *Rep. II*, p. 62; and for the Mithraeum (*ca.* A.D. 240), *Rep. VII–VIII*, Pl. XIV.

184. This scheme merely transforms into a principle of decorative arrangement the actual physical relationship of worshipers to a cult statue in the precincts of a temple.

185. On this see below, pp. 348f.

judge the question of their supposed relation to each other in thought or sequence of events. We shall deal with the panels register by register, beginning at the top of the room. In the case of Registers A and B, which are only partially preserved, we begin at either end of the extant series and follow the succession to the Central Group. In Register C, which is almost complete, we begin at the southeast corner of the room, where a partial

break occurs, and follow the series around the entire room. Our concern in the present context will be to present and describe as accurately as possible what remains of the several compositions and to identify the subject matter they depict. The systematic discussion of the style, composition, iconography, origin, and importance of the material belongs to the succeeding section.

2. THE PANELS OF REGISTER A

Jacob at Bethel

Panel NA 1 (fragmentary). H. *ca.* 1.20 m.; L. 1.43 m. (Pl. XXVI).[186]

Hopkins and Du Mesnil du Buisson, "La Synagogue," p. 248; Du Mesnil du Buisson, "Les Peintures," p. 110; *idem, Peintures*, pp. 28f.; Rostovtzeff, "Die Synagoge," p. 211; *Rep. VI*, p. 344; Grabar, "Le Thème," pp. 154–157; Schneid, *The Paintings*, pp. 10f.; Sonne "The Paintings," pp. 276–278; Sukenik, *The Synagogue*, pp. 111–113; Wischnitzer, *Messianic Theme*, pp. 73f.

The composition is poorly preserved. A triangular section representing about a third of the picture was cut away from the top at the right when the north wall of the building was reduced to the gradient of the embankment in which it was

buried.[187] Relative proximity to the surface of the embankment has dimmed outlines and colors all along the diagonal upper edge of what remains and has contributed to the breaking of the plaster in this area. Even when the building was still under a roof, however, the pressure of the fill behind the west wall of the building, transmitting itself to the north wall, produced a wide crack running down through the picture at the left and causing the loss of portions of the surface. Happily, the portions affected belong largely to the background and the frame of the composition.[188]

186. The designations of the several panels (here NA 1) give first the wall (north, south, east, west), then the register (A, B, and C, beginning at the top of the wall), and finally the number of the panel in the register, counting from the left end of each wall.

187. Cf. above, p. 5. Preserved to the very top of the panel at the left, the height of the painting exceeds that of the panels of Register A on the west wall by *ca.* 0.10 m., indicating a slight difference in the alignment of the registers. At the right the height of the portion preserved is only *ca.* 0.43 m.

188. The crack cuts down through the field parallel to and just behind the lower of the two figures mounting the ladder, turning back sharply at the level of his calf to the frame of the composition and continuing downward through the frame and the area of the corner pilaster. All such cracks and losses were necessarily repaired when the chamber was reconstructed in the Damascus Museum, but the repairs are clearly identifiable as such on the originals and can for the most part be spotted even on the photographs from which our plates are made.

What remains of the picture is enough to show that its elements were arranged in two ascending planes, each with a different background color; namely, green below and black above, the black indicating that the events portrayed occur at night.[189] Against the green of the lower plane the artist has set the recumbent figure of a man enfolded in a grayish-lavendar himation. Occupying the entire width of the field, he lies with his feet toward the left side of the panel and with his head toward the right. Up to the shoulders his body rests upon a broken reddish-brown mass, but his head is pillowed upon a large object of a lighter color. With this thoroughly static element of the composition that of the upper plane stands in sharp contrast. Here the eye is led diagonally upward from left to right along a large yellow ladder, up which two elaborately dressed figures are ascending rapidly. Whatever else the composition may once have contained, the sleeper in the foreground, the ladder with the men mounting it, and the nocturnal setting are sufficient to indicate that the scene portrays the familiar story of Jacob at Bethel (Gen. 28.10–17), which tells how the patriarch, resting in the open from his travels, had the dream of the ladder connecting heaven and earth and of the angels ascending and descending upon it.

It is important to note and to record the organization of the scene and the rendering of the details. From the use of two different background colors it is evident that the artist was familiar with the "stage space" convention[190] Yet being unable to contain his imagery within the space defined, he used what should have been a backdrop as a second plane of the field, falling back upon the ancient Oriental method of bringing more distant objects into view by representing them separately on a higher level.[191] The massive Jacob who lies in the foreground presumably wears the costume of chiton and himation that the later Orient had inherited from the Greeks, and that is familiar from the contemporary paintings and sculptures of Palmyra. It appears to greater advantage in other compositions and is used by the Synagogue artists for all males save children, servants, or the like, and members of the court and Temple personnel.[192] The himation, its folds boldly outlined in black and softened by the addition of brown shadow lines, envelops not only Jacob's body but his left arm and hand, from which its ends hang down in symmetrically arranged pleats.[193] The fact that on the upper part of his body the curves marking the folds of the garment are unbroken shows that his right arm does not rest upon his chest, suggesting that it probably was extended upward into the damaged part of the panel where, bent at the elbow, it supported Jacob's head.[194] Of the head itself nothing remains save a bright red color-mass with some slight indication of black about it, representing traces of the hair. The color associated with the face matches that of the projecting and unshod left foot, and the shape of the pigmented area suggests that the face was turned into a frontal position.

The reddish-brown mass upon which Jacob lies is hatched with angular brown lines. The lines are particularly clear at the left and are intended to emphasize the stony character of the place, to which the Biblical narrative alludes (Gen. 28.11). This rocky mass, however, is crossed at intervals by three or possibly four wide, curving bands such as commonly ornament the mattresses of beds, this being a simple device used to indicate that the

189. Black backgrounds are used to indicate nocturnal settings also in the upper left half of Panel NB 2 (Hannah and the Child Samuel at Shiloh) and in the central section of Panel EC 1 (David and Saul in the Wilderness of Ziph).

190. Most of the Synagogue murals have monochrome backgrounds, denying spatial depth. Yet the artists knew the "stage space" convention, which creates a limited spatial depth by setting aside a separate strip along the bottom of a composition. The convention occurs, for instance, in Panels WB 1 (Wilderness Encampment and the Miraculous Well of Be'er), WB 2 (Consecration of the Tabernacle and its Priests), WC 4 (Pharaoh and the Infancy of Moses), and NB 1 (Battle of Eben-ezer). The last-mentioned illustrates the use of the "stage space" convention most adequately. The necessary references to the literature on the subject are given in that connection. Cf. below, p. 95, n. 307.

191. The Oriental tradition is familiar from the ancient bas-reliefs of Assyria and the tomb paintings of Egypt.

192. The several details of the costume are clearly visible, for instance, in Panel WA 3 (Exodus and Crossing of the Red Sea). Cf. below, pp. 81 f.

193. For covered hands in other panels see below, pp. 166 f., 235.

194. The sleeping figures of the central section of Panel EC 1 (David and Saul in the Wilderness of Ziph) hold their right or their left arms in the position suggested. Cf. Pl. XXXII.

rocks serve the sleeper as his couch.[195] According to the story, Jacob took one of the stones of the place and used it as a pillow, later making of it a sacred *betyl*. This must originally have been prominently displayed at the right, behind Jacob's head and right arm, but all that remains of it today is a light gray or white mass apparently circular in form.

The ladder whose lower pole forms the dividing line between the green and the black sections of the background, at least at the left, and thus separates the two sections of the composition from each other, springs from the side of the panel. Yellow in color (hence golden) and outlined in brown, it is seen in profile quite like those of the Assyrian bas-reliefs of siege operations.[196] The two figures that mount it therefore place their feet upon the poles rather than the rungs. The first man at the left is the more clearly visible. His left leg is bent sharply at the knee, as would be proper if he were to be shown in profile striding confidently up the ladder. Actually, however, the right foot and the upper part of the body are portrayed in a frontal position. This reduces the bent knee to a cliché of motion unrelated to pose. The extended right arm gestures toward the sleeping Jacob, while the left is bent at the elbow with the hand gesturing upward toward the top of the ladder, as the position of the lines that mark the cuff of his sleeve indicates. The man wears high, soft, white boots; pink trousers whose folds are outlined in red; and a long-sleeved reddish-brown tunic, its lower end adorned with a band done in the brown that is used also to indicate its folds. The tunic is gathered at the waist with a narrow white belt and is decorated with a vertical band down the middle. This combination of tunic, trousers, and boots represents in the Synagogue paintings the costume of court and Temple personnel.[197] Here the man

wears in addition a yellow chlamys that is held in place on the right shoulder, presumably by a fibula, and that falls along the side of his body at the right.[198] Of the second figure it is clear only that his pose is identical, that he is somewhat shorter than his neighbor, and that he is similarly clad, with white boots and pink trousers.

From what has been said it should be evident that the scene of Jacob at Bethel as the Synagogue artist has presented it is a simple paratactic combination of certain elements essential to the story. This is characteristic of most of the Synagogue compositions. Though the artist knows conventions of the realistic tradition, such as those of space limitation, he is unable to use them effectively and finds no contradiction between them and devices like the mattress bands which he injects arbitrarily to make his meaning inescapably clear. In rendering the elements of his composition he falls back in part upon models that are ultimately classical in inspiration (e.g., Jacob's garments and pose), and in part upon prototypes that are Iranian in character (e.g., the figures on the ladder). In the treatment of faces, figures, and objects, frontality dominates. Gestures and leg motions are stiff, and the relation between garments and body outlines are unrealistic.

It would be interesting to know how the missing upper part of the composition was handled. In the Christian rendering of the scene Christ sometimes appears at the top of the ladder, replacing God, to whom the Biblical narrative alludes in this connection (Gen. 28.13).[199] In Jewish art a corresponding representation of God is altogether unlikely, and indeed in the monuments of Christian art that are most likely to represent the earliest iconographic types there is nothing at the top of the ladder.[200] It seems likely, therefore, that in the Synagogue also the ladder simply came to an end against the frame of the composition at the right. That an additional figure was shown ascending or

195. For actual ornamental bands on the mattresses in the Synagogue, see Panel WC 1 (Pl. LXIV). They are regular features of the mattresses on Palmyrene funerary reliefs; see e.g., *Syria*, XVII (1936), Pl. XLVI, 2.

196. Cf. e.g., H. R. Hall, *Babylonian and Assyrian Sculpture in the British Museum* (1938), Pl. XL (Ashurbanipal).

197. The costume, which is ultimately Iranian in origin, appears to better advantage, e.g., in Panels WB 2 (Consecration of the Tabernacle) and WC 2 (Mordecai and Esther). For a description and discussion of it, see below, pp. 92, 129, 161.

198. The chlamys is associated with persons of a martial capacity in, e.g., the third section of Panel NC 1 (Ezekiel, the Destruction and Restoration of National Life, Pl. LXXI).

199. E.g., the Codex Vaticanus Graecus 747, fol. 50r, among the octoteuchs.

200. Cf. e.g., the scene of Jacob at Bethel in the Paris Gregory (B. N. 510, f. 174v), H. Omont, *Miniatures des plus anciens manuscrits grecs de la Bibliothèque Nationale* (1929), Pl. XXXVII.

descending the ladder is possible, but by no means to be taken for granted. That more than three persons could have been accommodated all told is extremely doubtful.[201]

The recent scholarly discussion of the scene has turned about the question whom the figures on the ladder represent. The question was first raised in connection with a passage in the *Pirke de Rabbi Eliezer*, where Jacob's dream is interpreted as showing him the "princes" of the four pagan nations (Babylonia, Persia, Greece, and Rome) climbing up and falling down from the ladder, to symbolize the rise and the ultimate fall of their kingdoms.[202] This would give the scene an eschatological import.[203] More recently a group of statements in the *Midrash Rabbah* on Gen. 28.12 has been taken to imply, among other things, that for the artist the ladder represented Mount Sinai and the two figures mounting it, Moses and Aaron.[204] The suggestions made by no means exhaust the range of the interpretations available in the Haggadic tradition, and could be multiplied still further by recourse to Philo's allegorical treatments of the Jacob story.[205]

For the appraisal of all such suggestions and for the interpretation of the Synagogue's narrative scenes as a whole, a clear understanding of the artists' principles of costume-attribution is absolutely necessary. These principles can readily be inferred from the paintings and are rigorously applied throughout. Leaving aside for the present the representation of soldiers, women, and children, it can be said that the artists portray two basically different types of costume. The one consists of a long chiton, an ample himation, and sandals and is ultimately Greek; while the other consists of a short, belted, long-sleeved, jacket-like tunic, trousers, and boots or shoes, and is ultimately Iranian. The latter is regularly associated with court and Temple personnel, the former with the "lay" group, including patriarchs, prophets, and members of the people not associated with either the religious or the official classes.

In the present context this means that, of the two figures ascending the ladder, neither can possibly be Moses — who otherwise appears always in chiton and himation — and that therefore the identification of the men as Moses and Aaron is out of the question. They could, of course, be "princes," but the suggestion that they must be the "princes" of the foreign nations because they do not have the proper dress for angels is invalid. So far as angels are concerned, it must be said that unless the figures mounting the ladder are of this category of beings, angels do not appear at all in the paintings of the Dura Synagogue. The winged figures used as acroteria on the Temples of Panels WB 2 and 3 (Pls. LX, LVII) are simple Nikés, as their reappearance on the city gate in Panel WA 3 (Pl. LIII) clearly indicates. The [winged figures in Section 2 of Panel NC 1 (Pl. LXX) are Psyches coming to breathe life into dead bodies. Anyone wishing to form a judgment on the representation of angels proper to ancient Jewish art should not let himself be confused by statements about special types of angels like the Seraphim, or by developments in Christian or mediaeval Jewish iconography.[206] Instead he should recall

201. This is entirely a matter of space limitation. Parts of two persons are all that is visible. The second from the bottom of the ladder is set astride the axis of the composition. If the interval between figures remained constant the panel could be thought to provide space horizontally for one additional figure. But vertical space relations must also be kept in mind. Judging by the position of the lowest figure, the head of the second must have come to within 0.10–0.15 m. of the top of the panel. Even this head room was achieved only by a noticeable reduction in the size of the figure. Whether there was a third figure depends upon whether the artist was willing to reduce still further its size and to crowd the upper frame still more closely.

202. *Pirke de Rabbi Eliezer* XXXV, ed. D. Luria (Wilna, 1837). Available also in the English translation of G. Friedlander (1916), p. 265.

203. So A. Grabar, who first called attention to the passage in the *Pirke*, and who emphasizes the eschatological implications of the decorations in his excellent essay, "Le Thème," pp. 154–157.

204. So Sonne in his important essay, "The Paintings," pp. 276–287. The symbolic interpretation is part of Sonne's attempt to show that Register A has as its theme the "crown of the Torah." He also finds lesser allusions to the crowns of the priesthood and the kingship. The section of the *Midrash Rabbah* referred to by Sonne is Gen. Rabbah LXVIII, 12–14 (Trans., II, pp. 625–629).

205. Cf. particularly *De somniis* I, §§ 133–156. Philo thinks of Jacob as the type of individual whom experience molds as he develops from the Supplanter to the Man who sees God, and of the angels on the ladder as typical

of the souls that mount upward or sink downward depending on whether they are engrossed in things heavenly or earthly.

206. On this subject see now the excellent article of F. Landsberger, *Hebrew Union College Annual*, XX (1947), pp. 227–254.

that in Jewish thought angels are normally regarded as males and as members of the royal retinue of God, the heavenly King.[207] This means that the figures on the ladder are costumed with entire propriety to represent the angels of whom the Biblical text speaks in the story of Jacob's dream.

To say that the figures on the ladder are likely to be angels does not yet rule out the suggested allusion to the *Midrash Rabbah.* Indeed, a closer scrutiny of the story about the "princes" of the foreign nations will indicate that the persons in question are not earthly monarchs at all, but actually the guardian spirits or heavenly representatives of the kingdoms in question, and hence themselves of the order of angels.[208] The real difficulty with the supposed allusion is that the artists should, on this assumption and in keeping with their own graphic realism, have shown the "princes" tumbling from the ladder instead of mounting it successfully.

Perhaps the identity of the angelic visitors in our panel can be settled with the help of a passage in the Targum hitherto neglected. To understand the passage it is necessary to realize that the story of Jacob's dream presented a difficulty to rabbinical exegetes in so far as the angels are said to "ascend and descend" the ladder, rather than vice versa. This was taken to imply that they were not on hand in heaven as a part of the regular celestial retinue, and hence on duty in, or connected with, the world. Some suggested that they were the angels appointed to guard or represent the worldly kingdoms, as we have seen above.[209] Others, however, claimed that they were angels appointed to accompany Jacob on all his travels after his departure from his father's house, and to act, we must assume, as his guardians. Of these guardian

angels of Jacob, we hear in the Palestinian Targum that they were two in number and that at Bethel they ascended the ladder and said to their celestial associates that they should come down and see Jacob, the (truly) pious man.[210] This resolution of the problem presented by the Biblical text accounts for the number of angels seen ascending in the panel and explains perfectly the gesture of the angel most clearly visible in the picture, whose extended right arm points toward Jacob, while his bent left may be thought to be beckoning to his comrades above.[211]

If the version of the story echoed in the Targum was actually the one that determined the iconography, then the panel can be said to have suggested the thought of God's renewing to Jacob at this occasion the pledge given to Abraham that his seed would possess the land. Jacob's own outstanding piety is the justification of this divine act.

Exodus and Crossing of the Red Sea

Panel WA 3. H. *ca.* 1.16 m.; L. 4.66 m. (Pls. LII–LIII).

Hopkins and Du Mesnil du Buisson, "La Synagogue," p. 247; Du Mesnil du Buisson, "Les Peintures," pp. 110f.; *idem, Peintures,* pp. 30–41; Rostovtzeff, "Die Synagoge," pp. 210f.; *Rep. VI,* pp. 345–347; De Vaux, "Un Detail," pp. 383–387; Grabar, "Le Thème," pp. 146–148; Sukenik, *The Synagogue,* pp. 73–85; Wischnitzer, *Messianic Theme,* pp. 74–78.

The longest of the compositions on the entire west wall, Panel WA 3 is a combination of several scenes, each portraying a large number of figures. Nowhere else in the Synagogue is space at such a premium and are the figures so tightly packed together. Two vertical elements of the composition serve respectively as a starting point for, and as a temporary check to, the action portrayed. They are: first, at the extreme right of the panel, a section of a high crenellated city wall joined with

---

207. Any handbook on Jewish religion will supply the proper perspective upon the angels as members of the heavenly court. Cf. e.g., Bousset and Gressmann, *Religion des Judentums,* pp. 320–327.

208. This is made particularly clear in Lev. Rabbah XXIX, 2 (Trans., IV, p. 370). Basic to the idea of such heavenly representatives is ultimately the Iranian conception that every human individual and earthly entity has a spiritual counterpart (Fravashi) in the upper realm.

209. The idea can be traced back to R. Meir (on the authority of some) according to Lev. Rabbah XXIX, 2 (Trans., IV, p. 370) and Ex. Rabbah XXXII, 7 (Trans., III, p. 411).

210. *Fragment Targum, ad* Gen. 28.12, ed. Ginzburger, p. 16.

211. It would seem to follow from this interpretation that if there was a third angel on the ladder, he was descending.

a still higher, similarly crenellated gate tower; and second, near the middle, a broad body of water reaching from the base to the very top of the panel. Though static in themselves, these elements of the composition are enlivened by the artist; the former by descending cloud masses, falling hailstones, free-standing columns, the open doors of the gate, and the statuary decorating the arch of its passageway; the latter by swimmers in various poses, fish breaking from the water, and indications of waves and highlights in the water itself. Hence the static elements of the composition do not really disturb the action that moves on vividly to the left of each of them.

The action of the panel is developed by the instrumentality of three figures of heroic proportions, each of which dominates a separate scene and exercises authority over groups of smaller figures closely crowded together. The first scene shows a man of heroic proportions leading a host from a city toward a body of water. The second shows a man associated by his action with the immersion of a group of men in the body of water. The third shows a man conducting a throng alongside a thin strip of water. The two last mentioned represent events involving the divine intervention, for the Hand of God comes out of the clouds in token of his miraculous assistance. As if the pictures themselves were not enough to identify the scenes, the artist has added Aramaic titles which tell us that the three large figures are three representations of Moses, and that the events are the Exodus, the Drowning of the Egyptians, and the Crossing of the Red Sea, respectively, reading from right to left (Exod. 12–14).[212]

Considering its position in the uppermost of the three registers of paintings, the panel is very well preserved. The surface is broken by one large horizontal crack that traces an uneven course through the lower part of the panel, and by three vertical cracks that join it, one in each of the three scenes.[213] The cracks have led to the loss of sections

of plaster, but the losses are minimal and do not affect our knowledge of details save in one particular.[214] The only distressing feature is the loss of the extreme upper end of the panel which, while devoted to background, apparently provided a treatment quite different from that of the other paintings of the Synagogue. Normally in the Synagogue backgrounds are done each in a single color that varies from panel to panel and gives no indication of spatial depth. Here the general tone of the background, so far as we can judge today, is a dull gray, but the gray is overlaid with descriptive elements. In the scene of the Red Sea Crossing and in that of the Exodus a wide black band traces an irregular course through the background area. Brick red Hands of God emerge from it at the left; and at the right, where it drops to run at a level only a short distance above the city wall, hailstones appear. The band therefore represents a cloud, but not necessarily merely such a cloud as one might naturally associate with the coming of the plague of hail (Exod. 9.13–35). In both the Exodus and in the Red Sea Crossing the band representing the cloud is associated with narrower stripes of gray and pink. In the scene of the Exodus they appear above the cloud, and in the Red Sea Crossing below the cloud. Whether the change means anything is not clear, but it could be that the artist was endeavoring to portray the cloud that "removed from before them and stood behind them" (Exod. 14.19), having no other place to put it. What suggests this possibility is the

212. Cf. Inscrs. nos. 3–5 below, pp. 269–271.

213. The horizontal crack, cutting through the columns at the extreme right, continues across the doorway of the gate and across the file of soldiers in the company of the liberated host, reaching the level of Moses' left hand, from which it dips across the scene of the drowning Egyptians to the level of the second Moses' knee. Swinging upward from this point to the right hand of the third Moses, it

moves down again to follow the line made by the feet of the soldiers at his left virtually to the end of the panel. One vertical crack comes down along the right side of the gate tower, causing no little breakage in the red column, where it joins the horizontal crack. A second cuts through the drowning scene somewhat to the left of the center, and a third coming from the right Hand of God moves diagonally toward the shoulder of the third Moses and follows the general direction of his arm and staff down through the water in the foreground. This last has a separate branch that cuts across Moses' neck and turns upward to the border again.

214. There are missing a goodly portion of the upper part of the left door of the city gate, a small fragment on the chest of the first Moses, a piece of the left shoulder of the second Moses and of the right shoulder and staff of the third Moses. The loss of part of the staff of the third Moses, due to breakage of the plaster, has resulted in flaking of paint in the adjacent area and has disclosed underneath the staff a painted fish. See further p. 84 below.

fact that in the Biblical passage the cloud is both a source of darkness and of light, and that in the Targum pseudo-Jonathan it is actually described as having two sides, one of which was bright, the other dark. Conceivably the change in the relative location of the lighter gray and pink stripes was intended to show that the cloud presented its bright face to the Israelites, but its dark face to the Egyptians and their cities.

The city at the extreme right end of the composition is set in a frontal position, and therefore seems to be unrelated to the host supposedly issuing from it and moving toward the left. But this lack of relation is more apparent than real, the by-product of a tendency toward frontality that we shall have occasion to notice throughout the decorations, and that applies not only to persons but also to objects.[215] The gate tower is higher than the curtain, as is quite proper, and projects from the face of the wall, the projection being marked by a vertical division of the courses of masonry.[216] Curtain and tower alike are rendered in a dull gray, the course- and block-lines being done in dark brown with occasional dark gray shadows to mark the drafting of the blocks. Against the surface of the walls there are to be seen not only the round balls representing the huge hailstones, but also flecks of the fire that accompanies them.[217] At least at one point a small animal with an oval body, a small head, at least four longish legs and a long thin tail is depicted (Fig. 15). This is probably to be interpreted as a salamander, the animal supposedly generated by intensely hot fire and said by the Midrash to have been shown to Moses by

FIG. 15. Panel WA 3. Salamander

215. Cf., for instance, the Ark of the Covenant in Panels NB 1, WB 4, etc.

216. For the walled city in the early bas-reliefs of Asia Minor, and in the art of the Hellenistic and Roman periods, see F. Biebel in *Gerasa*, pp. 341–351.

217. For the unusual size of the hailstones, see Josephus, *Antiquitates* II, § 305, where he says they were larger than those known to dwellers in the polar region.

God.[218] Its presence here, where it could certainly not be seen from the floor of the House of Assembly, is probably the result of a whim of the artist, reflecting his own belief in the fiery origin of the animal or his effort to suggest that the fire mixed with the hail of the story was exceedingly hot.[219]

Before the curtain of the city wall stand two lofty columns, each with carefully molded bases and ornately carved Corinthian capitals. Their shafts are black and red respectively. They have no organic relation to the wall itself and fulfil no architectural function. Either they serve merely to call attention to the brilliance of the architectural monuments gracing the interior of the city behind its mighty walls, which seems doubtful,[220] or they have been added by the ambitious artist to a section of the panel not fully exploited in order to clarify the allusion contained in the red and black stripes in the sky, and hence represent in their monumental form the "pillar of cloud" and the "pillar of fire" respectively (Exod. 13.21–22). For such a physical concretion of its imagery, the terminology used by the Biblical account provides a natural basis and Christian iconography a clear analogy.[221]

The gateway leading through the tower the artist has embellished in particularly brilliant fashion. The jambs, the lintel, and the arch above the lintel are rendered in light gray and marked

218. The creature is simply outlined with the strokes of the brush. Du Mesnil du Buisson reproduces two (*Peintures*, p. 31, Fig. 26), which is entirely possible, though I could locate only one. The number of the legs indicated is probably irrelevant, but the long tail is not and argues strongly against his assumption of borrowing from a scene representing the *arob* of the fourth Plague. That the salamander is generated by intense fire was said to have been the belief of Rabbi Akiba (L. Blau in *Jewish Encyclopedia*, X, 1905, pp. 646 f., *s.v.* "salamander"). The reference to God showing Moses the salamander is contained in that part of the *Midrash Rabbah* that concerns Exod. 12.1. Cf. Ex. Rabbah XV, 28 (Trans., III, p. 202).

219. According to the earlier tradition, a fire must burn seven days and nights to produce a salamander. The miraculous nature of the association of the two opposites, fire and hail, is commented upon in the Midrash; e.g., Ex. Rabbah XII, 4 (Trans., III, pp. 146 f.); in the *Wisdom of Solomon*, 16, 15–23; and by Philo in the *Vita Mosis* I, § 118.

220. Cf. Sukenik, *The Synagogue*, p. 80.

221. The term used is Hebrew עמוד, Aramaic עמודה, which is naturally rendered in Greek by στύλος and κίων (Philo). For analogous representations of the "pillars" in Christian art, see e.g., Codex Vaticanus 747, fol. 89.

with brown lines to show their carefully cut moldings. The paneled yellow doors are thrown open to either side, leaving unobstructed the passageway, the interior of which is painted black. Blue was used, however, to fill the semicircular lunette enclosed by the arch above the doorway. To decorate the crown of the arch and its spring at either end, three figures rendered in solid black were introduced (Pl. LII). The figures at the spring of the arch are winged Nikés bearing wreaths and mounted on globes. They are identical in form with those used as acroteria upon representations of the Temple in Panels WB 2 and WB 3, where they apparently suggest that the structure which they decorate is "royal" in character or foundation.[222]

FIG. 16. Panel WA 3. Figure above Gate

The figure set upon the crown of the arch is that of a nude helmeted man in a graceful pose, whose right hand clutches a tall staff or scepter reaching to the ground by his feet, while in his extended left he holds a globe (Fig. 16).

The identity of the crowning statue has become the center of an interesting line of argument affecting vitally the interpretation of the scene at the right end of the panel.[223] The Targum pseudo-Jonathan, in dealing with a somewhat difficult verse of the story of the Exodus (Exod. 14.2), where Israel is said to camp "before" two places at one time (namely, Pi-hahiroth and Baal Zephon), turns the second into the name of an idol and offers the comment that among the many idols in Egypt, that of Baal Zephon was the only one still intact at the time.[224] If this comment is regarded as being definitive for the identification of the statue represented in our panel, it necessarily follows that the city portrayed is not the city of bondage from which the Exodus began, but that where the statue stood and before which the Israelites made their second camp after leaving Succoth, their last before crossing the Red Sea.[225] The obstacle which the falling hailstones might seem to offer to this identification is supposedly set aside by another passage of the same Targum where the phenomena of hail and fire reappear in close association with the Red Sea Crossing.[226]

Pl. XXXVI; *Rep. VI* pp. 63–67, Pl. XLI, 1; pp. 456–466, Pl. XXV A and Frontispiece; *Rep. VII–VIII*, p. 197, Fig. 50 and pp. 199 f.) none has this peculiarity, though all are of the same general type. For the general literature on the subject see the pages of *Rep. II* mentioned and H. Bulle in Roscher, *Lexikon*, III, 1 (1897–1902), cols. 305–358, *s.v.* "Nike."

222. Dancing on tip-toe, with the skirt of their Doric chiton gathered at the waist and billowing in sweeping curves behind the knees, the Nikés are in all respects but one identical with the countless examples of the same design and symbol found on the coins, the bas-reliefs, sculptures, and paintings of the Roman Imperial age, particularly in Syria. The one detail in which they differ is that the wreath is held by both hands. Among the several examples of Nikés from Dura itself (see *Rep. II*, Frontispiece, and pp. 181–193; *Rep. V*, pp. 153–156,

223. See Grabar, "Le Thème," pp. 147 f.

224. The thought that all the statues were destroyed has its roots in the conception that the plagues were a punishment for idolatry. See Ex. Rabbah XV, 15 (Trans., III, p. 178) Baal Zephon is excepted to make possible the escape from the supposed difficulty of Exod. 14.2, and the exception is subsequently explained as intended to lead the Egyptians the more surely to their destruction in the Red Sea.

225. For the itinerary see Exod. 13.20 and 14.2. The Targum pseudo-Jonathan substitutes the familiar Tanis for the otherwise unknown Pi-hahiroth, without thereby improving matters in the least.

226. Cf. the rendering of Exod. 14.24, where the Targum pseudo-Jonathan reads, "the Lord looked forth with anger upon the hosts of the Egyptians from the column of fire, to hurl upon them flakes of fire and hail, and from the column of cloud and confounded the host of the Egyptians."

The value of this line of thought is that it unifies the elements comprising the right section of the panel: everything happens on the very shores of the Red Sea. In the background lies the city before which the host makes its last camp in Egypt proper. Inside the city, we must assume, are the Egyptians, and from before the city Moses leads the Israelites out and across the water. Interesting as it is, the interpretation is open to a number of objections. The recurrence of the hail and fire phenomenon is really associated by the Targum, not with the period immediately preceding the Israelites' crossing of the Red Sea, but with the moment when the Egyptians, following the Israelites, are actually traversing the dry bed of the sea. In this connection it serves to confuse the Egyptian host, to make its chariots unusable, and to explain why those at the beginning and end of the column were not able to escape the returning waters. If the artist included it in his picture of the earlier events, we should have to assume that a transfer has been effected, which of course opens the doors also to other similar combinations. In the second place, the *titulus* of the scene (Inscr. no. **3**) mentions both the Exodus and the cleaving of the Red Sea, which, seen from the Jewish point of view, constitute two distinct and particularly memorable events, each accompanied by a special and different act of the divine intervention.[227] With the gates of the city actually portrayed as being wide open, it would seem much more logical to suppose that it is the city of bondage that is being portrayed, rather than that "before" which Israel encamped and which on the other assumption the Egyptian host has momentarily occupied. The former calls for an element of almost stenographic abbreviation in the technique of composition employed by the artist, for at the same moment that the host leaves the city of bondage it is already at the point of crossing the Sea; but this is quite the commonest among the devices of narration and compression used in the paintings of the Synagogue.[228] Finally, it seems almost too much to ask of the spectator that he should find in this small piece of statuary the clue to the proper identification of the city and the action portrayed. Actually, of course, both in its pose and by virtue of the fact that it holds in its hands a globe, the statue is a derivative of the type that in the later centuries of the Roman Empire had come into wide use to represent the emperor as pantocrator.[229] Interpreted in this sense its association with the two flanking Nikés is much more appropriate, and the decorative design applied to the doorway becomes a device by which an artist of the third century of our era might readily have thought to indicate that the city portrayed is a "royal" city, hence the city of Pharaoh and the Exodus.

Starting from the assumption that the decorations of the gateway are conventional and significant only in terms of existing traditions, it is necessary to conclude that, as the *titulus* actually informs us, the Exodus from the city of bondage is being portrayed in the right section of the panel, with the Red Sea crossing already imminent. The telescoping of the time sequence involved in this particular has its counterpart in the introduction of the plague of hail and fire (Exod. 9.22–26), which preceded the Exodus proper by some days, in the economy of the narrative. The choice of this particular plague as the one to be represented was probably quite pragmatic, for it lent itself more readily than the others to combination with the representation of a city. It should be noted, however, that the paradoxical combination of hail and fire elicited an extra amount of comment from ancient interpreters, and that in the ancient classification of the plagues common to Philo and the Midrash, hail and fire, the locusts, and the darkness are the three which Moses himself brings about without Aaron's

---

227. Cf. e.g., Ex. Rabbah XXII, 3 (Trans., III, p. 277), where the question of the difference between the Exodus and the dividing of the Red Sea is discussed, and where it is said that the Exodus was the more difficult (miracle). The differentiation is used to account for the requirement that both the plague of the first-born and the dividing of the sea are to be mentioned in the Benediction beginning with "True and firm" after the recitation of the Shema' in the morning.

228. Cf. especially Panels WB 4, NB 1, WC 1 and 4, EC 1, and SC 4.

229. For the use of the type in the Imperial statuary see the statue of Hadrian in the Hermitage (*Hermitage, Museum of Ancient Sculpture*, 4th ed., 1901, p. 104, no. 214). For its use on the coins see e.g., H. Mattingly, *Coins of the Roman Empire in the British Museum*, IV (1940), p. 785, Pl. 104, no. 6. On the earlier usage of the imagery see K. Sittl, *Jahrbücher für classische Philologie*, Supplementband XIV (1885), pp. 1–51.

assistance.[230] In a scene in which Moses is given such prominence, the inclusion of a reference to one of the plagues occasioned by him alone is particularly appropriate.

Immediately at the left of the city of bondage the artist has portrayed the host of those participating in the Exodus. They are arranged in four parallel companies reaching almost to the top of the panel, the nearest files of the lowest and the uppermost fully exposed to view, the second and the third partly concealed by overlapping with each other and with the lowest file. Among the several files, that in the foreground consists of civilians, all of whom are men. They wear long-sleeved chitons, all severely girded up so that they form pronounced *kolpoi* at the waist and reach only to the knees, and are shod with sandals, both in careful agreement with the Biblical directions for the Passover celebration, which are also those for the march.[231] White tunics with broad red clavi predominate, but others in plain red or green are added for variety. The company is two or three files deep, but only a single row of legs is shown, the left legs set at an angle to the side and rear, the right bent sharply at the knee in token of motion forward

FIG. 17. Panel WA 3. Israelite

(Figs. 17–18). The suggestion of motion conveyed by the position of the legs is further emphasized by the position of the right hands which reach out forward.[232] Yet the faces and the upper parts of the

FIG. 18. Panel WA 3. Israelite

bodies are seen in a frontal position. All of the figures hold the left hand close to the chest, where it normally clutches the end of a bag or a roll of cloth resting upon the left shoulder. This represents, of course, the unleavened dough which the Israelites took with them bound up in their clothes upon their shoulder, as the Biblical story has it (Exod. 12.34).[233] One man, near the end of the file, holds in his left arm a fluted circular bowl (Fig. 18) rendered in gray to show that it is made of silver, the detail being intended to illustrate "vessels of silver and vessels of gold" which the departing Israelites obtained from the Egyptians, despoiling them (Exod. 12.35–36). In a prominent place near the middle of the file the artist has portrayed a man leading a small child (Fig. 19). Dressed in a green tunic gathered up like that of its father, the child has his parent swung momentarily out of line, for the child is at the father's left while he tries to lead

230. For comment on the plague of hail and fire see Wisdom of Solomon 16.15–23; Philo, *Vita Mosis* I, § 118; and Ex. Rabbah XII, 4 (Trans., III, pp. 146f.). For the classification of the plagues see Philo, *Vita Mosis* I, esp. §§ 113–125; and Ex. Rabbah XII, 4 (Trans., III, p. 146). One might even imagine that the descent of the cloud over the city of the Exodus was intended as an allusion also to the plague of darkness, though this is quite unneccessary.

231. Exod. 12.11: "thus shall ye eat it, with your loins girded, and your shoes on your feet..."

232. For the posture as a cliché of later Imperial art, see the altar from Ostia (A.D. 124) with the representation of the finding of Romulus and Remus by the shepherds, and the Antonine fresco from Rome depicting the departure of the traveler, both reproduced in Wirth, *Römische Wandmalerei*, p. 56, Fig. 17, and p. 149, Fig. 77. See also the same iconographic detail in the Paris Psalter (H. Buchthal, *The Miniatures of the Paris Psalter*, 1938, Pl. IX, Fig. 9).

233. The same iconographic detail appears in the Paris Psalter; see previous note.

it with his right hand. This detail was probably introduced to bring to graphic expression what is said in Exod. 13.3, 5, 6, 8, "Remember this day in which ye came out of Egypt.... And it shall be when the Lord shall bring thee into the land of the

FIG. 19. Panel WA 3. Israelite

Canaanites, ... that thou shalt keep this service in this month ... seven days thou shalt eat unleavened bread... and *thou shalt tell thy son in that day*, saying, It is because of that which the Lord did for me when I came forth out of Egypt."[234]

In a composition of the size of Panel WA 3 the introduction of these manifold details in one small section of the imagery is a significant witness to the meticulousness of the artist and to the care which he lavished upon his product. While they do not have the same wealth of associations, the figures of the three upper files are at least drawn with the same painstaking devotion to detail. Of the upper files, the second and the last are made up entirely of soldiers in massed ranks at least three deep. For the representation of his massed infantry the artist employs a convention that must have developed in the late imperial period and to which the illuminations of the Joshua Roll provide the closest, though a much later, analogy.[235] The files to the

234. A child, it should be noted, is included in the representation of the departing Israelites in the scene of the Crossing of the Red Sea in S. Maria Maggiore. Cf. J. Wilpert, *Die römischen Mosaiken und Malereien*, III (2nd ed., 1917), Pl. 18. See also the Paris Psalter.

235. Cf. *Il Rotulo di Giosuè*, ed. U. Hoepli (1905), Pls., I VII, X, XI, XIV. The development of the convention can be observed by following the treatment of massed infantry from the Column of Trajan onward through the

rear are so closely packed that only rows of bell-shaped, knobbed helmets in red, gray, and green (cf. Fig. 20) and of projecting black spear tips are visible. Overlapping oval bossed shields colored red, gray, and blue and decorated with convention-

FIG. 20. Panel WA 3. Helmets

al designs cover the face and body of the entire file in the foreground (cf. Fig. 21).[236] But it is clear, particularly from the scene at the left end of the panel where the soldiery reappears, that the men wear a short cuirass over a pink tunic, close-fitting trousers that are alternately light green and red, and high black boots.

The presence of these files of armed men in the host of the departing Israelites both before and during the crossing of the Red Sea is one of the most unexpected features of the scene. It has no counterpart in the iconography of the Exodus in Christian art, but finds support in the Hebrew text of Exod. 13.18 as it was interpreted by some of the ancient rabbinical authorities and is sometimes

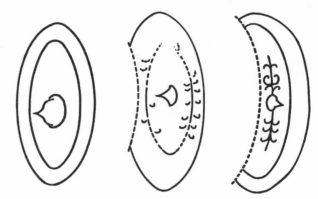

FIG. 21. Panel WA 3. Shields

official triumphal monuments of the Empire to the Arch of Constantine (see S. Reinach, *Répertoire de reliefs*, I, 1909).

236. The armament, particularly the shields and helmets, recalls that of the scenes of Trajan's column. Cf. K. Lehmann-Hartleben, *Die Trajanssäule* (1926), e.g., Pls. 37, 55, 61, 67, 70.

translated today; namely, "and the children of Israel went up armed out of the land of Egypt."[237]

Between the two files of soldiers, both clearly moving toward the left, there is represented a single row of civilians, seen in a frontal position. The figures are so arranged that the right shoulder of each man save the first is hidden by the left shoulder and arm of the man behind him. All wear chiton and himation, the costumes being colored alternately pink and white, the softer colors contrasting with the bright brick red of the faces and the black of the hair. Their central position in the host and the fact that they are guarded on either side by soldiers makes it evident that they represent the Elders of Israel whom the story of the Exodus mentions at one point (Exod. 12.21). Here, as elsewhere in the paintings of the Synagogue, they are twelve in number, one for each of the twelve tribes of Israel.[238]

At the head of the host the artist has portrayed in heroic proportions the figure of Moses. He strides confidently toward the left, his legs spread far apart, the right knee bent sharply and the left foot set at an angle to the right foot, while his right hand is raised over his head, holding the long knobby staff outlined in brown with which he is about to strike the water. The upper part of his body is turned into a frontal position, giving a full view of the rounded, carefully drawn face. Though damaged by a deep scratch at the left, the face is clear in all salient detail, showing the characteristic wide-open, well-placed eyes, the prominent, elongated nose, the full cheek- and chin-beard, and the well-developed round of brown hair outlined heavily in black. The color of the skin is a dull brick red throughout.

Moses is clad in the garb of a civilian; namely, a short-sleeved yellowish-gray chiton with wide blue clavi, and a himation of the same color draped over his left shoulder. The ends of the himation, rolled about the left wrist, hang down at his side carefully folded and reveal on their face the ends of blue bands terminating in a double-pronged ornament, and at their very tips a number of projecting threads, possibly but not necessarily the ritual *ṣiṣith* (Fig. 22).[239] By the introduction of white highlights the artist has endeavored to accentuate the folds of the himation as it drapes itself over the bent left knee. He follows in this particular, here as elsewhere, a series of established conventions familiar above all from the bas-reliefs of

237. The treatment of this passage by ancient authorities provides a test case of the sources of the Synagogue artists' inspiration and for the proper division of iconographic types, Jewish and Christian. The crucial word of the Hebrew text, namely, "armed" (חֲמֻשִׁים), the LXX renders "to the fifth generation" (πέμπτη δὲ γενεᾷ). This provides the occasion for the Hellenistic Jewish writers to deplore the utter defenselessness of the departing Israelites. So Ezekiel (αὐτοὶ δ'ἄνοπλοι) and Demetrius (fragments of their works quoted by Eusebius, *Praeparatio Evangelica* IX, 29, ed. E. H. Gifford, I, 1903, p. 555), Philo (*Vita Mosis* I, § 72), and Josephus (*Antiquitates* II, § 326). This conception carries over into early Christian iconography, being illustred, e.g., by the mosaics of Santa Maria Maggiore. See below, p. 83, n. 247. The same interpretation and others equally innocuous appear in the Fragment-Targum, the Targum pseudo-Jonathan and in the Mekilta (trans. J. Winter and A. Wünsche, *Mechiltha*, 1909, pp. 75f. and Ex. 13.18). But the Mekilta also knows another interpretation according to which the word חֲמֻשִׁים is rendered מְזֻיָּנִים, that is "armed" (*ibid.*). This can be followed further in the Jerusalem Talmud, Shabbat VI, 4 (Trans. M. Schwab, *Le Talmud de Jérusalem*, IV, 1881, p. 72) where a play on words provides an occasion for listing five types of arms carried by the departing Israelites; in Exodus Rabbah XX, 19 (Trans., III, p. 257); and in the Targum Onkelos, which rendered the crucial word with מְזָרְזִין, i.e. "girded" or "armed."

238. In the story of Exodus the number of the Elders is, of course, indeterminate. Other parts of the early tradition suggest that there were seventy (see e.g., Exod. 24.1). In view of the regularity with which the group of twelve appears in the Synagogue (see Panel WB 1 and probably the Upper Central Panel in the last stage of its development), it would seem that by the third century of our era the conception of the Elders and their function had developed in such a way as to associate them one with each Tribe and thus to create the fixed number twelve.

Josephus, it may be noted, already has a clear conception of the existence of twelve tribal chiefs or phylarchs (*Antiquitates* III, §§ 47, 220, 222), though he also speaks of the host that departed from Egypt as being ranged according to phratries (*ibid.*, II, § 312).

239. These hanging threads are a feature of the ends of some of the himatia of the Synagogue, but their absence is noticeable in certain cases; for instance, on the figures of Samuel and the sons of Jesse in Panel WC 3 and on Ezekiel in the third section of Panel NC 1. This may be sheer accident or may indicate that the threads are a convention rather than the ritual *ṣiṣith* of Num. 15.37–40. Analogous projecting threads are to be seen on the tips of the himatia in Syrian sculpture. Cf. the Palmyrene funerary relief of the third century reproduced by H. Seyrig, *Syria*, XVIII (1937), p. 25, Fig. 16. There is in the Synagogue naturally no indication of the "blue thread" included in the "fringe" that would make the identification absolutely certain. In all probability those viewing the paintings would take the threads to represent the "fringes," but whether they were included by the artists for this purpose is not entirely clear.

Palmyra, though not achieving any more than they a thorough and convincing correlation of body outlines and drapery.[240] On his feet he wears a type of sandal commonly portrayed in the paintings of the Synagogue.[241]

FIG. 22. Panel WA 3. *Ṣiṣith*

In portraying his figures of Moses the artist has abandoned his isocephalic convention, as he does elsewhere on occasion, emphasizing in this way the significance of the person for the action of the composition. It is interesting to note that Haggadah and iconography are in accord at this point, the former also speaking of Moses' unusual stature, and that the tradition of Moses' extreme height can be followed back to Rab, a contemporary of the Dura Synagogue in southern Mesopotamia.[242] It would be interesting to know whether this accord is accidental or the result of dependence, and in the latter instance whether the

Haggadic tradition developed from, or with the help of, other similar pictorial compositions, or vice versa.

Between the legs of the first figure of Moses there appears the almost superfluous *titulus*, "Moses, when he went out from Egypt and cleft the sea" (Inscr. no. **3**). While the gesture of Moses' uplifted right arm is appropriate to the statement of the *titulus*, and Moses actually stands at the very edge of the Red Sea itself, what is shown in the next section of the panel is not the "cleaving" of the Sea but the Drowning of the Egyptians, an event associated with a second figure of Moses on the farther side of the body of water. The inference that this is the result of extreme compression in the development of the composition is inescapable, and the simplest explanation is this: that of two separate scenes, each depicting the Sea, that part of one representing the water before it was cleft by Moses' staff has been omitted.[243]

In the second scene of the panel, depicting the Drowning of the Egyptians, the water is done in vertical perspective and therefore covers the entire field from the bottom to the top of the panel, but the men swimming about in it are seen horizontally.[244] Some of the men are nude, others wear yellow or pink tunics, some decorated with clavi. The flesh color is brick red throughout. Though the relative size of the swimmers does not diminish toward the upper part of the panel because of the nature of the perspective used, it is clear that their numbers increase toward the top and that heads alone appear more frequently, while toward the bottom of the panel entire bodies are more commonly shown. The basic color used for the water is black, but this is highlighted with streaks of light gray and yellow to represent the waves. Between the swimmers, particularly in the foreground, green and pink fish are to be seen, leaping from the water.

At the left of the irregularly outlined body of water stands Moses, somewhat shorter of stature

240. On the treatment of the Greek costume in Palmyrene and Syrian sculpture, see H. Ingholt, *Studier over palmyrensk Skulptur* (1928), esp .p. 23 ; and V. Müller, *Zwei syrische Bildnisse römischer Zeit (86. Winckelmanns-programm* 1927), pp. 30–33.

241. The sandal consists of a flat piece of leather attached by thongs that come up at the instep and between the first and second toe to join a band circling the ankle.

242. The Haggadah mentions Moses' height as ten cubits, approximately fifteen feet. For Rab's comment on the subject see Bechoroth 44a and in general W. Bacher, *Die Agada der babylonischen Amoräer* (1878), p. 12.

243. On the fundamental question of the prototypes of the Synagogue paintings, their nature and origin, and the procedure by which they were combined, see below, pp. 385–398.

244. Analogies to this type of combination in Roman Imperial art; e.g., on the Column of Marcus Aurelius (boats portrayed horizontally on a river seen vertically, see E. Petersen *et al. Die Marcus-Säule*, 1896, Pl. XLIa) have been pointed out by E. Hill, *Marsyas*, I (1941), pp. 1–15.

than in the other two of his appearances in the composition, but otherwise identical in dress and mien. The position of his feet and the gesture of his right arm, which crosses the body, clearly indicate his relation to what is going on in the water, over which he extends his long black staff. Above his right shoulder there is still dimly to be seen a faded dipinto which reads, "Moses" (Inscr. no. **4**). Above his head and from above the black band representing the column of cloud, a Hand of God with thin, elongated fingers, all but the thumb held closely together, reaches down in token of the miraculous divine intervention involved in the event.[245] Apparently the Hand is intended to be a left hand, but this does not necessarily imply that the event mediated by it is an expression of divine disfavor.[246]

In the artist's rendering of the scene the most striking feature is the absence of anything that would identify the swimmers as soldiers of the Egyptian army, and the omission of the horses and chariots that play so important a part in the Song of Miriam (Exod. 15.1), and are so familiar in the Christian representations of the event.[247] Conceivably the difference between the Christian and the Jewish iconography at this point is the result of a difference of emphasis. Whereas in Christian art the importance assigned to the half-submerged chariots and weapons suggests the seriousness of the threat from which the unarmed Israelites escaped, the absence of these features in the Jewish composition may suggest the utter impotence of the oppressors as compared with the might of the Lord and the strength of the Israelite armed force.[248] At all events there is to be noted a strong

resemblance between the resultant representation and Assyrian bas-reliefs such as that depicting the battle of Assurbanipal against the Elamites, where men, horses, weapons, and fish are spread indiscriminately about over a wavy background to show in vertical perspective how the king had driven his enemies into the sea.[249]

The third and last scene of the panel repeats five of the elements already used in the earlier parts of the composition; namely, the cloud, the heroic figure of Moses, the file of armed Israelites, the twelve Elders, and the Hand of God appearing from above the black cloud. Some differences in the representation of each of them are to be noted. The background gives the impression of being coloristic and realistic rather than monochrome, but this can scarcely be intentional considering the treatment of the background in the other panels. Rather, we must assume that the black cloud which elsewhere darkens the scene for the Egyptians is here brightened to show that it gives light to the departing Israelites.[250] The Hand of God is a right hand, the second of a pair, each betokening an act of divine intervention.[251] The Elders, while preserving their single file and their alternately light and darker costumes, are in this instance supplied each with a "standard" analogous in form to a Roman vexillum (Fig. 23). The square of cloth mounted upon the staff of the "standard" is pink,

---

245. For the Hand of God in the Sacrifice of Isaac see above, p. 57. For the difference between this rendering and those found on other panels see below, pp. 182, 229. The presence of the Hand is probably in part the explanation for the reduction in the size of the figure of Moses.

246. Rather the left hand appears in combination with the right to make a pair, both here and in the Upper Side Panels of the Central Group. See below, p. 229.

247. Cf. e.g., the mosaic of Santa Maria Maggiore (Wilpert, *Die römischen Mosaiken und Malereien*, III, Pl. 18) and the Ashburnham Pentateuch, fol. 68 r. (O. V. Gebhardt, *The Miniatures of the Ashburnham Pentateuch*, 1883, Pl. XVII).

248. In this connection it may be proper to mention the statement of R. Nathan who said, "The Egyptians, when they sank in the sea, were also punished naked, as

it says, *And with the blast of Thy nostrils they were stripped* (נֶעֶרְמוּ) *in the midst of the sea* (Ex. XV, 8)" (Esther Rabbah III, 14, Trans., IX, p. 55). R. Nathan derives the form from עָרַם meaning "to strip" instead of "to pile up."

249. H. Schäfer and W. Andrae, *Die Kunst des alten Orients* (*Propyläen Kunstgeschichte*), II (1925), p. 539. For similar details in a scene of Ramses III's battle with the Sea Peoples, see *Medinet Habu, I* (*Oriental Institute Publications*, VIII, 1930), Pl. 39.

250. Cf. above, p. 76.

251. In this connection it may be interesting to note the passage in Exodus Rabbah XXII, 2 (Trans., III, p. 276) where God's protection of Israel is compared to that of a father saving his son from robbers and taking his son in one hand while with the other he fights the attackers. His son expresses his gratitude in the words, "May I never lack [the protection of] those two hands." This is what Israel said to the Lord upon the destruction of the Egyptian army according to the Midrash; namely, "May peace be upon both Thy hands! Both on the one with which Thou dost save us from the sea and on the other with which Thou dost overthrow the Egyptians." The Midrash, however, regards both hands of God mentioned in the interpretation as right hands.

being set off against a grayish band of the cloud already described. The file of soldiers ranged in front of the Elders is identical with that represented in the first scene of the composition save that the colors are better preserved, making the coats of mail more distinctly visible, and save that the

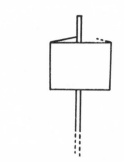

FIG. 23. Panel WA 3. Standard

first man in the file, at the extreme left, is turned into a frontal position, arresting the leftward movement implied in the cliché which the artist uses for his massed infantry. Moses, finally, is identical in every respect but one with the figure portrayed in the first scene of the composition. Here he moves calmly toward the left, but his right hand extends downward toward a narrow strip of water in the foreground into which his long black staff is directed.

To these elements of the last scene repeated from the first two must be added those that are new and therefore of outstanding importance for the identification of the episode portrayed. The first is the narrow strip of black water into which Moses' staff

FIG. 24. Panel WA 3. Shell

projects, from which red and green fish jump in large numbers and against which two gray seashells with white flutings are outlined (Fig. 24). The second is a group of lavender bands, probably twelve in number, that trace a fairly regular course

across the gray background on either side of the figure of Moses.[252]

Comment upon the scene as a whole has tended to conclude that it combines allusions to several episodes, among them the Numbering of the Twelve Tribes, the Sweetening of the Waters at Marah, and the Crossing of the Red Sea. Of these the first is suggested by the fact that the "standards" which the Elders bear are not actually found in the text of the Hebrew Bible before Num. 1.52, the chapter dealing with the Numbering of the Tribes.[253] But the Midrash frequently mentions the "standards" in describing the events at the Red Sea, making it unnecessary to imagine a conflation of scenes on their account.[254] Allusion to the episode of Exod. 15.22–26, when Moses sweetened the "bitter waters" of Marah by casting into it a "tree" (עֵץ, wood?), is said to be found, first, in the narrow body of water stretched across the foreground and, second, in the loose connection between Moses' hand and staff, supposedly indicating that Moses is "throwing" a staff into the water.[255] However, the gesture of Moses' hand can scarcely be described properly as one of "throwing" and a careful examination of the staff reveals that its lower end covers the better part of one of the fish leaping from the water (Fig. 25). This implies that the staff was omitted when the figure of Moses was executed, and was supplied only after the fish had been ren-

252. The bands continue also between the feet of the figure of Moses "closing" the sea. The number twelve is probably what was intended, though this count can be arrived at only by following the succession of bands between the two adjacent figures of Moses and by assuming that the lowest section of the foreground, below the Moses who "closes" the sea, represents the first band. Du Mesnil du Buisson suggests that the bands were originally blue (*Peintures*, p. 38).

253. Cf. Du Mesnil du Buisson, "Les Peintures," p. 111.

254. Cf. Exodus Rabbah XX, 5 (Trans., III, pp. 246f.), and Song of Songs Rabbah IV, 12, 1 (Trans., IX, p. 220). The last-mentioned of these passages speaks of the Israelites being "arranged in rows"; that is, in something like the files of the Synagogue painting. Numbers Rabbah II, 2, 7 (Trans., V, pp. 28f.), suggests that the nations (Romans) derived their use of the vexillum from Israel's "standards," indicating that the form of the "standard" was commonly conceived of in later times as being like that of the vexillum and hence like that of our scene.

255. Cf. Du Mesnil du Buisson, *Peintures*, p. 39 and p. 40, Fig. 34, where an accurate drawing of the relation between the staff and Moses' hand is given; Schneid, *The Paintings*, pp. 11f.; and E. R. Goodenough, *By Light, Light* (1935), p. 222.

dered. The dissociation of hand and staff are therefore accidental rather than intentional.[256]

To us it would seem that the scene represents one and only one episode; namely, the actual crossing by the Israelites of the Red Sea. With this

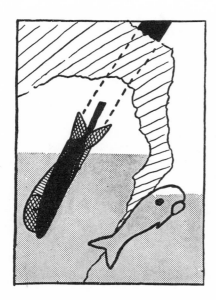

FIG. 25. Panel WA 3. Moses' Staff on top of Fish

the inscription at the left of Moses' head is in accord, for it repeats the words, "Moses when he cleft the sea" (Inscr. no. **5**), and with this the twelve strips at either side of Moses can alone be harmonized. Interpreted in the Preliminary Report as the pictorial representation of the waters standing "like a wall to the right and to the left" (Exod. 14.22), they are more properly to be associated with the Haggadic conception of the twelve paths through the sea to which several recent interpreters have alluded.[257] But the precise relation of the strips to the rest of the scene has still to be determined.

For the interpretation of the scene as a whole, two matters are of outstanding importance. The

first is the fact that the conception of the twelve paths arises from the thought, expressed, for instance, in the Targum pseudo-Jonathan, that Moses "divided" the sea into "twelve divisions," much as one might make twelve slices in a loaf of bread.[258] The second is that the scene as a whole is a combination of elements that have to be seen in a double perspective, partly horizontal and partly vertical. The strips are intended to be seen in a vertical perspective, the lavender bands indicating, not the "paths," but the several sections of water divided from each other and forming "walls" on either side of the twelve passageways. Of these several walls of water, the narrow body of water running along the bottom of the panel to the left is one example, as its continuation behind the feet of Moses in the widest of the lavender strips indicates. It too must be understood as being seen in a vertical perspective. Moses, the host, and the Elders are, however, to be seen in a horizontal perspective and must be thought of as moving in files toward the left, one file between each pair of these walls — Moses before the one illustrated in detail, the soldiers and Elders between those farther to the rear.[259]

From this interpretation of the composition a number of inferences can be drawn. The first is that the scene represents a single episode and can be interpreted as such without the assumption of conflation. The second is that the arrangement of the Israelite band in files, both here and in the first scene of the panel, is a natural corollary of the procedure by which it crosses the Red Sea. The third and last is that the staff, which, as we have seen, has caused so much difficulty and was apparently introduced into the composition late in its execution, is not really necessary to the intent of the artist and may actually be superfluous, the addition of one of his helpers.[260]

256. It will be noted from Pl. LIII that the staff of the Moses in the scene under discussion is not drawn with anything like the precision and regularity of those in the other two scenes, though there can be no doubt that the same object is represented.

257. Cf. de Vaux, "Un Détail," pp. 383–387; Du Mesnil du Buisson, *Peintures*, pp. 38 f.; Grabar, "Le Thème," pp. 146 f.; Schneid, *The Paintings*, p. 12; Sukenik, *The Synagogue*, pp. 83 f.

258. Cf. the Targum on Exod. 14.21. Allusions to the "twelve paths" or divisions are common in the Midrash; see Genesis Rabbah LXXXIV, 5 and 8 (Trans., II, pp. 772 and 775), Deuteronomy Rabbah XI, 10 (Trans., VII, p. 185), and Mekilta, *ad* Exod. 14. 16 (ed. Winter-Wünsche, p. 97 and note).

259. Note the cast shadows behind the two figures of Moses.

260. On the several artists of the Synagogue and on the reasons for and against the assumption that Panel WA 3 was not the work of the men who did the other panels of the Synagogue, see below, pp. 380 f.

From the foregoing examination of the details of the panel, important insights into the artist's abilities and idiosyncrasies are to be gained. It should be clear at the outset that his work is of a most meticulous character. He has done everything in his power to be exact even in the smallest detail. With his love of detail goes his interest in masses of people, an unusual phenomenon in the over-all picture of the Synagogue's decoration, there being actually only one other panel which even approaches the mass effects he has produced at both ends of his composition.[261] While his massed groups are sometimes conventionalized, as in the case of the soldiers, whose relatively formless legs contrast sharply with those of the civilians in the foreground of the Exodus scene, they are not inert, and add effectively to the element of movement visible in the panel as a whole. A counterpart to his love of masses in motion is provided by the three figures of heroic proportions which he introduces to crystalize and embody the meaning of the action, and upon whom he has lavished exceptional care. Wide in proportion to their height, shrouded rather than clothed in their garments, and frontal in their representation, the figures are nonetheless anything but dead, making rather the impression of strength of character, intentness, and power — a particular in which they contrast not only with most of the other figures of the Synagogue, but also with much of the contemporary art of the Orient.[262]

Quite casual and traditionalistic in his handling of perspective, the artist has allowed himself one liberty with the subject matter of the story that has already occasioned considerable comment. He has depicted the Drowning of the Egyptians before the Crossing of the Red Sea by the Israelites. Unheard of in any other similar continuous compositions, and indicative, it would seem, of the fact that continuity means something quite different to him than to the artists of the western schools, the procedure represented by the peculiar allocation of the drowning scene seems to be the result of the meeting of at least three factors. The first is the fact that the drowning scene, requiring the use of a vertical perspective, was bound to interrupt the open background of the other two scenes, and that for purposes of balanced composition a location at the center of the panel was therefore preferable. The second is that, with only a limited amount of space at his disposal, he could by this device place the Moses who leads the host in the scene at the right into immediate juxtaposition to a body of water and thus give at least a semblance of reality to his act of "cleaving the sea," without actually repeating the sea in its entire expanse twice. The third is that, since he was inclined to make the action of the scene move from right to left, the emplacement of the drowning scene at the very end of the panel would have left the Israelites still at the wrong side of the water. As he has arranged matters, the action may be thought to sweep on unobstructed toward the achievement of its purpose, the return of Israel to the Promised Land.

Unidentified Scene

Panel WA 1 (fragmentary). H. *ca.* 1.16 m.; L. 1.89 m. (Pl. XXVII).

Rep. VI, p. 349; Du Mesnil du Buisson, *Peintures*, p. 48; Grabar, "Le Thème," p. 6; Sonne, "The Paintings," pp. 279–281; Sukenik, *The Synagogue*, p. 87; Wischnitzer, *Messianic Theme*, pp. 70f.

The first of the panels of Register A on the west wall of the Synagogue, counting from the left, is at the same time the one most poorly preserved. The whole upper part of it was destroyed when the height of the building was reduced to that of the embankment. What remains is a long narrow strip of plaster no more than 0.43 m. high at the highest point, and on this strip traces of color are limited to a zone never more than 0.29 m. high, representing the bottom of the composition. The colors reveal very little more than a series of feet set against a yellowish-brown background. The feet are those of two unequal groups of people, of whom the larger comes from the left while the smaller

---

The omission of the staff does not make the miracle any the less real and the Hand of God unnecessary. The artist is merely representing the accomplished fact of the division of the waters or the last of the divisions being made.

261. Cf. Panel EC 1, Pl. XXXII.

262. This is largely a matter of pose and face. It should be noted in this connection that the flesh color is brick red throughout, as in Panel NA 1 and Wing Panel I of the Central Group, while in the other panels it is a lighter yellow or pink.

comes from the right. Since the two meet to the right of the center of the field, the action of the composition may be said to move from left to right; that is, from the southern end of the wall toward the middle.

Of the two groups of people participating in the encounter, the one at the right is more clearly identifiable because the lower ends of the garments which the men wear are still visible. The first man, beginning at the extreme right, is dressed in a white chiton and himation, the chiton having the usual dark clavi, and the ends of the himation the usual fringes or tassels. His legs are well modeled and rendered in reddish brown, but details are not sufficiently clear to show the sandals he should be wearing with the costume.[263] The second figure in the group at the right is of more exalted station, for he wears a costume with which we are thoroughly familiar from other well-preserved panels of the decorations.[264] It consists of high, soft, white boots, trousers ornamented with a wide vertical stripe, and a long-sleeved tunic with a broad border along the bottom and a wide stripe down the middle. This costume is reserved for members of the Temple and court hierarchy, being worn by priests, Levites, kings, generals, and members of the royal retinue. In this instance the garments are of a reddish color and the stripes and borders yellow. Portions of the feet of still a third figure in the group at the right are indicated in the Gute copies, but are no longer visible today. The position assigned to this third figure is to the right and the rear of the man in royal or priestly raiment. There is nothing to show what kind of garments he may have worn.

The group at the left side of the scene is larger and embraces in all probability five persons. They stand closely together, their figures probably overlapping in such a way that the left arm and shoulder are hidden by the right arm and shoulder of the next person forward in the file.[265] All have bare legs, some reddish brown, others perhaps lighter in color, and in one instance traces of a sandal can be seen. From the fact that they are bare-legged

and wear sandals, it follows that they are men and must be wearing either the combination of chiton and himation, or the simple chiton gathered by a belt at the waist familiar from other parts of the decoration.[266] Between the two possible forms of dress it is impossible to choose, for though the simple chiton usually leaves more of the legs exposed than the combination of chiton and himation, matching more closely what the panel seems to show, the traces of color are so few at the level of the calves that it is better to suspend judgment.

It may be that in the foreground between the two unevenly matched groups of people some object was originally depicted. Of this there are two slight indications: first, a change in the pigmentation of the area from the yellowish brown of the background to a dull reddish brown; and second, the presence of dark irregular lines, some of them radiating from a focal point, others turning back upon themselves. Unfortunately the lines do not add up to a recognizable shape or pattern.[267]

Several interpretations of the scene have been proposed, but none of them can be said to satisfy the iconography.[268] The important figure in the

263. A cast shadow taking the form of an inverted *V* is visible between his feet, as well as between the feet of the next figure toward the left.

264. Cf. Panels WA 2; NA 1; SB 1; WB 1; WB 2; WB 4; NB 1; NB 2; WC 2; WC 4; NC 1; EC 1.

265. For analogies to the handling of such groups see Panels WA 3, SC 3, and WC 2.

266. For the latter see e.g., Panel NB 1, left half.

267. Of these lines some were at one time traced by the writer and tentatively interpreted as an Aramaic *titulus* (*Rep. VI*, p. 391, no. 4). Du Mesnil du Buisson (*Peintures*, p. 162, no. 24) promptly supplied a reading of the tracing, which others in turn have modified as they saw fit (cf. Sonne, "The Paintings," p. 279, and Wischnitzer, *Messianic Theme*, p. 71). A re-examination of the area shows that some of the lines traced are still visible, but makes their interpretation as a dipinto very dubious. The one line that curves back upon itself just above the right foot of the man in white boots is too close to him to represent the foot of a third person in the group at the right of the panel. Persons wearing the costume of court and Temple personnel are not otherwise crowded by the Synagogue artist.

268. Du Mesnil du Buisson (*Peintures*, p. 48) proposed Joseph greeting his brothers in Egypt or presenting them to Pharaoh. In the former instance who is Joseph's associate at the extreme right, and in the latter instance why does not Joseph, because of his association with the king, wear the court costume? Sonne ("The Paintings," pp. 279f.) has suggested Jacob's burial, interpreting the episode in the light of the Haggadic narrative that tells how Husham the son of Dan (supposedly mentioned in the dipinto) decapitated Esau at this occasion. The suggestion does not do justice to the costume of the important figure at the right. Wischnitzer's proposal to see here a rendering of Saul among the prophets (*Messianic Theme*, pp. 70f.) runs afoul of the additional person in the group at the right, who, judging by his garments, cannot be Saul's servant.

group at the right is in all probability a king or a high Temple official. His one recognizable associate in "civilian" garb might either be a counsellor or a prophet.[269] This being so, an episode from the period of the Hebrew monarchy might properly be regarded as the most likely subject. Among the many episodes of this period, the Anointing of Solomon as told in I Kings 1.38–40 should not be overlooked, particularly in view of the subject matter of the next panel to the right (WA 2), Solomon receiving the Queen of Sheba. On this suggestion the group at the right would represent Zadok, the High Priest, accompanied by the prophet Nathan (at the extreme right of the panel) and by Benaiah, who appears also in the next scene. It would then be necessary to assume that Solomon headed the group in the left part of the composition, the others being those who acclaimed him at his consecration. The absence of any indication of "royal" garments in the left part of the picture is not necessarily fatal to this suggestion as the analogy of Panel WC 3 (Samuel Anoints David) shows.[270]

Solomon Receives the Queen of Sheba

Panel WA 2 (fragmentary). H. *ca.* 1.16 m.; L. 2.54 m. (Pl. XXVIII).

Rep. VI, pp. 348f.; Du Mesnil du Buisson, "Les Peintures," pp. 111f.; *idem, Peintures*, pp. 46f.; Grabar, "Le Thème," pp. 5f.; Leveen, *Hebrew Bible in Art*, p. 36; Schneid, *The Paintings*, p. 12; Sukenik, *The Synagogue*, pp. 85–87; Sonne, "The Paintings," pp. 281–284; Wischnitzer, *Messianic Theme*, pp. 71–73.

Only slightly better preserved than its neighbor at the left, the scene is known to us from a narrow strip of plaster, never more than 0.95 m. high, above the base line, a strip on which traces of the painting are limited to a zone only 0.19 m. high at the left and not more than 0.40 m. high at the right.[271]

Yet the difference is sufficient to render the subject of the composition intelligible, and to show that the scene was one of particular brilliance and interest, making the loss of the entire upper part of the picture all the more regrettable.

Fundamentally the composition is quite simple, being a combination of two unequal elements. The first of these, occupying fully three fifths of the panel beginning at the right, is static in character, depicting a king upon his throne with members of his court seated before him at either side. It is a noticeable feature of this part of the composition that, while the courtier at the left faces toward the right, correctly framing the assemblage at his end, the courtier on the right faces forward, leaving the scene open, as it were, at the other end. The lack of balance in this particular is explained by the empty chair which the artist has squeezed into the extreme right corner of the scene, for the person supposed to occupy it would naturally face left and thus complete the tableau. The second element of the composition, filling the remaining two fifths of the panel at the left, apparently portrayed but three persons. Two are women, who move from the extreme left toward the royal presence; the third is a man in court attire who stands full front between the women and the enthroned monarch, acting in some sense as the mediator of the king's will for those approaching him.

The scene has a close parallel in that forming the right part of Panel WC 2 (Mordecai and Esther), where also the identical throne with its elaborate dais reappears. This makes it possible to reconstruct much of the lost upper part of the composition and indicates that we are dealing here with a type of scene thoroughly familiar to the artist; namely, the audience scene. The type is one that has a long history in ancient imperial art, particularly Oriental and Byzantine, and lent itself readily to the illustration of certain Biblical materials, but the discussion of the type belongs properly to the context of the panels more fully preserved.[272] Whereas in the analogous part of Panel WC 2 it is the court of Ahasuerus that is depicted, here the scene is laid in the court of Solomon, as two Greek *tituli* supplied by the artist

---

269. For counsellors see Panel WA 2.

270. Other panels celebrating Solomon's reign include not only WA 2 (Solomon Receives the Queen of Sheba) but also SB 1 (Dedication of the Temple).

271. The surface is disturbed by one horizontal and four vertical cracks which trace irregular courses through the plaster, but none of these has produced appreciable losses or dislocations of the surface elements.

272. Cf. below, pp. 157f. and pp. 170–172. In its basic elements the audience scene appears also in Panel WC 4 (Pharaoh and the Infancy of Moses).

himself clearly indicate.[273] Two episodes of Biblical story have thus commended themselves especially as possible subjects of the composition. The first is that of Solomon's Judgment, the judgment between the two women who were rival claimants for the possession of a child (I Kings 3.16–28); and second, that of the visit of the Queen of Sheba to Solomon's court (I Kings 10.1–13).[274] For the choice between these two alternatives the details of the rendering, particularly in the left part of the composition, provide the necessary evidence.

The entire composition is developed against a monochrome background, of which, however, only a few traces remain. It was originally a bright yellow, and has now faded to a dirty grayish brown.[275] For the central feature of the static right portion of his composition the artist naturally chose King Solomon and his throne. Here he was presenting to worshipers in the Synagogue a person and an object that played prominent roles in Jewish legend, that did not cease to stir the imagination of the Oriental story-tellers even in late Islamic times, and that inevitably reappeared in later Jewish and Christian art.[276] All traces of the

king and of the upper part of his throne have disappeared. What remains is a portion of the dais painted in yellow and outlined in brown, suggesting that it was overlaid with pure gold, as the Biblical text says (I Kings 10.18). The dais had six steps, of which five are clearly visible, and the sixth can be inferred from random evidence, bringing it into correspondence in this particular also with the Biblical description (I Kings 10.19).[277] On the ends of the steps are mounted confronted animals, crouching lions and eagles with outstretched wings, all in yellow outlined in brown (Fig. 26). The eagles and lions alternate at either side but in such a sequence that every step has a lion at one end and an eagle at the other.

The animals on the dais of Solomon's throne became, as is well known, the occasion for the development of the legend about the mechanical

Fig. 26. Panel WA 2. Decoration of Solomon's Throne

273. Inscrs. nos. **30** and **31,** below, p. 279. Because of the inaccessibility of the panels of the upper registers it is quite unlikely that these *tituli* were added at a later time as Sonne suggests ("The Paintings," p. 284).

274. The former is supported by Du Mesnil du Buisson, *Peintures,* pp. 46f.; Grabar, "Le Thème," p. 6; Schneid, *The Paintings,* p. 12; and Wischnitzer, *Messianic Theme,* pp. 71–73. The latter is proposed in Du Mesnil du Buisson, "Les Peintures," pp. 111 f.; *Rep. VI,* p. 349; and Sukenik, *The Synagogue,* pp. 86f. Sonne ("The Paintings," pp. 281–284), disregarding the *tituli,* interprets the scene as Pharaoh receiving the midwives, but this episode is portrayed in Panel WC 4 (Pharaoh and the Infancy of Moses).

275. While monochrome backgrounds are common in the Synagogue, yellow is not characteristic of them. Its use in this instance may be intended to emphasize the splendor of King Solomon's surroundings. On the splendor of Solomon's throne-room, see I Kings 7.7, Josephus (*Antiquitates* VIII, § 134), and Islamic legend (see J. Walker in *Encyclopaedia of Islam,* IV, 1934, pp. 519–521, *s.v.* "Sulaiman").

276. The prominence of Solomon in the centuries before and after the beginning of the current era is indicated by the association of his name with various apocryphal and pseudepigraphical books. For his place in Haggadic narrative see Ginzberg, *Legends of the Jews,* IV, pp. 125–176, and for Islamic legend see M. Grünbaum, *Neue Beiträge zur semitischen Sagenkunde* (1893), pp. 198–236. On the throne of Solomon see G. Salzberger, *Salomos Tempelbau und Thron in der semitischen Sagenliteratur (Schriften der Lehranstalt für die Wissenschaft des*

Judentums, II, 1, 1912); J. Perles, *Mitteilungen der Gesellschaft für die Wissenschaft des Judentums,* XXI (1872), pp. 122–139. On the throne in Byzantine writers (Glycas and Constantine Porphyrogenitus) see M. Sachs, *Beiträge zur Sprach- und Altertumsforschung,* I (1852), pp. 70–72. For the later representations of the throne see the Machsor of the fourteenth century at Budapest (reproduced in *Encyclopaedia Judaica,* VIII, cols. 181–182) and the carvings above the central doorway of the west façade of the Strassburg Cathedral.

277. Above the tread of the fifth step a curved line is visible at the right side of the dais, forming a part of the outline of a bird such as reappears on alternate steps below. This implies the existence of a riser above the tread of the fifth step and therefore the existence of a sixth to complete the dais. On the riser of the fourth step is inscribed the *titulus*: Σλήμων, for the form of which see below, Inscr. no. **30,** p. 279.

contrivances of the throne by which the king was raised to the top of the dais without effort on his part. There is nothing in the representation of the Synagogue to show whether or not the artist knew the legend and thought of the animals as fulfilling a mechanical as well as an ornamental purpose. It is clear, however, that the identity of the animals has changed from that of the Biblical description where only lions are mentioned (I Kings 10.20). For the iconography of the Synagogue it is the tradition reflected in the *Targum Sheni* to Esther that is normative, for here we are told,

> "And there stood upon it (the dais of the throne) twelve lions of gold and over against them twelve golden eagles, a lion opposite an eagle and an eagle opposite a lion, so that each golden lion's right paw was opposite each golden eagle's left wing."[278]

Two men are seated at either side of Solomon's throne, one in a profile, the other in a frontal pose, as already indicated. Both occupy luxurious golden chairs, that at the left visibly supplied with a red cushion. The chair of the man at the left is of the folding variety, its legs crossed in the middle, in the fashion of the ancient δίφρος ὀκλαδίας.[279] The chair of the man at the right is largely hidden by his garments, but was undoubtedly of the same type. More imposing, by contrast, is the vacant chair in the extreme right corner of the scene, whose bowed front legs ending in lion heads recall at once the more formal type of *sella curulis* familiar from the consular diptychs.[280] It too has

a bright red cushion. The two men seated upon the chairs are dressed, not in court attire like their neighbor to the left, but in white chiton and himation.[281] Their sandal-shod feet rest upon red cushions that in turn seem to be resting upon the usual footstool (Fig. 27). Now the *Targum Sheni*

FIG. 27. Panel WA 2. Footstool

preserves the tradition that "beside the throne (of Solomon) stood... two golden chairs," but it goes on to say that they were reserved "one for the High Priest and one for the Chief Priest."[282] The Synagogue artist, while following the tradition of the two chairs, apparently knew it in a different form, for he identified the left occupant by a *titulus* as συνκάθαδρο[ς] (*sic.* Inscr. no. 31). In all probability he meant by the use of this otherwise rather rare noun to point to the men's judicial function, in which case we would probably not be far wrong in imagining that they represent the Great Sanhedrin, an interpretation that would explain their "civilian" attire.[283] Certainly the fact that the two

---

278. Edit. P. de Lagarde, *Hagiographa chaldaice* (1873), p. 227, lines 17–22. The *Targum Sheni*, it may be noted, has a full description of the mechanical function of the lions and eagles. For the description of the remaining features of Solomon's throne see the treatment of Panel WC 2 below, pp. 158 f.

279. For examples of this type of chair in ancient Greek art, see G. M. A. Richter, *Ancient Furniture* (1926), pp. 39–43, Figs. 109–121; and in Roman art, *ibid.*, pp. 126 f., Figs. 300–302. A couch or settee of the same type appears in the representation of Pluto and Proserpina in the painted tomb at Marwa in Transjordan. See C. C. McCown, *Quarterly of the Department of Antiquities in Palestine*, IX (1942), pp. 6 f. and Pl. I. A grave stele from Antioch depicts the same object. Cf. *Antioch*, III, Pl. 14, no. 344. The cross-piece that seems to transform the *X* of the legs into an *A* is actually, of course, the bar connecting the two rear legs.

280. Cf. R. Delbrueck, *Die Consulardiptychen und verwandte Denkmäler* (1929), pp. 63 f., and especially the diptych of Anastasius, Pls. 20–21.

281. The chiton projects below the edge of the himation in each case but lacks the clavi that would normally make it more readily identifiable. Probably the absence of the clavi is an oversight on the part of the artist.

282. Lagarde, *op. cit.*, p. 228, lines 1–2, 16–17.

283. In the Byzantine period συγκάθεδρος is used of officials whom we would call assessors (F. Preisigke, *Sammelbuch griechischer Urkunden aus Ägypten*, 1915, no. 2253, line 13). The verb συγκαθίζω, however, appears in earlier contexts in association with συνέδριον (*Hellenica Oxyrhynchia*, ed. B. P. Grenfell and A. S. Hunt, 1909, XI, 4) and with δικαστήριον (Xenophon, *Hellenica* V, 2, 35). In the LXX it is used in Exod. 18.13 in connection with the expression κρίνειν τὸν λαόν. The LXX of Esther 1.14 speaks of Ahasuerus having three πρῶτοι παρακαθήμενοι. On the existence of the Great Sanhedrin since the days of Moses in Jewish legend, see the *Jewish Encyclopedia*, XI (1905, 1909), p. 43. On the Sanhedrin in the legends concerning Solomon see the Midrash, Cod. Hebr. 222, Munich, as reported by M. Grünbaum, *Gesammelte Aufsätze zur Sprach- und Sagenkunde* (1901),

men in "civilian" dress are actually seated in the presence of the monarch adds to the traditional audience scene of imperial art an element foreign to its fundamental character and to the conception of Oriental monarchy. Here, we must suppose, there has been conflated with the iconographic prototype a scene of a different character, perhaps of an assembly or council.[284]

The two persons who move toward the throne from the extreme left end of the panel are identifiable without difficulty as women from the fact that their garments fall almost to the ground, covering all but the tips of their heavy-soled dark brown shoes.[285] The garments themselves differ in important respects from the large majority of those worn by women in other panels of the Synagogue. Their outlines, particularly at the bottom, are more gracefully drawn and curved. A larger variety of colors is used, whether to indicate contrasting borders or additional layers of clothing. Above all there is indicated, beginning at the right calf, an article of clothing whose hem or border sweeps gently upward toward the left knee and whose ends hang down, presumably from the bent forearm, along the left side of the figures. In the case of the woman at the extreme left this overgarment is a plain light blue. In the case of the woman preceding her toward the throne it is more ornate, for here it seems to have had a wide red and pink border and may have been ornamented with panel-like designs (Fig. 28). The garment finds its only analogy in the Synagogue in that which is draped

over Esther's lap and legs, and is clearly an ornamented shawl or cloak (Panel WC 2, Pl. LXV; Fig. 44). What is worn under this cloak or shawl is clearly not the loose, wide overgarment held in place over the left shoulder by a fibula and characterized by a wide roll around the hips, as in Panels

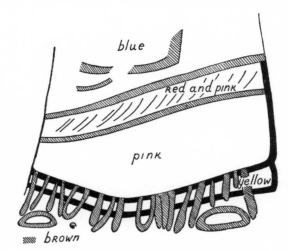

FIG. 28. Panel WA 2. Detail of Queen's Skirt

WC 1 and 4. Rather it would seem to be a garment with contrasting bodice and skirt such as Esther wears in Panel WC 2.[286] The skirt of the woman at the extreme left of our scene is yellow and has a broad pink border at the bottom. The woman who precedes her either wears two such skirts one over the other — the outer pink, the under yellow — or a single pink skirt with a yellow border.[287]

From the description of the garments which the women wear, two simple conclusions follow. The first is that they stand above the average station in the social order. Their dress is not the common garb found for instance in Panels WC 1 and WC 4, but that worn by heavenly beings (the Psyches of Panel NC 1), a queen (Panel WC 2), and the attendants of a princess (Panel WC 4). The second is that the garments of the woman who leads the way toward Solomon's throne are in each instance given

p. 57; and Perles, *Mitteilungen der Gesellschaft für die Wissenschaft des Judentums*, XXI (1872), pp. 132f. In the *Targum Sheni* gold chairs for the seventy members of the Sanhedrin stand on a gallery above.

284. Examples of such assemblies are to be found in Greek tradition; for instance, in the representation of the Assembly of the Gods in the east frieze of the Parthenon, and in the Roman tradition in the representation of the magistrates' college on the Tomb of C. Lucius Storax (see Reinach, *Répertoire de reliefs*, III, 1912, p. 334). The fusion of the two types leads in Christian art to the scenes of Christ and his apostles (see the apse mosaic in Santa Pudentiana, C. Diehl, *La Peinture byzantine*, 1933, Pl. I, and the Dijon ivory in Peirce and Tyler, *L'Art byzantin*, I, Pl. 125), and to scenes showing the Emperor presiding at Councils. Grabar's excellent observations on the latter (*L'Empereur dans l'art byzantin*, 1936, pp. 90–92, 207–209) may need to be adjusted in the light of the new material.

285. This is typical of the great majority of the female figures in the paintings of the Synagogue. Cf. e.g., Panels NB 2, SC 2, WC 1, 2, 4.

286. On this type of garment see below, p. 159. It is often supplied with a wide border of contrasting colors, as in Panels WC 4 and NC 1.

287. What causes the uncertainty in the latter instance is the presence of a further ornament that the dress of her associate lacks; namely, brown fringes that hang down from the edge of the pink skirt over the yellow zone below it (Fig. 28).

added ornamental features and are by that token intended to be regarded as more excellent than those of her associate. From this it follows that the women cannot be the two prostitutes who, as social equals of an inferior class, compete before Solomon for the possession of a child, but must be, on the contrary, the Queen of Sheba and a lady in waiting such as attends also Queen Esther (Pl. LXV).

The man who stands full front between the women and the throne scene wears soft white boots, baggy red trousers (each trouser leg ornamented with a vertical stripe down the front outlined in black), and a red tunic that comes down well below the knees and has a wide bluish border. The costume is probably Iranian in character, belongs to a type frequently represented in the Synagogue, and apparently stamps its wearer as a person of high station, frequently a member of the royal court.[288] On the assumption that the scene portrays the visit of the Queen of Sheba, the man can readily be identified as Benaiah, the son of Jehoiada, who appears in the Bible as chief of the host and in later Jewish tradition as chief of the palace guards and president of the Great Sanhedrin.[289] In either of these capacities he might readily be chosen to conduct the Queen into the presence of Solomon, as the *Targum Sheni* actually has him do, and in the latter capacity he would properly be associated with the vacant *sella curulis* at the right end of the composition.[290]

The dependence of the Synagogue artist upon Jewish legend in the development of the scene is typical of his point of view and procedure here as elsewhere, and shows that he portrayed the episodes as they were interpreted in his day, making no distinction between the written word and its Haggadic amplification. His dependence upon current iconographic tradition is equally clear and significant. What he presented in this panel illustrated to the worshipers at the Synagogue the brilliance of the Solomonic era, but above all, no doubt, the wisdom of the king; for tradition reaching back as far as the Biblical record itself (I Kings 10.3–4) made the visit of the Queen of Sheba a great contest of wits whose details later story-tellers were ever ready to supply.[291]

What actually remains of Register A of the Synagogue's decorations is little indeed. It is not surprising, therefore, that scholars have been cautious in discussing the problem of its unity even when they have ventured suggestions about the "theme" which it might be supposed to express. Indeed, only two suggestions of this type have been advanced: first, that it is an "historical cycle," intended to provide an introduction to those of a "liturgical" and "moralizing" character in the registers below; and second, that it seeks to express Israel's claim through Moses to the "crown of the Torah," quite as the lower registers express its claim to the "priesthood" and the "kingdom" respectively.[292] To discuss these suggestions and the problem of the register's unity without a knowledge of the rest of the decorations is manifestly impossible. We must content ourselves, therefore, with certain general observations, these being still further limited by the fact that the panels of the Central Group lying within Register A are reserved for separate treatment. The first observation is that in the compositions of Register A on the west wall, all of which are known, the action inside the individual panels moves from the ends of the wall toward the Central Group. The second is that, in time at least, the subject of Panel WA 3 (Exodus and Crossing of the Red Sea) is related to the subject matter of the two Wing Panels of the Central Group that lie within Register A (Panel I:

288. On its origin and its use at Dura and Palmyra see Seyrig, *Syria*, XVIII (1937), pp. 4–26.

289. I Kings 4.4; the LXX of III Reg. 2.46h, a supplement to the Hebrew text, refers to him as ἐπὶ τῆς αὐλαρχίας; on Benaiah in Jewish legend and as convener of the Great Sanhedrin, see Ginzberg, *Legends of the Jews*, VI, p. 302, n. 95, and the Munich Midrash, ed. Perles, *Mitteilungen der Gesellschaft für die Wissenschaft des Judentums*, XXI (1872), pp. 132f.

290. The *Targum Sheni* (ed. Lagarde, p. 232, lines 8–21) tells how, when Benaiah was sent to conduct the Queen into Solomon's presence, she first mistook him for the king.

291. Cf. Ginzberg, *Legends of the Jews*, IV, pp. 142–149.

292. The former suggestion is that of Du Mesnil du Buisson, *Peintures*, p. 16, the latter that of Sonne, "The Paintings," pp. 267–276, 285f. Grabar ("Le Thème," pp. 23f.) finds no common denominator other than the fact that all the scenes testify to divine intervention serving to inspire one of Israel's leaders. Wischnitzer also rejects an ideological unity (*Messianic Theme*, p. 78), while construing the whole as a "supralinear gloss" to the lower registers, particularly Register C, each scene of Register A supposedly reflecting a scene below. It should be noted that as Sonne handles the three "crowns," each is supposedly adumbrated in each of the registers.

Moses and the Burning Bush; Panel II: Moses Receives the Law). The third is that so far as Panel NA 1 (Jacob at Bethel) is concerned, the action unfolded in its upper part moves away from the west wall and the Central Group. That this panel forms the beginning of a "cycle" is possible but not demonstrable.[293] Indeed, from what is

known about the emplacement of the cycles contained in Registers B and C, it is more likely that if a comparable cycle appeared in Register A, it would have begun on the south wall and have continued on the south half of the west wall, ending with WA 1 and WA 2 (Solomon Receives the Queen of Sheba).[294]

293. The term "cycle" is applied here only to groups of adjacent panels of a single register depicting successive episodes from a given Biblical context. Such groups are to be seen in Registers B and C.

294. The cycle in Register B begins on the north wall and moves toward the Central Group, that in Register C begins on the south wall and moves toward the Central Group. A cycle in Register A should logically match that of Register C.

3. THE PANELS OF REGISTER B

Not counting the lower half of the Central Group, there is preserved of the decorations of Register B a total of seven panels. Five of them exist in their entirety and two in fragmentary state, but together they represent over half of the material originally presented in this zone. Among the seven panels a series of four on the north wall and the north half of the west wall is of particular interest. It follows a thread of narrative that begins with I Sam. 1 and develops this narrative as the panels follow each other from right to left; that is, from the east end of the north wall to the center of the west wall. Indeed, the fact that a relationship between the several elements of the series is recognizable is of primary importance for the identification of the fragmentary panel NB 2 with which the sequence begins.

Hannah and the Child Samuel at Shiloh

Panel NB 2 (fragmentary). H. *ca.* 1.53 m.; L. 2.69 m. (Pl. XXIX).

Rep. VI, p. 349; Du Mesnil du Buisson, *Peintures*, pp. 70–72; Grabar, "Le Thème," pp. 8f.; Wischnitzer-Bernstein, "Samuel Cycle," pp. 87f.; Schneid, *The Paintings*, p. 15; Sukenik, *The Synagogue*, pp. 114f.; Sonne, "The Paintings," p. 309; Wischnitzer, *Messianic Theme*, pp. 61–63.

Of the panel under discussion here, over half was destroyed when the walls of the chamber were cut down to the gradient of the embankment in which they were buried. What remains is a triangular piece representing the lower left half of the composition. Its surface is cut by a large number of diagonal cracks resulting from the pressure of the west wall upon the north wall, but these detract from a knowledge of the composition less than the weathering to which the colors of the panel were subject.

Among the various elements of the composition still dimly visible today, the most prominent is a long grayish-yellow city wall that extends across almost two thirds of the panel beginning at the left.[295] The outlines of its towers or crenelations are

295. The wall actually occupies 1.72 m. of the total panel length.

clear because they are set against an intensely black background, but those of its blocks and tiers of masonry are less so. Where the city wall ends, or rather begins, at the right, the lower portions of two figures are visible. The background behind them is dark, but apparently green rather than black. They occupy 0.68 m. of the remaining right part of the field, and are shown moving from the right toward the city at the left.[296] The one that leads the way is a woman of Junoesque stature. She wears high black boots or shoes; a pink, probably short-sleeved, chiton; and an overgarment of the type that is held in place over the left shoulder by a fibula and is draped around the hips in a heavy roll, from where it falls covering the legs like a skirt.[297] In this instance only the lower ends of the garments are visible. The overgarment has a checkerboard weave represented by lighter and darker red squares, and is embroidered over the right calf with a large black *H*-shaped ornament.[298] Walking behind the woman is a person of much smaller proportions, in all probability a boy. Only his high soft white boots and his red trousers are still visible; but with them he must originally have worn the knee-length, long-sleeved tunic, belted at the waist, that completes the costume in other scenes. So dressed, he could be either a member of the royal court or a part of the Temple personnel.

From the thread of the narrative which the panels of Register B on the north wall and the

north half of the west wall unfold, it is evident that the picture represents the pious Hannah bringing to the sanctuary at Shiloh the child Samuel who had been born to her in answer to her prayers and in fulfilment of the divine promise (I Sam. 1, esp. vv. 21–28). The scene thus brings before the eyes of the devout worshiper the very beginning of the career of a man who in difficult days played a crucial role in the life of his people as military leader, judge, zealous opponent of idolatry, and as anointer of kings.[299] It associates him with the noble figure of his mother in whose actions were portrayed in exemplary fashion faith in the answer to prayer, piety that is sure of divine reward, fidelity in the discharge of vows, and devotion — as later legend was quick to note — to the practice of religious pilgrimage.[300] More than that, Hannah came at a fairly early time to be regarded as having a prophetic spirit, a fact which is reflected in the rendering of I Sam. 2 by the Targum pseudo-Jonathan and is not unimportant for the understanding of the further development of the series of scenes which she introduces here.[301] In I Sam. 1.24f. Hannah is described as bringing with her bullocks and other sacrificial offerings for the sanctuary when she dedicated Samuel to the service of the Lord at Shiloh. Certain of these sacrificial offerings were probably originally represented in the space behind and above the boy.

About the wall that here represents the city of Shiloh two things are noticeable. The first is its extreme length, and the second the fact that it is so low compared both to the figure of Hannah and to the height of similar walls in other panels.[302] This is because the space above the wall was used by the artist to introduce a supplementary scene. The existence of this second scene is shown by the fact that the black background ends just above the crenelations of the wall in a line of rounded protuberances, and really acts only as a frame for an

---

296. The plaster breaks off short of the east end of the panel, but measurements show that there remained about 0.28 m. beyond the last of the two figures which could have been, and probably was, used by the artist in developing his composition.

297. For the details of this type of garment, familiar from other scenes of the Synagogue, see Panels WC 1 and WC 4 (Pls. LXIII, LXVII–LXVIII) and their description, p. 146, n. 532.

298. From the checkerboard effect of the garment and its analogy to those worn by Moses and Aaron in Panels WB 1 and WB 2 (Pls. LIX–LX) it has been inferred that the wearer is a man (so *Rep. VI*, p. 349; Grabar, "Le Thème," p. 8; Wischnitzer-Bernstein, *American Academy for Jewish Research, Proceedings*, XI, 1941, p. 87; *idem*, *Messianic Theme*, pp. 62 f.), but the treatment of the feet and of the hem of the garment preclude this, these having their only analogy in the Synagogue in figures of women. The checkboard design is the result of a type of weaving (chevron weft twill) of which examples have been found at Dura (no. 36 in *Final Report* IV, part II, p. 2; p. 5, Fig. 1; and Pl. XIII). For the *H*-shaped ornament, see *ibid.*, p. 11 and Pl. XI; and M. von Berchem and E. Cluzot, *Mosaïques chrétiennes* (1924), pp. xlvii–xlix.

299. Note that the child already wears the costume appropriate to the period of his service in the Temple at Shiloh.

300. Ginzberg, *Legends of the Jews*, IV, pp. 57–60.

301. Cf. below, pp. 111–113. On Hannah as one of the seven prophetesses of Israel see Megillah 14a (Trans., p. 82).

302. Including the crenelations the wall is only *ca.* 0.49 m. high, or approximately one third of the height of the panel. Cf. the much higher walls of Panels WA 3, SC 2, and WC 4.

area in which the basic colors were bright yellows and reds. Of what was originally portrayed inside the framed area nothing remains but a few angular lines in its lower left corner; but the subject of the scene can be inferred from the nature of its frame— black indicating the darkness of night — and from the subject of the next panel. It portrayed the experience of the boy Samuel told in I Sam. 3.1–14, when he slept in the sanctuary at Shiloh before the Ark of the Covenant and heard the voice that he mistook first for Eli's, but learned eventually to understand as that of the Lord himself, telling him of the impending punishment of the house of Eli. Among the necessary elements of the scene, we can therefore imagine a temple with the Ark in it, the light that burned before it, and the boy Samuel asleep in the foreground.[303]

The use of an inset would make this one of the more unusual of the compositions of the Synagogue and throw further light on the handling of narrative art. The artist employs here a technique familiar in Roman Imperial art, where, however, the inset usually introduces concomitant events or associated figures.[304] If it serves here to represent subsequent developments, this is probably only because the artist was being forced to compress his material severely as in Panel WA 3 (Exodus and Crossing of the Red Sea). The fact that he was able to combine vertical and horizontal perspectives, thus finding it entirely possible to portray above such a barrier as a wall the events transpiring behind it, undoubtedly stood him in good stead in organizing the composition. So too did the basic principle of the telescoping procedure, which makes elements necessary to one scene (here wall and temple) serve also for the rendering of the other.[305]

303. For the temple there is a fair analogy in Panel WB 2.

304. Cf. e.g., the two insets, one showing Father Danube, the other a mass of dead animals, in the bas-reliefs of the Column of Trajan (Lehmann-Hartleben, *Die Trajanssäule*, p. 133 [Höhlenprinzip]; Pls. 6, section III, and 17, sections XXIX/XXX); and in early Christian art the Dream of Pharaoh on the Maximianus Chair (C. Cecchelli, *La Cathedra di Massimiano*, 1936–1944, Pl. IV and p. 51).

305. These have already been encountered in the compositions of Register A. The fact that the black background which the artist commonly employs to indicate a nocturnal setting is here used in schematic fashion as a frame for the inset may be mentioned in passing.

The Battle of Eben-ezer

Panel NB 1. H. 1.53 m.; L. 3.835 m. (Pls. LIV–LV).

Hopkins and Du Mesnil du Buisson, "La Synagogue," p. 249; *Rep. VI*, pp. 349f.; Du Mesnil du Buisson, "Les Peintures," p. 114; *idem, Peintures*, pp. 72–74; Grabar, "Le Thème," pp. 6–8; Wischnitzer-Bernstein, "Samuel Cycle," pp. 88–91; Schneid, *The Paintings*, p. 15; Sukenik, *The Synagogue*, pp. 115f.; Sonne, "The Paintings," pp. 308–310; Wischnitzer, *Messianic Theme*, pp. 63f.

The longest among the compositions of Register B that are known to us, Panel NB 1 is at the same time probably the most spirited and provocative of the entire Synagogue. Save for relatively small portions of the two upper corners, it is preserved in its entirety; and, save for the right half, particularly at the top, where proximity to the surface of the embankment has caused weathering, the outlines and colors are fairly clear.[306] As his background color the artist has in this instance chosen a dull brick-red, but the lower 0.26 m. of the field are again treated as though he were creating an element of stage space and are rendered in green.[307]

306. The missing section of the upper left corner, where the plaster had been crumbled by stresses transmitted from the west wall, has been restored. The restored section includes the head, shoulders, and the upper part of the shield and sword of the last soldier at the left. A long, deep crack cuts through the panel, beginning at the level of the shoulder of the first Ark-bearer and dropping gradually to the level of the green foreground strip. It has occasioned the loss of several small pieces of plaster surface with portions of the third Ark-bearer's chiton. Where the feet of the first and second bearer come together, a larger circular piece of plaster has been lost (and the surface restored) as the result of a deep fissure visible in the upper portions of the next lower panel (Panel NC 1, *q.v.*). Apart from the multiple breakage in the upper right hand corner of the panel, two vertical cracks can be seen running down through the two riders. The one farthest to the left cuts diagonally through the soldiers in the foreground, where again small pieces of plaster are missing and where the surface has been restored (see particularly the third soldier in the foreground counting from the right).

307. On the use of space in Hellenistic and Roman art, see G. Rodenwaldt, *Die Komposition der pomejanischen Wandgemälde* (1909), esp. pp. 1–40; C. M. Dawson, *YCS*, IX (1944), pp. 11–24. On other aspects of the Synagogue artists' use of space, including cast shadows, see below, pp. 367–370.

Beginning his composition at the right, he found that the area set aside by the use of this technique was not sufficient to contain the action, and so developed part of it upon the red background above. In the left half of the panel the "stage space" was continued but is completely unrelated to the distribution of the figures.

The action of the panel is developed in two scenes. The first scene, presented in the larger right portion of the panel, depicts the progress of a mighty battle. The elements of the conflict are held carefully apart and arranged in three successive planes. Prominently displayed in the central plane are two horsemen, mounted on black and white steeds respectively, who charge toward each other with leveled lances, the moment of their fateful collision patently imminent. In the uppermost plane groups of three and four infantrymen confront each other with shields advanced and swords poised, ready for the shock of bodily contact. In the lowest plane, the concerted movement that brings opposing groups of combatants together in the center of the panel is abandoned, and the action is broken down into three separate episodes distributed across the entire field. Each episode shows infantrymen of the opposing forces engaged in single combat, the moment portrayed being that in which the outcome of their encounter is sealed by the bloody death of one or both of them.[308]

The second scene, developed in the left half of the panel, is more placid though not less warlike. Its central feature is a bejeweled chest with a round top, the Ark of the Covenant, mounted on a base of two steps and supported by long poles which four civilians bear upon their shoulders as they march toward the left; that is, away from the battle scene. In the foreground beneath the Ark, and on a higher plane at either side of the Ark, are pairs of soldiers with shields and drawn swords. From the point of view of the artist, the soldiers represent files of infantrymen that march in parallel columns with the Ark-bearers, forming its guard at either side.[309]

From the panel which precedes in the series (Panel NB 2) and from that which follows (WB 4), it is clear that what the Synagogue artist has portrayed in this instance is a part of the action of the important battle of Eben-ezer described in I Sam. 4.1–11. As viewed by the Biblical historian, the battle brought to fulfilment the divine oracle given to the boy Samuel in the sanctuary at Shiloh, for it ended with the defeat of the Israelites by the Philistines and with the death of the two sons of the priest Eli, forming a judgment upon the latter for the abuse of their priestly office. To the mighty loss of lives involved in the defeat there was added, according to the Biblical narrative, a loss equally tragic — that of the Ark of the Covenant, that was brought into battle on the second day to stem the tide, but fell into the hands of the Philistines. When the Philistines took the Israelite palladium with them to the cities of the coastal plain as part of the spoils of war, the pious, we are told, said, "the glory is departed from Israel" (I Sam. 4.22). With the battle itself and the transport of the Ark to Philistia by the victors, the two scenes of the composition can readily be associated.

Interesting as the panel is in its composition and its historical association, so interesting is it also in the execution of its details. The battle scene at the right, with which the examination of these details must begin, has as its central feature the combat of two confronted horsemen. For this feature the artist evidently used the same models as the Iranian hunting and combat scenes known to us from paintings, bas-reliefs, and silver dishes, and from regions as remote from one another as South Russia and Fars. Yet he did not need to go far in search of them, for they were available at Dura itself, whither they had apparently been brought

---

308. Between them the infantrymen in the lowest plane occupy the entire "stage space". From the placement of the left horse it would seem as though the artist or any model he may have been copying may have meant the upper edge of the foreground strip to be used as a base line for the cavalry combat of the second plane. The position of the right horse, however, shows how far he was from any sense of compulsion to adhere to such a scheme or intention.

309. Note that in this scene the "stage space" has lost its function entirely and that the arrangement in three ascending planes has broken down, all figures but the upper file of soldiers using the lower edge of the panel as a base line. Perhaps in the intention of the artist or in any model he may have been following, the Ark-bearers were originally assigned to a position on the upper edge of the foreground strip. If so, the insufficient height of the panel and the desire to bring the Ark closer to the middle of the composition caused the abandonment of the intention or of the original design.

in the Parthian period of the city's history.[310] The riders in the Synagogue scene wear blue belted tunics with elbow-length sleeves, red trousers, and low reddish-brown boots.[311] With one hand each of them grasps a lance with a long pointed tip, while the other is clenched and in position to hold the reins of the bridle.[312] A sword in a scabbard dangles beside the thigh of the rider approaching from the right. The fact that the arm holding the lance is extended toward the rear ready for the forward lunge naturally turns the upper part of the body into a three-quarter position in each instance. The mounts of the two combatants are in each case deep-breasted, spirited animals of the type familiar from Persian art, with bodies heavy in proportion to the thinness of the legs, with fine pointed heads, long flowing tails, and clipped manes.[313] They bear

a relatively simple harness consisting of a bridle, a saddlecloth held in place by a cinch, breastband, and crupper, all in red. The harness reappears on other scenes where its elements are more clearly visible and can be dealt with more advantageously.[314]

Like the riders and their mounts, the infantrymen of the panel are accoutred in identical fashion whether they are Philistines or Israelites. This is something which a national art, whether Roman or Sassanian, would probably have avoided, but which for the Synagogue artist was not a matter of concern. The uniform consists of a knee-length long-sleeved cuirass of scale armor (*lorica squamata*) belted at the waist, narrow trousers, and low boots — both of the latter analogous to those worn by the riders.[315] Sometimes, as in the scene at the left, a helmet or a coif covered with chain mail is added to the cuirass. The weapons are normally two in number; namely, a wide-bladed sword and a bossed, yellow, hexagonal shield, though lances are also in evidence at one point in the infantry combat.[316] Infantrymen in scale armor appear among Roman detachments in the monuments of Roman Imperial art, but the use of this type of equipment is Oriental in origin and in the form which appears here probably derives from Oriental, rather than Roman, models.[317]

310. Cf. e.g., the so-called Sassanian Fresco of Dura, *Rep. IV*, pp. 182–199 and Pls. XVII–XVIII. On the wider subject of the Iranian hunting and combat scenes see Rostovtzeff, *YCS*, V (1935), esp. pp. 262–272; and *idem, Revue des arts asiatiques*, VII (1931–1932), pp. 202–222. For the combat scene from South Russia (Panticapaeum), see Rostovtzeff, *Ancient Decorative Painting*, Pl. LXXIX; and for the combat scenes of Firuzabad, E. Herzfeld, *Iran in the Ancient East* (1941), Pl. CIX. In the western monuments of Roman art confronted riders are virtually nonexistent.

311. A narrow edge of white is visible at the neck, the ends of the sleeves, and at the hem of the tunic, which may represent either a narrow border or an undergarment. The low dark-colored boots worn by all the military in this panel, and here alone in the Synagogue, are analogous to those on the statue of Antiochus in the Nemrud-Dagh relief (see K. Humann and O. Puchstein, *Reisen in Kleinasien und Nord-Syrien*, 1890, Pl. XXXIX, 1, 2). The thongs on the feet of the infantrymen, particularly in the left half of the panel, do not mean that they are wearing sandals (as do the Ark-bearers), but represent straps attached to the trouser-legs and holding them in place by passing under the boot. For a similarly clothed mounted archer see the terracotta relief of the Parthian period in A. U. Pope, *Survey of Persian Art*, IV, Pl. 134 A.

312. Following the standard Oriental convention the artist makes one rider the mirror image of the other, so that the one at the right holds the lance in his left hand.

313. Professor Hopkins has noted that in the instance of the left horse, as also at various points elsewhere in the panel, the color of the subject depicted is superimposed upon the red of the background. This implies a departure from the procedure followed elsewhere in the Synagogue, for the background color was normally painted around the outlines of the figures and objects set against it, but before the outlines were filled in. It accounts for the liberal use of the background color in the trousers and the exposed body members of the persons represented, and suggests that the artist was using short cuts in executing his composition.

314. Cf. Panel WC 2, Pl. LXIV and below, p. 154. As recorded by Hopkins at the time when the panel was first uncovered, the elements of the bridle, now no longer clearly visible, comprise nose- and brow-bands joined at the side by cheek-straps, and a throatlatch that passes around the head behind the ears holding the bridle in place. The reins seem to be attached to the nose-strap. Tassels are recorded as having been visible on the breastband and crupper of the horse at the right. The cinch was also visible at that time on the belly of the horse at the right, but none is discernible on the photographs or on the wall today. There is no such difference between horses and riders as Wischnitzer imagines, *Messianic Theme*, p. 63.

315. The cuirass is always a dirty greenish gray; the trousers are reddish brown save in one instance when they are green. Black or reddish-brown fold lines are conspicuous throughout.

316. Cf. below, p. 98. The shields are probably to be thought of as being made of leather stretched on wooden frames whose ribs are indicated by the pairs of horizontal lines dividing the surface into zones. Hexagonal shields are used by Roman soldiers on the Arch of Septimius Severus; see Reinach, *Répertoire de reliefs*, I, p. 260.

317. Scale armor is usually worn by Roman troops without the trousers and low shoes of our scene. For early eastern examples of soldiers in scale armor, see the South

In contrast to the procedure followed in Panel WA 3 (Exodus and Crossing of the Red Sea), the artist has here resisted the tendency to mass his figures in serried ranks, and has even avoided the use of the mêlée type of composition. Instead he follows the principle common to Oriental and earlier Greek art of breaking the conflict up into a series of individual encounters, and presents his masses in groups of no more than four men, each separately drawn.[318] Among the individual encounters, those of the infantry in the foreground of this scene deserve a further word of comment. At the extreme left the artist has portrayed a man mortally wounded, who has fallen forward from a kneeling position and who pillows his head upon his forearms. At his right the swordsman who has dispatched him moves on to assist a comrade brought to his knees by an assailant who has come from the right and is ready to strike him from above. Still farther to the right are seen two soldiers who have wounded each other mortally and are *in extremis*. A lance has pierced the side of the first at the waist, and as he raises his hands above his head in agony, his sword falls from his hands to the ground. His scabbard hangs empty by his left side. The second man sags to the ground, pulling with his hands at a lance that has pierced his abdomen. His shield has fallen to the ground behind him.

In the left half of the panel there are to be seen

FIG. 29. Representations of the Ark of the Covenant. Panels SB 1, WB 4, NB 1

Russian tomb scene in Rostovtzeff, *Ancient Decorative Painting*, Pl. LXXIX; and for a horseman wearing the combination of scale cuirass, trousers, and boots, the relief from Tanaid in the Crimea now in the Hermitage Museum, *ibid.*, Pl. LXXXIV, 3. For examples of scale armor from Dura itself, see *Rep. VI*, pp. 439–452.

318. The group of four in the upper right hand corner of the scene is imperfectly preserved. The heads have disappeared entirely, but the body masses and the weapons are sufficiently distinct to make it evident that in pose and armament they match approximately the group of three at the left.

in addition to the soldiers the Ark of the Covenant and its bearers. The palladium appears again in two other panels of the same register (Panels WB 4 and WB 2). Its multiple representation shows how important the object was in the Biblical tradition and for the religious life of later Judaism. Wherever it appears in the Synagogue paintings, the Ark is depicted as a tall yellow chest with a rounded top (Fig. 29), but the details the artist felt entirely free to vary from scene to scene. In our panel indications of coffering were either omitted or have faded out. What remains are two dull reddish-brown bands representing garlands of leaves encircling the Ark, and a series of large and small jewels attached directly or by means of special mountings to the top and the end of the object and to its garlands.[319] Though it is actually being carried toward the left, the Ark is seen here, as elsewhere in the Synagogue, in a frontal position, this being apparently for the artist the canonical form of its representation.[320] It is mounted on a carrying device (*ferculum*) consisting of a yellow stepped base and a pair of long poles carried upon the shoulders of the bearers.[321] The bearers themselves are civilians, probably Philistines and certainly not Levites.[322] They wear long greenish-gray chitons with wide pink clavi and ordinary sandals. The chitons have elbow-length sleeves and are girded up at the waist by a belt, like those of the departing Israelites in the Exodus Panel, indicating that the men are on the march. All are turned three-quarters front, with their heads sometimes approximating a full frontal position; but by showing their knees slightly bent the artist has succeeded in conveying nonetheless the impression that they are carrying a heavy object while moving rapidly toward the left. In the case of the soldier guards, all of whom face full front, the impression of movement is not so well transmitted.

319. The same type of ornament appears on the Ark in Panel WB 4, but in a different arrangement. Cf. also the setting of the stones on the garment of the High Priest in Panel WB 2 (Pl. LX).

320. A three-quarter view is provided by the bas-relief on the frieze of the synagogue of Capernaum in Palestine. Cf. Kohl and Watzinger, *Antike Synagogen*, p. 34, Fig. 68.

321. The arrangements for carrying the Ark contradict those described in Exod. 37.1–5, the artist falling back in this particular upon his knowledge of religious and triumphal processions, in which cult statues and *tropaia* were carried upon *fercula* of the type represented. Cf. Daremberg-Saglio, II, 2 (1896), pp. 1040f. (P. Paris), *s.v.* "ferculum"; and V, pp. 486–491 (R. Cagnat), *s.v.* "triumphus"; and for an archeological example, the mosaic from Praeneste, E. Breccia, *Monuments de l'Egypte gréco-romaine*, I (1926), Pl. LVI, I.

322. Schneid protests correctly against their identification as "captured Levites," of which there is no indication in the Biblical text (*The Paintings*, p. 15). In Panel SB 1 the presumed bearers of the Ark are Levites, their garments being quite different from those worn here and quite in accord with the representation of the Levites in Panel WB 2.

7*

As the absence of the Levites indicates, the Ark has been taken from its rightful bearers and has passed into unconsecrated hands. The *ferculum* on which it is mounted shows that it is being borne in something approximating a triumphal procession. Were a welcoming crowd included in the picture, the analogy to other familiar scenes of triumph would be complete and the moment depicted clearly identifiable as that at which the Ark is received in Philistine lands. The absence of the crowds, the presence of the guard of soldiers, and the incorporation of the procession in one panel with a scene of combat make it more likely that what the painter wanted to portray was the Ark leaving the battlefield as a piece of booty in Philistine hands. Yet he did see fit to indicate that this was for the Philistines a moment of triumph and the beginning of a triumphal journey that would reach its climax when the Ark actually arrived in Philistia. That the Synagogue artists were free to include among the pictures they portrayed a representation of what was, after all, one of the great catastrophes in the early history of the Israelite people, is of the utmost significance for our knowledge of the nature and function of their decorative work, and a testimony to the depth, both of the Jewish faith and of its understanding of the historical process.

The Ark in the Land of the Philistines

Panel WB 4. H. 1.55 m.; L. 2.23 m. (Pl. LVI).

Rep. VI, p. 350; Du Mesnil du Buisson, "Les Peintures," p. 10; *idem*, "Une Peinture," pp. 192–203; *idem*, "Nouvelles observations," pp. 305f.; *idem*, *Peintures*, pp. 75–84; Wischnitzer-Bernstein, "The Samuel Cycle," pp. 91–94; Sukenik, *The Synagogue*, pp. 88–91; Wischnitzer, *Messianic Theme*, pp. 64f.

With the present panel the series of scenes in Register B that has been followed hitherto on the north wall, and the action of which has moved consistently from right to left, turns the northwest corner of the building and is continued on the west wall. Here again two scenes are combined in a single panel, this time quite successfully and with decided economy of presentation, due to the use of pictorial abbreviation. The first scene, at the right, is one of desecration and spoliation. It shows the façade of a temple of Imperial style, its despoiled interior exposed to view, and scattered about in the foreground, in what may represent the forecourt of the temple, all the wealth of its cult images and cult implements. The objects, like the means of their emplacement in the interior of the shrine, are yellow, and hence to be thought of as being fashioned of gold. Dominating the static scene of desolation at the right, and forming the most important element of the more dynamic scene at the left, is the Ark of the Covenant. Garlanded and bejeweled as before, it is mounted on a sumptuous cart bright with the colors of the cushions and the canopy that protect the palladium. The cart is shown making a sharp turn toward the left of the panel, away from the neighboring scene of destruction. It is drawn by a pair of oxen who are being conducted and goaded on by two drivers in Iranian dress. From the rear three men in Greek garments move forward, following the cart in its progress.

The two scenes are cast against a single monochrome background of yellowish gray, the color of which is varied at one point only; namely, under the cart and the oxen, for reasons that will appear shortly. The panel has suffered appreciably from falling objects that have marked the surface with long deep scars and scratches, and from cracks, both vertical and diagonal. Both types of accident have been the occasion for the loss by fragmentation and pulverization of elements of plaster surface, largely confined, however, to areas where they make little difference.[323] Of the subjects of the scenes represented there can be not the slightest

323. Most of the scratches were made after the paintings were executed, and may be associated in their origin with the unroofing of the chamber. They are particularly noticeable in the scene at the right, where they often end in deep vertical depressions suggesting that what scarred the surface had momentarily or finally lodged. Another such deep impression has brought about the loss of a piece of the surface in the area of the humps of the two oxen. One set of lesser parallel scratches directly over the left pedestal in the temple has given rise to the impression that a statue was shown mounted here. This impression is incorrect. There are four vertical cracks, none of them of great consequence, and one more serious horizontal fissure beginning in the lower right hand corner. The last-mentioned has led to the loss of a section of the surface below the cart, and to dislocations in the area of the lower of the two statues.

doubt. Continuing the thread developed on the north wall, they represent two further episodes from the history of the Ark as recounted in I Sam. 5 and 6. The first scene, at the right, depicts the damage done by the Ark in the Temple of Dagon at Ashdod, when the Philistines installed the captured palladium there beside the image of the god, and on two successive mornings found the statue fallen to the ground, once severely damaged by the fall (I Sam. 5.1–5). The second scene, at the left, presents the final episode in the disconcerting train of events to which the presence of the Ark gave rise in Philistine lands. After the Ark had been sent from one Philistine city to another, bringing misfortune wherever it went, so the story tells us, the princes of the land, upon the advice of the priests and diviners, arranged to have it and certain expiatory offerings placed upon a specially constructed cart drawn by two milch-kine, and sent away wherever the kine would take it. By watching whether the kine took the road toward Judea the princes were to know whether it was the God of Israel who had caused their misfortunes, and by returning it to its rightful owners they were to deliver themselves from further calamity (I Sam. 6.1–12). The artist has shown the Ark as it begins its unusual journey, with the princes of the Philistines observing from behind. In so doing he has balanced the seizure of the Ark already depicted in Panel NB 1 with the scene of its restitution. Moreover, by placing the Ark mounted on its cart in the very center of his composition, he has not only emphasized its significance for the Jewish community, but has also found an excellent way of combining the two scenes, suggesting the relation of the palladium to the havoc wrought in the temple of Dagon without reproducing the Ark a second time in the scene at the right. At the same time, by turning his oxen to the left, he has shown the imminent separation of the Ark from the Philistine environment, and has suggested that the train of action developed in the series of panels up to this point is to continue and find its conclusion in the next panel at the left.

While the subjects of the two scenes are thus entirely clear, there are a number of iconographic details that require elucidation: some of them because they contradict or supplement what the Biblical narrative tells us, and others because they

59093

have been interpreted as involving allusions to a particular pagan cult, the cult of Adonis.[324] These can be treated best in connection with the necessary analysis of the elements of the representation.

As it stands, the temple in the upper part of the scene at the right is an architectural monstrosity, comparing unfavorably with the building in the next panel to the left (Panel WB 3). In all probability — though this is not absolutely clear — the artist meant to represent here only the façade of the temple, spacing the columns of his portico in the arbitrary manner familiar from Roman coins to provide an unobstructed view of the interior of the cella.[325] The crepidoma, the columns of the Corinthian order, and the architrave (of which at least a portion is visible) are all rendered in white, and contrast with the yellow cella wall, whose courses of stones are clearly outlined.[326] Set into the cella wall, the doorway to the adyton is framed with dark yellow pilasters and lintel block, and is actually wider than it is high. Above the lintel a gable forms a pediment whose white tympanum is decorated with a yellow (gold) rosette.[327] Like most interiors in the Synagogue, that of the cella is shown in black. Against the black background are portrayed three yellow objects outlined in brown. The two at the sides are probably not altars, but the empty pedestals upon which the cult images now to be seen lying in the foreground must be

supposed to have stood.[328] The one in the center, seen in profile as a combination merely of two turned legs and a horizontal bar decorated with pairs of vertical stripes, has been interpreted as a bed for the *lectisternium* of the god on the assumption that the cult and the image portrayed are that of Adonis.[329] It may with greater propriety, in our estimation, be regarded as a table, the table upon which the Ark was placed when it was introduced into the temple and "set alongside of Dagon," as the Biblical narrative says (I Sam. 5.2).[330]

In the foreground of the scene and in what may from the artist's point of view have been the forecourt of the temple, implements and objects of the cult lie scattered about (Fig. 30). Most of the objects are readily identifiable, among them a

FIG. 30. Panel WB 4. Objects before the Temple of Dagon

324. For this interpretation see the several publications of Du Mesnil du Buisson listed in the bibliography of the panel, above, p. 95.

325. For the coins see, e.g., Mattingly, *Coins of the Roman Empire in the British Museum*, IV, Pls. 36–39 and *passim*. On the code of numismatic conventions in the representation of temples, see Bluma L. Trell, *The Temple of Artemis at Ephesos* (*Numismatic Notes and Monographs*, 107, 1945), pp. 3–6.

326. The courses and stones are outlined at both sides of the doorway, those at the right so lightly that the lines do not register well on the photographic negative. In all probability the white of the portico is really only the untouched plaster of the wall. The lowest step of the crepidoma is partly covered at the right by the wash used for the background color.

327. Above the pediment two architecturally unintelligible triangular areas, rendered in yellow, are introduced to complete the façade. It may be that the artist, not having sufficient room at the top for a pediment crowning the façade of the temple as a whole, decided that he could preserve this significant architectural feature by reducing its size and applying it to the doorway, and that in doing so he found himself left with the two triangular pieces in question.

328. They are certainly not "horned" altars as Hempel has suggested, *Zeitschrift für die alttestamentliche Wissenschaft*, LI (1933), p. 288. On the face of the die of each altar is represented a disc set in a circle (so correctly Du Mesnil du Buisson, "Une Peinture," p. 198); that is, probably a wreath (see the same design on the ceiling tiles, type 12, above, p. 46, and on the door reveals, below, pp. 253 f.). On the question why two pedestals and cult images, see below, p. 103.

329. Cf. the publications of Du Mesnil du Buisson in the bibliography for the panel.

330. The supposed iconographic allusion to the cult of Adonis is discussed below. All other beds of the Synagogue murals have mattresses (see Pls. LXIII, LXXIV). The horizontal member of the object in the cella is in our judgment not sufficiently wide to represent both rail and mattress. On tables in cult scenes and acts see Kruse in *RE*, XXIX (XV, 1, 1931), cols. 937–948, *s.v.* "mensa"; and H. Mischkowski, *Die heiligen Tische im Götterkultus der Griechen und Römer*, Königsberg dissertation (1917).

large, wide-mouthed storage jar (Fig. 30, no. 1), a hydria (no. 2), two shallow basins or bowls (nos. 3–4), three small jugs (nos. 5–7), three candelabra or lampstands (nos. 8–10), two larger thymiateria (nos. 11–12), two smaller thymiateria (nos. 13–14), and two altars (nos. 15–16). Many of these have analogies in other panels of the Synagogue and none of them poses a problem.[331] Less commonplace are two other objects, of which one (no. 17) is probably a snuff-shovel, and the other

whose scabbard can be seen projecting at his side.[333] His raised right hand grasps a long staff, the decorations of the upper end of which are only dimly visible but in one instance make it look suspiciously like a *thyrsos* (Fig. 32).[334] Both cult images have suffered damage, the one (no. 19) having lost its head, the other (no. 21) its foot. The lost elements are portrayed separately by the artist (nos. 20 and 22).[335] The head is that of a youthful figure with a heavy aureole of hair but no ornaments.

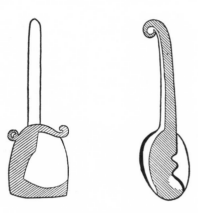

FIG. 31. Panel WB 4. Snuff Shovel and Musical Instrument

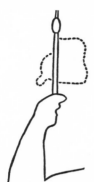

FIG. 32. Panel WB 4. Object held by God

(no. 18) a musical instrument (see also Fig. 31).[332] Among the paraphernalia of the cult the artist has represented two images (nos. 19 and 21). The god wears an Iranian costume consisting of a belted knee-length tunic, baggy trousers, and high soft boots. Thrown over his shoulder is a chlamys, one end of which hangs down at his right side. His left hand is held close to the body at the waist, where it probably clutches the pommel of the sword

331. For nos. 1–2 see Panel SC 4, Pl. LXII; for nos. 5–7 see Panel WC 4, Pl. LXVII; for nos. 8–14 see Panels WB 1 and WB 2, Pls. LIX, LX; the triangular shape of the altars (nos. 15–16) is probably an unintentional by-product of the rendering of their upper surfaces. For a similar (portable) altar see Panel WB 2, Pl. LX.

332. A number of shovels of this type, used probably in connection with the service of altars or the incense-burners, are to be seen in the National Museum at Damascus. Cf. M. Narkiss, *Journal of the Palestine Oriental Society*, XV (1935), pp. 14–28; and A. Reifenberg, *ibid.*, XVI (1936), pp. 167–169; and the same, *Palästinensische Kleinkunst* (1927), pp. 75 f., Figs. 97–98. The musical instrument known as the πανδοῦρα, which seems to be of Oriental origin and was a great favorite in Roman times, has a shape approximating that of the second object. Cf. Th. Reinach, in Daremberg-Saglio, III, 2 (1904), pp. 1437–1451, *s.v.* "lyra."

333. The lower end of the projecting object is rectangular, and the artist has apparently tried to indicate that its surface on each side is broken lengthwise into two planes. This would be entirely appropriate for the scabbard of a sword such as is shown in Panel NB 1 (Pl. LV), but scarcely for the λαγωβόλον with which Du Mesnil du Buisson has associated it (*Peintures*, pp. 77 f.). For another scabbard see Panel NC 1, Pl. LXXII.

334. Near the top is a knob, and below the knob another decorative element whose outlines are very indistinct, leaving only the impression of unequally balanced color-masses. Du Mesnil du Buisson has interpreted this second element as a pennant (see *Peintures*, p. 77, Fig. 56). In his color copy Gute has rendered it like a double-bitted axe. It might with equal propriety represent the traditional bundle of ivy or vine leaves, or the loops of the ribbons attached to the *thyrsos*. It is only the statue no. 19 on Fig. 30 that shows these details. The staff of the other statue (no. 21) is too poorly preserved to give any clear picture of its upper end.

335. It is to be noted that in the Hebrew text and in the Targum of it there is mentioned only damage to the head of the statue and to the "palms of his hands." The fact that the Synagogue artist has substituted for the loss of the hands the loss of a foot is probably of no great importance. It may be mentioned, however, that some versions (Armenian and Latin) and certain minuscules of the LXX substitute the breaking of the idol's feet for that of his hands, perhaps merely because the LXX uses ἴχνη to translate כַּפּוֹת (palms), a term more appropriate to the feet than to the hands. For the variants see A. E. Brooke, N. McLean, and H. St. J. Thackeray, *The Old Testament in Greek*, II (1935), p. 15 *ad* I Kings 5.4.

In the earlier discussion of the scene a good deal of attention has been paid to the question what deity it is that the artist has portrayed, the answer given by Du Mesnil du Buisson being that it is Adonis. The line of argument developed in support of this contention, and having as its supposed confirmation the discovery of an analogous representation of Adonis in the temple across the street from the Synagogue at Dura, does not seem convincing.[336] Indeed, the question itself seems inappropriate, introducing a type of short-range polemic into the decorations that in general appears to be alien to the rest of the work of the Synagogue artists. Since it can hardly be assumed that the artist knew much about Dagon, and since it is clear at the same time that the Adonis of the temple across the street at Dura was painted to suit local convention, having little but youthfulness in common with other known representations of him, it would seem more proper to suppose here that the artist merely drew upon the current vocabulary of form when required to paint a Dagon, and that he would have portrayed any other deity in identical fashion.[337]

More appropriate to the study of the scene is the question why two images should have been presented in the scene occupying the right portion of the panel. Here Du Mesnil du Buisson has undoubtedly found the correct answer in suggesting that the figures were duplicated to provide in visual form an allusion to the two separate occasions at which Dagon's statue fell to the ground before the Ark (I Sam. 5.3–4). Still more appropriate is the question why the artist should have added to the statues in the forecourt the full array of cult implements belonging to the temple. That they were affected by the misfortune that came to the image of the god is a possible inference from, but not to be accounted for on the basis of, the Biblical text.

A suggestion to explain how the artist came to draw this inference is therefore in order. It will be recalled in this connection that on monuments of an historical and triumphal character, victories over enemy forces are commonly signalized in Imperial Roman art by representations of the *tropaia* (shields, helmets, swords, etc.) whether grouped in masses for dedicatory purposes or left scattered about on the field of battle in disorder.[338] Perhaps the dispersed cult implements are for the Synagogue artist the *tropaia* of the Ark's triumph over Dagon.[339] If any weight attaches to the suggestion, it would imply that the artist conceived of the events in the temple of Dagon as a great victory of the God of Israel over the pagan gods — which would not only be intelligible in itself and comparable to what he does elsewhere, but would form from his point of view the appropriate counterpart to the disastrous defeat of Israel depicted on the preceding panel (NB 1).

The scene occupying the left half of the panel presents fewer problems. Overshadowing the composition in this area is the Ark mounted on its cart and drawn by two humped bullocks. In presenting this all-important element the artist has preserved the shape of the object familiar from the preceding panel, the jewels, and the garlands (to which in this instance the jewels are exclusively attached).[340] He has brought more clearly into view, however, the wooden paneling decorating the exposed end of the palladium, and has shown the sides covered by a bright red veil.[341] The cart on which the Ark is mounted is represented frontally with only two of its four wheels showing, and these are set in a quartering position, perhaps to provide an element

---

336. The argument involves the assumptions already treated above: namely, that the central object shown in the temple of the panel is a bed, and that the weapon at the god's side is a λαγωβόλον. On the further assumption concerning the nature of the cart, see below, p. 104, n. 343. In general it is argued: (1) that we are dealing with a youthful deity; and (2) that Dagon was interpreted as a god of vegetation in Syria (by Philo Byblos). On the representation of Adonis in the Temple of Adonis at Dura, see *Rep. VII–VIII*, p. 159, Fig. 44.

337. On the interpretation of the representation of Adonis at Dura, see *Rep. VII–VIII*, p. 160, n. 4.

338. For the former see e.g., the Column of Trajan (Reinach, *Répertoire de reliefs*, I, p. 331), and for the latter, e.g., the friezes of the Arch of Pola and of the Arch of Septimius Severus (*ibid.*, pp. 226, 272).

339. They are portrayed each as a separate object because as an Oriental the artist followed a tradition whose strength lay in analysis of detail rather than in composition; because scattered about they covered the field better; and because they could be joined with the representation of the statues better than if they had been arranged in a heap.

340. The jewels number seven in this instance, five of them red. Three rosettes take the place of the jewels on the upper rounded end of the Ark.

341. Cf. the veil covering the *aron* in Wing Panel III of the Central Group. Num. 4.6 requires for the Ark a covering of blue cloth.

of transition from the frontal view of the cart to the side view of the draft animals.[342] Inside the body of the cart with its flaring sideboards the Ark reposes on a pair of cushions, the upper green, the lower pink. The cart has a high rectangular back ending in a point well above the top of the Ark. This is draped with a pink cloth enclosing the palladium on all three sides, for which reason the interior is shown in black. Analogies to it are to be found in the carts used for religious and ceremonial processions, such as that depicted on one of the coins of Sidon, and above all in the wagons reserved for the use of the highest state officials.[343]

Prominently displayed in the foreground of the scene at the left are the draft animals pulling the cart. They are well-drawn examples of the hump-backed cattle found also on other scenes of the Synagogue (Panel WB 2) and familiar in the region of Dura.[344] The nearer of the two is white, the further brown. A yellow yoke held in place by a

strap rests upon their necks; each wears a halter in addition. The animals portrayed are bullocks rather than the milch-kine which the Biblical story demands, but deviation from the text in this detail is without doubt the result of the artist's use of standard conventions for the representation of draft animals.[345] The two men who attend directly upon the cart and its oxen are dressed in Iranian costume, from which it is clear that they cannot be mere stable-boys, but must be the "priests and diviners" of the story (I Sam. 6.2), who originally suggested the procedure adopted for the disposal of the troublesome Ark, and who here put their own suggestion into execution.[346] They wear long-sleeved tunics reaching to the knees, baggy trousers, and high soft boots.[347] One rests his left hand on the yoke borne by the oxen; the other is ready to strike the oxen with the thin switch that he holds in his uplifted right hand. The three men in the rear, dressed in chiton and himation, are moving forward, following the cart, and should represent the "lords" of the Philistines watching to see where the draft animals will take the Ark, as the diviners of the story instructed them to do (I Sam. 6.9, 12).[348]

One peculiar feature of the scene has still to be

---

342. By his failure to carry the axle across the rim of the wheel at the left the artist has made the wheels toe in, which was probably not intended. The wagon tongue is not connected with the axle. For a bas-relief showing a cart making a similar turn, see Reinach, *Répertoire de reliefs*, III, p. 269.

343. Du Mesnil du Buisson finds his analogies in two-wheeled funerary carts, and suggests a relation to the cart used in the rites re-enacting annually the death of Adonis (*Peintures*, pp. 82 f. and Fig. 62). What such funerary carts actually looked like can be seen from vases and terracottas reproduced in Daremberg-Saglio, II, 2 (1896), pp. 1375 f., *s.v.* "funus." Moreover, as practised at Antioch in Syria and at Alexandria, the ἐκφορά of Adonis apparently did not involve a funerary cortege, but only the display at specified localities of the cult statues set out on special cushions. Cf. Roscher, *Lexikon*, I (1884–1890), cols. 69–77, *s.v.* "Adonis." The procedure at Byblos is unknown. In any event representation of a funerary cart would have been most embarrassing in the present context. Wagons and carts used in religious and triumphal processions are common. Some, like the *tensa*, represent temples (see F. Staehlin, *Röm. Mitt.*, XXI, 1906, pp. 332–386); others are four-wheeled wagons on wich thrones are mounted (see R. Forrer, *Un char de culte à quatre roues et trône*, 1921, esp. p. 35, Fig. 19). For early prototypes see Ebert, *Reallexikon der Vorgeschichte*, XIV (1929), pp. 232 f. For the coin from Sidon see Daremberg-Saglio, I, 1 (1877), p. 95, Fig. 136. The cart has a top, but the protecting draperies are lacking because the image it contains is intended to be seen. On the use of wagons by the Roman emperors and other high officials, see A. Alföldi, *Röm. Mitt.*, XLIX (1934), pp. 103–110. For the wagon of the *praefectus praetorio per Italias* as portrayed in the *Notitia Dignitatum*, see *ibid.*, p. 115, Fig. 10.

344. Cf. the graffito from the house in Block C3, *Rep. VI*, p. 123, Fig. 4.

345. For bullocks drawing carts in processions see, e.g., the Column of Theodosius; Reinach, *Répertoire de reliefs*, I, p. 104, no. 3 and p. 105.

346. For an approximation of the stable-boy costume, see Haman in Panel WC 2 (Pl. LXIV).

347. The garments of the man at the extreme left are gray, with yellow and brown fold-lines and trimming, while those of the man farther to the right are reddish brown. In both cases the tunic has a wide yellow collar about the neck, such as appears elsewhere upon Levites; that is, Temple personnel (see Panel WB 2). A tie-string narrowing the opening at the collar is clearly visible on the tunic of the man at the left. Both men have heavy heads of brown hair.

348. The garments of the two men at the ends of the row are pink; those of the man in the middle are gray with reddish-brown shadow lines. A two-pronged ornament is visible on the ends of the himation of the figure at the extreme left. The fact that only three are represented when the text actually speaks of five "princes" (I Sam. 6.4) is probably due to lack of space. The use of civilian garments is unexpected and probably to be explained from the connotation which the Aramaic *tûrānîm* (the Targumic equivalent for the Biblical *šerānîm* in I Sam. 6.12) had in contemporary usage. A loan word, representing the Greek τύραννος, it had no regal connotation and was therefore loosely applied in contemporary Jewish usage; e.g., to Roman provincial officials such as Tinneius Rufus, governor of Judea under Hadrian.

mentioned. In the foreground of the scene forming the left half of the panel, a strip running along the lower border and reaching from the panel band to the level of the draft animals' hoofs is rendered in a color darker than that of the rest of the background. Underneath the belly of the oxen a somewhat narrower strip of even darker color runs down toward that of the foreground, the two meeting at right angles and forming an inverted *T*. That these are not shadow masses is evident from the artists' treatment of space and shadow in other panels. Instead, the strips in all probability represent roads, whose relation to each other corresponds to the relative positions of the cart and the oxen. What the artist is trying to indicate is that the cart, having come toward the foreground down one road, finds itself at a junction, and is now making a sharp turn to follow the road running parallel to the base of the panel. The detail is significant because it reflects a familiar Haggadic clarification of the Biblical story. In the Haggadic narrative the Philistines conduct the cart to a place where three roads meet and where the kine take the "straight" road, thereby bringing the Ark back to its Judean homeland.[349] Rabbinic legend has still further details to add to the event, the one most commonly reported being that, as the kine took what was for the Ark the homeward road, they broke forth into song, praising the Ark in the following words:

Sing, O sing, acacia tree,
Ascend in all thy gracefulness.
With golden weave they cover thee,
The sanctuary-palace hears thy eulogy,
With divers jewels thou art adorned.[350]

There is nothing in the picture to suggest that the artist knew the legend, but his representation of the Ark as a paneled chest covered by a veil and adorned with jewels matches the wording of the song. It would not be strange if such represen-

tations had played a part in popularizing the tale so oft repeated in Haggadic narrative.

From what has been said it will be evident that in the panel under discussion the artist has developed themes that were necessarily full of meaning to a people waging a continuous battle against idolatry and polytheism, and devoted to the belief that God can be trusted to take care of his own. If in organizing the imagery of the panel, the artist has started the Ark on its homeward journey, continuing here at the very end of the panel the sense of motion toward the left, it would seem that in the series of which this panel is a part there should follow another scene in which the thread is completely unwound and the Ark finds a resting place from its vicissitudes. Whether this is done, the discussion of the next panel will indicate.

Jerusalem and the Temple of Solomon

Panel WB 3. H. *ca.* 1.53 m.; L. 2.31 m. (Pl. LVII).

Rep. VI, pp. 350f.; Du Mesnil du Buisson, "Les Peintures," pp. 114f.; *idem, Peintures*, pp. 84–92; Grabar, "Le Thème," pp. 180–182; Wischnitzer-Bernstein, "The Samuel Cycle," pp. 95–98; Leveen, *Hebrew Bible in Art*, pp. 36f.; Schneid, *The Paintings*, p. 16; Sukenik, *The Synagogue*, pp. 91f.; Wischnitzer, *Messianic Theme*, pp. 65f.

Among the several panels of the Synagogue's decorations, this is clearly the most static, for it portrays no action, and lacks even the representation of a single person to give life and motion to the scene. The composition covers all but the last few centimeters of the surface enclosed by the panel bands and threatens by virtue of this fact to degenerate from a picture into a design. Well preserved save for a few incidental cracks, for the loss of two pieces of plaster, and for surface dislocations in the lower right corner, the composition comprises two basic elements.[351] The first of these

349. The clarification is already presupposed in the account of Josephus (*Antiquitates* VI, § 13) and is known also to pseudo-Philo (*Biblical Antiquities* LV, 8, trans. James, p. 227).

350. The detail arises from the derivation of the וַיִּשַׁרְנָה of I Sam. 6.12 from שִׁיר ("sing") instead of יָשַׁר ("to be straight"). The version of the incident quoted is that of Abodah Zarah 24b (Trans., pp. 123f.). For other occurrences of the legend see Ginzberg, *Legends of the Jews*, VI, p. 225, n. 36.

351. There are in the main four cracks: the first to the left of the left door, the second running down the entire panel on a line with the left door jamb of the central door, the third cutting through the middle of the temple façade and running diagonally through the right door, at the right side of which it joins with the fourth crack coming down vertically from above. Where it cuts through the pediment of the right door, the third crack has brought

is a series of seven crenelated walls, each of a different color. Spread across the entire panel and mounting to its very top, the walls form, as it were, the solid background upon which the second element of the composition is superimposed. The superimposed element, which the artist has not seen fit to relate organically with the walls in any way, is developed in two planes. The lower plane presents a formal triple gateway with heavy closed bronze or gilded doors; the upper exhibits a noble Hellenistic temple standing on a crepidoma two steps high, the doors of its cella also shut tight.

The fact that the scene lacks both action and actors, and is for this reason not so readily to be associated with a specific episode in Biblical narrative, has caused interpretations to vary. Two rival views have been advanced. The first is that the scene represents a temple of the sun that may be supposed to have stood at Beth Shemesh, whither the kine took the Ark when it left the land of the Philistines (I Sam. 6.12–21).[352] The second is that the scene represents the Temple of Solomon, where the Ark found for itself a more abiding resting place.[353] The choice between the two alternatives can be argued on general principles and in terms of the details of the rendering. The latter it will be well to make a part of the record before the choice is considered.

So far as the over-all design providing the background of the panel is concerned, it is evident that of the several walls constituting it only the first and lowest in the series is seen in its entirety. Of each of the others, the uppermost courses and the crenelations surmounting them are all that is portrayed. Arranged one above the other, and hence to be thought of as standing one behind the other, the

walls are given each a different color. Certain of the colors have been affected by the passage of time and are no longer precisely what they were originally. Others we have already learned to recognize as equivalents for certain metals; e.g., yellow for gold. Numbering the walls from 1 to 7 beginning at the bottom of the panel, and associating with the colors as they now appear the probable or implied ancient equivalents, we obtain the following list:

7. Pink
6. Dark gray (originally blue)
5. Dull white
4. Light gray (to represent silver?)
3. Yellow ochre (to represent gold)
2. Black
1. Dull red.[354]

The fact that the number of the walls is odd rather than even, and that the colors do not repeat at the top in a reverse order indicates that the artist's purpose in the over-all design is to suggest an arrangement comprising seven concentric rings of walls. Their sevenfold number and the variety of the colors used has inevitably, and quite properly, we believe, suggested also some relation between the design and the astrological lore of the ancient Orient. As is well known, the number seven owes no small measure of its importance in this area to the number of planets as they were counted in antiquity, and with the seven planets astrology associated from early times not only stones and flowers but also colors.[355] In the known lists the planetary colors vary from instance to instance, but in general it can be said that their range corresponds quite closely to that of the colors of our

about the loss of a fairly large piece of the surface (now restored), and where the third and fourth cracks meet in the lower right corner of the panel the surface is dislocated. At the left end of the cornice over the central portal one of a series of vertical scars (less in number here than in Panel WB 4 to the right) has caused the loss of a smaller section of the surface.

352. So first Du Mesnil du Buisson, "Les Peintures," pp. 114f. and more recently *Peintures*, pp. 84–92; his interpretation has been accepted with reservations by Grabar ("Le Thème," p. 181 and pp. 6f.), Wischnitzer-Bernstein ("The Samuel Cycle," pp. 95–98, most of which really argues against the accepted identification), and by Schneid, *The Paintings*, p. 16.

353. So *Rep. VI*, pp. 350f.; Leveen, *Hebrew Bible in Art*, pp. 36f.; and Sukenik, *The Synagogue*, p. 92.

354. Lines indicating the courses and the stones of the walls are done in various colors: 7, red; 6, black and red; 5, white and red; 4, reddish brown; 3, reddish brown; 2, white. The first wall is not blocked out into courses and stones, perhaps to avoid the suggestion that a wall supposedly seen in its entirety was actually shown to be only a few courses high. The crenelations of the uppermost, seventh wall are barely indicated, dark yellow being introduced in the spaces between them to cover the remaining unoccupied surface of the panel. This really represents all that remains of the open space of the field.

355. On the general subject see A. Jeremias, *Handbuch der altorientalischen Geisteskultur* (1913), pp. 84–86; W. H. Roscher, in Roscher, *Lexikon*, III, 2 (1897–1909), cols. 2518–2539, *s.v.* "Planeten"; and *idem, Abhandlungen der königlich sächsischen Gesellschaft der Wissenschaften, phil.-hist. Klasse*, XXIV, 6 (1906).

seven walls, though apparently the Synagogue artist has not attempted to follow or construct a particular order.[356] That astrological lore should by virtue of this correspondence be acknowledged to have entered into the imagery of the scene is not at all strange. The only question is precisely how the symbolism is to be interpreted. It has been suggested that the representation of the seven walls reflects current Mesopotamian ideas concerning the proper arrangement of an astral, or more specifically a solar, temple.[357] In other words the artist by the use of these walls has done what he could to help us identify the temple as that of the sun, supposedly located at Beth Shemesh. The reference made in this connection to the stepped temple-towers of Mesopotamia with their several steps, each given a different coloring, is not precisely helpful; for it is clear that not all temples with ziggurats are solar, just as it is probable that the Synagogue artist intended us to think of the temple he portrayed as being inside the seventh wall rather than beside a seven-stepped temple-tower.

In dealing with a seven-zone design such as our panel portrays, it is important to note that the scheme was used ultimately to describe the structure of cosmic reality in both the physical and the celestial spheres.[358] By virtue of this fact it could be applied wherever cosmic significance was to be suggested, even to the description of cities. What may be an early example of such an application is Herodotus' quite fantastic story that Deioces had the Medes construct for him a system of seven walls, each of a different color, around the city of Ecbatana, the colors again approximating those associated with the planets.[359] A late example is available in a Jewish Midrash where we find even the heavenly Jerusalem described as being surrounded with seven walls, each of its own particular color.[360] What makes it possible to transfer the scheme of the seven zones or planes from the sphere of mythical cosmography and celestial topography to the description of cities is of course the belief that these cities are of cosmic significance, whether as the capitals of world empires for the present order or as the abode of the blessed in the future order, and that microcosmos and macrocosmos must correspond. Once this is evident, it becomes possible to suggest that by his over-all design of seven concentric walls, each with a planetary color, the artist here endeavored to suggest, not a part of a temple, but a city that from his point of view was necessarily of universal significance. In a synagogue this could naturally be only the city of Jerusalem, whose significance as the world center the Haggadah, particularly of the Midrash Tanḥuma, develops quite fully.[361] We are inclined to assume, therefore, that in the panel under discussion the basic design seeks to do justice to the Biblical statements according to which David and Solomon built Jerusalem, surrounding it with walls (II Sam. 5.9 and I Kings 3.1), and that in representing these walls as seven in number, each with a different planetary color, the artist intended

356. Of the colors of the seven walls, (1) red is commonly associated with Mars; (2) black with Saturn; (3) yellow with the Sun; (4) probably silver with the Moon; (5) probably white with Venus; (6) probably blue with Mercury. Pink, no. 7, is not a planetary color but may represent purple, the color associated with Jupiter. Du Mesnil du Buisson's attempt to account for the order in which the yellow color appears (*Peintures*, p. 89) is unconvincing.

357. Du Mesnil du Buisson, *Peintures*, p. 88.

358. For the seven superimposed physical worlds see the Manichaean conception set forth in the Turfan Pehlevi fragment M 98–99 as interpreted by A. V. W. Jackson, *Researches in Manichaeism* (1932), pp. 22–71 and the diagrams on p. 73 and opposite p. 75. On the sevenfold division of the heavenly world, particularly in Judaism, see Bousset and Gressmann, *Religion des Judentums*, pp. 238f., 283–285.

359. *Historiae* I, 98. The colors are white, black, purple, blue, orange, silver, and gold, beginning at the bottom. Josephus' account of the twice three walls of Babylon (*Antiquitates* X, § 224) quoted from Berossos is more accurate, but irrelevant in the present context, save as it provides a part of the general background for the relation of multiple circumvallation to Oriental city construction. Cf. in general A. Billerbeck, *Der alte Orient*, I, 4 (1903), pp. 19–24.

360. *Parḳe Mešiaḥ*, ed. A. Jellinek, *Bet ha-Midrasch*, III, p. 74 (trans. Wünsche, *Aus Israels Lehrhallen*, III, p. 139). In the *Seder Gan ʿEden* the heavenly paradise is described similarly as a place surrounded by several walls of fire, each with a different color (*ibid.*, pp. 131–133). For late Jewish representations of cities surrounded by seven walls, see those of Jericho reproduced by A. Yaari, *Kirjath Sepher*, XVIII (1941), pp. 179–181 and Pls. I and III.

361. Ed. S. Buber (1885), Section קדושים, pp. 71 ff. Cf. in general A. J. Brawer, *Gesellschaft für Palästinaforschung*, VI (1920), where the whole conception of Palestine as the center of the world, Jerusalem as the center of Palestine, and the Temple as the center of Jerusalem is fully developed.

to portray the city as the capital of a world empire.[362]

The first of the two elements which the artist has superimposed upon his sevenfold wall design is the triple gateway depicted in the lower half of the panel. The gates are set into the outermost of the seven walls but overtop it, showing that they are organically unrelated to it, at least in composition. They may belong either to the city or to the court of the Temple above, depending on which they seem to suit best. Of the three gates, the two at either end are identical in execution, and at the same time smaller than, and different from, the one in the middle. Both are pedimented and have their architectural elements shown simply in gray. The lintel is carved with an egg and dart design and tapers beyond the line of the unmolded jambs as though it belonged to a cornice. At its ends it is met by raking cornices forming the pediment and framing the tympanum with its eight-pointed rosette.[363] Above, where the raking members meet, an irregularly shaped block is introduced that would serve well as the base of an ornamental statue. The larger central door, whose frame is also rendered in gray, has wider, molded jambs flanked at the top by consoles whose volutes are shown in profile, and a very narrow lintel.[364] Above the narrow lintel there is a dentilated cornice with a steep pitch, done in yellow. Below its dentils the cornice has a bed-mold carved with a vine scroll, its circular fields filled with leaves, flowers, and clusters of grapes.

Massive double doors done in yellow to represent gold or bronze close the passages of the triple gateway. Each door leaf is divided into three panels by the nail-studded members of the heavy frames. In the lesser doors at the sides, the upper and lower fields of each leaf are ornamented with groups of five eight-pointed rosettes, while the central field contains a conventional door-pull in the shape of a lion's head with a ring in its mouth, all done in brown. The panels of the central doors vary in height, the tallest being at the bottom; they contain more ambitious, figured designs also done in brown and representing low reliefs. In the panels at the top the two leaves portray crouching humped bullocks seen vis-à-vis. The tallest of the panels, at the bottom of the door, present standing figures of a nimbed Tyche holding in her right hand a rudder and in her left a large cornucopia (Fig. 33).[365] The designs in the central panels are somewhat more difficult to understand (Pl. XL, 1). They show in each instance a large nude figure with one hand upraised and the other at the hip, standing be-

FIG. 33. Panel WB 3. Figure of Tyche

---

362. On Solomon as one of the three or the ten monarchs who ruled over the entire world, see Ginzberg, *Legends of the Jews*, VI, p. 289, n. 40. It is possible to suggest also that the Holy City is here represented as the "throne of the Lord" (Jer. 3.17), and that the seven walls correspond to seven steps of this throne. Cf. *Genesis Rabbah* LXIV, 4 (Trans., II, p. 575). It does not seem possible to use Philo's statements about the one heavenly temple and the one Temple on earth (*De specialibus legibus* I, §§ 66–75) as a basis for, or a clue to, the development of the imagery, because the thread developed up to this point in the panels in Register B requires here a scene whose function it is to terminate a series of historical events rather than to point a parable.

363. The raking cornices are marked with curving diagonal lines that may indicate a cyma molding.

364. The ends of lintel and jambs are mitred.

365. The Tyche wears the garments of royalty. She is dressed in a bodice and skirt and has draped about the lower part of her body a cloak the ends of which are gathered over her left arm. Cf. the dress of the Queen of Sheba in Panel WA 2 (above, p. 91) and of Esther in Panel WC 2 (below, p. 159). On Tyches of this type see O. Waser in Roscher, *Lexikon*, V, cols. 1309–1380, s.v. "Tyche"; and Daremberg-Saglio, II, 2 (1896), pp. 1264–1277, s.v. "fortuna." Originally associated with Alexandria, the type was popularized by the Roman coins and appears in Syria, e.g., in a graffito of Baalbek. Cf. T. Wiegand, *Baalbek*, II (1923), p. 127, Fig. 180.

tween two smaller, equally nude figures, all facing front. The larger figure bears no identifying emblems but seems to wear a spreading ornament on its head. Rosettes fill the blank spaces in the upper part of the panel at either side of the head. In all prohability the artist intended the large central figure to be that of a male.[366] Perhaps a Zeus or a Helios type is indicated. In the related design on coin types of Marcus Aurelius, Lucius Verus, and Septimius Severus, the deity is clearly Zeus, but this association of the lesser figures with the brother emperors is so patently secondary that adaptation from some mythological context is likely.[367] A Helios with his two dutiful sons Ochimos and Kerkaphos, or possibly with the *Dioscuroi* would satisfy the iconography in the case of the Synagogue and may have served as the inspiration for the coin type.[368] Whatever be the symbolism of the reliefs, such bronze or gilded doors are commonly associated with the entrances to sanctuaries and their temene in antiquitity, including the later Temple at Jerusalem, where it was particularly Nicanor's Gate that stirred pious imagination.[369] At the top of the panel the artist has superimposed

upon his mural background an excellent Hellenistic temple. The lowest step of its crepidoma, rendered in pink, is set directly above the crenelations of the third wall and the dentilated cornice of the central gate.[370] Above this from the upper step of the crepidoma the bases, columns, entablature, and the raking cornices of the pediment outline the architectural decor of the temple in a dull white and set it off from the pink of the cella walls, of the tympanum, and of the tiled roof.[371] Here the artist has shown the façade and one whole side of the building, arranging four columns irregularly spaced across the façade and seven along the side. The order is Corinthian and uses bases with two heavy torus moldings above a plinth.[372] In the center of the tympanum (Fig. 34) stands a rosette

FIG. 34. Panel WB 3. Tympanum of Temple

of sixteen points or petals set in a circle.[373] Rinceaux fill the angles of the tympanum, as they do in related monuments from the earliest days of the Roman occupation of the Near East, providing room in their circular fields for at least two smaller rosettes.[374] Winged victories carefully painted in black and holding wreaths in their outstretched hands form the acroteria at the ends of the pediment. The great double doors of gold or bronze

366. No genitals are indicated in any instance, nor could their indication be expected in so minute a part of the composition. The outline of the torso under the uplifted arm begins with a curved line to suggest the breast, but this is also not decisive. It is the combination of absolute nudity and posture that will be taken as normative for the determination of sex.

367. On the coins Zeus wears only a cloak draped loosely behind him, while holding staff and thunderbolt in his hands. The smaller figures are fully clothed in the earlier issues, but nude in those of Septimius Severus. Cf. for the issues F. Gnecchi, *I Medaglioni romani*, II (1912), Pls. 63, 3–4 and 74, 6–7; and A. R. Bellinger, *The Third and Fourth Dura Hoards* (*Numismatic Notes and Monographs*, 55, 1932), Pl. XV, nos. 105–106; and *Final Report* VI, Pl. XVII: 924, 926.

368. If the ornaments on the figure's head are leaves, one might also think of Dionysos holding a bunch of grapes in his upraised hand.

369. As to the fact, see the inscription from the Temple of Bel at Palmyra, J. Cantineau, *Inventaire des inscriptions de Palmyre*, IX (1933), pp. 36f., inscr. 25; as to tradition, see the report about the golden doors presented to the Temple at Jerusalem by Queen Helena of Adiabene (Yoma 37a, Trans., V, pp. 174f.), and about Nicanor having brought with him from Alexandria the bronze doors of the Temple gate bearing his name (Yoma 38a, Trans., V, pp. 174f.). It may be noted that doors with panels of different heights, consoles at the top of the jambs, and lion heads with rings are familiar from Palmyra; see e.g., the tomb of Iarhai, R. Amy and H. Seyrig, *Syria*, XVII (1936), Pl. XXVIII.

370. At the left this lowest step is not extended sufficiently to project as it should beyond the upper step.

371. The upper step of the crepidoma extends so far beyond the last column of the portico as to suggest either that the stonework of the wall forming the background has not been extended sufficiently, or that it was at one time planned to add another column to the side of the building.

372. Here, where the artist is using black and what may have been his finest brush, the details are much clearer than on the panels of the doors below.

373. Du Mesnil du Buisson correctly interprets the rosette as a solar symbol (*Peintures*, p. 90). Cf. also the use of rosettes on Jewish ossuaries, Watzinger, *Denkmäler Palästinas*, II, Pl. 30, Figs. 69–70.

374. Cf. the pediments of the rock-cut tombs from the early Roman period near, and directly north of, Jerusalem, reflecting a flattened treatment of the same Hellenistic decorative motif, conveniently accessible *ibid.*, Pls. 28–29, Figs. 63–66.

giving upon the cella are closed, their leaves paneled but without representation of designs or animate objects.

From the details of the rendering it is possible to proceed now to the important question concerning the identity of the temple represented and therewith to the problem of the meaning of the panel. Since the last previous scene (Panel WB 4, left half) showed the Ark of the Covenant leaving Philistia on a cart, the suggestion that the present scene represents Beth Shemesh (literally: the House of the Sun), the next stopping place on the Ark's itinerary, is entirely appropriate and at first glance quite captivating.[375] There are, however, certain difficulties. The first is that neither the Biblical text nor the Haggadic tradition where they deal with the episode of the Ark at Beth Shemesh mention a solar temple as its repository, speaking instead of a large rock in the wheatfield of a certain Joshua (I Sam. 6.13–15). The second is that the visit of the palladium to Beth Shemesh is of no definitive significance for the termination of the series of events that begins with the scene at Shiloh (Panel NB 2). In that series, so far as it concerns the Ark, Beth Shemesh is but a brief stopping-place on the way to Kirjath Jearim, where the sacred chest finally comes into Israelite possession and remains for a period of twenty years (I Sam. 7.1–2). Given the wide variety of subject matter available to the artists for pictorial development, and given also their tendency to crowd a number of episodes into one composition, it may be questioned, finally, whether and by what means they could have been persuaded to devote an entire panel near the center of the important west wall of the chamber to the representation of so unimportant an episode, more particularly since, on the hypothesis suggested, it involved glorifying a pagan shrine.[376]

Under the circumstances it seems preferable to suppose that the scene represents the Holy City, Jerusalem, and its Holy Temple, the Temple of Solomon. On this assumption it is possible to suggest that the artist has limited so severely the number of the elements of the composition in order to suggest a connection of the picture with two episodes of Biblical history; namely, the building of the walls of Jerusalem by David (II Sam. 5.9), and the building of the Temple by Solomon (I Kings 6). In his effort to bring out the significance attaching to the city and its Temple in the history of the Israelite Kingdom and for mankind generally, the artist has employed a convention that is ultimately astrological, that of the seven concentric rings of walls. That a man such as he, using this type of convention and living in the middle of the third century of our era, should have incorporated other astrological and solar symbols in his composition when developing the details of his decorative treatment of the gate and the temple, is only what might be expected. This is not because he was trying to represent a solar shrine, but because in his day the solar element had penetrated so largely into the religious imagery of the Orient that in using the best models he knew to represent the finest possible temple and gates, he had necessarily to fall back upon examples strongly representative of the solar monotheism.[377]

The assumption that Jerusalem and its Temple

---

375. On this hypothesis, the left half of Panel WB 4 would represent I Sam. 6.1–12 and Panel WB 3 would adumbrate the events of I Sam. 6.13–21.

376. There have been two attempts to escape from this dilemma. The first is contained in the suggestion that the artist of this panel originally projected the scene of David being anointed King (Panel WC 3) for the place now occupied by the temple (WB 3), and that he was led by personal considerations for the Elder Samuel to change his plan, leaving the space available for a substitute scene, so to speak (so Du Mesnil du Buisson's *Peintures*, pp. 92–127). This scarcely commends itself for serious consideration. The second is the more interesting suggestion that, since the temple is shown closed and devoid of worshipers, the thought of the artist was to allude at one and the same time to the temple of the sun at Beth Shemesh and to the Temple of Solomon at Jerusalem in the period before the reforms of Josiah, and to suggest that all idolatry must cease (Grabar, "Le Thème," pp. 180–182). This line of thought is suggested by the identification of the adjacent Wing Panel III as a representation of Josiah (*ibid.*, pp. 178–180). The fact that such polemics are visibly a part of the point of view of the Synagogue artists gives the suggestion a measure of verisimilitude, but it must be said that here the artist has gone a long way to make his point, and that the closing of the doors can be interpreted also along other lines (see below). Moreover, we are not inclined to regard the subject of Wing Panel III as Josiah.

377. In such matters throughout the Synagogue the artists are not concerned as we are with problems of the historical origins of the design or cliché, but with the search for the most excellent pattern for the expression of their ideas. Hence, of course, a Hellenistic peripteros for Solomon's Temple, triple gateways and crenelated walls for ancient fortifications, and formal entrances.

are portrayed in the panel seems to give it the proper significance as a part of the decorations of the west wall and as a terminal panel of the series to which it belongs. Flanking the Central Group at the right, it balances the corresponding panel at the left (WB 2), where the inauguration of the Wilderness Tabernacle is shown, with the High Priest performing the sacrifice and the Levites in attendance. Terminating the series that began on the south wall with the scene of Hannah and Samuel at Shiloh, it provides the final and intended resting place for the Ark after its many vicissitudes, instead of merely a temporary one. In this connection an explanation for the fact that the doors of the city and the Temple are closed suggests itself. The suggestion is that the closed doors are meant to indicate the safekeeping and the security, both of the Ark itself, and of those who dwell in the city under the divine protection.[378] That the artist should have skipped so many chapters of Biblical history in I and II Samuel in providing this particular ending to his series is by no means strange: first, because he brings certain episodes of the intervening material in other contexts, and second, because he is pointing up history in the pragmatic, purposeful way of his day and generation.[379] Indeed, once it is admitted that the artist's historical perspective is sufficiently extensive to associate the founding of Jerusalem and the Temple with events from the early chapters of I Samuel, new horizons reveal themselves for the interpretation of the series as a whole.

In the earlier discussion of the scenes attention was focused upon the Ark of the Covenant as the feature that gives meaning to the series as a whole.[380] While this is correct in one sense, it appears to limit somewhat the range of the suggestions inherent in the compositions. More recently it has been suggested that greater importance

should be attached in the interpretation to the transition from Shiloh (Panel NB 2) to Jerusalem, this transition marking the ascendency of the Judean over the Israelite tribal units and the centralization of the cult in the Temple of Solomon, on the one hand, and the triumph of the divine purpose over adversity, on the other.[381] It is not clear to what extent the fundamental historical implications were evident to the artist or those who suggested this particular series of scenes to him, and perhaps it would be well not to project into the minds of those responsible for the work too much of our modern understanding of ancient Israelite history. But that at least some of the historical and theological implications were evident in the period of the Dura Synagogue can be shown from an interesting passage in the Targum of I Sam. 2.

In I Samuel Hannah, having brought the child Samuel to the temple at Shiloh, utters a prayer of thanksgiving in which she glorifies God for the help which he has given to the unfortunate, and expresses the firm conviction of her faith that he will protect and vindicate his own in the future as well, judging the ends of the earth and exalting the horn of his anointed (I Sam. 2.1–10). In the corresponding part of the Targum, where Ḥannah is transformed into a prophetess, we find the following passage substituted for the Biblical prayer:

"And Hannah prayed by the spirit of prophecy and said,

"Behold Samuel, my son, is destined to be a prophet over Israel. In his days they will be delivered from the hand of the Philistines, and by his hands there will be performed for them signs and wonders. Wherefore my heart is strengthened in the good portion which the Lord has given to me.

"And Heman too, the son of Joel, the son of my son Samuel, is destined to arise, he and his fourteen sons, that they may say praise with lyre and cither together with their brothers, the Levites, to glorify

---

378. The familiar story about the Temple gates refusing to open at the occasion of the dedication of the building (e.g., Shabbat. 30a, Trans., II, 1, pp. 132 f.) is probably not alluded to here and would have been more appropriately taken account of in Panel SB 1 (q.v.).

379. For other scenes from the Books of Samuel, see Panels SB 1, WC 3, EC 1, and the last scene of NC 1. For the rabbinical interpretation of history, see N. N. Glatzer, *Untersuchungen zur Geschichtslehre der Tannaiten* (1933).

380. So Du Mesnil du Buisson, for whom the series is part of the *cycle de l'alliance* ("Les Peintures," pp. 113–115).

381. So Wischnitzer-Bernstein, "The Samuel Cycle," pp. 96–98. The position taken would seem to require that the panel under discussion be interpreted as representing Jerusalem and the Temple of Solomon.

God in the Holy House. Wherefore my horn is lifted up because of the gift which the Lord has apportioned to me.

"And also (she prophesied) about the miraculous visitation destined to overtake the Philistines, who are to bring the Ark of the Lord on a new cart and together with it a guilt offering. Wherefore let the assembly of Israel say, I open my mouth to say great things over my enemies, because I rejoice in thy salvation.

"Over Sennacherib the king of Assyria she prophesied and said, It is destined that he and his whole army will arise against Jerusalem and much will be done to him. There there will fall the bodies of his soldiers, for which reason all the people, nations and tongues will confess and say, There is no Holy One but the Lord, for there is none other beside thee. And thy people will say, There is no one who is strong other than our God.

"Over Nebuchadnezzar the king of Babylon she prophesied and said, You Chaldeans and all the other peoples who are destined to rule over Israel, you shall no more speak boastfully, nor shall blasphemies proceed from your mouth because the Lord knows all and his judgment extends over all his creatures and you too he will requite for your sins.

"Over the Greek kingdom she prophesied and said, The bows of the Greek tyrants will be broken, and (as for) those (tyrants) of the house of the Hasmoneans, who are weak, there will be done for them signs and wonders.

"And over the sons of Haman she prophesied and said, (Those) who were filled with bread, overbearing in wealth and rich in money, they have been made poor. They have returned to being hired for bread and for the sustenance of their mouth. Mordecai and Esther, who were lean and poor, have grown rich and have forgotten their poverty. They have once more become nobles.

"So Jerusalem, which was like a sterile woman, is destined to be filled with the people of its captivities, while Rome, which was filled with many peoples, her armies will cease (and) she will be laid waste and destroyed."

The passage is highly instructive as a sample of the Targumic procedure and as an indication of the transformation that has taken place in the conception of Hannah. As one who could be thought to have spoken such words, she merits the stature and the prominence assigned to her in the opening panel of the series (Panel NB 2). More important for our purposes is the impression obtained from the Targum that the Philistine oppression and the return of the Ark, both of which are explicitly mentioned in the prophecy, are in the mind of the author analogous to other critical periods of Israel's history in which evident misfortunes were turned into, or may confidently be expected to become, the occasion for divine blessings. This is an excellent indication both of the reason why a series of scenes such as that under consideration here was given so large a place in the decorations of the Synagogue, and of the point of view from which the pictures were in all probability regarded by the worshipers who saw them.[382] It is perhaps even more important for our immediate purpose to note how readily the thought of the Targumist passes from the Philistine danger and its dissipation to Jerusalem and its Temple, about which some of the parallel episodes alluded to in the text turn, and with which the conclusion of the prophecy occupies itself. It is Jerusalem repopulated with returning Exiles that appears at the end as the counterpart of the sterile Hannah blessed at last with a child, and of this city of Jerusalem it is implied that it will endure as a world capital when Rome (Aram) is laid waste and desolate. Here we seem to have at one and the same time a confirmation and an explanation of the suggestion that the artist chose to conclude his Samuel series with the representation of Jerusalem as the world capital. From the representation of the capital he

---

382. One might even argue that from texts such as this an idea can be gained of the scenes portrayed on the parts of the Synagogue that have been destroyed. Note the fact that Haman, Esther, and Mordecai (Panel WC 2); the Levites in the Temple (Panel WB 2); and the return of the Exiles (Panel NC 1) — all mentioned in the prophecy — do appear at other points in the Synagogue.

could naturally not omit the Temple, the guarantee of the faith that made the historical narratives portrayed meaningful to the worshiper.

The Dedication of the Temple

Panel SB 1 (fragmentary). H. *ca.* 1.48 m.; L. 3.38 m. (Pl. LVIII).

Hopkins and Du Mesnil du Buisson, "La Synagogue," p. 249; Du Mesnil du Buisson, "Les Peintures," p. 114; *idem, Peintures*, pp. 69 f.; *Rep. VI*, pp. 354 f.; Grabar, "Le Thème," pp. 9–12; Schneid, *The Paintings*, pp. 14 f.; Sonne, "The Paintings," pp. 306–308; Sukenik, *The Synagogue*, p. 137; Wischnitzer, *Messianic Theme*, pp. 53–55.

Leaving the panels north of the Central Group, we turn now to the southern half of Register B and deal first with the only panel known to us in that register on the south wall. This was apparently an ambitious undertaking and may originally have extended the full length of the wall, though all that remains of it today is a triangular piece of the right part of the composition, a piece whose length is less than half that of the wall. Along the diagonal side, where the line of preservation follows the pitch of the covering embankment, traces of color are vague in a zone 0.20–0.30 m. wide. The surface has suffered noticeably throughout — from fragmentation along the diagonal upper edge, and from cracking, scratching, and even gouging elsewhere. At the extreme right and toward the center cracking has brought about the loss of three fair-sized pieces of plaster, necessitating a certain amount of restoration.[383]

Throughout the panel, wherever traces of color are visible, the background of the scene is monochrome, a dull reddish brown. Against this background the artist has set a company of people moving from right to left, which indicates at once that the scene cannot be part of a series running toward the panels of the Central Group. Among the figures preserved, those that provide the clearest indication of the subject and nature of the composition are two symmetrical pairs of men dressed in Iranian costume. The pair on the right carries the end of a pole at shoulder height, in analogy to the Ark-bearers of Panel NB 1. The pair at the left, however, is set at a slightly higher level and seems to be drawn to a somewhat larger scale, and it is difficult to see how these men could have carried the other end of the pole. But since the poses of the two pairs are so similar, and the need for some extension of the pole toward the left so clear, it is almost impossible to escape the assumption that they did carry some object between them. This object is represented by a light-colored area above the level of the assumed carrying-poles, and in all probability is the Ark of the Covenant carried in a procession similar to that on the north wall.[384] There are, however, important differences between the two, seen not only in the dress of the Ark-bearers and in the fact that one of them at least has leaves or flowers in his hair, but also in the figures of the children whom the artist has introduced beneath the Ark and behind and above its bearers. All of the children are dressed in elaborate costume and those most clearly visible hold branches in their hands. Before the Ark, in what remains of the panel at this end, the extreme

383. The most noticeable crack is that which runs at knee height along the lower right part of the panel. This is joined by several vertical fissures, the most important of which traces an irregular course down from the top through the first two figures at the extreme right of the panel, causing the loss of a section of the background to the right of the head of the upper, and the loss of the face and the upper part of the left arm of the lower. These have been restored and are so shown in the Plates. In the area of the second Ark-bearer, counting from the left, at the level of his hip and directly behind him fragmentation resulting from another vertical fissure has caused the loss of a further piece of the plaster surface. The break has been filled in and a few lost details have been restored. A number of deep vertical scars and some surface

scratches are noticeable near the head of the fourth Ark-bearer. Holes have been gouged in the surface in his vicinity, two of them in his cheeks just below the eyes. The last mentioned are probably to be associated with intentional eye disfigurement undertaken probably by workmen when the first phase of the embankment within the chamber was constructed. Additional instances of this are found in Panel WB 1 and in the panels of Register C against which the embankment was set. In this instance the disfigurer did not quite achieve his objective. On the general subject see below, p. 338.

384. The shape of the color-mass and the interval between the carriers allows for the representation of an object shown vertically, but not for the horizontal bier required by the interpretations of Wischnitzer (*Messianic Theme*, pp. 53–55) and Sonne ("The Paintings," pp. 306 f.).

lower portions of two other large figures can still be distinguished. They either stand still in a frontal pose or are moving with the Ark-bearers toward the left as a part of the procession, and are both clothed in the formal costume of court and Temple dignitaries.

From the purely formal point of view the artist has succeeded here to a far greater degree in creating the impression of an actual procession than he did on the north wall. While he never attains the excellence of his models of Roman Imperial art such as the triumphal procession on the Arch of Titus, he has grouped his figures more closely in this instance, has given them a certain amount of animation, and has succeeded in conveying a mood of joyous celebration, the very antithesis of the austerity and martial atmosphere of the triumph depicted on the other side of the chamber. Using this mood as a criterion, it is clear that there are really only two incidents of Biblical narrative which the picture could portray. The first is the episode recounted in II Sam. 6.12–15 when David brought the Ark of the Covenant into that part of Jerusalem that was called the City of David. The second is that told in I Kings 8.1–11, when Solomon dedicated the Temple he had built and at that occasion brought the Ark of the Covenant from the City of David to its final resting place in the Holy of Holies of the new sanctuary. Both are described as events of great rejoicing and of popular participation, and interpreters of the scene have connected the panel now with the one, and now with the other. If the left part of the composition had been preserved, the scene could no doubt have been identified with certainty. But the fact that less than half of it remains does not mean that the issue must be left undecided, for a close study of the details of what is preserved gives enough evidence, it would seem, for a judgment of probability on the subject portrayed. These details have now to be analyzed.

The central motif of the Ark and its bearers should be compared in all particulars with its counterpart on the north wall (Panel NB 1, Pl. LIV), to which it is analogous. The carriers here seem not to reflect in the position of the knees the weight of the burden they bear; but their pose is identical, with the right leg advanced and in profile, while the left leg and the body are in a three-quarter position

and the head is turned virtually full front.[385] What distinguishes the bearers in the two instances is the extent of their hair masses and the type of garments worn. Whereas in the scene to the north the hair of the bearers is like that of the soldiers — sufficient but not luxuriant — here it is developed as a heavy aureole and is decorated with what appear to be leaves or flowers (Fig. 35). The change in the

FIG. 35. Panel SB 1. Flowers in Hairdress

hair styling is not accidental, but the necessary concomitant of a difference in costume, coiffure and garments being carefully correlated by the Synagogue artists as indications of the rank and standing of the persons in question. As to the costume worn in this instance, it consists of soft white boots, trousers tucked into the boots, and a long-sleeved knee-length tunic that is belted at the waist and slit at the sides from the hips down. The lower edges of the tunics are occasionally supplied with borders of a different color, while vertical bands run down the middle of the tunic and trousers.[386] In spite of minor variations, the cos-

385. The relation of the hands to the poles on their shoulders and of the poles to the Ark resting upon them is equally poor in both cases. Only one pole is actually visible on the scene on the south wall, and from the direction it takes one would infer that its other end would cut across the forward bearers at the level of the elbow instead of the shoulder. Two things should be noted in this connection: first, that the patch in the plaster at his back makes the nearer of the forward bearers seem taller than he really is; and second, that the poles on Panel NB 1 do not run in a single plane either, tending to reach a peak in the middle, where here they apparently sag.

386. In this instance the vertical tunic decoration occurs only on the first and second bearers counting from

tume is readily recognizable as one that occurs on many panels of the Synagogue and is proper to cult and court officials of all but the very highest rank. In this instance it is undoubtedly intended to identify the Ark-bearers as the Levites whose special privilege it was to carry the palladium, thereby telling us that the Ark is here in the hands of its proper owners rather than in those of unworthy slaves or servants.[387] But this is not enough by itself to identify precisely the episode depicted.

If there is nothing about the Ark-bearing Levites that would serve to identify the scene portrayed, the same is not true of the minor figures which the artist has introduced above, below, and behind the Ark.[388] These are all by reason of their stature and their dress children.[389] Their presence provides us with an unusually favorable opportunity to study children's costume, and contributes essentially to both the joyous spirit and the proper identification of the scene.[390] On the part of the panel still preserved no less than five children were depicted, three in line along the base of the panel and two on a higher plane above and behind the Ark-bearers, the two above being much more indistinct than the three below. All apparently wear sandals, short-sleeved, knee-length tunics, and an unidenti-

fied undergarment.[391] All of the tunics are elaborately ornamented with designs woven into the fabric of the garment, and of these designs some have reappeared upon textiles discovered in the excavation of the city.[392] The last child on the right in the series along the base of the panel is the one whose tunic is best preserved in all its details. It is made of white cloth whose fold lines are shown in pink and is decorated along the hem and the neck with reddish-brown ornamental borders outlined in black. At the neck the border consists of a wide band from which strips run down at the shoulders, each ending in an arrowhead design.[393] At the hem the border is serrate and ends at either side in a vertical two-pronged ornament. The garments of all the other four children are analogous save that the first of the two under the Ark has hanging down over its tunic the end of a sash or cloak decorated with a checkerboard of intersecting red lines.[394]

So far as the position of their feet, their bodies, and their heads is concerned, the children are drawn in the same manner as the Ark-bearers, showing that they are participating actively in the joyous procession, while preserving the frontality that brings them into association with the spectators. The one in the lower right corner apparently wears in its hair flowers or leaves like the last of the

---

the left and that of the trousers only on the third. The colors of the garments of the four men, counting again from the left are as follows: (1) tunic white with red fold lines and a vertical stripe outlined in black, trousers grayish yellow with black fold lines; (2) tunic dark blue with red border and vertical stripe, trousers green with black fold lines; (3) tunic green with pink border and white belt outlined in black, trousers gray with a vertical stripe outlined in black, shoes outlined at the top with a narrow red line; (4) tunic grayish white with a red border and a black belt outlined above in white, trousers green. Fold lines on the garments of (3) and (4) are in black throughout.

387. Num. 4.1–15; Deut. 10.8.

388. The fact that the artist has made room for standing figures behind the last of the Ark-bearers is an indication, it would seem, of the amount of room he had at his disposal.

389. What was said above in connection with Panel NA 1 (Jacob at Bethel) precludes the possibility of their being angels as Sonne has suggested ("The Paintings," p. 308).

390. The best analogies for children's garments in the Roman phase of the art of the Near East are provided by the funerary reliefs of Palmyra (see e.g., H. Ingholt, *Berytus*, II, 1935, pp. 57–75), and the paintings and bas-reliefs of Dura (see e.g., the paintings in the Temple of Bel, Cumont, *Fouilles*, Pls. XXXV–XLI).

391. The undergarment projects as a triangular piece of material from under the tunic where, by virtue of the raising of the child's right arm, the lower hem of the tunic is pulled up. The artist seems to have exaggerated the extent to which it covers the legs in attempting to show it at all. For a more conservative rendering of the same garment on Palmyrene bas-reliefs, see Ingholt, *op. cit.*, Pls. XXXIII, 2; XXXIV.

392. Cf. *Final Report* IV, II, esp. Pls. V–XII.

393. Cf. *ibid.*, Pl. IX, and for an analogy at Palmyra, Seyrig, *Syria*, XVIII (1937), p. 21, Fig. 12.

394. A similar effect is to be seen on the garments of the young men shown in Ingholt, *op. cit.*, Pl. XXXIV, where, however, a different garment seems to be worn. As to the costume of the four children in question the following details may be noted: (1) the first of the children under the Ark (counting from the left) wears a white tunic with pink fold lines and a serrate pink border ending in vertical prongs; (2) the second child under the Ark has a white tunic with a border outlined by two black lines and ending in vertical two-pronged ornaments; (3) the first of the two children above the Ark, counting from the left, has a white tunic with pink fold lines; (4) the second of the children in the upper row wears a yellow tunic with red bands on the sleeves, a reddish-brown collar band with pendants outlined in black, and a border of the same color at the hem.

Levites, from which it may be legitimate to infer that originally all other figures in the scene did likewise. The difference between the Levites and the children comes to expression especially in the treatment of their arms and hands. Of the three

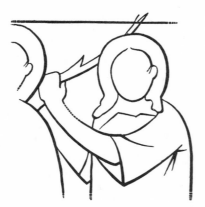

FIG. 36. Panel SB 1. Palm Branch

children in the lower row, the last two, counting from the left, wave long slender curving objects which can scarcely be anything but conventionalized palm branches (Figs. 36–37). In the clearer

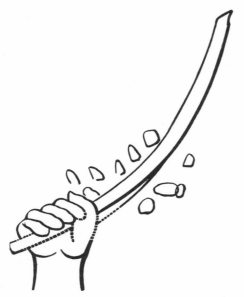

FIG. 37. Panel SB 1. Palm Branch and Myrtle Leaves

of the two instances the branch has associated with it a scattering of small irregularly shaped lobes that must be the leaves of a plant or tree other than the palm. The last child in the row holds a

palm branch in its right hand and a second branch with multiple twigs and lanceolate leaves in its left (Fig. 38).

The rendering at this point, so far as it involves the use of foliage or flowers in the hair and different

FIG. 38. Panel SB 1. Willow Branch

kinds of branches in the hands, is necessarily of decisive significance for the interpretation of the scene. In the Orient almost any kind of a procession could be accompanied with the cutting, strewing, and waving of branches.[395] But in the portrayal of historical scenes, especially scenes of a Biblical character, artist and interpreter alike have naturally to consider first the association of such foliage with specific events of the normal festival calendar, in particular with the Feast of Tabernacles. With the requirements for the celebration of Tabernacles, moreover, the details of the scene portrayed in the panel are in perfect accord. The children bear in their right hands the lulab, with

395. The most familiar analogy is in the narrative of Jesus' entry into Jerusalem, Mark 11.8 and parallels.

which the palm and myrtle and willow are associated, and the one child has in addition in its left hand what seems to be the willow branch that played a separate role in the ritual.[396] As for wreaths or crowns worn in the hair, their connection with Tabernacles is confirmed by Jubilees XVI.30. Finally, the presence of children in the procession itself suggests an allusion to Tabernacles, for according to the Torah all males are required to participate in the Temple observances at this occasion (Exod. 23.17; Deut. 16.16), and the children represented are by their garments shown clearly to be boys.[397] If, then, reference to the Feast of Tabernacles seems inescapable, the scene must depict the Dedication of the Temple by Solomon: first, because the event as described in the Bible actually occurred at the beginning of the feast; and second, because the celebration of the feast in later days was consciously associated with the memory of the Temple and with the hope of its rebuilding.[398]

As a scene representing the Dedication of the Temple by Solomon, the panel naturally has many overtones for the worshipers at the Synagogue. It serves as a visible witness to the associations of the feast, just as the scene representing the Exodus and the Crossing of the Red Sea serves as a reminder and a witness of the Feast of the Passover. It reflects the same interest in the movement of history toward its destined end that has already come to expression in the series of scenes connected with the narrative of I Samuel. And if, in the

period that had transpired since the event of the Dedication, both the glory of Temple and city and their function as the religious and national center of human life had been destroyed, the confident assurance remained that the God who had guided the course of events in the days of the Philistine dangers, and sanctioned the work of Solomon, would fulfil the expectation that sanctuary and city would be rebuilt and that the nations would come to Jerusalem to worship the Lord of Hosts and to keep the Feast of Tabernacles as Zechariah had prophecied (Zech. 14.16).

If Panel SB 1 actually represents, as seems probable, the Dedication of Solomon's Temple, the two remaining figures of the scene and even the part that has been lost can be described and interpreted with some degree of assurance. In front of the first of the Levites, it has already been noted, dim outlines of the feet and legs of two persons are still to be discerned. Both men wear soft white boots and trousers that seem to have been gray or blue with black and red fold lines. They belong therefore to the priestly or royal classes and may represent either Solomon and Zadok or the two priests Zadok and Abiathar.[399] Ahead of the two men leading the procession the red background may have been interrupted by a yellow object, perhaps an altar, as Du Mesnil du Buisson has suggested, and as the story itself would imply.[400] If this be so, the scene must have continued at this point with the sacrifice performed by Solomon before the Temple, and with the Temple itself in all its magnificence. Between them these two additional elements would undoubtedly have filled the space remaining in Register B on the south wall, giving the movement of the procession both direction and a goal, and making the composition probably one of the most successful in the entire Synagogue.

396. On the basic requirement for "taking" at the festival the boughs and fruit of goodly trees, including palm and willow and by interpretation myrtle, and the ethrog (citron), see Lev. 23.40. Of the "four species" required, only the ethrog is not represented in the part of the scene preserved. Willow, myrtle, and palm are normally tied together to form the lulab, and are held in the right hand. The lulabs are much more realistic in the present scene than on the façade of the Torah Shrine (see Pl. XVI). Minors who know how to wave the lulab are subject to the obligation to use it (Sukkah 42a, Trans., p. 191). On the separate part played by the willow branch in the ritual of the celebration see Sukkah 42b–43b, Trans., pp. 193–200.

397. For the distinction between boys' and girls' garments, see not only the murals of the Temple of Bel (Cumont, *Fouilles*, Pls. XXXV–XLI), but at Palmyra itself, e.g., the reliefs from the Tomb of Iarhai (Amy and Seyrig, *Syria*, XVII, 1936, pp. 239, 241, and Pl. XXXVI).

398. Cf. Sukkah 41a, Trans., pp. 184f. and the *Haftaroth* (lessons) of the feast, which are taken from I Kings 8.2–21 and Zech. 14.1–21, respectively.

399. Of the two men, the first in line may have been portrayed as the taller, judging by the spread of his feet, but this is only in keeping with the position assigned to him and does not help in choosing between Solomon and Zadok.

400. Cf. Du Mesnil du Buisson, *Peintures*, p. 69 and I Kings 8.62–64. Of the tent which Du Mesnil du Buisson believed he could see somewhere behind the procession, no traces have been noted either by Hopkins in his field notes or by other observers. A tent would have required a black interior, and of a black color-mass no traces are visible. Perhaps Du Mesnil du Buisson regarded as a tent the first of the two children in the upper plane behind the Ark.

Wilderness Encampment and the
Miraculous Well of Be'er

Panel WB 1. H. 1.44 m.; L. 1.90 m. (Pl. LIX).

Rep. VI, pp. 353f.; Du Mesnil du Buisson, *Peintures*, pp. 64–69; *idem, Revue de l'histoire des religions*, CXI (1935), pp. 110–117; Goodenough, *By Light, Light*, p. 209; Ehrenstein, *Die Fresken*, pp. 12f.; Leveen, *Hebrew Bible in Art*, pp. 39f.; De Vaux, *Revue biblique*, XLIX (1940), p. 140; Grabar, "Le Thème," pp. 190–192; Sonne "The Paintings," pp. 305f.; Wischnitzer, *Messianic Theme*, pp. 55–58.

The first panel on the west wall in Register B, beginning at the left, is a static composition, the basic elements of which are organized about a central axis. Reading from top to bottom, the elements of this central axis are: first, an aedicula composed of a pair of columns supporting an architrave and a pediment; second, a group of ceremonial objects in front of the aedicula, including a seven-branched lampstand, a table, and two other appurtenances of the cult; and third, below the ceremonial objects, the curbstone of a well. Symmetrically arranged on either side of this axis is a series of tents, two pairs of three each set in diagonal lines running from the central aedicula toward the sides of the panel, and two similar pairs of three each in vertical lines along the edges of the panel. Small figures in Iranian dress, their hands upraised, are associated one with each of the twelve tents. In the left half of the composition, as the one important asymmetrical element, stands the tall bearded figure of a man dressed in Greek garments. Like all the other men, he faces full front; but with his left hand he gestures toward the well-curb beside him, and with the staff held in his right hand he reaches over to touch the waters of the well. These flow forth from the curb in twelve winding streams that trace their courses directly to the twelve tents along the periphery of the composition.

Like most of the scenes in the lower registers of the west wall, that of the panel under discussion is well preserved save for a few not very disturbing cracks, some vertical scars, and the defacement of

the eyes of two of its figures.[401] Since the picture was first uncovered, it has been clear that the scene has something to do with the Biblical stories telling how the Israelite people was miraculously supplied with water during its Wilderness wanderings, and that the large figure with the staff is that of Moses. There has been some uncertainty, however, as to which of the five Biblical episodes involving the supply of water the artist meant to depict.[402] This is largely because there is so little in the composition that reflects circumstances peculiar to but one of the incidents in question. In addition, however, there is incorporated in the composition a good deal of material for which there is no immediate justification in any of the Biblical narratives directly concerned. In the Preliminary Report attention has already been called in this connection to the miraculous Well of Miriam that appears in Jewish legend, and of which it is said that rivers flowed from it dividing the camp into twelve parts.[403] The reference is not without its importance for the imagery; but it cannot suffice by itself, partly because it does not do full justice to the elaborate setting which the artist has supplied, and partly because the legend can have been used only as a medium for the interpretation of one or the other of the Biblical incidents. Only a closer study both of the major elements of the composition and of the treatment of the relevant Biblical narratives in later Jewish tradition can determine precisely the subject matter and the meaning of the scene.

Of the elements used to fashion the frame and setting for the central feature of Moses and the Well, the most important is without doubt the aedicula at the upper end of the central axis. This

401. One large horizontal crack runs across the entire panel on the level of the lowest tents at either side. Three other cracks beginning at the top trace irregular courses downward; two in the vicinity of the columns of the aedicula, a third in the upper right corner. The first and last of these, counting from the left, develop diagonal offshoots cutting through the large standing figure at the level of the forehead, the right elbow, and wrist respectively. Narrow pieces of plaster surface are occasionally lost along the line of the cracks. Scars resulting from the impact of falling bodies are noticeable, particularly in the right half of the panel. The eyes of the large figure at the left of the *puteal* and of the small figure below it at the right have been gouged out, as in various other panels.

402. The episodes are those of Marah (Exod. 15.22–25), Elim (Exod. 15.27), Rephidim (Exod. 17.1–6), Meribah (Num. 20.2–11), and Be'er (Num. 21.16–18).

403. Cf. *Rep. VI*, p. 354.

can only be the artist's conception of the Wilderness Tabernacle, a much simplified version of the portable sanctuary described in Exod. 35–38. It consists of two white Corinthian columns set on plinths and molded bases and fluted along the upper two thirds of their shafts, and a simple superstructure whose pink architrave and gable frame a light-colored pediment.[404] The interior of the sanctuary is, like almost all interiors elsewhere in the Synagogue, shown in black; but the black, it should be noted, is carried down only approximately two thirds of the distance to the base of the columns. The forepart of the interior is rendered in yellowish brown. The departure from a monochrome treatment at this point requires explanation, and the analogy to the battle scene of Panel NB 1 suggests that the function of the change is to provide "stage space" within the Tabernacle. The "stage space" in turn can best be explained on the assumption that it furnished an emplacement for the ceremonial objects connected with the outer part of the sanctuary according to Exod. 40.2–4; namely, the candlestick, the altar of incense, and the table of shew-bread. These are actually represented outside the Tabernacle in the scene, but only because the artist found it desirable to display them singly and in a size proportionate to their dignity and importance. In providing the "stage space" in the Tabernacle he has done what his conventions permitted to indicate that the objects are really to be associated with the interior of the sanctuary.

Of the four cult objects before the Tabernacle, the Menorah is the one most prominently displayed. Fashioned of alternating discs and balls to represent the required flowers or cups and the knobs respectively, the straight narrow shaft and its three semicircular arms give the candelabrum a shape quite different from that found on the façade of the Synagogue's Torah Shrine (cf. Pl. XVI), but more in line with the traditional representation.[405] The shaft rises from a fluted circular base mounted on three feet. At the top of shaft and arms the artist has shown the seven lamps, which in this instance are white and seem to be tumbler-shaped glass vessels.[406] At either side of the Menorah stands a tall cult object also fashioned of alternating discs and balls similarly rendered in yellow.[407] These could be additional lampstands, but in view of the intended Biblical allusion the probability is that in this instance they are thymiateria, and represent the "altar of incense" that stood in the interior of the sanctuary and is here duplicated for purposes of balance of composition.[408] Before the large Menorah stands still a fourth object, which, if it belongs to the interior of the Tabernacle, can only be the table of shew-bread. Triangular in shape, it represents the artist's conception of an ornate ceremonial table.[409]

On either side of the Tabernacle the scene depicts six tents. These are of a type commonly used for military purposes,[410] and differ from the one rep-

404. According to the early notes of Hopkins, the pediment originally showed traces of blue color and was set with a black circle in the center. These are no longer visible. The pink and blue of the aedicula's superstructure are perhaps the artist's concession to the Biblical description of the veil of the Tabernacle (Exod. 26.31 f.).

405. Cf. Goodenough, *Jewish Symbols*, IV, pp. 71–98.

406. They are definitely not candles. For tumbler-shaped lamps from early Christian churches, see e.g., P. Baur in *Gerasa*, pp. 521 f.

407. The one at the left is mounted on three feet.

408. Analogous objects identified above as lampstands are to be seen in Panel WB 4 (see p. 102). In other scenes of the Synagogue thymiateria are normally of a different shape and size (see Panels WB 4 and WB 2). However, tall thymiateria analogous in design to those represented here do exist (see two in bronze in the Vatican illustrated by H. T. Bossert, *Geschichte des Kunstgewerbes*, I, 1928, p. 223, nos. 4–5). The association of the objects with the interior of the sanctuary and the fact that the shaft ends at the top in a flat dish (clearly visible in the example at the left), suggests that in this instance not lamps, but thymiateria are represented. The doubling for purposes of symmetry is a device already met in the representation of the temple of Dagon in Panel WB 4.

409. Like all the other objects, the table is done in yellow to represent gold. Its well-molded legs are strengthened near the foot with a circular supporting rod. The shape is that of the *mensa delphica* (see Daremberg-Saglio, III, 2, 1904, pp. 1723–1725), and corresponds in this particular to the fanciful description given by Josephus, who says that the table in question was like those at Delphi and had legs such as the Dorians affix to their couches (*Antiquitates* III, § 139). For the actual form of the table in the last days of the Second Temple, see the relief on the Arch of Titus (H. Holzinger, *Zeitschrift für die alttestamentliche Wissenschaft*, XXI, 1901, pp. 341 f.).

410. For this type of tent see e.g., the reliefs of the Column of Aurelian (Reinach, *Répertoire de reliefs*, I, p. 305, nos. 45–46; and Daremberg-Saglio, V, p. 119, Fig. 6806). The same type of tent occurs on the scene at the extreme right end of Panel NC 1 (Pl. LXXII). The difference between it and the tent on the façade of the Torah Shrine is explained in part by the fact that a different hand, using its own conventions, was at work, and in part by the difference of function to be explained shortly.

resented on the façade of the Synagogue's Torah Shrine in connection with the Sacrifice of Isaac (Pl. XVI). They are constructed of cloth woven with alternate wide and narrow stripes, and are supported by poles that give them straight sides and peaked roofs. Guyropes attached at the eaves hold them erect. To enrich the scene the tents are rendered in various colors — black, green, red, pink, and yellow — with the stripes in black, white, or reddish brown.[411] Except in two instances the interiors are shown in black, the exceptions being tents 6 and 8 of the series, counting from the left, where the use of black for the tent itself required light colors, pink and yellow, for the interior.

The setting which the tents with the Tabernacle in their midst give to the scene of the Well is more elaborate than any of the Biblical narratives having to do with the miraculous supply of water in the desert actually requires. Nor is it probable that the artist would have gone to this length to do justice to an incidental element of the later legend of Miriam's Well. Some separate source of inspiration for this framing element of his composition is therefore needed. Attention must be called in this connection to certain unusual aspects of grouping and of the use of space in the panel as a whole. The first is the arrangement of the tents themselves into four groups of three each, two groups in diagonal lines at the right and the left of the Tabernacle respectively, and two further groups in vertical lines along the sides of the panel. The second is the fact that the artist has carried the pink color of his "foreground" up to within 0.20 m. of the top of the panel, where finally he limits his horizontal plane by a narrow zone of yellow "background."[412] His

departure in this particular from the practice of using a narrow zone at the base of the panel as "stage space" is very significant. It would seem to imply, not that he had suddenly begun using the "high perspective" characteristic of so much of Roman landscape painting, but rather that he wished the larger part of the composition to be viewed vertically rather than horizontally. Precisely what it is that he wished us to see vertically in such great depth is indicated by a third unusual feature in his treatment of grouping and the use of space. This is the substitution of yellow for pink in certain sections of the "foreground" area. The sections in question are noticeably wide strips that run around all four sides of the area enclosed by the tents, and form a hollow square, framing the scene at the Well (Fig. 39).[413]

These unusual departures from the monochrome and the narrow "stage space" treatment of backgrounds and foregrounds, while they do not achieve

FIG. 39. Panel WB 1.
Features suggesting Form of Encampment

411. Beginning at the lower left hand corner the colors of the tents and their stripes are as follows: (1) reddish brown with black, (2) pink with reddish brown, (3) green with black, (4) reddish brown with black, (5) reddish brown (?), (6) black with white, (7) reddish brown with black, (8) black with white, (9) pink with reddish brown, (10) yellow with reddish brown, (11) pink with reddish brown, (12) green with black. On the roofs of tents 4, 5, 6 the stripes are not visible on the photographs. On the originals the white stripes of tent 6 can still be seen. Hopkins' notes record black stripes for the roofs of 4 and 5.

412. The extension of the pink of the "foreground" to the height indicated is visible at the right and the left in the angles made by the two diagonal lines of tents, and also in the small triangles that appear along the sides of the panel between the base of one tent and the sloping roof of its neighbor, where the pink color reappears.

413. Notice how the artist has contrived to indicate the regularity of the delimited zone by using the base of the panel at the bottom as one side of his square, and by terminating the black indicating the interior of tents five and seven on a line with that of the Tabernacle, creating here a single horizontal plane that represents the opposite side of his square. The irregularity of the other two sides is occasioned by the unequal arrangement of the tents and of the figures associated with them. The strips forming the sides of the square are to be thought of as forming a continuous design in spite of the slight inconsistency which developed directly before tent six, where the pink of the interior was continued, probably by error, to include the small triangular area bounded by the column of the Tabernacle and Moses' left shoulder.

a completely unified and convincing result judged by our own conceptions of perspective, undoubtedly have a significant basis in the artist's intention. They may be taken to imply that the tents and the Tabernacle together were to him more than merely a setting for the scene at the Well. Instead we must assume that his composition combines two elements of equal importance, and once this is assumed it becomes clear that the only valid reason for the attention paid to space in the development of the framing element is the desire on the artist's part to portray a typical encampment of the Israelite host in the Wilderness as described in Num. 2.[414] The Biblical description, it will be recalled, divides the tribes into four groups of three, precisely as the Synagogue artist has done, and assigns to the several camps of each group a position on one of the four sides of a hollow square surrounding the tent of the Tabernacle. It is this square for which room had to be provided in our composition, and whose shape had to be indicated. Christian artists of the earlier period have also attempted to depict the *schema* of the Wilderness encampment, and if the Synagogue artist has given a more plastic rendering of the subject, it is because he has added to the plan seen in vertical perspective the Tabernacle and tents seen in horizontal perspective, sacrificing something of the geometric regularity of the plan in so doing.[415]

Leaving aside for the moment the small figures associated with the several tents, we turn now to the central scene of the Well, dominated by the heroic figure of Moses. The figure was drawn with unusual care, with close attention to the arrangement of the folds of the garments and must have had, before the eyes were gouged out, a particularly pleasing oval face. The head with its dark hair, its well-groomed beard and mustache, and its soft yellowish flesh tones highlighted with white, faces full front, but the rest of the body is turned

slightly toward the left. This is reflected in the position of the feet, of which the left is shown in profile while the right is turned outward and slightly to the rear, and was made necessary by the gesture of the right arm, which reaches across the body to touch the waters of the Well with its staff while the left arm is held close by the side of the body.[416] Moses wears the combination of chiton and himation familiar from the Exodus Panel (WA 3), but the material is represented in this instance as being woven in a checkerboard pattern.[417] The weave is apparently of no importance save as an indication of the excellence of the material and the garments, a fact which is brought to further expression in the extent of the ornament used. The yellow chiton, whose black tie-string is clearly visible at the shoulder, is supplied with dark lavender bands at the neck and the hem, wide lavender bands about the forearm of the long sleeve, and similar clavi of such width that they cover almost the entire front of the garment and all of the shoulder. The himation, clearly of the same material, adds to the wide two-pronged band that comes up diagonally over the left thigh a similar ornament on the left shoulder and a series of squares on the ends hanging down from the left arm. No other single instance of the combination of chiton and himation in the Synagogue contains all of these ornamental features, suggesting that the artist had some special reason for providing his hero in this instance with such sumptuous apparel.[418] This reason still remains to be discovered.

From Moses' left hand his knobby yellow staff extends downward into the well that lies on the

414. Since the encampment was fundamentally military, tents of the type used by the Roman army were distinctly in order.

415. For early Christian parallels see Cod. Vat. Graec. 699 (Cosmas Indicopleustes) fol. 52ʳ (ed. C. Stornajolo, *Le Miniature della topografia cristiana di Cosma Indicopleuste,* 1908), and Cod. Vat. Graec. 747 (Vatican Octateuch) fol. 160ᵛ. To introduce the horizontal factor the artist has left one side of his square open, pushing his four groups of tents together in such a way as to create the diagonal and the vertical arrangement already discussed.

416. In the color of the hands and feet yellow continues to play an important part, but there are strong indications of modeling with the use of brown, and some white highlights. Sandals are indicated on the feet in early copies and photographs, but are no longer clearly visible on the originals and later photographs made from them.

417. Cf. the comment on the garment of Hannah in Panel NB 2, above, p. 94, where the same pattern reappears.

418. Clavi of the width indicated are rarely found on the long chiton. Perhaps the best examples are those on certain of the figures portrayed in the Temple of Bel (see Cumont, *Fouilles,* Pls. XLV-XLVII). A band on the sleeve of the tunic is shown on the painting from the Temple of Zeus Theos, *Rep. VII–VIII,* Pl. XXV. The two-pronged ornamental band cutting diagonally across the himation is common on the Synagogue paintings and reappears in Palmyrene sculpture (see Seyrig, *Syria,* XVIII, 1937, p. 25, Fig. 16).

axis of the composition inside the rectangular patch of pink "foreground."[419] The Well is done in yellow and takes the form of a *puteal* with a square base and a circular throat.[420] Black loops outlined against its yellow interior indicate that the water is bubbling up, thus accounting for the twelve streams which run in undulating bands to the tents at the right and the left.[421] Here they pass the small standing figures associated one with each of the twelve tents. All but one figure stand directly in front of the tent to which they belong. The exception, placed in the lower right foreground, probably owes his unusual position to nothing more significant than the carelessness of the artist in handling proportions in the right half of the composition.[422] Except for one detail in the rendering of one of the figures, all the men wear the Iranian costume of white boots, trousers, and long-sleeved, knee-length belted tunic that is otherwise connected with members of court and Temple personnel.[423] Details of color and costume have become obscure in a number of instances.[424] Ornamental

bands on collar and hem of the tunics and down the center of tunic and trouser leg suggest, however, that the costume is quite as ornate as that of Moses himself.[425]

From the analysis of the details it is possible to proceed profitably to a discussion of the nature and significance of the episode represented in the center of the composition. Two facts have already been recorded bearing upon this question; namely, first, that no one of the five relevant episodes in the form in which they are told in the Bible satisfies all the details of the iconography; and second, that the legend of Miriam's Well, which alone accounts for the twelve streams, cannot itself be regarded as of sufficient weight in the artist's mind to have been taken as the sole and direct subject of the entire composition. Various suggestions have been made to provide an escape from the difficulties thus posed, but only a full examination of the developing tradition about the wilderness water supply can provide a firm basis for the interpretation of the imagery.

The earliest indication of the further development of the Biblical stories in question is to be found in the work of the Jewish tragic poet Ezekiel, who, writing in the pre-Maccabean days, spoke of Elim, the scene of one of the episodes (Exod. 15.27), as so fertile that it draws twelve springs from a single rock.[426] This introduces a rock into the Elim story and relates the twelve springs to each other by virtue of their common relation to the rock, yet

419. From the fact that the staff merely abuts upon the hand, whose fingers are shown tightly closed, it has been inferred that Moses is throwing rather than holding the staff (Du Mesnil du Buisson, *Peintures*, p. 66). This seems improbable because the gesture of throwing should be more violent and the dissociation of hand and staff more patent. Instead, we are probably dealing here with an imperfect rendering of detail.

420. The type is among the commonest of well and cistern curbings. For examples see Winter and Pernice, *Die hellenistische Kunst in Pompeji*, V, pp. 12f., Pl. VII, 1, 3; and J. Chamonard, *Le Quartier de théatre* (*Exploration archéologique de Delos*, VIII, 2, 1924), pp. 323–351 and p. 348, Fig. 213.

421. The yellow streams are outlined in black and white and are occasionally continued into the interior of the tents.

422. The figure actually belongs to the next to the last tent at the right. There was no room for him there because the man associated with the fourth tent from the last was given too much height, forcing the artist to move the man associated with the third tent down into the position which the man of the second tent should have occupied.

423. The one exception is the man in the doorway of the first tent in the lower left corner, who, strangely, wears sandals instead of boots and therefore has no trousers. Note also the apparent absence of the large aureole of hair usually associated with the Iranian costume.

424. In the several figures beginning in the lower left corner the following details can be made a matter of record: (1) pink tunic with black ornament, light-colored belt, no trousers; (2) light-colored tunic, black belt, pink trousers; (3) reddish-brown tunic, white belt, pink trousers; (4) light-colored tunic with black band on hem,

pink belt, pink trousers; (5) pink tunic with black ornament, lavender trousers; (6) yellow-brown tunic, dark belt, lavender trousers; (7) pink tunic with black ornament, white belt, yellow trousers; (8) reddish-brown tunic, pink trousers; (9) grayish-blue tunic, pink trousers; (11) man out of position: pink tunic with black ornament, light belt, pink trousers; (12) grayish-blue tunic, pink trousers.

425. One detail of the costume, an angular extension of the band decorating the neck of the tunic, visible particularly on the fifth and seventh men of the series counting from the lower left, has already been commented upon by Seyrig in connection with a fragment of Palmyrene sculpture (*Syria*, XVIII, 1937, p. 17 and p. 18, Fig. 9). This detail is identifiable as the representation of a rever or flap by the bas-relief published by Ingholt, *Berytus*, II, (1935), Pl. XXXVII. On more ornate garments, it would seem, this flap took the place of the tie-string in closing and opening the aperture on the neck of the knee-length tunics.

426. Ezekiel quoted by Eusebius, *Praeparatio evangelica* IX, 29, first referred to in this connection by Père R. de Vaux, *Revue biblique*, XLIX (1940), p. 140.

it falls short of suggesting a single source with twelve channels.[427] Philo mentions at least four of the five relevant Biblical episodes in the *Vita Mosis* (Marah, Elim, Rephidim, and Be'er) but finds only one, that of Rephidim, miraculous.[428] This he interprets in the light of the allusion in Deut. 8.15 as providing a spring of water which gushes forth from a steep rock like a stream.[429] With this interpretation it would be entirely possible to associate the iconography of the early Christian representations of the Water from the Rock, but scarcely that of the Dura scene.[430] The one further passage, in the *De fuga*, where Philo deals at some length with the Elim episode, using it to provide supplementary material for the allegorical interpretation of the "spring" of the Hagar story (Gen. 16.7), might conceivably provide suggestions for a speculative interpretation of the Dura scene, but can hardly be regarded as a sufficient source for its iconography.[431] Josephus, who mentions only three of the five "water" episodes, seems to follow an interpretative tradition not unrelated to that of Philo in emphasizing the importance of Rephidim over Marah and Elim (neither of which he regards as in any sense miraculous), and in using the term "river" to describe the water of the spring that issued from the rock.[432] There is, however, no basis in the account for either a well or twelve streams.

While the writers of Hellenized Judaism speak consistently of a "spring" and emphasize the importance of Rephidim and Elim, those representing Oriental Judaism seem to follow another tradition. One group of witnesses to this Oriental tradition is that of the Targumim, where the episodes at Marah, Elim, Rephidim, and Meribah are reported without any elaboration upon the Biblical narrative, but where instead it is the episode at Be'er (Num. 21.16–18) that receives supplementary interpretative treatment. The interpretative additions to the narrative of the episode take different forms in Onkelos, pseudo-Jonathan, and the Fragment Targum, but all concern themselves with a Well rather than a spring.[433] What the Targumim tell us about the Well is: (1) that from the time it was given it went up hill and down dale with Israel; (2) that it had already been given to Israel at a previous time, but had been hidden and was now being restored to them (pseudo-Jonathan and the Fragment Targum only); (3) that it was originally "digged" or seen by Abraham, Isaac, and Jacob, and by the seventy Elders constituting the original Sanhedrin; and, having been found by Moses, Aaron, and the scribes with their rods, it was given to them from the desert as a gift (pseudo-Jonathan and the Fragment Targum only).

It is evident from these supplementary elements of the Targumic account that the legendary story of Miriam's Well was well known to the paraphrasers, and, what is more important, that they tended to associate the story with one specific episode of Biblical narrative; namely, the story of the well at Be'er in Num. 21. The same general picture can be gathered from the Midrashim where the story is often alluded to, though never recounted in detail, and where — as in the Midrash Rabbah, for instance — Marah, Elim, Rephidim, and Meribah tend to elicit little or no Haggadic comment, while Be'er is the occasion of lengthy discussion of the relation between the details of

427. The question is whether "rock" in this instance really means "well," and whether the twelve "springs" may be thought of as twelve "streams."

428. For Marah, see, *Vita Mosis* I, 181–186; Elim, *ibid.*, 188–190; Rephidim, *ibid.*, 210–211; and for Be'er, *ibid.*, 255–257.

429. Cf. the note of Thackeray on *Vita Mosis* I, 210 and the passage in *De somniis* II, 222. The reference in Deut. 8.15 is clearly to Rephidim and not to Meribah.

430. Cf. e.g., the frescoes of the catacombs of Priscilla (*capella graeca*), Domitilla (chamber III), and Callixtus (chapel A 6) in Wilpert, *Die Malereien der Katakomben Roms*, Pls. 13, 55, and 46.

431. *De fuga*, 183–187. Certainly in a composition inspired by the Philonic allegory one would expect to find the representation of a "gateway" (the gateway to knowledge which Philo finds suggested in the name Elim) and twelve springs rather than one well with twelve rivers. Moses and his staff would need to be omitted, because the process of imbibing wisdom on the lower level of the educational procedure is described in the passage as a natural result of the people's thirst for learning. For the opposite of the position taken here, see Goodenough, *By Light, Light*, pp. 209f. For a discussion of the question of principles of interpretation for the Dura scenes, see below, pp. 349–351.

432. Josephus reports the story of Marah in *Antiquitates* III, 4–8; of Elim, *ibid.*, 9–32; and of Rephidim,

ibid., 33–38. The account of Rephidim contains an allusion to Num. 21.

433. Perhaps it was the fear of the paradox of a well "bubbling" or "springing up" that caused the LXX to omit the reference to this phenomenon in rendering the text of Num. 21.17.

the legend of the Well and the statements of the Biblical text.[434]

From what has been said it will be evident that the tradition concerning the miraculous supply of water during Israel's Wilderness wanderings developed in the post-Biblical period along two different lines. The one line, associating itself particularly with Rephidim, using the imagery of a "steep" rock yielding a single "stream," and reflected in the more Hellenized Jewish writers, may be the source of the iconography reflected in Christian catacomb art. It is with the other line that uses the episode of Be'er (Num. 21.16–18) as a base and speaks of a Well which, strange to say, "bubbled up," that we should in all probability associate the iconography of the Dura scene. This would agree with the conclusion already reached in the discussion of the encampment, which is also taken from Numbers, and would explain the use of the *puteal* or well-curb as the source from which the water proceeds, not to mention the bubbling itself.[435] The fact that it is the Be'er episode to which in rabbinical texts elements of the legend of Miriam's Well are regularly attached, prepares the way for the introduction into the scene of details borrowed from that legend. The two details most clearly derived from the legend are the position of the Well in the midst of the encampment, directly in front of the Tabernacle, for which there is support both in the Midrash and in the Tosefta, and the twelve streams of water flowing from it to the several camps, which the tradition preserved in the Tosefta comes closest to explaining.[436] Confirmation

of the suggestion that the imagery of the scene is to be associated fundamentally with the Be'er episode is provided by two details not previously discussed. The first is the dress of the twelve figures connected with the twelve tents. They are in some sense representatives of the twelve tribes, and the tendency has been to identify them with the twelve Elders who appear, for instance, in the Exodus Panel (WA 3). It should be noted, however, that whereas the Elders wear Greek dress, the men represented in the scene under discussion have the costume associated normally with court and Temple personnel. The difference is explained by the allusion in the Song of the Well (Num. 21.18) to the "nobles of the people," an allusion which carries over into the later rendering of the Be'er episode and makes the "princes" of Israel those who sing the Song at the occasion.[437] The second detail is that of the gesture used by the twelve "princes." Each holds his arms outstretched and bent at the elbows, the open hands at shoulder level, palms outward. The gesture appears in only one other scene of the Synagogue (Panel NC 1, Section C), where also it is properly to be interpreted as the gesture of song and praise.[438]

The presence in our composition of so many features explicable only from the story of the epi-

434. Numbers Rabbah XIX, 25–26, Trans., VI, pp. 773–777. So far as the details of the later part of the legend are concerned, it would seem that the Well had been "hidden" upon the death of Miriam when Israel first entered Moabite territory, and was not "revealed" again until Israel was at the Arnon, the northern boundary of Moab. This is in punishment of Israel's attitude toward the Moabite women and explains the dearth of water complained of at Meribah. So far as the earlier details of the legend are concerned, it is the opinion of the Rabbis that Israel had the Well during the forty years of the Wilderness wandering. Cf. on the general subject Ginzberg, *Legends of the Jews*, III (1911), p. 308; and VI, p. 107, n. 602.

435. There is, of course, a basic difference in the architectural treatment of wells and springs in antiquity, as there are also differences in the iconography of their pictorial representation.

436. Cf. Numbers Rabbah I, 2 (Trans., V, p. 5), where it is said that the Well was a rock shaped like a bee-hive

and that wherever Israel journeyed it rolled along and came with them. When the standards halted and the Tabernacle was set up, the rock would come and settle down in the court of the Tent of Meeting and the princes would come and say "Rise up, O Well" (Num. 21.17), and it would rise. It is with this form of the tradition that the statement of the Apostle Paul about the rock which followed the Fathers in the Wilderness (I Cor. 10.4) should be connected, furnishing incidentally a clear indication of the antiquity of the tradition. Similarly the Tosefta to Sukkah 3, 11–16 (trans. A. W. Greenup, *Sukkah, Mishna and Tosefta*, 1925, p. 76) where we are told that the Well which followed Israel during its Wilderness wanderings settled down in front of the Tabernacle whenever the host stopped, and that when Moses and the Elders appeared from their tents and sang the Song of the Well, it would gush forth rivers of water that were said to divide the camp into twelve parts. In the Dura scene the twelve streams, instead of dividing the camp into twelve parts (by flowing between the tents), enter directly into the tents. This comes closer to the conception of the Targum pseudo-Jonathan where it is said that the Well gave Israel to drink, everyone at the door of his tent (*ad* Num. 21.19).

437. So e.g., in Numbers Rabbah I, 2 (Trans., V, p. 5).

438. See also below, p. 193 n. 756. Gestures of acclaim and surprise are made regularly with one hand in the Synagogue paintings.

sode at Be'er provides the proper perspective for the appearance in the scene of the staff of Moses. This should not be regarded as normative for the basic allusion, but rather as the sign of authority carried by Moses in the course of the Wilderness wandering of the people, and therefore as something which the artist introduced into the scene without the immediate justification of the story itself, so far as we know its Targumic and Midrashic development. Fundamentally, then, the panel develops two elements of Biblical narrative, both taken from Numbers, and paves the way in this particular for the panel which follows at the right.

The Consecration of the Tabernacle and its Priests

Panel WB 2. H. 1.43 m.; L. 2.55 m. (Pl. LX).

Rep. VI, pp. 352f.; Du Mesnil du Buisson, "Les Peintures," pp. 112f.; *idem, Peintures*, pp. 55–64; Leveen, *Hebrew Bible in Art*, pp. 37–39; Grabar, "Le Thème," pp. 186–190; Sukenik, *The Synagogue*, pp. 92–98; Sonne, "The Paintings," pp. 301–305; Wischnitzer, *Messianic Theme*, pp. 58–60.

Judged solely by artistic standards, the scene under discussion here is among the less successful compositions of the Synagogue. It conforms to the standards of its immediate neighbors at the right and the left in that it is entirely static and frontal, telling no story, so it seems, and developing no action, but falls even below their level in failing to combine the figures and objects portrayed into a unified, well-organized composition, distributing them about instead in various parts of the space enclosed by the frame and at various levels from bottom to top. It may seem strange, at first glance, that the artist should have chosen to assign static scenes of this type to what is clearly one of the choice locations in the entire Synagogue, immediately beside the Central Group. The reason is, of course, that his criteria for determining location were not necessarily the artistic potentialities of a given subject, a fact which suggests that in this instance the composition presents a matter of outstanding importance in the exercise and tradition of ancient Hebrew religion.

Save for the usual number of cracks and for the far more disturbing vertical scars — some deep and short, others wide and long, and all now repaired — the panel is well preserved and presents its materials in legible fashion.[439] Seen in the light of the methods for handling space and perspective used by the Synagogue painters, the relation of the several elements of the composition to each other becomes quite intelligible.

The center of the lower half of the scene is taken up with a crenelated wall built of white stones, whose bosses are outlined in dark yellow and whose well-dressed edges are marked in brown. Three yellow doors surmounted by conches or fans are let into the wall — somewhat awkwardly, if the truth be told.[440] The paneling and the door frames (the latter having jambs with molded jamb caps and lintels) are all outlined in black. From the lintel of the middle gate a green curtain with a pink border is suspended. It is shown as though blown by the wind, revealing a part of the paneled door behind it.

The wall with its triple gateway is to be thought of as enclosing a temenos, for what is shown in the upper half of the composition represents what lies directly behind the wall. The scene here extends

439. The following elements of damage or disfigurement may be noted: (1) a horizontal crack continuing from Panel WB 1 at the left and cutting across the lower part of the entire composition at a level slightly below the belly of the heifer at the left and above the back of the ram at the right; (2) four diagonal cracks: two passing across the face and chest of the first figure in the upper row, counting from the left; a third coming down through the pediment of the Temple and passing through the heifer at the left; and a fourth cutting through the neck and chest of the last two figures in the upper row, from where it crosses Aaron and descends via the altar to the central door of the triple gateway; (3) a vertical crack running down through the right shoulder of the fourth person in the upper row of figures and on through the animals below; (4) a number of heavy, deep scars made by falling objects, visible at the base of the Temple and on the wall below it from the central door of the gateway to the heifer at the left; (5) a wide continuous vertical abrasion running down as a band through the left part of the Temple façade, the altar, the adjacent thymiaterion, and the central door of the gateway. Repairs of the damage have brought with them some retouching of the painted surface.

440. The spacing is uneven, the door at the extreme right is too high compared with that at the extreme left, and the semicircular head of the central doorway reaches to the very top of the highest course of stones in the wall, leaving no support for the surmounting crenelation. Clearly the artist had trouble trying to crowd into the picture all the elements he wished to portray.

the full width of the panel, the artist feeling entirely free to give the more remote interior of the temenos more space than to the wall in the immediate foreground. Primary importance attaches on the higher level to two parts of the imagery: a figure designated "Aaron" in the Greek dipinto at the right, and a sanctuary portrayed at the left. The sanctuary takes the form of a temple, of which the portico and one side are both equally visible, as in Panel WB 3. Here, however, the structure is of more modest proportions, with but two columns across the face and four along the side of the building, and no indication of a crepidoma, of the entrance wall of the cella, or of the door closing the entrance. Instead, the terminal columns of the portico frame the black interior directly, where a pink veil and the paneled Ark of the Covenant are to be seen. The "veil" that divides the two parts of the cella of the Israelite sanctuary is shown behind the Ark instead of before it as Exod. 36.35–36; 40.20–21 demands, purely for pragmatic reasons. The Ark takes the paneled form familiar from other scenes (Panels NB 1 and WB 4), and may itself be covered at the sides by a veil. The design on its rounded cover is varied to include in this instance two rosettes and a circular line that Du Mesnil du Buisson has interpreted as part of a seven-branched candlestick.[441] The architectural ornament of the sanctuary consists of white columns set on plinths and molded bases and surmounted by Corinthian capitals which support a narrow architrave. On the façade the framing members of the pediment are crossed by diagonal lines and the white tympanum has within it the typical rosette.[442] Black Nikés holding wreaths serve as acroteria at the corners of the edifice, quite as in Panel WB 3. The only surprising feature of the entire structure is the fact that its cella walls and roof, though marked with lines to represent the individual blocks and tiles, are none the less rendered in dark brown. The brown of the walls, it will be noted, is carried out beyond the last columns to the rear of the building and in a band below the plinths of the columns. These features will require further explanation.

In front of the building, though actually superimposed upon the crenelated temenos wall and its

central doorway, stand four ceremonial objects. Three of them belong to the interior of the cella; namely, the golden seven-branched candelabrum depicted in the same form as on Panel WB 1 with tumbler-shaped lamps at the top of its seven arms; and two short golden thymiateria analogous in form to those of Panel WB 4, representing, no doubt, the altar of incense. To the right of this group of three stands a portable golden altar whose square, paneled die is set upon a molded base supported by short gracefully curved legs.[443] This is not the golden altar of incense, as one might infer from its shape, but an altar of burnt sacrifice; for atop it lies a sacrificial animal, in all probability a ram, judging by the treatment of the part of its tail that is still visible (Fig. 40).[444] The victim on the altar, the burning incense, and the lighted lamps indicate that a cult act is in process.

Alongside the altar stands the well-proportioned

FIG. 40. Panel WB 2. Altar

441. *Peintures*, Pl. XXVI, 1.

442. Analogies to these details are to be found in the temples and gates of Panels WB 3 and WB 4.

443. On the paneled surface of one face of the die a curved space is marked off. Du Mesnil du Buisson interprets this as part of a larger design (see *Peintures*, Pl. XXVII, 4).

444. For the altar of incense see Exod. 37.25–26. Bullocks on the altars of Panels SC 3 and SC 4 have their long tails laid over and around a hind leg when shown in a crouching position, quite as do the crouching animals of the dado (Pls. XXXVII, 4; XXXVIII, 1). Here the tail hangs free behind the animal and widens perceptibly toward the end, apparently to curl outward as does the tail of the ram in the lower right corner of the panel.

and relatively tall man to whom the Greek dipinto gives the name Aaron.[445] He is arrayed in the sumptuous ceremonial robes of the High Priest which enfold him so completely that only his hands, his neck, and the pleasing regular features of his face with its mustache and its well-groomed brown beard are visible.[446] The fact that these garments (Fig. 41) are described in detail in the Bible (Exod.

ΑΡШΝ

FIG. 41. Panel WB 2. Garments of High Priest

ing what the Synagogue artist has portrayed it is important to bear in mind that he was not an antiquarian, and that he is likely to have come only as close to a rendering of the Biblical description as his repertory of design and his knowledge of contemporary vestments and terminology would allow.

The High Priest wears on his head a reddish-brown bell-shaped cap with a cape that covers the back of his neck and falls over his shoulders. It represents the mitre (מִצְנֶפֶת) of the Biblical description, but lacks the plate of gold (נֵזֶר or צִיץ) supposed to be attached to it, and bears no direct resemblance to the description of Josephus save in its general shape.[448] Instead, it is decorated with chains of pearls the ends of which fall down at either side of the High Priest's face, recalling in its shape as in its ornament the bell-shaped headdress sometimes appearing on Parthian coins and Sassanian bas-reliefs.[449] Over his shoulder the High Priest wears a sleeveless reddish-brown cloak edged with a yellow band and fastened across the chest by an elliptical yellow buckle. The cloak opens progressively as it reaches the level of his feet, revealing more and more of the lower vestments. The outer garment is undoubtedly intended to represent the Biblical ephod (אֵפוֹד), which Hellenistic Jewish writers regularly refer to as an ἐπωμίς; that is, a cloak thrown over the shoulders.[450] As rendered here it recalls the cloak worn by Iranian monarchs much more closely than the typical Greek *epomis*.[451] Instead of having upon each shoulder a single gem inscribed with the names of six of the sons of Jacob, the cloak is studded with twenty separate jewels, each held in place by four

28.1–39; 39.1–26) and elsewhere, particularly in Josephus (*Antiquitates* III, 151–187), but are not otherwise depicted save in Christian contexts until the period of the Renaissance, makes their appearance here in a Synagogue of the third century a matter of particular importance.[447] In interpret-

445. Inscr. no. **29,** below, p. 279.

446. Aaron's beard, already the subject of comment in the Psalter (Ps. 133.2), is mentioned also in Jewish legend. Cf. Leviticus Rabbah III, 6 (Trans., IV, p. 43).

447. For the description and symbolical interpretation of the garments by Philo see *Vita Mosis* II, 109–135, and *De specialibus legibus* I, 85–95.

448. Cf. Exod. 28.36–37 and Josephus, *Antiquitates* III, 157–158, 172–178. Josephus does indicate that the shape of the headdress is that of a cap without a peak (πῖλος ἄκωνος).

449. Cf. e.g., the headdress on a coin of Mithradates III whose form is outlined by chains of dots, probably representing jewels (Pope, *Survey of Persian Art*, IV, Pl. 142, B), and that worn by followers of Shapur I in the Naksh-i-Rajab relief (*ibid.*, Pl. 154, B).

450. For the Biblical description of the ephod see Exod. 28.6–14.

451. Compare the cloak billowing out behind mounted royal figures in Sassanian bas-reliefs, which is reinterpreted as a coat in Panels WC 2 and EC 1 (below, p. 158). For the Iranian garment shown hanging down over the wearer see e.g., the figure at the right in the Tak-i-Bostan relief, Pope, *Survey of Persian Art*, IV, Pl. 160, B.

lesser stones. Except for the two on the shoulders, they were apparently set in rows above and below white bands that were woven into the fabric and divide the cloak horizontally into zones. One such band is still visible on the middle of the garment at the right (Fig. 41, Pl. LX). Whether or not additional decorations were woven into the cloak between the bands can unfortunately no longer be decided one way or another.[452]

Below the buckle the aperture between the two sides of the cloak is spanned by a series of ovoid jewels, apparently set in a chain and probably four in number. They seem to represent the artist's effort to cope with the "breastplate" (חֹשֶׁן) of the Biblical text (Exod. 28.15–29), and are typical of his inability to visualize even with the help of a detailed description anything for which there was no parallel in his own experience and training.

Underneath the ephod the High Priest wears a blue tunic decorated at the collar, down the middle, and at the hem with a yellow band, and encircled by a white belt. In shape and general character it is reminiscent of the tunics worn by royal personages in various panels of the Synagogue (e.g., Panels WC 2, WC 4, and the upper Central Panel) and is clearly borrowed from royal Iranian art.[453] Even so it approximates quite closely the "robe" (מְעִיל) of the Biblical text (Exod. 28.31–35), which the Hellenistic commentators describe as a ὑποδύτης or a χιτών,[454] save that the artist has omitted the Biblical ornament of pomegranates and bells along the hem and has added a belt, both in keeping with the court attire that served him as a model.

Below the hem of the "robe" are visible the ends of a pair of baggy blue trousers ornamented with

vertical yellow stripes, and the upper part of a pair of soft white boots.[455] Trousers and boots go with the royal garment which the artist is copying, and while the boots are probably not a part of the high priestly costume and the priests must be assumed to have officiated barefoot, the trousers may well represent the "linen breeches" (מִכְנְסֵי־בַד) of Exod. 28.42, even though the latter are in reality an undergarment.[456] At either side of the trouser legs and between them are areas that are rendered in a checkerboard design of green and brown squares.[457] Already recognized in other panels as the indication of a type of cloth woven in a special way, the design might seem to represent merely the lining of the High Priest's ephod. But since linings are by no means typical of ancient clothing, it may be that the artist has used this device to suggest the "coat" (כְּתֹנֶת) of Exod. 28.39, which is described as being woven in checkers and is in reality an undergarment that is said to reach to the ankles.[458] That the use of the device yields no convincing picture of the garment in question was probably less important to the artist than the indication of something that could be associated with it by virtue of the type of weave. On this analogy the belt that goes regularly with the royal tunic but not with Aaron's "robe" can have served to represent the "girdle" (אַבְנֵט) which the High Priest wore around his checkered "coat" (Exod. 28.39) and which would naturally be hidden by the "robe."

From what has been said it would appear that the artist has done his very best to portray with what models and devices he had on hand all six of the garments of the Israelite High Priest. The efforts he put forth to accomplish this end suggest that to show them fully was necessary if the panel was to convey its full meaning to the worshiper.

In the upper half of the composition the artist has portrayed besides the High Priest four helpers, two at either side of the central group.[459] All wear

452. Du Mesnil du Buisson in his rendering of the garment (*Peintures*, p. 59, Fig. 46) has indicated the presence of wreath-bearing Nikés, and other winged genii not visible there today, in the zones between the bands. It is clear that any such figures would have been indicated in fine white lines like those marking the bands, which last have now largely disappeared from view. But the existence of these winged figures was not noted by Hopkins in the field notes recording his careful description of all elements of the panel nor in the color copy of M. Le Palud, both made directly after the panel was unearthed. Besides, it is doubtful whether the gems applied to the garment, when properly distributed, leave enough room between the bands for the introduction of the figures in question.

453. On this royal costume see below, p. 153.

454. The former is the expression of Philo, *Vita Mosis* II, 109 and the latter that of Josephus, *Antiquitates* III, 159.

455. The High Priest's feet are not actually shown, perhaps to prevent the inference that he is standing upon the wall.

456. Josephus says that they are put on like ἀναξυρίδες, the Iranian trousers (*Antiquitates* III, 152).

457. Cf. Fig. 41.

458. Cf. Josephus, *Antiquitates* III, 153, who calls it a chiton.

459. Note the indications of cast shadows behind the two figures at the left.

the costume of lesser court and Temple personnel, consisting of white boots, trousers, and long-sleeved belted tunics that are slit at the waist so that their lower part falls to the knees in apron fashion.[460] The colors of the garments are varied, but the two men nearest the High Priest both have analogous combinations of blue trousers and a pink or reddish-brown tunic with a yellow border attached at the hem and the sides.[461] All four of the assistants hold short, slightly curved trumpets in their right hands, the two at the right as though they were about to blow them. In spite of their size and number, they probably represent the חֲצוֹצְרֹת blown in the wilderness for the convocation of an assembly and at the breaking of camp (Num. 10.1–2), and in the Temple at the New Moon, at the daily sacrifices, and at stated occasions between the sacrifices (Num. 10.10; II Chron. 29.26–28).[462] The first of the assistants at the left holds in his outstretched left hand in addition a small round object (Fig. 42). Perhaps this represents the half-shekel paid by each member of the Israelite community toward the conduct of the cult (Exod. 30.11–16). In the background of the scene at the top are hung green

FIG. 42. Panel WB 2. Object in Hand of Attendant

460. The tunics of the men at the right have the rever-like flap already noted on Panel WB 1 (see above, p. 122, n. 425), while at least the man at the extreme left has the tie-string to close the slit at the neck like that shown on Panel WB 4 (see above, p. 104, n. 347).

461. The tunic of the man at the extreme left is blue with a yellow band at the hem, while that of the man at the extreme right is green with a red hem. The pink trousers of the former have a vertical black stripe but those of the latter are apparently a plain red.

462. Num. 10.1 mentions only two such trumpets, but the number was subsequently increased to at least 120 in the days of Solomon (II Chron. 5.12). Josephus describes them as being slightly less than a cubit long (*Antiquitates* III, 291) but those represented on the Arch of Titus must be at least four times that length. Cf. the reproduction in the article of Holzinger cited above, p. 119, n. 409. In spite of the confusion of terminology in the later period of which Sukkah 34a (Trans., p. 152) speaks, it is not probable that the more secular *shofar* is represented here, as has been suggested.

and pink curtains, some with black stripes. Such curtains appear elsewhere in the Synagogue and in contemporary art in an ornamental capacity.[463]

In the lower half of the composition, as we have already seen, the crenelated wall surrounding the temenos of the sanctuary occupies only slightly more than half of the length of the panel. The wall is so placed that sections of the foreground remain available at either side of the picture, and these the artist has developed as elements of "stage space" by substituting for the yellowish gray of the background used above a reddish orange in a well-delimited zone 0.40 m. high. By creating this zone the artist undoubtedly meant to indicate that the area in question does not belong to the temenos depicted above, and therefore lies outside the precincts of the sanctuary. This is a fact of some importance in the interpretation of the subject matter portrayed in it. At the left the zone is developed with a cliché familiar from Roman Imperial art.[464] It shows a man in the vestments of court and Temple holding or swinging a long-handled axe over his right shoulder, while his left hand grasps the horn of a humped reddish-brown heifer. The heifer is properly garlanded for the sacrifice and is drawn rather successfully in a three-quarter position.[465] In the space at the right two further animals are depicted, both done in gray. Both are seen in profile and are excellently drawn. The lower of the two is a spotted ram placed on the base line of the panel, the upper a bullock whose feet are set directly upon the line dividing the "stage space" from the background of the scene. That they provide additional victims for the sacrificial cult of the sanctuary is obvious.[466]

463. For the synagogue see Panels WC 1 and WC 4. For contemporary art see e.g., in the Antioch mosaics, *Antioch*, II, Pls. 40, 55, 60 and *Antioch*, III, Pl. 81. The draperies on the tombstones of Palmyra (e.g., Cantineau, *Inventaire des inscriptions de Palmyre*, VIII, 1932, pp. 20 and 31) probably are more than ornamental in their significance.

464. For analogous scenes in Roman art see e.g., Reinach, *Répertoire de reliefs*, I, pp. 60, 271, 275, 344.

465. There can be no question about the sex of the animal in view of the care with which genitals are otherwise indicated. Note the cast shadows under the heifer and the attendant.

466. The relation of "stage space" to background and of the gray bullock to the "stage space" has its analogy in the Synagogue in the combat scene of Panel NB 1, where the technical aspects of the matter have already been discussed. Cf. above, pp. 95 f.

From a description of the details of the composition it is possible to proceed now to the all-important question: What does the scene illustrate? Clearly it has to do with the Israelite cultus, and forms in this connection a counterpiece to the Holy City and Temple of Panel WB 3 as interpreted above.[467] Yet in view of the artist's tendency elsewhere to associate his compositions with specific incidents of Biblical narrative, it is unlikely that he created this scene to depict the cultus as such. Some particular episode must be alluded to. In searching for a specific event with which to connect his picture, interpreters find themselves confronted with a basic contradiction in the rendering. The contradiction is that between the dipinto "Aaron," which would associate the scene with the period of Israel's Wilderness wandering, when the sanctuary was a portable affair of planks, poles, and curtains (Exod. 36), and the rendering of the temenos wall and the sanctuary itself in a form that is decidedly monumental and permanent in its implications. To resolve this contradiction it must be assumed either that the dipinto "Aaron" is generic in its use, or that in portraying what was described as a sanctuary with an enclosed courtyard the artist could not emancipate himself from his architectural clichés sufficiently to do justice to the portable character of the Wilderness Tabernacle. Of the two alternatives the latter is clearly in closer accord with his normal procedure, as even his treatment of the High Priest's vestments has shown. It seems likely therefore that the scene represents the Wilderness Tabernacle and Aaron himself, and once this is accepted as being the case, a number of details of the rendering become intelligible. The first is the curtain before the central door of the triple gateway, a curtain that is mentioned in the description of the Tabernacle (Exod. 27.16; 38.18), but has no place in the monumental Temple at Jerusalem. The second is the curtains hung in the background of the scene, which represent the artist's effort to show that the construction of the court involved also, as he understood it, the use of "hangings" (Exod. 27.9–15).[468]

The third and most important is the fact that the roof and walls of the Tabernacle are rendered in dark brown and that the brown is extended beyond and below the line of the columns. For the use of this color there can naturally have been no precedent in his knowledge of how temples are to be portrayed. In all probability he has deviated from his models in this particular in order to do what justice he could to the Biblical statement that the Tabernacle was covered with curtains of goats' hair (Exod. 26.7; 36.14).[469]

Once the allusion to the Wilderness Tabernacle has become plain, it is possible also to identify the particular Biblical episode which the scene is supposed to represent. It is the episode described in Exod. 40 and Num. 7 when the Tabernacle was finally erected and Aaron, the priests, and the Levites were installed in office. The event took place on the first of the month of Nisan; that is, at the beginning of the religious year. The day is celebrated in the Midrash as one that had ten distinctions, the most important of which are that it was the day on which the Divine Presence found an abiding place with men, and that on this day through the establishment of the divinely ordained cult the reconciliation of man and God through the removal of guilt could begin.[470] What identifies the episode is not so much the blowing of the trumpets, though they were sounded at New Moons and hence at the beginning of the month of Nisan, but the number and identity of the sacrificial animals portrayed. The consecration of the priests as described in Exod. 29.1 requires the sacrifice of one bullock and two rams, and the animals in question are actually depicted, two in the right foreground and one on the altar respectively. In the left foreground a further animal is shown which can be only the "red heifer" of Num. 19.1–13, whose ashes were used in the "water of purification" to restore ritual purity to those contaminated by contact with dead bodies.[471] The introduction of the "red

467. Cf. above, pp. 110–113.

468. That is, having presented the enclosing medium of a temenos in the only way that made sense to him if it was to be identified as such, he compensated for the inadequacy of his rendering by adding curtains, hoping in this way to do justice to the Biblical description.

469. That is, if he had depicted a tent of goats' hair, the object would not have been identifiable as a sanctuary. Hence he presented what would be recognizable as a sanctuary and varied the rendering in such a way as to take in what he could of the Biblical description. Analogous is the superimposition of the bolster stripes upon the rocks in Panel NA 1; see above, p. 71.

470. Numbers Rabbah XIII, 6 (Trans., VI, p. 517).

471. Some account of the use of the "water of purification" is given in Num. 19.11–22 and Deut. 21.1–9.

heifer'' into the scene would be strange on any assumption that the normal sacrificial cultus is being depicted. On the assumption that the consecration of Aaron and his priestly associates is portrayed the matter is quite intelligible, for according to Num. 8.7 the sprinkling of the Levites with the "water of purification" was a part of the procedure of consecration.[472] It had therefore to be prepared especially at this occasion. Moreover, the artist has followed precisely what is said about the procedure involved in the killing of the "red heifer," for the animal is not permitted to be brought inside the area of the sanctuary and is slaughtered with the use of a hatchet.[473]

What we hear about the killing of the "red heifer" in Num. 19.3 raises one further question; namely, whether the identity of Aaron's assistants in the scene can be determined. According to the passage in question it is actually Eleazar, one of Aaron's four sons, who is commissioned to perform the act that prepares the material for the "water of purification." He is therefore the figure in the lower left corner of the scene. Aside from him there are four assistants portrayed in the court above. Since on the day the Wilderness sanctuary was consecrated two of Aaron's sons, Nadab and Abihu, perished for reasons not to their credit (Lev. 10.1–2), it is questionable whether the four brothers are actually shown here side by side in the Tabernacle courtyard. Conceivably we have in the courtyard alongside Aaron, Ithamar, the second of his surviving sons, and one representative of each of the three important families of Levites; namely, Gershon, Kohath, and Merari.

The interpretation suggested satisfies the details of the iconography, associates the panel with the period of the Wilderness wanderings — making it thus a proper neighbor of the scene of the Encampment and the Miraculous Well (Panel WB 1) — and at the same time explains its relation to Panel WB 3 at the other side of the Center Panel. What the Encampment and the Wilderness Tabernacle inaugurated only foreshadowed, from the later point of view, what Jerusalem and its

Temple brought to monumental and perfect expression.

* * * * *

What has been said about the individual panels of Register B naturally raises the question whether the register as a whole may be said to express some central idea or illustrate a special theme. Already there have been several attempts to answer this question, especially by Du Mesnil du Buisson, Grabar, Sonne, and Wischnitzer-Bernstein; but the interpreters differ, emphasizing liturgical, eschatological, polemical, and Messianic interests, and there is disagreement both about the propriety of including Wing Panels III and IV in the cycle and about the identification of individual scenes.[474]

In dealing with the material from this angle two facts must be kept clearly in mind. The first is that our knowledge of Register B, though superior to that of Register A, is, nonetheless, only partial; for about one third of its paintings have perished and must remain unknown. The second is that a consistent progression of scenes can be established for the register as a whole only by doing violence to the subject matter of certain panels and is in

---

472. Cf. also Sifre to Numbers 7.1, trans. K. G. Kuhn in *Rabbinische Texte, Tannaitische Midraschim,* ed. G. Kittel (1933), pp. 141–143.

473. Cf. Num. 19.3 as interpreted in Abodah Zarah 46b (Trans., p. 229) and Sotah 45b (Trans., p. 235).

474. Du Mesnil du Buisson (*Peintures,* p. 16) includes in the cycle the two Wing Panels and Panel WC 3 (Samuel Anoints David) which he believes was "displaced" to permit the introduction of the Lower Center Panel. He calls the series the "liturgical cycle," indicating by this term that it deals with those relations between Israel and God that are established on the basis of the sacred covenant and come to expression in official cultic acts. Grabar ("Le Thème," pp. 20–23, 28–32), suggesting as the principle of arrangement the "correspondence of the scenes by antithesis" and seeing in the decorations of the Synagogue as a whole a tribute to the sovereignty of Yahweh, finds in Register B a cycle illustrating the *sacra* of the cult and thus a testimony to the conviction that Temple and cult will play an important part in the Messianic age. Sonne ("The Paintings," pp. 290–292, 302) takes Panel WB 2 (Consecration of the Tabernacle) as normative for the theme, and with this as a starting point constructs a sequence of scenes moving about the entire register. The series expresses Israel's claim to the "crown of the Priesthood" and serves to combat the Christian position that with the destruction of the Temple in A.D. 71 this "crown" had been forfeited to the Church. Wischnitzer (*Messianic Theme,* pp. 66–69) argues that the action of the scenes moves from either end of the series toward the Center Panel and displays both the glorious beginnings and the subsequent misfortunes of the Ark of the Covenant, thus illustrating the assurance of the coming of a Messianic age and the element of "travail" that will precede its establishment.

9*

effect impossible.[475] This is by no means to imply that such a progression does not exist in the northern section of the register, but only that the southern section cannot be pressed into the same pattern. Even the suggestion of Grabar that the scenes of the southern section are chosen individually to form contrasting counterparts to those of the northern section does not commend itself as a comprehensive principle of organization, though it does reflect an observable phenomenon.[476]

Once this has been said, it must be affirmed that all interpreters of the material have been right in noting an emphasis on the cultic in the scenes of the register. The Jerusalem Temple occurs at least once and probably twice, the Wilderness Tabernacle twice, the Priesthood twice, and the Ark probably four times. Yet it should be evident also that the register contains scenes whose subject matter is not easy to reconcile with the cultic interest. The least germane to the cultic interest is the scene of the Wilderness Encampment and the Miraculous Well of Be'er (WB 1). Next, perhaps, is the scene of Hannah and the Child Samuel at Shiloh (NB 2). Finally the emphasis in WB 3 on Jerusalem, the site of the Temple, as a world capital can be said at least to exceed the strictly cultic principle.

Whether and by what extension of the interest in the *sacra* a comprehensive and satisfactory basis for the choice of the known scenes can be developed, is the real question at issue. The validity of the suggested eschatological, Messianic, and even symbolic involvements can best be examined in the light of what is known also of Register C. In the meantime it should be evident that the "tone" of the register is determined by the scenes assigned to

the two most important fields of the register at either side of the Central Group, the scenes portraying the Consecration of the Wilderness Tabernacle and its Priests (WB 2) and Jerusalem and the Temple of Solomon (WB 3). Conceivably it is only the allocation of these two scenes that is programmatic, the others having suggested themselves by a process of association more or less clearly discernible. The scenes from I Samuel that form a continuous series on the north wall and on the northern part of the west wall may well have recommended themselves for inclusion on various grounds: because of the Ark, because of the lessons to be learned from the jealousy of God's protection of it and the futility of the nations' efforts to possess it, because of the eminent contrasts between the sanctuaries at Shiloh and Ashdod and the Temple at Jerusalem, because of the contrasts between the faithful and the undeserving priests, and because of the importance of Samuel and Hannah themselves. But above all it must not be forgotten that the entire series lent itself to association with Panel WB 3 (Jerusalem and the Temple of Solomon) by virtue of the Targumic interpretation of the Prayer of Hannah, and that the scenes develop a narrative thread determined by the sequence of episodes in the Biblical text. The element of historical continuity cannot be ruled out and may provide a clue also to the inclusion of the Wilderness Tabernacle and the Miraculous Well of Be'er (WB 1) in the register. Clearly, if the Consecration of the Wilderness Tabernacle (WB 2) was to provide a correlative to the scene of Jerusalem and the Temple of Solomon (WB 3) in the second of the two most important scenes of register B, judged by position, the tendency must have been to look for a series of episodes connected with the Wilderness sojourn that would serve to lead up to it as the series from I Samuel had led up to the scene of the Temple. Actually at least one other scene representing this period was included in the register — that of the Wilderness Encampment and Well (WB 1), which is in fact drawn from the same Biblical context (Numbers) as the scene of the Consecration of the Tabernacle and its Priests. Indeed, in terms of the principle of selection, the representation of the Encampment may take precedence over the Well, the former providing the pendant to that part of

---

475. As when Wischnitzer interprets Panel SB 1 (Dedication of the Temple) as depicting how Joseph's bones were carried to Canaan, and Sonne as portraying the death of Aaron.

476. The difficulty is that if, according to Grabar, Panels WB 1 and 2 balance WB 4 and 3, while SB 1 balances NB 1, the entire group of paintings on the east wall of the chamber must be thought of as balancing NB 2, which, as an introductory scene of the "Samuel Cycle," it scarcely deserves. The fact that contrasting scenes were occasionally placed on opposite walls of the building is evident also in Register C (see Panels WC 2 and EC 2). This is clearly not fortuitous, as the assignment of WC 1 (Elijah Revives the Widow's Child) to a position directly vis-à-vis the door through which the women entered the House of Assembly shows. The only question is whether it is possible from these phenomena to develop a comprehensive principle for an entire register.

Panel WB 3 that portrayed the city of Jerusalem, as the scene of the Tabernacle and its Priests provided the pendant to the part that showed the Temple of Solomon.

Three things might seem to follow from this exploratory discussion of the organization of Register B. The first is that the choice of at least the two scenes flanking the Central Group and calling attention to the Tabernacle, the Priesthood, and the Temple is significant and reflects the intention of the artist to illustrate the formal aspects of Israel's covenant relation to God. The second is that the principle governing the choice of additional scenes may well have been — in part, at least — the result of happy combinations suggested by a wealth of available material, the Dedication of the Temple in SB 1, being a particularly apt selection on historical grounds and in terms of the Festival Calendar. The third is that historical and Biblical context is not without significance for the choice and arrangement of the supplementary material. Further light should be shed on these observations by a study of the panels of Register C.

4. THE PANELS OF REGISTER C

Register C is the last of the Synagogue's decorative zones devoted to the representation of Biblical scenes. Its base line runs about the House of Assembly at eye-level, being separated from the tops of the benches only by the height of the dado. The register is therefore interrupted in its course by the Torah Shrine at the center of the west wall and by the two doorways irregularly placed in the east wall. The wall spaces between these natural breaks, the artists laid out into eleven panels, and of the compositions contained in these panels, seven are preserved in their entirety and the remaining four at least in part. The very extent of its preservation makes Register C the most important in the entire Synagogue, especially when it is recalled that, aside from the Central Group, the two upper registers between them preserve only an equal number of panels. Yet is not only the number of its compositions that makes the register so important. Here for the first time it becomes possible to study the organization of an entire register and thus to obtain perspective upon theories about its supposed theme and function. Here, too, the wealth of the artists' decorative and iconographic vocabulary, and their use of the "continuous style" of narrative composition are illustrated with exceptional clarity in compositions that are not only among the largest, but also the most complex of their entire repertoire so far as we know it today.

While something at least is known of every Panel in Register C, there are regrettable losses. Along the east wall and the eastern half of the south wall, the height of the covering embankment was not sufficient to preserve more than a fraction of the zone devoted to Register C, and on much of this color and outline have largely disappeared. Even where, as on the west wall, the protection afforded by the embankment was at its best, one scene (WC 4) is considerably damaged, apparently by water seeping through the wall from the adjacent street while the room was still in use. During the very last years of the history of the structure, moreover, certain persons who came to visit the building under circumstances not entirely clear to us were permitted to record their visits and reactions in Middle Iranian graffiti and dipinti executed upon the surface of some of the paintings, not without detriment to their artistic intention. Finally, in the last phase of its history, when the great room was being filled with earth in connection with the erection of the embankment in its earlier phases, superstitious or hostile workmen gouged out the eyes of some of the persons represented in the paintings, thereby further disfiguring the compositions. Yet, saving these details, the panels of Register C provide a highly impressive body of wall decoration, vivid in execution, brilliant in color, and expressive in the subject matter they communicate.

Among the several panels, those on the south wall and the first on the southern half of the west wall are related and form a narrative cycle analogous to that in the northern half of Register B. Conceivably this alternation between north and south wall as the emplacement of such cycles implies that if Register A had a similar cycle, it began on the south wall of the building and ended with the scene of Solomon receiving the Queen of Sheba (WA 2). However this may be, the cycle in Register C forms an obvious starting point for the description of the several panels of the register, even though this means beginning with the composition that is the most poorly preserved of all; namely, SC 1. Starting from this point we shall follow the scenes from left to right about the entire room without wishing thereby to prejudice decisions on arrangement beyond the panel WC 1 with which the narrative cycle ends.

Elijah Proclaims a Drought and Leaves for Cherith (?)

Panel SC 1 (fragmentary). H. *ca.* 1.33 m.; L. 1.84 m. (Pl. XXX, 1).

Sukenik, *The Synagogue*, p. 145.

At the southeast corner of the chamber in the vicinity of the south door, the filling of earth introduced into the House of Assembly in the construction of the embankment rose to a height of only about 2.50 m. above floor level. Since it sloped upwards only gradually at first before mounting steeply toward the west, what is preserved of the decorations of this register immediately adjacent to the south doorway is necessarily little. On the

south wall all that remains of the first panel (SC 1) is a narrow strip of plaster *ca.* 0.16 m. high at the left and not more than 0.46 m. high at the right.[477] The surface of the strip is traversed by numerous cracks, horizontal, vertical, and diagonal. It is inscribed at the right with the beginning of a pictorial graffito that extends into the adjacent panel, and, what is more important in this context, has preserved only scant traces of the colors with which it was painted.[478] Enough random traces of pigment remain to show that the background was red, but of the scene or scenes developed against this background, only one small detail is still visible. It is a pair of feet in the lower right corner of the panel. The feet are dark red and seem originally to have been shod with sandals. The person portrayed was not a member of the court or of the Temple hierarchy, since such dignitaries always have their feet encased in soft boots, but he could have been either an ordinary individual or a prophet, and probably wore a chiton and himation.

Of the two feet, the one is in profile, the other in a three-quarter frontal position, which is the common rendering for erect figures throughout the Synagogue, whether standing or moving. If motion is implied, it would have to be motion toward the right, for it is the left foot that is seen in profile; and two facts suggest that this was indeed the case. The first is the position of the figure at the extreme right end of the panel, so close to the frame that the man's garments must have touched the border all the way up to his shoulder. The second is the fact that the artist used the lower edge of the panel as his baseline in drawing the figure, causing the tip of the right foot to project into the framing panel band, which is in itself unusual. It would be doubly strange for the artist to have assigned a figure to this corner position, to have shown his left foot in profile rather than his right, and still to have intended that he should share in whatever action the rest of the scene was supposed to por-

---

477. The benches and the dado account between them for the difference between the height of the filling and that of the strip of plaster belonging to Register C.

478. For the graffito see below, Inscr. no. **68,** p. 320. The surface preserves in addition dim traces of the scratch line that ran the length of the wall and has been commented upon above (see pp. 65 f.), and is pockmarked with holes, as is the surface of the next panel at the right (*q.v.*).

tray. The most reasonable assumption is that he was dissociated from the rest of the action because he was supposed to be moving away from the scene depicted and toward the right.[479]

There is nothing about these insignificant details that would identify the scene depicted. But the panel is the first on the south wall in Register C, adjoins the south door that breaks the continuity of the field available for decoration, and is at the same time adjacent on the right to a series of four related compositions. It is entirely possible under these circumstances that it was associated in subject matter with the panels at its right, forming the first of the series in question. An examination of the other four will show that something is required at their left to introduce the sequence, and will explain our suggestion that the panel portrayed a meeting of Elijah with Ahab and Hiel (I Kings 16.29–17.1), and ended with Elijah leaving for the brook Cherith (I Kings 17.2–3).

Elijah at Cherith and Zarephath

Panel SC 2 (fragmentary). H. *ca.* 1.33 m.; L. 1.69 m. (Pl XXXI).

Hopkins and Du Mesnil du Buisson, "La Synagogue," p. 251; *Rep. VI*, p. 364; Du Mesnil du Buisson, "Les Peintures," p. 116; *idem, Peintures,* pp. 109f.; Grabar, "Le Thème," pp. 14f.; Leveen, *Hebrew Bible in Art,* p. 44; Sukenik, *The Synagogue,* p. 144; Sonne, "The Paintings," p. 326; Wischnitzer, *Messianic Theme,* pp. 22–24.

Of the plaster upon which this panel was painted, much more is preserved than of its neighbor at the left. The line of breakage, following that of the mounting embankment, begins in this instance at the left at a point *ca.* 0.67 m. above the lower border of the panel and rises in a series of irregular jogs to the level of the upper border, which it reaches approximately 0.12 m. before the end of the composition at the right. There are at least three systems of fissures that trace their course through the plaster, two of them at the right being of sufficient depth to produce dislocations and losses of

narrow strips of the surface.[480] Deep holes made with a sharp metal instrument pockmark the plaster and disfigure the one face within reach of the vandals.[481] The end of the large pictorial graffito that begins in Panel SC 1 and the end of a large, still more deeply incised Middle Iranian graffito that begins in Panel SC 3 mar the lower third of the surface at the left and the right respectively.[482]

These defects in the preservation of the plaster upon which Panel SC 2 was painted would be less distressing were more of the composition itself still visible. Actually only a small area in the lower right corner of the scene, an area *ca.* 0.90 m. wide and *ca.* 1.00 m. high, shows elements of outlines sufficiently clear to make an intelligible picture. For the rest we have to content ourselves with color-masses lacking outline, and with tantalizing fragments of outlines that raise more questions than they answer. Two facts, however, these fragmentary remains bring to our attention; namely, first, that the composition embraced two scenes, of which the second is identifiable; and second, that the background color was lighter than that of Panel SC 1.

At the extreme right side of his composition the artist depicted a white city wall whose blocks are outlined in red. The upper part of the wall has faded out, leaving no trace of the crenelations in which it undoubtedly ended, but enough remains to reveal the presence of a tall, narrow gateway the

---

479. The movement is not violent, as in the case of the Exodus Panel (WA 3), for the feet are quite close together.

480. The first system of cracks, beginning at the left, is horizontal with extensions upward toward the top of the panel. The other two systems are vertical. Of these the next in order has an arm that cuts through the figure of Elijah at the hip and descends by way of the projecting ends of his himation to the base of the panel, where it follows an irregular horizontal course to the right. Surface dislocations are particularly apparent in connection with this arm. The last system comes down through the city wall to enter the area of the gate, cuts across the shoulders of the woman before the gate and joins the horizontal extension of the crack farther to the left. The loss of small pieces of plaster is common in the area of this system. All losses and dislocations were repaired when the plaster was remounted at Damascus.

481. The face is that of the woman bending over before the gate. The holes were probably made by the workmen who constructed the embankment in the interior of the chamber. They are common to all panels along the southern part of the chamber.

482. Cf. Inscrs. nos. **68** and **56,** below, pp. 320 and 315–317.

interior of which is done in black.[483] The doorway is framed at the top by a narrow brown lintel capped by an arch, and has brown doors simply paneled in reddish brown that are flung back at either side. In front of the gateway at the right and at the left the artist has portrayed human figures. The one at the right is that of a woman dressed in a short-sleeved white chiton with a red border at the hem, and a reddish brown overgarment that covers the chiton from the armpits to the calves and his gathered about her hips in a wide fold.[484] The woman bends from the waist and reaches toward the ground with her left hand, while her right hand is upraised in a gesture of salutation to the person approaching from the other side of the gate. The results of the artist's effort to show her in this unusual pose are very awkward. He has given her torso in profile, turning it into a three-quarter position at the shoulders to permit the introduction of a frontal face. But for all the profile torso, the legs are drawn frontally, as the width of the skirt and the placement of the black shoes that project dimly below the white chiton testify. Clearly, the frontality that dictated his rendering did not make it easy for the artist to handle narrative materials involving actions of such a character.

At the other side of the doorway a man advances toward the woman from the left. His height is remarkable, being identical with that of the gateway, as a dark color-mass representing the hair of his head indicates, but from the elbow upwards the outlines of his figure have largely disappeared. Above his reddish-brown feet, shod with sandals, the bottom of a white chiton with red clavi outlined in black is visible, together with the folded ends of a white himation ornamented with red two-pronged ornaments. The left arm about which the ends of the himation are rolled was apparently hidden by the right arm that reaches across the man's body toward the woman, the right shoulder being turned slightly forward to permit this gesture.

From the elements of the scene described up to this point, its identification becomes quite clear. The picture represents the meeting of Elijah and the widow of Zarephath, whom he had been divinely instructed to seek out for his own sustenance and whom he met at the gate of the city as she was gathering sticks to build a fire according to I Kings 17.8–16. It will be recalled that in making his request for sustenance the prophet discovered that the widow had at home only enough flour in her jar (כד) and oil in her cruse (צַפַּחַת) for a single meal. These supplies she and her son were about to consume, although knowing that because of the drought no more was to be had. By the intervention of the prophet, we are told, and in view of her act of faith in preparing the meal for him instead of for herself, the jar and the cruse were miraculously made to furnish a continuous supply of flour and oil till the end of the drought. The jar and the cruse the artist has depicted behind the widow, giving them the form of a wide-mouthed brown amphora[485] and a round-bellied white bottle respectively, and placing them one on top of the other. The vessels overlap to its full width the band dividing the scene from its neighbor at the right. This is for the Synagogue artist a highly unusual procedure and suggests that the introduction of the vessels was an afterthought.[486]

At the left of the gate Gute's field copy of the scene suggests the presence alongside of Elijah of another man similarly clad (Pl. XXXI, 1). This second figure was not seen by Hopkins and Du Mesnil du Buisson, and is somewhat embarrassing because in the Biblical story Elijah is quite unaccompanied on his journey and visit to Zarephath. As rendered in the Gute copy, the two figures overlap each other in the manner characteristic of the Synagogue artists when dealing with groups, but since the upper portion of both figures is hope-

483. The black is carried down in the form of a wide band past the end of the door leaves to the very base of the composition. Whether this is anything more than a simple error of rendering, is not clear. It should be noted that wall and gate occupy only a relatively narrow part of the panel compared with the gates of Panels WA 3 and WC 4.

484. The same combination of garments is encountered again in Panel WC 1, where the details are clearer and the costume is more fully discussed. See below, p. 146.

485. The amphora with its tall angular handles is reminiscent of one of the common Dura forms of green glazed amphorae, see *Final Report* IV, I, 1, Pls. I–VII.

486. Along the framing panel band the white of the city wall was overlaid with a vertical red band, now largely faded out but clearly indicated in the earliest photographs and noted by Hopkins in his field notes. This is more than wide enough to contain the projecting contours of the two vessels but may have been introduced simultaneously with them. If so, it may have been added either to set them off, which seems less likely, or to suggest the widow's house where they properly belong.

lessly indistinct, it is virtually only in the area of the feet and the lower part of the garments that the correctness of the copy can be tested. From a re-examination of the painted surface and the earliest negatives it would appear that the presence of a second figure is indeed possible. Two things point in this direction. The first is that the faint haze of color representing the remains of the background does not close in on the figure of Elijah from the left as close to the probable line of his garment as one might expect, leaving room here for part of another light garment. The second is that dark color-masses to the right and left of Elijah's right foot where the feet of the other figure would have to be, correspond in general to the suggestion of the copy. But today no clearly identifiable outlines of any part of the second figure are visible. If it actually existed, the figure can only have represented Elisha, Elijah's pupil and successor, with whom as a "second Elijah" he could readily be associated in such intimate fashion.[487] The fact that Biblical record brings the two men together only at a later period (I Kings 19.19–21) does not invalidate the identification, for in Jewish legend Elisha is already serving as Elijah's pupil in the episode of the contest on Mount Carmel (I Kings 18).[488]

The portion of the composition examined up to this point covers only approximately 0.90 m. of the length of the panel, leaving some 0.79 m. at the left still unaccounted for. Of this smaller left portion of the composition, only the meagerest traces have survived. The most clearly recognizable are the diagonally folded ends of a himation still visible beginning at a point only 0.11 m. to the left of the right foot of Elijah's probable associate, albeit on a much higher level.[489] At the appropriate distance above these folded ends, which are out-lined in reddish brown, there are to be seen the contours of the roll which the ends of the himation make as they are wound around the left arm before dropping at the side of the figure. Their position is such as to indicate that originally a goodly

portion of the arm was to be seen held tightly against and across the left side of the body. In terms of the Synagogue artists' repertoire of forms, the extent to which the left arm is visible would necessarily imply that the figure, though frontal, was turned slightly and was associated with some action taking place at its own right, that is in the left half of the panel.[490]

Farther to the left the copy records the existence at one time of still other details, among them the sandaled left foot of what can only be a second figure in a similar pose closely associated with the first, and above this foot what may be the roll of the himation about the left arm of the figure in question. Two lines meeting at an angle still farther to the left convey no meaning. Of these additional details no identifiable traces are visible on the plaster today.

Since we are dealing here inevitably with a separate scene, a part of an Elijah Cycle, as we shall see, it seems proper to conclude that the picture originally showed Elijah being fed by the ravens at Cherith (I Kings 17.5–7), the place from which he went to Zarephath. If the copy is correct here also, he was shown already accompanied by Elisha at this time.

The Prophets of Baal on Mount Carmel

Panel SC 3. H. 1.31 m.; L. 1.95 m. (Pl. LXI).

Hopkins and Du Mesnil du Buisson, "La Synagogue," p. 251; *Rep. VI*, pp. 363f.; Du Mesnil du Buisson, "Les Peintures," p. 116; *idem, Peintures*, pp. 110f.; Grabar, "Le Thème," pp. 14f.; Leveen, *Hebrew Bible in Art*, p. 44; Sukenik, *The Synagogue*, pp. 139–144; Sonne, "The Paintings," pp. 326–330; Wischnitzer, *Messianic Theme*, pp. 24f.

Panel SC 3 is the first on the south wall of the chamber the plaster surface of which is completely preserved, and where all the essential features of the composition are still clearly visible. Slightly longer than any of the other three in the same area,

---

487. The designation Διπλοῦς Ἐλίας is that of Chrysostom, *Homilia in Heliam et Viduam, Patrologiae Graecae*, LI, col. 343.

488. Cf. below, p. 143, n. 517.

489. Actually 0.31 m. above the base of the panel and *ca.* 0.19 m. above the corresponding part of Elijah's garment.

490. Cf. e.g., the way in which the free right hands of the figures in the neighboring panel SC 3 are inclined toward the central altar from both right and left.

it is at the same time one of the most crowded in the entire Synagogue and one of the most static and schematic. Carefully balanced, the composition is organized about a central axis; namely, a large yellow altar on which a humped bullock lies. At either side of this axial feature stands a group of men. Their height scarcely exceeds that of the altar and their thin, elongated bodies overlap in regular fashion as they stand stiffly and in identical poses, giving rigid symmetry to the major outlines of the scene. The only departure from the lifeless balance thus achieved is provided by a small animated human figure set against a black recess in the die of the altar and by a large serpent, whose uncoiled body stretches across the entire right half of the scene in the foreground, and whose head is raised to strike the small figure in the recess of the altar.

From the relation of the panel to the one that precedes and particularly to the one that follows it, it is evident that we are dealing here with the first of a pair of compositions which taken together illustrate the familiar contest between Elijah and the prophets of Baal on Mount Carmel, described in I Kings 18.17–40. As in the Biblical narrative, the contest follows the visit of Elijah to the widow of Zarephath (I Kings 17) and divides itself naturally into two episodes, one involving the futile efforts of the prophets of Baal to call down fire from heaven upon their sacrifice (I Kings 18.25–29), and the other the success of Elijah in doing, in spite of obstacles, what his opponents had failed to do. The fact that the two episodes assigned to Panels SC 3 and 4 follow the meeting with the widow at the gate in SC 2, shows that we are dealing with a series in which the action moves steadily from left to right; that is, toward the west wall and the Torah Shrine, providing in this way a counterpart to the series already described in Register B, and lending support to the suggested interpretation of the fragmentary scenes of Panels SC 1 and 2.

How the artist proceeded in putting together the elements of his composition, a more detailed study of the scene will show. To the knowledge of these details, the several deep horizontal and vertical cracks in the surface, the dimming of outlines in the upper left corner and at the base of the altar, and the general distortion of the figure of the

sacrificial animal at the top of the altar provide no effective barrier.[491] But the surface generally speaking is uneven, the result of severe pressures in the core of the wall, and the deeply incised Middle Iranian graffito that begins at the knee of the third prophet from the end at the left and continues into Panel SC 2 helps to disfigure the artist's work.[492]

The scene is set against a reddish-brown background with no indication of space and depth. By dint of much crowding the artist has succeeded in portraying four prophets at either side of the altar, the crowding being no doubt intentional to show the numerical strength of Elijah's opponents in the contest, a fact which the Biblical narrative itself underlines.[493] The men are so arranged at the left that the one nearest the altar is seen in his entirety, while each of his associates has the left half of his body hidden by the right half of the body of his predecessor. On the right side of the altar this arrangement is not reversed, as symmetry would require, but actually continued, making the man most remote from the altar, at the end of the file, the one who is seen in full. The arrangement is occasioned, it would seem, by the artist's desire to bring into view in each instance the prophet's right hand which extends limply downward and outward. The gesture contrasts sharply with that of

491. The most noticeable of the vertical fissures is that at the extreme left of the panel, running down through the first of the prophets of Baal at that end. Two major horizontal systems are distinguishable. The first cuts through the left part of the panel at elbow height, runs through the upper part of the altar, where its vertical ramifications disturb the outlines of the bullock, and continues from this area toward the right at the level of the prophets' necks and shoulders. The second reaches knee level at the left, and after passing through the base of the altar continues along the base of the panel. Several minor vertical cracks are visible in the right half of the composition, the most important being one that passes through the first of the prophets of Baal at the right of the altar, disfiguring his face, and moves toward the right at elbow height to run down the garment of his neighbor. Scarcely any of the surface was lost by virtue of this fission, so that the cracks could be repaired without affecting the subject of the composition. Numerous vertical scratches are to be seen along the upper and lower borders, some associated perhaps with the construction of the embankment, others with the dismantling of the ceiling. Instances of eye-disfigurement are mentioned below.

492. Inscr. no. 56, below, pp. 315–317.

493. Cf. I Kings 18.22, Elijah alone against 450 prophets of Baal.

Elijah in the companion scene (Panel SC 4), and may either signify exhaustion and failure, or call attention to the serpent in the foreground.

In executing the painting the artist lavished particular care upon the faces of his eight subjects. Some of them are now rendered indistinct by cracking and abrasion, but all of them were originally done with painstaking attention to a simple formula for frontal rendering. The faces are generally oval, rather than round, and are framed at the top with a goodly but not excessive head of curly brown hair outlined in black. The hair recedes over the eyes but descends between the points of recession to form a semicircular bang over the center of the forehead. The eyes are wide open and heavily browed, a single curving brush stroke being used to paint the highly arched right brow and the outline of the longish, straight nose. The mouth is firm and straight, save where the upper lip is on occasion drawn in one stroke with a mustache, while the chin is round and sometimes heavily shaded.[494] In contrast to the heads, the feet are poorly executed. They are awkwardly drawn, particularly those intended to be seen in a three-quarter position, are insufficient in number, and are often improperly placed in relation to the bodies with which they are to be associated.

Static by reason of the rigid frontality of its figures, the composition is, nonetheless, given a certain vividness by the treatment of the garments which the prophets wear. The garments themselves are as much alike as the figures, consisting of the proper chiton with brown clavi and the himation with a broad two-pronged brown ornament shown diagonally over the left thigh. But the colors are bright and purposely varied, alternate figures on either side of the altar being clothed entirely either in pink or in white.

Between the two files of prophets stands the tall yellow altar, drawn in accordance with a pattern that appears not only in the neighboring Panel, SC 4, but also across the room in NC 1. It has a wide rectangular base and cap from which simple beveled surfaces lead over to the narrow

die.[495] Atop the altar there is a layer of faggots and on these reposes a now much mutilated humped bullock. Enough remains to show that the animal was drawn exactly as on the companion piece, Panel SC 4: its head to the left, green garlands about its neck and its body, the left foreleg doubled back on itself, while the right is extended and hangs over the edge of the altar, and the tail drawn under the body and laid around the outside of the left hind leg.[496] Needless to say, no fire comes down from heaven upon the sacrificial animal in answer to the cries of the prophets.

Up to this point all of the elements of the rendering are explained by the Biblical story as narrated in I Kings 18. For the two remaining details no basis of this kind exists. They are the small figure set against a black field in the face of the altar and the huge serpent in the right foreground. From what is known of the Synagogue artists' conventions, it is clear that the black field represents an interior, and hence that the small figure is standing in an aperture in the altar. The figure itself is indistinct in its details, partly because of the abrasion of the colors, and partly because its face has been disfigured, apparently by the action of those who constructed the embankment. It is clear, however, that the man wears a pink knee-length tunic, pink trousers, and white boots.[497] This

494. As will be seen more clearly on other panels, the mustache divides at its ends. The flesh color here is much lighter than in the upper registers, particularly Register A. The condition of the painting makes it impossible to say whether the faces are bearded.

495. This is of course a simplification of the typical altar form, the bevels replacing the more elegant moldings with which such objects were in fact usually carved.

496. The position of the sacrificial animal is apparently canonical for the Synagogue artists, being identical in all three instances where the immolation of a victim is portrayed. Complete analogies are scarce, for Roman Imperial art usually portrays the animals in procession on their way to the altar, but the several elements of the rendering can readily be recognized in other representations. For a bull on an altar of a coin of Caligula, see H. Cohen, *Médailles impériales*, I (1859), Pl. IX, 18 (where the left foreleg hangs down over the edge of the altar). The position of the animal's legs in the Synagogue paintings is typical of those of the bull in Mithraic reliefs (see e.g., at Dura, *Rep. VII–VIII*, Pl. XXIX), and of dying animals generally in scenes of the chase and of animal combat (see e.g., Reinach, *Répertoire de peintures*, 1922, p. 303). Garlands are more commonly found encircling the horns of sacrificial victims, while in Roman Imperial art the *dorsuale* ornaments the body.

497. The tunic has a dark brown border at the hem and the neck and a single ornamental band running vertically up the front to the neckband. Over the left side of the chest directly at the neck there are to be seen the remains of the rectangular flap already noted on the lesser figures in Panel WB 1 and discussed on p. 122, n. 425.

identifies him as a member either of the court or the priesthood. He faces front and has his right arm extended stiffly downward, while his left is bent at the elbow. In his left hand he seems to hold a round object. The serpent coming from the right raises its head directly at his side, ready to strike him in the leg.[498] Its uncoiled body, rendered in green above and pink below, with black spots superimposed upon the scales of the back, indicates the rapidity of its motion as it passes in front of the prophets at the right.[499]

The interpretation of these details suggested in the Preliminary Report[500] has found general acceptance and can be no longer in doubt. We are dealing with material borrowed from the Midrashic elaboration of the Biblical story and alluded to in both the *Midrash Rabbah* and the *Yalkut Shimeoni*. According to the tradition preserved by these compendia, the prophets of Baal, recognizing from the outset the impotence of their prayers, evolved a cunning stratagem to win their contest with Elijah. The stratagem involved the services of Hiel, the man who is mentioned in I Kings 16.34, as having rebuilt Jericho and who appears here as a member of Ahab's military staff, judging by his Iranian dress. Hiel agreed to hide in an aperture especially provided in the altar and to ignite the faggots from underneath with a "fire" which he held in his hand, as soon as he heard the voices of the prophets raised in supplication. The plan was frustrated by the Lord, who sent a serpent that bit Hiel, "and he died."[501] Since the appearance of the Preliminary Report, a fuller form of the story has come to light in an Oxford manuscript of the *Midrash Debarim*

Rabbah, supplying at one point details that are helpful in interpreting the artist's rendering. The relevant portion of the text reads:

> And the Prophets of Baal knew that Baal was unable to cause fire to come forth of its own accord. What did Hiel do? He stood before the Prophets of Baal and said to them, "Take courage and oppose Elijah and I will make it seem to them that Baal sent fire for you." What did he do? He took two stones in his hands and hatcheled flax and entered inside of Baal, because he was hollow. And he struck the stones one against the other so that the flax was ignited.[502]

Whether or not Baal is equated in this version of the story with the altar, the reference to the procedure by which Hiel expected to ignite the fire elucidates the Synagogue iconography. Hiel probably holds in his left hand the stone against which he has just struck a second stone in his right hand, expecting the spark to ignite the flax held also in the left hand.[503]

The story is interesting in itself as an example of how the effort to answer obvious questions causes older narratives to grow.[504] Its appearance in the Synagogue paintings of Dura makes it doubly important: first, as an indication of the antiquity of Midrashic materials, in this instance a tale hitherto known only from tenth century sources and now shown to have been current in the middle of the third; and second, as an example of the point of view of those who produced the Synagogue paintings. The materials which the artists reproduced in pictorial form were clearly not part of a dead, alien tradition, immutably fixed by the words of a book, but rather a part of a living popular heritage of which the written word was the essential core, but which could and did

498. The serpent's head was mutilated before the embankment covered it.

499. The rendering differs from that common to Hellenistic and Roman art, where the bodies of snakes are usually heavily coiled, and approximates that of the hunting scene from the Dura Mithraeum. Cf. *Rep. VII–VIII*, Pls. XIV–XV, where the animal is in flight.

500. *Rep. VI*, p. 364.

501. Cf. Exodus Rabbah XV, 15 (Trans., III, p. 180) and the *Yalkut Shimeoni* on I Kings 18.26 (Warsaw ed., 1877, II, p. 758 § 214). Ginzberg (*Legends of the Jews*, VI, p. 319, n. 15) suggests that the story was known to Chrysostom, who says that he has seen with his own eyes pits under altars from which priests ignite fires to deceive the credulous and make them think that fire comes from heaven (*Homilia in Petrum et Heliam, Patrologiae Graecae*, L, col. 733). It would seem, rather, that Chrysostom was familiar with temple practises that suggested the development of the Midrashic narrative.

502. S. Liebermann, מדרש דברים רבה (1940), p. 132. Later in the account we are told that the serpent struck Hiel in the heel.

503. To show Hiel under or inside the altar, the artist has apparently adapted to his use the design of altars with single standing figures represented on recessed fields of the die (see e.g., W. Altmann, *Die römischen Grabaltäre der Kaiserzeit*, 1905, p. 246, Fig. 193) transforming the field into a recess by rendering it in black.

504. In this instance the obvious question was: How could the prophets of Baal have been so stupid as to believe that Baal could ignite the fire?

undergo the elaboration of all folk narrative in the best sense of the word. The same phenomenon has already brought itself to our attention in other scenes. Here we find its clearest and most vivid manifestation.

Elijah on Mount Carmel

Panel SC 4. H. *ca.* 1.27 m.; L. 1.75 m. (Pl. LXII).

Hopkins and Du Mesnil du Buisson, "La Synagogue," p. 251; *Rep. VI*, p. 363; Du Mesnil du Buisson, "Les Peintures," pp. 116f.; *idem, Peintures*, pp. 111f.; Grabar, "Le Thème," pp. 14f.; Leveen, *Hebrew Bible in Art*, p. 44; Sonne, "The Paintings," pp. 326–330; Sukenik, *The Synagogue*, p. 138; Wischnitzer, *Messianic Theme*, pp. 25–27.

As already indicated, the last of the panels in Register C on the south wall of the chamber is a companion piece of its neighbor at the left and depicts the success of Elijah's efforts to call down fire from heaven where the prophets of Baal had failed, following closely in this connection the narrative of I Kings 18.30–38. The composition is developed against a monochrome green background and has suffered extensively from cracks, from the dislocation and even the loss of certain sections of the plaster, from wide vertical scars, particularly at the left, and from scratching with sharp instruments in the center and at the right.[505]

505. The most important fissure is that which comes up diagonally from the lower right corner and divides just below the left elbow of the small figure in chiton and himation at the right of the altar. From here one branch continues upwards through the water carrier just above, a good part of whose body is missing and has been restored. The crack creates the impression that the figure below him at the right of the altar is carrying a shepherd's crook, which is not the case. The other branch passes through the altar and turning upward divides once more, one part cutting across the figures at the left of the altar, the other running upward into the mass of fire above the altar. Wide scars, apparently made by falling objects, are to be seen on the face and the clothes of the figure next to the altar at the left. Deep scratches appear at the ends of the tongues of fire, as though someone had tried to emphasize them. Shallow scratches, perhaps forming a pictorial graffito, cover the water carrier in the lower right corner (see Inscr. no. 69, p. 320). The Iranian dipinto, which refers to the scene of the adjacent panel (WC 1), is written upon the figure in chiton and himation at the right of the altar (see Inscr. no. **51**, pp. 310–312).

A Middle Iranian dipinto has been superimposed upon one of the figures at the right. Still, the several elements of the pictures are all clearly distinguishable, and interpretation is not difficult save in one particular.

At the center of the picture the artist has placed a large altar, quite as in the preceding composition. Shape and color are the same, but better preservation brings into view a detail which the counterpart in Panel SC 3 lacked. This is the accentuation of the structural elements and molded surfaces of the altar by the use of wide bands of yellow ochre, a device probably intended to suggest that Elijah built it of twelve stones, "after the number of the tribes of the sons of Jacob," as the Biblical text explicitly states (I Kings 18.31). The white bullock atop the altar is identical with that of the previous scene, only more clearly discernible. For the tongues of fire the artist has used the brightest red on his palette.[506]

Beginning with this axial element the artist has developed the left half of his composition on the same pattern as the preceding scene. He shows here a group of men closely crowded together, dressed in chiton and himation and wearing sandals. The garments are alternately gray and pink, but all have reddish-brown clavi and two-pronged ornamental bands.[507] The men are of somewhat smaller proportions than in Panel SC 3 and their number is reduced to three. The altar too is smaller, and this is in all probability merely because sufficient room had to be saved, both vertically and horizontally, for an adequate rendering of the flames at the center of the picture. The men's faces are analogous in type to those of the preceding panel. Only their pose is somewhat different, for their right hands are raised to the level of their heads and even above it in what is probably a gesture of acclamation, and the left leg of at least the foremost of the group is advanced and bent at

506. The outline of the bullock was corrected at the hump, but the correction was not completed. Similar lapses, apparently on the part of the artists' assistants, are noticeable elsewhere in the Synagogue; for instance, on the hind legs of Mordecai's horse in Panel WC 2, and in the left shoulder line of the figure immediately to the left of the altar in the present scene.

507. The gray garments in the panel all have a slightly greenish tinge, deriving perhaps from the inadvertent mixture of the color with that of the background, and are highlighted in white.

the knee so that the foot actually rests on the base of the altar, apparently indicating, as in the case of the Moses who leads the Exodus (Panel WA 3), the initiation of action.[508] If the pose of the man at the head of the group truly has this significance, it is indeed highly probable that he is Elijah, and that the figures behind him are "the people" whom he summons to come near to him (I Kings 18.30) and for whose sake the miracle is requested and performed (I Kings 18.37).

In the right half of the composition the balance that we would expect, after the analogy of Panel SC 3, is suddenly disturbed. Here the proportions are changed and the field is divided horizontally into two zones, each with a row of figures much reduced in size. Four of the figures are dressed in short-sleeved, knee-length tunics girded up at the waist by a belt, but they apparently wear no sandals.[509] Each one carries a yellow vessel; those in the upper row are two-handled yellow amphorae decorated with red bands and held in such a position that the contents must run out; those in the lower row are large round-bellied water jars similarly decorated which they hold upright on their shoulders.[510] The four figures have been introduced by the artist, without doubt, to illustrate the action resulting from Elijah's thrice repeated instruction: "Fill four jars with water and pour it on the burnt offering and on the wood" (I Kings

18.33). Why the artist attached such importance to the detail should be obvious. Like the original story-teller, he wanted to emphasize Elijah's efforts to raise his miracle above suspicion, a matter that was particularly relevant to him because in the companion piece he had showed the prophets of Baal engaging in a deceitful strategem with the help of Hiel. The four figures whom he has introduced to underline this point are servants, or possibly pupils, of Elijah; their size is a by-product of the composition and does not indicate that they are boys.[511]

The right, unbalanced half of the composition contains yet a fifth figure, the identity and significance of which is in doubt. It is that of a man dressed in gray chiton with reddish-brown clavi and a himation of the same color as the chiton ornamented with a reddish-brown two-pronged band on the ends that hang down from the left arm.[512] The left arm is bent sharply at the elbow, bringing the open hand into position before the shoulder, while the right hand is upraised to a slightly higher level at some distance from the body.[513] The right foot is seen in profile, indicating relation to, or movement toward, the altar and actually reposes on the base of the altar, like the left foot of the man at the left of the altar. The figure is proportionally much larger than those of the servants carrying the water jars, but at the same time a good deal smaller than the three men in the left half of the composition.

In the Preliminary Report it was suggested that the mysterious figure might be that of Elijah's servant, whom the prophet sends to the top of Mount Carmel to look for signs of the approaching rain immediately after the dispatch of the discredited prophets of Baal (I Kings 18.42–44), and who could therefore be thought to have been present also in the earlier stages of the action on the mountain.[514] This suggestion has been rejected quite correctly by Leveen who remarks that as

508. The artist apparently did not find room to portray the uplifted right arm of the second figure. The feet are executed with more care than in Panel SC 3. Elements of the scratch line that runs the length of the wall and whose existence has already been noted above (p. 66) can be seen where it crosses the altar and the feet of the figures at the left.

509. In the top row the tunics are gray and pink respectively and have reddish-brown and black vertical clavi. The figure at the left has a plain narrow border at the hem of his tunic. In the bottom row the tunics are reddish brown, but the colors are so poorly preserved in this area that details of ornamentation are no longer visible. Cracks have obscured the faces of two of the four smaller figures. They seem to be rounder and provided with heavier heads of hair than those of the large figures at the left.

510. The four figures provide an interesting example of the care with which the artist handles such matters as pose. Those with the amphorae in the pouring position are drawn with the right knee bent and the foot advanced, indicating intense action as they move toward the altar, while those carrying the round water jars on their shoulders, though moving toward the left as the profile rendering of the right foot indicates, are walking at a leisurely pace.

511. In the *Seder Eliyahu Rabbah* 17 (*Tanna debe Eliyahu*, Warsaw, 1873, p. 116), Elijah's pupils bring the water.

512. The Iranian dipinto mentioned above is written on the himation at the level of the stomach. It does not concern the scene depicted.

513. The impression that the figure holds a shepherd's crook in its left hand is an illusion caused by a crack in the plaster. Cf. above, p. 141, n. 505.

514. *Rep. VI*, p. 363.

Elijah's servant the man would need to wear garments of another type. Leveen's own suggestion, however; namely that he is a "(young) priest" (like the two on the other side of the altar with Elijah) is unacceptable for the same reason.[515] Du Mesnil du Buisson has made a passing allusion to Elisha,[516] and in view of the second figure conceivably associated with Elijah in the panel dealing with the widow of Zarephath, which we have said might be Elisha, this allusive suggestion is not to be dismissed lightly. As a matter of fact, rabbinical legend, which transforms the relationship of Elijah and Elisha into that of a rabbi and pupil, actually brings the two men together before the period to which I Kings 19.19–21 assigns their meeting, and tells the story of a special miracle associated with the presence of Elisha at the contest on Mount Carmel.[517]

While in the present form of the composition the figure in white at the right of the altar should probably be taken to represent Elisha, it may originally have been none other than Elijah himself.[518] A plausible basis for this suggestion can be developed from a study of the "telescoping" illustrated by this and other panels. The discussion of this matter belongs properly to another context and to the consideration of the compositions as examples of "narrative art."[519]

Taken together, the two panels depicting the contest on Mount Carmel illustrate in graphic style the traditional confidence in the superiority of the faith of Israel over pagan religion, falling in line on this count with the scene of the Ark in the land of the Philistines (Panel WB 4), and deserving in the eyes of the local Jewish community the prominence and the space assigned to them.[520]

515. *Hebrew Bible in Art*, p. 44. Priests do not wear civilian garments in the Synagogue, nor is size in this instance an indication of age, as has been pointed out above.

516. *Peintures*, p. 112.

517. On Elijah and Elisha discussing the words of the Torah, which made it impossible for the angel of death to gain control over them, see *Seder Eliyahu Rabbah* 5, (*Tanna debe Eliyahu*, p. 42.) On the presence of Elisha at Mount Carmel, *ibid.*, 17, *op. cit.*, p. 116.

518. So Schneid, *The Paintings*, p. 21, and Du Mesnil du Buisson, *Peintures*, p. 112. The suggestion was also advanced independently by Kurt Weitzmann, whose line of reasoning is here followed.

519. See below, pp. 385–390, especially p. 388.

520. The artist and the community were apparently not disturbed as some of the rabbis were by the fact that the

Elijah Revives the Widow's Child

Panel WC 1. H. 1.30 m.; L. 2.42 m. (Pl. LXIII).

Rep. VI, pp. 362f.; Du Mesnil du Buisson, "Les Peintures," p. 117; *idem, Peintures*, pp. 113–115; Grabar, "Le Thème," pp. 14f., 18, 20, 29; Leveen, *Hebrew Bible in Art*, pp. 43f.; Sonne, "The Paintings," pp. 326–330; Wischnitzer, *Messianic Theme*, pp. 28f.

With the panel under discussion here, the series of scenes from the life of Elijah turns the corner of the room and continues on the more important west wall quite as did the series from I Samuel in Register B. The turn is associated with a significant change in the nature and quality of the compositions, for whereas on the south wall the panels were crowded with figures and showed on occasion a lack of balance, here in Panel WC 1 in a much longer field only three adult persons are portrayed, arranged in perfect balance, and used to develop an action that moves from left to right with the utmost clarity and simplicity. The composition begins at the left with the tall buxom figure of a woman in somber clothing holding a nude limp child in her outstretched arms. The limpness of the child implies that it is dead, and the woman's gesture that she is handing it to someone. The center of the composition is taken up with the figure of a man on an elaborate couch. It is he who has received the child, which he now holds upright in his arms, presenting it to view, as the Hand of God appears from the right above him in token of the miracle of the child's revivification. At the right the woman reappears, this time in clothes of a gayer color, holding the active, clothed infant in her left arm, while with her right she gestures toward the man on the couch who has restored it to her alive. Nothing could be simpler or more direct than this rendering of a very dramatic episode of Biblical story.

So far as Biblical narrative goes, the picture could illustrate either Elijah reviving the son of the widow of Zarephath (I Kings 17.17–24) or Elisha restoring to life the child of the Shunamite woman (II Kings 4.18–37). The stories are virtually identi-

sacrifice occurred at a place other than in the Temple at Jerusalem. Whether the relation to the *minḥa* was at all considered is quite beyond our knowledge.

cal, each telling how the prophet takes the child to his bed and how, after the prayer of intercession has evoked the divine intervention, he returns it to its mother. That the artists intended the scene to be understood as referring to Elijah is indicated by the Aramaic *titulus* inscribed on the rail of the bed, containing merely the name "Elijah."[521]

The composition with its dull red background has suffered damage and disfigurement of various kinds, as a study of its details, otherwise particularly rewarding in this instance, clearly reveals. Heavy fissures may be seen tracing a horizontal course through the plaster at the level of the bed rail and in the background above the heads of the figures. These have occasioned the loss of parts of the plaster surface in the upper part of the panel and are associated with a number of minor shallow diagonal cracks.[522] Vertical scars are visible especially along the upper part of the scene, where they have disfigured Elijah's face and have helped to render unrecognizable the figure of the child held in his arms. The eyes of the widow and the child at the left, and the left eye of the widow at the right have been gouged out; a Middle Iranian graffito has been incised deeply upon the background above the couch; another may be more superficially inscribed upon the footstool under the bed. Middle Iranian dipinti appear upon Elijah's foot and on the foot of the revived child.[523]

Of the three major figures in the composition, that of the widow at the left side of the panel is by all odds the most interesting. The artist is apparently anxious to show the woman's attachment to the dead child, and possibly to indicate her confident reliance upon the prophet to whom the child is being given. For this reason, it would seem, he

has departed from his usual frontal rendering and has shown her face in profile. Certain limitations in his ability to handle profile figures are indicated, for from the waist down he seems to revert to his frontal conventions. The widow is dressed in a dark brown garment that is wrapped around the lower part of her body, one end being draped over her head. The normal arrangement of this garment is illustrated at the right side of the panel where she reappears.[524] It is actually a woman's himation, an overgarment. Over the hips the garment is arranged in a broad horizontal fold that adjusts it to the height of the person and prevents it from dragging on the ground. The end thrown over the head, the folds of which recall those of the end of the men's himation, is held in place by what seems to be a close-fitting white band or cap. The fact that in this head-covering we have a part of the overgarment and not a veil is proven by the identity of the color in which they are rendered.[525] Her feet and the entire upper part of her body are bare, as is the body of her dead child. The partial nudity of the woman and the dark color of her garments provide an important witness to the preservation of ancient Oriental mourning customs by the Jews of Mesopotamia in the late Roman period.[526] On the bare left breast of the widow, clearly outlined above her left arm, Du Mesnil du Buisson believes that he saw three marks representing incisions such as were commonly made in token of grief and are found on occasion in Palmyrene sculptures.[527] The

521. Cf. Inscr. no. **7**, below, p. 271.

522. A good bit of the background above the widow's head in the upper left corner of the panel has been restored, together with all of the lower part of the Hand of God, sections of the body and head of the revived child at the right, and elements of the background above it. Smaller gaps in the plaster occur in the mattress of the bed just below the instep of Elijah's foot and in the draperies hung above the bed. Six lesser cracks can be counted running diagonally downward from right to left: through the upper left corner of the panel, through the skirt of the widow at the left, through the body of Elijah (two), through the body of the widow at the right, and through the lower right corner of the composition.

523. Cf. Inscrs. nos. **55, 49, 50,** and **71,** below, pp. 309 f., 314 f., 320.

524. For analogies, see below, p. 146, n. 532.

525. For actual veils see the Panels of Mordecai and Esther (WC 2) and Pharaoh and the Infancy of Moses (WC 4), pp. 159, n. 593; 174, n. 674.

526. Among the monuments the clearest analogy is that of the bas-relief published by Seyrig, *Syria*, XXI (1940), Pl. XIX (third century B.C.). For literary material see J. Wellhausen, *Reste arabischen Heidentums*, 2nd ed., (1897), p. 181; and A. Marmorstein, *Studi e materiali di storia delle religioni*, X (1934), esp. pp. 80–94. The removal of the sandals is mentioned occasionally in the Bible as a sign of mourning (see II Sam. 15.30; Ezek. 24.17, 23). The removal of garments and sandals may be alluded to in Micah 1.8 (Qeri), where the text should probably be read, "For this will I wail and howl. I will go barefoot and stripped" (LXX: ἀνυπόδετος καὶ γυμνή). The use of dark garments, still the most common feature in western mourning costume, is not unknown in the Judaism of the Talmudic period (see J. D. Eisenstein in *Jewish Encyclopedia*, IX, 1905, pp. 101–103, *s.v.* "Mourning").

527. Examples are to be found in collections at Beirut, Istanbul, and Copenhagen. Cf. H. Ingholt, *Berytus*, I (1934), pp. 40 f.

marks are not visible now and were not otherwise noted at the time of excavation. If they actually existed, their existence would probably tell us more about the extent to which the artist depended upon the patterns currently used in his day to depict scenes of mourning than about the official attitude of the local Jewish congregation toward the Torah, for the latter strictly forbade self-mutilation on behalf of the dead (Lev. 19.28).

Half of the panel at the center is taken up by the massive couch and the figure of the prophet reclining upon it. Seated animals, probably lions, mounted on square plinths form the legs that support its paneled rails. Like the elongated footstool beneath the bed, the frame is yellow, suggesting gold overlay. Upon the frame lies a thick rounded mattress and bolster, both in green, the cloth showing an over-all pattern of diamonds formed by groups of four black dots. The mattress is either decorated or held in place by wide green bands edged in pink. More ornate than any of the other beds and couches portrayed in the Synagogue, it exceeds in its magnificence even those shown on Palmyrene funerary reliefs, whose general character it does, however, vividly recall.[528] Elijah reclines upon the couch in the conventional pose, his left leg doubled back under his right thigh, the right leg extended but bent at the knee. He is dressed in a chiton with elbow-length sleeves and pink clavi, and a himation that has pink bars on its ends and pink two-pronged ornaments at the right knee and the left thigh. The garments are painted a grayish white, but the folds are olive green and the highlights pink. The himation has fallen from the upper part of the body to the waist, where its extra folds are visible, but the artist has apparently over-

emphasized the additional folds caused by the raising of the knee, making it seem as though the garment has two sets of ends, one set laid over the left knee, the other set hanging from the left arm.[529] Cracks and scars have greatly disfigured the image of the child associated with the reclining prophet. Little more can be said about it than that it sits erect in Elijah's extended arms and faces front quite as he does. The features of Elijah's head are similarly marred, but the face is clearly beardless though crowned with a goodly head of brown hair arranged in curls and outlined in black. The type is different from the aged, gray-bearded Elijah of later Christian art, as others have already noted, but is not immature or youthful. Fundamentally it is identical with that of all save one of the men of the Synagogue paintings.[530]

Above the figure of Elijah on the couch, gray cloths or curtains are hung, their folds indicated in black, their surfaces decorated with pink bands. Attached at the upper edge of the panel, they are arranged to form festoons, the second ending at the right behind the Hand of God extended toward the prophet from above. The Hand of God serves here as elsewhere to indicate the divine intervention involved in the revivification of the widow's child. Its flesh color, like that of the other figures in the scene, is lighter than that used in the parallel occurrences of Register A. The fingers of the hand are spread more widely, and the forearm is stockier. The nail of the thumb is indicated, and the fingers are shaded in pink and brown. Whether the hangings beside it are merely decorative or suggest how

528. For a good example of the typical Palmyrene bed or couch see Seyrig, *Syria*, XVIII (1937), Pl. IV, opp. p. 16. The mattress is thinner and more ornate, but the pillow and the figure upon the bed are in the identical position. On the bands around the mattress see above, p. 72, n. 195. All the known couches and beds of Palmyra and both the other couches of the Synagogue paintings (Panel EC 2, Lower Center Panel) have the turned legs familiar from pictures of Roman *lecti*. For the latter see Richter, *Ancient Furniture*, pp. 130–135; and C. Ransom (Williams), *Studies in Ancient Furniture* (1905), pp. 33f., Figs. 15–16. For tables and as the support of backless thrones, legs in the form of seated animals were common in the West and the East. Cf. Winter and Pernice, *Die hellenistische Kunst in Pompeji*, V, p. 2, Fig. 1; and Sarre and Herzfeld, *Iranische Felsreliefs*, p. 214, Fig. 102; p. 218, Fig. 107.

529. The basis for the exaggeration can be seen in the folds created by the raising of Jacob's left knee in Panel NA 1 (Pl. XXVI).

530. The exception is the gray-haired figure of Wing Panel IV of the Central Group (Pl. LXXVIII). Typical chin and lip beards are noticeable particularly on Moses (Panel WA 3) and Aaron (Panel WB 2). Lighter chin beards and mustaches go with important figures in Iranian dress, but can also be seen on the figure in Wing Panel III of the Central Group and on Samuel in Panel WC 3. In the entire Elijah series beards are noticeable by their absence, though mustaches are common. Where chin beards are absent the artist uses a different technique for setting off the face properly; namely, that of shading it heavily at the right (so here). In Panel WC 3 the bearding and shading conventions are used to distinguish between Jesse's oldest and younger sons (Pl. LXVI). It should be noted, however, that in Panel WC 3 the younger sons do not have the mustache commonly found on the Elijah panels and probably on Elijah in this instance.

the three scenes should be divided, it is difficult to say.[531]

In the third and last section of the composition, the widow and her child are again presented. This time the artist has rendered the woman in a frontal pose, with the child comfortably seated in the crook of her left arm and her right outstretched toward the prophet. She has now abandoned her mourning, is therefore completely clothed, and wears bright colored garments. The garments include a gray chiton with elbow-length sleeves and clavi, and a yellow overgarment, the women's himation, wrapped loosely about her, one end fastened over the left shoulder, the other thrown over her head as though it were a veil.[532] On her feet she has solid brown shoes that extend at least as high as the ankle.[533] Her face is an irregular oval and this, together with the firm line of the nose and the mouth, and the heavy outlines of eyes and eyebrows, gives

531. It is noticeable, of course, that the artist has simplified the Biblical narrative in his rendering, for according to the story Elijah takes the child up to the chamber where he sleeps and brings him down again from the chamber when returning him to his mother (I Kings 17.19, 23).

532. For other instances of this costume in the Synagogue, see e.g., Hannah and the Child Samuel at Shiloh (NB 2) and Pharaoh and the Infancy of Moses (WC 4). The end of the himation fastened over the left shoulder and held in place by a fibula is most clearly visible in WC 4. The garment is commonly reproduced in Palmyrene funerary reliefs (see Ingholt, *Studier over Palmyrensk Skulptur*, Pl. XIII). It is worn loose with one end thrown over the head. The head coverings associated with this garment are commonly interpreted as veils (e.g., *ibid.*, p. 67), but the fact that in all instances in the Synagogue the color of the head covering is identical with that of the overgarment argues to the contrary. For the horizontal folds in the garment across the hips there is apparently no parallel at Palmyra, where the common form of sculpture is the bust. The fold may be the *marzab* mentioned in the Talmud (Shabbat 147a, Trans., p. 746). Literally a "gutter," the *marzab* is a roll or pouch that can be made in a garment either for ornament or with the intention of gathering it up. The pink strip running down from the widow's right shoulder is the clavus of the chiton. Such clavi are not otherwise found on the type of chiton worn by women, though they are common on that worn by men. The fact that clavi are present here is indicated by their reappearance on the lower end of the chiton below the overgarment, where their color has inexplicably changed to brown, and is at the same time an indication of the excellence of the garment itself.

533. Solid shoes of ankle height are characteristic of the costume worn by women in the Synagogue paintings. In the case of royal personages, such as Esther (Panel WC 2) and the Queen of Sheba (Panel WA 2) only the tips of the shoes are shown.

her a sober, solemn mien quite in contrast with the happier lively expression on the face of the child, where the features are better placed and executed. The child itself wears a shortsleeved pink tunic that reaches to the knees. Its left arm is outstretched, its right hand, palm open, is raised to the height of its mother's shoulder.[534]

The Elijah Cycle

Before discussing the other scenes of Register C, it will be advisable to consider briefly and in its entirety the group devoted to events from the life of the prophet Elijah. The group forms a counterpart to that which in Register B develops a thread of narrative taken from the early chapters of I Samuel. The cycle from I Samuel, it will be recalled, began on the north wall and continued on the west wall of the Synagogue to the area of the Central Group. It portrayed a series of colorful events associated not so much with the life of an individual person as with the life of the nation under God, pointing to the several circumstances and factors, human and divine, that either disturb or guarantee the eventual fulfilment of the national hope based upon the divinely ordained Covenant. The Elijah group stops one panel short of the all-important central area of the west wall, clearly not so much because of a lack of material or of general importance, but rather, it would seem, because the space immediately adjacent to the Torah Shrine on the south half of the west wall (Panel WC 2) had been reserved by the artist for the scene of Esther and Mordecai. The Elijah scenes so far as we can identify them give much more prominence to the prophet as an individual and to the part which he plays in alleviating the distress of other individuals, but this is only what must be expected, because Elijah's person dominates the Biblical account of his period much more distinctly than Samuel may be said to dominate the events of the early chapters of I Samuel. Yet the prominence of the individual in the Elijah scenes by no means rules out the interest in the nation, as the space allotted to the contest on Mount Carmel indicates; and besides, the national interest expressed is not such as to

534. On a line with the widow's feet can be seen the scratch line that runs the full length of the wall at this height. Cf. above, pp. 65 f.

require the suppression of the individual, thriving instead where, by the instrumentality of men such as Elijah, the welfare of the individuals who make up the nation is furthered.

Studied as a group the Elijah scenes raise certain problems, among them, for example, the problem of order. The most patent departure of the scenes from the Biblical order of the incidents portrayed is the interposition of the two pictures depicting the events on Mount Carmel (Panels SC 3–4) between those dealing with the widow of Zarephath (SC 2 and WC 1). In I Kings 17 the episode of the raising of the widow's son follows directly that of the multiplication of her supplies of oil and meal, and precedes the conflict with the prophets of Baal. The question is why the artist departed from the natural association of the scenes in this particular. It is interesting to note in this connection how the Haggadic tradition related to each other the episodes involving the use by Elijah of miraculous powers. His action in punishing Ahab for his idolatry by suspending the normal rainfall, the action that caused the famine distressing the widow of Zarephath, was regarded in later legend as having been undertaken without previous divine sanction. Legend therefore has it that when, upon the death of the widow's child, Elijah requested of God the power to bring the child back to life, God was loath to grant his request, deeming it improper that of the powers reserved for Himself, too large a proportion should reside even temporarily in the hands of one of His agents. Hence before the child could be brought back to life by the prophet, he had first to resign his power over the rainfall, which meant that he had hurriedly to unwind his affairs with Ahab and the idolaters.[535]

It is possible that the arrangement of the scenes by the Synagogue artist presupposes some such interpretation of the early part of the Elijah story, the point being that in a pictorial rendering of the material the only way to make the allusion patent was to bring the revivification scene after those portraying the contest on Mount Carmel, a contest which marks not only the defeat of idolatry, but also the end of the drought that Elijah had pro-

claimed.[536] It is equally possible, however, that the dissociation of the two scenes dealing with the widow is the result merely of pragmatic considerations, and that the space required for the panels and the relative importance of the several scenes was the determining factor in their allocation.[537]

More important than the problem of order is that of the choice of the scenes portrayed. What can be learned on this score has no small bearing upon the identification of the subject matter of Panel SC 1, and upon our understanding of the function of the Elijah Cycle as a whole. The one thing that will be evident in this connection is that the series stresses the events at the beginning of Elijah's career. The whole later period of his work, including many episodes that might have provided fairly good subject matter for pictorial compositions, is left aside, unless it was used in that part of the Synagogue's decorations that was destroyed, which seems unlikely.[538] The identical phenomenon, it should be noted, appears also in later legend, where the call of Elisha is dated back by implication into the period preceding the events on Mount Carmel, and where, of the events following the contest with the prophets of Baal, only the episode on Mount Horeb and Elijah's translation are developed more fully.[539] Why legend should have focused the attention of the pious so largely upon the earliest events of the prophet's career

535. For the general outline of the story and its many variants see Ginzberg, *Legends of the Jews*, IV, pp. 196f. and VI, p. 318, n. 12. Among the original sources see especially Sanhedrin 113a (Trans., p. 780).

536. In the written form of the legendary rendering no such transfer is, or has to be, made.

537. It can be argued quite properly that Panel WC 1 would have had to be much compressed to take the place now occupied on the south wall by Panel SC 3; that to have separated Elijah's sacrifice from the attempted sacrifice of the prophets of Baal even by the turn of the wall was deemed improper, since together they form a pair; and that for the prominent position on the west wall, immediately vis-à-vis the women's entrance, the scene of the reviving of the widow's child was deemed more appropriate than that of Elijah's sacrifice. Certainly the visitors responsible for the Iranian dipinti found the scene of the widow's child among the more significant of the scenes of the Synagogue. For a different approach to the matter of order, see Wischnitzer, *Messianic Theme*, pp. 33f.

538. The most important of the later episodes from the life of Elijah thus passed over are: Elijah on Mount Horeb, Elijah and Elisha, Elijah's protest to Ahab on the death of Naboth, Elijah's refusal to receive the emissaries of Ahaziah, and Elijah's translation.

539. That Elijah's translation should have interested the later Jewish story tellers is natural because it forms the prelude to the second phase of Elijah's career, about which so many stories cluster and in which he reappears upon the scene of history as teacher, guide, and helper of

when dealing with the historical Elijah can be understood at least in part. The stories narrated in I Kings 17–18 bring to expression much more clearly and graphically than those of I Kings 19, 21 and II Kings 1–2 the essential character and function of the prophet as helper of the distressed and champion of the cause of God in his battle against idolatry. Their value in this particular can scarcely have escaped the Synagogue artists, suggesting that they too were interested in calling attention to these aspects of Elijah's career and significance.

It should be noted that later Jewish legend in relating to each other the episodes of Elijah and the widow of Zarephath, and Elijah and the prophets of Baal, as previously reported, provided them with a fitting preamble in the form of a story, expanding the Biblical account of the meeting of Elijah and Ahab (I Kings 17.1). This meeting occurred, we are told, at the house of none other than Ahab's general, Hiel, whose sons had died in punishment for their offense against Joshua's command forbidding the rebuilding of Jericho. At the meeting, presumably at Jericho, Ahab suggested that the sons' death was not to be construed as a divine punishment, for he himself had committed many so-called idolatrous acts without incurring the punishment threatened by Moses; namely, that God would let no rain descend upon the earth if Israel served the idols (Deut. 11.16–17). It was this remark that caused Elijah to suspend further rainfall, thus paving the way, not only for his own distress at the brook Cherith and for the difficulties of the widow of Zarephath, but also for the contest with the idolaters that occurred on Mount Carmel.[540]

The fact that legend not only has thus concerned itself especially with the earlier events of Elijah's earthly career, but has developed elaborate means for the coördination and motivation of them, may not be without some bearing upon the interpretation of the Dura Synagogue murals. It will be recalled in this connection that we have at the beginning of the group of the Elijah scenes not less than one half-panel and one whole panel where

the subject matter is so poorly preserved that the identity of the scenes once depicted here can no longer be determined with certainty from the paintings themselves. The half-panel, forming part of the composition depicting Elijah's encounter with the widow of Zarephath (Panel SC 2), must of necessity belong to the Elijah series and can well be taken to have depicted Elijah fed by the ravens at the brook Cherith. In view of its position at the beginning of the south wall and directly beside an interruption in the east wall, it is inherently likely that Panel SC 1 also belongs to the Elijah cycle. What has been said above about the preamble with which the Cherith-Zarephath-Mount Carmel episodes were supplied in the Haggadic expansion of I Kings 16.29–17.1 provides a feasible basis for the identification and interpretation of Panel SC 1. It should have portrayed the encounter between Elijah and Ahab (I Kings 17.1), where the rainfall was suspended and where the whole series of events, including Elijah's sojourn at the brook and the widow's distress, is begun. If the artist conceived of the meeting of Elijah and Ahab as having turned upon the issue of idolatry, as the legend suggests, the pictorial association of this meeting with scenes depicting, not only the effects of the famine, but also the contest on Mount Carmel, where Elijah routed the forces of idolatry, would have been entirely logical, and the series would assume a unity analogous to that of the cycle suggested by I Samuel. That the artist did actually follow the lead of the legend — which, it will be recalled, makes Elijah's attitude toward Ahab turn upon the latter's attitude toward Hiel — is confirmed by one particular; namely, the appearance and punishment of the selfsame Hiel under the altar in the scene portraying the prophets of Baal on Mount Carmel.[541] The following, therefore, suggests itself as a possible organization of the material in the Elijah Cycle. First, in the larger part of Panel SC 1, beginning at its left the artist depicted the meeting of Elijah and Ahab in the house, or in

the faithful of all ages, and as the one who prepares the way for the coming of the Messiah. Its absence from the Synagogue cycle is not without significance, as will appear later.

540. For the legend see Sanhedrin 113a (Trans., p. 780) and Ginzberg, *Legends of the Jews*, IV, pp. 195f.

541. The possible appearance of Elisha beside Elijah in the scene depicting the prophet's encounter with the widow at the gate (SC 2), and the possibility of Elisha's presence in the scene of Elijah on Mount Carmel (SC 4, see above, pp. 137, 143) follows the example of later legend in dating the relation of the two men back to the earlier days of Elijah's career, as we have already seen. See above, p. 143.

the presence, of Hiel, where, to enforce the threats of Deuteronomy 11.16–17 against idolaters, the prophet bids the rainfall to cease (I Kings 17.1). At the extreme right of the panel, as the remains described above indicate, he showed Elijah leaving the place of meeting under divine orders to seek the brook Cherith (I Kings 17.2). Next, in the left half of Panel SC 2, he portrayed Elijah in a standing position receiving from the ravens the food promised by God (I Kings 17.6) and then in the right half of Panel SC 2, as already indicated, Elijah coming under divine orders to meet the widow of Zarephath (I Kings 17.8–10) to relieve her distress.[542] There follows next the contest on Mount Carmel in which both Hiel and the idolatrous priests are disposed of, and once the contest is concluded, Elijah gives up the "keys of rain," to use the terminology of the Haggadah. Hence there now follows the scene in which the prophet employs the "keys over life and death" in revivifying the widow's child.

To what has thus been said about the beginning and the general development of the Elijah Cycle, a word must be added about its ending. Two matters require brief consideration in this connection. The first is the especial elegance of the bed upon which Elijah reclines in Panel WC 1. The point about the bed is that its ornate character is quite out of keeping with the requirements of the Elijah story, for it belongs to the widow, who is herself so poor that she has to gather sticks outside the city gate to build a fire. The failure of the artist to keep his imagery in line with the requirements of the narrative in this particular may well be the result largely of his lack of concern for verisimilitude in such matters. The position of the scene on the prominent west wall in the lowest and most directly visible register may have suggested to him to depict here a bed more ornate than any of the

others portrayed in the Synagogue. There is, however, a further factor that may conceivably have played a part in determining the iconography. We have already noted above that the story of Elijah and the widow's child has its counterpart in that of Elisha and the son of the Shunamite woman (II Kings 4). In the latter story, it will be recalled, we are dealing with a household of such wealth that it could provide Elisha with a chamber especially constructed and furnished by the family for his use. If in dealing with the origin of these pictures representing scenes from the Bible, we have of necessity to keep in mind the possibility of prototypes, and if in such prototypes a cycle of Elisha scenes, including a virtual duplicate of Elijah bringing a child back to life, has of necessity to be postulated, it is entirely possible that the artist borrowed his iconography of the scene in the bedroom from the Elisha parallel, perhaps for no other reason than that it provided a more sumptuous rendering of the scene and one more appropriate to the prominent position which the picture was to enjoy on the west wall of the Synagogue.

Finally, it is only proper to consider in this connection, at least in preliminary fashion, the function of the entire Elijah Cycle. Much has recently been said on this subject by interpreters of the paintings, to emphasize the eschatological and Messianic associations of Elijah himself and to develop the thesis that either Register C as such, or indeed the entire body of the Synagogue paintings, is intended to demonstrate and strengthen the Messianic hope. Seen from this angle the scene of Elijah on Mount Carmel can be thought to teach the final destruction of the wicked; Elijah's altar becomes the symbol of the ultimate reëstablishment of the cult, or of the reunion of the Twelve Tribes; the encounter with the widow at the gate becomes the occasion for Elijah to instruct her that his own return will precede the coming of the Messiah ben Joseph, who is in fact her son; the revivification of the widow's child becomes a token of the final resurrection; and its position alongside the scene of Mordecai and Esther (WC 2) is determined by the reappearance of Elijah in Babylon in the guise of Harbonah.[543]

---

542. The fact that the artist in portraying Elijah and the widow has chosen to depict the encounter at the gate rather than a scene in the widow's house, where the multiplication of the oil and the meal might have been given more prominence, suggests that the preceding scene was static, requiring the element of motion toward Zarephath in the sequel. If this is so, SC 1 and SC 2 as interpreted would be analogous, for each would begin with a static element (Elijah and Ahab, Elijah and the ravens) and would continue with an element indicating motion (Elijah leaving for the brook Cherith, and Elijah arriving at Zarephath).

543. Grabar, "Le Thème," pp. 14f., 18, 29; Sonne, "The Paintings," pp. 324–330; Wischnitzer, *Messianic Theme*, pp. 21–34.

Three things must be said at the outset in discussing even in preliminary fashion the views advanced by scholars in these matters. The first is that the Messianic and eschatological element of the Jewish faith can scarcely be thought to have been disregarded entirely by those who planned the decorations of the Dura Synagogue, though this does not necessarily mean that the element dominated either the entire system of decoration, or even Register C, in preference, let us say, to the pictures of the Central Group. The second is that, since in Haggadic literature generally a given Bible verse or story can and does conjure up the most amazing variety of associations in the Haggadists' minds — such being the ingenuity of preachers of all times and faiths — any given scene of the Synagogue's decorations undoubtedly had, and was represented in part at least because it could have, many different applications. But this does not prove that a given interpretation was in fact decisive for the choice of the scene by the Synagogue artists and those who advised them. A governing principle must first be established, which means, in the third place, that only after the complete examination of the Synagogue material can a final judgment be hazarded in matters of this sort.

Nonetheless, certain points have emerged from our examination of the Elijah material itself which should be recorded in this context. The first is that the Synagogue decorations, like the Haggadah, emphasize the early phases of Elijah's career, omitting or subordinating the very episodes, such as Elijah's translation, that have the strongest eschatological potential. The second is that the interpretation offered here for the two scenes of Panel SC 1 and of the first scene of Panel SC 2, gives to the Elijah series a greater degree of inner coherence and narrative significance than has hitherto been recognized, and requires of those who would correlate the material of the individual panels with the supposed "theme" of the register, or of the decorations of the Synagogue as a whole, much more careful attention to this narrative factor. So far as the individual panels are concerned, it is obvious that much more weight must be attached in the interpretation of Panels SC 3 and 4 to the thesis that idolatry is subject to divine punishment than has hitherto been done. To what

extent Panel WC 1, like SC 2, as parts of the series, should be thought of as going beyond the complementary thesis that God rescues the righteous from catastrophe, remains to be seen. Only this need be said here, that Haggadic interpreters tend to use narratives such as I Kings 17.17–24 and Ezekiel 37 in different ways. The former serves primarily to attest God's power over life and death in an absolute sense, and thus to show the feasibility of return to life at his pleasure under all circumstances and at any time. The latter is the one that really carries the specific burden of an eschatological restoration, usually in a national sense.[544] It is unwise under these circumstances to generalize too readily about the eschatological significance of the Elijah panels, especially when stories like that of Elijah's translation have been disregarded by the artist, and when other panels of the Synagogue may with greater propriety be said to express the eschatological hope. Of course the intention of the artist and the reactions of preacher and layman to the artist's work are not necessarily identical, but the writer of the Iranian grafitto on the panel is not far wrong when, confronted with the scene, he praises God as the one who gives life in the absolute sense and then goes on to describe this life as "life to all eternity."[545]

So far as the identity of the widow's child is concerned, finally, there appears to be no simple procedure by which one can demonstrate that the artist understood him to be the Messiah son of Joseph rather than the prophet Jonah, or that in fact he was anything more than himself.[546]

---

544. On the interpretations of I Kings 17.17–24, see e.g., *Tanḥuma*, Nosse § 30 (ed. Buber, 1885, p. 41), and on Ezek. 37 the discussion of Panel NC 1 below. The same distinction is made by Christian interpreters between the story of the raising of Lazarus, as showing Jesus' power over life and death in an absolute sense, and the stories of his own resurrection, which make him the "first-fruits" of them that sleep (I Cor. 15.20) and thereby the guarantor of an eschatological resurrection.

545. Inscr. no. **55**, below, pp. 314 f. On Elijah as the one who raises the dead at the end of time see, e.g., *Mishnah*, Sotah IX, ult., and Midrash Daniel, ed. Jellinek, *Bet ha-Midrasch*, V (1873), p. 128 (trans. Wünsche, *Aus Israels Lehrhallen*, II, 1908, p. 74).

546. On the tradition that the child was the prophet Jonah see Ginzberg, *Legends of the Jews*, VI, p. 318, n. 9; and among the texts, e.g., J. Sukkah 5, 1, fol. 55a; Gen. Rabbah 98, 11 (Trans., II, p. 959) and *Pirke de Rabbi Eliezer* 33 (trans. Friedlander, p. 240).

Mordecai and Esther

Panel WC 2. H. 1.30 m.; L. 3.52 m. (Pls. LXIV–LXV).

Du Mesnil du Buisson, "Nouvelles découvertes," pp. 553f.; *Rep. VI*, pp. 361f.; Rostovtzeff, *Dura-Europos and its Art*, pp. 112f.; Du Mesnil du Buisson, *Peintures*, pp. 116–120; Wodtke, "Malereien," p. 61; Grabar, "Le Thème," p. 18; Leveen, *Hebrew Bible in Art*, pp. 42f.; Schneid, *The Paintings*, p. 29; Sukenik, *The Synagogue*, pp. 105f.; Sonne, "The Paintings," pp. 320–324; Wischnitzer, *Messianic Theme*, pp. 29–34.

That a Jewish community living near the frontier of Sassanian Mesopotamia, once it had decided to decorate its House of Assembly with pictures of Biblical scenes, should have included in those decorations a composition depicting episodes from the book of Esther, is probably almost inevitable. The position which those who planned the arrangement of the scenes assigned to it, immediately at the left of the Torah Shrine in the center of the west wall of the chamber, shows how important the subject matter was for them, no doubt both by reason of its connection with the annual celebration of Purim and because it testified to the recognition by a Persian monarch of rights for which Judaism inside the boundaries of the Roman Empire was still struggling.

By all odds the most striking and ornate of the compositions in the lower register of the west wall, Panel WC 2 is fortunately in a relatively good state of preservation, considering the vicissitudes to which it was exposed. Among these vicissitudes, the two most clearly visible in their effects are the settling of the west wall of the House of Assembly, and the pressure exerted against the wall by the fill of the embankment in the street behind the Synagogue. The settling process is reflected in a deep fissure that traces a horizontal course along most of the wall on a level with the top of the aedicula block, and that is particularly noticeable here because it descends temporarily from the register band into the pictorial field, cutting through the faces of a number of the persons represented at the right.[547] Subsequently the pres-

sure of the embankment caused an inward movement of the entire upper part of the wall amounting to several centimeters, a movement that has still further distorted the faces in question and has occasioned the loss of at least one large piece of the plaster surface near the middle of the panel.[548] To these misfortunes suffered by the painting must be added the fact that the eyes of at least two of its figures were gouged out, probably by workmen constructing the embankment, and that at a still earlier time, while the building was still in use, visitors using the Middle Iranian language incised and inscribed records of their visits upon its surface.[549]

Set against a monochrome green background, the composition consists of two scenes readily distinguishable from each other by a change in the relative proportions of the persons depicted.[550] Each scene begins with a strong indication of motion from the left, and ends with a static terminal element by which the motion is arrested. Yet the composition does not for that reason break apart, because at least one person seems to be common to both scenes, and because the emphasis that falls upon the figures in motion in the scene at the left shifts at the right to those that are static, giving an over-all balance and unity. The fact that the direction of the movement in the two scenes matches and continues that of Panel WC 1 and of the four panels of Register C on the south wall,

547. The settling of the aedicula block is indicated by additional diagonal cracks, such as those cutting downward

through Mordecai's flying cloak, through Mordecai's face and right shoulder, through the neck of Mordecai's horse, between Haman and the horse's head, across the chest of the first bystander, through the head of Esther's maid, and along the edge of Esther's left arm. In the lower part of the panel these cracks are occasionally linked by lesser horizontal fissures, such as those that cut across the bodies of the bystanders at the level of their left hands and their thighs, and across Mordecai's horse at the level of its back. The large horizontal fissure in the upper part of the panel probably followed approximately the level of the street behind the building as it was at this time.

548. Because of the prior settling of the lower part of the wall the movement was both inward and downward. Narrow strips of the plaster surface in the area affected are now in a diagonal or horizontal rather than in a vertical plane. Missing near the middle of the panel is a section of the green background and parts of the faces of two of the men attending the scene at the left.

549. Inscrs. nos. **42–48,** below, pp. 300–309. On the particular preference shown for the Esther Panel by the visitors writing in Iranian, see below, p. 337.

550. The same change in proportions can be observed in Panel WC 4, and must originally have been most marked in Panel NB 2.

suggests that the whole arrangement is purposeful, being intended to lead the eyes of the worshipers on from the sides of the chamber to the all-important Torah Shrine in the center of the west wall. At the same time, the fact that in both scenes of this panel the movement begins at the left suggests that the scene at the right should follow that portrayed at the left, both in time and in the narrative of the book of Esther, which is not without bearing upon its identification.[551]

In the first scene, beginning at the left, the Synagogue artist has depicted a man sumptuously attired in regal Iranian garments and mounted upon a magnificent white steed. The horse is being led by a bare-legged figure in an abbreviated tunic, the spread of whose legs continues the motion observable in the hind legs of the horse and in the coat that billows out to the rear of its rider. Witnessing the action is a group of four men in chiton and himation, closely crowded together at the right, each with his hand uplifted in a gesture of acclamation.[552] As to the identity of the scene, there cannot be the slightest doubt. It represents the familiar episode from Esther 6, where the pious Jew Mordecai is finally rewarded for having saved Ahasuerus' life some years earlier. The reward, it will be recalled, takes the form suggested by the Jew-baiter Haman under the impression that it is he whom the king has in mind when posing the question, "What shall be done unto the man whom the king delighteth to honor?" (Esther 6.6). What Haman suggests for such a man is that "royal apparel be brought which the king useth to wear, and the horse that the king rideth upon, ...and let the apparel and the horse be delivered to the hand of one of the king's most noble princes, that they may array the man therewith whom the king delighteth to honor, and cause him to ride on horseback through the streets of the city, and proclaim before him: Thus shall it be done to the man whom the king delighteth to honor" (Esther 6.8–9). This suggestion Haman is required in the story, as in the Synagogue scene, to execute to the advantage, not of himself, but of Mordecai, whom he despises; while the inhabitants of Susa, represented by the four figures at the right, offer their acclamation.[553]

Far from being a pure invention of the Synagogue artist, the composition in its major elements is inspired by a type of composition belonging to standard repertory of monumental imperial art. The type is that of the imperial triumph. In the Imperial art of Rome itself, scenes of triumph normally show the Emperor riding in a *quadriga* followed by detachments of his soldiery.[554] In the East, however, the imperial triumph takes a very different form. On the monuments of Byzantine and early Christian art, triumphing emperors and even saints are frequently depicted riding on horseback, carrying a spear or labarum and accompanied by wreath-bearing victories or angels.[555] Earlier examples of this iconography are to be found on the monuments of imperial Sassanian art, particularly the familiar bas-reliefs of Naqsh-i-Rajab and Shapur, where the triumphant monarch on his charger is accompanied or met by ranks of marching or standing figures.[556] Closely allied to these

551. The Esther story comes to us in a great variety of forms and has received much Haggadic comment and elaboration. Variant texts are available in Hebrew, in two Greek versions, the so-called "standard" and the so-called "Lucianic" (see Brooke, McLean, and Thackeray, *The Old Testament in Greek*, III, 1, 1940), and in two Targumim, the "First" and the "Second" (see de Lagarde, *Hagiographa chaldaice*). Josephus renders the text freely in *Antiquitates* XI, 6 = §§ 184–296. Among the Haggadic treatments the more important are those of the *Midrash Rabbah* and of the *Midrash Megillat Esther* (ed. Jellinek, *Bet ha-Midrasch*, I, pp. 18–24). See also the smaller Midrashim, ed. S. Buber, *Siphre di-Agadath al- Megillat Esther* (1886).

552. The association of the four figures with the action in the left half of the panel (rather than with the scene farther to the right, as some have thought) is required by their proportions and is indicated by the position of the men's feet. Here, as elsewhere in the Synagogue, the fact that the weight of the figure is on the right foot, the foot in question therefore being shown in profile, implies that its primary relation is to the events at its right, hence in this instance to the man on the horse at the left end of the panel.

553. Mordecai is identified in the scene by an Aramaic *titulus* placed under the belly of the horse and giving merely his name. Inscr. no. 8, see below, p. 271.

554. Cf., for instance, the triumph of Titus on the Arch of Titus, that probably identified correctly as the triumph of Marcus Aurelius on a bas-relief in the Palazzo dei Conservatori, and that on the Arch of Constantine (see conveniently Reinach, *Répertoire de reliefs*, I, pp. 274, no. 1; 374, no. 2; and 256, no. 1).

555. Cf. e.g., Peirce and Tyler, *L'Art byzantin*, II, Pls. 1 and 72a (Barberini ivory and gold medallion of Justinian), and the representation of St. Phoibammon in a chapel at Baouit, Diehl, *La Peinture byzantine*, Pl. 4.

556. Cf. Sarre and Herzfeld, *Iranische Felsreliefs*, Pls. XI and XLII.

Sassanian renderings, in all probability because of a common dependence on Parthian prototypes, are the works of the Dura artists, not only the artists of the Synagogue, but also the man who executed in the Temple of Azzanathkona the drawing probably representing Odenath's triumphal reception in the city.[557] The historical importance of the iconographic type for our knowledge of Byzantine art, of Parthian art, and of imperial art generally would in itself make a closer examination of the details of its rendering in the Synagogue desirable. The fact that certain of its elements — for instance, the costume worn by Mordecai and the ensemble of the man and his mount — recur in other parts of the Synagogue decorations make it absolutely imperative.[558] For the interpretation of these details there are available not only monuments of imperial art such as those mentioned above, but the materials of religious, private, and funerary art in which they reappear; for instance, the paintings and graffiti of Dura, the bas-reliefs of Palmyra, the silverware and bronzes of Sassanian origin, and the tomb decorations of Panticapaeum.[559]

Mordecai sits astride the stallion, his left hand holding the reins on the right side of the horse's neck, his right held in front of his chest with the index finger advanced and crooked. The position of the right index finger is meaningless in the present context but perpetuates clearly the models which the artist was copying, where it results from the holding of an object, in all probability a short sword, on the pommel of which the finger rested.[560] Mordecai's shoulders are shown in a three-quarter perspective, permitting his head to be turned full front in accordance with the artist's own preference for frontality and with certain contempo-

rary, and most later, modifications of the basic designs.[561] Mordecai wears on his head neither the heavy military helmet nor the elaborate crown familiar from Parthian coins and Sassanian bas-reliefs, but the soft, slightly pointed cap of the type familiar from Mithraic reliefs and paintings, from satrapal coins, and from Achaemenian sculpture.[562] It is rendered in reddish brown and surrounded at its rim by a white diadem whose ends are represented by zigzag white lines at either side of the large aureole of brown hair, the curls of which are outlined in black. Intentional disfiguration of the features, particularly the eyes, has made the details of the face uncertain; but the outline was heavily shaded at the right, the mouth apparently had a slight mustache, and the chin may have had the thin stringy beard that appears also on Ahasuerus in the right half of the panel.[563]

Over his shoulders Mordecai wears a long-sleeved reddish-brown coat that billows out behind him as he rides. The coat is ornamented along its edges with wide yellow bands and at the wrists of the sleeves with two narrow bands of the same color.[564]

557. See *Rep. V*, pp. 153–156 and Pl. XXXVI; and Rostovtzeff, *YCS*, V, p. 251.

558. The costume is that of all royal figures. It undoubtedly appeared upon the figure of Solomon once depicted on Panel WA 2 and now destroyed, and is further illustrated by Ahasuerus in the right half of the panel under discussion here, by Pharaoh in Panel WC 4, by Saul in Panel EC 1 (where the king is mounted), and by the royal figure in the upper Center Panel.

559. See particularly Seyrig, *Syria*, XVIII (1937), pp. 4–26; Rostovtzeff, *YCS*, V, pp. 219–288; and C. Hopkins, *Berytus*, III (1936), pp. 1–31.

560. Cf. e.g., the index finger of Ahasuerus' left hand at the right end of the panel (Pl. LXV). The omission of the sword is significant, indicating the peaceable nature of the triumph that is being depicted.

561. Among Sassanian representations of imperial triumphs only that of Naqsh-i-Rajab departs from a profile rendering, see Sarre and Herzfeld, *Iranische Felsreliefs*, p. 92 and Pl. XI. In the relevant monuments of Byzantine art; e.g., the medallion of Justinian and the painting of St. Phoibammon, frontality has become standard.

562. The cap appears again on the head of Ahasuerus at the right end of the panel and on the harpist in the lower Center Panel (Figs. 43, 59), but was omitted from the rendering of Pharaoh in WC 4, though his costume is otherwise the same. Whether or not it appeared in the upper Center Panel and in EC 1 is not clear. The cap is probably closer to the *kyrbasia* than to the *bashlyk* or the stiffer *tiara*. For analogies see the reliefs and paintings of the Dura Mithraeum (*Rep. VII–VIII*, Pls. XIII–XVIII), the tetradrachms of Bagadat (G. F. Hill, *British Museum: Catalogue of the Greek Coins of Arabia, Mesopotamia and Persia*, 1922, pp. 195f. and Pl. XXVIII, nos. 7–8), and the discussion of Sarre and Herzfeld, *Iranische Felsreliefs*, p. 52.

563. See below, p. 158.

564. Hopkins' field notes indicate that the coat was ornamented with lines in a deeper red. Traces of these lines in vertical and horizontal pairs still remain but they do not combine to yield an intelligible pattern. Mordecai's coat replaces the billowing cloak common in representations of Sassanian monarchs on horseback. Cf. e.g., Sarre and Herzfeld, *Iranische Felsreliefs*, Pl. VII. The cloak reappears on the hunting scenes from the Dura Mithraeum (see *Rep. VII–VIII*, Pls. XIV–XV), where it is properly worn like a chlamys and is held in place about the neck by a brooch (*ibid.*, Pl. XVI). Above the coat an Iranian graffito is incised in the background of the scene. Inscr. no. **54**, below, p. 314.

Under the coat there appears the typical dark blue tunic held together at the waist by a narrow white belt. It is ornamented at the neck, the hem, and vertically along the front with yellow bands. Dark blue trousers with similar vertical yellow bands and high soft white boots complete the costume. Tunic, trousers, and boots differ only in elegance from the Iranian costume worn by other figures of the court and the Temple personnel in scenes already described, and commonly represented elsewhere both at Dura and at Palmyra.[565]

The white stallion upon which Mordecai rides has already been admired by others as an especially fine example of the work of Oriental, Iranian artists. Typical of many of the best renderings of this favorite animal, both at Dura and in the painted, sculptured, and modeled monuments of the eastern world in general, are the heavy body, the proportionately slender legs, the gracefully arched neck, and the dainty intelligent, closely reined head. Commonly, as on the Sassanian reliefs, the further front leg of moving horses not shown in the jump or the "flying gallop" is advanced and raised, sharing with the further hind leg in the motion of the next forward step. In this particular the Synagogue artist has departed from the most common type of representation, following another convention, quite familiar from other monuments of Dura, in which both front legs are placed firmly on the ground parallel to each other.[566] Carefully outlined in red, the white body of the horse is shaded in green, short supplementary strokes of red, white, pink, and gray being used occasionally; for instance, to render the mane and to show the movement of the hair. On the neck the folds of the hide are carefully outlined, as are also the muscles of the chest. To give this feature particular prominence, the artist rendered it in what is almost a frontal position.[567]

The horse's harness consists of a saddlecloth, here entirely concealed by the rider's garments, an ornamented breastband and crupper that hold the saddlecloth in place, and a bridle.[568] Bow case and quiver are attached to the saddlecloth directly behind the rider. The reddish-brown quiver flares slightly toward the top and is decorated with three yellow bands. It contains a sheaf of white arrows, their ends held together by a thin red cord. The white bow case is marked with diagonal brown spots, intended perhaps to suggest that it was covered with leopard skin.[569] Missing is the scabbard of the long broadsword usually found on the Iranian prototypes of the cliché.

In introducing at the right of the rider the man

565. As worn by royalty in the Synagogue, the costume is noticeably less elaborate in its ornamentation than on the Palmyrene funerary reliefs, in the Dura Mithraeum, or in the drawing from the Temple of Azzanathkona. Yet the basic pattern is one and the same throughout.

566. Hopkins has gathered the material and derives the convention from Assyrian art. See *Berytus*, III (1936), pp. 20f.

567. Emphasis on the muscles of horses' chests is a regular feature of Sassanian bas-reliefs (see e.g., Sarre and Herzfeld, *Iranische Felsreliefs*, Pls. XLI–XLII), but the change in perspective is typical only of the freedom of the Synagogue artists. It should be noted that the artist or

his assistant in filling in the green background has changed the contours of the horse's further hind leg, making it narrower at the thigh. The projected contour line has been brought to light again by the fading of the green background color. Similar unevennesses of execution have already been noted in connection with Panel SC 4, see above, p. 141, n. 506. For an analogy to the rendering of the horse's tail, the several strands of which are here outlined in red, see the drawing in the Temple of Azzanathkona (*Rep. V*, Pl. XXXVI, 3).

568. Fundamentally the conventions used for harness in this scene are identical with those of EC 1, the hunting scenes of the Mithraeum, the drawing of the Temple of Azzanathkona, and the Sassanian bas-reliefs. The only real difference is the degree of elaboration of detail. Here the flying tassels typical of the more ornate Sassanian compositions are missing, and the phalerae are reduced in size and number. The crupper, decorated with a single phalera, is done in brown and is duplicated by a green shadow line. The breastband and bridle are rendered in pink. The two gold phalerae that adorn the breastband, one on each shoulder, where the strap divided before meeting the saddlecloth, are both actually visible, showing the extent of the artist's change of perspective in rendering the horse's chest. The bridle consists of a crown piece, a brow band, and a nose-strap joined by a cheek-piece. The convention which permits the artist to represent both the right and left rein of the bridle on the right side of the horse's neck, bringing the latter down to and under the breastband, is familiar from the hunting scenes of the Mithraeum, from the drawing found in the Temple of Azzanathkona (see *Rep. V*, Pl. XXXVI, 3, and *Rep. VII–VIII*, Pl. XIV), and from Palmyra (see Ingholt, *Berytus*, II, 1935, p. 65 and Pl. XXVI).

569. Quivers of analogous form, though frequently larger, are commonly found on battle and hunting scenes of Parthian and Sassanian origin as well as on scenes of military triumph (see e.g., Sarre and Herzfeld, *Iranische Felsreliefs*, Pl. XLII). Details such as the handling of the arrows are not so clearly represented elsewhere. Attached bow cases curved at the lower end to conform to the shape of the bow are not commonly represented. But see the figurine of the rider reproduced by F. Sarre, *Die Kunst des alten Persien* (1923), Pl. 54; and the bas-relief from Block L8 of Dura, *Rep. VI*, Pl. XXX, 1–2.

who leads the horse, the artist has made his most significant departure from the traditional composition of scenes of imperial triumph. But analogies to the iconography of this detail are by no means hard to find; for instance, in the funerary sculptures of the Tomb of 'Atenatan at Palmyra, where in the blank space beneath the couch of Maqqai the artist has depicted three of Maqqai's servants, one of them leading his master's favorite horse.[570] In both instances the figure of the man leading the horse is shown frontally, but whereas in the Palmyrene relief the horse is led by a halter rope which the servant holds in his right hand, in the Synagogue scene the man grasps the horse's bridle with his right and holds the halter rope loosely gathered in his left.[571] Two other details show significant departures from the Palmyrene analogy. The first is the method by which the artist conveys a sense of the attendant's motion. At Palmyra this is accomplished in classical fashion by putting the figure off balance. There the feet are kept close together, but the legs are set at a distinct angle to the torso, being inclined in the direction of the horse's movement. In the Synagogue scene the artist has used again his typical device for the indication of rapid movement, showing the man's feet spread far apart, the right seen frontally, the left in profile, with the right leg in a firm diagonal line to the body and the left bent sharply at the knee.[572] The second departure

is in the attendant's dress. In the Palmyrene analogy the attendant who leads the horse, even though he is a servant, wears an elaborate Iranian costume of soft high boots, and sumptuously embroidered tunic and trousers, like his master.[573] In the Synagogue he has the scantiest costume of any figure in the entire range of its pictorial material known to us. His feet have neither boots nor sandals and his legs, carefully modeled and shaded and painted in a light brownish flesh color, are bare almost to the hips. To cover his body he has only a reddish-brown long-sleeved tunic ornamented with red wristbands, a vertical band of the same color outlined in black running down the middle of the garment, and a wide yellow border with a red stripe at the hem. About the waist it is held tight against the body by a broad white girdle or sash, which shows gray shadow lines and is ornamented with two red bands that divide it into three unequal parts. At the bottom the tunic is either cut in apron fashion or gathered up at the hips. In the Synagogue the closest analogies are the costumes of the water-carriers in Panel SC 4, which also consist merely of a tunic. But these tunics are not as severely abbreviated or gathered at the hips, and have the typical narrow belt instead of the wide one. For better analogies we must go, it would seem, to the stable and the race track, of which some impressions are recorded in the Roman mosaics of the second century portraying representatives of the circus factions, each with a highly abbreviated tunic held tight against the body by a wide harness-like girdle that covers abdomen and chest alike.[574] Since in these mosaics the charioteers wear high boots, tight-fitting leg- and arm-protectors, and caps, the inference would seem to be that the more scantily clad attendant of the Esther Panel is by contrast to them portrayed as a groom or stable-boy.[575]

To identify Mordecai's attendant by his costume

570. See Ingholt, *Berytus*, II (1935), Pls. XXVI and XXVII, 1.

571. Du Mesnil du Buisson has suggested that the three wavy black lines projecting from the man's left hand represent a whip with which to disperse the crowd or the cord with which Haman had expected to hang Mordecai upon the gibbet (*Peintures*, pp. 117 f.), but this seems less likely. The halter rope, used when the horse was being led riderless to Mordecai, was removed as soon as he mounted it, and is therefore carried properly in Haman's hand. On halter ropes see B. Shabbath 54a (Trans., p. 249). For Achaemenian renderings from the bas-reliefs of the staircase of the imperial *apadana* at Persepolis, see Pope, *Survey of Persian Art*, IV, Pl. 93B.

572. The same stance and device is used, as we have already seen, in Panels NA 1, WA 3, NB 1, SB 1, and SC 4. It reappears in the right half of the Esther composition and in Panel EC 1. A scene from the Alexander Romance in Cod. Graec. 479, f. 8ʳ of the Bibl. Marciana, Venice, closely parallels the iconography (see K. Weitzmann, *Illustrations in Roll and Codex*, 1947, Fig. 133). The legs of the attendant in the scene under discussion are inscribed at the calf and the thigh with Iranian dipinti (Inscrs. nos. **43, 44**, see below, pp. 301–305).

573. Cf. the careful argument on the identity of the figure of the attendants developed by Ingholt, *Berytus*, II (1935), pp. 66–73.

574. See Wirth, *Römische Wandmalerei*, Pl. 12. Analogous is the costume of certain figurines from Seleucia; see W. van Ingen, *Figurines from Seleucia on the Tigris* (1939), p. 142, nos. 425–426, Pl. XXIX, nos. 210–211.

575. The gold bands at the lower end of the tunic might, however, suggest that the wearer is attached to the royal stables, as the king's stable-boy, so to speak.

as a stable-boy seems at first merely to create further difficulties, but leads in actual fact to a clear understanding of the artist's intention. The difficulties are two in number. The first is that the attendant's beardless face, now disfigured by virtue of the fact that the eyes have been gouged out, is surrounded by a heavy aureole of brown hair, its curls outlined in black. This type of coiffure is normally reserved by the Synagogue artist for members of the court and of the Temple hierarchy.[576] It is strange to see it on a stable-boy. The second difficulty is that the Biblical form of the Esther story, while identifying the attendant leading Mordecai's horse as Haman himself, contains not the slightest suggestion that in doing so Haman loses his status as a member of the court.[577] Where, then, did the artist get the inspiration for his rendering? Our suggestion is that the Synagogue artist depended here upon an oral development of the Esther story, upon a form of the narrative known to us from the Midrash Rabbah. In this form of the story, Mordecai, to make Haman's task doubly bitter for him, demands of the courtier services usually performed only by menials; namely, a bath, a haircut, and assistance in mounting the horse. The result, the story tells us, is that Haman has to perform for Mordecai four servile offices; those of bath attendant, masseur, groom, and herald.[578] The allusion to, and the irony of, this later form of the Esther narrative was without doubt clearly apparent to the artist's contemporaries, familiar as they were with the conventions of the day, when they saw in the picture the contradiction implied in the rendering of Haman's hair and in the rendering of his costume.

The third and last element of the scene with which the Esther Panel opens is the group of four figures in the familiar costume of chiton, himation,

and sandals, closely crowded together near the middle of the composition and forming the static mass by which the action of the triumphal procession is set off. Of all the figures of the panel, these are the least plastic and most lifeless. In pose, height, and physiognomy each is exactly like the other, recalling in this connection the rendering of similar groups in Panels SC 3, WC 3, and NC 1. The figures overlap in what is for the artist a standard pattern. Their legs are shapeless cylinders. The left hands and forearms, encircled by heavy rolls of garment-ends, are shapeless and dead. Of the right arms raised in acclamation, only that of the man at the extreme left end of the group is acceptably executed. Right hands for two of the remaining three figures are stuck in at odd places alongside the heads of their neighbors. Only seven feet are actually portrayed.

To vary the monotony of the rendering and to enliven the group, the artist has resorted to two devices. He has supplied two of the figures with light beards, and he has rendered the costumes of the four in various colors: the first white with pink ornaments, the second and fourth pink, and the third yellow with brown ornaments.[579] Even in the execution of these compensating details, poor workmanship is to be noted. The dark lines framing the clavi and the two-pronged ornamental bands are occasionally left incomplete, creating an impression of illusionistic treatment that was clearly unintentional; for instance, on the left shoulder of the man at the right end of the group.

The text of Esther contains no explicit statement in chapter 6 that would account for the presence of this group of people in the scene of Mordecai's triumph. But of course the assumption of the narrator is that Haman's proclamation, "Thus shall it be done unto the man whom the king delighteth to honor," is heard by the crowds who line the streets to watch the unusual procession, and this assumption the *Targum Sheni* transforms into a statement of fact, mentioning particularly partici-

576. On the treatment of the hair in general, see below, pp. 371–374. The other exception is found in Panel NC 1 and will be described below, p. 188.

577. In the Biblical narrative Haman does not lose his rank until in chapter 8 Esther reveals his plot to exterminate the Jewish people.

578. Cf. *Midrash Rabbah* to Esther X, 7 (Trans., IX, p. 118) and for other occurrences of the same narrative Ginzberg, *Legends of the Jews*, VI, p. 477, n. 174. The *Targum Sheni* VI, 11 (trans. A. Sulzbach, 1920, p. 86), in dividing the four offices among four people, reflects a later stage in the development of the legend.

579. The face of the second figure from the left is so poorly preserved that it is impossible to be sure whether he did or did not have a beard, but the latter seems the more likely. The shadow lines marking the folds of the garments are rendered in green, reddish brown, and red. An Iranian dipinto is inscribed upon the himation of the first figure. See below, Inscr. no. **42**, pp. 300f.

pation of the House of Israel in the proceedings.[580] From the point of view of the artist, the association of the group with the triumphal procession, indicated, as we have seen, by the position of the men's feet, is both logical and necessary. The bystanders serve to render objective the fact of the triumph, just as do the flying Nikés of the Hellenized counterparts, and the accompanying hosts of the Sassanian bas-reliefs. It should be noted that the ornamentation of the bystanders' dress is particularly lavish.[581] This may mean only that the artist regarded a more ornate rendering of himation and chiton appropriate to a scene of such regal magnificence, or that he wished to emphasize the dignity and importance to which the Jews of Susa could legitimately, and did by virtue of Mordecai's elevation actually, lay claim.

Compared with the first, the second scene of the Esther Panel occupies a relatively small amount of space. This does not imply that the scene is unimportant. It is in all probability a by-product of the demands made upon the artist by the previous scene, and of the fact that the events in the throne room lent themselves quite readily to a condensed rendering.[582] Into this compact scene the artist has managed to crowd no less than six persons, three of them clearly of outstanding significance. The central figure is that of a king seated upon a magnificent throne. At his left upon a separate throne is seated his queen, arrayed in sumptuous royal garments. From his right a courtier advances toward the king, holding in his outstretched right hand an important document. Upon these three persons and their attitudes the interpretation of

the scene depends. The other three are attendants, naturally associated with the royal presence and with the circumstances of the event portrayed.

King and queen are identified by Aramaic *tituli* inscribed on the dais of the king's throne and under the footstool of the queen's throne as Ahasuerus and Esther respectively.[583] The courtier approaching from the left is unfortunately not identified by a *titulus*.

In its essential elements the throne room scene at the right end of the panel, like the triumphal procession at the left, reflects the iconographic tradition of imperial art. It portrays an audience with a king and belongs to a type of which we have examples also in Panels WA 2 and WC 4, and for which analogies are to be found in the imperial monuments of both East and West. In Roman Imperial art the closest analogies are those of the sculptured fragments from the balustrade of the Roman Forum depicting a seated emperor receiving in audience a female figure, possibly Roma herself; the scene of the seated *Augusti* on the Arch of Galerius; and the scene of the Emperor receiving the submission of the German chieftain on the Arch of Constantine.[584] In the imperial art of the Orient this type of scene has a tradition that can be followed back from the bas-relief of Bahram II holding court at Shapur to the reception of Antiochos I of Commagene by Zeus Oromazdes at Nemrod Dagh and to the audience portrayed on the reveal of the west door of the Hall of the Hundred Columns at Persepolis.[585] The iconographic type as the Synagogue artists knew it is reflected most clearly in Panel WC 4 (Pl. LXIX), where the constituent elements are kept in perfect balance. In the scene under discussion here they have been thrown out of balance by the addition of a feature distinctly foreign to the earlier iconographic tradition; namely, that of the queen with her attend-

---

580. *Targum Sheni* VI, 11 (trans. Sulzbach, p. 85).

581. The clavi on the chitons are especially wide and the two-pronged ornaments appear not only on the lower part of the himation, but also on the part draped over the left shoulder. Single, double, and triple bars appear upon the hanging ends of the garment. The right sleeve of the man at the extreme left has a wide ornamental band on the forearm and another at the wrist. The closest parallel to these lavish ornaments in the Synagogue is to be found on the figure of Moses in Panel WB 1.

582. In the panel as a whole the lack of balance between the two halves of the composition is scarcely to be felt because of the neutral rendering of the bystanders, who, while belonging to the scene at the left, create the impression of a balancing central element separating Haman, Mordecai, and the horse from the throne room scene at the right, the two terminal elements being of approximately equal length.

583. Inscrs. nos. **9–10**, below, pp. 271 f.

584. The material is conveniently accessible in Reinach, *Répertoire de reliefs*, I, pp. 278, 390, and 248. For allusions to the iconographic type, see Grabar, *L'Empéreur dans l'art byzantin*, pp. 85–88.

585. See Pope, *Survey of Persian Art*, IV, Pl. 157A; Humann and Puchstein, *Reisen in Kleinasien und Nordsyrien*, Pl. XXXIX; and Pope, *op. cit.*, IV, Pl. 88. At Nemrud Dagh the audience scene is used to indicate Antiochos' acceptance by the god as the instrument of his epiphany, and therefore involves exchange of the handclasp.

ant.[586] How the artist redistributed the typical figures of the king's own entourage will be evident if the two scenes are compared with each other.

Ahasuerus, at the center of the scene, wears a royal costume similar to that which, in accordance with Haman's suggestion, he has bestowed upon Mordecai in the scene at the left; namely, a soft red cap with a diadem,[587] a long-sleeved red coat, blue tunic and trousers, and soft white boots. The only difference between them is that the king's garments are more ornate, their ornamental yellow bands being woven with continuous scrollwork designs, the surface of the coat bearing in addition conventionalized flower designs and an arm-band apparently mounting a jewel (Fig. 43). Surrounded by a heavy mass of brown curly hair outlined in black, the king's features are regular, though somewhat pointed, this fact being emphasized by the stringy beard and the long pointed mustache. Like all the other static figures of the group, the

FIG. 43. Panel WC 2. Ahasuerus

586. For the association of emperor and queen on the coins and the "family portraits" of Byzantine origin, see Grabar, *L'Empéreur dans l'art byzantin*, p. 27. In the earlier period the analogies are to be found rather in religious art, in the associations of deities and their consorts, as for instance in the bas-relief of Hadad and Atargatis from Dura; see *Rep. III*, Pl. XIV.

587. The zigzag ends of the diadem are to be seen just above the king's shoulders.

king faces full front, his left hand holding the hilt of a long black sword, his right extended toward the courtier who advances from the left.

As for the throne upon which Ahasuerus is seated, this is to all intents and purposes identical with the one portrayed by the artist in Panel WA 2, above. It has a yellow (golden) dais of five steps at the ends of which golden eagles and lions are mounted alternately in opposing pairs.[588] On the dais stands a chair whose seat is supported at either side by golden lions and whose high straight back ends at the top in a horizontal pole or rail. The chair has upon it a soft red striped cushion, and is draped with a cloth of the same color that covers completely both the legs and the back, being rolled over the rail or pole at the top. It is somewhat more ornate than the other thrones depicted in the Synagogue, they being normally, like that of Esther immediately at the king's left, chairs with turned legs and draperies covering only the back rest.[589]

That the Synagogue artist rendered the throne of Ahasuerus like that of Solomon in Panel WA 2, and at the same time differentiated these two so carefully from those occupied by Pharaoh (WC 4), and by the harpist and the royal figure of the Center Panels, was of course not accidental, but the result of intention. He was familiar with the legendary description of Solomon's throne already outlined above, and apparently also knew the tradition preserved in both *Targumim* of Esther, according to which the throne on which Ahasuerus

588. Actually only three pairs of animals are indicated, the artist having failed to watch his proportions as carefully in this instance as in Panel WA 2.

589. Cf. Panels WC 4, the upper Center Panel, and the harpist in the lower Center Panel. See Pls. LXVIII, LXXIV–LXXV, and Fig. 55. The cushion of Esther's throne is blue, and the cloth covering the back yellow. With the throne goes a yellow footstool. The typical throne of the Synagogue differs radically from the backless thrones of Sassanian art, being closer at the same time to the chair-thrones depicted on Achaemenian and Assyrian monuments. (See E. Herzfeld, *Jahrbuch der preußischen Kunstsammlungen*, XLI, 1920, pp. 1–9.) From these it probably derives its high straight back, its cushion, and the cloth with which it is draped. The turned legs, the absence of high arm rests, and the method of draping the cloth over the back recall the chairs of the Hellenistic period. Thrones flanked by lions are typical of deities and are common in the Orient in the period of the Synagogue and earlier. At Dura see the bas-relief of Hadad and Atargatis (*Rep. III*, Pl. XIV) and that of Azzanathkona (*Rep. V*, Pl. XIV).

sat (Esther 1.2) was not his own and not that of his fathers, but that of King Solomon, the one which Hiram of Tyre had built for him with great artifice, and which Nebuchadnezzar had originally brought to Mesopotamia.[590]

The fact that Ahasuerus' throne had to be shown standing upon a dais made it necessary for the artist to assign Esther to a position high above the base line of the panel, lest she seem to occupy an inferior position at the king's feet. This the artist was quite free to do because he had established no

FIG. 44. Panel WC 2. Esther

base-line for his composition.[591] Esther's garments are of a type that reappears in Panels WC 4 and NC 1, and are of unusual interest because they represent the costume of the ladies of the court, a costume not commonly depicted on the monuments (Fig. 44). She wears a tight-fitting blue bodice and a flowing pink skirt that falls from below her breast to the ground, leaving only the tips of her white shoes exposed. Across her lap is draped another garment, reddish brown in color, apparently gathered in a roll at the top and provided with a wide border at the hem. Its ends hang in a series of loose folds beside her left leg. The fabric is ornamented with white dots that form rows at either side of the hem and are arranged in rosettes elsewhere upon its surface.[592] The garment is apparently a cloak that would, if she were standing, be draped about her shoulders. On her head Esther wears a golden mural crown encircled at its lower rim by a wreath. A long white veil ornamented with cross-bands is draped over the back of the crown and falls to her waist.[593] With her left

590. On the legends describing the construction of the throne, see above, p. 89, n. 276. The two Targums explain how the chair came to Ahasuerus in commenting upon Esther 1.2. For a translation of the *Targum Sheni ad loc.*, see Sulzbach, *op. cit.* pp. 19–26. In the First Targum, Ahasuerus, finding it impossible to use the original Throne of Solomon, has a duplicate made which serves him in its stead. In the Second Targum he uses the original. See also the *Midrash Rabbah* to Esther 1.12 (Trans., IX, p. 28) and Ginzberg, *Legends of the Jews*, IV, pp. 159f.

591. If in actual fact her throne stands on a level slightly higher than that of Ahasuerus, this is probably the result of practical considerations, such as the best use of the space available, rather than of the desire to show her superiority over the king.

592. White dot ornaments and patterns are frequently seen on Sassanian textiles. See e.g., Pope, *Survey of Persian Art*, I, p. 694, Fig. 241a, and p. 695; but see E. Kitzinger, *Dumbarton Oaks Papers*, 3 (1946), p. 39. Iarhibol wears a cloak with an analogous pattern of dots in the drawing from the Temple of Azzanathkona (*Rep. V*, Pl. XXXVI, 3).

593. Two types of veil appear in the Synagogue: the one short (as in Panel WC 4; the attendant of Pharaoh's daughter), and the other long, as here. For the long veil there are said to be parallels in Palmyrene funerary reliefs (see Ingholt, *Studier over Palmyrensk Skulptur*, Pls. X–XVI), though it seems probable that the supposed veil is merely the end of the overgarment thrown over the head and used as a veil (see above, p. 146, n. 532). In bas-reliefs of procession scenes found in the Temple of Bel at Palmyra and its Agora, figures of women entirely veiled by their overgarments are shown (H. Seyrig, *Syria*, XV, 1934, Pl. XIX, opp. p. 158; and XXII, 1941, Pl. I, 1, opp. p. 34). To bring the *palla* or the himation over the head was virtually the only form of "veiling" used by the women of Greece and Rome. Where "veils" are referred to in literary texts, usually with a loose use of the term *mitra*, the allusion is often to Orientals (see Preisendanz in *RE*, XXX [XV, 2, 1932], cols. 2217–2221, *s.v.* "Mitra"). In the Orient the veil was more common (see A. Jeremias, *Der alte Orient*, XXXI, 1931), but whether among the Jews it was regarded as an essential part of women's dress is not clear (see S. Krauss, *Talmudische Archäologie*, I, 1910, pp. 189f., 195f.; and Oepke in Kittel, *Theologisches*

hand she touches the edge of the veil in a gesture familiar from Palmyrene sculpture,[594] while her right is held loosely before her. Esther's carefully curled hair is held close to the outlines of her head, its end falling in large rolls to her shoulders. She wears pearl pendants as earrings, a necklace with a double row of beads or pearls, a large jewel or brooch at the center of the neckline of her bodice, armbands and bracelets, and perhaps a ring on the fourth finger of her right hand. The lavishness of her jewelry; the excellence of her costume; the dignity of her pose; and the careful shading of her oval features, neck, and arms, suggest that the Synagogue artist has endeavored to make her the model of queenly bearing and propriety, in keeping with the suggestions of the writer of the Book of Esther himself.

With Esther the Synagogue artist has associated a maid or a lady-in-waiting. Only the upper part of the attendant's body is visible, as she stands behind and to the left of the queen's throne, her right arm extended across the draperies on the back of the throne, adjusting the right side of Esther's veil. The maid's face has been severely damaged by the displacement of the plaster surface in this area already described, but it is evident that her coiffure was somewhat simpler and fuller, though analogous to that of her lady.[595] She wears a light-colored garment, perhaps a sleeveless chiton, its surface heavily marked with loose, curving folds.[596] "Maidens" are mentioned in Esther's ret-

inue at three points in the Biblical form of the Esther story, all three instances belonging to contexts which have no relation to the scene portrayed here.[597] Though pious Jews would doubtless find in the attendant of the scene an allusion to these "maidens," the probability is that she is introduced by the artist largely because of his sense of what was proper for a queen.[598]

Ahasuerus is attended in the scene by two courtiers, both standing at his right. They are beardless but wear the typical heavy head of hair and are dressed in the normal court costume of long-sleeved, knee-length tunic, trousers, and soft white boots. The one behind the throne, only the upper part of whose body is visible, wears a blue tunic. The one farther to the left is seen full front, his right hand lifted in what appears to be a gesture of acclamation.[599] His tunic, embroidered at the cuff, on the sleeve, and down the front with bands set off in black, is pink, but ends in a blue border at the hem line, just above the white trousers. The identity of the two men and their function can be inferred from the analogous scene in Panel WC 4 (Pl. LXVIII), where they are placed one at each side of the throne. The one who has been moved to a place behind the throne because of the introduction of Esther at the right side of the scene, has in his left hand what by comparison with the analogous composition can still be identified as a diptych, his right hand being poised ready to write. He is therefore the king's scribe. The one who still occupies his proper position beside the throne holds in his left hand a short black object with a knob at the top and a flat surface at the base, represented by a straight line (Fig. 45). The same object appears again in the hand of one of the two sleeping attendants of King Saul in Panel EC 1 (Pl. XXXII), and was apparently to be seen originally in the

Wörterbuch, s.v. ad I Cor. 11.6). If veiling was required, the Synagogue suggests that the veil was not normally a separate garment. Pictorial representations are scarce, perhaps the closest analogy being provided by a funerary relief from Edessa (E. Littmann, Zeitschrift für Assyriologie, XXVII, 1912, Pl. opp. p. 382). The long veil depicted in this panel may be the sabnitha mentioned, e.g., in Shabbat 147b (Trans., p. 749) which Rashi interprets as a large cloth falling over the shoulders, the ends of which were sometimes tied together to prevent it from falling off.

594. So already Du Mesnil du Buisson, Peintures, p. 118, n. 1. For examples of the gesture on Palmyrene funerary reliefs, see Ingholt, Studier over Palmyrensk Skulptur, Pls. XI, 2; XII, 1, 3; XIII, 1, 2, 4, etc. The official character of the scene is probably responsible for the absence of any symbol of her domestic authority, which after the analogy of the Palmyrene sculptures, she should be holding in her right hand.

595. The features of the face are less carefully picked out and the face completely unshaded.

596. The garment is identical in treatment, and probably identical in character, with that which the women of the Palmyrene funerary reliefs wear under

their enveloping himation. See Ingholt, Studier over Palmyrensk Skulptur, Pl. X and p. 54.

597. Esther 2.9; 4.4, 16; Josephus (Antiquitates XI, 6, 4, 234); and the Lucianic text of the Greek Esther (Esther A, 6, 2, see Brooke, McLean, and Thackeray, The Old Testament in Greek, III, 1, 1940) mention the maidens also at other occasions; e.g., when Esther went to seek audience with the king.

598. The Queen of Sheba in Panel WA 2 appears before Solomon with an attendant, as we have seen above, pp. 91 f.

599. Cf. the gesture of the attendant in the audience scene of Bahram II at Shapur (Pope, Survey of Persian Art, IV, Pl. 157A).

hand of the left attendant in Panel WC 4.[600] This object could be regarded as a dagger only on the assumption that the artist neglected to complete its rendering in every instance. It is more probable therefore that it represents an object of special

FIG. 45. Panel WC 2. Key

significance entrusted to a specific member of the court. Its shape suggests a key rather than anything else, implying, if the suggestion is correct, that the man is the royal treasurer or chamberlain.[601] Pious readers of the Book of Esther would undoubtedly associate him with one of the "chamberlains" (*sarim*) singled out for approval or disapproval in the text and its legendary renderings, but the probability is that he owes his presence in the scene to the iconographic convention used by the artist rather than to the details of the story.[602]

The scene at the right end of the Esther Panel contains still one further figure, the one in the left

foreground. It is that of a man also dressed in court costume; namely, in a long-sleeved reddish-brown tunic with a wide yellow border at the hem line, white trousers, and high soft white boots.[603] The man's right leg overlaps the legs of those watching Mordecai's triumphal journey at the left, showing how severely the artist has compressed his composition. His left leg is far advanced and sharply bent at the knee. The resultant pose has been taken to imply the performance of an act of obeisance before the king, but is more properly to be interpreted as an indication of rapid or significant movement.[604] The fact that the courtier is actually approaching the king's presence is emphasized by two additional details. The first is the profile rendering of his face, this being one of the few exceptions to the Synagogue artist's observance of frontality.[605] The profile is excellently done, showing that it was not the artist's inability to draw this type of face that caused him normally to use the frontal rendering. Nose, mouth, and chin are well proportioned and highlighted in white. The sweep of the jaw back toward the ear is firm and graceful.

600. On the peculiar circumstances involved in the scene in Panel WC 4, see below, p. 172, n. 657.

601. Because of the angular projection at the base of the object, it cannot be a stylus. Seals of the form and size suggested are apparently unknown. For the fiscal officials of the Persian court see A. Christensen, *L'Iran sous les Sassanides* (1936), pp. 117f.

602. The chamberlains in question include the familiar Hathach whom the I Targum connects with Daniel (Esther 4.5; see also *Midrash Rabbah* to Esther VIII, 4, Trans., IX, p. 105) and Harbonah "of blessed memory" (Esther 7.9; see also *Midrash Rabbah* to Esther X, 9, *ibid.*, IX, p. 119). The *Targum Sheni* VI, 1 (trans. Sulzbach, p. 80) is the only one to mention by name the associated scribe Shimshai.

603. The tunic has a narrow stripe down the front and is held together at the waist by a white belt. From the waistline down, the parts of the cloth forming the front and the back of the garment are not sewed together at the side, giving the lower part of the garment an apron-like character. This is undoubtedly typical of all other instances of the garment, explaining its tendency to flare at the hem, but comes to particularly clear expression in this instance because of the unusual pose of the figure. The border at the hemline continues upward along the sides of the garment to the waist as in Panel WB 2.

604. A formal act of obeisance seems to be implied in Sukenik's description of the scene (*The Synagogue*, p. 106). For actual renderings of *proskynesis*, see the bas-relief of Valerian kneeling before Shapur (Sarre and Herzfeld, *Iranische Felsreliefs*, Pl. VII), and for the later development of the iconography, for instance, the mosaic in the narthex of Sancta Sophia showing Basil I (?) kneeling before the Pantokrator (Diehl, *La Peinture byzantine*, Pl. XXII). The Synagogue artists apparently did not choose to emphasize *proskynesis* as an element of the proper approach to royalty. The midwives stand erect in the presence of Pharaoh in Panel WC 4. Instead, *proskynesis* is associated with supplication to the deity, as in the case of the man clinging to the horns of the altar in Panel NC 1, third part. The pose of the courtier approaching Ahasuerus has its counterpart in the figure of Moses leading the Exodus (Panel WA 3), of David approaching the sleeping Saul (Panel EC 1), and of the Psyche revivifying the dead bodies (Panel NC 1, second part). In each case it merely suggests rapid motion.

605. The other exceptions are the first appearance of the widow in Panel WC 1 and the Psyche revivifying the dead in Panel NC 1, second part.

The head of hair is identical with that assuming the aureole form on members of the court seen frontally. The profile rendering makes it clear that the aureole really represents a mass of hair gathered together in a bun at the back of the head. The second suggestive detail is the position of his hands, of which the left rests on the pommel of the short sword hanging at his side, while the right is extended upward and outward toward the right hand of the king. In the extended right hand the courtier holds a rolled white object that must be a parchment or papyrus document. It occupies in the scene a position directly above and slightly to the left of the open palm of Ahasuerus' extended right hand. On the right sleeve of his tunic the courtier wears an exceptionally ornate arm-band, decorated apparently with a ring of pearls.[606]

The interpretation of this second scene of the panel has given rise to a wide diversity of opinion, at least four different views having been advanced to date. One associates the scene with the episode Esther 3.8–15, where Haman obtains from Ahasuerus permission to destroy the Jews throughout the provinces of the kingdom.[607] A second connects it with the narrative of Esther 6.1–3, when the king, in the course of a sleepless night, had the "book of records" read before him and discovered in this way that Mordecai had never been rewarded for having saved the king's life.[608] According to a third view, the scene despicts Ahasuerus "revoking"

(hoshib: literally "causing to come back") the letter issued by Haman, the one authorizing the Persians to exterminate the Jews in the provinces of the kingdom.[609] Finally, the scene is said to have something to do with "the letter" (hassepher), presumably the Purim letter, which the "lad" (na'ar) is said to be receiving from the king, though precisely how this is to be related to the text is not said.[610]

That no one of the suggestions advanced satisfies the iconography should be evident. There is no reason why the Synagogue artist should have given so much prominence to the attempt of Haman to destroy the Jews, when other more edifying episodes were available in the narrative. The scene depicted is not a bedroom scene, but one of a royal audience. The letter issued to Haman was never revoked, but counteracted by supplementary letters. No one of the several "letters" mentioned in the book was ever issued by the king himself and given to courtiers. The man with the jeweled arm-band cannot be a servant, but must be a courtier of great prominence, and the action which he is performing must be that of presenting a document to the king, not that of receiving a document from the king.[611]

For the interpretation of the scene, the courtier in the left foreground who carries its action is undoubtedly of decisive significance. All reference to the "letters" of Esther 3, 8, and 9 being excluded so far as he is concerned by reason of the fact that he is apparently handing his document to the king, it seems to follow that the action depicts the episode narrated in Esther 9.11–14. Here we are told:

---

606. White dots are used elsewhere by the Synagogue artists to indicate pearls used as jewelry (see e.g., Panel WC 4, the daughter of Pharaoh). The several types of arm-bands that appear in the Synagogue paintings, especially in this scene, are probably to be taken as insignia of rank. See the passage in the *Cyropaedia* (VIII, 2, 8) where it is said that in Achaemenian days no one among the Persians was allowed to have such things as bracelets, necklaces, and gold-studded bridles for horses except as a gift of the king. For the later period see Procopius, *De bello Persico* I, 17, 28. Similar jewel-studded arm-bands appear upon the Magus at the north side of the niche in the Dura Mithraeum (*Rep. VII–VIII,* Pl. XVI, 1).

607. Schneid, *The Paintings,* p. 23. The "pained expression" on Esther's face to which Schneid alludes in this connection is sheer imagination and reads into the art of the Dura Synagogue a subjective element that is quite out of its reach and manner.

608. So originally Du Mesnil du Buisson in *Revue biblique,* XLIII (1934), p. 553. The assumption in this case would necessarily be that the king is seen verifying the scribe's rendering of what was written in the "book of records." For this there is no justification in the text.

609. So Du Mesnil du Buisson, *Peintures,* p. 118, "with some hesitation," and Grabar, "Le Thème," p. 18.

610. So Sukenik, *The Synagogue,* pp. 105f. In view of his bejeweled arm-band, which he wears as a sign of rank (see above), the courtier with the letter cannot be a mere servant. Needless to say, the Hebrew text of Esther nowhere speaks of the king issuing any letter, and the natural inference from the rendering is that the courtier is presenting rather than receiving the document.

611. So far as the four episodes suggested are concerned, there are no variations in their rendering by the two Targums and in the Midrashim (*Midrash Rabbah* and *Midrash Megillat Esther*) that would account for the details of the scene. To make a connection with the Lucianic Greek text of Esther, where the king does not give his ring to Mordecai, would provide too recondite an explanation.

On that day the number of those slain in the palace was brought before the king. And the king said unto Esther the queen, The Jews have slain and destroyed five hundred men in Shushan the palace, and the ten sons of Haman; what then have they done in the rest of the king's provinces? Now what is thy petition and it shall be granted thee, or what is thy request further and it shall be done. Then said Esther, If it please the king, let it be granted to the Jews that are in Shushan to do to-morrow also according to this day's decree, and let Haman's ten sons be hanged upon the gallows. And the king commanded it so to be done, and a decree was given out in Shushan and they hanged Haman's ten sons.

How the artist arrived at his rendering on the basis of this passage is not difficult to understand. The episode suggests as its setting a royal audience at which the king receives the reports of his ministers, permitting the artist to show the king seated upon the Throne of Solomon surrounded by his courtiers. The presence of Esther herself is required by the development of the narrative, and she acts in this instance, not as a suppliant, but as a participant in the development of imperial policy, the matter of further action upon the report being referred by the king directly to her. Hence she can appear seated on a throne beside that of the king, precisely as the artist has rendered her. The presentation of the "number of the slain" the artist has dramatized by showing a man actually handing a document containing the list to the king. For this dramatization the artist's familiarity with the type of document known as *apographē* and with the essentially documentary character of administrative procedure in the Hellenistic monarchies is all that is required.[612]

Why the artist should have chosen to portray this particular episode should be evident in part from what has already been said, but two additional points may be mentioned. First, the episode and the scene representing it bring to expression in a delicate way the fact of the revenge upon those who have threatened the very existence of the Jews in the Persian empire, showing this revenge sanctioned by the king himself. Second, by an easy combination, the episode permits the introduction into the composition of a further detail about Mordecai. The first scene of the panel showed only a passing phase of Mordecai's elevation, his triumphal journey through the streets of Susa. In the earlier verses of the very chapter from which the second scene is taken we are told that "Mordecai was great in the king's house and his fame went forth throughout the provinces, for the man Mordecai waxed greater and greater" (Esther 9.4). If, as a result of his rise, all the princes, satraps, and governors of the kingdom stand in fear of him (9.3), the natural inference is that, as the First Targum actually says, Mordecai has become the "*epitropos*, chief and prince of the house of the king." It is Mordecai, the prince of the court, who might be most readily thought to have presented the "number of the slain" to the king, and whom the artist has in all probability found it possible to include in the audience scene, identifying him for us by the bejeweled arm-band.[613]

In one particular only does the choice of the scene raise any question; namely, in the apparent absence of a reference to the inauguration of the Feast of Purim. Even this the artist may readily be thought to have suggested by the scene, if, as other panels have already shown, he interpreted the episode in terms of its Targumic rendering. It should be noted in this connection that the First Targum of Esther departs from the Hebrew text in reporting Esther's response to the query "What is thy petition?" (Esther 9.12). Instead of having her request permission for further revenge, as in the Biblical text quoted above, it has Esther say, "If it please the king may permission be given to-morrow also to the Jews who are in Susa to celebrate a day of festivity and rejoicing, as it is fitting to do on the day of a miracle." This means that from the point of view of the Targumic tradition, the episode depicted is actually the one authorizing the celebration of Purim, and that

612. A documentary presentation of the evidence to the king might, of course, be said to follow logically from the fact that in the text the king has to transmit the number of the slain orally to the queen at his side.

613. In the hierarchy of the Persian court he would thus represent in all probability the "prime minister." See Christensen, *L'Iran sous les Sassanides*, pp. 108–110.

this authorization, suggested by Esther herself (rather than by the second letter of Mordecai), is effected by the action of King Ahasuerus. If the scribe behind the royal presence was intended by the artist to have an actual part in the action portrayed, which is by no means certain, he should be thought of as ready to take down the festival decree which the king issued in acting upon Esther's request after he had received the "number of the slain." At least, the Jews of Dura, knowing their Targumic tradition, could readily see in the scene the episode authorizing the Feast of Purim.

Thus interpreted, the panel portraying Mordecai and Esther takes its place as the first in a long line of pictures suggested by the Festival Scroll. It is interesting to note with what regularity seventeenth and eighteenth century illustrators of Esther Scrolls fell back upon identical or related episodes in choosing the materials for their pictorial compositions.[614] Lacking the Purim play of the later centuries and being still in precarious outward circumstances, the Jews of Dura dramatized on the walls of their Synagogue those episodes of the narrative that showed most effectively the benevolent attitude of the Achaemenid monarch, placing the panel where it would serve the worshiping community best both in its observance of the festival and in expressing to outsiders the Jews' desire for, and claim to, freedom and security.[615] The brilliance of the court of the benevolent Ahasuerus to which the composition testifies makes this scene the foil to the one directly opposite, where,

as we shall see, the disastrous end of the hostile Nebuchadnezzar and of the Babylonian empire is portrayed (Panel EC 2). If, as has been suggested, the second scene of Panel WC 2 represents the events of Esther 9.11–13, the action of the composition as a whole moves from left to right, continuing uninterruptedly the movement that has been followed in the Elijah cycle, the movement which, in this panel, comes to its natural conclusion at the edge of the Torah Shrine in the center of the west wall.

Samuel Anoints David

Panel WC 3. H. 1.31 m.; L. 1.67 m. (Pl. LXVI).

Rep. VI, pp. 360f.; Du Mesnil du Buisson, "Nouvelles découvertes," pp. 551f.; *idem*, *Peintures*, pp. 126f.; Grabar, "Le Thème," pp. 172–176, 16–19; Wischnitzer-Bernstein, "Samuel Cycle," pp. 95f., 100; Leveen, *Hebrew Bible in Art*, pp. 41f.; Schneid, *The Paintings*, pp. 22f.; Sukenik, *The Synagogue*, pp. 103–105; Sonne, "The Paintings," pp. 316–320; Wischnitzer, *Messianic Theme*, pp. 50–52.

At the right of the Torah Shrine the pictorial decorations continue with what is actually the shortest single composition of Register C, but not for that reason the least important. From the more animated scenes of Panels WC 1 and WC 2, with their more liberal use of space, we return here momentarily to the more hieratic, more compact typè of composition familiar from Panel SC 3 on the south wall (The Prophets of Baal on Mount Carmel). Against a monochrome green background matching that of the panel at the left of the Torah Shrine (WC 2, Mordecai and Esther), he has portrayed a group of eight men closely crowded together and seen in unrelieved frontality. Seven of their number, their heads in a single plane, their bodies stiff and relatively lifeless, occupy two-thirds of the space at the right. The eighth, head and shoulders taller than the rest, stands in a line with them at the left, but extends his unduly elongated right arm across his body and over the heads of the nearest members of the group, touch-

---

614. See, for instance, the scenes depicting Ahasuerus and Esther, and Mordecai riding upon the horse in MS A 6 of the Landesbibliothek Fulda reproduced by Wischnitzer-Bernstein in her article "Esther Rolle," *Encyclopaedia Judaica*, VI (1930), opp. cols. 811–812, Fig. 3. The second scene of the Dura Synagogue provides the background for the hanging of Haman's ten sons, which also is commonly found in illustrations of the Megillah. For the Throne of Solomon in later Jewish art, see the Machsor formerly in the Kaufmann Collection, the relevant page of which is reproduced in *Encyclopaedia Judaica*, VIII, cols. 181–182.

615. The position of the Esther scene on the west wall of the Synagogue beside the Torah Shrine, where it was clearly visible from the women's benches, may, among other things, have been suggested by the position taken in the third century, that women should be required to attend synagogue services on the Festival of Purim (B. Megillah 4a quoted by Leveen, *Hebrew Bible in Art*, p. 43 and n. 1).

ing with the horn in his hand the head of the third in the company at his side.[616]

The scene is crowded against the right side of the panel, as though to keep the large figure of the man at the extreme left out of the shadows of the Torah Shrine. What it represents would not be difficult to guess and is explicitly stated in the Aramaic *titulus* that reads: "Samuel when he anointed David."[617] The composition takes us back, therefore, to I Samuel, the book which the Synagogue artist used previously in developing the scenes assigned to the north wall and to the north half of the west wall in Register B (Panels NB 1–2, WB 3–4). It continues in this book with chapter 16.1–13, where Samuel, having turned away from Saul in anger because of the latter's failure to follow God's instructions to the letter, is sent to Bethlehem to anoint a new king, in this instance from among the sons of Jesse. The story, it will be recalled, goes on to tell how Samuel was led to reject one after another of Jesse's sons as the intended recipient of the unction, until David, the youngest, was summoned from his keeping of the sheep. Upon seeing David, we are told, Samuel anointed him "in the midst of his brethren."

The artist has taken very literally, it would seem, the Biblical statement that David was anointed "in the midst of his brethren," for he has portrayed him as a member of a larger group, moving him as near to the center of this group as he could without putting him beyond Samuel's reach, and keeping his stature on a par with that of his brothers.

David is distinguished from the group to which he belongs in but two ways: first, by the color and arrangement of his himation, of which more will be said later; and second, by the fact that he is set out from the files in which his brothers are arranged at either side of him.[618] Like his brothers he stands with his weight on the right foot, indicating his relation to the figure of Samuel at the left of the panel. But while all the rest overlap each other at the right, so that in each case only a part of the person is actually visible, David is set out from the others, his entire person being brought thereby into view. David's prominence in the group forming the right part of the scene is matched by that of Samuel, who moves toward the group from the left, indicating that from the point of view of the artist it is the relation of these two figures upon which interest is focused.[619] If Samuel's stature exceeds that of David, this is probably the result largely of practical considerations, the difference making it possible for Samuel to reach over the heads of the two nearest brothers in anointing David with the oil from his horn.

Of the several figures in the scene, Samuel is by all odds the most animated. In part this results from his stance, the right leg being set out slightly from the vertical line of the body and providing an opportunity to show the contours of the calf, the hips, and the shoulder. In part it derives from a more careful handling of the lines marking the folds of the garments he wears, particularly on the sleeve of the chiton and over the right thigh on the himation. Both garments are grayish-white, and have the usual ornaments: clavi on the chiton, and two-pronged bands on the hanging ends of

616. The panel has suffered no defacement at human hands. In the upper right background a number of heavy horizontal fissures are noticeable, from which two vertical cracks run down to the base of the panel: one directly at the right of David's head, the other cutting through the head of the last of the figures at the right. A smaller diagonal crack crosses Samuel's right leg. In the lower part of the panel, particularly at the right, the background color has suffered appreciable damage, due apparently to water seepage. On the damage from water seepage in this area, see the discussion of Panel WC 4 below, p. 169. In the extreme upper right corner a deep scar that begins in Panel WB 3 above, cuts down through the frame of the scene, continuing in the field of the adjacent composition (Panel WC 4).

617. Inscr. no. **11**, below, p. 272. The dipinto was written on the green background in the free space at the left of Samuel's right shoulder. It was partly effaced by the abrasion which the surface suffered when the paintings were transported from Dura to Damascus, but had been previously recorded and is still quite unambiguous.

618. For another example of the file arrangement, see Panel SC 3, and above, p. 138. The tendency toward homogeneity of figure and rendering can be seen entering the treatment of groups in Western art; e.g., in twelve men represented on the lunettes of the arcosolium of the Tomb of the Aurelii at Rome (see Wirth, *Römische Wandmalerei*, Pl. 49), but does not come to anything like the artificiality of the Synagogue scene until a later date; e.g., in the familiar mosaics of Justinian and Theodora and their retinue in San Vitale at Ravenna (van Berchem and Clouzot, *Mosaïques chrétiennes*, pp. 154 f., Figs. 197–198).

619. In Christian iconography the emphasis falls even more exclusively upon these two figures. See e.g., the silver dish of the sixth century in the J. P. Morgan Collection, now in the Metropolitan Museum (O. M. Dalton, *Byzantine Art and Archaeology*, 1911, p. 102, Fig. 60) and the Paris Psalter (Buchthal, *The Miniatures of the Paris Psalter*, Pl. III, Fig. 3).

the himation.[620] Samuel wears the sandals that normally go with his costume. He has a head of short curly hair outlined in black, a thin mustache, and a close-cropped beard indicated by a succession of short straight lines. The ear is shown at the left and the face is set off from the hair at the right by a curving white line.[621] The face is much more competently done than the hands, of which the left is held clenched at the side while the right reaches out with the horn toward David's head. The horn is done in reddish brown; it is outlined in a darker brown and heavily shaded underneath at the wider end in the same color.[622]

Beardless, but with his face and the right side of his neck heavily shaded, David stands near the center of the panel in a less animated pose. His hair makes a smooth narrow circle about his head; and he wears the same combination of sandals, chiton, and himation as Samuel and all the other figures in the scene. In two particulars, however, the treatment of the himation departs from that found in most of the scenes: namely, first, that the garment is rendered solidly in purple, its folds highlighted in pink; and second, that it is drawn over both shoulders and is held together before the middle of the body, where it covers completely both hands, its folded ends hanging down between the legs from this point, rather than at the left of the body.[623] The departure of the artist from his usual conventions in these details is naturally of no small importance for the understanding of his intention, and is intimately connected with the nature of the scene depicted. As to the use of the purple color, this may be intended to indicate that David has at the moment of his unction become king, even though

he still wears a himation like his brothers.[624] The way in which David wears his himation; namely, drawn over both shoulders, is probably a by-product of the artist's desire to show David's hand held crossed before him and covered entirely by the folds of the garment. The same convention was used by the Synagogue artists in at least one other composition, Wing Panel IV of the Central Group (Pl. LXXVIII), where its occurrence is perhaps the best single clue to the identification of the scene. Hence its appearance here requires more than passing notice.

Involved in the representation are two distinct elements: first, the crossing of the hands at the wrist, and second, the covering of the hands by the garment. Of these the former is apparently an old *gestus* of adoration and submission familiar in Oriental sculpture since the days of the Sumerians.[625] That it was still used and clearly understood in the early centuries of our era is attested by a passage in the *Babylonian Talmud* which deals with the proper preparation for confronting God in prayer. It reads:

Raba removed (שדי) his cloak, clasped (פכר) his hands and prayed saying, '[I pray] like a slave before his master.' R. Ashi said: I saw R. Kahana, when there was trouble in the world, removing his cloak, clasp his hands, and pray, saying, '[I pray] like a slave before his master.' When there was peace, he would put it on, cover and enfold himself and pray,

620. The fold lines are gray, shaded with pink and red, and the highlights white. Particularly clear in this instance is the elbow length of the sleeve of the chiton.

621. Note the extension of the upper eyelid beyond the eyeball and the close proximity of the eyebrow to the eyelid, details which make this and the other faces of Panel WC 3 superior by far to those of Panel SC 3 (Prophets of Baal on Mount Carmel).

622. As in a rhyton, the contents are dispensed from the thin end of the vessel. The distance separating Samuel and David makes it necessary for the former to hold the vessel horizontally, closing the upper end with the palm of his hand, rather than vertically as in Christian iconography (see e.g., the silver dish from Cyprus referred to above, p. 165, n. 619).

623. Under the purple himation David wears a white chiton, its folds outlined in gray and pink.

624. It will be noted that David wears the court costume (red tunic and trousers) in Panel EC 1 and in the lower Center Panel. The contrast that exists between the purple of David's himation in the present scene and the reds and blues of the royal garments worn by Ahasuerus, Pharaoh, and Mordecai cannot be said to express a judgment about the character of David's kingship. On the colors designated "purple" in antiquity, and on the relation of purple and kingship, see A. Dedekind, *Ein Beitrag zur Purpurkunde*, 1898–1906; and M. Besnier in Daremberg-Saglio, IV, 1 (1907), cols. 769–778, *s.v.* "purpura." For the ancient Jewish acceptance of the association of purple and imperial authority, see Krauss, *Talmudische Archäologie*, I, pp. 147, 555.

625. The first to call attention to the *gestus* was L. Heuzey, *Les Origines orientales de l'art* (1892), p. 26. For subsequent discussions see e.g., R. Heidenreich, *Zeitschrift für Assyriologie*, XL (1931), p. 106; G. Contenau, *Revue d'assyriologie*, XXXVII (1940), pp. 125f.; *idem*, *Manuel d'archéologie orientale*, I (1927), p. 385.

quoting, 'Prepare to meet thy God, O Israel.' (Amos 4.12).[626]

If under particularly difficult circumstances R. Kahana thought it proper to shed his cloak (in a partial simulation of servile nudity) when appearing before the deity in prayer, the more normal procedure was undoubtedly that of covering oneself in the presence of deity.[627] In Judaism the custom eventually gave rise to the use of the *tallith* worn over the head and the shoulders as a "prayer-shawl." In the period of the Dura Synagogue the *tallith* was apparently not yet a separate religious vestment, but the standard overgarment of the adult Jewish male; that is, in terms of the Synagogue murals, the himation.[628] That the act of covering performed with it should in this instance have involved the hands rather than the head is in all probability to be connected with the old Persian practice that eventually invaded even Roman court ceremonial and is reflected in the monuments of ancient art, pagan and Christian.[629] In the form in which the *gestus* is most commonly portrayed, the covered hands are extended to receive a gift from a deity or a king. Here, where the gift received was not an object but the kingship, the hands did not need to be extended and could thus be shown crossed in prayer.[630] But the

fact that they are covered seems to suggest that David is in the divine presence.[631] Samuel, of course, appears in the scene merely as the instrument of the divine action, for the kingship is really conferred upon David by God himself.[632]

In contrast to David, his brothers received only a moderate amount of attention at the hand of the artist. They are aligned in identical pose at either side of David himself, frontal, stiff, and lifeless, each overlapping the right shoulder of his neighbor. The six of them share nine feet, all carefully sandaled but unrealistic in their rendering and occasionally superimposed one upon the other. All of them are to be thought of as raising their right hands in an appropriate gesture of acclamation, but the artist found room between the heads of the men for but three hands, and these are very poorly drawn. With one exception, to be mentioned later, the faces of the brothers are all alike, oval and beardless, but heavily shaded at the right and highlighted on the lips, the nose, and the forehead.[633] To relieve the monotony of the rendering the artist has again resorted to his favorite device of varying colors and insignificant details. Here he has distributed to the brothers alternately smooth and curly heads of hair, and has given them garments of different shades: to the first and last pink, to the second and fourth (counting from the left) yellow, and to the third and fifth combinations of one white and one pink garment.

Among the brothers the one at the head of the file, in immediate proximity to Samuel, is singled out for special treatment in one particular: the man is bearded and has the familiar thin mustache. In the rendering of the beard short vertical black and white strokes are used, and of these the latter recur in the treatment of his hair. The purpose of these details is undoubtedly to represent him as older than the others. Who the oldest of the brothers was

626. Shabbath 10a (Trans., p. 34). I owe the reference to Prof. L. Ginzberg. The meaning of the word פכר in the passage is commented upon by Maimonides in his Code (Tefillah V, 4) and is taken to imply that the right hand crosses the left, as in the scene before us. For a discussion of the passage see J. Berman, *Mitteilungen der Gesellschaft für die Wissenschaft des Judentums*, LXXIX (1935), pp. 330f., where survivals of the *gestus* in Islamic usage are listed. See also the statement of Jonah Ghirondi (*Sepher ha-Yirah* 41c) quoted by Sonne ("The Paintings," p. 294): "When a man wants to recite the prayer, he should stand up and put his hands under his garment, the right one over the left."

627. For the group of women participating in the procession on the Palmyrene bas-relief, completely enveloped in their garments, see H. Seyrig, *Syria*, XV (1934), pp. 164f., Pl. XIX.

628. See Krauss, *Talmudische Archäologie*, I, pp. 167f.

629. Hands were kept covered in the presence of the Persian monarch, according to the familiar statements of Xenophon (*Hellenica*, II, 1, 8; *Cyropaedia*, VIII, 3, 10). On the rite and monuments see among others A. Dieterich, *Kleine Schriften* (1911), pp. 440–448; F. Cumont, *Memorie della Pontificia Accademia Romana di Archeologia*, III (1932), pp. 93–99; Alföldi, *Röm. Mitt.*, XLIX (1934), pp. 33–36.

630. Abraham receiving the Promise in the Vienna Genesis (W. von Hartel and F. Wickhoff, *Die Wiener Genesis*, 1895, Pl. XI) is a familiar example of the *gestus* used in connection with the receipt of an immaterial gift.

631. See on Wing Panel IV (below, p. 238), but cf. Panel NA I (above, p. 71).

632. I see nothing in the representation to suggest that David at this moment became both priest and king as Grabar suggests ("Le Thème," p. 175). Sonne, on the other hand, appears to underestimate the importance of the gesture ("The Paintings," pp. 316f.).

633. Note the occasional shadow cast by the head upon the neck and the shoulder. This is particularly clear in the case of David.

is not stated in I Samuel, but the Chronicler (I Chron. 2.13) provides the necessary information on this point, indicating that it was Eliab. Eliab, it will be recalled, is the brother whom Samuel first thought to anoint until he was divinely instructed not to judge a man's suitability for kingship by "countenance" or "outward appearance" but by "the heart" (I Sam. 16.6–7). The artist, no doubt following some Haggadic tradition, has apparently interpreted the reference to the "countenance" and the "outward appearance" in I Samuel in the light of the Chronicler's statement that Eliab was the oldest of the brothers, indicating his greater age graphically by the beard with its gray hairs.[634]

One further feature of the composition is worthy of note; namely, the fact that the number of the sons of Jesse as they appear in the scene is seven, rather than eight as the story of I Samuel would require. Here again it is the later tradition that is normative for the artist; for the smaller number, already found in I Chron. 2.13–15, is adopted subsequently, for instance, by Josephus.[635]

Much has been made of the place to which the artist assigned the panel that portrays Samuel anointing David. The composition is located just above the raised seat probably occupied during the services of worship by the Elder or Archon of the community, whose name also happened to be Samuel, as the inscriptions tell us.[636] From this it was originally inferred that the panel had been given its location to do honor to the Elder Samuel, putting him in immediate juxtaposition to the picture of his renowned namesake.[637] Subsequently it was even suggested that the panel really belonged to the Samuel Cycle of Register B, and that it was "displaced" to honor the Elder of the community and because its subject was in accord with the thought of Register C, its place being taken above by the scene of the Temple with the seven

walls (Panel WB 3).[638] More mature reflection has led to the conviction that the coincidence in names, however pleasing it may have been to those who determined the arrangement of the scenes, cannot itself have been the determining factor in the allocation.[639] The emphasis must naturally fall in this connection upon the importance of David himself, and upon the importance which his house and kingship had for loyal Jews. This importance was partly historical, for David and Solomon between them provided the norm and standard by which the intention and the program of Jewish national history was, from the Jewish point of view, to be judged.[640] In still larger measure, however, it was eschatological, for in the Messianic hope, by no means dead, the Davidic house and the Davidic ideal played by all odds the most important role.[641] For the members of the Jewish community of Dura to see before them at the very right of the central Torah Shrine of the House of Assembly a scene depicting the anointing of David, was inevitably a reminder of the divine promises concerning the Messianic king who was to come, the Lord's Anointed, himself a "shoot out of the stock of Jesse" (Isa. 11.1) and a son of David. In all probability the scene received its prominent position in order to perform precisely this function. What bearing this conclusion may have upon our understanding of the arrangement of the scenes in the register as a whole, must be left for discussion in a later context.[642]

634. The Haggadic tradition preserved does not, to my knowledge, make this combination; instead it says that Eliab, whom God had himself at first singled out as Saul's successor, was rejected because of his violent temper (*Midrash Samuel* 19, 5, ed. S. Buber, 1893, p. 103, trans. Wünsche, *Aus Israels Lehrhallen*, V, 1910, p. 109).

635. *Antiquitates* VI, 8, 1, §§ 158–163.

636. On the raised seat see above p. 17 and Pls. V, XXIV–XXV. For the inscriptions (nos. **1, 23, 24**), see below, pp. 263 f., 277 f.

637. So originally Du Mesnil du Buisson, "Nouvelles découvertes," p. 558.

638. So Du Mesnil du Buisson, *Peintures*, p. 127.

639. So explicitly or implicitly Grabar, "Le Thème," pp. 175 f.; Wischnitzer-Bernstein, "The Samuel Cycle," p. 96, n. 19; Sukenik, *The Synagogue*, pp. 104 f.; Sonne, "The Paintings," p. 316. This disposes simultaneously of the "displacement" hypothesis, which is awkward to begin with, since Register C contains still another scene from I Samuel; namely, EC 1, and since there is no standard of placement by which "displacement" could be judged.

640. For the historical importance of David see, e.g., the Haggadic utterances of Rab, a contemporary of the Dura Synagogue in lower Mesopotamia (Bacher, *Die Agada der babylonischen Amoräer*, pp. 9 f.).

641. See e.g., P. Volz, *Jüdische Eschatologie von Daniel bis Akiba* (1903), pp. 197–199 and Bacher, *op. cit.*, p. 23.

642. See below, pp. 212 f. All recent discussions of the over-all meaning of Register C have turned upon, or have been inspired by, the more mature reflection upon the significance of the panel under discussion here. See e.g., Grabar, "Le Thème," pp. 17 f.; Wischnitzer-Bernstein, "The Samuel Cycle," p. 101; and Sonne, "The Paintings," pp. 316–320.

Pharaoh and the Infancy of Moses

Panel WC 4. H. *ca.* 1.29 m.; L. 4.01 m. (Pls. LXVII–LXVIII).

Rep. VI, pp. 359f.; Du Mesnil du Buisson, "Nouvelles découvertes," pp. 550f.; *idem, Peintures*, pp. 120–125; Leveen, *Hebrew Bible in Art*, p. 41; Schneid, *The Paintings*, p. 22; Sukenik, *The Synagogue*, pp. 101–103; Sonne, "The Paintings," pp. 313–316; Wischnitzer, *Messianic Theme*, pp. 46–50; Wodtke, "Malereien," pp. 56–59.

The panel under discussion here takes up by far the largest part of the north half of Register C on the west wall of the Synagogue. It recalls in this connection the long composition depicting the Exodus and Crossing of the Red Sea (Panel WA 3) above it in Register A, a composition with which it is associated in more than merely its length. Like its neighbor above, it contains a number of scenes adroitly joined together to tell a story, and draws upon the Book of Exodus for its inspiration, portraying episodes from the first and second chapters of the book. The story there recorded tells about the new king who arose over Egypt "knowing not Joseph," and who afflicted the children of Israel in twofold fashion. He set taskmasters over them who made them build the store-cities of Pithom and Ramses, and he issued instructions to the Hebrew midwives Shiphrah and Puah that all male children of the Hebrews were to be killed at birth. The familiar story goes on to tell how the mother of Moses contrived to save her newborn son from this fate by depositing him in an "ark" laid in the flags by the river bank, where he was watched by his elder sister; how the Pharaoh's daughter, coming to bathe in the river, discovered the child; and how at the sister's suggestion the child's mother was called and given the child to nurse and rear for the princess (Exod. 1.8–2.9).

The story of how the oppressor's ruthlessness was thwarted by the tender-heartedness of his own daughter, preserving the life of the very one who was to deliver his people from their oppression, the artist has found it possible to portray in four scenes combined in a single panel. Unfortunately the composition suffered no little damage in the period between its execution and its burial in the depths of the embankment. The damage began

with water seeping through the wall in the period when the Synagogue and the thoroughfare behind the chamber's wall were still in use. The seepage brought about a general deterioration of the painted surface in the lower part of the panel, and eventually removed all traces of color and design from a wide strip along the bottom in the center and at the right. The damage continued with the cracking of the plaster under the thrust of the fill introduced into the street behind the wall, a process that occasioned the loss of some sizable pieces of the surface; and included scratching and scoring and the execution of at least one pictorial dipinto in connection with the erection of the buttressing embankment inside the chamber.[643] The damage along the bottom was necessarily repaired when the panel was remounted in the Damascus Museum, a certain amount of patching and retouching of the rest having been undertaken in this connection. In general, however, the vicissitudes which the composition suffered have not affected seriously our knowledge of its subject matter and, save in one particular, the process of retouching and repair has not obscured the details of the original rendering.[644]

643. The large horizontal fissure caused by the settling of the wall and already commented upon in connection with Panel WC 2, continues along the top of the panel. Among the larger vertical subsidiaries of this, two are of sufficient importance to be mentioned, the first cutting through the nude princess in the water, the second through the last of the women standing in the presence of Pharaoh. The latter crack has a horizontal extension running across the royal group at the right with its own vertical subsidiaries. The cracking, associated at the top with an inward movement of the surface, has occasioned the loss of larger and smaller elements of the plaster at the following points: on the seat and back of Pharaoh's throne above the king's right knee, on the second and third of the draperies along the top of the panel and in the space between them, along the right side of the princess in the water, including her right hip and armpit, across the left arm and the skirt of the third of the princess' attendants, and across the entire waist of the next to the last woman in the composition. A deep diagonal scratch coming from the adjacent panel cuts through the lower part of the skirt of the last woman in the panel at the left. On her skirt was drawn a large dipinto of a lion (see below, Inscr. no. 59). Additional short scratches were originally to be seen pock-marking the gate at the right end of the composition and the lower part of the royal group before it.

644. The wide strip of fresh plaster supplied along the bottom at the right is clearly identifiable as a supplement. Patches replacing pieces of the surface lost from the upper part of the panel, while painted to continue the design, are carefully outlined in white as elsewhere, so that there is never any question in the examination of the original

With its liberal use of space and the elements of setting incorporated in it, the composition is among the most pleasing of all the Synagogue's panels. It combines a larger number of scenes than any other known mural of the chamber, excepting only Panel NC 1 (Ezekiel, the Destruction and Restoration of National Life). Of the four scenes to be portrayed, two were associated directly with a river, presumably the Nile, while two were not. To combine them effectively in a single composition the artist divided his field horizontally into two unequal zones. The narrower, at the bottom, he developed as a river running the entire length of the panel. The river itself is rendered as a broad white band, marked at one point with red lines to indicate the ripples caused by the descent of the princess into the water. A near, as well as a far, bank is indicated, the first taking the form of a yellowish-brown strip in the immediate foreground, the second suggested by the beginning of the reddish-brown background of the upper zone.[645] Each bank is set out descriptively with lines of straight-stemmed water plants rendered in black with long drooping leaves and intended to represent the "flags" of the Biblical story (Exod. 2.3).[646] The appearance of parts of two such plants at the extreme right end of the panel, where they are outlined against the base of a city wall, shows that the river actually extended the full length of the panel as originally composed.

The upper two thirds of the panel, beginning at the farther edge of the stream, the artist painted a reddish brown, using it as a field for the represen-

tation of the majority of the figures belonging to the several scenes. As in the panel portraying the Battle of Eben-ezer (Panel NB 1), the limited space created in the foreground serves as the emplacement of but a part of the action.[647] If in the panel under discussion here the artist seems to have coped with the problem of space more successfully, this is only because the river with its reeds is more convincing as a foreground, and because the combination of city and river is familiar to us from other types of compositions.[648] Of the four separate incidents portrayed in the composition, the first two are arranged in horizontal planes at the right. The third cuts vertically through the entire panel from top to bottom, and the fourth shows a return to the horizontal plane. The scene vertically developed in the middle of the composition serves to tie foreground and background together, thereby providing the composition with a unifying factor that is absent from the battle scene.[649]

Following the scenes in their natural order, an order which moves here from right to left, but by that token again toward the Torah Shrine in the center of the west wall, we begin necessarily with the episode portrayed in the upper plane in the right half of the composition. In developing this scene the artist has used approximately three fifths of the length of the entire panel. The constitutive elements in the rendering of the episode are two groups of figures: the one a king seated upon a throne attended by two courtiers, the other a group of two standing women. The unity of the two groups and their separation from each other is indicated by two ornamental draperies suspended

---

where the repainted area begins and ends. The one instance in which retouching may have altered a detail of the composition is the sword placed in the left hand of the courtier standing at the right of Pharaoh. On this see below, p. 172, n. 657.

645. To mark the upper edge of the near bank the artist has used the lower of the two scratch lines that originally ran the entire length of the wall in this area. See above, pp. 65 f.

646. The schematic treatment and paratactic arrangement of the water plants contrasts markedly with the realistic handling of the vegetation in Nilotic landscapes (see e.g., G. E. Rizzo, *La Pittura ellenistico-romana*, 1929, Pls. CLXXXVII–CLXXXIX), recalling that of Assyrian bas-reliefs (see e.g., A. Paterson, *Assyrian Sculptures, Palace of Sinacherib*, no date, Pls. 51, 92). The plant is not the papyrus, but the straight *mappas* or *maḥselet* of Talmud and Midrash (see I. Löw, *Die Flora der Juden*, I, 1928, pp. 678 f.) commonly used for roofing, etc., as at Dura itself.

647. Gute's color-copy suggests the presence of dark wavy lines in the reddish-brown background. The accuracy of this rendering can no longer be checked. The element of depth which it suggests would be surprising, especially in view of the development of the foreground in the "stage-space" manner.

648. The association of the walled city and the river in the foreground is probably entirely fortuitous and does not serve to unify the composition, for the imagery is definitely not that of Hellenistic landscapes generally or of Nilotic landscapes in particular. For cities and bodies of water in the latter vein, see the Pompeian wall painting of the Flight of Icarus (Rizzo, *op. cit.*, Pl. CLXVII) and the mosaic from the Church of St. John the Baptist at Gerasa (Kraeling, *Gerasa*, Pl. LXVIII).

649. The same type of vertical interlude reappears in the Exodus Panel (Panel WA 3), where, however, it serves to separate, rather than combine, the several elements of the composition.

from the edge of the frame of the panel and filling the vacant background above them.[650]

The group comprising the king and his courtiers is already familiar to us from the scene of Mordecai and Esther (Panel WC 2), where, however, the iconographic convention was disturbed by the introduction of the dais of Solomon's throne and of the queen and her attendant. Here, where Pharaoh is represented, the convention appears in its elementary, balanced form. The king wears the same costume as Ahasuerus and Mordecai, save that the color scheme is reversed. Pink and reddish brown are used for the trousers and the belted tunic with its yellow bands respectively, while the coat is rendered in blue.[651] White boots and the white diadem whose zigzag ends project at the sides of the neck complete the costume. The king holds a short sword close to his side in his left hand, the sword outlined in white, probably for no other reason than to set it off from the dark blue of the coat. His open right hand is extended in what may be a gesture of the acceptance of those coming before him, or of their acclamation, or a gesture of instruction.[652] He sits upon a throne with turned legs and a straight, square back. The back is draped with a green cloth identical in color with the cushion upon which he sits. His feet rest upon a yellow, bench-like footstool, of a type already familiar from other scenes of the Synagogue.

650. The cloth draped above the royal group is white and is decorated with yellow bands. That above the standing women is green. It too has ornamental bands which are outlined in black, but the color of the material does not appear to change in the area of the bands. The appearance of analogous draperies in Panels WB 2 (Consecration of the Tabernacle) and WC 1 (Elijah Revives the Widow's Child) has been pointed out above. The draperies serve as space-fillers, testifying to a measure of *horror vacui*, but add also to the ornateness of the decorations on the all-important west wall (to which, so far as we know, they are limited), and are usually in some sense appropriate to the scene in which they appear. See above, p. 145. In this instance the element of propriety may be the baldachin associated with royal audience scenes in the iconography of the ancient Orient. See the audience scene on the pillar of the doorway leading to the Hall of the Hundred Columns at Persepolis (Sarre and Herzfeld, *Iranische Felsreliefs*, p. 143, Fig. 65) and on the general subject A. Alföldi, *Röm. Mitt.*, L (1935), pp. 127-132.

651. The pink trousers have red bands down the front.

652. A scratch running vertically across the palm of the hand makes it seem as though he were holding an object, but this is not the case. The hand is open and the fingers are only slightly bent.

At the right and the left of the king stand the two courtiers who have appeared also in the scene of Mordecai and Esther (Panel WC 2). They wear the typical court costume of long-sleeved tunic, trousers, and white boots, and have the heavy head of hair that goes with this costume. In portraying them the artist has again followed a set scheme of color variation, giving to the one pink trousers and a light blue tunic, and to the other light blue trousers and a pink tunic.[653] Of the two men the one at the right holds in his hand a diptych with a brown surface set in a yellow frame. He is seen writing upon it, but the stylus in his right hand is no longer clearly visible. Occupying here his canonical position, from which he was moved to a place behind the throne in the Mordecai and Esther Panel (WC 2) for reasons already indicated, he is in both instances the royal scribe who takes down the king's utterances that are the law of the land.[654] The man at the left of the throne is identical in pose and position with the comparable figure in the Mordecai and Esther Panel. The two should represent one and the same official.[655] He extends his right arm and raises his right hand in what is probably a gesture of acclamation, and holds his left before his chest with the last three fingers clenched and the index finger extended but slightly crooked. In the Mordecai and Esther Panel (WC 2) the comparable official holds what we have been led to interpret as a key, an object that would identify him as the royal treasurer or chamberlain.[656] In the scene under discussion here there is

653. The yellow bands decorating the cuff and the skirt of the tunic, the vertical band down the front of the garment, and the belt around it are the same in each instance. The tunic of the courtier at the left has the flap at the neck familiar from other representations of the costume (see above, pp. 122, n. 425; 129, n. 460).

654. For the recording of the utterances of oriental monarchs, see Esther 6.1 and Pseudo-Aristeas, §§ 298-299. The last-mentioned passage is particularly informative, telling us that "it is the custom from the moment the king begins to transact business until the time when he retires to rest, for a record to be taken of all his sayings and doings." In the hierarchy of the Sassanian court the figure depicted would probably represent the Chief Scribe (*dibhēran mahisht*), the head of the department of state (see Christensen, *L'Iran sous les Sassanides*, p. 129).

655. See above, p. 160. Note also the identical armbands indicating court rank.

656. In terms of the organization of the Hellenistic monarchies of the Orient, this would make him a *dioiketes*. In the hierarchy of the Sassanian court, he would probably bear the title *ganzvar* (Christensen, *op. cit.*, p. 118).

a regrettable uncertainty whether he has a short sword in his right hand or at his side, or both, or neither. This uncertainty can no longer be removed, but in our own judgment it is probable that the man had no weapon at all, and possible that the left hand held the object identified in the comparable scene as a key.[657] However this may be, the figure of the king seated on his throne and attended by courtiers standing at either side of him is clearly one of the standard designs in the repertoire of the Synagogue artists, deriving in all probability from the iconography of audience scenes in the royal art of the Orient. The same arrangement of the king and the chief dignitaries can be inferred from the audience of Darius portrayed on the pillar of the entrance to the Hall of the Hundred Columns at Persepolis, if due allowance is made for the profile rendering.[658] Late echoes of the frontal rendering used in the Synagogue are perhaps to be seen in the gold medallion showing Constantine flanked by two soldiers and

the diptych presenting Probianus between two secretaries.[659]

When an audience scene is developed frontally, the persons approaching the royal presence have of necessity to be represented at one or the other side of the throne. This is the case, not only in the Mordecai and Esther Panel, but also in the composition under discussion here. At the left of the throne, the Synagogue artist has depicted two women approaching the king. They appear before him in the proper standing position.[660] They are seen full front but extend their right arms across their bodies and toward the king in what must be a gesture of acclamation. The costume they wear is identical with that of the women in Panels NB 1 (Hannah and the Child Samuel) and WC 1 (Elijah Revives the Widow's Child), consisting of a chiton with elbow-length sleeves and a women's himation, one end of which is fastened over the left shoulder, while the other is draped over the head to form a veil.[661] The first of the two has a white undergarment and a yellow overgarment, the second a reddish-brown undergarment and a white overgarment.[662] Both wear their brown hair closely gathered against the head, with short tresses falling to the shoulder and two single strands curving down from the temple across the cheek. The second wears pearl earrings, represented by three white dots.[663] In the left hand, hanging at her side, she

657. In Damascus the panel today shows the courtier with a sword (not a scabbard) hanging at his right hip and another in his left hand. This is manifestly too much of a good thing. The color-copies of Gute show, and the description of Du Mesnil du Buisson (*Peintures*, p. 122) implies, a sword in the left hand but none at the belt. The early photographs (made before the surface had been fully cleaned!) yield no information concerning the sword at the side because of the dark background, and show no trace of the sword held in the hand. Hopkins' field notes made contemporaneously with the early photographs mention no weapons at all. This is the more noteworthy because they describe the figure in detail even down to the position of the relevant left hand, which is said to be "on the chest with the fore-finger slightly advanced," as we have already seen. The fact that the panel was retouched has been indicated above (p. 169, n. 644). If the original form of the rendering has been interfered with in these particulars in the course of retouching, it is a rare, if not the only, occurrence of such interference. The probability and possibility suggested in the text derive from a consideration, first, of the analogous figure in the Mordecai and Esther panel, and second, of the likelihood that the sword introduced into the left hand was suggested by the key, whose form is similar to that of the hilt of a sword.

658. Sarre and Herzfeld, *Iranische Felsreliefs*, p. 143, Fig. 65. Note the comment of the authors: "alles was nebeneinandersteht und daher im Profil sich decken würde, ist hintereinandergestellt. Die wirkliche Anordnung dagegen muß folgende sein: Hinter dem Thron stehen die beiden Diener, sowohl der Fächerträger, wie der ganz rechts angebrachte Diener mit Tuch und Napf. Zu seiten des Thrones stehen die beiden Würdenträger, vor dem Throne, vielleicht gerade schon unter dem Baldachin, steht der Audienzhabende...."

659. For the former see Alföldi, *Röm. Mitt.*, L (1935), p. 60 and Pl. 16; for the latter Peirce and Tyler, *L'Art byzantin*, I, Pl. 82.

660. Whatever be true about the performance of an act of prostration or of *proskynesis* at the moment of entrance into the royal presence, the proper position for persons accepted in audience and represented as such is the standing position. See again the audience scene from the Hall of the Hundred Columns (Sarre and Herzfeld, *Iranische Felsreliefs*, Pl. XXIV) and the bas-relief from Nemrud Dagh showing Antiochos of Commagene in the presence of Zeus (Humann and Puchstein, *Reisen in Kleinasien und Nordsyrien*, Pl. XXXIX). On the question of court etiquette in these matters, see Alföldi, *Röm. Mitt.*, XLIX (1934), pp. 42–44.

661. See above, p. 136, n. 484, and p. 146, n. 532.

662. The undergarment of the first of the two women has black stripes around the sleeves; the overgarment of the second is decorated at the side with a black two-pronged ornament of angular design. For these designs in the actual textiles of Dura, see *Final Report* IV, II, Pl. XII, 23–24.

663. Their absence in the case of the first woman is probably no more than an oversight on the part of the artist.

seems to hold a long spoon-shaped instrument (Fig. 46).

The identity of the two women and of the audience scene in which they participate can scarcely be questioned. The women are the two midwives, and the scene that in which they receive

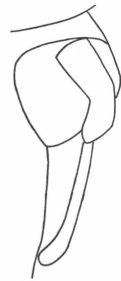

FIG. 46. Panel WC 4. Object held by Midwife

instructions from the Pharaoh to kill the male offspring of the Hebrews (Exod. 1.15–16).[664] This being so, it is entirely possible that the object which the second woman seems to hold in her hand is an obstetrical instrument, perhaps a simple type of vector, the mark of her profession.[665]

At the right of the king the scene contains yet a third element that requires a word of comment. It is a city which, as in the Exodus Panel (Panel WA 3), the artist has represented by a gate tower

664. Sonne ("The Paintings," pp. 313–316) suggests that the Synagogue artist showed the midwives before Pharaoh twice, once in Panel WA 2 (which we interpret as Solomon receiving the Queen of Sheba) and once here. From this he infers that the verses portrayed are not Exod. 1.15–16 but 1.18–21, the second appearance of the midwives before the Pharaoh. The suggestion is not borne out by the remains of Panel WA 2, and the inference would appear to the writer to spoil the dramatic force of the composition, substituting for the Pharaoh's threat to the lives of the Hebrew children (including Moses) a scene that could only illustrate the futility of his efforts to work through the midwives in trying to accomplish his purpose. Why the Pharaoh's efforts were in vain, the artist has made evident in another way. See below, p. 174.

665. For ancient obstetrical instruments, see T. Meyer-Steineg and K. Sudhoff, *Geschichte der Medicin im Überblick* (1922), p. 118, Fig. 76.

and a section of the city wall adjacent to it. Against the white of the wall its several stones and its crenelations are outlined in light brown. The gray doors of the gate, their panels outlined in black, stand open, showing the interior of the passageway in black. Above the level of the doors, the arch of the vaulted passageway is closed by a grillwork indicated by diagonal lines set against a gray background. It has been suggested that the city owes its presence in the scene to the artist's knowledge of the Oriental custom in accordance with which justice was administered and judgment rendered "in the gate."[666] Intriguing as the suggestion is, it seems to impute to the artist too great a competence in matters historical and too great an interest in the verisimilitude of his setting. It seems preferable, therefore, to see in the city an allusion to the "treasure-cities of Pithom and Ramses" which the Israelites were required to build for the Pharaoh according to the very chapter of Exodus that the artist is illustrating (Exod. 1.11). So interpreted, the city contributes directly to the theme of oppression that the audience scene seeks to develop.

Immediately at the feet of the first of the midwives a third woman is partially visible. The entire lower part of her body has been obliterated by water seepage, making the character of her action and the precise nature of her relation to the river slightly vague. She wears a pink chiton with black bands on its short sleeves and a brown overgarment. The loose end of the overgarment is not draped over her head as in the case of the standing women, leaving exposed her dark brown hair, which falls from her head to the neck and over her right shoulder. Though her face is turned into three-quarter position, her body is rendered in profile as she bends from the waist and reaches forward with her outstretched arms.

The fact that the audience scene is complete without this third woman, that two different postures for those coming into the royal presence would be unlikely unless one were in some sense a suppliant — for which the story provides no justification — and that the number of the midwives mentioned in accounts of the Biblical episode never exceeds two, makes it necessary to conclude that

666. See e.g., Amos 5.15; Zech. 8.16; and II Sam. 19.8. So already Du Mesnil du Buisson, *Peintures*, p. 122.

the third woman belongs to a separate scene. From her proximity to the zone occupied by the river, it is natural to infer that she is actually kneeling at the river bank, and from the position of her arms, that she is depositing in the river something held in her outstretched hands. Hence it is only logical to suppose that she represents Jochebed, the mother of Moses, depositing her infant son in the ark which she hides in the reeds at the river bank according to the Biblical story (Exod. 2.3). This interpretation is borne out by the subsequent development of the composition.[667] If correct, it implies that the artist has acted quite drastically and fearlessly in placing in two planes two consecutive scenes whose actions clash so violently with each other; the one showing the Pharaoh issuing the orders for the destruction of the Hebrew infants, the other showing Moses' mother saving her child from the Pharaoh's anger. In all probability it was the compelling need for compression that produced the close juxtaposition, but the resultant composition is not without an element of irony in exhibiting the futility of the king's efforts.[668]

As already indicated, the third scene of the composition, occupying only a fifth of the panel, cuts vertically across the field.[669] The continuity of the panel was preserved since the subject of the scene — the daughter of Pharaoh bathing in the river — allowed its major figure to be portrayed standing in the water which provides the connecting element for all four scenes.

The upper portion of the scene portrays the princess' attendants, who are three in number.[670]

They are set in a row, and face full front. The maids wear an ornate court costume consisting of three garments: first, a short veil that reaches no farther than the shoulders; second, what looks like a sleeveless, tight-fitting bodice; and third, a long skirt with a wide border at the bottom.[671] The skirt has one unusual feature; namely, an upper part, also bordered, that falls apronlike from the waist to the hips, projecting at the side and forming a box pleat in the middle. Judging by the way in which the artist distributed his colors, applying black borders to both sections of a pink skirt in two instances, and pink borders to a yellow skirt in the third, the upper part should be of a piece with the lower. The antecedents and the character of the costume are not entirely clear. It is related without doubt to that worn by Esther (Panel WC 2) and by the winged figures of the panel of Ezekiel and the National Restoration (Panel NC 1).[672] The relation to the last-mentioned suggests derivation by gradual distortion from a Greek *peplos* with a high-girded *kolpos*, as this garment appeared, for instance, on the Parthian renderings of the typical Greek Niké. The Nikés of Dura itself provide intermediate stages in the development.[673]

The veil which the maids wear clearly has nothing to do with the Greek costume copied here, being in all probability an Oriental addition. So too is their jewelry, consisting of pearl earrings represented by pairs of white dots, armbands, and bracelets.[674] In pose the maids are differentiated

667. Sonne's interpretation ("The Paintings," pp. 315f.), making her one of the Hebrew women in childbirth, the facility of whose parturition is described (and supposedly here demonstrated) to the Pharaoh according to Exod.1.19, seems highly improbable.

668. As in the Exodus Panel (WA 3) and in the Battle of Eben-ezer (NB 1), the foreground strip is to be viewed in a vertical perspective and the actors set against it in a horizontal perspective (see above, p. 86).

669. See above, p. 170.

670. The artist has made some attempt to vary the height of the figures, the one at the center being the shortest, but their heads lie in the same plane, preserving the principle of isocephalism. In drawing the figure at the left end of the group, the artist or his assistant has apparently made a slight slip, extending unduly the dark border at the bottom of her garment, and thereby giving the figure a stilted appearance. A similar slip has already been noted in Panel SC 2 (Elijah at Cherith and Zarephath), see above, p. 136, n. 483.

671. Black shoes complete the costume.

672. See above, p. 159 and below, pp. 183 f.

673. See *Rep. II*, pp. 181–193, and Frontispiece; and *Rep. VI*, pp. 63–67; Pl. XLI, 1. The basis of the development may well have been a misinterpretation of the heavy shadow line marking the lower end of the *kolpos*. This could have been interpreted as a border marking the end of one part of the costume. On the painted panel from the Palmyrene Gate the whole upper part of the costume including the *kolpos* is interpreted as one garment, while the skirt below it is another. Hence the colors change from white to green where the skirt begins to show. In the Synagogue the *kolpos* is associated with the skirt, leaving the upper part of the costume to be interpreted as a separate garment.

674. See the veil worn in combination with chiton and himation by the widow of the deceased at the banquet scene in Room W6 of Block M7 (*Rep. VI*, p. 154; Pl. XLII, 1) and those covering the elaborate tiaras of Bithnannaea and Baribonnaea (Cumont, *Fouilles*, Pl. XXXVI; *Rep. VII–VIII*, Frontispiece). All are longer than those worn by the maids. Conceivably length of veil is determined by social status. Pearls and pearl-

from each other only by the position of their arms and hands, with which they hold the princess' toilet accessories. The first, beginning at the left, carries a small gold jug of the type familiar from

FIG. 47. Panel WC 4. Pitcher

the inventory of the Temple of Dagon (Panel WB 4, the Ark in the Land of the Philistines), and a fluted gold bowl (Figs. 47, 48). The second holds before her chest a paneled ivory casket (Fig. 49), her right hand ready to open its characteristic

FIG. 48. Panel WC 4. Bowl

fishing are said to have come to the attention of the western world through Alexander's conquest and the operation of his fleet in the Persian Gulf. On the use of pearl earrings in the Roman period, see Rommel in *RE*, XXVIII (XIV, 2, 1930), col. 1696.

pyramidal cover. The third carries a fluted gold dish (Fig. 50).[675]

In the foreground the scene shows the daughter of Pharaoh, variously called Bithiah or Thermuthis

FIG. 49. Panel WC 4. Castet

in later Jewish legend, as she finds the child Moses in the ark. She stands up to her thighs in the water of the river, facing full front and already holding the child in her left arm. The artist has placed her slightly to the left of the center of the scene,

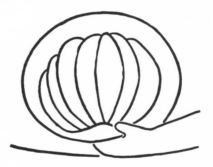

FIG. 50. Panel WC 4. Bowl

675. For ivory caskets of this type, see e.g., A. Venturi, *Storia dell'arte italiana*, I (1901), pp. 412f., Figs. 376–378 (covers), and p. 505, Fig. 442 (entire casket). A discussion of the later monuments of this type will be found in K. Weitzmann, *Die Elfenbeinkästen aus der mittel-byzantinischen Zeit* (Diss. Leipzig, 1930). Fluted bowls and dishes are common in the Orient from the Persian and the Hellenistic periods onward. For some early examples see J. H. Iliffe, *Quarterly of the Department of Antiquities in Palestine*, IV (1935), pp. 182–186 and Pl. XC (Palestine, Persian period); E. S. Vernier, *Bijoux et orfèvreries* (*Catalogue général des antiquités égyptiennes du Musée du Caire*, XXX, 1927), nos. 53.267; 53.275; 53.277 (Egypt, Ptolemaic period); and J. de Morgan, *Délégation en Perse, Mémoires*, VIII (1905), Pls. II–III (Achaemenian).

bringing her thereby closer to the two women in the next scene at the left, toward whom she gestures with her extended right arm. At her side there is to be seen the empty ark. The princess and the child are entirely nude. For the color of their bodies, as for the faces and arms of the other figures in the panel, the artist has used a flesh-tint probably composed of yellow, brown, and red, but with less red than in the panels of Register A.[676] The princess is depicted as an adult, her well-developed breasts with dark brown nipples being outlined in white. She and the child have brown hair outlined in black, but while that of the child is short and curly, that of the princess encircles her head smoothly and falls to her shoulders in loose tresses. The faces of both have suffered in the deterioration of the painted surface of the panel, but that of the princess was clearly in the same technique as those of her three maids; namely, fully front and almost entirely unshaded, the line of the nose forming a single stroke with the left eyebrow, the eyes wide and staring, their black pupils set high in the white eyeball, highlights on the chin and the lips represented by white dots. Indicative of her social position and determinative of her identity is the comparative wealth of her jewelry, comprising earrings, two necklaces (one with a double row of beads, white above and black below; the other supporting a circular pendant set in a frame), two pairs of armbands (one a flat band, the other composed of jewels strung together), and a pair of bracelets.[677]

The ark by the princess' side is represented as a yellow chest, its shape defined by black lines, its framing structural members and the ledge that serves as a handle at the end being indicated by wide strokes of ochre. From the triangular gable shown at the one end we are to infer that the chest

has a peaked lid hinged on the ridgepole, the end of which appears as a circle at the top of the gable.[678] The ark is encircled by what may be two reeds (Fig. 51), perhaps representing the artist's effort

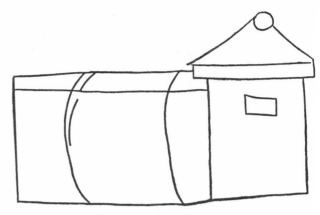

FIG. 51. Panel WC 4. Ark

to associate with the ark in some way the "bulrushes" or "papyrus" of which it is made in the Biblical story.[679]

The scene at the river, as we have described it, departs in one particular from the Biblical story; namely, in that it shows the daughter of Pharaoh actually retrieving the child from the river herself. The Biblical narrator states that the princess went to the river to bathe, but so far as the discovery of the child is concerned, this intention serves merely to motivate her presence at the river bank.

676. Neither here nor in the panel depicting Ezekiel, the Destruction and Restoration of National Life (NC 1) do the artists and the Jewish community which they serve show the slightest feeling that nudity would be improper in the pictorial decorations of a religious House of Assembly. This does not imply an absence of personal modesty, as the lack of raised footrests before the benches occupied by the women of the congregation clearly indicates (see above, p. 16).

677. The nature and arrangement of the jewelry is closely paralleled on the Palmyrene bas-reliefs representing women. See e.g., Ingholt, *Studier over Palmyrensk Skulptur*, Pls. XV–XVI.

678. Save for the absence of legs, the shape of the ark recalls that of the Hellenistic wood coffins from Egypt published by C. Watzinger, *Griechische Holzsarkophage aus der Zeit Alexanders des Großen* (*Wissenschaftliche Veröffentlichungen der Deutschen Orient-Gesellschaft*, VI, 1905). In these coffins the round ridgepole that acted as a hinge for the sloping sides of the cover is still clearly visible, being emphasized at the gable ends by attached discs. The similarity to the coffins is incidental, ark and coffins alike copying the style of Hellenistic chests. For the latter see E. G. Budde, *Armarium und Kibotos* (Diss. 1940). Early Torah Shrines in the form of standing chests have the same peaked top. See e.g., Sukenik, *Ancient Synagogue of Beth Alpha*, p. 26, Fig. 27 (Na'aran).

679. We have seen him resort to a similar device in dealing with the Wilderness Tabernacle (Panel WB 2, see above, p. 130). Where the object he is asked to portray is to him essentially unfamiliar, he uses the closest familiar analogy suggested by the object (there a temple, here a chest) and modifies it by an attribute supposed to do justice to the actual Biblical description (there the dark color representing the cloth of which the Tabernacle was made, here the reeds laid about the chest).

Hence, when she spies the child in the ark among the flags, we are told that "she sent her handmaid to fetch it" (Exod. 2.5). The difference between the Hebrew text and the picture at this point has raised doubts concerning the fidelity and comprehensiveness of the artist's rendering. It can be explained, however, by assuming that the artist depended upon the Targumic version for his inspiration, for in the Targum Onkelos the statement "she sent her handmaid to fetch it" is rendered "she stretched out her arm and seized it," implying that she was herself involved in the act.[680] The artist has made a simple combination of her intention to bathe and her act of reaching for the ark, showing the result of the act in his picture.[681]

The last section of the panel adds a fourth and final scene to the composition. It shows two women dressed in the familiar costume of the short-sleeved chiton and the himation, the latter draped over the left shoulder, around the body, and over the head. Both wear black shoes, those of the woman farthest at the left giving us a particularly clear impression of the type of footwear in question (Fig. 52).[682] The woman nearest the princess holds the child Moses in her right hand, steadying it at the shoulder with her left as she passes it on to the woman behind her. The latter has already placed her left hand under the child's body and grasps

Fig. 52. Panel WC 4. Shoes

680. The change in the interpretation results from a simple substitution of 'amthah (her arm) for 'ammathah (her maid). The change was familiar to R. Judah (see T. Soṭah 12b, Trans., p. 62).

681. It is important to note that neither the LXX nor the tradition used by the authors who follow it, could have produced the artist's rendering of the scene. Philo has the princess command that the child be brought to her (*Vita Mosis* I, § 14) while Josephus has her send swimmers to fetch it (*Antiquitates* II, 9, 5 = § 224).

682. The shoe is black and has a decorative red band irregularly notched above the ankle. Above this band the leg is rendered in white, whether to indicate the upper part of the shoe or to represent a sock worn with it. In any case the footwear is Oriental.

12

its right arm with her own right, ready to draw it to herself and take it in her arms. What the scene represents is quite apparent. It shows the result of the activities of Moses' sister Miriam, who, it will be recalled, had kept watch over the ark, had offered to call a nurse for the child when it was found by the princess, and had brought the child's own mother to the scene in this capacity. Here, then, Miriam is seen returning the infant to its mother on behalf of the princess, terminating the jeopardy in which it had been by virtue of the king's edict and the child's own exposure, and thus providing a suitable ending to the narrative composition.

A number of details in the rendering of the scene require a further word of comment. Above it the artist has introduced a yellowish-white drapery, apparently for no other reason in this instance than to fill a blank part of the background. The faces of Miriam and Jochebed are identical in execution with those of all the other women in the composition, even down to the jeweled earrings; but they are turned more to the right than those of the three maids, following in this particular the orientation of the faces of the two midwives. The first of the two, Miriam, stands with her left foot actually in the water. If the line of the river's farther bank visible in the previous scene were extended straight to the end of the panel, Moses' mother also would be standing in the water. Actually, however, the artist has extended the red background (bank?) into the zone set aside for the river, thus obtaining for the action a location intermediate between the two planes used at the right end of the composition.

About Miriam and Jochebed as they appear in the final scene, two additional details are worthy of note. The first is that the colors of their garments are identical with those of the two midwives who appear in the presence of the Pharaoh. Miriam has the reddish-brown undergarment and the white overgarment of the second midwife, and Jochebed the white undergarment and the yellow overgarment of the first midwife.[683] This may be quite accidental, but the probability is that it is intentional, for the Targum of Jonathan, the Frag-

683. A rampant lion has been drawn in black upon the skirt of Jochebed's overgarment (Inscr. no. 59, see below, p. 318). The dipinto belongs to the period of the chamber's desecration.

mentary Targum, and the Midrashic tradition identify Shiphrah and Puah, the two midwives, with Jochebed and Miriam respectively.[684] The second detail worthy of note is the peculiar contradiction between the pose and the gesture of Miriam. She stands with her left knee sharply advanced from the line of the body, a pose for which analogies have already been seen in the Mordecai and Esther Panel (WC 2, Mordecai approaching the king) and in the Exodus and Red Sea Panel (WA 3, Moses leading the van). In the artist's repertory of form, the pose indicates rapid motion and significant relationship on the part of the person in question toward a person or an object before him. Here it is combined in contradictory fashion with a gesture moving in the opposite direction; namely, that of handing the child Moses back to its mother, who approaches from the rear. The contradiction is the result, in all probability, of a process of abbreviation and compression, but the discussion of the possibilities and procedures involved belongs more properly to another context and to the interpretation of the compositions as examples of narrative art.[685]

Ezekiel, the Destruction and Restoration of National Life

Panel NC 1. H. *ca.* 1.26 m.; L. *ca.* 7.46 m. (Pls. LXIX–LXXII).

Du Mesnil du Buisson, "Les Peintures," pp. 117f.; *idem, Peintures*, pp. 94–103; *Rep. VI*, pp. 355–359; Wodtke, "Malereien," pp. 52–56; S. Blank, *Hebrew Union College Annual*, XII–XIII (1937–1938), pp. 327–346, esp. p. 343, n. 34; Sukenik, *Journal of the Palestine Oriental Society*, XVIII (1938), pp. 57–62; E. G. Kraeling, "Meaning of the Ezekiel Panel," pp. 12–18; Wischnitzer-Bernstein, *Journal of Biblical Literature*, LX (1941), pp. 43–55; M. H. Ben-Shammai, *Jewish Palestine Exploration Society*, X (1942), pp. 93–97 (in Hebrew); Grabar, "Le Thème," pp. 148–154, 12–15; Leveen, *Hebrew Bible in Art*, pp. 45–51; Schneid, *The Paintings*, pp. 16–19; Sukenik, *The Syna-*

gogue, pp. 117–136; F. Landsberger, *Hebrew Union College Annual*, XX (1947), pp. 227–254, esp. pp. 248f.; Wischnitzer, *Messianic Theme*, pp. 36–46; Sonne, "The Paintings," pp. 330–335.

The panel under discussion here presents the largest and most ambitious among the known paintings of the Dura Synagogue. To it the artist devoted the entire length of Register C on the north wall of the chamber. He subdivided the area into three parts by changing the background color from grayish white to reddish brown and from reddish brown to grayish yellow, but enclosed the three sections thus created within a single frame. Each of the three sections, here designated Sections A, B, and C respectively, beginning at the left end of the panel, in turn portrays several scenes.[686] To set out the seven and one half meters of this field in such a way as to make the sections and scenes develop a single theme required on his part, not only sustained effort, but also unusual powers of composition. The prominence of the panel in the lowest of the three registers, the amount of space allotted to it, and the thought and labor manifestly expended in planning and executing it are justified only by the outstanding importance that its subject had in the minds of those responsible for the Synagogue's decorations.

Quick to recognize its importance, scholars have already devoted a great deal of attention to the painting. Interpretation has ranged far and wide, and opinions have differed so sharply that there is scarcely a figure or detail in the composition for which two or more explanations have not been offered. Even the question whether the action of the whole should be read from left to right or from right to left is the subject of much controversy. In some measure this divergence of opinion stems from difficulties that are inherent in Section C of the composition and are not entirely surmountable. The difficulties are twofold: first, to find a proper

---

684. For the Midrashic tradition see T. Soṭah 11b (Trans., pp. 56f.), Exodus Rabbah I, 13 (Trans., pp. 16f.), and Midrash Samuel 23, 5 (ed. Buber, p. 113; trans. Wünsche, *Aus Israels Lehrhallen*, V, p. 124).

685. See below, pp. 389, 398.

686. The actual lengths of the three sections are: A, 2.27 m.; B, 3.06 m; and C, 2.13 m. Du Mesnil du Buisson's suggestion that Section C is in reality a separate panel, the artist having neglected to supply the vertical band necessary to complete its frame at the left (*Peintures*, p. 100) is a counsel of despair that is both unnecessary and unjustified. It may be noted, however, that under quite different circumstances the artist omitted terminal members of frames on the panels of the east wall (see below, pp. 204, 208, n. 829).

association between Section C and the rest of the panel; and second, to cope with a body of material that in its present state is somewhat confused. It appears that the right half of Section C as originally executed proved unsatisfactory, whether to the artist or to those who commissioned his work. The area was therefore repainted, some figures undergoing a change of pose, others being added — not, of course, without affecting the meaning of the scene. Flaking and the disintegration of the painted surface have transformed what was once visible here into a medley of the two versions, the interpretation of which is made more difficult by the confusion in which they are mingled.

On one point, however, most interpreters are agreed; namely, that in Sections A and B the artist has taken his inspiration and subject matter from the prophetic part of Biblical record, more specifically from Ezekiel's account of the events in the Valley of Dry Bones (Ezek. 37). Perhaps the most graphic of the narratives of Ezekiel, chapter 37 was also one of the best known portions of the book. Jews and Christians alike heard it read annually in public worship.[687] Jewish sages and Christian Church Fathers commented upon it frequently, though not always in the same sense. Beginning in the fourth century representations of its subject matter appear in the extant monuments of Christian art: first on the sarcophagi, then on a gold glass and possibly on an ivory, and finally in a group of illustrated manuscripts the most distinguished member of which is the Paris Gregory.[688] But the Book of Ezekiel was not commonly made the subject of systematic treatment by Jewish scholars in antiquity, largely because of the especially sacred character of the opening vision (Ezek. 1), so that for our understanding of the pictures representing Ezekiel 37 we are dependent upon incidental references in rabbinical literature and upon the comments of eastern Christian Church Fathers.[689]

So far as the technical and most of the interpretative problems posed by Panel NC 1 are concerned, they can, in our judgment, be solved if due consideration is given to the artist's procedures and conventions as known from other panels, and if Sections A and B be regarded as presenting "in a parable" the revival of the Jewish State.[690] On this interpretation Section C should portray a selection of those acts of violence that brought Jewish national life to a disastrous end and ushered in the Exile, thus requiring an act of divine intervention such as that symbolized in Ezekiel 37 if the promises made to the Fathers were to hold good. That Section C actually permits of this interpretation can, we believe, be demonstrated from the scenes portrayed, though the meaning of some details must remain obscure. The panel as a whole would then portray the Destruction and Restoration of National Life, but would not by virtue of that fact represent a complete departure from the rest of the Synagogue paintings, the abandonment of narrative for didactic art. This is prevented by the importance attaching to Ezekiel himself in the composition, especially in Sections A and B, and

687. A saying of R. Huna, made in the name of R. Shesheth shows that the present use of Ezek. 37.1–14 as a *haftarah* (Prophetic Scripture lesson) for Passover was already well known in the fourth century (Megillah 31a, Trans., p. 189). For the Christian Church, see Jerome's statement: "Famosa est visio, et omnium Ecclesiarum Christi lectione celebrata" (*Commentaria in Ezechielem*, XI, 37, *Patrologia Latina*, XXV, col. 346).
688. For the sarcophagi see Garrucci, *Storia della arte cristiana*, V (1879), Pls. 312, 1; 372, 2; 376, 4; 398, 3. The gold glass from Cologne is frequently reproduced, e.g., in H. Leclercq, *Manuel d'archéologie chrétienne*, II (1907), pp. 488–490, Fig. 327. The ninth-century ivory that has been taken to show some part of the scene is that of the British Museum (O. M. Dalton, *Catalogue of Early Christian Antiquities etc.*, 1901, Pl. XI, no. 299). For the Paris Gregory (f. 438ᵛ) see Omont, *Miniatures des plus anciens manuscrits grecs de la Bibliothèque Nationale*, Pl. LVIII. For the other codices see W. Neuss, *Das Buch Ezechiel in Theologie und Kunst* (1912).

689. For early Jewish interpretation see the detailed comment on the identity of those resurrected; e.g., in Sanhedrin 92b (Trans., pp. 620f.), and on the resurrection of the dead generally in the *Midrash Rabbah* (Eccl. Rabbah III, 15, 1, Trans., VIII, pp. 98f.). More explicit as witnesses to contemporary Jewish interpretation of the chapter are eastern Church Fathers like Jerome, who apologizes for applying the vision to the restoration of Israel contrary to prevailing Christian tradition (*Commentaria in Ezechielem*, XI, 37, *Patrologia Latina*, XXV, col. 349), and Polychronios, a Syrian bishop of the late fourth or early fifth century, who is said to render the text in Jewish fashion when he speaks of it as portending the return of the Jews from captivity (see Mai, *Nova Patrum Bibliotheca*, VII, 2, 1854, p. 92). The more typical Western Christian interpretation applying the vision to the general resurrection, can be seen in Justin Martyr (*Apologia*, I, 52) and Tertullian (*De resurrectione*, 30). Theodoret of Cyrrhus supports both interpretations (*Patrologia Graeca*, LXXXI, col. 1192).
690. The basis for this interpretation is provided by Sanhedrin 92b, Trans., pp. 618f.

12*

by the fact that in the days of the Dura Synagogue the events recorded in Ezekiel 37 were commonly believed actually to have occurred, being thus both fact and parable.[691] Structurally the panel with its several sections and scenes can on the interpretation suggested be said to be patterned after the centralized compositions familiar from other parts of the building (e.g., SC 3 and 4). The organization of its scenes and the development of the action within the composition as a whole can be set forth in diagram as follows:

A 1, A 2, A 3, | B 1, B 2, B 3, | C 1, C 2, C 3

————————————→ /\ ←—— ←————————

In view of the extent of the panel and of the wide variety of opinion about the meaning of its parts, we shall describe the several sections before attempting to interpret them. To assist the reader further, we add here in full the text of those parts of Ezekiel 37.1–24 that are illustrated in Sections A and B, arranging them in paragraphs corresponding to our understanding of their use in the scenes portrayed.

Scene A 1　1. The hand of the Lord was upon me, and the Lord carried me out in a spirit, and set me down in the midst of the valley, and it was full of bones; 2. and He caused me to pass by them round about, and, behold, there were very many in the open valley; and, lo, they were very dry.

Omitted　[3. And He said unto me: 'Son of man, can these bones live?' And I answered: 'O Lord God, Thou knowest.']

Scene A 2　4. Then He said unto me: 'Prophesy over these bones, and say unto them: O ye dry bones, hear the word of the Lord: 5. Thus saith the Lord God unto these bones: Behold, I will cause breath to enter

into you, and ye shall live. 6. And I will lay sinews upon you, and will bring up flesh upon you, and cover you with skin, and put breath in you, and ye shall live; and ye shall know that I am the Lord.' 7 a. So I prophesied as I was commanded;

Scene A 3　7b. and as I prophesied, there was a noise, and behold a commotion (ra'aš: earthquake), and the bones came together, bone to bone. 8. And I beheld, and lo, there were sinews upon them, and flesh came up, and skin covered them above; but there was no breath in them.

Scene B 1　9. Then said He unto me: 'Prophesy unto the breath, prophesy, son of man, and say to the breath: Thus saith the Lord God: Come from the four winds, O breath, and breathe upon these slain, that they may live.' 10a. So I prophesied as He commanded me,

Scene B 3　10b. and the breath came into them, and they lived, and stood upon their feet, an exceeding great host. 11. Then He said unto me: 'Son of man, these bones are the whole house of Israel; behold, they say: Our bones are dried up, and our hope is lost; we are clean cut off. 12. Therefore prophesy, and say unto them: Thus saith the Lord God: Behold, I will open your graves and cause you to come up out of your graves, O my people; and I will bring you into the land of Israel. 13. And ye shall know that I am the Lord, when I have opened your graves, and caused you to come up out of your graves, O my people. 14. And I will put my spirit in you, and ye shall live, and I will place you in your own land; and ye shall know that I the Lord have spoken and performed it, saith the Lord.

Omitted　[Vss. 15–20 give divine instructions concerning the two sticks, symbolic of Joseph and of Judah respectively, which are to become one stick in the prophet's hand.]

Scene B 2　21. And say unto them: Thus saith the Lord God: Behold, I will take the children of Israel from among the nations, whither they are gone, and will gather them on every side, and bring them into their own land; 22. and I will make them one

691. See the discussion about the identity of those who were raised and about the place where they were brought back to life, especially in Sanhedrin 92b (Trans., pp. 620f.), and also allusions in *Targum pseudo-Jonathan* on Exod. 13.17–18; *Midrash Rabbah* on Song of Songs VII, 9, 1 (Trans., IX, pp. 295–297); *Pirke de Rabbi Eliezer*, XXXIII (trans. Friedlander, pp. 248f.); and *Yalkut Shimeoni*, II, 375, p. 844. Rab and Samuel, Mesopotamian contemporaries of the Dura Synagogue, participate in the speculation. The fact that the dead were by some said to have been raised "in the plain of Dura" should not give rise to idle speculation on our part, since the Dura in question was certainly not Dura-Europos.

nation in the land, upon the mountains of Israel, and one king shall be king to them all; and they shall be no more two nations, neither shall they be divided into two kingdoms any more at all; 23. neither shall they defile themselves any more with their idols, nor with their detestable things, nor with any of their transgressions; but I will save them out of all their dwelling-places, wherein they have sinned, and will cleanse them; so shall they be My people, and I will be their God. 24. And My servant David shall be king over them, and they all shall have one shepherd; they shall also walk in Mine ordinances, and observe My statutes, and do them.

Sections A and B

Description. In Section A of the panel (Pl. LXIX), the surface is marred by the beginnings of a series of horizontal cracks that trace an irregular course through its entire length and are crossed at intervals by vertical fissures. These cracks are the result of a thrust transmitted to the north wall by the west wall of the chamber and caused by the pressure of the fill behind the latter. The thrust has dislocated entire sections of the north wall, moving them eastward several centimeters, disturbing the continuity of the lines painted upon the inner surface, and bringing about the loss of some of the plaster.[692]

692. In the section under discussion here, the systems of horizontal cracks are three in number: near the top, the middle, and the bottom of the field respectively. The third and lowest drops below the level of the field halfway along the section, joining another that runs in the frame separating the register from the dado below. Vertical fissures are to be noted cutting down through the face of the first figure counting from the left, and on either side of the third figure. The two last-mentioned are joined by a horizontal crack disfiguring the third man's face. The effects of dislocation are to be seen in the discontinuity of the contours of the third Hand of God, counting again from the left. Sizable sections of plaster have been lost in both corners of the field at the extreme left, particularly the upper. Smaller gaps have been filled in along the top of the field (between the second and third Hand of God), in the garments of the three men (for instance, above the belt and on the lower part of the tunic of the first), as well as on the second ridge of mountains (to the left of the inverted house) and in the tree surmounting it. The

The artist's development of his field in this area is markedly static and shows complete disregard of both balance and proportion in the representation of the materials. In the left half of the section he has extended his neutral grayish-white background to the very bottom of the panel, giving room for the representation of three large human figures whose arms, outstretched in different directions, provide the only element of movement in this whole part of the composition. At the right the background is reduced to a narrow strip by a double range of mountains that takes in almost half of the width of the field and is pyramided upward so that the trees surmounting it crowd the upper border of the panel. A series of divine hands above, and a series of human heads, hands, feet, and even entire bodies ranged along the lower part of the field, tie the imagery of the section together at top and bottom. The section, in our judgment, presents three scenes.

The imagery of the composition begins at the extreme left with a large pollarded tree, whose trunk, branches, and leaf-masses are rendered in black, its fruits or blossoms represented by gray discs contained within circles of radial gray lines.[693] The tree actually belongs to the upper part of the field, the base of its trunk projecting sharply from the frame halfway up the side of the panel. The three men who stand between the tree at the left and the mountains at the right are identical in every particular save height and pose. All three face directly front and are dressed in the same costume. They wear long-sleeved, reddish-brown tunics, green trousers, and soft white boots. The tunics are more highly ornamented than any of the comparable garments in the other Synagogue paintings; for they not only have white belts, white vertical stripes down the front, and wide yellow bands at the cuffs and along the hem and the slit sides — all of which are typical — but are also

surface of the field is very uneven throughout, elements of it projecting inward and out of plumb by as much as two and three centimeters.

693. The pollarded fruit tree, common in paintings of more formal garden scenes from the early days of the Roman Empire (see the familiar garden scene from the House of Livia at Rome), lives on in the East in the repertoire of decorative design till a late date. For an example of the sixth century from the Church of SS. Peter and Paul at Gerasa, see Kraeling, *Gerasa*, Pl. LXXVa.

woven in white with intricate palmette designs.[694] All three heads are rendered in identical fashion: the faces surrounded by thick masses of curly brown hair outlined in black, the lip showing the familiar narrow, two-pronged mustache, and the entire circuit of the jaw a short beard indicated by lines of vertical brush strokes.[695]

The first of the three men, beginning at the left, stands with his arms extended. The hands show no tendency to gesture. From above the Hand of God descends upon him. The Hand is partly closed, differing in this particular from the four others of the panel, its fingers grasping the hair of his head. The man stands in the midst of a collection of parts of human bodies; namely, four heads (one of them between his feet), three arms (one of them partly obscured by the second figure to the right), and three legs. The heads are carefully drawn and have short brown hair that falls uncurled over the temples and the occiput. The faces are unbearded, and the eyelids are closed. The second man is shorter than his two companions, no doubt merely because the artist has had to fit him into the space between the other two, whose pose and position were the first to be determined.[696] His left arm extends upward, its fingers relaxed and slightly bent, like those of the hands scattered about in the foreground of the scene, and therefore probably not pointing. Slightly to the left of it a second Hand

of God appears, palm outward, coming from the right. The man's right arm extends downward. With his open hand he gestures toward the *disjecta membra* in the first part of the scene. The third man raises his right arm upward toward still another Hand of God that comes directly toward it from above the mountains, palm outward, while his left arm gestures at chest level toward the mountains beside him.[697]

The mountains in the right half of Section A are reddish-brown masses built up out of a succession of semicircular lobes or ridges with brown contours and dull brown shadow areas. The ridges mount in scale-like succession to a peak, where they are surmounted by black trees.[698] In its simplest form the iconographic pattern that the artist uses for his mountains appears at the end of Section B of the panel.[699] In that simpler form it preserves almost unchanged a convention that had existed for millennia in the history of Mesopotamian art.[700] Here the artist has varied the pattern, doubling the ridges, no doubt on purpose, to introduce between them a deep cleft that he has rendered in black. Since elsewhere he uses black masses to indicate interiors we must infer that what he has tried to show us is one ridge torn apart, revealing the bowels of the earth. Scattered about upon the two halves of the riven mountain are various objects. On the right half near the top he has represented an inverted masonry structure with crenelated walls, a door, and a window — a structure that is probably a house, but might also be a miniature city.[701] Below it lie three nude male corpses ranged

---

694. The designs originally covered the tunics entirely, as the earliest photographs show, but later faded out. Some of them were retouched when the Synagogue was reconstructed at Damascus. The retouched designs visible on the Plates are basically in accord with the originals, judging by the earliest photographs, but do not bring out fully the richness of the over-all development of the design. In the Synagogue the closest analogy is the design woven into the cloak of Ahasuerus (Pl. LXVI). Rabbinical texts occasionally interpret such work as embroidery, indicating for instance that the "richly woven work" mentioned in Ezek. 16.10 was translated "embroidered garments" ('*aphaqleṭôrîn* = ποικιλτά) by Onkelos (read: Aquila). See *Midrash Rabbah* on Lam. I.1 (Trans., VII, p. 67), and in general Krauss, *Talmudische Archäologie*, I, p. 525, n. 51.

695. The eyes of all three were gouged out, probably when the embankment was constructed.

696. Note the way he steps on the third man's foot. The fact that such matters as height are quite immaterial to the Synagogue artists is evident from the two Mordecais of Panel WC 2 and the three Moseses of WA 3, making it impossible to infer in this instance that because of its lesser height the figure in question is that of Benjamin (against Wischnitzer-Bernstein, *Journal of Biblical Literature*, LX, 1941, p. 48).

697. The index finger of the man's right hand is extended, but it is questionable whether the hand can be said to point. Rather, it would seem, we have here the relaxed hand of the second figure and of the *disjecta membra* seen from a different angle.

698. In the color copies these are also shown bearing fruits or flowers, like the pollarded tree at the left. On the originals no traces of such fruits or flowers are visible today.

699. See also a further variation of the pattern in the central section of Panel EC 1 (David and Saul).

700. In glyptic art see, e.g., H. H. von der Osten, *Ancient Oriental Seals in the Collection of Mr. Edward T. Newell* (1934), p. 113, Fig. 8; and Frankfort, *Cylinder Seals*, Pls. XVII a, j, k; XIX a. In bas-reliefs see, e.g., Paterson, *Assyrian Sculptures, Palace of Sinacherib*, Pls. 17–18, 32–33, 34–35, 67, 71–73.

701. E. G. Kraeling calls attention to clay models of houses, analogous in shape, found in the Ishtar Temple at Ashur. See "Meaning of the Ezekiel Panel," p. 13; and

one above the other, their heads toward the right side of the picture, their size quite out of proportion to that of the trees, the house, and the mountain. At the left and overhanging the cleft additional parts of human bodies are to be seen: two legs, three heads, and four arms. One of the arms overhanging the cleft from the right has been so badly damaged by the cracking and dislocation of the plaster that it is difficult to recognize. Along the base of the mountains are scattered four rib bones. At two points Iranian dipinti have been written upon the surface of the ridges.[702] In the upper right corner of the section a fourth Hand of God is to be seen, coming from the left instead of the right, the back of the hand showing, as the finger nails indicate. The change in direction from which the hand comes is probably of no consequence, a by-product of the arrangement of the scenes, for the hand is associated with the first figure in the next section of the panel, having been placed where it is for the sake of economy of space. What is important is that the artist in changing direction has departed from his usual procedure of showing the palm of the hand. The departure shows that he wanted to continue representing only a right hand.

In Section B (Pls. LXX–LXXI) the background changes to a reddish brown, making less visible the ramifications of the horizontal and vertical fissures that enter from the left and become particularly numerous toward the center of the section.[703] The composition is less static here,

at least in the left half of the section, where the artist has shown a group of three winged figures flying through the air from left to right. The movement thus imparted is not sustained, but is turned back upon itself by the action of a fourth Psyche, who moves along the base of the panel from right to left and in the direction of the three corpses that lie on the ground before her. From the way in which the action reverses itself, it is evident that the Psyches, the corpses, and the man standing to the left of them constitute a single complete scene. At the extreme right end of the section the artist has presented another scene, completely static in character. It shows a large man standing beside a range of mountains with ten smaller men ranged in three rows by his side. Their relationship to each other is indicated by the gesture and posture of the large figure and by the positions of the men's feet.[704] Crowding the ten smaller figures at the left is a second tall man, identical in all but gesture with the one at the right end of the section. The position of his feet indicates that he is not a part of the scene at the right. Conceivably he may belong to the scene with the Psyches at the left; but for this he is not absolutely necessary, the action of this scene being complete in itself, as we have already seen. Actually he stands not only in the middle of the section, but by virtue of that fact also in the middle of the whole panel. Conceivably, therefore, he may need to be regarded as a separate element of the composition, in which case Section B might be said to contain three different scenes. Only the interpretation of the material can indicate which of the alternatives is to be preferred.

Of the figures represented in Section B, the most interesting are the Psyches. The three that fly through the air in the upper part of the field at the

W. Andrae, *Die archäischen Ischtar-Tempel in Assur* (*Wissenschaftliche Veröffentlichungen der Deutschen Orient-Gesellschaft*, XXXIX, 1922), Pl. 15.

702. Underneath the hand overhanging the left half of the mountain at the left (Inscr. no. **53**) and underneath the overturned house (Inscr. no. **52**).

703. Of the horizontal cracks that begin in the previous section, those along the top and through the middle of the field continue uninterruptedly. The former, having moved upward to leave the flying figures untouched, descends sufficiently toward the right end of the panel to disfigure the head of the last man in the top row of the small standing figures, and to cut through the last of the Hands of God. It has several systems of branches running diagonally downward at the extreme left and in the center of the panel. The lower of the horizontal cracks, after running at thigh level through the Psyche on the ground, rises to disfigure the faces of the first two men in the bottom row of small standing figures, descending again from this area toward the base of the panel. The most important of the vertical fissures descends just behind the Psyche on the ground. Small sections of the plaster

surface were broken out in antiquity across the body of the Psyche on the ground, in the empty space just behind her, in the last of the Hands of God, and along the right hip of the last figure in the section. Severe dislocation of line can be observed in the first and second man in the bottom row of small standing figures, where the lower part of the face has disappeared and head and neck are out of line by several centimeters, the upper section of the wall having been pushed eastward.

704. The large man at the left rests his weight on his right foot, the ten smaller men at the right rest their weight on their left foot. On the importance of stance as an indication of relationship of figures, see what was said above in connection with Panel WC 2 (Mordecai and Esther), p. 152, n. 552.

left are done simply in gray, with black used for the outline of details. Of all the figures in the entire Synagogue, they preserve most clearly the details of Greek prototypes after which they are modeled. The relation to these prototypes, especially to Paionius' famous Niké, is visible in the inclination of the figure as a whole; in the graceful position of the hands and legs; in the nature of the costume; in the way the costume is draped, leaving one shoulder bare and revealing the thigh and calf of one leg through the slit in the side of its skirt; and finally in the arrangement of the hair.[705] As in the case of the court costume for women portrayed in Panels WC 2 (Mordecai and Esther) and WC 4 (Pharaoh and the Infancy of Moses), the *kolpos* of the Doric chiton has been transformed into an overskirt worn in combination with a bodice.[706] In the flying Psyches, however, the transformation is not as evident as in the Psyche on the ground, because of the absence of color differentiation in the rendering of the several parts of the garment. Further indications of Oriental influence are to be seen in the curls that surround the carefully combed hair and in the bracelets, armbands, and anklets with which, like the Niké of the painted panel, the figures are adorned. Following the type of Psyche that was particularly beloved in the East and that appears commonly on Syrian sarcophagi, their wings are of the triangular, slightly lobed, butterfly type.[707]

Larger in size than the three who fly through the air, the Psyche on the ground is rendered after the same model but with less fidelity, providing an excellent example of the way in which a change of situation leads inevitably to the transformation of iconographic prototypes. She has the same butterfly wings, and the same type of garment, both here rendered in yellow, wears the same jewelry, and bares one of her legs in traditional fashion; but the

total effect of the figure is quite different. The difference is due in part to the fact that the upper part of her garment, being rendered in black, is transformed into a bodice, while the black bands common to the lower border and the end of the *kolpos* visibly transform the latter into an overskirt. In much larger measure, however, the difference is due to the change in the pose of the Psyche. She strides energetically toward the left instead of being lightly poised. Her face is seen in profile, the artist abandoning his tendency toward frontality in her case, as in the case of the widow in Panel WC 1 and of Mordecai in Panel WC 2, apparently to indicate intensity of motion or purposeful action.[708] Her action is directed toward the uppermost of the three nude male bodies that lie before her at the left, for her hands are poised at either side of its head ready to grasp it. Bending forward to this end, she loses the relaxed nobility that is typical of her classical prototype.[709]

The standing figure enclosed within the framework of the Psyches' action wears the costume normally associated with court and Temple personnel, a long-sleeved pink tunic with a yellow band along the bottom and at the sides, green trousers, and white boots.[710] His face is lightly bearded. He wears a thin mustache and a heavy head of brown hair outlined in black; his eyes have been gouged out. Facing full front, he gestures with his open left hand toward the Psyche and the three bodies on the ground beside him, while his right hand reaches upward into the corner of Section A, where the Hand of God comes down toward it.[711]

The man in the very center of the section and panel is of slightly larger proportions than those described thus far. He is dressed in grayish-white

---

705. For the details in the representation of the Psyche and of the Niké with which she was occasionally combined, see O. Waser in Roscher, *Lexikon*, III, 2 (1897–1909), cols. 3201–3256 (*s.v.* "Psyche"); and H. Bulle, *ibid.*, III, 1 (1897–1902), cols. 305–358 (*s.v.* "Nike").

706. The transformed chiton appears on the painted Niké of *Rep. II*, Frontispiece. For the discussion of her garment see *ibid.*, pp. 189–193. For the court costume of the Synagogue, see above, pp. 159, 174.

707. See e.g., M. Meurdrac and L. Albanèse, *Bulletin du Musée de Beyrouth*, II (1938), p. 82, Fig. 4; and III (1939), pp. 49f. and Pls. IV d and VII c, d.

708. The visible left eye of the Psyche was found disfigured.

709. It may be noted in this connection that the Psyche's dark hair with its curls at the neck lacks the careful grooming of the traditional coiffure, and that in transforming the upper part of her garment into a bodice the artist has departed from the convention requiring one shoulder to be entirely bare. In this particular he has compromised by keeping the necessary two shoulder straps, but showing the left one out of position over the upper arm.

710. The tunic has the usual white belt and a vertical band down the front outlined in black.

711. The palm of the man's hand is open; his fingers do not point.

chiton and himation, and wears the sandals that go with this costume. The chiton has dark clavi that were originally probably blue. Green was used liberally to make the shadow- and fold-lines of the garments and has accidentally given them a greenish tinge.[712] The man faces full front, wears a light chin beard and mustache and a heavy head of curly brown hair outlined in black. He stands with his weight on his right foot, the left set between those of two of the smaller figures beside him, whom he appears to crowd. The most important feature of the man is the gesture of his uplifted right hand. In this gesture the palm is turned outward and the second and third fingers are held extended while the thumb, the fourth, and the fifth fingers are doubled back against the palm. In actual fact the gesturing hand is close to the wings of the first of the flying Psyches. Whether by his gesture the man means to call attention to the Psyches or not is one of the issues about which interpreters are divided.[713]

The final scene of the section ends, as we have already seen, in a single range of mountains identical in pattern with those of Section A. Their color is slightly lighter, largely no doubt because the reddish brown used in the previous case serves in this section as the color of the background. The tree atop the pyramid of ridges is more conventionalized and is pollarded. As to the man standing beside the mountain, he is the exact duplicate of the one just described in pose, features, and coloring — the only difference being that he gestures toward the ten smaller figures at his right with his open right hand.[714] From above a final Hand of God comes down toward him. It is again a right hand and, coming from the unfilled background at the left, its back is what the artist has portrayed.

The ten men toward whom the larger figure gestures are drawn to the smaller scale that the artist uses occasionally when persons are to be shown in multiple ascending ranks. The patent analogy is the scene of the Exodus and Red Sea

Crossing (Panel WA 3), where those whom Moses leads are similarly differentiated from him in size for practical reasons. Here the figures are crowded closely together and arranged in three rows, with four in the first row and three in each of the upper two rows, all facing front. All wear the identical costume of chiton, himation, and sandals, and have heads of short curly brown hair outlined in black. To relieve the monotony of the group, the artist has resorted to various devices. He has alternated between yellow and grayish white in the rendering of the costumes, and between red and brown in the fold lines, and has even given light chin beards to two members of the group, the first and last in the middle row.[715] It was evidently the intention of the artist to portray all ten men with both hands upraised, palms forward. In this he did not succeed completely, largely because of a lack of space caused by the severe crowding of the figures. But the arrangement in the top row, where the background provided additional latitude and where six raised hands are actually visible, strange though their distribution may be, reveals the nature of his purpose. Below, a lack of space, or carelessness, or both, have caused him to be satisfied with seven feet distributed among the four figures.[716]

Only one further detail has still to be added to make the description of Section B complete. Between the ten smaller figures and the large man at the end of the section the artist has introduced another collection of parts of human bodies. The members are scattered about indiscriminately and comprise one head, two hands, and four legs. Their rendering is identical with that of those in Section A of the composition.

Interpretation. The only part of this large body of material about which there is even a measure of agreement among interpreters is the first scene of

712. Whether this tinge was imparted in the painting process or developed from the spread of elements of the pigment when the surface was varnished for purposes of preservation in the reconstruction of the chamber at Damascus is not clear. Only this is evident, that the garments were not originally intended to be green.

713. Cf. below, pp. 187 f., 194.

714. One of the man's eyes was found disfigured.

715. Counting from the left, the garments of the first and third figures in the first and third rows are done in yellow. The others are grayish-white. The fold lines of the garments of all three men in the middle row are rendered in red, those of the others in brown. The clavi on the chitons are black, this color being occasionally supplemented with brown. Black bands appear at the end of the sleeves of the chitons, and diagonal two-pronged ornamental bands in brown and black upon the himatia of the men in the first row.

716. The phenomenon is one that we have already met at several other occasions; e.g., Panels SC 3 (Prophets of Baal) and WC 2 (Mordecai and Esther).

Section B (Scene B 1). With this scene, interpretation will therefore do well to begin. Here, it will be recalled, the artist has represented three winged creatures flying in the upper part of the field, while in the lower part a fourth prepares to take into her hands the head of one of the three corpses lying before her. The scene has been associated universally and quite properly, we believe, with Ezekiel 37.9, where the prophet is instructed to say "come from the four winds, O breath, and breathe upon these slain that they may live." We are dealing therefore with the final stage in the process by which the dry bones of Ezekiel 37.1 are transformed into living human beings.

While the subject of the scene is generally agreed upon, the meaning of its details is hotly debated, and the precise relation of picture and text is in need of clarification. One of the questions at issue is the identity of the three corpses on the ground before the Psyche. Are they generally symbolic of the larger company of those to be brought back to life, or are they to be associated with the bodies and parts of bodies in Section A to make up a fixed and significant number?[717] The matter is not unimportant, but the discussion of it must be reserved for a later context.[718]

More immediately relevant here is the question about the identity of the winged beings depicted in the scene. According to the interpretation advanced originally by Du Mesnil du Buisson and subsequently favored by most commentators, they are the "four winds" of Ezekiel 37.9, and by virtue of this fact the agencies through which the "breath of life" comes into the dead bodies.[719] The interpretation is suggestive, particularly because the

idea that man has within himself a bit of "air in motion," implanted and ultimately also dissipated by action of the wind, is familiar from ancient Greek philosophy, and is known to have been shared also by speculative Jewish thinkers like Philo.[720] Moreover, the idea has found expression in contemporary Roman funerary art, where winds appear frequently as the guides of the soul.[721] Meanwhile two other interpretations have been proposed. The first is that of Landsberger, who regards the winged creatures as a special class of angels, serving, of course, to represent the winds and the "breath."[722] The second is that of Sukenik, for whom they are precisely what their shape suggests; namely, three souls or Psyches on their way to enter three human bodies. The fourfold number of the Psyches he explains by the assumption that the artist has repeated in the foreground one of the three souls to make their imminent association with the bodies more explicit.[723]

To interpret the scene properly, we must distinguish between two conceptions of how man becomes a living being and the representation proper to each of them. According to the first conception, animation occurs when a soul enters the lifeless body. This is normally portrayed in late classical art by showing a Psyche approaching a rigid, commonly upright body from the front, ready to enter into it through its mouth.[724] According to the

717. Compare in this connection the interpretation of Sukenik (*The Synagogue*, p. 130), who champions the first alternative, and that of Wischnitzer (*Messianic Theme*, p. 44), who adopts the second, arriving at the number fourteen, which suggests to her the eleven tribes and the two half-tribes that make up the Israelite nation, plus David.

718. Cf. below, p. 194, n. 755.

719. Cf. Du Mesnil du Buisson, "Les Peintures," p. 117; *Rep. VI*, p. 356; Du Mesnil du Buisson, *Peintures*, pp. 96f.; E. G. Kraeling, "Meaning of the Ezekiel Panel," p. 16; Wischnitzer, *Messianic Theme*, p. 43. See also R. Dussaud's review of F. Cumont, "Une Terre cuite de Soings," in *Revue de l'histoire des religions*, CXX (1939), p. 219; and C. Picard's review of Du Mesnil du Buisson's *Peintures* in *Revue archéologique*, 6th ser., XVII (1941), p. 306.

720. Cf. E. Rhode, *Psyche*, II, 7–8 ed. (1921), p. 212; Cumont, *Recherches sur le symbolisme funéraire des romains*, p. 112. For Philo see *Quod deterius potiori insidiari soleat*, 46–48 = §§ 134–139; *De somniis* I, 22 = §§ 135–145; and in general E. Brehier, *Les Idées philosophiques et religieuses de Philon d'Alexandrie*, 2nd ed. (1925), pp. 133–135.

721. Cf. F. Cumont, *Pisciculi, Antike und Christentum, Ergänzungsband* (1939), pp. 70–75; idem, *Revue archéologique*, XV (1939), pp. 18–59; and *Symbolisme funéraire*, pp. 146–176. As Sukenik has correctly pointed out, however (*Journal of the Palestine Oriental Society*, XVIII, 1938, pp. 59f.) the allusion to the "four winds" in the text of Ezekiel is probably quite metaphorical, in keeping with the use of the same expression in Zech. 2.6 and Dan. 11.4, and need imply no more than that the "breath" comes from beyond the ends of the earth where the winds have their home. Cf. the monuments reproduced in the relevant sections of Cumont, *Symbolisme funéraire*, pp. 146–176. The exception here is Aura, who appears, naturally, as a female (*ibid.*, Pl. XXIII,2).

722. *Hebrew Union College Annual*, XX (1947), pp. 248f.

723. *The Synagogue*, pp. 130f.

724. This rendering develops in connection with representations of the Prometheus myth. See Weitzmann

second conception, enlivenment occurs when a permanently independent divine being breathes into man, causing him to breathe also. For this conception, which comes to clearest expression in Genesis 2 and is reflected also in Ezekiel 37, there probably was no established iconographic convention in late classical art.[725] As reflected in Christian art, the composition appropriate to this conception shows Christ approaching a prone body from behind and stooping down to take its head in his hands, ready to breathe into its mouth or nostrils.[726] Fundamentally, this is what the Synagogue artist has shown at a much earlier time, the possibility of confusion arising in connection with his rendering from the fact that he has used a Psyche as the enlivening agent. In all probability this is merely because there was no standard representation for the "breath" or "spirit" which his text required him to portray. He fell back, therefore, upon the Psyches he had seen in examples of the other type of animation scene, knowing that the Hebrew word for "breath" was feminine and would allow the use of the Psyche form. Yet the Psyche on the ground in Scene B 1 must represent the "breath" of his Biblical text, for she is in the proper position to breathe upon the bodies, but not in the position to enter into them. So far as the three corresponding figures above her are concerned, they apparently represent the artist's effort to show that the "breath" comes from (among) the four winds (Ezek. 37.9). Since the Hebrew word for "breath" is also properly used in the Ezekiel passage to mean "wind," he felt free to employ the Psyche form to represent the winds, thinking perhaps to safeguard his representation of enlivenment against misinterpretation, but clearly ignoring or ignorant of the artistic convention that renders winds as males. The Psyche on the ground should therefore be understood in the first instance as the one "breath" that enlivens man and second-

arily as one of a group of four winds. Throughout the artist has tried to follow literally his Biblical text, the ambiguities of his rendering arising from his ignorance or the absence of established conventions for certain basic elements of the conception underlying his text.

In the area under discussion here the two men standing at either side of the Psyche and the three corpses are also the subject of controversy. The one at the right, it will be recalled, is dressed in chiton and himation, the one at the left in tunic and trousers. The immediate questions here are twofold: first, do both men belong to the scene; and second, who are they? On both points opinion is divided, the second having elicited wider discussion.[727] The figure at the left has been identified variously as Ezekiel, as one of the revived dead, as David the Messiah, and as the Lord's Servant.[728] The figure at the right has been called Ezekiel, the Messiah, Gabriel or Michael.[729] The difference of opinion exhibited here is more than a petty squabble about the identities and associations. It reflects a difference of opinion about the reading of the panel as a whole. Fundamentally the question is: should Sections A and B in their entirety be read continuously from left to right as a record of the developing sequence of events in Ezek. 37, or should Section A and the scene of the revivification by the Psyche be taken together as a series to be seen from the vantage point of the man standing directly at the right of the Psyche? What raises this fundamental problem is the fact that the scene of the Psyche and the corpses forms the dividing line between the use of two different types of costume. To the left of the Psyche and the corpses

(*Illustrations in Roll and Codex*, pp. 176f., Figs. 179, 181, 182), who has developed also the distinction in terminology between animation and enlivenment. Additional representations are cited in Roscher, *Lexikon*, *s.v.* "Psyche" (Schmetterling) and "Prometheus." The procedure by which the soul leaves the body is analogous to that of her entry into the body.

725. Weitzmann takes the opposite position, *op. cit.*, pp. 176f.

726. So in the Grandval Bible (B.M. add. 10546) as shown by Weitzmann, *ibid.*, Fig. 178.

727. Those who separate the figure at the right from the scene of the revivification include Leveen, *Hebrew Bible in Art*, pp. 47f.; E. G. Kraeling, "Meaning of the Ezekiel Panel," p. 16; Grabar, "Le Thème," p. 150; and *Rep. VI*, pp. 357f.

728. Ezekiel: Du Mesnil du Buisson, *Peintures*, p. 96; E. G. Kraeling, "Meaning of the Ezekiel Panel," p. 15; Grabar, "Le Thème," pp. 149f.; Leveen, *Hebrew Bible in Art*, p. 47. One of the revived dead: Sukenik, *The Synagogue*, p. 131. The Davidic Messiah: Wischnitzer, *Messianic Theme*, p. 43. The Lord's Servant: *Rep. VI*, p. 358.

729. Ezekiel: *Rep. VI*, p. 358; Du Mesnil du Buisson, *Peintures*, p. 97; Grabar, "Le Thème," p. 149; Sukenik, *The Synagogue*, p. 129; Wischnitzer, *Messianic Theme*, p. 43. The Messiah: E. G. Kraeling, "Meaning of the Ezekiel Panel," pp. 16f. Gabriel or Michael: Leveen, *Hebrew Bible in Art*, p. 48.

all the standing figures are clothed in the Persian costume of tunic and trousers, while at the right all the figures wear the Greek costume of chiton and himation. Those interpreters for whom the latter costume is the only proper dress for a prophet restrict the representations of Ezekiel himself to the right part of Section B, and thus tend to interpret all of Section A and the left part of Section B as a composite rendering of the contents of the prophet's vision. Those, on the other hand, who begin with the assumption that the standing persons in Section A represent Ezekiel, and who find A and B developing a progression of scenes moving from left to right, each requiring the presence of Ezekiel, have then to explain or explain away the change of costume in the right half of Section B.

If these differences of opinion are to be surmounted, three things must be kept in mind. The first is that the Synagogue artists are very careful in the attribution of costume, as we have had ample opportunity to see. This implies that no explanation of the panel not doing full justice to the distribution of costume types will prove satisfactory. The second is that, while in other compositions chiton and himation are commonly worn by prophets, and tunic and trousers are reserved for court and Temple personnel, the costume situation in the panel under discussion here is not as simple as interpreters have imagined.[730] The one fact hitherto overlooked in this connection is that the costume of chiton and himation is invariably associated elsewhere with the short head of hair, while that of the court and Temple personnel always goes with the large aureole of hair. In the two large standing figures at the center, and in the right half of Section B, the artist has departed from his established convention, associating with the chiton and himation the heavy coiffure. This departure is unique in his work so far as we know it, and must be given due consideration in the discussion of the change of costume. The third thing to be kept in mind is that in any successful interpretation full justice must be done also to other details of the rendering, such as composition and particularly the handling of the gesture.

For the identification of the man at the left of the Psyche and the corpses, it is important to note

his gestures. He reaches upward with his right hand into the corner of Section A where a Hand of God comes down toward him, while his open left is extended in the direction of the Psyche on the ground beside him. This same combination, it will be noted, recurs in the second and third figures of Section A, being associated there also with the appearance of a Hand of God. Now it is clear that in the other panels of the Synagogue where the Hand of God appears, no such gestures are attributed to the persons involved in the action.[731] In each of the other panels we are dealing with the performance of a miracle, and the rendering suggests that miracles are to be understood as acts of God, occurring perhaps at human request but without significant human mediation. Here, where the appearance of the Hand is combined with gestures on the part of the person concerned, we must conclude from the fact itself that the emphasis is not upon the miracle of the revivification, but upon some divine act requiring human participation, and from the nature of the gestures that this participation involves both the receipt and the transmission of what the Hand communicates. The basis of the rendering is supplied by the words of Ezek. 37.9–10:

> Then said He unto me: Prophesy unto
> the breath... and say to the breath:
> Thus saith the Lord... So I prophesied
> as He commanded me.

Here, as in the comparable statements of vv. 4–7, the prophet acts simultaneously as the recipient ("He said to me") and as the agent for the transmission of a divine utterance ("So I prophesied"). With this interpretation of the double gesture, both the scene under discussion here and related parts of Section A are in perfect accord. The open Hand of God denotes the communication of a divine revelation, the upward reach of the human hand

730. For prophets in chiton and himation, see especially the Elijah cycle, Panels SC 1–4, WC 1.

731. See Panels WA 3 (Exodus and Crossing of the Red Sea), WC 1 (Elijah Revives the Widow's Child), and Wing Panel I (Moses and the Burning Bush). In early Christian art, too, the appearance of the Hand of God is not accompanied by an upward gesture of the person or persons involved in the event. Cf. Wilpert, *Le Pitture della Catacombe Romane* (1903), Pls. 196, 201, 237; Garrucci, *Storia della arte cristiana*, III (1876), Pls. 112, 1 and 2; 118, 1; 147, 1; etc.; Wilpert, *Die römischen Mosaiken und Malereien*, III, Pls. 8, 27; von Hartel and Wickhoff, *Die Wiener Genesis*, Pls. I, VIII, XXV; and in general Leclercq in Cabrol, *Dictionnaire*, as cited on p. 57, n. 121.

its receipt, and the outward reach of the other human hand its transmission.[732]

If our interpretation of the gestures is correct, two important conclusions can be drawn about the scene at the left end of Section B. The first is that the man at the left of the Psyche and the corpses is not one of those raised from the dead, but Ezekiel receiving the divine instruction to speak to the "breath" and actually addressing the Psyche with the words: "breathe upon these slain that they may live." The second is that the man at the right of the Psyche is not a part of Scene B 1, but belongs to another scene, B 2. For this there are a number of reasons. One is that Scene B 1 is already complete in itself, a fact borne out by the way in which the movement of the Psyches turns back upon itself, giving a natural terminus to the action at a point just short of him.[733] Another is that the gesture which he makes with his right hand is of another type and too important in its own right to imply merely that he is pointing to the Psyches in the air.[734] Still another is the central position he holds in the panel as a whole, which reserves for him a separate role still to be determined.

If the figure at the left of the Psyche and the corpses is actually Ezekiel, it becomes necessary to explain why he is wearing Persian garb. The explanation would seem to be that in terms of the Synagogue artist's application of convention, he has a twofold claim to the costume: first, because in the book that bears his name Ezekiel calls himself a priest (Ezek. 1.3); and second, because in later Jewish legend he appears as one of the princes of his people.[735]

Using the interpretation of Scene B 1 as a starting point, it is possible now to undertake an explanation of the scenes of Section A. Here, it will be recalled we have three further standing figures. Of these figures the second and third, counting from the left, are identical in gesture with the person of Scene B 1 just identified as Ezekiel. All three men of Section A also wear the same costume as the Ezekiel of Scene B 1, with only this distinction: that the colors have been changed slightly, and that in Section B indications of elaborate woven designs in the tunic have been omitted. These changes being readily intelligible as the natural concomitants of a change in the color of the background, and hence of no importance for iconography,[736] it would seem likely that, because of the similarities between them, all three figures should be taken to represent Ezekiel, each being the central factor of a separate scene. The only question is whether the imagery can be interpreted convincingly on the basis of this supposition, and whether the juxtaposition of so many Ezekiels can be motivated.

In Section A, as we have seen, the background is a bright grayish-white, and the standing figures are set between a double range of mountains at the right and a tree placed far in the background at the left.[737] The background color and in a measure also the arrangement of the physical details suggest that this could well be the artist's effort to represent the "plain" or "valley" in which the action

732. The association of gesture and wording of the Biblical text was pointed out first by Grabar, "Le Thème," pp. 149f.

733. Cf. above, p. 184.

734. On the character and meaning of the gesture see below, p. 194. For the suggestion that he is pointing to the Psyches, see e.g., Wischnitzer, *Messianic Theme*, p. 43; and Schneid, *The Paintings*, p. 17.

735. Later tradition has it that Ezekiel was transported to Babylonia by Nebuchadnezzar as one of three hundred (or thousand) men of distinction in the days of king Jehoiakim. So already Josephus, *Antiquitates* X, 6, 3, § 98. Josephus' οἱ ἐν ἀξιώματι corresponds to the *sarîm* (princes) of II Kings 24.14, the tradition holding the deportations under Jehoiachin and under Jehoiakim in confusion. See in general, Ginzberg, *Legends of the Jews*, VI, pp. 379f., nn. 132–133. The Biblical statements implying that, though an exile, Ezekiel had a house in Babylonia (Ezek. 8.1), and the later tradition about his

magnificent tomb on the banks of the Euphrates are part of this picture. For the tomb of Ezekiel see *ibid.*, IV, pp. 325f.; and *Benjamin of Tudela* (ed. Grunhut and Adler, 1904, I, pp. 66f., trans. A. Asher, I, pp. 107–110).

736. In Section A, it will be recalled, the tunics of the standing figures are a reddish brown, and the figures are set against a white background. In Section B the background changes to a reddish brown. Here the artist had perforce to change the color of the tunic to a lighter shade (pink) if the figure was to be visible, though he could and did keep the green of the trousers. Why the woven design does not reappear, it is almost useless to inquire. We know that such details were supplied (or omitted) by the artist when the final touches were added, as the irregular distribution of tassels at the ends of himatia and of tie-strings on the shoulders of tunics indicates. This makes their presence or absence often a matter of momentary impulse. The absence of the design in the Ezekiel of the first scene of Section B may be the result of simple negligence or of the feeling that the white of the design went better with the white background of Section A than with that of Section B.

737. Cf. above, pp. 181f.

of the revivification of the "dry bones" takes place (Ezek. 37.1).[738]

Of the three men set against this background the one at the extreme left stands somewhat apart from the other two. It is he whom the divine Hand grasps by the hair and who holds his own arms extended in a limp, unusual pose. On the supposition that the man is Ezekiel, the action portrayed can only be that described in the very first words of Ezek. 37, "The hand of the Lord was upon me, and the Lord carried me out in a spirit and set me down in the midst of the valley and it was full of dry bones" (Ezek. 37.1). The Hand of God is literally upon him, and the effect of his being carried by the Lord or his Hand is visible in the position of his arms, which approximates that of the wings of a bird.[739] The artist has portrayed the terminal moment of the action, when Ezekiel is being set down upon his feet and is adjusting his balance. The position of the *disjecta membra* in this part of the composition lends further support to the interpretation suggested, for instead of being distributed equally among all three figures, they are grouped directly about the first, one head being actually between his feet.[740] The artist could scarcely have indicated more clearly how Ezekiel was set

down in a valley that is "full of bones," or that the imagery makes up one complete scene, Scene A 1.[741]

On the assumption that all three standing figures of Section A represent Ezekiel, the proper association of the second and third figures with the text of Ezek. 37 poses a problem that has caused even careful interpreters to come to different conclusions.[742] The fundamental questions at issue are two: whether the conversation between God and Ezekiel in v. 3 deserves to be connected with Scene A 2, and if not, how to explain the use of two scenes (A 2 and A 3) for vv. 4–8 where one might seem to have been sufficient. As to the question which God asks of Ezekiel in v. 3, "Can these bones live?" and the answer, "Thou knowest," the likelihood is that it would not have been portrayed in the composition, partly because it would probably not have seemed especially edifying to the local Jewish community, and partly because it had nothing to add to the action of the composition.[743] To determine the proper association between the second and third figures and the text it is best to begin with the mountains at the right side of Section A.

The complicated imagery developed in connection with the mountains of Section A has proven highly suggestive to interpreters from the very first. Some have found a proper basis for the mountains in Ezek. 37; others have preferred to draw upon chapters 6, 35–36, or 38.[744] Some have given them a direct part in the revivification process, such as the opening of the tombs. Others have interpreted them as part of the general setting di-

738. The composition of this Section is important for the understanding of the artist's position in respect to landscape painting. His use of an over-all monochrome background is a denial of spatial depth and thus also of the basic element of landscape composition. The mountains at the right are introduced for their own sake to explain a part of Ezekiel's prophecy, as will appear presently. Only the position assigned to the pollarded tree at the left and the way in which in this area the *disjecta membra* are confined to a zone along the base of the panel suggest that he is trying to portray a low-lying plain.

739. The gesture of the divine Hand in seizing the man by the hair recalls, of course, the passage Ezek. 8.3, where the prophet says that he was taken "by a lock of his head" and transported to Jerusalem, but an allusion to the related passage such as was suggested by Du Mesnil du Buisson ("Les Peintures," p. 117), and has commonly been found here also by other interpreters (*Rep. VI*, p. 356; Leveen, *Hebrew Bible in Art*, p. 45; E. G. Kraeling, "Meaning of the Ezekiel Panel," p. 12) is quite unnecessary, there being scarcely any other way in which the statement of Ezek. 37.1 could have been rendered by the artist. Moreover the assumption that the composition is a conglomerate of elements gathered from many parts of Ezekiel (see Leveen, *op. cit.*, p. 45) seems very dubious.

740. E. G. Kraeling ("Meaning of the Ezekiel Panel," p. 12) suggests in this connection that the artist may have taken the words *wěhe 'ĕbhîranî 'ălêhem* literally; i.e., "he caused me to walk upon them (the bones)."

741. On the question why flesh-covered limbs and not bare bones are represented, see below, p. 192 and n. 752.

742. The following table shows how Du Mesnil du Buisson (*Peintures*, pp. 95 f.), E. G. Kraeling ("Meaning of the Ezekiel Panel," pp. 12 f.), and Grabar ("Le Thème," pp. 149 f.) apportion the first verses of Ezek. 37 among the first four scenes of the panel:

Scene	Du Mesnil du Buisson	E. G. Kraeling	Grabar
A 1	v. 1	vv. 1–2	vv. 1–2
A 2	vv. 2–7a	vv. 4–8	v. 3
A 3	vv. 7b–12	vv. 9–10	vv. 4–8
B 1	v. 8	v. 12	v. 9–10

743. Cf. e.g., *Pirke de Rabbi Eliezer*, XXXIII (trans. Friedlander, p. 249) where Ezekiel is criticized for the evasive nature of his reply, for which he was punished by dying and being buried in Babylonia instead of returning to Palestine. The same tradition is found elsewhere also. Cf. *Yalkut Shimeoni*, II, 375, p. 844.

744. E.g., *Rep. VI*, p. 357; Du Mesnil du Buisson, *Peintures*, p. 98; Leveen, *Hebrew Bible in Art*, p. 46.

viding several regions or groups from each other.[745] Among the details, the inverted masonry structure on the right ridge and the trees atop both ridges have elicited comment more frequently — the former suggesting allusions to Jerusalem, the "high places," "the house of Israel," or being interpreted as a Palmyrene tower tomb; the latter recalling the trees of Ezek. 17 or even the two "sticks" (literally: woods or even trees) of Ezek. 37.15–20.[746] The suggestion that the imagery of the scene to which the mountains belong contains allusions to a variety of passages raises a problem of fundamental importance for the understanding of the pictures of the Dura Synagogue; namely, to what extent didactic considerations have affected the rendering of the narratives. The question will be dealt with more fully below.[747] Here it can only be said that in each of the panels hitherto examined, it has been possible to interpret all salient details as essential to the development of a single narrative thread, leaving the didactic purpose to be served by the panels as entities or as parts of larger groups. These findings suggest that it would be advisable to begin by trying to find for the mountains a place in the development of the narrative of Ezek. 37.

In the text of Ezek. 37 the only detail not bearing upon the fate of the bones themselves that the artist could render concretely is that contained in the statement of v. 7: "behold a commotion," or, "behold a shaking." The Hebrew word used here; namely, *ra'aš*, is that commonly applied to an earthquake (cf. e.g., Amos 1.1). If for any reason the Synagogue artist wanted to depict at this point the earthquake of which the text may be said to speak, the imagery that would be most likely to suggest itself is that supplied by the metaphor employed for instance in Zech. 14.4, "And the mount of Olives shall be cleft in the midst thereof," where the inhabitants of Jerusalem are urged to flee "as ye fled from before the earthquake (*ra'aš*) in the days of Uzziah king of Judah" (Zech. 14.5).

It is perfectly possible therefore to assume that the divided mountains are intended merely to indicate the earthquake of Ezek. 37.7, as E. G. Kraeling was among the first to point out.[748] To make sure that the black cleft in the mountains was correctly understood, the artist can be said to have added at the right the overturned building, for which, therefore, no separate interpretation is necessary. Why the earthquake should have been so important to the artist is not immediately evident. Père de Vaux and Grabar have taken a statement of the *Pirke de Rabbi Eliezer* to imply that in its interpretation of Ezek. 37.7 the earthquake played an essential part; namely, that of bringing the scattered portions of the human bodies together.[749] The fact that the first completely reunited bodies are represented at the right of the cleft in the mountains may serve to substantiate this view.

The imagery of Scene A 3 therefore associates itself logically and satisfactorily with Ezekiel 37.7b–8, showing the "commotion" or earthquake and how the bodies are assembled. If the artist has included in the imagery of this scene everything from rib-bones to flesh-covered limbs and assembled bodies, this is because in the verses in question all three stages of the process are described. At the end the bodies are ready for the next stage in the development, that described in v. 9 and portrayed in the first scene of Section B. Here, in this case, is Ezekiel himself, receiving the divine inspiration with his right hand and pointing with his left to the developments that transpire in accordance with the words he has spoken.

Returning now to Scene A 2, it follows from what has been said that the person portrayed in it is Ezekiel, and that the portion of the text of Ezekiel 37 illustrated is in all probability vv. 4–6, where again, as in v. 9, we have the divine com-

745. For the latter position, see e.g., Wischnitzer, *Messianic Theme*, p. 45; and more fully, "Conception of the Resurrection," p. 49.

746. On the inverted structure see Wischnitzer, *Messianic Theme*, p. 45; *Rep. VI*, p. 357; Du Mesnil du Buisson, *Peintures*, p. 98; Sukenik, *The Synagogue*, p. 132. On the trees see *Rep. VI*, p. 357, and Sukenik, *op. cit.*, pp. 132 f.

747. Cf. below, pp. 350 f., 354–356.

748. "Meaning of the Ezekiel Panel," p. 13. It will be evident that two mountains were required to show the "rent" between them. Since the iconographic model for a mountain included a tree at the top, as the range at the right end of Section B and the comparative materials listed in n. 700, above, p. 182 indicate, it is unnecessary to look for a separate significance for the trees themselves, or to speculate about the contrast between the two trees in Section A and the single tree in Section B as Sukenik does (*The Synagogue*, pp. 132 f.).

749. Cf. *Pirke de Rabbi Eliezer*, XXXIII (trans. Friedlander, p. 249); de Vaux's review of Du Mesnil du Buisson, *Peintures* in *Revue biblique*, XLIX (1940), p. 141; and Grabar, "Le Thème," p. 150.

mand to prophesy. On this interpretation Scenes A 2 and A 3 both concern the same step in the progress of the action, the one showing how Ezekiel is inspired and prophesies, the other how, as he prophesies, the prophesy is fulfilled. To depict in two separate scenes the initiation and the culmination of the same action is intelligible as a procedure of narrative art and in line here with the religious premises of the subject matter, where everything turns upon the divine initiative. Examples of the same method of presentation will be found not only in other compositions of the Synagogue,[750] but also in this panel in the relation between Scenes B 1 and B 3.

As far as it has gone, the interpretation suggested provides for continuity and progress of action in the left half of Panel NC 1 and offers an association of Biblical text and iconographic detail that satisfies the major demands of both. Clearly the several standing figures of Scenes A 1–3 cannot be ordinary people or end-products of the process of revivification. For this their clothing and gestures are too eloquent, and besides the final stage in the procedure of resurrection has not been reached in this part of the artist's composition.[751] That Ezekiel himself should appear so often in so short a compass is not really strange if the analogy of the Exodus and Red Sea Crossing (WA 3) be kept in mind, and was in fact almost inescapable if the element of prophecy inherent in the subject matter was to be brought out. The one detail for which no truly satisfactory explanation has been found is that of the appearance of flesh-covered limbs and heads about the feet of Ezekiel in Scene A 1, in place of the "dry bones" which the text would lead one to expect. Was this change made to avoid offending the worshipers, or has some perfectly obvious interpretation escaped us?[752]

Returning now to Section B, it can be said that if Scene B 1 shows the initial phase of the enlivenment of the assembled bodies, with Ezekiel receiving and uttering the prophecy and the Psyche ready to breathe into the bodies the breath of life, the section should contain as a sequel a scene in which the result of the action is portrayed. This complementary scene is presented at the right end of Section B in Scene B 3. Here, it will be recalled, we see a tall figure clothed in chiton and himation standing beside a ridge of mountains, his open right hand gesturing toward a group of ten smaller similarly clad figures, while the Hand of God comes toward him from above. The group of smaller figures in the left part of the scene should represent the dead of Section A as they finally "stand on their feet" (37.10) once the breath has actually come into them. The single large figure at the right could only be Ezekiel participating in this final phase of the action after the manner familiar from the last scene of Section A, his participation being expressed by the gesture of his right hand, while the Hand of God above indicates that the action is the fulfilment of divinely inspired prophecy uttered by him. Most interpreters are in general accord with this interpretation, but there are several details in the rendering that must be explained satisfactorily before the interpretation can be accepted.[753]

One elementary detail can be dismissed with but a few words. This is the fact that, contrary to the example of the second, third, and fourth scenes, the large standing figure at the end of Section B does not raise one of his arms in the direction of the Hand of God appearing from above. This departure probably need not be taken too seriously, for it is readily intelligible as a by-product of the change in garments, the use of the himation requiring that one arm (the left) be held close to the side of the body to receive the garment ends rolled about it.[754]

750. E.g., Panel WA 3 (Exodus and Crossing of the Red Sea) where one scene shows Moses about to divide the waters and another the Israelites marching through the divided waters.

751. Against Sukenik, *The Synagogue*, p. 132, and Wischnitzer, *Messianic Theme*, pp. 43f.

752. Bones, it will be recalled, do appear in Scene A 3, where all the various phases of the procedure by which they are transformed into bodies are represented because alluded to in the relevant text. In Scene A 1 they are strangely absent and the flesh-covered hands and heads are out of place. Did the artist deem it too difficult to articulate properly the bones of hands and feet?

753. The exception among the interpreters at this point is Sukenik (*The Synagogue*, pp. 128f.) for whom the scene portrays Ezekiel acting as mentor of the "elders" of the Jewish community in Babylonia (see Ezek. 8.1; 14.1).

754. The extreme limit of the arm's mobility is apparently reached in the case of the ten smaller figures of the scene. Their gesture of the left hand would not have sufficed for the upward reach toward the Hand of God. Actually, then, the artist may have been forced to choose whether to have the large figure reach upward toward the Hand of God or reach outward toward the group beside

But if the large figure be Ezekiel, why the change of garments, why the larger number of figures standing beside him, and why the mountains and the renewed appearance of *disjecta membra* in the scene?

The answers to these several questions are to be found in the divine utterance communicated to Ezekiel in vv. 11–14, where we are told that the events of the Valley of Dry Bones are a parable. Those revived represent the whole House of Israel which in its present exiled state is cut off, is without hope, and complains that its "bones are dried up." The people are, so to speak, already in their graves but God promises to open their graves, to place his spirit in them so that they will truly live again, and to bring them back to their own land, quite as he has revived the dead in the Valley of Dry Bones. Since the action described in Ezek. 37. 1–10 was a "parable," the artist in showing the culmination of the event initiated by the coming of the "breath" (Scene B 1), actually had two choices. He could either stay within the framework of the parabolic narrative as he had developed it in scenes A 1–B 1, or he could pass over into a representation of the thing symbolized; namely, the return of the House of Israel to its own land. Since the former would have left the parabolic import of the earlier scenes unexplained, and since the return of Israel was in effect the supreme culmination, he apparently adopted the second alternative. The ten figures in Scene B 3 do on this interpretation represent the nation.[755] They are dressed in the garb appropriate to their role as free men and seem by their gestures to be shown in an attitude of thanksgiving or praise.[756] The mountain in the right part of the

scene, of course, provides an allusion to the land of Israel, to which one always "goes up" from Babylonia.[757] The *disjecta membra* in the foreground of the scene are troublesome in the sense that the reason for their occurrence is difficult to pin down exactly, but it seems doubtful that they represent the artist's attempt to distinguish between the resurrection of the righteous and the eternal death of the wicked, or that added to those of Section A they make up a number significant in itself.[758] Rather, it may be, we should think of these members as a device of the artist intended to remind us that those restored to their homeland are brought up out of their graves, according to Ezek. 37.12–13, and thus to make sure that the scene is understood as a continuation of those that have gone before. So far as Ezekiel's own garment is concerned, this is entirely appropriate to him as a prophet, but the change would seem to be motivated by the transition to a new context and by his association with the redeemed community of which he is a part. The heavy aureole of curly hair not usually found with chiton and himation is preserved to identify him as the figure represented in Scenes A 1–B 1.

With Scene B 3 the action that has moved consistently from left to right in Scenes A 1 to B 1 is already reversed and moves in the opposite direction, for the figures of Scene B 3 all have their weight on their right foot and the mountain pro-

him. In choosing the latter alternative, which made it necessary to station the large figure at the right of the group, he may have been guided by the thought of providing in this way a terminus for the development of the action of Sections A and B.

755. The suggestion that the tenfold number of the persons represented is inspired by the conception of the return of the Ten Tribes (see especially Grabar, "Le Thème," pp. 150–152; and Wischnitzer, *Messianic Theme*, p. 44) is interesting but scarcely in line with what we know about the rabbinical attitude toward that conception. See especially in the *Mishnah*, Sanhedrin XI, 3; in the *Talmud*, Sanhedrin 110b (Trans., pp. 759f.); and Moore, *Judaism*, II, pp. 368f.

756. The artist clearly wished them to be thought of as having both hands raised, though for technical reasons his rendering falls short of communicating this fact clearly. See above, p. 185. The gesture has been inter-

preted to mean that they are praying (Du Mesnil du Buisson, "Les Peintures," p. 118) but this the Synagogue artists indicate in a different way. See Panel WC 3, above, pp. 166f., and Wing Panel IV, below, p. 238. The song gesture of Panel WB 1 is closer (see above, p. 124) and Sanhedrin 92b (Trans., II, p. 619) suggests that the dead whom Ezekiel raised broke forth in song, singing I Sam. 2.6. This would confirm Leveen's suggestion (*Hebrew Bible in Art*, p. 47). The relation to the Orans gesture of Christian art is patent, and in the light of the evidence now available it may be asked whether it is not properly a gesture of *eucharistia* or *eulogia*, and hence a derivative of the song gesture.

757. See e.g., Ezra 1.5; 2.59; Neh. 7.6. The imagery is entirely clear without bringing in Ezek. 36.1 etc.

758. For the former suggestion see Du Mesnil du Buisson, *Peintures*, p. 97, and in more detailed fashion with the use of a passage from the *Pirke de Rabbi Eliezer*, XXXIII (trans. Friedlander, p. 250), Grabar, "Le Thème," p. 153. For the latter see Wischnitzer, *Messianic Theme*, p. 44. The procedure of counting heads across Sections A and B implies a compositional coherence and unity in excess of that typical for narrative composition in the continuous style.

vides a terminal feature at the right of the scene. This indicates that the solitary person in the very center of Section B, whom we have not been able to assign to the scenes on either side of him, has in fact the pivotal importance proper to him as the central feature of the entire panel, and does deserve and need to be considered separately as one unit (Scene B 2) of the entire composition. If what has been said above is correct, the fact that he wears chiton and himation, but has also the elaborate coiffure normally associated with Persian dress, necessarily identifies him as Ezekiel.[759] As to his function there is but a single clue, that represented by the gesture of his uplifted right hand. This he holds in such a way that the index and the middle fingers are extended and the thumb and the last two fingers are folded back upon the palm of the hand. The gesture has no counterpart elsewhere in the Synagogue so far as we can know it, and must therefore be interpreted with the help of outside sources. In general it can be said that the gesture does not readily lend itself to the interpretation that the person employing it is pointing, this being accomplished usually either with the open hand or with the extended index finger.[760] The most familiar analogy is the so-called gesture of benediction, typical among others of Christ as Pantokrator in Byzantine art.[761] The gesture in question, without its later refinements of detail, is used also in later Roman art, for instance by the senators who appear before the tribunal addressing themselves to the magistrate seated upon it in the Probianus diptych.[762] In the same sense, as a gesture of address, though in the later refined form, it is used appropriately by the prophets of the Codex Ros-

sanensis.[763] In the scene under discussion here it lends itself well to this same interpretation. The Ezekiel to whom it is appropriate is thus one who addresses himself in words of wisdom and authority to his own people through the medium of his prophetic work and specifically in Ezek. 37.21–28, where we have a long series of instructions issued by God to Ezekiel as to what he shall do and what he shall say when the children of his people speak to him asking the meaning of his acts. What he is to say not only reaffirms the promise of the return to the land of Israel, but tells of the coming of God's servant David as their king, of the establishment of the new covenant of peace, and of the restoration of the Lord's sanctuary in their midst. In view particularly of the desperate situation portrayed in Section C, these words are of the utmost importance as the expression of the larger Jewish hope for the future. It is only natural that the artist should have made some attempt to bring them to expression in the composition. He did it appropriately at the very center of the panel by the simple expedient of showing the prophet addressing himself to his people as their authoritative spokesman.[764]

Section C

The third section of this remarkable composition (Pl. LXXII) presents two problems: first, how to construe its relation to the other two sections of the panel; and second, how to interpret adequately the imagery that repainting and subsequent severe

---

759. He has been interpreted also as the future David seen in a prophetic capacity (E. G. Kraeling, "Meaning of the Ezekiel Panel," p. 17), as either Gabriel or Michael (Leveen, *Hebrew Bible in Art*, p. 48), and as either Ezra or Zerubbabel (*Rep. VI*, p. 358). His dress excludes most of these interpretations.

760. For the gesture with the index finger see, e.g., the cupid pointing to the departing ship in the scene of Ariadne's grief in the House of Meleager (Rizzo, *La Pittura ellenistico-romana*, Pl. CIX) and in early Christian art, Abraham pointing to the ram in the bush in the scene of the Sacrifice of Isaac from the Catacomb of Priscilla (Wilpert, *Pitture*, Pl. 78).

761. Cf. e.g., Diehl, *La Peinture byzantine*, Pls. I, III, XXII, XXXV.

762. Delbrueck, *Consulardiptychen*, pp. 46f., Figs. 16 a and b.

763. A. Haseloff, *Codex Purpureus Rossanensis* (1898), fols. i–iv and vii, and in the text, p. 73, where the gesture is correctly interpreted as one of address (*Anrede*). Cf. also, e.g., Joshua addressing the Archangel in the Joshua Roll (ed. Hoepli, Pl. 4). It is entirely possible that what has become in Byzantine iconography a gesture of benediction began as one of address. Used by persons of authority it becomes, naturally, one of pronouncement, as already on the medal of Constans in Peirce and Tyler, *L'Art byzantin*, I, Pl. 20.

764. Christian art provides a good analogy to the reappearance of Ezekiel as authoritative spokesman in the center of a narrative composition dealing with events in which he plays a part. A full-page miniature of the Vatican Cosmas shows at the left and right a series of scenes portraying elements of Paul's conversion experience, while in the center, prominently displayed, stands Paul himself holding the book of his letters. Cod. Vat. Graec. 699, fol. 83ᵛ. See Weitzmann, *Illustrations in Roll and Codex*, Fig. 130.

cracking, flaking, and weathering have made obscure at so many crucial points.[765] In general it can be said that the artist has developed here against a grayish-yellow background a composition with three parts and two or three scenes, depending on how the central feature is interpreted.[766] The lower element of this central feature is a large yellow altar of the type familiar from the Elijah Panels on the South Wall, the outlines of whose die, cap, base, and beveled members are drawn in dark ochre.[767] Above the altar there is to be seen as the second element of the central feature, a green tent. The tent is identical in shape with those portrayed in Panel WB 1 (Wilderness Encampment), its fabric shot through with black stripes, its frame supported by guy-ropes attached at the ends of the peaked roof. The interior of the tent is rendered in black as usual, the dark surface providing a back-

ground against which four objects are outlined. The two at the bottom are round yellow objects inscribed with a reddish-brown band, the area contained within the band showing in reddish brown the flutings that converge toward the top and identify the objects as golden bowls (Fig. 53).[768]

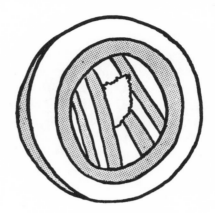

FIG. 53. Panel NC 1. Bowl

Above the bowls is a rectangular white object, badly damaged by the cracking of the surface, that rests on legs and may therefore be regarded as a table.[769] Upon the table stands a yellow object, its wide low base supported on three short legs, its tapering body marked horizontally and ending at the top in a cup or dish. Though badly distorted by the movement of the wall surfaces, it is in all probability to be identified as a *thymiaterion*.[770]

To the left of altar and tent in the smaller left part of the field the artist has portrayed two figures. The one in the foreground kneels on his right knee, at the same time clinging with both hands to the

765. Cf. above, p. 181. The weathering is due to the fact that the Section was not so deeply buried in the embankment as the other two. Flaking arises from the superimposition of several layers of paint. Resistance of the east wall of the chamber to the thrust transmitted by the north wall from the west has multiplied the vertical and diagonal fissures running between the large horizontal cracks along the top and bottom of the field. Two such fissures run down through the soldier at the extreme left end of the section; a third, coming through the tent, passes along the left side of the altar. This has a branch that crosses from the tent to the right side of the altar, divides at the level of the altar's die, and runs diagonally downward to the right and the left. A fourth, crossed by diagonal branches of the horizontal crack coming out of the area of the tent, cuts through the second of the four soldiers at the right of the tent. A fifth traces an irregular course downward just beyond the last of the four soldiers, while a sixth runs through the figure at the extreme right end of the composition. The horizontal cracks have occasioned severe dislocations, disturbing continuity of line by as much as several centimeters. Losses of plaster surface are small and confined largely to the lower central section of the field.

766. In organization the section recalls such axial compositions as Panels SC 3 (Prophets of Baal on Mount Carmel) and SC 4 (Elijah on Mount Carmel).

767. Along the bottom of the die the surface of the altar is badly cracked and has been patched to fill wide gaps in the plaster. In the photograph used for the color plate, the altar seems to rest at the right upon a small rectangular block serving as a foot. In the final rendering this part of the altar must have been covered by the foot of the man at the right of the altar. Perhaps what appears in the plate as a small block is the remains of a basal member once extending the full width of the altar, all of which had faded out when the photograph was made, save for the section protected by the man's foot that had eventually flaked off. Nothing at all is visible in this area today.

768. There is a patch in the plaster at the center of the bowl. A similarly fluted bowl seen in a different position appears in Panel WA 3; see above, Fig. 18, p. 79.

769. The left leg is clearly visible; the right can be seen on early detail photographs, its upper and lower portions dissociated from each other by the horizontal movement of the respective parts of the wall.

770. For other short, three-legged *thymiateria* see particularly Panels WB 2 (Consecration of the Tabernacle) and WB 4 (The Ark in the Land of the Philistines). For Roman *thymiateria* of similar shape see Bossert, *Geschichte des Kunstgewerbes*, I, p. 223, nos. 4–5. F. Landsberger reproduces a rendering of the brass laver of the Temple in a form analogous to the object depicted here, taken from a fifteenth-century Jewish manuscript. Cf. *Hebrew Union College Annual*, XVIII (1943–1944), p. 293, and Fig. 5.

side of the altar.[771] He wears a reddish-brown tunic, ornamented down the front with the usual band outlined in black, belted at the waist, and finished at the hem with a border in a color no longer distinguishable.[772] Like all other garments of this type, the tunic is slit at the sides as far as the waist. In showing how the front half of the tunic falls between the man's legs as he kneels, the artist has brought the slit too far forward, making the back half of the garment go most of the way around the man's waist. With the tunic go green trousers and boots that are darker in color than usual.[773] The hilt of the dagger hanging from the belt of the tunic is visible at his left side. Though his legs are shown in profile, his body is turned into three-quarter perspective and his head almost full front. The chin is lightly bearded, but the features of the face are not clearly recognizable and the eyes have been gouged out. A peculiar character is given to the head by the fact that the hair-mass is unevenly distributed, being much wider than necessary at the right and narrower than usual in this type of coiffure at the left.[774] Poorly drawn from the outset because of his unusual pose, the figure has apparently been daubed over by someone thinking to make "improvements."

The second figure, at the left of the first, is much better drawn and wears military garb. On his head is a yellow (golden?) helmet with pink plumes. Coming from beneath it there can be seen at the left one end of a pink fillet or diadem. A pink chlamys, fastened over the right shoulder, hangs down over his left arm, its end also visible by his right side. His body is covered with a yellow (golden?) breast plate to which are attached

lamboys forming a skirt. The cuirass as a whole (*cuirasse à lambrequins*) is worn over a long-sleeved blue tunic fringed at the hem, and has about it an ornamented belt (*cingulum militare*). Greaves and black shoes complete the costume, which, while similar at some points to Roman military dress, is perhaps in part quite fantastic, and has its closest analogy in that assigned to military deities.[775] The man stands to the left of and slightly behind the kneeling figure, whose shoulders he grasps with his hands as though to remove him by force from the altar.

At the right of the altar and the tent the imagery is highly confused due to the fact that parts of two superimposed renderings are visible simultaneously. The parts are separated out in Fig. 54, with which Pl. LXXII should be compared. Perhaps the most distinct element of the composition in this area is the group of four soldiers who stand alongside the tent in the upper part of the field. They are drawn at half scale, but their equipment is similar to that of the larger figure at the left, only less magnificent. As elsewhere, the artist has varied details and colors to enliven the group. The first and third soldiers, counting from the left, have yellow helmets with pink plumes and skirted cuirasses of yellow scale armor, over which they wear at the waist a wide belt and at the shoulder a yellow chlamys. The second and fourth lack the chlamys, have light gray helmets and gray scale armor, and hold both hands palm outward before their chests in what looks to

771. A vertical movement of the plaster has pushed the parts of his right forearm out of line. The fingers of the left hand come up over the upper edge of the altar in awkward fashion.

772. It is recorded in the Gute copies as light brown. Hopkins' field notes indicate green cuffs on the tunic. A note made at the time of discovery by Du Mesnil du Buisson indicates that the tunic had "white embroidery" in addition to the white belt (*Peintures*, p. 101 and n. 1).

773. Du Mesnil du Buisson states that he wears, not white boots, but black shoes (*Peintures*, p. 101). A reexamination of the dim traces remaining suggests that he does wear boots and that while the right was gray, the left was reddish brown, which is unusual, to say the least.

774. The hair-mass, perhaps insufficient on all sides at first, seems to have been supplemented at the right beyond the proper measure, giving the unbalanced appearance.

775. For Roman armor of the later Empire see P. Couissin, *Les Armes romaines* (1926), pp. 403–469. For the costume in question here, compare the representations of Bel, Iarhibol, and Aglibol in the fresco of the sacrifice of the Roman tribune Terentius from the Temple of Bel at Dura (Cumont, *Fouilles*, Pl. L) and that of the god Aphlad in the bas-relief from his temple (*Rep. V*, Pl. XIII), the former being the closer. While the belt, the *cuirasse à lambrequins*, and the plumed helmet recall Roman military equipment of the later period, the form of the helmet in particular is unusual. Instead of cheek-pieces (*paragnathides*) it seems to have a face-guard of one piece that passes under the chin and is attached to the helmet by a hinge at the back. Helmets giving fuller protection to the face were developed particularly for gladiators (see examples from Pompeii reproduced by G. Lafaye in Daremberg-Saglio, II, 2, 1896, p. 1582, Fig. 3574, *s.v.* "gladiator"; and later examples entirely covering the face, e.g., in L. Robert, *Les Gladiateurs dans l'orient grec*, 1940, Pls. VI, XIII–XV) but no exact counterparts are known, and the few gladiators found in the Dura graffiti (*Rep. V*, Pl. XXXIII, 3; and *Rep. VI*, p. 483, Fig. 31) do not wear analogous headgear.

FIG. 54. Panel NC I. Section C. Two stages of Design at Right of Altar

be a gesture of horror or amazement. Parts of the third and fourth soldiers have flaked or faded out entirely, leaving a reddish-brown mass that belongs to the underpainting.

At the extreme right end of the panel stands a large figure clad in a light-colored, long-sleeved tunic with red and black fold lines, reddish-brown trousers, and light gray boots.[776] The tunic is slit to the waist, has an extra-wide yellow band at the hem, is decorated with vertical black bands down the front, and is worn with the white belt.[777] A large sword or empty scabbard done in reddish brown hangs from the belt at his left, its lower end projecting between the man's wide-spread legs.[778] The legs are seen in profile, with the right far advanced and sharply bent at the knee to indicate rapid movement toward the left, but the upper part of the body is turned into a frontal pose, giving a full view of the face with its heavy aureole of brown hair outlined in black.[779] At present no less

than three arms are to be seen, indicating that the position of one of them was changed when the scene was repainted. In both versions the right arm was raised high over the man's head, where it now holds, and may originally have held, a heavy pointed sword with a thick round pommel. In the first rendering of the scene the left arm was drawn back, where it was in position to rest upon the sword or the scabbard at his side.[780] This arm was later covered by the background color, but flaking and fading have brought it to light again. In the second rendering of the scene the left hand was brought forward so as to grasp the hair of the remaining figure in the scene.

This last figure, apparently the one most re-painted, is a jumble of the worst order. In both versions the man represented was dressed in a reddish-brown tunic and green trousers. In the final rendering the lower part of his body was seen in profile, the right hip in close proximity to the altar, the left leg far advanced and sharply bent at the knee. The upper part of the body in this rendering was doubled over from the waist, bringing the head into position to be grasped by the man at the right. Of the head, whose features are today quite indistinguishable, having flaked off to

776. Du Mesnil du Buisson (*Peintures*, p. 102) and Hopkins' field notes indicate that the tunic was white! The Gute copy renders it in light pink.

777. On the left shoulder the tie-string of the garment is clearly visible.

778. The Gute copy (Fig. 54) records at the man's right side near the belt a peculiar excrescence, the nature and meaning of which is not certain.

779. The eyes were disfigured, probably when the embankment was constructed. Apparently the man was lightly bearded, but details are obscure.

780. Actually the arm seems to continue above and beyond the top of the scabbard. The Gute copy shows a cuff at the end of this scabbard.

reveal a mass of reddish brown belonging to the underpainting, only this can be said: that it had a heavy mass of hair, which the man at the right grasps with his extended left hand, and that the face was turned full front. This contortion brings the right arm into view, hanging loosely downward in the direction of the knee of the man at the right. The position of the left arm is difficult to distinguish. In its final form, then, the scene showed the man at the right about to decapitate the contorted figure before him. Between the feet of the two of them there have been sketched in light pink the outlines of a basket that stands ready to receive the head of the victim.[781] Yet the victim was apparently not entirely defenseless, for between his legs lines that suggest a sword or scabbard hanging by his side have been noted.[782]

In the earlier rendering this same figure, instead of being bent over at the middle, was erect. Elements of the reddish brown of his tunic extend into the area occupied by the third and fourth of the soldiers above. Below, between the right leg of the swordsman and the left leg of his victim, the remains of the left trouser leg of the earlier figure are to be seen. From the position and angle of the trouser leg it is evident that the man was striding toward the left in the same manner as the swordsman behind him. His right leg, therefore, must have been well advanced toward the altar. On either side of the calf of the swordsman who follows there have been noted parallel lines running diagonally across the field. These may well represent the outlines of a scabbard or sword hanging at the left side of the figure in the van.[783] Conceivably the man's left hand rested upon the object by his side, as did that of the man behind him.

The earlier rendering of the scene at the right of the altar, therefore, contained in all probability but two figures, being analogous in this respect to the scene at the left of the altar. The four soldiers alongside the tent cannot have been part of it, for the space they now occupy was taken by the head and shoulders of the man nearest the altar with

just enough space between him and the tent to balance the scene at the left and to allow for the guy-rope that must originally have been shown holding the tent at this side. The two men in the scene were closely matched in costume, both with each other and with the figure clinging to the altar in the scene at the left, though the tunic of the one at the extreme right was lighter in color. From the relative position of their respective right and left legs it seems that the one was following directly upon the heels of the other. If in this earlier form of the scene the man to the rear also held his sword poised over his head, as seems probable, he can be said to have been in a position to bring it down directly upon the head or neck of the man before him, attacking him from the rear.

On the basis of such general information as has been available hitherto, the subject matter of Section C has been interpreted in three different ways. The first interpretation takes its cue from the figure clinging to the altar at the left. In the Bible there is but one story that can provide a concrete explanation of this detail; namely, that of I Kings 2.28–34. The story tells how Solomon used Benaiah, the captain of his host, to put to death Joab, the erstwhile captain of David's army. Joab, anticipating Solomon's enmity, "fled to the Tent of the Lord and caught hold on the horns of the altar." Benaiah, finding him there, hesitated to kill him until he had received more explicit instructions from Solomon. When these instructions were forthcoming, Benaiah returned and killed Joab in the Temple in spite of the sanctity of the place. In terms of this story, the scene at the left has been said to represent Benaiah or one of his soldiers removing Joab from the altar, while that at the right shows Joab's execution.[784]

The interpretation has several advantages; above all, the association of the detail of the man at the altar with a specific Biblical story, and the logical progress of the action from the one scene to the other. At the same time there are numerous difficulties; for instance, the introduction of the soldier in the scene at the left to replace Benaiah,

---

781. For the use of baskets as containers for severed heads see II Kings 10.7 and Josephus, *Antiquitates* IX, 6, 5, § 127.

782. So Hopkins' field notes and the Gute copy. At present these lines are no longer distinguishable.

783. So both Hopkins' field notes and the Gute copy. At present these lines are no longer distinguishable.

784. Suggested first by Hopkins and Du Mesnil du Buisson (*CRAI*, 1933, p. 252), this interpretation is still favored by Du Mesnil du Buisson (*Peintures*, pp. 100–103), Grabar ("Le Thème," pp. 12 f.), Sonne ("The Paintings," pp. 330–335), and Wischnitzer (*Messianic Theme*, pp. 36–38).

or the change in Benaiah's own dress from the first to the second scene, if he be the soldier in the first scene; the use of a tent to represent the Temple of the Solomonic era, or the character of the tent as compared with the Tabernacle in WB 1 and 2; and above all, the problem how to connect the story from I Kings with the scenes taken from the Book of Ezekiel. Solutions for most of these difficulties have already been proposed and more could readily be developed to account for the earlier version of the scene at the right.[785] Those who find these solutions less convincing can take recourse to another suggestion, originally made by Sukenik; namely, that Section C represents the death of Zechariah in the Temple.[786] The historical event of the death of Zechariah occurred several centuries before the days of Ezekiel, being connected by II Chronicles 24.20–21 with the reign of Joash, king of Judah, but the story does indeed play a part in the traditions connected with the period of the exile. Tradition has it that Nebuzaradan, Nebuchadnezzar's general, coming to destroy Jerusalem and the Temple, found the innocent blood of Zechariah still seething beside the altar and calling for vengeance, which he finally supplied.[787]

The difficulty is that the Biblical form of the story about Zechariah gives no basis for the scene of the man clinging to the altar, and is in flagrant disagreement with the imagery at the right, for according to II Chronicles 24, Zechariah was stoned.

More recently a third suggestion has been advanced; namely, that Section C should be connected with the episode described in Ezek. 9.1–6.[788] This episode is part of Ezekiel's symbolic vision of the punishment of Jerusalem for its sinfulness. In it the prophet sees six men (the six angelic "guardians" of the city) coming into the Temple and standing beside the brazen altar. All six are described as having a "destroying weapon" in their hands. With them is a man clothed in linen with a writer's inkhorn at his side. The man in linen garments is ordered to go through the city and make a mark (*taw*) upon the foreheads of those who lament the city's wickedness. These are to be spared, but the rest are to be slain without pity by the six men, who are to begin at the sanctuary itself, defiling its courts with the slain.

The interpretation has much to recommend it, particularly the fact that it makes applicable to the scene the words of Ezekiel, such as were used also for Section A and B. Yet there are difficulties here too. On the assumption that the soldiers in the scene represent the "men" with the "weapon of destruction" in their hands, we must suppose that the artist has reduced their number from six to five; on the assumption that the person at the extreme right is the man "clothed in linen," that he has changed the man's function by making him join in the slaughter. From these difficulties an escape may be provided by the *Midrash Rabbah* on Lamentations 2.1, where apparently the number six is interpreted to include the man "clothed in linen," and where it is said of the latter, who is none other than Gabriel, that he served in three capacities: as scribe, executioner, and High Priest.[789] But the fact remains that no one of the soldiers actually has in his hands the distinguishing "weapon of destruction," this being monopolized by the figures in the foreground, and that on the hypothesis suggested, the artist must have invented the scene of

785. Du Mesnil du Buisson (*Peintures*, p. 100) assumes that the artist forgot to introduce the vertical band necessary to divide the Joab scenes from these representing Ezek. 37, which is a counsel of despair. Wischnitzer (*Messianic Theme*, p. 37) makes a good point in this connection in suggesting that the scenes are related to those of Panel EC 1 (David and Saul in the Wilderness of Ziph). Her explanation of the introduction of the soldier in the scene at the left; namely, to avoid showing Benaiah turning away from the niche when seizing the evildoer, is unconvincing (*ibid.*, p. 38). Grabar finds a connection between Ezekiel and the Joab story in the moral sphere (Joab the type of those who do not have a claim upon eternal life; see also Du Mesnil du Buisson, *Peintures*, p. 103) and associates the latter also with the demands of the covenant relationship ("Le Thème," pp. 12f.). Sonne explains the connection eschatologically, finding in the Joab scene a "symbolic-homiletical" allusion to the slaughter of the "Prince of Edom," who represents the Roman Empire, and obtains in this connection a basis for the imagery of the scene at the right, where the victim is grasped by the hair of his head ("The Paintings," pp. 330–335).

786. *Journal of the Palestine Oriental Society*, XVIII (1938), p. 61. The same interpretation was proposed independently by S. H. Blank, *Hebrew Union College Annual*, XII–XIII (1937–1938), pp. 343f., n. 34.

787. The full story is frequently repeated, for instance in the *Midrash Rabbah* on Lamentations 2.2 (Trans., VII, pp. 163–166, see also Proem XXIII, pp. 32–34) and on Ecclesiastes 3.16 (Trans., VIII, pp. 101f.).

788. So first Leveen, *Hebrew Bible in Art*, pp. 48–51; and more recently Sukenik, *The Synagogue*, pp. 126–128.

789. Trans., VII, p. 153.

the man being dragged from the altar as a way of expressing in graphic fashion the effort of the doomed Jerusalemites to escape from the imminent retribution. This is possible but not likely.

The problems posed by all of the interpretations hitherto suggested indicate that an adequate understanding of the imagery has not yet been reached. Other solutions must therefore be sought, and to have the highest degree of probability they should start from two assumptions: first, that Section C is part of the Panel NC 1; and second, that for the explanation of what goes on in Section C, the imagery of A and B is more immediately important than anything else. Proceeding inductively from this basis, it would appear that if A and B really develop the thought of Israel's return from exile, Section C might properly be expected to illustrate some theme to which the return could be regarded as a foil. The most likely area from which to draw such a theme is that of the end of the Jewish national life and the capture and destruction of Jerusalem in the days of Nebuchadnezzar. The importance attaching both to the celebration of the Ninth of Ab, and to the hope of national restoration in the period after the destruction of Jerusalem by Titus would make this particularly appropriate. From what we know about the artist's treatment of the Samuel Cycle (Panels NB 2, 1; WB 4, 3) we may even expect such a juxtaposition of scenes to bring to expression the thoughts of the Prophets themselves; namely, that the destruction of Jerusalem and the end of Jewish national life are a divine punishment visited upon the people for their infidelity to the divine Law and its ethical implications, and that the restoration expresses God's mercy and his abiding fidelity to his promises.

Interpretation would do well to begin with the tent and the altar in the middle of the section. The former is probably not the "Tent of the Lord" mentioned in the Joab story (I Kings 2.28), as a glance at the Tabernacles of Panels WB 1 and 2 will show, but rather a military tent like those used by the armed tribes when they came up from Egypt, as depicted in Panel WB 1. The objects portrayed in it — the bowls, the table, and the thymiaterion — should be the sacred vessels, whose removal from the Temple is so constantly referred to in accounts of Jerusalem's last days, whose return is a part of the eschatological hope, and

whose desecration by Belshazzar the Synagogue artist was portraying in another composition (Panel EC 2). If this interpretation is correct, it provides a point of orientation for the rest of the imagery, associating the composition with the period of the fall of Jerusalem and of the campaigns of Nebuchadnezzar. From the position assigned to the military tent, the artist would probably wish us to infer further that the Temple had already been destroyed, and that in the sacred enclosure in which his scene is laid, nothing remained but the altar and the tents of the conquerors. Perhaps he found it difficult to convince his sponsors that in the combination of these two elements he had composed a scene giving an effective representation of the destruction and spoliation of the Temple. Hence when the scene at the right end of the composition (Scene C 3) had to be repainted, he used the additional space provided to present alongside the tent the members of the conquering host. This was the best he could do to enliven the scene (C 2).[790]

If Scene C 2 portrays the events that are recorded in II Kings 25 and are associated in religious thought and observance with the Ninth of Ab, what suitable interpretation can be offered for the actions of Scenes C 1 and 3? Two facts must be evident in this connection: first, that the actions are deeds of violence; and second, that of the persons involved, the three in tunic and trousers are by their costume identified as members of the priesthood or the nobility — in all probability the latter, since they all carry weapons. In dealing with Scene C 3, the problem is to inquire which king or peer could be thought to have been slain in the Temple by his equal in connection with the events that led to the nation's downfall. The episode should, moreover, be of such a kind that the artist could in repainting his rendering of it properly make the action more drastic. On these points the Bible helps us not at all, but Midrashic narrative does in its elaboration of the story about the death of Jehoiakim at the hands of Nebuchadnezzar.

What the Bible tells us about Jehoiakim is only that he was bound in fetters by Nebuchadnezzar to be carried off to Babylonia (II Chron. 36.6), and

790. Perhaps, of course, the stenographic brevity of Scene C 2 was one of the reasons for the repainting of Scene C 3.

that he slept with his fathers while his son Jeho-iachin reigned in his stead (II Kings 24.6). From this there eventually developed the story that Nebuchadnezzar took Jehoiakim about with him through all the cities of Judah before actually killing him.[791] Another form of the Midrashic version happens to be presented by Josephus, who tells us that Jehoiakim received Nebuchadnezzar in Jerusalem, expecting that the Chaldean king would do him no harm. Nebuchadnezzar, however, once he was in the city disregarded his agreements and slew all those that were of outstanding vigor and beauty, together with King Jehoiakim, whose body he ordered to be thrown unburied outside the walls of the city.[792] With this last version of this story it seems possible to associate Scene C 3 at the right end of our panel. King Jehoiakim, still possessing his sword, is unexpectedly put upon by Nebuchadnezzar and killed at Jerusalem in the very Temple precincts from which his body could most readily be thrown over and outside the city walls, to lie unburied. Indeed, this particular story is the only one that would permit the two successive renderings developed by the artist. The first, in which the one royal person comes up behind the other with his sword ready to deal the fatal blow reflects the unexpected nature of the attack, while the second in which Nebuchadnezzar grasps Jehoiakim's head emphasizes with equal propriety the brutality of the assault. The basket supplied in the second rendering suggests that while the body is to be disposed of, the victim's head is to be preserved as a trophy and shown to those who could be impressed by the death of their king.[793]

Scene C 1, at the left side of this section of the panel, provides even greater difficulties for the interpreter. Perhaps this is because at the present time we do not have the material needed to place the allusion properly. Clearly an important, proba-bly royal, person is to be dragged from the horns of the altar where he has taken refuge, but the chances are that he is not Joab. Rather we must look to the period of the nation's downfall, and from this period neither the Bible nor the more well-known *Midrashim* record any episode that could have inspired the rendering. The only clue as to the historical context is supplied by the large figure of the soldier involved in the action. He wears the same military costume as the soldiers introduced into Scene 2 at the side of the tent, and should on this score be Nebuzaradan, Nebuchad-nezzar's "captain of the guard." Whether the allusion in our scene is to some specific act, or merely to those whom he took from Temple and city into captivity and exile (II Kings 25.18–20), it is impossible to tell. Only this would follow: that the episode portrayed in Scene C 1 follows in time the destruction of the Temple (Scene C 2), which in turn follows the slaying of King Jehoiakim by Nebuchadnezzar (Scene C 3). Section C of the composition would therefore show a series of events whose proper order runs from right to left, and which would combine with Scene B 3 to develop in the right half of the panel the same consistency of movement toward the center as that already discovered in the left half, making the whole a balanced, centralized, composition.[794]

In Section C of our Panel we thus have before us a typical and significant selection of those acts of violence that mark the end of national life, including the destruction of the Temple, the removal of the sacred vessels, the violence done to the members of its royal house, and the exile of its men of note. All this was viewed by the prophet Ezekiel as a divine punishment, but not as a mark of final and complete rejection. It therefore serves as a foil in his work to the glories of a new age, when Israel will return to its own land and when the life of the nation will be restored. The Syna-

791. See the *Midrash Rabbah* on Leviticus XIX, 6 (Trans., IV, pp. 245–248) and for the same story in more abbreviated form Genesis Rabbah XCIV, 9 (Trans., II, p. 879). In general see Ginzberg, *Legends of the Jews*, IV, pp. 284f., and VI, p. 379, n. 128.

792. *Antiquitates* X, 6, 3 = § 97.

793. This would be an effective way of reconciling the version of the story depicted here with that of the *Midrash Rabbah*, the explanation being that it was the king's head that was taken around the cities of Judah, not the king himself.

794. The fact that in the right half of the panel the subject matter changes between Scene B 3 and Scene C 1 does not affect the fact of consistency of movement from the right in the direction of Scene B 2. It is interesting to note, however, how cleverly the Synagogue artist has extricated himself from a potential difficulty at this point by combining a division into three sections with consistency of movement from two directions toward the middle. Scene B 3 by the direction of its movement belongs to the right half of the panel, but stands within its own subject matter context in Section B.

gogue artists, in voicing Israel's hope of a better future, could not have made a happier choice than to combine in one magnificent composition, turning on the person of Ezekiel himself, scenes depicting the end of national life and the graphic narrative of the Valley of Dry Bones, understood as a parable of the nation's rebirth under God. What they produced in presenting this material will doubtless continue to be regarded as their greatest and most important composition. Particularly noteworthy is the fact that they succeeded in dealing with prophetic material and serving didactic purposes within the limitations of a framework provided by narrative art.

David and Saul in the Wilderness of Ziph

Panel EC 1 (fragmentary). H. *ca.* 1.29 m.; L. 4.88 m. (Pls. XXXII, LXXIII).

Rep. VI, pp. 365f.; Du Mesnil du Buisson, "Nouvelles découvertes," pp. 555f.; *idem, Peintures*, pp. 103–107; Grabar, "Le Thème," pp. 15f.; Leveen, *Hebrew Bible in Art*, p. 45; Sukenik, *The Synagogue*, pp. 147–149; Sonne, "The Paintings," pp. 339–342; Wischnitzer, *Messianic Theme*, pp. 34–36; Wodtke, "Malereien," pp. 59–61.

On the east side of the Synagogue's House of Assembly the space devoted to Register C was broken by the main doorway let into the wall near its mid-point. Two fields were thus formed of which the one to the north was longer, the length of the one to the south being diminished by the width of the smaller doorway set into the wall at its extreme southern end (Plan XII). These fields the artist developed as two separate compositions (Panels EC 1 and EC 2), both of which are now fragmentary and poorly preserved, the latter especially so. Of Panel EC 1 an irregular strip along the top, 0.10–0.20 m. wide, is missing. This was broken off along with the entire upper portion of the wall when the parts of the building projecting from the embankment were razed by the city's defenders. In the area immediately below the line of breakage the plaster that remains consists of large fragments. In a zone along the top, *ca.* 0.20 m. wide at the left and as much as 1 m. at the extreme right,

it has preserved almost no trace of the color applied to it because of its proximity to the surface of the embankment and to the resultant weathering.[795] Elsewhere, particularly in the central element of the composition, there have been losses of parts of the surface due to cracking. That what remains of the painting suffices for the identification of most of its subject matter is fortunate indeed, for the composition was developed with great care by the artist because it provided opportunities for the presentation of materials in which apparently he took great delight.

The inspiration for the picture comes in this instance from the historical books of the Bible, and there more particularly from the cycle of stories told in I Samuel about the relations of Saul and David.[796] One of the more colorful narratives of this cycle relates how Saul in his anger at David, hearing that David was in the wilderness of Ziph, marshalled 3,000 men against him, encamping finally on the hill of Hachilah (I Sam. 26). David, having ascertained Saul's whereabouts, came to the camp with Abishai, the brother of Joab, at night and found Saul "within the barricade" and Abner and the host bivouacked round about, all sound asleep. Abishai, realizing that David had his enemy at his mercy, asked permission to kill Saul with the king's own spear, conveniently accessible beside his head. David, however, refused to do harm to the Lord's Anointed and merely took from beside the sleeping monarch his spear and a cruse of water. With these he crossed over to a high hill from which he called back to Abner and Saul, upbraiding the former for his failure to protect the king and offering to return the spear if the king would send one of his young men over to fetch it (I Sam. 26.1–22).

Certain parts of this story the artist has presented in a composition made up of three scenes

795. The reduction of color intensity at the right has made it impossible to reproduce that section of the composition in color.

796. This is doubted today only by Sukenik and Sonne. The former associates the composition with events in the period of David's war with the Philistines, more particularly with the episode of II Sam. 23, when some of David's "mighty men" brought water to him from the well of Bethlehem, while he was camped in the cave of Adullam (*The Synagogue*, p. 148). The latter connects it with the wars of Gog and Magog ("The Paintings," pp. 339–342).

set off from each other by changes in the color of the background. Of these scenes the one at the left is the longest (approximately 1.87 m.), the one at the right the shortest (*ca.* 0.97 m.).[797] The only question is whether the scene at the right is taken from, or is supplied as a foil to, the narrative of I Sam. 26. In the one instance the action must be said to move continuously from left to right, in the other from both ends toward the middle. In either case Saul and his men should be thought to come consistently from the left and David consistently from the right.

The first scene, beginning at the left, is set against a solid reddish-brown background and shows a large company of horsemen moving toward the right. The members of the company have been so disposed by the artist as to give particular prominence by his size to one of their number who is presented in the foreground, near the center of the scene. Behind him at the left and somewhat higher up in the field is the largest part of the company, drawn to smaller scale, closely packed and possibly numbering originally as many as seven men. At the right of the central figure, but also higher up in the field and therefore really in the background, are two additional riders of intermediate proportions. In the empty spaces in the foreground at the right and left of the central figure are shown dogs moving with their master to the right.

In spite of certain differences between them, all members of the company are drawn in accordance with one and the same pattern, that exhibited in full detail by the important person at the center. The pattern has already been encountered in the representation of Mordecai in Panel WC 2, where it is rendered with equal delight and care by the artist and where its elements and its associations with Sassanian art and with the art of Dura have already been pointed out.[798] It is that of a man in the court costume of tunic, trousers, and soft boots seated on an elegantly caparisoned and beautifully proportioned white stallion. The man faces full front and the horse's chest is shown in a three-quarter view in spite of the fact that the movement

is toward the right. So far as the horse is concerned, the only differences from WC 2 to be noted are that the head is here held higher, which is to be expected since it is being guided by the reins of the rider and not by an attendant, and that one of the forelegs is off the ground, both details indicating more rapid movement.[799] The horse's harness and accoutrement, including quiver and bow-case, are the same as in Panel WC 2, the only difference being that the important breastband and crupper are reddish-brown and, instead of being decorated with phalerae, are fringed.[800] The rider's tunic and trousers, ornamented with the usual yellow bands and set off against the white boots, are here done in red. Like the quiver, the coat that billows out behind the rider and identifies him as a king is rendered in green.

Of the other figures in the scene, the king's associates are identical with him save in a few particulars. They naturally lack the coat that he wears, and have trousers that are green and quivers that are sometimes red and sometimes white. All face directly front in spite of the fact that they move toward the right. Both forelegs of their horses are set firmly on the ground, following the convention used for Mordecai's horse in Panel WC 2, the left hind leg being the only one that is advanced and showing motion.[801] The two dogs in the foreground are of one and the same type, that of the saluki, a gazelle hound still bred in the Near East, and occasionally represented also on hunting sarcophagi of Asia Minor.[802] Their long sleek bodies are done

797. The scenes overlap slightly where they meet, making all measurements approximate.

798. Cf. above, pp. 152 f. For groups of horsemen in Oriental scenes of martial character, see the left half of Bas-relief VI at Shapur, Sarre and Herzfeld, *Iranische Felsreliefs*, Pl. XLV.

799. That the position of the forelegs in Panel WC 2 is unusual has been noted above. On the bas-reliefs horses, when not shown in the "flying gallop," usually have the leg nearest the background raised and advanced, for obvious reasons. Cf. Sarre, *Die Kunst des alten Persien*, Pls. 70, 71, 73, 74. Painters were not subject to the same limitations as sculptors in this particular and could show the leg nearest the spectator raised. So, by way of exception, also the late bas-relief, *ibid.*, Pl. 86.

800. The shadow lines on the horse are done throughout in red.

801. On the parallels to this rendering elsewhere, see above, p. 154, n. 566. Note in the case of the two riders to the right of the king an instance of inverted perspective. The body of the horse farthest to the rear has been elongated so that, while its head and chest project at the right beyond the horse in the foreground, its rider sits to the left of his companion.

802. Cf. the sarcophagus in Limyra reproduced by G. Rodenwaldt, *Sitzungsberichte der preußischen Akademie der Wissenschaften* (1933), Pl. II, 5.

in white, with parallel dark lines along the backbone suggesting ribs and similar lines along the neck to indicate the mane. They wear a harness consisting of two bands that go around the neck and the chest respectively meeting above the shoulders.[803] Both forefeet are off the ground as they advance in bounds toward the right. Their presence in the picture shows its association, not only with scenes of a martial character, but also with the hunting scene tradition that played so important a part in the royal art of Persia and the inner Orient.[804]

Reasonably clear in its essential import in spite of the fading along the top, the cracks, and the graffiti that mar its surface occasionally,[805] the scene is readily intelligible as the product of the artist's effort to show Saul and his host of 3,000 men setting out for the wilderness of Ziph to capture David and his band. The scene does more than ample justice to this theme and to the importance of Saul in the later tradition, a fact that has raised the question whether David and the band that he had gathered about him during Saul's time in his constant fighting with the Philistines (I Sam. 18–25) should not be regarded as the subject of the painting.[806] On this point the observation that in the other scenes of the panel David comes from the right and Saul from the left must be taken as decisive. The probability is that the artist gave so much space to the scene and developed it in such splendid fashion, not because of the importance of Saul, but because the subject offered opportunities for him to display his skill along lines particularly familiar to him.[807] It may be noted in this connection that at the extreme left end of the scene the figures are incomplete, only the riders and the foreparts of their horses being visible, something quite without parallel in the other known panels of the Synagogue. It is possible that as first sketched in outline the figures were complete at the left and that the thigh and buttock of the last horse were covered by the vertical panel band subsequently introduced. If so, the artist's original intention was to leave the field without vertical framing members at the left, as apparently he did also at the right.[808] The reasons for his departure from the normal practice of framing his panels at the sides are naturally to be found in the demands which the subject of the composition

803. The same harness appears on the animals of the dado. For the comparative material see below, p. 246, n. 983.

804. On the hunting scene as a part of the art tradition of the Orient see in general Rostovtzeff, *YCS*, V, esp. pp. 276–283; *Rep. IX, 3*, pp. 46–50; G. Rodenwaldt, *Journal of Hellenic Studies*, LIII (1933), pp. 195–211. The hunting scenes of Dura are those of the Mithraeum (*Rep. VII–VIII*, Pls. XIV–XV) and that of the private house in Block M7 (*Rep. VI*, Pl. XLII, 1). Neither shows dogs accompanying the hunters. For Assyrian hunting scenes with dogs (mastiffs), see the famous relief from the period of Assurbanipal in the British Museum (Hall, *Babylonian and Assyrian Sculpture in the British Museum*, Pl. LIII, 2). For Persian counterparts, see, e.g., the Sassanian or Parthian silver dish reproduced by Sarre (*Die Kunst des alten Persien*, Pl. 118), the Sassanian tapestry in the Musée Guimet, and the funerary stele from Dascylium in Lycia, reproduced by Rostovtzeff (*YCS*, V, Figs. 69 and 65).

805. The most important of the cracks in this section of the panel is that which comes down diagonally from the upper right corner of the panel, cutting through the right hind leg of Saul's horse and continuing in the same direction to the area of the dado below the panel. Three graffiti are incised on this part of the composition: a horse plainly visible in front of the thighs of the forelegs of Saul's horse (Inscr. no. **63**), a harp or lyre below the dog ahead of the horse (Inscr. no. **64**), and a crude image of a human being to the right of the left hind leg of the same horse (Inscr. no. **62**). Cf. below, p. 319.

806. So originally *Rep. VI*, p. 366; and more recently, Wischnitzer, *Messianic Theme*, pp. 34–36. Sukenik's interpretation to the effect that the scene shows the "mighty men" coming to David with Abishai in the lead (*The Synagogue*, p. 148) moves along the same lines, but is ruled out by the fact that the rider in the middle of the scene wears the mantle reserved for kings.

807. Roman hunting sarcophagi, especially those representing Attis as a huntsman, commonly have an introductory scene of some length, showing the hunter's departure. Cf. e.g., C. Robert, *Die antiken Sarkophag-Reliefs*, III, 1 (1897), Pls. II–III. That the portrayal of Israelite monarchs in the setting of Parthian hunting scenes would not be offensive to the Jews can be demonstrated from the story of Rab, a contemporary of the Dura Synagogue in lower Mesopotamia. The story tells how Satan once appeared to David in the form of a deer while he was devoting himself to the sport of falconry, and how David shot at him with arrows and pursued him to the Philistine lands. Cf. Sanhedrin 95a (Trans., p. 640) and Bacher, *Die Agada der babylonischen Amoräer*, p. 9 and n. 48. Here the Israelite ideal of kingship has been translated entirely into Persian forms.

808. The vertical panel band at the left end of this scene is of unusual character. The north wall, being of extra thickness near the bottom, met the east wall on a diagonal line in the lower part of the field. In consequence the vertical band framing Panel EC 1 at the left tapers from its normal width at the top to a sharp point near the bottom. It may have been introduced only to hide the irregularity of the wall construction in this area.

made upon the limited space at his disposal in this instance.[809]

The all-important central scene begins under the very legs of the horses and dogs in the scene at the left. No formal division is made, the change from one scene to the other being indicated by the pose of the persons represented and by changes in the nature of foreground and background. In the foreground the reddish color against which the figures are portrayed has superimposed upon it a series of heavy semicircular brown lines that ascend in scale pattern to indicate mountain ridges after the convention familiar from Panel NC 1. In the upper part of the panel the background is dark, and was perhaps originally black.[810] The mountain ridges, while stretching across the entire foreground of the scene, continue upward in the field only at the right, providing in this way a resting place for the head and shoulders of a man whose large reclining figure takes in the full width of the scene along the bottom. He rests in the conventional position, his body inclined, his left leg doubled back and under the outstretched right, his right arm lying limp along the right side of his body, the left bent back at the elbow to support his head, which faces full front.[811] He wears the usual court costume of tunic, trousers, and boots. The boots are white and the trousers are green, matching those of Saul's companions in the scene at the left; but the tunic, while gray rather than red or blue, has one feature otherwise associated only with members of the royal court. This is the wide, dark yellow band that comes down the front of the garment connecting with those that ornament the neck and the hem.[812]

He is therefore either a king or a member of the court hierarchy not met hitherto in the paintings.[813]

Above the unusually large figure in the foreground at least three others were represented, arranged in two ascending zones. The first zone contains two men drawn to a greatly reduced scale, both sitting on the ground and facing full front. The one pillows his head on his left arm, the other on his right arm, indicating that both are also asleep. Because of their diminutive size, no doubt, the artist has not been able to develop in all detail the decoration of the costumes they wear, contenting himself with the indication of light-colored (white?) tunics and of trousers that are green in the case of the man at the left and pink in the case of the man at the right. The man at the left is shown on the Gute copy holding in his right hand an object that has a rectangular black projection at the top (Pl. XXXII).[814] The uppermost of the three zones preserves only dim traces of the fourth figure. It is that of a man identical in pose with the large figure in the foreground, hence probably also asleep. Of smaller proportions than the latter, he wears nonetheless an identical costume. In this instance, however, the tunic is red decorated with light-colored bands at the collar, down the front, and at the hem, while the trousers are apparently of a lighter color. The unusual feature connected with this fourth figure is the fact that he reclines upon a rectangular object apparently consisting of a frame of poles to which a cloth is attached by cords. This has been interpreted by Du Mesnil du Buisson as a camp bed.[815]

To complete the description of the scene it is necessary to include two additional persons who come from the right out of the next section of the composition, where the background is a light green, toward the large sleeping figure in the central foreground. Both are shown with their right legs advanced and bent sharply at the knee, indicating

809. Cf. also Panel EC 2 below. The evidence of the east wall cannot be used to argue that the artist neglected to supply the vertical panel bands between Sections B and C of Panel NC 1. See above, p. 178, n. 686.

810. So Du Mesnil du Buisson, *Peintures*, p. 106. The surface of the original in its present stage permits no judgment in the matter. For another scene in which the whole upper portion is developed against a black background, see Panel NA 1 (Jacob at Bethel).

811. The identical pose was used by the artist in Panel NA 1 (Jacob at Bethel); cf. Pl. XXVI. A large diagonal fissure in the plaster, running downward from beside his head through the length of his body has caused the loss of several pieces of plaster, particularly at the neck, on the chest, and at the hem of his tunic.

812. Cf. Panels WC 2 (Mordecai and Esther) and WC 4 (Pharaoh and the Infancy of Moses), Pls. LXIV–LXV, LXVIII. The costume has the usual white belt about the tunic.

813. For the king's stable boy see above, p. 155.

814. This may be either a short sword or dagger (of which only the pommel has been spotted), or, since no extension is visible below, the object depicted in the hand of the courtier beside the throne in Panel WC 2 (Mordecai and Esther, see Pl. LXV) and identified in that connection as a key (see p. 161). The detail is not visible today on the original.

815. *Peintures*, p. 106.

rapid motion toward the left, but their faces are turned into a frontal position. The man in the lead is somewhat smaller than his companion and has his right foot planted on the first ridge of the hills upon which the sleeper lies. Both men wear the familiar court costume and have a short sword hanging from the belt at their left side, but their garments are rendered in different colors.[816] Weathering, cracks, and gaps in the plaster have reduced to a vague outline their heads and necks, but the position of their arms can still be ascertained.[817] The second of the two men has his right hand raised, while holding in his left, close to the side of his body, a globular bottle with a long thin neck. The first apparently rests his left hand upon the hilt of the sword at his belt and reaches out with his right in the direction of the large sleeping figure in the foreground. The Gute copy indicates that his hand grasps there a long straight staff extending diagonally upwards from the mountain masses directly behind the sleeper's head.[818]

The scene thus described lends itself readily to interpretation on the basis of the narrative of I Sam. 26. The central section with its indication of mountain ranges shows Saul and his host encamped on the "hill of Hachilah" (I Sam. 26.3). It is night, hence the dark background in the upper part of the scene; and all the members of the company, including those supposed to be guarding the king, are sound asleep. The two men who approach from the right are David and Abishai, come to reconnoiter the camp in the darkness. If they advance from a green area toward the mountains, this is because the story tells us that the hill of Hachilah was "before the wilderness (yešîmôn),

by the way" (I Sam. 26.3).[819] We prefer to assume that the man in the van, showing the greater daring, is David himself, which would be in accord with the more elegant red color of his tunic. But it is possible, also, that he is Abishai and that David is given second position. This would provide a good way of interpreting the gesture of the second figure, a warning to Abishai not to do violence to the Lord's Anointed (I Sam. 26.8–11). Yet there are difficulties here on the score of the "cruse" held in the second figure's hand — since it is removed only after Abishai has been persuaded to desist — and on the score of the left portion of the scene.[820]

The encampment forming the left part of the scene presents one very difficult problem. Since in the Biblical narrative David takes the cruse and spear from beside the head of Saul (I Sam. 26.12), it is natural to suppose that the large sleeping figure in the foreground toward which David moves is that of the king himself. The tunic which the man wears seems to be in accord with this perfectly natural interpretation. The difficulty is that, while the man in the foreground bivouacs on the hard ground, the analogous reclining figure in the second zone above him, who would of necessity be Saul's general, Abner, sleeps on a specially prepared surface. This would appear to be a reversal of proprieties. The imperfect preservation of the upper part of the panel makes it difficult to say precisely what the object on which the upper sleeper reclines actually is. It will be recalled that in the Biblical narrative Saul is said to sleep *bamma'gāl*, which is commonly translated "within the barrier." This makes little sense and does not seem to be what the artist has represented. The root meaning of the word, however, would permit the artist to think of a "litter" or of any type of conveyance used also as a bed (Latin: *carruca*), which is precisely what he seems to have tried to indicate.[821] The fact that such a litter was provided

816. The first of the two men wears a red tunic, gray trousers, and white boots. The boots of the second man are darker, but his garments seem to be lighter, though their original color is no longer clearly distinguishable. The Gute copy indicates a reddish brown for both tunic and trousers. The tunics are decorated down the front with narrow stripes outlined by black lines.

817. Two cracks coming diagonally downward from above meet in the area where the head of the first of the two men was portrayed. The cracks have occasioned the loss of extensive pieces of the plaster surface. Most of the head of the first man is gone and part of the head of the second. There are additional gaps (now patched) between the two figures, where the crack continued downward, and on their respective right knees.

818. No longer visible on the original, but scarcely to be doubted.

819. Du Mesnil du Buisson aptly points to the color contrast between the plains and the hills of the Syrian uplands in spring (*Peintures*, p. 105).

820. We therefore prefer to suppose that Abishai, in second position, holds out his hand to receive from David the spear to add to the cruse.

821. The root *'agal*, meaning "to roll," has as its derivative the noun *'ǎgālāh*, meaning "wagon." Wagons used as beds at night are familiar even in Jewish tradition (see Krauss, *Talmudische Archäologie*, II, p. 337). The

for the upper of the two reclining figures would seem to suggest that he, not the man in the foreground, is Saul. By putting Saul into the background, the artist could in this case be thought to have indicated that, as the story tells us, Saul's army was actually "pitched round about him." To make the more prominently displayed of the two reclining figures the less important is contrary to the canons of Oriental art and seems even to offend against the text of the Biblical story, where it is from the king's own side that cruse and spear are taken (I Sam. 26.12). But the latter detail is not decisive, for Jewish legend provides versions of the story in which David takes the objects away from Abner's keeping and is momentarily pinned down by the giant general as he moves in his sleep.[822] In balancing the pros and cons of the decision that has eventually to be made on this point we prefer to regard the reclining figure in the foreground as Abner, in which case Saul reclines on the bed above, being guarded by his giant general and attended by the two courtiers who are part of the artist's convention in rendering royalty, and who reappear on Panels WC 2 (Mordecai and Esther) and WC 4 (Pharaoh and the Infancy of Moses).[823]

If the first and second scenes of the composition offer no great difficulties when interpreted in the light of contemporary Jewish legend, the same cannot be said of the third (Pl. XXXII). Here, it will be recalled, the surface is so poorly preserved that only faint traces of the subject painted upon it survive, these being confined to a narrow strip along the very bottom on the panel. What remains to be seen in an area less than a meter long is portions of the legs of two men who come toward

each other from opposite directions. The artist has changed his scale in this scene, so that the figures are large in proportion to David and Abishai.[824] Both men wear the costume of the royal court; namely, tunic, trousers, and soft boots. The tunic of the man at the left, of which only the lower part is visible, is of a light color, the trousers are red, and the boots white.[825] The man is shown moving rapidly to the right, for his left leg is bent sharply at the knee. From the position of his left foot it would be possible to infer that, like the David of the previous scene, he is stepping up upon higher ground. Of the man who comes toward him from the right only a few traces remain. In the extreme lower right corner of the panel there are visible the elements of a booted left foot. Some distance above the foot a reddish color-mass can be seen, the lower edge of which sweeps downward toward the right. This can properly be taken to represent the remains of his red tunic.[826] The position of the man's right foot was on a higher plane than that of his left. Its outlines seem to be preserved at some distance from his left foot and on a higher level, directly opposite the shin of the man who advances toward him from the left. This position is possible only if his right knee was sharply bent, projecting from the slit in the side of the tunic as in the case of David and Abishai in the previous scene.[827] He was therefore in rapid motion toward the left and must himself have been shown mounting to a higher level.

To identify the scene with any degree of certainty is by no means easy in view of the scanty traces that remain, but is of the utmost importance for the understanding of the structure of the composition as a whole. Judging by the costumes of the two men portrayed, we are dealing with an episode involving members of the royal court or retinue, and judging by the position of their legs, it is an episode in which an elevation plays a part. The scene at the center of the composition, showing

LXX translated *bamma'gal* with *en lampene*, which also means "in a covered wagon." On this assumption the wagon would need to be seen in a vertical perspective, as a bed. There may, of course, have been uses of the noun *'ăgālāh* unknown to us which could have yielded to him the meaning "stretcher," "cot," or any portable type of bed.

822. *II Alphabet of Ben Sira* 24b (ed. M. Steinschneider, אלפא ביתא, *Alphabetum Siracidis*, 1858, p. 24 b). For further details of the story see Ginzberg, *Legends of the Jews*, IV, p. 91, and VI, p. 253, n. 48. The royal costume with the wide yellow bands that Abner wears in the picture must be appropriate to him as "captain of the host."

823. On Abner's abnormal size and strength, aptly portrayed on the choice made, there is a whole series of stories, for which see Ginzberg, *Legends of the Jews*, IV, p. 73.

824. The scenes are crowded so closely together here also that the right foot of the man moving toward the left is set behind the left foot of Abishai.

825. Hopkins' field note suggests a white tunic with a yellow band along the hem.

826. To judge by the remains of colors in the area below the reddish mass, his trousers were probably of a lighter color and had red shadow- and fold-lines.

827. A dim color-mass in the appropriate area verifies this inference.

David removing the spear from beside Abner's head, suggests as a logical sequel the incident that follows in the story of I Sam. 26. After the raid on Saul's camp, we are told, David crossed over from the hill of Hachilah and stood on top of another mountain. From here he called back to the camp of Saul, chiding Abner for his failure to keep watch over Saul and offering to return the king's spear if some one were sent to fetch it (I Sam. 26.13–22). The scene might then be thought to depict David at the right returning the spear to one of the king's "young men" coming up from the left to the adjacent mountain. In this case the panel as a whole would be a succession of episodes following each other in chronological order from left to right. The difficulty with the interpretation suggested is that the Bible does not tell us whether David's offer to Saul was ever accepted, and that in general we do not find the Synagogue artists inventing scenes for which there is no factual basis in the Biblical text. It seems preferable, therefore, to look for another episode that might have been associated at least in locality with the events depicted in the other parts of the panel.

Now it is evident from his indication of a mountainous terrain that the artist is conscious of the geographic locale of action portrayed in the scenes at the left. This locale the Bible identifies as the hill of Hachilah in the wilderness of Ziph. In the wider context of I Sam. 26 there is only one other story that has the same locale; namely, that of I Sam. 23.15–18, where Saul's son, Jonathan, hearing that David was in the wilderness of Ziph, came down to visit David to reassure him, and made with David a covenant before the Lord. The idyllic nature of the friendship between David and Jonathan in Biblical narrative suggests that to introduce some representation of it into his decorations would have had a great appeal to both the Synagogue artist and his audience. A scene showing this meeting, moreover, would act as a foil to the representation of Saul's own murderous intent revealed by the display of his military might at the left end of the panel. If, as we are inclined to believe, the scene under discussion here did probably portray the meeting of David and Jonathan, with David coming from the right and Jonathan from the left, the panel as a whole becomes a centralized composition in three parts, of which

the two terminal scenes represent episodes each antecedent to the central element in time, the movement thus developing from the outer limits of the composition toward the middle. This is a type of structural pattern familiar to us from other portions of the Synagogue.

Belshazzar's Feast and the Fall of Babylon(?)

Panel EC 2 (fragmentary). H. *ca.* 1.29 m.; L. 3.78 m. (Pls. XXIII, XXX,2).

Hopkins and Du Mesnil du Buisson, "La Synagogue," p. 253; *Rep. VI*, p. 365; Du Mesnil du Buisson, *Peintures*, pp. 107f.; Grabar, "Le Thème," pp. 157–159; Leveen, *Hebrew Bible in Art*, p. 45; Schneid, *The Paintings*, p. 20; Sukenik, *The Synagogue*, pp. 146f.; Sonne, "The Paintings," pp. 336–339; Wischnitzer, *Messianic Theme*, pp. 21f.

On the east wall Register C contained yet one additional composition; namely, that occupying the area between the main door of the House of Assembly and the smaller door at the extreme southern end of the east wall. What remains of the surface upon which the scene was painted is a long strip of plaster no more than 0.90 m. high at its highest point. It is crossed by many horizontal and diagonal cracks and marred by one large, and many small, holes. A short illegible graffito and a small pictorial graffito are incised upon it near the center.[828] Traces of color and outline appear only upon the lower left part of the plaster in a zone less than 2 m. long and no more than 0.60 m. high. This means that only about half of the picture is to be known at all, a fact that needs to be kept in mind in trying to infer from the scant remains the nature of the composition as a whole.[829] In the lower left corner over a section of the picture some

828. Cf. Inscrs. nos. **57** and **66**, below, pp. 317, 319. The former has no bearing upon the subject of the panel, as interpreted by Du Mesnil du Buisson, *Les Peintures*, p. 161, No. 17.

829. It is indicative of the ruinous condition of the painting that we are not in a position to tell even whether it was framed at the ends by vertical panel bands. The chances are that it was not so framed, which would be unusual but in agreement with the treatment of the dado in the area and suggestive, both of the artist's need of space, and of his reliance upon the doorways as terminal factors serving to set off the composition.

0.38 m. high the background of the scene was red. It is entirely possible that above and at the right the background changed to a lighter shade, transforming the red along the bottom into an element of "stage space," but here certainty can not be achieved. Against the red background at the left the artist has portrayed a series of bright yellow objects. Beginning at the left we have first a curved object with a wide mouth, in the shape of a horn or a rhyton; next an amphora with a finely tapered body, whose wide foot or stand is visible though its handles are not; and then an oval object set a short distance above the base line of the picture and crosshatched in brown, which can be only a basket. Farther to the right there follows a rectangle with a molded surface resting on the base of the panel, and possibly another oval object somewhat above and to the right of the rectangle. Of the two last mentioned, the first may be a footstool, such as is commonly associated with couches in the Synagogue, and the second a low table of the type regularly set before couches in ancient banquet scenes.[830] Just beyond the end of this series of objects can be seen a short section of a typical turned leg. Above the series the red background comes to an end against a yellow strip outlined in black. This is the rail of a couch to which the turned leg belongs.[831] Horn, amphora, and basket are therefore to be thought of as placed before the couch, together with the usual footstool and table.

Above the yellow rail the elements of color and outline disappear very rapidly in the neutral gray of the plaster, but just enough of them remains to give a vitally significant indication of the further development of the scene. Above the frame of the couch the artist depicted a dark-colored mattress and upon this he showed a man reclining. Only a small part of the man's body is visible, but fortunately it is the section at the knees where the folds of the garments follow a pattern familiar from other scenes, being used whenever the artist wants to show that the left leg is doubled under the right and the right knee is slightly elevated.[832] From the position of the color-masses it is evident that the man had his feet toward the left end of the scene; that is, toward the main door of the building, and was therefore, reclining on his left elbow. From the nature of the fold-lines it is clear, furthermore, that he wore, not a chiton and himation, but light-colored trousers whose folds were shown in reddish brown. At the right the folds of the left trouser leg come to an end against a heavy diagonal line marking the edge of a reddish-brown band from which a mass of red sweeps upward and to the right. This indicates that with his light-colored trousers he wore a dark red tunic. The costume makes it clear at once that we are dealing here with a member of the priesthood or the court, more probably the latter because of the nature of the scene.

To the right of the couch, elements of the red background continue along the base of the panel, though it is possible that it changes to a lighter color on the general level of the couch rail. Here, beginning at the level of the base line, two large birds are drawn. They have long reddish legs and similarly long, erect necks. The breast is well rounded, and the wings are extended in the manner typical of runners, a category to which these birds can readily be assigned by virtue of the length and pose of their legs. The color of neck, body, and wings is white. Wing feathers are picked out in a dark color. The animal recalls nothing so much as the common bustard (*otis tarda*) that still haunts the open spaces of the East, but almost any other similar land bird of the larger sort may have been intended. About the birds one fact of importance is to be noted; namely, that they face toward the right, being associated therefore not with the banquet scene at the left but with whatever the right half of the composition contained.

830. For footstools under couches see Panels WC 1 and the underpainting of the lower Center Panel. The shape of the object in this instance is quite indistinguishable and may be slightly different from that suggested by the outlines of the Gute copy. For tables at banquet scenes, see funerary bas-reliefs, and mosaics such as those of *Antioch*, II, Pl. 40.

831. A similar leg must have been represented at the extreme left end of the scene. It is the fact that no trace of the leg is to be seen where the last vestiges of the red background stop some centimeters from the doorway that suggests the absence of a vertical panel band at the end of the composition. It is not clear that there would have been room here for both the couch leg and a framing band.

832. Cf. e.g., Panels WC 1 and EC 1. The pose is typical of the funerary banquet scenes of Palmyra; cf. e.g., Ingholt, *Berytus*, II (1935), Pl XXVI. The mattress is indicated at the extreme right of the bed by a dark mass ending in a curved line as on Panel WC 1.

14

Above the head of the bird at the left one further element of the picture is still dimly visible. It is part of a light-colored area, the full extent of which can no longer be determined.[833] Beginning near the head of the left bird a section of this lighter area is bounded by a single red line that mounts in a gentle curve upward as it moves from left to right. The line is characteristic of the hems of garments as they are portrayed in the Synagogue, but there are no traces at the right of diagonally folded ends, nor remains below of feet, such as would be expected if the garment were the himation of a man. Instead there are to be seen just above the delimiting red hem a series of vertical lines in light red, two at the left joined by a cross line at the bottom as though forming the end of an ornamental band or stripe. These vertical lines appear to stop just short of what we have called the hem. Toward the right end of the hem and inside the part of the light-colored field bounded by it, a small area in the shape of a flattened semicircle is set off, outlined in reddish brown and filled with other dark lines. This is reminiscent of the way in which the Synagogue artists render the shoes of ladies in court attire as they protrude from beneath their long trailing robes.[834] With this detail to help us, the other traces of color and outline in the vicinity become intelligible as vestiges of the garb of a lady whose costume matches that of the man on the couch.

At the present time all traces of color and outline come to an end near the tip of the wing of the right bird; that is, at a point *ca.* 1.63 m. from the left end of the panel. Farther to the right Du Mesnil du Buisson noted at one time the existence of vertical bands which appear to him to belong to an architectural construction, and early photographs seem to attest the accuracy of his observation.[835] For all practical purposes, however, the remainder of the field is blank, and this remainder constitutes the larger part of the area covered by the composition, having a length of *ca.* 2.15 m.

Opinion has naturally differed widely as to the identity of the scene or scenes depicted in the panel. Hopkins and Du Mesnil du Buisson were the first to suggest some connection with Noah, the animals, and the Ark, a suggestion which the latter eventually developed further in his *Peintures*.[836] On this suggestion the action would move from right to left, the composition beginning at the right with the Ark, continuing with the animals leaving the Ark, and ending at the left with the drunkenness of Noah (Gen. 8–9). The difficulties in the way of the acceptance of this interpretation are numerous. The birds face the wrong way, the costumes are of the wrong type, the presence of any garments on the drunken Noah would be surprising, the vessels under the couch are explicable only in part and do not seem to deserve the prominence assigned to them; and the subject, whatever its propriety or lack of propriety in this kind of a setting, belongs to a part of Biblical narrative not otherwise drawn upon by the Synagogue artists so far as we know their handiwork.[837] In the Preliminary Report the attempt was made to associate the scene with the Elijah cycle on the south wall, the thought being that the artist had tried to represent Elijah being fed by the ravens with food supplied, as in Jewish legend, from the table of the pious king Jehoshaphat, which might account for the presence of the sumptuous vessels beneath the couch.[838] The difficulties here are, of course, that the birds cannot be ravens, that the garments of the man on the couch revealed by an examination of the originals are not proper to the person of Elijah, and that this scene was in all probability represented on Panel SC 2. Leveen, who was quick to spot the ineptness of the suggestion, has proposed an allusion here to the occasion when Abraham frightened the birds away from the sacrifice of the divided "pieces" that sealed the covenant between God and himself (Gen. 15.8–21).[839] Even though the sacrifice might have suggested to the artist a sacrificial meal, thus introducing the couch,

833. The fact that the extent of the light color-mass can no longer be defined makes it necessary to keep in mind the possibility that the red background along the lower part of the panel may be no more than the "stage space" of the composition.

834. Cf. the Queen of Sheba in Panel WA 2 and Esther in Panel WC 2.

835. Cf. *Peintures*, p. 107, Fig. 79.

836. Cf. *CRAI*, 1933, p. 253; Du Mesnil du Buisson, *Peintures*, pp. 107f.

837. In no other known composition of the Synagogue artists do they go back beyond the period of Abraham.

838. On this variation of the Biblical story, see also Genesis Rabbah XXXIII, 5 (Trans., I, p. 265), Sanhedrin 113a (Trans., pp. 779f.).

839. *Hebrew Bible in Art*, p. 45. Sukenik prefers this interpretation, *The Synagogue*, p. 147.

the proposed interpretation is difficult to accept, for the birds are not birds of prey such as the story requires, and the garments worn are not those appropriate to the patriarch.[840]

The variety of the interpretations offered illustrate the difficulties which the scene presents to anyone trying to make sense out of the fragmentary remains of the composition. In view of these difficulties all interpretations, including the one to be advanced here, must be regarded as tentative and exploratory. For the view submitted here, dependent as it is in part at least upon incidental suggestions supplied by Du Mesnil du Buisson and Grabar, three things are significant. The first is the probability that the birds, since they face toward the right, should be associated with a separate scene forming the right half of the composition; the second is the discovery of the details concerning the clothes worn by the two identifiable figures in the scene at the left as described above; and the third is the conviction that special importance must accrue to the vessels so prominently displayed under the couch.

As regards the vessels, Grabar has already advanced a fruitful suggestion. Tradition has it that certain sacred vessels of the Temple originally associated with the Ark and removed as spoils by the Chaldeans were not restored with those which Sheshbazzar brought back with him to Jerusalem following the decree of Cyrus. They were lost, and are to be restored ultimately by none other than Elijah. The vessels in question are the horn of oil used at the consecration of Aaron, the jar of the water of purification prepared for the first time at that occasion, and the basket of manna preserved from the days of the Wilderness sojourn — that is, precisely such vessels as appear under the couch alongside the table and footstool.[841] The fact that

the vessels appear here at a banquet with a woman in attendance is sufficient to cast doubts upon Grabar's inference that the scene gives expression to the eschatological aspects of Elijah's career, showing him as the one who brings about the return of the missing objects. By the same token it does suggest that the scene represents Belshazzar's feast (Dan. 5) when the king profaned "the golden vessels that were taken out of the temple of the house of God which was at Jerusalem" (Dan. 5.3). The artist has identified the vessels used by Belshazzar with those which later legend said were lost and would be restored by Elijah.

With the suggestion already considered in passing by Du Mesnil du Buisson,[842] the other details of the scene are in perfect agreement. The figure on the couch is that of a royal personage, and his position is such that above him the artist could well have shown the hand writing upon the wall the famous words, "Mene, mene, tekel upharsin." The lady of the court depicted at the right of the couch would also be appropriate, for she would be the queen (or the king's mother) who proposed to Belshazzar that he call Daniel to read the writing on the wall (Dan. 5.10–12).[843]

From the foregoing analysis of the possible meaning of the scene all reference to the birds has been omitted because they belong to the second half of the composition overlapping the first along the base of the panel. The problem of the birds is to find a separate scene that might properly be associated with the episode of Belshazzar's feast and to which they would be appropriate. For the solution of this problem, it would seem, the most important clue is to be found in the fact that the feast of Belshazzar marks the last night of his life, the night in which, as Daniel tells us, Darius the Mede received the kingdom (Dan. 5.31). With the broader implications of this event the narrative of Daniel does not concern itself, but the implications were perfectly familiar to all pious Jews from the story of Ezra and from the prophecies of Isaiah (43–47) and Jeremiah (25.50–51). This material offered a perfect gold mine to an artist seeking a *pendant* to Belshazzar's feast, and from it, we sug-

840. Still more difficult is the suggestion of Schneid, who tries among other things to associate the scene with the events from the careers of Saul and David, more particularly with I Sam. 15.9, the thought being that Panel EC 2 is connected somehow with Panel EC 1. The presence of the birds is a barrier to all attempts to connect the imagery with David playing before Saul at his court (I Sam. 18.10–11), with Jonathan's trespass in eating after Saul had enjoined abstinence (I Sam. 14.24–30), and with the army's failure to dispose of all of the Amalekites' possessions as commanded by the Lord (I Sam. 15).

841. Grabar, "Le Thème," p. 158. Grabar has already suggested that the first vessel is shaped like that used by Samuel in anointing David (Panel WC 3, Pl. LXVI).

842. See his *Peintures*, p. 108.

843. There is room at the right of the woman for Daniel, whom the artist would on this suggestion have been likely to include in the composition in a central position.

gest, he chose the subject of the second half of his composition. From the artist's point of view, the important event to associate with the scene of Belshazzar's feast would undoubtedly be the fulfilment of the prophecy written on the wall by the mysterious hand; and in view of the significance of the event, this fulfilment should take an objective form involving, not so much the end of Belshazzar himself, as the end of the kingdom which he represented. One would therefore expect at the right of the panel the destruction of Babylon so eloquently described in Jer. 50–51. In terms of the standard designs of the Synagogue this would require nothing more elaborate than a crenellated wall in a ruinous condition, and of remains of such an architectural construction, Du Mesnil du Buisson believes he has seen traces in the right half of the composition.[844] Now in Jeremiah the important characteristic of the fallen Babylon is its utter desolation. She becomes "a wilderness, a dry land, and a desert" (50.12), and as such, the haunt of the wild animals of the open places. Jer. 50.39 describes the scene of desolation in the words:

> Therefore the wild beasts of the desert
> with the wolves shall dwell there, and the
> ostriches shall dwell therein, and it shall
> be no more inhabited forever, neither shall
> it be dwelt in from generation to gene-
> ration.

In the desolation of the city of Babylon as Jeremiah visualizes it, we seem to have the best explanation of the only element the right half of the composition actually preserved; for to the ruined city the artist can well be thought to have added along the base of his panel a whole series of desert animals of which the birds are merely the last, representing either the bustards which the artist naturally associated with the desert regions, or the ostriches of the text itself, drawn as faithfully as his knowledge of the actual animal permitted and at a size proportionate to the space available and to the size of the remaining animals in the series.

Interpreted as a panel depicting Belshazzar's feast and the destruction of Babylon that followed

it, the composition is one that would naturally appeal to a Jewish community of Mesopotamia. It would do justice in a very graphic way to an event of outstanding importance for the life of the nation, the event that provided the occasion for the return of the Jews from the Exile. At the same time it would fall into line with other scenes depicting the divine punishment meted out to the enemies of the Lord and his people and would provide a fitting antithesis to the scene of Ahasuerus and Esther across the room (Panel WC 2).

* * *

Before leaving the panels of Register C entirely, it would seem desirable to comment briefly upon their supposed relation to each other and upon the so-called "theme" of the decorative zone to which they belong. With so large a proportion of the total number of its panels sufficiently well preserved to permit of positive identification, Register C should provide genuine indications of the artists' program, if such there were. Already, as the growing literature on the Synagogue shows, several efforts have been made to set forth such a program. The earlier attempts were relatively modest in character, Du Mesnil du Buisson being satisfied to suggest that Register C was "moralizing" in tone, showing how God protected his own while punishing the wicked and rewarding the good; while Grabar developed a thesis of thematic correspondences between the scenes on either side of the panel that shows Samuel anointing David (WC 3).[845] Later attempts have been more thoroughgoing and seek to define the "theme" of the register in doctrinal,

<hr>

844. The traces as they seem to appear upon early negatives of the area are at a distance sufficient to permit the introduction of the figure of Daniel alongside that which we have interpreted as Belshazzar's queen.

845. Du Mesnil du Buisson, *Peintures*, p. 17; and Grabar, "Le Thème," pp. 16–20. According to Grabar's hypothesis, the corresponding pairs group themselves at either side of Panel WC 3 (Samuel Anoints David), in such a way that WC 2 (Mordecai and Esther) matches WC 4 (Pharaoh and the Infancy of Moses) in showing how the plans of hostile rulers are put to shame; while WC 1 (Elijah Revives the Widow's Child) and NC 1 (Ezekiel, the Destruction and Restoration of National Life) plus SC 4 (Elijah on Mount Carmel) bear upon the subject of resurrection and the reunion of the tribes; SC 3 (Prophets of Baal on Mount Carmel) and NC 1, Section C (interpreted as the death of Joab) upon the death of the evil plotters; and SC 2 (Elijah at Cherith and Zarephath) together with EC 1 (David and Saul in the Wilderness of Ziph) upon the special protection afforded the pious in difficult times.

especially Messianic and eschatological, terms while constructing more or less comprehensive schemes to show sequence of thought and movement of action from panel to panel throughout the entire register.[846]

What strikes the careful reader about these several hypotheses is not so much the extent to which they cancel each other out or will require revision now that the material is made more fully available, but rather the extent to which they find a hidden meaning for everything, including facts and phenomena that permit of much simpler explanation. It should be obvious, for instance, that in view of the importance of David for the Jewish understanding of both the historic and Messianic kingship, the scene of David's consecration (WC 3) should be given a prominent place immediately at the right of the Torah Shrine. It does not necessarily follow from this that the panel in question gives the tone of, or is the organizing principle for, the entire register; or that it, the scene of Mordecai and Esther (WC 2), and Pharaoh and the Infancy of Moses (WC 4) form a "kingship cycle," or have a common Messianic theme. Indeed it is difficult to believe that the dominant reason for the juxtaposition of WC 3 (Samuel Anoints David) and WC 4 (Pharaoh and the Infancy of Moses) is to be found in the thought that the descendants of the midwives would have "houses of kingship," or that Mordecai and Esther (WC 2) follows the scene of Elijah reviving the Widow's Child (WC 1) because in the former Elijah reveals himself in his eschatological role by appearing in the guise of Harbonah and saving the situation for the Jewish people. The word "cycle" applied in such narrow arbitrary limits is misleading; the picture of the infancy of Moses is important in its own right because of the story which it tells, and the appearance of Esther and Mordecai in a position of prominence alongside the Torah Shrine is for a Parapotamian synagogue at least quite as intelligible on grounds of local interest as the appearance of the consecration of David by Samuel is on historical and theological grounds.

Now it must be admitted that the Synagogue artists have assigned to the lowest and most

clearly visible register materials that are of outstanding interest or importance for the congregation and its faith. David, Moses, Mordecai and Esther, Jonathan, Daniel, Elijah — these were names to conjure with. What is more, in the great composition dealing with Ezekiel, the artist ventured more clearly than elsewhere in the Synagogue into the difficult but tremendously important area of the national hope and its ultimate fulfilment. Finally, inside the individual composition, and, as we have had occasion to see, in the Elijah Cycle, he does make use of materials reflecting the tendency of Haggadists and preachers to weave tenuous nets of relationships between Biblical episodes. The only question is, how far may one legitimately go in using the facts of juxtaposition and association to develop reliable conceptions of a comprehensive program or theme?

On this important and difficult point the following observations may be apposite. There is more in Register C that associates it with the other two registers of the Synagogue than divides it from them and sets it apart. There is more in the presentation of a single narrative composition made up of several scenes, or of a series of panels portraying episodes from successive chapters of the Bible, than merely the theological or doctrinal idea possibly to be assigned to them. There are practical exigencies and considerations in the allocation of any given panel or group of panels of such force as to make unlikely the achievement of a perfect correspondence between an intended program, a given body of wall space, and a group of Biblical stories, especially when the wall space is angular and interrupted by structural features. Register C must be in more than one respect a compromise between intention and feasibility. Keeping these generalizations in mind, we can say about Register C: that it contains a narrative cycle (the Elijah Cycle); that it has assigned the scenes of Saul anointing David (WC 3) and of Mordecai and Esther (WC 2) to the positions of greatest prominence on the west wall; that it has in the great Ezekiel Panel (NC 1) applied itself seriously to the question of the national hope; and finally that, in common with the other registers of the building, it portrays through incidents from the lives of important men the divine guidance and protection of the righteous, and the punishment and defeat of

---

846. See Sonne, "The Paintings," pp. 311–342; and Wischnitzer, *Messianic Theme*, pp. 33 f., 51 f.

the wicked. We cannot speak with absolute as-surance of a sequence of panels except in the case of groups such as the Elijah Cycle; we cannot be sure that Haggadic suggestions of the meaning of episodes apply legitimately save in the explanation of iconographic detail in a single composition, or in the choice and correlation of successive episodes of Biblical story; and we must realize that it is always easier to find sensible reasons for all manner of association *ex post facto* than to be sure that the association was intentional.

5. PANELS OF THE CENTRAL GROUP

Above the Torah Shrine the west wall of the Synagogue exhibits a group of panels that re-quires separate treatment. In its final form the group was made up of six units: the two large Center Panels, one above the other; and four nar-row Wing Panels so arranged that they flank the Center Panels. When the register decorations were originally laid out, the area comprising the two Center Panels was first treated as a single vertical field extending through Registers A and B. At this time, then, the group had but five elements.

Some scholars, dividing the group horizontally, have compared the two sets of three panels each, located in Registers A and B respectively, with open triptychs.[847] The comparison is suggestive but ignores the erstwhile unity and the ultimate vertical association of the two Center Panels. Other scholars in turn have dissociated the flanking Wing Panels from the central group, connecting them instead with the narrative cycles of the registers in which they stand, the "themes" of which they are sup-posed to illuminate.[848] This ignores the fact that, but for the presence of the central area which the artist sought to frame, there would have been no occasion for the use of the narrow Wing Panels, and disregards the unity of the central group as a whole.[849] Only a full examination of the subject matter of the scenes can show how they are related to each other and to the register decorations. Meanwhile it is important to keep in mind that the five or six panels constitute a symmetrically arranged group without parallel in any other part of the Synagogue, and one that by its symmetry creates in the decorative scheme a focal element analogous to, and in the same axis with, the one that the Torah Shrine provides in the architectural organization of the west wall and of the chamber.[850]

847. So originally Rostovtzeff, *Dura-Europos and its Art*, p. 108.

848. So Grabar, "Le Thème," pp. 17/f.

849. The Dura Mithraeum, with its representations of Zarathustra and Ostanes alongside the niche and its cult reliefs (see *Rep. VII–VIII*, Pl. 2), provides a partial analogy and urges caution in the treatment of the problem.

850. It is very noticeable in the building itself and can be seen on Pl. XXIV and Plan IX that the Central Group is not accurately centered upon the axis of the Torah Shrine, the Lower Center Panel at its base pro-jecting no less than *ca.* 0.30 m. beyond the end of the

The presence of such a centralizing element in the decorations of the Synagogue, and its vertical development as one part of a scheme which otherwise through its register divisions emphasizes the horizontal so continuously, is highly interesting and of great importance for the proper understanding of the origin and history of such decorative schemes. In an earlier chapter there have already been pointed out the analogies to the use of register divisions that exist at Dura in the Temple of Bel, in the Temple of Zeus Theos, and in the Christian Chapel.[851] In these shrines the horizontal register division also gives way at one point to a vertical element; namely, the painted cult image of the god or his representative, which usually occupies the entire rear wall of the naos. The function of these vertical interruptions in the horizontal scheme of wall division is, of course, to supply the worshipers with a point of orientation.

Now the transverse construction of the pagan naoi of Dura is such that the focal representation of the cult image usually occupies one of the long walls of the naos, rather than one of the short walls, but in no case is the wall in question as long as the west wall of the Synagogue. It is natural, therefore, that in the Synagogue the vertical centralizing element of the decorations should fill only a portion of the west wall, the part just above the Torah Shrine. The nature of the Jewish religion precluded the representation of the deity itself in this central area, necessitating the development by the artist of another type of subject matter appropriate to this function. The fact that the area

of the Center Panels was repainted repeatedly, as has already been pointed out above and will be shown in more detail immediately, suggests that at this point the artist and his advisers were uncertain in their own counsels, because they were launching out into uncharted waters. The Christians of Dura, facing the identical problem, had an easier solution, for in their Chapel they could portray in the focal area the Lord of the cult, who was the representative and incarnation of the deity.[852] It is important to note, however, that in the corresponding area of the Christian Chapel the decorations substitute a symbol for the representation of the historical person, portraying Christ in the form of a shepherd pasturing his flock. An analogous symbolic form of representation, the Tree of Life, was chosen for the first decorative design developed by the Synagogue artists in the area above the Torah Shrine, as we have already seen.[853] Whether this tradition was adhered to in the later stages of the decorative process, and what the relation of the symbolic and the historical in the art tradition of the Jewish community may be, only the full analysis of the material can indicate. This analysis necessarily must begin with the Center Panels.

The Area of the Center Panels

Upper (fragmentary): H. *ca.* 1.14 m.; L. 1.82 m.; Lower: H. 1.43 m. (at left) and 1.50 m. (at right); L. 1.83 m. (top) and 1.86 m. (bottom). (Pls. XXXIII–XXXV, LXXIV–LXXV).

Hopkins and Du Mesnil du Buisson, "La Synagogue," p. 246; Rostovtzeff, "Die Synagoge," p. 209; Du Mesnil du Buisson, "Les Deux synagogues," pp. 81f., 86–89; *Rep. VI*, pp. 367–371; E. R. Goodenough, *Journal of Bible and Religion*, V (1937), pp. 11f.; Rostovtzeff, *Dura-Europos and its Art*, pp. 108f.; Du Mesnil du Buisson, *Peintures*, pp. 27f., 43–45, 48–52; H. Pearson, *Guide*, pp. 28f., 33–35; Grabar, "Le Thème," pp. 159–172, 33f.; Leveen, *Hebrew Bible in Art*, pp. 24–31; Schneid, *The Paintings*, pp. 8–90; Sonne, "The Paintings," pp. 342–355; Sukenik, *The Synagogue*, pp. 58–64; Wischnitzer, *Messianic Theme*, pp. 91–99.

Torah Shrine toward the south. This means that at this level the axis of the Central Group of panels is 0.15 m. to the south of the axis of the Torah Shrine. In part this discrepancy is due to the architect who, as we have already seen (see above, p. 14, n. 56), placed the Torah Shrine *ca.* 0.10 m. to the north of the center of the west wall. In part it is chargeable to the artist, who must have begun his division of the wall at the top, under the rafters, without considering where the dividing lines would come with respect to the Torah Shrine, and who would have made an even worse fit had he not widened the Lower Center Panel by several centimeters toward the base at the expense of the Wing Panel toward the north. Similar inaccuracies in alignment; e.g., between the axis of the Torah Shrine and that of the main door (see above, p. 17, n. 75), and between the main door and the intercolumniations of the portico (see Plans V–VI), show that in all such matters we are dealing with typical results of the Oriental way of doing things.

851. Cf. above, p. 69.

852. *Rep. V*, Pl. XLIX.
853. Cf. above, p. 63.

For purposes of description and interpretation the area of the two highly important Center Panels unfortunately provides greater difficulties than any other part of the entire Synagogue. The difficulties arise from a combination of two factors: the poor condition of the wall surface, and the successive stages of the decoration. In the demolition of the structure to the gradient of the embankment covering it, a triangular strip along the top of the Upper Center Panel was removed, so that at the left its plaster is preserved to a height of no more than 0.83 m.[854] Directly below the line of demolition the plaster is badly broken, and here the action of the elements has so affected both the surface and the pigments that in a zone *ca.* 0.30 m. high only dim traces of the subject matter can occasionally be seen. Additional cracking, caused by the pressure of the fill behind the wall in the earlier stages of the embankment, is noticeable in both the Upper and Lower Center Panels.[855] At some time the painted surface was exposed to a good bit of abrasion, most of it represented by short narrow scars, occasioned perhaps by the erection of the embankment, some of it taking the form of long diagonal scratches, particularly in the upper left quarter of the Lower Center Panel (cf. Pl. XXXIV,

overlay). Still earlier, perhaps, a graffito representing a krater was incised near the base of the field at the right of the tree.[856] To these disturbances of the field must be added those produced by the rubbing of the surface along clearly defined lines, and the introduction of a large number of holes that have been drilled through the plaster into the wall behind it. Some of the smaller holes seem to have contained pegs to which rosettes were at one time affixed, as has been explained above.[857] The rubbing and the rest of the holes were occasioned by the mounting of a canopy or baldachin that covered part or all of the Torah Shrine directly below. Perhaps a rather large gap in the plaster of the Lower Center Panel, close to the middle near the bottom, was caused by the efforts to anchor the canopy or by the strain which the canopy placed on its mountings.[858]

More disastrous in their consequences for the understanding of the panels are the vicissitudes suffered by the area in the process of decoration. In the course of a relatively brief period of time it was painted, not merely once, but several times. Under other conditions the earlier design might have remained quite unknown; but fading and flaking, particularly where the surface was most heavily covered, have brought it again into view. The flaking seems to have begun soon after the decorations were completed, for some of the blemishes it occasioned were repaired in antiquity.[859] It probably continued, however, down to the destruction of the building, making it impossible to arrive at a satisfactory development of the lower parts of the area.

As seen today (Pls. LXXIV, LXXV) the Center Panels present a combination of four different elements in extreme confusion. A dull reddish cover coat overlies most, but not all, of the field; groups

854. At the right the plaster is apparently preserved almost to the top of the panel, the height from the base line of 1.14 m. comparing favorably with that of 1.13 m. for the Wing Panel I (Moses and the Burning Bush) and that of 1.16 m. for Panel WA 3 (Exodus and Crossing of the Red Sea). Cf. above, p. 74. In no case is any trace of the painted register band along the top of these panels preserved.

855. In the Upper Center Panel a continuous horizontal crack cuts across the field. At the right it runs at waist level across the row of figures in the foreground; dipping below the footstool of the throne, it continues at knee level across the figures at the left. Four vertical cracks are to be noted here; one each at the extreme left and right sides of the field, one at the right of the four figures in the lower left corner of the scene, and the fourth at the right of the enthroned king. The last has caused the loss of a small piece of plaster where it intersects with the horizontal fissure at the lower right corner of the king's footstool. The vertical cracks of the Upper Center Panel continue through the Lower, showing a tendency to veer somewhat to the left. They are crossed by a horizontal fissure running at mattress level across the beds, and end, naturally, in the large fissure running across the entire west wall of the Synagogue just above the top of the niche block of the aedicula, but just below the base of the Lower Center Panel. Pieces of plaster have been lost from the mattress of the bed at the left, where the cracks intersect, and from the base of the panel directly below.

856. For the tree, see above, pp. 62 f., and for the graffito Inscr. no. **58** below, p. 318.

857. Cf. above, p. 63.

858. The gap was old and not connected with the cracking of the wall, and may have been painted over. On the canopy see below, pp. 258 f.

859. Efforts to remedy flaking in its earlier stages can be seen, for example, in the upper right corner of the Lower Center Panel, where successive covering layers peeled off right down to the leaves of the original Tree of Life. Repairs consisted of the re-introduction of the tree design, the new leaves being painted partly over the old and partly over the red cover coat that had expunged them.

of figures, animals, and objects are distributed in various parts of the panels and largely visible only dimly through the red; there is a scattering of foliage, mostly in a green dulled by red; and there is a similar scattering of blank spots that represent the plaster surface laid bare by flaking and turned from white to a dirty brown by the coat of varnish that has been applied to the painted surface of the entire Synagogue for purposes of preservation. The chains of irregular blank spots continue across the register band dividing the Upper from the Lower Center Panel, showing that the entire area was at one time a unit of decorative embellishment.

To disentangle the maze of positive and negative evidence for the decorations of the area in such a way as to obtain complete assurance about every detail of the representation in every stage of its development is apparently quite beyond the range even of modern technical equipment, supposing that it could be brought to bear upon the study of the surface. The best that can be expected under the circumstances is an understanding of the main stages in the treatment of the field and a fair appraisal of the major elements belonging to each of them. That this expectation has been so largely realized is the result of the preparation of a good photographic record, of the efforts of technicians and scholarly interpreters, and of repeated close and prolonged examinations of the originals. The finds of the most recent re-examination happily confirm in their major outlines the earlier analyses save in one particular, as will shortly appear.

How the area was handled in the first stage of the decoration of the Synagogue has already been described above (pp. 62–65) but may be recapitulated briefly here. The entire west wall of the chamber was at this time a single white field broken only by the Torah Shrine set against it midway, and above this in approximately the area included in the two later Center Panels there was represented, as a free-standing design, a tree, its green leaves and branches studded with rosettes affixed to pegs embedded in the wall (Pl. XVII). Below the tree, at either side of its vertical brown trunk, stood objects rendered in yellow. The object at the left was probably a throne. On it lay a cushion and on the cushion a round object, perhaps a royal diadem. The object at the right was probably a table whose top was supported by two lions or lion

cubs confronting each other in the rampant position.

The tree and the symbolic objects beneath it having been executed simultaneously with the decorations of the Torah Shrine, the room was put into use as a house of worship before the dado completing the scheme could be executed, and in this connection there was probably erected for the first time the canopy that covered the Torah Shrine and shielded the *aron* or Scroll Chest placed within it. The cloth of the canopy was anchored to the wall above the Torah Shrine with the help of the nails driven into wooden pegs set into the wall, and may have obscured part of the trunk of the tree, except perhaps when the curtains were thrown open.

(*a*) *Redecoration, First Phase: The Lion and the Promised King of Judah.* During the second stage in the decoration of the Synagogue, while it was being adorned with the magnificent murals upon which its fame rests, the area directly over the Torah Shrine was treated not once but several times. Some of the treatments were preparatory or corrective, but two represent positive efforts to incorporate it in the new scheme of development. The conclusion that the work of incorporation was not a single operation but developed in two successive steps, here spoken of as the first and second phases of the redecoration, is a necessary correction of the position taken in the Preliminary Report, based upon a further and minute examination of the entire area.[860]

In the first phase of the redecoration, the artist thought to contain the design of the tree and the symbolic objects in a single vertical field of his system of register decoration, with only slight changes.[861] Since this field running through

860. *Rep. VI*, pp. 367f. Aside from the many matters of detail, the fundamental reason for the assumption of two phases in the second stage of the decoration of the central area is that certain figures are superimposed upon the earlier design of the tree, thus succeeding this in time, but remained undisturbed during the preparation for the final recasting of the field, thus preceding the latter in time.

861. The fact that the tree had been developed originally as a free-standing design whose elements were not distributed equally in both directions was apparently one of the reasons why the field incorporating it in the register system is off-axis both in relation to the Torah Shrine and to the west wall as a whole, as already noted. See above, p. 62, n. 147.

Registers A and B was higher than it was wide, he framed it appropriately with four similarly proportioned Wing Panels, thus creating a Central Group of five units and providing an acceptable transition to the horizontal emphasis of the register divisions. The changes he introduced in the design were simple and affected only its central area (Pl. XXXIII). In the center directly above the end of the heavy trunk, he superimposed upon the foliage the figure of a large lion. At the top above the tree a king was represented, seated upon a throne, with two persons below and before him at either side. The king's footstool and attendants were superimposed upon the foliage, and the introduction of the throne required the removal of a certain number of the plaster rosettes that originally adorned the tree (Fig. 55).[862]

Fig. 55. Central Area. Position of Holes near King's Feet

As for the figures portrayed, the lion was done in bright yellow and outlined in reddish brown (Fig. 56). White lines following the inner edge of the darker outlines; for instance, along the belly,

Fig. 56. Central Area. Lion

were added to give the figure more plasticity.[863] Noteworthy is the animal's lack of ferocity, a trait that distinguishes it from most of the representations of lions in ancient art, including a dipinto and a graffito on the walls of the Synagogue.[864] The explanation of this departure is not to be found in the assumption that the artist intended to portray a female, but rather in that he used a pattern coming from an iconographic tradition other than that used in hunting and combat scenes.[865] The pattern is apparently that used in the representation of animals as guardians and as the servants of deities.[866] For the symbolic purposes

862. In the Preliminary Report (*Rep. VI*, pp. 367f.) the lion, the king, and his associates were assigned to the First Stage in the decoration of the Synagogue, hence to the original design of the tree. This assignment was disproved by a closer examination of the evidence for the distribution of the foliage and by a study of the holes pockmarking the field. The holes in question are those made to receive the wooden pins that held the rosettes adorning the tree and that anchored the cloth of the canopy covering the Torah Shrine. Of the former the majority was open and had been heavily daubed with the red paint of the cover-coat applied in the second stage of the redecoration when the tree design was abandoned entirely. At least three, however, representing points on an arc, had been filled with plaster and painted over. They are located in the area covered by the king's throne and are marked with *F* on Fig. 55. Their treatment, like the distribution of the foliage, requires the assumption of a separate first stage in the redecoration of the area, the rosettes having been removed to prepare the surface for the addition of the new elements. For an artist to combine figures of human beings and animals with a vegetal design was by no means unusual. See e.g., the triumph of Liber Pastor in the mosaic from el-Djem, *Africa Italiana*, VI (1935), p. 148, Fig. 35, and the familiar Antioch Chalice.

863. As originally seen, the lion was not covered at any point by leaves but was painted over them, the thought of an animal realistically hidden behind foliage being quite foreign to the point of view of the Synagogue artists, as all their other paintings clearly show. The leaves that partly conceal the lion in the painting as it appears today belong to a later stage in the development of the decoration. Cf. below, p. 227, n. 898.

864. Cf. Inscrs. nos. **59** and **68**, below, pp. 318, 320, and for a still better illustration of the ferocious type, the lion on the Roman shield from Dura (*Rep. VI*, Frontispiece). For typical lions from elsewhere, see the mosaics of Antioch (*Antioch*, III, Pls. 52 and 76) and of North Africa (e.g., S. Aurigemma, *I Mosaici di Zliten*, 1926, p. 181, Fig. 111a and p. 192, Fig. 120).

865. The animal has consistently been called a lioness by Du Mesnil du Buisson (e.g., *Peintures*, pp. 28, 49) and others. For this there is no basis in fact. In the Synagogue, as in ancient art generally, females are clearly identified by their rows of udders. Cf. the tigresses of the dado of the Synagogue (Pl. XXXVII,2), their counterpart on the Antioch mosaic now in the Worcester Museum (see C.R. Morey, *The Mosaics of Antioch*, 1938, Pl. XX; *Antioch*, II, Pl. 73), and the lioness on the late Sassanian dish (Sarre, *Die Kunst des alten Persien*, Pl. 122). Cf. also below, n. 867.

866. Familiar examples of lions that probably serve as guardians are those of the Ishtar Gate and those from Susa. For the later period see the lion frieze of the 'Arak il-Emir, *Publications of the Princeton University Archaeo-*

he had in mind, the Synagogue artist undoubtedly found this pattern more appropriate. As to the meaning of the symbol there cannot be the slightest doubt. What we have before us is the earliest known example of the familiar Lion or Judah, the symbol that derives from the familiar passage in the Blessing of Jacob, where it is said of Judah:

> Judah is a lion's whelp;
> From the prey my son, thou art gone up.
> He stooped down, he couched as a lion,
> And as an old lion, who shall rouse him up?
> (Gen. 49.9)[867]

As for the three figures above the lion, two standing and one seated, they all face full front, and form a nicely balanced group. The king occupies a position higher than his companions and must therefore be thought of as seated somewhat behind them. His head is no longer visible, but his pose and his robes are analogous to those of other enthroned monarchs in the Synagogue; for instance, Ahasuerus in Panel WC 2 (Mordecai and Esther) and Pharaoh in Panel WC 4 (Infancy of Moses). He wears a long-sleeved red coat and a dark blue tunic, the latter belted at the waist and ornamented down the front and at the hem with yellow bands.[868] His trousers are similarly ornamented and are tucked into the usual soft white boots. In this instance, however, the king wears over these boots a pair of dark shoes (Pl. XXXIII).[869] His feet rest

on an oblong yellow footstool outlined in brown as he sits upon a throne with yellow turned legs and a high back. The seat is covered with a cushion, which, like the cloth that is draped over the back of the throne, seems to have been green. Equally typical of the cliché which the artist has used throughout his work are the gestures of the king's hands: the right extended with the palm open, the left held close to the chest with the index finger extended and crooked. But the artist has apparently omitted here the sword to which the position of the finger is appropriate.[870]

The king is drawn to almost exactly the same scale as his counterparts in other panels. The two figures set before him at either side of the throne supply, in proportions proper to their rank, the associates without which a king cannot be thought to appear. They differ from the courtiers of corresponding scenes in two particulars: first, in their position in the foreground, and second, in their dress. The dress consists of a white chiton and himation, the former ornamented in one instance at least with wide clavi, and the latter with a two-pronged band shown in a diagonal position on the skirt of the garment. Each man keeps his left arm close by his side to hold the rolled ends of the himation; the right arm of the man at the left is extended downward and outward, while that of his associate at the right is indistinct but may have been held before his chest.[871]

For the identification of the king and his associates we have only two clues; namely, first, the

---

logical *Expeditions to Syria in 1904–5 and 1909*, II, A (1910), Pl. I. For lions as draft animals of the chariots of deities, see, e.g., the familiar bas-relief of Cybele (Reinach, *Répertoire de reliefs*, III, p. 134).

867. On the lion as a Jewish symbol, and particularly as a symbol of Judah, see Sukenik, *Ancient Synagogue of Beth Alpha*, pp. 32–34; and Wischnitzer-Bernstein, *Gestalten und Symbole der jüdischen Kunst*, pp. 42, 129–131. There is nothing to indicate that ancient Jewish interpreters, including the Targumists, followed the example of modern translators in rendering the Hebrew word *labhî* of Gen. 49.9 "lioness." The word could mean "lioness" if vocalized *lĕbhiyyā'*, but is probably merely a synonym of *'aryēh*, "lion." The translation "old lion" given above is a rendering commonly suggested and a means of compensating for the paucity of synonyms for "lion" in the English language.

868. Similar bands at the side of the tunic, where the skirt of the garment follows the line of the king's lap, represent the ornament of the cloak. Cf. Panels WC 2 and 4.

869. The color of the shoes is no longer clearly identifiable. They belong, of course, to the state costume of royalty, being analogous in this particular to the *campagia regia* of late Roman and Byzantine Emperors

(see A. Alföldi, *Röm. Mitt.*, L, 1935, pp. 65 f.), which in turn have their antecedents in the shoes worn by Persian kings, by Alexander, and by the Diadochoi (see Delbrueck, *Die Consulardiptychen*, pp. 37 f.; idem, *Die Antike*, VIII, 1932, esp. pp. 5–8; A. Alföldi, *Röm. Mitt.*, XLIX, 1934, esp. pp. 16 f.). Exact counterparts to the form of the shoes depicted in the Synagogue painting are apparently not available in the monuments of later imperial art. The shoes of the later Byzantine Emperors are much higher (see the miniature of Basil II in the Venice Psalter, graec. 17, fol. 1, J. Ebersolt, *La Miniature byzantine*, 1926, Pl. XXIV). Those of the earlier period are low, but substitute for the characteristic tongue a strap going across the ankle (see shoes of the mounted emperor on the silver dish from Kertsch in the Hermitage Museum, Peirce and Tyler, *L'Art byzantin*, I, Pl. 27).

870. Cf. the figure of Ahasuerus in Panel WC 2 (Mordecai and Esther), Pl. LXVI.

871. So the Gute copy. Whether the men may be said to gesture is not clear. If they are gesturing, the man at the right can only be pointing downward toward the lion and the one at the left upward toward the king.

relation of the group to the lion below it, and second, the departure from convention in the kind of garment worn by the two lesser figures. The connection between the lion as a symbol of Judah and Gen. 49.9 leads very naturally to the assumption that the allusion in the royal figure is to the famous words that follow in the Blessing of Jacob:

> The sceptre shall not depart from Judah,
>> Nor the ruler's staff from between his feet
> Until Shiloh come
>> And unto him shall the obedience of the
>> people be (Gen. 49.10).

Whatever the words "until Shiloh come" may originally have meant, it is clear that for the Targumists their connotation was Messianic.[872] According to the prophecy, then, the house of Judah is to supply a line of kings that is to continue unbroken until it reaches its apex in the person of the Messianic ruler to whom the people will be obedient. The suggestion to be drawn from the words of this prophecy for the interpretation of the royal figure in the painting is that it represents the promised king, whether as a single historical individual (David), as an abiding element of the nation's life, or as the Messiah who is to come.[873]

Confirmation of the suggestion connecting the king with the Shiloh prophecy of Gen. 49 can apparently be found in the detail of his associates' unusual dress. In the *Targum pseudo-Jonathan*, one of the very works that provide the Messianic interpretation of the Shiloh prophecy, the first half of Gen. 49.10:

> The sceptre shall not depart from Judah
>> Nor the ruler's staff from between his feet,

is rendered:

> Kings and rulers shall not cease from the house
> of Judah
>> Nor scribes (*saphrin*) and teachers of the
>> Law from among his descendants.[874]

Now the interpretation of the Targum was well known to the Tannaim and Amoraim of Palestine and Babylonia, becoming the occasion for utterances defining the relative importance of the Babylonian exilarchs, who claimed Davidic descent, and the Palestinian rabbis, as the spiritual descendants and successors of Hillel.[875] The assumption that the additions to the design of the tree were inspired by Gen. 49.9–10 thus explains the lion, the enthroned king, and his civilian attendants, who are Scribes or teachers of the Law and not typical courtiers. It is important in this connection to recall what was said above (pp. 63f.) about the objects portrayed under the tree in the original design; namely, that they seemed to be symbolic representations of the throne and table prepared for the Messianic king. The interpretation offered for the supplements added in the first phase of the redecoration of the area suggests that the Synagogue artist was merely trying to render the intended allusion more vivid by associating the eschatological symbols with the elements of a Biblical prophecy. The conservatism displayed by him in this particular may assist us in interpreting also the next phase in the development of the area.

(b) *Redecoration, Second Phase.* Long before the Synagogue was buried in the covering embankment additional changes were made in the central area, much more extensive and drastic in character. There must have been dissatisfaction with the effort merely to enliven and clarify an old design. The reasons for that dissatisfaction are not hard to guess if the brilliance of the neighboring panels, each a narrative unit set against a monochrome background, be kept in mind. Clearly the area over the Torah Shrine deserved the most brilliant treatment of all; and clearly, as a design painted directly on plaster without a background and with but few figures to enliven it, it could not compare with the rest of the walls of the chamber. So the decision was

---

872. So in the *Targum Onkelos*, "until the Messiah (or, the Anointed) comes, whose the kingdom is"; in the *Targum pseudo-Jonathan*, "until the time when the King Messiah comes, the youngest of his sons"; and in the *Fragmentary Targum*, "until the time when the King Messiah comes, whose the kingdom is." See in general, A. Posnanski, *Schiloh, ein Beitrag zur Geschichte der Messiaslehre* (1904).

873. The last is the choice of most interpreters, save Wischnitzer, *Messianic Theme*, p. 97.

874. Similarly the *Targum Onkelos*, "Not shall he who exercises dominion pass from the house of Judah, nor the

scribe (*saphra'*) from his children's children." Note that in the *Midrash Rabbah* the "scribes" of the Targum on Gen. 49.10 are described as being two in number (Gen. Rabbah XCVIII, 8, Trans., II, p. 956). They are likened to those who stand before the Sanhedrin, one to the right and the other to the left.

875. See Sanhedrin 5a (Trans., pp. 15f.) and Horayoth 11b (Trans., p. 81), together with the comment of Sonne, "The Paintings," p. 346.

made to redecorate the area, and at the same time to divide the large vertical field horizontally into two panels by extending across the field the register band separating Registers A and B. The first step in this direction was to take down the canopy covering the Torah Shrine and to remove the remaining rosettes from the surface of the wall. The next was to cover the design of the tree and its symbolic objects with a red wash. This last was necessary to provide a homogeneous color base, but contrary to the artists' normal procedure and fraught with unfortunate long-range consequences. Plans had, of course, been made meanwhile for the new compositions that were to occupy the two Center Panels, and in these plans the lion, the enthroned king, and his two associates continued to play a part. They were therefore exempted from the red wash that was spread over everything else. For purposes of composition the Upper Center Panel was treated as a single field, but the Lower Center Panel was not. It was developed to show three separate scenes, two in one plane near the base line, and a third, not centered, at a higher level.[876] The reasons for this peculiar treatment of the Lower Center Panel cannot be fully known, but in all probability the decision to preserve the Lion of Judah had something to do with it.

Lower Center Panel: *The Blessings of Jacob and David, Pious King* (Pls. XXXIV, LXXIV). The two scenes in the lower portion of the Lower Center Panel are homogeneous in character, for they represent in each instance a person reclining upon a couch with various figures gathered about him (Figs. 57–58). Of their import there cannot be the slightest doubt, for they portray Jacob blessing his two grandsons and his twelve sons respectively. Both scenes are only dimly visible at the present time.

As they are recorded in Gen. 48–49, the stories upon which the scenes are based tell how when Jacob had spent seventeen years in the Land of Goshen as a guest of Pharaoh and Joseph, he fell

sick. The news was transmitted to Joseph, who took his two sons, Ephraim and Manasseh, to visit their grandfather and found him "sitting upon the bed" (Gen. 48.2). Jacob took this occasion to adopt his two grandchildren so that they became equal in rank to his own twelve sons, and to bless them, giving unexpected preference to the younger, Ephraim, by blessing Ephraim with his right hand and Manasseh with his left. Then he summoned all twelve of his own sons, uttered a prophecy over each of them, and blessed them also.

Throughout, the artist has held himself closely to the details of the Biblical story. He placed the scene of the blessing of Ephraim and Manasseh (Gen. 48) in the right part of the field, and that of the blessing of the twelve sons (Gen. 49) in the left. In both instances Jacob reclines on a couch with a green mattress, a yellow rail, yellow turned legs, and a long yellow footstool beneath it.[877] With his feet extended toward the left, the patriarch in both scenes leans with his left arm upon a cushion,[878] quite as do figures in contemporary banquet scenes, holding his body more erect, however, than is usual in such cases. His face is either beardless or only very lightly bearded; but the details of his features, like those of his costume, are quite obscure, only this being evident: that he faces full front, and that his head is surrounded by a heavy aureole of dark hair.[879]

876. The division between the upper and the lower zones in the Lower Center Panel is marked by a scratch line upon which the feet of the musician at the left clearly rest. The scratch line is not parallel to the register band. The lower zone is 0.85 m. high at the left and 0.88 m. high at the right, while the upper zone is 0.58 m. high at the left and 0.62 m. high at the right.

877. Cf. in the Synagogue apparently the couch in Panel EC 2 (Belshazzar's Feast), and elsewhere the banquet scenes familiar on funerary bas-reliefs. The Biblical text does not mention Jacob's lying on the bed in Gen. 49, but this may readily be inferred from the previous story, more especially from Gen. 48.2. The *Targum pseudo-Jonathan* not only mentions the bed in rendering Gen. 49.1, but describes it as a golden bed.

878. In the scene at the left the cushion is yellow and ornamented with parallel black stripes, while in the scene at the right it is green.

879. From the way in which Jacob's foot projects from his garment, it seems to follow that he is wearing a chiton and himation, rather than tunic and trousers. In this case the ornament on the left shoulder of the outer garment in the scene at the left should be interpreted after the analogy of that on the garment of Moses in Panel WB 1 (Wilderness Encampment and Miraculous Well of Be'er). We have already noted, however (see above, p. 188), that this type of garment is not associated normally with the heavy coiffure the patriarch clearly wears. Either the inference from the projecting foot is incorrect (and for this conclusion the vertical stripes down the center of the patriarch's chest in the scene at the right, as recorded in the Gute copy, give some

In the scene at the left, representing the events of Gen. 49, the twelve sons of Jacob are seen standing behind the patriarch's couch, arranged in two groups of six each (Fig. 57). All face directly front,

Joseph and the two children stand before and to the right of the couch, all facing front, in spite of the direct personal relation with Jacob into which their receipt of his blessing places the children.

FIG. 57. Central Area. Jacob and Sons

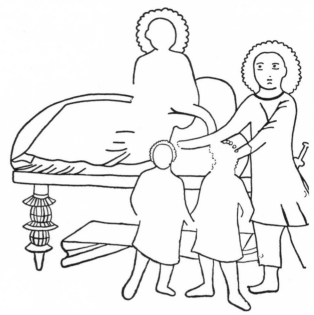

FIG. 58. Central Area. Jacob and Grandsons

have heavy heads of dark curly hair, and seem to wear the court costume of tunic, trousers, and soft white boots. The figures are stiff, lifeless, and closely crowded together, particularly at the right of Jacob's head.[880] In the scene at the right (Fig. 58)

justification), or special circumstances have dictated the unusual combination, as in the case of the second and third Ezekiel of the second section of Panel NC 1. These circumstances could readily be the patriarch's association with the other figures in the scenes, all of whom wear the court costume, probably because of their supposed connection through Joseph with the Pharaonic court.

880. As to details of the rendering, now often quite obscure, some information can be provided with the help of the field notes and the Gute copies. Counting from left to right, the men in the back row of the group at the right of Jacob's head wear yellow, red, and green tunics respectively, while those in the front row wear red, yellow, and red respectively. At the left of Jacob's head the tunics of the four men in the rear row are red, red, green, and yellow; while those of the two men in the front row are yellow and red. The fourth man in the rear row of the group at the left of Jacob has a series of light vertical fold lines inscribed upon his tunic, a detail not elsewhere duplicated in the Synagogue, for which there may, however, be foundation in Palmyrene sculpture. Cf. the vertical folds in the costume on the bas-relief reproduced

Joseph wears a red tunic, trousers, and soft white boots, and has at his left side the sword that is proper to his position at the Pharaonic court. His heavy coiffure is appropriate to the costume he wears; his arms are extended toward the left, his hands seeming to touch the heads of the two children as, in accordance with the Biblical narrative, he arranges them so that Manasseh, the first born, will be in the correct position to be blessed by the right hand of Jacob (Gen. 48.13).[881] The children wear long-sleeved belted tunics comparable to that of their father, though with two vertical clavi down the front instead of the single decorative band normal in the court costume of

by H. Seyrig, *Antiquités syriennes*, III (1946), p. 136, Fig. 11. This style of representation is relatively archaic. In our scene the tunics are generally belted and have vertical decorative bands down the middle, though such a band is noticeable by its absence in the case of the man with the vertical fold lines in his garment.

881. Since in the scene Joseph and the children face forward instead of toward Jacob, Joseph takes Ephraim in his right hand and Manasseh in his left, contrary to the Biblical narrative.

adults.[882] Their legs and feet, only dimly visible, seem to be bare. Their hair is short but curly. Each holds one hand at his side, the other slightly extended. Of Jacob's part in the benediction only one detail is observable; namely, that by means of a peculiar elongation of the arm the artist has contrived to make the patriarch's right hand approach the head of Ephraim, the child actually most accessible to his left hand. This is enough to indicate that the artist has kept in view the important detail of the story according to which Jacob crossed his arms, blessing with his right hand the younger of the two sons, contrary to Joseph's wishes (Gen. 48.14–19).

The representation of the two scenes from the life of Jacob in the lower half of the Lower Center Panel constitutes no problem if the interpretation offered above for the details added in the preceding stage of the development of the area is accepted. The artist has merely provided in these two scenes the historical setting for the very Benediction of Jacob from which the Shiloh prophecy comes. This is important in showing us the direction in which his mind was moving in the redecorative enterprise. It should be noted, moreover, that by virtue of his choice of subject matter, so far as we have studied it, he has brought Jacob, the third patriarch, and his descendants into immediate proximity to Abraham and Isaac as they are represented on the façade of the Torah Shrine immediately below, and that in this way he has begun a narrative sequence running upwards.

The upper half of the Lower Center Panel presents a number of problems, not all of which can be solved with the evidence available. About this area in the second phase of redecoration two things are quite certain: first, that the artist preserved the lion from the first phase; and second, that he added at the extreme left the seated figure of a royal musician.

The musician (Fig. 59) is superimposed upon both the foliage of the tree and the red wash with which this foliage was expunged. As he sits upon his throne, the tips of his feet are planted directly

upon the scratch line that divides the panel horizontally. He wears the familiar royal costume, perhaps originally red in color, consisting of a long-sleeved tunic ornamented down the front and at the hem with yellow bands, trousers similarly orna-

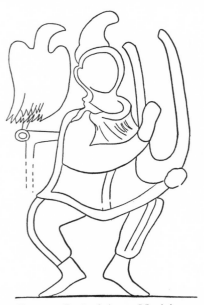

FIG. 59. Central Area. Musician

mented, and soft white boots. With this costume go two articles of clothing found also in other scenes of the Synagogue: the soft "Phrygian" cap worn by both Mordecai and Ahasuerus in Panel WC 2, and a chlamys thrown over the left shoulder.[883] The latter appears with the court costume in NA 1, but replaces here the more typical coat seen in WC 2 and EC 1. In his left hand the man holds a well-proportioned lyre, the arms of which curve gently to the left at the top. His right arm reaches across his chest as he touches the strings with his right hand. Beside the man's right shoulder there is visible the end of the horizontal rail in which the back of the throne terminates at the top.[884] Upon it is perched a large yellow bird, probably an eagle, with his wings partly opened out and his head turned toward the right.

882. The children's costume differs from that of the youths in Panel SB 1 (Dedication of the Temple), being similar, however, to that of the two boys in the foreground of the Conon Fresco (Cumont, *Fouilles*, pp. 52–54; Pls. XXXI, XXXV). This may be a second indication of archaism in the rendering.

883. Judging by details visible on the man's left shoulder, the chlamys also had a yellow border. This suggests that the yellow band following the contour of the right side of his body represents the edge of the chlamys hanging down behind him, rather than additional trimming on the tunic.

884. The same rail appears in the thrones of Ahasuerus (Panel WC 2) and Pharaoh (Panel WC 4).

The combination of pose, lyre, "Phrygian" cap, and chlamys has, since the painting was first brought to light, called to mind the figure of Orpheus, and properly so, for there can be no doubt that Orpheus has served the artist in part at least as the model of the representation.[885] The presence of animals in the upper half of the Lower Center Panel in the immediate vicinity of the royal musician raises the further question whether an allusion to Orpheus charming the beasts with his music was intended. The question could be answered with less reserve were greater certainty to be had as to the number and identity of the animals represented. In addition to the lion and the eagle, one observer has thought to see in the confused tangle at the immediate right of the musician a seated animal (monkey, hyena, bear, or dog), but neither the field notes, photographs, Gute copies, nor a reëxamination of the original bears this out.[886] More difficult is the problem presented by the bird or birds that several observers have seen, particularly at the right, but also at the left of the lion.[887] That something suggesting part of a bird actually appears just above the lion's tail, can be verified from Pl. LXXIV. Yet the peculiar fact is that what looks like a bird on the photographs is actually on the wall only an area devoid of the red wash. It is not outlined by brush-strokes or painted

in color. How this peculiarly shaped break in the red wash is to be explained, is not clear. What is clear is that of all the animals supposedly associated with the royal musician, there is positive, incontrovertible evidence only in the case of the lion and the eagle.[888] But if the eagle, being rendered in yellow, belongs more properly to the insignia of royalty with which a throne can be decorated than to the living creatures of field and forest, it would appear that all we can really be sure of is the association of the lyre-player with the lion. Since the lion himself belongs to the first phase of the redecoration of the area, the question whether an allusion to Orpheus charming the beasts was intended in the second can be answered properly only in the light of the purpose the artist had in mind in introducing the figure of the musician.

To what we can know about the identity of the musician two facts are relevant. The first is that he wears under the chlamys a form of the Persian habit that the Synagogue artists reserve for kings and the highest officials of the court and Temple.[889] The second is that in the second phase of the decorative development of the central area the artist can be said to have been illustrating in narrative form the prophecy of Gen. 49 that had been used

885. So already Hopkins and Du Mesnil du Buisson, *CRAI*, 1933, p. 246. On the representation of Orpheus in Greek, Roman, and Christian art see K. Ziegler in *RE*, XXXV (XVIII, 1, 1939), cols. 1311–1313, *s.v.* "*Orpheus in der bildenden Kunst*"; O. Gruppe in Roscher, *Lexikon*, III, 1 (1897–1902), cols 1172–1207; and Leclercq in Cabrol, *Dictionnaire*, XII, 2 (1936), cols. 2736–2755. R. Eisler believes to have seen in a cubiculum of the Jewish Catacomb on the Via Appia at Rome under the Vigna Randanini some slight remains of another Jewish representation of Orpheus (see his *Orphisch-dionysische Mysteriengedanken in der christlichen Antike, Vorträge der Bibliothek Warburg, 1922–23*, II, 1925, p. 4, Figs. 2–3). According to his sketch this showed a horse, the head of a man, and a lyre. There are no iconographic connections with the type under discussion here, so far as the evidence available permits us to judge.

886. Cf. the drawing of Du Mesnil du Buisson, "Les Deux synagogues," p. 88, Fig. 11 and his comment in *Peintures*, p. 49. Hopkins' field notes describe the area in question as containing a "series of black and dark brown splotches marred by white where the paint has chipped away." It may be noted that in the area one of the branches of the tree makes the type of reverse curve that could have been taken as the outline of a seated animal.

887. Cf. the drawing of Du Mesnil du Buisson cited above; *Rep. VI*, p. 368; and Pearson, *Guide*, p. 33.

888. The additional animals shown in the sketch of Du Mesnil du Buisson, "Les Deux synagogues," p. 88, Fig. 11, at the right side of the panel have not been noted by others and are not visible today, any more than the "swords and the head of a serpent" which Pearson's *Guide* (p. 33) mentions among the additional subjects that the observer seems to distinguish. The bird in front of the lion, of which Pearson speaks and the head of which seems to appear on the photographs, has no substance and would, if it existed, cancel out Du Mesnil du Buisson's seated animal. The confused condition of the painted surface in this area gives no positive support to any additional representations.

889. On the traditional costume of Orpheus on Greek vase paintings and the change that develops in the fourth century B.C., giving the singer the more formal priestly dress of long-sleeved chiton, mantle, and "Phrygian" hat, see Ziegler in *RE* cited on p. 224, n. 885. In the earliest of the Christian catacomb paintings, a short tunic and trousers replace the χίτων ποδήρης, suggesting the existence of an Oriental prototype closer to that found in the Synagogue. Cf. the description of Wilpert, *Pitture*, I, pp. 222–224, and II, Pl. 37, as well as Leclercq in Cabrol, *Dictionnaire*, cited on p. 224, n. 885. While the combination of knee-length, long-sleeved tunic and trousers is widely used in the Synagogue for Temple and court personnel, the particular form of it worn by the lyre-player is that which reappears on the king in the Upper Center Panel, on Ahasuerus (Panel WC 2), and Pharaoh (Panel WC 4).

also in the earlier phase. From the combination of these two facts it would seem to follow that the lyre-player must be David, the classic historical representative of the "kings... in the house of Judah" (hence his association with the lion) and the ancestor (and prototype) of the "King Messiah" of the future (Gen. 49.10, Targum).[890] If David appears in this context as a musician, rather than in the more warlike guise of Panel EC 1 (David and Saul in the Wilderness of Ziph) or the distinctive civilian garments of Panel WC 3 (Samuel Anoints David), the purpose in all probability is to emphasize the religious significance of the divinely instituted kingship by portraying him as the pious king, the author and singer of psalms.[891] The historical approach to the representation of the Shiloh prophecy expressed by the introduction of the two episodes from the life of Jacob in the lower part of the panel suggests that here too an allusion to a Biblical narrative may be intended. If so, it would be entirely proper to refer to II Sam. 22, which tells how David sang a long Psalm of Praise on the day that he was delivered from the hands of Saul and of all his enemies. In view of the uncertainties about many of the details of the area, the only inference that can safely be drawn from the upper part of the Lower Center Panel about

the influence of the Orpheus tradition upon the Synagogue paintings is that the artist fell back upon the best-known and most appropriate of the many clichés for musicians as a happy device for portraying David in the rôle assigned to him by II Sam. 22.[892]

Upper Center Panel: David, King over All Israel. Divided from the scenes below by an extension of the horizontal band that separates Registers A and B, the area containing the upper part of the tree, the king, and his two associates was developed in the second phase of its redecoration as the Upper Center Panel. The branches of the tree were expunged by the red cover-coat, but the king and his associates were kept, being made the nucleus of a larger group of figures which the artist proceeded to arrange about them in symmetrical fashion (Pls. XXXV, LXXV). What he was apparently trying to depict was a throne-room scene showing the king and his court, a type of scene that has a long and significant history in the later development of ancient art.[893] If he has been less successful than usual in this composition, it is probably because the position of three of the figures was already fixed in a way not entirely suited to the further development of the area.

The figures grouped about the throne are arranged in two ascending rows. All face full front,

---

890. It is David's unique importance in this connection that probably accounts for the absence of a balancing figure in the right part of the upper half of the Lower Center Panel.

891. How clearly this was recognized as a separate aspect of David's activities as king can be seen from Josephus, *Antiquitates* VII, 12, 3 = §§ 305–306, and from the Midrashim (see Ginzberg, *Legends of the Jews*, IV, p. 101, and VI, pp. 262 f., where further details concerning David's harp are to be found). In view of the care which the Synagogue artist has taken not to assign to David when he is anointed by Samuel the royal garments appropriate to his later career as king, it is unlikely that the particular allusion in the Lower Center Panel is to David as the shepherd who pastures and protects his flocks (so particularly Grabar, "Le Thème," p. 170, on the basis of Micah 5.4). A distinction must therefore be made between the Synagogue representation and that of the Christian Psalters, where at the outset, at least, David is clearly portrayed as shepherd (see especially the Paris Psalter, Buchthal, *The Miniatures of the Paris Psalter*, Pl. III; and Eisler, *Mysteriengedanken*, pp. 11–23). This alternative iconographic tradition known from the fresco in the catacomb of Callixtus (Wilpert, *Pitture*, II, Pl. 37) to be at least as old as that of the Synagogue, permits a much fuller use of the Orpheus prototypes and seems to reflect a more romantic interest than that of the Synagogue.

892. Standing and seated musicians, male and female, playing stringed instruments are commonly represented in ceramic art. Figurines of this type were well liked in the Orient; cf. E. D. Van Buren, *Clay Figurines of Babylonia and Assyria* (1930), pp. 235–240. One was found directly behind the Synagogue at Dura, in the fill between it and the city wall. The object is reproduced by Rostovtzeff *YCS*, V, Fig. 21.

893. Developed perhaps from the audience scene of which we have examples in Panels WC 2 (Mordecai and Esther) and WC 4 (Pharaoh and the Infancy of Moses), the representation of the seated king and his standing entourage is found, for instance, on the Arch of Constantine in the scene of the *congiarium* (Grabar, *L'Empereur dans l'art byzantin*, Pl. XXXI); in scenes of the Virgin and the apostles or angels and saints (e.g., at Baouit, Diehl, *La Peinture byzantine*, Pl. III); and Christ with angels and bishops (at Ravenna, in the apse of San Vitale, *ibid.*, Pl. VIII). Where the scene has a juridical character, the entourage is seated (see the apse mosaic of Santa Pudentiana, *ibid.*, Pl. I; the final judgment scenes at Torcello; and the comment of Grabar, *L'Empereur*, pp. 249–258, and "Le Thème," pp. 32 f.). Where it has a processional character, the monarch is himself standing, as in the scene showing Justinian and his court in San Vitale at Ravenna (Diehl, *op. cit.*, Pl. IX).

and those added to the scene in the final stage of its development all wear the court costume of belted, long-sleeved tunic, trousers, and soft white boots. With the costume goes the heavy hair appropriate to it. The gestures of the men's hands are only dimly discernible, but apparently were neither homogeneous or particularly meaningful. The men in the lower row are set in a plane with the two standing figures preserved from the earlier composition. Seven seem to have been added here, four at the left and three at the right.[894] The men in the upper row stand slightly above the level of the king's throne, the lower part of their legs sometimes being hidden by the heads of the men in the front rank. Here the artist has either varied the height of the figures (as at the right) or given them a slightly lower position (as at the left) so as to taper the files somewhat toward the sides of the panel. The number of the men in this file is six, three at each side of the throne. In most cases only the lower parts of their bodies are still visible.[895]

If the number of the supplementary figures is correctly fixed at thirteen, there can be little doubt as to their identity. They are the representatives of the eleven tribes and the two half tribes that together make up the entirety of the Hebrew nation. In other words they correspond to the sons of Jacob and the two sons of Joseph, Ephraim and Manasseh, whom Jacob adopted to replace their father, precisely as portrayed in the two scenes in the lower part of the Lower Center Panel. The correspondence shows the unity of the upper and lower elements in the second phase of the development of the area, and provides the essential clue for the interpretation of the scene. If the pictures showing Jacob blessing his sons and grandsons provide the setting for the utterance of the Shiloh prophecy (Gen. 49.10), that of the Upper Center Panel shows the fulfilment of the final words of that prophecy; namely, "unto him shall the obedience (or, the gathering) of the peoples be" — "the peoples" being interpreted here as the tribes of Israel.[896]

That the use of the Shiloh prophecy in the area of the Center Panels was inspired by its eschatological import, goes without saying. But the procedure followed in Panel NC 1 (Ezekiel, the Destruction and Restoration of National Life) in handling material of eschatological import, and what we have learned about the approach to the Shiloh prophecy in the organization of the Lower Center Panel, bid us keep in mind the possibility of an historical situation for the scene of the fulfilment in the Upper Center Panel. The basis for such a situation does in fact exist in II Sam. 5, where representatives of all the tribes of Israel come to Hebron, and where David is finally anointed and recognized as king over the entire united nation. The scene should therefore probably be thought to show the representatives of all the nation's tribes grouped about the enthroned David at that occasion.[897] As such it would, like the events of Ezek. 37, constitute both a fulfilment and a "parable" of events alluded to in the prophecy of Gen. 49.10–11, the events being in each case in the first instance matters of national importance.

In the redecoration of the area over the Torah Shrine, then, the Synagogue artist endeavored to bring the quality of its material and treatment up to the standard set by the remainder of the decorations. That, after the canopy over the Torah Shrine had been remounted, the area continued to

---

894. The Preliminary Report (*Rep. VI*, p. 368) and Du Mesnil du Buisson's drawing (*Peintures*, Pl. XX) put the number of the supplementary figures at eight, but the Gute copy indicates only seven and this number is confirmed by a reëxamination of the original. Du Mesnil du Buisson himself states that the supposed fourth figure at the extreme right is scarcely to be discerned (*Peintures*, p. 44, n. 2). The colors of the men's garments, each with two black stripes down the middle, are still recognizable, though the details are often quite obscure. Beginning at the extreme left of the file, the seven supplementary figures are rendered as follows: (1) yellow tunic; (2) green tunic; (3) pink tunic and green trousers; (4) dark brown tunic; (5) pink tunic and green trousers; (6) brown tunic, yellow trousers; (7) –?– tunic, pink trousers.

895. The figures of the upper file immediately adjacent to the throne on either side are perfectly clear and wear pink tunics. At the left the second figure from the throne had pink trousers. Of the third on this side the right elbow and the left leg are still visible. At the right the second figure from the throne is today identifiable only from the remains of the heavy head of hair, while of the third only a part of the left trouser leg is visible, where it is tucked into his boot. Where it can be checked against the original today, the Gute copy is entirely reliable in the rendering of the scene.

896. For the interpretation of 'ammîm as "tribes," see the rendering of Deut. 33.3 by the *Targum Onkelos* and the comment of the Jewish interpreters Ibn Ezra and Rashi *ad loc*.

897. In this event the two figures in civilian garments before the throne might, if necessary, be thought of as two of David's counsellors.

provide difficulties, was due to technical reasons and to the inherent conservatism of the procedure by which the decorative changes were made, and should not diminish our respect for the good intentions.[898] The very conservatism of treatment that played a part in the physical deterioration of the painted surface is at the same time the prime factor in permitting us to reconstitute the process, to distinguish the elements, and to understand the meaning of the successive compositions. Only because we can see the original design being changed by stages can we reconstruct the thread of eschatological reference that leads from the Tree of Life with its Messianic symbols via the symbolic adumbration of Gen. 49 to the presentation of the circumstances under which the prophecy was given, received its initial fulfilment, and developed its normative character. At the same time we obtain in this connection an insight into changes in the point of view normative for the decoration of the Synagogue. In the first stage of the decorative process the symbol is regarded as the prime object of representation and medium of instruction. In the second stage of the decorative process, after an attempt to develop a compromise position, historical narrative is regarded as the proper subject of representation and medium of instruction. This is of fundamental importance for the interpretation of the function and the nature of the narrative decorations of the Synagogue as a whole.

The Wing Panels

Panel I. Moses and the Burning Bush (upper right, virtually complete): H. *ca.* 1.16 m.; L. 0.68 m.

Panel II. Moses Receives the Law (upper left, fragmentary): H. *ca.* 1.16 m.; L. 0.67 m.

Panel III. Ezra Reads the Law (lower right): H. 1.52 m.; L. 0.67 m. (top), 0.62 m. (bottom).

Panel IV. Abraham Receives the Promise (lower left): H. 1.43 m.; L. 0.69 m.

(Pls. XXXVI, LXXVI–LXXVIII).

Hopkins and Du Mesnil du Buisson, "La Synagogue," p. 246; Rostovtzeff, "Die Synagoge," p. 209; Du Mesnil du Buisson, "Les Peintures," pp. 111f., 115; Goodenough, *By Light, Light*, p. 242; *Rep. VI*, pp. 347f., 351f.; Rostovtzeff, *Dura-Europos and its Art*, pp. 108f.; Du Mesnil du Buisson, *Peintures*, pp. 41–43, 45f., 53–55, 92–94; Pearson, *Guide*, pp. 28f., 33f.; Grabar, "Le Thème," pp. 176–186; Leveen, *Hebrew Bible in Art*, pp. 32–35; Schneid, *The Paintings*, pp. 9f.; Sonne "The Paintings," pp. 273, 290–301; Sukenik, *The Synagogue*, pp. 64–73; Wischnitzer, *Messianic Theme*, pp. 79–86.

Around the two Center Panels the Synagogue artist has grouped four narrow Wing Panels that serve to frame them and to enhance in the focal area of the decorations the symmetrical arrangement of scenes. Analogies to such balanced arrangements, in which narrow fields frame and set off a central composition, are common in ancient painting, including the later phases of Pompeian decorative art; and the arrangement carries over naturally into mosaic decoration and ivory carving because of its pleasing character and its usefulness in the treatment of square and rectangular areas.[899] At Dura the closest analogy is that provided by the Late Mithraeum, where the seated figures of Zarathustra and Ostanes adorn the outer faces of the piers at either side of the cult niche.[900] In the Preliminary Report these Wing Panels of the west

---

898. That the canopy was restored to its position is evident from the existence of peg holes that are completely free of paint. The deterioration of the repainted area derives from the superimposition of multiple layers of paint. Since the paint was unable to penetrate the plaster, those elements of the first and second phases of the redecoration that were superimposed over parts of the original design tended to flake off. This had the effect of bringing to light again the original tree and the symbols beneath it. It is possible that before the Synagogue was buried in the embankment, its elders, bowing to necessity, sanctioned a re-introduction of the tree design in the central area, if only by systematizing the blemishes to make their character and effect less obvious. As to the time and extent of this operation there must inevitably be great uncertainty.

899. For examples of Pompeian wall paintings suggesting such tripartite arrangement, see V. Spinazzola, *Le Arti decorative in Pompei* (1928), Pls. 106, 117, 118, 119, 173, 174. For single persons in separately framed panels in mosaic see, e.g., D. Levi, *Antioch Mosaic Pavements*, I (1947), Fig. 2; and more particularly the prophets and saints on the north and south walls of S. Apollinare Nuovo (*Tavola storiche dei mosaici di Ravenna*, IV, 1934, Pls. XXI–XXVIII). For illustrated manuscripts see the representation of Ezra in Codex Amiatines (G. Biagi, *Reproductions from Illustrated Manuscripts*, 1914, Pl. VI). For the ivories see the book covers reproduced in Peirce and Tyler, *L'Art byzantin*, II, Pls. 2 (Barberini Ivory), 165, 169.

900. *Rep. VII–VIII*, Pls. XVI–XVIII.

wall of the Synagogue were referred to as "portrait panels," in view of the fact that each portrays but a single standing figure. In each instance, moreover, the head of the person represented is separately framed by a device that destroys the simplicity of the monochrome background normally associated in the Synagogue with narrative composition, and recalls nothing so much as the rectangular panels upon which are rendered the familiar mummy portraits of Hellenistic Egypt.[901] Yet it is clear that portraiture, even if suggested, was neither feasible nor achieved, and that each of the Wing Panels, as we now prefer to call them, contains enough supplementary material to connect the figure represented with a particular historical episode. The panels are therefore probably narrative in origin, but the historical reference is severely abbreviated so that the emphasis falls primarily on the person involved. This sets them off from the other panels of the registers and permits them to serve the purposes of a special group. As parts of this group of panels, they call attention to certain persons who, by virtue of events associated with them, are of particular significance for the theme the group develops.

(a) Panel I: Moses and the Burning Bush

(Pl. LXXVI).

Preserved almost to its full height, the Wing Panel in Register A at the right of the Upper Center Panel has suffered mainly from the cracking of its plaster base and the loss of certain color elements, especially at the top.[902] What it represents; namely, the scene of Moses at the burning

901. So already Rostovtzeff, *Römische Quartalschrift*, XLII, p. 210; and more explicitly Grabar, "Le Thème," p. 176, n. 2, quoting also de Vaux's review of Du Mesnil du Buisson, *Revue biblique*, XLIX (1940), p. 139.

902. One vertical crack can be seen coming down through Moses' right shoulder and tracing an irregular course through his garments and alongside his figure till it passes from the panel near the tip of his right foot. This is crossed by three horizontal fissures; at the level of the crown of Moses' head, of his hip, and his knee respectively. The last-mentioned extends across the entire panel, dividing into two branches at the right and joining another vertical crack that comes down through the panel band at the right. Pieces of plaster have been lost in the panel band at the right, to the left of Moses' head, and in the panel band at the left near the bottom. Cracking has brought about dislocation of the painted line in the lower part of Moses' himation.

bush (Exod. 3), has never been in doubt. The story of the event as told in the Bible is one of a theophany that occurred while Moses was tending the flock of his father-in-law at the "mountain of God," Horeb. Both the "angel of the Lord" and God himself appeared to Moses in the midst of the bush that burned but was not consumed, Moses hiding his face because he was afraid to look upon God, and removing the shoes from his feet as instructed because the place was "holy ground." The occasion of the theophany, it will be recalled, is that of Moses' commission to lead his people out of Egypt into the land flowing with milk and honey.

In his rendering of the episode the Synagogue artist has abbreviated sharply. There is no sign of the mountain or of the flock and only a symbolic representation of the presence of the divine visitors. By far the largest part of the field is taken up by the large, stocky figure of Moses, who stands at the right side of the panel, facing front and resting his weight upon his right foot. His right hand is extended as he gestures toward the tall bush that fills the space at the left of the panel almost to the top. His shoes stand before him at the bottom, while from above at the left the Hand of God comes down toward him.

Moses is dressed in the familiar costume of chiton and himation, both of which are rendered in yellow, with white highlights and brown fold-lines. The chiton has blue clavi and the himation two-pronged blue ornamental bands on the ends that hang down over the left arm. In comparison to its height and to the man in the panel just below, the figure is very wide at the hips, corresponding in this particular to the representations of Moses in Panel WA 3 (Exodus and Red Sea Crossing). As in the other scenes of this register, a dull brick red serves as a flesh color, this being considerably darker than the red used in the lower registers. Moses' head as it appears today seems to be both beardless and bald, but this is only because weathering has caused the heavy layers of paint that represented the hair to disintegrate or flake off. From traces still visible along the edges of the area they covered, it is clear that Moses here had the same heavy pointed black beard and the head of curly hair he wears on Panel WA 3. The face is expressionless, with heavy arched eyebrows, the line of one of which is continued to form the nose;

wide-open eyes; and a relatively small mouth, above which some trace of a mustache has been detected. At the bottom of the panel, against the light pink of the background, can be seen elements of a dull cast shadow taking the form of an inverted *V*, and the high white boots ornamented and outlined in brown and tied at the top with laces. They are never associated elsewhere in the Synagogue with the costume that Moses wears, and are intended, no doubt, to represent the *caligae rusticae* of farmers and shepherds rather than the *caligae militares*, which they also resemble — serving in this capacity to provide an allusion to Moses' momentary occupation without requiring the artist to portray him in a costume unsuited to his importance and to the decorative context to which he belongs.[903]

For the bush at the left the artist has used the convention that serves also to render the reeds at the side of the Nile in Panel WC 4 (Pharaoh and the Infancy of Moses), save that he has increased the height of the plant. Between the long drooping black leaves that radiate from the straight stem there are to be seen wavy red lines and short black strokes that represent the fire burning in the bush without consuming it. Above the bush the Hand of God emerges from the frame of the panel at the left, extending through the vault of heaven toward the figure of Moses. It is rendered in the same brick red used for flesh tones throughout the composition, and with its long arm and the close juxtaposition of all fingers but the thumb recalls the Hands represented in Panel WA 3 (Exodus and Red Sea Crossing).[904] Apparently the Hand is a left hand. This is evidently not because something infelicitous is portended, but probably because it was one of

a pair, the other (right) hand being shown originally in the complementary Wing Panel at the left.[905]

The upper part of the panel the artist has treated in an unusual manner. In the rectangular field he has inscribed here the vault of heaven, rendering it in black and thus continuing the effect of the black clouds that border the scene of the Exodus and Red Sea Crossing at the right. The curve of the vault, however, does not span the entire panel, but comes to an end at the left in the space occupied by the fingers of the Hand of God. The presence of the hand obscures the termination of the vault, but from the tips of its fingers the lower edge of the inscribed black area runs in a horizontal line to the frame of the panel at the left. Precisely why the vault was not made to span the entire field is not evident, but the effect of the shortened span is to deëmphasize the narrative elements of the scene that come to expression through the bush, and to accentuate the importance of Moses as a person by setting him into a niche-like field. The segment of the field contained within the arc of the vault of heaven was further subdivided by wide black lines that drop perpendicularly from the perimeter to the chord and return to the perimeter on the chord. The areas fashioned by these lines were painted a light color, but apparently remained blank.[906] Even the Aramaic *titulus*: "Moses son of Levi" (Inscr. No. 6), that could have been placed in one or the other of them is carefully set below and outside of the one at the left. It would seem therefore that the function of these subdivisions is really negative rather than positive, and that they serve to restrict the space about Moses' head to a narrow rectangular field, thus creating the effect of a frame without actually drawing one.[907] The whole procedure looks like that of an artist who knows at least the

903. Cf. in general H. Blümner, *Die römischen Privataltertümer* (I. Müller, *Handbuch der klassischen Altertumswissenschaft*, IV, 2, 2, 1911), pp. 226f. For military shoes at Dura see the graffito representing Iarhibol (*Rep. V*, Pl. XXXVI, 3) and the Sacrifice of Terentius Tribunus (Cumont, *Fouilles*, Pl. L). While different in form, the footwear of the Good Shepherd in the catacomb frescoes illustrates the shepherd's need of such protection as the high, laced shoes of the Synagogue painting give. Cf. Wilpert, *Pitture*, pp. 92f. and Pls. 51, 1–2; 61 etc. David as shepherd wears the high laced shoe in later representations; e.g., in the Paris Psalter (Diehl, *La Peinture byzantine*, Pl. LXXVI).

904. By the same token it is different from the Hands of God in Panel NC 1 (Ezekiel, the Destruction and Restoration of National Life).

905. Cf. below, p. 232. In Panel WA 3 (Exodus and Crossing of the Red Sea) the two Hands of God also make a pair.

906. Du Mesnil du Buisson gives the color as bluish gray (*Peintures*, p. 42) while Hopkins' field notes indicate white. Today the original color can no longer be determined accurately.

907. Hopkins' field notes suggest that the part of the field within which Moses' head lies was painted blue, but there is today no change from the pinkish lavender of the field as a whole, and this color Du Mesnil du Buisson assigned to the space in question (*Peintures*, p. 42).

basic techniques for rendering portraits and for representing effigies in niches and who feels the propriety of the application of these techniques to this part of his work, but is trying to avoid making their use too apparent.

(b) Panel II: Moses Receives the Law

(Pl. XXXVI, 1; Fig. 60).

Of the complementary Wing Panel at the left of the Upper Center Panel in Register A, only the lower 0.86 m., or less than three quarters, is actually preserved, the rest having been destroyed

FIG. 60. Wing Panel II. Moses Receives the Law

when the upper part of the west wall of the Synagogue was razed to the level of the embankment in which it was buried. Two systems of horizontal cracks with numerous vertical offshoots cut through the upper and lower parts of the plaster that remains, and at the top, particularly at the right, the colors have become very dim. Yet certain essentials of the representation are still clearly visible. The panel contains again a single standing figure dressed in a gray chiton and himation whose fold-lines are indicated in white. The chiton has blue clavi and the himation two-pronged ornamental bands on the ends that hang from the man's left arm. The ends of the himation are supplied with tassels. The position of the man's feet it is important to note, for while the left bears the weight of the body and is therefore seen in profile, indicating association with something at the right, the right foot is set far back and is turned three-

quarters front rather than back. This is a departure from the standard convention used by the artist in showing standing persons engaged in events toward the right. It denotes intensity of movement and in most cases goes with a profile rendering of the face.[908] Here motion is clearly implied, but the vertical position of the left leg shows that the motion has reached its terminal stage and has been arrested. Similarly a departure from frontality is indicated, but the probability is that the artist did not go beyond the three-quarter pose in his handling of the body, thus making it possible to keep the head in a frontal position.[909] That there should be indications both of movement and of a three-quarter pose in a panel of the Central Group is quite unexpected and requires explanation. The explanation is provided by the position of the man's hands, both of which must have been extended toward the right — the left hand because of the prominent display of the ends of the himation that were rolled over it, and the right because the upper edge of the sleeve can be seen passing across the body. The man was thus shown in motion and in a three-quarter pose because he was to be seen approaching and either giving something to, or receiving something from, someone at the right. This inference is verified by the existence at the appropriate place of traces of a large whitish object, squarish in shape, which the man was holding in his outstretched hands.[910]

The upper part of the standing figure and the object which he holds are set off against a background that is bright red. At the base of the panel, however, the red has been exchanged for a sandy yellow. The yellow of the foreground sweeps upward from left to right to form two ridges, one behind the other, each outlined in pink. Above the

908. For the standard convention see the second figure of Moses in Panel WA 3 (Exodus and Crossing of the Red Sea). For three other instances of the departure from this standard, see Mordecai approaching the throne of Panel WC 2 (Mordecai and Esther), the Psyche approaching the dead bodies in Panel NC 1, Section 2 (Ezekiel, the Destruction and Restoration of National Life), and Moses approaching the Red Sea in Panel WA 3.

909. In a strictly profile rendering the ends of the himation, prominently represented at the right, would have been hidden by the body.

910. So the Gute copy and Hopkins' field notes. Cf. also Du Mesnil du Buisson, *Peintures*, p. 45: "objet rectangulaire gris, bordé de noir." Only a change from the darker background color is visible today.

first of the ridges traces of a simple green plant have been observed.[911] Between the legs of the standing figure elements of what seems to be a cast shadow are visible. Before his left foot stand two high shoes, analogous to those in the previous panel, though more simply rendered and consisting merely of red outlines painted against the yellow background.

The subject of the scene has been a matter of controversy, opinion being divided largely between two alternative interpretations. Some interpreters find here a representation of the episode from the life of Joshua when the successor of Moses, having just crossed the Jordan with the Israelites, is confronted by the angelic "captain of the host of the Lord," whose presence portends the divine assistance in the impending capture of Jericho and the occupation of the Promised Land (Josh. 5.13–15).[912] Others connect the scene with one or the other of the two instances at which Moses ascends Mount Sinai to receive at the hand of God the commandments of the Law written upon the stone tables (Exod. 24.12–18; 31.18; and Exod. 34). Two considerations have given particular force to the first of these interpretations. One is that, aside from the narrative of Moses and the burning bush, the story of Joshua and the angel is the only one in which there appears the explicit demand, "Put off thy shoes from off thy feet" (Josh. 5.15). Another is the supposed relation of the panel to one or the other of the group of four to which it belongs.[913] More recently analogies from Christian art have also been brought into the picture, particularly the scene of Joshua and the angel as rendered in the mosaics of Santa Maria Maggiore.[914]

In the interpretation of the scene too much stress should not be laid upon the fact that the man represented has removed his shoes. According to

Jewish tradition the receipt of the Law occurred on the same mountain as the episode of the burning bush.[915] Since the reason for the removal of the shoes in the latter instance was the sacredness of the place itself, the artist might well have concluded that other events occurring at the same place, such as the receipt of the Law, were subject to the same requirement and have rendered the scene accordingly.[916] For purposes of interpretation attention should be focused upon the essential features of the scene; its organization, its background, and the pose and dress of the person depicted. In this connection it will be apparent that none of the essentials favors the Joshua hypothesis. Even though it be granted that in later Christian art Joshua is not always shown falling on his face as the Biblical text requires, it is clear that there is no room in the panel for the "captain of the Lord's host," without whom the allusion would be obscure, and that both the costume and the background are unsuited to the scene of Joshua and the angel.[917] On the contrary, all the details of the rendering agree perfectly with the suggestion that the scene represents Moses receiving the Law: the mountain, the garments, the position of the man's hands, the indication that a square object was actually being held, and even the color of the background, whose red can be thought to be suggested

911. So the Gute copy and Hopkins field notes. The plant is not clearly visible today.

912. So more recently particularly Leveen, *Hebrew Bible in Art*, pp. 33 f.; and Sukenik, *The Synagogue*, pp. 70 f.

913. The argument is developed in different ways. Some find it unlikely that Moses would have been represented twice in a group of four panels, supposing that III and IV portray other and different persons, and hence prefer to find Joshua in Panel II. Others in turn, associating Panel IV with Joshua and III with Moses, see in the supposed balance of II and IV an additional reason for interpreting II as Joshua and the angel.

914. Sukenik, *The Synagogue*, pp. 70 f.

915. Cf. Josephus, *Antiquitates* III, 2, 5 = § 62; and in general Ginzberg, *Legends of the Jews*, II, p. 302; V, p. 415, n. 113.

916. In Christian manuscript illustration, Moses is commonly barefoot when receiving the Law on Mount Sinai, his shoes sometimes being shown separately. Cf. e.g., the Cosmas Indicopleustes (Stornajolo, *Le Miniature*, Pl. 25; Garrucci, *Storia della arte cristiana*, III, Pl. 143, 1) and the Paris Psalter (Omont, *Miniatures des plus anciens manuscrits grecs de la Bibliothèque Nationale*, Pl. X). Sonne, "The Paintings," p. 258, n. 4 properly points to the rendering of Exod. 3.5 by the *Targum pseudo-Jonathan* in this connection.

917. In Santa Maria Maggiore Joshua merely bows before the angel (Wilpert, *Die römischen Mosaiken und Malereien*, III, Pl. 24) while in the Joshua Roll, for instance, he falls to the ground (Hoepli, *Il Rotulo*, Pl. 4; see also the Octateuchs in K. Weitzmann, *The Joshua Roll*, 1948, Pl. 4). Though in the scene from Santa Maria Maggiore Joshua has temporarily abandoned his military costume, he still wears the chlamys as an indication of his rank. It is quite unlikely that the Synagogue artist would have shown Joshua in chiton and himation. Moreover, there is in the Joshua story no basis for the indication of the mountain, and such background elements were not included by the Synagogue artists in their compositions without good reason.

by the allusions to fire and smoke in the description of the mountain in Exod. 19.18.[918] The monuments of Christian art, on which the scene of the receiving of the Law appears quite frequently, support rather than contradict the identification.[919]

It can scarcely be doubted, therefore, that our scene represents Moses receiving the Law on Mount Sinai, in which case we must supply at the right the Hand of God holding the upper end of the "table" to make the picture complete.[920] The two uppermost of the Wing Panels, then, bring a pair of scenes that are closely associated with each other and balance each other nicely, a fact that is evident from the reappearance of both the arrangement and the combination in monuments of Christian art.[921]

(c) Panels III and IV: Ezra Reads the Law; Abraham Receives the Promise

(Pls. XXXVI, 2; LXXVII–LXXVIII; Fig. 61).

The fact that Panels I and II of the Central Group form a pair does not necessarily mean that III and IV are similarly related, yet practical considerations suggest that they be treated together. Of the two, Panel III, at the right of the Lower Center Panel in Register B, is among the finest products of the Synagogue artists' work that has been preserved to us. In part this is because the subject lent itself to representation along lines already highly developed in classical art, and in part because the artist lavished upon the composition particular care, especially in the rendering of detail.

918. Wischnitzer's suggestion that the scene represents Moses receiving "the signs" (*Messianic Theme,* p. 82) rests upon a misunderstanding of the nature of the white object at the right side of the panel.

919. See e.g., the early Christian sarcophagi, particularly that of the Two Brothers (G. Wilpert, *I Sarcofagi cristiani antichi,* II, 1932, Pl. LXXXXI) and that of Adelphia (O. Wulff, *Altchristliche und byzantinische Kunst,* I, 1914, p. 124, Fig. 110) and among the manuscripts, e.g., the Cosmas Indicopleustes and the Paris Psalter quoted above, p. 231, n. 916.

920. The Hand would be a right hand, making a pair with that shown in Panel I, quite as in Panel WA 3 (Exodus and Red Sea Crossing).

921. It should be noted that in Christian sarcophagi with central medallions the canonical position of Moses receiving the Law is at the left of the medallion, and that in both of the manuscripts referred to above the scene of Moses receiving the Law is paired with that of the burning bush.

Panel III presents the figure of a man dressed in chiton and himation and facing full front as he stands reading from a wide scroll. Beside his feet at the left is an object rounded at the top and covered with a cloth. The man is tall and slender. His pose, as he rests his weight on the right foot, bringing the right hip into slight relief and thus adding grace and fluidity to the lines of the body, is familiar from the portrait statues of orators, statesmen, and philosophers that decorated the public places and building of ancient cities everywhere at this time.[922] The type as it comes to us in the Synagogue has been orientalized, with loss of plasticity and vigor, and has here been adapted to the needs of the scene represented by the introduction of the extended scroll, but its basic features are still clearly recognizable.[923]

Fortunately the surface of the composition has not been marred or disfigured by heavy cracking.[924] Color intensity may have been affected slightly by deterioration of the binding medium, but it is clear that the artist has endeavored here as in Wing Panel IV[925] not to make too sharp a contrast between the background colors and those used in the rendering of the figure. The over-all background against which the figure is set is a light gray. Through the gray there are to be seen at the left, above and below the level of the man's hip, the green tips of branches of the tree belonging to the first stage in the development of the Synagogue's decoration.[926] The area behind the man's head the

922. The classic examples of the type are the Lateran Sophocles, the Vatican Demosthenes, and the Augustus *togatus* in the Louvre (see in general A. Hekler, *Greek and Roman Portraits,* 1912).

923. The more immediate analogy is therefore to standing figures in chiton and himation in Palmyrene art. See e.g., Ingholt, *Studier over Palmyrensk Skulptur,* Pl. I, 3; and *idem, Acta archaeologica,* III (1932), p. 10, Fig. 3 and Pl. II. Normally extended scrolls are to be found in the classical tradition only in representations of seated philosophers.

924. One thin fissure runs down vertically at the left of the man's head, cutting through the middle of the scroll and of the lower part of the himation, from which point it turns sharply to the right, running over into the adjacent panel. A further horizontal crack cuts across the panel just below knee level.

925. See below, p. 235.

926. These traces have apparently been brought to light by the thinning of the gray background pigment, and are one of the indications that the tree preceded the panel and register organization of the decorations, extending even beyond the band framing the Center Panel.

artist has developed as a vertical panel, setting it off at the right and the left with vertical black lines and coloring it a light yellow. Thus he creates a favorable background for the brown of the hair and frames the head in bolder fashion than he had ventured to do in Panel I. The man's garments are fundamentally gray in color, but are heavily overlaid with yellow. To indicate the folds of the draperies brown is used and to show the highlights, white. Nowhere in the Synagogue are the folds more carefully drawn to follow the contours of the body, and nowhere do we find as careful and appropriate a deepening and concentration of drapery- and shadow-lines as at the man's right hip, below his left arm, and above the folded lower edge of the himation where it sweeps upward from the right calf to the left knee. Tassels ornament the tips of the upper garment and two-pronged bands its ends, while clavi adorn the chiton. Clavi and bands are black but are outlined in white, a special feature of this particular composition. The yellow scroll is of exceptional height and very long, as the heavy rolls at either end indicate, each of which seems to have at its center a rod or "pillar."[927] Only a long and significant text can be thought to have required so massive a product of the ancient *scriptoria*. Upon the scroll the artist has traced a series of continuous wavy lines that represent the inscribed text.[928] That these lines are on the reverse of the parchment and run the full length of the exposed portion of the manuscript did not bother him in the least, for they serve merely to suggest something belonging in its proper form to the obverse.

For the hands which hold the scroll, the feet, legs, and face of the man the lighter yellowish flesh color generally employed in the lower registers of the Synagogue has been used. The fingers of the hands are individually drawn, with the fingernails clearly indicated, and the legs carefully shaded and even modeled at the calf and the ankle. The man wears on his feet the sandals that go with the costume, and these again are rendered with such

927. The left rod is indicated by a brown dot at the top of the scroll, while the right seems to be indicated by a circular projection at the bottom. On the 'ammûd or "pillar" of the Hebrew scrolls, see e.g., Sukenik, *Ancient Synagogue of Beth Alpha*, pp. 30–32.
928. Du Mesnil du Buisson (*Peintures*, p. 93) suggests that the writing moves from left to right.

care, even to the laces, that the sole of the sandal on the right foot is separately visible. It is the face, however, that is the measure of the artist's success in the rendering of the scene. Turned slightly to the right so that the outline of one ear is visible against the hair, the face is well proportioned and drawn with a sure, steady hand. Its dark brown hair outlined in black encircles the head from the nape of the neck at the left to the ear at the right, curls showing not only in outline at the top but still more prominently over the forehead, where they form a regular pattern. A tufted or curled brown beard outlined in black encircles the lower part of the face, coming to a point below the chin, and a thin two-pronged mustache continues the line of the upper lip at either side of the mouth. Brown is used for the outline of the eyes with their white eyeballs, and for the irises that are set high in the eyeballs to give the eyes a steady outward look. The upper lids and their lashes are separately indicated in brown, as are the eyebrows. The line of the right eyebrow is continued downward to form the outline of the nose. The mouth is small and not prominent, but the cleft of the upper lip and the curve of the lower are shown by short dark strokes. White highlights appear on the nose and the lips, and a dark yellow shadow on the cheek at the right. The shadow reappears in the appropriate position on the neck, which is carefully modeled and doubly outlined at the ends, probably to show where the chiton passes over the shoulders. The mien is sober and dignified, but registers no emotion.

The object depicted alongside the standing figure in the lower left corner of the panel is not easy to identify. It is tall with a round top, and must be sacred in character because it is covered with a reddish-brown veil whose folds and edges are outlined in brown. From what is visible below the veil it appears that the object ended at the bottom in a horizontal member and was supported on two short legs, here outlined simply in brown.

Interpreted by scholars in no less than six different ways, the composition affords only three clues to the identity of the person and the episode depicted. The clues are the garments which the man wears, the excellence of his rendering, and the monumentality and character of the scroll from which he reads, coupled with the presence at his side of what can scarcely be anything other than a Scroll Chest, the cabinet in which the sacred scriptures are kept and from which the scroll in hand must be presumed to have been taken.[929] The garments serve only to exclude from the list of the persons and episodes supposedly portrayed here that of Josiah reading from the newly discovered text of the Law as reported in II Kings 23.1–3; II Chron. 34.29–31.[930] As king, Josiah would have required a different costume. The excellence of the rendering implies that the person represented was of outstanding significance in the eyes of the artist and the local congregation. That he should for this or other reasons be identified as Samuel, the Elder of the local congregation[931] seems unlikely. His preëminence must be historical, for the emphasis in the decorations as a whole is too patently upon the significant aspects of a heritage of guidance and leadership that has become classical and canonical, to permit of such "modernizing" intrusions.[932] The monumentality of the scroll, finally, and its association with a Scroll Chest implies that the event portrayed was a particularly important instance of the reading of the Law.[933] This would rule out the suggestions that the scene represents the Biblical Samuel or Jeremiah, and narrow the field down in the last analysis to Moses and Ezra.[934]

If it is Moses whom Panel III presents, the episode referred to is in all probability that of Exod. 24.7 when Moses, having come down from Mt. Sinai, is said to have taken the "Book of the Covenant" and have read it to the people, who promised forthwith to observe its ordinances. The allusion as the *Targum pseudo-Jonathan* understood it is to Exod. 20–23, which is all it believes Moses wrote while on the mountain.[935] But since according to another Haggadic tradition Moses received and wrote down the entire Pentateuch while on Mt. Sinai, it is entirely possible to assume that if the man was shown reading the Law the figure could be that of Moses.[936]

If it is Ezra whom the panel presents, the allusion is necessarily to the episode reported in Neh. 8, where the Babylonian sage, finding that the returned exiles are not adhering to the commands of the divine Law, gathers the people together in the open place before the Water Gate of Jerusalem and reads to them the Book of the Law from early morning to midday, causing them in this connection to rededicate themselves to the observance of its demands. Important as the event was in itself, Babylonian Jews were particularly proud of the fact that at this, as at other subsequent occasions, men from among their own number were the instruments for the revival of Israel's knowledge of the Law. Ezra's importance for them was not limited, however, to the part he had played in the episode narrated. He was, of course, the first and most outstanding representative of Scribal learning and piety, and is said to have written with his own hand the copy of the Law that he brought to Jerusalem, being responsible for the type of script used in all later codices. So great was his concern and importance for the Law that it was said of him, "If Moses had not anticipated him, Ezra would have received the

---

929. The form of the cabinet is that of the Ark of the Covenant as portrayed especially in the panels of Register B and on the façade of the Torah Shrine. So already Wischnitzer, *Messianic Theme*, pp. 84 f., who is wrong, however, in suggesting that it is seen from the rear. For the "veil" over Torah Shrines see Krauss, *Synagogale Altertümer*, pp. 376–384. It will be noted from the Lateran Sophocles that a scroll case is traditionally associated with the model which the artist was following in the development of the composition.

930. Suggested by Grabar, "Le Thème," pp. 178–180.

931. Suggested by Sonne, "The Paintings," p. 300.

932. The historical character of the subject depicted in the decorations as a whole makes improbable the suggestion of Sonne, that the scene portrays the reading of the *Shema*. The analogy between the scene and elements of the Synagogue worship could, of course, make the scene significant didactically, even though the episode portrayed was historical.

933. If the scroll depicted actually had two "rods" ('*ammudîm*), as seems likely, its identification as a Torah scroll would be the more probable because such scrolls were rolled toward the center and had a "pillar" at each end, while other scrolls had but one. Cf. Baba Bathra 14a (Trans., p. 67).

934. The Biblical Samuel has been proposed by Wischnitzer (*Messianic Theme*, pp. 84–86), and Jeremiah

at one time by Du Mesnil du Buisson ("Les Peintures," p. 115). So far as the Biblical evidence is concerned, the case for both Samuel and Jeremiah is not too strong, resting on no better foundation than that each of them is said to have *written* a scroll, the former having in addition laid up his book before the Lord (see I Sam. 10.25 and Jer. 36.2).

935. See the *Targum pseudo-Jonathan* on Exod. 24.4.

936. See Exodus Rabbah XLVII, 7 (Trans., III, pp. 542 f.). The Midrash has not affected the account of Josephus or the rendering of the Biblical text in the Targumim.

Torah."[937] In the light of the veneration in which he was held and in view of the appearance of the "scribes" of the Targum of Genesis 49.10 in the Upper Center Panel, it would by no means be strange if Ezra were to find a prominent place in the decorations of a synagogue on the borders of Mesopotamia.[938] The final choice between Moses or Ezra, however, must await the discussion of the last of the four Wing Panels.

Panel IV, the last of the group, is even less explicit in its imagery than those already considered, but was not for that reason any more enigmatic to the worshipers at the Dura Synagogue. It is not quite as well preserved as Panel III, but all essential elements remain perfectly clear.[939] The picture portrays a venerable old man dressed in chiton, himation, and sandals, facing full front as he stands under the vault of heaven and holds his hands crossed before him covered by the folds of his outer garment.

The background against which the figure is set is divided into two unequal parts, as in Panel II directly above. At the bottom, as high as the lower end of his garments, the background of the scene is a yellowish brown. Against this bit of "stage space" the dark brown inverted V of his cast shadow stands out with unusual clarity.[940] Above

937. For these and other elements of the later Jewish tradition about Ezra, see Ginzberg, *Legends of the Jews*, IV, pp. 354–359, and VI, pp. 441–449.

938. So now particularly Du Mesnil du Buisson, *Peintures*, pp. 92–94. The objection of Wischnitzer (*Messianic Theme*, p. 83) that the figure cannot be Ezra because of the absence of the "pulpit" on which Ezra stands in Neh. 8.4 and because of the absence of the crowd addressed, does not seem to be fatal. The hearers are excluded by the nature of the composition. To have introduced a platform would have been awkward, requiring a reduction in the size of the figure. By using a neutral background the artist avoided committing himself in any way in the matter of place and circumstance.

939. A single large crack comes upward into the panel at the left from the adjacent scene WB 2 (Consecration of the Tabernacle) at the level of the knees of the man portrayed here. This soon divides into several branches, of which two cut across his legs at the level of the knees and of the thighs respectively; while the third, running upwards in the open field, enters the figure at the man's right elbow and continues diagonally across his chest, leaving at the top of his left shoulder. The cracks have caused some displacement of painted lines and the loss of a small piece of plaster in the upper left background. There are numerous small scratches and abrasions on the surface of the panel.

940. On the cast shadows of the Synagogue murals see below, p. 370.

the level of the lower end of the man's garments the background was originally a bright blue, but the color has lost much of its intensity, appearing now as a light bluish haze. At the top the blue of the background comes to an end against the gray vault of heaven with its astral bodies; but on the axis of the panel, between the vault and the shoulders of the standing figure, a vertical panel has been introduced, breaking the monochrome background and setting off the man's head against an intense black field.

The garments of the standing figure are rendered in light gray and the clavi of the chiton, like the two-pronged ornaments of the himation ends, in black. The tassels at the tips of the himation ends and the fold-lines of the under- and the overgarment are indicated by brown lines of varying thickness, while the highlights are done in white. The fact that he had to show the himation worn in an unusual way; namely, draped over both shoulders, covering both arms, and brought together in front of the body where the folded ends hang down from the crossed and covered hands, prevented the artist from following the conventions he commonly used in molding the garments to the outline of the body and in arranging their folds. The result is that the figure lacks grace and that the himation has an unusually baggy appearance, contrasting vividly in this particular with Panel III.

For the visible members of the man's body the artist used the lighter flesh tones found throughout the lower registers of the decorations. The legs and feet are carefully shaded at the right, and the sandals are done with the same attention to detail as in the corresponding panel at the other side of the central area. The position of the feet is that of persons standing at rest, but the fact that the left foot is seen in profile indicates that the figure is related to something at the right, rather than to the scenes at the left. Particular interest necessarily attaches to the rendering of the head (Pl. XLVIII, 2), for in one particular it departs from all other heads in the Synagogue. The hair, held close against the side of the head, is done in white instead of brown and black, and lacks all indications of curls. In place of the curls, rows of short brush strokes surround the head of hair, perhaps representing stray locks, those at the outer edge being white and those along the inner edge brown. The brown strokes go around three sides of the face, joining on the cheek and at the chin with irregular lines that represent the mustache and the well-developed beard. Mustache and beard are also rendered in brown, but the brown is heavily overlaid with white dots and lines, continuing the emphasis on the color used for the hair of the head. There are white highlights on the forehead, the cheeks, and the lips, and heavy shadows at the side of the nose and the face. The face is sober but expressionless.

Upon the gray vault of heaven that fills the upper part of the panel the artist has inscribed a group of astral bodies, including the sun, the moon, and seven stars (Fig. 61). Set apart from the moon

FIG. 61. Wing Panel IV. Detail of Background

and the stars, the sun at the left is represented by a pink disc upon which are inscribed two concentric red circles, and from which there radiate sixteen rays, each taking the form of a ladder.[941] Balancing the sun at the opposite end of the vault of heaven, the moon is rendered as a white crescent outlined in black. The black lines form two com-

plete circles coinciding at the left.[942] About the moon are grouped seven white stars, each composed of a central dot and eight tapering rays that terminate in dots.[943] The close association of stars with the moon in the right half of the panel is entirely natural, but their sevenfold number poses something of a problem, for the seven planets are usually taken to include the sun and moon rather than to be supplementary to them.[944] The probability is, however, that we are dealing here with another instance of what Ronzevalle has called the

941. The combination of red and pink used in the orb of the sun is repeated in the rays, which were first drawn in pink and then outlined at the sides with red. The form of representation is by no means common. On Babylonian monuments the classic representation of the sun is that of a disc from which project four tapering rays and four striated bands (e.g., the Naram-Sin Stele), but this scheme permits of much variation, particularly in the increase of the number of rays. Cf. H. Prinz, *Altorientalische Symbolik* (1915), pp. 74 f. In the Hellenistic period the familiar rayed head was introduced into the Orient, but the simple disc with multiple rays survives, as, e.g., in the smaller and earlier Mithraic relief at Dura (*Rep. VII–VIII*, Pl. XXIX). This commonly becomes conventionalized as the sixteen-point rosette; for instance, in the ornament on the tympanum of the temple pediment in Panel WB 3 (Jerusalem and the Temple). For the ladder type of ray there is a very early analogy in a pottery fragment from Tepe Moussian; cf. J. de Morgan, *Délégation en Perse, Memoires* VIII (1905), p. 111, Fig. 178.

942. The form of representation is a departure from the old horizontal rendering of the new moon, a rendering that arises in the ancient Orient, is commonly used on Western funerary monuments of later date (see Cumont, *Recherches sur le symbolisme funéraire des romains*, pp. 204–246), and still survives at Dura, e.g., in the earlier of the two Mithraic reliefs and in the relief of the Dromedary God (*Rep. VII–VIII*, Pls. XXIX, 1 and XXXI, 2). Even where the crescent is contained within a complete circle, as in the bas-relief reproduced by Prinz (*Altorientalische Symbolik*, Pl. X, 5), and probably in the later Amrit Stele (Contenau, *Manuel d'archéologie orientale*, III, p. 1474, Fig. 895), it appears in a horizontal position at the bottom of the circle. On the rendering of the moon in the phase of the *lumière cendrée*, see most recently Cumont, *op cit.*, p. 204, n. 2, where the other literature is cited. In the light of the Dura Synagogue example it would appear that Cumont dismisses the possibility of such a rendering too quickly, and that the distinction made by Dussaud between the conjoined disc and crescent as a symbol of the moon alone and as a symbol of sun and moon combined should be upheld. Cf. R. Dussaud, *Revue archéologique*, Ser. 4, I (1903), pp. 125 f. Vertical crescents lacking the disc are to be seen on Parthian coins.

943. Without the terminal dots this type of star is common on the monuments of the East in the Hellenistic and the Roman periods. Cf. the terracotta head of Alexander from Amisus in Pontus (Cumont, *op. cit.*, Pl. XVI, 1), and the horoscope of Antiochos of Commagene (Humann and Puchstein, *Reisen in Kleinasien und Nordsyrien*, Pl. XL). It appears elsewhere at Dura in the Mithraeum (*Rep. VII–VIII*, p. 102) and in the Christian Chapel (*Rep. V*, p. 255).

944. So clearly in Jewish tradition as exemplified by Philo (*Vita Mosis* II, §§ 102–103) and Josephus (*Antiquitates* III, §§ 144–145). Cf. in general Ginzberg, *Legends of the Jews*, III, p. 151. The fact that the seven planets were distinguished from sun and moon in Persian belief (see A. V. W. Jackson, "Sun, Moon and Stars [Iranian]" in *Encyclopaedia of Religion and Ethics*, XII, 1922, pp. 85–88) and in certain forms of syncretistic religion; for instance the Manichaean (see *idem, Researches in Manichaeism*, p. 38, n. 1), is irrelevant here, for the stars represented in the Synagogue are probably not to be regarded as malevolent. The Pleiades are probably to be excluded from consideration in this context because they play no great part in Hebrew and Jewish thought (see the supposed reference in Job 38.32 and in general Ginzberg, *Legends of the Jews*, I, p. 162).

"tautology of oriental art," a trait which elsewhere also permits the seven planets to appear alongside of representations of the sun and moon.[945]

In the interpretation of the person and the scene depicted scholars have again reached different conclusions. Some have identified the man as Joshua, others as Moses, others as Jacob, and still others as Abraham, the difference of opinion stemming partly from the relative importance attached to one or the other of the salient details of the rendering, and partly from divergent conceptions of the association of this panel with others. Those who favor Joshua find here an allusion to the episode Josh. 10.12–14, when the Israelite commander ordered the sun and moon to stand still until the nation had revenged itself upon its enemies in the battle for the relief of Gibeon. The interpretation recommends itself particularly to those who see in Panel II the scene of Joshua and the Angel.[946] Those who favor Moses see a reference here to the episodes Deut. 32 and 33, where are recounted the Song and the Blessing that Moses addressed to his people just before the ascent of Mount Nebo, from which he did not return.[947] For those who think of Jacob, the allusion is to the event in Gen. 28.10ff., where Jacob coming from Beersheba stays the night at the place Bethel, because the sun was set.[948] For

those, finally, who see here the figure of Abraham the reference is to the episode in Gen. 15.15 where the Patriarch is asked by God to count the stars and is told that as the multitude of the stars, so shall his seed be.

The case for Joshua and Jacob is rendered dubious from the outset by two general questions: namely, whether the Synagogue artist would have represented Joshua, the great military leader of Israel in the civilian garb of chiton and himation; and whether, with all the wealth of the Biblical material to draw upon, he would have used the episode of Jacob at Bethel twice, once here and once in Panel NA 1.[949] Ultimately, however, the identification of the scene must depend upon the proper interpretation of the three salient details of the rendering: the white hair of the man's head and beard, the gesture of the covered hands, and the combination of the vault of heaven with the black background against which the head is set.

As regards the white hair, one thing can be said with some assurance. In all probability it is not used here to suggest that the man in question is now at a more advanced age than in other representations of him elsewhere in the murals. This is improbable because of the artist's remoteness in all other particulars from the realism and the understanding of individuality that comes to expression in Hellenistic and Roman portraiture. For him people are fundamentally types; and where he varies his rendering of types, his purpose is either to accommodate his representation to changes of outward circumstance and function or to make the person identifiable.[950] In the present instance the white hair is probably a special feature or attribute of the person in question, and one that by its uniqueness helps to identify him. It therefore lends

945. Cf. the bas-relief from Argos reproduced by Cumont, *Symbolisme funeraire*, p. 242, Fig. 62, and note 3, where the reference to Ronzevalle is given. In one early detail photograph of the upper part of Panel IV (Pl. XXXVI, 2), there is to be seen a gridiron of horizontal black lines within which the stars are comprehended. Of this nothing is visible today. The several fields of the grid can be thought to represent the "courses" or "paths of heaven" along which the planets move. Cf. e.g., *Ps. Sol.* XVIII, 12.

946. Cf. above p. 231; Leveen, *Hebrew Bible in Art*, p. 34; and Sukenik, *The Synagogue*, pp. 72f.

947. This is the Biblical context of the interpretation suggested by Goodenough (*By Light, Light*, pp. 222f., 242), who, however, interprets the event as the "translation" of Moses, following Philo, *Vita Mosis* II, §§ 288–292 and *De sacrificiis*, §§ 8–10. It may be noted that while Moses' "translation" was widely affirmed in antiquity, it was as widely combatted and denied. Cf. e.g., Josephus, *Antiquitates* IV, § 326 and *Assumption of Moses*, I, 15; and in general Ginzberg, *Legends of the Jews*, VI, pp. 151f., n. 904 and 161f., n. 951.

948. Cf. Sonne, "The Paintings," pp. 291–298. Sonne obtains help for his interpretation from the reference to Jacob as "the hoary Israel" and from the rabbinical and Targumic interpretation of *paga'* as "pray" rather than as "light upon."

949. Cf. above, pp. 70–74.

950. Because people are considered as types, there is no distinction, e.g., between Pharaoh and Ahasuerus among the kings and between Moses, Samuel, and Elijah among the "laity." For changes in the rendering of an individual corresponding to changes in circumstance and function, see e.g., the three representations of David in Panels WC 3 (Samuel Anoints David), EC 1 (David and Saul), and the Lower Center Panel (David as the royal lyre-player). For departure from type as an identifying medium, see the Ezekiel of the second scene of Section B of Panel NC 1, where the heavy aureole of hair is used to show that he is identical with the important figure of Section A (see above, p. 193).

no support to the suggestion that the person represented is Moses or Joshua, for it is not clear that either of them was regarded in any sense as "graybeards," and Moses at least is represented with dark hair elsewhere in the murals.[951] So far as Jacob is concerned, it has been pointed out that in Jewish tradition he is called *Israel Saba*, "the hoary" Israel, which certainly would be in accord with the artist's rendering.[952] It must be pointed out, however, that so far as Abraham is concerned, there is available a much more imposing tradition of the same sort; namely, that he was the first person ever to have had gray hair.[953] This would seem to provide at least an equally acceptable basis for the iconography.[954]

So far as the gesture of the crossed and covered hands is concerned this has already been discussed in connection with Panel WC 3 (Samuel Anoints David) where it recurs.[955] The crossing of the hands is clearly an indication of adoration and supplication, but the covering is most likely to imply at this stage in the historical development of gesture the significant presence of God and the receipt of a divine gift or favor. So interpreted, the detail lends itself particularly to association with Abraham, who at the occasion of the episode re-

counted in Gen. 15 received not only the promise of the birth of Isaac, but also the favor of the divine covenant guaranteeing the inheritance of the land.

As far as the vault of heaven with its astral bodies is concerned, this would seem to lend itself to any one of the four interpretations that have been offered, for it would have been quite as natural for the artist to parade the full range of celestial luminaries if the text illustrated had spoken only of "the heavens" as it would have been for him to include the stars had the text mentioned only the sun and moon, or vice versa. Only the fact that the vault of heaven is associated with a black panel framing the head of the standing figure serves as a limitation in this connection. Granted that the panel itself is a device borrowed from portrait painting, the fact that it here appears as a black field may itself imply that the episode portrayed is connected with the coming of darkness. This is because elsewhere the Synagogue artist has used black only for interiors and night scenes.[956] An allusion to the story of Moses addressing himself to the heavens in his final song (Deut. 32) is less likely on this account.

Judging by the salient features of the rendering, the episode of Abraham receiving the promise is most likely to be the subject of the scene. Abraham is the white-haired patriarch *par excellence*. He is taken out into the open to view the stars of heaven, and in this connection receives not only the promise that his offspring will be as the stars in number, but also at night, when the sun has set, the covenant that guarantees the possession of the land by his descendants.[957] It is only natural under the circumstances that the earliest Christian rendering of the episode shows the same characteristic features.[958]

951. It is interesting to note that in the nave mosaics of Santa Maria Maggiore, where white hair is a common sign of age and venerability, Moses and Joshua are the only two outstanding characters whose hair is dark throughout — in the case of the former, even at his final appearance on Mt. Nebo.

952. So Sonne, "The Paintings," pp. 297 f.

953. Cf. *Pirke de Rabbi Eliezer*, LII (trans. Friedlander, pp. 421 f.): "From the day when the heavens and the earth were created there never was a man upon whom grey hairs were sprinkled until Abraham came. The people were astonished because they had not seen any one like him from the day when the world was created." The statement is based upon the traditional interpretation of the passage Gen. 24.1, which, as reflected, e.g., in Sanhedrin 107b (Trans., p. 737) and Baba Mezi'a 87a (Trans., pp. 502 f.), indicates that until Abraham there was no old age. People continually confused Abraham and Isaac until Abraham prayed to God that there should be (some distinguishing feature of) old age, and his prayer was granted. See also Midrash Rabbah on Gen. 24.1 (Trans., II, pp. 516–520) and Ginzberg, *Legends of the Jews*, I, p. 291, and V, p. 258, n. 272.

954. The fact that Abraham has dark hair in the scene of the Sacrifice of Isaac on the façade of the Torah Shrine does not militate against this conclusion, because the scene was done by another artist at a different time and with less opportunity for the graphic rendering of such details. Cf. above, p. 40.

955. Cf. above, pp. 166 f.; see also pp. 71, 238.

956. For the former see, e.g., the temple of Dagon in WB 4; and for the latter, Panel NA 1 (Jacob at Bethel) and EC 1 (David and Saul).

957. As R. Levi interpreted the passage Gen. 15.5, God showed Abraham the "courses" or "paths of heaven" along which the planets move (*Midrash Rabbah* on Gen. 15.5, Trans., I, pp. 367 f.). The fact that such "courses" were originally to be seen in the painting has been indicated above.

958. Cf. von Hartel and Wickhoff, *Wiener Genesis*, Pl. VIII, where at the receipt of the covenant Abraham is shown as a white-haired man holding his hands covered before him and looking up toward the star-studded orb of heaven.

If Panel IV probably represents Abraham receiving the Promise, the chances that Panel III portrays not Moses, but Ezra reading the Law are greatly heightened; for it is more likely that the Synagogue artist would have chosen for his Wing Panels two representations of Moses and one each of two other figures than that he would have showed three Moseses and one additional figure. The only question is whether the panels as we have interpreted them are appropriate to their position and can be said to express a single theme. It should be evident in this connection that all four scenes are related in some way to the covenant between God and his Chosen People. Panel IV tells how the covenant was originally made between God and Abraham. Panel I shows Moses being called to deliver his nation from bondage so that it may return to the Land of the Promise, call and deliverance being the expression of God's fidelity to the covenant he has made.[959] In Panel II, where Moses appears before God on Mount Sinai, he receives at God's hand the "words of the covenant" (Exod. 34.28) written upon the stones that are called the "tables of the covenant" (Deut. 9.11), words to which the people pledged allegiance when they accepted the "book of the covenant" before the mountain (Exod. 24.7). In Panel III, finally, we are reminded that Ezra by his reading of the Law caused the people to rededicate themselves to the provisions of the covenant, their representatives signing a formal document to this effect (Neh. 9.38; 10.1). All four Wing Panels, therefore, illustrate through historical persons and in connection with specific events in their lives, the fact and the history of the covenant relationship in which God and Israel stand.

Two things follow from this analysis of the Wing Panels. The first is the unity of the Central Group to which we have assigned them. The covenant is the basis upon which the prophecy about the abiding kingship rests and has come to partial fulfilment in the past. Indeed, it is only within the framework of this covenant that it can find its ultimate fulfilment in the future. The second is that the panels of the Central Group by their

witness to the prophecy and the covenant serve a didactic purpose; namely, that of setting forth the foundations, the character, the requirements, and the assurance of the Messianic hope. From the second of these observations, important inferences can be drawn about the procedure of the Synagogue artists in handling the didactic and narrative aspects of his undertaking, observations which will serve to guide the interpreter in assessing the nature and the meaning of the artists' work in its entirety.

959. The Biblical narrative is explicit in its statements that the call of Moses occurred because God remembered his covenant with Abraham, Isaac, and Jacob (Exod. 2.24; 6.2–8).

6. THE DADO

(Pls. XVIII–XXIV, XXXVII–XXXIX; Figs. 62–69)

Of the four zones into which the decorations of the later Synagogue's House of Assembly were divided, the lowest was developed as a dado. In the large literature that the decorations have already occasioned, this has hitherto received scant attention.[960] While naturally it cannot compete with the narrative scenes in the scope of the interest they arouse, it deserves careful attention at least on this account: that it is among the most elaborate and ambitious examples of purely decorative wall painting known to us from the Roman period of Near Eastern history.

In character the dado is a painted imitation of marble incrustation and inlay work (*opus sectile*) developed with great care as to the balance of its elements, the richness of its designs, and the variety of its colors. It occupies the upper 0.65–0.75 m. of the space between the lower border of Register C and the top of the benches, and forms a band that runs around the entire chamber, broken only by the Torah Shrine on the west wall and the two doors in the east wall of the room.[961] Structurally it is intended to suggest a porphyry plinth into which rectangular marble panels are set at regular intervals. The panels have an average height of 0.45 m., but their length varies from approximately half a meter to a full meter.[962] In part this difference is due to the space requirements of the subjects developed within the panels. In part, however, it results from the structural irregularities of the chamber, for which the artist had to compensate if regularity of design was to be maintained, and a pleasing effect was to be created.[963] Particu-

larly disturbing to the artist, no doubt, was the fact that the east and west walls of the chamber were broken at different points, the former by the two doorways irregularly placed (Plan XI), and the latter by the Torah Shrine near the middle. This precluded the possibility of making the design on the east wall in its entirety match the design developed on the west wall in its entirety.

The artist had before him, then, six sections of wall space; the opposing north and south walls, the two corresponding halves of the west wall, and the two portions of the east wall, unequal in length. In planning his treatment with an eye to the proper symmetry of elements, he developed the north and south walls as a pair, matching panel for panel across the entire width of the room. In dealing with the east and west walls, however, he matched the northern portion with the southern portion of the same wall. The northern and southern walls, since they provided the longest uninterrupted surfaces, were so laid out that each had nine panels inset into the dado, while the two parts of the west wall each had seven, and the two parts of the east wall each had five (Fig. 62). All panels were rectangular, but the rectangles were alternately longer or shorter; and to vary the design, a circle was drawn in each shorter panel for development in medallion form.[964] On the north and south walls it was the odd-numbered panels that contained circles, while on the matching sections of the east and west walls it was the even-numbered. This resulted in a regular alternation of panels with and without circles about the entire room, the series beginning and ending with a panel without a circle at either side of the main door on the east wall.[965]

960. Du Mesnil du Buisson, "Les Peintures," pp. 109f.; Rostovtzeff, *Römische Quartalschrift*, XLII (1934), p. 208; *Rep. VI*, pp. 342f.; Du Mesnil du Buisson, *Peintures*, pp. 127–130; Wischnitzer, *Messianic Theme*, pp. 18f.

961. Between the bottom of the dado and the top of the benches a strip varying from 0.25–0.35 m. remained blank. The Elder's Seat encroached upon the zone of the dado some 0.10 m., but not enough to interfere with the regularity of its pattern.

962. The reddish-purple strips framing the band at top and bottom are normally 0.15 m. high. Those between the inset panels are occasionally narrower.

963. As the description of the building indicates (see above, pp. 14, 17), no two walls of the room had the same length; nor did the tops of the benches run about the

room in a single plane, due to irregularities in their own height and in the level of the floor. An element of batter noticeable in the lower portion of the walls has affected the regularity of the dado, especially in the northeast corner of the room, where the vertical terminal strip of the north section of the east dado is wedge-shaped.

964. The artist prepared for the medallions by having circles incised in the appropriate fields with a compass, but the medallions as painted were in every instance larger in diameter than the incised circles. The diameter of the incised circles was 0.37 m., and that of the medallions normally about 0.41 m.

965. Peculiarly, the panels of the dado on each side of the main door are not framed at the end by a vertical purple strip, leaving the sections incomplete, so to speak. The reason for this peculiarity is not clear, but perhaps the artist wished to suggest that the two fields on either side of the door formed one panel, and that therefore the

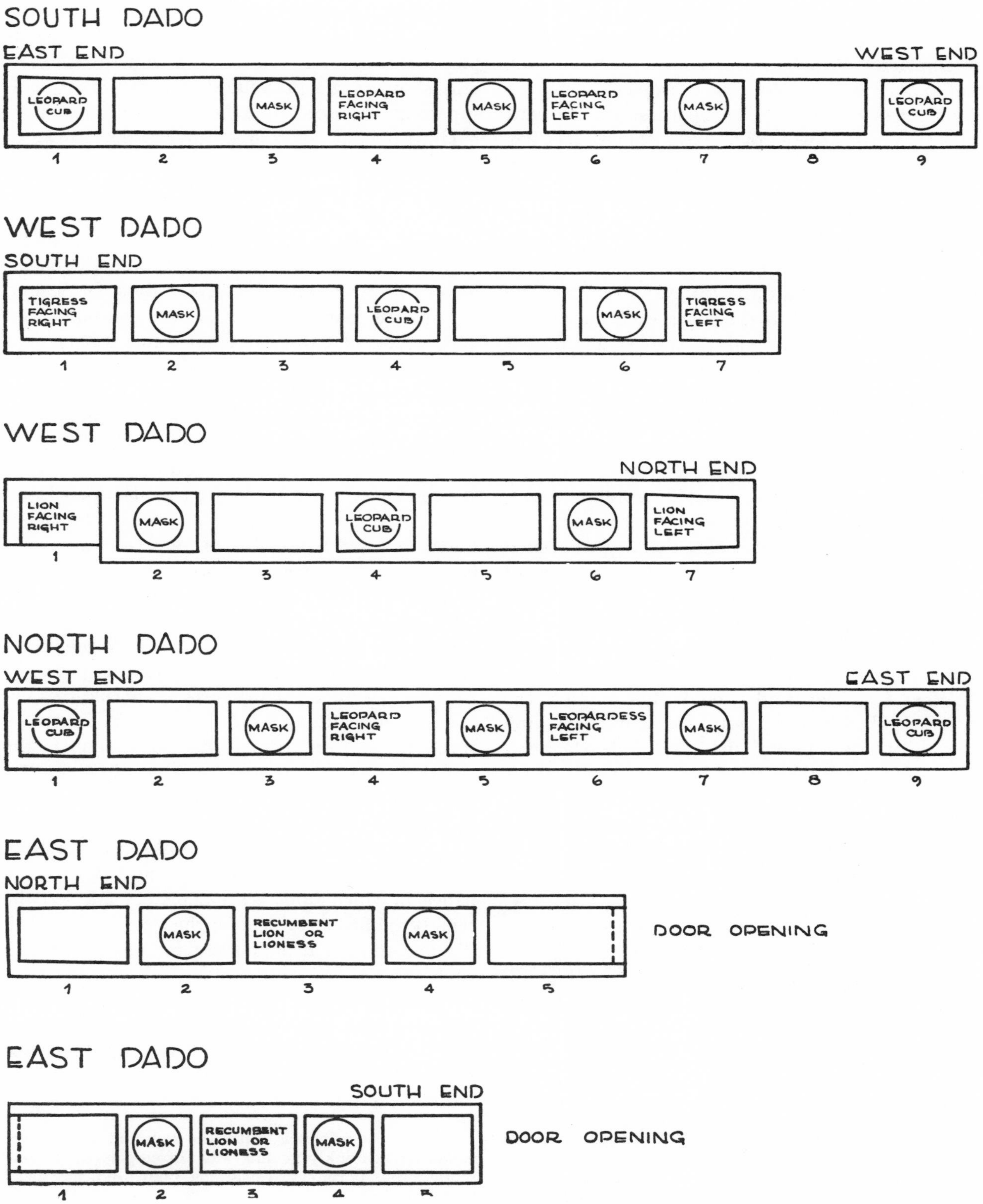

SOUTH DADO

EAST END   WEST END

| LEOPARD CUB | | MASK | LEOPARD FACING RIGHT | MASK | LEOPARD FACING LEFT | MASK | | LEOPARD CUB |
| 1 | 2 | 3 | 4 | 5 | 6 | 7 | 8 | 9 |

WEST DADO

SOUTH END

| TIGRESS FACING RIGHT | MASK | | LEOPARD CUB | | MASK | TIGRESS FACING LEFT |
| 1 | 2 | 3 | 4 | 5 | 6 | 7 |

WEST DADO

NORTH END

| LION FACING RIGHT | MASK | | LEOPARD CUB | | MASK | LION FACING LEFT |
| 1 | 2 | 3 | 4 | 5 | 6 | 7 |

NORTH DADO

WEST END   EAST END

| LEOPARD CUB | | MASK | LEOPARD FACING RIGHT | MASK | LEOPARDESS FACING LEFT | MASK | | LEOPARD CUB |
| 1 | 2 | 3 | 4 | 5 | 6 | 7 | 8 | 9 |

EAST DADO

NORTH END

| | MASK | RECUMBENT LION OR LIONESS | MASK | | DOOR OPENING |
| 1 | 2 | 3 | 4 | 5 | |

EAST DADO

SOUTH END

| | MASK | RECUMBENT LION OR LIONESS | MASK | | DOOR OPENING |
| 1 | 2 | 3 | 4 | 5 | |

FIG. 62. Dado. Diagram

To enliven the forty-two panels that he had projected, the artist introduced into them representations of animals and masks.[966] Of animals, the dado contains sixteen examples, including lions, tigresses, leopards, a leopardess, and leopard cubs; of masks, there are fourteen. This leaves but twelve panels to be developed simply in imitation of marble slabs, two in each of the six sections of wall surface. The masks are invariably assigned to the panels inscribed with circles, but the animals appear in both rectangular and circular fields. Animals and masks alternate in each section of the dado, but on the north and south walls and on the two sections of the east wall they are so distributed as to form compact central groups of panels, each with a representational element.[967] This enriches the middle of the design. On the two corresponding sections of the west wall, however, there is no such concentration. Here there are never more than two consecutive panels with figured representations, and these occur at the ends of the sections, not in the middle. This is undoubtedly an intentional arrangement; for it prevents the creation of secondary centers of interest on the wall containing the Torah Shrine, concentrating the panels with pictorial materials instead in the very area of the Torah Shrine, two on either side.

What has been said should indicate that the artist applied himself with great industry and ingenuity to the formal and graphic development of the dado. A further word is necessary about his use of color, which he also handled with great care and forethought in the effort to give symmetry and variety to his product. For the basic structure of the plinth in which the panels were set he used a

rich reddish purple to represent porphyry. For the panels developed simply as marble slabs he employed his lighter colors — a whitish gray, a grayish green, a light yellow, and a light green — superimposing upon the solid color irregular diagonal lines of black, dark green, and reddish brown to simulate the veins of the marble. For the panels containing pictures of animals he chose his darker colors to set off the tawny bodies of the lions, tigresses, and leopards. A light green, heavily stippled with black dots, alternates here with black, heavily stippled with light green dots. In dealing with panels that were inscribed with medallions he had, of course, to use different colors for the field of the rectangular panel and the field of the medallion into which the mask or animal was set. Here he had recourse to three combinations; namely, yellowish orange for the panel and red for the medallion, yellow for the panel and green for the medallion, and a deep red for the panel and black for the medallion. It was only in the longer north and south sections of the dado in panels inscribed with circles and portraying animals that the third of these combinations was employed, the black again serving to set off the animals properly.

Part and parcel of the artist's care in the use of color was the treatment of the veining of his panels. All surfaces intended to represent porphyry were correctly left without indication of veins. Otherwise three types were employed: the diagonal, the crinkled, and that represented by stippling. The diagonal was limited in its application to those rectangular panels that were not further developed with figures of animals or masks, as has been indicated above. Stippling was limited to those panels in which animals are depicted. This left the crinkly veining as typical for the treatment of both the field and the medallion of panels inscribed with circles.[968]

In the absence of color plates for the dado the following table will show the distribution of figure representation, of color, and of veining among the panels of the six sections of the dado.[969]

alternation of panels with and without circles was unbroken around the entire chamber. Preservation is so bad at the southern end of the east wall that it is quite impossible to say whether the terminal panel of the east dado north of the smaller door was, or was not, framed at the end. If there is any value in the above suggestion, it should have been framed.

966. It may be noted in this connection that in one instance only, in the central panel of the southern section of the west dado, a series of smaller circles had been incised in the inscribed circle, forming a quatrefoil (Pl. XXXVII, 4). This suggests that the artist had originally projected a more geometric development of the dado, but had given this up in favor of a livelier treatment.

967. On the north and south walls we have in the center five consecutive panels decorated alternately with animals and masks, while on the two sections of the east wall there are three.

968. In those panels with the red and black color combination crinkly veining was not employed, the red, representing porphyry, remaining plain and the black being stippled.

969. The symbols used to identify the panels indicate first the wall (north, south, east, west); then, after the

PANEL NUMBER	PART OF PANEL	BASIC COLOR	TYPE OF VEINING	COLOR OF VEIN	FIGURE INSET
		North and South Walls			
ND 1, SD 1	rectangle	red	plain		
	medallion	black	stippled	dark green	leopard cub
ND 2, SD 2	rectangle	white	diagonal	black & brown	————
ND 3, SD 3	rectangle	yellow	crinkly	red	
	medallion	lt. green	crinkly	dark green	mask
ND 4, SD 4	rectangle	lt. green	stippled	dark green	leopard
ND 5, SD 5	rectangle	red	plain		
	medallion	gray-white	plain		mask
ND 6, SD 6	rectangle	lt. green	stippled	dark green	ND 6 leopardess SD 6 leopard
ND 7, SD 7	rectangle	yellow	crinkly	red	
	medallion	lt. green	crinkly	dark red	mask
ND 8, SD 8	rectangle	lt. green	diagonal	dark green	————
ND 9, SD 9	rectangle	red	plain		
	medallion	black	stippled	dark green	leopard cub
		West Wall, Northern and Southern Sections			
WD 1(S), WD 1(N)	rectangle	black	stippled	green	WD 1(S) tigress WD 1(N) lion
WD 2(S), WD 2(N)	rectangle	yellow	crinkly	brown	
	medallion	green	crinkly	black	mask
WD 3(S), WD 3(N)	rectangle	green	diagonal	dark green	————
WD 4(S), WD 4(N)	rectangle	yellow	crinkly	brown	
	medallion	red	plain		leopard cub
WD 5(S), WD 5(N)	rectangle	wh. gray	diagonal	black	————
WD 6(S), WD 6(N)	rectangle	yellow	crinkly	brown	
	medallion	green	crinkly	black	mask
WD 7(S), WD 7(N)	rectangle	black	stippled	green	WD 7(S) tigress WD 7(N) lion
		East Wall, Northern and Southern Sections			
ED 1(N), ED 1(S)	rectangle	gr. white	diagonal	gr. black	————
ED 2(N), ED 2(S)	rectangle	yellow	crinkly	brown	
	medallion	green	crinkly	dark green	mask
ED 3(N), ED 3(S)	rectangle	black	stippled	dark green	recumbant lion or lioness
ED 4(N), ED 4(S)	rectangle	yellow	crinkly	brown	
	medallion	green	crinkly	dark green	mask
ED 5(N), ED 5(S)	rectangle	wh. gray	diagonal	dark green	————

letter *D* for "dado," the number of the panel in the section, counting from left to right; and finally, because the east and west walls are divided into two corresponding sections, in parentheses the letters *N* or *S* to show which section is being referred to. Hence WD 1 (S) means west dado, panel 1 counting from the left, southern section.

16*

The decorations that constitute the dado have suffered extensively from cracking, from loss of portions of the plaster surface — especially on the north section of the west wall — from their proximity to air and moisture in the area of the east wall, and from the wear and tear occasioned by their location directly above and behind the benches.[970] Yet, due to the correspondence of its elements, these damages do not interfere with our knowledge of all parts of the design or detract from the importance of the dado as an example of decorative art in the third century of our era. The general background for the interpretation of such decorative designs — including their relation to the "structural style" as reflected in the Hellenistic tombs of Alexandria, the transition to a real "incrustation style" in the Koiné of Roman Imperial art, and the known examples of incrustation dadoes in the later Roman Orient — has already been sketched in connection with our treatment of the earlier Synagogue and need not be rehearsed here.[971]

The design used in the dado of the earlier building had, as we have seen, found an echo in the treatment of the Torah Shrine in the first phase of the decoration of the later House of Assembly, and may even have been the model for the dado projected for the walls of the later building but never executed.[972] In the context of the second phase of the decorations, however, there was not sufficient room for a dado whose panels were arranged vertically in accordance with the older orthostate tradition; and besides, the narrative development of Registers A, B, and C called for the use of figured representation in the dado to assure uniformity of treatment throughout. Indeed the stronger emphasis upon the pictorial element in the wall decoration of the Roman Imperial period makes the departure from a purely geometrical treatment entirely logical, and suggests that the Synagogue artist was merely following the developing fashions of his day and age in the introduction of animals and masks. The destruction of all but the lowest parts of house walls in the cities of the Roman Orient, as excavation brings them to light, deprives us of most of the evidence for such changes in fashion, making the material from Dura doubly important for the reconstruction of the process. To gauge the course of the development we have, as in the earlier period, to fall back upon tomb painting; and here at least the Tomb of the Three Brothers at Palmyra is helpful, with its row of animal scenes in the very lowest zone of the decoration, below the geometric incrustation dado.[973] To this, however, can now be added information coming from the mosaics of private houses of the Near East, particularly at Antioch, for mosaics tend during this very period to reflect in their pictorial development the character and wealth of wall decoration. It is not strange, therefore, to find in mosaics, especially in the strips that were needed to fill blank spaces in irregularly shaped rooms, designs that contain the same basic elements as the Dura Synagogue dado and probably are merely copies of dadoes transferred from wall to floor.[974]

970. Along the east wall the plaster is broken in all directions because of the destruction of the upper two thirds of the wall, and indications of colors and designs are vague and fragmentary, save in the center of the northern section. On the north wall the surface is affected by the eastward movement of the entire wall under the thrust from the fill in Wall Street (see above, p. 5). The major cracks are therefore horizontal, tracing an irregular line down through Panels ND 2–4, upwards through ND 5–6, downward through ND 6–7, upwards through ND 7–8, and down again in ND 9. There are losses of plaster surface in Panels ND 3, 6, and especially in ND 9, where the upper fourth of the panel has been restored, including the head and neck of the couchant leopard cub. On the north section of the west wall preservation is at its worst. Much of the destruction here results from the water seepage that has affected also the lower part of Panel WC 4 (see above). Here virtually all of Panel WD 5 (N), half of Panels WD 4 and 6 (N), and about one third of Panels WD 2, 3, and 7 (N) have been lost. In no case, however, has the loss affected our knowledge of the design of the panel in question. Along the southern half of the west dado preservation is much better. Here there are to be noted horizontal and diagonal cracking, occasioned by the pressure which the fill outside the building exerted upon the wall. In Panels WD 3–7 (S) they are only slightly disturbing. In Panels WD 1–2 (S), however, and especially in the former, cracking of the plaster is extensive and has led to the loss of irregularly shaped pieces of the plaster belonging to the body and the head of the tigress and to the medallion and the field of Panel WD 2 (S). All losses have been restored with great care, restored sections being clearly identifiable as such in the Synagogue as rebuilt in the Damascus Museum.

971. See above, pp. 36–38, where also the literature is given in the footnotes.

972. See above, pp. 59, 66.

973. Farmakowski, *Proceedings of the Russian Archaeological Institute, Constantinople*, VIII (1903), Pls. XXIV, XXVI.

974. See e.g., *Antioch*, II, Pl. 35, no. 48, Panel A (from room 3 of a villa at Daphne), where in a strip

Of the two types of figures portrayed in the Synagogue dado the animals (Pls. XXXVII to XXXVIII, 1) are, of course, a familiar element of the vocabulary of Oriental art since time immemorial. Their location in a dado puts them in line ultimately with the monsters in high relief at the entrances to Assyrian and Persian palaces, and the animals of the basreliefs that formed the wainscoting of their important chambers. If, on the one hand, the animals scenes in the decorative friezes of ancient Oriental palaces reflect the hunt and the combat between weaker and stronger animals in the struggle for survival, the great bulls of the palace entrances are, on the other, symbolic transformations of the wild animals that were in older times chained at the gates of cities and palaces to guard the premises.[975] The animals of the Synagogue dado are, of course, a long distance removed from these older Oriental prototypes, yet their presence in the design and the form of their rendering are not fully intelligible without reference to the older tradition and materials.

Between the animals of the Dura Synagogue dado and those depicted elsewhere in the contemporary art of the Roman Near East there are striking differences. It is not that the animals belong to species usually neglected; for with the wide interest in hunting scenes, lions, tigers, and leopards are among the animals most commonly represented. Nor is it that the artist was unable to produce a convincing likeness or to render properly the flowing lines of the feline form so typical of the better examples in the mosaics of the later Orient.[976] Quite on the contrary, it must be said that animal forms were among the most successfully

and lovingly handled by the Synagogue artist. The real difference is one of pose and attitude. Male lions, tigers, and leopards of the later Oriental art are usually represented in their fiercest mien. One has only to recall in this connection the lions of the Antioch hunting mosaics, the one on the leather shield from Dura, or even the figured graffito from Panel WC 4 of the Synagogue.[977] The animals of the Synagogue dado are by contrast quite subdued and almost tame in their demeanor. The only reminiscence of their relation to scenes of combat between the stronger and the weaker in the struggle for survival is to be found in the fact that the standing animals of the north, south, and west walls are shown with a forepaw resting upon the head of a weaker animal seized as prey.[978] But this is, of course, merely an inherited cliché deriving in all likelihood from the decorative vocabulary of funerary sculpture.[979]

The really significant feature of the Synagogue artist's rendering of the animals in his dado is that all but the cubs wear harnesses.[980] These are represented by two pink bands that run about the neck and the body of the animals respectively, meeting above the shoulders. The animals are thus in effect captive, the only question being whether

composed of alternate rectangles and squares, inscribed with diamonds and circles respectively, faces and animals are portrayed.

975. This older practice produces the standard formula of historical inscriptions in referring to the servitude of captured kings, as for instance in the text of Assurbanipal, "ein Halsband legte ich ihm an, band ihn mit Bären und Hunden und ließ ihn die Stadttore bewachen." See B. Landsberger, *Abhandlungen der sächsischen Akademie der Wissenschaften, phil.-hist. Klasse,* XLII, (1934), p. 81.

976. It may be noted here that the lions and tigers of the Synagogue dado are rendered in a rich golden yellow. The lions are outlined in brown and have brown manes. The tigers and tigresses have black stripes. Leopards are done in gray. Their spots, their ears, and the noticeable ring of curls at the neck are, like their bodies, outlined in black. Tongues are indicated in red.

977. See *Antioch,* II, Pls. 66, 71–74; *Rep. VI,* Pls. XXV–XXV A and below, Fig. 111.

978. The heads of these victims are not always clearly distinguishable, and seem to vary at the artist's pleasure. The head in Panel WD 7 (S) has antlers and may be that of a deer, while that of WD 1 (S) has horns that curve only slightly and is probably that of a bull. The heads of Panels WD 1 and 7 (N), as well as of Panels SD 4 and 6, seem to belong to rams. By contrast, the heads of Panels ND 4 and 6 lack horns, the artist emphasizing instead their long ears. Perhaps they are intended to be goats. Red is commonly used to show that the neck has been severed from the body. Otherwise the heads are usually done in gray.

979. See especially C. Robert, *Journal of Hellenic Studies,* XX (1900), pp. 81–98, Pls. IX–X; W. Altmann, *Architectur und Ornamentik der antiken Sarkophage* (1902), pp. 48f., and *idem,* art. "Sarkophage" in *RE.* The cliché develops from a scene in which the entire body of the victim is shown, together, it should be said, with a human being who may be either a hunter or a keeper. For later examples see, e.g., K. Lehmann-Hartleben and E. C. Olsen, *Dionysiac Sarcophagi in Baltimore* (1942).

980. The absence of the harness and the pose is the justification for calling the couchant leopards of Panels ND 1 and 9, WD 4 (S), and WD 4 (N) cubs. It may be noted in passing that the artist failed to complete one element of his design in forgetting to add the necessary spots to the leopard cub of Panel ND 1.

the nature and circumstances of their captivity can be divined to give us the source of the artist's inspiration. Captive wild animals were apparently quite common in the ancient Orient and appear occasionally on the monuments of ancient art.[981] But the medium of restraint is normally a simple collar rather than a harness. The same collar appears on dogs, panthers, and even tigers in the monuments of Hellenistic art.[982] Harnesses of the type represented in the Synagogue dado seem to occur especially in hunting contexts, whether of the normal hunt in the open or in the *venationes* of the amphitheater.[983] In the present instance the pink color used for the harness suggests that it is ornamental, and that the animal either belongs to a private zoo or is decked out for appearance in the arena.[984]

More interesting than the animals are the masks that appear in the circular fields of the Synagogue dado (Pls. XXXVIII, 2–XXXIX). It is tempting to call them heads or faces rather than masks; for the former have a long and distinguished history in Oriental and Hellenistic art, and the ultimate prototype for the setting in which they appear in the dado is the *imago clipeata* of the Hellenistic and Roman portrait tradition.[985] But at least one of

the likenesses portrayed in the Synagogue's lowest zone is clearly a theatrical mask, making it altogether likely that the others belong to the same category.[986] Of the fourteen masks represented, four are those of men and ten those of women. The male character in the four instances mentioned is always the same. He appears near the opposite ends of the northern and southern sections of the west dado; namely, in Panels WD 2 (S), WD 6 (N); and twice on the southern section of the east dado; namely, in Panels ED 2 and 4 (S).[987] On the west dado he is balanced in each section by the same female character, who appears twice again in the northern section of the east dado.[988] The two are thus clearly a pair. This selfsame female character appears once more as one of six women's masks represented on the north and south dadoes, the six forming a second group.[989] All told, we therefore have one male character represented four times, one female character represented five times, and five additional female characters each represented but once.

981. Captive leopards and bears appear in the representation of tribute from Syria and Nubia on ancient Egyptian monuments (see W. Wreszinski, *Atlas zur alt-ägyptischen Kulturgeschichte* I, 2, 1923, Pls. 269–270) and panthers or guepards and lions in Mesopotamian art. For the former see H. Friedrichs, *Der alte Orient*, XXXII, 3–4 (1933), Figs. 12, 24, 26 (Maikop vase); O. W. Weber, *Altorientalische Siegelbilder*, Fig. 515; and for the latter, E. Herzfeld, *Archaeological History of Iran* (1935), Pl. XIII (Bishapur relief).

982. For a panther with a neck piece and a tiger with a decorative collar, see the mosaics in the House of the Masks at Delos, *Exploration archéologique de Delos*, VIII (1922), Pl. LII; and XIV (1933), Pl. III.

983. For harnesses on hunting dogs see Panel EC 1 (Pl. LXXIV) and Robert, *Die antiken Sarkophag-Reliefs*, III, 2, Pl. LXXV, nos. 223a and b. For wild animals with harnesses, see the lion, panther, and bear in a bas-relief of the Palazzo Torlonia, the background of which is the amphitheater (*Monumenti inediti dall' instituto di corrispondenza archeologica*, III, Pl. XXXVIII). The relief shows the ring at the top of the animals' shoulders, where the two bands of the harness meet, to which leashes could be attached.

984. On the animals in private zoological gardens, their trappings, and their study by ancient artists, see L. Friedlander, *Darstellung aus der Sittengeschichte Roms*, 10th ed., II (1922), pp. 78, 85f.

985. See in general Rostovtzeff, *YCS*, V, pp. 183–185. The material is widely scattered; for human likenesses

appear in the Roman Orient on capitals, voussoirs, pilasters, lintels, dadoes, mosaics, sarcophagi, and pottery, and no adequate treatment of the material exists. Indeed, there is need for a clear definition of terminology and for a basis of distinction between face and mask. Perhaps the basic distinction should be between bust and mask. The former seems to appear where deities, personifications, and living persons are to be represented. Faces might be interpreted as death masks in a funerary context (where they are attached to coffins or appear in graves), and should be taken elsewhere to represent theatrical masks.

986. Masks must have begun to enjoy the favor of Orientals as decorative materials in the Hellenistic period and are widely represented in the Roman Orient. See the masks at Antioch, *Antioch*, II, Pls. 21 (no. 227), 35 (no. 48, Panel A), 36 (no. 48, Panel F), 40 (no. 53, Panel A), 61 (no. 85, Panels C, D, E, F); in Southern Syria, *Publications of the Princeton University Archaeological Expeditions to Syria in 1904–5 and 1909*, II, A, p. 89, Fig. 68; and in Jordan, *Gerasa*, Pl. LXXXVa.

987. Only in Panel WD 2 (S) is the face well preserved. Most of WD 6 (N) has been destroyed, as indicated above. Traces of the end of the roll of hair establish the presence of the mask in ED 2 (S) and traces of the exaggerated mouth serve the same purpose in ED 4 (S).

988. Preservation of this mask is best in Panel WD 6 (S). In WD 2 (N) the lower part of the face is indistinct. In ED 4 (N) much of the color has been lost, but the design is clear. ED 2 (N) preserves only elements of the basic design.

989. Her location in this group is in Panel ND 3. Slight damage has been done to her face by the loss of a small piece of plaster. The other masks occur in Panels ND 5 and 7, SD 3, 5, and 7.

The mask of the male character, clearly identifiable as such by its caricature of the human face, is marked by a thick roll of hair that follows closely the line of the forehead, covers one ear, and hangs

FIG. 63. Dado. Mask

down beside the neck, ending in a curl at shoulder level (Fig. 63; Pl. XXXVIII, 2). The mouth with its beard roll is exaggerated into a wide crescent-shaped maw. The eyes are wide and staring and the nose ends in an oval button set against a wide bridge. In terms of Pollux' *Onomasticon* and its catalogue of the *personae* of the New Comedy (IV, 143–154), this could be either the Leading Servant (ἡγεμὼν Θεράπων), whose status is that of a freedman, or the ἐπίσειστος ἡγεμὼν, who is seventh on Pollux' list of the servants.[990] The two are said by Pollux to be much alike save as regards the hair. The difference in hair is interpreted by Robert as applying to the absence of curls under the hair roll, but — more properly, we believe — by Bieber,

990. On the importance of the New Comedy, especially Menander, in the Orient, see A. M. Friend, *Antioch*, III, pp. 248–251. For the interpretation of Pollux' list and of ancient masks generally, see the fundamental essay of C. Robert, *Die Masken der neueren attischen Komoedie* (*25 Hallisches Winckelmannsprogramm*, 1911); and M. Bieber's two major publications, *Die Denkmäler zum Theaterwesen im Altertum* (1920), and the article "Maske" in *RE*, XXVIII (XIV, 2, 1930), cols. 2070–2120. In this instance, examples of the first mask are reproduced by Robert, *op. cit.*, p. 4, Figs. 2 and 4 (see also Bieber, *Denkmäler*, Pl. XCVIII, 3) and an example of the second Robert, *op. cit.*, p. 6, Fig. 12.

to the length of the hair.[991] Since the mask of the Synagogue has a roll of short hair which, like the short beard about the mouth, is done in yellow, we conclude that the *persona* in question is the Leading Servant, who is specifically described by Pollux as a youthful "red-head."

The female *persona* bracketed with the above Fig. 64; Pl. XXXVIII, 3) is somewhat more difficult to identify. The mask is normally tilted slightly either toward the right or toward the left, and is characterized by its high head of hair, carefully parted in the middle and built up in ascending layers into two peaks. Stray hairs are shown on the forehead and the temples, and long curling strands fall down beside the face to shoulder level. The hair is brown, outlined in black. The features are regular and show no indication of age. Flesh tints are light and must originally have been pinkish. The eyes are wide open under the well-marked brows.[992] Conceivably we have here a representation of the courtesan known as "Little Torch," of whom

FIG. 64. Dado. Mask

991. Robert, *op. cit.*, pp. 7, 26; and Bieber in *RE*, *op. cit.*

992. In one instance (Panel ND 3) the mouth seems to be open, but this may well be the result of an improper allocation of the shadow line under the lip. See WD 6 (S). The part in the hair is occasionally carried up in white above the level of the top of the head. See WD 2 (N).

Pollux says that her name derives from the shape of her coiffure, which mounts to a peak, somewhat like the flame of a torch. Robert has pointed to examples of this coiffure in the Tanagra figurines, and reproduces an example of a terracotta mask at Berlin with an analogous hair arrangement.[993]

For the remaining five masks the means of positive identification are still more difficult to find. Of the three on the north dado, the one in Panel ND 5 (Fig. 65; Pl. XXXVIII, 4) is the most poorly preserved. The features have been washed or rubbed off, leaving only the impression of a round face, against the outlines of which the scant head of hair is tightly held. The distinguishing feature of

Fig. 65. Dado. Mask

the coiffure is a small roll of hair or row of curls running around the head with a curved bang covering a large portion of the forehead. A close examination of the field indicates that in all probability the hair originally had a decoration mounted in it. This appears today as a light mass, but seems to have the outlines of a flower and leaf design. The mask in Panel ND 7 (Fig. 66; Pl. XXXIX, 1) has its hair parted in the middle and pulled up at either side to form peaks, but these are widely separated, leaving a trough between them. Tresses fall down over the ears to the shoulders at either side. The trough at the top of the coiffure seems originally

993. Robert, *Masken der neueren attischen Komoedie*, pp. 43 f., Figs. 76–77.

to have been filled with a decorative element whose nature is no longer distinguishable. Projecting into it from the hair are several black lobes. If these were originally connected with a dark oval mass

Fig. 66. Dado. Mask

that appears in the middle of the part in the hair directly above the forehead, one might guess that they represent the ends and the knot of a band encircling the head. On the south wall the mask in

Fig. 67. Dado. Mask

Panel SD 3 (Fig. 67; Pl. XXXIX, 2) has an unparted head of brown hair encircling a pink face. The hair is either brushed back at the sides or fashioned into a roll. Above the temples at either side of the face large yellow discs ornament the hair. These

seem to be attached to a white band outlined in
pink that encircles the head. The mask in Panel
SD 5 (Fig. 68; Pl. XXXIX, 3) is notable for the lack of
any particular arrangement of the hair. The brown

FIG. 68. Dado. Mask

hair masses are unbalanced, and are allowed to fall
irregularly on either side of the head with tresses
extending to the line of the shoulders. Into the
coiffure there is as set an ornament at the top, a

FIG. 69. Dado. Mask

trumpet-shaped object rendered in pink and outlined in black. The mask in Panel SD 7 (Fig. 69;
Pl. XXXIX, 4) has, like the one in Panel SD 3, a well-
organized hair arrangement. In this instance it is

clear that the brown hair is carefully combed back
to form a solid roll around the entire head. There
is, therefore, no indication of tresses falling to the
shoulders, but the artist has enlivened the picture
by showing a single strand out of position and
hanging down over the forehead. Again the coiffure
is ornamented, this time with a crescent-shaped
object set into the hair and another in the shape
of a mushroom arising from it. Both are rendered
again in pink.

The standardization of the Synagogue artists'
treatment of faces and heads of hair observable in
the narrative panels makes it necessary to conclude
that each of these five masks represents a well-
defined type, rather than an arbitrary variation of
a single theme. In certain particulars the masks in
question have affinities with the *personae* of Pollux
and with the representation of masks elsewhere.
Using as a criterion merely the arrangement of the
hair, it is simple to divide them according to the
presence or absence of a part in the hair or according to the types of rolls into which the hair is
arranged, and to record which have a ribbon or a
braid of hair tied about the forehead. From this
analysis a line of argument can be developed to
suggest that the mask of Panel SD 5 is the Virgin
(κόρη) of the New Comedy, that of Panel ND 5 the
second Demi-Virgin (ψευδοκόρη), that of Panel
SD 7 the Concubine (παλλακή), that of Panel ND 7
the Little Courtesan (ἑταιρίδιον), and that of
Panel SD 3 the Gilded Courtesan (διάχρυσος
ἑταίρα).[994] The difficulty with these identifications
is that the applicability of the other details of
Pollux' description of the several masks cannot

994. See in this connection especially Robert's discussion of the masks of female *personae* of the New
Comedy, *ibid.*, pp. 36–49. In Pollux' list the Virgin is said
to have her hair brushed straight or left uncurled, but
parted in the middle; for discussion and suggested
occurrences see *ibid.*, pp. 40 f. and Fig. 69. The Second
Demi-Virgin has her hair bound about her forehead but
not parted (*ibid.*, pp. 41–43); Robert is certainly correct
in maintaining that Pollux' description does not call for
a ταινία on the forehead, but he may be limiting the
interpretation unduly by considering only a σφενδονή.
The Concubine is described as having a roll of hair
(περίκομος), but is in other respects like the Constant
Talker (see *ibid.*, pp. 38 f. for discussion of the term, and
Fig. 68 for a suggested example); the Little Courtesan has
her hair bound with a band (for discussion see *ibid.*,
pp. 40 f., and for suggested examples Figs. 70–71); the
Gilded Courtesan is said merely to have much gold in her
hair (for discussion see *ibid.*, p. 45).

always be checked, and that all five of the masks of the Synagogue have elements that do not appear in either the account of the *Onomasticon* or in the examples or representations of masks found elsewhere. The elements in question are especially the ornaments, floral or otherwise, that appear in the hair. Some of these might be Dionysiac in origin or connotation — as, for instance, the floral ornament (if such it be) on the mask of Panel ND 5, and the circular yellow objects of SD 3, supposing they too were to represent flowers.[995] The masks in question might thus represent characters of the later Dionysiac festivals and processions rather than the New Comedy.[996] The wealth of ornament worn in the hair in the later Orient not only in the cult acts and by cult deities (e.g., Isis), but also generally by personifications and in scenes of religious and other banquets, makes it entirely possible, however, that in this region the traditional masks of the New Comedy acquired additional decorative elements such as those which the Synagogue dado shows.[997] It will be wiser, therefore, to hold fast to the sphere of derivation suggested by the masks of the Leading Servant and the Little Torch, and to allow for variations upon the repertoire of the traditional *personae*, than to wander too far afield in the search for analogies in other contexts.

From what has been said it should be apparent that the figures represented in the Synagogue dado probably derive from two well-developed decorative traditions, which are here made to complement each other. There is an orientalizing element in the rendering of the materials from both traditions, whether in perpetuation of iconographic clichés that are ultimately of Oriental origin, or in the modification of Hellenistic patterns under Oriental influence. But this serves only to render the more uniform a blend of two artistic traditions, both of

which reflect the life of the wealthier, pleasure-loving classes of the later Roman Empire. The Synagogue dado therefore represents a type of wall decoration that was no doubt found commonly in the villas of the wealthier inhabitants of the larger cities of the Roman Orient. It probably appears here in a Synagogue because, in the absence of a clearly defined tradition for the decoration of synagogues, the artists fell back upon the most advanced models of dadoes known to them from contemporary decorative art.

995. See e.g., the masks on the Bacchic cantharos in the Cabinet des Medailles at Paris (P. Gusman, *L'Art decoratif de Rome*, II, n.d., Pl. 63), and for other examples of similar hair ornament H. von Rohden and H. Winnefeld, *Architektonische Terrakotten der Kaiserzeit* (*Die antiken Terrakotten*, IV, 1911), Pl. XXXIX; and J. Loeb, *Die Terrakotten der Sammlung Loeb*, II (1916), Pl. 115.

996. Compare the Orthonobazos frieze at Dura, Cumont, *Fouilles*, p. 237, Pl. LXXXVI.

997. The evidence is as widely distributed as the materials for our knowledge of Oriental cults in Italy, the mosaics of Antioch, and the ivories of Begram are separated from each other geographically.

7. DECORATIVE FRAMEWORK: PANEL BANDS, CORNER PILASTERS, DOOR REVEALS

In describing the narrative paintings of the Synagogue, we have of necessity left aside the frame within which they are comprehended. This and such incidental decorations as were applied to the door reveals must therefore be considered briefly here.

The first — immediately more noticeable, though relatively less important — element of the frame within which the narrative decorations are comprehended is the system of bands by which the individual panels are enclosed and arranged in ascending zones or registers. From the way in which they cut in upon the peripheral detail of the narrative compositions,[998] it is clear that the panel bands were executed after the scenes themselves had been completed, though of course their introduction had been anticipated from the outset. Since each wall was painted separately from the top down, even the register bands did not always meet at the same level in the corners.[999] Fundamentally the panel and register bands are heavy black strips of a type and width (*ca.* 0.15 m.) common also elsewhere in the decorations at Dura, whether plain or embellished.[1000] To relieve their severity they were in this instance inscribed with a wavy white line, the loops of which were then filled to half their depth with solid color, producing a twisted ribbon design. On bands running horizontally the loops open to the top were filled halfway with white, as were the loops opening to the left in vertical bands. Loops opening to the right

on vertical bands, and loops opening toward the bottom of horizontal bands, were filled halfway with pink. Pink and white areas were delimited by a simple red line that consequently runs as an almost continuous element through the middle of the ribbon. Opposite each half-filled loop of the ribbon, the black of the band was marked with three light-colored dots. This twisted ribbon replaced the running designs that Hellenistic wall painting had taken over from monumental architecture, and became a great favorite in the Roman Orient, no doubt because it was so easy to execute.[1001] It is important to note, however, that the artist has added to the ribbon a system of dot triads. Used here only as a filler, they are in fact appropriate to a quite different pattern; namely, the vine scroll, whose grape clusters they represent.[1002] But this combination of ribbon and dot clusters is by no means unique here, occurring numerous times in the known mosaics of Antioch.[1003]

The careful framing of pictorial materials is as common on the smaller monuments of ancient Oriental art as their arrangement in long strips is on the walls of royal palaces.[1004] Abandoned for a while under the impact of Hellenistic systems of decoration, such frames emerge again at Dura, perhaps only in the third century of our era, as a means of defining outwardly the fields which the background colors limit in depth. In this respect they have a positive and significant function to fulfil.

---

998. See, for example, the vessels belonging to Panel SC 2 (Elijah at Cherith and Zarephath), which were set so close to the next scene that the panel band had actually to be painted around them. See also the way in which the panel band overlaps the hind end of the horse in Panel EC 1 (David and Saul in the Wilderness of Ziph).

999. So e.g., in the northwest corner of the room there is a difference of about 0.10 m. between the levels at which the bands between Register B and C run. There is a noticeable rise in the register band dividing the two Center Panels. This is due to the difference in the height of Wing Panels I and II, whose frame the register band eventually continued and connected.

1000. In the Temple of Bel (Cumont, *Fouilles*, Pls. XLVIII–XLIX, LIV); the Christian Chapel (*Rep. V*, Pls. XLI–XLII, XLVIII, LI); the Temple of Zeus Theos (*Rep. VII–VIII*, p. 197, Fig. 50); and the Mithraeum (*ibid.*, Pls. XIV–XVII). The width of the bands in the Synagogue actually varies between 0.06 m. and 0.18 m.

1001. For examples of architectural running designs from Pompeii, see, e.g., H. G. Beyen, *Die Pompejanische Wanddekoration vom zweiten bis zum vierten Stil*, I (1938), Figs. 191–192, 211, 215. Examples of the ribbon meander are common, e.g., in the Antioch mosaics. See Morey, *The Mosaics of Antioch*, Pl. XIII; *Antioch*, II, Pls. 27, 31, 48; *Antioch*, III, Pls. 53, 57, 61, 66.

1002. The vine scroll is among the oldest and most widely used decorative designs of the Hellenistic and Roman periods. In the general vicinity of the Dura Synagogue its earliest known examples seem to belong to the Parthian period. See Andrae and Lenzen, *Die Partherstadt Assur*, Pls. 27 and 34; and L. Legrain, *Terra-cottas from Nippur (University of Pennsylvania, Publications of the Babylonian Section of the University Museum*, XVI, 1930), Pl. LXXVI, 442a.

1003. *Antioch*, II, Pls. 23, 27; *Antioch*, III, Pl. 57.

1004. For the former see, e.g., the limestone plaques from Khafajah and Tell Asmar, H. Frankfort, *Sculpture of the Third Millennium B.C. from Tell Asmar and Khafajah (Oriental Institute Publications*, XLIV, 1939), Pls. 105–114, and for the latter, the bas-reliefs from the palaces of Nineveh and Khorsabad.

The second — less noticeable, but intrinsically by far more important — element of the frame within which the narrative panels of the Synagogue are comprehended is that of the painted pilasters set into the four corners of the room (Fig. 70; Pls.

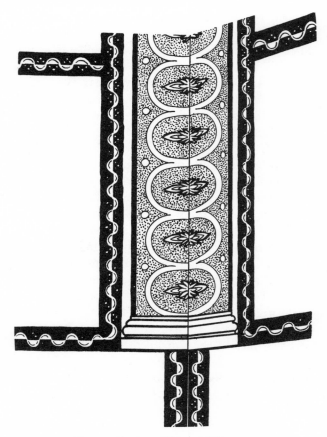

FIG. 70. Design of Corner Pilasters, Register and Panel Bands

XVIII–XXI; Plans IX–XII). What restricts their prominence is a combination of three factors; namely, first, the more sober colors in which they were executed; second, the fact that they begin only at the bottom of Register B; and, third, the fact that so much of the upper part of the Synagogue's decorations has been destroyed. Since no part of Registers A and B is preserved in the northeast and southeast corners of the room, we can know of the existence of the pilasters only from the northwest and southwest pair, yet it can scarcely be doubted that the design was repeated in all four corners of the building.

For the development of the corner pilasters the

Synagogue artists set aside at both ends of each wall a vertical strip 0.30–0.40 m. wide, beginning at the top of Register A and running down to the base of Register B. The two adjacent strips in each corner of the room were treated as one field, about 3 m. in height. In developing it the artist first painted the last 0.25–0.35 m. of each wall a reddish brown to represent the shaft of the pilaster. The outer ends of the shaft were outlined by a strip of black *ca.* 0.05 m. wide, suggesting the projection of the shaft from the surface of the wall. This in turn was separated from the adjacent panel bands by a white strip of approximately the same width. At the bottom the pilaster rested upon a yellow base with a double torus molding set upon a simple plinth.[1005] Upon the shaft of the pilasters the artist inscribed a succession of orange loops that meet in the corners of the room and represent intertwined vine scrolls. Poor workmanship makes the loops anything but symmetrical in shape and turns the resultant design into a series of compressed ovals rather than circles. Into the ovals created by the loops were set identical floral designs that spring from the corners and consist of conventionalized clusters of four yellow and white leaves from which a pointed bloom in red and white projects. Outside the ovals in the interval between the loops, small yellow discs are occasionally visible.

Imitations of columns and pilasters are recognized features of the architectural development of the Structural Style in Hellenistic paintings.[1006] If they appear here inscribed with double vine scrolls, this is no doubt the result of the use of such designs upon so many of the vertical members of archi-

1005. The profile described is especially clear on the southwest pilaster. Base and plinth run through the area otherwise devoted to the register band separating the pictures of Registers B and C. Inequalities in the level at which the register bands run on adjacent walls created difficulties for the artist; for instance, at the west end of the north wall, where the base of the pilaster is some 0.08 m. lower than on the adjacent north end of the west wall (see Pl. XIX). The elements of the profile are indicated by red lines superimposed upon the yellow base. On the north face of the northwest pilaster some confusion has developed in the rendering of the base, perhaps as the result of retouching.

1006. See in general Beyen, *Pompejanische Wanddekoration*, I, Figs. 1–3, 47, 50 etc.; and for an excellent example of a pilaster carried around a corner, E. Pfuhl, *Malerei und Zeichnung der Griechen*, III (1923), p. 315, Fig. 707 (Boscoreale Villa).

tectural structures, especially in the Hellenistic East.[1007] Originally the pilasters of the Synagogue must have ended in painted capitals, which in turn lent imaginary support to a painted architrave encircling the room above the windows and just under the beams of the roof. All traces of this superstructure have of course disappeared, but without it the design would not be complete. In its fully developed form this columnar frame for the decorations of the four walls of the Synagogue becomes recognizable as a survival of a type of wall organization best known to us in the Orient from the painted tombs at Marissa and from the frescoes of the Temple of Bel at Dura.[1008] Since the days of these earlier paintings the architectural element had ceased to be part of the internal development of wall space, and was relegated to the periphery. Here, however, it could still fulfil a function, as in the present instance; namely, to provide the vertical supports of an imaginary trellis. The horizontal element of this trellis was the grid of ceiling beams, to which the pilasters gave the fiction of support and within which the fruits, flowers, personifications, and zodiacal symbols of the ceiling tiles were with some element of propriety distributed.[1009]

The last of the decorative materials to be considered here is the design applied to the door reveals in the east wall of the chamber (Fig. 71). We know this design solely from the larger central doorway, and there only from its lower ends. Yet the pattern is so simple that its upward continuation provides no problem, and the uniformity of the Synagogue's decoration is such that it can safely be thought to have been applied also to the women's doorway. In actual fact the decoration of the reveals was the second step in the treatment of the doorways, since the rubble walls that framed the opening had received a coat of red paint before the trim was put in place and the reveals con-

structed.[1010] Bnt there can be no question that the reveals themselves were decorated in one operation with the rest of the building.

Again, as on the corner pilasters, the central element of the design is a double scroll. This is set

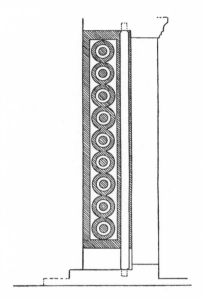

FIG. 71. Design on Door Reveals

into a long white rectangular field carefully framed in red. On the side of the reveal nearest the chamber the vertical framing strip was 0.12 m. wide, but on the side nearest the door jamb its width was more than double (*ca.* 0.26 m.), clearly to allow for the thickness of the door leaves and to provide behind them a strip sufficiently wide to balance that nearest the chamber. Into the field thus framed there were set intertwining bands 0.08–0.09 m. wide, creating circles 0.43 m. in diameter. These were rendered in pink, but had dark red edges. Into the center of each loop was set a disc *ca.* 0.11 m. in diameter, also done in pink and outlined in red. The white field into which the overlapping circles were set began *ca.* 0.45 m. above the reveal floor —

1007. See e.g., on the Temple of Baal Shamin at Siʻ, *Publications of the Princeton University Archaeological Expeditions to Syria in 1904–5 and 1909*, II, A, Pl. XXVIII; on the Nabataean doorjambs, *ibid.*, p. 113, Fig. 90 and p. 89, Fig. 68; and at Palmyra again on a vertical member, Wiegand, *Palmyra*, p. 95, Fig. 108.

1008. See Peters and Thiersch, *Painted Tombs in the Necropolis of Marissa*, p. 17, Fig. 2; Cumont, *Fouilles*, Pls. XXXI–XXXII, XLV; and C. Hopkins, *American Journal of Archaeology*, XLV (1941), pp. 18–29.

1009. See above, p. 53.

1010. See above, p. 18. The application of simple coats of red paint even to finished door reveals has a parallel at Dura in a house in Block E4 (*Rep. VI*, p. 17). The painting of the wall against which the reveal was later set was a part of the first phase in the decoration of the chamber and prepared the room for use while it was still not entirely finished. During this time the door opening was probably covered with a curtain. On such curtains in the doorways of houses, whether of cloth or of reeds, see Krauss, *Talmudische Archäologie*, I, p. 39 and n. 509.

the height of the red frame at the bottom of the design — and allowed sufficient space, it would seem, for a series of about nine consecutive loops between that point and a framing element at the upper end of the reveal wall.[1011]

The design thus described suggests at first glance an imitation in color of the paneling of wooden door trim. Such imitations exist in plaster on antae and at entrances to chambers.[1012] Yet the impression created by the frame of the design is not necessarily decisive, for the intertwined bands are probably to be regarded as flower garlands. In color and execution they recall nothing so much as the ceiling tiles with a disc set into a wreath.[1013] The artist may thus have enlivened his panel by introducing an element intended to carry the thought of celebration, as flower garlands readily do.[1014]

1011. Actually, of course, the design was painted from the top down, and on the south reveal of the main door carelessness in the spacing and dimension of the rings resulted in the series ending at the bottom of the field with three quarters of a ring instead of a complete ring.

1012. Long rectangular fields broken up into squares, each inscribed with a circle, decorate the antae of the Kasr Firaun at Petra. See G. and A. Horsfield, *Quarterly of the Department of Antiquities in Palestine*, VII (1938), Pl. XXX. For similar paneling on the entrance to the *tablinum* of a house in Pompeii see A. Mau, *Röm. Mitt.*, XVI (1901), p. 336 and p. 337, Fig. 2.

1013. See above, p. 46.

1014. On garlands in scenes of celebration at Dura, see the banquet scenes (Rostovtzeff, *YCS*, V, Figs. 72–73) and the paintings in the Temple of Bel (Cumont, *Fouilles*, Pls. LVI, LVIII, etc.).

FURNISHINGS AND INTERIOR APPOINTMENTS

The two successive Synagogues of Dura were not destroyed and buried by enemy action, nor did they fall into ruins by neglect. Rather they were systematically razed by the inhabitants of the city, the earlier in order to pave the way for the construction of a newer and larger edifice, and the later in the course of the city's efforts to prepare itself for an expected siege. In both cases, therefore, the members of the Synagogue had ample opportunity to remove from the building in advance of its abandonment all of its interior furnishings. On that account, no doubt, no minor finds of any consequence were made in the complex, strange as that might otherwise seem. For the minor disappointment this provides, the remarkable series of decorations preserved on the walls of the later building is more than ample compensation.

While the Synagogue building as excavated was in effect an empty shell, there are nonetheless certain details in our knowledge of it, all carefully recorded by the members of the expedition staff, that permit of inferences about the furnishings and appointments of at least the later building. Some of these have already been mentioned in the Preliminary Report.[1]

It is a matter of record that the uppermost of the two floors of the Synagogue, like the thresholds, showed definite signs of wear at certain points and not at others. On the floor the signs of wear appeared, as might well be expected, immediately in front of the benches set against the four walls of the room. But in these regions they were limited to a zone that stopped abruptly *ca.* 1.40 m. from the edge of the benches. The proper inference from this fact is that the central section of the floor was covered with mats or rugs, while the zone of wear was not. Similarly it was observed that the surface of the benches themselves was unusually well preserved, and that on the benches when excavated there could still be seen spots of paint that had dropped upon them when the murals were being executed. The natural inference is that the benches

1. *Rep. VI*, pp. 322, 324f., 331.

were also covered with rugs or cushions during the short life of the building.

The examination of the floor revealed also the existence in it at certain points regularly distributed of holes that could only have been fashioned intentionally when the floor was laid. Fig. 72 shows the location of these holes, alto-

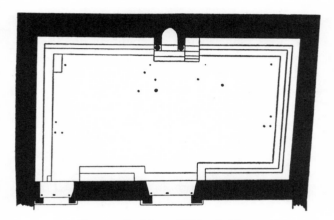

FIG. 72. Position of Holes in Floor

gether sixteen in number. Ten of them were identical in shape and were arranged in a roughly symmetrical pattern in the area adjacent to the benches and thus within the zone left free of matting or rugs. Four of the ten formed a straight line along the benches of the west wall; namely, one in each corner and one at either side of the central feature comprising the Torah Shrine and the raised seat built upon the benches at its side. The remaining six appeared in groups of three next to the north and south benches, approximately two thirds of the way across the room toward the east wall. All ten holes were octagonal in shape, 0.04 m. wide and tapered to a point at a level 0.16 m. below the surface of the floor. Most of them were found broken out at one side, as though what they contained was put in place when the floor was poured and had eventually to be broken out of their plaster and pebble seat by force. It has been inferred from their position that these ten holes held upright lampstands. The lamps along the west wall were in this view mounted upon simple straight rods, while those along the north and south walls were mounted on stands with three feet. Our best source of information for ancient lampstands is Pompeii, where a large number has come to light.[2] Examples of the type used in the Orient are represented in the Synagogue itself in Panel WB 4 (The Ark in the Land of the Philistines) among the scattered furnishings of the Temple of Dagon (Fig. 30, nos. 8 and 10). We should probably be quite safe in visualizing the lampstands of the Synagogue as the counterparts of those drawn by the artist.

The six remaining holes in the floor (Fig. 72) were not homogeneous in shape or depth, and provided no easy clue to their significance. Located in the western half of the room, they formed two groups — one of four holes, the other of two — set at either side of the Torah Shrine and its raised seat. Of the group to the left (south) of the Torah Shrine, the two forward holes were set about 1.60 m. from, and roughly parallel to, the benches; and of these in turn the hole farthest toward the north was found to contain a quantity of oily soot. We cannot know precisely what items of furniture were anchored to the floor in these two groups of holes, nor what was the material of which the furniture was made, but the probability is that the items were two in number. Among items of synagogue furniture that deserve special consideration in this connection, the first and foremost is naturally the *bema*. This was the raised podium from which the weekly scripture lesson was read and some of the prayers recited.[3]

The earliest literary references to the *bema* indicate that at first it was made "of wood," which explains why none of the earlier examples has been preserved. The group of four holes to the south of the Torah Shrine might be thought to have held the legs of such a wooden *bema*, which in that case had the form of a trapezium. The peculiar shape would be the result merely of a desire to set the

side nearest the Torah Shrine, from which the *bema* would normally be approached, at the angle most convenient for access from the repository of the sacred scrolls. Scarcely a meter wide, the *bema* of the Dura Synagogue would probably have been similar in construction to, though much smaller in compass than, those of the mediaeval synagogues of Palestine, merely providing standing room for one person and a reading desk at elbow height before him.[4] We would, of course, need to imagine that the uprights supporting the platform continued above its floor to support also the railing enclosing it on three sides, and the board across the railing that served as a reading desk. In this connection it would be possible to find an explanation for the larger size of the hole that held the left front support and was filled with a quantity of oily soot. Perhaps this support was larger because it extended above the platform, the rail, and the reading desk of the *bema* and had mounted on top the lamp required in exactly this position for the flawless reading of the lessons.

If the four holes at the southern side of the Torah Shrine can thus properly be said to mark the position of a raised wooden *bema* with lampstand, the two at the northern side are enigmatic. One might expect here either the "chair of Moses" or "chair of Elijah," but two holes seem scarcely sufficient to anchor the legs of such a piece of furniture.[5]

In the monumental Torah Shrine at the center of the west wall of the Synagogue there undoubtedly stood during the life of the building as its most sacred treasure an *aron* or Scroll Chest. It must have been of the portable variety, and thus in all probability also made of wood. Scroll Chests of the portable type, reproduced on gold glass, in catacomb paintings, on stone surfaces, and in mosaics, taking the forms of ancient chests generally, are commonly either square, peaked, or round

---

2. Winter and Pernice, *Die hellenistische Kunst in Pompeji*, IV (1925), pp. 43–57, Figs. 53–74.

3. On the *bema* see, among others, Krauss, *Synagogale Altertümer*, pp. 384–387; *Jewish Encyclopedia*, I (1907), pp. 430f.; Sukenik, *Ancient Synagogues in Palestine and Greece*, p. 57.

4. For the wooden *bemas* of old Palestinian synagogues, see J. Pinkerfeld, *Synagogues in the Land of Israel* (in Hebrew) (Jerusalem, 1946), Figs. 53, 56, 64, 65. The famous *bema* of the sixth century of our era in the al-Hayyat Mosque at Aleppo may well be a stone copy of such a small wooden *bema*, as the columnar supports of its platform suggest. A drawing of the Aleppo *bema* is conveniently accessible in Sukenik, *Ancient Synagogues in Palestine and Greece*, p. 58, Fig. 17.

5. On the "chair of Moses" see *ibid.*, pp. 57–61; and Krauss, *Synagogale Altertümer*, pp. 386–388.

at the top.[6] It may be entirely idle to speculate about the type used at Dura, yet it is obvious that a rounded-headed chest would have been more appropriate to the architectural form of the Synagogue's Torah Shrine, and it may well be that in the shape normally given to the Ark of the Covenant in the paintings we have a close approximation of the shape of the Synagogue's Scroll Chest.[7]

From a relatively early time there is mention in rabbinic sources of draperies used to screen the sacred Scroll Chests from casual inspection. The analogy is, of course, to the veil which in the Temple of Solomon separated off the Holy of Holies and hid the Ark of the Covenant. We have already seen how careful the Synagogue artists were in supplying curtains at the proper places in the representation of the Wilderness Tabernacle (Panel WB 2), and in covering the Scroll Chest with a red veil in the picture of Ezra reading the Law (Wing Panel III). There is good evidence to show that the elders of the Synagogue were equally careful in providing the proper appointments for the Scroll Chest in the Torah Shrine of the building. The first piece of evidence comes from the façade of the Torah Shrine itself (Fig. 73). It consists of four holes, each about a centimeter in diameter and at least equally deep, let into the surface of the crowning member near the top of the field with the pictorial decorations. Two of the holes appeared at the upper right in the blue background beside the tent in the scene of the Sacrifice of Isaac (Pl. XVI). The other two appeared in the opposite corner of the field, above and upon one of the lamps of the golden Menorah. The last two mentioned were also broken out, indicating that whatever they held had been violently removed when the building was dismantled.

It seems a likely inference that the holes were associated with the mounting of a veil hiding the Scroll Chest from view. The veil in this case was not a piece of cloth placed over and upon the Scroll Chest, but a curtain hanging straight down and

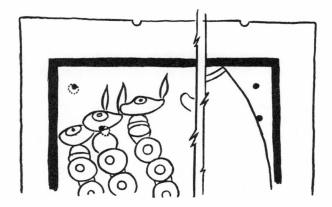

FIG. 73. Position of Holes in Torah Shrine Façade

screening the front of the niche in which the Chest stood. This is in accord with the statements of the sources about the function of the פריסא, a word used especially in the Babylonian Talmud in place of the more common Biblical *paroketh*.[8] It is somewhat difficult to visualize the way in which a simple curtain could have been hung with the help of the four holes mentioned, especially when those at the left side of the façade are not in a straight line vertically. Palmyrene funerary reliefs frequently show such simple veils or curtains, and in one instance at least indicate that they are hung from two round-headed pins.[9] But it is not probable that such veils could be moved. Rabbinical sources speak of veils or curtains being "rolled up" on "staves" with the help of woolen or linen cords.[10] We should therefore probably imagine that in the Synagogue the veil with its rod attached at the lower end was fastened to the Torah Shrine by dowels or pins set into the lower of the two holes on either side. The cords by which it was rolled up, coming down behind the veil, could then have run up in front through rings or eyelets set in the upper holes on either side, from where their ends could have been made con-

6. On ancient chests generally, see Budde, *Armarium und Kibotos*. For Torah Shrines on gold glass, see Garrucci, *Storia della arte cristiana*, VI, Pl. 490, Figs. 1–6; Sukenik, *Ancient Synagogue of Beth Alpha*, Pl. I,a, and p. 31, Fig. 35. For Torah Shrines on stone, see Kohl and Watzinger, *Antike Synagogen*, p. 40, Fig. 76 (Capernaum); I. Ben-Zevil, *Palestine Exploration Fund, Quarterly Statement*, 1930, pp. 213f. and Pl. II, Fig. 2, opp. p. 215; and Maisler, *Beth She'arim*, Pl. XXXIII. For Torah Shrines in mosaics, see Sukenik, *Ancient Synagogue of Beth Alpha*, Pl. VIII, and p. 26, Fig. 27.

7. See Panels WB 2, WB 4, and NB 1, and the discussion of the decorations on the façade of the Torah Shrine, above p. 60.

8. See Krauss, *Synagogale Altertümer*, pp. 380f.

9. Cantineau, *Inventaire des inscriptions de Palmyre*, VIII (1932), pp. 20f.

10. Krauss, *op. cit.*, pp. 379f.

veniently accessible to those officiating at the Shrine (see Fig. 73). It was noted when the building was excavated that on the right (northerly) column of the Torah Shrine in a zone several centimeters wide the paint was unusually well preserved, as though something had once encircled the column at this point, protecting its surface from light and wear. Conceivably whatever it was that went around the column provided an anchorage for the ends of the cords when the veil was pulled up.

For our knowledge of the appointments in the area of the Torah Shrine still further information is available. It is supplied by sundry bits of evidence that came to light on the top and the sides of the Shrine and on the surface of the Lower Center Panel just above it. Atop the crowning member of the Torah Shrine's facade there are to be seen two small channels gouged into its outer edge at either side and shown on Fig. 73. On the horizontal upper face of this same member, immediately alongside the channels, two sockets for poles are visible, with the plaster that set the poles in place still marked with the grain of their wood. In the Lower Center Panel there is, in addition to one area where the plaster has broken away entirely, a large number of holes drilled in the wall, some of which must be connected with the embellishment of the Torah Shrine. The sides of the Torah Shrine again, though clearly visible from the benches, were found never to have been decorated, but marked with spots of paint that had dropped down from above when the murals were being executed. Clearly, then, the Torah Shrine had an over-all ornamental and protective covering that completed it at the top and lessened the awkward angular effect of a crowning member rising above the body of the aedicula to which it belongs (Pl. XL, 2). This covering must have been a baldachin (כילה) of the type mentioned in rabbinical sources.[11]

It is somewhat difficult, if not impossible, to reconstruct from the holes drilled in the plaster of the Lower Center Panel the form and arrangement of the baldachin anchored in them. The difficulty here is that the entire surface of the panel is pockmarked with holes, some representing the emplacement of the gilt rosettes applied originally to the tree in the first phase of the chamber's decoration, others representing the mounting of the baldachin when the Synagogue was first dedicated, and still others representing the remounting of the baldachin after the completion of the second phase of its decoration.[12]

The distinction between the last and the first two is that between holes in which the white plaster is clearly visible and holes painted red when the area was prepared to receive the new scenes in the second phase of the chamber's decoration.[13] (For the latter, see the overlay of Pl. XXXIV.) Neither set provides a convincing design, no doubt because of a variety of factors — mistakes, repairs, changes of organization — which we cannot control.

For a tentative reconstruction of the Synagogue's baldachin, we have therefore to fall back upon two complementary pieces of information. The first is supplied by representations of Torah Shrines on gold glass, on stone, and on mosaic pavements, the other by another feature of the Lower Center Panel area.[14] Many of the details of these representations that have hitherto been regarded as elements of the superstructure of scroll chests do on closer examination in the light of the Dura Synagogue problem reveal themselves as elements of jewel-studded baldachins. These are sometimes rounded but more often peaked, and normally have the curtains descending from them thrown back or pulled away from the front of the chest.[15] The second piece of information is supplied by two

11. Krauss, *Synagogale Altertümer*, p. 381. It is said to be mentioned especially in Palestinian sources. For a discussion of the baldachin in the history of art, see Bratschkova, "Die Muschel," pp. 18–30.

12. See above, pp. 63, 216.

13. See above, p. 221.

14. Modern and mediaeval Torah Curtains, representing under the name *Paroketh* rather an elaborated form of the inner "veil" moved sidewise rather than rolled upward, are of no assistance in this particular. See the excellent article of F. Landsberger, *Hebrew Union College Annual*, XIX (1945–1946), pp. 353–387.

15. Because of the curving lines I am inclined to regard the crowning elements of the scroll chest representations in Garrucci, *Storia della arte cristiana*, VI, Pl. 480, nos. 3 and 6 and on the gold glass at Berlin (Sukenik, *Ancient Synagogue of Beth Alpha*, Pl. I, a) as inspired by baldachins attached to a Torah Shrine with heavy round-headed studs, rather than as pediments of scroll chests. Garrucci nos. 1 and 2 would reflect more heavily studded and bejeweled baldachins of a rounded shape. The dots over the scroll chest in the Na'aran mosaic (Sukenik, *op. cit.*, p. 26, Fig. 27) might be a reminiscence of the same installation.

diagonal strips on the surface of the Lower Center Panel along which the paint has been disturbed and which meet at a point close to the middle of the field.[16] They can well have resulted from the application of the cloth of the baldachin to the surface of the panel before the paint had dried entirely, and from the consequent absorption of some of the paint by the cloth.[17] In this case it would appear that the baldachin added to the Torah Shrine a prismatic superstructure whose upper edge met the surface of the west wall just below the Lion of Judah on the Lower Center Panel (Pl. XL, 2).[18] From the upper part of the baldachin two curtains must have been suspended, covering the unpainted but paint-spotted sides of the Torah Shrine and simultaneously also its entire front. The forward part of the curtains could have been opened upwards and outwards by cords attached to their edges at a proper distance from the top and running up over the crowning member of the Torah Shrine in the channels still visible there.[19]

It is a disturbing feature of the arrangements suggested, both for the inner veil and the outer curtain, that they conceal parts of the painted surfaces we would expect to remain exposed to full view. This is either a matter in which our modern expectations are not in accord with the point of view of the Synagogue community of Dura, or one in which we have the results of poor coördination between those who were responsible for the artistic embellishment and for the proper liturgical appointments of the building. In either event the application of these appointments to the Torah Shrine not only improves its appearance but adds a significant fact to our understanding of its character. With the baldachin added, the Torah Shrine

16. Overlay of Pl. XXXIV.

17. The repainting of the Lower Center Panel was in all probability among the last of the operations undertaken by the Synagogue artist. See above, pp. 220 f. Similar marks and abrasions above the major diagonal lines would on this suggestion merely represent further temporary contact of the cloth with the not fully dried surface, produced in the process of mounting the baldachin.

18. Pl. XL, 2 shows the result of several efforts to mount a baldachin experimentally upon the Torah Shrine of the Synagogue as rebuilt in the National Museum at Damascus. Other arrangements were less satisfactory. The material used in the experiments was common burlap.

19. The picture shows the curtains pulled back and is deficient only in not indicating also the veil that remained under the curtains and was rolled up separately and vertically.

17*

is transformed into an example of just such structures as are represented in Panel WB 1 (Wilderness Encampment and the Miraculous Well of Be'er), whether the tents of the Twelve Tribes or the Wilderness Tabernacle itself.[20] Quite possibly this similarity is not unintentional, especially since we have found so many points at which the imagery of the paintings and furnishings of the Synagogue, so far as we can know them, bear close resemblance to each other.

Under the baldachin in the Scroll Chest set in the Torah Shrine, reposed the sacred scrolls of the Law and the Prophets. These were naturally removed for safe-keeping when the building was evacuated, and no trace of them has, or could have been expected to, come to light in the excavations. In the fill of Wall Street, however, more precisely in Section W8 behind the neighboring Block L8, a piece of parchment was discovered in 1932 which may have some relation to the furnishings of the Synagogue (Pg. 25).[21] The text, written in Hebrew, is related in content to the Birkat ha-Mazon, but according to Torrey should not be regarded either as a prayer or as a "liturgical" document. His suggestion is that what we have in the parchment is a fragment of a tract on the eating of animal food, and that it may have been prepared for use in the Jewish school of Dura. If so, it may have belonged to the materials used in the Synagogue, though kept in the Elder's residence or the school room. His translation is as follows:

Blessed is our God, the Eternal King. . . .
a portion of food He appointed. . . . .
the children of men. Cattle . . . .
He created man to eat of . . . .
carcasses innumerable of . . . .
blessing (?) them all, cattle . . . .
. . . .
[cl]ean . . . .
. . providing . . . .
. . both small and great . . . .
. . . . all beasts of the field . . . .
. . . . . . to eat their carcasses . . . .
. . . . and we kill (?) . . . .

20. So already on other grounds, Landsberger, *Hebrew Union College Annual*, XIX (1945–1946), p. 360.

21. See C. B. Welles in *Münchener Beiträge*, XIX (1934), p. 395, no. 2 (DPg. 25); Torrey in *Rep. VI*, pp. 417–419; and Du Mesnil du Buisson, *Syria*, XX (1939), pp. 23–34.

To the interior appointments of the Synagogue belong also the benches and the raised seat at the right of the Torah Shrine that were constructed as integral parts of the building. Benches are frequently found in basilical synagogues, but the raised seat superimposed upon them has no parallel in the known monuments.[22] Two synagogues, in Hammath (Gadara) and Delos respectively, have yielded recognizable portions of heavy stone chairs that at one time were parts of their equipment, and undoubtedly served purposes analogous to the raised seat of the Dura building.[23] The chairs have been interpreted as examples of the "seat of Moses," using the term applied to an article of synagogue furniture in the New Testament (Matt. 23.2). At Dura, however, should the two holes to the north of the suggested location of the *bema* provide for the emplacement of a wooden chair or bench, we would need to distinguish between two especially prepared seats and the question is: to which of them would the term "seat of Moses" be more properly applicable?

It has long since been suggested by Du Mesnil du Buisson that the raised seat atop the benches at Dura was occupied by Samuel, the builder of the Synagogue, and that for this reason his namesake is represented in the scene of Samuel annointing

David just above.[24] While this can scarcely be regarded as a sufficient motivation for the allocation of the painting, it does fit the situation in one particular. Samuel was the "elder" of the Synagogue, and his eldership was in some sense eponymous for the community, as the building inscription indicates (Inscr. no. **1**). At the same time we know that elders in synagogues sat with their faces to the congregation and with their backs to the *aron* or Scroll Chest.[25] We should, therefore, probably be correct in supposing that Samuel as "elder" sat beside the Torah Shrine, near but slightly above any others who were archons with him. For this reason we have preferred to call the raised seat the Elder's Seat rather than the "seat of Moses." The latter term could as well apply to a chair from which instruction was given and the lessons were expounded, and to a chair with that function a position on or near the *bema* was more appropriate.[26] Of the two seats especially prepared in the Dura Synagogue, the raised seat, then, provided for the leader of the congregation and community, the other possibly for a special participant in the worship services. Naturally this distinction would not have prevented Samuel, if he chose to do so, from taking part in the services of worship.

24. Du Mesnil du Buisson, *Peintures*, pp. 92, 127, followed by Grabar, "Le Thème," pp. 175 f.

25. Tosephtah to Megillah IV, 21 (ed. Zuckermandel, p. 227, 10–11); see also Krauss, *Synagogale Altertümer*, p. 393.

26. For the fact that exposition in worship services was given seated, see Luke 4.20. For an entirely different suggestion about the meaning of the term "seat of Moses," see C. Roth, *Palestine Exploration Fund, Quarterly Statement*, 1949, pp. 100–111.

22. For the benches in the basilical synagogues, see Kohl and Watzinger, *Antike Synagogen*, Pls. II, IV, VII, and VIII; and Sukenik, *Ancient Synagogue of el-Hammeh*, pp. 32–34.

23. Drawings of the stone chairs are conveniently accessible in Sukenik, *Ancient Synagogues in Palestine and Greece*, pp. 59–61, Figs. 18, 19.

INSCRIPTIONS

I. THE ARAMAIC TEXTS

Among the epigraphic materials that came to light in the rooms of the two successive Synagogues of Dura and were identifiable as writing, rather than mere scratches or crude drawings, there are twenty-two Aramaic texts. The most important of these is the building inscription (Inscr. no. **1**), which was recorded on three ceiling tiles. Of the others, the great majority was found on the walls of the building or on fallen fragments of their plaster coating. The texts include several interesting epigraphical specimens, particularly Inscr. no. **4**, but also Inscr. no. **2** and certain of the graffiti in the group between Inscrs. nos. **12** and **22**. Inscrs. nos. **4**, **6**, and **17** contain important examples of the Mesopotamian Jewish dialect, the texts showing the actual pronunciation. The originals of Inscrs. nos. **12–22**, belonging to the earlier Synagogue, have unfortunately been lost, under circumstances concerning which there is little information and over which the excavators had no control. The loss is compensated for by the excellent copies which had been made by Du Mesnil du Buisson when they were discovered, and which are faithfully reproduced in the present publication.

A. The Building Inscription

The building inscription (Inscr. no. **1**), already the object of no little discussion, gives the date of the later building, the names of those who had charge of the work, and some additional information. It is recorded in a long, a short, and an intermediate form (Inscrs. nos. **1a**, **1b**, and **1c** on three ceiling tiles, here designated Tiles A, B, and C respectively).

Tile A (Pl. XLI, 1) contains the greater part of the long form of the inscription; namely, the first fourteen lines of its text. The tile was badly broken when found; but the several fragments have been skilfully joined, and no part of the text appears to have been hopelessly lost by reason of this breakage. The entire inscription was painted in black with a brush. Some parts of the text that had been distinct at first, when the tiles were first brought to light at Dura, faded out almost immediately. By the time the tiles reached New Haven very much of the text had become indistinct, while also the surface of the tiles was gradually deteriorating. Excellent photographs were promptly made by Dr. Toll; and through the use of infra-red photography much that had been nearly, or quite, invisible was brought back. Even so, a large part of the text remains illegible, the writing of lines 10–13, for instance, being more than half obliterated.

Tile B (Pl. XLI, 2), containing eight lines, continues the long form of the inscription to its end. On this tile more than half of the text originally written has completely vanished, and it is only by good fortune that the few words that can be read are such as to give some idea of what the text was intended to say.

Tile C (Pl. XLII, 1–2) contains merely two copies of the first part of the inscription, corresponding to the first five and the first seven lines on Tile A and giving the short and the intermediate forms of the text. As will be seen, one of the copies (Inscr. no. **1b**) is a graffito, very lightly traced but almost completely legible; the other, painted in black (Inscr. no. **1c**), is imperfectly preserved.

The language of the building inscription is of a pure type of Jewish Aramaic with no unusual features. The orthography is that of the rabbinical writings, with great use of the vowel letters *waw* and (especially) *yodh*. The letters of the alphabet are rapidly drawn but well formed, and are plainly the work of a skilled hand. *Waw* and *yodh* are generally simple perpendicular strokes, and often are distinguishable from each other only by context; but where they are in juxtaposition, *yodh* is made shorter. Occasionally the one or the other has a hook or barb at the top, as in the name "Samuel" in line 7 on Tile A or (both characters) at the beginning of line 8. *Nūn* may closely resemble *waw*, but in such cases there is always in some part of the letter a more or less distinct curve to the left; thus, for example, in the first word of line 1 and in the middle of line 6, just before the *aleph*. *Hē* and *ḥēth* are made precisely alike; see, for example, the second line on Tile A. *Daleth* and *rēsh* are regularly distinguished from each other as in line 5. *Zayin* is made like *waw*, as in the word at the end of the sixth line. *Gimel* appears three times: near the end of line 6, at the beginning of line 8, and in the first word of line 5 in Tile B. *Ṭēth*, the regularly formed "square" character, occurs once, near the end of line 10 on Tile A. The only letter of the alphabet which is not found in the portions of the inscription that have been preserved is *ṣadhē*.

Since the text has so many wide gaps, while the letters or parts of letters that remain are often indistinct or ambiguous, there is great temptation to conjecture, and the interpreters will differ, often widely. The decipherment has indeed been a slow process thus far, and is certainly not yet complete.

The first attempt to present the text of any portion of the building inscription was made by Prof. J. J. Obermann in 1936 in a brief note contributed to *Rep. VI*.[1] This offered a tentative text of the first seven lines, with a translation giving the well-assured date of the building and the clearly written names of three of the leaders, but making no claims to have permanent value beyond these few items. It was a mere *prodromos*, intended to serve until closer study, with more adequate material, should make possible a thoroughgoing interpretation of the entire document. My own preliminary attempt, published in 1938 under the title "The Beginning of the Dura Synagogue Inscription," while perhaps a slight improvement over Obermann's, was nevertheless a failure.[2] Both Obermann and I misinterpreted (in different ways) three or four fragmentary or obliterated characters, of which the true reading is now furnished by Tile C, at that time quite unknown to both of us.[3]

1. Pp. 389f.
2. *Jewish Quarterly Review*, n.s. XXVIII (1938), pp. 295–299.
3. The inscriptions of Tile C came to light only when the painted floral decoration with which they were overlaid flaked off while the object was being transported.

Obermann's final publication appeared in 1942 under the title "Inscribed Tiles from the Synagogue of Dura."[4] This is, first of all, an elaborate corpus of the epigraphic material: texts, translations, critical notes, facsimile drawings, and four plates; every part of the material is fully described. The investigation includes much more than this, however, the greater part of it being taken up with an excursus in which the wider questions are discussed: the classification of the inscriptions of the Dura Synagogue, both Greek and Aramaic; sanctuary inscriptions in general; the external and internal evidence for successive phases in the history of the building, etc. Since many of these matters lie outside the range of the present discussion, and since some of them are treated elsewhere in this volume, only the epigraphic results will be considered here.[5]

The treatment of the main body — the well-preserved part — of the inscription on Tile A calls for no special comment. There may be argument over a few small details, but in general only agreement. In the fragmentary lines — the part of the inscription where each decipherer makes his own conjectures — two words of lines 9 and 10, on the interpretation of which much depends, have been misunderstood by Obermann. The last legible word in line 9 is *shaddarū*, "they sent," not *Ṭedros*, a personal name. The misreading of a badly smeared letter (*shīn*) had the result of bringing an otherwise unknown and unlikely personage into the number of those who had charge of the work. The last word in line 10 is the verb "they ran," not the noun "beams" or "columns."

The text on Tile B Obermann divorces from the one on Tile A, making it an entirely separate composition. It is interpreted by him as a liturgical text; namely, a prayer for the dead, or the conclusion of such a prayer. At the same time he freely admits the possibility that his reading and interpretation might be "completely mistaken."[6] The little fragments of lines on this tile may indeed lend themselves to various interpretations, and no solution conjectured thus far can claim more than a certain degree of plausibility. But the evidence showing that the text of Tile B is the

4. *Berytus*, VII (1942), pp. 89–138.
5. See below, p. 329, n. 41.
6. *Berytus*, VII (1942), pp. 112–117, especially p. 116.

direct continuation of that of Tile A is compelling, as will appear presently. Obermann himself accepted this conclusion at first, and it is unfortunate that it was afterward abandoned by him.[7]

The inscriptions on Tile C, as they have been variously deciphered and explained, will be discussed presently.

I. TILES A AND B

In the transcription of the Aramaic texts which follows, a dot under a letter indicates that its reading is doubtful. In either text or translation, the use of square brackets indicates that the portion thus enclosed has been obtained by conjecture and rests on no other authority, while double brackets indicate an erasure.

Inscr. no. **1a** is a dipinto on two ceiling tiles found in the embankment inside the House of Assembly of the later Synagogue. The tiles are now in the Yale University Art Gallery (Tile A, 1933.255; Tile B, 1933.256). Tile surfaces *ca.* 0.42 m. × 0.42 m. (standard for all the ceiling tiles of the later Synagogue building). Tile A: fifteen lines of text written with black paint. Letters 0.016 m. –0.028 m. high (Pl. XLI, 1); Tile B: nine lines of text in black paint. Letters *ca.* 0.020 m. high (Pl. XLI, 2).

Du Mesnil du Buisson, *CRAI*, 1933, p. 202; *idem*, "Nouvelles découvertes," pp. 556 f.; *Rep. VI*, p. 389; Du Mesnil du Buisson, *Biblica*, XVIII (1937), pp. 163–169 and Pl. IV, 1–4; C. C. Torrey, *Jewish Quarterly Review*, XXVIII (1938), pp. 295–299; Du Mesnil du Buisson, *Peintures*, p. 158, Pl. LIX, 1; J. J. Obermann, *Berytus*, VII (1942), pp. 95–112, Pl. XVI. The above deal only with Tile A. For the only discussion of the text of Tile B, see *ibid.*, pp. 112–117, Pl. XVIII.

556 Seleucid Era   A.D. 244/245

(Tile A)

ה
1   הדין ביתאתבני
2   בשנה חמש מאה חמשין
3   ושית דאינן שנת תרתן לפלפוס

7. See *Rep. VI*, p. 389.

4   ⸢ויוליס⸣] קסר בקשישותה דשמואל
5   כהנה בר ידעי ארכון· ודקמו
6   על עיבידה הדין אברם גיזב־
7   רה ושמואל ⸢בר⸣ ספרה ו .....
8   גיורה· ברוח ⸢מיתרעיה שוין למיבני⸣
9   בשנת שית וחמשין אילין ושדרו ל ..
10   .... ר .. .. ורהטו
11   ..... ב .... תה ועמלו ב ...
12   .... ברכתה מן שביה
13   וכל בני .... עמלו ולאין ...
14   שלמה ⸢ולהון ולנ⸣שיהון ובניהון כלהון·
15   וכשים

(Tile B)

1   וב
2   וכשים כלהון דעמְלוֹ ⸢כך אחיהון⸣ ...
3   .... כלהון דבכספה
4   ובחמידת נפ⸢ושהון⸣
5   אגרהון כלמה .... עלמה ⸢ההבא⸣
6   .... דאתי ה .
7   קימה להון .... שם ....
8   בכל שבת .... פרסיָן ⸢וידיהון⸣
9   בה·

(Tile A) "This house was built in the year 556, this corresponding to the second year of Philip Julius Caesar; in the eldership of the priest Samuel son of Yeda'ya, the Archon. Now those who stood in charge of this work were: Abram the Treasurer, and Samuel son of Sapharah, and ..... the proselyte. With a willing spirit[8] they [began to build] in this fifty-sixth year; and they sent .... and they made haste .... and they labored in .... a blessing from the elders and from all the children of .... they labored and toiled .... Peace to them, and to their wives and children all. (Tile B) And like all those who labored [were their

8. The mention of the "spirit" in which these leaders undertook their task, and the adjective used to characterize it, were probably intended to remind the reader of the passage in the Targum of Exod. 35.21 ff., the story of the building of the Tabernacle. In that passage, as also in the present inscription (see below), praise is given to those who assisted in the work by their contributions of precious metal and other treasure.

brethren ....], all of them, who with their money .... and in the eager desire of their souls .... Their reward, all whatever .... that the world which is to come ....

.... assured to them .... on every sabbath .... spreading out [their hands] in it (in prayer)."

From these fragments, meager as they are, it is perhaps possible to see the main features of the entire inscription, and the fact that it was a well-constructed and concisely worded document. The loss of a connected text is especially painful in the second part (Tile B), where the few bits that have been preserved are sufficient to show that the original must have been an eloquent and impressive composition.

Tile A: line 1. The letter ה above the line, possibly added by the original hand, is hardly necessary. There is some good reason to think that the text as at first written illustrated a habit of Hebrew scribes which has often been discussed; namely, that they felt free to write but once a letter which is both the final consonant of a given word and the initial consonant of the next following word.[9] Final *ā* is regularly written with ה in this inscription, but in the case here supposed א would serve. The same thing precisely takes place in line 5; see the note there and also the note on line 1 of the intermediate text, Inscr. no. **1c**.

Line 2. Most of the second מ is missing because of the fracture in the tile.

Line 3. The letter nearly obliterated by the chipped surface of the tile was variously guessed at, until the belated appearance of Tile C showed it to

9. On this "habit of Hebrew scribes," see Felix Perles, *Analekten zur Textkritik des Alten Testaments* (1895), p. 44, n. 2, and under the same title, as *Neue Folge* (1922), p. 25, where he gives references to Luzzatto as far back as 1847 and to other scholars; F. Delitzsch, *Die Lese- und Schreibfehler im Alten Testament* (1920), pp. 5, 7, 10 f.: "Denn nach altem Schreiberbrauch wurde dann der Buchstabe nur einmal geschrieben." It is obvious that the juxtaposition of two *alephs* would be especially common in Aramaic texts. I have found five examples of this custom in the Aramaic which underlies the Greek text of the Fourth Gospel. In the passages 4.25; 5.27; 8.56; 11.2; 14.31, the single *aleph* (certainly attested) makes acceptable sense only when it is read twice. See C. C. Torrey, *Our Translated Gospels* (1936), pp. 139, 142, 144, 148.

be *yodh*. The plural of the demonstrative pronoun was unexpected. At the end of the line, where a piece of the tile was broken away, a portion of the ס can be seen in the photograph made before the tile was repaired.

Line 4. The name "Julius" seems to have been purposely obliterated. In the earliest photographs each of the five letters can be distinctly made out.

Line 5. The reading ידעיא ought not to be questioned. Aside from the fact that it is the only form of the name to be expected, there is no other possible reading. The obliterated third letter could only be ע, and its slanting main stroke can be seen in the photographs and on the tile. No one would have questioned this but for the fact that the א is the initial consonant of the following word ארכן. Certainly it is; this seems to be another example of the procedure described above in the note on line 1. If it had not been for this following word, the scribe would have written ידעיה. Here also a ה might have been written above the line for the sake of exactness, but there is no need of supposing any omission.

The word *archon* appears to be treated simply as Greek with no attempt to make it Aramaic (cf. Targum 2, Chron. 28.7). I at one time thought it possible to regard the letter following the crack as *aleph*, but that was before I had seen Tile C, where the same letter appears as *nūn*. And indeed the long vowel (*o*) in the final syllable of this foreign word could not have been left unrepresented. The half-preserved letter in the crack is certainly *waw*, and only one form of the word is attested in these inscriptions.

Line 6. The characters in the middle of the line have been nearly destroyed, but repeated examination of the remaining traces seems to show that the original reading was עיבידה הדין. Secondary marks across the head of the first *daleth* made it resemble a *tau*. The reading of the *bēth* at the end of the line is practically certain, though only a part of the top of the letter can be seen.

Line 7. Among the tiles of the Synagogue which are inscribed in Greek there is one which names Σαμουῆλ Βαρσαφάρα as one of the "founders" of the building (Inscr. no. **24**, see below p. 277). The "Samuel" of this line is evidently the one intended, for the name "Sapharah" is almost entirely preserved, and there is just room for the *bar*, "son."

The name of the father of "Abram the Treasurer" (lines 6 and 7) is not given. This Abram is named on one of the painted tiles inscribed in Greek in a list of those who "assisted" in the building (Inscr. no. **25**, see below p. 278). The strange reading here has made some trouble (see *Rep. VI*, p. 388, and below pp. 278f.). The text reads Ἄβραμ καὶ Ἀρσάχου καὶ Σίλας κὲ Σαλμάνης ἐβοήθησαν. Now Ἀρσάχου is certainly genitive, not nominative. It is a plausible supposition that the painter of the tile was given a list containing merely the names, and that the insertion of the first καί was his mistake. Ἄβραμ Ἀρσάχου would then have been the Greek rendering of אַבְרָם בַּר אַרְשַׁךְ. This transliteration of the royal name (conjectured also by Obermann) makes no difficulty; compare Σῶβαχ for שׁוֹבַךְ in I Chron. 19.16 and 18 (Cod. A) In Syriac the adjective "Arsacid" is regularly written with *kaph*, not *qoph*.

Line 8. The first word, "the proselyte," is clear. Beyond this point conjecture plays a major part, for the greater part of the original text is hopelessly destoyed. The reading "*and* they sent" in the next line shows that another verb had preceded, and that something is being told about the beginning of the actual work of building. "In the year" at the beginning of that same line (9), followed soon by the plain remnants of the words "and fifty" (compare line 2), makes the matter still more certain. The conspicuous *bēth*, the sixth letter in line 8, appears to introduce the new subject.

While it might seem useless to attempt to fill out the line, there are nevertheless two portions of it that can be guessed at with much probability. The word בְּרוּחַ is plainly suggested, since three of the letters are clear, and *rēsh* could easily fill the vacant space after *bēth* (see the *rēsh* four times in lines 7–9). A phrase descriptive of the "spirit" in which the leaders just named began their work would be in place here. Either שְׁלִימָה or מתרעיה might have been suggested by Targ. Exod. 35.21; but the possibilities are numerous. Also it would seem that this eighth line must have contained the words "they began to build." The restoration here conjectured has also the advantage that it fills exactly the given space.

Line 9. After the word וחמשין there is space for five letters, of which the last was certainly *nūn*. The missing word must have been אילין or אינך, "*this* year 56," see line 3. The reading "and they

sent" at the end of the line is certain, though the letter *šīn* is somewhat blurred.

Line 10. The only word which can be made out is at the end of the line. The verb "run," in Aramaic as in Hebrew, is often used to indicate eager haste.

Line 11. "And they labored" is the only sure word, though a number of scattered letters can be identified.

Line 12. Here again it is only the end of the line that has been preserved. It is to be noticed that the author of the inscription wrote שָׂבַיָּא "elders," with *sīn*, as the word appears in the Aramaic of Ezra and in the Elephantine Letters. The ב in the word is clear, not at all like מ; the horizontal base line extended to the right (see Pl. XLI,1) makes the reading quite certain.

Line 13. The fourth letter in the line looks most like *bēth*, because of the form of the top; *kaph* is possible, however, and Obermann, reading thus, plausibly conjectures כנישתה[. At the end of the line the second verb can only be לאין, even though the last letter cannot be made out.

Line 14. The word שלמה is certain, and so are the words which make up the second half of the line, the last one of them running uphill. The line can be restored with certainty, with its "peace upon them and their wives and children all," by inserting ועליהן ולנשיהון, the nine letters in brackets just filling the vacant space.

Line 15. This "line," if I am not mistaken, consists of only five letters, whose province is to make the immediate connection with the second part of the inscription, contained in Tile B. In my first study of the inscriptions I was struck by what seemed to be a device for showing that the text of Tile B is the continuation of the text of Tile A. Further study confirmed this, though the writing on the tiles is not easily legible. At the bottom of Tile A is written the first word of the main inscription on Tile B, while at the top of the latter is seen the indication to the reader that its text is a continuation (see below and Fig. 74). The word which stands at the beginning of line 15 is וכשים. The second letter is distinct and yet puzzling, as it is also at the beginning of line 2 in Tile B, where it was evidently written by the same hand.

Tile B: line 1. This consists merely of the two letters וב, "And the second (part)." Both letters are quite distinct, and the *waw* has the hook or barb at the top which the writer of this inscription so frequently uses.

Line 2. The reading of the first word is difficult. It is followed by כלהן, after which the writing is almost entirely obliterated. The first letter in the line is *waw*, with the usual hook at the top (see

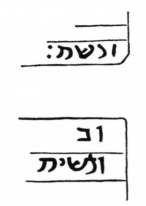

FIG. 74. Inscr. No. **1a**, Detail

Fig. 74). The second letter looks something like *nūn* (which would hardly be possible here), but is more like *kaph*, with its regular curve. Observe that in Obermann's facsimile drawing of Tile A (*op. cit.*, p. 96) the letter is clearly *kaph*. At the top of the letter is a short horizontal mark which might be accidental, but looks intentional. Very possibly it was added in order to make the reading of the *kaph* certain. The reading וכשים, "and like," appears to be just what is required here. The context shows that the third word in the line, now illegible, must have been דעמלו: "And like all those *who toiled*, so also [were their brethren in Dura] all those who with their money..." A single letter, *hē* or *ḥēth*, appears in the second half of the line, and this might be a letter in אחיהון — a mere guess.

Line 3. "All of them who with money..." The reading is clear, except that the *d* which stands for the relative pronoun is wanting (though there is space for it), and that the *h* at the end is indistinct. The rest of the line is obliterated.

Line 4. Here again the beginning of the line is legible, while the rest is lost. The reading of the first six letters shows that we have here a literary phrase taken from Targ. Isa. 26.8. The word *naphshehōn*, "their souls," must be conjectured, though the initial letter, *nūn*, is perhaps clear enough.

Line 5. The first half of the line appears to present no difficulty as far as the decipherment is concerned, though the seventh letter might possibly be *mēm*, or even *bēth*. In the second half of the line near the end the word *'almah*, "world," seems plain; and in the remaining space may be supplied ההוא, the continuation of the familiar phrase "that world which is to come" being supplied by the word at the beginning of line 6 — the only word which can be made out in that line.

Line 7. קימה להן, "assured to them," is a possible decipherment of the indistinct characters, and nothing more plausible suggests itself. Near the end of the line several letters appear more or less distinctly, but no word has thus far been made out.

Line 8. The line begins with the phrase "on every sabbath." In the second half of the line the two letters רס are distinct. Since the suffixed pronoun at the beginning of line 9 presumably refers to the Synagogue, it is tempting to conjecture that the two letters named belong to some form of the verb פרס, which is so often used in the phrase "spreading out the hands in prayer." This is mere conjecture and very possibly wrong; if it is right, there are several ways in which the clause could have been worded. In this much-used phrase, "the hands" is often omitted, and this is true also of "in prayer." A good example of the omission of both words is Targ. I Sam. 9.13. In our inscription there is plenty of room for one of the words at the end of the line.

Line 9. The two noticeably large letters at the beginning seem to mark the end of the main inscription. Something more was written in this line, in smaller characters and perhaps by another hand. No plausible guess at what this may have contained has thus far been made.

The lower half of the tile contained no writing and had always been blank.

2. TILE C

Tile C, as was said above, contains two inscriptions, a graffito and a dipinto, each of them copied from the beginning of the inscription on Tile A. The manner of their arrangement may be seen from the accompanying drawing taken from Obermann's publication (Fig. 75).

The graffito (Inscr. no. **1b**), indicated in the drawing by dots, consists of six lines and reproduces almost exactly the first sentence of Inscr. no. **1a**; namely, the text contained in the first five lines of Tile A. The dipinto (Inscr. no. **1c**), done in ink,

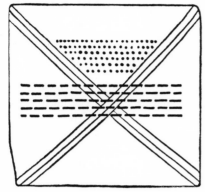

FIG. 75. Plan of Inscrs. Nos. **1b** and **1c**

consists of five lines running the whole width of the tile. It is indicated in the drawing by lines of dashes, and reproduces with some variation the text of the first seven lines of the inscription on Tile A. The position occupied by the dipinto shows that it was preceded on the tile by the graffito; otherwise it certainly would have begun higher up. It is probable that the two inscriptions were made at no great distance from each other in time.

1b. Graffito on a ceiling tile (Tile C) from the fill of the House of Assembly, now in the Yale University Art Gallery (1938.4881). Six lines; letters *ca.* 0.008 m.–0.010 m. high. (Fig. 76, Pl. XLII, 1).

Du Mesnil du Buisson, *Biblica*, XVIII (1937), pp. 163 f., Pl. III; *idem, Peintures*, p. 158, Fig. 109; Obermann, *Berytus*, VII (1942), pp. 93 f., Pl. XVII, 2.

הדין ביתה בני בשנת חמש 1

מאה חמשין ושית דאינין 2

שנת תרתן לפלפוס ק[וסר] 3

בקשישותה דשמו[אל] 4

כהנה בר[ידעיה] 5

ארכ[ון] 6

The variations of this short text from the long form (Inscr. no. **1a**) are such as are incident to reproduction from memory. The following points may be noted. Instead of אתבני, "was built," the graffito has the passive participle בני, treated here as a perfect tense. The proper name "Julius" is omitted; but here it must be remembered that the name is canceled in Tile A (though left barely legible), and the cancelation had probably taken place before this copy was made. Lines 3–6 are partly obliterated at the left: lines 3 and 4 have each lost the last two letters; at the end of the fifth line the name of Jedaiah, the father of Samuel, cannot be made out; in line 6, which consists of the single word ארכן, only the first three letters are distinct. In general the inscription seems to have been somewhat hastily scrawled.

1c. Dipinto on the same tile with the preceding text. Five lines, black ink; letters *ca.* 0.010 m. high (Pl. XLII, 2).

Du Mesnil du Buisson, *Biblica*, XVIII (1937), pp. 163 f.; Obermann, *Berytus*, VII (1942), pp. 94 f., Pl. XVII, 3.

The writing of this dipinto has one curious feature. The crossed ribbon-like bands which appear on the surface of the tile occupy considerable space, and the author of the inscription elected to keep these strips free of writing as far as possible.[10] In fact, he broke his rule but once — in the first line, where otherwise it would have been necessary to cut a word in two (Fig. 77). Accordingly, each of the other lines shows a wide gap, where the writing leaps over the spaces occupied by the

FIG. 76. Inscr. No. **1b**

FIG. 77. Inscr. No. **1c**

bands. This is all the more noticeable because in the similarly marked Tiles A and B the writer of the inscription has paid no attention to the crossed bands. In the transcription the gaps left by the author are indicated by empty parentheses: ( ).

1 הדין בית ( ) אתבני בשנת חמש מאה

2 חמשין ושית ( ) דאינין שנת ⟨תרתן⟩ לפלפ־

3 וס . . . . . קסר ( ) בקשישותה דשמואל

4 כהנה ובר ידעזי ארכון ( ) ודקמו על מלאכתיה כהוניה

5 ואב]רם גיזברה] ( ) ושמואל בר . . . .

The readings which call for comment are the following:

Line 1. It is interesting to see that in this copy, as in the original text, a single *aleph* is made to do double duty in ביתאתבני (see also ידעיארכון in line 4). Compare the notes on lines 1 and 5 of Tile A and Fig. 77.

Line 2. The numeral *tartēn*, "the second year," was carelessly omitted. At the end of the line there is no space for the last two letters of "Philippos," but at the beginning of the next line they can be recognized, the *samekh* being especially clear.

Line 3. Between the וס just mentioned and the word קסר there is plenty of space for the name "Julius," and it is hardly to be doubted that this, and nothing else, occupied the space.

Line 4. The latter half of the line makes difficult and uncertain reading; some letters are rubbed out of shape, others are lost. Instead of the עיבידה of Tile A, the word for "work" seems to be מלאכת (a word much used in the Bible for the work of building the Temple: I Kings 5.30; II Kings 12.12; Ezra 3.8; Neh. 2.16, etc.). The next to the last letter in the line is *kaph*. It has been read as *nūn*, but wrongly; *nūn* never has this form in these documents, but the letter is a very good *kaph* (compare the one in the word *archon*). How to interpret the resulting text is a problem. Employment of the adverb כָּה, "here," is not to be thought of. It is tempting, as a last resort, to conjecture an unfinished כְּהֻנָיה, "the priests." There is room at the end of the line for the remaining letters of this

word, which might have been obliterated; or the careless writer may have forgotten to put them at the beginning of the next line. Presumably Abram the Treasurer and Samuel bar-Sapharah *were* priests.

Line 5. It does not appear that the author of the dipinto finished his task.

It remains to explain Tile C. How did it come to be given the two partial copies of the building inscription? It might be supposed that the repetition of the first sentences was a precaution to guard against the possibility that through some accident to the original text, its important information might be lost to the world and especially to the Jewish people. Some such theory as this must be accepted if the two scrawls are supposed to be the work of responsible persons. The explanation hardly satisfies, however. It does not account for the two inscriptions on the tile, nor for the careless manner of their execution. Neither of the two was finished; the graffito fails to include the names of those who had charge of the work, while the dipinto not only leaves out the numeral of one date but also appears to break off in the middle of a sentence, as if interrupted. The more probable theory, therefore, appears to be that while the tile was lying on the ground it was used for epigraphic exercises by rival artists. The first of the two scratched the opening sentence of the now familiar inscription in the angle formed by the bands on the tile. It was a rather poor performance. His successor undertook to improve on this, using ink and brush and including more of the important information. Like his predecessor, he left the bands on the tile undisturbed. His memory of the original was slightly imperfect, and he was interrupted before he had quite finished his task. This theory can at least account for all the facts. Nevertheless, the two efforts have given real help to modern interpreters of the inscription, as has been shown. That the two efforts on this tile were not the work of responsible persons appears to be shown by the fact that the tile was straightway painted over and made use of for another purpose. It was only after the whitewash and the floral decorations flaked off from it that the inscriptions came to light.

---

10. On the nature and origin of these bands, found also on other tiles of the Synagogue, see above, p. 41.

B. The Other Inscriptions

2. Graffito on the façade of the aedicula at the left, below the base of the Menorah. Two lines, letters *ca.* 0.01 m. high (Fig 78; Pl. XLII, 3).

Rep. VI, p. 392 (Aramaic graffiti, no. 1); Du Mesnil du Buisson, *Peintures*, p. 161 (no. 16).

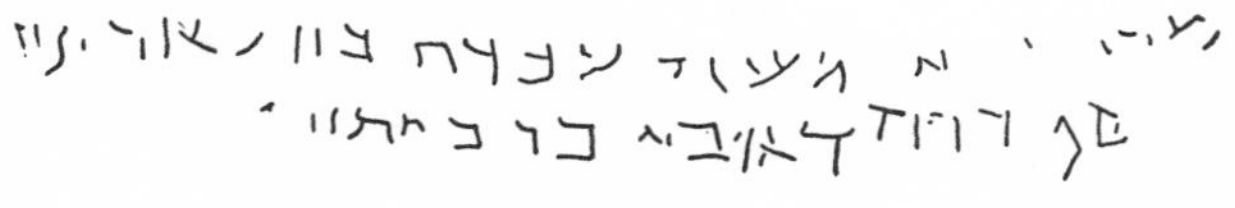

ווירואא /יוז בוד העבע י /א   יעיד
׳יתתיב וב איבאד׳תיו ד ז אא

FIG. 78. Inscr. No. **2**

אנא עזי עבדת בית ארונה ....
מ
ה . . . ב עבד דאבא ברה יוסף

"I, 'Uzzī, made the repository of the Torah Shrine."
"Joseph, son of Abba, made the . . . ."

The two lines appear to have been inscribed at the same time and by the same hand. Kraeling, who discovered the graffito in Damascus, thought that possible traces of letters might be seen in the first line as far to the right as the beginning of the second line, though nothing can be made out distinctly until the first ע (preceded by a somewhat doubtful א). Most of the characters in both lines are well made and distinct. Even so, the present attempt at an interpretation is very precarious.

Line 1. One of the copies gives both *alephs* of the pronoun אנא with space left for the *nun*. The name *'Uzzī* is very common. The horizontal part of the stroke forming the top of the *beth* in the word בית is missing. Of the *waw* of ארונה only a small section is visible in the tracing. The expression בית ארונה, evidently referring to the aedicula upon which the graffito was inscribed, may appear also in an inscription at Nawe published by J. Braslawski.[11]

Line 2. The two letters סף are clear and certain; the *pē* with the little hook at the top is the duplicate of one published in Julius Euting's *Tabula scripturae aramaicae* (1890). On the right Kraeling saw uncertain traces of letters, but recognized the *yodh*; the photograph seems to show also *waw* in

[11] *Jewish Palestine Exploration Society, Bulletin* IV, 1–2 (1936), pp. 8–12 (in Hebrew).

just the right place. The letter which follows is indistinct. It can hardly be anything else than *bēth*, but if so, the bottom stroke is all but obliterated. The name *Abba*, otherwise common, appears elsewhere in the inscriptions from Dura. Traces of the *'ain* in the next word are very slight and uncertain; there is plenty of room for the letter. A series of five to seven letters at the end of the line begins with *mēm* or *bēth* and ends with *hē*. The attempt to identify the intervening characters, each and all of them indistinct, has not thus far been successful.

3. Dipinto on Panel WA 3 between the legs of the first figure of Moses (counting from the right). Four lines, white paint; letters *ca.* 0.025 m.–0.030 m. high (Fig. 79).

Rep. VI, pp. 395f.; Du Mesnil du Buisson, *Biblica*, XVIII (1937), pp. 154f., Fig. 1; *idem*, *Peintures*, p. 159 (no. 7).

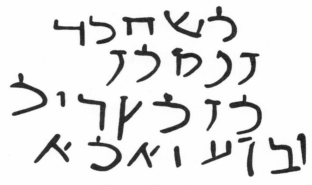

FIG. 79. Inscr. No. **3**

משה כד | נפק מן | מן מצרים | ובזע לאמה

"Moses, when he went out from Egypt and cleft the sea."

The inscription occupies the space between Moses' right foot and the tassel which hangs from his robe. The Aramaic letters are interesting in form and carefully made. The preposition *min*, "from," is repeated, evidently as the result of some error. Apparently the artist who painted the inscription intended to arrange the words in three lines, but miscalculated the space in the first line. The letters in the last line are quite indistinct at the bottom (and there has been progressive deterioration, see below), but the reading is certain.

The verb *bĕzaʿ* is regularly used for this "cleaving" of the Red Sea in the Aramaic texts; see not only the Targums of Exod. 14.16, 21, but also Psalm 78.13 and Isa. 63.12.

The reading אמא "sea," is interesting and important. It is found also in the abbreviated form of the inscription dealing with this same scene which occurs in another place; see Inscr. no. **5** below. It represents the Babylonian-Mesopotamian pronunciation of the word which in Palestine and the western lands was spoken and written as יָם. This could have been known at any time since the publication of the *Additamenta ad librum Aruch Completum*, edited by Samuel Krauss and others (Vienna, 1937). On p. 425, Prof. Louis Ginzberg, discussing אמא, אם, demonstrates the dialectic form in both the Aramaic and the Hebrew of Babylonia, showing especially that the אַמָּה, "pond, lake, etc." of the Babylonian Talmud, is a feminine form of (western) יָם, corresponding perfectly in its use to Syriac *yammĕthā*.

The phonetic habit thus illustrated is familiar in the Assyrian and Syriac languages, in which the open palatal consonant, English *y*, is very sparingly employed. The dialectic peculiarity has other examples in the Dura inscriptions: thus, *Iddaʿya* (Εἰδδαίας on one of the Greek tiles, Inscr. no. **24** below), אדעיה for *Yedaʿya*, יְדַעְיָה, Jedaiah; also ארמיה (Inscr. no. **17**, below) for ירמיה, Jeremiah; compare the Syriac from of the name, Ēramyā, apparently identical with the eastern Jewish form. The Babylonian Jews, as a matter of course, employed the classical orthography in their written Hebrew, while retaining their own pronunciation. As a result, their use of a Mesopotamian dialect could not be proven, and remained virtually unknown to modern scholars. Even in the Talmud, be it noted, there is an example of a Biblical name written as it was pronounced with initial *aleph* instead of *yodh*. In Baba Meṣīʿā, 39b, a Babylonian Jew of the fourth century bears the name מרי בר איסק. Doubtless the name "Isaac" was always thus pronounced in that region, though of course written in the usual way, יִשְׂחָק.

4. Dipinto on Panel WA 3 to the left of the head of the second figure of Moses. One line, bluish-white paint; letters *ca.* 0.020 m.–0.026 m. high (Fig. 80).

Rep. VI, pp. 345, 391 (Aramaic dipinti, no. 1); Du Mesnil du Buisson, *Biblica*, XVIII (1937), pp. 154f., Fig. 2; *idem*, *Peintures*, p. 159 (no. 7).

FIG. 80. Inscr. No. **4**

משה

"Moses"

The middle consonant of the name is almost obliterated.

5. Dipinto on Panel WA 3 to the left of the head of the third figure of Moses. Two lines, light blue paint; letters *ca.* 0.018 m.–0.028 m. high (Fig. 81).

Rep. VI, pp. 346, 391 (Aramaic dipinti, no. 2); Du Mesnil du Buisson, *Biblica*, XVIII (1937), pp. 154f., Fig. 3; *idem*, *Peintures*, p. 159 (no. 7), Fig. 110.

FIG. 81. Inscr. No. **5**

משה כד בזןוע | לאמא

"Moses, when he cleft the sea"

All of the first line is distinct as far as the letter *bēth*, after which there is a break in the plaster. The word בזע seems certain (cf. Inscr. no. **3**), but the *zayin* is nearly or quite lost, and the *ʿain* is hardly clear.

Regarding the אַמָּ of the eastern dialect for western יַמָּא, see the comment on Inscr. no. **3** above. Because of the belief that the word must begin with *yodh*, Du Mesnil du Buisson wished to read יאמא (!), but in the original painting and the oldest photographs of Inscr. no. **5** enough of the foot of the *lamedh* is visible to make the reading certain.[12] On the other hand, some later photographs show only the upright shaft of the letter.

6. Dipinto on Wing Panel I, to the right of Moses at the level of his shoulder. Two lines, white paint; letters *ca.* 0.02 m.–0.023 m. high (Fig. 82).

Rep. VI, p. 391 (Aramaic dipinti, no. 3); Du Mesnil du Buisson, *Biblica*, XVIII (1937), p. 159, Fig. 4; *idem, Peintures*, p. 42, Fig. 36, and p. 160, no. 8.

FIG. 82. Inscr. No. **6**

משה בר | לֵוִי

"Moses, son of Levi"

The letters in the second line are very indistinct, but the above reading seems the only possible one, emphasizing the priestly origin of Moses. Du Mesnil du Buisson gives this reading in his article in *Biblica*; but in his *Peintures* (p. 42) he has inserted also the name *Amram* — strangely, for on the wall (as Kraeling insists) there are no traces of an additional name.

7. Dipinto on Panel WC 1 on the rail of Elijah's bed. One line, brown paint; letters *ca.* 0.015 m. high (Fig. 83).

Rep. VI, pp. 363, 391 (Aramaic dipinti, no. 9); Du Mesnil du Buisson, *Biblica*, XVIII (1937), pp. 161f., Fig. 6; *idem,* "Les Peintures," p. 177; *idem, Peintures*, p. 115, Fig. 83, and p. 160 (no. 11).

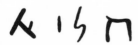

FIG. 83. Inscr. No. **7**

הליא

"Elijah"

The writing of the name with initial *hē* instead of *aleph* is noticeable. The *lamedh* has a form familiar in both Aramaic and Iranian of about this period.

8. Dipinto on Panel WC 2 under the belly of Mordecai's horse. One line, reddish-purple paint (Fig. 84).

Rep. VI, pp. 361, 391 (Aramaic dipinti, no. 8); Du Mesnil du Buisson, *Biblica*, XVIII (1937), pp. 160f., Fig. 5; *idem, Peintures*, p. 120, Fig. 88, and p. 160 (no. 12).

FIG. 84. Inscr. No. **8**

מורדכי

"Mordecai"

The letters are indistinct and partly obliterated.

9. Dipinto on Panel WC 2, on the third step of Ahasuerus' throne. One line, reddish-purple paint (Fig. 85).

Rep. VI, pp. 361, 391 (Aramaic dipinti, no. 6); Du Mesnil du Buisson, *Biblica*, XVIII (1937), pp. 160f., Fig. 5; *idem, Peintures*, p. 120, Fig. 88, and p. 160 (no. 12).

FIG. 85. Inscr. No. **9**

חשהורש

"Ahasuerus"

Thus the dipinto is transcribed by Du Mesnil du Buisson; see also *Rep. VI*, p. 361, and the presumption is therefore strong that this is the correct reading. There are grave reasons for questioning it, however. The letter ה is very strange here, indeed quite inexplicable. The local pronunciation of the

---

12. Thus in the photograph published by Du Mesnil du Buisson in *Biblica, l.c.,* p. 168a, Pl. I, the *lamedh* is unmistakable; no one who looks at it could question it. So also in Pl. XVIII of his *Peintures.*

royal name was obtained, in any case, from memory of the public reading; and this could give no suggestion of an extra syllable. The written form to be expected at Dura would unquestionable be חשוירוש(א). In all the Biblical passages the chief accent in the name is on the long *ō* of the final syllable; it is hardly conceivable that the *waw* could have been omitted in a transcription so loaded with the vowel letters. As for the syllable *wĕ*, also sure to be written *plene*, a slight rub across the tops of its two characters could easily produce the semblance of the letter *hĕ*. The somewhat unusual form of the supposed letter (see also the facsimile in *Biblica*, p. 160) adds to the probability that we should read here the two letters וי rather than the one letter ה.

How to interpret the complex of badly rubbed brush strokes which follow is a problem. That which was entrusted to the painter to transcribe must have been רו. If ור was written, as Du Mesnil du Buisson decides, it would seem that the painter blundered. There is at all events good reason to interpret the inscription as חשוירוש.

10. Dipinto on Panel WC 2 under Esther's footstool. One line, reddish-purple paint (Fig. 86).

Rep. VI, pp. 362, 391 (Aramaic dipinti, no. 7); Du Mesnil du Buisson, *Biblica*, XVIII (1937), pp. 160f., Fig. 5; *idem*, *Peintures*, p. 120, Fig. 88, and p. 160 (no. 12).

FIG. 86. Inscr. No. **10**

אסטיר

"Esther"

A good illustration of the fact that the proper names in the Dura inscriptions are not copied from sacred scripture, but transcribed from the current pronunciation. The Biblical form in this case is אֶסְתֵּר; see Inscr. no. **7** above.

11. Dipinto on Panel WC 3 to the left of Samuel at the level of his shoulder. Two lines, brown paint (except last word in first line, where lighter brown is used); letters *ca.* 0.01 m.–0.02 m. high (Fig. 87).

Rep. VI, pp. 361, 391 (Aramaic dipinti, no. 5); Du Mesnil du Buisson, *Biblica*, XVIII (1937), pp. 160–162; Fig. 5; *idem*, *Peintures*, pp. 126f., Fig. 94, and p. 160 (no. 13).

FIG. 87. Inscr. No. **11**

שמו[ל] כד
משח [ד]ויד

"Samuel anointing David"

At the time when Du Mesnil du Buisson copied the inscription all the letters were distinct, but since then portions of the text have been obliterated.

It would seem that in the popular pronunciation the usual phonetic development had taken place, *Shămŭ'ēl* becoming *Shămūwēl*, for there is not room for an *aleph*.

A later reader, choosing to read בר instead of כד, inscribed at the left (in a different color) the name חנה, making the line read, "Samuel, son of Hannah" (I Sam. 1.20). Du Mesnil du Buisson takes account of this in his *Peintures*.

The texts that follow, occurring on dislocated materials, are known only from the tracings of Du Mesnil du Buisson made at Dura. The materials remained in the storage rooms of the expedition house, which was partially destroyed during the war.

12. Graffito on a fragment of a door jamb found in the debris of the Forecourt. One line (Fig. 88).

Du Mesnil du Buisson, *Peintures*, p. 161 (no. 18, second part).

FIG. 88. Inscr. No. **12**

חיא בר[
"Ḥiyā, son of ..."

The very common name *Ḥiyā* occurs several times in these graffiti. The way in which it is written here (the work of an expert hand) and in Inscr. no. **15** illustrates the fact that the letters *waw* and *yodh* are often not distinguished from each other in these inscriptions; though if they happen to occur together, *yodh* is always made shorter than *waw*.

13. Graffito on the same fragment of a door jamb. Two lines (Fig. 89).
Du Mesnil du Buisson, *Peintures*, p. 161 (no. 18).

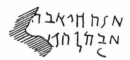

FIG. 89. Inscr. No. **13**

אנה חיא ברו
אבה להון

"I, Ḥiyā, son of...
am their leader."

Both lines of the graffito are defective on the left. This is a good example of the frequent use of אב, "father," to mean "chief, counsellor, etc." in both Hebrew and Aramaic. Important examples in the Hebrew Bible are Gen. 45.8; Isa. 9.5; II Chron. 2.13 and 4.16.[13] The usage has still other illustrations in the Bible and the apocryphal literature.

14. Graffito on the same fragment of a door jamb. One line, parts of letters only (Fig. 90).

FIG. 90. Inscr. No. **14**

איוֹו

"Jo[b]"?

Possibly the name איוב "Job" stood here, if a guess is worth while.

13. These last examples are almost universally misunderstood; see *Journal of Biblical Literature*, XXXI (1912), pp. 151–155.

18

15. Graffito on a fragment of a door jamb found in the embankment covering the Synagogue in the northwest corner of the House of Assembly. One line, letters *ca.* 0.03 m.–0.035 m. high (Fig. 91).
Du Mesnil du Buisson, *Peintures*, p. 162 (no. 21).

FIG. 91. Inscr. No. **15**

אנא חיא
"I am Ḥiyā."

Observe by comparison with Inscr. no. **13** that it is a matter of indifference whether final *ā* is written with *aleph* or with *hē* in the pronoun of the first person singular. There is constant variation in these graffiti.

16. Graffito on the same fragment. Two lines, letters 0.012 m.–0.02 m. high (Fig. 92).
Du Mesnil du Buisson, *Peintures*, p. 162 (no. 21, second part).

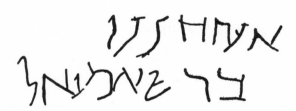

FIG. 92. Inscr. No. **16**

אנה חנני
בר שאמואל
"I am Ḥananī,
son of Samuel."

The name *Ḥananī* is familiar from the Old Testament, as well as from inscriptions. The name *Samuel* is here carelessly written with *aleph* as the second letter. This certainly does not represent any actual pronunciation, nor is it elsewhere written in this way.

17. Graffito on a piece of stone trim found in the embankment. Two complete lines, letters *ca.* 0.025 m. high (Fig. 93).

Du Mesnil du Buisson, *Peintures*, p. 160 (no. 14).

FIG. 93. Inscr. No. **17**

אנא פינחס
בר ארמיה ברו

"I am Phinehas,
son of Jeremiah, son ..."

Interesting here is the example of the Mesopotamian dialect, avoiding initial *yodh* and substituting for it *aleph*; see the long note on Inscr. no. **3** above. Instead of the *Yirmĕyā* of the Biblical Hebrew, the form here is *Ermĕyā* (or *Eremyā*, like the Syriac pronunciation).

The form of the letter *mĕm*, almost or quite a parallelogram, is familiar from both Palmyrene and Nabataean inscriptions.

18. Graffito on a fragment of plaster (wall-coating or door jamb?) found in the core of the west wall of the House of Assembly, together with others preserving elements of the decorations of the earlier Synagogue building (see above, p. 14). One line, letters 0.025 m.–0.04 m. high (Fig. 94).

Du Mesnil du Buisson, *Peintures*, p. 157 (no. 2).

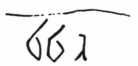

FIG. 94. Inscr. No. **18**

גטט

gṭṭ

The characters are clearly drawn, but without their context are quite meaningless.

19. Graffito on a similar plaster fragment also found in the core of the west wall of the House of Assembly and belonging probably to the earlier Synagogue building. Three lines (?), letters *ca.* 0.008 m.–0.025 m. high (Fig. 95).

Du Mesnil du Buisson, *Revue biblique*, XLV (1936), p. 77 and Fig. 4; *idem, Peintures*, p. 157 (no. 3).

FIG. 95. Inscr. No. **19**

This looks like a boy's scrawl, and such it probably is. Above is written אב, "father," (the subject of the portrait?). Below, the letters appear to be אבלמי (?), which might possibly be intended for "Abram," known as an Aramaic proper name.[14] It is not easy to make any other guess.

20. Graffito on a fragment of a plaster door jamb still showing traces of red paint, found in room 7 of the earlier Synagogue building, and perhaps part of the trim of the south door giving upon its assembly chamber (room 2, see Plan IX). Four lines, letters *ca.* 0.01 m.–0.02 m. high (Fig. 96).

14. M. Lidzbarski, *Ephemeris für semitische Epigraphik*, II (1903–1907), 247; *idem, Répertoire d'épigraphie sémitique*, III (1900–1905), No. 1794. The name *Abramū* listed in Lidzbarski's *Handbuch der nordsemitischen Epigraphik nebst ausgewählten Inschriften*, I (1898), p. 206, is the result of a false reading; see his *Répertoire*, II, No. 1168.

Du Mesnil du Buisson, *Revue biblique*, XLV (1936), p. 76 and Fig. 3; *idem, Peintures*, p. 157 (no. 1, first part) and Fig. 108.

FIG. 96. Inscr. No. **20**

הדין | כתבה | דיכתב | מתני

"This is the writing which Mattĕnai inscribes."

The name *Mattenai* is known especially from the books of Ezra and Nehemiah, but it appears also in the Aramaic inscriptions of this time.

21. Graffito on the same fragment. Three lines, letters *ca.* 0.01 m. high (Fig. 97).

Du Mesnil du Buisson, *Revue biblique*, XLV (1936), p. 76 and Fig. 3; *idem, Peintures*, p. 157 (no. 1, second part) and Fig. 108.

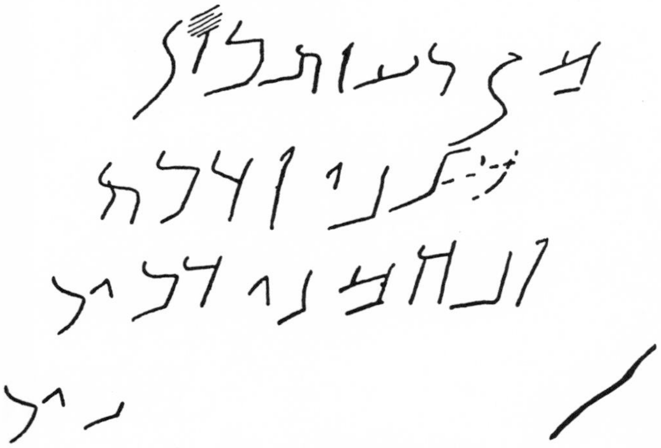

FIG. 97. Inscr. No. **21**

מן רעותכון

חנני ודכה

ונחמני דכיר

"By your leave;
Ḥananī and Dakkā;
and Naḥmanī may be remembered."

The polite formula was indispensable, as Naḥmanī was inscribing names other than his own. On the name *Ḥananī*, see Inscr. no. **16**. The name *Dakkā* is known from a Palmyrene inscription in the Metropolitan Museum in New York City.[15] The name *Naḥmanī* is found once in the Old Testament, Neh. 7.7.

22. Graffito on the same fragment. Parts of three lines, letters *ca.* 0.01 m. high (Fig. 98).

Du Mesnil du Buisson, *Revue biblique*, XLV (1936), p. 76 and Fig. 3; *idem, Peintures*, p. 157 (no. 1, third part) and Fig. 108.

FIG. 98. Inscr. No. **22**

דכיר מנימן

אפותיקי

"Remembered be Minyāmīn
commissary"

On the debated question whether the name *Minyamin*, familiar from the cuneiform records, is the same as Benjamin, see the article "Binjamin-Minyamin" by R. de Vaux in *Revue biblique*.[16]

15. See *Journal of the American Oriental Society*, XXVI (1905), pp. 110f., where the true interpretation in lines 3f. is "Yarhai [son of] Dakkā." See also Lidzbarski, *Handbuch*, p. 255; *Répertoire*, II, No. 761.
16. XLV (1936), pp. 400–402.

The word אַפּוֹתִיקִי occurs frequently in the Talmud and elsewhere with the meaning of the Greek word which it transliterates, ἀποθήκη, "repository, magazine, warehouse, etc." But here, whether the text is complete or not, it is the title or description of the man just named, and this seems to be the first known example of such usage. The post-classical Latin *apothecarius* is used of a man in charge of a magazine or warehouse; and in late Greek ἀποθηκάριος occurs with the meaning "commissary" of an army; see the reference in Sophocles, *Lexikon, s.v.* In the present case, the word designates either such a commissary or a person in charge of some important repository. The vocalization was then presumably *apothēqāi.*

There are in all nineteen Greek texts from the Synagogue: three formal painted decorative notices on ceiling tiles; three repetitions of the same rough graffito, perhaps a maker's mark, on other tiles; three identifying labels on frescoes of the west wall, and perhaps a fourth (inscr. no. **34**) of very doubtful Greek; three graffiti on the wall plaster; and six graffiti or dipinti on pottery fragments. Except for their contribution to the history of the building, they are not remarkable. From them, however, we learn the names of the leading members of the Jewish community at Dura — Hebrew, Aramaic, and in one instance Iranian (Arsaces) — and find a rather unnecessary *terminus post quem* in the form of the date A.D. 247/8. Palaeographically, only the painted texts are important, showing as they do a rather fine calligraphic "book-hand" as an addition to our rather slim list of literary hands at Dura.[18] The simple shapes and plump aspect fit well into the mid-third century. Grammatically there is nothing remarkable; ΕΙ for Ι and Ε for ΑΙ (both in Εἰδέου, Inscr. no. **24**) are current.

23. Dipinto framed by wreath on ceiling tile. Five lines, black paint; letters *ca.* 0.028 m. high. Now in the National Museum at Damascus (Pl. XLIII, 1).

Rep. VI, p. 388, no. 798; Du Mesnil du Buisson, *Biblica*, XVIII (1937), p. 162, Fig. 7,1; Obermann, *Berytus*, VII (1942), Pl. XV, 1; Hopkins and Du Mesnil du Buisson, *CRAI*, 1933, p. 244; Du Mesnil du Buisson, *Peintures*, p. 159, no. 5, and Pl. LX, 1; *idem, Revue biblique*, XLIII (1934), p. 556.

> Σαμουὴλ
> Εἰδδέου
> πρεσβύτερος
> τῶν Ἰουδέ-
> ων ἔκτισεν

17. For unfailing guidance and help in the field of Aramaic and Hebrew proper names I have to thank my colleague, Professor Harald Ingholt. The errors, however, are my own.

18. Cf. Welles, *Transactions of the American Philological Association*, LXX (1939), pp. 203–212.

"Samuel, son of Idaeus, elder of the Jews, built it."

For the names, see above, p. 270, and Obermann's discussion, *op. cit.*, pp. 102f. The LXX has the same nominative case of Σαμουήλ. The shortened form of the Aramaic name ידעיה, ידי, is followed by the Greek, which renders the full form with Ἰεδ-. The name is common in the Middle East, especially at Palmyra, where we have the full theophoric form, Ἰεδειβῆλος, "Known by Bel."[19] Cumont believed he could read Ἰαδα[ῖος in a graffito in the Temple of Bel at Dura, *Fouilles*, no. 40, pp. 396f., but the reading is uncertain.

24. Dipinto framed by wreath on ceiling tile. Five lines, black paint; letters *ca.* 0.028 m. high. Now in Yale University Art Gallery (1933.257) (Pl. XLIII, 2).

Rep. VI, pp. 388f., no. 800; Obermann, *Berytus*, VII (1942), Pl. XV, 2; Du Mesnil du Buisson, *Peintures*, p. 159, no. 5, and Pl. LX, 3.

> Σαμουὴλ
> Βαρσαφάρα
> μνησθῇ ἔκ-
> [τ]ισεν ταῦ-
> τα οὕτως

"Samuel, son of Sapharas:[20] may he be remembered! He built this (building) thus (as you see)."

In the Aramaic text (Inscr. no. **1a**) Samuel, Sapharah's son, appears among those who superintended the work. The Greek expresses both his part and that of the Elder Samuel by the verb ἔκτισεν. Earlier commentators have been disturbed by the idea that two different persons might be

19. E.g., Cantineau, *Inventaire des inscriptions de Palmyre*, IX (1933), no. 32, of A.D. 127. Cf. e.g., M. Noth, *Die israelitischen Personennamen im Rahmen der gemeinsemitischen Namengebung* (1928), p. 181; F. Rosenthal, *Mitteilungen der vorderasiatischen Gesellschaft*, XLI (1936), p. 66.

20. The genitive ending -α presumes a Greek nominative ending in -ας, as commonly at Dura. Cf. Karl Dieterich, *Untersuchungen zur Geschichte der griechischen Sprache von der hellenistischen Zeit bis zum 10. Jahrhundert n. Chr.* (1898), p. 171.

said to have "founded" the Synagogue, but such an idea strains the meaning of the verb. It is used in the Syrian inscriptions along with ἔτευξεν, ἐποίησεν, ἀνήγειρεν, ᾠκοδόμησεν, ἐτελειώθη, etc. of building operations in which many might take part; while, as Professor Kraeling reminds me, it is translated in the Palmyrene bilinguals by בנא.[21] Cf. *Inscriptions grecques et latines de la Syrie*, 359 = Prentice, *Princeton Expedition*, III, B, 1175 from Brâd in the Jabal Sim'an country, dated to A.D. 207/8: Οὔρβικος Ἀνδρόνικος καὶ Μάρκος οἱ Λογγίνου υἱοὶ σὺν τέκνοις ἔκτισαν .... Ἀντώνιος καὶ Σώπατρος ἀδελφοὶ ἔκτεισαν, κτλ.

The final words of the text have made difficulties also. Du Mesnil du Buisson thought to read ταῦτα ὁ υἱός — "this the son," but the reading seems impossible. The demonstrative οὗτος or ὅδε is common in building inscriptions, though normally with an explanatory noun (τὸ κτίσμα τοῦτο, etc.). For an exception, one may compare Prentice, *American Expedition*, 217 (Serjilla in the Jabal Ruha region southwest of Aleppo, A.D. 473): ὁ δεῖνα τόδ' ἔτευξεν, where the building, a λουτρόν, has already been mentioned. The adverb οὕτως can mean both "as follows" and "thus." I incline to the latter interpretation because its sweeping vagueness is no more ambiguous than that of the ταῦτα itself, and because the text was, seemingly, not continued on other tiles. But I have no epigraphical parallels.

The patronymic Βαρσαφάρα is a literal rendering of the Aramaic (בר ספרה; cf. above, pp. 263 f.). A similar pleonastic use of Βαρ- occurs in an inscription from the Main Gate, *Rep. II*, pp. 126 f., no. D 41: Σηλαῖος Βαρβαρνέος for שאילא בר ברני.[22]

25. Dipinto framed by wreath on ceiling tile. Five lines, black paint; letters *ca.* 0.028 m. high. Now in the National Museum at Damascus (Pl. XLIII, 3).

Rep. VI, p. 388, no. 799; Obermann, *Berytus*, VII (1942), Pl. XV, 3; Du Mesnil du Buisson, *Peintures*, p. 159, no. 5, and Pl. LX, 2.

Ἄβραμ
καὶ Ἀρσά-

χου καὶ Σιλᾶς
κὲ Σαλμάνης
ἐβοήθησαν

"Abram and Arsaces (?) and Silas and Salmanes assisted."

This text has already been discussed above (p. 265). The first name occurs in the Aramaic text (Inscr. no. **1a**), if this person is actually the Treasurer. The genitive form of the second name is awkward. Perhaps a second *Abram* has slipped out. Perhaps Professor Torrey was right in suggesting Ἄρσα[ς Μί]χου for which there is room, although no trace of the missing letters remains,[23] or that the καί in line 2 was written in error (above p. 265). On the other hand, the graffiti and rough inscriptions with lists of names at Dura are sometimes careless as to grammatical form.[24] It may be that the occasional alternation of nominative and genitive is due to a conflation of ideas. These are usually contribution lists, and one can say ὁ δεῖνα (i.e. ἔδωκεν) or (ἀπὸ) τοῦ δεῖνος. This is true of the list of the φυλὴ Ζεβεινᾶ in the parchment which Cumont published as no. VII.[25]

Of the names, *Arsaces* is Iranian, but spelled with *chi* because of the Semitic setting; ארסך would give Ἀρσάχης. *Salmanes* is very common in the North Semitic area, and is found often at Palmyra and at Dura. *Abram* is primarily Hebrew.[26] The name Σιλᾶς occurs in the classical authors, especially Josephus,[27] and in *Acts* as the name of Paul's companion, whom Paul calls by the Latin "Silvanus."[28] The same name occurs in Syriac, and with preservation of the א as Σεειλᾶς at Palmyra.[29]

21. Cantineau, *Inventaire des inscriptions de Palmyre*, IV, nos. 6, 9, 27.

22. See also H. J. Cadbury in *Amicitiae Corolla, A Volume of Essays Presented to James Rendel Harris* (1933), p. 46, n. 2.

23. *Rep. VI*, p. 388.

24. So the lists, *Fouilles*, p. 444, no. 123; pp. 446 f., no. 127, mix names in the nominative and in the genitive.

25. *Fouilles*, pp. 317–320.

26. Noth, *op. cit., s.v.*

27. W. Pape, *Wörterbuch der griechischen Eigennamen*, 3rd. ed. (1884), p. 1390.

28. II Cor. 1.15; I Thess. 1.1; II Thess. 1.1; I Pet. 5.12. This use of similar Aramaic and Latin names is common among the Orientals, where such names as Marinus, Germanus, and Bassus are ambivalent. The accent in the manuscripts is Σίλας; but cf. e.g., Friedrich Blass, *Grammatik des Neutestamentlichen Griechisch*, 2nd. ed. (1902), p. 74.

29. Cantineau, *Inventaire des inscriptions de Palmyre*, III, 14, 15; *Répertoire d'epigraphie semitique*, II (1907), 742; cf. Th. Nöldeke, *Zeitschrift der deutschen morgenländischen Gesellschaft*, XXIV (1870), pp. 96 f.; Rosenthal, *op. cit.*, p. 28, n. 5.

The interpretation of similar names at Dura is uncertain.[30] This individual may have been a Jew, if we assume that the weakened form was especially popular in Palestine. This is the view also of Cadbury,[31] who points to the Talmudic spelling שׁילא. The spelling Σειλᾶς occurs in Emesa, A.D. 78/9.[32]

26–28. Graffito inscribed upon three ceiling tiles during process of manufacture. One line each; letters *ca.* 0.04–0.12 m. high. One in Yale University Art Gallery (1933.288), two in National Museum in Damascus (Pl. XLIII, 4).

Rep. VI, p. 389, no. 801; Du Mesnil du Buisson, *Peintures*, p. 159, no. 6, and Pl. LX, 4; *idem*, *L'Illustration*, July 29, 1933, p. 456.

Ὄρβαζ

"Orobazus"

The meaning of this graffito has been disputed. The original suggestion of Professor Torrey[33] was that of a connection with the place Herbaz, near Samosata. More recently Du Mesnil du Buisson has recognized the Iranian name Ὀρόβαζος, "Having Ahura as his arm."[34] A personal name is easier to understand, though this name, whether of the maker of bricks or not, has not before been recognized at Dura. On the other hand, it is now possible to see the name in a retrograde stamp on the handle of a "yellow, bitumen-lined pot" found in the second season of the Yale excavations,[35] and this interpretation seems assured. Iranian names, while rarer than the Greek and Semitic, are not infrequent at Dura.[36]

29. Dipinto on Panel WB 2 to the right of Aaron's head. One line; letters *ca.* 0.025 m.–0.032 m. high. Black paint (Pl. LX).

Rep. VI, p. 392 (Greek dipinti, no. 3); Du Mesnil du Buisson, *Biblica*, XVIII (1937), p. 162, Fig. 7,3,

30. Cf. *Rep. II*, pp. 115f., no. D 3, with Torrey's comment; and *Rep. VI*, p. 135.
31. *Amicitiae Corolla*, pp. 50f.
32. *Corpus Inscriptionum Graecarum*, 4511 = P. Le Bas and W. H. Waddington, *Voyage archéologique en Grèce et en Asie Mineure* (1847–1870), 2567.
33. *Rep. VI*, p. 389.
34. A. H. M. Stonecipher, *Graeco-Persian Names* (1918), p. 54.
35. It lacks the final *zeta*; see *Rep. II*, p. 47.
36. Cf. my comments in *Studies in Roman Economic and Social History in Honor of Allan Chester Johnson* p. 270; *Rep. IX*, 3, p. 49.

and Pl. 2 on p. 168b; *idem*, *Revue biblique*, XLIII (1934), p. 112; *idem*, *Peintures*, p. 160, no. 10, and Pl. XXIX.

Ἀρών

"Aaron"

According to Hatch and Redpath's *Concordance to the Septuagint*, this spelling of the name occurs rarely in the LXX beside the usual Ἀαρών.

30. Dipinto on Panel WA 2 on fourth step of dais to Solomon's throne. One line, black paint; letters *ca.* 0.025 m.–0.030 m. high (Pl. XXVIII).

Rep. VI, p. 392 (Greek dipinti, no. 1); Hopkins and Du Mesnil du Buisson, *CRAI*, 1933, p. 248; Du Mesnil du Buisson, *Revue biblique*, XLIII (1934), pp. 111f.; *idem*, *Peintures*, p. 160, no. 9.

Σλήμων

"Solomon"

I do not know any other instance of this Greek spelling of the Hebrew name, which here appears, not only with the final *nun* of Aramaic-Greek, but with practically the Syriac vocalization.[37]

31. Dipinto on Panel WA 2 underneath chair at left of throne. One line, black paint; letters *ca.* 0.023 m.–0.028 m. high (Pl. XXVIII).

Rep. VI, p. 392 (Greek dipinti, no. 2); Du Mesnil du Buisson, *Biblica*, XVIII (1937), p. 162, Fig. 7, 2; *idem*, *Peintures*, p. 160, no. 9.

συνκάθαδρο[

"Counselor(s)"

The loss of the final letter makes the number uncertain, whether singular or plural. The word is of a late Greek character, and rare in our sources. Liddell and Scott translate by "assessor" or "colleague." On the other hand, the grammarian Ulpian uses it in his commentary on Demosthenes, XXI, 178, to explain the Attic πάρεδρος. The spelling with *alpha* is presumably due to assimilation.[38]

32. Graffito on dado, west wall, WD 7 (S). Two lines; letters *ca.* 0.04 m.–0.097 m. high (Fig. 99).

37. I have to thank Professor Kraeling for this information.
38. Cf. Dieterich, *Untersuchungen zur Geschichte der griechischen Sprache*, pp. 19–21.

FIG. 99. Inscr. No. **32**

Βόηθος
"Boethus"

This Greek personal name occurs here for the first time at Dura, and it is a little surprising to find it, the only Greek name in the Synagogue. While not a typical soldier's name,[39] it is common in general in all parts of the Roman Empire, and is associated with a Jewish High Priestly family of the period of the Second Temple (see B. Pesachim 57a). The form of the final *sigma* is strange, but I suppose there is no doubt that the reading is correct. On the basis of the ἐβοήθησαν in Inscr. no. **25**, and the συνκάθαδρο[of Inscr. no. **31**, one might perhaps argue that it was a common, and not a proper, noun.

33. Graffito on Panel NC 1, section 4, on the hem of the tunic of the man being executed. Two lines; letters *ca.* 0.025 m. high (Fig. 100).

FIG. 100. Inscr. No. **33**

Numerals: ρξε′ = 165, and πβL′ = 82½. If the remaining mark is writing, it may be the numeral

39. It does not occur otherwise at Dura or in L. R. Dean, *A Study of the Cognomina of Soldiers in the Roman Legions* (1916), and only once in Dessau's index to the *Inscriptiones Latinae Selectae*, no. 6974, from Narbo.

λ = 30 or F = 6. Cf. for the latter the examples in the accounts in the House of Nebuchelus.[40]

34. Possible dipinto in panel band at right of aedicula directly over WD 1 (N). Two or three letters, *ca.* 0.07 m. high (Fig. 101).
Du Mesnil du Buisson, *Peintures*, p. 161 (no. 19).

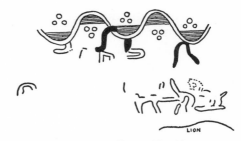

FIG. 101. Inscr. No. **34**

[The remains of painted letters visible in this area have suggested to Du Mesnil du Buisson the Greek word δοβ and the Aramaic שַׁחְלָא, both meaning "lion" and referring to the animal painted below. The vagueness of the remains makes even this doubtful. C.H.K.]

35. Graffito on a fragment of plaster found in the embankment covering the Synagogue. Traces of paint indicate that it belonged at one time to the wall of the House of Assembly. Five lines; letters *ca.* 0.013 m. high (Fig. 102, copy of Du Mesnil du Buisson).
Rep. VI, p. 392 (Greek graffiti, no. 1); Du Mesnil du Buisson, *Peintures*, p. 162, no. 22.

FIG. 102. Inscr. No. **35**

40. *Rep. IV*, pp. 79–145.

Μνησθ[ῇ]
᾿Α]μαθβήλ-
]ΕΙ καὶ ἀδελ-
]ΟΣ αὐτοῦ
]γ καὶ ΑΙΤΟ

"Let there be remembered Amathbel ... and brother (or sister) .... of him — — and — —"

The copy makes it seem as if the text were complete on the right. In any case, the loss on the left is hard to estimate. It is possible to combine lines 3/4 with the loss of a single letter, ἀδελ|[φ]ός but 2/3 and 4/5 show that the loss is greater than this.

The name אמתבל occurs at Palmyra[41] and at Dura in the form ᾿Αμαθθαβείλη.[42] Perhaps the full form here was ᾿Αμαθβήλη, with the Greek inflectional ending. On the other hand, the spelling Μαθβήλ without the initial A would also be possible.[43]

36. Dipinto on jar fragment in the embankment covering the Synagogue near the west wall of the House of Assembly, close to the ground. Two lines, black paint; letters *ca.* 0.01 m. high (Fig. 103, copy of Du Mesnil du Buisson).

FIG. 103. Inscr. No. 36

Apparently a date, θνφ′ = S.E. 559 = A.D. 247/8. It is not impossible that the second line should be read ΑΥΔ for Αὐδ[ιναίου or Αὐδ[ιναῖος, the month of January in the Roman calendar at Dura.

37. Dipinto on a jar fragment found in the core of the north wall of the House of Assembly. Parts of one line, black paint; letters *ca.* 0.02 m.–0.03 m. high (Fig. 104, copy of Du Mesnil du Buisson).

41. *Corpus Inscriptionum Semiticarum*, III, 1, 4081.
42. DP 73 of A. D. 251; cf. *Rep. VI*, p. 437.
43. Cf. the note of H. Immerwahr, *Rep. IX, 1*, p. 226, n. 44.

FIG. 104. Inscr. No. 37

Seemingly the letters ΟΣΗ or ΟΣΙΣ.

38. Seal-impression on a jar fragment found in the core of a wall in the House of Assembly. Letters *ca.* 0.01 m. high (Fig. 105, copy of Du Mesnil du Buisson).

FIG. 105. Inscr. No. 38

The very common name Βαρναῖος is clear, and assuming a mixture of square and round characters, the letters at the end may be ҶΛ = S.E. 430 = A.D. 118/9. For the rest, we may perhaps read ῾Ερμαίου, with a flat-topped M. For the script, see *Rep. III*, p. 65, no. D 164, of the same year, and other texts from the Temple of Artemis in the same report, pp. 59–65. See further the table in *Gerasa*, p. 359. It is possible that the same stamp has occurred elsewhere; see the description and the end of an inscription, ΑΙΟΣ in *Rep. II*, p. 47.

39. Dipinto on a jar fragment in the fill under the floor of the later building. One line, red paint; letters *ca.* 0.028 m. high (Fig. 106, copy of Du Mesnil du Buisson).

FIG. 106. Inscr. No. 39

This is seemingly the end of a theophoric name in -γ]ιννᾶιος or -αίας; e.g., 'Αβιδγ]ιννᾶιος or Βαργ]ιννᾶιος, the former read by Cumont on a seat in the Temple of Artemis, and the latter occurring several times among the Dura soldiery, notably in the roster of the Twentieth Palmyrene Cohort, DP 12 of A.D. 219–222. These theophoric names have occurred only at Dura, and presumably derive from the particular Bedouin stock which included Dura in its *dira*.[44] The deity Ginnai occurs in the inscriptions of the Jebel Sha'ar, in the orbit of the same Bedouin;[45] and the name may be present on the coins of Characene.[46] Cf. further *Rep. II*, pp. 133f., no. D 81; *Rep. VI*, p. 509, Indices, *s.v.*[47]

44. Welles, *Studies ... in Honor of ... Johnson*, p. 267.

45. H. Ingholt, J. Starcky, in D. Schlumberger, *La Palmyrène du Nord-Ouest* (*Institut français d'archéologie de Beyrouth, bibliothèque archéologique et historique*, XLIX, 1951), texts listed in index, p. 186. Schlumberger, *ibid.*, pp. 135–137, would take the term to be a common noun equivalent to the Arabic جن "spirit"; but see R. Mouterde, *Mélanges de l'Université Saint-Joseph*, XXIX (1951–1952), pp. 311f. Cf. further W. F. Albright, *Journal of the American Oriental Society*, LX (1940), pp. 292f.; H. Seyrig, J. Starcky, *Syria*, XXVI (1949), pp. 236–257.

46. So Lidzbarski; see Cumont, *Fouilles*, pp. 431f., no. 97.

47. This remains true, whatever be the solution of the puzzling Dura inscription *Rep. VI*, pp. 238–240, wherein F. E. Brown (*ibid.*, pp. 234–238) recognized the word נויא in this sense. C. C. Torrey, however, the editor of the Palmyrene text, took the word to mean "gardens." Subsequently a revision of the text by H. Ingholt in Damascus caused him to revise his interpretation (*Rep. VII/VIII*, p. 442), leaving, however, the meaning of this word uncertain. At all events, it is impossible to follow his theory and see in the divine name a borrowing from the Latin *Genius*; this could never produce the early theophoric compounds of the Dura onomasticon.

40. Dipinto on a jar fragment found in the core of the benches in room 2 of the earlier building. Parts of one line, black paint; letters *ca.* 0.015 m.–0.032 m. high (Fig. 107, copy of Du Mesnil du Buisson).

FIG. 107. Inscr. No. **40**

It is difficult to make anything certain from the tracing, beyond the obvious observation that the final symbol resembles that for ¼.

41. Graffito on a jar fragment found in the core of the benches in room 2 of the earlier building. Incised before baking. Two letters, *ca.* 0.02 m. high (Fig. 108, copy of Du Mesnil du Buisson).

FIG. 108. Inscr. No. **41**

"Three denarii"
The denarius sign occurs frequently in Roman Dura, notably in the accounts of Nebuchelus.[48]

48. *Rep. IV*, Indices, p. 288.

III. THE MIDDLE IRANIAN TEXTS.[49]

A. Introduction

I. HISTORY AND PRINCIPAL RESULTS OF THE PRESENT INTERPRETATION

The present edition of the Iranian or, more accurately, Middle Iranian inscriptions of the Synagogue of Dura-Europos; i.e., of a group of twelve dipinti in Pārsīk (Middle Persian) and of three graffiti in Parthian (Pahlavīk) script and language,[50] is not quite complete. It contains only the transliterations, readings, and translations of the inscriptions, preceded by short introductory remarks and accompanied by brief explanations and by the best available photographs. Because it was necessary to condense my contribution to this Final Report as much as possible, a complete *tabula scripturae* and my own very careful tracings of the inscriptions, which are naturally more reliable than free-hand drawings, could not be included in the present edition, though they are necessary for a full understanding of the inscriptions and for the justification of many details of my interpretations. In these tracings I have reproduced also, as far as it was technically feasible, a number of letters written by later hands above or beneath the text

lines or even between or inside the letters of words of the text in some of the inscriptions. These later inserted letters are rarely visible in the small-sized photographs which were taken at the time of the excavations. But in some excellent photographs taken in recent years in the Museum of Damascus a considerable number of these letters are distinctly recognizable. Some of them are written rather clumsily, while others are examples of beautiful and expert handwriting, and some are so tiny and thin that, in order to recognize them with certainty, the eyes had to be strained to the utmost. I found it very surprising that none of those who have made tracings of the dipinti on the spot have noticed any of the letters inserted by later hands. Here we have to emphasize that these additional letters are by no means to be considered as idle scribbling. Though there are cases in which such letters were needlessly repeated by a second or even by a third hand, there is no doubt that in most instances they were added only for the purpose of correcting or identifying an incorrectly written or damaged or indistinct letter of a text word. Sometimes a letter written inside a letter or between two letters of a word in a text is to indicate the kind of letter that follows in the word. As a matter of fact, these inserted letters proved to be of invaluable help to me in so far as they furnished in quite a number of difficult cases the final confirmation of my readings.

As a result of the decision to condense my contribution to the Report as far as possible, the tracings, the *tabula scripturae*, and a more detailed discussion of certain important problems had to be reserved for another context. We contemplated the preparation of a separate *editio major*. It is very fortunate that in the meantime the projected *Corpus Inscriptionum Iranicarum* has become a reality and that I have been given the opportunity to publish the *editio major* as part of the *Corpus*. The tracing and a tentative reading of a badly preserved Pārsīk inscription on a doorjamb at the

49. I wish to express my sincere thanks to the American Philosophical Society in Philadelphia for a grant bestowed upon me which helped me continue and complete the present work. Owing to outward circumstances the work was frequently interrupted and resumed at longer intervals.

50. Previously scholars who have dealt with the Iranian inscriptions of the Synagogue have used the term "Pahlavi (Pehlevi) inscriptions," though the language and the script of the three graffiti cannot be subsumed under this term. Nowadays, however, Iranian scholars are replacing this term with two others: "Pārsīk" or "Middle Persian" for the southern dialect, in which the Zoroastrian literature ("the Books"), one version of the Sasanian inscriptions, and the Sasanian seals and coins are written; and "Pahlavīk" or "Parthian" for the northern dialect, which is the language of the other version of the Sasanian inscriptions and of some parchments and ostraca. In the Turfan fragments many Pahlavīk texts are preserved as well as texts in Pārsīk. This remark is, of course, meant only to give scholars outside the group of specialists in Iranian studies the necessary information about the character of the languages and scripts in which our dipinti and graffiti are composed.

entrance of the Synagogue, which starts with the words *zwt'n Y'TWN*, "Quickly ye come!" will be included in this *editio major*.

The first draft of my readings and interpretations of almost all of these inscriptions I presented in a lecture to the Oriental Club of New Haven in 1942. It was based on partly insufficient, often indistinct photographs and on tracings that were mostly unsatisfactory. For some of the inscriptions only tracings and no photographs were available at that time. Later a number of mostly very accurate tracings by Professor Jakob Polotsky became available and these often proved vey helpful. Still later, the reading of difficult passages and the clarification of epigraphical details were facilitated by a number of excellent new photographs and enlargements of photographs, for which I am indebted to Professor Carl H. Kraeling and Dr. Nicholas Toll. It is to be noted, however, that sometimes single letters or whole words are better preserved and more distinct in the older photographs and that in some cases the more recent photographs fail to provide additional help, when letters or words present themselves in about the same poor condition in which they appear in the old photographs. But in general the new photographs often proved to be of valuable help. We have especially to acknowledge the important fact that without their support the complete restoration and final interpretation of Inscrs. nos. **43** and **44** would not have been possible.

Since the present work sheds new light on the contents, the meaning, and the purpose of the Middle Iranian inscriptions, it is appropriate to give in this introduction a short survey of the major results achieved. I wish in this context to stress the fact that nearly all the essential details of readings and interpretations were already contained in the first draft of my work, being afterwards fully confirmed by the new photographs and the discovery of the inserted letters, and that only slight changes have subsequently proved to be necessary. Only one major error required radical elimination. This concerned the last word of the Inscr. no. **42**, which I then read and still read, *ptčyt*, against the seeming *psčyt* of the photographs. Unfortunately I connected this word with Middle Persian *pačēn*, Armenian *patčēn*, "a copy," and therefore rendered it by "it was copied." This interpretation, according to which "this picture" (*ēn nikār*) would have been "copied" by the *dipīr* when he came to the Synagogue, is sharply contradicted and definitely excluded, as I shall prove later, by the fact that in the parallel passages of other inscriptions verbs with the meanings "it was looked at (viewed, beheld)" correspond to the verb *ptčyt* of Inscr. no. **42**. It is, therefore, evident that *ptčyt* must have the same meaning as the corresponding verbs. As a matter of fact, even in the first draft I indicated that possibly *ptčyt* might be composed of the preposition *pat-* and the preterite of the Old Indic and Avestan root ²*či-* (*kay-*), "to discern." Shortly afterwards I abandoned my earlier, erroneous explanation and adopted the interpretation "it was observed (beheld)." As a result of this interpretation we are able finally to solve the problem of the function exercised by the *dipīrs* when they came to the Synagogue.

Another major result of the present effort is that it succeeds in providing an entirely satisfactory interpretation of the rather difficult and important Inscr. no. **52**, written on the panel inspired by Ezekiel 37 (NC 1). For, in contrast to the dated inscriptions, it turned out to be a general sentence with a bearing upon the meaning of the picture on which it was written. The sentence reads: "This make ye known that joyous ye are, and to God's voice listen! Then peace [will be] upon us." I had already found this type of inscription in the graffito Inscr. no. **55**, written in the Parthian (Pahlavīk) script on the second panel of the Elijah series (SC 2), which in translation reads: "Praise to God, praise! For life, life eternally he gives." But I discovered still a third instance of such a general sentence in the dipinto Inscr. no. **53** on the Ezekiel panel. Though the reading of the first word of line 2 is uncertain and the sense of the phrases '*ZLWN 'yny'* and '*L 'ZLWN 'yny'* is not quite clear, there is hardly any doubt that my translation is otherwise a true rendering of the original text.

On the other hand my interpretation of the dipinti Incrs. nos. **49** and **51** furnished the result that they combine both types of inscriptions. They not only date the visits of *dipīrs* to the Synagogue like almost all of the dipinti, but also add to the dates a brief explanation of the meaning of the paintings — in this instance the revival of the dead child of the widow by the prophet Elijah.

In a passage of the badly preserved Inscr. no. **44** the highly interesting and important fact could still be ascertained that among those who came to the Synagogue on the date of this inscription there was also an official (*zandak*) of the Jews; i.e. of the Jewish community. It is striking furthermore that in this text the Synagogue is called "the edifice of the God of the Gods of the Jews," and noteworthy that here and in two other dipinti (Inscrs. nos. **45** and **47**) the Middle Persian word *patrastak* was used as a designation of the Synagogue instead of the Aramaic *BYTʾ*. There is still one more item that deserves to be included in the list of major results. It is the successful deciphering of the phrase *dipīwarē ī zahmē* in Inscrs. nos. **42**, **44**, and **45**. Indistinct or damaged letters and the hitherto unknown form of the initial letter *z* of the word *zahmē* made the reading rather difficult. Fortunately this reading proved to be certain beyond doubt, and the important result is that we have obtained knowledge of the existence and the title of one more otherwise unknown official who came to the Synagogue with the *dipīr* and certain other persons.

The fundamental problem with which we are confronted in these inscriptions concerns the function of the *dipīr* (*dipīwar*) and turns on the question whether he is a scribe or a painter. This problem will be discussed later on in this introduction and will be brought to a conclusive solution. Finally, I have to call attention to the fact that the present work also contains results important from the epigraphical point of view. The script of these inscriptions, which represent some of the oldest extant examples of cursive Pārsīk and Pahlavīk writing, shows interesting ligatures and a number of peculiar, hitherto unknown forms of letters. Some of them could be restored only through comparison of parallel passages or with the help of letters inserted by later hands. Details concerning these epigraphical facts are to be reserved for the *editio major*, where they will be illustrated by my tracings and the *tabula scripturae*.

2. THE PREVIOUS EDITIONS

Up to the present the few attempts that have been made to read and interpret the Middle Iranian inscriptions of the Synagogue have dealt with only parts of the material, and unfortunately almost all of the attempts turned out to be quite unsuccessful. It will become evident from the present work that two of the more extensive contributions to the interpretation of these inscriptions end in complete failures and present an entirely wrong idea of the contents and the meaning of the texts. Only one contribution, though only partly satisfactory, stands on a higher scholarly level and is distinguished by a relatively considerable number of correct readings. But this is unfortunately fragmentary and remains unpublished. At first Professor Antonio Pagliaro published a preliminary, tentative reading and translation of the dipinto Inscr. no. **42**. This was in 1936.[51] However, his reading of the last four lines: "...*ZNDANT*...(?) *i dipīr* 2 (?) *dipān i* (?) *purr ō ēn χānak i ap(ā)dan i ēn šahr pas(ā)čet*," andh is translation: "...Zand ...(?), the painter, executed for this Synagogue of this city two complete pictures,"[52] is almost entirely wrong and shows an inadequate acquaintance with the epigraphical alphabet. The only positive and acceptable result of Pagliaro's initial effort is his undoubtedly correct interpretation of the years in the dates of the inscriptions as the regnal years of Šāhpuhr I.

Five years later Pagliaro published an extensive edition of ten of the dipinti under the title "Le Iscrizioni Pahlaviche della Sinagoga di Dura-Europo."[53] The numbers 1–10 in his arrangement of the dipinti correspond to the numbers **49**, **50**, **46**, **45**, **47**, **48**, **43**, **44**, **42**, and **51**, respectively, in the succession of the dipinti in the present work. Our dipinti Inscrs. nos. **52** and **53** are missing in Pagliaro's work and, apart from one occasional note which will be mentioned afterwards, he did not deal with the three Parthian graffiti. Furthermore, attention must be drawn to the fact that Pagliaro offers on p. 613 the photograph of an obviously damaged text of the inscription which is our no. **51**. The first word of the first line (*BYRX*)

51. *Rep. VI*, p. 395.

52. I wish to state here that the readings *dipīr*, *dipān*, *MLMN* (*sic*!), allegedly representing *MʾLḪ* — the Aramaic ideogram with the Iranian equivalent *pur(r)*, "full" — *ap(ā)dan* (i.e. *apad(ā)n*), and *šahr* (instead of *nikār*) are sharply contradicted by the letters of the original text.

53. *Atti della R. Accademia d'Italia, Rendiconti della classe di scienze morali e storiche*, Series 7, 2 (1941–1942), pp. 578–616.

and the first word of the second line (*'MT*) appear in this photograph as the initial words of the second and the third line, respectively. They apparently have slid down as a result of a crack in the plaster. In later photographs and in Polotsky's tracing these words are standing in their proper places, probably as the result of a later restoration of this piece of plaster.

In Pagliaro's study we are presented with reproductions of photographs that are mostly very inadequate, with free-hand drawings (as a substitute for tracings), with transliterations, readings, and translations of the texts, and full commentaries, abundant in quotations from the Middle Persian literature and other sources in support of the author's interpretations. All this is preceded by an introduction which is devoted largely to the discussion of the problem concerning the identity and the functions of the *dipīr* (*dipīwar*). As in his "Preliminary Note," Pagliaro regards the *dipīrs* as painters and the inscriptions written on the paintings of the Synagogue as commemorative notes and as signatures of the painters (*dipīrs*). This interpretation of the *dipīr* originated and developed under the influence of the erroneous opinion advanced by Du Mesnil du Buisson[54] that כתב in the Aramaic inscriptions of the Synagogue means "to paint." Hence, according to Pagliaro, these inscriptions are intended to tell us which parts of the paintings the *dipīrs*, "painters," were doing or had completed on a certain date. We even learn that they report having performed part of the work at dawn on a certain day and another part at night (!).

Pagliaro concluded from his interpretation of the dipinti, from the use of the Zoroastrian calendar in their dates, from the way they counted by the years of the reign of Šāhpuhr I, from the Iranian names of the *dipīrs* themselves, and from the fact that their "commemorative notes" are written in Middle Persian, that these *dipīrs* were Iranian artists. In his opinion the paintings were not the work of only one master-*dipīr*, but of a greater number of artists, headed by a chief ("capo dei pittori").[55] He thought that they constituted a

"school" of Iranian painters who were not resident at Dura, but probably were called from Persia to Dura for the work in the Synagogue. From the fact that there are no inscriptions for a period of six months — between the last inscription of the year fourteen and the one inscription of the beginning of the year fifteen — Pagliaro infers that the Iranian *dipīrs* interrupted their work during the hot season in order to return to the Iranian plateau. On the other hand Pagliàro regarded[56] the two graffiti reproduced by Du Mesnil du Buisson,[57] because they are in Pahlavīk (Parthian) script and language,[58] as the work of "Iranized Hebrews" who hailed from the northwestern provinces of Iran and were not painters, "but visitors or patrons of the Synagogue or coadjutors of the painters proper..."

Pagliaro made special reference to the *dβyr* of the Manichaean fragments of Turfan in order to add strength to the theory that the *dipīrs* of our inscriptions are painters. He pointed[59] to the fact that the period in which the painters of the Synagogue were at work is identical with that in which the Manichaean scribes were copying the Manichaean hymns and embellishing the Manichaean books with miniatures, and he asserted that the Manichaean *dβyr* was both the writer of the texts and the painter of the miniatures of the books and that there did not exist a special name for the miniature painter. He therefore considered it likely that also in the Zoroastrian Iranian art of the Sasanian period no real distinction between the scribe and the painter was made by using different words for each of them. To back up his theory that the *dipīrs* of our inscriptions were painters Pagliaro went to great trouble and pointed to a number of "technical terms," such as *dip*, "pittura," plural *dip(ā)n*, "figure," and the derivatives *nidipīt, nidipis[t]*, and *nipist* with the meaning "(il) dipinse," which he believed to have found in these inscriptions and which he thought to have a bearing upon painting.

---

54. *Peintures* p. 160, nn. 2 and 3. Cf. Pagliaro, p. 585, note 1.

55. The reading *dipīr(ā)n masist* ("the painters' chief") in *Rendiconti*, p. 606, is quite wrong. The correct reading of the passage in Inscr. no. **43**, lines 3–4, is *dpywr Wd[p]ywr*

= *dipīwar ut dipīwar*, "the *d.* and the *d.*" The second *dipīwar* is followed by the genetive *ZY ldky* = *ī radakē*, "of the *radak.*"

56. *Rendiconti*, p. 582, n. 1.

57. *Peintures*, pp. 161 f.

58. There are in reality three graffiti; the third of them (our Inscr. no. **56**) was interpreted by Du Mesnil du Buisson as an Aramaic inscription (*ibid.*).

59. *Rendiconti*, p. 584.

As to Pagliaro's assertion that in the Manichaean fragments *diβīr* is used as a designation of both the scribe and the painter, it is easy to show that this assertion is entirely wrong. In the passages to which Pagliaro referred,[60] the word *diβīr* undoubtedly denotes the professional scribe, according to the contexts. Indeed, there are additional texts in which *diβīr* occurs in this same sense. In one of them the *diβīrs* are mentioned together with books (*niβēγ*), among them the "Evangeliyon."[61] In a Parthian text[62] the addressee of a letter is asked to receive the beloved son of Mar Mani like his own son and to educate him well in the art of writing and in wisdom: *uδ frahenjāh paδ diβīrīft uδ paδ χraδ*. Here the *diβīrīft* corresponds exactly to the Pārsīk *dipīrīh*, the art of writing, which is one of the parts of higher education in which young Artaχšēr was educated according to the *Kārnā-mak*.[63] In another passage we are told that Mani's apostle Mari Amu knew *pahlavā[nī]γ diβīrī [u]δ ʿzv[ān]*, "the Parthian script and language."[64] What Pagliaro did not notice is that there are passages in Manichaean texts where clear distinctions are made between writing and painting and between the scribes and the book painters or painters of pictures. Such are the passages: *brāδa-rān diβīrā[n] niβēγān niγār aβāγ*, "the brethren scribes together with the painter of the written (books);"[65] *niγārgar kē...až rang ē gōnaγ gōnaγ pahikar niγārēδ*, "the painter who ... from various colors paints a picture,"[66] *ayāβ niβēγ niβištan ayāβ niγār niγārdan...*, "either to write a written (book) or to paint a picture."[67]

Thus, as a matter of fact, the Manichaean texts distinguish between *diβīr*, "the scribe," *niβištan*, "to write," *niβēγ*, "the written (book)" on the one hand, and *niγārgar*, "the painter," *niβēγān niγār*, "painter of written books," *niγārdan*, "to paint," on the other. Accordingly Pagliaro's conclusion that the Zoroastrian Iranian art of the Sasanian period probably made no distinction between the scribe and the painter, is without any foundation whatsoever. In reality, in the Sasanian inscriptions neither the Pārsīk *dipīwar*, *dipīr*, nor their Parthian equivalent, the Aramaic word ספרא, show the slightest relation to the art of painting. They designate the scribe exclusively as a high-ranking official, the secretary of the king or of the state. And the ספרא of the Aramaic literatures and the Hebrew סופר as well as the *dipīr* of the Middle Persian literature, the *dipīr* in the Christian Sogdian translation of Matthew 20.18 (for γραμμα-τεύς) the Armenian *dpir*, the *dabīr* of Modern Persian literature, in particular of the *Šāhnāma* of Firdousī, and the *dabīr* of Arabic sources[68] refer only to the scribe in the above-mentioned meanings, never to the painter. It is, therefore, quite evident that like the *dipīrs* of our dipinti, the *SPRʾ Aparsām* of the Parthian graffito, Inscr. no. 54 is a scribe, and not a painter.

As to the "technical terms" *dip(ā)n*, "figure," *nidipīt*, "(il) dipinse," etc., which Pagliaro produced in favor of his theory that the *dipīr* is a

---

60. F. W. K. Müller, *Ein Doppelblatt aus einem mani-chäischen Hymnenbuch (Abhandlungen der preußischen Akademie der Wissenschaften, phil.-hist. Klasse*, XCVI, 1913), p. 17, lines 220–227 (but also p. 14, lines 118f.); and W. B. Henning, *Ein manichäisches Bet- und Beicht-buch*, Glossary, p. 110 (referring to lines 220, 271, 352).

61. F. C. Andreas and W. B. Henning, *Mitteliranische Manichaica*, II, p. 301 with n. 2.

62. *Ibid.*, III, p. 859.

63. Ed. by Sanjana, I, 23. Much additional information about the role which the art of writing occupied in the higher education of Sassanian times is to be obtained from other Middle Persian and from Arabic and Modern Persian sources, to which I shall refer at another occasion.

64. Andreas and Henning, *op. cit.*, II, p. 303. The objection raised by Schaeder (*Iranica*, I, p. 19, n. 1) against the translation "Schrift" by the editors of the text is not justified. Here the word *diβīrī* in close con-nection with the word for "language" evidently means "the writing" (i.e., the art of writing), and is not used in the wider sense which includes the endowment of the literary man with higher qualifications ("Schriftgelehr-samkeit") and with the requirements for the high office of scribe (secretary) in the royal administration. The expression *diβīrī uδ ʿzvān* is obviously to be understood in the same sense as סֵפֶר וּלָשׁוֹן, "script and language (of the Chaldaeans)," which Israelite boys are to be taught, according to Daniel 1.4. Cf. *Šāhnāma*, ed. J. Mohl, V, p. 501: *yakē tā dabīrī biyāmōzadaš*, "one (Mōbad), that he should teach him (the art of) writing."

65. *Ibid.*, II, p. 303.

66. *Ibid.*, I, p. 203.

67. W. B. Henning, *Zeitschrift für Indologie und Iranistik*, IX (1933–1934), p. 251.

68. In the works of the Arabic writers Al-Nadīm, Masʿūdī and al-Khvārazmī the forms دفیریه, دبیره, دفره, which go back to Middle Persian *dipīrīh (diβīrīh)*, are used to mean "the writing," especially on religion (*dēn*), and as a designation of the office of the secretary (of justice, finance, etc.), and are explained by the Arabic words *al-kitābah* and *al-khaṭṭ*, "the writing." Cf. also H. W. Bailey, *Zoroastrian Problems* (1943), pp. 153, n. 3, and 170.

painter, we shall later demonstrate that these words owe their existence only to the most arbitrary reading of the letters of the photographs.

Indeed, as it has turned out, Pagliaro's reading and interpretation of all ten of his dipinti — with the exception of a few recurrent and easily legible words, such as *BYRX* ("month"), *YWM* ("day"), *BYT'* ("house") etc. — is a complete failure. I regret that I am compelled to make this statement about the work of a scholar who otherwise has made valuable contributions in the field of Middle Persian studies. His failure in the present case is to be attributed largely to his strange and improper approach to an epigraphical study, which naturally requires the same accuracy and strict philological method that is to be applied to the critical edition of a literary text. He barred his way to correct and acceptable readings by arbitrarily distorting in his free-hand drawings letters that were easily legible on the photographs, and showed thereby that such drawings are very insufficient substitutes for accurate, reliable tracings. The natural consequence of this unmethodical procedure is a variety of fantastic readings, including a considerable number of imaginary Aramaic ideograms in the place of evidently Iranian words, and extremely far-fetched interpretations.

About ten years after Pagliaro's publication, Professor Franz Altheim, without a sufficient background in Iranian, and in particular without an adequate acquaintance with the inscriptional alphabet, undertook in his book *Asien und Rom*[69] to interpret not only two parchments of Dura, but also two entire dipinti of the Synagogue and a few lines, or parts of lines, of certain others.[70] He completed this work, which deals also with other topics, within a few months; that is, between the end of 1951 and the autumn of 1952. I must make it quite clear from the outset that Altheim's interpretations and the conclusions which he bases on them are, with the exception of a few readily legible words, such as *BYRX* ("month"), *BYT'* ("house"), etc.,

entirely wrong in every respect, arbitary, and fantastic. He leaps lightly over obstacles which are difficult to surmount and creates problems and far-reaching theories out of the simplest passages of the dipinti. One of these theories is concerned with his alleged discovery of an ever-increasing penetration of "East Aramaic" elements into the "Reichs-Aramäisch" ("Imperial Aramaic") idiom represented by the Pārsīk and Pahlavīk inscriptions. He believed to have found an abundant treasure of hitherto unknown East Aramaic intruders precisely in the Middle Iranian inscriptions of Dura, in the two parchments, and in the few lines of the dipinti which he tried to interpret. This, like some of the other theories which Altheim has advanced, quickly dissolves into thin air when it is more closely examined.

Though Altheim expresses himself in very derogatory terms about Pagliaro's work — he says that Pagliaro's readings and interpretations sometimes border on the fantastic[71] — he has adopted and considerably amplified Pagliaro's theory that the *dipīr* was a painter. But whereas Pagliaro assumed that the *dipīrs* who where working in the Synagogue were Iranian artists, Altheim declares that the painters (*dipīrs*) were Jews of Persian descent, hardly Zoroastrians, though they used the Zoroastrian calendar and dated their inscriptions by the regnal years of Šāhpuhr I.[72] In support of this theory of the Jewish faith of the painters Altheim points to a passage in Inscr. no. **48**, line 1, in which the "painters" are said to "speak of a dating according to the heathen," which is taken to mean that the "painters" regarded the Zoroastrians as heathen. This leads Altheim to the conclusion that those who speak to us in the inscription were Jews who had been brought from Persis to decorate the Synagogue. However this interpretation turns out immediately to be a very grave blunder. The reason is that the phrase "nach den Heiden" applied to the dating procedure is offered as the translation of a reading *'pw ḤNP'YN*, and that this reading is utterly absurd. Altheim points out that "there exists *in Aramaic* the preposition *'YPW* = ὑπό," and that *'pw*, "which is attested here for the first time is to be identified either with

---

69. F. Altheim and R. Stiehl, *Asien und Rom. Neue Urkunden aus sasanidischer Frühzeit* (1952).

70. Our Inscr. no. **42** (complete): p. 24; Inscr. no. **52**, lines 1–2: p. 24; part of Inscr. no. **48**: pp. 26f.; part of Inscr. no. **46**: p. 27; three words of Inscr. no. **45**: p. 28; part of Inscr. no. **51**: pp. 28ff. and 61f.; Inscr. no. **47**: pp. 66f.

71. Altheim, *Asien and Rom*, p. 23.
72. *Ibid.*, p. 27.

'YPW = ὑπό or with Greek ἀπό."[73] This very strange looking hodge-podge, consisting of the preposition ὑπό — which is used in certain Aramaic texts in the form *'YPW* — or of the preposition ἀπό, and the objectionable Aramaic plural form *ḤNP'YN*, falls apart in the light of the correct interpretation of the relevant part of this inscription. For there the word *'MT*, "when" — always wrongly interpreted by Altheim as "until" (German "bis") — is followed by the three words *nχy'ťp*, *Whwp't* (i.e., "and *Hupāt*"), *Wplχwy* (i.e., "and *Farraχvē*"),[74] which are the names of three persons — probably at least one of them being a *dipīr* — who came to the Synagogue. Altheim connected the two final letters *'p* of *nχy'ťp* with the initial *W* ("and") of *Whwp't* into *'pw* and made out of the undoubtedly genuine and characteristic Zoroastrian name *Hupāt* (meaning "*Well-protected,*" sc. "by the gods")[75] the monstrous "Aramaic" word *ḤNP'YN* "the heathen," which is also irreconcilable with the letters of the original.

However, Altheim discovered still another aspect of the activities of the *dipīrs*. He asserts that the painters of the Synagogue "boasted" in some of the inscriptions of having worked "for (or: on) the castles," or — more explicitly — "for (or: on) the castles of the great ones (*RBN* [*sic!*])"; i.e., the castles of the Sasanian high nobility ("Hoch-Adel"). It is *a priori* quite incredible that these "painters," being Jews of Persian descent, bearing almost throughout Zoroastrian names, using the Zoroastrian calendar in the datings of their inscriptions, and nevertheless daring to call the Zoroastrians "the heathen," should have been chosen to work on the castles of the Sasanian high nobility. And it must arouse distrust and suspicion when we are told by Altheim that one of his "painters" says in his inscription (no. **46**) that at

a certain date the astonishing number of thirty(!) painters (*dipīr*) were "on the castles of the great ones (BBYL'T RBN [*sic!*])..."[76] In another inscription (no. **51**, lines 2–3) one "painter" is said to write: *dpyr/Y'TYNY//////* *šhpwr* *'L BYLDYT'Y'*, which Altheim translates: "ein Maler kommt *zu mir*[77] ////////// Schāhpuhr für die (auf den) Burgen."[78] We are told that Šāhpuhr [the painter?] was himself one of the great ones "who were sitting on the castles,"[79] and that in another inscription (no. **45**, line 3) a *d]py[r]* *ZY* *Š'pwr*, "der Maler des Schāhpuhr," is mentioned.[80]

However, like *Ḥnp'yn*, "the heathen," "the painters" working in the castles of the Sasanian nobility are figments of Altheim's imagination and have no other basis in fact than entirely incorrect readings and interpretations of the respective passages of the inscription. In fact, none of these passages says anything about castles. The word which Altheim translates by "the castles" is the one which he reads as *BYL'T* in Inscr. no. **46** and as *BYLDYT'Y'* in Inscr. no. **51**. Both are supposed to be plural forms of Aramic *BYRT'*. We can dispense here with Altheim's twisted and extremely far-fetched explanations of these two forms. It suffices to state with absolute certainty that his *BBYL'T*, "in the castles," is a fantastic reading of the very distinctly written *Wbwlj'tw[r]*; i.e., *ut Burz-ātu[r]*, "and Burzātur,"[81] the companion of *Rašnakē*, the *dipīr*, and that his reading *šhpwr* *'L BYLDYT'Y'* (in Inscr. no. **51**) with the translation "Schāhpuhr auf den Burgen" is an even more amateurish reading of *ZNḤ nyk'l*

73. *Ibid.*, pp. 25 and 27. The "Aramaic" אֵיפוֹ = ὑπό is obviously taken from G. H. Dalman, *Aramäisch-neu-hebräisches Woerterbuch zu Targum, Talmud und Midrasch* (1901), p. 31.

74. Altheim quite incorrectly read *dpl XWY* instead of *Wplχwy* (i.e. *ut Farraχvē*). Here *dpl* (which could not have been written for *dpyr*) is rendered by "Maler" [plural!]. For *XWY* he referred to Herzfeld, *Paikuli*, no. 359, although *XWY* is there listed as the Parthian form of the auxiliary verb "to be" (Pārsīk *XWḤ*).

75. Cf. Avestan *ātərəpāta-* and other names composed with *-pāta-*, which are listed in Justi's *Iranisches Namenbuch*, p. 505.

76. Altheim, *Asien und Rom*, p. 27, does not give the reading and translation of the words which follow his "RBN".

77. One would like to ask to whom the painter comes! In a completely wrong translation of Inscr. no. **52**, lines 1–2, we find (*ibid.*, p. 24) the phrase "Zu uns ist gekommen der Maler."

78. *Ibid.*, p. 28.

79. *Ibid.*, pp. 28 and 30.

80. *Ibid.*, p. 28.

81. It is inconceivable how Altheim could mistake the very distinct initial *W* of the word for a *B* and write *BBYL'T* instead of *Wbwlj'tw[r]*; i.e., *ut Burz-ātu[r]*. He obviously does not know that the Aramaic preposition *B*, "in," occurs only in Parthian inscriptions (Paikuli and Ka'ba), in Pārsīk *BYRX*, "month," and Parthian באתר (Pārsīk אחר = *pas*), "after." As to the name *Burz-ātur* see the remarks on my transliteration of Inscr. no. **46**, below p. 306.

n̊ẙkldyt ˀP-š ...; i.e., "the picture was looked at, and by him ..."[82]

The "thirty painters" working on the castles of the Sasanian high nobility are doomed to share the fate of the imaginary castles. For the two letters *ky* after *lšn*; i.e., *Rašn*, which Altheim interpreted as the number for XXX, are in reality the final two letters of *lšnky*; i.e., *Rašnakē*, the name of the *dipīr*.

We have to add here that, like the castles, so also the alleged designation of the high Sasanian nobility as *RBN* (sic!), "the great ones" ("die Grossen"), which Altheim believed to have discovered, is without any foundation. It is one of the most elementary facts of Pārsīk writing that the Aramaic ideogram *RAB(B)Ā*, "great," is always written *LBˀ*, with *L* = *R*, in the Pārsīk of the inscriptions and of the literature, and that the plural form is, of course, *LBˀN* (= *RBˀN*), with *aleph*, in the inscriptions. Even in the first draft of my work I stated that the correct reading of this slightly damaged word is the Aramaic preposition *BYN*, Iranian *andar*, "in, into," and that in connection with the following word *YˀTWN* it corresponds to Modern Persian *andar āmad*, "came into."

As previously mentioned, Altheim thought to have discovered in Inscr. no. **45**, line 3 the words *d]py[r] ZY šˀpwr*, which he translated "der Maler des *Schāhpuhr*." However, I have ascertained through comparison with the corresponding passages of two other inscriptions, (nos. **42**, line 4, and **44**, line 2), and through the well-established explanation of the strange initial letter of the third word as a form of the letter *z*, that the correct reading of the three words in Inscr. no. **45**, line 3 is *dpywry ZY zhmy*; i.e., *dipiwarē ī zahmē*, "the scribe of the building."[83] The passage has therefore no bearing whatsoever on any Šāhpuhr.

Under these circumstances we are highly surprised to learn that Altheim has assigned to this imaginary "Maler des Šāhpuhr" an important political role. But it is significant that this assignment is based solely on his entirely wrong interpretation of the first two lines of the Inscr. no. **52**.[84] Though all nine words of these lines have been totally misread by Altheim, his reading of the last word of the first line as *ŠNT XIIX*; i.e., "the year 18," is especially harmful and misleading. From this allegedly "latest date," which is three years later than the date ("year fifteen") of Inscr. no. **42**, Altheim unhesitatingly drew the conclusion that in the eighteenth regnal year of Šāhpuhr; i.e., in the year 258/259, Dura was still standing and that its conquest therefore took place in 259/260, not in 256 or 257. From this statement he proceeded to the further conclusion that these Persians of Jewish faith, who boasted to have been working in the castles of the Sasanian nobility, were not only painters but were also acting as part of the Jewish community of Dura which stood in secret understanding with the Persians before the siege and fall of the city, and that only under this presupposition the continuing activity of the painters in the Synagogue during the critical years 255/256 and 258/259 and their "marked pro-Persian attitude" are understandable. One would hardly exaggerate — says Altheim — in declaring that "der Maler des Schāpur" was a Persian agent.

Altheim assumed that a strong pro-Persian gesture of the painters — and of the whole Jewish community — is expressed in the very prominent part which the representation of the triumph of Mordecai occupies among the paintings of the Synagogue. "The Book Esther tells of the glorious connection between Jews and Persians. Referring to it meant expressing, more, or less distinctly, whose side one was taking." But it is far-fetched to imagine that the Jewish community of Dura should have singled out the pictorial representation of one of the Biblical stories in order to show its sympathy with the enemy of the Romans. For there are many other paintings, depicting such Biblical stories as that of the Prophet Elijah and the widow (WC 1) and that of the resurrection of the dead in the Valley of Dry Bones (NC 1) that

---

82. Altheim mistook the word *ZNH* for *šh* (i.e., *šah-*), the letters *nyk* for *pwr* (i.e., *pur*), אל (the last two letters of *nykˀl*) for the Aramaic preposition על ("upon") — attributed by him to the "East Aramaic" interchange between א and ע —, and the two words *n̊ẙkldyt ˀP-š* ("it was looked at, and by him") for *BYLDYTˀYˀ* ("castles"), with a "suffix" *ˀYˀ* instead of *ˀP-š*. Though he himself calls (p. 28) his *ˀL BYLDYTˀYˀ* a misformation ("Unform"), he takes great pains to explain and to justify this "Unform."

83. See the remarks on my transliteration of Inscr. no. **42**, below p. 301.

84. Altheim abstained (pp. 24f.) from the reading of the rather difficult third line.

are displayed in equally prominent positions, and are in some respects more venerable than the story of the Book of Esther, but have not the slightest bearing upon political events. The choice of the subjects for the decoration of the Synagogue was certainly dictated by the desire to represent the most remarkable and distinguished episodes of the Holy Scriptures, not by the desire to uphold a political conspiracy. In view of the importance of the historical problem which is involved in Altheim's reading *ŠNT XIIX*, we must emphasize very strongly the fact that this reading is decisively refuted by the very letters of the original. My reading *š'ty*; i.e., *šātē*, "joyous," is, like that of all the other words of this inscription, in strictest accordance with the letters.[85]

The facts presented on the preceding pages have illustrated some of the gross deficiencies of the method and results in the hitherto published interpretations of our inscriptions. More facts will be presented in the following discussions to show how completely Pagliaro's and Altheim's studies have

obscured the real meaning of these inscriptions and that they are misleading and without any value for the interpretation of these documents.

At this point it is appropriate to call attention to an unpublished contribution by Professor Jakob Polotsky. The task of publishing the inscriptions had been tranferred to him some time after Pagliaro published his "Preliminary Note." But Polotsky had to discontinue his work, and after I had been entrusted with the publication, I received from the Dura Editors his tracings and his manuscript. This consists of only seven pages and contains tentative and sometimes incomplete transliterations and translations of Inscrs. nos. **42**, **43**, **45**, **46**, **47**, **48** (complete), and **49**. Inscr. no. **52** lacks a translation, and Inscr. no. **53** lacks both transliteration and translation. Inscr. no. **44** is mentioned, but not dealt with, and Inscrs. nos. **50** and **51** are entirely missing. The three graffiti are not included. In spite of its very fragmentary condition this manuscript constitutes a very valuable contribution and stands high above Pagliaro's and Altheim's achievements. Though it contains a number of erroneous readings and wrong interpretations and though the transliterations and translations show many gaps, we are on the other hand, as we had to expect, presented with a relatively considerable number of correct readings of difficult words and passages, which give evidence of a perfect philological method and of sound judgment.

In his very short manuscript Polotsky does not discuss any of the problems with which we are confronted by the inscriptions of the Synagogue. We learn, however, from Rostovtzeff's *Dura-Europos and its Art*[86] that even before 1938 Polotsky interpreted these inscriptions as commemorative texts recording the visits to the Synagogue by several Iranians in the years 255 and 256, the last years of the existence of the Synagogue. We are further told that according to Polotsky's opinion the inscriptions "were written by professional scribes [the *dipīrs*], who recorded their own names and the names of the visitors[87] in the inscriptions," and that "the visitors may have been members of the retinues of ambassadors sent

---

85. Altheim has recently — in Franz Altheim and Ruth Stiehl, *Ein asiatischer Staat*, I (1954), p. 246, n. 1 — tried in vain to defend his reading *ŠNT XIIX*, after it had been questioned by A. Maricq. In order to prove the correctness of his reading, he gives at the end of the volume an enlarged photograph of the inscription and beneath it in Abb[ildung] 8 an "Umzeichnung," a drawing in which he separates the alleged components of the *aleph* in the word *š'ty* — which is the correct reading — into the letters *NT*, the *t* into the ciphers *IX*, and the final letter *y* into the ciphers *XI*; i.e., the second half of the alleged numeral XIIX. However, his letters *NT* are merely products of imagination and have not the slightest resemblance to the letters *n* and *t* of the inscriptional alphabet. In reality this *NT* is undoubtedly our letter *aleph*. In my photographs and partly also in the tracings of Pearson and Polotsky there is still to be seen a distinct trace of the left part of the *aleph*; i.e., of the slanting stroke. And this *aleph* is followed by an indisputable *t*, and the following sign is the pointed form of a final *y* (= *ē*), with a blur at the bottom on the left side. In Altheim's opinion his *ŠNT XIIX* is confirmed by his reading *ŠNT MWTN* of the last word of line 2. This he interpreted as "das Jahr des Wankens, Zitterns" (Hebrew and Aramaic מוֹט) and very arbitrarily identified with the plague, "Jahr der Seuche," which broke out in the army of Valerian. This far-fetched reading *ŠNT MWTN* and its interpretation are ruled out completely by the absolutely certain reading *'ŠMYTN*; i.e., "ye listen!" which I discovered at the very beginning of my work on these inscriptions. In the meantime Henning has shown in *Gnomon*, 26 (1954), pp. 477 f., that Altheim's reading *ŠNT LMWT* with the translation "(im) Jahr des Wankens" in the Dura Parchment 12 (*Asien und Rom*, pp. 9 ff.) is also without any foundation.

86. Pp. 113 and 149 f., n. 57.
87. It would be quite correct to say "of the other visitors."

by Shapur to Dura before and during his great invasion of the Syrian provinces of the Roman Empire." Rostovtzeff at that time was still wavering between Polotsky's theory and that of Pagliaro, who interpreted the inscriptions as signatures of the artists, the painters. Polotsky's interpretation of the inscriptions in his manuscript shows that he upheld his opinion even at a later date, though he failed to explain the last word of the Inscr. no. **42**, which provides one of the clues to the solution of the problem of the *dipīr*, and which is, in my opinion, inaccurately written *psčyt* instead of *ptčyt*. And as a matter of fact, Polotsky's theory of the *dipīr* as a professional scribe is fully confirmed by the results of the present work.

When these inscriptions are read faithfully letter by letter and with an adequate background for epigraphical studies, it should not be too difficult to arrive first of all at an understanding of the pattern according to which the dated inscriptions are worded. In them we are told that on a certain date (month, day, year) a *dipīr* (*dipīwar*), either alone or accompanied by another *dipīr* (the *dipīr ī zahmē* or the *dipīr ī radakē*) or by some other persons, came to this house; i.e., the Synagogue, and by him (*'P-š = u-š*) or by them (*'P-šn = u-šān*) this picture (*nikār*, or *by'm'y*) was looked at (beheld, viewed). In Inscrs. nos. **46** and **47** we find *Wby'm'y* (no. **46** incorrectly *Wbym'y*) *ndyšyt*; i.e. *ut by'm'y ndyšyt*, "and the *by'm'y* was beheld," with *W* (= *ut*), "and," instead of *'P-šn*, *'P-š*, "and by them" or "and by him," respectively, whereas Inscr. no. **48** has *'P-šn by'm'y nykylt* (i.e., *nikīrīt*), "and by them the *by'm'y* was looked at."[88]

These expressions *'P-š* ("and by him") and *'P-šn* ("and by them"), which are composed of the Aramaic conjunction *'P* and the Iranian enclitic pronouns of the third person and stand at the beginning of the clauses, postulate, like the corresponding *W* (= *ut*), "and," as predicates forms of the third singular of the preterite with passive meaning. In the texts these are, in fact, the three verbs *nkylyt* (*nikīrīt*), *ndyšyt*, and "*psčyt*."

The word *nikīrīt* is very well known from the Middle Persian of the literature and appears very frequently in Modern Persian as *nigarīd*. The reading *nkylyt* is certain beyond doubt. In Inscr. no. **48** only the initial *n* has lost some of its color, but it is still very easily recognizable even on the oldest photographs. It is, therefore, inconceivable how Pagliaro and Altheim could go so far astray as to offer for this unmistakable verbal form the readings *tlys = thares* and *šylwyn = sīrōīn*, respectively[89]. Polotsky has, of course, the right reading *nkylyt*. However, the verb *nkylyt* (*nikīrīt*) does not occur only in Inscr. no. **48**. I found it also in Inscr. no. **43**, which the confused scribe has thrown for the most part into complete disorder and the original text of which I have restored, in the phrase [*'P-šn ZN*]*Ḥ nk'l nkyl*[*yt*], "and by them this picture was looked at." I have, furthermore, identified it with the strange-looking verbal form *nykldyt*, written with a pseudo-historical *d* for *y*, in the phrase *'P-š* [*Ż*]*ṄḤ* ⟨*nyk'l*⟩ [*ny*]*kldyt*

---

88. The correspondence of *by'm'y* with *nikār*, "picture," in a number of parallel passages (cf. Inscrs. nos. **46, 47,** and **48** with nos. **42, 43, 44, 49,** and **51**) shows clearly that they must be synonymous, although I have tried in vain to ascertain the etymology of *by'm'y*. This word was sometimes wrongly identified with βῆμα by Pagliaro and Altheim. Polotsky has no explanation.

89. Cf. *Rendiconti*, pp. 602 f.; *Asien und Rom*, pp. 26 f. *Thares* is supposed to be the chamberlain תֶּרֶשׁ of Esther 2.21 and 6.2, who together with his fellow-conspirator בִּגְתָנָא sought to lay hand on the king. Pagliaro believed to have found the name of this companion in the plot in the preceding word which he read *bg't'n = bagathan* [sic!], though it is in reality the distinctly written word *by'm'y*, the synonym of *nikār*, "picture." The three words by which *by'm'y* is preceded; namely, the words *Y'TWN HWḤ*[*ṅ*]*d 'P-šn* ("they came and by them"), he rendered as follows: *Y'TWN* by עאמן (= המן), "Haman"(!), the letters *HWḤ* of the auxiliary verb as Mid.Pers. *hōš*, "the mind"; the last two letters [*ṅ*]*d* of this verbal form as *viy-*, which he connected with the following word *'P-šn*, wrongly rendered as *'p'n*, into [*viy*]*āpān* ("confusing, deluding"). Thereby he arrived at the interpretation of this part of the inscription as "Haman che ha traviato la ragione a Bagathan e Thares," instead of "they came and by them the *by'm'y* was looked at." In reality Haman did not have anything to do with the plot against the king! We meet Haman also in Inscr. no. **47**, where Pagliaro read עאמן *Wbgmwrdky*(?) = *Haman u bay-mordekai*(?), with the translation "Haman e il divo Mardocheo(?)," instead of *Y'TWN Wby'm'y*, "came and the *by'm'y*." For *by'm'y nkylyt* Altheim offers the fantastic reading *Bb'm'y šylwyn* with the translation "bei dem βῆμα der *Šīrōīn*" and the explanation that this βῆμα is named after a woman *Šīrōīn*, who bears the same name as the celebrated wife of Khosrau II. Parvēz and probably founded the βῆμα. It is this βῆμα "to which the painters go and where they perform their prayers." In addition we have to state that Altheim's reference to Noeldeke, *Tabari*, p. 283, n. 2, is not justified, as Noeldeke quotes the only existing form *Šīrīn* — not "*Šīrōīn*" — from Greek and Oriental sources.

of Inscr. no. **49**, and in the corresponding phrase [ʾ]*P-š ZNH̱ nykʾl ṅykldyt ʾP-š* ... *ny[k̇]ldyty*... of Inscr. no. **51**. Finally, the verb *nkylyt* appears in the difficult Inscr. no. **44** where I discovered it in the final passage, which is, at least from line 5 on, written by a later hand in rather clumsy and partly blurred, but otherwise unmistakable letters. This passage reads as follows: (line 4) *ʾP-[šṅ]* [...] *ZNH̱ nkʾl ndyšyt* (line 5) *ʾP-šn nkylyt Wṅdyšyt*... Although the words of lines 5 and 6 are obviously a later addition, the close association of *nkylyt* (*nykylyt*) with *ndyšyt* would be sufficient to prove that *ndyšyt* is a synonym of *nkylyt*.

That *ndyšyt* and *nkylyt* are synonymous, is confirmed by the fact that the phrase *nykʾl ndyšyt* of line 4 of Inscr. no. **44** corresponds to *nykʾl ṅykldyt* of Inscrs. nos. **49** and **51**, to the reconstructed *nkʾl nkyl[yt]* of Inscr. no. **43** and to *byʾ mʾy nkylyt* of Inscr. no. **48**, which stands in exchange for *byʾmʾy* (*bymʾy*) *ndyšyt* of Inscrs. nos. **46** and **47**.

The identity of meaning of *ndyšyt* and *nkylyt* can also be proved from the linguistic point of view. As a matter of fact, Polotsky had already explained *ndyšyt* correctly as a pseudo-historical spelling, with *d* for *y*, for *niyīšīt*, which is identical with the preterite *nyyšyd*; i.e., *nīšīδ*, "he looked, beheld," in the Middle Persian texts of Turfan.[90]

The results reached in our investigation into the meaning of the two verbs *nikīrīt* and *ndyšyt* (*niyīšīt*, *nīšīt*) have paved the way for a satisfactory and final solution of the problem presented by the verbal form which stands at the end of Inscr. no. **42** and in a context similar to or identical with the passages in which the verbs *nkylyt* and *ndyšyt* appear. The last sentence of Inscr. no. **42** reads: *ʾP-š*[91] *ZNH̱ nkʾl ps(?)čyt*; i.e., "and by him

this picture was ...." The last word, which must be a third singular of a preterite ending in -*īt* and standing in a passive construction, is still unexplained. Pagliaro in his "Preliminary Note"[92] read it *pas(ā)čēt*. But this reading was properly rejected by Polotsky, who pointed out that this word would be a form of the present tense, and that the preterite would have been *psʾχt*. He should have pointed out also that *pasāčēt* would have been written *psʾčyt*, not *psčyt*. In this context we must call attention to the fact that both Pagliaro and Altheim in numerous instances arbitrarily and wrongly introduce the long *a*-vowel, transliterating it by "(ā)," where the text does not offer the *mater lectionis aleph*, because it does not contain an *ā*. They did not bear in mind that in the Pārsīk inscriptions, not only in those of the Synagogue, the *ā* is as a rule — with certain exceptions which will be mentioned later[93] — expressed by the *mater lectionis aleph*. Altheim's reading *psχt = passāχt*, which he translates "ausgeführt" ("executed") and makes a separate sentence,[94] betrays its incorrectness by being spelled without an *aleph*. The reading is definitely excluded, moreover, by the fact that the *χ* of Altheim's *psχt* is in reality an unmistakable *č*, and that the "dot" ("Punkt") before the *t*, which Altheim does not know how to explain, is a *y*!

Later, Pagliaro replaced his earlier reading *pas(ā)čēt* by *pargast*, which is even worse, and to which he assigned the meaning "was terminated" ("porto a termine"). It is sufficient to state that this reading is sharply contradicted by the letters of the photographs, where one looks in vain for the *r* or the *g* or the *s* (which last is in reality a *č*). Pagliaro, on the other hand, disregarded the *y* before the final *t*.[95]

90. Polotsky referred to Henning, *Zeitschrift für Indologie und Iranistik*, IX (1933–1934), p. 168, where the passages of the Turfan texts are listed and where P. Tedesco's remarks on *īš-* and *nīš-* (preposition *ni* and √*īš-*, = OldInd. *īkṣ-*), "to see," in Modern Iranian dialects (*Monde Oriental*, XV, 1921, pp. 237f.) are referred to. However W. Geiger, *Grundriß d. Iran. Philologie*, I/2, has not only the Māzandarānī *īš-*, "to see" (p. 364), but also Tāt *dänširän*; i.e., *dä-nīš-īrän*, explained by *nigāh kardan*, "to observe, pay attention" (*ibid.*, p. 377: Tāt, line 2, and p. 378, n. 71). C. Salemann, *Manichaeische Studien*, I (*Memoires de l'académie impériale des sciences de St. Pétersbourg*, 8th series, VIII, no. 10, 1908), p. 100 had already pointed to Judaeo-Pers. *nīšīdan* and Tāt *de-nišire*.

91. In the original text the word *ZNH̱* must have been preceded by the two words *YʾTWN ʾP-š*, ("came and

by him"), but in the photographs only one word is to be seen, and it is difficult to decide which one is missing, for besides a well preserved ʾ only remnants of the other letters are visible. But for epigraphical reasons it is more likely that it is the word *YʾTWN* which the scribe has erroneously omitted.

92. *Rep. VI*, p. 395.

93. See below, p. 297, n. 115.

94. *Asien und Rom*, pp. 24 and 28.

95. Pagliaro (*Rendiconti*, p. 592) believed to have found the same word in the form *prks[t] = parkast* with the meaning "was completed" in Inscr. no. **50** as the last word of line 1. However, though the letters or their remnants are difficult to identify, there is no doubt that the word is not *prks[t]*, but *dpyr* (*dipīr*), especially since

Polotsky did not offer any explanation of the word which he transliterated by *psčyt*. He merely said "unknown word." Only recently Prof. P. J. de Menasce in a review of Altheim's book[96] has proposed the reading *psynyt* (*pēsīnīt*), with the translation "a peint" (i.e., "has painted"). This interpretation is, however, impossible in view of the fact that the *yn* of "*psynyt*" is an indisputable *č*, that *pēs*- would have been expressed by *pys*- (not *ps*-)[97], and that after our clarifications of the meanings of the verbs *nkylyt* and *ndyšyt* the synonymy of *psčyt* with these two verbs is firmly established.

Now there still remains the task of determining whether it is possible to explain the word *psčyt* epigraphically and linguistically in a way consistent with the postulated meaning. It seems to me that this possibility exists, and that the explanation which I propose will prove convincing and will stand the test. Even in the very first draft of this work, as mentioned above, I suggested that we should read *ptčyt* instead of *psčyt*. It can not be denied that the second letter of the word is an *s*. But it seems upon closer inspection very likely that, owing to a somewhat inaccurate, hasty manner of cursive writing, the left part of the letter *t* was not written in a vertical line, as we might have expected, but curved in the direction of the following letter *č*, and that in consequence of this irregularity the horizontal bottom stroke of the *t* was omitted, so that the *t* became an *s*. This conjecture is supported by the fact that in the preceding line of Inscr. no. **42**, just above our word, the scribe in connecting the letter *Y* with the following *T* of the word *BYT'* also omitted the horizontal bottom stroke of the *T*.[98] It is of great interest and an additional confirmation of my reading that I subsequently discovered in some of

the most excellent photographs of the text, under the space between the *p* and *s* of *psčyt* two extremely tiny and hardly visible letters which I could identify with certainty as the *pt*. I have reproduced them in my tracing of this inscription made for the *editio major*. It is noteworthy that I had previously found a word *ptčyt*; i.e., *patčīt*, in the Pārsīk Dura parchment 37, Verso, line 3. I consider it very likely that this word coincides in its meaning with the *ptčyt* of the dipinto.[99]

As to the linguistic aspect of the problem, I have already mentioned that in my first draft I indicated the possibility of explaining the word *patčīt*, which I had conjectured instead of the inexplicable *psčyt*, as a compound of the third singular preterite of the Old Indic and Old Iranian root ²*či*-, "to discern," and the preposition *pat*-. Abandoning my wrong combination of the word with Middle Persian *patčēn*, "the copy," I interpreted *patčīt* henceforth as a derivative of the root ²*či*- with the meaning "it was observed (viewed)." The same root is used in OIndic and in OIranian with the prepositions *vi*- (in the Avesta *vī-čidyāi*, *vī-čiϑa-*, *vī-čira-*, *vī- δčoišta-*, etc.) and *ni*- (in OInd. *ni-či-*, *ni-čira*, *ni-četṛ*-). This composition of ²*či*- with the preposition *ni*- represents a verbal compound of the same kind as the above-mentioned *ndyšyt*; i.e., *niyīšīt*, *nīšīt*, "it was beheld," from *ni*-√*īš* (OInd. √*īkṣ*-), which occurs in three of our dipinti. We are reminded also of MidPers. *nikās* (ModPers. *nigāh*), "observation," from *ni*- and OIran. √*kas*-, "to see." Our reconstructed verbal compound *pat-čīt* itself has parallels in Avestan *pati-dī-*, "to look at," Middle Parthian *pd-gs-* (from **pat-kas-*), "to look at," Parthian epigraphic *pātkāsē*, "visible," and OInd. *prati-īkṣ-*, *prati-cakṣ-*, *prati-paś-*, all three

---

its letters are, in accordance with the fixed pattern, preceded by '*MT*, "when," and by a word which obviously is the name of a scribe, and are followed by the words *Y'TWNt HWḤnd*, "they [instead of "he"] came."

96. *Journal asiatique*, CCXL (1952), p. 516.

97. Pagliaro and Altheim sometimes also disregard the fact that the long vowels *ī*, *ē* would have to be expressed by the *mater lectionis y*. One of the former's gravest errors is his reading *mčrnn* = *mečr(ē)n(ā)n*, "the Egyptians," in line 4 of the inscription under discussion, instead of the correct *zhmy* = *zahmē*, "the building."

98. We may even say that owing to this lack of accuracy the *T* of *BYT'* is, in some degree similar to the seeming *s* of *psčyt*.

99. A photographic reproduction of the parchment is to be found in Altheim's *Asien und Rom*, p. 74, fig. 3. The letters *pčyt* of the word in the fragment are beautifully written and very distinct. Only the initial *p* is not wholly preserved, having lost some of its color, but there is no doubt that it is the letter *p*. Altheim offers the fantastic reading ...]*ḥr WKYNYT* with the translation "und auf gerechte Weise" (*ibid.*, p. 20). His *ḥr* is in reality the initial *p* of the word, the letters *WK* are mistaken for the letter *t*, and the letters *YN* for *č*. He explains (p. 21) *KYNYT* as an adverbial form of Syriac *kēnā*, "gerecht," with the "East-Aramaic" ending -*īt*, so that — according to Altheim — here for the first time an East Aramaic form appears in the "Imperial Aramaic" of the ideograms. In reality the word is the genuinely Iranian *patčīt*.

meaning "to look at," and *prati-dṛś-*, in the middle and passive "to be looked at, to be visible." From all these facts we are entitled to draw the conclusion that my reading *patčīt* and its interpretation are well established both from the epigraphical and the linguistic point of view and in perfect harmony with the two parallel verbs *nikīrīt*, "it was looked at," and *ndyšyt* (*niyīšīt*, *nīšīt*), "it was beheld."

In an earlier part of this introduction I remarked briefly that Pagliaro in his extensive work[100] has referred to a number of alleged technical terms which he claimed to have found in these inscriptions and which he quoted in support of the theory that the *dipīrs* were painters. Let me therefore clarify here briefly the actual state of affairs. The word *dipān* he explained as a plural form of *dip*, asserting that it means "figure" (paintings). But the reading *dipān* is absolutely impossible in all three passages of the inscription where the word is said to occur. In Inscr. no. **43**, line 6 (*Rendiconti*, p. 606) *dipān* is wrong and the word must be read *'P-šn* (*u-šān*), and by them"; in Inscr. no. **42**, line 4 (*ibid.*, p. 612) the correct reading is undoubtedly only *dpywr* (*dipīwar*); and in no. **49**, line 3 (*ibid.*, p. 589) the reading *dipān* is quite irreconcilable with the letters of the word, which obviously is *zywndk*, "living."

Pagliaro has himself pointed (p. 584) to the well-known fact that in the Pārsīk of the literature the word *dip* is attested only in the meaning "the written document," especially "the legal document"; i.e., one to which a seal is affixed, but he inferred from his imaginary *dipān* that *dip* in our inscriptions means "pittura" (p. 590). Since this conclusion has turned out to be wrong, all his attempts to trace and to ascertain derivatives or denominatives of *dip-*, like **dipist*, *nidipīt*, *nidipist*, with the meaning "he painted," (p. 584) were bound to end in failure. The first of these forms, **dipist* ("hypothetically") or "*nipist*(?)" is supposed to render the monstrous ideogram *KYTBWstww* [!], "*dipinse*"[101] in Inscr. no. **49**, line 2 (*ibid.*, pp. 589 ff.),

whereas the photographs unmistakably show the two words *dpywr Y'TWN*, "the scribe came!" The form *nidipīt* (*ibid.*, p. 595) — or "possibly *nidipist*" according to p. 596 — incorrectly reproduces *ndyšyt*, "it was beheld," in Inscr. no. **46**, line 5; and *ndypš . . . = nidipis[t]* (p. 597) is in reality the word *dpyr*, "the scribe," which has its correct and regular place after the name of the man in Inscr. no. **45**, line 2. As to the word *nipist*, we must point out that on p. 606 [*nipis*]*t* is misread for ['P-šn ZN]*H̱*, "and this" (Inscr. no. **43**, line 7); that on p. 603 ("fu dipinto") it misrepresents the letters *wp't* of the personal name *hwp't* (*hupāt*) (Inscr. no. **48**, line 1); that on p. 615 [*nipi*]*st* replaces the correct *'mt* (*āmat*), "he became" (Inscr. no. **51**, line 5). There is finally Inscr. no. **47**, line 3, where the very distinctly written word *ndyšyt*, "it was beheld," was quite wrongly rendered by Pagliaro (p. 600) as *nikārt*, "it was painted."

Finally, the expressions *'P-š* (*u-š*), "and by him," and *'P-šn* (*u-šān*), "and by them," which have been completely misunderstood by Pagliaro and Altheim, require a few supplementary critical remarks to clarify the sense of the inscriptions. Only Polotsky has recognized these expressions, except in the Inscrs. nos. **44** and **51**, which he did not try to interpret at all. In Pagliaro's transliterations *'P-š* of Inscr. no. **49**, line 3, becomes *BYN PRG* (Iranian *andar nēm*), "inside" (*Rendiconti*, pp. 589 f.); the *'P-šn* of Inscr. no. **48**, line 2, becomes -*'p'n*[102] (pp. 603 f.); the *'P-šn* of Inscr. no. **43**, line 5, becomes -*sp'n*; and *'P-šn* in the same inscription, line 6, becomes *dyp'n = dipān*, "figure" (pp. 606, 608).

Altheim's readings stand on the same level. He failed to recognize the *'P-š*, "and by him," in those of the passages with which he has dealt. In Inscr. no. **42**, line 5 he reads,[103] quite inconsistently with the letters of the original, the "East Aramaic" *BBYT* ("inter," "within") instead of *'P-š*[104]; in

---

100. *Rendiconti*, pp. 584 f., 590, and elsewhere in his comments.

101. It is well known that the ideogram for *nipištan*, "to write," occurs in the Sasanian inscriptions, Pārsīk *YKTYBWN*, Parthian *KTYBt* (in four passages of the Ka'bah inscription), and in the Middle Persian literature *YKTYBWNt* or *YKTYBWNst*.

102. Supposed to be the second part of a word with the meaning "[con]fusing." See above p. 292, n. 89.

103. *Asien und Rom*, pp. 24 and 28.

104. The epigraphical explanation of this reading (*ibid.*, p. 28), according to which "die beiden *b* sind in ihrer unteren Querhasta, wie auch sonst, verbunden. Daß das darüber befindliche *y* davon durch einen kleinen Zwischenraum verbunden ist, erkennt man....," is sharply contradicted by the letters of the original. Two *b* letters are never connected by an "untere Querhasta" in the Sasanian inscriptions (e.g. in the ideogram בבא). In the dipinti there

Inscr. no. **51**, line 3, first word, he did not recognize the partly distinct traces of 'P-š[105]; and in the end of the same line he reads -'Y' as the ending of the monstrous word *BYLDYT'Y'*, to which he assigned the meaning "the castles."[106]

As to 'P-šn, "and by them," Altheim declares[107] that "the word 'pšn is attested only in Syriac." Unfortunately he had discovered in Brockelmann's *Lexicon Syriacum*[108] a "Syriac word" אפשׁין ('afšīn) which Brockelmann quoted from a collection of Syriac liturgical texts found in a village north of Damascus and described by Eduard Sachau.[109] The word 'afšīn appears there among a number of liturgical technical terms explained as εὐχή, "prayer," and it is evident that the "Syriac" word 'afšīn is nothing but a reproduction of the Greek word or rather of its accusative εὐχήν. It is, therefore, an utterly wrong idea to identify the 'P-šn of Inscr. no. **48**, line 2 in the passage *Y'TWN HWH[ṅ]d 'P-šn by'm'y nkylyt*; i.e., "they came and by them the *by'm'y* was looked at," with the "Syriac" 'afšīn and to assign it together with other "Syriac" words of the same kind to Altheim's imaginary list of "East Aramaic" elements within the "Reichs-Aramäisch" of the "Pehlevi" ideograms. He did not even take into consideration the fact that this 'afšīn would undoubtedly have been reproduced by 'PŠYN, with Y in Iranian script. The

absurdity of Altheim's explanation of our 'P-šn[110] manifests itself most clearly in his reading and interpretation of the passage in Inscr. no. **48**, line 2, the only correct interpretation of which I have just presented. Altheim reads *Y'TWN HWH[nd B]'PŠN Bb'm'y šylwyn*, and translates it by: "sie kommen (und) sind[111] zur εὐχή bei dem βῆμα der Šīrōīn." I have already stated (above, p. 292, n. 89) that the woman called *Šīrōīn* is in reality the verb *nikīrīt*, "it was looked at," and that *Bb'm'y* incorrectly renders *by'm'y*,[112] the synonym of *nikār*, "the picture." Furthermore, Altheim's assertion that between *HWH* and 'P-šn not only the traces of *nd*, but also that of the *B* are visible, is undoubtedly wrong; and *B'PŠN*, "zur εὐχή," proves to be a most arbitrary reading for 'P-šn, "and by them."

According to Altheim (p. 26) this "'pšn" [= Syriac אפשׁין] "is in the Synagogue inscription regularly connected with βῆμα." In reality our 'P-šn ("and by them") — his 'afšīn = εὐχή — appears only once, in Inscr. no. **48**, line 2, in the neighborhood of our *by'm'y* (= *nikār*), his *b'm'y* = βῆμα. However, Altheim found one more case of the connection of his 'PŠN (= 'PŠYN) with the βῆμα; namely, in Inscr. no. **47**, line 3, where he reads:[113] *Y'TWN Bb'm'y 'PŠNYN* and translates: "sie kommen [und sind] bei dem βῆμα der Gebete." But *Bb'm'y* is in reality *Wby'm'y* ("and the *by'm'y*"; i.e., the picture), and his 'PŠNYN ("prayers"), which he makes a plural of his "Syriac" 'PŠYN with a "remarkable" initial 'ayin instead of the *aleph* of the singular[114] is like

---

did not even exist any opportunity for such a connection, as the succession of two *b*'s occurs in none of them. Altheim's *Bb'm'y*, p. 26 — our Inscr. no. **48** — is in reality *by'm'y*; his *BBYL'T*, p. 27 — our Inscr. no. **46** — is *Wbwlĵ'tw[r]*; and his *Bb'm'y*, p. 66 — our Inscr. no. **47** — is *Wby'm'y*. Pagliaro, in *Rep. VI*, p. 395 and *Rendiconti*, pp. 612 f., offers the far-fetched reading '*pd(')n*, and in connection with the preceding word *BYT'* the phrase *BYT'* (= χānak) [i] *apad(ā)n*, to which he assigns the meaning "casa di riunione" as a designation of the Synagogue. We are presented with the same reading *BYT'* [i] [apad(ā)]n, instead of *BYT'* [*Y'TW*]*N* of Inscr. no. **43**, lines 5 f., in *Rendiconti*, pp. 606 and 608. In Pagliaro's opinion the original meaning of the Old Persian *apadāna*-, reflected in Middle Persian *apadān*, is "audience hall"; i.e., "place of assembly." In reality the original meaning is "palace, castle," which is still preserved in the loanwords in Aramaic, Arabic, and Armenian.

105. Cf. the more distinct 'P-š in the corresponding passage of Inscr. No. **49**, line 3.

106. See my criticism of this form above, p. 289.

107. *Asien und Rom*, pp. 26 f. and 58 f.

108. C. Brockelmann, *Lexicon Syriacum* (2nd ed., 1928), p. 43b.

109. *Sitzungsberichte der berliner Akademie der Wissenschaften* (1899), p. 506.

110. This explanation is still upheld in Altheim-Stiehl, *Ein asiatischer Staat*, I (1954), p. 248.

111. This translation is an offence against one of the most elementary facts of grammar. *Y'TWN* (or complete *Y'TWNt*) *HWHnd*; i.e., *āmat hēnd* (Modern Persian *āmad-and*) is the third plural preterite, composed of the participle preterite and the plural of the present of the auxiliary verb (*HWHnd*) and of course means, "they came," not "they come [*sic*!] (and) are." Strangely enough, Altheim (p. 67) translates in Inscr. no. **47**, line 3 [not 4!]*Y'TWN Bb'm'y* [*sic*! instead of *Wby'm'y*], though there is no *HWHnd* (= *hēnd*) after *Y'TWN*, by "sie kommen [und sind] bei dem βῆμα....."

112. It is inconceivable how the two letters *by* so beautifully and clearly written, could be mistaken for two *b*'s.

113. *Asien und Rom*, pp. 66 f.

114. Altheim says only "Hervorzuheben ist die Schreibung '*pšnyn* mit Aiyin statt Aleph." He obviously thought that this his substitution of ע for א is to be

the above-mentioned woman *Šīrōin* — properly the verb *nikīrīt*, "it was looked at" — an ordinary verbal form; namely, *ndyšyt* (*niyīšīt, nīšīt*), "it was beheld," which we already know as a synonym of *nikīrīt*.[115]

In closing I wish to point to the interesting fact that the wording of the dated dipinti, according to which on a certain date (month, day, year) a *dipīr*, either alone or accompanied by other persons, came to the Synagogue and "by him (or by them) a picture was looked at," is strikingly reminiscent of two passages of the Middle Persian inscriptions of Persepolis.[116] The first, Pers. I, reads: *BYRX spnd[r]mt QDM ŠNT* ... (line 2) ... *'MT* ... *MLK'* ... (line 5) ... *'L st stwny* ("to the Hundred Columns") *Y'TWN 'P-š* (line 7) ... *'plyny 'BYDWN* ("came and by him blessing was made"). The second, Pers. II, has: *BYRX tyr QDM ŠNT* ... *YWM 'whrmzdy 'MBYN* (?) ... (line 2) ... *'L st stwny Y'TWN HWH̱-m* (line 3) *'P-m HNH̱ n'mky* ... (line 4) ... *plm'ty ptpwrsyt 'P-m* (line 5) *'plyny krty* ("... when (?) to the Hundred Col-

umns I came and by me this document ... was ordered to be read and by me blessing was made"). This close similarity of wording makes it evident that the *dipīrs* of our dated dipinti followed a customary, traditional formulation used by professional Iranian scribes.

3. THE VISITORS TO THE SYNAGOGUE

The facts which I have presented in the earlier part of this introduction fully justify and firmly establish the conclusion that the *dipīrs* were scribes and at the same time visitors. This conclusion is confirmed by additional facts that can be gathered from some of the inscriptions. As I have previously stressed, it is obviously of special significance that the *dipīrs* have typical Zoroastrian names, such as *Yazdāntaχ[m]-Far[n]bay* (Inscr. no. 42), "Through the Gods Strong-Having Glory (Fortune) as his Share"[117]; *Yazdān-pēsē* (Inscr. no. 43), "Having

---

explained in the same easy way as that of א for ע in his reading *'L BYLDYT'Y'*, with אל for the preposition על (see above, p. 290 with n. 82). In reality the ע of Altheim's *'PŠNYN*; i.e., *'afšnīn*, is an unmistakable *n*, the alleged *P* (= *f*) is represented in the photographs by the two clear and well-formed letters *dy*, the *N* (after the *š*) is a partly blurred *y*, and the two final letters *YN* are in reality the one unmistakable letter *t*. The whole word is, therefore, not *'PŠNYN*, but the verb *ndyšyt*! The word *ndyšyt* is distinct enough in Altheim's photograph (p. 84, Abbildung 30), but it is still clearer in his two photographs (p. 76, Abbildung 9a–b) of our Inscr. no. 46. One wonders why Altheim did not transliterate and translate the last three words *Y'TWN Wbym'y ndyšyt* of Inscr. no. 46 on p. 27 of his book.

115. It seems necessary to add a few words here about the writing of the word *'P-šn = u-šān*, "and by them," after it has been so badly treated in the previous publications dealing with these inscriptions. It is well known that *'P-šn*, like the combinations of Aramaic *'P* with other enclitics such as *-am, -at, -aš*, etc., occurs innumerable times in the Pārsīk of the literature and in the Sasanian inscriptions. To be sure, the enclitic *-šn* is written *-š'n* (שאן) in the Pārsīk of the literature and in the Manichaean fragments from Turfan. But the Pārsīk versions of the Sasanian inscriptions always write the enclitics *-šān* and *-tān*, the plural of the enclitic of the second person, without א; i.e., *-šn* and *-tn*, like the Parthian *-šn* and *-tn* (also Sogdian *-šn*, etc.). Moreover we still find the enclitics *-m'n, -t'n* and *-š'n* in the defective writing *-mn* (*-m'n* only at the end of a line), *-tn* and *-šn* in the Pahlavī Psalter, where *'P-mn, 'P-šn* (with the singular *-š* in *'P-š*) occur often also in passive constructions ("and by us," etc.).

116. E. Herzfeld, *Paikuli* (1924), pp. 121f.

117. In the course of repeated examinations of this word, which stands between *'MT*, "when," and *dipīwar* and must therefore necessarily be the name of the scribe, I always arrived at the result that this reading is absolutely correct, although it met with a number of difficulties. The *z* is blurred, the *n* is shorter than usual and similar to a *w* (= *r*), the *m* is damaged (a trace still visible and part of an *m* is to be seen above the line), the *p* (= *f*) is partly blurred and disfigured, the *r* is written with a *w* (= *r*) instead of *l* (= *r*), the following *n* is either effaced or incomplete, and is followed by a beautifully written ligature of two letters which can only be a combination of *b* and *y*. It is this ligature which proves conclusively the correctness of the reading *Farnbay* as the second element in the name, although on Sasanian seals the last letter is always a *g* (in the Pārsīk of the literature the originally different letters *g* and *y* have fused into one sign), and in the Pārsīk of the Sasanian inscriptions and coins the word *bay* (*bayē*), "God," is always written with a *g*. There are only a few cases to be found in Pāzänd where derivatives of *bay* show *y* instead of *g*. It seems possible that Parthian *bg* was taken over into the Pārsīk dialect and here obtained predominance over the Pārsīk *by*. Only in the Manichaean fragments from Turfan do we find the Parthian *bg* and its derivatives sharply distinguished from the Pārsīk *by* (*bay*) and its derivatives. However, I believe to have found another case of the writing *by* in our Inscr. no. 44, end of line 3, where I arrived at the result that the correct reading of the difficult passage is *by ZY by'n*, "the God of the Gods." My long and intensive study of the peculiarities of the script of these inscriptions has convinced me that the final sign of the name in Inscr. no. 42 is not a ligature of *b* and *g*, but can only be a combination of *b* and *y*; this will be demonstrated with more details in the *editio major*. As to the second letter of the *pr[n]by = Far[n]bay*, it seems surprising that it is here written with *w*, whereas the Pārsīk of the literature always uses *l* (= *r*). However, this should not be cited as

the Gods as his Ornament"; *Hormazdē* (Inscrs. nos. **44**, **49**, and perhaps **50**); *Rašnakē* (Inscr. no. **46**); *Artāv* (Inscr. no. **51**); *Mahrspandē* (Inscr. no. **47**). Only the names *Pakōrē* (Inscr. no. **45**) and *Aparsām* (*SPR'*) (Inscr. no. **54**) are of a different kind, and the origin and meaning of the name *Syh'r* (Inscr. no. **56**), which is not known from other sources, cannot be determined.

However, in two inscriptions (Inscrs. nos. **44** and **45**) we have alongside the *dipīr* another *dipīr* (*dipīwar*), called the *dipīwarē ī zahmē*, among those who came to the Synagogue. Instead of *dipīwarē ī zahmē* one inscription has the expression *dipīwar ī radakē* (Inscr. no. **43**), and it seems most likely that *radakē* is a synonym of *zahmē*, the meaning of which will be discussed later. I must point out in this connection that in the last three of the inscriptions just mentioned the proper names of the *dipīwarē ī zahmē* and that of the *dipīwar ī radakē* are not given. It is, therefore, not unlikely that in Inscr. no. **42**, where the name *yzd'ntχ[m]-pr[n]by* is immediately followed by *dpywr ZY zhmy*, the scribe has mistakenly written the passage the way it appears in the photographs. Very likely he meant to write *yzd'ntχ[m]-pr[n]by dpyr Wdpywr ZY zhmy*; i.e., the *dipīr Y.* and the *dipīwar ī zahmē*. Our suspicion that the scribe has omitted the letters *dpyr W*, seems to be justified by the fact that he has erroneously omitted also the word *Y'TWN* in line 5 between *BYT'* and *'P-š*, as I have stated above in n. 91. In Inscr. no. **46** the *Burzātu[r]* of *Rašnakē dipīr ut Burzātu[r]* is probably not a *dipīwarē ī zahmē*, but a different person who accompanies the *dipīr* to the Synagogue. In another instance, in Inscr. no. **48**, perhaps due to an accidental omission, even the word *dipīr* does not occur, and only the names *Nχy'ľ'p*, *Hupāt*, and *Far(r)aχvē* are listed as names of the persons who visited the Synagogue. It seems, however, that after *Far(r)aχvē* the words *ZY dpyr* have been added by a later hand. In any case, it is noteworthy

that the otherwise unidentified companions of the *dipīrs*, such as *Burzātur, Hupāt, Far(r)aχvē*, probably also *Nχy'ľ'p*, have typically Zoroastrian names. In my opinion the names of the *dipīrs* and of their companions give a strong presumption that the bearers of these names, in particular the *dipīrs*, were for the most part persons of a higher social rank and, in all likelihood, "members of the retinues of ambassadors sent by Shapur to Dura before and during his great invasion of the Syrian provinces of the Roman Empire."[118]

In some of the dipinti the *dipīr* goes to the Synagogue alone. In three other cases, as we have seen, he is said to have been accompanied by a *dipīwar(ē) ī zahmē* or a *dipīwar ī radakē*. As I have already mentioned, the word *zahmē* begins with a strange, hitherto unknown letter which I have identified as a form of the letter *z*. As far as the etymology and actual meaning of the word are concerned, there are two words, or rather two forms of one word of the Middle Persian literature with which this *zhmy* could be connected. They are *ztm*; i.e., *zϑm*, an historical writing for *zhm* = *zahm*; and *zhm* or *zχm*; i.e., *zahm, zaχm*. Both words mean "striking, stroke, blow" and are continued in Modern Persian *zaχm*, "blow, wound."[119] However, in Modern Persian *zaχm* has the further meaning of "the erection of a building, structure, edifice," and there is no doubt that in this meaning the word goes back to the same origin as *zaχm*, "blow," that is to the root OIran. *jan-*, Middle and Modern Persian *zan-*. This root was obviously used also in the sense "to strike into the ground, to erect a building," as is proved by Modern Persian *sarāparda*, or *χaima, zadan*, "to erect a (royal) tent" (*Šāhnāma*). This *zaχm* occurs five times in Firdousī's *Šāhnāma*. In four of these passages it is connected with *binā, ēvān*, or *kār*, in the sense of the erection of a building, a palace or an (architectural) work.[120] The fifth passage refers to the erection of a palace for *Xosrou Parvēz*, which is praised with the words: *kas andar jihān zaχm-i čunān na-dīd*, "Nobody in the world saw a structure (edifice) like that."[121] If this identifi-

---

an argument against my reading. Here I point only to the fact that in this same inscription the word *fravartin* is written *pwwwtyn* (as in the Šāhpuhr inscription published by R. Ghirshman, *Revue des arts asiatiques* X, 1936, p. 124, line 1) instead of *plwltyn*, as it is always written in the literature. In the *editio major* I am giving a few additional remarks concerning *yzd'ntχ[m]*, and there I shall have to deal with Pagliaro's and Altheim's entirely wrong readings of the name of the *dipīwar*.

118. Rostovtzeff, *Dura-Europos and its Art*, p. 113.

119. Cf. Chr. Bartholomae, *Über ein sasanidisches Rechtsbuch* (*Sitzungsberichte der heidelberger Akademie der Wissenschaften*, 1910, No. 11), p. 22.

120. Ed. J. Mohl, VII, pp. 322–324, vvs. 3807, 3826, 3832, 3852.

121. *Ibid.*, p. 326, v. 3861.

cation of *zahmē* is correct, as it is most likely to be, the expression *dipīwar ī zahmē* means "the scribe of the building," though we do not know what kind of building is meant. In any case, the *dipīwar ī zahmē* is a Persian official, perhaps of an even higher rank than the ordinary *dipīr*; and *zahmē*, "the building," should by no means be considered identical with *BYT'* and *patrastak*, the words which in our inscriptions designate the Synagogue. As to the *dipīwar ī radakē*, by whom the *dipīwar* is accompanied in Inscr. no. **43**, I have in my commentary to line 3 of this inscription given reasons in support of my opinion that *radakē* means "erection, structure, building" and is a synonym of *zahmē*.

The official character of the two kinds of *dipīrs* and of their functions and the fact that, at least in one inscription (no. **48**), even persons who are not *dipīrs*, go along with them to the Synagogue, is strikingly illustrated by the highly interesting and important Inscr. no. **44**, which I was fortunate enough to interpret satisfactorily in spite of the poor state of preservation of some of its parts. Here we read to our great surprise that with a *dipīr* and a *dipīwar ī zahmē* a certain *zandak ī yahūdān*, "the *zandak* of the Jews"; i.e., undoubtedly a high representative or the head of the Jewish community of Dura, went to the Synagogue, "and by them this picture was beheld." This proves that E. L. Sukenik was wrong in asserting that when the Persian visitors came to the Synagogue, the Jews had long since left Dura.[122]

This inscription is also important in that it provides us with a better insight into the circumstances under which these inscriptions were written so prominently and strangely on the paintings of the Synagogue. The fact that the head of the Jewish community accompanied the Iranian visitors to the Synagogue can only be interpreted to mean that he was supposed to explain to them the meaning of the paintings which they beheld. We may even suggest that at all the other visits recorded in inscriptions the visitors were also guided by a representative of the Jewish community. For the Iranians would hardly have understood the subjects of the pictorial representations without an explanation given by a Jew, nor would they have

been able unaided to describe the meaning of the paintings such as those dealing with Ezekiel and Elijah as they did in the interpretative sentences of the Inscrs. nos. **52**, **53**, **55**, and in part also in Inscrs. nos. **49** and **51**. We cannot escape the conclusion that such descriptions and general sentences can only rest on information given to the Persians by Jews, or that they merely translate sentences of Jewish texts into Pārsīk and (No. **55**) Parthian. The opinion that the *dipīrs* were Jews, is, of course, quite erroneous. Bearing this in mind, we shall not be misled into believing that only a Jew could have written the words in line 3 of Inscr. no. **44**: *patrastak[ē] ī bay ī bayān [ī] yahūdān*, "the edifice of the God of the Gods of the Jews," which here designates the Synagogue, whereas other inscriptions speak of the Synagogue merely as *BYT'* ("the House") or just *patrastakē* ("edifice")[123] without any special qualification. In Inscrs. nos. **49** and **51** the expressions *ZNḤ* ⟨*nyk'l*⟩ [*ny*]*kldyt zyw*[*n*]*dk kydly* (?) *YMYTN* ("the picture was looked at: alive [was] the dead child (?)") and *ZNḤ nyk'l ṅykldyt 'P-š kydly* (?) *ny*[*k*]*ldyty 'YK zyw*[*nd*]*ky* (?) *YMYTN 'mt* ("this picture was looked at, and by him the child (?) was looked at thus: 'Living the dead became'") remind us to some extent of the words of Elijah in the Hebrew text of I Kings 17.23: רְאִי חַי בְּנֵךְ, "See, thy son liveth."[124] But unfortunately all efforts to identify the general sentences of other inscriptions with the underlying Jewish texts have been in vain.

It is furthermore regrettable that Inscr. no. **44** does not provide more information about the representative of the Jews of Dura. His name, *Kantak*, is not known from any other available source, and the exact meaning of his title *zandak* in *kantak ī zandakē* ("Kantak, the *zandak*") and *zandakē ī yahūdān* ("the *zandak* of the Jews") can only be guessed to be that of the head of the community. However, while I was searching for a plausible explanation and etymology of the word *zandak*, Professor Saul Lieberman of the Jewish Theological Seminary kindly called my attention to a passage of Aggadath Esther (ed. S. Buber, p. 37) where a word זנדיקין occurs, to which he assigns

---

122. *The Synagogue*, p. 163.

123. Details about the writing of the word *patrastakē* and the expression *bay ī bayān* will be given in the *editio major*.

124. In Syriac חזי דחיא ברכי.

a meaning similar to that which we postulate for the *zandak* of the inscription. In this passage Haman is said to have complained that the Jews cheated the Pharaoh. These are Haman's words: נכנסו אצלו אנשים בחורים זנדיקין ובאו עליו בעלילה. Lieberman does not accept the late Prof. Louis Ginzberg's interpretation of אנשים בחורים זנדיקין[125] as "unverschämte Jünglinge" ("insolent young men"). Ginzberg regarded זנדיק as identical with Arabic *zindīq* (MidPers. *zandīk*), "the heretic," and assumed the Jews might have used this word as a term of abuse. According to Lieberman it was the intention of Haman to emphasize that it was the Jewish "dignitaries" who deceived the Pharaoh, and the context in which the above-mentioned sentence stands seems to be very much in favor of this interpretation. Haman points out that the Pharaoh treated the Jews well and fed them in the years of famine, but when he asked them to build a palace, אנשים בחורים זנדיקין "gathered in his presence and came upon him with a false pretext," saying they were going to sacrifice to their God and would return after three days. When they had obtained permission to borrow jewels of silver and gold and did not return them, they were pursued by the Pharaoh. It is most unlikely indeed that the persons who appeared before the Pharaoh were persons who could have been characterized as insolent youngsters or as heretics. The only natural explanation is therefore that the persons

who appeared before the Pharaoh were official representatives of the Jews and that אנשים בחורים זנדיקין means "selected men, officials." Consequently, there is a high degree of probability that this זנדיקין, incorrectly written instead of זנדקין, is the plural of the word *zandak* of our inscription. The word *zandak* might be an Iranian word.

Among the new facts with which we are presented by Inscr. no. **44**, one is of very great importance. I refer to the three words which I have found in a specially circumscribed, nearly rectangular dark space underneath the last word (*ndyšyt*) of line 4 of the inscription, but without any connection with, and without any bearing upon, the inscription itself. I at once read these words *DYN' nzdyk YHWWN*; i.e., *dātistān nazdīk bavēt*, which means "Judgment is near!"[126] For some time I hesitated about the reading of the first three letters, *nzd*, of the second word, because they are blurred and seemed to be uncertain. But my reading was strikingly confirmed by the scarcely visible, but still distinct and absolutely certain, letters *nzdyk*, which a later hand wrote above the word of the line of text. The only possible and proper conclusion to draw from these ominous sounding words is that they express a warning attached to the inscription by one of the Iranian visitors sent to Dura by the Sasanian king before the fall of the city as members of his retinues of ambassadors.

B. The Inscriptions

42. Dipinto on Panel WC 2, on the himation of the first bystander, counting from the left. Six lines, black paint, Pārsīk script. Dimensions 0.105 m × 0.09 m. (Pl. XLIV, 1).

Rep. VI, p. 395; Pagliaro, *Rendiconti*, pp. 611–613; Polotsky's manuscript, partial transliteration and translation. Tracings by Pearson and Polotsky.

Transliteration

(1) BYRX prwrtyn QDM
(2) ŠNT 15 WYWM lšnw
(3) 'MT yzd'ntχ[m]pr[n]by
(4) dpywr ZY zhmy 'L
(5) ZNḤ BYT' 'P-š ZNḤ nk'l
(6) +ptčyt

Reading

māh fravartīn apar
sāl 15 ut rōč rašnu
kaδ yazdāntaχ[m]-far[n]bay
dipīwar ī zahmē ō
ēn χānak u-š ēn nikār
+patčīt

---

125. *In Festschrift Adolf Schwartz* (1917), p. 349.
126. The meaning "(last) judgment" is especially preserved in the Iranian loan word in Armenian *datastan*; e.g., Hebrews 19.27.

"The month Fravartīn in
the year fifteen and the day Rašnu,
when Yazdāntaχ[m]-Farnbay,
the scribe of the building, to
this house [came], and by him this picture
was observed."

Lines 1–2. *QDM ŠNT*; i.e., *apar sāl*, "upon (in) the year," occurs not only in the Sasanian inscriptions,[127] but also much later as *'br s'r* in a Middle Persian text of Turfan.[128]

Line 3. *yzd'ntχ[m]pr[n]by/* It will be evident from n. 117 (above p. 297) and from the tracing that my reading of this name is correct, and is at least partly confirmed by letters written by later hands above and below the line and even between the letters of the text line. I wish to emphasize here only that the sign at the end of the line is a ligature of *b* and *y*, by no means of *b* and *g*, as one might expect.

Line 4. *dpywr ZY zhmy*. After I had discovered that the phrase *dpywry ZY [?]hmy* occurs also in Inscr. No. 44, line 2, and No. 45, line 3; that instead of the strange initial letter which the present inscription has in common with Inscr. No. 45, Inscr. No. 44 offers the distinct trace of a *z*, which

is confirmed by a nicely written ligature *zh* beneath the line; and that furthermore in Inscr. No. 45, line 4, the word *ZNH̱* has instead of *Z* the same strange letter which stands initially in [?]hmy of the present inscription, it became evident that this strange and hitherto unknown letter is an imaginative or ornamental form of the letter *z*. As to the etymology of this word and the presumable function of the *dipīwarē ī zahmē*, see above pp. 298 f.

Line 5. Between the words *BYT'* and *'Pš*; i.e., Iranian *χānak* and *u-š*, the scribe omitted the word *Y'TWN*, Iranian *āmat*, "he came." See above, p. 293, n. 91.

Line 6. *ptčyt*. The reasons for my reading *ptčyt*, instead of the seeming *psčyt* of the photographs, and for my interpretation of the word as "it was observed" are given above pp. 293 f. About the word [*p*]tčyt in the Dura parchment 37, Verso, first word of line 3, with which I have identified the *ptčyt* of the dipinto, see above, p. 294, n. 99.

43. Dipinto on Panel WC 2, on Haman's left leg, the text proper on the thigh and the "tag" on the calf. Eight lines, black paint, Pārsīk script. Dimensions 0.05 m. × 0.08 m. (Pl. XLIV, 2).

Pagliaro, *Rendiconti*, pp. 605–608; Polotsky's manuscript, attempted transliteration and translation. Tracings by Pearson, Du Mesnil du Buisson, and Polotsky.

The text of the inscription from the last word

(*Y'TWN*) of line 4 until the end of line 7 is in a state of utter disorder as a result of mistakes and awkward corrections made by the scribe. I have restored the original text underlying the corrupted and confused text of lines 4–7, and I am presenting here the restored text of these lines immediately after the transcription of the text as it is offered by the photographs.

Transliteration	*Reading*
(1) BYRX mtry QDM ŠNT	māh miθrē apar sāl
(2) 14 WYWM št[r̄yw̄r̄]	14 ut rōč šaθ[rēvar]
(3) 'MT yzd'ṅpysy dpywr	kaδ yazdānpēsē dipīwar
(4) Wd[p]ywr ZY ldky Y'TWN	ut di[p]īwar ī radakē āmat
	ō
'L	
(5) H[WH̱]d 'P-šn ZNH̱ BYT'	h[ēn]d u-šān ēn χānak
(6) [Y'TW]N 'P-šn nkyl	[āmat] u-šān nikīr
(7) ['P-šn ZN]H̱ nk'l [*vacat*]	[u-šān ē]n nikār
(8) ['P-š]n ['p]lyny krty	[u-]šān [āf]rīnē kartē

127. Persepolis I,1 and II,1 in Herzfeld, *Paikuli*, pp. 121 f.

128. Müller, *Abhandlungen der preußischen Akademie der Wissenschaften, phil.-hist. Klasse*, XCVI (1913), lines 160, 235 f.

Corrected text of lines 4–7

Transliteration	*Reading*
(4) Wḋ[p]ywr ZY ldky	ut dipīwar ī radakē
(5) ʽL ZN<u>H</u> BYTʼ	ō ēn χānak
(6) YʼTW[N] H[W<u>H</u>]d	āmat h[ēn]d
(7) [ʼPšn ZN]<u>H</u> nkʼl nkyl[yt]	[u-šān ē]n nikār nikīr[īt]

The following translation is based on the original
text of lines 1–3, the corrected text of lines 4–7, and
the original text of line 8.

"In the month *Miθr*, in the year
fourteen, and on the day *Šaθrēvar*,
when Yazdānpēsē, the scribe,
and the scribe of the *radak*
to this house
came
[and by them] this picture [was looked at]
[and] by them praise was made."

A considerable distance beneath this inscription
are to be seen two letters, the first of which seems
to be only partly preserved. I am inclined to take
this for the word ʽD, Iranian *tāk*, "until." It seems
to have been added by a later hand as a connecting
link between the inscription proper and the "tag"
consisting of two lines a short distance below the
word ʽD. The text of these two lines reads as
follows:

Transliteration	*Reading*
(1) Byrx mtry	māh miθrē
(2) Q̇DM — ŠNT 1[4]	apar sāl 1[4]

"In the month of *Miθr*
in — the year 1[4]."

Line 2. *štrywr*. In this name of the day only the
first two letters *št* are quite certain. This is, however, sufficient to prove that the complete name
was *štrywr* (*šaθrēvar*). The remaining letters are
damaged and blurred and their restoration is partly
difficult.

Line 3. *ʼMT*. The letters of this word are only
partly preserved.

yzdʼnpysy. I read the name of the *dipīwar yzdʼn-
pysy* (*yazdān-pēsē*), which would mean, "having
God as his ornament." The decipherment of this
word met with great difficulties. This is especially
true with regard to the first part of the word, as
its letters with the exception of the *z* are blurred
and not easy to recognize. My reading was fortunately confirmed by letters written by later hands
above and below the line, as will be seen from my
editio major and from the tracing. I think also that
my reading of the second part (-*pysy*) of the name
is free from objections. The reading *yzdʼn-pysy*
can, of course, not be questioned on the ground
that this name is hitherto not known from any
other source.

Line 4. *Wḋ[p]ywr*. This word is not completely
preserved. The initial *W* is blurred but quite certain. The following sign looks as if it were only the
upper part of a *d*, but it might as well be a blurred
complete letter *d*. The *p* is effaced.

ldky. Polotsky read this word *lwdy*, but there is
no doubt that the second letter is not a *w* but a *d*,

the lower half of which is somewhat blurred owing to the interference of the end of the preceding *l*, nor that the third letter is an unmistakable *k*. I therefore read *ldky*; i.e., *radakē*, and consider it possible that this word has here the meaning "structure, building"[129] and that it is the Pārsīk form ($\sqrt{rad}$-) corresponding to the Parthian word *rāz*, "building," with which I have dealt in connection with other derivatives of the root *rad-*, *raz-*.[130] We may also point to the word *ptrstky* (*patrastakē*) which I have found and restored in Inscrs. nos. **44**, **45**, and **47**, although this word designates the Synagogue, whereas the *radak* of the present inscription must be some other building. My interpretation of *ldky*: *radakē* as part of *Wdpywr ZY ldky* is moreover supported by the fact that this phrase is obviously identical with the phrase *Wdpywry ZY zhmy* of Inscrs. nos. **44** and **45**; for the *dipīwar* of the *radak* as well as the *dipīwar* of the *zahm* are mentioned after the *dipīwar* proper in the lists of those who have come to the Synagogue.

44. Dipinto on Panel WC 2, on Haman's right leg, the text proper on the thigh, the "tag" on the calf. Both texts run along the length of the leg, appearing vertical from the standpoint of the spectator. Six lines, black paint, Parsīk script (Pl. XLIV, 3).

Pagliaro, *Rendiconti*, pp. 608–610: attempted transliteration and translation of a few words. Not in Polotsky's manuscript. Tracings by Pearson, Du Mesnil du Buisson, Kraeling.

The photographs show at some distance to the left of the text proper a tag written by a different hand, and at the right margin a few partly indistinct words which were added later and turned out to be repetitions of some words of the text. Their reading will be given in my *editio major*. Furthermore, beneath the last word of line 4 there are three words which have no bearing on the

Y'TWN. Here the confusion of the scribe begins. Between *ldky* and *Y'TWN* he forgot the words *'L ZNH BYT'*, "to this house," and after *H[WH]d* in line 5, the auxiliary verb belonging to *Y'TWN*, he continued erroneously with a new and grammatically impossible sentence in lines 5–6: *'P-šn ZNH BYT' [Y'TW]N*. A later hand has corrected this error with regard to the omission of *'L ZNH BYT'* by writing the two letters *WL*; i.e., *'L* (Iranian *ō*), above the word *ZNH* of the following line, the W (= ꙮ) below the *y* of *ldky*, and the *L* below the *Y* of *Y'TWN*. It seems also that a curved dotted line leads up from the lower end of the W (= ꙮ) of the inserted *WL* = *'L* to the *Y* of *Y'TWN* in order to indicate that this *WL* and *ZNH BYT'* should be inserted before *Y'TWN*.

Line 6. Instead of *'P-šn ZNH nk'l nkylyt*, the scribe wrote erroneously in utter confusion *'P-šn nkyl ['P-šn (line 7) ZN]H nk'l* (corrected out of *nkyl*), which is followed by an empty space to the end of the line.

inscription, and which will be mentioned later.

This proved to be one of the most difficult Middle Iranian inscriptions of the Synagogue, as a great number of letters are destroyed or very indistinct, and beautifully written words alternate with words which show a very awkward and careless handwriting. The inscription proper contains only four lines, whereas the last two lines contain only words which are repetitions of, or additions to, those of the text.

When I began my study there were only two unsatisfactory, almost entirely illegible, tracings by Pearson and Du Mesnil du Buisson, in which only a few words could be recognized. My impression that the decipherment of this inscription might be of special importance was later confirmed by some excellent photographs taken by Dr. N. Toll and Professor Kraeling in Damascus. In fact, they enabled me to read and understand virtually the whole text of this most interesting and important Middle Iranian inscription of the Synagogue, although the bad state of preservation made the reading and interpretation still extremely difficult. An older photograph, that which is badly reproduced in Pagliaro's edition, proved helpful in a few cases and gave additional evidence for some of my readings.

---

129. Not "line, row, range," as *rdg* in W. Henning, *Bulletin of the School of Oriental Studies (University of London)*, IX (1937–1939), p. 87; and XI (1943–1946), p. 57, § 40.

130. *Wiener Zeitschrift für die Kunde des Morgenlandes*, XLI (1934), p. 120; *Archiv Orientalni*, X (1938), pp. 210f. Cf. now also Buddhist Sogdian *ptr'z* in E. Benveniste, *Textes Sogdiens* (1940), text 2, 964, which I prefer to translate by "erection, building up," instead of Benveniste's "dimension."

It is of great interest and importance that the Synagogue is called in this inscription "the edifice of the God of the Gods of the Jews," and that an official (*zandak*) of the Jews is mentioned as having come to the Synagogue with the scribes and looked with them "at this picture." It is furthermore very surprising that beneath the last word of line 4 the words *dyn' nzdyk YHWWN*; i.e., *dātistān nazdīk bavēt*, "judgment is near," have been added by a later hand. These facts and the meaning of the words are discussed above, p. 300.

Transliteration

(1) BYRX mtr[y] [Q̇ḊṀ ŠNT] 14 WYWM [ṗṙẇṙ]-t[ẏṅ]

(2) 'MT hwṙmzdy dpyr Wkntk ZY zndky Wd[ṗẏẇṙ]y ZY zhm[y]

(3) WZṄḤ zndky ZY yhwd'n 'L ZNḤ pt[l]st-{k}[y] ZY by [ZY] by'n ZY

(4) yhwd'n Y'TWN 'P-[šṅ] [*v.v.*] ZNḤ nk'l ndyšyt

(5) 'P-šn nykylyt Wṅdyšyt [......] ṅ[y]kylyt

(6) [............] nk'l [....]

Reading

māh miθr[ē] [apar sāl] 14 ut rōč [fravar]t[īn]

kaδ hormazdē dipīr ut kantak ī zandakē ut di[pīwar]ē ī zahm[ē]

ut ēn zandakē ī yahūdān ō ēn pat[r]astak[ē] ī bay [ī] bayān ī

yahūdān āmat [hēnd] u-šān [*v.v.*] ēn nikār niyīšīt

u-šān nikīrīt ut niyīšīt [......] nikīrīt

[............] nikār [....]

"In the month *Miθr*, in [the year] fourteen, and
  on the day [*Fravar*]*tīn*
when Hormazd, the scribe, and Kantak, the *zandak*,
  and the scribe of the building,
and this *zandak* of the Jews to his edifice of the
  God [of] the Gods of
the Jews came, and by them [..] this picture was
  beheld,
and by them it was looked at and beheld [......],
  it was looked at,
[............] the picture [.....]"

The tag written by a later hand contains only the three words: *BYRX mθry YWM*; i.e. *māh, miθrē rōč*, "in the month *Miθr*, on the day."

Line 1. The first line is very badly preserved. The words *QDM ŠNT* are blurred and hardly to be distinguished. Of the numeral only the curve representing the number "ten" is still distinct. It is doubtful by how many vertical strokes marking the units it is followed, as these strokes are partly blurred and incomplete; but we obviously have to expect the number "fourteen." It is not quite certain whether the name of the day is *prwrtyn*, but the traces of the word, as far as they are still visible, are in favor of this reading.

Line 2. The reading of all the words of this line are absolutely certain, although sometimes only rather indistinct traces of the letters are preserved.

Here I wish to call attention only to the following facts. It has been rather difficult to recognize the name *hwrmzdy*. The definite identification of the *h* was not possible until I discovered that it is to some extent disfigured by an extremely tiny *h* written by a later hand as an explanation and placed close to the initial letter of the word. The remainder of the *m* is followed by a nicely written and very distinct, but not easily recognizable, ligature of the three letters *zdy*. The reading *Wd[ṗẏẇṙ]y* is sufficiently justified by the scanty traces still remaining, and is corroborated by the corresponding phrase *Wdpywry ZY zhmy* in Inscr. no. **45**, and *dpywr ZY zhmy* in Inscr. no. **42**.

Line 3. It is strange and probably due to a mistake of the scribe that he continues the list of the visitors to the Synagogue, which consists of Hormazd the scribe, Kantak the *zandak*, and the *dipīwar ī zhm[y]*, by adding *WZNḤ zndk ZY yhwdʾn*, "and this *zandak* of the Jews," although the latter is obviously the same person as Kantak the *zandak*. It seems most likely that the scribe erroneously omitted the words *ZY yhwdʾn* after *Kntk ZY zndky*, and then corrected himself awkwardly by adding the whole phrase after the title of the third visitor. The reading *WZNḤ* is quite certain, although the *N* is blurred and illegible.

ptlstky. This word (written with two *k*'s) is very badly preserved. Fortunately I succeeded in restoring it completely after recognizing that it is the same word which occurs in corresponding passages of Inscrs. nos. **45** and **47**, as a synonym of *BYTʾ* (the Synagogue). More details will be given in the *editio major*. As to the etymology of the word, see above, p. 303 and n. 130.

45. Dipinto on Panel WC 2, on the chest of Mordecai's horse. Four lines (the fourth standing alone at the right side), black paint; Pārsīk script. Dimensions: lines 1–3, 0.084 m. × *ca.* 0.025 m.; line 4, 0.062 m. × *ca.* 0.04 m. (Pl. XLV, 1).

by, byʾn. As in the case of -*prnby* instead of -*prnbg* in Inscr. no. **42**, line 3, we should have expected here *bg* and *bgʾn* instead of *by* and *byʾn*; but I tried in vain to find any, however remote, resemblance between the letter after the initial *b* and the Pārsīk *g* of the inscriptional alphabet.

Line 4. There is an empty space between *ʾP-[šn]* and *ZNḤ*, although no word is missing.

ndyšyt. Very blurred and badly written by a different hand, but quite certain. About the etymology and meaning of this word see above p. 293, with n. 90.

Line 5. *Wndyšyt*. Partly blurred and badly written; the *n* is badly preserved. This is followed by another empty space. The last word of the line is perhaps *nk[y]lyt*; the first visible letter is probably *n*.

Pagliaro, *Rendiconti*, pp. 594, 596–598; Polotsky manuscript, attempted and incomplete transliteration and translation. Tracings by Du Mesnil du Buisson, Pearson (three copies), Kraeling.

Transliteration

(1) BYRX mtry QDM ŠNT 14
(2) WYWM mtrspndy ʾMT pkwry ŻẎ dpyr
(3) Wdᵖywry ZY zhṁẏ
(4) ʿL ZNḤ ᵖtlsᵗky YMYTN

Reading

māh miθrē apar sāl 14
ut rōč mahrspandē kaδ pakōrē ī dipīr
ut dipīwarē ī zahmē
ō ēn patrastakē ⁺āmat

"In the month *Miθr* in the year fourteen
and on the day *Mahrspand* when Pakōr, the scribe,
and the scribe of the building
to this edifice ⁺came."

Line 2. *mtrspndy*. It is surprising to find here for the first time the name of the twenty-ninth day of the month written *mtrspndy*, with *t*. This way of spelling, in contrast to the usual writing *mʾrspnd* (*mārspand*) in the Middle Persian of the literature, might lead to the conclusion that the former represents historical writing for *mhrspndy*; i.e., *mahrspandē*. As a matter of fact, *mahraspand* appears as the name of the twenty-ninth day of the month in a Manichaean text,[131] and *mahr*, "hymn," (from Avestan *mąθra*) occurs elsewhere in Pārsīk Mani-

chaean texts. However, one might be inclined to doubt the correctness of the writing *mtrspndy*, although we meet it again in Inscr. no. **47** in the name of the day and in the name of a scribe. Further details will be given in the *editio major*.

pkwry. This is a predominantly Parthian name. There is hardly any other reading possible, although the initial *p* is not as well preserved and as distinct as the following letters.

ZY. These postulated letters are not easy to identify. The *Z* seems to be disfigured by a blur on top, the *Y* by a blur beneath the letter. This reading, however, seems to be confirmed by at least one tiny ligature *ZY* written by a later hand beneath the *Z* of the text line.

---

131. F. W. K. Müller, *Handschriften-Reste in Estrangelo-Schrift aus Turfan, Chinesisch-Turkistan*, II (*Abhandlungen der preußischen Akademie der Wissenschaften, phil.-hist. Klasse*, LXXXVIII, 1904, Anhang II), p. 95.

dpyr. This word is written in large and vigorously drawn letters which seem to have been added by a later hand. It is possible, although not certain from the photographs, that this word has one or two more letters, making it *dpyry* or even *dpywry*.

Line 4. *ptlstky*. For the reading of this word, see above, p. 299. Here I wish to add only that in the present inscription only the horizontal bottom stroke of the second *t* is preserved, and that the letter *k* is blurred.

YMYTN. The scribe committed a gross and puzzling blunder in writing *YMYTN*; i.e., *murt*, "died," instead of *Y'TWN*; i.e., *āmat*, "came." It is probably only by mistake that the sentence "and by him (them) this picture was beheld," which in all the dated inscriptions except no. **50** follows the sentence about the coming to the Synagogue, is missing at the end of the present inscription.

46. Dipinto on Panel WC 2, on the shoulder of Mordecai's horse. Five lines, black paint, Pārsīk script. Dimensions 0.105 m. × *ca.* 0.065 m. (Pl. XLV, 2).

Pagliaro, *Rendiconti*, pp. 594–596; Altheim, *Asien und Rom*, p. 27; Polotsky's manuscript: transliteration and translation. Tracings by Du Mesnil du Buisson, Pearson (two copies), Polotsky.

The photographs show several cracks in the plaster, which made parts of the left side slide down a little so that in several places letters which were crossed by the cracks were split in two parts. In these cases the original letters can easily be restored by piecing the separate parts together. We have only to imagine that we push the parts on the right side of the cracks down to the point where they have been torn away from the parts on the left. This refers to the *B* of *BYRX* in line 1, to the *l* (= *r*) in *prwltyn* in line 2, to the *d* of *dpyr* in line 3, and to the *N* of *BYN* in line 4.

In a number of excellent photographs of this inscription which have been recently taken, the first word of line 1, *BYRX*, is only partly distinct, and of *prwltyn*, the first word of line 2, almost nothing but the initial *p* is preserved; whereas these words are quite distinct in an older photograph. The letters of these two words are still to be seen in the tracings of Du Mesnil du Buisson and Pearson, although the tracings are not quite accurate. However, Polotsky says in his manuscript in a note to the word *prwltyn*, "now obliterated save the *p*." From this we have to conclude that all the letters of both words were still well preserved when Du Mesnil du Buisson and Pearson made their tracings.

Transliteration	*Reading*
(1) BYRX 'mʷldt WYWM'	māh 'murdat ut rōč
(2) prwltyn 'MT	fravartīn kaδ
(3) ršnky dpyr Wbwlǰ'tw[r]	rašnakē dipīr ut burz-ātu[r]
(4) BYN Y'TWN Wbym'y	andar āmat ut bym'y
(5) ndyšyt	niyīšīt

"Month *Amurdat* and the day
Fravartīn, when
Rašnak, the scribe, and Burz-ātu[r]
came in and the *bym'y*
was beheld"

Line 1, *'mʷldt*. A small *w* is inserted between the upper part of the initial stroke of the *m* and the *l* (= *r*).

WYWM'. The final *aleph* of this word is unusual, as Polotsky has stated. The writing with *aleph* is discussed in my *editio major*.

Line 3, *Wbwlǰ'tw[r]*. A distinct trace of the *w* after the *t* is preserved in all photographs, whereas the last letter is no longer visible. My reading is therefore absolutely certain. The name *burz-ātur* is well known to us from the *Kārnāmak*,[132] where it is preceded by the name *bwrǰk*; i.e., *burzak*, and from the Sasanian Code of Laws (*Mātīkān ī Hazār Dātistān*)[133], where the name *burzātur-farnbay* oc-

132. ed. Sanjana, VII, 2.
133. vol. I, pp. 16,3; 72,6; 100,16. See also Bartholomae, *Sitzungsberichte der heidelberger Akademie der Wissenschaften*, 1910, No. 11, part V, p. 24.

curs. Pagliaro offers an extremely far-fetched reading which he interprets as "i pannelli sopra," whereas Altheim presents us with the fantastic reading *BBYL'T*; i.e., *BBYR'T*, which is supposed to mean "in den Burgen." (See above, p. 289.)

Line 4, *BYN*. Only Polotsky has the correct reading. The word can easily be restored when one realizes that as a result of the crack in the plaster, the bottom stroke of the *N* was moved out of its former place toward the right. Pagliaro reads *b'n* (*bān*), "tetto" ("roof, ceiling"), whereas Altheim offers *RBN* (*sic*), "der Grossen."

Wbym'y. Here written *bym'y*, whereas Inscrs.

47.
Dipinto on Panel WC 2, on the flank of Mordecai's horse directly below the rider. Three lines, black paint, Pārsīk script. Dimensions 0.095 m. × 0.03 m. (Pl. XLV, 3).

nos. **47** and **48** have *by'm'y*. Both forms show clearly that this word can by no means represent Greek βῆμα, as Pagliaro and Altheim have assumed. Unfortunately I am not in a position to offer a convincing etymology. Nevertheless it can be asserted with a high degree of likelihood that this word means something like "picture," for in Inscrs. nos. **42, 43, 44** the word *nikār*, "picture," occurs in the very same context as *bym'y*, *by'm'y* in Inscrs. nos. **46, 47, 48** as the thing which was looked at (beheld) by the person or persons who came to the Synagogue.

Line 5. *ndyšyt*. (See above, pp. 293 and 305.)

Pagliaro, *Rendiconti*, pp. 598–601; Polotsky manuscript: attempted transliteration and translation. Tracings: Du Mesnil du Buisson (two copies) and Pearson (two copies).

Transliteration	*Reading*
(1) BYRX štrywl YWM mtlspndy 'MT štwlyly	māh šaθrēvar rōč mahrspandē kaδ šaθvarērē(?)
(2) mtlwlwspn(?) dydpyr 'L [ŻN]Ḥ ptlstky	mahrspandē dipīr ō ēn patrastakē
(3) Y'TWN Wby'm'y ndyšyt	āmat ut by'm'y niyīšīt

"Month *Saθrēvar*, day *Mahrspand* when
Mahrspand the scribe to this edifice
came, and the *by'm'y* was beheld."

Line 1, *BYRX*. This word is written on a lower level than that of the following words of the line. Of the letters *Y* and *W* (= *R*), only the blurred upper parts are visible.

The word *štrwyl* (*šaθrēvar*) was badly and very inaccurately reproduced beneath the line by someone who did not understand the word which he copied and therefore confused the letters. In the best photographs the third letter of the copy looks like a *w*, but this is not to be seen in the older photographs. If this *w* stands for *r*, then the following *l* (= *r*) is superfluous. The last three letters: *y*, *l* (= *r*), *y*, are obviously the poor result of an ignorant person's attempt to copy or to correct the last three letters: *ywr* (*ēvar*) of the text word. Polotsky transliterated this inserted word wrongly *W Ktwly-dy*, which makes no sense.

mtlspndy. Here the word is written with an *l* (= *r*) after the *t*, in contrast to the *w* (= *r*) in Inscr. no. **45**, line 2. Concerning the reading of *mtlspndy*, see above p. 305.

Line 2. The same word that in the preceding line designated the name of the day appears here as the name of the scribe. However, we are here confronted with a very confused and faulty writing of the word. The *s* is preceded by an *l* (= *r*) and a *w*, whereas in line 1 the word correctly has only an *l*. It is very difficult to ascertain the form and meaning of the letter, or two letters, between the *t*, the second letter of the word, and the above-mentioned *lw*. It seems to me that these indistinct characters are remainders of an *l* and a *w*, so that the scribe would have written *lw* twice. My suspicion that this strange and nonsensical writing of the first part of the word was due to confusion and ignorance is confirmed by the fact that the last two letters, the ligature *dy*, are separated from the word and closely attached to the following word *dpyr*. We have to add that the right part of the *t* was moved upwards a little as a result of the crack in the plaster, and at the same time the two or three following letters may also have been affected.

[ŻṄ]Ḥ. The Z and N have almost entirely faded out. There are still faint traces of these two letters to be seen, but it is rather difficult to localize them accurately.

48. Dipinto on Panel WC 2, on the hind leg of Mordecai's horse. Two lines, black paint, Pārsīk script. Dimensions: line 1, 0.208 m.; line 2, 0.15 m.; line 3, 0.065 m. × 0.035 m. (Pl. XLV, 4).

Pagliaro, *Rendiconti*, pp. 601–604; Altheim, *Asien und Rom*, pp. 25 f.; Polotsky's manuscript: transliteration and translation. Tracings: Du Mesnil du Buisson (two copies), Pearson, Polotsky.

Transliteration

(1) BYRX mtry WYWM ršnw ᵓMT nχyᵓtᵓp
Whwpᵓt Wplχwy [ŻẎ ḋṗẏṙ]
(2) YᵓTWN HWḪ[ṅ]d ᵓP-šn byᵓmᵓy nkylyt
BYRX mtry WYWM ršny

Reading

māh miθrē ut rōč rašnu kaδ naχē-ātāp(?) ut hupāt
ut farraχvē [ī dipīr]
āmat hē[ṅ]d u-šān byᵓmᵓy nikīrīt
māh miθrē ut rōč rašnē

"Month *Miθr* and day *Rašnu*, when Naχē-ātāp(?)
and Hupāt and Farraχv, [the scribe,]
came and by them the *byᵓmᵓy* was looked at."
"Month *Miθr* and day *Rašn*"

Line 1, *lšnw*. It is obviously this, with *w* as the final letter, as in Inscr. no. **42**, line 2. The pointed end of the letter is certainly not intentional, but caused by a spread of the paint or a smudge.

nχyᵓtᵓp. This is, of course, the first of the names of three persons who came to the Synagogue. Unfortunately, it is hardly possible to give an etymological explanation of this name, which was hitherto unknown. One might be inclined to consider it as a compound with *ātāp*, perhaps in the meaning "splendor," as its second member, although in the only place where *ātāp* occurs — in Psalm 135.8 of the Middle Persian fragments of the Psalms — this word means "sun." The form and meaning of *nχy* (or *nhy*), the first part of the compound, are still more obscure. It is, of course, not permissible to connect it with Middle Persian *naχvist*, "first," as did Pagliaro. It is only with great reserve that I render *nχyᵓtᵓp* by *naχē-ātāp*.

Whwpᵓt. This very distinctly written, unmistakable, and obvious name was rendered by Altheim as Aramaic *ḪNPᵓYN* (*sic*), which together with the alleged preceding *ᵓpw* (supposed to repre-

ptlstky. See above pp. 299, 305 f.
Line 3, *Wbyᵓmᵓy*. See above, pp. 292 with n. 88, 296.
ndyšyt. See above, p. 293.

It is not correct to say, as did Pagliaro and Polotsky, that this inscription consists of three lines. What they considered as the third line is nothing but a kind of tag beneath the beginning of the second line of the text, which repeats the first four words of the inscription and is undoubtedly written by a later hand.

sent Greek ἀπο or Aramaic *ᵓYPW*, Greek ὑπό) was translated by "nach den Heiden;" i.e., "according to (the era of) the pagans (the Zoroastrians)." (Cf. above, pp. 288 f.).

Wplχwy. The word *plχw*; i.e., *far(r)aχv*, "having glory or fortune," Modern Persian *farruχ*, occurs frequently as a personal name; e.g., in a number of passages in the Sasanian Code of Law (*Mātīkān ī Hazār Dātistān*).[134]

ZY dpyr. The word *Wplχw* is followed by a few letters rather clumsily written by a later hand. The first two are very indistinct, but it seems still possible to recognize in some of the photographs the letters *ZY*, which were repeated at the right and left sides and also above the line by later hands as ligatures of *ZY*. The following letters *dpyr*; i.e., *dipīr*, are easily legible. Polotsky did not see these letters; he has in his tracing above the end of the first line only the remark, "erasure 6.5 cm."

Line 2, *HWḪ[ṅ]d*. The vertical stroke of the *n* looks partly damaged in most of the photographs.

byᵓmᵓy. See above, p. 296.

134. See also F. Justi, *Iranisches Namenbuch* (1895), p. 94.

nkylyt. About *nkylyt* and the other verbs used in these inscriptions in the meaning "to look at" the pictures of the Synagogue, see above, pp. 292f.

49. Dipinto on Panel WC 1, on Elijah's foot. Four lines (the first entirely blurred and illegible), black paint, Pārsīk script. Dimensions: 0.075 m. × 0.02 m. (Pl. XLVI, 1).

There I have also discussed the wrong interpretations of these verbal forms by Pagliaro and Altheim.

Pagliaro, *Rendiconti*, pp. 588f.; Polotsky manuscript: transliteration and translation of the second line and of the first word of the third line. Tracing: Pearson (?)

Transliteration

(1) illegible
(2) 'MT hwrmzdy dpywr Y'TWNt
(3) 'P-š [Ż]ṄḤ ⟨nyk'l⟩ [ny]kldyt zyw[n]dk
(4) kẏdly(?) YMYTN

Reading

— — — — — — — — — — — — — —
kaδ hormazdē dipīwar āmat
u-š ēn ⟨nik'r⟩ [ni]kardīt zīvandak
kydly(?) murt

"......................................
When Hormazd the scribe came
and by him this [picture] was looked at: "Living the child(?) that had been dead."

Line 1. This is obliterated to such a degree that not even one letter can now be recognized. The only sign I could discover was near the end of the line, a curve of the form which is the sign for the number "ten" in dates; and this curve is followed by perhaps four vertical, very blurred strokes. Accordingly the year in this inscription seems to have been "fourteen."

Line 2, *Y'TWNt.* Among the numerous photographs at my disposal there are only two enlarged ones which show the Iranian suffix *t* after *Y'TWN*. It is a very distinct, fat letter, the left part of which covers the uppermost part of the vertical crack in the plaster which crosses the prophet's toe. The other Synagogue inscriptions except Inscr. no. **50** have *Y'TWN* without a final *t*, like the Sasanian inscriptions.

Line 3, *'P-š.* The *š* is written somewhat irregularly, but it is quite certain.

[*Ż*]*ṄḤ.* It was extremely difficult to identify the letters of this word except for the *Ḥ*, and it too is partly blurred in some of the photographs. The second letter is most probably an epsilon-like *N*. Only the *Z* seems to be entirely lost by fading out; but in older photographs there are still traces to be seen, from which we may conclude that it was a rather low-lying *Z*, similar to that of the word *ZNḤ* in the corresponding passage (line 3) of the closely related Inscr. no. **51**.

nyk'l. This word was omitted by the scribe, whereas in Inscr. no. **51** it is written *nyk'l*, with *ny* instead of only *n*.

[*ny*]*kldyt.* The first two letters seem to have faded out entirely. From Inscr. no. **51** we have to infer that the *k* was preceded by the letters *ny*, which are not visible in any of the photographs. But on the right side of the space which must have contained the *ny* one sees what seems to be one or more epsilon-like letters, obviously written by later hands. The letters *kld* are only partly preserved, but certain. The *y* and *t* are blurred. The form *nykldyt*; i.e., *nikardīt*, is quite unusual. It corresponds to the word *nkylyt*; i.e., *nikīrīt*, of other inscriptions, and has undoubtedly the same meaning: "it was looked at." Its *d* might represent an inserted pseudo-historical *d*. Or is it the result of a contamination of the word *dīt*, "it was seen"?

zyw[n]dk. This word is quite certain. The *n*, which is now missing, has faded out. The corresponding word in Inscr. no. **51**, line 4, looks like *zywky*, but it might perhaps stand for an original *zyw[nd]ky*; see below, p. 311.

Line 4, *kydly(?).* Repeated attempts at the identification of this word, which occurs also in Inscr. no. **51**, line 4, did not lead to a definite result, although the context leaves no doubt that the word must mean "child" or "son." In any case, my reading can claim to be in full accord with the epigraphical facts which can be ascertained through comparison of the forms visible in the various photographs of Inscrs. nos. **49** and **51**. Besides, letters, often very tiny and hardly visible, written by later hands above and beyond the text line in Inscr. no. **49** as well as in no. **51** proved to be most helpful.

50. Dipinto on Panel WC 1, at the foot of Elijah's bed. Two lines, black paint, Pārsīk script (Pl. XLVI, 2).

Copy of a tracing by Du Mesnil du Buisson bearing the remark "Elija [corrected into 'Élie'] resurrection vers le bas à dr[oit] au pied du lit." According to a note of Professor Kraeling, Polotsky did not find the inscription. And in 1946 Kraeling stated after examining the painting in Damascus, "no trace on West Wall in panel indicated." As a

For details see the *editio major* and the tracings.

YMYTN. So also in Inscr. no. **51**, line 4. We should expect *ZY* between *kydly*(?) and *YMYTN*. The meaning of *zyw[n]dk kydly*(?) *YMYTN* must be the same as that of *zyw[nd]ky YMYTN 'mt* in Inscr. no. **51**.

matter of fact, the inscription is not to be seen anywhere at the foot of Elijah's bed in any of the recent photographs. However, the existence of the inscription is attested by an older photograph which Pagliaro has reproduced in *Rendiconti,* p. 591. His photograph is followed by a transliteration, translation, and commentary, which are entirely wrong.[135] Du Mesnil du Buisson's tracing proved to be very unsatisfactory.

Transliteration

(1) BYRX mtry QDM ŠNT 14 'MT [hwr]mzdy(?) [ZY(?)] dpẏṙ
(2) Y'TWNt HWḪnd

Reading

māh miθrē apar sāl 14 kaδ [hor]mazdē(?) [ī?] dipīr

āmat hēnd

"Month *Miθr* in the year fourteen, when Hormazd
(?) the scribe
they [*sic*] came."

Line 1, [*hwr*]*mzdy*(?). The letters of the name of the scribe are partly faded out, partly blurred and indistinct. However, there is still so much left which can be identified at close examination that my conjectural reading [*hwr*]*mzdy* can be considered probable. The first two letters, *hw*, are not visible. The third letter, *w* (= *r*), could be part of the thick vertical stroke. What follows the *m* seems to me to be a ligature of *zd*, or even *zdy*, similar to the ligature *zdy* in the name *hwrmzdy* in Inscr. no. **44**, line 2.

ZY. At first glance this sign looks like a *g*, which would, however, be entirely out of place here. After repeated examination I was able to recognize that this sign consists of the letters *ZY* written in ligature, with another and smaller *ZY* super-

imposed on the *Y*. Under these circumstances the horizontal stroke which seems to form the end of the sign is to be considered meaningless and not belonging to the sign. It is to be admitted that we should not expect the *ZY* to stand so close to the name [*hwr*]*mzdy*. However, in view of the poor handwriting shown by the following word *dpyr*, we should not attribute any weight to the unusual position of *ZY*. Furthermore, we must point to the fact that sometimes, as in Inscrs. nos. **45**, line 2, and **48**, line 1, *ZY* is found between the name and the word *dpyr*.

Line 2. The surprising fact that the singular subject of this sentence as followed by a verb in the plural is discussed in the *editio major*.

51. Dipinto on Panel SC 4, on the himation of the small figure standing at the right of the altar. Five lines, black paint, Pārsīk script (Pl. XLVI, 3).

Pagliaro, *Rendiconti,* pp. 613–616: transliter-

ation and translation. Tracing: Polotsky.

Transliteration

(1) BYRX ['wrtwhšt ?] YWM hwrmzdy
(2) 'MT 'ṙt'w dpyr Y'TWN[ṫ]
(3) [']P-š ZNḤ nyk'l ṅẏkldyt 'Ṗ-š
(4) kẏdly(?) ny[k̇]ldyty 'YK zyw[nd]ky(?)
     YMYTN
(5) 'mt

Reading

māh [urt-vahišt ?] rōč hormazdē
kaδ Artāv dipīr āmat
u-š ēn nikār nikardīt u-š
kydly(?) nikardītē ku zīva[nda]kē(?) murt

āmat

"Month [*Urt-vahišt* ?], day *Hormazd*,
when Artāv, the scribe, came
and by him this picture was looked at and by him
the child (?) was looked at thus: 'living the dead
(be)came.'"

The strange fact that this inscription, although referring only to the resuscitation of the widow's child by Elijah, was written on a panel which represents the sacrifice of Elijah on Mt. Carmel is discussed in my *editio major*. There I have pointed out that, according to my reading and interpretation of Inscrs. nos. **49** and **51**, it is evident that these two inscriptions are closely related as regards their contents, their awkward wordings, and their use of strange grammatical forms. I arrived at the conclusion that Inscr. no. **51** is only an enlarged and deteriorated copy of no. **49**.

Line 1. A few traces of letters still to be seen between *BYRX* and *YWM* seem to favor the conclusion that the badly damaged word for the month was 'wrtwhšt; i.e., *urt-vahišt*, the second month.

Line 2, 'rt'w. The last letter is undoubtedly a *w*, not a *k*. The name of the scribe is therefore *Artāv*, not *Artāk*.

Y'TWN[ṫ]. The *N* of *Y'TWN* is perhaps followed by a *t*; see above, p. 309.

Line 3. The word '*P-š* at the beginning of the line is partly blurred, but quite certain; cf. Inscr. no. **49**, line 3.

nykldyt. The first two letters are damaged, but there is hardly any doubt that the original letters were *n* (probably an angular, not an epsilon-like *n*) and *y*. This is proved by the *nyk'l*, and probably also by *ny*[*k̇*]*ldyty* in the following line. See above p. 309 for discussion of the corresponding word in Inscr. no. **49**.

Line 4, *kydly* (?). The first three letters are blurred, but the comparison with the corresponding letters of the same word as they appear in Inscr.

no. **49** (see above, p. 309) shows clearly that they must be the letters *kyd*.

ny[*k̇*]*ldyty*. In the space between the *y* of *ny* (with an epsilon-like *n*) and the letter *l*, we expect to find the letter *k*. Consequently the strange-looking large curve which stands between the two letters must be considered as part of a blurred and not completely preserved *k*. The photographs seem to support this explanation, as there are traces recognizable inside this large curve which make it possible to reconstruct the original *k*. In this case the initial part of the curve up to its highest point would be meaningless and would not belong to the letter.

zyw[*nd*]*ky* (?). The letters of which this word consists seem to recommend the reading *zywky*; i.e., *zīvakē*. However, this word is not attested in Middle Persian, although a derivative *zīvakē* from Avestan *ǰīva-*, "living" (opposite to *mərəta-*, "dead")[136] is possible. In this case the stroke across the space between the letters *w* and *k* would be meaningless. Nevertheless I should prefer to consider this word as wrongly written instead of *zyw*[*nd*]*ky*, which would correspond exactly to the word *zyw*[*n*]*dk* of Inscr. no. **49**, line 3. Then the seeming stroke across the space between *w* and *k* might consist of remainders of the missing letters *nd*.

YMYTN. *Sic*! Like the last word of Inscr. no. **49**.

Line 5. The *aleph* and *t* are incomplete and partly blurred, but quite certain. The use of the Iranian instead of the Aramaic word is surprising.

136. Christian Bartholomae, *Altiranisches Wörterbuch* (1904), pp. 609f.

52. Dipinto on Panel NC 1, in the first section counting from the left, near the second range of mountains directly below the overturned building. Three lines, black paint, Pārsīk script. Dimensions 0.08 m. × 0.023 m. (Pl. XLVI, 4).

Polotsky manuscript: transliteration but no translation; Altheim, *Asien and Rom*, pp. 24–26. Tracings: Pearson (two copies), Polotsky, Kraeling.

Transliteration	*Reading*
(1) LŻṄH̱ ’[Ż]DH̱ ‘BYDWN ’YK š’ty	im azd kun[ēt] ku šātē
(2) YHWWN Wyzd’n K’L’ ‘ŠMYTN	bav[ēt] ut yazdān vāng āšnav[ēt]
(3) ’DYN ŠWM⟨m⟩’n QDM	aδak drōt-mān apar

"This make ye known, that joyous
ye are, and to God's voice listen;
then peace upon us [will be]."

Line 1, *LZNH̱*. Even with the best available photographs, it was extremely hard to arrive at a satisfactory reading of this word, until it seemed to me most likely that we have here before us the Aramaic ideogram *LZNH̱*, corresponding to the *LDNH̱* of the Middle Persian of the literature and the *Frahang ī Pahlavīk*; i.e., Iranian *im*, "this." The reading seems to me quite certain, although the *n* is somewhat disfigured, as I shall show in my tracing. I have still to point to the fact that LZNH̱ (= *im*) and *LZNH-č* (= *im-ič*), "this too," is to be found in Pārsīk texts of the Sasanian inscriptions,[137] and that the Iranian *im* occurs often in the Middle Iranian, mostly in Parthian, texts of Turfan.

Lines 1–2. The Aramaic verbs *‘BYDWN, YHWWN,* and *‘ŠMYTN* appear here without the Iranian personal endings. After repeated deliberation I arrived at the conclusion that these ideograms probably represent forms of the second person plural of the imperative. This interpretation is postulated especially by the sentence *Wyzd’n K’L’ ‘ŠMYTN*. For only if we take these words in the sense of "and listen ye to God's voice"! does the concluding sentence, "then there will be peace upon us," stand in a proper connection with the preceding part of the passage. The word *‘ŠMYTN* requires an additional remark. Not even Polotsky has noticed that this word begins with a *w* (= 𐭥).

137. As to the Sasanian inscriptions, cf. the passages quoted by Herzfeld, *Paikuli*, p. 210; and M. Sprengling, *American Journal of Semitic Languages and Literatures*, LVII (1940), p. 387, at the bottom.

The photographs show that only the lower half of the vertical part of the letter preceding the *Š* is preserved. This is important as it proves that we have here a form of the Aramaic ideogram for the Iranian verb *āšnūtan*, "to hear." It is, furthermore, remarkable that this form of the present stem, *‘ŠMYTN-*, appears here for the first time, whereas we know from the Pārsīk texts of the literature and of the Pahlavī Psalter the form *‘ŠMH̱N-* and from the Sasanian inscriptions the Pārsīk form *‘ŠMH̱WN-*. Our *‘ŠMYTN-* differs in the second part from the usual Pārsīk formations. It is formed like the ideogram *ZRYTN-* of the Pahlavī Psalter and *ZRYTWN-* of the literature, "to sow," after the verbs *tertiae Y*, as *XZYT(W)N-* from *XZY*, "to see," and *RMYT(W)N-* from *RMY*, "to throw." The verb *YD‘*, "to know," is treated in the same way in *YD‘YTN-* of the Pārsīk of the Sasanian inscriptions and of the Pahlavī Psalter, but it has preserved the *‘ayin.*

Line 3, *ŠWM’n*. I have succeeded in identifying the last but one word of the third line of this inscription as *ŠWM’n*, with *W = L*, and therefore *ŠLM’n*, and in explaining it as a word composed of *ŠLM*, "peace, blessing" (which is also in the texts of the literature written *ŠWM*), and the Iranian enclitic pronoun of the first person plural *m’n*. This word *ŠWM’n* is written with only one *m*, instead of *ŠWMm’n*. Consequently *ŠLM’n* is Iranian *drōt-mān*, and *ŠLM’n QDM = drōt-mān apar* means "blessing-us upon"; i.e., "blessing upon us" [will be given]. The construction of *apar* (*aβar*) as a postposition connected with a preceding enclitic pronoun is well attested in the Turfan fragments. Here I only mention *u-mān aβaχšāyišn.... aβar kun*, "and upon us do mercy,"[138] *aβaχšād-[mā]n aβar*, "have mercy upon us," which is preceded by *tāk-mān aβaχšāδāy aβar*, "until thou wilt have mercy upon us." And with another postposition: *āfrīn-t(ā)n ZY MRWXY LWTḤ*, "the Lord's blessing with you (-*tān.... LWTḤ* [= *aβāy*)."[139]

My transliteration and interpretation of this rather difficult inscription is in perfect accord with the letters of the text. It might be instructive to contrast my reading with that offered by Altheim. I here present the words of his text of the first two lines beneath the corresponding words of my text, the only difference being that I am writing his Aramaic, or allegedly Aramaic, words in capital letters:

53.
Dipinto on Panel NC 1, on the first range of mountains counting from the left directly below severed hand. Three lines, black paint, Pārsīk script. Dimensions 0.08 m. × 0.03 m. (excluding the tall vertical stroke at the beginning of line 1,

Transliteration

(1) vs'n Y'TWN LK 'ZLWN 'yny'
(2) 'ŻLYN(?) 'L 'ŻLWN 'yny'
(3) [yzd'n(?)] sp'sy YXSŃWN

Reading

vasān āyēnd tō šau ēnyā
šavēnd(?) mā šau ēnyā
[yazdān(?)] spāsē dār

"Many are coming, thou go otherwise!
They go (?), do not go otherwise!
To God give ye thanks!"

Line 1, '*yny*'. This word is here and in the following line so distinctly written that the problem of the pronunciation of the corresponding word in the Middle Persian of the literature, which was read *ēnīh* by Bartholomae and by me,[140] is now definitely settled.

Line 2, '*ZLYN*. I have tried in vain to find a satisfactory reading and interpretation of this word. However, one can hardly escape the impression that we have here after the '*ZLWN* of the

(1)   LŻŃḤ 'ŻDḤ 'BYDWN 'YK š'ty
A.: LN   'TH WBYRḤ 'bn ŠNT XIIX
(2)   YHWWN Wyzd'n K'L' 'ŠMYTN

Altheim: Wḥwrwmwzdy dpyl' ŠNT MWTN
Altheim's translation: (1) "Zu uns ist gekommen, und zwar im Monat Abān des Jahres 18 (2) und im Hormizd der Maler (im) Jahre der Seuche..."

I wish to add here only that Polotsky read part of the words of this inscription, as '*ZDḤ, 'BYDWN, 'YK, Wyzd'n, 'DYN*, quite correctly. About *K'L'*, which is certain, he made the remark "possibly *K'L'* ('voice')." On the other hand he transliterated *LZNḤ* wrongly by *l'/*, *š'ty* by *š'try*, *YHWWN* by *yhdwy*(?), '*ŠMYTN* by *ŠMYTWN*, and *ŠWM'n* [= *ŠLM(m)'n*] by *r'm'n*. He did not translate the inscription.

which is not a letter) (Pl. XLVII, 1).

Polotsky's manuscript contains only the remark: "I am unable to read more than *LK* ('thou') in l. 1, and '*L* ('don't') in l. 2." Tracings: Pearson (two copies), Polotsky, Kraeling.

first line and before the '*ZLWN* near the end of the second line a form of the same verb '*ZL* (Aramaic אֲזַל). The first letter is obviously a *w* (= ﻌ), which, as can be seen distinctly in one of the photographs, was moved away from its original place upwards to the right as the result of a crack in the plaster. The following letter is a little blurred, but can hardly be anything but a *Z*. The following three letters are very distinct. However, if the reading '*ZLYN* is correct, we are at a loss to explain this form, the more so as the context and the meaning of the other parts of the first two lines are not clear. My tentative translation of these two lines is also open to doubt on account of the fact that '*yny*' (*ēnyā*) seems to be used only in the sense of "or

138. Andreas-Henning, *Mitteliranische Manichaica*, II, p. 24, lines 7 f.

139. Pahlavī Psalter, 122,2 and 3; 128, 8.

140. *Wiener Zeitschrift für die Kunde des Morgenlandes*, XL (1933), p. 117, n. 1.

else," if we may judge from the sentences quoted by Bartholomae.[141] The first letter of *'ZLWN*, the last word but one of line 2, looks like a *Y*, but there is no doubt that it is a *W* (= ע), the horizontal bottom stroke of which was effaced.

Line 3. The first of the three words of line 3 seems to be entirely destroyed. However, it is beyond any doubt that a letter which looks like an *aleph* and stands on the right side of the inscription on a level between the second and third lines was originally the first letter of line 3. The only possible explanation of its present position is that it, like the first letter of line 2, was displaced as the result of a crack in the plaster. After I had succeeded in reading the other words of line 3 as *sp'sy YXSNWN*; i.e., *spāsē dār* (or rather the plural *dārēt*), "extend ye thanks," I concluded that the preceding damaged word should be the word for "God." As neither אלהא, the Aramaic ideogram in

Pahlavīk texts, nor *WWHY'*; i.e., (אלהיא עלהיא) used in the Pārsīk texts, nor the word *bay* can be considered here, only the word *yzd'n* (*yazdān*) could be imagined to fit in. And as a matter of fact, repeated painstaking examination of the seeming initial *aleph* and of the other letters, among them very tiny and almost invisible letters written by later hands, led me to the conviction that the damaged word is indeed to be restored *yzd'n*. Here I have to confine myself to the statement that the initial sign which looks like an *aleph* turns out at closer sight to consist of two separate and very blurred letters *y* and *z*, that this *z* is followed by a *d*, and that there is in the end still a trace of a ligature *'n* to be recognized.

As to the following two words *sp'sy YXSNWN*, the photographs show clearly that these words have been reproduced very inaccurately in the existing tracings.

54. Graffito on Panel WC 2, above Mordecai's billowing cloak. One line, Pahlavīk (Parthian) script (Pl. XLVII, 2).

Du Mesnil du Buisson, *Peintures*, p. 162, no. 23; *Rep. VI*, p. 392, where this inscription is erroneously listed as Aramaic.

Transliteration

[N?]YYNY 'prs'm SPR'

Reading

[?] Aparsām dipīwar

"This is I (?), Aparsām, the scribe"

The initial *N* which Du Mesnil du Buisson supplemented in his tracing is not visible in any of the excellent photographs. It is, however, very distinct and absolutely certain in two other inscriptions in Parthian script.[142] In these *NYYNY* is followed

by a proper name, just as in the present inscription. My efforts to identify this *NYYNY*, which Du Mesnil du Buisson rendered by "c'est moi," with an Aramaic or Iranian word have been in vain.[143]

55. Graffito on Panel WC 1, above Elijah's right thigh. Two lines, Pahlavīk (Parthian) script (Pl. XLVII, 3).
Du Mesnil du Buisson, *Peintures*, p. 161, no. 20.
Some of the letters of this inscription, which is in general beautifully written, are not reproduced

quite accurately by Du Mesnil du Buisson. Two of his letters are barely visible in my otherwise excellent photographs, and another one is wrong, as I shall mention later. It is surprising that the scribe wrote the letter *p* throughout in a quite unusual way: very rounded, to some extent similar to the Pārsīk *p* and different from the characteristic form

141. *Über ein sasanidisches Rechtsbuch (Sitzungsberichte der heidelberger Akademie der Wissenschaften,* 1910, No. 11), p. 10. Cf. the text of *Šāy. nē šāy.* (ed. Tavadia) 2, 66, with n. 4; and the passages in Herzfeld, *Paikuli*, pp. 119 and 132.

142. Both are from the still unpublished Temple of Zeus Megistos at Dura, the one painted in black on a sherd (O. Yale. Inv. 2), the other inscribed on a seat block. They are illustrated in F. Altheim and R. Stiehl, *Das erste*

Auftreten der Hunnen (1953), Figs. 6 and 17. For the seat block, see also *YCS*, XIV (1955), pp. 143 f.

143. As to the name *Aparsām*, see Kaabah inscription: ed. by M. Sprengling, *American Journal of Semitic Languages and Literatures*, LVII (1940), pp. 404, 413: Pahlavīk *Apursām*, Pārsīk *Apursān*; Arabic *Abarsām* (Nöldeke, Tabari, p. 9); Armenian *Aprsam* (H. Hübschmann, *Armenische Grammatik*, 1897, p. 21); Justi, *Iranisches Namenbuch*, p. 1.

of the letter as it occurs in all the Pahlavīk (Parthian) inscriptions we possess. The typical, original form of this letter is also to be found in inscriptions of the Synagogue, as in the graffito on the Panel of the prophets of Baal (SC 3) and in some of the parchments and ostraca of Dura. The *p* of our

present inscription obviously represents an oversimplified and very cursive variant of the letter. The forms of the *p* in the word *'prs'm* and *SPR'* in Inscr. no. **54** come nearer to the regular form, but are still by no means its normal shape.

Transliteration

(1) 'pryn 'L 'LH['] [']pryn MḤ gy'n
(2) gy'n L'LMYN *YNTN(WP?)*

Reading

āfrīn ō bag [ā]frīn čē gyān
gyān yāvētān dahēt..(?)

"Praise to God, praise! For life,
life eternally he gives (..?)"

Line 1, *'LH*[']. There is no doubt that we have here the word *'LH'*, "God." However, it is very difficult, or rather impossible, to ascertain the places and the outlines of the *L* and of the final *aleph*. It is of no help that they are properly written in the reproduction of the inscription offered by Du Mesnil du Buisson.

[']*pryn* (second instance). Du Mesnil du Buisson's reproduction presents here the reading *npryn*, with the remark "(sic)". As a matter of fact, *npryn*; i.e., *nafrīn*, is quite impossible in this context, as it is the opposite of *āfrīn* and means "malediction, curse." It is beyond any doubt that only *'pryn*, "praise," can be expected in this context, and that the alleged initial *n* is in reality only one of the meaningless curves and strokes which are to be

seen before the *p*. This statement holds true in spite of the fact that all efforts to ascertain the exact place and the outlines of the *aleph* which must have preceded the *p* at a proper distance, proved to be in vain.

Line 2. The final *N* of *YNTN* is closely followed by two letters which might be *wp* or, less likely, *pp*.[144]

It may be noteworthy that in the text of this inscription the words *āfrīn* and *gyān* are repeated. This could have happened without any special reason. In particular, the word *gyān* at the end of line 1 might have been repeated inadvertently by the scribe at the beginning of line 2. However, the two repetitions might as well be an expression of the solemnity of the language, and might have been taken over from some original text.

56. Graffito deeply incised, beginning in the thigh of the first prophet of Baal to the left of the altar in Panel SC 3 and continuing into Panel SC 2. One line; Pahlavīk (Parthian) script. Letters 0.05-0.08 m. high (Pl. XLVII, 4).

Rep. VI, p. 392 (listed as Aramaic); Du Mesnil du Buisson, *Peintures*, p. 161, no. 15, where an obviously quite unsuccessful attempt is made to interpret the whole inscription as Aramaic, although the reading ... הוא עד כתוב בבו is advanced with "quelques réserves." Moreover, two excellent photographs at my disposal do not justify Du Mesnil du Buisson's statement that the script is "très négligée."

In some notes made at Damascus Professor

Kraeling gives the following description of the letters of this graffito: "The incisions are very deep and regular and may have been made when the plaster was still wet. Certainly the paint goes right through the trough created by the letters, in certain instances. No part of the inscription mars the scenes painted in Panels SC 2–3....." Kraeling considered it possible that the letters which appear in my transliteration and in my tracing as the last letters of the inscription were followed by more letters, but this seems to me very uncertain and unlikely. If my interpretation of the inscription is correct, we do not have to expect any continuation of the text of the line.

144. Cf. Herzfeld, *Paikuli*, p. 202: *YNTNW*.

Transliteration

syh'r
syh'[r?] dpyr RB' dnk(?) RBRB'

Reading

syh'r
syh'[r?] dipīr vazurk d(ā)n(ā)k (?) mahist

"Syh'r, the great scribe, the very great wise man."

As the final letter of the first word of the text was wrongly written (there is no such letter in the Pahlavīk alphabet), the scribe himself corrected this mistake by writing the same word above the line and replacing the wrong letter with a correct *r*.

I am advancing this interpretation of the inscription with some reluctance, after repeated attempts to reach more conclusive solutions of some of the difficulties with which we are confronted here. However, I still feel to some extent confident that my reading *RB' dnk RBRB'*, being in almost perfect agreement with the letters of the inscription, can claim a rather high degree of likelihood, in spite of the fact that there are two or three points which still might remain open to doubt. It is first of all absolutely evident that we have here an Iranian, not an Aramaic, inscription. The fact that this line is written in the Parthian script implies that the inscription is also Iranian in language. Unfortunately, only one Iranian word is absolutely certain. It is the second word in the line, the beautifully and elegantly written word *dpyr* (*dipīr*), "the scribe," which Du Mesnil du Buisson transliterated wrongly by כתוב ("qu'a fait peindre"). Even the little stroke below the letter *d* by which this letter is distinguished from *r*, is to be seen very distinctly.

The preceding word is undoubtedly the name of the scribe. I read it first *pyh'r* or *pyχ'r*; but in view of the perfect *p* in the following word *dpyr*, it is more likely that the first letter of the first word is not a *p* but an *s*, although the scribes are often not reliable in drawing the letters. Accordingly, the name of the scribe is obviously to be spelled *syh'r* or *syχ'r*. Unfortunately, a name of this form is not known from any Iranian or Aramaic source.

My interpretation of the words that follow the word *dpyr* is to some extent conjectural. This is especially due to the fact that, in contrast to the word *dpyr*, which represents a model of exact and careful calligraphic writing, the remaining letters of the line are drawn in a rather rough — or even clumsy — manner which made it difficult to ascertain the real value of the second letter of the word which I propose to read *RB'*, and the second letter of the word which I am inclined to read *RBRB'*. I think that these readings are favored by the fact that in both words the *r*'s are absolutely certain, and that the letter after the second *r* of the second word (my *RBRB'*) is undoubtedly a huge *B*,

which is obviously connected in ligature with a final *aleph*. Between the two upper arms of the *aleph* there is to be seen a hole, which Kraeling mentions in his description of the graffito. The *aleph* of the word *RB'* is less distinct. It is difficult to recognize and to reproduce it accurately because of the interference of several strokes which cannot possibly belong to the letter. As to the letter *B* of *RB'*, it can be stated with certainty that there is no letter in the Parthian alphabet with which it could be identified but *B*. It is awkwardly written and a little smaller than we should have expected. But its ductus is obviously in general similar to that of the huge second *B* of *RBRB'*. There remains only the form of the second letter of this word as a seemingly insurmountable obstacle to my reading, for it looks more like a *K* than a *B*. However, this may be due only to inaccuracy. Such suspicion is justified in view of the above-mentioned error of the scribe in writing the final letter of the first word of the inscription (*syh'r*). In any case the conclusion seems to be inevitable that the word consisting of the letters *R[?]RB'* can only represent *RBRB'*, and that a word *RKRB'* is out of the question.

However, my reading of the three letters between the words *RB'* and *RBRB'* as *dnk* (= *dānāk*), "wise," might constitute the most dubious part of my interpretation of this inscription, as it is open to an apparently very serious objection. It seems very unlikely that in an inscription written in the Parthian script a Parsīk word like *dānāk* should have been used. In the Parthian dialect only a word with initial *z* is possible, as we know from the Parthian texts of Turfan, which offer the preterite *z'n'd*, the present stem *z'n-*, "to know,"[145] and *prz'ng*, "wise,"[146] which appears as a loan-word, *frazānak* (modern Persian *farzāna*), also in Pārsīk besides the regular *dānāk*. And yet it seems to me possible and likely that the scribe has used *d(ā)n(ā)k* against the rule, owing to inaccuracy or for some other similar reason. This suspicion is apparently supported by the fact that the scribe wrote here

145. Carl Salemann, *Manichaeische Studien*, I (*Mémoires de l'académie impériale des sciences de St. Pétersbourg*, 8th series, VIII, No. 10, 1908), p. 78; Andreas-Henning, *Mitteliranische Manichaica*, III, p. 64 (909).
146. Carl Salemann, *Manichaica, III–IV* (*Bulletin de l'académie impériale des sciences de St. Pétersbourg*, 6th series, VI, 1912), pp. 24, 47.

an abnormal *dpyr*, whereas other Parthian inscriptions[147] always have the Aramaic *SPR'* corresponding to the *dpyr* or *dpywr* of the Pārsīk version.[148] It is understandable that in the composition with *pat*, "chief, lord," the Parthian does not offer *SPR'* but, like the Pārsīk, *dpyr* in *dpyrwpt*, *dpyrpty*.[149] It is therefore abnormal when our Parthian graffito offers *dpyr* instead of the Aramaic *SPR'*, and this irregularity may be taken as an indication that the use of the Pārsīk form *dnk*, written in the manner peculiar to the Parthian

writing without the *aleph* letters, is due to the same kind of error.

In the present edition of the Middle Iranian inscriptions of the Synagogue I have had to restrict myself to the attempt to clarify as far as possible the problems offered by Inscr. no. **56** merely from the epigraphical point of view. A considerable number of facts derived from different literary sources concerning the scribe, which might endorse my interpretation of this inscription, will be advanced in my *editio major*.[150]

57. Graffito on Panel EC 2 under the couch to the left of its right leg and above the yellow vessel. Two lines (Fig. 109).
Du Mesnil du Buisson, *Peintures*, p. 161, No. 17.

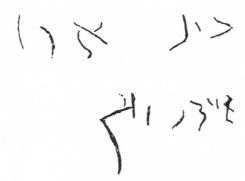

FIG. 109. Inscr. No. **57**

Illegible, language unknown.

147. E.g., our graffito, Inscr. no. **54** (*Aparsām SPR'*); the Kaabah inscription (Sprengling, *American Journal of Semitic Languages and Literatures*, LVII, 1940, p. 415, no. 55): Parthian *SPR'*, Pārsīk *dpyr*; the Sāhpuhr inscription (ed. R. Ghirshman, *Revue des arts asiatiques*, X, 1936, pp. 123–129) line 9: Parthian *SPR'*, Pārsīk *dpywr*, further Pārsīk *dpywr* in line 15 of the Pārsīk version; in Paikuli (Herzfeld, p. 102): line 4, *χšθr-'hmr SPR'*.

148. Herzfeld substituted in the missing passage of the Pārsīk version from Paikuli a Pārsīk *SPR'* as corresponding to the *SPR'* of the Parthian version, but he corrected this error (*Paikuli*, p. 247).

149. Sprengling, *op.cit.*, p. 405, no. 18, and p. 414, no. 45.

150. Editors' note. It should be mentioned that early records report the presence of two more Iranian dipinti — one on the leg of the revived child in Panel WC 1, and one on the figure to the right of the altar in Panel SC 4 (in addition to our Inscr. no. **51**) — but give no details. These are no longer visible, and have never been studied. A graffito on a doorjamb will he published by Professor Geiger; see above pp. 283 f. There are also sets of scratches — across the foot of the altar in Panel SC 4, on the footstool in Panel WC 1, and on Panel EC 2 — which might have been intended as inscriptions, but which are completely illegible.

IV. THE PICTORIAL DIPINTI AND GRAFFITI

In addition to the epigraphic materials presented by Torrey, Welles, and Geiger, there are on the walls of the Synagogue numerous graffiti and at least one dipinto that represent objects or figures. The dipinto was of course executed after the murals had been completed, but the large majority of the graffiti was incised on the walls either at the time of construction or during the period prior to their decoration. They are therefore now covered with paint, and so hard to see that it is difficult to know whether all have been recorded. A close study of the surface of the walls as reconstructed in Damascus revealed several that had not been noticed at the time of the excavation. It is difficult to know where figured representation stops and mere scratching begins, but every effort has been made to exclude the latter.

58. Graffito on Lower Center Panel, to the right of center near the bottom, hidden behind the façade of the Torah Shrine (Fig. 110). Vessel.

FIG. 110. Inscr. No. **58**

59. Dipinto on Panel WC 4, painted in black on the skirt of Moses' mother at the left end of the panel (Fig. 111). Lion.

FIG. 111. Inscr. No. **59**

60. Graffito on Panel ND 6, over the figure of the leopard (Fig. 112). Scale 1:5. Torah Shrine or tent.

FIG. 112. Inscr. No. **60**

61. Graffito on Panel ND 6 to the right and above the preceding (Fig. 113). Scale 1:5. Wall, ladder, *klimax*?

FIG. 113. Inscr. No. **61**

A somewhat similar design from G7 B8 was published in *Rep. V.*, p. 94, and interpreted as a *klimax* design (pp. 95–97).

62. Graffito on Panel EC 1 to the right of het hoof of the left hind leg of Saul's horse, extending into the register band (Fig. 114). Scale 1:5. Human figure.

FIG. 114. Inscr. No. **62**

63. Graffito on Panel EC 1, directly in front of Saul's horse (Fig. 115). Scale 1:5. See also Pl. LXXIII. Horse.

FIG. 115. Inscr. No. **63**

64. Graffito on Panel EC 1, just below the dog in front of Saul's horse (Fig. 116; Pl. LXXIII). Scale 1:5. Lyre.

FIG. 116. Inscr. No. **64**

65. Graffito on Panel EC 1 and its register band above Panel ED 3 (N) (Fig. 117). Scale 1:5. Eye.

FIG. 117. Inscr. No. **65**

66. Graffito on Panel EC 2, at the right of the second bird from the left (Fig. 118). Scale 1:5. Bird.

FIG. 118. Inscr. No. **66**

67. Graffito on Panel SD 2 (Fig. 119). Scale 1:5. Tent?

FIG. 119. Inscr. No. **67**

68. Graffito running across Panels SC 1 and SC 2 (Fig. 120). Scale 1:5. Hunting scene.

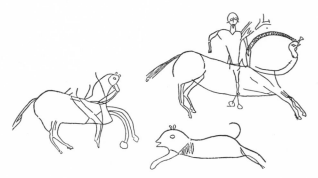

FIG. 120. Inscr. No. **68**

Cf. Du Mesnil du Buisson, *Peintures*, p. 163, Fig. 112.

69. Graffito along extreme right side of Panel SC 4 (Fig. 121). Scale 1:5. Human figure or demon?

FIG. 121. Inscr. No. **69**

70. Graffito on a fragment of a doorjamb found in the excavation of the Forecourt (Fig. 122). Plant or tree.

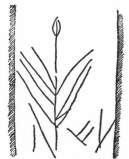

FIG. 122. Inscr. No. **70**

71. Graffito on the face of the south bench of the Earlier Building (Fig. 123). Scale 1:2. Torah Shrine.

FIG. 123. Inscr. No. **71**

Cf. Du Mesnil du Buisson, *Revue biblique*, XLV (1936), p. 75, Fig. 2; *idem, Peintures*, p. 7, Fig. 4.

72. Graffito on a plaster fragment found among the remains of the Earlier Building (Fig. 124). Scale 1:2. Torah Shrine?

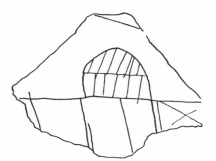

FIG. 124. Inscr. No. **72**

INTERPRETATION

"Dura-Europos," Rostovtzeff has aptly said, "was never an important centre of ancient life. First a Seleucid fortress, then a Parthian caravan-city, and finally a stronghold on the Euphrates frontier or *limes* of the Roman Empire, Dura-Europos played no momentous part in the history of its time; nor was it ever distinguished for independent creative activity."[1] The statement applies with equal force to both the general and the particular and can thus be paraphrased in the present context to say that Dura was never a prominent center of ancient Jewish life and played no important role in the history of contemporary Judaism. But if, as Rostovtzeff goes on to say, Dura has none the less added immensely to our general knowledge of the Hellenistic and Roman Orient because of "the scientific importance of the material that its ruins yield," the same is true also for our knowledge of ancient Judaism. Quite out of proportion to anything we might have expected is the contribution that Dura makes to our under-standing of the synagogues, the religious life, the art, and the institutions of the Judaism of the Dispersion in the third century of our era and through this fact also to our picture of the con-temporary scene.

The preceding chapters have set forth with some

1. *Dura-Europos and its Art*, pp. 1 f.

measure of illustrative comment the essential facts about the Dura Synagogue: its architecture, its decorations, its furnishings, and its inscriptions. The report would not be complete, however, with-out some attempt to interpret the factual evidence and thus to assess the contribution it makes. To deal comprehensively with this subject would require an undue amount of space and would inevitably command also the efforts of specialists in many fields, working over a long period of time. We can therefore only deal summarily here with some of the more important aspects of the matter. Indeed, since we have already discussed above what the successive buildings tell us about the origin and development of ancient synagogue architecture generally, we can focus our attention upon four subjects:

    I. The history of the Jewish community at Dura;

   II. The interpretation of the paintings and the religious orientation of the local Jewish community;

  III. The technique, style, and composition of the paintings; and

  IV. The origin and antiquity of the Synagogue's Biblical scenes.

We begin here with the discussion of the first of these topics.

I. THE HISTORY OF THE JEWISH COMMUNITY AT DURA

For the history of the Jewish community at Dura there are available as evidence certain important, and many of the seemingly trivial, facts revealed by the excavation of the Synagogue buildings, as well as a few pieces of information from other parts of the city. The bulk of the material belongs to the Roman period of the city's history; namely, to the period from the capture of Dura by Lucius Verus in A.D. 165 to the destruction of the city by the Sassanians in A.D. 256.[2] Since at best the evidence is fragmentary, it will be well to have at the outset a general perspective upon Dura and Judaism in the second and third centuries of our era.

A. Dura and Judaism in the Period of the Dura Synagogue

Anyone dealing with the later history of Dura will soon realize that Roman influence did not begin there only with Lucius Verus. There are in effect two periods of Roman influence in the city, the first being that in which, while still under Parthian domination, it felt the effects of the Roman control of Syria; the second, that in which it was incorporated officially into the Roman Empire. Of these two periods, each approximately a century long, it was the first, strangely enough, in which Roman influence had the most beneficial impact upon the city's life, sending its impulses rapidly down along the trade routes into the interior. The quickened tempo of Syria's economic life in the Flavian and Antonine periods meant for Dura's Macedonian *Europaioi* and their Oriental *paroikoi* the end of an era of decline and stagnation that had begun even before the Parthian conquest (*ca.* 113 B.C.) and had lasted through the early days of the Julio-Claudian emperors. One indication of this change is the large increase in the coin yield of the site beginning with the reign of Claudius, the new money being largely Roman bronze from the provincial mint at Antioch.[3] Put into

a position where it was able to expand and to enrich its life for the first time in some centuries, Dura began to erect new temples, to rebuild and redecorate others, to improve the palace on the citadel and the *strategeion* on the acropolis, to increase the number of its private houses, to establish a bath, and to develop and expand the *sukh* that replaced the Hellenistic agora. With all classes and sorts of residents being given opportunity to benefit from the changes, it is evident that for large scale entrepreneurs, lesser merchants, priests, artists, craftsmen, and even the simple day-laborers, the century from *ca.* A.D. 50–165 was perhaps the happiest and most affluent in all of the city's history.[4]

From this earlier period of Roman influence, the one that begins with the Roman occupation in A.D. 165 and to which the buildings of the Dura Synagogue belong is to be distinguished sharply. In spite of the titles of *municipium* and *colonia* which it acquired at Roman hands, Dura was no longer as a city a strong autonomous organism. In the space of a little more than fifty years it was transformed into a Roman frontier fortress and a military post whose civilian residents served in the main to minister to the needs of the garrison. The changes in its life are subtle but nonetheless of great meaning. There was much building going on,

2. The evidence for the capture of Dura by the Sassanians in A.D. 256 or soon thereafter has been presented by Rostovtzeff and Bellinger in *Berytus*, VIII (1943), pp. 17–71. More recently Altheim, *Asien und Rom*, p. 39, has argued for a date of A.D. 260, influenced mainly by his reading and interpretation of Dura Parchment 12. This parchment was found in the Main Gate and belongs to the level prior to the siege, but Altheim's reading of its date is both doubtful and isolated. Unless it can be confirmed, we must abide by the date inferred from the mass of the evidence, especially the coins.

3. Cf. Bellinger's catalogue in *Final Report* VI, pp. 74–76 and his comment, p. 203. Among the cities of

Syria the effects of the *Pax Augusta* were of course even more noticeable. At Gerasa the change also becomes apparent only in the middle of the first century, as is indicated by the adoption of the new ambitious city plan, Kraeling, *Gerasa*, p. 35.

4. On Parthian Dura, see Rostovtzeff, *Dura-Europos and its Art*, pp. 18–23.

but largely in the northern fourth of the city, which had been expropriated by the army and was being equipped with the structures necessary to the administration of the military affairs of the post and the *limes*. Civilians were probably more numerous and living quarters at a greater premium than ever before, but the space available to them was proportionately less because of expropriation and because of special provisions made for the offices of army supplies outside the military zone. Money continued to abound but the coins either represent small bronze issues of the mints of northern Mesopotamia, testifying to Dura's participation in a regional rather than an Empire trade; or they are the silver denarii, tetradrachms, and Antoniniani of the type that ultimately represents soldier pay.[5] The descendants of the original Macedonian settlers no longer appear by name in the inscriptions, and the members of the community made up largely of Orientals now speak of themselves as *Dourani* (adopting the local Semitic name) rather than as *Europaioi*.[6] Whether among the military or in the civilian population, the relation between race and nomenclature seems to have disappeared and in general the city had become "an undistinguished part of the Roman Levantine world, sharing that uniformity toward which the Empire led."[7]

While in certain respects there were thus vast differences between the Dura of the Severi and the Dura of the Flavian and Antonine Emperors, there were certain aspects of its life that showed a remarkable degree of continuity throughout. Typical of Dura's life under both Parthian and Roman domination is the intermingling of different cultural forces and of their respective forms of expression. This is nowhere more clearly illustrated than in the sphere of art where elements deriving ultimately from familiar traditions of Hellenistic painting and sculpture are regularly combined with others reflecting typically Iranian models, on the one hand, and perpetuating patterns and procedures of long standing in the Semitic Orient, on the other.[8] The fundamental combination had

already been established when the long succession of wall paintings and sculptures known to us from Parthian and Roman Dura begins; and save for degrees of technical proficiency and for the relative emphasis upon one or the other element, there is no essential difference between the components of the paintings from the Temple of Bel and those from the Synagogue, though they are all of two hundred years removed from each other in time. In a real sense the same thing is true also of the religious and secular, particularly domestic, architecture of the city. Here again uniformity is observable throughout Parthian and Roman days in the ingrafting of lesser Greek and Hellenistic elements into a structural pattern that is traditionally Oriental. Finally, there is a persistent homogeneity in the religious history of the city. Whatever the names applied to them, the gods of Dura during Parthian and Roman days are fundamentally Oriental in character. Their number increases steadily and the importance of their shrines grows as the need for security rises, whether because more is being ventured or because life loses more and more of its essential satisfactions for the individual. From the nature of the cults represented it is clear, furthermore, that in religion the individual was seeking association with the highest gods, giving occasion in this connection for solar henotheism to make itself felt as a powerful harmonizing force in the diversity of the cults, and that religions requiring the greatest amount of personal commitment were growing continuously in importance. Of this fact the presence and development at Dura of Judaism, Christianity, and Mithraism are the best indication.[9] In other spheres of life also — in the laws by which social relations were governed, in the procedures of buying and selling, in jewelry and ornament, and in the arrangements made to safeguard travelers and caravans on the highroads north-east and south-west — large elements of continuity are visible, because these too were features determined by the geographical position of Dura and by the abiding character of the cultural forces to which it was subject. The interpreter of any monument of Dura can disregard its relation to this setting only at the risk of going utterly astray in his own work

5. Bellinger, *Final Report* VI, pp. 207–209.
6. See Welles, *Studies in Roman Economic and Social History in Honor of Allen Chester Johnson*, pp. 251–274.
7. *Ibid.*, p. 274.
8. Cf. in detail, Rostovtzeff, *Dura-Europos and its Art*, pp. 63–99; and Cumont, *Fouilles*, pp. 145–164.

9. Cf. in general Rostovtzeff, *Dura-Europos and its Art*, pp. 57–63 and 100–134.

and of confusing a larger picture otherwise perfectly clear and intelligible in its outlines.

For ancient Judaism the century of the Roman occupation of Dura was by no means as dark as anyone focusing his attention upon the wars under Vespasian and Hadrian might be led to believe. Yet the peak of its impact upon ancient life had passed, and the beginnings of the transition that leads toward its medieval configuration and that reflects the change from state to church were already visible in certain spheres. So far as numbers are concerned, no great change can have been apparent; for while the disastrous wars in Palestine undoubtedly greatly diminished the Jewish population there, the region had apparently recouped most of its losses by the Antonine period, and the tragic developments had changed scarcely at all either the general distributional picture or that of the major areas of concentration. Flourishing Jewish communities still existed in all of the larger cities of the Empire; and in Palestine, lower Mesopotamia, Alexandria, Rome, Antioch, and the petty frontier kingdoms of Roman Syria and Parthian Mesopotamia they were still very numerous.[10] Nor had the official status of Judaism throughout the Roman Empire undergone a radical transformation, for fundamentally the traditional privileges were still being upheld.[11] What did happen as the result of the several wars, apart from local pogroms and certain population displacements, was that inside the boundaries of the Empire the exercise of the traditional privileges was limited for shorter or longer periods of time to those who were born Jews and was hedged about with restrictions that tended to reduce the expansiveness of Judaism's relation to its environment.[12]

The effects of the change in Judaism's relation to its environment were gradual but not for that reason any the less real, and because of the paucity of our sources for the literature and piety of the Dispersion can best be seen in terms of long-range developments. The efforts to reconcile revelation and philosophy that we associate naturally with Philo and the allegorists of Alexandria diminished, to reappear again only at a much later time under the Islamic influence in the work of Saadia Gaon. Neoplatonic speculation which meanwhile had so profoundly affected the main stream of Christian theology registered its impression on Judaism only in the esoteric traditions that came to expression ultimately in the Kabbalah. If then Philonic theology and mysticism were disappearing from the Jewish sphere of interest, how much more so the attempts at syncretism that we associate with the names of Artapanos and the other Jewish writers of the Hellenistic period whose fragments are preserved by Eusebius.[13] Even the Wisdom literature comes to an end and only the dire prophecies of the Sibyl continue.

It is hard to escape the impression that in the second and third centuries of our era, in spite of their considerable numerical strength and their continuing fidelity to the ancestral faith, the Jews of the Mediterranean Dispersion, including those of Alexandria and Antioch, played a less important role in the larger pattern of Jewish life than they had during the first century. Certainly it was in the Near East, among the less effectively Hellenized Jewish communities of Palestine and of Mesopotamia, that the two features of greatest significance for the further development of Jewish life were being created at this very time. The first was the codification in the Mishnah and ultimately in the Talmud of a great body of what had long been oral commentary on Biblical laws and injunctions, with which there went side by side the growth of a vast reservoir of Haggadic material expounding and interpreting the Biblical text for devotional and inspirational purposes. The second was the creation of a central authority, vested in Palestine in the Patriarch and in lower Mesopotamia in the Exilarch, by which the larger community could be represented and through which certain aspects at

10. The material bearing upon the distribution of the Jews throughout the ancient world is gathered in J. Juster, *Les Juifs dans l'empire romain*, I (1914), pp. 179–212. See also A. v. Harnack, *Die Mission und Ausbreitung des Christentums*, 3rd. ed. (1915), I, pp. 3–10.

11. See especially Juster, *Les Juifs*, I, pp. 243–251.

12. Cf. *ibid.*, pp. 253–290, 338–408. The more drastic acts that denied by implication the essential privileges; for instance, Hadrian's interpretation of the Lex Cornelia, were all eventually modified. That prosecutions on the charge of "atheism" which, in view of the Jewish rejection of idolatry and of Emperor-worship, might have had disastrous consequences were ever very numerous, seems quite unlikely.

13. *Praeparatio Evangelica* IX, 17–29; cf. in general J. Freudenthal, *Hellenistische Studien* (1875).

least of its religious and social life could be administered.[14] Through these developments Judaism regained some measure of the unity it had lost in the wars with the Romans, albeit a unity of a new type. At the same time it tended to turn more and more away from the world and back upon itself, concerning itself ever more exclusively with the vast body of tradition its scholars and preachers had created for it out of their study of the sacred book.

If in the period between Hadrian and Septimius Severus the outward conditions for a rectilinear development along these lines were sometimes unfavorable, so that Judaism seemed occasionally to be threatened in its essential juridical status, from at least the reign of Alexander Severus on the situation was greatly improved and there was ample opportunity for the development to come to full fruition.

It is an interesting phenomenon of the history of Judaism in the early centuries of our era, that the period which saw it turning in and back upon itself most clearly is also the period from which there come to us the most elaborate monuments of Jewish architecture and art: the Galilean synagogues, the Jewish catacombs of the Western Mediterranean, and the Dura Synagogue. It is a nice question whether the existence of these monuments implies a larger measure of Jewish outreach toward contemporary culture than what has just been said about the major trend in the development of Jewish thought might seem to suggest. If it did, the position taken above would need to be revised. Our personal inclination, however, is to interpret these monuments as tokens of greater economic competence and communal strength and well-being, but not as signs of a return to the programmatic "Kulturfreundlichkeit" of the early Hellenistic period.[15] The reason is that all of the monuments in question seem to be intended primarily, not to enhance the position of Judaism in the life of an enlightened society, but rather to help express a fundamental conviction about the importance of Jewish religious observance and tradition. Inter-

preted as a means of exalting the value of what the Law and the tradition, worship and piety meant for the Jewish people, these monuments are in accord with what has been said about the direction in which Jewish interests were moving in the period under discussion.

The particular importance naturally attaching in the present context to the Judaism of lower and upper Mesopotamia in the early centuries of our era makes a brief word of orientation on that subject unavoidable. Numerically the Jewish population of lower Mesopotamia in the period of the Dura Synagogue must have been stronger than that of Palestine. A peculiar feature of its life was the fact that it was concentrated in a series of towns along the great canal running from Babel to Nippur, towns that were predominantly Jewish.[16] Representing largely the descendants of the exiles brought from Palestine by Nebuchadnezzar, together with such refugees as had left Syria and Palestine in the years of the Jewish revolt against Rome and of Hadrian's repressive edicts, the communities guarded with great zeal the purity of their racial stock and flourished increasingly in the Parthian and Sassanian periods.[17] Devoted largely to agriculture, the Jews of southern Mesopotamia were in Sassanian times very wealthy and were under the control of an Exilarch who was acknowledged to be of Davidic descent and was a recognized official of the Sassanian court.[18] Per-

14. For the major developments in the history of Judaism during the second and third centuries of our era, the best comprehensive treatment is still that of H. Graetz, *Geschichte der Juden*, 3rd ed. (1893), IV.

15. Save in so far as they may involve a repristination of older forms and materials.

16. On the distribution of the Jews in lower Mesopotamia see especially A. Neubauer, *La Géographie du Talmud* (1868), pp. 292–399; J. Obermeyer, *Die Landschaft Babylonien* (1929); A. Berliner, *Jahresberichte des Predigerseminars zu Berlin* (1882–1883). Josephus speaks of there being "not a few" or again "untold myriads" of Jews in lower Mesopotamia (*Antiquitates* XV, 39; XI, 133), while Philo suggests that Petronius, the legate of Syria in the days of the Emperor Gaius, feared lest powerful Jewish influence might bring about a Parthian attack upon Rome's eastern provinces (*Legatio ad Caium*, §§ 216–217).

17. See Graetz, *Geschichte der Juden*, IV, p. 251; and for the purity of the priestly families, S. Funk, *Die Juden in Babylonien* (1902), I, p. 5, n. 1. Herod the Great, it will be recalled, brought a Babylonian Jew, Ananel, to Palestine as high priest.

18. On the background of Jewish life in Mesopotamia, see J. Newman, *The Agricultural Life of the Jews in Babylonia* (1932). The earliest known Exilarch is Huna, a contemporary of R. Judah ha-Nazi in the late second century (Jer. Killaim 32b). On the regal splendor and descent of the Exilarch, see in general Graetz, *Geschichte der Juden*, IV, pp. 254–257.

petuating the tradition that goes back ultimately to Ezra the Scribe, Babylonian Judaism of the Parthian period gave no less a light to Palestinian Judaism than Hillel, and produced a succession of scholars whose opinions were recorded by the Palestinian sages. Beginning in the second century of our era it sent to Palestine a succession of students who were educated at the great academies there and most of whom returned again to their home land.[19] Eventually, as the Palestinian

academies declined in importance, comparable institutions of learning developed in lower Mesopotamia itself. This development belongs in general to the early years of the third century. It brings to the fore two important personages, both outstanding among the intellectual leaders of ancient Judaism; namely, Rab, the founder of the academy at Sura, who died in A.D. 247; and R. Samuel, who succeeded R. Shila as head of the academy at Nehardea and who lived until 255. With these men the weight of rabbinical authority began to shift from Palestine to lower Mesopotamia, in consequence of which students began to come from the west to the east instead of vice versa as heretofore.[20]

19. On the tradition that Hillel had been a student of the interpretation of the Law before coming to Palestine see Moore, *Judaism*, I, pp. 77f. Among the scholars resident in Babylonia whose opinions were quoted in the West were R. Judah ben Bathyra of Nisibis and R. Nehemia of Beth Deli in Nehardea (Pesachim 3b; Sanhedrin 32b; and Yebamoth 122a). Among those who came to study in Palestine and eventually rose to prominence are R. Nathan, R. Haninah, Rabba ben Hana, Rab, R. Hiyya and his two sons, and eventually R. Samuel himself.

20. On Rab and Samuel and their exegetical tradition, see particularly Bacher, *Die Agada der babylonischen Amoräer*, pp. 1–45.

B. The Beginnings of the Jewish Community at Dura

Turning now from the wider background to the local community itself, it is interesting to note that the earliest evidence for the presence of Jews at Dura comes not from the earlier of the two Synagogue buildings mentioned above, but from the coins of the city as a whole. The coins in question are pieces representing an issue of John Hyrcanus, the Maccabean King who ruled Palestine from 135 to 104 B.C.[21] Found in various parts of the city, they have already and quite properly been taken to imply the passage through Dura of a military expedition which Hyrcanus is known to have led from Palestine to Babylonia in 130 B.C., to assist Antiochus VII in his campaign against the Parthians.[22] The yield of Jewish coins at Dura increases somewhat in the period of Alexander Jannaeus (103–76 B.C.) and continues sporadically with issues of the Herodians, going down ultimately to the period of the Jewish Revolt (A.D. 66–71). In all likelihood the later pieces, like those of John Hyrcanus, also testify largely to the transit through Dura of Jews from Palestine. But the period to which they belong was the one in which the Jewish

Dispersion achieved its greatest strength and influence, and at the same time the one in which relations between Palestinian and Babylonian Judaism, long interrupted and tenuous, began to be resumed.[23] Under the circumstances and in view of Dura's position on the Euphrates road, it would have been unusual if a small resident colony had not developed in the city during the late Parthian period.

Once Palestinian coinage ceases there is no further indication of the presence of Jews at Dura until we come to the earlier building of the Synagogue. It is therefore important to fix the date of this building as closely as possible. Unfortunately the evidence available for this purpose is largely indirect, consisting of information about the beginnings of construction work in the area and about the probable date of a row of three houses in Block L7; namely, Houses A and B and the earlier Synagogue building.[24] Construction in the area

21. For the list of all the Jewish coins of Dura see *Final Report* VI, p. 11, and for their interpretation the comments of Bellinger, *ibid.*, p. 199.

22. On the expedition see Josephus, *Antiquitates* XIII, 250–251, quoting Nicolaus of Damascus.

23. On the Dispersion in general see Juster, *Les Juifs dans l'empire romain*, I, pp. 179–212. On the relations between Palestinian and Babylonian Jews in the centuries before and after the beginning of our era, see above.

24. The coin yield of the block, which is not inconsiderable, is useless for dating the individual buildings of the block because of the fact that the area was disturbed so much in antiquity in the erection of the embankment.

begins with an edifice which was not organic to the building lines of Block L7 as finally drawn, and of which scattered elements were re-used in House C and in the earlier Synagogue building.[25] It belongs apparently to the early Parthian period.[26] This then is the *terminus a quo* for all construction in the block. As regards the building adapted to Synagogue use, this is known to have been erected in Block L7 at the same time as the adjacent dwelling, House B, and probably not much earlier than House A.[27] All three had long been in existence when the city was destroyed, for all gave evidence of long occupation and all seem to have undergone changes in the emplacement of their doorsills to compensate for a steady rise in the level of Wall Street.[28] This and the oldest architectural member of House A, a jamb capital, suggest for the group a date in the late first or the early second Christian century.[29] In general the date proposed

agrees with what has been said above about the prosperity and growth of Dura during the century between A.D. 50 and 150.[30]

That the dwelling which eventually became the earlier building of the Synagogue was originally erected by Jewish inhabitants of Dura for their own use is possible but not demonstrable. Its actual relation to the Jewish community becomes evident only when it was adapted to synagogue use as described above. Of the date of this adaptation, important as it is for present purposes, only two indications are available. The first is implied in the fact that the doorsill of the house and the floor of its entrance passageway were raised approximately to the height of that of House B; namely, 1.73 m. above the level of the interior courtyard, when the building was remodeled for religious use[31]. This would probably put the remodeling into the period after A.D. 150.[32] The second is a plaster cornice belonging to the building itself which is assigned to the late second or early third century.[33] Allowing for later alterations inside the adapted house and extensive indications of long use by worshipers, it seems most likely that the dwelling became a Jewish house of worship in the early days of the Roman occupation of Dura, that is in the period between A.D. 165 and 200.

When through its possession of a house of worship the Jewish community of Dura first comes concretely into our field of vision, some simple facts about it become recognizable. The community must already have numbered ten or more adult males, for this is the minimum necessary for the establishment of a synagogue. Some of those who were members of the community in these earlier days are known to us by name from the graffiti inscribed on a door jamb of room 7,[34] but the names themselves — Mattenai, Hanani, Dakka, Nahmani and Minyamin — tell us nothing unusual, and only the designation apparently attached to one of them as interpreted by Professor Torrey;

What coins were not displaced or brought in with the fill can have been dropped by workmen erecting the embankment. The hoards from the area are all late deposits.

25. The outer wall of the building is that which now separates rooms 18 and 22 from rooms 19 and 27 in House C of Block L7 (Plan II). A jamb capital probably from this building was embedded in the bench of the earlier Synagogue structure. See p. 30, n. 140 above; and in *Rep. VI*, p. 213.

26. A date in the first century B.C. is assigned to the jamb capital by Shoe, *Berytus*, IX (1948), Pl. IV, no. 85.

27. Houses A and B were much pulled about in the later period of the city's history. For their original forms see *Rep. VI*, pp. 224–227, 274f., and Pl. XI. Since the doorway of House B was constructed as an integral part of the south wall of the earlier Synagogue building, the two structures are of the same date. House A was built against House B, but since it was affected in equal measure by the rise in the level of Wall Street (see below), it must be almost as old as House B.

28. In House A the sill of the original doorway, first set at 0.85 m. above Wall Street, was raised 0.95 m. above its original level; and when this proved insufficient to cope with a further rise in the level of the street, the door was blocked up and a new entrance provided on Street 2 (see *Rep. VI*, pp. 274f.). In House B and in the earlier building of the Synagogue the doorways were approximately 1.73 m. above the level of the interior court. In neither case is the position of the original doorsills known, but since the drop in the Synagogue building from doorway to courtyard (1.73 m.) approximates the rise in the emplacement of the doorway of House A (0.85 m. + 0.95 m. = 1.80 m.), the inference is that House A, the Synagogue building, and House B were erected when Wall Street was at approximately the same level, and thus at about the same time. At that time one entered from street to courtyard without an appreciable change in level.

29. On the capital see Shoe, *Berytus*, IX (1948), Pl. VI, no. 139.

30. See above p. 325.

31. See above p. 27, n. 123.

32. In his analysis of the relation between the fill in Wall Street and the changes in the fortification of the city, von Gerkan assigns the first 1.65 m. of fill to the period before A.D. 160 (*Rep. VII–VIII*, p. 36 and p. 41, Fig. 18.)

33. *Berytus*, IX (1948), Pl. VIII, no. 180.

34. Inscrs. Nos. **20–22** above, pp. 274–276.

namely, *apotheqai*, suggests that the man in question was the overseer of certain stores, or perhaps merely a shopkeeper.[35] More important for our purposes are the inferences that can be drawn from the building itself. It was a structure of modest proportions, located on one of the less desirable streets of the city. The city wall just across the street acted as a barrier to the cooling winds from the desert, and the rapid accumulation of debris and sand in the street itself may have caused the water of the winter rains to saturate the plaster walls of the adjacent houses at street level, thus bringing discomfort to users and inhabitants. The community was therefore originally not wealthy, nor was it numerous, for the number of persons that could have been accommodated in the meeting. room was distinctly limited.[36]

Nonetheless, it seems that the community had developed sufficient resources to improve the property by creating the one large chamber (room 2) for worship services, by making special provision for attendance of the women, by paving the court, supplying the laver basin in its northeast corner, and erecting the colonnaded porticoes. From the arrangement of the other rooms it would appear that some members of the group, perhaps the owner of the house or a *hazzan* (superintendent), continued to inhabit the premises, occupying rooms 4 and 5 and protecting the property.[37] The additional chamber, room 6, may also have been at the disposal of the occupant, or more probably it may have served to provide lodgings for such Jewish travelers as passed through the city on their way up or down the Euphrates, whether on commercial or other errands.

From the organization of room 2, it is evident that the community held in highest esteem the sacred scrolls that it possessed, providing a special repository to house them. In the matter of the attendance of women at the services of worship, it took approximately the same position as that reflected in the contemporary Galilean synagogues.

Women were permitted to attend and provision was made for their attendance, but this was in an area separate from that used by the men. In the Galilean synagogues that separate area was a gallery above the main floor of the house of worship.[38] In the earlier building of the Dura Synagogue it was a special chamber alongside the assembly room.

The two chambers intimately associated with the conduct of worship were appropriately decorated as previously indicated, in keeping with the best traditions of non-pictorial art in the period and the locality.[39] Whether the absence of representations of animate objects implies a more conservative orientation than that which obtained in the later period, or is merely a sign of a lower economic status, it is impossible to say. It is not even clear whether the decorations were applied to the earlier building when it was first adapted to synagogue use or at some later time. About the further history of the earlier building only these two facts are known: first, that it saw a great deal of use; and second, that eventually the seating capacity was enlarged slightly when the low aperture in the north wall of room 2, the one that gave access to the cellar under the entrance passage (room 3), was closed up. This made it possible to carry the benches around the northeast corner of the chamber.[40]

The picture of the Jewish community at Dura that we get from the earlier building of the Synagogue is therefore that of a modest ethnic and religious group, living at some distance from the centers of its faith and its people. It constitutes an insignificant minority in a thoroughly pagan environment, but is being permitted to provide for itself, apparently without interference from the civic authorities or the Roman military. What it did to provide for itself shows distinct limitations of size and of financial competence but it also reflects sobriety, judgment, and an undeniable element of enterprise. Contacts with the outside the group may well have had occasionally, but one would imagine that they were limited to individual

---

35. See above p. 275, Inscr. no. **22.**

36. Allowing 0.45 m. per person, a maximum of forty-one men could have been accommodated in room 2 on the benches as originally constructed, and seventeen women in room 7.

37. Synagogues having a dwelling for a *hazzan* are mentioned in 'Erubin 55b (Trans., p. 389). See also Krauss, *Synagogale Altertümer*, p. 192.

38. Cf. the arrangement at Tell Hum (Capernaum), where the gallery of the basilica provides for the attendance of the women. Kohl and Watzinger, *Antike Synagogen*, Frontispiece and p. 140.

39. See above, pp. 34–36.

40. See above, p. 30.

travelers along the Euphrates road. Beyond this there is nothing whatsoever to suggest that the community was anything but Oriental in its life and outlook — identical, we may imagine, with countless others that existed in the smaller cities and settlements along the commercial and military highways of the Near East.

C. The Jewish Community at the Height of its Prosperity

At some time during the period between A.D. 165 and 256, presumably toward the latter part of the period, at least some of the circumstances of Dura's Jewish community underwent a radical change. This we know fundamentally from the erection of its ambitious later building, the date of which, according to the Aramaic commemorative inscription, is the year A.D. 244/245.[41] But even before the new building was erected a number of houses in the neighborhood had already passed into Jewish hands. Among them we have certainly to number House H, the largest and best in the entire block, which was subsequently absorbed into the precincts of the new Synagogue building. At least two others; namely, Houses C and D, seem to belong in the same category, and perhaps at one time also House I.

To explain this contention it is necessary to digress briefly to a discussion of the laws of Sabbath observance. One of the many labors forbidden on the Sabbath by the commandment to keep the day holy and to do no work therein was that of transportation (Exod. 20.8–10; Jer. 17.22). As commonly interpreted this meant that objects could be moved about freely only inside the physical boundaries of a single piece of private property. There was naturally much discussion among Jewish scholars on this account about the nature of private property, and about the distinction be-

tween it and public domain, and about a third type of domain that was partly private and partly public. The results of this discussion are set down in the massive tractate 'Erubin of the Babylonian Talmud.

In the discussion of the difference between private and public property it sometimes appears that an entire city could be regarded as private domain, in which case there was no restriction upon the transportation of objects on the Sabbath within the circuit of its walls.[42] We must be careful, however, not to read into the life of normal cities of the Dispersion conditions supposed to have existed ideally in Palestine before the Revolt, and actually, no doubt, in the completely Jewish settlements of lower Mesopotamia or by special arrangements in medieval Europe. What is said in 'Erubin itself in connection with Sabbath limits on the distinction between "new" and "old" cities, and the extent of the legislation on the "joining of courtyards," indicates that normally conditions were quite different, and that in particular the open streets of cities of the Hellenistic and Roman type were public domain.[43] This being so, at Dura it would have constituted a transgression of the Law for any Jew residing in Block L7 to have carried an object on the Sabbath from House A into House B by way of Wall St. But there was a way, under certain circumstances, to alleviate the restrictions imposed by the Law. Among the circumstances two are worthy of a mention in the present context. The first is the existence of a passageway connecting

41. See Inscr. No. **1**, above, pp. 263 f. In *Berytus*, VII (1942), pp. 89–138, Obermann has developed the hypothesis that the date should be taken to refer to the earlier building. This is ruled out by a number of factors: (1) It is unlikely that there would have been occasion to build two successive structures on the same site inside a period of eleven years. (2) The hypothesis makes it entirely impossible to account adequately for the signs of long wear and usage visible inside both buildings (see above pp. 19, 30) and for the remainder in the rise of the level of Wall Street, from above the 1.73 m. level (see von Gerkan's diagram, *Rep. VII–VIII*, p. 41, Fig. 18). (3) The earlier building did not use tiles of the size that bear the inscriptions, but the later building did. For most of the questions raised there are much simpler answers than those which Obermann suggests.

42. Tractate 'Erubin 6b (Trans., pp. 32 f.) speaks of Jerusalem and Mahuza (in lower Mesopotamia) as being removed from the restrictions of public domain in the eyes of certain rabbis by virtue of the fact that the gateways in their walls were closed at night, thus transforming them into courtyards.

43. The distinction between "new" and "old" cities is that between cities whose walls were built before they were settled and those supplied with walls after settlement ('Erubin 26a, Trans., pp. 177 f.). It is essentially that between planned cities of Hellenistic and Roman foundation and older Oriental towns.

two or more houses, and the second, the existence of a doorway at the entrance of an alley leading to two or more houses. Where such passageways or such a doorway existed the adjoining establishments could for purposes of Sabbath observance be transformed into a single piece of private domain by the agreement of the owners and by the emplacement at a proper place in the passageway or the alley of a dish with a quantity of food contributed to by each of them. The mingled food was known as the 'erub and the procedure as the "union of courtyards."[44]

Lacking archaeological evidence for Jewish residential quarters in the centers of Babylonian Judaism that produced the legislation of the Babylonian Talmud, it has hitherto been extremely difficult to visualize the application of the rabbinical decisions about the use of the 'erub. In Block L7, however, we now have possible examples of the circumstances described. The first example is provided by the fact that the alley leading to House H (which was ultimately incorporated in the later building of the Synagogue and thus clearly Jewish property) and to House C had a doorway where it left Street A (see Plan II). The second example is provided by the fact that the courtyards of Houses C and D (i.e., rooms C23 and D24) are joined by a passageway, just as are also the outer and inner suites of House H, and just as House I was at one time joined with House C.[45] In any of these cases the decision of the inhabitants and the proper use of the 'erub could have transformed the property on either side of the alley, including the later Synagogue and the adjacent houses, into a single private domain for purposes of Sabbath observance.

While passageways between courtyards and alleys running into blocks of houses are not unknown in other parts of Dura, their occurrence in the immediate vicinity of a synagogue should not be regarded as fortuitous, especially not when they provide circumstances so favorable to the religious life of possible Jewish inhabitants. Hence we are inclined to infer from the nature of the circumstances that Houses H, C, D, and at one time also House I were actually inhabited by Jews, and find in this indication of the changes in the circumstances of the Jewish community since the earlier Synagogue building was erected, and of the increase of its numbers and its financial competence.

What the circumstances were that permitted the Jewish community thus to grow and flourish at Dura during the early third century, we can see at least in part. The role played in this connection by the improved conditions inside the Roman Empire, by the removal of certain of the restrictions, the re-affirmation of ancient privileges, and the closer contact between the Babylonian and the Palestinian centers of Jewish intellectual life has already been outlined above.[46] To this we may add here the fact that the coins of Dura belonging to the period suggest a close economic relationship at this time with the cities of northern Mesopotamia, especially with Nisibis and Edessa, where there were also strong Jewish colonies. Perhaps Jewish merchants and traders had no small share in the development of this regional commerce, and some of them may have established themselves at Dura, defense headquarters for the whole region, the better to sell the country's products to the army's service of supplies. Finally, conditions in lower Mesopotamia may have contributed their share. As long as imperial Roman policy pursued a course hostile toward the Jews, their institutions, and their missionary efforts, and imposed upon them special taxes like the *fiscus Judaicus*, there was undoubtedly a tendency of those not too far removed from the Empire's borders to move to the territory of friendlier states, such as the Parthian kingdom is known to have been.[47] The rise of the Sassanian kingdom, and particularly the religious policy of Ardashir, through whom the Magian cult received a larger measure of recognition and became an instrument of national policy, seemed for a time to provide a greater threat to Judaism than it had faced inside the Roman Empire.[48] Conditions having meanwhile improved greatly in the

---

44. On the regulations concerning the use of the 'erub, as set forth in the tractate 'Erubin, see the article of D. J. Bornstein in *Encyclopaedia Judaica*, VI, cols. 735–741.

45. On the door at the entrance of the alley leading to House H and House C, see above p. 7. On the doorways connecting Houses C and D, see *Rep. VI*, p. 215.

46. See above, pp. 325 f.

47. See in general Graetz, *Geschichte der Juden*, VI, pp. 254–259.

48. See, e.g., Christensen, *L'Iran sous les Sassanides*, p. 261; and Graetz, *Geschichte der Juden*, VI, p. 259.

territory under Roman rule, nothing would have been more natural than for those who had much to lose to seek to escape from the new dangers by leaving lower Mesopotamia and taking refuge in Roman lands. Dura, as the southernmost frontier outpost of Rome in the Mesopotamian area, might well have benefited from such an exodus.

When in the middle of the third century the Jewish community of Dura thus comes again into view we can not only appraise its growth from the size and elegance of the new building, but also discern with the help of inscriptions and graffiti some members of the group and some elements of its organization.

Random graffiti scattered about upon the walls or their remains bring us a series of proper names, such as Boethus, Amathbel, Hiya, son of –––– , Job (?), Hanani son of Samuel, and Phinehas son of Jeremiah son of –––– ;[49] but there is nothing remarkable about the names, not even that of Amathbel, and, so far as we can tell, nothing noteworthy about the people in question. At the opposite pole from these apparent nonentities stands the one man who more than anyone else represents the community, and in his official capacity as well as in his personal dignity gives expression to its character and purpose. This is Samuel the son of Yeda'ya, whose name appears in all three versions of the Aramaic commemorative inscription and in a separate Greek inscription of the same type.[50] He is a man of high religious station, being proudly referred to as priest in all three Aramaic texts. The particular priestly family of which he was a member is apparently one of great antiquity and prominence, for it is probably the familiar one from the books of Chronicles, Ezra, and Nehemiah.[51] In the Dura community Samuel held the office of קשיש which the Greek inscription renders πρεσβύτερος. The Aramaic title has not hitherto appeared in synagogue inscriptions, but this is probably quite accidental, for it is common in Syriac usage and really replaces the Hebrew זקן.[52] In the Aramaic commemorative inscription Samuel's "eldership" is of such import for the historical and

chronological life of the community that it is in effect eponymous, Samuel as Elder being mentioned in one breath, so to speak, with the Emperor Philip Julius Caesar. The office is therefore not one which he shares with others, but a position that he holds alone and that stamps him, in all probability, as the highest authority of the community, here regarded as a *genos*. It is analogous to that of the "Elders" who, as phylarchs, were believed to have administered tribal affairs in the Biblical history of the people, and who appear in Panel WA 3 of the Synagogue's decorations (Exodus and Crossing of the Red Sea).[53]

In the Aramaic inscriptions Samuel the Elder has a second title; namely, that of Archon. The title appears as a loan word in Talmudic tractates, and commonly in Jewish catacomb inscriptions.[54] From its long history in Greek usage, we know that it refers frequently to a collegiate magistracy. Since Samuel's archonship is mentioned after his eldership, it may be that he shared it with a group of persons (ἄρχοντες) who in concert administered the affairs of the community.[55] If there was such a body, Samuel as Elder would probably have been its chairman.

In the Iranian dipinti the titles of two other officials appear. One, "the scribe of the building" (*dipivar i zahme*), occurs repeatedly (Inscrs. Nos. **42, 43?, 44, 45**) while the other, "the *zandak* of the Jews," occurs but once (Inscr. No. **44**). Geiger believes that the first is not the title of a synagogue official; and in this he may well be correct, especially since it is applied to several persons within a short period of time.[56] But if we knew more about the function of the mysterious *dipivars* of the dipinti generally and enough about the "scribes of the house" in particular to associate any one of the latter with the Synagogue, the result would be merely to confirm what is known about the existence of "scribes" as synagogue officials elsewhere.[57] Like the γραμματεῖς of Greek civic and

---

49. Cf. above, Inscrs. Nos. **32, 35, 12–13, 14, 15**, and **17**.
50. Inscrs. Nos. **1** and **23**, above, pp. 263–268, 277.
51. See Obermann, *Berytus*, VII (1942), p. 103, and n. 19.
52. See Payne Smith, *Thesaurus Syriacus*, *s.v.*, where there are listed examples of "elders of the synagogue," and of an "elder of the City."

53. See above, p. 81, n. 238.
54. See the passages (e.g., Baba bathra 164b) quoted by J. Levy, *Chaldäisches Wörterbuch über die Targumim* (1867), *s.v.*; and J. B. Frey, *Corpus Inscriptionum Judaicarum*, I (1936) Index, *s.v.*
55. See in general Krauss, *Synagogale Altertümer*, pp. 146–149.
56. See above, p. 299.
57. See Krauss, *Synagogale Altertümer*, pp. 149–151.

communal organizations, synagogue "scribes" probably acted merely as recorders of official synagogue business.[58] The *zandak* of the Iranian inscription, here a man named Kantak, is also something of a mystery. Clearly he ranks above the "scribes of the building," but whether he is an official of the local Jewish community or has another, more extensive, competence and relationship, it is impossible to say.

The building enterprise of the year A.D. 244/245 brings to our attention another aspect of the organizational life of the community, one that was probably only *ad hoc*, but is not for that reason of less interest. No great importance attaches in this connection to the ʿUzzi who "made" the Torah Shrine and to the Joseph son of Abba who "made" another object no longer identifiable, according to the graffito on the lintel block of the Torah Shrine itself, since in all likelihood they were merely donors.[59] What is important is the occurrence in the Aramaic commemorative title of the names of three men who "stood in charge of this work" (i.e., the construction work); namely, Abraham the Treasurer, Samuel bar Saphara, and –––––– the Proselyte, whose name is lost, and the existence of a separate Greek commemorative tile which lists Abraham, Arsaces, Silas, and Salmanes as persons who "assisted" (Inscrs. Nos. **1** and **25**). In these names there is reference probably to some sort of a building commission, or technically to a group of ἐπιμεληταί, such as were commonly appointed by ancient communities to supervise structural and other enterprises and are mentioned elsewhere in numerous dedicatory inscriptions.[60] There are difficulties, however, in the interpretation of the information we have about this commission. According to the Aramaic commemorative tile, the commission would have consisted of three men working under the general supervision of Samuel the Elder, but the Greek commemorative inscriptions give a different overall picture. They

agree with the Aramaic text in doing honor to Samuel the Elder as "founder" or "builder" (Inscr. No. **23**), but award a separate palm also to Samuel son of Saphara for having "built this (building) thus (as you see)" (Inscr. No. **24**). Only then in a third text do they go on to give honorable mention to the group of four as persons who "assisted" (Inscr. No. **25**). The difficulties here are twofold; namely, how to understand the role of Samuel son of Saphara, and how to reconcile the divergences between the two lists of people who "assisted" or "stood in charge."

What is involved here is, of course, not merely a proper distribution of honors, but rather a proper insight into the workings of a synagogue of the Dispersion in which representatives of various cultural backgrounds coöperated in an enterprise serving their common religious persuasion and interests. That we are dealing with such a situation is indicated by the very existence of two sets of commemorative inscriptions, one in Aramaic and the others in Greek, and by the mention of a proselyte in one group and of a man with an Iranian name (Arsaces) in the other. Since what we know about the difficulties and tensions within such mixed groups from literary documents is usually quite general, it seems wise to try to formulate here as clear as possible a picture of the situation.[61]

The situation presented in our commemorative inscriptions permits of three possible explanations. The first is that those honored by the Greek element of the Dura community as having "assisted" constituted a sub-committee, working under the commission appointed by the Elder Samuel. This would account for the difference in personnel, but would scarcely help with the special accolade given in the Greek texts to Samuel son of Saphara, who in the Aramaic texts appears merely as one of the group of three commissioners. The second explanation would be that there were in effect two separate commissions, one for the Aramaic-, the other for the Greek-speaking, element of the Synagogue, each having received special mention in its

---

58. See Schulthess in *RE*, *VII* (1912), cols. 1708–1780.

59. See Inscr. No. **2** above. The fact that the lower left corner of this block, where the graffito occurs, was left void of figured representation implies that some importance was attached to the commemorative text recorded there.

60. See in general J. Oehler in *RE*, VI (1909), cols. 162–171; and for specific examples from the Near East his inscriptions nos. 40, 46, 114, 146, and those published by Welles in *Gerasa*, pp. 393, 396, 417, 426, etc.

61. From literary material we know of difficulties created by the presence of extremists in one or another synagogue; for instance, by a certain Antiochus, son of an Archon of the synagogue at Syrian Antioch, who turned informer against his own people (Josephus, *Bellum* VII, 3, 3 = §§ 46–52) and by the visits of Christian apostles, such as Paul, to synagogue communities.

own commemorative texts. The difficulty in this case is that Samuel the son of Saphara appears in both the Greek and the Aramaic texts, and that perhaps the same is true also of the Greek Abraham, supposing he is the Treasurer of the Aramaic tile. The third, and in our judgment the most likely, explanation is that the differences between the two groups of texts reflect changes that occurred in the constitution and membership of the commission in the course of the progress of the work. We may imagine that the commission was the first established under the benevolent supervision of Samuel the Elder, with Samuel son of Saphara as chairman and with the membership given in the Greek commemorative text. Subsequently dissatisfaction may have developed with the work of the group and a reorganization was effected by virtue of which Samuel the Elder replaced Samuel son of Saphara as director of the undertaking, the latter serving henceforth with Abraham the Treasurer and the Proselyte ..... merely as one of the members of a reconstituted smaller commission. If something like this actually happened, the change must have occurred between the time the painted tiles with the Greek inscriptions were executed and mounted and the time when the Aramaic tiles were executed. Indeed, the existence of more than one version of the Aramaic commemorative text, and the fact that the inscriptions of the Aramaic tiles were executed in a somewhat hasty manner, lacked the decorative embellishment of the Greek tiles, and were thus out of keeping with the ornateness of the rest of the ceiling decorations, may indicate that they were added at the last minute in consequence of such a change in the administration of the undertaking as has been suggested.[62] In any event both groups did equal honor to Samuel the Elder, so that, in the event of any disagreements in the enterprise, it must have been he who by his wisdom and authority held the two groups together and brought the work to a successful conclusion.

What is evident from the epigraphic material about the officers and appointees of the Jewish community at Dura is of exceptional importance for our knowledge of synagogue organization generally. This is not only because Aramaic, Greek, and even Iranian names here stand side by side in the texts, but because the texts give us an unusually complete picture of the range of the officials and their activities. As to the particular hierarchy which the list of the known officers reflects, this is one that probably recommended itself to the local community for various reasons. By vesting supreme authority in a single person, the Elder, it could express its allegiance to the age-old principle that men of years and representatives of divinely instituted classes such as priests were in a very special sense directors and guardians of community life. That such an Elder as Samuel, the priest, should have at his side both a council and a commission entrusted with a specific enterprise is in some measure at least only what tradition and circumstances required. Yet it is interesting and important to note that officials of the type and with the titles familiar from the organization of the Greek city states and civic and private corporations also appear among the officers of the Synagogue.[63] More clearly at Dura than elsewhere we see how valuable the Jewish communities of the Dispersion found the civic and religious communes of their environment as models of group organization, and how they adapted them to their own use.[64]

The year A.D. 244/245 mentioned in the commemorative inscription is that of the roofing of the House of Assembly of the later building. This is because the ceiling tiles bearing the commemorative inscriptions were in all probability, like those with figured representations, prepared upon the ground before being mounted on the poles and rafters.[65] But the date A.D. 244/245 scarcely marks the completion of the whole building enterprise. Since most of the materials for the

---

62. Of course the changes made could also have been the reverse of those suggested here, but this would leave the informal rendering of the Aramaic texts unexplained.

63. On the administration of Greek cities and private corporations, see in general K. F. Hermann, *Lehrbuch der griechischen Staatsaltertümer* (ed. H. Swoboda, 1913); and on the private organizations, F. Poland, *Geschichte des griechischen Vereinswesens* (1909).

64. Naturally synagogue organization in Palestine and in southern Mesopotamia must be supposed to have differed at many points from that of cities of Hellenistic or Roman origin.

65. See above, p. 41. When the chamber was roofed, Tile C with its two shorter forms of the Aramaic commemorative text had already changed its function, having been covered with a white wash and decorated with a floral design; in other words, recaptured for decorative use.

Forecourt and the House of Assembly had of necessity to be brought through House H, the latter must be imagined to have been in only the first stage of its adaptation to duplex residential use; namely, with its northern end torn down but not yet rebuilt as a separate suite. Here as well as in the addition of the trim to the House of Assembly proper, work may well have gone on for an additional period of time. But even before the work on the trim was completed, the House of Assembly was put into service, as the layer of dirt under the sill and the coat of red paint applied to the wall surface behind the trim clearly indicate.[66] The minimum preparation before dedication, therefore, involved some decoration and probably included also the painting of the Torah Shrine and of the tree and the symbolic objects on the wall above it, as well as the mounting of the first canopy over the Shrine.

The erection of the new larger building of the Dura Synagogue marks a milestone in the history of the community. From its size, from the greatly enlarged piece of property that it covers, from the size of its House of Assembly and the spaciousness of its Forecourt we can see how the wealth of the community had increased and how it had grown in numbers. Seats were now provided in the building for at least sixty-five persons. In comparison with the community that we know from the earlier building it was now no longer an insignificant minority group, but one that held considerable property in the vicinity of its house of worship and through the excellence of its house of worship stood on a par with, or even eclipsed, other competing religious groups. Among those eclipsed was the Christian group in the more southerly part of the city. It is of course impossible to determine how many of the later members of the community were born at Dura as descendants of the older Jewish nucleus, how many had come in from outside, and what proportion of the more recent arrivals represented the old Babylonian stock. But it is obvious from the Greek dedicatory inscriptions and from the appearance of a proselyte with a Greek name on one of the Aramaic tiles that a new element brought up in a more Hellenized environment had joined the community, had helped to swell its ranks, and had gained in the group a

66. See above p. 18 and n. 76.

position of some influence and dignity. If what was said above about the changes in the building commissions is valid, it would seem to follow that there may have been differences of some sort between the newcomers from the more Hellenized areas and the rest of the community.

Seen in retrospect the growth of the Jewish community at Dura in wealth and numbers during the Forties of the third century is at first glance difficult to understand. In these very years Rome received the first of the blows that were to dim and finally destroy for all time Rome's prestige in the Near East. With the opening of the decade Shapur I had succeeded Ardashir on the throne of the new Persian Empire and with his accession a new active force entered upon the scene. Rome lost its Armenian bastion almost at once and officially declared war. But the effort of Gordian III to cope with Shapur in the field failed and he was mortally wounded in a battle along the lower course of the Euphrates. Probably in the very year when the new building of the Synagogue was begun, the inhabitants of Dura saw the remains of the beaten Roman army streaming up along the farther bank of the Euphrates past the city, with the dying Gordian in their midst. A monument was erected in his honor only a short distance up the river and a peace treaty was signed by his successor Philip in which high ransom was paid by the Romans for the release by the Persians of their prisoners. This was only the beginning of the long series of campaigns which finally saw the Roman Emperor Valerian made captive by Shapur, Antioch looted, and the last vestiges of military authority in the region pass to the Palmyrene Odenath and his wife Zenobia.

If at first glance the period seems suited more to discourage than to enhance the expansion of the Jewish community and of its enterprise, the opposite is not by any means inexplicable or strange on second thought. Under the Romans Dura was, as we have seen, essentially a military base and whatever wealth was accumulated by any of its inhabitants, Jewish or pagan, was bound to stem from the service of supply to the Roman military. With military activity and the number of military units committed increasing drastically, it necessarily followed that for the procurers of the necessary supplies and services the period was one of enormous increase in revenue. It would be no more than fair to suppose that members of Dura's Jewish community profited as much as the pagans under these circumstances. Indeed it may be that part of the increase in the community's numbers is related to the same developments. With the enemy active in the south, it was naturally the more fertile and well-watered regions of the upper Khabur, the very region whose coins increase noticeably at Dura during the third century, that provided the best markets for the purchase of provisions. Jews born in the larger cities of the region, such as Edessa and Nisibis, can well be thought to have had that closer contact with the Hellenistic civilization that is reflected in the importance of the Greek commemorative inscriptions of the Dura Synagogue. Perhaps some of the newcomers in Dura's Jewish community came from there in connection with the service of supply.

The suggestion that the Roman-Persian war was one source of the growing wealth and strength of the Jewish community at Dura is confirmed by an additional fact; namely, that in the period after A.D. 244/245 when the military situation became most tense, the growth seems to have continued with an even greater tempo. The city and the Synagogue had at that time only about ten years more to live, and the number of facts available to us about the history of the Synagogue during that period is limited to three. But two of the three point in this direction. The three facts are three events in the life of the Synagogue building; namely, (1) the raising of the floor level in the House of Assembly; (2) the execution upon the walls of the House of Assembly of the narrative compositions that form the second stage in the decorative embellishment of the room; and (3) the superimposition upon certain of these paintings of a series of Iranian dipinti (Inscrs. Nos. **42–53**). In time the three events form a series. How close they are to each other and to the beginning (A.D. 244/245) or to the end (A.D. 256) of the period into which they fall, is a matter of conjecture. More important by far is the proper understanding of their meaning for a knowledge of the life of the community.

The introduction of the new floor into the House of Assembly at a level some 0.24 m. above the first has already been commented upon above.[67] What-

67. See above, p. 17.

ever else the change involved, it had the effect of transforming a construction consisting of a podium with a bench mounted upon it into two ascending rows of benches, thereby raising the seating capacity of the room from 65 to 124 persons. We may therefore have here a token of the continuing rapid growth of the community even beyond the measure provided for by the construction of A.D. 244/245.

The second of the three events, the execution of the magnificent wall decorations of its Synagogue, is still more revealing. Since the work was undoubtedly long and costly, it tells us something about the economic situation of the group. Clearly the extensive building operations that had preceded it had not drained the financial resources of the group. It had the means to launch its most ambitious new enterprise. Equally important, of course, is what the wall decorations tell us about the religious life and thought of the community, its attitude toward the Law, toward the historical tradition, and toward the religious observances of the Jewish people. Such insights are extremely rare in the context of archaeological discovery and when provided at all are commonly conveyed by written documents, as in the case of the Dead Sea Scrolls. Where the evidence comes through the written word, it is usually relatively unambiguous. Where, as here, the medium of transmission is a group of narrative paintings, principles of interpretation have first to be established before their meaning can be inferred. On this account and because the inferences to be drawn are so important, the discussion of the frescoes as sources of knowledge of the religious life of the Dura community is reserved for the next chapter. Suffice it to say here that if our understanding of the pictures is correct, they reveal on the part of those who commissioned them an intense, well-informed devotion to the established traditions of Judaism, close contact with both the Palestinian and the Babylonian centers of Jewish religious thought, and a very real understanding of the peculiar problems and needs of a community living in a strongly competitive religious environment and in an exposed political position.

The third and last of the items of information available for our knowledge of the later history of the Jewish community at Dura is that provided by the Middle Iranian dipinti executed upon the surface of some of the Synagogue's pictorial panels (Inscrs. Nos. **42–53**). With these we move into the very last years of the life of the group, and through them we catch a glimpse of an episode the meaning of which is far from being clear and the problems of which can be assessed only in connection with a knowledge of the contemporary political situation.

D. The End of the Jewish Community at Dura

From the careful work which Geiger has done on the material over a period of years, and upon which a more complete report is to be published separately, it would appear that the majority of the dipinti (no less than ten) has one and the same burden. With minor variations they tell us that on a certain day of a certain Persian month in the fourteenth of fifteenth regnal year of Shapur[68] such and such persons, called *dipivars* (scribes) and bearing good Mazdean names, came to the Synagogue (once clearly in company with a Jewish official) and "looked at" a specific picture. Simple as the formula is, it raises a host of questions. Who were these visitors with Mazdean names — Sassanian Persians or Persian Jews? What is the competence or office which the title *dipivar* describes? Why were there so many *dipivars* at Dura? What were the circumstances under which they were permitted to execute these inscriptions upon the paintings in the first place? What purpose did the record serve? Is there any significance in the fact that the dipinti are applied primarily to three panels?

Now the fact that the dipinti are written in the Middle Iranian idiom, that the visitors dated their inscriptions by the regnal years of the Persian king, and that they bore recognizable Mazdean names favors the inference that the texts were inscribed, not by Persian Jews, but by men who were ethnically and religiously Persians, perhaps Sassanian officials. What we know about the contemporary political situation makes this extremely puzzling. The battle that had turned out so disastrously for the Romans in the second year of the reign of Shapur — the one that brought about the death of Gordian III and the retreat of the Roman armies up the Euphrates — was but one element of a long and destructive first campaign of the Sassanian king against the Romans. This we know especially from the now famous Shapur Inscription on the so-called Ka'abah of Zarathushtra.[69] Emboldened as he was by his initial successes, there was no telling when the Sassanian king would take the field again, perhaps to strike at the rich province of Syria itself. As it turned out Shapur did conduct a second and third campaign against the Romans, of which the third belongs to the years A.D. 254–259/260, brought about the destruction of Dura, and was of most disastrous consequences for Rome's hold on the eastern frontier. The second campaign must be assigned to the period between 244 and 254, probably to the latter part of the period; and the problem is how, with the situation so tense, a succession of Sassanian *dipivars* could have been admitted to the Roman garrison city of Dura. The problem might be brought nearer to a solution if the dates of the dipinti could be determined more closely.

Of the texts that give a complete date (month, day, and year), the earliest was written on the fourth day of the seventh month of the fourteenth year (Inscr. No. **43**) and the latest on the eighteenth day of the first month of the fifteenth year (Inscr. No. **42**). The interval between the two is six and one half months. But there are reasons for assuming that the period covered by the inscriptions is longer. Among the texts in which the month or the month and the day are all that is given or legible, three mention the second, the fifth, and the sixth month respectively (Inscrs. Nos. **51, 46, 47**). Since none of these months falls into the period between the earliest and the latest of the texts with the full formula, the period covered by the inscriptions

68. On the fundamental assumption that the numbered years referred to in the dipinti are regnal years and apply to the reign of Shapur I, see Rostovtzeff, *Berytus*, VIII (1943), p. 49.

69. Discovered by the Persepolis Expedition of the Oriental Institute of the University of Chicago and first published (in part) by M. Sprengling (*American Journal of Semitic Languages*, LVII, 1940, pp. 341–419), the inscription is already the subject of a large literature. For a recent bibliography see E. Honigmann and A. Maricq, *Recherches sur les Res Gestae divi Saporis* (1953).

must actually be longer. The absence of the regnal year in Inscrs. Nos. **46**, **47**, **48**, and **51** leaves us free to assign them to any period whatsoever after the completion of the Synagogue paintings, but the chances would seem to be that they are closely related in time. Are we to assume that where the reference to the year was omitted it was because the scribes intended to associate their visits with others already recorded in which the regnal year had been indicated? Or did the scribes merely choose to omit the year? The first alternative would imply that the texts with the full formula came first and suggests that the inscriptions lacking the regnal year be assigned to the period after the eighteenth day of the first month of the fifteenth year (Inscr. No. **42**). The second would permit us to place them before the seventh month of the fourteenth year (Inscr. No. **43**). The period covered by the texts would in either case amount to approximately a calendar year, but the period covered would begin and end at a different time.

Before the texts can be considered in their relation to the Jewish community their dates have still to be translated into Julian equivalents. At this point we face a further uncertainty. For the beginning of Shapur's reign we have currently four different calculations; namely, March 1, A.D. 240 (W. Ensslin);[70] A.D. 241/242 (A. Maricq);[71] March 20/21, A.D. 242 (Th. Nöldeke);[72] and April 9, A.D. 243 (S. H. Taqizadeh).[73] This is clearly not the place to discuss in detail the relative merits of the several calculations, even if this were within our competence. But it will be obvious that the longer the period to any part of which the Synagogue dipinti can be assigned, the more difficult it is to dissociate them from the days of Dura's military jeopardy. The easiest escape from this predicament would be to attribute the dipinti to the year A.D. 253, which would mean adopting the acession date proposed by Ensslin. This would fit

with the hypothesis advanced by Rostovtzeff that in A.D. 253 Dura was temporarily occupied by the Sassanians without a siege.[74] If we were to assume that the Iranian dipinti of the Synagogue belong to a period in which the Sassanians were actually in possession of the city, at least some of the questions raised by the texts could be answered. The *dipivars* could be understood to be Sassanian officials who came to inspect the premises, perhaps even at the invitation of the Synagogue Elders. The dipinti would in this case be in effect certificates of inspection conferring upon the Jewish community and its newly completed structure a measure of safety and immunity during the period of occupation. This would explain why they were permitted to display their dipinti so prominently on the walls of the building, and might have some bearing also upon the application of the dipinti to a certain group of panels. Most of the dipinti, it will be recalled, were inscribed upon the panel showing Mordecai and Esther (WC 2), and the rest upon the scene of Elijah reviving the Widow's Child (WC 1) and that of Ezekiel, the Destruction and Restoration of National Life (NC 1). Of these, the first documents the favor and protection extended to the Jews by Persian monarchs in earlier days, to which the attention of Sassanian visitors would certainly have been called by the Synagogue officials, while the second and third express the community's faith in the doctrine of resurrection to which the Persians also subscribed.[75]

Should it be necessary on other grounds to abandon the hypothesis of a temporary Sassanian occupation of Dura or to move the date of the Iranian dipinti upward beyond the range of that occupation, they would present a problem which only the discovery of additional evidence would

70. *Sitzungsberichte der bayerischen Akademie der Wissenschaften, phil.-hist. Klasse* (1947), Heft 5, pp. 6–8.

71. Honigmann and Maricq, *Recherches sur les Res Gestae divi Saporis*, pp. 37, 141, n. 2.

72. *Geschichte der Perser und Araber zur Zeit der Sassaniden* (1879), p. 412.

73. *Bulletin of the School of Oriental and African Studies, University of London*, XI (1943–1946), pp. 13–17. [Editorial note. W. B. Henning, *Asia Major*, III (1952), p. 201, calculates that the coronation of Shapur took place on 12 April, A. D. 240.]

74. See *Berytus*, VIII (1943), p. 53. M. Sprengling has recently found reason to support this hypothesis in his reading of the text of the Shapur inscription. See his *Third Century Iran, Sapor and Kartir* (1953), p. 88. The Dura Papyrus Inv. DP 90 shows that the Romans were in control of the city on April 30, A.D. 254.

75. On the double assumption that the dipinti belong to the year A.D. 253/254 and that Dura was during this period temporarily in Sassanian hands, it would, of course, follow that the paintings had been executed between A.D. 244/245 and 253, say roughly about A.D. 250. One could also take the graffiti (Inscrs. Nos. **54–56**) as the records of Sassanian visitors unaccompanied by representatives of the Jewish community or less considerate of decorations they were defacing.

clarify. Either the date of the capture of Dura would need to be revised, or we would need to postulate for the period before the siege special conditions of which there are at present no clear indications. Even so it must remain something of a mystery who or what the *dipivars* were, and why so many of them were available in the vicinity of this particular time.

The three events whose bearing upon the history of the Jewish community have just been discussed; namely, the raising of the floor level of the House of Assembly, the inauguration of the revised scheme for its decoration, and the application of the Iranian dipinti, brought other less important events in their train. The canopy over the Torah Shrine was dismounted and replaced after the completion of the decorative work.[76] The new floor was supplied during its construction with holes to receive the legs of the lamp stands and the reading desk that belonged to the new furnishings of the chamber.[77] While the scaffolds for the painting of the walls were in place, occasion may have been taken to blot out the name Julius on the ceiling tile with the Aramaic commemorative inscription.[78] A patch was set into the reveal floor of the main doorway to compensate for the unevenness caused by extensive wear.[79]

The community enjoyed the possession and use of its newly decorated House of Assembly only for a brief period,[80] during which time water seeped in from Wall Street, disfiguring the lower part of Panel WC 4 (Infancy of Moses) and certain sections of the dado below it.[81]

What remains to be told of the life of the Jewish community at Dura and of the history of its building after these events is little indeed. The story is tragic and largely to be gleaned from the several phases in the erection of the embankment in which the building was engulfed. The events which transpired belonged, it seems, to a single year. Shapur, as a part of his third campaign against the Romans, decided to destroy the most westerly defenses of the Roman *limes* and sent an army northward on the farther bank of the Euphrates. Dura was one of the first fortresses to be attacked, and its Roman garrison proceeded to create behind the city walls a zone of defense with earthworks intended to guard the wall against Persian siege operations. The preliminary steps in the development of the embankment were, as we have seen, made with a view to the preservation of the buildings involved in it. There was even a subsequent effort to counteract a certain amount of damage actually done in spite of all precaution by the initial measures.[82] Those who introduced into the Synagogue's House of Assembly the masses of earth needed to hold its walls in place were by no means friendly toward the owners and worshipers. In the course of their work they took occasion to gouge out the eyes of such painted figures as came within their reach.[83] Eventually, no doubt under the pressure of the siege itself, these moderate measures were abandoned, and the upper part of the House of Assembly was razed together with the Forecourt; while House H was destroyed even below its foundations, all in the effort to increase still further the height and depth of the embankment and to create behind it an open zone of defense for the continuation of the combat, should the walls be breached. Herculean as these labors of the garrison and the citizenry were, they did not suffice to stem the tide

---

76. See above, pp. 258 f.

77. See above, pp. 255 f.

78. Other instances of a *damnatio memoriae* applying to Philip are known. See E. Stein in *RE*, X (1919), cols. 755–772. The hostility toward Philip in Mesopotamia may have arisen from the confiscatory taxation imposed by his brother Priscus in the latter's capacity as *praefectus Mesopotamiae*. This brought about the uprising in the course of which Jotapianus was declared emperor.

79. See above, p. 19.

80. This is indicated by the fact that the paintings were still fresh when buried in the embankment, and that on the parts of the benches covered by rugs or mats (see above, p. 255) the paint spots were still preserved.

81. This must have happened before the embankment was introduced into Wall Street, and is important as an indication of the height to which the street level had risen in the interim between the remodeling of the house that became the earlier Synagogue and the end of the city's history. Actually the water seepage begins at a level

ca. 2.27 m. above the upper floor of the later building, which, it will be recalled, lay between 0.69 m. and 0.89 m. above the floor of the earlier building. If the level of the street had already risen to *ca.* 1.73 m. when the house on the site became the earlier building of the Synagogue (perhaps in the last half of the second century, see above, p. 27), enough time must be allowed for the additional deposit of 1.23 m. before the destruction of the city. This argues conclusively against the suggestion that both buildings were erected inside the space of eleven years. See above, p. 329, n. 41.

82. See above, p. 5.

83. Eye-gouging has been recorded above, pp. 113, 121, 139, 140, 144, 156, 182, 184, 185.

and the city was captured, apparently near the end of the year A.D. 256.

What the fate of the members of the Jewish community was during this difficult year, we cannot say. That they removed from the House of Assembly even before the erection of the first phase of the embankment all the treasures it contained; namely, the Torah Shrine with its scrolls, the canopy over the aedicula, the wooden *bema*, the lamp stands, and the mats or carpets that covered the floor and perhaps the benches, is evident from the condition in which the building was found. What eventually became of these objects when House H was demolished is unknown. Perhaps the Elder and some of his companions succeeded in escaping with the sacred scrolls to the Persians, and found their way to southern Mesopotamia. More probably, like all the other people dispossessed by the razing operations in the zone of defense along the city wall, he and his fellow Jews became part of a mixed company that found grudging shelter in the houses and temples in the eastern part of Dura, and being indistinguishable from the rest of the populace, shared the fate that overtook them all when the Persians finally captured the city.

II. THE INTERPRETATION OF THE PAINTINGS AND THE RELIGIOUS ORIENTATION OF DURA'S JEWISH COMMUNITY

As the preceding pages have marshalled the archaeological, numismatic, and epigraphic evidence for our knowledge of the history, growth, and organization of Dura's Jewish community, so the present chapter will endeavor to set forth what can be learned about its religious convictions, attitudes, and traditions from the decorations of the Synagogue. That these paintings provide an unusual opportunity for insight into such matters has already been indicated above. This is because they deal with Biblical narratives and prophecy and thus lead directly to the source and fountainhead of Jewish religious belief. But still more it is because their choice and arrangement is not entirely haphazard, and because in their rendering of the Biblical stories they exhibit some elements of current interpretation and application.

Before the pictures can be made to speak to us about the community that authorized their execution and was edified by their existence, it is necessary first to establish the principles for their interpretation — a matter of no small difficulty. Since for us the knowledge of Jewish pictorial art is relatively new, there is always the prior question whether by their very existence the pictures of the Dura Synagogue do not set the local community apart from other Jewish groups. Only after a position has been taken on this question can the problem be raised from what angle the paintings are to be approached, whether from the mystical angle or the rabbinic-homiletical angle, and whether a particular set of theological ideas underlies their arrangement and inner organization. There is great danger in this connection of letting our eyes be blinded to, or by, the novelty of the material, and thus of losing perspective either upon the paintings themselves or upon the picture of ancient Judaism as it has been developed from the study of other types of evidence by the scholars of the last hundred years. Since the matter is so difficult, the discussion both of presuppositions and of the principles of interpretation will undoubtedly need to go on for many years to come, and adjustments will need to be made in many different directions until a just and comprehensive appraisal of the Dura paintings can be reached. What needs to be avoided most under present circumstances is the attempt to exploit the material for the benefit of extraneous hypotheses and to impute partisanship and obscurantism to other interpreters where as yet there is much reason for honest differences of opinion. Instead of this, the materials must be permitted as much as possible to speak for themselves; and if what they tell us cannot at all points be reconciled with what is currently known, judgment must be suspended till it becomes clearer what the significance of the divergences may be. Obviously reality will always be more complex than any system man can devise for comprehending it.

A. The Paintings and the Prohibition of Images

The first question that needs to be clarified in the present context is that of the possible contradiction between the very existence of the Dura Synagogue paintings and the Jewish proscription of images out of fear of idolatry. How we view the supposed contradiction will necessarily determine whether in our judgment the community that commissioned them was atypical or sectarian in its religious life and thought.

The familiar proscription of images is recorded for the first time in the second commandment of the Decalogue, "Thou shalt not make unto thee a graven image, nor any manner of likeness of anything that is in heaven above, or that is in the earth beneath, or that is in the water under the earth" (Exod. 20.4; Deut. 5.8). Almost equally familiar are the stories recounted by Josephus about the heroic young men of Jerusalem who pulled down the eagle that Herod the Great had had mounted over the entrance of the Temple (*Bellum* I, 33, 2–3 = §§ 648–650; *Antiquitates* XVII, 6,2 = § 151), and about the disturbance that arose when Pontius Pilate had an army detachment come to Jerusalem bringing with it its military "standards" upon which the image of the Roman Emperor appeared (*Antiquitates* XVIII, 3, 1 = §§ 55–59). In the passage of the *Jewish War* as well as elsewhere in his works Josephus explicitly says that it was unlawful for the Jews both to make and to have images, this being taken to apply not only to images of persons but also those of animals.[84] On the strength of this evidence, coupled with what was then known about the Jewish coins and in general about the Jewish fear of idolatry, Benzinger, writing in the *Jewish Encyclopedia*, could say that the religion of the Jews precluded the full development by them of the art of sculpture, and that the commandment forbidding the representation of living beings could not have been carried to its ultimate consequence had the Jewish people not lacked artistic inclination, creative power, and formative imagination.[85]

What Benzinger was saying in 1902 had already been contradicted in 1897 by David Kaufmann when he wrote that, the divergent opinions of the sages and rabbis to the contrary notwithstanding, the Synagogue had at all times availed itself of the services of the painter and the sculptor without further reflection.[86] While it is true that on the strength of the evidence then available, Kaufmann was perhaps overstating the case, it is also true that the evidence brought to light since that time has come closer to confirming his judgment than that of Benzinger.

Most important for our immediate purposes, of course, is what archaeological exploration has added to our knowledge of ancient synagogues, beginning with the work of Kohl and Watzinger in Galilee between 1905 and 1907. Since that time additional structures have come to light not only in Palestine itself but in eastern and western Syria,

in the Aegean, and in North Africa, and most of them add in some particular to our knowledge of the ancient Jewish use of representational art.[87] Even in Palestine the use of representational art eventually went far beyond the sculptured figures and designs on door lintels and on pulvinated friezes, as the floor mosaics with their zodiacal designs, their representations of the seasons and the solar chariot, and their portrayal of Biblical episodes have shown.[88] Second in importance only to the synagogues as sources for our knowledge of the ancient Jewish use of art are the burial places of the dead. These include the monumental tombs preserved in the neighborhood of Jerusalem, the ubiquitous underground chambers with their supply of ornamented ossuaries, lamps, and simple private possessions — the sources in many instances of ancient charms and engraved ringstones — and the labyrinthine catacombs.[89] Of the last-mentioned, a well-developed series with interesting painted decorations has been known at Rome for almost a century, and of this series at least two; namely, those of the Monteverde and of the Villa Torlonia, have meanwhile been accurately described.[90] So also the fragments of Jewish gold

84. See further the less well-known episodes of the trophies in the theater at Jerusalem (*Antiquitates* XV, 8, 1–2 = §§ 276, 279) and of the statue of Caligula (*ibid.*, XVIII, 8, 2 = §§ 261–263), and the comment on the destruction of Antipas' palace in Tiberias (*Vita* 12 = § 65).
85. *Jewish Encyclopedia*, II (1902), p. 141.
86. *Gesammelte Schriften*, I (1908), p. 97.

87. Most of the individual monuments and publications are referred to above in the discussion of the architecture of the Dura Synagogue. For a brief history of synagogue excavation see Sukenik, *Ancient Synagogues in Palestine and Greece*, pp. 2–7; and for the most recent discoveries *Bulletin I* and *II* of the *Louis M. Rabinowitz Fund for the Exploration of Ancient Synagogues* (Jerusalem, 1949 and 1951).
88. Particularly important for our knowledge of floor mosaics with figures are the synagogues of Beth Alpha, Na'aran (see Sukenik, *Ancient Synagogue of Beth Alpha*), and Gerasa (see F. M. Biebel in Kraeling, *Gerasa*, pp. 318–323 and Pls. LXIII–LXIV) in Palestine; and that of Hammam Lif (Naro) in North Africa (see more recently the article by F. M. Biebel, *Art Bulletin*, XVIII, 1936, pp. 541–551, where also a full bibliography is given, and the covenient, if partial, reproductions in Krauss, *Synagogale Altertümer*, Fig. 7, opposite p. 266).
89. On the Jewish tombs in general and the monumental tombs near Jerusalem in particular, see Watzinger, *Denkmäler Palästinas*, II, pp. 59–76; and K. Galling, *Biblisches Reallexikon* (1937), *s.vv.* "Grab, Ossuar, Sarkophag," etc. E. R. Goodenough, *Jewish Symbols in the Greco-Roman Period*, 4 vols. (1953–1954), now brings together a great deal of the evidence for the form and contents of Jewish tombs and for charms and talismans otherwise widely scattered. For the one Palestinian catacomb known to date, the full extent of which is not yet entirely explored, see Maisler, *Beth She'arim* (1944).
90. For the former see N. Müller, *Die jüdische Katakombe am Monteverde zu Rom (Schriften der Gesellschaft*

glass and of figured sarcophagi ultimately derived from such Roman catacombs and treasured in museums of Europe and America.[91]

While archaeologists have thus been adding increasingly to material available for an understanding of the Jewish use of representational art in the Greco-Roman world, art historians have contributed in like measure to our knowledge of the monuments of Jewish art from the Mediaeval and Renaissance periods of the history of eastern and western Europe. Here, too, attention has been given to the earliest of the synagogue buildings and their appurtenances, to the stones marking the location of Jewish graves, and to ceremonial objects, in this case especially the silverware used in ritual and liturgical contexts.[92] More important than any of these, perhaps, is the large number of illuminated and illustrated Hebrew manuscripts about which precise information has become available in the last fifty years. They range all the way from a Hebrew Bible codex of the tenth century with its schematic representations of the Tables of the Ten Commandments and the implements of the Tabernacle to the relatively recent illustrated Esther Scrolls.[93] Bible codices continued to be

written through the fifteenth century, but their illustrative embellishment did not normally exceed the elements already contained in the earliest known examples.[94] By contrast pictorial illustration came to play a prominent part in the special prayer book prepared for home use in connection with the Passover Seder. This is the Passover Haggadah, the ultimate origins of which may lie in Egypt and of which the most important single manuscript is that of Sarajevo with a cycle of pictures covering Biblical history from the creation to the Blessing of Moses.[95] Eventually other types of illustrated manuscripts came into existence until all but the scrolls actually used in the worship services of the synagogues were open to embellishment of a pictorial nature. And once such material came to be familiar in the better Jewish homes, it was only a matter of time until representational art invaded the synagogue once more and was used for the embellishment of the house of worship.[96]

During the last fifty years, then, a good insight has been obtained into not only one, but two successive episodes in the history of Jewish use of representational art, thus affording the advantage of a broader outlook upon the most fundamental of the questions which the paintings of the Dura Synagogue raise. Indeed, the question itself, posed also in the earlier years of the century, has already been discussed afresh in the light of the newest

zur Förderung der Wissenschaft des Judentums, 1912); and for the latter Beyer and Lietzmann, *Die jüdische Katakombe der Villa Torlonia in Rom*. The materials reproduced by Garrucci in *Storia dell' arte cristiana*, VI, Pl. 489 are from the Vigna Randanini on the Via Appia. Of the use of artistic representation in the Jewish burial places of the Dispersion, there is no more complete account than in Goodenough's *Jewish Symbols*, II, pp. 3–69.

91. Most of the familiar pieces are reproduced in such general works on Jewish art as E. Cohn-Wiener, *Die jüdische Kunst* (1929). On a new piece of gold glass, see M. Schwabe and A. Reifenberg, *Rivista di archeologia cristiana*, XV (1938), pp. 319–329.

92. On mediaeval synagogues see R. Krautheimer, *Mittelalterliche Synagogen* (1927). Among the treatises on synagogue appurtenances see, e.g., the article of F. Landsberger, *Hebrew Union College Annual*, XIX (1945–46). On tombstones see, e.g., A. Levy, *Jüdische Grabmalkunst in Ost-Europa* (1924). On ritual objects, see, e.g., H. Frauberger, *Über alte Kultusgegenstände in Synagoge und Haus* (1903), and Wischnitzer-Bernstein, *Gestalten und Symbole der jüdischen Kunst*. For a general survey there is now available also F. Landsberger's *History of Jewish Art* (1946). Articles on individual objects and structures, well illustrated, will be found in *Encyclopaedia Judaica*.

93. For the Leningrad manuscript of the Hebrew Bible, found in the Cairo Ginizah and dated A.D. 930, see the excellent facsimiles in V. Stassov and D. Günzbourg, *L'Ornement hébreu* (1905). The pictures are often reproduced; e.g., in Wischnitzer-Bernstein, *Gestalten und Symbole der jüdischen Kunst*, Pl. I and Fig. 18; and Lands-

berger, *History of Jewish Art*, Fig. 124. On the Esther Scrolls see especially the article by Wischnitzer-Bernstein in *Encyclopaedia Judaica*, VI, cols. 810–814, where their type and distribution are outlined. On the general subject of Jewish manuscript illustration, see now especially Leveen, *The Hebrew Bible in Art*, pp. 66–117.

94. Such manuscripts exist today in libraries at Munich, Paris, Copenhagen, London, and Oxford.

95. D. H. Mueller and J. Schlosser, *Die Haggadah von Sarajevo* (1898). Additional important manuscripts of the type are the Darmstadt Haggadah (A. Schmidt, *Zeitschrift für Bücherfreunde*, VI, 1903, pp. 487–491; and B. Italiener, *Die Darmstädter Pessach-Haggadah*, 1927); and the Cincinnati Haggadah (F. Landsberger, *Hebrew Union College Annual*, XV, 1940, pp. 529–558). Other Haggadahs exist in libraries and private collections in Parma, Turin, Berlin, Nuremberg, Frankfort, Paris, and London. Kaufmann mentions a fragment of a Haggadah from the Ginizah at Cairo with representations of the Bitter Herb and the Mazoth, *Gesammelte Schriften*, III (1915), p. 231.

96. For the use of pictorial decorations and sculpture in synagogues of central and western Europe in the post-Renaissance period, and for the disputes about their permissibility, see Kaufmann, *Gesammelte Schriften*, I, pp. 87–103.

materials, making it possible to estimate the lines along which scholarly opinion is currently developing and to benefit from the observations that have been made.[97]

It will be evident that so far as the Palestinian Judaism of the Second Temple is concerned, the evidence supplied by Josephus about the opposition to images on the part of the observant groups cannot be read out of court. What we know about the contemporary coinage, and what the ossuaries and the small artifacts of the period show, confirms the written testimony to show that the representation of animate beings was avoided and that objects, plants, and designs, some of them symbolic, were all that was commonly used. It is probable that the strict and literal observance of the Biblical commandment became a dominant feature of the Palestinian scene beginning in the period of the Maccabean revolt, and that it persisted as such until well down into the Mishnaic period. That observance of the prohibition was complete among the Jews of Palestine during this period, including those who had returned from the Dispersion, not to mention half-Jews, sectarians, proselytes, and the non-Jews of Galilee and the coastal cities, is too much to expect. A special position must also be reserved for the representatives of ruling houses who, as always in the Orient, commonly stood above the law. It is likely indeed that certain at least of the representatives of the Maccabean family, once it had established itself, found no reason to be as literal in their outlook toward representational art as the observant circles. Not that in such public monuments as that erected to Jonathan at Modein (*I Macc.* 13.27–30) we should suspect the representation of more than the weapons and the ships of which the report speaks, but we know of at least one golden vessel described as being adorned with representations of stags and lions among the family treasures of Alexander

(presumably Jannaeus).[98] As far as the Herodian family is concerned, its disregard of the prohibition is indicated in the episode of the eagle over the Temple gate, and in what Josephus tells about the decorations of Antipas's palace at Tiberias.[99] But with such exceptions the prohibition against the images of living beings must be thought to have been dominant in Palestine during the period specified, so long indeed as the fear and hatred of non-Jewish and non-observant forces remained acute.

In Palestine itself the attitude on the question began to change as early as the second century. Not all the circumstances of this change are now evident. For one thing, the extinction of the Jewish national state altered the approach to this ever-present problem, making observance not so much a matter of national policy as of individual conduct. Then, too, the leadership of the religious community was consolidated, and there were fewer cross-currents and less fanatical extremism. Among the rabbis to whom the faithful now looked consistently for guidance there was a greater tendency to consider such matters as idolatry systematically and analytically and thus to enforce the prohibition against images only where real danger of idolatrous acts was involved. Of course even among the rabbis there continued to be rigorists who, like R. Menahem ben Simai, refused to look even at the image on a *zuz*.[100] But there were also scholars like Rabban Gamaliel II who kept in his upper chamber a lunar diagram used for obtaining precise testimony for the occurrence of moon phases, in spite of the unfavorable comment which it elicited in certain circles.[101] The same Gamaliel, using a bath at Acco

97. Among the earlier discussions see, e.g., D. Kaufmann, *Jewish Quarterly Review*, IX (1897), pp. 254–269; S. J. Solomon, *Jewish Quarterly Review*, XIII (1901), pp. 553–566; Kaufmann Kohler, *Jewish Encyclopedia*, II, pp. 141–143. Among more recent discussions see S. Krauss, *Mitteilungen der Gesellschaft für die Wissenschaft des Judentums*, LXV (1921), pp. 211–220; J. B. Frey, *Biblica*, XV (1934), pp. 265–300; E. Bevan, *Holy Images* (1940); Leveen, *The Hebrew Bible in Art*; Goodenough, *Jewish Symbols*, I, pp. 23–32 in an autobiographical vein.

98. The reference is to the *terpolē*, mentioned by Josephus, *Antiquitates* XIV, 3, 1 = §§ 34–36, and described in greater detail by Pliny the Elder, *Hist. Nat.* XXXVII, 2 = § 12, which was presented to Pompey by the representatives of the Hasmonean factions seeking his approval, and thus became a temple treasure at Rome. Since it bore an inscription connecting it with this Alexander, it was not made for Pompey's benefit but belonged to the family heirlooms and was offered to Pompey as a gift. On the type of vessel in question, see Wreszinski's article in *Orientalistische Literaturzeitung*, XXVII (1924), no. 10, cols. 570–573.

99. See above, p. 341 n. 84.

100. A small coin. See Abodah Zarah 50a (Trans., p. 251).

101. *Ibid.* 43a–43b (Trans., pp. 214–216). The passage also refers to a statue set up in the synagogue at Nehardea without offence to R. Samuel's father.

in which there was a statue of Aphrodite, found it possible to distinguish between a cult image set up in a pagan temple, which it would have been idolatrous to approach, and a statue set up in a non-cultic environment and thus to be regarded as merely an ornament.[102] It is interesting to see how, beginning in the still difficult second century of our era, rigorous dicta such as that of Rabbi Meir were relaxed by school opinion.[103] Reflection on what had idolatrous potential, and what idolatry consisted of, was in process, and functional distinctions were being made.

Thus when, beginning with the Severan period, outward conditions improved for the Jewish communities and religious structures requiring decorative embellishment could be built in Palestine, the permissive statements for their embellishment were forthcoming. Familiar are the two commonly quoted from Abodah Zarah 48d of the *Palestinian Talmud*, "In the days of Rabbi Jochanan men began to paint pictures on the walls, and he did not hinder them," and "In the days of Rabbi Abbūn men began to make designs on mosaics, and he did not hinder them."[104] To these passages, reflecting developments in the late second and the early fourth centuries respectively, we may add the one from the *Targum pseudo-Jonathan* included in its rendering of Lev. 26.1, where after paraphrasing the prohibition against the making of idols and graven images and such figured stones as men bow down to, the text makes the following exception: "but a stone column carved with images

and likenesses you may make upon the premises of your 'sanctuaries,'[105] but not to worship them."

What we thus learn about the relaxation of the prohibition against images in Palestine indicates that even there, by the third century of our era, pictorial representation was permitted by the dicta of the religious leaders of Judaism. What is not indicated is that pictures representing Biblical narratives were known at that time (though they are attested there later) or that painted synagogues existed. Also not implied is any suggestion that with the relaxation the Judaism of Palestine had become any the less Jewish than it had ever been. Rather, this entire episode in the application of the prohibition, running from the official strictures of the Maccabean and post-Maccabean period to the relaxing dicta of the second and third Christian centuries, exhibits the range within which responses to an established commandment may be expected to move. This becomes evident when the episode is seen in its proper perspective.

In the history of Palestine it is possible to define at least two earlier occasions at which analogous variations in attitude toward images occurred. The first is the period that runs from the beginning of the monarchy to the Exile, and the second that which runs from the days of the restoration to the days of "acute Hellenization" under Seleucid hegemony. At the beginning of the first period it was entirely proper for Solomon to adorn the Temple with dedicatory gifts like the Brazen Sea, the character of which, as described in the Bible, so horrified Josephus.[106] At the end of the same period the prophetic denouncement of luxury and idolatry coupled with the Deuteronomic reforms had so far affected local conditions that even the representation of animals on the seal rings, particularly in Judea, seems virtually to have disappeared.[107] After the Exile the economic condition of the reestablished community was such as not to encourage artistic production; and, besides, the effort of the community to preserve its identity, the impact of its scribal leadership and of the teachings

102. *Ibid.*, 44b (Trans., pp. 220f.).

103. The passage *ibid.*, 40a–41b (Trans., pp. 202f.) is an excellent case in point. R. Meir's basic statement that all images are prohibited because they are worshipped once a year is later limited in its application to images that have a staff or bird or orb in the hand; that is, to imperial statues. Rabbi Meir's position is that since most images will receive some form of worship or adoration at least once a year, therefore it is better to outlaw all lest one run the risk of countenancing idolatry. The sages take the position that annual worship applies to imperial statues, involving the observance of the day of the ruler's accession, and that therefore only those are prohibited which are marked by the insignia of imperial rule and authority. Rabbi Johanan goes further and indicates that statues (on the streets) inside a city are permitted (presumably because they would probably be either honorific or ornamental), while those at the entrance of a city are prohibited (presumably because, as at Dura, they would be tutelary representations of the Good Fortune or the Gad of the place).

104. See, e.g., Leveen, *Hebrew Bible in Art*, p. 12.

105. The Aramaic word ṣuṭin applies to columns, porticoes, and stoas alike.

106. Note that he characterized Solomon's use of the animal figures on which the Brazen Sea was mounted as a sin in *Antiquitates* VIII, 7, 5 = § 195.

107. See Reifenberg, *Palestine Exploration Quarterly*, LXXI (1939), pp. 195–198.

of the Priestly Code, must be thought to have given a fresh impulse to the literal observance of the Second Commandment. But even in the Achaemenian period Jewish coins with human faces or the Athenian owl begin to appear.[108] The Greek period of Jewish history, witnessing as it did a decided change in the economic life of the community and the development of strong philhellenic attitudes on the part of some elements of the community, must have encouraged the production and use of objects of representational art. Archaeological evidence for these developments is still relatively scarce, but *Sirach* gives an interesting picture of local gem-cutting in the passage,

> "Likewise the maker of carving and
>   cunning device
> Who by night as by day hath no rest,
> Who engraveth signet-engravings,
> And whose art is to make variety of design
> He is careful to make the likeness true
> And his anxiety is to complete his work"
>   (38.27).

Across the Jordan, moreover, the remains of the 'Arak el-Emir with its sculptured lion frieze still give evidence of the mixture of Alexandrian and Oriental influences and elements in the life of the Tobiads of Palestine.[109]

The fundamental impression created by the evidence for the use and disuse in Palestine of representations of living beings is that attitudes on this subject varied from period to period in proportion as internal forces and external pressures conspired to make an issue of the prohibition. The same conclusion follows also from an understanding of the history of western Judaism after the period of the Jewish catacombs of Rome, of southern Italy, and of North Africa. Again sharp restrictions seem to have been imposed, the ultimate effects of which are to be seen in protests occasioned by the introduction of pictorial decorations and of elements of sculpture in the synagogues of central and western Europe during the period of the Renaissance.[110] In

this whole matter, of course, Judaism does not stand alone, as the familiar iconoclastic controversy in the history of eastern Christendom indicates, and as the changes in the attitude and practise of the Islamic peoples and individuals from the days of the Omayyads to those of the Abbasids and on to the personally disenfranchised moderns demonstrate. Indeed the difference of usage that persists in Judaism on the subject even today suggests that we should avoid before everything the assumption that at any one time in history any one pattern of observance or nonobservance can be taken as completely normative for the entire people and its religious life.

Returning to the period of immediate concern to us here, and turning now from Palestine to the Dispersion, it is obvious that an exact appraisal of attitudes prevalent there is still more difficult, largely because our evidence is fragmentary and sporadic, and because the Dispersion covered so wide a territory and embraced communities established at such different times. In general it would seem reasonable to suppose that Jewish communities existing in immediate contact with Greco-Roman culture would have acquired from their surroundings a tolerant view of the question at issue, as the paintings of the Dura Synagogue themselves may be thought to indicate. Indeed, we have evidence for another synagogue with mural decorations of some sort from Erciş in Phrygia, where an inscription has been found commemorating the work of a group of synagogue officials, who, among other things, are said to have caused the walls to be painted (γραφεῖν).[111] True, the Dispersion was the area in which the most notable Hellenization of Judaism developed, and we have no reason to believe that such Hellenization was limited to theology. But the fact remains that, save in a few instances such as the Synagogue of Dura and possibly that of Erciş, certain tombs in North Africa, and some sarcophagi at Rome, the decorative material associated with Jewish monuments is to my knowledge limited to the representation of things and does not include animate beings. This may be the result merely of the lamentably incomplete nature of the evidence, or it may suggest

108. See Watzinger, *Denkmäler Palästinas*, pp. 6f.; and A. Reifenberg, *Palestine Exploration Quarterly*, LXXV (1943), pp. 100–104.

109. See H. C. Butler, *Princeton University Archaeological Expeditions to Syria in 1904–5 and 1909*, II A (1919), pp. 1–25.

110. See Kaufmann, *Gesammelte Schriften*, I, pp. 87–103.

111. W. H. Buckler and W. M. Calder, *Monumenta Asiae Minoris Antiqua*, VI (1939), p. 97, no. 264. No date is given for this text.

that here too we must guard against over-hasty generalizations. After all, it was always possible in a strange environment to have two opposite reactions, one of attraction to, the other of extreme revulsion against, the environment; and there were undoubtedly times and seasons, such as that of the Jewish War and of the repressive edicts against the Jews, when developing tensions, either local or general, might and probably did cause as distinct a reaction against the use of representational art forms as they did against the political and civic authorities.

If we actually had even a good part of the evidence that was once available for a knowledge of the life of the Jewish Dispersion, we would in all probability find that here too observance and attitude on the subject of the use of representational art differed, and that not only from time to time, but also from place to place. This would seem to follow in part from the separate origin of the settlements in lower Mesopotamia, in the Hellenistic and Roman cities near Palestine such as Alexandria and Antioch, and of those more remote in Greece and Italy, some being older in point of establishment, some being relatively stable and closely associated with the continuing life of the home land, even though later in point of origin, and some derivative and mixed as to the origin of their members. It would seem to follow also from the fact that in certain civic communities the Jews were exposed to popular malice and hatred, while in others conditions were more tranquil. Particularly important for any judgment in these matters, and interesting for our purposes, would be some archaeological information about the long-estab-

lished Jewish settlements of lower Mesopotamia, whose inhabitants prided themselves upon the purity of their stock and upon their knowledge of the Law, and about the large Jewish communities of the smaller kingdoms along the eastern fringes of Syria — in Emesa, Commagene, Osrhoene, and Adiabene — where connections of the ruling families with the Jewish faith must have created especially favorable local conditions. Until these and other gaps in our knowledge have been filled, we would do well not to generalize too hastily. Besides, it is important to keep in mind that in the Dispersion, apart perhaps from lower Mesopotamia, controls were by no means as strong as in the more closely knit community of Palestine, and that under these circumstances opposing attitudes on such questions as the use of representional art may have co-existed in diverse Jewish groups of one and the same city, or even within a single group.

In fine, there is apparently no reason why decorations such as those of the later Dura Synagogue could not have been used in the mid-third century either in Palestine or in the Dispersion in a synagogue that intended to be observant of the Law. The question which the very existence of the pictures has posed is a question, not of the history of Judaism, but of our own failure hitherto to have understood the wide range within which the observance of the prohibition against images has at various times and places and under various conditions tended to move. But since the Dura Synagogue is still in a very real sense an extraordinary monument, the one thing we cannot say today is that the use of pictorial decorations was typical of the synagogues of the Dispersion generally.

B. The Paintings and the Religious Thought of the Community

I. SUGGESTED INTERPRETATIONS OF THE PAINTINGS

Once the mind has accustomed itself to the thought of the existence of the Dura Synagogue decorations, the question of their meaning comes more naturally to the fore. On this subject several suggestions have already been made by interested scholars, and more are certainly to be expected. The earlier and simpler among these suggestions have already been reviewed briefly in the treat-

ment of the supposed "themes" of the several registers and of the Central Group of panels.[112] The simplest suggestion is that which contents itself with a classification of the compositions by subject matter and maintains, for instance, that Register A is historical; Register B, liturgical; and Register C, moralizing in its function and choice of material.[113] If correct, this would indicate that the Jewish

112. See above, pp. 92f., 131–133, 212–215.
113. So Du Mesnil du Buisson, *Peintures*, pp. 16f.

community at Dura had a thoroughly pragmatic and abstract approach to the understanding of its religious tradition.

Another group of scholars endeavors to comprehend the entire body of decorative material in some kind of a unified ideological scheme. One instance of this approach is the analysis of Grabar, who finds an analogy here to the material and the programs of the official monuments of late Roman imperial art, and sees the authority of Yahweh, represented in the Central Group of Panels by the enthroned Anointed and his symbol, brought to victorious expression through the power of the Ark as a sacred palladium (Register B), demonstrating its effectiveness by bringing to naught the opposition of hostile rulers and by providing a more glorious future for his people (Register C), all in fulfilment of a covenant promise guaranteed by certain events and persons of the distant past (Register A).[114] Another instance is the suggestion of Sonne, for whom the decorations of the three registers exhibit the "three crowns" on which the abiding claims of Judaism as the authoritative and divinely revealed religion are traditionally said to rest; namely, the "crown of the Law" as exhibited in Register A, the "crown of the priesthood" set forth in Register B, and the "crown of the kingdom" dramatized in Register C. The theme of the third "crown" is in his judgment developed Messianically in the Center Panels.[115]

Even more ingenious is the suggestion of Wischnitzer-Bernstein, for whom the Messianic theme pervades the entire body of the decorative material, so that Register C presents the heroes of the Messianic drama (especially the Messiah, son of David, and Elijah), and Register B gives in an historical allegory, so to speak, the trials and tribulations that will precede the Messianic era, while Register A sets forth in simple illustrative and paratactic manner a series of witnesses to the coming salvation. The three registers as a whole form a unit of material that is to be associated with the Central Group, the Center Panels of which show the ancestors of the coming salvation and the Wing Panels the prophets of the coming salvation, while the Messianic Temple on the façade of the Torah Shrine acts as the focal element in the entire

scheme of decorations, holding all together like the keystone of an arch.[116]

To these interpretations it will undoubtedly soon be necessary to add that of Goodenough in which the material is to be given a mystic interpretation. So far as we can judge from what he has published to date, he will interpret the decorations as expressing the thought-world of the Jewish mysticism that he has recreated from the pages of Philo and now seems to regard as the most potent element of contemporary Judaism generally, a replacement for the "normative" Judaism of the rabbinic tradition.[117] Hence it is to be expected that the several compositions will on this hypothesis reflect different phases and representations of the soul's mystic ascent to true being. In accordance with this scheme of things he has already interpreted Wing Panels II (Moses Receives the Law) and IV (Abraham Receives the Promise) as portraying in effect the giving of the Mystic Torah and the Assumption of Moses respectively. Panels WB 2 (Consecration of the Tabernacle) and WB 3 (Jerusalem and the Temple of Solomon) have been taken to depict two contrasting sanctuaries, probably representing the lower and higher forms of the mystery rite, the latter with its seven walls showing the seven steps of the mystic ascent, while Panel WB 1 (Wilderness Encampment and the Miraculous Well of Be'er) is said to illustrate the mystic fount of the higher knowledge.[118]

Each of these several interpretations ascribes to the Jewish community at Dura a different religious outlook and point of view. Since all of them cannot be true at the same time, the question naturally arises how to choose between them, or, more properly, on what basis the validity of an interpre-

---

114. "Le Thème," pp. 30–35.
115. "The Paintings," pp. 267–276, 345.

116. *Messianic Theme*, especially p. 100.
117. The doctrines of the mystic Judaism of Philo are carefully developed in Goodenough's *By Light, Light*. That Philo's intellectualized and subjectivized interpretation of the traditional Jewish faith, turned into a mystic cult, had become in Hellenistic and Roman times the most potent element of Judaism generally is suggested, it would seem, by Goodenough's rejection of the power of "normative" (rabbinic) Judaism (*Jewish Symbols*, I, pp. 33–58) and by the effort made in the publication mentioned to show that Jewish symbols are the same the world over. Indeed, it would be necessary to any demonstration of the impact of a Philonic type of Judaism upon the Dura paintings.
118. For these details see Goodenough, *By Light, Light*, pp. 209f., 242; *Jewish Symbols*, I, pp. 93f.

tation can be established. The answer to this question must inevitably be that an interpretation to be valid must be appropriate to the historical context of the Dura Synagogue, and must be arrived at inductively from a study of the paintings themselves. It is along these lines that we propose to discuss the subject here.

2. THE SYNAGOGUE AND THE PAINTED TEMPLES OF DURA

One of the elements of the historical context of the Dura Synagogue that should not be neglected in this connection is that of the painted sanctuaries of the city generally — the temples of Bel, Atargatis, Aphlad, Azzanathkona, the Gaddé, Mithras, Zeus Theos, Adonis, and the Christian Chapel. Clearly the fact that the interiors of temples were painted at Dura has some relation to the fact that the Synagogue was decorated. What the relation was we should be able to understand more clearly if we knew more about the origin of the painted temple as such. Ancient classical authors provide occasional references to paintings executed or hung on the walls of Greek and Roman temples in more westerly lands, but these are properly *ex votos* and make no great contribution to a solution of the problem.[119] What we know about the Roman temples of Syria indicates that a tradition of painting cellas probably did not exist there either.[120] In plan, of course, the temples of Dura are closely akin to the traditional shrines of ancient Mesopotamia, but the use of painting is less typical of the religious structures of Babylonia and Assyria than it is, for instance, of the palaces of their kings.[121] All that can therefore be inferred from this about the reason for the existence of a painted Synagogue at Dura is that those who decided the matter must have been aware of a local tradition making this customary

for religious edifices, and that they saw good reason for following this tradition.[122]

The meaning of the relationship between the painted temples and the painted Synagogue at Dura can be further developed from a study of the subject matter of their decorations. In the choice and organization of their decorations the religious edifices of Dura suggest the existence of a single basic type, varied in two degrees or stages. The basic type is best exhibited in the Temple of Zeus Theos, and fundamentally also in the Temple of Bel.[123] Here the image of the cult deity is shown on the cella wall facing the entrance doorway, and on the side walls are shown worshipers offering incense to the deity through the agency of his priests. The simplest variation of this pattern provides for the addition of a modicum of narrative material, usually from the cult myth of the god or of other gods. The classic example here is the Temple of Mithras, where Mithras the hunter appears on the side wall, and where over the cult image on the all-important end wall there is added a whole cycle of scenes from the life of Mithras.[124] From what is known about the decorations of the Temple of the Gaddé it too had at least one scene of this type, an encounter between Ba'al Shamin and Malakbel, while in the Temple of Bel similar scenes were eventually added in the pronaos.[125] In the extreme variation of the pattern, represented by the Christian Chapel and the Synagogue, the narrative element predominates, and in these two structures alone appears the active intervention of the deity in the affairs of mortals to whom he is particularly beholden.[126]

The appearance of the narrative element in the religious art of Dura does not distinguish the

119. For Greece see Pausanias, I, 17, 2 (Athens); I, 18, 1 (Athens); and IX, 4, 1 (Plataea). For Rome see Varro, *de lingua*, 7, 57; Pliny, *Hist. Nat.* XXXV, 136; Plutarch, *Pompey* II, 8.

120. See Krencker and Zchietzschmann, *Römische Tempel in Syrien*. True there is evident here a manifest interest in lavish interior display, but this takes architectural form as in the small temple at Baalbek.

121. On the plans of the temples of Dura see Cumont, *Fouilles*, p. 34; *Rep. III*, pp. 23f.; Rostovtzeff, *YCS*, V (1935) p. 205; Hopkins, *Berytus*, VII (1942), pp. 1-18.

122. The same is not necessarily true of the earlier building, whose decorations approximate those of domestic and non-religious structures.

123. See *Rep. VII–VIII*, p. 197, Fig. 50; and in Cumont, *Fouilles*, compare the diagram of the arrangement, p. 42, Fig. 10, with Pls. XXXI, XLIII, XLV, XLIX.

124. See *Rep. VII–VIII*, especially pp. 105–110, and Pls. XIV, XV, XVIII.

125. See *Rep. VII–VIII*, pp. 272–274; and Cumont, *Fouilles*, pp. 114–119.

126. This generalization would imply that the function of the scene of the three women at the tomb in the Christian Chapel is not primarily dogmatic (to demonstrate the resurrection of Christ), for the lid of the sarcophagus is still in place, but rather to suggest that God plans to reward the women for their piety in coming to the tomb to anoint the body of Christ.

several sanctuaries from each other completely. In the organization of the decorations of the Christian Chapel, Christ, in the symbolic form of the Good Shepherd, occupies the canonical position of the painted cult image of the temples. And in the Synagogue, where of course the representation of the deity was excluded, the principle of a focal organization of the decorations was preserved, and the Messianic King of the House of David surrounded by the representatives of the Twelve Tribes becomes in the final repainting of the Central Area the substitute for the prohibited deity. On the other hand the fact that the new element comes to strongest expression in the structures of communities which require a personal commitment on the part of their members implies that the decorations have a didactic function. They are intended to testify to, or remind the believers of the grounds for and the substance of, the faith they profess. If in form these decorations are narrative, the assumption is that the substance of the faith can be made explicit in a recital of events.

3. THE BIBLICAL SUBJECT MATTER OF THE PAINTINGS

Leaving the matter of context aside for the time being, we turn now to a closer examination of the paintings and inquire how they handle the Biblical subject matter and what this tells us about the religious outlook of the community that authorized their execution. In so doing we shall take as the basis of our discussion our own identification of that subject matter, but there is enough common consent among interpreters on this score to prevent the individual points of divergence in identification from necessarily vitiating our conclusions.

So far as the decorations of the Dura Synagogue are preserved, Biblical narrative has been drawn upon in them to portray or allude to approximately fifty-eight different episodes comprehended in twenty-eight separate spaces or panels. Arranged according to the sequence of the Biblical material, the narratives are as follows:

Gen. 15   Abraham Receives the Promise (Wing Panel IV)

Gen. 22   The Sacrifice of Isaac (Torah Shrine façade)

Gen. 28   Jacob at Bethel (Panel NA 1)

Gen. 48.13–19   Jacob Blesses Ephraim and Manasseh (Lower Center Panel, left)

Gen. 49.1–28   Jacob Blesses his twelve Sons (Lower Center Panel, right)

[Gen. 49.9–10   Jacob's Prophecy over Judah; The Lion and the Messianic King (Central Area)]

Exod. 1–2   The Infancy of Moses. 4 or 5 scenes (Panel WC 4)

Exod. 3   Moses and the Burning Bush (Wing Panel I)

[Exod. 9.22–26   The Plague of Hail mixed with Fire (Panel WA 3)]

Exod. 12–14   The Exodus and Crossing of the Red Sea. 3 scenes (Panel WA 3)

Exod. 34   Moses Receives the Law (Wing Panel II)

Exod. 40 and Num. 7   Consecration of the Tabernacle and its Priests (Panel WB 2)

Num. 2.21   Wilderness Encampment and Miraculous Well of Be'er. 2 scenes (Panel WB 1)

I Sam. 1   Hannah and the Child Samuel at Shiloh (Panel NB 2)

[I Sam. 2   Hannah's Prophecy Fulfilled (Panel WB 3)]

I Sam. 3   Samuel's Dream in the Temple at Shiloh (Panel NB 2)

I Sam. 4   The Battle of Eben-ezer. 2 scenes (Panel WB 4)

I Sam. 5   The Ark in the Land of the Philistines (Panel WB 4)

I Sam. 6   The Ark Released for Return to its Owners (Panel WB 4)

I Sam. 16   Samuel Anoints David (Panel WC 3)

I Sam. 23.15–18   Jonathan Warns David (Panel EC 1, extreme right)

I Sam. 26   David and Saul in the Wilderness of Ziph. 2 scenes (Panel EC 1)

II Sam. 5   David, King over All Israel (Upper Center Panel)

[II Sam. 5   David Builds the Walls of Jerusalem (Panel WB 3)]

II Sam. 22   David, Pious King, Singer of Psalms (Lower Center Panel)

I Kings 1   Solomon Anointed King? (Panel WA 1)

I Kings 6   Solomon Builds the Temple (Panel WB 3)

I Kings 16.34–17.3   Elijah Proclaims a Drought and Leaves for Cherith. 2 scenes (Panel SC 1)

I Kings 17.4–16   Elijah at Cherith and Zarephath. 2 scenes (Panel SC 2)

I Kings 17.17–24   Elijah Revives the Widow's Child. 3 scenes (Panel WC 1)

I Kings 18.25–29   The Prophets of Baal on Mount Carmel (Panel SC 3)

I Kings 18.30–38   Elijah on Mount Carmel. 2 scenes (Panel SC 4)

II Kings 25.8–10   The Temple Desecrated by Nebuzaradan (Panel NC 1, scene C 2)

II Kings 25.18–20   Priests Forcibly Removed into Captivity (Panel NC 1, scene C 1)

II Chron. 36.6   Jehoiakim Executed (Panel NC 1, scene C 3)

Jer. 50   The Fall of Babylon (Panel EC 2, right half)

Ezek. 37   Restoration of National Life. 6 scenes (Panel NC 1, section A and section B)

Dan. 5   Belshazzar's Feast (Panel EC 2, left half)

Neh. 8   Ezra Reads the Law (Wing Panel III)

Esther 6   Mordecai Honored (Panel WC 2)

Esther 9.11–14   Vengeance Reported and Purim Instituted (Panel WC 2)

This tabulation of the scenes represented shows that the material is of a single cast, and bears upon a single theme. It begins with the patriarchs, with Abraham and Jacob in particular, and extends to the re-establishment of the exiled and dispossessed nation in the Land of Promise in the Messianic era. Its concern is with the sacred history of the Chosen People seen in the light of the Covenant promise made to Abraham and confirmed to Jacob, and ultimately brought to fulfilment in its original intent on this earth, in spite of internal and external obstacles.

How adequate is this as a basis for interpreting the function of the paintings and the religious outlook of those who commissioned the decorations? Granted that only slightly more than half of the decorations of the building are preserved, a combination of two facts makes it clear that the missing elements were probably only a further elaboration of the same theme. The first is the fact that on all four walls a wide variety of Biblical contexts is drawn upon, and second the fact that in spite of this variety of Biblical reference, the focus remains one and the same throughout. If there had been involved in the full development of the artists' program some interest in a type of material other than that bearing upon the history of the Covenant People, the chances are very high that it would have revealed itself at least once in the extant part of the decorations. Hence the representation of any of the material from Gen. 1–14; i.e., from the Creation to Abraham, is quite unlikely, and what remains can well be taken as typical of the entire program.

A closer examination of the treatment of Israel's sacred history as presented in the Synagogue painting leads to a number of inferences that will help to appraise the community's religious outlook and to define further the principles of interpretation. These include the following:

a) There is a very real sense in which the paintings testify to an interest in the actual continuity of the historical process to which the sacred record testifies. This is evidenced by the fact that they do not illustrate interest in the Covenant relationship by a combination of scenes chosen from some one segment of sacred history, but provide instead a well-organized progression of scenes from the period of the Patriarchs and Moses and Aaron, from the early days of the monarchy, through the prophetic period, the exile, the post-exile period, to the expected Messianic age as visualized by prophecy. Indeed in certain contexts they insist on presenting Biblical narratives episode by episode, giving rise to what have above been called "cycles" of compositions.

b) There is a very real sense in which the history portrayed in the paintings involves not only certain individuals, but concretely the nation as a whole, and in which the course of events in time and space are for the individuals and the nation a full and completely satisfactory expression of their religious aspirations and ideals. This is shown by the extent to which the nation is represented in the paintings, whether in its entirety or by its "princes"; by the fact that so large a proportion of the scenes shows an individual contributing to the welfare of the people, this being taken as the measure of his importance; and by the fact that the course which history takes, while not achieved without repeated divine intervention, leads properly to the safety and assurance of national life in a national home under a divinely given Anointed King.

c) There is a very real sense in which the piety exhibited in, and inculcated by, the paintings finds a full expression in the literal observance of the Law. This comes to light in the effort to provide the historical documentation for the origin of the religious festivals, a documentation which fixes their ritual and observance; in the attention paid to the cult and its *sacra*, including the sacrifices; and in the opposition to idolatry.

d) Because they have this interest in the historical process, in the people of Israel, and in the literal observance of the Law, the paintings can and do properly include scenes showing how those nations and individuals that oppose God's purposes and His people are set at naught or destroyed. At the same time they also include scenes showing how Israel and its leaders are divinely punished because of their failure to abide by the ordinances of the Covenant and the Law.

Two general conclusions follow from our characterization of the paintings. The first is that any community decorating its House of Assembly with material so chosen and orientated cannot be said to have regarded itself, or to have been in fact, remote from religious life and observance of the Judaism that we know from the Bible and the Mishnah. The second is that the paintings give emphasis to materials and ideas not typical of the allegorists of the school of Philo. This we see in the way in which the later phases of Israel's history are included in their purview, in the importance given in the Central Area to the traditional form of the Messianic hope, in the interpretation of Ezekiel 37 as a prophecy looking toward the re-establishment of the nation in its homeland, in the acceptance of the Deuteronomistic conception of history, in the conviction that sin and accountability for sin are also national, and in the related belief that salvation is of the national and mundane order of events. In other words, the religious problem which the Synagogue paintings reflect is not that of the individual's search for participation in true being by the escape of the rational soul from the irrational desires to a higher level of mystical experience, but rather that of faithful participation in the nation's inherited Covenant responsibilities as a means of meriting the fulfilment of the divine promises and of making explicit in history its divinely determined purpose.

What thus emerges as the meaning of the decorations in their entirety is suited to the circum-

stances and the competition in which the Jewish community at Dura found itself. Dura, we have said above, was in the period of its Roman occupation more than ever before an Oriental city, albeit with a Roman military garrison. Judaism, meanwhile had fallen back visibly upon the Biblical sources of its religious life as the means of recruiting its strength in a world in which it no longer had a home. It could hope to survive and to compete effectively in an Oriental environment, as at Dura, only in proportion as it reassured itself and others about the operation of the divine will in what was, after all, part of the history of the Orient and in the exigencies of human life as it was lived there. The pictures of the Dura Synagogue give this reassurance directly, explicitly, and graphically. Therein their purpose can be said to be expressed fully.

So far as the pictures themselves are concerned, it would be possible to escape from the force of this conclusion by assuming that the compositions as they appear at Dura are copies of much earlier works, the original intent and meaning of which was different and lay in the sphere of a mystic Judaism. That some of them are probably in some respects copies, and that their origins are remote both from Dura and from the third century of our era, is in our judgment a hypothesis worthy of serious consideration. What their meaning in such an earlier form would have been, however, would depend upon the context in which they originated, a matter which will receive further attention below.[127] Here our concern is with the paintings as they appear at Dura and in this setting they do not in our judgment have a mystic connotation.

4. MIDRASH AND TARGUM
IN THE SYNAGOGUE PAINTINGS

For our understanding of the paintings and of the Jewish community at Dura another characteristic of the compositions is of importance; namely, their use of Midrashic and Targumic material. The treatment of this subject really belongs to those who have especial competence in the handling of what is in effect a vast separate continent in the world of the Jewish tradition.

127. See below, pp. 392–398.

ICONOGRAPHIC DETAILS RELATED TO THE TARGUMIC TRADITION

(*Fragmentary Targum*; *Pseudo-Jonathan*; *Onkelos*; *First* and *Second Targums to Esther*)

TEXT	BIBLICAL LOCUS	PANEL	SUBJECT	REFERENCE	RELATIONS
Frag. Targ.	Gen. 28.12	NA 1	Jacob's guardian angels	p. 74	
Onkelos	Exod. 13.18	WA 3	Departing Israelites armed	p. 81	Ex. Rab., Mekilta
Jonathan	Exod. 14.21	WA 3	Twelve paths in the Sea	p. 85	Gen. Deut. Rab., Mekilta
Sheni	Esther 1.2	WA 2 (WC 2)	Animals on Dais	p. 90	
Sheni	Esther 1.2	WA 2	Chairs beside Throne	p. 90	
Sheni	Esther 1.2	WA 2	Benaiah escorts Queen	p. 92	
Jonathan	I Sam. 2	NB 2 (WB 3)	Hannah's Prophecy	pp. 111 f.	
Jonathan	Num. 21.19	WB 1	Water flows to Tents	p. 124	Tosefta to Sukkah
Sheni	Esther 6.11	WC 2	Israel acclaims Mordecai	pp. 156 f.	
Sheni	Esther 1.2	WC 2	Ahasuerus on Solomon's Throne	p. 159	I Esther
I Esther	Esther 9.13	WC 2	Purim request of Esther	p. 163	
Onkelos	Exod. 2.5	WC 4	Princess fetches child	p. 177	
{ Jonathan { Frag. Targ.	Exod. 1.15	WC 4	Identity of Midwives	pp. 177 f.	Ex. Rab. et al.
{ Frag. Targ. { Jonathan { Onkelos	Gen. 49.10	Upper Center	Shiloh is Messianic King	p. 220	
{ Jonathan { Onkelos	Gen. 49.10	Upper Center	Scribes with Shiloh	p. 220	

Here only a simple preliminary attempt can be made to appraise for a specific purpose the meaning of the findings already recorded.

From what was said earlier, it would appear that there is a considerable number of instances in which Targum and Midrash have influenced the pictures. These instances it will be well to list here under separate headings for the Targums and the Midrashim respectively. Overlapping attestation will be noted where it exists, but no effort will be made to develop a complete list of witnesses to a given interpretation.

The fact that Targumic and Midrashic materials can be said to have been included in the paintings of the Dura Synagogue is again highly informative. We cannot stop to expand here upon its importance for our knowledge of the Midrash itself, its antiquity, and the distribution of its elements. What it tells us about the community which possessed the paintings is that it understood its Bible, not as an artificially restricted body of material, but as the basic element of a living native tradition, the vehicle for the communication of which was in all probability the Aramaic language. The type of interest which Midrash and Targum reflect has been described above as particularly characteristic of the Judaism of the second and third centuries of our era.[128] This is because it accepts the tradition as the living and abiding source of Israel's strength and character and serves to enhance its importance in Jewish religious life. By using Targum and Midrash the Synagogue paintings again reveal their relation to the contemporary scene.

It is, of course, obvious and well known that the tradition reflected in Targum and Midrash cannot be identified strictly as to its provenience either in time or in space. But not all of it is prevalent everywhere and what we know about its regional associations is sometimes revealing. So, for instance, the range of the materials used in the Synagogue

128. See above, pp. 325f.

ICONOGRAPHIC DETAILS RELATED TO THE MIDRASHIC TRADITION

TEXT	PANEL	SUBJECT	REFERENCE	RELATIONS
Exod. Rab. XV, 28 (Exod. 12.1)	WA 3	God shows Moses the salamander	p. 76	
Exod. Rab. XX, 19 (Exod. 13.18) Mekilta	WA 3	Departing Israelites armed	p. 81	Onkelos
Esther Rab. III, 14	WA 3	Egyptians drown naked	p. 83	(R. Nathan)
Exod. Rab. XX, 5 S.o.S. Rab. IV, 12, 1	WA 3	Standards at Red Sea	p. 84	
Gen. Rab. LXXXIV, 5, 8 Deut. Rab. XI, 10 Mekilta (ad Ex. 14.16)	WA 3	Twelve Paths in the Sea	p. 85	Jonathan
Seder Eliyahu R. 5	SC 2 (SC 4)	Elisha companion of Elijah	p. 143	
Exod. Rab. XV, 15 Deut. Rab.	SC 3	Hiel and the Serpent	p. 140	
Esther Rab. X, 7	WC 2	Haman as Stable Boy	p. 156	
Esther Rab. 1,12	WC 2	Ahasuerus on Solomon's Throne	p. 159	Sheni
Exod. Rab. I, 13	WC 4	Identity of Midwives	pp. 177 f.	Frag., Jonathan
II Alph. Ben Sira 24b	EC 1	Spear and jug with Abner	p. 207	
Gen. Rab. XCVIII, 8	Upper Center	Scribes with Shiloh	p. 220	Onk., Jonathan
Gen. Rab. on Gen. 24.1	Wing IV	White-haired Abraham	p. 238	(Pirke R. El.)

paintings seems to reflect the general location of the Jewish community at Dura. The affinity with the tradition that was incorporated in *Targum Onkelos* and in *Targum Sheni* points to relations with Babylonian Judaism, while the affinity with the tradition incorporated in *Targum Pseudo-Jonathan* and in the *Fragmentary Targum* points to Palestine. The combination of the two suggests relations with both centers and confirms the contention that the Dura community was not foreign to the developing religious thought of its environment.

From these general observations it seems possible to proceed to the further statement that the Haggadic tradition embodied in the Dura Synagogue paintings was, broadly speaking, distinct from the one that was normative for Philo and for that part of the ancient Jewish world that he represents. There are thus two instances in the Synagogue paintings in which iconographic details would have been completely different if the tra-

dition that was current in his circles, so far as we know it, had been used. The first of these is that of the "armed" Israelites as they appear in the scene of the Exodus and Red Sea Crossing (Panel WA 3). Here as we have seen in detail above, not only Philo but the LXX, the Hellenistic Jewish authors Ezekiel and Demetrius, Josephus, the *Fragmentary Targum*, pseudo-*Jonathan*, and one element of the *Mekilta* follow a tradition that maintains and deplores the utter defenselessness of the Israelites departing from Egypt; while a second element of the *Mekilta*, the *Palestinian Talmud*, *Onkelos*, and *Exodus Rabbah* so render the Biblical word *hamushim* in Exod. 13.18 as to imply that they were "armed."[129] The second is that of the Pharaoh's daughter actually retrieving the child Moses from the Ark in Panel WC 4, where again, in following one reading of a word in Exod. 2.5, Philo, the LXX, and Josephus would require the act to

129. See above, p. 81, n 237.

23

be performed by others, while *Targum Onkelos* and the Hellenistic author Ezekiel have her stretch out her own arm to grasp it.[130]

To avoid misunderstanding it should perhaps be repeated that what can be said about the Dura Synagogue paintings in the light of their use of Midrashic and Targumic material is illustrative rather than definitive. The use of this material does not prove that such pictures could have been painted only at Dura, or that they were first painted at Dura, or that they must have been conceived and executed for the first time in the middle of the third century of our era. It is entirely possible that there existed earlier paintings of all or part of this identical cycle of legends in which certain or all of the Midrashic and Targumic elements now found there were omitted. It is equally possible that there existed in other parts of the Jewish world other cycles using quite different materials and serving quite different ends. What is meant is that this particular cycle as it is known to us at Dura moves within a definable orbit of the Haggadic tradition, that this orbit has Palestinian-Babylonian rather than Egyptian relations, that while not a few of the Haggadic details incorporated in the paintings may have been available for use at a much earlier time, the aggregate belongs to the time and place of the execution of the paintings.

With the presentation of the evidence for the influence of Midrash and Targum upon the Dura Synagogue pictures, we have moved closer to the angle from which they are interpreted by Sonne and Wischnitzer-Bernstein. The next question is, therefore, what can be said on the score of these interpretations.

5. PRACTICE AND PRINCIPLES IN THE USE OF THE HAGGADIC MATERIAL FOR THE INTERPRETATION OF THE PAINTINGS

Perhaps the most interesting feature of the interpretations advanced by Sonne and Wischnitzer-Bernstein is the extent to which the homiletic materials of the Midrashic tradition can actually be drawn upon to demonstrate both the thesis of the "three crowns" and that of the Messianic ex-

pectation as the unifying theme of the Synagogue decorations. This very fact must itself give us pause and lead us to inquire whether the principles governing the interpretation of the paintings can be further clarified. It will be obvious in this connection that the continuous homiletic use of a given body of sacred scripture leads inevitably — and that not only in Judaism — to the discovery by preachers of an almost infinite variety of connotation and association in any one statement or episode. Indeed, this is constitutive of the procedure of homiletic exposition everywhere, as the homilies of the Christian Church Fathers, or for that matter of the sermons of contemporary rabbis and preachers, clearly show. Hence it is to be expected that if one were to look hard and long enough in the vast treasure house of Jewish homiletic tradition of which the Midrashim are a part, one could develop a basis for the association of almost any episode with any other along a great variety of lines, and thus with good fortune arrive at many different formulae for the interpretation of such a body of material as the Dura Synagogue paintings. It is in order, therefore, to inquire whether any restrictions need be imposed upon the synthesizing and correlating opportunities provided by the Midrashic materials, and whether the syntheses advanced are in effect appropriate to the particular time and place with which we are dealing.

In this connection it is desirable in the first place to illustrate two tendencies that develop when the Pandora's box of homiletic material is opened and examined.

There is first the tendency to give special and wide significance to a single detail of a picture on the strength of suggestions provided by the Midrashic materials. So, for instance, the ark (or scroll chest) seen by the side of the reader in Wing Panel III (for us, Ezra; for Wischnitzer-Bernstein, Samuel) is said to provide an allusion to the tradition that the Ark of the Covenant will be returned with the coming of the Messianic age.[131] Similarly, the red heifer portrayed in Panel WB 2 (Consecration of the Tabernacle and its Priests) is taken to symbolize the slaying of the Prince of Edom by the Priest Messiah, a theme also said to be adumbrated in the execution of Joab sup-

---

130. See above, p. 177 and n. 681.

131. *Messianic Theme*, p. 86.

posedly presented in Section C of Panel NC 1 (Ezekiel, the Destruction and Restoration of National Life).[132] Similarly, the absence of the rope on the ram in the scene of the Sacrifice of Isaac (Torah Shrine Façade) is thought to indicate that the Dura artist was inclined to make less of the belief in the enslavement of Israel than the artist of the Beth Alpha mosaics, where the rope actually appears.[133] Again the conical tent in the same scene is taken as the Sukkah of the Holy One on Mount Zion, and its green color is explained by the fact that according to the tradition the Sukkah was made of olive branches.[134]

There is in the second place the tendency to use details or implications suggested by the Midrashic tradition as a means of relating panels to each other, thus bringing unity into the decorative scheme. So, for instance, Abraham's posture and dress in Wing Panel IV (Abraham Receives the Promise) are said to show his relation to the Messiah David, who also has his hands covered under his himation.[135] Similarly the theme of Panel NA 1 (Jacob at Bethel) is associated with the theme of the pictures representing events in the life of Moses in the same register (WA 3 and Wing Panels I and II) by virtue of the fact that the Midrashic tradition makes Jacob's vision symbolize Mount Sinai, leading to the suggestion that the angels on the ladder are Moses and Aaron.[136] In like manner the central figure in the group of three at the middle of Panel WC 2 (Mordecai and Esther), once it is identified as Harbonah — one of Ahasuerus' chamberlains according to the Midrashic tradition — makes it possible to associate this panel with a Messianic cycle, since Harbonah in another part of the tradition is in effect Elijah returned as the forerunner of the Messiah.[137] In the same way the representation of Haman in the same panel is said to relate the panel to the theme of the "wars against Amalek" and hence to the eschatological drama, because it is suggested that as the Agagite he is a descendent of the Agag against whom Saul contended (I Sam. 15–16).[138]

This procedure eventually leads to the point where something not explicitly represented in the compositions can become decisive for their meaning, as when the fact that Elijah demanded a "cake" from the widow of Zarephath is used to make Panel SC 2 imply that Elijah will precede the Messiah into Babylon, or when the promise of "houses" made to the midwives of Panel WC 4 (Pharaoh and the Infancy of Moses) suggests that the composition helps to develop the theme of the "kingdom" as one of Israel's "crowns."[139]

The use of such interpretative procedures leads to formulas for the coördination of the decorations as a whole that seem completely fanciful. Thus the Samuel Cycle of Register B, since it depicts among other things the fatal battle of Eben-ezer, is taken to suggest the trials and tribulations that are to precede the Messianic era, and, combined with the reminiscences of happier days of the past (the scene from the wilderness sojourn in the rest of the register), is said to characterize the procedure leading to the fulfilment of the Messianic hope.[140] Similarly a so-called Moses cycle and a so-called Jacob cycle in Register A are said jointly to express Israel's claim to the crown of the Torah and to illustrate Deut. 33.4, where it is said, "Moses commanded us a Law, an inheritance of the congregation of Jacob."[141]

The application of what Sonne has called the "homiletic symbolic" method of interpretation to the paintings of the Dura Synagogue leads in our judgment to the same difficulty as the application of the allegorical method. Both methods make interesting combinations, assume a similar mentality in those who commissioned the paintings, and create a situation in which almost everything can mean something else and in which almost anything can mean almost everything.[142] Leaving aside for the moment the question of the genuine expressions of apologetic and Messianic interest in the choice of the Synagogue's decorative subject matter, we must return to what has been said

132. "The Paintings," pp. 304 f., 334.
133. *Messianic Theme*, p. 90.
134. "The Paintings," p. 361.
135. *Messianic Theme*, p. 80.
136. "The Paintings," p. 277.
137. *Messianic Theme*, pp. 31 f.
138. "The Paintings," p. 320.

139. For the former see *Messianic Theme*, pp. 23 f., and for the latter "The Paintings," pp. 314–316.
140. *Messianic Theme*, pp. 61, 67–69.
141. "The Paintings," p. 286.
142. This is literally true in the study of Sonne, where allusions to all three of the "crowns" are eventually seen to appear in almost every register. See "The Paintings," pp. 277 f., 318, 319, 327.

23*

above about the sense in which the paintings express an interest in the actual continuity of Israel's sacred history.[143] If this observation is correct — and their very organization in registers, panels, and scenes would seem to make it so — the decorations of the Synagogue must have an historical purpose, no matter what stimulus they may also have given to homiletic syntheses and flights of fancy. Because they seem above all to document, to narrate, and to move within a given frame of reference — sometimes to the point of tracing a series of events — we would be inclined to maintain as proper principles of interpretation the following:

1. That details of compositions have relevance only to the subject of the composition as a whole, and that what is not represented should not be imputed;

2. That relations between compositions can safely be said to exist only when they:

    a) Adjoin one another in the same register and represent successive episodes in Biblical narrative;

    b) Adjoin one another in the same register and can be said to have as their major concern the same person, place, object, or doctrine;

    c) Are arranged in symmetrical groups or perhaps positions;

3. That Midrashic or Targumic material should be used in the interpretation of a composition only where it helps to explain elements of the iconography not otherwise clear.

If the application of these principles would differentiate our understanding of the paintings from those of both Sonne and Wischnitzer-Bernstein, so also would the questions we should be inclined to raise about the theses that develop from their inquiries. The former, it will be recalled, finds in the Synagogue's emphasis upon Israel's inalienable right to the "three crowns" a defense against the efforts of the Christians to usurp these prerogatives.[144] The latter regards the rebirth of the Persian kingdom and the threat it represented to Rome's supremacy as the occasion for that intensification of the Messianic expectation that makes this expectation the dominant theme of the entire range of the Synagogue's mural decorations.[145] What we would question here is not so much the fact of apologetic and Messianic interests in the choice, and perhaps even in the organization, of some of the material, but rather the extent to which the "theme" of the decorations can be clarified by reference to either one or the other of these interests. Two things should be kept in mind in this connection. The first is that what we know about homiletic interests and materials in the period in question gives us no grounds to expect more than a passing concentration upon either the apologetic or the Messianic interest such as is thought to be monumentalized in the Synagogue paintings. Rather the picture is one of a wide range of interests on the part of the preachers with only the usual proportion of references to the topics in question, however important they may have been in themselves.[146] The second thing to be kept in mind is that at Dura the Christian community was scarcely of sufficient importance to rival the Jewish either in numbers or in influence, and that if the upheaval ushering the Messianic era had in fact been expected by the Jews of the city they would scarcely have created so imposing and expensive a monument as the Dura Synagogue, or have advertised their anti-Roman feelings in its decorations as freely as suggested.

6. POSSIBLE INFERENCES ABOUT THE CHOICE AND ORGANIZATION OF THE SYNAGOGUE'S BIBLICAL PAINTINGS

The question may properly be asked at this point whether the choice and organization of the Dura Synagogue paintings can be explained at all satisfactorily on the basis of the observations made above and in keeping with the rules of procedure proposed. Clearly the answer depends upon what is meant by "satisfactorily," for if the word is taken to imply the establishment of a comprehensive and canonical scheme, the answer will in our judgment and at the present state of our knowledge probably have to be "No." For those who would be satisfied with less, an attempt should none-

---

143. See above, pp. 350 f.
144. "The Paintings," pp. 267–269.

145. *Messianic Theme*, pp. 11 f., 100.
146. See Bacher, *Die Agada der babylonischen Amoräer*, especially the sections on Rab and Samuel, contemporaries of the Dura Synagogue, pp. 1–33; 37–45, and by the same author, *Die Agada der palästinensischen Amoräer*, I (1892).

theless be made to formulate what seems to us to be demonstrable at the present time.

As to the selection of materials, we may say that the Synagogue artists or those who commissioned the work chose:

1. To exhibit in a medley of pictorial compositions those events, persons, institutions, and objects that are important for the knowledge and understanding of the historical covenant relationship between God and His people, a relationship established with Abraham and terminating in the fulfilment of the promises in a future Messianic era;

2. To illustrate the punishment or reward of those (especially the Gentile nations as represented by their rulers) who oppose or further the divine will and purpose in their relation to God's people, and to show that Israel itself is not exempt from such divine punishment for failure to observe the terms of the covenant and the Law;

3. To give adequate attention to the historical antecedents of the festivals of the religious year and the institutions and paraphernalia of the cult;

4. To provide individuals and the nation alike with the assurance of divine succor and protection in times of dire need.

As to the organization of the subject matter, the Synagogue artists or those who commissioned them chose:

1. To set forth in the focal area of the decorations, in connection with the Shiloh Prophecy (Gen. 49) and through a selection of scenes and symbols, the substance, the personages, the basis, and the nature of the Messianic expectation, and to develop in the registers the material illustrating the broader reaches of the historical covenant relationship, its episodes, persons, and institutions;

2. To use groups of adjacent panels in the two lower registers to present successive historical episodes from two different Biblical contexts (the so-called cycles);

3. To allocate other scenes of their choice to particular places in the scheme of decorations in accordance with practical considerations, special local interests, and didactic purposes or combinations of them. Among the practical considerations, we may identify that of space requirements; among local interests, those of proximity to certain Gentile nations and exposure to the dangers of idolatry; and among didactic purposes, those of

teaching by the examples of great men, of maintaining the proper respect for the institutions and monuments of national life, and of giving full assurance of divine assistance and ultimate salvation for all.

Is it illogical to conclude that the organization of the Synagogue's pictorial decorations does not follow a single comprehensive and unified plan? How quickly and under what circumstances may unified programs of interior decoration be thought to have developed? In the case of Oriental, Classical, and Christian art, such programs are the result of long periods of experimentation and do not gain general acceptance until the form of the building to which they are applied has itself been standardized. The form of the synagogue, however, had not yet been stabilized in the third century, even though a most important step toward the development of a structural element, the Torah Shrine, had already been taken.[147] It therefore seems much too early for a comprehensive and canonical program of synagogue decoration in which each element had a predetermined or meaningful location and in which purely practical considerations did not affect choice and location of subject matter. In view of the restrictions under which the Jews were forced to live in the period that begins with Theodosius, the question may well be raised whether for wall decorations a canonical scheme of this sort was ever developed in ancient Judaism.[148]

If in interpreting the organization of the Dura Synagogue decorations, we must think of a scheme borrowed from outside sources — itself a much more reasonable hypothesis — there is no adequate reason for giving preference to the programs of the official monuments of late Roman imperial art, as Grabar has done.[149] This would be to misjudge the sphere in which the Dura artists can properly be supposed to have operated. Preference should rather be given to the decorative pattern familiar to us from the temples of Dura, as has already been suggested.[150] Here, the basic plan was first to

147. See above, pp. 22 f.

148. What we know about the mosaic of the synagogues of Palestine suggests that there something approximating a canonical scheme of floor decorations did develop at a later time, perhaps even in advance of the solution by the Christians of the problem of dealing properly with the decoration of floor space in the churches.

149. See above, p. 347.

150. See pp. 348 f.

develop the central area of the west wall focally, and then to organize the remainder of the decorations in registers. The former concept was in line with the structural and decorative treatment of the Torah Shrine already established in the earlier phase of the history of the building, while the latter was suited to the subject matter of the narrative compositions. How little else was actually determined in advance we can see from the recomposition and repainting of the Central Area, where if anywhere the artists must have had a canonical scheme. Here the artists and those who commissioned the work labored diligently and long to arrive at a formula that would utilize some of the earlier decorations and would at the same time give the area a treatment corresponding to the prototype in effect. Since the restrictions which they faced made their problem much more difficult than that of the Christians at Dura, their solution is more remarkable than that of the Christian Chapel. It was only when they saw the possibility of taking the Sacrifice of Isaac scene not only symbolically but also historically, and thus as the starting point for a procession of historical scenes moving vertically upward, that they came out at the top with the Messianic King receiving the homage of the representatives of the Twelve Tribes and thus with a close approximation to the subject matter presented in the local scheme of temple decoration.

These conclusions, if they are correct, provide an important witness to the religious life and to the status of the Jewish community at Dura. The congregation subscribed sincerely to the beliefs and value judgments that are traditional in Judaism, and endeavored by the decoration of its House of Assembly to memorialize and inculcate reverence for the historic tradition to which it adhered. Consciousness of such an objective would doubtless provide the strongest possible support for the conviction that in using representational art it was not transgressing a sacred commandment. The intention was the reverse of idolatrous, and expressed precisely those feelings that had come to be normative for the relaxation of the proscription of images in the minds of the Jewish authorities since the time of the destruction of the Temple.[151]

To find at Dura a Jewish community so orientated in its religious outlook provides a welcome

addition to our knowledge of the history and status of Judaism in the third century of our era. Indeed, what we know about the Judaism of the period would lead us to expect precisely this type of orientation, even though we might not have hoped to see it set forth with such eloquence in a pictorial medium of religious self-expression. It is doubtless no coincidence that Rab, the famous sage of the Babylonian Jewish communities, a contemporary of the Synagogue, had exactly the same type of historicizing interest, showed himself equally impressed by the great figures of Israel's past — including especially Moses, David, and Solomon — and used Haggadic procedure, not to allegorize, but to fill gaps in the narrative record and to develop allusions contained in it.[152]

7. SIDELIGHTS FROM THE BIBLICAL SCENES ON ASPECTS OF CONTEMPORARY JUDAISM

The narrative compositions of the Dura Synagogue do more than merely provide another link in a familiar chain. They also provide insight into many matters on which we have been ill, or only partly, informed by the literary tradition.

One such is the interpretation of scripture itself. Interesting in this connection is not only the treatment given to the Shiloh Prophecy of Gen. 49, but also and especially the representation of Ezekiel 37. On the interpretation of the vision dealing with the Valley of Dry Bones, as in fact on the interpretation of the Book of Ezekiel as a whole, rabbinical authorities were inclined to be uncommunicative. In the Synagogue painting we have an eloquent testimony to the way in which the chapter was understood in Jewish circles in the third century, and we obtain from this in turn insight into the derivation of some of the interpretative material used by the Christian Church Fathers in their commentaries.[153] Equally interesting and important historically is what the paintings tell us about the availability of Targumic materials at this particular time and place. *Targum Onkelos*, having in all likelihood been codified by this time, was current in Babylonian Jewish circles and perhaps also known at Dura, but with it there seems to have

151. See above, p. 343.

152. See Bacher, *Agada der babylonischen Amoräer*, pp. 8–16.

153. See above, p. 179, n. 689.

gone even at this time an extensive knowledge of the Targumic materials for Esther, in whatever form, and of the Targumic rendering of other books of the Bible in both the older and the later phases of the Palestinian Targum. What we have learned about the applicability of pseudo-Jonathan's version of Hannah's prayer (I Sam. 2) to the so-called Samuel Cycle in Register B is worthy of special note in this connection.[154]

Still more important is what the paintings tell us about the nature and extent of the Midrashic material familiar to the Jews of Dura in the middle of the third century of our era. Save for some affinities with the *Mekilta*, the Tannaitic Midrashim have no important echoes in the paintings of the Dura Synagogue and in view of the nature of their material this should probably not be expected. But the importance which the traditions of Exodus Rabbah and Genesis Rabbah have in the decorations where they embroider upon the Biblical narrative is a welcome confirmation of scholarly opinion that these were among the first to be codified and contain the oldest materials. Besides, with the pictures in hand, we obtain in some instances a much clearer conception of the nature and implications of the Midrashic narrative; so for instance, in the Hiel episode, in that of the twelve paths through the Red Sea, and in that of the well of Be'er and its streams of water.[155] In connection with the last instance we have in addition an opportunity to see how the more easterly and the more westerly Midrashic traditions diverge from each other, the one applying its efforts to the Be'er incident, the other to what happened at Rephidim and Elim.[156] In these and in many similar matters we shall undoubtedly have occasion to profit greatly from the treatment of the material in the years ahead once it comes under the scrutiny of those who are experts in the field.

An entirely different area in which we may expect the painting of the Dura Synagogue to make an important contribution to our knowledge of ancient Judaism is that of the representation of individual objects and aspects of Jewish religious life and usage. Especial importance attaches in this connection to the *sacra* of the cult, for the knowledge of which we are otherwise so largely dependent on word pictures, at least in the period before the tenth century of our era. The frequent representation of the Ark of the Covenant is worthy of particular note, since it provides impressions of its form and decoration, the devices used to carry it, and the veils with which it was covered.[157] With the representations of the Ark go those of the other vessels and implements of the cult and above all those of the cult personnel; for instance, that of Aaron in his official vestments in Panel WB 2. To them in turn must be added what the paintings tell us about such matters as the "fringes," about ceremonial and religious gestures (acclamation, benediction, reverence or prayer, and song), and about the customs of mourning. All this is most important and greatly welcome.

At this point a word of caution is in order. The representations have their own limitations. They portray the objects and usages largely as they were understandable to the people of the middle Euphrates region in the middle of the third century of our era. The objects are therefore not necessarily represented as they were in fact, or as they were understood in earlier periods and at other places. This is because neither the artists nor those who commissioned the paintings were trained antiquarians. They had of necessity to use their own contemporary knowledge and their limited supply of iconographic formulae to represent whatever it was that composition of the scenes required. In some particulars their contemporary knowledge seems to have included also acquaintance, whether direct or indirect, with older representations of the same objects. This is demonstrated by the close relations between the Ark of the Covenant as it appears at Dura and on the walls of the somewhat earlier Capernaum synagogue. It is demonstrated even more effectively by the relation between the Temple on the façade of the Torah Shrine and the device on the coins of the Bar Kochebah uprising. There may be other points of contact with iconographic forms of an earlier period which we cannot at the present time document. However this may be, the bulk of the representation, especially in the

154. See above, pp. 111 f.
155. See above, pp. 85, 123 f., 140.
156. See above, pp. 122 f.

157. A special study of the Torah Shrine, with which the representation of the Ark is closely connected, has already appeared. See C. Wendel, *Der Thoraschrein im Altertum (Hallische Monographien* XV, 1950).

narrative compositions, had to be executed in forms corresponding to the sources of the artists' training and to the range of their own experience. This is to say for instance that civilians have inevitably to be clothed in chiton and himation, since this is an element of the vocabulary of contemporary art. It may be that chiton and himation were also actually worn (on special occasions?) by the local citizenry of Dura and at earlier times in the Orient, but of course the dress has nothing to do with the historical persons to whom it is applied. The extent to which garments and coiffures are portrayed with strict application to certain categories of people is a further expression of the use of patterns and conventions, and explains, for instance, why all kings — whether Egyptian, Achaemenian, or Israelite — appear in the same costume. Of course, the patterns extend beyond the sphere of dress to that of pose and posture, but the discussion of this matter belongs to a different context. In the specific case of Aaron's robes, it must therefore be remembered that whatever the artists may have known or learned about the Biblical description of these sacred garments, they were still bound of necessity to fall back upon images familiar to them in giving form to their impressions. It is therefore likely that the Aaronic vestments as shown in Panel WB 2 owe more to the typical royal garment as we see it in other panels than to a real understanding of the Biblical text on its own terms, as would be much more evident if either Aaron had been shown seated or mounted, or one of the kings in the decorations had been shown standing. The use of the decorations of the Dura Synagogue has therefore the same limitations that are inherent in mediaeval illustrated Jewish manuscripts, those arising from the use of a certain repertoire of artistic form. But they do show what a Jewish community of the third century of our era was willing to believe the Biblical antiquities had looked like, and in this particular are not only interesting and valuable, but sometimes closer to the objects themselves than anything hitherto available.

8. THE INCIDENTAL DECORATIONS OF THE SYNAGOGUE

In the preceding pages our attention has been focused on the narrative compositions that make up the bulk of the wall paintings of the Dura Synagogue. Some comment on the incidental decorations is therefore still in order, the particular question in this context being: What do they tell us about the Jewish community that commissioned them and accepted them as part of the decorations of its House of Assembly? The incidental decorations, it will be recalled, bring certain materials that we otherwise might not have expected to see in such a setting. Noteworthy among them are the Persephone of the ceiling tiles, the animals from the private zoos or the arena in the dado, and the masks of the New Comedy that go with them.[158]

It is clear that if these materials were all we knew about the decoration of the building we would not be able to identify it as a synagogue, and it should also be clear that if one were to take these materials as a starting-point for the development of the principles by which the entire body of the decorations are to be judged, one might conceivably come out with a picture altogether different from that presented above. But the procedure followed is the one that does the fullest justice to the most important and informative body of the decorative material, and with the findings as we have recorded them the interpretation of these incidental materials can, we believe, be combined without doing them either violence or injustice.

The important point to keep in mind in this connection, in our judgment, is what has just been said about the use by the artists of a repertoire of artistic form. That such a repertoire existed with respect to the materials of the ceiling decorations and the imitated incrustation work of the dado and the Torah Shrine, has already been pointed out above with the help of materials from other structures at Dura itself.[159] The representation of Persephone in a setting of ceiling tiles depicting, at least in large part, the fruits of the field is not strange in itself. She goes well with the rest of the materials, so far as existing conventions and the repertoire of form is concerned.[160] But why did the Jews of Dura not object to her? The answer is probably

158. See above, pp. 41 f., 245–250.
159. See above, pp. 51, 55 f.
160. It is important to note in this connection what was said about the necessity to which the artists were put in providing a variety of tile designs for so large a surface. See above, p. 52.

the same as that applying to the representation of the seasons and even of the chariot of the sun in the mosaics of the later Palestinian synagogues.[161] Seasons went with a zodiac, and a Persephone associated with the fruits of the field may well have been regarded more as a symbol than as a person. In any event, she was not there to be worshiped, and the functional distinction between a cult image and an ornament applying to the statue in the synagogue at Nehardea and to the Aphrodite in the bath at Acco could apply to her as well.[162] In other words she was not inconceivable as a part of a synagogue ceiling at this time if she belonged to a well-decorated ceiling in accordance with the current repertoire of design.

The Persephones were painted and put in place in the first phase of the decoration of the later House of Assembly, and go with the work done on the façade of the Torah Shrine. The animals and the masks belong with the second phase of the decorations, but the problem they present is no different. About the animals it will be noted that the standing lion is addorsed to the Torah Shrine at its right side, but no symbolic pattern emerges since he is balanced at the other side of the Torah Shrine by an addorsed tigress. We would probably be right, therefore, in regarding the animals as an integral part of the decorative scheme of the dado as a whole, rather than as a series whose further development was suggested by a convention for the adornment of Torah Shrines, such as existed in later times and may already have been used in the Kefr Birim synagogue of Palestine.[163] By whatever chain of circumstances animals and masks were brought together in the first place in such dados, the probability is that here they too are a part of a repertoire of design for an elaborately decorated interior, and that the Jewish faithful were no more disturbed or personally affected by them than they were by the *adventus regis* cliché used for the triumph of Mordecai (Panel WC 2).[164]

We take the same position also with regard to the foundation deposits discovered in the door-sockets of the Synagogue's House of Assembly.[165] It is not entirely clear under what circumstances they were placed there, nor what they included. That their implications are magical and that they thus stand in conflict with the highest religious standards of Jewish life and practice, and hence with what has been said above about the orientation of Dura's Jewish community as reflected in the Biblical paintings, is perfectly clear. The same thing applies equally to the representation of the evil eye on one of the ceiling tiles of the building. Certainly due consideration must be given to such matters in the appraisal of the religious orientation of the community. The only point we would make here is that conformity to what was after all a traditional part of a very different world does not necessarily fix entirely the horizon of those belonging to it or require us to judge all their efforts in the light of such conformity.

9. ELEMENTS OF A TRADITION OF SYMBOLIC ART IN THE DECORATIONS OF THE SYNAGOGUE

We have concluded that historical interest predominated in the great system of Biblical scenes executed in the House of Assembly some years after the completion of the building, presumably about A.D. 250. As has been pointed out above, there was also an earlier phase in the decoration of the chamber, coinciding with the construction and dedication of the building. To this earlier phase we have assigned the ceiling tiles, the decorations of the Torah Shrine, and the design on the wall directly above it; that is, the underpainting of the Central Area. Some care was taken in that context to describe the differences in the repertory of form and in brushwork, and it was discovered that the decorations on the Torah Shrine were done by other artists than those responsible for the great body of the Synagogue murals. It was further disclosed that the decorations of the Torah Shrine at least, and of the design on the wall above it, were fundamentally symbolic. This can now be seen to indicate that the materials belong to quite another tradition in the history of ancient Jewish art than the one represented by the great body of the narrative compositions; namely, the tradition to the

161. See for these Sukenik, *Ancient Synagogues of Palestine and Greece*, p. 30, Fig. 5; p. 33, Fig. 8.

162. See above, p. 343, n. 101.

163. On the Kefr Birim lion see, e.g., Sukenik, *Ancient Synagogues in Palestine and Greece*, Pl. VIII.

164. That the cliché had religious significance in official imperial art seems evident from its later usage. See, e.g., Grabar, *L'Empereur dans l'art byzantin*, p. 19.

165. See above, pp. 19 f.

knowledge of which so much has been added by the recent studies of Goodenough and Wischnitzer-Bernstein.[166] In this tradition most if not all of the materials represented in the first phase of the decoration of the Synagogue reappear in a wide variety of places and with a wide variety, no doubt, of connotations.

We have already suggested that by virtue of their association with each other and with the area of the Torah Shrine, the symbols used in the Dura Synagogue must be thought to exhibit here the guarantees of the divine forgiveness and to show how reliance upon them as communicated in the revealed Law gives assurance of participation in the Messianic banquet under the tree of life in the world to come.[167] If this interpretation is correct, it supports what has been said earlier in this chapter about the religious orientation of the local Jewish community. The outlook is the same as that inferred from the large mass of the pictorial decorations, only the statement is more theological because the form of its presentation is abstract and symbolic rather than narrative.

The co-existence at Dura of two different traditions of ancient Jewish art and their relation to each other is an interesting historical phenomenon worthy of brief additional comment. That there should have been more than one tradition is by no means stranger than that there should have been more than one cycle of pictorial compositions representing Biblical scenes. The large repertoire of narrative compositions at Dura and the decorations on and above the Torah Shrine actually represent two separate traditions. They make a separate appearance and perform different functions, and had different origins in time and place. The ultimate clarification of this point so far as the large narrative cycle is concerned must depend upon the argument to be developed in the last chapter.[168] Here only two points relevant to the larger question are to be touched upon. The first concerns the origin of the repertoire of symbolic Jewish art, and the second the appearance of individual Biblical scenes in the context of the symbolic art tradition.

The two most salient facts about symbolic Jew-

166. See Goodenough, *Jewish Symbols*, and Wischnitzer-Bernstein, *Gestalten und Symbole der jüdischen Kunst*.

167. See above, pp. 64 f.

168. See below, pp. 398–402.

ish art, now heavily underscored by the work of Goodenough, are: first, that so many of the symbols appear simultaneously in so many localities, having an almost universal acceptance; and second, that not a few of them can be traced back as far as the Maccabean period of Palestinian Jewish history. It will also be noted that the symbols appear in a great variety of contexts, and are applied to many different types of objects. From these facts it follows that their origin must go back sufficiently early in time to make their wide distribution possible. In all probability it should also be inferred that their place of origin must have been sufficiently central to make them generally acceptable. It is hard under the circumstances to escape from any other conclusion than that their origin goes back to Palestine and at least to the beginning of the Maccabean period. How large the repertoire was at the outset and what the medium was in which the symbols were created and presented, are questions on which we must await the opinions of those currently dealing with the problem. It seems probable, first, that the repertoire of symbolic form was added to in the course of time, as the Menorah and the device on the coin of the Second Revolt indicate; and second, that virtually all of the earliest symbols are capable of separate representation in relatively limited special contexts. How this may be thought to differentiate the symbolic tradition in Jewish art from that represented by such a cycle of narrative paintings as those of the Dura Synagogue will appear presently.

The fact that the repertoire of symbolic Jewish art was gradually enlarged provides the proper perspective upon one point that may have seemed contradictory. This is the appearance of the Sacrifice of Isaac on the Torah Shrine of the Dura Synagogue. Its subject matter, of course, is narrative; but, as already indicated, its function is clearly symbolic. The question arises in this connection, why, if narrative material can be used for symbolic purposes, any narrative scenes could not be interpreted symbolically, and why the existence of two different traditions in ancient Jewish art should be postulated. The answer to these questions so far as the Dura Synagogue is concerned involves judgments both as to the facts about, and the origins of its narrative compositions. Our conclusion has been that the body of the register compositions is in fact not symbolic or allegorical, but narrative and historical in intent. The further suggestion will be made below that the pictorial compositions derive ultimately from illustrated manuscripts.[169] This hypothesis provides a context of origin and a medium of communication other than that which can be presumed for symbolic Jewish art, and one to which the simple narrative function of pictorial composition is also most appropriate. How context and medium can help us differentiate between the function and meaning of scenes can be illustrated in the history of Jewish art from the developments in the post-Renaissance period. Here the *Akedah*, the Sacrifice of Isaac, continues to appear; for instance, on ceremonial silver and in illustrated manuscripts such as the Sarajevo Passover Haggadah. On the silverware the function of the scene is clearly symbolic, but it would be quite incorrect to conclude that for this reason it must have the same meaning and function wherever it appears at this time. In the Passover Haggadah the scene is equally clearly non-symbolic, because in the manuscript it is part of a cycle narrating the events from the creation to Moses. Of course scenes can pass from one type of context to another, but in changing context they are also likely to change function.

169. See below, pp. 392–398.

In antiquity the scene of the Sacrifice of Isaac appears not only in the Dura Synagogue but also in the Beth Alpha mosaic and on a hitherto unpublished gem. (Pl. XL, 4).[170] In all three contexts its symbolic character, as the classic instance of the exemplary piety that merits the divine forgiveness, is assured. Indeed we may presume that when Biblical scenes appear separately, their value is normally symbolic.[171] But as we see from the analogy above, this does not imply that all Biblical scenes portrayed anywhere in ancient Jewish art are necessarily symbolic in character and function. Indeed where scenes appear in large cycles the presumption would be the opposite, especially if it seems probable that they come out of a manuscript tradition and in this manuscript tradition served to illustrate a sequence of historic events. In the Dura Synagogue once the Sacrifice of Isaac had acquired its new relation to the narrative scenes in the second phase of the decorations, it also took on a new, second function. It became part of a narrative sequence leading from the Promise to its fulfilment in the days of the Messianic King.[172]

170. See above, p. 58, n. 130.
171. So, e.g., the scene of Daniel in the lions' den in the Na'aran mosaic and that of the sons of Noah in the Gerasa mosaic.
172. See above, p. 223.

III. TECHNIQUE, STYLE, AND COMPOSITION OF THE SYNAGOGUE PAINTINGS

Beyond doubt the paintings of the Dura Synagogue are among the most important monuments of the late Roman wall decoration that we know today. This will be evident in a rudimentary way to anyone who has visited the National Museum at Damascus, where the Synagogue's House of Assembly has been rebuilt in its entirety and where the full impact of the richly colored wall surfaces and the comprehensiveness of their decorations are clearly revealed. But to appraise in all its details the nature of their importance and the contribution they make to the history of art generally will take many years and require the services of experts in many fields. The present chapter is intended to supply the material for that appraisal by describing the more salient features of the style and composition of the scenes. Since their number and the excellence of their preservation makes it possible to know something also about the techniques which the artists used in their execution, a brief word on this subject will be in order at the outset.

A. Technique and Materials

The Synagogue paintings are executed upon a plaster base made of a rather crude grade of burned gypsum or calcium sulphate, containing a considerable amount of clay and silica impurity and many small particles of a variety of calcium sulphate known as anhydrite.[173] The paint was applied to the plaster by the use of the *al secco* method, but what the vehicle was is not precisely known. In all probability it was of the gum or egg-white type. In preparing to execute their paintings, the artists first laid out the surface of each wall horizontally into registers and then vertically into panels. The registers and fields were apparently not outlined by scratch lines, but seem to have been defined with charcoal or thin painted lines which were later covered by the heavy painted panel and register bands. Scratch lines do appear inside the fields of Register C and of the Lower Center Panel, presumably as part of the preparation for the first phase of the decoration of the chamber.[174]

Working from the top of each wall down toward the base,[175] the artists first sketched the outlines of the several figures and objects projected for each composition in charcoal or with a paint brush, apportioning space in accordance with the type of subject matter presented and with the number of scenes needed to complete the action. A good demonstration of the use of this procedure is provided in Wing Panel I (Moses and the Burning Bush) where a series of dark lines, partly correcting one another and outlining the round of Moses' hair, have been brought into view by the flaking of the paint representing the hair itself. In setting out their material the artists moved with great assurance and with a particularly clear understanding of how to reduce a scene to its minimum essentials and still make it tell its story. There are relatively few points in the entire series of compositions where the meaning of scenes can have been obscure to their contemporaries, and none showing bad judgment in the distribution of the component elements. What recomposition occurred at the east end of Panel NC 1 (Ezekiel, the Destruction and Restoration of National Life) and in the area of the Center Panels is to be ascribed to changes in the instructions issued to the artists rather than to any dissatisfaction with the original organization of the material. Whether in developing their compositions

173. The chemical analysis of the plaster has been supplied by Mr. Rutherford J. Gettens, formerly of the Fogg Museum.

174. There are no traces of scratch lines under the painted register and panel bands. It will be recalled that the artists responsible for the first phase of the decoration of the room were others than those who executed the murals (see above, p. 65), and that they never completed the original program. It should be noted that scratch lines were used by the artists of the second phase of the decorations in shaping the circular medallions of the dado (see above, p. 240, n. 964).

175. See above, p. 68.

the artists worked from sketches is of course not known, but certain features of their work suggest that they knew or visualized more extensive series of episodes which they here abbreviated and combined to produce the resultant pictures.[176]

Once a given composition, its elements tentatively outlined, had gained the approval of the artists and their employers, the outlines were firmly drawn in color and thereby fixed as parts of the picture. The use of such painted outlines is shown by the occasional departure from them; for instance, in the rendering of the left hind leg of Mordecai's horse in Panel WC 2, where the background color was extended over the area originally outlined, the leg thus being reshaped. As the third step in the execution of each panel the areas outside the figures and objects were painted with washes of varying intensity to provide a colored background. After the background had been filled in, the artists next proceeded to paint the figures and objects, working here without benefit of much detail in the underlying design.[177] The several major elements of each figure or object were first supplied with the basic color selected for its further rendering; for instance, the head, neck, hands, and feet of human beings with red; the garments with the color chosen as appropriate, especially white in the case of many occurrences of chiton and himation. Upon the areas thus coated with the basic color, other colors were superimposed to delineate detail. Brown or black strokes set against the red background outlined the eyes, nose, and mouth. Darkened basic colors, complementary colors, or contrasting colors were applied in wide sweeps to show the drapery. Shading was provided by applying additional strokes of darker colors, particularly at the right of the head and legs. Finally accents and highlights to enliven the figures were scattered about in black and white as the artists' fancy dictated, and patterns woven into the cloth of the robes were indicated.

The execution of the face is a particularly good example of the procedure used by the Synagogue artists (Pl. XLVIII). Faces are never modeled but are built up by the addition of element after ele-

ment, and are never individualized but only varied by the introduction of supplementary materials to suit the artists' purpose and their iconographic patterns.[178] In shape faces are basically oval, the chin continuing the rounded contours of the upper part of the head. Normally they are shown frontally, but there is usually enough departure from absolute frontality to bring one of the ears into view.[179] What the formula was for the rendering of the features can best be seen from the company of the redeemed in Section B of Panel NC 1, where it appears in its simplest form (Pl. XLVIII, 3). To provide the features of the face the artist had to superimpose upon the prepared flesh-colored surface eleven brush strokes and two dots, the latter for the pupils of the eyes. The brush strokes in question are: the one outlining the chin, the one outlining the one eyebrow and going on to provide also the outline for the nose, the one for the second eyebrow, the four that frame the eyes at the top and bottom, the two that outline the upper eyelids, and the two that mark the line of the mouth and the projecting underlip. The formula is used throughout the Synagogue, and dependence upon such formulae is typical of the style of its artists.

The differences that exist between faces in the Synagogue derive from the addition of supplementary detail. Some supplements are added indiscriminately at the artists' pleasure. Others go with certain types of persons and with certain types of dress. They are not difficult to list. One of the commonest supplements is the application of a darkened form of the flesh color to the cheek, the chin, and the shoulder at the right side of the face to provide an element of shadow. Good examples are to be found in the scene of the Prophets of Baal (Panel SC 3) and of Samuel Anointing David (Panel WC 3). In certain instances (for example, in the Wing Panels portraying Ezra and Abraham, Wing Panels III and IV) the nose also receives a shadow line at the right, but this is rather unusual. Hair is supplied in accordance with the demands of sex and of type of costume. For all men wearing chiton and himation (with one exception) and for all women save the flying Psyches a short head of

---

176. See below, pp. 387–390.
177. Where the helpers participated in the rendering of detail, execution sometimes falls below the standards of composition (see below, p. 381).

178. On the latter see below, pp. 371–373.
179. On the few instances of profile rendering in the Synagogue, see below, p. 374.

hair is provided.[180] It consists of a cap-like mass of the type found also in the Antioch mosaics, to which short projecting strokes are added at top and bottom to represent curls or separate strands.[181] In the case of men wearing the Iranian dress (short tunic and trousers) the hair is a large aureole that frames the entire face, rather than merely the top of the head. The coiffure is represented at an earlier date at Dura in the Konon frescoes and is now known also from the sculptures of Hatra.[182] Here it is built up with great care on a brown base surcharged with dark brown curls often outlined in black.

The techniques used in the execution of their paintings are by no means the invention of the Synagogue artists. At Dura these techniques had already been observed and described by Hopkins in dealing with the Banquet and Hunting Scene of the private house in Block M7 before the Synagogue was discovered, and they have since been recognized as typical for all mural decorations at the site.[183]

The colors available to the Synagogue artists were distinctly limited in number, consisting apparently of black (lamp or soot black), brick red (red ochre), light red (ferric oxide), pink, bright yellow, brown (brown ochre with hydrous ferric oxide), blue (blue copper frit), and green (not copper, but green clay earth different from terre verte).[184] The basic colors were varied by being darkened or by being reduced to washes, but at Dura they were not mixed to provide the gradations of shades that were used in the West where figures or objects were modeled.

At least two different types of brushes were available to the artists, of which the smaller, used in delineation of outline and detail, is the more noteworthy. This seems to have been a medium soft-pointed brush *ca.* 7.5 mm. in diameter that held sufficient paint to execute strokes up to half a meter in length without replenishing. Normally it drew lines *ca.* 3 mm. wide, but it could also be used for lines half or twice as wide. Brush strokes are usually continuous and flowing, rather than short and dauby, and all objects and figures are invariably contained within finished and closed outlines, emphasizing the linear aspect of the artists' style.[185]

B. Composition and Style

Even a cursory inspection of the Dura Synagogue paintings will yield a clear impression about one essential element of their character; namely, the forcefulness with which they address themselves directly to the viewer. As others have already pointed out, we are leagues removed here from the picturesque, naturalistic art of the Hellenistic world with its gracefully poised and charmingly draped figures, its rich and varied landscapes, its interplay of light and shade, and its effort to find and enjoy beauty in and above all things.[186] Similarly we are leagues removed from the realistic and descriptive art of the historical Roman bas-reliefs with their painstaking attention to accuracy in the rendering of setting, racial types, and the dress, arms, and equipment proper to them. Instead we are confronted, purposely so, with a galaxy of hieratically posed or solidly massed figures whose basic function it is to impress and to communicate the importance and the grandeur of the personages and events portrayed. In this respect the Synagogue paintings belong essentially to the age-old tradition of ancient Oriental art.

180. The exception, Ezekiel in his fourth and fifth appearances in Panel NC 1, has been explained above, p. 194.

181. See Doro Levi, *Antioch Mosaic Pavements*, I, p. 552. Abraham in Wing Panel IV provides a good example of the cap-like mass of hair (Pl. LXXVIII).

182. See Cumont, *Fouilles*, Pl. XLVII. For the Hatra sculptures, see now the report by H. Ingholt, *Memoirs of the Connecticut Academy of Arts and Sciences*, XII (1954).

183. See *Rep. VI*, pp. 163–167; and for a more comprehensive statement, Rostovtzeff, *YCS*, V (1935), pp. 256 f. Hopkins has noted that the same procedure was followed in the paintings of the Assyrian palace at Tell Ahmar (*Rep. VI*, p. 164).

184. A full analysis of Dura pigments has been prepared by Mr. R. J. Gettens, formerly of the Fogg Museum, for the comprehensive final report on the paintings of the city.

185. The material for these observations on technique was provided by Messrs. Nicholas Toll, Herbert Gute, and Andrew Petryn of the staff of the Yale University Art Gallery and of its School of Design.

186. M. Aubert, *Gazette des beaux-arts*, LXXX (XX) (1938), pp. 1–24.

But it will also be obvious that the Synagogue paintings reflect the artistic tradition of the ancient Orient in their own particular way. Between them and the last great imperial art of the Near East, the Achaemenian, lie centuries of development. During the intervening period the Orient had changed, and traditions stemming from, or developed in, various parts of the world had had occasion to meet and intermingle in a great variety of ways. Only an analysis of the major features of their style and composition can indicate the nature of the peculiar fusion represented by the Synagogue paintings and thus help assign them to their rightful place in the development of the art of the later Orient.

I. STRIP ORGANIZATION AND COMPARTMENTALIZATION

To organize the decoration of the Synagogue the artists decided to divide the large wall surfaces of the House of Assembly horizontally into a succession of registers. In so doing they adopted a scheme appropriate to the pictorial compositions and in keeping with the time-honored traditions of ancient decorative art.[187] Those traditions were still being honored generally at Dura, as the paintings of the Temple of Bel, the Temple of Zeus Theos, and the Christian Chapel show. But in the Synagogue, as in the latest additions to the decoration of the Temple of Bel, the divisions between the pictorial zones are indicated not by architectural or other suggestive means, but by heavy black register bands that leave no illusion as to their purpose. At the same time the artists divided the registers into compartments by similarly uncompromising panel bands. Thus each pictorial composition is completely framed and contained, and the fields are strictly delimited in accordance with a practice not unfamiliar in the older Orient but certainly especially well-known from its later monuments.[188] But with this pattern of wall organ-

ization the Synagogue artists have combined an element projected originally as a part of the earlier scheme of the chamber's decoration; namely, the painted corner pilasters represented at the ends of each of the four walls in the two upper registers. In combination with the painted architraves along the top of the walls, the beams, and the decorated tiles of the ceiling, they represent a vine trellis. Such trellises we know from quite different systems of wall decoration, in which they had the opposite function; namely, of acting as a frame for efforts to break down spatial limitation and to create the illusion of distant prospects and open vistas.[189]

2. BACKGROUND. SPATIAL DEPTH, AND CAST SHADOWS

How they treated the space they had so carefully enclosed in their panels is one of the interesting aspects of the Synagogue artists' work. Naturally one would not expect them to paint landscapes and wide panoramas, for these are typically the products of other parts of the ancient world and had nothing to contribute to the purposes of synagogue decoration. Instead, in the majority of cases we find figures and objects represented against a monochrome background without any indication of depth of space. The colored backgrounds drop like curtains from the upper edges of the frames, shutting the figures in from the rear quite as effectively as they are shut in by the frames of the panel. This has the effect of giving the compositions a two-dimensional character. Of the figures represented, those presumably closest at hand are assigned positions near the base of the panel, while those more remote are placed in the upper parts of the field. This is, of course, the common practice in ancient Oriental art generally and finds its best example in the Synagogue in the arrangement of the files of soldiers guarding the Ark in the scene of the Battle of Eben-ezer (Panel

187. Cumont (*Fouilles*, pp. 147 f.) and others have already pointed in this connection to the decorations of the Babylonian and Assyrian palaces and monuments.

188. Others have already pointed to the obelisk of Shalmaneser and the votive plaques as examples of the early appearance of compartmentalization. For the later period reference can be made to the Hellenistic temples of Egypt. See G. Jéquier, *Les Temples ptolémaïques et romains* (1924), Pls. 6, 7 (Karnak); 27, 30 (Edfu); 45, 46,

50 (Kom Ombo); 70 (Denderah); and in general, R. Hamann, *Ägyptische Kunst* (1944), p. 297. See also the reliefs of Shapur I at Shapur (Sarre and Herzfeld, *Iranische Felsreliefs*, esp. Pl. XLIII); and the scenes from the life of Buddha in the stupas at Sikri and Sanchi (H. Buchtal, *Journal of the Royal Asiatic Society*, 1943, pp. 137–148 and Pls. V–XIV). On the tendency of later Roman art to break down wall surfaces into geometric fields, see Wirth, *Römische Wandmalerei*, pp. 129–142.

189. See above, p. 38, n. 14.

NB 1). Naturally there is no attempt either to maintain a consistent proportion between the size of objects and persons or even between the several persons of a composition in relation to their distance from each other.

While fifteen of the Synagogue compositions had monochrome backgrounds to begin with, and the two Center Panels received them in the last stage of their decoration, there are eleven in which the treatment of the background is varied somewhat. These deserve separate consideration.

Of the group of eleven, three invite attention at the outset if only because they are the simplest to understand. In each instance a relatively narrow strip along the base of the composition is rendered in a color different from the rest of the background. So, in Panel NB 1 (Battle of Eben-ezer) we have a green strip 0.26 m. high running along the base of a composition with a red background; in Panel WB 2 (Consecration of the Tabernacle and its Priests) there is a zone some 0.40 m. high before and on either side of the temenos wall of the Tabernacle, reddish in color and darker than the yellow used to set off the rest of the composition; and finally in Wing Panel IV (Abraham Receives the Promise) a strip of yellowish brown running up to the lower tips of Abraham's himation contrasts with the faded blue of the background color used above. In all three instances we seem to have examples of a simple form of depth representation known as "stage space," a device familiar from Hellenistic and Roman wall painting and perhaps typical especially of the earlier efforts to achieve depth and perspective in Hellenistic art.[190] It should be noted in this connection, however, that the element of "stage space" thus provided is actually used only in the right half of Panel NB 1 where the green field serves as the background for a file of warring infantrymen, and its upper edge provides a base line for the emplacement of the confronted riders.

In a second group of panels; namely, NA 1 (Jacob at Bethel), EC 1 (David and Saul in the Wilderness of Ziph), Wing Panel II (Moses Receives the Law), and WC 4 (Pharaoh and the In-

190. On the early date of its appearance and the monuments attributable to the third century B.C. upon which "stage space" is found, see C. Dawson, *YCS*, IX (1944), pp. 16–21.

fancy of Moses), the narrow band of foreground is painted descriptively and in keeping with the demands of the narrative. In the first of these the green foreground, which stops short at the ladder mounting to heaven, is overlaid with a reddish brown area upon which angular brown lines appear to show that the place was stony, as the story explicitly says. A similar convention is used in the central section of Panel EC 1, where Abner is shown asleep in the Wilderness of Ziph, guarding Saul. It being night, the background of the upper part of the scene is again dark, probably black. The foreground, done in red, has superimposed upon it a series of semicircular brown lines to indicate mountain ridges. It is upon this mountainous terrain that Abner and the host are supposed to rest, and this for a very compelling reason; namely, because the Biblical story says that the host encamped "upon the hill of Hachilah" (I Sam. 26.3). In both cases, then, the artists have developed the foreground descriptively in an effort to do the maximum justice to the details of the Biblical narrative.

Not greatly different, but perhaps interesting is the descriptive element in Wing Panel II, where the lower, yellow part of the composition is not an area artificially defined by a horizontal or diagonal line but a mass whose outlines curve toward a peak at the right. If, as we have every reason to believe, the Gute copies are correct, there was even an indication of a plant or shrub upon the upward slope near its peak. The intention of the artist in this instance is scarcely debatable. He was trying in simple but effective manner to make his composition include a representation of the locale of the episode, which occurred, of course, on Mount Sinai.

Perhaps the most descriptive in this group of panels is WC 4 (Pharaoh and the Infancy of Moses). Here, it will be recalled, we have along the base of the composition a representation of the Nile. It flows along as a horizontal band between a foreground strip that is yellowish brown and the background of the picture as a whole, which is red. The foreground strip may have been included to make sure that the water would be interpreted as a stream, and its color may even have been chosen with due regard to proprieties for river banks. Certainly the artist went to some trouble to convey his meaning by indicating the presence of reeds along the banks of the river, and even added reddish lines to suggest ripples in the water. He is obviously trying to construct the proper setting for the Biblical story but goes beyond the necessities in one particular; namely, in supplying a city at the right end of the composition. That in terms of the wider context of the story portrayed it must represent one of the cities built by the Children of Israel, we have already indicated.[191] But since the specific events depicted do not actually require the inclusion of a city, it seems possible to argue that its representation was suggested by a traditional landscape pattern familiar to the artist.[192]

Still a third group of compositions requires attention here because of its treatment of background. The group comprises the Panels WB 4 (Ark in the Land of the Philistines), WA 3 (Exodus and Crossing of the Red Sea), and WB 1 (Wilderness Encampment and the Miraculous Well of Be'er). In the left half of the first of these we find the Ark mounted upon a cart being drawn by two oxen. The notable features of this part of the panel are two; namely, first the fact that the oxen, their drivers, and the attending princes or diviners of the Philistines are so arranged as to overlap each other in ascending planes; and second, the representation under the cart and the oxen of darker brown strips arranged in the form of a *T*. These strips represent the fork in the road of which the popular rendering of the Biblical narrative speaks.[193] To be properly understood in relation to the rest of the composition they must be interpreted as a cartographic rendering.

The panel depicting the Exodus and Crossing of the Red Sea (WA 3) also contains unusual features. We need not linger over the heavy black band outlined above and below with red which the artists have introduced to represent the cloud. It is not part of a realistic rendering of the sky, for the scene lacks a horizon line, but serves merely as a descriptive part of the setting required by the narrative. The important feature for us here is the succession of horizontal stripes in the third scene of the panel, representing the walls of water into

which the Red Sea was divided. These walls are to be thought of as standing at either side of parallel files of soldiers and Elders as they march through the sea.[194] Here again the rendering is cartographic, and the composition must therefore be viewed horizontally and vertically at the same time to be properly understood.

The panel showing the Wilderness Encampment and Miraculous Well of Be'er is analogous to the foregoing. Its tents and persons are rendered *en face*, but the space occupied by the encampment is not. The encampment, it will be recalled, is carefully described in the Biblical narrative as a square with tents on all four sides. The laws of frontality may have prevented the artists from arranging the tents in accordance with the demands of the story, but to compensate for this they introduced into the composition the yellow zones or stripes that frame the pink background on all four sides of the central feature. These give the shape of the encampment, which is thus also rendered cartographically.

The treatment of backgrounds in the Dura Synagogue compositions is therefore by no means uniform or elementary. Those painted solidly with a single color predominate, but alongside them we have an almost equal number in which supplementary features have been added. The supplementary features are not the invention of the Synagogue artists but conventions which have a history in other and earlier phases of ancient art. The earlier appearance of the device of "stage space" in Hellenistic art, with or without the addition of descriptive detail, has already been mentioned above.[195] The combination of vertical and horizontal perspective in rendering the elements of a single scene is known from Roman monuments of the second century and from the third-century mosaics of Antioch and has been followed as a factor in the developments of the post-Constantinian period by Doro Levi.[196] Here, then, methods

---

191. See above, p. 173.

192. On architectural landscapes see the article of Rostovtzeff, *Röm. Mitt.*, XXVI (1911), pp. 1–185; and Dawson, *YCS*, IX (1944).

193. See above, p. 105.

194. See above, p. 85.

195. See above, p. 368, n. 190.

196. See Hill, *Marsyas*, I, p. 4; and Levi, *Antioch Mosaic Pavements*, I, pp. 608–614. Contemporary with the Synagogue paintings at Antioch is the simultaneous representation of the elements of a ceiling and of the brackets of a wall under the ceiling in a mosaic on the triclinium of the House of the Boat of the Psyches, *ibid.*, II, Pl. XXXV.

and devices not traditional in the Orient are used by the Synagogue artists in their handling of background, but the use to which they are put is entirely descriptive. They were needed to bring out the salient points of the Biblical stories. In presenting these stories the artists never went out of their way to create settings imaginatively. They were not tempted to develop the interior of the upper room to which Elijah takes the widow's child (Panel WC 1), or the street of Susa along which Mordecai rides in triumph (Panel WC 2), or the audience chamber in which Ahasuerus receives Mordecai (*ibid.*). Instead their approach was analytical, and if analysis of the story showed that a certain element of setting was required, they proceeded to cope with it using whatever means were available to them to represent it.

As to the monochrome background used in the majority of the scenes, we would not wish to imply that it has only a negative function, the denial of a positive interest in space. This might be true if all had the same color. Actually, of course, they are done in a great variety of colors: red, green, bright yellow, black (to indicate night), and even white. From this it would seem to follow that they also had a positive function to fulfil; namely, to add richness to the total effect of the decorations. If so they represent another step in the direction of mediaeval art, where color as applied to background is so important a factor in decorative work.[197]

A word must be added here on the subject of cast shadows. Familiar as features of late Hellenic and early Hellenistic painting, they represent one of the earliest steps along the road that leads to naturalism in the rendering of pictorial subject matter. In the Synagogue their occurrence is distinctly noticeable, but quite unpredictable. So, for instance, they are used in Wing Panels I and IV, but not on II and III. We have no knowledge of their presence in the paintings of the east, south, and north walls, though this may be due to chance. On the west wall they appear in WA 1 (unidentified scene), WA 3 (Exodus and Crossing of the Red Sea), and WB 2 (Consecration of the Tabernacle and its Priests). An examination of the relation between occurrence and non-occurrence suggests that they are never employed where dark backgrounds are used, that they are never used in connection with objects or seated figures, and never in the representation of women. Their normal use would seem to be with individual standing male figures set against a light background. When the artists at their discretion decided to introduce cast shadows, they did so consistently throughout a given panel. So, for instance, in WB 2 (Consecration of the Tabernacle and its Priests) each of the men except Aaron and each of the standing animals has his own cast shadow. It would appear from use and disuse that, while the artists knew the convention well, other factors than those of the representation of spatial depth could and did affect its use. Here it is important only to point out that in the contemporary development of pictorial art in Italy, and as close to Dura as Syrian Antioch, the representation of cast shadows, and indeed of light and shade elsewhere than in the impressionistic rendering of figures and objects *per sè*, had been reduced to a triviality and was soon to disappear entirely.[198] The form that cast shadows seem normally to take in the middle of the third century is that of separate short dark masses attaching themselves to the heels of standing or striding figures.[199] The shadows shown in the Synagogue are of a different character, in effect an inverted *V*, and seem fundamentally unrelated in form to the figure to which they are attached. They are evidently a cliché at this time, but originally would have been applicable to figures shown in movement and either nude or wearing only a short chiton. In view of the care with which cast shadows are rendered in such compositions as the Alexander Mosaic, and of what we know further about the development of skiagraphy as applied to the human body itself, it is interesting to speculate whether the cast shadows of the Synagogue are not borrowed ultimately from Hellenistic paintings (military funerary stelae?) and preserved as a stereotype in the Eastern repertory of form.[200]

197. See in this connection what Levi has said about the function of light in the post-Hadrianic period, *ibid.*, I, p. 606.

198. See especially *ibid.*, p. 608.

199. See, e.g., Wirth, *Römische Wandmalerei*, Pl. XLI, b; and Levi, *Antioch Mosaic Pavements*, II, Pls. XLVIII, a, b; XLIX, a, b.

200. In the Alexander Mosaic note, for instance, the accuracy with which the shadow of the boot and trouser of the man directly in front of the wheel of Darius' chariot

3. REPRESENTATION OF HUMAN FIGURES

The absence of all but a minimum of setting makes the figures of the Dura Synagogue paintings loom particularly large, as their most important elements. This is, of course, in keeping with the traditions of all ancient art, save only for the brief episode of impressionistic landscape painting, and is only natural in a narrative context in which so much depends upon the actors if the action is to be portrayed convincingly. Seen in its entirety the Synagogue's House of Assembly presents a galaxy of the great and near-great of Biblical record, including Abraham, Isaac, Jacob, Joseph and the rest of Jacob's sons, Moses and Aaron, Hannah, Samuel, Saul, David, and Solomon among those who helped establish the kingdom; Elijah, Ezekiel, Mordecai, and Esther among those who saw it subjected to unusual strains from without and within; Ezra, under whom the nation was finally rededicated to the piety of its founders; and the company of the faithful of the entire post-patriarchal period.

The artists labored diligently to make this great array of historical persons identifiable to the beholder and apparently found their efforts so successful that they gave up the practice of labeling the figures with *tituli* before they had gone far in their work. Even today we have in general no great difficulty in determining the *dramatis personae* of a given composition. The procedure by which this end is achieved is worthy of closer scrutiny. There was never in the artists' minds any thought of individualized, portrait-type representation, and all efforts to find in any one of the faces or figures the likeness of an historic person, such as the Elder Samuel, are thoroughly misguided.[201] Nor was there ever any consideration of realism in the modern sense of the word; that is, any thought of representing various persons in the costume proper to the period and the nationality to which they belonged. Hence in the Battle of Eben-ezer,

the Philistine and the Israelite infantry and cavalry are identically attired and armed; Pharaoh, David, and Ahasuerus are interchangeable; and Moses, Samuel, Ezra, and the Prophets of Baal are rendered in the same way as the people of Susa. The artists commonly determine the size of persons by the amount of space available and the number of people to be represented in it, using the principle of isocephalism in the rendering of groups. They give no thought either to perspective or to the relative size of persons and objects such as city walls, temples, and tents.

If the absence of a realistic tendency does not lead to monotony and rigid uniformity of representation in the Synagogue paintings, this is because other factors are involved which have yet to be considered. So in matters of size isocephalism can be and is abandoned if the Biblical narrative specifies a person of unusual size, or if the artist wishes to imply that a given person is of paramount importance for the events portrayed. A good example of the former is Abner in Panel EC 1, and of the latter, Moses in the scene of the Exodus and Crossing of the Red Sea (Panel WA 3). In other respects variety is introduced by the use of separate iconographic patterns for various types or categories of persons. From a knowledge of the type of person represented, from size as an indication of relative importance, and from the relation between the action or the objects portrayed and the Biblical story, it is usually quite easy to identify the subject of a given composition.

For men the artists have available basically four different patterns. The first and to us the most familiar type is that of the men wearing chiton, himation, and sandals. They are normally seen standing, facing full front, the left arm held close to the side of the body to manage the ends of the himation rolled about it, the right performing some gesture.[202] With this garment there goes normally a short head of hair. Facial hair is optional and may consist either of mustache alone or of mustache and full beard. The type is used for prophets, elders, civilian leaders, and laymen — in fact, for all but members of special classes still to

is rendered (see Pfuhl, *Malerei und Zeichnung*, III, pp. 267f.). On the development of modeling by color gradation and its application at first only to male figures, see, e.g., *ibid.*, pp. 120–123. Shadows seem to appear on some of the painted military stelae found at Sidon; e.g., *Revue biblique*, N. S. I (1904), Pl. XII, 4. It is not entirely clear whether the cast shadow in Levi, *Antioch Mosaic Pavements*, II, Pl. L, d, is of the same type as that used by the Synagogue artists.

201. See above, p. 234.

202. Exceptions to the standing position are the reclining Elijah of Panel WC 1, the Jacob of the Lower Center Panel, the recumbent Jacob of Panel NA 1, and the seated counsellor of Panel WA 2.

24*

be specified. It is obvious that the type is ultimately Greek in origin, representing a Western contribution to the art of the Near East. It could have been adopted in the Orient from the direct observation of those among the Macedonian settlers who upheld the tradition and dress of the Greek citizen. But with equal facility the type could have been copied at the outset from statues or other works of art imported or fashioned by imported artists in honor of distinguished citizens of the Greek cities of the Orient. The fundamental uniformity of the type and the close analogy that it shows to such familiar classical prototypes as the standing orator, philosopher, and dramatist (compare the well-known Sophocles and Demosthenes) suggests the latter alternative.

For men the second iconographic type is that used for all court and Temple personnel. In this instance the costume consists fundamentally of a short belted tunic, trousers, and soft white boots. Where kings are portrayed there is added to this basic costume a wide flowing coat, or in the case of special messengers a chlamys. In the one exceptional case of Aaron a cloak covers the sleeved coat. With this costume goes a short dagger worn at the left hip, save in the case of Temple personnel. Kings wear with the costume a diadem or soft pointed cap or both, and courtiers of higher rank armbands. The hair of those who wear such costumes is invariably arranged in curls to form a large aureole about the entire head. It hangs down behind the head at the neck, where in one instance we see it gathered into a roll (Mordecai in the audience scene at the right side of the Esther panel, Panel WC 2). The costume is found in Western art only where Oriental figures are portrayed (e.g., Mithras), but is commonly represented on the monuments of Palmyra, Commagene, Edessa, Dura, Hatra, Persia, Elymais, and Turkestan and has properly been said by Seyrig to have gained its vogue in the Near East under Parthian influence and during the period of Parthian supremacy.[203]

For the representation of soldiers of the line the artists had three different iconographic patterns, no doubt a witness to the clash of political interests in northern Mesopotamia in the early centuries of our era and at the same time a testimony to the wide diversity of the units currently serving in the Roman frontier forces along the Euphrates. Of the three, that employed in the scene portraying the Battle of Eben-ezer (Panel NB 1) and consisting of a sleeved mail or scale hauberk descending to the knees, close-fitting trousers, and short boots, is probably Iranian in origin.[204] The other two, that of the execution at the right end of Panel NC 1 and that of the Exodus (Panel WA 3), are probably Roman adaptations of Hellenistic and Greek prototypes. The former consists of cuirass with *pteryges*, high plumed helmet, and chlamys; while the latter brings together a shirt of mail or scale armor, knobbed helmet, spear, oval shield, high boots, and close-fitting trousers.

In the case of servants the iconographic formula called for a simple belted tunic, normally supplied with two *clavi* and girded up at the waist, and for the one "royal" servant or stable-boy (Haman in Panel WC 2), an extra short tunic with a single *clavus* and a wide belt.

Among the women several types of rendering must again be distinguished. Here we have first of all the "mothers in Israel," such as the widow with the dead child (Panel WC 1), Hannah (Panel NB 2), and Jochebed and Miriam (Panel WC 4). Their dress consists of a plain chiton with elbow-length sleeves, a woman's himation with one end fastened over the left shoulder with a brooch and the other end draped over the head to form a veil, shoes, and either stockings or long drawers. The type is common at Palmyra and elsewhere and is definitely of Oriental origin.[205] For queens such as Esther (Panel WC 2) and presumably the Queen of Sheba (Panel WA 2) a sleeveless bodice, a long flowing skirt, a cloak, and a veil are indicated. The costume seems to be inspired by Hellenistic models and may not be unrelated in part to that represented on the famous Tyche of Antioch, as the mural crown that Esther wears suggests. So far as undergarments are concerned, the costume is analogous to that worn by the ladies-in-waiting who attend Pharaoh's daughter in the scene of the Infancy of Moses (Panel WC 4), which in turn, as we have seen, is an Oriental adaptation of the Greek peplos with high-girded kolpos. With all of these costumes goes

203. *Syria*, XVIII (1937), pp. 4–31.

204. See *Rep. VI*, p. 451.
205. See Ingholt, *Studier over Palmyrensk Skulptur*, p. 52.

a simple coiffure in which the ends of the hair hang in curls at the base of the neck. In the flying Psyches of Panel NC 1, finally, we have a thoroughly Greek garment, the Greek peplos of Paionius' Nike, represented with only slight modification and with a coiffure that is equally traditional.

A combination of Eastern and Western elements, of types taken from Iranian, Greek, and Roman art, the repertoire of form used by the Synagogue artists was wide indeed and provided a convenient way of differentiating between not a few of the persons whom they were called upon to portray. For our purposes here, it is important to determine how these types were handled stylistically and whether the treatment is homogeneous throughout or differs with the different models.

In the proportions of their male figures the Synagogue artists have generally hit a happy medium between elongation and compression. Scale is varied to indicate importance, as has been pointed out above, but proportions are varied only in the direction of a certain stockiness noticeable, for instance, in the thick-set Moses of the Burning Bush Panel (Wing Panel I), and of the Exodus composition (Panel WA 3). As for the women it will be evident that of those whom we have called "mothers in Israel," Hannah (Panel NB 2) and the widow of the Elijah scenes (Panels SC 2 and WC 1) are unusually buxom and broad-hipped, compared for instance to the Psyches, Pharaoh's daughter, and her ladies-in-waiting. The difference may well go with the model that was being followed: the one Oriental, the other ultimately Hellenistic.

The figures of the Synagogue paintings can further be said to be fundamentally linear in character, each person being carefully outlined, fully contained within a solid frame, and sharply defined as to all his major features. Linearity is a standard phenomenon at Dura, as we have seen, can be traced back there to the earliest of the Konon frescoes, and has its roots in old Oriental usage.[206] With linearity there goes a certain rigidity of pose. By far the greatest number of the figures stand stiffly vertical facing the beholder, the weight of the body resting on one foot, which is seen in profile, while the other is *en face* and appears to

point downward, the left arm held close to the body, and the other making some kind of simple gesture.[207] Departures from the standard pose can readily be itemized. In the case of men wearing chiton and himation the most common departures are those which show them reclining, as noted above.[208] The reclining figure is a separate iconographic type, forming the central feature of the banquet scenes familiar from countless funerary reliefs at Palmyra and throughout the Greek world.[209] So far as the figure in chiton and himation is concerned, it would therefore seem probable that the Synagogue artists had two iconographic types at their disposal: the reclining figure and the standing figure, the former familiar to them from banquet scenes, the other essentially that of the standing philosopher or man of letters.[210] Throughout their work the Synagogue artists followed these models with only slight deviations.

So far as the figures in Iranian dress are concerned, the artists were seemingly less narrowly bound. The tunics they wear leave the men somewhat freer to move their arms, and a much greater variety of poses results. The way in which the arms sway loosely in the Ezekiel Panel (NC 1) is perhaps extreme. More characteristic is the pose in which the right arm is doubled back against the body while the left rests akimbo (e.g., Panel WB 2). More important still, these figures can hold objects (keys, writing tablets, trumpets), swing an axe or a whip, and move in processions. Though seen largely *en face*, they occasionally depart from the rigid perpen-

206. See Cumont, *Fouilles*, p. 49, Pls. XXXII–XXXIII.

207. As to which foot carries the weight of the body, this is determined by practical considerations of position in the decorations, or by the relations between two or more persons in a given composition. So in the Wing Panels the figures at the right of the Center Panels have their weight on the right foot, and those at the left on the left foot. In the Mordecai and Esther panel (WC 2), the people of Susa, intended to be taken as witnesses to Mordecai's triumph at their right, rest their weight on their right foot. The diagrammatic rendering of the foot which makes it seem to point downward is as old at Dura as the earliest Konon frescoes (see Cumont, *Fouilles*, Pl. XXXI).

208. See above, p. 371, n. 202.

209. See now Seyrig, *Les Annales archéologiques de Syrie*, I (1951), pp. 32–40.

210. In the example of Ezra reading the Law (Wing Panel III) the relation to the prototype becomes particularly clear from the way the head is held, from the way the right hip is set out from the perpendicular to give grace to the pose, and from the relation between the figure and the scroll chest standing beside it.

dicular, a slight sway coming into the body, and can even be shown three-quarters front when moving.[211] In addition there are in Iranian dress, confidently executed as to pose, kings mounted on chargers and seated on thrones in audience, charging cavalrymen and infantrymen engaged in single combat, ox-cart drivers, and stable-boys. What this greater variety of pose and mobility in the figures wearing Iranian dress means with respect to the artists themselves, to the richness of their Iranian pattern-book, or to the character of late Iranian art itself, is not clear. It has been suggested by Hopkins that Iranian costume appears with two different types of trousers, the one baggy and full, the other close-fitting — the former being Sassanian, the latter Parthian.[212] Such a difference occurs also in the Synagogue, and can be illustrated by the contrast between the representation of Mordecai in the audience scene of Panel WC 2 or the Ezekiels of Section A of Panel NC 1, on the one side; and Aaron's sons in Panel WB 2 or the drivers of the ox-cart in Panel WB 4, on the other. Conceivably, the variety of pose and rendering in the figures wearing Iranian costume reflects the confluence of several iconographic traditions. While there is variety in this particular element of the repertoire of form and pose, there is visible in the rendering a lassitude and flabbiness quite as marked as the rigidity of the forms that are ultimately of Greek origin, betokening an equal lack of interest in the physical reality that underlies the garments worn.

The female figures of the Synagogue are equally puppetlike, whether clad in the local or in the misunderstood Greek costume, the only exceptions being the flying Psyches (Panel NC 1), in the rendering of whom the fluttering of the drapery and the careful modeling of the exposed leg is faithfully copied from the prototypes.

One further point of a general nature invites comment here; namely, that of frontality. In the Synagogue as in the other monuments of Dura frontality is the order of the day. The figures almost never look in the direction of their gestures,

or of any movement in which they are involved, but normally out into space over the heads of the beholders. The extent to which the Synagogue artists were ready to go to preserve frontality is to be seen in the execution scene of Section C of Panel NC 1, or in the scene of the widow before the gate of Zarephath in Panel SC 2, where even stooping figures turn their faces full front. In the West and as far east as Syrian Antioch frontality does not begin to loom as a factor in representational art until post-Severan times.[213] At Dura and at Palmyra it is a dominant feature as far back as we can trace the local artistic development; that is, to the first century of our era, while elsewhere in certain sections of the Near East there seems to be a special preference for it as early as the beginning of the Hellenistic period.[214] Whatever the ultimate origin of this form of rendering (and it is not typical of ancient Near Eastern art), it is for the purposes of the Synagogue paintings a regional Oriental rather than an imported Western element of style. It is interesting to note, however, that for all their devotion to frontality the Synagogue artists are nonetheless able and ready to depart from it in certain instances. The three most important departures are in the rendering of the Widow of Zarephath as she hands her child to Elijah (Panel WC 1); of Mordecai as he presents the "list of the slain" to Ahasuerus (Panel WC 2); and of the Psyche who, standing on the ground, is ready to breathe upon the corpses to revivify them (Section B of Panel NC 1). Common to all three is the connotation of forceful action, but whether this fact determines the departure from frontality in these instances is not clear. In one other scene; namely, that of the Battle of Eben-ezer (Panel NB 1), there may be in the rendering of the infantrymen a departure from frontality, but preservation here is so poor that details can no longer be made out clearly.

Coming now to the details of the figure rendering, we note that the faces are normally homogeneous, wide-eyed, and vacuous, the product of an analytic formula style that is Oriental in origin. But there are, especially on the west wall of the House of Assembly, faces to which the artists apparently de-

211. For the former see, e.g., the fourth Ezekiel in Panel NC 1, the figure with the red heifer in Panel WB 2, and the first of the ox-drivers in Panel WB 4. For the latter see Panel SB 1.

212. *Rep. IV*, p. 193.

213. See Levi, *Antioch Mosaic Pavements*, I, p. 548.

214. See in general Rostovtzeff, *YCS*, V (1935), pp. 238–241; Hopkins, *Berytus*, III (1936), pp. 9f.

voted unusual care, and which are worthy of closer attention. They include the faces of the first and third Moses of the Exodus Panel (Panel WA 3), Moses at the Burning Bush (Wing Panel I), Ahasuerus (Panel WC 2), and Ezra (Wing Panel III). The basic conventions are by no means modified in any of these instances, but greater care is taken in their application and some few details are added. What results the artists could achieve in this way can best be seen in the rendering of Ezra (Pl. XLVIII, 1) Here the lines defining the features of the face are drawn with more care, the shadows applied to the right side of the face are executed in a color more carefully adapted, additional shadows are provided at the right side of the nose, the cleft of the upper lip is indicated, highlights are supplied on nose, underlip, and forehead, and symmetry of feature and form is sought and obtained. At the same time the hair is given careful treatment, the underlying cap-like mass receiving deft overpainting. The eyes are still wide open, and the pupils are set high in the eyeball as elsewhere in the Synagogue so that the face looks upward rather than straight at the beholder, but here where execution is at its best the face has an aspect of wonder and of timelessness rather than of vacuity. It suggests an element of repose in, and of quiet devotion to, the supernatural powers whose earthly purposes and workings the person represented accepts and furthers.

The nature of the garments which the persons of the Synagogue paintings wear has been described above. So far as matters of style are concerned, the important fact about them is that they are for the artists not adjuncts of the body, used at their convenience to hide or reveal torso and members, but ends in themselves. Hence the emphasis falls upon the correctness of their representation in all particulars. We have noted elsewhere the occurrence of the tie-string at the neck of the short Iranian tunic (for instance, on the more advanced of the two ox-drivers, Panel WB 4) and of the angular collar-flap on the same garment (for instance, on the nearest of Aaron's assistants, Panel WB 2). Designs woven into the cloth are carefully recorded on the cloak of Ahasuerus (Panel WC 2), and on the tunic of Ezekiel (Panel NC 1). The chitons have their proper clavi, and the himations are decorated with two-pronged ornaments near the ends and with supplementary ornaments where they are draped over the knees and the shoulders. Tassels are common, hanging from the very ends of the himation, and the lower ends of short tunics are made to flare out from the top of the slit. Still another element of the artists' efforts to achieve correctness in all matters of dress is that of the fold lines, which are supplied with great regularity and according to specific patterns. On the Iranian costumes the folds on trousers and tunics seem generally to run vertically save in one or two particulars. The exceptions are the rounding of the lines over the abdomen on the short tunic to show the gathering created by the belt, and the circular folds that go around the sleeves of tunics; for instance, on the three Ezekiels in Section A of Panel NC 1.[215] Save for the flying Psyches, the folds of the women's costumes are handled very much like those of the men wearing Iranian dress; that is, the folds tend to run vertically, save over the abdomen and on the sleeves of the chiton. The chiton and himation of the men wearing Greek dress follows a separate convention, quite uniformly applied throughout. *V*-shaped strokes mark the folds of the chiton over the chest, and deeply hooked or indented lines those of the himation over the lower part of the body. The upper edge of the himation, where it returns across the body in the direction of the left arm, shows deep horizontal folding, the roll around the left forearm a heavy concentration of the material, and the ends of the garment as it hangs down at the left side of the wearer a schematic diagonal organization. In the Dura Synagogue paintings, therefore, the fold lines are definite, linear, and uncompromising. Moreover, the basic color of the garment remains the same throughout, there being no recognizable areas of an interplay of light and shade, so that the folds exist largely as calligraphic forms on the surface of the fabric. Only in certain instances in which the artists have supplemented dark fold lines with lighter shadow lines and have added bright — often white — lines representing highlights, is any tradition of plasticity reflected. Ezra (Wing Panel III) and the upper part of Samuel's himation (Panel WC 3) are good examples of this.

215. The peculiar nature of this circular fold, sometimes extended to the entire garment, has been commented on by Hopkins, *ibid.*, p. 26.

It is interesting to note that the Synagogue artists have introduced into their rendering of the garments so wide a variety of basic colors. While in the Iranian costumes blues and the deep reds that represent purple are fairly standard for kings, the costumes of all the lesser personages of court and Temple are done in various shades of pink, blue, and yellow with frequent color contrasts between tunic and trousers and between the basic colors of the tunics and the colors of their borders and collars. Similarly in the Greek costume of chiton and himation, pinks, yellows, and grays appear quite as frequently as white. It may well be doubted whether the colored garments worn at Dura were actually quite as varied or as bright in color as the artists have suggested.[216] More likely the artists have exaggerated in their efforts to make the decorations look richer. It may well be that the Iranian costume has also been treated freely in this respect, though here our ignorance of the costume itself makes it more difficult to judge.

A few additional comments on gestures and indications of action will complete what needs to be said here in summary fashion about figure representation. Gestures — that is, movements of the hands not involving the manipulation of instruments or objects — break down into several types, most of which can be readily interpreted. Perhaps the commonest is that of pointing, in which the arm with the palm of the hand wide open is directed toward an object or the representation of an event to bring it to the beholder's attention. Examples are the second, third, and fourth Ezekiels (Panel NC 1), the widow with the revived child (Panel WC 1), and Moses at the Burning Bush (Wing Panel I). Next in order of frequency is undoubtedly the gesture of acclamation that we see used by David's brethren in the anointing scene (Panel WC 3) and by the people of Susa (Panel WC 2). This is expressed by the right arm bent at the elbow with hand held up, palm

open, at or above shoulder level. Related to this in form is the gesture of song in which both hands are held palm open at or above shoulder height, as in the case of the Elders in their tents around the well of Be'er (Panel WB 1) and of the repatriated faithful in Panel NC 1. For prayer the two hands are held crossed underneath the overgarment, as in the Anointing of David (Panel WC 3) and in the scene of Abraham receiving the Promise (Wing Panel IV). Not clear in their meaning are the gestures of the Princes of the Philistines in Panel WB 4 and of the Prophets of Baal in Panel SC 3. In both cases the arm hangs downward and the hand is half-open. It would be natural to regard this as an "at ease" gesture, were it not for the special arrangement of the Prophets of Baal which permits this gesture to be seen at both sides of the altar. Perhaps it should be regarded as a gesture of failure or dismay. In the case of the midwives before Pharaoh (Panel WC 4) the import of the gesture is also not entirely clear, but it may be that Pharaoh's gesture implies he is giving orders and that the midwives' gesture implies receipt of his orders. In any event, it should be clear that as in all other particulars the artists of the Synagogue have for the handling of gesture certain very recognizable conventions and follow these conventions faithfully. In no instance do the persons performing the gestures seem actually to participate in them. Indications of muscular action are wholly absent. Instead the gestures are limp and abstract, schematic and mechanical in execution.

Action, involving the movement of the body from one place to another or the manipulation of objects, is similarly handled in the few places where it occurs. Neither Miriam nor Jochebed can really be said to be holding the infant Moses, who is passing from one to the other (Panel WC 4), the ox-driver swinging his whip cannot be said to be putting much force into his stroke (Panel WB 4), and neither can the man with the red heifer and the sacrificial axe (Panel WB 2) or the executioner in Section C of Panel NC 1. The artists have one specific convention to indicate rapid movement; namely, that of advancing one leg and showing the knee bent sharply forward. It is used on many different occasions: in portraying the executioner in Panel NC 1, Moses leading the Exodus (Panel WA 3), Haman leading Mordecai's horse (Panel

216. Dura Papyrus 74 (unpublished) lists garments that are white, undyed, crimson, and purple. Color was also a feature of certain of the textiles representing parts of garments brought to light in the excavations (see *Final Report* IV, II, pp. 29–31). Undyed cloth seems to be represented by yellow in the Synagogue paintings; for instance, on the figure of Moses in Panel WB 1. The extent to which the yellow exaggerated the actual color of the undyed material will be obvious.

WC 2), Mordecai delivering the "list of the slain" to Ahasuerus (*ibid.*), Elijah advancing toward the burning altar from one side and the water-carriers coming from the other (Panel SC 4), Miriam advancing(?) toward Pharaoh's daughter (Panel WC 4), the Psyche advancing toward the reassembled bodies (Panel NC 1), and the soldiers with drawn swords advancing toward each other in the Battle of Eben-ezer (Panel NB 1). The results here are not naturalistically convincing either, sometimes because the body is not inclined forward sufficiently to continue the sense of motion implied, sometimes because the feet are placed too firmly or too artificially upon the ground, and sometimes because the leg not carrying the weight and action lags or is extended too far behind. There are, however, one or two instances in which the illusion is achieved, especially where we see Mordecai delivering the "list of the slain" to Ahasuerus (Panel WC 2). What gives the convention the effect of naturalism in this instance is partly the care taken in its execution, and more particularly the fact that it is associated with a forward movement of the right arm and with a profile rendering of the head.[217]

4. ANIMALS

A word must be added in this connection about the representation of animals in the Synagogue paintings. The repertory is by no means as negligible as one might think. Apart from the lions, tigers, and leopards of the dado, there are in the narrative panels the lion of the Lower Center Panel, the humped bullocks of Panel WB 2 and of the scene showing the Ark in the Land of the Philistines (Panel WB 4), the red heifer of Panel WB 2, the ram from the same composition and its parallel on the façade of the Torah Shrine, the horses of Mordecai (Panel WC 2), of the Battle of Eben-ezer (Panel NB 1), and of Saul (Panel EC 1), not to forget the birds in Panel EC 2, the snake before the feet of the Prophets of Baal (Panel SC 3), the fish in the Red Sea scene (Panel WA 3), and the salugis that run with Saul as he journeys toward the Wilderness of Ziph (Panel EC 1). About most of these animals it can be said that they are executed

with great care, as though the artists took particular delight in their rendering. While most of them are domesticated, as the narratives depicted require, it is noticeable that even when wild animals are introduced they are rendered in anything but a ferocious manner. There is thus an element of uniformity in the animal rendering that indicates a method of treatment and a repertory of form other than those used in the hunting scenes of the mosaics and the sarcophagi. This is somewhat strange in an environment and in a city like Dura where so much emphasis was otherwise placed in painting and graffiti on hunting scenes and on dangerous wild animals.

So far as the lions, tigers, and leopards of the dado are concerned, we have already suggested that they represent the animals of the amphitheater or of the private zoos.[218] The horses are associated in the Synagogue either with battle scenes or with the approach of royalty. For both these settings iconographic counterparts exist in the sphere of royal Sassanian art and in those paintings and graffiti of Dura itself that are inspired by the Iranian tradition.[219] The horses are actually rendered after the approved models of the Iranian tradition, with the head held back firmly against the neck, the neck gracefully arched and the hairs of the mane and forelock sharply delineated, the breast seen in a three-quarter perspective, the thin legs firmly set or poised, the body heavily outlined, the fold lines of the hide carefully indicated on the neck and breast, and the tail gracefully arched. In all these particulars they compare favorably with the horses of the Palmyrene sculptures.[220] Though the artists had excellent models to work from and have made a

217. On the use and associations of frontality, see above, p. 374.

218. See above, p. 246.

219. For the confronted riders see, e.g., the Sassanian reliefs of Firouzabad and Naksh-i-Rustum (Herzfeld, *Revue des arts asiatiques*, V, 1928, Pl. XXXVI, 4; and Sarre and Herzfeld, *Iranische Felsreliefs*, Pl. LI), and the Sassanian fresco at Dura (*Rep. IV*, Pls. XVII–XVIII). For the king approaching on horseback, see Sarre and Herzfeld, *op. cit.*, Pls. V, VII; at Dura, the cult scene of Iarhibol, *Rep. V*, Pl. XXXVI, 3; and in general for the mounted figure, Hopkins, *Berytus*, III (1936), pp. 10–26.

220. See e.g., the horse represented on the reliefs in the third-century tomb of Maqqai (*Syria*, XVIII, 1937, Pl. IV, opp. p. 16), and note there the identical delineation of the tail. Horses are not available in the Antioch mosaics until the fourth century, but see Levi, *Antioch Mosaic Pavements*, I, pp. 589f.

great effort to achieve a circumstantial rendering, even to the details of the harness, they have nonetheless become involved in difficulties and contradictions in their execution. The reins that should hold the horses' heads back are not taut, and the three-quarter view of the breast is really appropriate to the bas-reliefs on which the foreleg farthest from the beholder is for reasons of ease of execution the one that is raised, and where, therefore, the muscles of the breast can come prominently into view.[221] At the same time the legs, which the models undoubtedly also showed slender compared with the weight of the body, here become tubular, just as the body itself loses roundness and plasticity.

Next in the order of painstaking execution are the ram, the heifer, and the bullock of the Aaron scene (Panel WB 2). On the bullocks here as elsewhere in the Synagogue, and notably also in the later Antioch mosaics, there is visible the tendency to reinforce outline with heavy shadow lines.[222] The folds of the skin and the shadow masses on the rest of the body give a naturalistic illusion of firmness and roundness not otherwise so well achieved in the Synagogue.

About the lesser animals little needs to be said. The birds of the scene of Belshazzar's Feast (Panel EC 2) are quite as linear as are their counterparts on the graffito from Room D5 in Block C3.[223] The fish are extravaganzas of color, as so often in the mosaics and paintings that derive their inspiration from Hellenistic models. The serpent of the Prophets of Baal scene (Panel SC 3) with its undulating body, its carefully executed scales, and the bright colors that are no longer sufficiently opaque to register on the color plate, seems to belong in the same tradition. Here as elsewhere, therefore, different sources are drawn upon to provide material for the compositions.

As to the animals of the dado, they are shown in the traditional Hellenistic pose, ready to rip the flesh off the head of one of their natural victims. The form is loose and lithe; no little attention is devoted to the manes of the lions, the stripes of

the tigresses, and the spots of the leopards, but the bodies are virtually devoid of modeling, and indications of muscular structure or tension are completely absent.

5. ACCESSORIES

The artists of the Dura Synagogue, as we have seen, regularly provide the descriptive materials necessary for the rendering of a Biblical narrative, but make no serious effort to organize these materials into a unified pattern. In a very real sense, therefore, these materials may be classified as accessories. Their range is not extensive. Interior furnishings of dwellings are limited to the draperies that fill the empty space along the tops of three panels of the west wall (Panels WC 1, 2, 4); the couches of the Lower Center Panel, of Belshazzar's Feast (Panel EC 2), and of Elijah reviving the Widow's Child (Panel WC 1); the Throne of Solomon in Panels WA 2 and WC 2; the chair reserved for Benaiah in Panel WA 2; and the Scroll and Scroll-Chest that go with Ezra (Wing Panel III). Equipment for other than domestic use includes the altars of the Elijah and the execution scenes (Panels SC 3 and 4, NC 1), the tents of the execution scene and of the Wilderness Encampment (Panels NC 1, WB 1), the statues and the vessels of the Philistine temple (Panel WB 4), the cart from the same scene, and the *ferculum* on which the Ark is carried (Panel SB 1).

Elements of scenery are limited to the mountains of the Ezekiel scenes and of the Wilderness of Ziph (Panels NC 1 and EC 1), the sea of the Exodus (Panel WA 3), the river Nile in the Infancy of Moses (Panel WC 4), the sky of the scene in which Abraham receives the Promise (Wing Panel IV), the trees in the Ezekiel scenes (Panel NC 1), and the Burning Bush of the Wilderness of Midian (Wing Panel I). By far the most common accessories are temples (Panels WB 2, WB 3, NB 2, Torah Shrine Façade) and city walls and gates — the latter in the encounter of Elijah and the Widow of Zarephath (Panel SC 2), in the Exodus (Panel WA 3), in the representation of the ideal Jerusalem (Panel WB 3), in the Aaron scene (Panel WB 2), in the Infancy of Moses (Panel WC 4), and in the scene in which Hannah brings the child Samuel to Shiloh (Panel NB 2). Of the various types of material used

---

221. See, e.g., the relief showing Aurelian kneeling before Shapur at Naksh-i-Rustum (Sarre and Herzfeld, *Iranische Felsreliefs*, Pl. VII).

222. *Antioch Mosaic Pavements*, II, Pls. LVII, b; LXII, a; LXIV, b.

223. See *Rep. VI*, p. 127, Fig. 12.

as accessories, that represented by the walled city, with or without gates, is the one the history and development of which are most readily traceable. For comparison we have available here not only the cities of the Assyrian reliefs,[224] but also those on monuments of the Hellenistic period,[225] those that occur on the historical monuments of the Roman period, especially the Columns of Trajan and Aurelius, and those in the mosaics of the Byzantine period.[226] It is obvious from a perusal of this material that the cities of the Synagogue paintings are all seen frontally as in the Assyrian bas-reliefs, and not from the high viewpoint that brings the entire circuit of their walls into view, as we know it from the illusionistic tradition of later Hellenistic and Roman decorative art. But the forms of curtains and towers and their crenelations are modeled, not on the Assyrian reliefs but on those shown in the earlier Hellenistic monuments and such Roman materials as the relief in the Capitoline Museum where the same frontal approach is maintained.[227] Throughout the use of all these conventions, of course, relative proportions between walls and gates and walls and persons are disregarded, as in the Synagogue. It should be noted, however, that in the Synagogue, in spite of the application of occasional shadow lines, the walls have no real depth, being essentially two-dimensional; that the gates of the city of Jerusalem (Panel WB 3) and of the Tabernacle enclosure (Panel WB 2) so far exceed the height of the wall represented that they lose organic relation to the wall; and that the organization of the separate stones in the courses of the walls is haphazardly

executed. Save in the representation of what may be supposed to be the Nicanor Gate in Panel WB 3, all portals show a combination of archway and lintel, a regular feature of the architecture of Roman Syria and perhaps a witness here to the local variation of the traditional pattern.[228] The leaves of the open doors in the scene of the Exodus (Panel WA 3) and of the Infancy of Moses (Panel WC 4) are shown inclined upwards in token of the low viewpoint, rather than downwards as normally on representations of shuttered pictures in Pompeian and Roman wall decoration and in the Antioch mosaics.[229] It would appear, therefore, that while the convention of the walled city is being schematically treated, it represents in the Synagogue a Hellenistic type modified in accordance with a well-established local tradition.

What holds true of the walled city can with certain reservations be said also of most of the other accessories in the Synagogue paintings. These will therefore require only a few words of comment. In the one instance in which the artists felt they could with due respect to the text actually represent a temple; namely, in the panel showing Jerusalem as the world capital with the Temple of Solomon in its midst (Panel WB 3), it was a good typical *peripteros* that they used as a model, with its tympanum decorated in the Hellenistic manner.[230] But while in this instance two sides of the structure are shown, they are not actually rendered in perspective, so that the structure appears as a flat design.[231]

The dislocated pediment of the temple of Dagon (Panel WB 4) and the peculiar representation of the Wilderness Tabernacle underscores what has been said above about the casual and utilitarian treatment of the inherited patterns. So do the altars of the two scenes from the Elijah sequence

224. See P. Botta and E. Flandin, *Monument de Ninive* (1849–1850), II, Pls. 90, 93, 97, 141, 145, 147.

225. For instance, the Homeric cup from Tanagra (C. Robert, *50. Winckelmannsprogramm*, 1890, p. 46), the Pompeian fresco representing the Fall of Icarus (Pfuhl, *Malerei und Zeichnung der Griechen*, III, p. 335); and the Tabulae Iliacae (H. S. Jones, *Catalogue of the Museo Capitolino*, 1912, pp. 165f.).

226. The material has been collected and discussed in Biebel's treatment of the walled cities in the mosaics of Gerasa (see Kraeling, *Gerasa*, pp. 341–351). For the walled cities of the Synagogue paintings, see also Hill, *Marsyas*, I, pp. 5–8.

227. For the relief in the Capitoline Museum and in general, see T. Schreiber, *Die hellenistischen Reliefbilder* (1894), Pl. XLI (cited and reproduced by Biebel in Kraeling, *Gerasa*, p. 344 and Pl. LXXXVIII, b). Note in the Roman relief the regular courses of the stones and the small towers corresponding to our crenelations.

228. For the arches over the lintels of doors and gateways in Syria, see, e.g., *Princeton Archaeological Expedition to Syria*, II, A, 6, Fig. 332 (Theatron of Siʿ of the early first century of our era).

229. See, for instance, the wall decoration from the House of Livia (*Monumenti inediti*, XI, Pl. 22); and Levi, *Antioch Mosaic Pavements*, II, Pl. VIII, b.

230. See above, p. 109.

231. E. Hill provides a parallel at Rome from the period of Marcus Aurelius for the loss of perspective in the rendering of the two sides of a building (*Marsyas*, I, Pl. VII, Fig. 13). It is a relief from the Palazzo dei Conservatori.

(Panels SC 3, 4) and from the execution scene of Panel NC 1, which are linear and two-dimensional and where the established form provides no obstacle to the sudden introduction of a structurally ambiguous cavity as required by the Prophets of Baal scene (Panel SC 3) or for the addition of molded stones below the proper base in the scene of Elijah on Mount Carmel (Panel SC 4). Similarly two-dimensional are such objects as the throne of Solomon, the *ferculum* and the cart upon which the Ark is carried, tables, beds, and chairs, all of which involve the rendering of only one side of the object and of one set of legs or wheels. Guyropes and stripes in the fabric may suggest a naturalistic intention for the tents in Panels WB 1 and NC 1; but the structures are completely rigid, the black interiors are thoroughly schematic, and what sometimes looks like a perspective treatment is probably merely to be interpreted as a fortuitous lengthening or reduction of the respective vertical sides of the object. Similarly schematic are, of course, the orb of the sky, the sea and river, the mountains, the bush, and the trees. Only some of the smaller objects like the thymiateria, candlesticks, bowls, pitchers, spoons, and the like in the scenes of the Ark in the Land of the Philistines and the Consecration of the Tabernacle (Panels WB 2, 4) show plasticity by virtue of the introduction of shadows and include such details as flames fanned sideways by the action of the wind.

In general it can therefore be said about the accessories of the Synagogue compositions that they are occasional, intended for some special purpose, and not a part of an effort to create unified settings. So far as we can tell, the only elements that could conceivably have been omitted are the curtains along the top of certain panels of the west wall and the pollarded trees at the left end of Panel NC 1. Here *horror vacui* or the artists' love of color may have caused them to produce from a repertoire what is needed to provide a setting for the actors and the action; and while their pattern book seems to be of good ancestry, they handle its elements in a manner and a style that is linear, without depth, graphic but not plastic, descriptive but not structural.

C. The Artists

In the earlier phases of the discussion of the Synagogue the thesis was advanced that the three registers of its decorations were executed each by an artist of a different nationality: Register A by a Semite, Register B by a Greek, and Register C by an Iranian.[232] It was in particular the admittedly Iranian formulae for the rendering of Mordecai's triumphal ride through Susa, of the scene of Mordecai's audience with Ahasuerus, and of the midwives' audience with Pharaoh that created the impression of an Iranian style in Register C. In Register A it was the close attention paid to ceremonial matters and traditions in the Exodus Panel, especially the noticeable presence of the "fringes" on the ends of Moses' himation, that invited reference to a Semitic painter; while in Register B the appearance of a peripteral temple with its Hellenistic tympanum may have suggested a Greek. The hypothesis was of no small service in sharpening the interpreters' eyes and making them conscious of the variety of artistic traditions and clichés represented. It had also certain unfortunate effects in leading to suggestions about the "displacement" from one register to another of compositions that were not supposed to have the stylistic peculiarities assigned to a particular artist or register.[233] But the matter of the three independent artists of different nationality and style has quite properly been disposed of by the judicious observations of M. Aubert[234] on the stylistic unity of the compositions; and in view of the obvious way in which Iranian, Greek, and Semitic elements can now be seen to combine freely, not only in each of

232. So Du Mesnil du Buisson, first in *Revue biblique*, XLIII (1934), p. 561; and later in *Peintures*, pp. 150–154.

233. So first with regard to the scene of Samuel anointing David, *ibid.*, p. 127.

234. *Gazette des beaux-arts*, LXXX (XX) (1938), pp. 1–24. One other suggestion originally advanced; namely, that the separate scenes were executed on individual order, so to speak, after the analogy of those in the Temple of Bel (so Rostovtzeff in *YCS*, V, 1935, pp. 254 f.), needs to be abandoned in the light of what is now known about cycles of scenes and about the brief time available for the completion of the entire undertaking.

the registers but sometimes in a single composition, it is doubtful whether even the original proponent of the suggestion would still wish to adhere to it. More recently the number of the artists has been increased again to no less than thirty by a proposed reading of a Middle Iranian text.[235] This seems almost to verge on the fantastic.

In the Synagogue we have only a few scattered pieces of evidence that bear on the question of the number of artists employed. The first is that the façade of the Torah Shrine shows a type of brush work and a series of iconographic patterns different from those of the rest of the wall decorations. The chances are that the entire Torah Shrine, with the Tree of Life above it, was executed by an artist other than those responsible for the later pictorial compositions.[236] Whether this artist or others working under a separate contract decorated the ceiling tiles before they were put into place on the joists during the construction of the building, is not clear.

Among the great mass of the pictorial compositions later added to the decorations of the Synagogue, the picture of the Exodus and Crossing of the Red Sea (Panel WA 3) stands apart from all the rest. The difference is not one of style. Rather it comes to expression most forcibly in the meticulous attention to detail. Nowhere else in the building has so much attention been lavished on minutiae as in the representation of the massed infantry of the Red Sea Crossing, in the file of the civilians in the Exodus, the sculptures that adorn the gate of the City of Pharaoh, the divided waters with their fish and their sea-shells, and the rain of hail and fire mixed. It is obvious, of course, that if the rest of the decorations had been executed in similarly painstaking fashion the work would have taken much longer. This being so, it is tempting to suppose that the Exodus and Crossing of the Red Sea may have been the first picture to be executed, and that the differences between it and the others are the result not of a change of artists, but of a change in the orders of those who commissioned the undertaking. The difficulty is that with greater attention to detail there go also certain minor differences such as the use of deeper flesh tones and of a somewhat different rendering of the Hand of God. What to make of these is not clear. All we can say, therefore, is that if a different artist executed the scene of the Exodus and Crossing of the Red Sea, he belonged to the same school as those responsible for the rest. What gave rise originally to hypotheses about artists of different nationality; namely, the presence in the compositions of patterns borrowed from different artistic traditions, we regard rather as an indication of the eclecticism of the artists and of their special position in time and place.

It is probable, nonetheless, that more than one man was involved in the decoration of the synagogue. Aubert has made what is perhaps the best suggestion in this connection; namely, that the decorations are the work of a master and one or more helpers.[237] The master was responsible for composing and outlining the scenes and added most of the finishing touches to them. The helpers filled in the basic colors of the backgrounds and of the individual figures. Occasionally, it would seem, the master permitted his helpers to assist in the rendering of detail, this being the explanation of the fact that in some parts of the work composition excels execution. In this sense it seems entirely proper to speak of the Synagogue artists in the plural as we have done above. Their names individually and collectively remain unknown.

D. Summary

Leaving for the next chapter the discussion of the use of the continuous method in the handling of the narrative material, it remains here only to summarize the results of the foregoing analysis.

As a monument of ancient art the Synagogue falls readily into line with the succession of painted sanctuaries found at Dura, not only because the decorations are similarly arranged and are religious in subject matter, but also because the style is basically the same. Like the other buildings the

235. See Altheim, *Asien und Rom*, pp. 24–35.
236. See above, p. 40 on the distinction between the two phases in the decoration of the Synagogue's House of Assembly.

237. *Gazette des beaux-arts*, LXXX (XX) (1938), pp. 18f.

Synagogue brings us large, loosely jointed compositions in which impressive figures are presented, sometimes isolated, sometimes paratactically arranged, sometimes massed or shown engaged in action. The figures are presented with a certain number of accessories, the minimum needed to indicate the time, the place, and the nature of a given event or action; but these accessories are not combined to produce a unified setting, and the figures themselves seem unrelated to their environment. For each type of person, as also for each type of action, the artists have a separate pattern, part of a relatively large universe of form. The several representatives of this repertoire of form repeat and multiply, but only in a single plane as copies of each other. The figures therefore are without animation, modeling, or individuality. Bodily form is constructed with complete disregard of plausibility and of the living organism of flesh and bone, nor is there any relation between the garments that cover the body and its actual shape and movement. Participating not at all in the actions in which they are involved, the figures have a hieratic detachment that is offset, however, by the frontal pose through which they are made to communicate with something outside and above themselves. To frontality as an element of effective communication must be added the great variety of color in costume, accessories, and backgrounds, as well as the great emphasis upon the veristic rendering of detail and the inclusion of much finery for the adornment of persons and animals. Youthful and radiant as to type, the figures so enriched and posed impress the beholder vividly as the favored instruments and recipients of a divine revelation, and thus accomplish the didactic purpose for which they are intended in this context.

That in the religious art of Dura generally and in that of the Synagogue in particular we are not dealing with an isolated phenomenon but with a style and type of composition spread through many parts of the later Orient, has already been pointed out repeatedly.[238] The closest analogies so far as they are known today are those that appear in the sculpture and painting of Palmyra, but Hatra and Edessa are currently producing comparable material from the more immediate vicinity.[239] From the date of the earliest known monuments of this style it is clear that the style itself existed in the Orient long before the advent of the Romans, certainly as early as the period of Parthian domination. So early a date is necessary to explain the wide distribution of its examples in later times and the relations that exist in matters of style; for instance, between the art of Palmyra and that of the Ghandara school. But the context of time and place thus assigned to the style is important also for the understanding of the elements which together give it its character. Three are commonly pointed out; namely, the Iranian, the Greek, and the generally Oriental or Semitic.

From the Greek sphere there ultimately come to the Synagogue artists the dress worn by the civilian males and the standing philosopher type represented by Ezra (Wing Panel III); the spear and shield armament of the soldiers of the Exodus (Panel WA 3) as well as the cuirass and crested helmets of the soldiers in the execution scene (Panel NC 1); the temple forms and the Nikés, whether as acroteria or as decorations of the gateway of Pharaoh's city; the related Psyches and the costumes worn by ladies-in-waiting; the stage space device; the cast shadows; and the Persephones, with at least some of the fruits and flowers of the ceiling tiles. From the Iranian sphere there derive ultimately the costume of tunic and trousers worn by all members of the court and Temple personnel, the costumes of all royal figures, the magnificent horses and their riders, the hunting dogs of Panel EC 1, and the animals of the chase found on the ceiling tiles. From the local or the generally Oriental environment come the basic elements of the two-dimensional linear rendering, the neglect of naturalism and realism, the interest in ornament and in veristic detail, certain features of the architectural tradition, and perhaps the dress used by women other than those of the court. To the Hellenistic phase of the history of Oriental art it seems proper

238. See especially Cumont, *Fouilles*, pp. 145–157; and Rostovtzeff, *YCS*, V (1935), pp. 257–261.

239. On the art of Palmyra see especially Ingholt, *Studier over Palmyrensk Skulptur*; *idem*, *Acta Archaeologica*, III (1932), pp. 1–20; Seyrig, *Syria*, XV (1934), pp. 155–186; Rostovtzeff, *YCS*, V (1935), pp. 234–242. On Hatra see the monograph of Ingholt, *Memoirs of the Connecticut Academy of Arts and Sciences*, XII (1954). On the newly found mosaics of Edessa, see the *Illustrated London News*, 21 February 1953, pp. 28f.

to ascribe the use of the principle of frontality; but to the Roman phase it is possible to attribute only some few details such as the tents of Panels WB 1 and NC 1, the *ferculum* of NB 1, and the scattered *tropaia* of WB 4, as well as such devices as the picture within a picture in Panel NB 2. The list could be expanded, but the examples given will suffice to illustrate the point at issue.

The fact that the pictures of the Synagogue are so many and so complex and that they range over so wide a variety of subject matter throws certain sidelights upon the religious art of Dura not provided in equal measure by the paintings of the other structures. We have already seen how the very size of the ceiling in the Synagogue's House of Assembly caused the artists to bring in from other sources decorative design materials not otherwise found on ceilings at Dura. Similarly on the walls of the Synagogue we find a much greater repertoire of pictorial material than in the other religious edifices of the city. But the most interesting fact is the extent to which the artists reveal their dependence upon a fixed set of stereotypes. They have fixed conventions, in the first place, for different types of persons: for the civilian male and female, for the king, the courtier, the queen, the servant, the messenger, and the Temple personnel, and perhaps more than one convention for foot soldiers and cavalrymen.[240] Even clearer is the use of fixed conventions for objects such as temples, city walls, gates, tents, altars, thymiateria, lampstands, and utensils. Important above all is a precise set of conventions for gestures of pointing, of acclamation, song, and prayer; for the representation of the rapid movement of persons; and for the indication of the relation between standing persons by resting the weight of the body on the appropriate foot. The existence of this mass of formulae in the pictorial compositions of the Synagogue indicates that the artists learned their profession by absorbing and practicing the elements of pattern repertoires. They inherited thus the well-known and ancient Oriental custom of having to learn from "trial pieces," and their art deserves in some respects to be called "copy-book" art. Because they incorporated in their renderings elements of such diverse artistic traditions, their art also deserves to be called "synthetic."

The analysis of the Synagogue paintings suggests the artists' dependence on still other patterns than those for individual objects or persons. Its repetition in more than one panel implies the existence and use of an iconographic stereotype for at least one type of scene, the audience scene. The type is seen at its best in WC 4 (Pharaoh and the Infancy of Moses). In the basic pattern the king is seated frontally with a courtier on either side, while those being received in the audience approach from the left. The same pattern was used in representing the visit of the Queen of Sheba (Panel WA 2) and in the scene showing Mordecai reporting the "list of the slain" to Ahasuerus (Panel WC 2). In the latter instance existence of the stereotype is demonstrated with particular clarity by the changes which the artist made to accommodate an intrusive element required by the story; namely, Esther and her lady-in-waiting. The courtier who should have stood at the right of the throne, in the space occupied by Esther, was not omitted but was moved to a position behind the throne, though he had to be reduced in size to be accommodated alongside his fellow courtier at the left.

Putting together what we have in the Synagogue with what is known from related monuments of ancient art generally, it is possible to suppose that the repertoire of iconography for entire scenes available to the artists was still larger. Not unrelated in type are the Battle of Eben-ezer (Panel NB 1) and the so-called Sassanian Fresco of Dura.[241] Mordecai's triumphal ride through Susa we have ventured to call an example of the *adventus regis*.[242] The scene of Belshazzar's Feast (Panel EC 2) may well have been a typical banquet scene, just as there may well be a common iconographic archetype behind the two sacrifice scenes on Mount Carmel (Panels SC 3 and 4).[243] If there be any value in these observations, they would tend to confirm what Rostovtzeff has said in connection with the Sassanian Fresco about the dependence of the art of Dura upon imperial Parthian and Sassanian art.[244]

---

240. If they had a fixed convention for priests, it must have been judged unsuitable for use in the rendering of Aaron, who appears in what we have described as fundamentally a royal costume. See above, p. 127.

241. See above, pp. 96 f.
242. See above, p. 152.
243. See above, pp. 141 f., and below, p. 388.
244. *YCS*, V (1935), pp. 283–288.

The reason is that the repertoire of compositional form is clearest where we have scenes such as would be appropriate to an imperial art; that is, the decoration of palaces and national memorials. But separate repertoires may have existed also for religious and ordinary secular materials. We shall be in a better position to understand the iconography of late Roman imperial art and of early Byzantine art as we learn more about such repertoires of scenic form in the Near East, and if by good fortune more examples of the types of scenes represented are provided from other sites and earlier periods.

Applied to a large body of narrative material, the "synthetic" style of the Dura Synagogue artists had the special advantage of permitting the quick execution of a great number of scenes and of making their meaning obvious from the constant return of stereotyped detail. As applied to the sacred history of a people, it had the further advantage of safeguarding the precious heritage by ruling out the subjective factor and of escaping from the danger which the pious undoubtedly would have seen in any attempt to approach the material imaginatively and to go beyond the limited essentials of the Biblical narrative. Its very formalism and repetitiveness made it acceptable to the purposes of the Synagogue community and served as a safeguard against charges of abetting idolatry or of departing from the tradition of the written and oral Word. In the Synagogue, therefore, an art that was of necessity purposeful found an ideal opportunity to serve a community that needed what it had to give. This is what makes the Dura Synagogue with its decorations one of the finest and most fitting monuments of ancient Judaism.

Chance has preserved this one example of formalistic and synthetic art in the Jewish synagogues of antiquity, but we do know that very soon under other circumstances this same type of rendering and composing became equally useful to the Christian communities, especially in the eastern half of the Mediterranean. This is why the paintings of Dura can properly be called forerunners of Byzantine art.[245] The question which the Synagogue poses is whether what went over into Christian usage was only the style and an established repertoire of iconographic form, or whether the Christians took their Biblical scenes themselves from earlier Jewish prototypes. To this question we shall return in the final section.

245. Breasted, *Oriental Forerunners of Byzantine Painting*.

IV. THE ORIGIN AND ANTIQUITY OF THE SYNAGOGUE'S BIBLICAL SCENES

We began the interpretative section of this report by quoting a statement of Rostovtzeff which suggested among other things that Dura was never distinguished for its creative activity.[246] The truth of the statement has been underlined by the analysis of the style and composition of the paintings in the previous chapter. But if, as a Roman garrison city and frontier post leagues removed from the great centers of Jewish life in antiquity, Dura cannot be expected to have pioneered in the development of Jewish narrative art, what shall we say about the origin of the Synagogue's Biblical scenes? The natural conclusion is that they were not painted here for the first time in history but were copied from, or based upon, prototypes that once existed elsewhere. Several questions naturally arise in this connection. Is there any evidence in support of this conclusion? How old may these prototypes have been, and in what medium were they first created? Where can we suppose that the prototypes existed, in Syria or in Babylonia? Did they affect the use of Biblical scenes in non-Jewish circles? These are all highly interesting questions, but it is obvious from their nature that at the present state of our knowledge any attempt to answer them represents a venture into the realm of the hypothetical and must be treated accordingly.

From what has been said above, it is clear that we have today no evidence earlier than the Dura Synagogue for the representation of scenes from the Bible by Jews. The scenes that do appear in the mosaics of Jerash, Beth Alpha, and Na'aran are all later and belong, as we have suggested, to a different, symbolic tradition of ancient Jewish art.[247] Conceivably there may have existed synagogues with representations of Biblical scenes at an earlier date in the great Jewish centers of the ancient world; but these centers either have not been or cannot be explored archaeologically, and it is questionable whether in any of them circumstances for the preservation of synagogue decorations would have been as favorable as they were at Dura. In trying to answer the fundamental question about the evidence for the existence of prototypes we are therefore thrown back upon the paintings of the Dura Synagogue themselves. An examination of the paintings as examples of the so-called "cyclic" or "continuous" method of pictorial representation will be in order here, for it lends support to, and throws further light upon, the conclusion that they are indeed for the most part copies of earlier works.

A. The Synagogue Paintings as Examples of Progressive Narration in Art

Since it was first discussed by Wickhoff in his famous work on the Vienna Genesis, the "cyclic" or "continuous" method of pictorial representation has received more attention at the hand of students of manuscript illustration than from those concerned with the monuments of sculpture and painting.[248] This leaves an element of uncertainty in our knowledge of its application. Above all, the relations between the late classical and Christian monuments and the narrative bas-reliefs and tomb paintings of the ancient Orient have not been clarified. Much still remains to be done, therefore,

246. See above, p. 321.

247. See above, p. 363 and n. 171.

248. For the discussion of the cyclic method in illustrated manuscripts, see especially von Hartel and Wickhoff, *Die Wiener Genesis*; G. Thiele, *Antike Himmelsbilder* (1898); J. Strzygowski, *Eine alexandrinische Weltchronik* (*Kaiserliche Akademie der Wissenschaften zu Wien*, *Denkschriften*, *Phil.-Hist. Klasse*, LI, 2, 1906); T. Birt, *Die Buchrolle in der Kunst* (1907); W. Schubart, *Das Buch bei den Griechen und Römern* (2nd ed., 1921); K. Preisendanz, *Papyrusfunde und Papyrusforschung* (1933); E. Bethe, *Buch und Bild im Altertum* (1945); Weitzmann, *Illustrations in Roll and Codex*. For the use of the cyclic method in other media of ancient art, see C. Jahn, *Griechische Bilderchroniken* (1873); C. Robert, *Homerische Becher* (50. Winckelmannsprogramm, 1890); and *idem*, *Archaeologische Hermeneutik* (1919).

before the characteristics of the method can be fully described and before we can be sure about inferences to be drawn from them. The study of the use of the cyclic method in Greek illustrated manuscripts suggests that in them pictures appear first as separate scenes, each associated with a particular section of the text. It further suggests that where there are polyscenic illustrations, the elements are dependent upon each other and cannot stand alone; abbreviation can be assumed to have taken place; and older archetypes can be postulated in which each scene formed a complete and independent unit. The question is whether these inferences apply also to the Synagogue paintings.

In an earlier chapter we mentioned that Biblical narrative has been drawn upon to portray or allude to approximately fifty-nine different episodes, presented in twenty-eight fields or panels.[249] The following list gives the episodes in their Biblical sequence, brackets enclosing those to which there is allusion, but which are not complete or separable iconographic units.

Of the twenty-eight panels created by the artists, eleven portray each a single scene and deal with a single episode. Adopting the terminology developed by Weitzmann, we speak of them as "monoscenic" panels.[250] They can be listed as follows:

WA 1. Unidentified scene: Anointing of Solomon (?)
WA 2. Solomon Receives the Queen of Sheba
WC 3. Samuel Anoints David
NA 1. Jacob at Bethel
SB 1. The Dedication of the Temple
SC 3. The Prophets of Baal on Mount Carmel[251]
Wing Panel I.   Moses and the Burning Bush
Wing Panel II.   Moses Receives the Law
Wing Panel III. Ezra Reads the Law
Wing Panel IV.   Abraham Receives the Promise
Upper Center Panel. David, King over all Israel

All the other panels of the Synagogue use the "cyclic" method of representation, but for our purposes the group of "cyclic" compositions may be broken down further into those that have two, three, and more than three scenes. In these categories we have ten, three, and two compositions; namely,

1. Panels with two scenes each:
WB 1. Wilderness Encampment and the Miraculous Well of Be'er
WB 3. Jerusalem and the Temple of Solomon
WB 4. The Ark in the Land of the Philistines
WC 2. Mordecai and Esther
NB 1. The Battle of Eben-ezer
NB 2. Hannah and the Child Samuel at Shiloh
EC 2. Belshazzar's Feast and the Fall of Babylon
[SC 1. Elijah Proclaims a Drought and Leaves for Cherith]
SC 2. Elijah at Cherith and Zarephath
SC 4. Elijah on Mount Carmel.[252]

2. Panels with three scenes each:
WA 3. Exodus and Crossing of the Red Sea
WC 1. Elijah Revives the Widow's Child
EC 1. David and Saul in the Wilderness of Ziph.

3. Panels with more than three scenes each:
WC 4. Pharaoh and the Infancy of Moses (4 or 5 scenes)
NC 1. Ezekiel, the Destruction and Restoration of National Life (9 scenes).

In addition to these twenty-six compositions there are two which should in all probability be regarded as examples of the "simultaneous" method of representation; namely,

WB 2. The Consecration of the Tabernacle and its Priests
Lower Center Panel. The Blessings of Jacob, and David, Pious King.

Of the two panels in this category, the first deserves this classification because it brings together into the context of the Consecration of the Taber-

249. See above, p. 349.
250. See Weitzmann, *Illustrations in Roll and Codex*, especially pp. 12–36.
251. The fact that Panel SC 3 also depicts the death of Hiel does not remove it from the category of monoscenic panels, because the Midrashic accretion is an addition to the very verses of scripture represented. See above, pp. 139 f.

252. On the special circumstances suggesting that Panel SC 4 is a combination of two scenes, see above, p. 142, and below, p. 388.

nacle elements from several passages of Exodus and Numbers.[253] The second has of necessity to be listed here because of the peculiar mixture of materials resulting from the recomposition of the area.[254]

To understand what bearing method of representation may have upon the question of prototypes, we must try to determine what is typical of the Synagogue artists' rendering of a single episode and then see how the rendering is varied and for what reason. Two things are important to note in this connection. The first is that panels with one or at most two scenes form by all odds the largest part of the decorations of the Synagogue. Between them they account for twenty-one out of twenty-eight compositions. The second is that of the ten panels containing two scenes, five could readily be divided into pairs of monoscenic compositions without damage to, or change in, the rendering.[255] The only question that might arise in case of such a division is whether the scene would be as readily identifiable. But this is not a question of the method of rendering, but of interpretation and does not need to concern us in the present context.

What was said above about the style and composition of the Synagogue paintings indicates that a typical scene consists of nothing more than the person or persons engaged in an action and of such accessories as the action, the event, or the person requires for the occasion. So, for example, to portray the story of Jacob at Bethel (Panel NA 1) the artist needed to show Jacob asleep upon the stony ground of Bethel, the stone he used for a head rest, the ladder ascending to heaven, and the angels upon the ladder. Similarly the scene of Mordecai's triumph in the panel representing Mordecai and Esther (Panel WC 2) required that Mordecai be shown, clad in the king's clothes, mounted upon a royal charger, led by Haman, and acclaimed by the citizens of Susa. These scenes are typical of the Synagogue artists' work of composition. But some Biblical incidents required very little besides the central figure of the action. So in

the case of Moses and the Burning Bush (Wing Panel I) all that needed to be shown besides Moses were his shoes and the Bush, or in the representation of Abraham receiving the Promise (Wing Panel IV) Abraham and the Orb of Heaven studded with stars. On the other hand, in the case of Solomon receiving the Queen of Sheba (Panel WA 2) the reverse was true. Here the artist had to show Solomon and his throne, his counsellors (because what was involved was a test of wisdom), the Queen herself and the lady-in-waiting without whom the queen could not appear in public, and Benaiah to present the queen to Solomon, both undoubtedly in accordance with protocol. All these additional accessories were dictated by the iconography of court scenes. Not iconography but the importance of the episode itself may sometimes have prompted an expansion of the accessories, as in the case of the Dedication of the Temple, which apparently takes up all of Register B on the south wall of the building. These variations from maximum to minimum, however, should not obscure the basic character of a typical scene as it occurs in the bulk of the monoscenic and cyclic compositions.

Keeping in mind what has been said about the typical individual scene, we can see with greater clarity where the basic pattern has been varied under various circumstances. Here the character of the five two-scene compositions which are not readily separable into their elements must come under scrutiny. In the panel dealing with the Ark in the Land of the Philistines (WB 4) it is clare that the havoc created in the Temple of Dagon (I Sam. 5.1–5) required the representation of the Ark that caused it. This representation the artists spared themselves by placing the scene of the return of the Ark (I Sam. 6.1–12) alongside that of the havoc, making the one appearance of the Ark do for two by simple juxtaposition of the scenes. In the panel showing Hannah taking the child Samuel to Shiloh (Panel NB 2) a different device leads to the same result. By decreasing the height of the wall representing Shiloh, the artists gained enough space at the top to introduce another scene, that of the child Samuel receiving in the temple at night the declaration about the punishment of the house of Eli (I Sam. 3.1–14). The added scene is by no means unimportant to the development of

253. See above, p. 130f.
254. See above, pp. 221–225.
255. The five in question are WC 2 (Mordecai and Esther), NB 1 (Battle of Eben-ezer), EC 2 (Belshazzar's Feast and the Fall of Babylon), SC 1 (Elijah Proclaims a Drought and Leaves for Cherith), and SC 2 (Elijah at Cherith and Zarephath).

the narrative which the paintings trace, for it explains the destruction that overtakes the Israelite army in the adjacent scene of the Battle of Ebenezer (Panel NB 1) and the loss of the Ark to the Philistines. Since the Synagogue artists did not have enough room to place the scene in a separate panel, they have combined it with the scene showing Hannah and Samuel coming to Shiloh, abbreviating both parts of the composition. The technique they used in this instance is the "framework" technique, familiar also from the monuments of Roman narrative art.[256]

Still another technique, that of superimposition, comes into play in the interest of economy of space in Panels WB 1 and WB 3. In the first of these, as we have seen, the diagrammatic rendering of the Wilderness Encampment as described in Numbers 2 is superimposed upon and made to surround the scene of Moses and the Elders conjuring water from the Well at Be'er (Numbers 21.16–18). In the latter, Solomon's Temple described in I Kings 6 is placed directly against the representation of the city of Jerusalem whose walls were built by David and Solomon, as told in II Samuel 5.9 and I Kings 3.1 respectively.

In all these instances, then, the artists have found short cuts for presenting in one panel what on the basis of their normal treatment of a scene would have required two separate compositions. The logical inference is that they had available a larger repertoire of scenes which they were condensing to accommodate their work to the size of the chamber and to the requests of their employers. That such was indeed the case can perhaps be seen best from Panel SC 4, which shows Elijah on Mount Carmel. The scene is that in which Elijah succeeds in making the burnt sacrifice where the Prophets of Baal had failed (I Kings 18.30–33a, 36–38). What the basic pattern for such a sacrifice scene was in the Synagogue artists' repertory of iconographic form, we can see from the adjoining composition (SC 3). The typical sacrifice scene had a central feature; namely, the altar with the bullock upon it, and therefore also required an element of balance on either side, in this case two groups of four of the Prophets of Baal. Given this pattern, it would have been natural for the Synagogue artists to have composed the scene of Elijah's sacrifice

256. See above, p. 95.

(Panel SC 4) along the same line with the altar in the center, Elijah alone on one side in view of his importance, and on the other representatives of the people who had not bowed their knees to Baal, the fire coming down from heaven between them in answer to Elijah's prayer. Actually in Panel SC 4 the altar has the central position which the basic pattern demands, and Elijah stands at the left, with hand upraised as the fire descends. But Elijah does not stand alone as we would expect, and the composition is unbalanced. Unexpectedly at the right side of the panel the scale of the persons represented is reduced by half and what we see is two ranks of two servants pouring water upon the altar. The action thus portrayed really precedes in time the performance of the sacrifice (I Kings 18. 33b–35). How the unbalanced composition was arrived at can be explained if we assume that the prototype had two separate pictures which the artists here consolidated for the sake of economy. Both compositions were balanced at the outset and had an altar in the middle. The first showed Elijah standing beside the altar alone, with two servants bearing water containers approaching the altar from the right and two from the left. The second showed Elijah alone on one side of the altar and the representatives of the people of Israel on the other. To combine the two compositions the artists reduced the size of the water-carriers by half and thus were able to place all four of them on one side of the altar. To make room for them they moved the representatives of the people of Israel over to the left side of the altar, where they now stand with Elijah. In combining the two compositions they either neglected to omit, or were prevented from omitting, the Elijah of the water-pouring scene, who still stands at the right of the altar as a supernumerary but in this new combined rendering may represent Elisha.[257] The picture in this instance not only suggests but demands the assumption that the artists were combining two separate balanced scenes to produce what the panel shows. Thus the argument for monoscenic prototypes becomes cogent.

Coming now to the cylic compositions that represent three or more episodes of Biblical narrative, we find the indications of crowding and abbreviation even more clearly in evidence. The best ex-

257. See above, p. 143.

ample of abbreviation in this group is the panel showing how Elijah revives the Widow's Child (WC 1). Here artistic stenography is at its best. The minimum requirements for the rendering of the story would be three scenes, somewhat as follows. In the first scene a standing Elijah would be seen receiving the dead child from the widow. In the second he would be seen upon the couch, reviving the child. In the third he would be standing again, and the mother would would be seen receiving the living child back from him. In combining the three the artists have kept the second and all-important scene intact but they have omitted the standing Elijahs of the first and third scenes and have kept only the widow and the child. In so doing they have saved a great deal of space and have avoided repetition without sacrificing clarity of meaning.

In the Infancy of Moses (Panel WC 4) similar abbreviations occur, and in this case lead to departures from the known forms of the Biblical story. The probability is that here five separate scenes were combined in one composition. The first presented Pharaoh giving his orders to the Hebrew midwives for the destruction of all male children (Exodus 1.15–17). The second showed Moses' mother placing her child in the ark of bulrushes (Exodus 2.1–3). For reasons of economy of space the second was telescoped with the first and assigned to a place along the base of the composition, immediately below the first scene. The third scene was, of course, that of the princess finding the child (Exodus 2.5–60), but what follows is ambiguous. As we have already seen, the ambiguity arises from the fact that Miriam's pose shows her to be coming with haste to the princess.[258] The best interpretation of the use of this pose is that it belonged to a separate scene in which she approached the princess and asked whether she should go and call a nurse from among the Hebrew women (Exodus 2.7–8). This was abbreviated by omitting the princess. The same omission was made in the final scene, in which the princess was originally shown giving the child back to its mother (Exodus 2.9). By representing the princess once instead of three times the artists were able to combine five scenes in one panel, at the cost, however, of having Moses' mother receive the child back from Miriam,

contrary to the Biblical story, and of representing Miriam in a pose unsuited to the action she is performing.

In the most complicated and ambitious of the panels of the Synagogue; namely, the one that represents Ezekiel and the Destruction and Restoration of National Life (NC 1), the same compression and abbreviation appear, again with resultant ambiguities in the development of the narrative. The most striking piece of abbreviation is in Section A, where the identity of the three figures that stand in a row has not ceased to plague interpreters.[259] By far the simplest solution of the problem is to suppose that all three represent Ezekiel and that the artists have by this juxtaposition endeavored to represent three successive groups of verses at the beginning of Ezekiel 37; namely, vvs. 1–2, 4–7a, 7b–8. In the prototype, we must imagine, there were three separate scenes, each laid in the Valley of Dry Bones with just enough accessories to identify the location in each case. By omitting in this instance the accessories that located the scenes in a valley the artists were able to compress the material into one section of the panel. In so doing they not only brought the three Ezekiels surprisingly close together but disturbed the sequence of development so far as it concerns the bones. The Biblical text demands that the bones be shown first separated and bare, then assembled, and only after this covered with flesh and sinews (Ezekiel 37.7–8). In relation to the text the imagery of the separate scenes may well be thought to have been clear and explicit. In the combined rendering it is confused, for the bodily members are seen covered with flesh before the skeletons are reassembled.

From what has been said about the method of presentation, it would indeed seem likely that the Dura Synagogue artists not only had sets of formulae for the rendering of detail and conventions for certain types of scenes, but also knew more extensive cycles of Biblical scenes which they rendered and combined as circumstances dictated. This being so, it is entirely possible, though not demonstrable, that many of the characteristics of the Synagogue artists' style and composition were inherited from, or duplicated in, the prototypes. Whether they only copied and abbreviated or

258. See above, p. 178.

259. See above, pp. 189 f.

sometimes improvised we cannot know. The fact that in two instances they fell back upon the synthetic method of representation suggests the latter. Indeed what we know about the history of the one synthetic composition; namely, the Lower Center Panel, gives little choice in the matter. Be this as it may; the probability is that behind the narrative compositions of the Synagogue stands as a source a repertoire of Biblical scenes even larger than that which we know. This is an important inference, but by no means surprising when the size and the geographical position of the Jewish community at Dura are given proper consideration.[260]

B. *The Prototypes of the Narrative Compositions as Elements of Synagogue Decoration*

If the characteristics of the narrative compositions themselves and the nature of the geographic and social environment in which they came to light both suggest that the Dura Synagogue paintings are copied from elsewhere, where shall we suppose that the sources of their inspiration lay? Again the answer to the question must be hypothetical.

From what has already been said above it appears that the orbit of thought and tradition represented by the paintings moves between the two poles of Palestinian and of Babylonian Judaism.[261] The immediate question is therefore whether the prototypes can be assigned to either of these areas. So far as Palestine is concerned we have already noted that the painting of walls was permitted by R. Johanan in the third century of our era, and that while this does not necessarily apply directly to synagogues and no painted Palestinian synagogues are known, the door must at least be said to have been opened for the creation of such structures there.[262] The difficulty is that if, with Leveen, we assign the origin of all synagogue painting to the third century and to Palestine, there is not enough time for the effects of this development to transmit itself to the remote sections of the Roman Orient, for the large cycles of compositions that serve as prototypes for the Dura paintings to come into being, and for them to be adapted to the needs and dimensions of a frontier structure such as that of Dura.[263] Indeed the Dura Synagogue paintings, by contrast for instance with those of the Christian Chapel, give the impression of belonging to a long-established artistic tradition. The prototypes which they copy and emend should therefore be much older than the days of R. Johanan. Besides, in Palestine the tempo of developments leading to the use of representational art may well have been relatively slow because of earlier strictures in force there, and it would not be unreasonable to suppose that the Jews of other lands had used wall painting long before it was permitted in Palestine by R. Johanan.

As for the other pole of the Synagogue's orbit, we have no way of gauging its potentialities. There is nothing comparable in the Babylonian tradition to the statement of R. Johanan, but this might mean either that the use of wall painting had never been questioned there or that it had never been proposed. We have already quoted above the statement about the statue set up in the synagogue of Shaph-weyathib in Nehardea before the days of the Dura Synagogue.[264] To this may be added here the anecdote about R. Hiyya, who is reported to have said, "But that I would be dubbed a Babylonian who permits forbidden things, I would permit more."[265] But it may well be asked whether these things are typical, for the Babylonian Jews prided themselves greatly upon purity of stock and tradition. If we knew more about the *dipivars* of the Synagogue's Middle Iranian dipinti, they might give us at least an indirect perspective upon conditions among the Jewish communities in Babylonia, for the inscriptions suggest that when they come to the Synagogue and "see" the pictures, this is for them something of an unusual experience.[266] If, as we should imagine, the *dipivars* came

260. See above, p. 346. There is, of course, no way of telling which of the features of the Synagogue paintings reflect the immediate prototype directly or are variations upon it. We know the tradition only in relation to an hypothetical archetype.

261. See above, p. 354.

262. See above, p. 344.

263. See Leveen, *Hebrew Bible in Art*, p. 57.

264. See above, p. 343, n. 101.

265. Shabbat 60b (Trans., II, 1, p. 284).

266. See above, Inscrs. Nos. **42, 44, 46, 48, 49, 51.**

from the Sassanian lands down the Euphrates, they could not in this case have been familiar with painted synagogues there.

With the case for the south Mesopotamian origin of the Dura Synagogue paintings at least ambiguous, the mind turns naturally to Palmyra, where there was a strong Jewish colony and where Dura had connections in so many fields, including that of art. Of the synagogue at Palmyra nothing remains, and the Hebrew inscription sometimes assigned to it should in all probability be attributed to a private house.[267] Another inscription recording the building and "decoration" of a tomb at Palmyra by the members of a Jewish family is suggestive, but there is no way of telling whether the decor was architectural or painted.[268] Clearly the Palmyrene Jews were not highly regarded by their Palestinian co-religionists, for they were deemed to be of impure stock, their proselytes were regarded as unacceptable, and in general it was felt that the destruction of Palmyra would be a good thing.[269] Because the Palestinians' suspicion of the Palmyrene Jews may well have been inspired also by their attitude toward decorative art, the derivation of the Dura Synagogue paintings must remain possible. The only argument against it, as also against derivation from Palestine, is the relative strength of the Iranian element in the style and especially in the iconography of the paintings. A source closer to the centers of Parthian and Sassanian art might be preferable on this account, if it could be identified.

One fact should not be lost sight of in this connection; namely, that the period of the greatest numerical growth in the Jewish community of Dura was also the one in which the coins testify to increasingly close relations between the city and such north Mesopotamian centers as Edessa and Nisibis. We have already taken occasion above to suggest that the two things may be related, and certainly the area has much to recommend it as the source of the prototypes of the Synagogue paintings.

The potential importance of these northerly regions for our purposes rests upon a combination of three facts. The first is that during the earlier days of Roman rule many sections of the vast inland area reaching from Ituraea in the south to Commagene, Osrhoene, and Adiabene in the north and east were administered and organized as small vassal kingdoms on a more or less friendly footing with Romans and Parthians alike.[270] The second is the fact that Syria in general and many of these states in particular are known to have had large numbers of Jewish inhabitants.[271] The third is that, partly because of the large numbers of Jewish inhabitants, many of the ruling families of these petty kingdoms either adopted or sought to adopt the Jewish faith or entered into marital alliances with the Herodian family. The most familiar story in this connection is that of Queen Helena of Abiabene and her son Izates, who were converted to Judaism about A.D. 30. This same Izates subsequently also governed Nisibis as a gift of Artabanus II.[272] Not to be forgotten, however, is the fact that Azizus, king of Emesa, married Drusilla,

267. On the inscription in question see S. Landauer, *Sitzungsberichte der königlich preußischen Akademie der Wissenschaften* (1884), pp. 933f.; and E. Mittwoch, *Beiträge zur Assyriologie*, IV (1902), pp. 203–206. On Jewish names in Palmyrene inscriptions see J. B. Chabot, *Choix d'inscriptions de Palmyre* (1922), pp. 102–105; P. Le Bas and W. H. Waddington, *Voyage archéologique en grèce et en asie mineure. Inscriptions grecques et latines* (1870), no. 2619; and Cantineau, *Inventaire des inscriptions de Palmyre*, VII (1931), pp. 11f., no. 4. On the Jewish religion at Palmyra see J. G. Février, *La Religion des palmyréniens* (1931), pp. 219–223.

268. The expression used is תצביתה כלה.

269. See, e.g., the passages Yebamoth 16a, 16b, 17a (Trans., pp. 88f., 92, 93), and H. P. Chajes, *Rivista Israelitica*, I (1904), pp. 171–180, 238f.

270. On the history of these small city states, see in general Cumont in *Cambridge Ancient History*, XI, pp. 606–648; A. H. M. Jones, *The Cities of the Eastern Roman Provinces* (1937), pp. 216–295.

271. See the general statement of Josephus that there were more Jews in Syria than in any other part of the ancient world (*Bellum* VII, 3, 3 = § 43) and the collection of references in Juster, *Les Juifs dans l'empire romain*, I, pp. 199–202. For the Jews in Edessa see the statements of Melito of Sardis about the importance there of the Hebrew woman Kuthbi (W. Cureton, *Spicilegium Syriacum*, 1855, p. 25, lines 12 ff.), and what the Syriac *Doctrine of Addai* says about Jewish traders in fine cloths who became converts (idem, *Ancient Syriac Documents*, 1864, p. 14, lines 21–24, and p. 21, lines 3–5); in general see the article of R. Gottheil in *Jewish Encyclopedia*, V, pp. 39f. On the Jews in Adiabene see Josephus, *Bellum* I, 1, 2 = § 6; and II, 16, 4 = § 388; and what he tells in *Antiquitates* XX, 2–4 = §§ 17–96 about the ruling house of the region. The existence of a second Nisibis, in Babylonia, makes it difficult to know which statements refer to the Jews in the northern city by that name.

272. See Josephus' long account, *Antiquitates* XX, 2–4 = §§ 17–96.

the sister of Agrippa I, accepting circumcision as a condition of marriage;[273] that Chalcis ad Libanum was governed in succession by Agrippa I, his brother Herod of Chalcis, and Agrippa II;[274] that Abila on the Chrysoroas (Barada) above Damascus was given to Agrippa I by Caligula and to Agrippa II by Claudius;[275] and that Apamaea is said to have been particularly considerate to its Jewish inhabitants during the period of the Jewish Revolt.[276] Other projected or attempted marital alliances between the Herodians and the local princes include that between Epiphanes, the son of Antiochus of Commagene, and Drusilla, the daughter of Agrippa I; and that between Polemon, king of Cilicia, and Berenice, the sister of Drusilla.[277]

This unusual combination of circumstances provides by all odds the best background for the development and execution of the suggested prototypes of the Dura Synagogue paintings. The region represented by the names Commagene, Chalcidice, Osrhoene, and Adiabene was open both to Greek influence from such coastal centers as Antioch and to Iranian influence from the mountains eastward and the plains southward. Here the cultures that contributed most to the style and composition of the Dura Synagogue paintings can be assumed to have been intimately combined. At the same time the large concentrations of Jews in this region argues for the existence of the larger synagogues that are suggested by the larger repertoires of pictures. Finally the personal interest of the local ruling houses in Judaism could well have been the occasion at one time for the vassal kings to exhibit their benevolence toward their Jewish subjects by erecting synagogues for them. This was in line with royal munificence during the entire history of the Near East. And if their predecessors had erected painted temples to the pagan gods, what would have been more natural than that such proselyte kings should have built pictorially decorated synagogues at their own expense for the local Jews?

If, then, we look for prototypes of the Dura Synagogue with its paintings, the most natural assumption is that they existed in upper Mesopotamia and eastern Syria, perhaps as creations of local dynasts and erected as counterparts in elegance to the pagan shrines of the cities in question. This would imply, of course, that the prototypes may go back to a date as early as the first century of our era, and that the Dura Synagogue may well be merely a late imitation of the royally favored synagogues of the north, inspired by the closer associations between Dura and the region in question. There is nothing that we know about the history of the Jewish dispersion and its attitude toward art that would gainsay this suggestion, and indeed what we learn about the composition of the Dura Synagogue paintings argues that they had been in existence for some time.

C. The Synagogue Paintings and Manuscript Illustration

It seems only reasonable to suppose that the immediate prototypes of the Dura Synagogue paintings existed in other larger and even more elegant synagogues of the neighboring region. But the material as we have it raises the further question whether wall decoration was the medium in which the scenes were first executed. To understand what is involved here we must return to the paintings themselves and to the Biblical narratives with which they concern themselves.[278]

It should be clear from what has been said above that the subject matter of the Dura paintings is not chosen at random from all the different parts of the Bible and therefore cannot be said to illustrate the Bible as such or as a whole. Instead the paintings illustrate individual books of the Bible. Some, like Leviticus, Deuteronomy, Joshua, Judges, and the writings of most of the Prophets, they pass over entirely, so far as we can tell. Those that they do deal with, they are inclined to treat rather fully and in a particular manner. Listing the scenes represented in the order of their occurrence in the Biblical text, we obtain the following picture of the use of this Biblical material:

273. *Ibid.*, XX, 7, 1 = § 139.
274. *Ibid.*, XIX, 5, 1 = § 277, and XX, 4, a = § 103.
275. *Ibid.*, XIX, 5, 1 = § 277, and XX, 7, 1 = § 138.

276. *Bellum* II, 18, 5 = § 479.
277. *Antiquitates* XX, 7, 1 and 3 = §§ 138 and 145.
278. See above, pp. 349 f.

Genesis	15.1–6	Abraham receives the Promise (Wing Panel IV)	Exodus	[37.17–24	Construction of Lampstand] (Panel WB 2)
	22.1–14	Sacrifice of Isaac (Torah Shrine Façade)		[38.1–7	Construction of Altar of Burnt Offering] (Panel WB 2)
	28.10–17	Jacob at Bethel (Panel NA 1)		[39.1–26	Garments of Aaron] (Panel WB 2)
	48.13–20	Jacob blesses Ephraim and Manasseh (Lower Center Panel)		40 or Numbers 7	Consecration of the Tabernacle (Panel WB 2)
	49.1–28	Jacob blesses his twelve Sons (Lower Center Panel)	Numbers	2	Wilderness Encampment (Panel WB 1)
	[49.9–10	The Shiloh Prophecy] (Central Area)		[7	Consecration of the Tabernacle] (Panel WB 2)
Exodus	1.8–11	Israelites build Treasure-City of Ramses (Panel WC 4)		[19.1–13	Preparation of the Red Heifer] (Panel WB 2)
	1.15–16	Pharaoh gives Orders to Midwives (Panel WC 4)		21.16–18	The Well of Be'er (Panel WB 1)
	2.1–3	Exposure of the Infant Moses (Panel WC 4)	I Samuel	1.21–28	Hannah takes Samuel to Shiloh (Panel NB 2)
	2.5–6	Egyptian Princess finds the Infant Moses (Panel WC 4)		[2.1–10	Hannah's Prophecy] (Panel WB 3)
	2.7–8	Miriam accosts the Princess (Panel WC 4)		3.1–14	The Child Samuel in the temple (Panel NB 2)
	2.9–10	Moses is returned to his Mother (Panel WC 4)		4.1–10	The Battle of Eben-ezer (Panel NB 1)
	3.1–16	Moses and the Burning Bush (Wing Panel I)		4.11	Capture of the Ark by the Philistines (Panel NB 1)
	[9.22–26 or 14.24–25.	Plague of Hail and Fire] (Panel WA 3)		5.1–5	The Ark in the Temple of Dagon (Panel WB 4)
	12.37–39	Exodus from City of Ramses (Panel WA 3)		6.1–12	The Ark returned to Israel (Panel WB 4)
	14.21–22	Crossing of Red Sea (Panel WA 3)		16.1–13	Samuel anoints David (Panel WC 3)
	14.24–25	Pillar of Cloud and Fire (Panel WA 3)		23.15–18	The Meeting of David and Jonathan (Panel EC 1)
	14.26–28	Drowning of Egyptians (Panel WA 3)		26.2	Saul seeks David in the Wilderness of Ziph (Panel EC 1)
	24.12–18 or Exod. 34.	Moses receives the Law (Wing Panel II)		26.7–12	David spares Saul's Life (Panel EC 1)
	[27.16	Curtains before Gate of Court] (Panel WB 2)	II Samuel	5.1–5	David King over all Israel (Upper Center Panel)
	[30.11–16	Half-shekel Offering] (Panel WB 2)		[5.9	David builds the Walls of Jerusalem] (Panel WB 4)
	[35	Construction of the Tabernacle] (Panel WB 2)	I Kings	1.38–40	Solomon anointed King (Panel WA 1)
	[36.35–36	Veils of the Tabernacle] (Panel WB 2)		6	Solomon builds the Temple (Panel WB 3)
	[37.1–9	Construction of the Ark] (Panel WB 2)		8.1–11	Dedication of the Temple (Panel SB 1)

Whatever uncertainty may exist about the identification of the subject matter of individual compositions, it is entirely clear that the Synagogue artists tend to focus their attention upon certain individual books of the Bible and that in their treatment of these books they follow the thread of the Biblical narrative episode by episode. This is reflected in the existence of the Samuel and Elijah cycles in Registers B and C and in the panels with the largest number of scenes (Panels WC 4 and NC 1). The Moses scenes also follow the order of the Biblical narratives closely even though they are scattered about in various parts of the decorations. The interest of the artists in the sequence of episodes in a given Biblical book, moreover, does not end when they have developed such series of panels as those that bring the Samuel and the Elijah cycles. The cycles reach an end determined by the didactic purposes which the artists had in mind.[279] But other scenes from the same books are found outside the areas set aside for the development of the cycles, showing that the artists' interest in the books was not exhausted by the rendering of the cycles.

We are confronted, then, with a combination of three facts. The first is that the Synagogue artists had specific books of the Bible as the sources of their inspiration. The second is that in handling the subject matter of these books they tended to follow the thread of the Biblical narrative episode by episode. The third is that in at least two instances they began their rendering of the narratives with a scene representing the first chapter of the book.[280] The conclusion suggested by these three facts is that the bulk of the pictures was first conceived for and rendered in illustrated manuscripts of parts of the Bible or of its narratives in their Biblical sequence. From the manuscripts they

279. This is clear, for instance, in the Samuel cycle, where the terminus is reached when the Ark is ready to find a resting place in the Temple of Solomon at Jerusalem, and when through the establishment of the Israelite capital the prophecy of Hannah in the Targumic version of I Samuel 2.1–10 goes into fulfilment. Other series are terminated by didactic foils, especially the compositions with a central focus. So in the Ezekiel series, the scenes representing the end of national life at the destruction of Jerusalem provide a counterweight to those showing its rebirth, and in so doing terminate the use of the Ezekiel material.

280. This is clear in Exodus and I Samuel; it may also be true of I Kings.

passed into mural decoration, and through the mural rendering of the material they have come to us.

The suggestion implicit in this conclusion; namely, that there existed in antiquity in Jewish circles illustrated manuscripts with pictures representing Biblical scenes, is quite as strange at first as the existence of the actual Dura Synagogue paintings themselves. Like the paintings it raises a variety of questions for which an answer has yet to be found. But the transfer of material in general from manuscript illustration to wall decoration seems necessary. An analogy is provided by what the Venerable Bede tells us about Benedict Biscop who brought with him from Rome large collections of books and thus obtained material for the wall decorations of the chapel in the monastery of St. Peter at Canterbury.[281] Similarly students of Christian manuscript illustration have long believed that the mosaic decorations of the narthex of St. Mark's in Venice were taken from a manuscript such as the Cotton Bible and use these mosaics today to restore the cycle of the illustrations of the Cotton Bible.[282] The particular form in which the Dura Synagogue material may be said to have existed in earlier illustrated manuscripts can be conjectured from a knowledge of the history of book illustration and from what has been observed about the relation of the Cotton Genesis and the mosaics of St. Mark. As to the former it would appear from the study of Weitzmann that even in Egypt, where "strip" organization of manuscript illustration had earlier been in use, this tended to disappear in the Hellenistic period in favor of the individual scene inserted in columns of written text.[283] The inference would seem to be that if the suggested manuscript from which the Biblical scenes of the Dura composition were taken was produced in the Hellenistic period, the scenes would have existed as separate

entities in the text and would have been combined when they were transferred for the first time to wall surfaces. As to the latter, it would appear that in adapting the miniatures of the Cotton Bible to the decoration of the narthex of St. Mark's, the artists of the thirteenth century produced in their mosaics phenomena of combination, condensation, conflation, and selection similar to those in the paintings of the Dura Synagogue. The extent to which monoscenic compositions and compositions that bring together two scenes readily separable from each other predominate in the Synagogue, would therefore seem to show that in the projected manuscript source each scene originally stood alone. At the same time, the remoteness of Dura from libraries in which such manuscripts could conceivably have existed makes it inherently probable that as they are presented at Dura the compositions are copied from wall decorations in synagogues elsewhere, and that the postulated manuscript source is at least two steps removed from the form in which we have the picture.

But what shall we say about the basic suggestion that in the days before the Dura Synagogue and the synagogues of northern Mesopotamia there already existed manuscripts with illustrations of Biblical narratives? The suggestion must be received with great caution, because it relates to a holy book and one that was hedged about with many safeguards. True, we have in mediaeval Jewish manuscripts decorative and pictorial material. The manuscripts are scattered about among the great libraries and collections of Europe and America, and among them they present a wealth of illustrations of many different types. Those that provide the closest analogies to the Dura pictures are the Passover Haggadahs, the Esther Rolls, the Maḥzors and Siddurs with their hagiographic and Haggadic supplements. But in none of these do we find anything like the range of the interest represented in the Dura Synagogue, with its attention to such books as I Samuel and I Kings. Moreover, all of these illustrated books are types that cannot be presumed to have existed in antiquity. From the post-Renaissance period Hebrew Bibles with individual illustrations are known, and the use of illustrative material in Hebrew Pentateuchs can be traced back to the tenth century of our era. But in the earliest manuscripts the illustrations are

281. *Patrologia Latina*, XCIV, cols. 716–718. These decorations constituted an innovation in England at the time, and included pictures of the Evangelists and the visions of the Book of Revelations. That they were copied out of the manuscripts is a logical inference.

282. See J. J. Tikkanen, *Die Genesis-Mosaiken von S. Marco in Venedig und ihr Verhältnis zu den Miniaturen der Cottonbibel* (*Acta Societatis Scientiarum Fennicae*, XVII, 1889); and Weitzmann, *Illustrations in Roll and Codex*, p. 140. This and the previous reference I owe to Weitzmann.

283. See *ibid.*, pp. 57–69.

carefully restricted to the representation of the cult and Temple paraphernalia,[284] and they represent Bible codices rather than scrolls and are thus irrelevant for our purposes.

What we know about the preparation of Hebrew Bible manuscripts in antiquity bids us beware of supposing that there ever existed scrolls intended for official synagogue use that had any illustrations whatsoever. The rules and regulations covering their preparation were carefully laid down and observed, and if there was objection even to the use of gold for the letters of the tetragrammaton, there can be no doubt that even schematic representations such as occur in the Hebrew codices of the tenth century were quite out of the question.[285] In antiquity the beauty even of scrolls intended for private use was measured by the excellence and accuracy of the execution of their text.[286] It is not surprising, therefore, that in the large collection of books owned by the Essene community of the Dead Sea region, not a single fragment of an illustrated scroll has come to light.

If it were folly to imagine that illustrated scrolls containing books of the Bible in Hebrew ever existed, what can be said about translations and paraphrases? More particularly what can be said about the Septuagint and the Targumim? As regards the Targumim there is always the prior question of the date at which the text of these renderings was finally set down; and while, as we have seen above, dependence upon Targumic tradition is a feature of the decorations of the Synagogue, the interval between the earliest possible codification of the Targums and the Synagogue paintings is scarcely sufficient to make them the source of the pictures. In the case of the Septuagint and the other Greek translations, the situation is certainly quite different, and eventually evidence for the existence of illustrated copies of the text, prepared as luxury scrolls for Hellenized Jews, may be forthcoming. At the moment, however, it still seems as though some basis would first need to be established for the illustration of part or even all of the Septuagint, for at the outset it was still a holy book and as such not the kind of work into which illustrations would readily be placed.

Some attention should be given in this connection to what has recently been said by Weitzmann about the origin of book illustration generally in the Hellenistic world. He has advanced the thesis that book illustration begins in the Hellenistic period with the preparation of illustrated editions of the scientific works, magical books, and luxury editions of the epics and the works of the dramatists. Among literary works it is especially the Homeric epics and the tragedies of Euripides that existed in illustrated luxury editions. Evidence for this is provided by the Megarian bowls.[287]

Now it will be recalled that in the period of the closest *rapprochement* between Judaism and the Hellenistic world, the period between Alexander the Great and the Maccabean Revolt, efforts were made by Jewish writers to bring the contents of their Biblical books to the attention of the cultured Greek-reading public. To do this the writers in question had of necessity to take the material out of the category of sacred literature and to present it as secular literature in accordance with the literary taste of the age. In their original form all works produced in this connection and for this purpose have perished, as the result perhaps of the purist reactions of later periods. But particularly through Eusebius of Caesarea we have preserved to us lengthy quotations from several of them that represent the type of product in question. Apparently the works produced in the effort to bring the Biblical material to the attention of Greek readers generally took at least three forms. The first was that of historical prose narrative, and we know about and have fragments of several works "About the Kings who ruled in Judea" or "About the Jews." Some of these, like the writings of Artapanos, Kleodemos (or Malchos), and Pseudo-Eupolemos are definitely syncretistic and combine

---

284. The material is conveniently assembled in Stassof and Günsbourg, *L'Ornement hébreu*.

285. On the general subject of ancient Hebrew manuscript production, see L. Blau, *Studien zum althebräischen Buchwesen* (1902); and *idem*, *Soncino-Blaetter*, I (1925–1926), pp. 16–28.

286. See, e.g., Shabbath 133b (Trans., II, 2, p. 670): "Make a .... beautiful scroll of the Law, and write upon it with fine ink, a fine reed pen and a skilled penman and wrap it about with beautiful silks." The statement is ascribed to Rabbi Johanan, and parallels what he says about making beautiful Sukkahs, shofars, lulabs, and fringes.

287. See *Illustrations in Roll and Codex*, pp. 65–81.

Jewish and pagan religious beliefs and traditions.[288] These seem to have been written in Egypt. Some have nothing that we can associate either with a specific time or place, but others again, like the writings of Demetrius and Eupolemos, have contacts with the Palestinian Haggadah and may have originated there.[289] They are credibly assigned to about the years 200 and 150 B.C. respectively.[290] Alongside these prose narratives there existed also versions of Biblical narratives that took the form of epics and were written in hexameters. Eusebius has preserved twenty-four verses of an epic written by a certain Philo (called Philo the Elder) which recounted the history of Jerusalem and expatiated upon things as early as the Sacrifice of Isaac and as late as the history of the Jewish kings.[291] For this a date about 200 B.C. is suggested. Finally, one important part of the Biblical narrative; namely, that of the Exodus and Wilderness Wandering, was rendered as a tragedy written in iambic pentameters by a certain tragic poet Ezekiel in the second century B.C., of which 269 verses are preserved.[292] It was called "The Exodus."

These remains of an early Hellenistic-Jewish literature adopt the forms of Greek literary usage. If on other grounds it would appear that manuscript illustration began in the third century B.C. with the preparation of luxury editions of the Greek epic and tragic poets, it is entirely possible that the illustration of Bible narratives among the Jews began in those versions of the stories that presented them in the literary forms borrowed from the classical authors. This would be all the more likely since the works in question were written for promotional and propagandistic pur-

poses. Writers pursuing these purposes would be the more inclined to give their products all the attractiveness of the illustrated editions of the comparable works in the classical field.

The train of thought that we have followed in trying to answer the questions raised by the study of the Synagogue paintings suggests the following as an hypothetical development. The pictorial representation of Biblical narratives began in the pre-Maccabean period with cycles of individual scenes in works composed by Jews in the forms used in secular Greek literature and prepared as luxury editions to rival those of illustrated Greek classics. From these works the use of illustration spread into rolls representing the text of parts of the Bible also prepared as luxury editions for the private use of men of means or of political importance. From manuscripts of this type the material was taken several centuries later for the interior decoration of synagogues such as may have been built under princely auspices in the Dispersion. The transfer to the new medium was suggested by the desire to make the synagogues rival the painted pagan temples in the excellence of their interior appointments, and thus occurred in the region in which the painted temple was an established institution. This was certainly true of upper Mesopotamia, as Dura itself indicates. In being transferred from manuscript to wall, individual scenes were occasionally combined in large compositions, abbreviation, conflation, and selection permitting the representation of larger bodies of subject matter on limited wall surfaces. From larger synagogues existing in areas more densely populated with Jews, the paintings passed to remote frontier posts such as Dura, as the contacts with the areas in which they already existed became more continuous and close.

One additional aspect of the Dura Synagogue paintings seems to deserve consideration in this connection; namely, that of the direction of movement in the compositions. There are of course many compositions and scenes among the paintings that lack all indication of movement in one direction or another. They are either completely static and frontal, or they have a central axis toward which movement develops from either side. Examples of the former are the representation of David installed as king over all Israel (Upper Center Panel) and

288. For the material see Clement of Alexandria, *Stromata* I, 153; Eusebius of Caesarea, *Praeparatio Evangelica* IX, 26, 30–34 (Artapanos); Josephus, *Antiquitates* I, 15 = § 240f.; *Praeparatio Evangelica* IX, 20 (Kleodemos or Malchos); *ibid.*, IX, 17–18 (Pseudo-Eupolemos). For the entire range of literature represented, see O. Stählin in W. Christ, *Geschichte der griechischen Litteratur*, II, 1 (6th ed., 1920), pp. 588–591.

289. For the material see Clement of Alexandria, *Stromata* I, 141; and Eusebius, *Praeparatio Evangelica* IX, 21, 29 (Demetrius), 30–34 (Eupolemos).

290. On Demetrius see Freudenthal, *Hellenistische Studien*, I, pp. 35–82. On Eupolemos and an unnamed Samaritan writer confused with him, see *ibid.*, pp. 82–103.

291. For the material see Eusebius, *Praeparatio Evangelica* IX, 20, 24, 37. Another epic by a certain Theodotus is excerpted by Eusebius, *ibid.*, 22.

292. For the material, see *ibid.*, 28.

Abraham receiving the Promise (Wing Panel IV), and examples of the latter are the first scene of the Battle of Eben-ezer (Panel NB 1, right half) or the Prophets of Baal on Mount Carmel (Panel SC 3). Static or centralized scenes of this type could have stood in any manuscript and are familiar in all media and periods of Christian art. But there are also in the Synagogue scenes showing motion in a given direction, some to the right and some to the left, and the question is, whether this fact has any bearing upon the hypothesis deriving the prototypes from illustrated manuscripts. What makes the question relevant is the possibility that in an Aramaic scroll, whose text would be unrolled and read from right to left, we might well expect the action of any illustrations it contained to move with the eye from right to left, whereas in a Greek scroll the opposite might well be the case.

Now it stands to reason that any artist copying material could change direction of movement at will, by merely reversing the representation of his archetype, so that no general inference can be drawn from direction of movement to archetype. Especially is this so if at the same time he was combining, conflating, and generally abbreviating. But there is one longer composition in the Dura Synagogue the peculiarities of which may bear noting in this connection; namely, that portraying Pharaoh and the Infancy of Moses (Panel WC 4). Whereas in this composition as a whole the sequence of events moves from right to left, the individual scenes that are not static always show motion from the left toward a terminus at the right.[293] Leaving aside the static frontal scene showing the princess discovering the Ark in the Nile, we find that the midwives come into the presence of Pharaoh from the left, that Miriam approaches the princess from the left, and that Moses' mother approaches Miriam (or in the prototype the princess) from the left. At the same time the fact that we find Moses' mother stooping toward the right when she places the child Moses in the ark of bulrushes seems to imply that the ark will move toward the right in the direction she is facing. Thus we see that while the Synagogue artist found it desirable to have the action of the panel as a whole move from right to left — that is, toward the Torah Shrine — he was using scenes composed to show motion in the opposite direction. This not only argues that the scenes originally had a separate existence, but also suggests that we have here evidence for the direction of movement in the prototypes. In all other instances the original direction of movement could have been changed by the Synagogue artists by reversing the pattern for the scene. Here it had to be preserved, even though the sequence of events in the composition as a whole was changed, because otherwise the material could not have been abbreviated and compressed into the space available. If the direction of movement in the separate scenes was fundamentally from left to right, this would be most suitable in a scroll written in Greek, which was unrolled and read from left to right.

D. Biblical Scenes in Jewish and early Christian Art

We cannot suppose that the Dura Synagogue paintings themselves ever had any effect on the further development of ancient art, Jewish or Christian. They were too remote from the centers of ancient life and had too short a span of life.[294] The suggestion that they are copies of earlier prototypes and that behind them lie illustrated manuscripts reaching back to the pre-Maccabean period of Jewish life, however, inevitably raises the question whether the tradition they represent may not have influenced the development of early Christian art. The question is one that in its larger compass must be the concern of the historian of Christian art. Yet it cannot be ignored here entirely because the answer has a necessary bearing upon the understanding of the character of the different traditions in Jewish art discussed above.[295]

In approaching the materials of early Christian art it will be wise to avoid two common but highly debatable generalizations; namely, that the Christians adopted the use of art easily, and that the earliest monuments of Christian art — the catacomb frescoes — belong to the immediately post-

293. See above, Pls. LXVII–LXVIII.
294. The period between their execution and the construction of the embankment in which they were buried is not more than about five or six years.

295. See above, pp. 361–363.

apostolic period. A close study of the literary tradition indicates that the Christians, having adopted the Bible of the Jewish people, had to grapple with the selfsame prohibition of the use of images that had so much preoccupied the Jews of the post-Maccabean period, and found no easy solution.[296] Even after Palestinian Judaism had found the way toward a more liberal interpretation of the Biblical commandment, Christian writers were still taking a conservative position in their discussion of it. At the same time a close study of catacomb construction and of the style of the catacomb paintings has demonstrated the complete falsity of the views assigning the earliest of the decorations to the late first and early second centuries of our era.[297] But the fact remains that approximately by the time of the Dura Synagogue paintings, Christian catacomb art was already in existence and that with the Dura paintings in hand we can no longer avoid the question of the relation between early Christian and Jewish representative art.

One fact about Christian catacomb decorations has been evident since they began to receive serious attention; namely, that among the subjects chosen for representation those from the Old Testament far outnumber those from the New. Indeed, in the earliest phases of Christian catacomb art we find no representations of New Testament episodes, except the symbolic Good Shepherd. Everything else with historical associations comes from the Old Testament. This fact has led to suggestions by students of early Christian art that the Christians of Rome may have taken their inspiration from a Jewish art tradition.[298] With the Dura Synagogue material in hand the presumption of such a dependence can no longer be denied categorically.[299]

This does not necessarily mean that the antecedents of the Christian catacomb paintings are to be found in Jewish catacombs. It may well be doubted whether Jews were even inclined to portray Biblical scenes in such contexts. Nor is it likely that the paintings passed from the decorations of private houses to the catacombs, as Styger has suggested,[300] and that we would have to assume the existence of similar paintings in Jewish private houses to establish the connection. The only domestic context in which either Christians or Jews can be assumed to have used Biblical paintings is that of the house-church and house-synagogue; that is to say, in the context of a single room especially set aside for religious use.[301] This is not what Styger had in mind and in effect takes us back to a quite different milieu. Either we must associate the Christian and the Jewish use of Biblical scenes with synagogue decoration or with manuscript illustration.

For an understanding of the possible relation between the Old Testament materials in Christian catacomb decoration and those represented by the Dura Synagogue it is important to have a clear picture of the subjects represented in the former. Leaving aside the otherwise unidentifiable "prophets" who appear as solitary individuals in the Christian catacombs, or the identifiable prophets connected with New Testament scenes, we find the following Old Testament materials most commonly represented:

> Moses striking Water from the Rock (68 examples)
> Jonah and the Whale (58 examples)
> Daniel and the Lions (40 examples)
> Noah in the Ark (33 examples)
> The Sacrifice of Isaac (22 examples)
> The three Men in the Fiery Furnace (17 examples)
> Moses on Mount Sinai (15 examples)
> Job forsaken by his Friends (11 examples).[302]

296. See now N. H. Baynes' essay in *Byzantine Studies and other Essays* (1955), pp. 116–143; and W. Elliger, *Die Stellung der alten Christen zu den Bildern in den ersten vier Jahrhunderten* (*Studien über christliche Denkmäler*, n.s., 20, 1930–1934).

297. See especially P. Styger, *Die römischen Katakomben* (1933); and Wirth, *Römische Wandmalerei*, pp. 166–176.

298. See, e.g., O. Wulff, *Altchristliche und byzantinische Kunst*, I (1914), pp. 68 f.; and C. R. Morey, *Early Christian Art* (1942), pp. 58–77 among the Christian scholars; and among the Jewish scholars, D. Kaufmann, *Revue des études juives*, XIV (1887), pp. 33–48, 217–253; and Landsberger, *History of Jewish Art*, p. 171.

299. W. Elliger in his *Zur Entstehung und frühen Entwicklung der altchristlichen Bildkunst* (*Studien über christliche Denkmäler*, n.s., 23, 1934), pp. 45–48, still passes

over the subject much too lightly in our judgment. More acceptable is the position taken by Goodenough in *Jewish Quarterly Review*, n.s., XXXIII (1942–1943), pp. 403–417.

300. P. Styger, *Die altchristliche Grabeskunst* (1927), pp. 74, 90; *idem*, *Die römischen Katakomben*, pp. 356 f.

301. On house-church and house-synagogue, see above, p. 33.

302. The number of occurrences is that given by Leclercq in Cabrol, *Dictionnaire*, s.v. "Catacombes, Art des."

It will be noted that while the list of the subjects treated in the Christian catacombs overlaps with that of the subjects treated in the Dura Synagogue, there are fundamental differences between them. The first and most obvious difference is that the Synagogue paintings do not illustrate the Bible as such; they follow the narratives of individual books of the Bible.[303] The Christian catacomb paintings give the opposite impression. They seem to be a *florilegium* that brings together from the Bible as a whole the most graphic incidents and the ones that were bound to make the most profound and immediate impression on the beholder. In other words, the approach to the material is basically of a different character, even though the choices overlap. It is implied in this fact that the catacomb paintings do not normally follow the thread of development in rendering an episode, as do the Synagogue paintings. They do not, for instance, show how the king ordered Daniel to be thrown to the lions or how he was released after having escaped from their violence. Indeed the disregard of context can even go so far in the case of the "prophets" as to omit all accessories and thus leave some doubt as to the identity of the person represented. In the Synagogue even the individual figures shown in the Wing Panels are still associated with enough setting to identify the narrative portrayed. This relation to setting is even more pronounced in the representation of prophets like Elijah and Ezekiel. In the catacombs there is one exception to this disregard of the larger narrative context; namely, the representation of the fate of Jonah. Here the rendering involves at least the scenes of Jonah swallowed by the whale and Jonah spewed up by the whale. This we are inclined to regard as the exception that proves the rule, because the jeopardy which Jonah faced could not readily have been presented without showing both parts of the action.

More important still for our purposes is the difference that we note in the particular tradition about the jeopardy of the Wilderness Wandering used in the Christian catacombs. What the catacombs portray with complete consistency is the scene of Moses striking water from the rock. The reference is clearly to the episode that occurred at Rephidim, as told in Exodus 17.1–6. We have already had occasion to follow in the literary sources the two different traditions about the water supply of the Wilderness period, and to show how among the Hellenistic Jewish writers the emphasis falls on the Rephidim and Elim episodes, making certain iconographic demands upon the artists, and how among the Haggadic writers the emphasis falls upon Be'er and the miraculous well.[304] From this analysis it is clear that the catacomb representation follows a different tradition from the one used in the Dura Synagogue.

The fact that there are such fundamental differences between the Old Testament scenes of the Christian catacombs and the paintings of the Synagogue by no means indicates that the former are completely independent of Jewish art. It suggests that the particular tradition of Jewish art that provided the prototypes for the Christian catacomb paintings is different from the one represented in the great body of the Dura paintings. The former lacks the characteristics of a body of material prepared ultimately to illustrate manuscripts of individual parts of the Bible. Instead it has the characteristics of the tradition of symbolic Jewish art to which we have referred above.[305] Here, as we know from the synagogues of Gerasa, Na'aran, and Beth Alpha, individual Biblical scenes are occasionally used to emphasize or symbolize a particular concept or a range of associated ideas, and this is precisely what the Christian catacomb paintings do. That this tradition was much older than the period of these synagogues is demonstrated by the appearance of the Sacrifice of Isaac in a symbolic context on the façade of the Torah Shrine at Dura, a separate and earlier element of the Synagogue's decoration. The same scene appears in similar isolation in the Christian catacombs.

When in Christian art we pass from the period of catacomb decoration to that of pictorial mosaics in the churches and so from the third to the fifth century, the problem of the relation of Jewish and Christian art changes its character radically. Now New Testament material begins to take precedence over Old, but this does not mean that any influence of Jewish pictorial material upon Christian representational art is necessarily at an end. What is

---

303. See above, p. 392.

304. See above, pp. 122–124.
305. See above, pp. 361–363.

significant in this connection is the fact that the mosaic decorations of the churches bring long and increasingly detailed cycles of pictures representing successive episodes of Biblical history rendered in narrative form. Scene follows scene in a given composition and panel follows panel as the sequence of events in the development of the sacred history and the plan of salvation is developed. Here we have clearly left the art tradition that chooses an individual scene at random and presents it in isolation as a symbol of a range of ideas. If the Old Testament scenes of these mosaics have Jewish prototypes, those prototypes belong to an entirely different tradition than the prototypes of the catacomb frescoes. Their manner of presentation suggests that the prototypes are illustrated manuscripts.

Because so much of the interior decoration of the earliest Christian churches has long since disappeared and much of what existed has to be reconstructed by inference from ancient descriptions and from the filiation and provenience of illustrated Christian manuscripts, the question about the relation between the Dura Synagogue paintings and the later Christian art requires special investigation and may be left to others to answer. Two things, however, may be said here. The first is that with the sarcophagi, the mosaics, and the illustrated manuscripts of the early Byzantine period we come closer to the type of tradition represented in the Synagogue. The narrative interest and the narrative procedure in representation are common to both. The second is that in the tradition followed at Rome, to the extent that we see it in the mosaics of Santa Maria Maggiore, we may be dealing with quite a different type or family of illustrated Jewish manuscripts than the one reflected in the Dura paintings. The basis for this statement is what has been said above about the iconography of the Exodus and the Crossing of the Red Sea composition.[306] The fact that in the Synagogue this was so rendered as to show the Israelites armed and Pharaoh's army, while in the Christian counterpart the opposite is the case, indicates two different literary traditions, the Haggadic Jewish and the Hellenistic Jewish respectively. The inference is not that Christian and Jewish renderings are inde-

pendent even in this later period, but that the Jewish source would have been a body of manuscript illustration different in origin from that represented in the Dura paintings. If the illustrated manuscript tradition reflected in the Dura paintings had an echo in early Byzantine art, this might well be found in such products of eastern Christian art as the Octateuchs and their relatives and in the decorations of eastern Christian churches long since destroyed.[307]

The basic characteristics of Christian art before and after the peace of the Church serves to confirm our earlier suggestion that there were two fundamentally distinct types of ancient Jewish art.[308] The one tradition is symbolic, the other explicitly narrative. The narrative tradition, we have indicated, seems to come out of illustrated manuscripts of parts of the Bible and perhaps we need to visualize two separate cycles or families to account for the full range of the relevant material. The one is lost and could conceivably be restored from a study of such Christian monuments as Santa Maria Maggiore and its relatives, but goes with an interpretative tradition connected with the Judaism of Egypt and the Mediterranean basin. The other is known to us from the Synagogue of Dura and is perhaps reflected in the Christian Octateuchs. It belongs to the general region that has Palestinian and Babylonian Judaism as its two poles and the Haggadic tradition as its earmark. Perhaps in origin it is somehow to be associated with Syria or its neighborhood toward the east. It would clearly be wrong to suppose that these various traditions lived perpetually shut off from each other and never influenced each other, but the cross-fertilization that must have occurred should not be permitted to obscure the basic differences or to confuse or oversimplify the picture.

Its Synagogue thus bears out magnificently the truth of the statement of Rostovtzeff about Dura with which we began the final section of this report. Once more we see how a single building of a frontier city adds immensely to our knowledge of the ancient world generally because of the scientific importance of the material that its ruins yield.[309] The

307. Professor Weitzmann will have more to say on this in his publication of the Octateuchs.

308. See above, pp. 361–363.

309. See above, p. 321.

306. See above, pp. 80 f., n. 237.

26

Dura Synagogue is in a very real sense a chance discovery, an incident and an accident that could not be predicted and cannot be expected to occur soon again. But this by no means belittles its importance. The Synagogue brings to vivid expression the vigor and the piety, the high aspiration and the dignity of a relatively small and unimportant Jewish community of the eastern Dispersion in a frontier garrison city. At the same time through this one structure we can look out into a vast panorama of historical development and relationships, finding new insights suggested everywhere.

Here we find new suggestions for an understanding of the growth and development of synagogue architecture. Here the history of Jewish piety and of the development of its interpretative tradition is freshly illumined. Here the ancient Jewish use of art is restored to its rightful place in the total picture of ancient Judaism. Here we see in a new light the common front which Christianity and Judaism held against paganism, and the relationship between Jewish and Christian art. These are the things that give the Dura Synagogue its scientific importance.

Prolegomenon

Index

Addendum

Prolegomenon

by   HARALD INGHOLT

The origin of the Index goes back to the year 1970 when the Associate Provost of Yale University, George D. Langdon Jr., appointed a committee of four "to review all matters concerning Dura-Europos". The four were: Professors Ramsay MacMullen, Adam Parry (†), Jerome Pollitt, and Harald Ingholt, Acting Curator Dura-Europos Publications, Chairman. Their report was submitted to Mr. Langdon in November, 1972, recommending in its final remarks that the Dura publications be resumed. Of the eight *Final Reports* planned only one has been completed, four are incomplete and three have not even been started. It is most important that the remaining volumes of the *Final Reports* be finished as some of them contain much entirely new material.

For the proposed new publications funds would have to be raised and in order to help, even in a small way, the Committee already in March 1971 requested that Carl H. Kraeling's brilliant work on the Dura Synagogue should be reissued. It had been published in 1956 and the 800-copy edition had been quickly sold out. Fortunately 1000 extra sets of the color plates were made at the time of the first edition, so that the new issue could be manufactured for less than the current price. Mr. Langdon approved the request "contingent upon the funds being available to cover the full costs of printing the second edition".

Throughout the scholarly world Kraeling's book was cited for its excellence. However, the distinguished Curator of Judaica in the British Museum, Jacob Leveen, concluded his laudatory review with these words: "Our felicity would have been complete, if the book had included an index, so necessary when text and notes are thickly studded with references to notes".[1] He no doubt voiced a general desideratum, the fulfilment of which would add considerably to the usefulness of the book.

Already in 1971 three friends of Dura had decided to add an index to the reissue, the funds collected to be deposited in the Dura Publication Fund.

Mrs. Betty Ellis, guest-docent at the Yale University Art Gallery, when approached, volunteered to do the General Index, the larger part of the task. Stanley Insler, Professor of Sanskrit at Yale, volunteered to make a list of the Middle Iranian words and proper names, and Harald Ingholt a similar list from the Hebrew, Aramaic, Greek and Latin inscriptions, at the same time acting as general supervisor of the entire undertaking.

In drawing up a plan for the Index of the Kraeling book it seemed important to draw attention to the fact that Kraeling was not actually the sole author, but had inserted into his text contributions from three specialists: Charles C. Torrey on the Aramaic texts (pp. 261–276), C. Bradford Welles on the Greek (pp. 277–282) and Bernhard Geiger on the Middle Iranian (pp. 283–317). How should the references to these writers best be treated: integrated with the references from the Kraeling text in due alphabetic order, or listed separately?

The latter plan was chosen as being both fairer and clearer. In the case of one of the main subdivisions of the Kraeling material, the *General Index*, only the Kraeling text would be considered by the indexer. In like manner the texts of each of the linguists would be treated individually. In the two other main subdivisions of the Kraeling material, the *Citations* and the *Glossaries*, the same rule would be followed.

In favor of the accepted plan one may mention two special features. It has the advantage of distinguishing between the common Aramaic of the region and the Aramaic of the inscriptions from the Dura synagogue. Secondly, it would prevent a "hypothesis" or "conclusion" from being ascribed to Kraeling when it should have been attributed to one of the three linguists (see an article in *Syria*, XL (1963), pp. 305–309).

One problem was the large number of notes. Should they all be listed in the Index? In the editor's mind they were all so important to Kraeling's book that they should indeed be included. The notes may be divided into two categories

---

[1] Journal of Semitic Studies, III (1958), p. 315

according to important differences in their content. Some are "source notes"; others, by far the most numerous, give a background or a further development of the text in question. A couple of examples will, I think, make the difference clear. A good example of the source variety we find on p. 204 where the hunting tradition is mentioned and the source of the tradition given in n. 804.[2] As a sample of the "development note" we would cite p. 101 and its note 328, the former mentioning two pedestals, the latter discussing another identification.[3] Kraeling could, I suppose, have placed the contents of the "development notes" in the text, but preferred not to have his line of presentation broken.

In conclusion I want to render thanks to the many persons who in various ways have helped the double enterprise, the reissue of Kraeling's book and the creation of the Index. Our sincere thanks are due to George Langdon, now President of Colgate University, to John E. Ecklund, Treasurer of Yale University, and to William J. Feeney, Associate Treasurer of the University. Among the Yale colleagues who have been helpful with the Index in various ways Professor E. D. Francis, Curator of the Dura Collection from 1972 to 1975 should be mentioned; also Professor Sid Leiman, now of Georgetown University, Washington, D.C. who was always ready to give advice in the field of Judaica. To J. J. Augustin, the printer of the Index, I owe a sincere debt of gratitude for the patience and expert advice in dealing with the technical problems inherent in the archaeological, historical, linguistic and typographical aspects of the Index.

The printing costs of the Index was taken care of partly by the three authors, partly by a wider group of "Friends of Dura": A. Elizabeth Chase, Docent in the Yale Art Gallery emeritus, Millar Burrows, Liston Pope (†), Professors emeriti at Yale; and last but not least, Mrs. Prescott W. Townsend, without whose support this work would never have been accomplished.

[2] Another example: p. 148, Elijah and the widow's son, the source in n. 435.
[3] Another example: p. 173, the two midwives, the note 664 giving another identification. The "development notes" have the page number plus the note number, e.g. 101 n. 328, and 172 n. 660.

The work on the Index took much longer than at first anticipated. Unforeseen obstacles which had nothing to do directly with the work of the Index, and difficulties based on the multifacetted character of the Kraeling opus were mainly responsible for the delays. However, behind the years of work lay a genuine desire on the part of the authors to make this small contribution to the Dura bibliography worthy of the man without whom there would never have been a Yale excavation at Dura, Professor Michael Rostovtzeff.

What happened on the site of Dura in the few years *before* the joint excavation of Yale and the Académie des Inscriptions et Belles-Lettre explains when and why Yale became involved. In March of 1920 the region of Dura was administered under the British Mandate, and it was on this spot overlooking the Euphrates, that a British officer, Murphy, discovered some frescoes in remarkable state of preservation. He alerted his general who was unable at that time to do anything about them. That year it happened that James Breasted, Director of the Oriental Institute in Chicago, was travelling in the Near East and with the help of the British Army he was able to reach Dura; but because of the military situation he and his staff had but one day, May 4th, in which to examine and photograph paintings and temples.

When peace was declared Dura had passed from the British to the French Mandate, and it was first in July of the year 1922 that Breasted lectured before the French Academy, with the result that the Academy decided to excavate the site. The excavations were led by the Belgian scholar, Franz Cumont, whose book "Les Fouilles de Doura-Europos 1922–23" (Paris 1926) quickly became a "classic". Unfortunately, no further excavations were planned after his two campaigns.

At this point Yale entered the picture. In 1927 the General Education Board of the Rockefeller Foundation accorded to Yale the sum of $195,000 "in order to stimulate graduate research in the Ilumanities". Of this sum "Yale chose to invest a large sum of the fund in the efforts at Dura to secure a fuller and more rewarding insight into the history and culture of the Hellenistic-Roman period in the eastern Mediterranean". With the constant support of President James R. Angell,

Rostovtzeff saw the chance and had the first joint Dura campaign started already in the spring of 1928.

All the rest is well known. President Angell continued to help Rostovtzeff to obtain supplementary funds and during the years 1929–1944 volumes I–VIII and IX,1 of the "Preliminary Reports" were published under the aegis of Rostovtzeff. Important contributions were also made by some of his former students, notably Professors A. R. Bellinger, F. E. Brown, C. Hopkins, Carl H. Kraeling and C. Bradford Welles who would all agree with a remark of Cumont in which he characterized Rostovtzeff's learning in these words: "ressources inépuisables de son vaste savoir" (Cumont, *op.cit.*, p. viii).

Rostovtzeff died in 1952, and after 1959 only one larger publication appeared: *The Christian Building*, 1967 by C. Kraeling. Three smaller volumes were published as follows: in 1963 *Glass* by C. Clairmont, in 1968 *Commonware Pottery* by S. Dyson and in 1969 *Heracles Sculpture* by S. Downey. That these four *Final Reports* could appear at all was mainly due to the persistent efforts of the editors, Ann Perkins and C. Bradford Welles who, since the former endowment was exhausted, had to raise new capital for the Dura Publication Fund among friends of Rostovtzeff and Dura. Similar efforts will have to be made if a reasonably complete edition of the remaining Finals is to be published. There could be no more fitting memorial to Rostovtzeff for the incomparable contribution he made to Yale.

HARALD INGHOLT
Professor emeritus of Archaeology, Yale University

Index

to Pages xvii–xviii. 1–260, 261–317, 318–402

by BETTY ELLIS and HARALD INGHOLT

CONTENTS

PART I

Mithras, the hunter, 398b; iconographic type, 153b and n. 562; 372a; life of, cycle of scenes, 348b

Mitre, 127b

Mittwoch, E., 391 n. 267

Moab, 124 n. 434

Modein, 343a

Modeling by color gradation, 371 n. 200

"Monoscenic" panels at Dura, 386, 387, 388b

Monumenti inediti dall' instituto di corrispondenza archeologica, III: 246 n. 983

Moon, 107 n. 356; 236 Fig. 61 and n. 944

Moore, G. F., 33 n. 155; 193 n. 755; 326 n. 19

Morey, C. R., 218 n. 865; 251 n. 1001; 399 n. 298

Mordecai, 112a and n. 382; 146b, 149b, 151a–164b, 166 n. 624; 171, 172b, 207a, 212 n. 845; 213, 337b, 370a, 374a, 380a, 383b, 387a; costume of, 153b and n. 564; 154a and n. 565; 171a; hair of, 372a

Morgan, J. de, 175 n. 675; 236 n. 941

Morgan, J. P., collection, 165 n. 619

Moriah, land of, 58; Mount, 58b, 59 n. 134

Mosaic, 244b, 344a; Alexander, 370b and n. 200; of Antioch, 42b, 45 n. 60; 48 n. 86; 218 nn. 864, 865; 227 n. 899; 244b and n. 974; 245b, 366a, 369b and n. 196; in Christian churches, 400b–401a; from el-Djem, 218 n. 862; in floor, 341b and n. 88; see also Beth Alpha, Gerasa, Hammam-Lif, Na'aran; of No. Africa, 218 n. 864; of Palestine synagogues, 357 n. 148; 361a; from Pompeii, 38 n. 17; 47a and n. 77; from Praeneste, 99 n. 321; at Ravenna, 165 n. 618; 227 n. 899; Roman, late, 62 n. 149; 155b; Sabratha, 62 n. 149; S. Maria Maggiore, 80 n. 234; 81 n. 237; 83 n. 247; 231a and n. 917; 238 n. 951; 401a; in S. Pudentiana, 91 n. 284; 225 n. 893; in S. Vitale, 165 n. 618; 225 n. 893; of Uthina (Tunis), 45 n. 62; see also S. Mark, S. Sophia

Moses, 73, 76a, 78b, 79b, 92b, 123b, 124 n. 436; 142a, 148a, 213b, 234, 235a, 237 and nn. 947, 950; 238a and n. 951; 239a and n. 959; 350b, 355, 358b, 371; Assumption of, 347b; and burning bush, 93a, 227a, 228a–230a, 364b, 373a, 375a, 387b; in Christian art, 399b, 400; costume of, 81b–82a, 122b, 228b, 380a; in Exodus, 75a, 81b–86b, 161 n. 604; 228b, 230 n. 908; 371, 373a, 375a; infancy of, 169a–178a, 389a; receives the Law, 93a, 230a and Fig. 60, 347b, 368a; seat of, 260 n. 26; staff of, 81b, 82b, 84b, 85a Fig. 25 and n. 256; 125a; stature of, 82a and n. 242; at Well of Be'er, 118b, 121, 125a, 157 n. 581

"Mothers in Israel," see Hannah, Jochebed, Miriam, Widow of Zarephath

Mount Carmel, contest on, 137–142a, 146b, 148a, 149a; Elijah on, 141a–143a, 147; Elisha on, 137a, 143a and n. 517; Prophets of Baal on, 137b–141a, 147, 148b, 388a

Mount Horeb, 147 n. 538; 228b

Mount Moriah, 58b, 59 n. 134

Mount Nebo, 237a, 238 n. 951

Mount Sinai, 73a, 231a, 355a, 368b

Mount Zion, 355a

Mountain, 378b, 380a; in bas-reliefs, 182 n. 700; in Ezekiel panel, 182b, 191; in glyptic art, 182 n. 700; in Mesopotamian art, 182b

Mourning, 144b–145a, 359b

Mueller, D. H., 342 n. 95

Müller, I., 229 n. 903

Müller, N., 341 n. 90

Müller, V., 82 n. 240

Munich, 342 n. 94

Mūsaf, prayer, 59a and n. 134. See also Index I, 2b

Musical instrument, 101 Fig. 30a no. 18; 102a and Fig. 31; 225 n. 892

Musician, in Center Panel, 223 and Fig. 59; 224, 225; figurine of, 225 n. 892. See also Orpheus

Mustache, 139a, 145 n. 530; 167b, 371b; of Aaron, 127a; of Abraham, 236a; of Ahasuerus, 158a; in Ezekiel panel, 182a, 184b, 185a; of Ezra, 233b; of Mordecai, 153b; of Samuel, 166a

Mustapha Pasha, tomb, 37 n. 9; 68b, 69a

Myrtle, 116a Fig. 37; 117a

Na'ana, 60 n. 142

Na'aran, Synagogue, 24 n. 112; 50b, 60 n. 142; 258 n. 15; 341 n. 88; 385b, 400b; mosaic, 363 n. 171

Naboth, 147 n. 538

Nadab, 131a

Naḥman ben Isaac, (R.), 63 n. 155

Naksh-i-Rustum, 377 n. 219; 378 n. 221

Naos, 22a and n. 97; 215a

Naples, Museum, 47 n. 77

Naqsh-i-Rajab, relief, 127 n. 449; 152b, 153 n. 561

Naram-Sin Stele, 236 n. 941

Narkiss, M., 102 n. 332

Nathan, prophet, 88a

Nathan (R.), 83 n. 248; 326 n. 19

Nebuchadnezzar, 112a, 159a, 164b, 189 n. 735; 199a, 200, 201, 325b

---

[1] *Present numbers:* P Dura, 30 and 32 (H.I.)
[2] *Present numbers:* P Dura, 11 and 153 (H.I.)

2. GLOSSARY BY HARALD INGHOLT

a. HEBREW

אַבְנֵט   128b

'ammathah   177 n. 680

אֵפוֹד   127b

'aron   58b   217b

'aryēh   219 n. 867

מִכְנְסֵי בַּד *see* בַּד

hassepher   162b

he'ebhirani   190 n. 740

hoshib   162b

זָקֵן   331a and n. 51

חֲמֻשִׁים   hamushim   81 n. 237   353b and n. 129

חֲצוֹצְרוֹת   129a

חֹשֶׁן   128a

yešîmôn   206a

יְשֻׁרְגֶה   105 n. 350

כַּד   136b

כֹּה   58 n. 128

כַּפּוֹת   102 n. 335

כֻּתֹּנֶת   128b and n. 458

labhî', lĕbhiyyā'   219 n. 867

סֵפֶר *see* לְשׁוֹן

מִכְנְסֵי־בַד   128b and n. 456

minḥa   143 n. 520

ma'gāl   206b and n. 821

מְעִיל   128a and n. 454

מִצְנֶפֶת   127b

נֵזֶר   127b

na'ar   162b

סְבָך   57 n. 122

עַד   58 n. 128

עַמּוּד   76 n. 221; 'ammûd, 237 n. 927

'ammudîm, 234 n. 933

'ammîm   226 n. 896

עֵץ   84b

paroketh   257b   258 n. 14

perah, perahim   59 n. 135. *See* Index III

צִיץ   127b

ṣîṣith   81 n. 239   82a, Fig. 22

צַפַּחַת   136b

ra'aš   191a

sarîm   161a   189 n. 735

שִׁיר   105 n. 350

šerānîm   104 n. 348

b. ARAMAIC

'orah   58 n. 132

אִילָנא   57 n. 122

'amthah   177 n. 680

'aphaqleṭôrîn   182 n. 694

zuz   343b and n. 100. *See* Index III

Zikronoth   59a

טוּבה   49 n. 92

ṭallith   167a

כִּילָה   258a and n. 11

mezuzah   11 n. 35

מזוזינים   81 n. 237

מְזָרִין 81 n. 237

maḥselet and *mappas* 170 n. 646

marzab 146 n. 532

musaf 59a and n. 134. *See* Index III

נֶעֱרְמוּ 83 n. 248

sabnitha 160 n. 593

saphra', saphrin 220a and n. 874. *See* Index III

עִין 49 n. 92

עמודה 76 n. 221

'*erub* 330a and n. 44

paga' 237 n. 948

פכר 166b 167 n. 626

פריסא 257b and n. 8

ṣeriph 57 n. 124

ṣuṭin 344 n. 105. *See* Index III

קשיש 331 and n. 52

רעה 49 n. 92

שדי 166b

ṭûrānîm 104 n. 348. *See* Index III

תצביתה 391 n. 268 (Palmyrene)

C. GREEK

ἄκωνος 127 n. 448

ἀναξυρίδες 128b and n. 456

ἄνοπλοι 81 n. 237

ἀνυπόδετος 144 n. 526

ἀξιώματι, ὁι ἐν 189 n. 735

ἁπλοῦς 49 n. 92

apographé 163a

archon 11b

ἄρχοντες 331b and n. 55

ἀυλαρχίας 92 n. 289

bema 256b and n. 4 260

γενεᾷ 81 n. 237

genos 331b

γραμματεῖς 331b

γραφεῖν 345b and n. 111

γυμνή 144 n. 526

διάχρυσος 249b

δικαστήριον 90b n. 283

dioiketes 171 n. 656

Dioscuroi 109a

διπλοῦς 137 n. 487

δίφρος 90a

ἐκφορά 104 n. 343

Ἐλίας 137 n. 487

ἐπιμεληταί 332a

ἐπίσειστος 247a

epitropos 163b

ἐπωμίς 127b

ἑταίρα 249b

ἑταιρίδιον 249b

eulogia 193 n. 756

Europaioi 322a 323a and n. 6

eucharistia 193 n. 756

Exilarch 325 n. 18

ἡγεμών 247a

θεράπων 247a

θηρίον 43a and n. 43

thymiaterion 195b and n. 770

thyrsos 102b and n. 334

ἴχνη 102 n. 335

κίων 76 n. 221

kolpos 174b and n. 673 184 372b

κόρη 249b

κρίνειν 90 n. 283

λαγωβόλον 102 n. 333 103 n. 336

λαόν 90 n. 283

lampéné 207 n. 821

mitra 159 n. 593

ὀκλαδίας 90a

ὀφθαλμὸς 49 n. 92

d. LATIN

3. CITATIONS BY BETTY ELLIS AND HARALD INGHOLT

The Books of the Bible follow the order of the Version of King James

a. OLD TESTAMENT FROM THE HEBREW, THE GREEK, THE LATIN AND THE ARMENIAN

I. From the Hebrew

2. From the Greek

b. APOCRYPHA AND PSEUDEPIGRAPHA

c. TARGUMS

1. *Pentateuch*

a. Fragmentary Targum

Genesis 22:14   58 n. 133
         28:12   74b and n. 210
                 (Palestinian); 352
         49:10   220 n. 872   235a
Exodus   1:15   178a   352   353
           2:5   178 a
        13:18   81 n. 237

b. Onkelos

Genesis 22:13   57 n. 122
         49:10   220 nn. 872, 874   235a
                 352a   353b
Exodus   2:5   177a   352a   353b
        13:18   81 n. 237   352a   353b
        20–23   234b
     21:16–18   57 n. 122
         24:4   234 n. 938
Deuteronomy 33:3   226 n. 896

c. Pseudo-Jonathan

Genesis 49:10   220 n. 872   235a   352a
Exodus   1:15   177–178   352a   353b
     13:17–18   180 n. 691
        13:18   81 n. 237
         14:2   74b and n. 224
       14:21   85b   352a   353b
       14:24   77 n. 226
       20–23   234b
        24:4   234 n. 935

Leviticus 26:1   344a
Numbers 21:16–18   123b
         21:19   124 n. 436   352a

2. *The Prophets*

Targum Jonathan

I Sam. 2, (*see* Index III) 94b, l. 20
      2:1–10   111b–113a   352a
                 394 n. 279
        5:4   102 n. 335

3. *The Hagiographa*

First Esther   158b
      1:2   158b   159a and n. 590   352   353
        3   162b
      4:5   161 n. 602
      7:9   161 n. 602
        8   162b
        9   162b
     9:12f.   163   352a

Second Esther (Targum Sheni) 91 n. 283   158b
    I:2   Sulzbach, 19–26   159a and n. 590
    II:1   Lagarde 227, ll. 17–22   90 n. 278
               228, ll. 1–2, 16–17   90b and
                             n. 282
               232, ll. 8–21   92a and n. 290
    VI:1   Sulzbach 80   161 n. 602
    VI:11   Sulzbach 86   156 n. 578   157 n. 580

II Chronicles 3:1   58 n. 131

For separate tabulation under the Fragmentary Targum, Onkelos, Pseudo-Jonathan, Targum Jonathan, *see* Targums, I, 1, 3c

d. NEW TESTAMENT

Matthew
     6:22–23   49 n. 92
     23:2   260a
Mark 11:8   116 n. 395
Luke 4:20   260 n. 26

I Corinthians
     10:4   124 n. 436
     15:20   150 n. 544
Revelations
     22:2   63 n. 155

e. JEWISH WRITERS

1. Hellenistic Period

The central columns indicate the source: Eusebius, *Praeparatio Evangelica*[1]

Artapanos	IX, 26, 30–34	397 n. 288	Kleodemos (Malchos)	IX, 20	397 n. 288
Artapanos and group	IX, 17–29	324b and n. 13	Philo the Elder	IX, 20, 24, 37	397a and n. 291
Demetrius	IX, 21, 29	81 n. 237 397 n. 289	Pseudo-Eupolemos	IX, 17–18	397 n. 288
			Theodotus	IX, 22	397 n. 291
Eupolemos	IX, 30–34	397 n. 289			
Ezekiel	IX, 29	81 n. 237 122 n. 426 353b			

2. Roman Period

Josephus

Bellum, I, 1, 2 = § 6	391 n. 271	VI, 8, 1 = §§ 158–163	168 n. 635
I, 33, 2–3 = §§ 648–650	341a	VII, 12, 3 = §§ 305–306	225 n. 891
II, 16, 4 = § 388	391 n. 271	VIII, § 134	89 n. 275
II, 18, 5 = § 479	392 n. 276	VIII, 7, 5 = § 195	344 n. 106
V, 5, 4 = § 211	63 n. 150	IX, 6, 5 = § 127	198 n. 781
VII, 3, 3 = § 43	391 n. 271	X, 6, 3 = § 97	201 n. 792
VII, 3, 3 = § 46–52	332 n. 61	X, 6, 3 = § 98	189 n. 735
Antiquitates, I, 224–26	58 n. 131	X, § 224	107 n. 359
I, 15 = § 240f.	397 n. 288	XI, 6 = §§ 184–296	152 n. 551
II, 9, 5 = § 224	177 n. 681	XI, § 133	325 n. 16
II, § 305	76 n. 217	XIII, §§ 250–251	326 n. 22
II, § 312	81 n. 238	XIV, 3, 1 = §§ 34–36	343 n. 98
II, § 326	81 n. 237 353 n. 129	XV, 8, 1–2 = §§ 276, 279	341 n. 84
		XV, § 39	325 n. 16
III, 2, 5 = § 62	231 n. 915	XVII, 6, 2 = § 151	341a
III, 4–8, 9–32, 33–38	123 n. 432	XVIII, 3, 1 = §§ 55–59	341a
III, §§ 47, 220, 222	81 n. 238	XVIII, 8, 2 = §§ 261–263	341 n. 84
III, 139	119 n. 409	XIX, 5, 1 = § 277	392a nn. 274, 275
III, § 144–145	236 n. 944		
III, 151–187	127a	XX, 2–4 = §§ 17–96	391 n. 272
III, 152	128 n. 456	XX, 4a = § 103	392 n. 274
III, 153	128 n. 458	XX, 7, 1 = § 138	392 n. 275
III, 157–158, 172–178	127 n. 448	XX, 7, 1 and 3 = §§ 138 and 145	392 n. 277
III, 159	128 n. 454	XX, 7, 1 = § 139	392 n. 273
III, 291	129 n. 462	*Vita*, 12 = § 65	341 n. 84
IV, § 326	237 n. 947	*Contra Apionem*, I, 22 = § 192	22 n. 97
VI, § 13	105 n. 349		

[1] *See* below on p. 453 under I, 3h

Philo Judaeus

De fuga, §§ 183–187	123 n. 431	*Vita Mosis*, I, 210	123 n. 429
De sacrificiis, 8–10	237 n. 947	I, § 14	177 n. 681; 354 n. 130
De somniis, I, §§ 133–156	73 n. 205	I, § 72	81 n. 237
I, 22 = §§ 135–145	186 n. 720	I, §§ 113–125, 118	79 n. 230
II, § 222	123 n. 429	I, § 118	76 nn. 219, 221
De specialibus legibus, I, §§ 66–75	108 n. 362	II, 109	128 n. 454
§§ 85–95	127 n. 447	II, 109–135	127 n. 447
Legatio ad Gaium, §§ 216–217	325 n. 16	II, §§ 102–103	236 n. 944
Quod deterius potiori insidiari sole-		II, §§ 288–292	237 n. 947
bat, 46–48 = §§ 134–139	186 n. 720		

Pseudo-Philo,

Biblical Antiquities, LV, 8	105 n. 349	(trans. M. R. James, p. 227)

f. GREEK AND ROMAN WRITERS

1. Greek

Herodotus, *Historiae*, I, 98	107 and n. 359
Nicolaus of Damascus, *apud* Josephus, *Antiquitates*, XIII, 250–251	326 n. 22
Pausanias, I, 17, 2 18, 1 IX, 4, 1	348 n. 119
Plutarch, *Pompey*, II, 8	348 n. 119
Pollux, *Onomasticon*, IV, 143–154	247 n. 990
	249b n. 994

Xenophon, *Hellenica*, II, 1, 8	167 n. 629
Cyropaedia VIII, 2, 8	162 n. 606
VIII, 3, 10	167 n. 629

2. Roman

Pliny, *Hist. Nat.*, XXXV, 124	53 n. 107
XXXV, 136	348 n. 119
XXXVII, 2 = § 12	343 n. 98
Varro, *De lingua*, VII, 57	348 n. 119

g. RABBINICAL WRITINGS

1. Mishnah

Berakoth, IV, 5, *24 n. 114*
Ta'anith, II, 4, *59 n. 134*
Megillah, III, 3, *23 n. 106*
Menahoth, 11b, *64 n. 162*
Sotah, IX, ult., *150 n. 545*
Sanhedrin, X, 3, *193 n. 755*
Abodah Zarah, I, 5, *47 n. 79*

2. Tosephta

Sukkah, III, 11–16, *124 n. 436*
Megillah, IV, 21, *260 n. 25;* IV, 23, *23 n. 104*

3. Jerusalem Talmud

Killaim, 32b   *325 n. 18*
Shabbat, VI, 4   81 n. 237
Aboda Zarah, 48d   344a and n. 104

4. Babylonian Talmud

Berakoth, 30a, *24 n. 114*
Shabbath, 11a, *23 n. 105;* 30a, *111 n. 378;*
   54a, *155 n. 571;* 147b, *160 n. 593;*
   10a, *167 n. 626;* 147a, *146 n. 532;*
   60b, *390 n. 265;* 133b, *396 n. 286*

4. PICTORIAL DIPINTI AND GRAFFITI BY BETTY ELLIS

PART II

INSCRIPTIONS

1. THE ARAMAIC TEXTS BY *CHARLES C. TORREY*

a. LIST OF NUMBERS WITH REFERENCES

1 261–268. *See also* 168 n. 636   329 n. 41   331 n. 50   332
Also 1a (AB) 263–266b   277b   278b
1b(C) 266b–267a. *See also* 46 n. 68   54 n. 111
1c 267b–268.

2 269, also 261. *See also* 54 n. 111   56 n. 117   332 n. 59

3 269–270. *See also* 75 n. 212   78a   82b

4 270, also 261b. *See also* 75 n. 212   83a

5 270–271. *See also* 75 n. 212   85a

6 271, also 261. *See also* 229b

7 271

8 271. *See also* 152 n. 553

9 271–272. *See also* 157 n. 553

10 272. *See also* 157 n. 583

11 272–273. *See also* 165 n. 617

12 272–273, also 261. *See also* 12 n. 39   331 n. 49

13 273, also 261. *See also* 12 n. 39   331 n. 49

14 273, also 261. *See also* 12 n. 39   331 n. 49

15 273, also 261. *See also* 331 n. 49

16 273, also 261 and 275b

17 274, also 261 270a. *See also* 331 n. 49

18 274, also 261. *See also* 14 n. 55

19 274, also 261. *See also* 14 n. 55

20 274–275, also 261. *See also* 31 n. 144   327 n. 34

21 275, also 261. *See also* 31 n. 144   327 n. 34

22 275–276, also 261. *See also* 31 n. 144   327 n. 34   328 n. 35

b. GENERAL INDEX

C. GLOSSARY OF ARAMAIC WORDS AND PROPER NAMES FROM THE SYNAGOGUE

I. Words:

אב 274 **19**, 1

אבה 273 **13**, 2

אגרהון 263 **1a** (B), 5

אילין 263 **1a** (A), 9

אינין 263 **1a** (A3); 268 **1c** (C), 2

אמא 270 **5**, 2

אמה 269 **3**, 4

ארונה 269 **2**, 1

ארכון 263 **1a** (A), 5; 268 **1c** (C), 4

אנא 269 **2**, 1; 273 **15**, 1; 274 **17**, 1

אנה 273 **13**, 1; **16**, 1

אפותיקי 275 **22**, 2. *See also* p. 276a: *apothecarius*, 276b: ἀποθηκάριος

אתבני 263 **1a** (A), 1; 268 **1c** (C), 1. *See also* 264 n. 9

אתי 263 **1a** (B), 6

ב 1a (A), 2.4.8.9; **1a** (B), 3.4.8; **1b** (C), 4; **1c** (C), 1.3

בז' 269 **3**, 4; 270 **5**, 1

בית 269 **2**, 1

ביתא 268 **1c** (C), 1. *See also* 264 n. 9

ביתה 263 **1a** (A), 1; 267 **1b** (C), 1

בני 267 **1b** (C), 1

בר 263 **1a** (A), 5; 267 **1b** (C), 5; 268 **1c** (C), 5; 271 **6**, 1; 272 **12**; 273 **13**, 1; **16**, 2; 274 **17**, 2

ברה 269 **2**, 2

ברכתה 263 **1a** (A), 12

גטט 274 **18**

גיזברה 263 **1a** (A), 6-7; 268 **1c** (C), 5

גיורה 263 **1a** (A), 8

ד 263 **1a** (A), 3; 267 **1b** (C), 2.4; 268 **1c** (C), 2.3.4; 269 **2**, 2

די 275 **20**, 3

דכיר 275 **21**, 3; 275 **22**, 1

הדין 263 **1a** (A), 1.6; 267 **1b** (C), 1; 268 **1c** (C), 1; 275 **20**, 1

חמידת 263 **1a** (B), 4

חמש 263 **1a** (A), 2; 267 **1b** (C), 1; 268 **1c** (C), 1

חמשין 263 **1a** (A), 2.9; 267 **1b** (C), 2; 268 **1c** (C), 2

כד 269 **3**, 1; 270 **5**, 1; 272 **11**, 1

כהנה 263 **1a** (A), 5; 267 **1b** (C), 5; 268 **1c** (C), 4

כה[נ]יה 268 **1c** (C), 4

כל 263 **1a** (A), 13

כלהון 263 **1a** (A), 14; 263 **1a** (B), 2.3

כלמה 263 **1a** (B), 5

כספה 263 **1a** (B), 3

כשים 263 **1a** (A), 15; 263 **1a** (B), 2; 266a

כתב 275 **20**, 3

כתבה 275 **20**, 2

ל **1a** (A), 3; **1a** (B), 7; **1b** (C), 3; **1c** (C), 2; **13**, 2

לאין 263 **1a** (A), 13

מאה 263 **1a** (A), 2; 267 **1b** (C), 2; 268 **1c** (C), 1

מן **3**, 2.3; **21**, 1

מלאכתיה 268 **1c** (C), 4

מצרים 269 **3**, 3

משח 272 **11**, 2

נפק 269 **3**, 2

נפ[שהון] 263 **1a** (B), 4.

עבד 269 **2**, 2

עבדת 269 **2**, 1

עיבידה 263 **1a** (A), 6; 264b

על **1a** (A), 6; **1c** (C) 4; **3**, 4; **5**, 2

עלמה 263 **1a** (B), 5; 266b

עמלו 263 **1a** (A), 11; 266a

פרסין 263 **1a** (B), 8

קימה 263 **1a** (B), 7; 266b

קמו 263 **1a** (A), 5; 268 **1c** (C), 4

קשישותה 263 **1a** (A), 4; 267 **1b** (C), 4; 268 **1c** (C), 3

רהטו 263 **1a** (A), 10

רוח 263 **1a** (A), 8; 265a

רעותכון 275 **21**, 1

שביה 263 **1a** (A), 12; cf. Ezra VI:8 and Elephantine Letters, 265b

שבת 263 **1a** (B), 8

שדרו 263 **1a** (A), 9; 262b

שים *See* כשים

שית 263 **1a** (A), 3; 267 **1b** (C), 2; 268 **1c** (C), 2

שלמה 263 **1a** (A), 14; 265b

שנה 263 **1a** (A), 2

שנת 263 **1a** (A), 3; 267 **1b** (C), 1.3; 268 **1c** (C), 1.2

תרתן 263 **1a** (A), 3; 267 **1b** (C), 3; 268a

2. Proper Names

אבא (Abba) 269 **2**, 2 332a

אבלמי (Abram?) 274 **19**, 2

אברם	(Abram)	263 **1a** (A), 6; 268 **1c** (C), 5; 332a
אי[וב]	(Jo[b])	273 **14**
אסטיר	(Esther)	272 **10**. Cf Hebrew אֶסְתֵּר
ארמיה	(Jeremiah)	274 **17**, 2. As in Syriac Eremyā, in contrast to Hebrew Yirmĕyā
ד[ו]יד	(David)	272 **11**, 2
דכה	(Dakkā)	275 **21**, 2
הליא	(Elijah)	271 **7**
חיא	(Ḥiyā)	272 **12**; 273 **13**, 1; **15**
חנני	(Ḥananī)	273 **16**, 1; 275 **21**, 2
חשהורש	(Ahasuerus)	271 **9**
ידעי	(Yeda'ya)	263 **1a** (A), 5
[יול'ס]		**1a** (A), 4
יוסף	(Joseph)	269 **2**, 2; 332a
לֵ[ו]י	(Levi)	271 **6**, 2

מורדכי	(Mordecai)	271 **8**
מנימן	(Minyāmīn)	275 **22**, 1
משה	(Moses)	269 **3**, 1; 270 **4**; 270 **5**, 1; 271 **6**, 1
מתני	(Mattĕnai)	275 **20**, 4
נחמני	(Naḥmanī)	275 **21**, 3
ספרה	(Sapharah)	263 **1a** (A), 7
עזי	**2**, 1 (Uzzi) 269
פינחס	(Phineḥas)	274 **17**, 1
פלפוס	(Philip)	263 **1a** (A), 3; 267 **1b** (C), 3; 268 **1c** (C), 2–3
קסר	(Cesar)	263 **1a** (A), 4; 267 **1b** (C), 3
שאמואל	(Samuel)	273 **16**, 2
שמואל	(Samuel)	263 **1a** (A), 7; 267 **1b** (C), 4; 268 **1c** (C), 3
שמול	(Samuel)	272 **11**, 1

d. CITATIONS

1. Old Testament, Hebrew

Genesis 45:8   273a, **13**
1 Samuel, 1:20   272b, **10**
1 Kings 5:30   268a, **1c** (C)
2 Kings 12:12   268a, **1c** (C)
2 Chronicles 2:13   273a, **13**
            4:16   273a, **13**
Ezra, book of 275a, **20**
Ezra 3:8   268, **1c** (C)
Ezra 6:8   265b
Nehemiah, book of 275a, **20**
Nehemiah 2:16   268a, **1c** (C)
            7:7   275b, **21**
Isaiah   9:5   273a, **13**

2. Old Testament, Greek

I Chronicles 19, 16.18 (Codex A) 265a, Σῶβαχ **1a** (A 1)

3. Targums

Pentateuch:	Exodus 14:16, 21	270a
	" 35:21f.	263 n. 8 265a
Prophets:	I Sam. 9:13	266b
	Isaiah 26:8	266a, **1a** (B), 4
	" 63:12	270a, **3**
Hagiographa:	Psalm 78:13	270a, **3**
	2 Chronicles 28:7	264b. *See* Index III

4. Rabbinic Writings

Babylonian Talmud, Baba Meṣī'a 39:5   270a

5. New Testament

John 4:25; 5:27; 8:56; 11:2; 14:31 264 n. 9

e. UNUSUAL SPELLINGS OR RARE MEANINGS OF WORDS FROM THE SYNAGOGUE

1. אבה 273a, **13**,2. Here the word אב, father, probably means "chief counselor, leader", as also in Hebrew.

2. אמא 270, **5**,2; אמה 269, **3**,4. The usual word for "sea" in Aramaic is *yammâs* with initial *yod*, not *aleph*. Our two words are, however, just dialectic variants pointing to a source in Babylonia. The same linguistic peculiarity has other examples in Dura: ארמיה, **17**,2, for the Biblical ירמיה, and Εἰδδέου, **23**,2, for ידעי (**1a**, A,5), these last two representing the same person.

3. **אפותיקי** 276, **22**,2. This word occurs frequently in the Talmud with the meaning of the Greek word which it transliterates, ἀποθήκη, "repository, warehouse". The context here would, however, rather require the sense "a man in charge of the repository, the warehouse". In favor of this interpretation is the post-classical Latin *apothecarius*, the man in charge of a warehouse, and the late Greek ἀποθηκάριος, the "commissary" of an army. The vocalization of our word was then presumably apothēqai.

4. **חשהורש** 271b, **9.** Torrey prefers the reading **חשוירוש** 272a

5. **מלאכה**, "Work", see p. 268, **1c** (C), 4

6. **פָּרְסִין**, 263b, **1a** (B), 8. **פרס**, see 266 b.

These two verbs are sometimes used in the phrase "spreading out the hands in prayer". However, in one case, in the Targum to I Samuel 9:13, the two words for "hands" and "prayer" are omitted, yet the sense is evidently the same. Our **פָּרְסִין** may therefore have the same elliptical meaning as that in the Targum passage.

2. THE GREEK TEXTS BY *C. BRADFORD WELLES*

a. LIST OF NUMBERS WITH REFERENCES

<table>
<tr><td>23</td><td>277. See also 49 n. 94; 168 n. 636; 331 n. 50; 332b</td><td>33</td><td>280</td></tr>
<tr><td>24</td><td>277–78, also 264, 280. See also 49 n. 94; 168 n. 636; 332b</td><td>34</td><td>277a 280b</td></tr>
<tr><td>25</td><td>278–79, also 280. See also 49 n. 94; 332b</td><td>35</td><td>280–81. See also 12 n. 39; 331 n. 49</td></tr>
<tr><td>26–28</td><td>279. See also 45 n. 65</td><td>36</td><td>281</td></tr>
<tr><td>29</td><td>279. See also 127 n. 445</td><td>37</td><td>281. See also 14 n. 55</td></tr>
<tr><td>30</td><td>279. See also 89 nn. 273, 277</td><td>38</td><td>281. See also 14 n. 55</td></tr>
<tr><td>31</td><td>279, also 280. See also 89 n. 273; 90 n. 283</td><td>39</td><td>281–82</td></tr>
<tr><td>32</td><td>279–80. See also 331 n. 49</td><td>40</td><td>282. See also 16 n. 67</td></tr>
<tr><td></td><td></td><td>41</td><td>282. See also 16 n. 67</td></tr>
</table>

b. GENERAL INDEX

C. GLOSSARY OF GREEK WORDS, PROPER NAMES AND NUMBERS FROM THE SYNAGOGUE

1. Words:

ἀδελ[φ]ος	281a	**35**, 3–4
ἐβοήθησαν	278	**25**, 5
ἔκτισεν	277	**23**, 5; **24**, 3–4
Ἰουδέων	277	**23**, 4–5
καὶ	278	**25**, 2–3
κὲ	278	**25**, 4
μνησθῇ	277	**24**, 3; 281 **35**, 1
οὕτως	277	**24**, 5
πρεσβύτερος	277	**23**, 3
συνκάθαδρο[	279	**31**
ταῦτα	277	**24**, 4–5

2. Proper Names

Ἄβραμ	278	**25**, 1, also 332a
Ἀ]μαθβήλ	281	**35**, 2 (perhaps Μαθβήλ)
Ἀρσάχου	278	**25**, 2–3; 332. This Ἀρσάχου is most probably the father of the Abram who in the year 244–245 was the Treasurer of the Dura Synagogue, see Torrey, 265a. Unusual is the transliteration with a χ (*chi*) instead of the usual κ (*kappa*): Ἀρσάκης. Two similar examples are, however, pointed out by Torrey, *loc. cit.*

Ἀρών	279	**29**
Αὐδ[ιναῖος]	281	**36** (= January)
Βαρνᾶιος	281	**38**
Βαρσαφάρα	277b and n. 20	**24**, 2
Βόηθος	280a and n. 39	**32**
Γ]ιννᾶιος	281–282	**39**
Εἰδδέου	277	**23**, 2
Ἑρμαίου	281	**38**
Ὄρβαζ	279. Iranian name, **26–28**	
Σαλμάνης	278	**25**, 4, also 332a
Σαμουήλ	277	**23**, 1 **24**, 1
Σιλᾶς	278	**25**, 3. *See also* 278 n. 28; 332a
Σλήμων	279b	**30**. Vocalization practically as in Syriac: Šlēmōn

3. Numbers

Ϥ Λ	281	**38** = Seleucid era 430
Ͷνφ'	281	**36** = Seleucid era 559, but see above under Ἀυδ
⳨ Γ	282	**41** = 3 denarii
πβλ'	280	**33**, 2 = 82½
ρξε'	280	**33**, 1 = 165

d. CITATIONS

1. Old Testament in Greek

Septuagint 277b, **24**: Σαμουήλ, same nominative case as in LXX, see I Kings, 7:3

279b, **29**: ᾽Αρών, rare for ᾽Ααρών

2. New Testament

Acts, chps. 15–18, passim 278b, **25**: Σιλᾶς, the companion of St. Paul. It is of interest that the same person is called Silvanus by Paul in his letters:

2 Corinthians 1:15 278 n. 28: Silvanus
See *Index* III
I Thessalonians 1:1 " : Silvanus
2 Thessalonians 1:1 " : Silvanus

3. Rabbinic Writings

Babylonian Talmud, Pesachim 57a, 280a, **32**: Βοηθός

---

e. ARAMAIC, GREEK, LATIN AND ARABIC WORDS AND PROPER NAMES NOT FROM THE SYNAGOGUE

Aramaic

1. Words:

בנא 278a and n. 21 (**24**). Palmyra
גניא 282 n. 47 (**39**). Palmyra

2. Proper names:

אמתבל 281 a and n. 47 (**39**). Palmyra
ארסך 278b (**25**). See *supra II, c 2 sub* ᾽Αρσάχον
בר ברני 278a (**24**). Dura Main Gate
שילא 279a (**25**). Talmudic spelling of Σιλᾶς

Greek

1. Words:

ἀδελφοί 278a (**24**). From Brâd
ἀνήγειρεν 278a (**24**). Syria
ἔκτεισαν 278a (**24**). Syria
ἔκτισαν 278a (**24**). Syria
ἐποίησεν 278a (**24**). Syria
ἐτελειώθη 278a (**24**). Syria
ἔτευξεν 278a (**24**). Syria
λουτρόν 278a (**24**) From Serjilla
πάρεδρος 279b (**31**) Attic, see under Ulpian
τέκνοις 278a (**24**) Brâd
υἱοί 278a (**24**) Brâd
φυλή 278b (**25**) Dura, Parchment VII[1]
ᾠκοδόμησεν 278a (**24**) Syria

2. Proper names

Αβιδγ]ιννᾶἴος 282a (**39**). Dura
᾽Αμαϑϑαβείλη 281a and n. 42 (**35**). Dura papyrus DP 73[2]
᾽Ανδρόνικος 278a (**24**). Brâd
᾽Αντώνιος 278a (**24**). Brâd
Βαρβαρνέος 278a (**24**). Dura
Βαργ]ιννᾶἴος 282a (**39**). Dura
Ζεβεινᾶ 278b and n. 25 (**25**). Dura, Parchment VII[2]
᾽Ιαϑα[ἴος] 277b (**23**). Dura
᾽Ιεδειβῆλος 277b (**23**). Palmyra
Λονγίνου 278a (**24**) Brâd
Μαϑβήλ 281a and n. 43 (**35**). Dura
Μάρκος 278 (**24**). Brâd
᾽Ορόβαζος 279 n. 34 (**26–28**). Iranian name
Οὔρβικος 278a (**24**). Brâd
Σεειλᾶς 278b (**25**). Palmyra
Σειλᾶς 279a and n. 32 (**25**). Emesa
Σηλαῖος 278a (**24**). Dura
Σιλᾶς 278b (**25**). Occurs in classical authors, especially Josephus, and in Syriac
Σώπατρας 278a (**24**). Brâd

---

[1] Present number: P Dura 47 (H. I.)
[2] Present number: P Dura 29 (H. I.)

3. THE MIDDLE IRANIAN TEXTS BY *BERNHARD GEIGER*

a. LIST OF NUMBERS WITH REFERENCES

b. GENERAL INDEX

[1] Present number is now PDura 153 (H.I.)
[2] Present number is now PDura 154 (H.I.)

C. CITATIONS

1. Old Testament from the Hebrew

Esther 2:21   292 n. 89
6:2   292 n. 89
6:4   292 n. 89
Daniel, 1:4   287 n. 64

2. Syriac version of the Old Testament
Peshitta: I Kings 17:63   299 n. 124

3. Middle Persian version
Psalms 135:8   308a

Pehlevi Psalter   312b
122:2–3   313a and n. 139
128:8   313 a and n. 139

4. New Testament

Armenian version: Hebrews 19:27 300 n. 126
Sogdian Christian version, *dipīr* translated
by γραμματεύς, Matthew 20:18   287b

5. Rabbinical Writings. Other Midrashim:

Aggadat Esther, ed. Buber, p. 37 299b, 300a

d. HEBREW, ARAMAIC, SYRIAC AND GREEK WORDS, NOT FROM THE SYNAGOGUE

1. *Hebrew*

בִּגְתָנָא   292 n. 89
בְּנֶךְ   299b
חַי   299b
לְשׁוֹן   287 n. 64
סוֹפֵר   287b
סֵפֶר   287 n. 64
רְאִי   299b
תֶּרֶשׁ   292 n. 89

2. *Aramaic*

אזל   313b
איפו   289 n. 73
אנשים   300
אצלו   300a
ב   preposition, 289 n. 81
באו   300a

בחורים   300
זנדיקין   (Iranian) 300
נכנסו   300a
ספרא   287b 317a
עלילה   300a
עליו   300a

3. *Syriac*

אפשין   296a
חזי   299 n. 124
ברכי   299 n. 124
חיא   299 n. 124

4. *Greek*

ἀπό   289 n. 73
γραμματεύς   287b
εὐχή   296a (אפשין)
ὑπό   289 n. 73

PART III

CORRECTIONS BY BETTY ELLIS AND HARALD INGHOLT

PART I, PAGES 1–260 AND 318–402 (KRAELING)

P. 6 n. 7	*For* hakenneṣet *read* hakenneset
11 n. 33	*For* Vetii *read* Vettii
22a, last line	*For* like the pronaoi *read* not like the pronaoi
23 n. 105	*For* Shabbath 10b *read* Shabbath 11a
41 n. 28, l. 6	*For* private house *read* private house W
43 n. 49	*For* Ceteus *read* Cetus
57, Fig. 14	Hand should point to the left
59 n. 135	For *peraḥ, peraḥim,* read *peraḥ, peraḥim*
72 n. 195	*For* LXIV *read* LXIII
81b, l. 3 from bottom	*For* left knee *read* right knee
83a, l. 23	*For* Miriam *read* Moses
94b, l. 20	*For* Targum pseudo-Jonathan *read* Targum Jonathan
104 n. 348	For *tûrānîm* read *ṭûrānē*
107 n. 360	*For* Parḳe *read* Pirḳe
146 n. 532	*For* marzab *read* marzeb
150 n. 544	*For* Nosse *read* Nasso. *See also* Index I, 3g
152 n. 555, l. 2	*For* 72a *read* 72c (gold medallion of Justinian)
162 b, l. 7	*For* na'ar *read* na'ar
170 n. 646	*For* mappas *read* mappaṣ
177b	*For* Targum Jonathan *read* Targum Pseudo-Jonathan
186 n. 720	*For* Rhode, E., *read* Rohde, E
190 n. 740, l. 3	*For* wĕhe 'ĕbhîranî *read* wĕ he'ebhîranî
193 n. 755, l. 7	*For* XI *read* X
211b, l. 3 from bottom	*For* Jeremiah (25. 50–51) *read* Jeremiah (25 and 50–51)
219 n. 870	*For* Pl. LXVI *read* Pl. LXV
228b, l. 17	*For* visitors *read* visitor
237b, l. 2	*For* Genesis 15,15 *read* Genesis 15:5
257 n. 6	*For* Ben-Zevil *read* Ben-Zevi
319b, **67**, l. 1	*For* Panel SD2 *read* SC2
324 n. 13	*For* 17–29 *read* 17, 2, 9. The writer is Eupolemos, not the group of Artapanos
325, n. 18	*For* Judah ha-Nazi *read* Judah ha-Naśı

327b, last line	*For* Torrey; *read* Torrey,
342 nn. 93, 95	*For* Ginizah *read* Genizah
342 n. 95	*For* Mazoth *read* Maṣṣôt
343a, l. 6 from bottom	*For* Jonathan *read* Jonathan, his father and brothers
343 n. 98	*For* Hist. Nat., XXXVII, 2, § 12 *read* Hist. Nat., XXXVII, 2, § 14
344 n. 105	*For* ṣuṭin *read* סטיו (the Greek στοά)
348 n. 119	*For* Pausanias, IX, 4, 1 *read* IX, 4, 2
352	In the list of Targums to the left, *for* Jonathan *read* in ll. 3, 9, 15, 18, 20 Pseudo-Jonathan
353	Under the heading RELATIONS, to the right, *for* Jonathan *read* in ll. 3, 9, 18, 20, Pseudo-Jonathan
359a, l. 6	*For* pseudo-Jonathan *read* Jonathan
369, n. 196	*For* Hill, *read* E. Hill
378 n. 221	*For* Aurelian *read* Valerian
379 n. 226	*For* Hill, *read* E. Hill
389, l. 16 from bottom	*For* (Exodus 2. 5–60) *read* (Exodus 2, 5–6)
397 n. 288	*For* 26, 30–34 *read* 26, 30, 34. The writer is Eupolemos, not Artapanos whose chapters are 18, 1; 23, 1 and 27. The corrections conform to the Eusebius edition of E. H. Gifford from 1903, undoubtedly that used by Kraeling.
397 n. 289	*For* 21, 29, 30–34 *read* 21, 29, 30, 34. Chapters 21 and 29 are of Demetrius, 30 and 34 of Eupolemos

PART II, PAGES 261–276 (TORREY)

264b, middle	*For* Targum 2, Chron. 28, 7 *read* Targum, 2 Chron. 28, 7
265b	*For* שָׁבְיָא *read* שָׁבְיָה (1a, A, l. 12)
270a, l. 6	*For* Psalm 78:13 and Isaiah 63:12 *read* those of Psalm 78:13 and Isaiah 63:12
270a, middle	*For* inscr. **24** *read* inscr. no. **23**
274 n. 14, l. 2	*For* idem *read* J. B. Chabot
274 n. 14, l. 6	*For* his *read* Chabot's

PART III, PAGES 277–282 (WELLES)

278 n. 28, l. 1	*For* II Cor. 1.15 *read* II Cor. 1:19

Addendum

by STANLEY INSLER

MIDDLE IRANIAN WORDS AND PROPER NAMES

Note that references to the inscriptions are given first (e.g., 44.2, 45.3), followed by page references to the text where the forms are discussed (e.g., 285, 290, etc.).

A. MIDDLE PERSIAN

'DYN (= aδak) 52.3

'L (= mā) 53.2; 284

'MT (= kaδ) 42.3, 43.3, 44.2, 45.2, 46.2, 47.1, 48.1, 49.2, 50.1, 51.2; 286, 289, 297, 301

'mt (āmat) 51.5; 299, 310

'mwldt (əmurdat) 46.1; 306

'plyntn (āfrīn-tān) 313

'plyny (āfrīnē) 297

'P-m (= u-m) 297

'P-š (= u-š) 42.5, 49.3, 51.3; 290, 292f., 295–99, 301, 309, 311

'P-šn (= u-šān) 43.7, 44.4,5, 48.2; 292f., 295f., 303, 305

'rt'w (artāv) 51.2; 298, 311

't'p (ātāp) 308

'whrmzdy (ohrmazdē) 297

'wrtwhšt(?) (urt-vahišt) 51.1; 311

'YK (= ku) 51.4, 52.1; 299

'yny' (ēnyā) 53.1,2; 284, 313

'ZDH (= azd) 52.1

'BYDWN (= kunēt) 52.1; 312. (= kard) 297

'D (= tāk) 302

'L (= ō) 42.4, 43.5, 44.3, 45.4, 47.2; 297, 303

'ŠMḪN- 312

'ŠMḪWN- 312

'ŠMYTN (= āšnavēt) 52.2; 291 n. 85, 312f.

'ZLWN (= šau) 53.1,2; 284, 313f.

bwlǰ'twr (burz-ātur) 46.3; 289, 298, 306

by (bay) 44.3; 299, 305

by(')m'y 46.4, 47.3, 48.2; 292f., 296, 307f.

by'n (bayān) 44.3; 299, 305

BYN (= andar) 46.4; 290

BYRX (= māh) 42.1, 43.1, 44.1, 45.1, 46.1, 47.1, 48.1,2, 50.1, 51.1; 285, 288, 297, 304, 306f., 311

BYT' (= xānak) 42.5, 43.5; 285, 288, 294, 298f., 301, 303, 305

dpyr (dipīr) 44.2, 45.2, 46.3, 48.1, 50.1, 51.2; 284–89, 292f., 295, 298f., 306–08, 317

dpywr (dipīwar) 42.4, 43.3,4, 49.2; 285–87, 292, 295, 298f., 301–06, 310, 317

dpywry (dipīwarē) 44.2, 45.3; 285, 290, 298, 301, 304, 306

dydpyr (dipīr) 47.2

DYN' (= dātistān) 300, 304

HNḪ (= im) 297

HWḪd (= hēnd) 43.6

HWḪm (= hēm) 297

HWḪnd (= hēnd) 48.2, 50.2; 296, 308, 310 n. 135

hwp't (hupāt) 48.1; 289, 298, 308

hwrmzdy (hormazdē) 44.2, 49.2, 50.1(?), 51.1; 298, 310

K'L' (= vāng) 52.2; 312f.

kntk (kantak) 44.2; 299, 305

krty (kardē) 297

kydly(?) 49.4, 51.4; 299, 309–11

ldky (radakē) 43.4; 286 n. 55, 292, 298f., 302f.

LDNH (= im) 312

LK (= tō) 53.1

lšnw (rašnu) 42.2

LWTḪ (= aβāɣ) 313

LZNḪ (= im) 52.1; 312f.

LZNḪ-č (= im-ič) 312

-m'n (-mān) 52.3

m'rspnd (mārspand) 305

mhrspndy (mahrspandē) 305

MLK' (= šah) 297

MRWXY (= xvatāy) 313

mtlspndy (mahrspandē) 47.1; 298, 307

466

mtlwlwspn(?) (mahrspandē) 47.2 (dittography for mtlwspnd ?)

mtrspndy (mahrspandē) 45.2; 305

mtry (miϑrē) 43.2, 44.1, 45.1, 48.1,2, 50.1; 301

n'mky (nāmakē) 297

ndyšyt (niyīšīt or nīšīt) 44.4,5, 46.5, 47.3; 292–94, 297, 300, 305, 307

nxy't'p (naxē-ātāp?) 48.1; 289, 298, 308

n(y)k'l (nikār) 42.5, 43.7, 44.4,6, 51.3; 289, 292f., 303, 307, 309, 311

nykldyt (nikardīt) 49.3, 51.3; 290, 292f., 299, 309

nykldyty (nikardītē) 51.4; 293, 299, 311

n(y)kylyt (nikīrīt) 43.7, 44.5, 48.2; 292f., 295f., 303, 305, 309

nzdyk (nazdīk) 300, 304

pkwry (pakōrē) 45.2; 298, 305

plm'ty (framātē) 297

plxwy (farraxvē) 48.1; 289, 298, 308

prwltyn (fravartīn) 46.2; 306

prwrtyn (fravartīn) 42.1, 44.1; 304

*ptčyt (patčīt) 42.6; 284, 292–95, 301

ptlstky (patrastakē) 44.3, 45.4, 47.2; 285, 299, 303, 305f., 308

ptpwrsyt (patpursīt) 297

QDM (= apar) 42.1, 43.1, 44.1, 45.1, 50.1, 52.3; 297, 300, 312

RMY 312

RMYT(W)N- 312

ršnky (rašnakē) 46.3; 289f., 298

ršnw (rašnu) 48.1; 308

ršny (rašnē) 48.2

sp'sy (spāsē) 53.3; 314

spndrmt (spandarmad) 297

st (sat) 297

stwny (stūnē) 297

š'ty (šātē) 52.1; 291, 313

ŠLM (= drōt) 312

ŠNT (= sāl) 42.2, 43.1, 44.1, 45.1, 50.1; 290f., 297, 301

štrywl (šaϑrēvar) 47.1; 307

štrywr šaϑrēvar) 43.2; 302

ŠWM (= drōt) 52.3; 312f.

tyr (tīr) 297

vs'n (vasān) 53.1

W- (= ut) 42.2, 43.2,4, 44.1,2,3,5, 45.2,3, 46.1,3,4, 47.3, 48.1,2, 52.2; 298, 302–08, 312

WWHY' 314

XZY 312

XZYT(W)N- 312

Y'TWN (= āmat) 43.4, 43.6, 44.4, 46.4, 47.3, 48.2; 295–98, 301f., 306f. (= āyēnd) 53.1 (= āyēt) 284

Y'TWNt (= āmat) 49.2, 50.2, 51.2; 309–11

YD' 312

YD'YTN- 312

yhwd'n (yahūdān) 44.3,4; 299, 305

YHWWN (= bavēt) 52.2; 300, 304, 312f.

YMYTN (= murd) 45.4 (mistake for Y'TWN), 49.4, 51.4; 299, 306, 310f.

YWM (= rōč) 42.2, 43.2, 44.1, 45.2, 46.1, 47.1, 48.1,2, 51.1; 288, 297, 304, 306, 311

YXSNWN (= dār) 53.3; 314

yzd'n (yazdān) 52.2, 53.3(?); 312, 314

yzd'npysy (yazdānpēsē) 43.3; 297, 302

yzd'ntxmprnby (yazdāntaxm-farnbay) 42.3; 297, 298, 301

zhm (zahm) 298, 303

zhmy (zahmē) 42.4, 44.2, 45.3; 285, 290, 292, 298f., 301, 304f.

zndky (zandakē) 44.2,3; 285, 299f., 304f.

ZNH̱ (= ēn) 42.5, 43.5,7, 44.3,4, 45.4, 47.2, 49.3, 51.3; 289, 292f., 299, 301, 303, 305, 308f.

ZRYT(W)N- 312

ztm (zahm) 298

zwt'n (zōtān) 284

zxm (zaxm) 298

ZY (= ī) 42.4, 43.4, 44.2,3, 45.2,3, 48.1, 50.1(?); 286 n. 55, 290, 298f., 301, 303–05, 308, 310, 313

zywndk (zīvandak) 49.3; 295, 299, 309f.

zywndky(?) (zīvandakē) 51.4; 299, 309–11

B. PARTHIAN

'LH' (= bag) 55.1; 315

'prs'm (aparsām) 54.1; 287, 298, 314–315; 317 n. 149

'pryn (āfrīn) 55.1; 315

'L (= ō)   55.1

dnk (dānāk?)   56.2; 316f.
dpyr (dipīr)   56.2; 316f.
dpyrpty (dipīrpatē)   317
dpyrwpt (dipīwarpat)   317

gy'n (gyān)   55.1,2; 315

L'LMYN (= yāvētān)   55.2

MḤ (= čē)   55.1

NYYNY(?)   54.1; 314

p'tk'syy (pātkāsē)   294

RB' (= vazurk)   56.2, 316
RBRB' (= mahist)   56.2; 316

SPR' (= dipīwar)   54.1; 287, 315, 317
syh'r   56.1,2; 298a, 316a

YNTNWP(?) (= dahēt)   55.2; 315

C. TURFAN MIDDLE IRANIAN

'b'g (aβāγ)   287
'br (aβar)   313
'bxš'd'y (aβaxšāδāy)   313
'bxš'dm'n (aβaxšāδ-mān)   313
'bxš'yšn (aβaxšāyišn)   313

'č (až)   287

'wd (uδ)   287
'wm'n (u-mān)   313

'y'b (ayāβ)   287

'y (ē)   287
'zw'n (izvān)   287

bg (baγ)   297 n. 117
br'dr'n (brāδarān)   287

dbyr (diβīr)   287
dbyr'n (diβīrān)   287

PLATES

PLATE I

1

2

1. SITE OF THE SYNAGOGUE BEFORE EXCAVATION.   2. INTERIOR OF THE SYNAGOGUE WITH REMAINS OF EMBANKMENT

Plate II

1

2

I. BLOCK L7 FROM SOUTH.   2. ROOMS H3, H4, AND H5 AND FORECOURT FROM NORTHEAST

PLATE III

1

2

1. ROOMS H8, H9, H7, H6, AND H5 AND FORECOURT FROM SOUTHEAST.   2. FORECOURT, SHOWING STYLOBATE AND COLUMNS,
WITH CAPITAL IN FOREGROUND

PLATE IV

I

2

3

4

I. MAIN DOORWAY TO HOUSE OF ASSEMBLY, FROM FORECOURT.   2. MAIN DOORWAY TO HOUSE OF ASSEMBLY, INTERIOR.
3. MAIN DOORWAY TO HOUSE OF ASSEMBLY, SHOWING DIFFERENT FLOOR LEVELS.   4. SOUTH DOORWAY TO HOUSE
OF ASSEMBLY, SILL WITH SOCKET AND LOCK BAR HOLE

PLATE V

1

2

1. HOUSE OF ASSEMBLY, WEST WALL WITH TORAH SHRINE, ELDER'S SEAT, AND BENCHES.   2. EARLIER BUILDING, REMAINS OF SOUTH WALL AND BENCH

PLATE VI

I

3

4

I. CORNER OF FORECOURT, AS RECONSTRUCTED IN THE NATIONAL MUSEUM, DAMASCUS.   2. FORECOURT: LEFT, STYLOBATE OF EARLIER BUILDING; RIGHT, STYLOBATE OF LATER BUILDING.   3. DOORWAY TO HOUSE OF ASSEMBLY, AS RECONSTRUCTED IN THE NATIONAL MUSEUM, DAMASCUS.   4. SOUTH CORNER OF HOUSE OF ASSEMBLY, SHOWING REMAINS OF EARLIER BUILDING

PLATE VII

CEILING OF HOUSE OF ASSEMBLY, AS RECONSTRUCTED IN THE NATIONAL MUSEUM, DAMASCUS

PLATE VIII

1

2

3

CEILING TILES

PLATE IX

1

2

3

4

CEILING TILES

PLATE X

1

2

3

4

CEILING TILES

PLATE XI

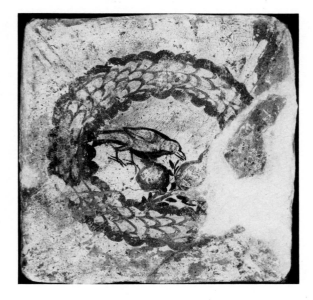

1

2

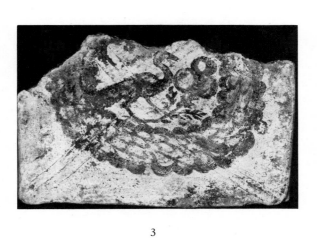

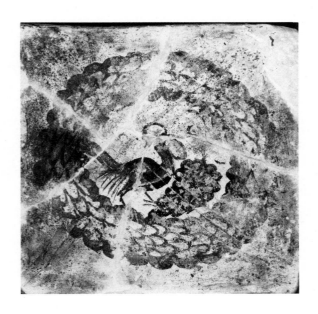

3

4

CEILING TILES

PLATE XII

1

2

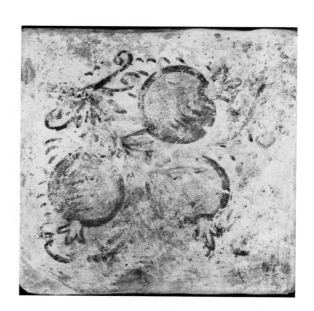

3

4

CEILING TILES

PLATE XIII

1

2

3

4

CEILING TILES

PLATE XIV

1

2

CEILING TILES

PLATE XV

I

2

3

I. TORAH SHRINE, DESIGN AT BASE OF NICHE.   2–3. TORAH SHRINE, ELEMENTS OF DESIGN ON INTRADOS

PLATE XVI

TORAH SHRINE, DECORATIONS OF FAÇADE

PLATE XVII

WEST WALL, CENTRAL AREA, ORIGINAL DESIGN (BY H. PEARSON)

PLATE XVIII

WEST WALL, SOUTH HALF, RECONSTRUCTED IN THE NATIONAL MUSEUM, DAMASCUS

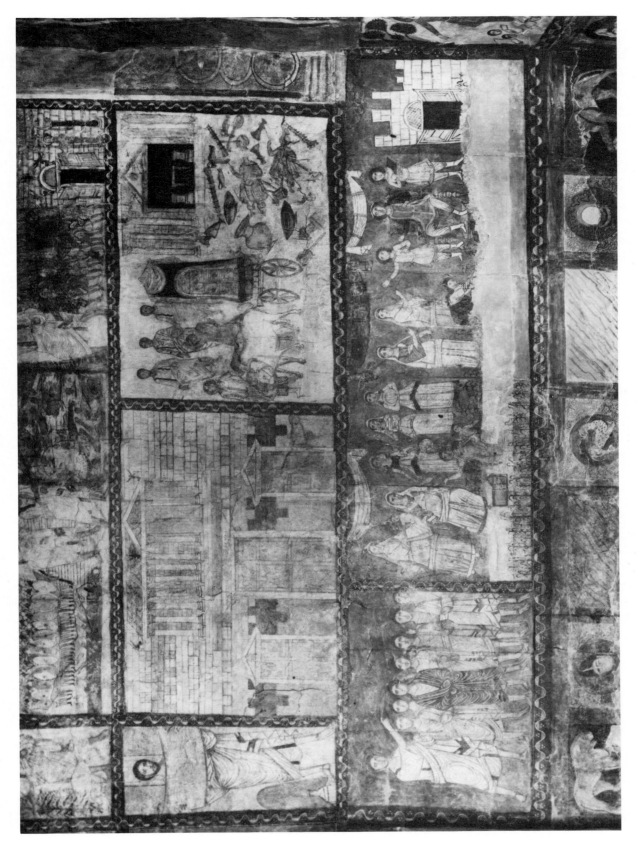

PLATE XIX

WEST WALL, NORTH HALF, RECONSTRUCTED IN THE NATIONAL MUSEUM, DAMASCUS

PLATE XX

SOUTH WALL, RECONSTRUCTED IN THE NATIONAL MUSEUM, DAMASCUS

PLATE XXI

NORTH WALL, RECONSTRUCTED IN THE NATIONAL MUSEUM, DAMASCUS

PLATE XXII

EAST WALL, NORTH HALF, RECONSTRUCTED IN THE NATIONAL MUSEUM, DAMASCUS

PLATE XXVII

PANEL WA I. UNIDENTIFIED SCENE

PLATE XXVIII

PANEL WA 2. SOLOMON RECEIVES THE QUEEN OF SHEBA

PLATE XXIX

PANEL NB 2. HANNAH AND THE CHILD SAMUEL AT SHILOH

PLATE XXX

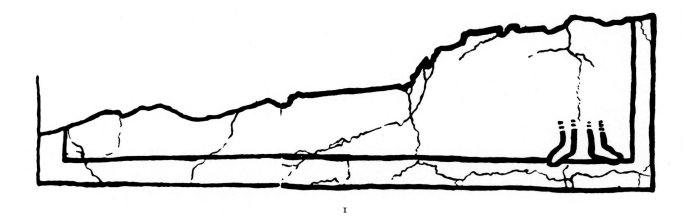

1

2

1. PANEL SC 1. ELIJAH PROCLAIMS A DROUGHT AND LEAVES FOR CHERITH (?).
2. PANEL EC 2. BELSHAZZAR'S FEAST AND THE FALL OF BABYLON (?)

PLATE XXXI

PANEL SC 2. ELIJAH AT CHERITH AND ZAREPHATH

PLATE XXXII

PANEL EC I. DAVID AND SAUL IN THE WILDERNESS OF ZIPH

PLATE XXXIII

CENTRAL AREA, FIRST STAGE OF REDECORATION

PLATE XXXIV

LOWER CENTER PANEL, FINAL STAGE. THE BLESSINGS OF JACOB AND DAVID, PIOUS KING (WITH OVERLAY SHOWING POSITION OF HOLES AND SCRATCHES)

PLATE XXXV

UPPER CENTER PANEL, FINAL STAGE. DAVID, KING OVER ALL ISRAEL

PLATE XXXVI

1

2

1. WING PANEL II. MOSES RECEIVES THE LAW.   2. WING PANEL IV. ABRAHAM RECEIVES THE PROMISE, DETAIL

PLATE XXXVII

2

4

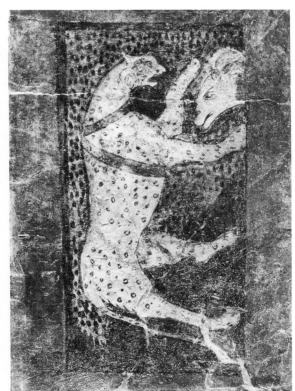

1

3

DADO PANELS

PLATE XXXVIII

3

1

DADO PANELS

4

2

PLATE XXXIX

I

2

3

4

DADO PANELS

PLATE XL

1

2

3

4

I. PANEL WB 3, DOOR OF TEMPLE.   2. RECONSTRUCTED TORAH SHRINE WITH CURTAIN.   3. COIN WITH REPRESENTA-
TION OF TEMPLE AND ARK OF COVENANT (FROM G. F. HILL, CATALOGUE OF THE GREEK COINS OF PALESTINE, BRITISH
MUSEUM, PL. XXXII, I).   4. GEM SHOWING SACRIFICE OF ISAAC (FROM THE COLLECTION OF C. C. TORREY)

PLATE XLI

1

2

1. INSCR. NO. 1a. TILE A.   2. INSCR. NO. 1a. TILE B

PLATE XLII

1. INSCR. NO. 1b.   2. INSCR. NO. 1C.   3. INSCR. NO. 2

1

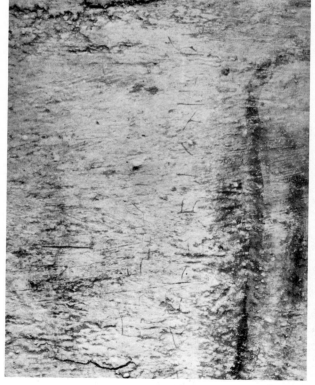

3

2

PLATE XLIII

1

2

3

4

1. INSCR. NO. 23.   2. INSCR. NO. 24.   3. INSCR. NO. 25.   4. INSCR. NOS. 26–28

PLATE XLIV

1

2

3

1. INSCR. NO. 42.   2. INSCR. NO. 43.   3. INSCR. NO. 44

PLATE XLV

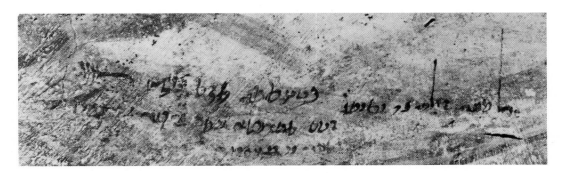

1

2

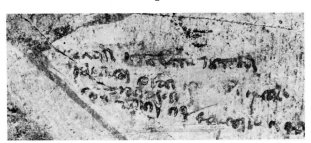

3

4

1. INSCR. NO. 45.   2. INSCR. NO. 46.   3. INSCR. NO. 47.   4. INSCR. NO. 48

PLATE XLVI

1

2

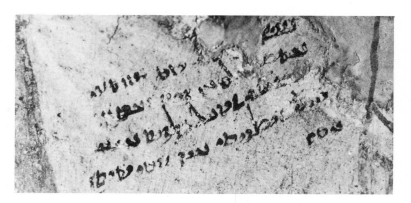

3

4

1. INSCR. NO. 49.　　2. INSCR. NO. 50.　　3. INSCR. NO. 51.　　4. INSCR. NO. 52

PLATE XLVII

1

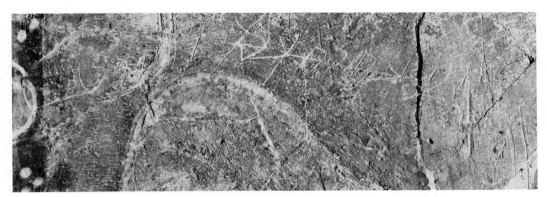

2

3

4

1. INSCR. NO. 53.   2. INSCR. NO. 54.   3. INSCR. NO. 55.   4. INSCR. NO. 56

PLATE XLVIII

I

2

3

4

I. WING PANEL III, DETAIL.   2. WING PANEL IV, DETAIL.   3. PANEL NC I, DETAIL.   4. PANEL WB 2, DETAIL

PLATE XLIX

EARLIER BUILDING, RECONSTRUCTION OF WALL PAINTING

PLATE L

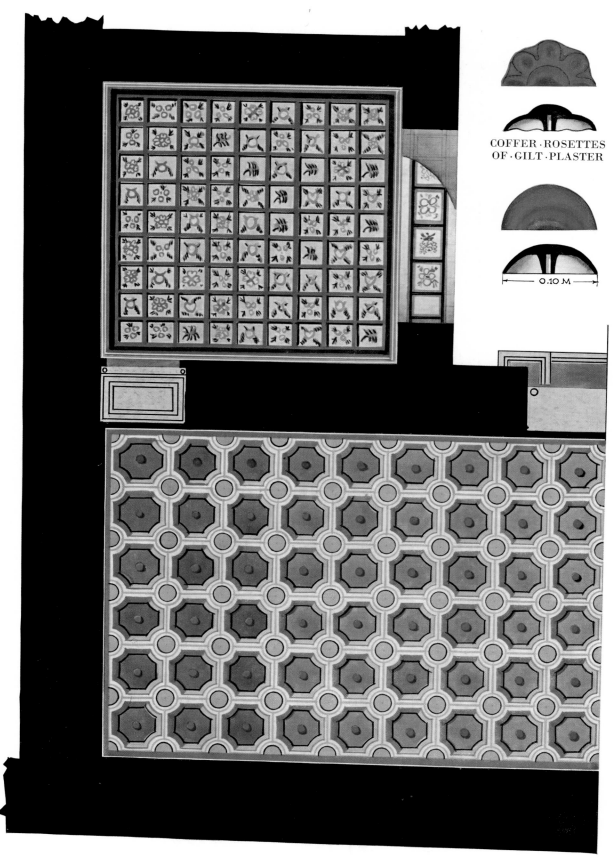

COFFER·ROSETTES
OF·GILT·PLASTER

0.10 M

EARLIER BUILDING, RECONSTRUCTION OF CEILINGS

PLATE LI

TORAH SHRINE

PLATE LII

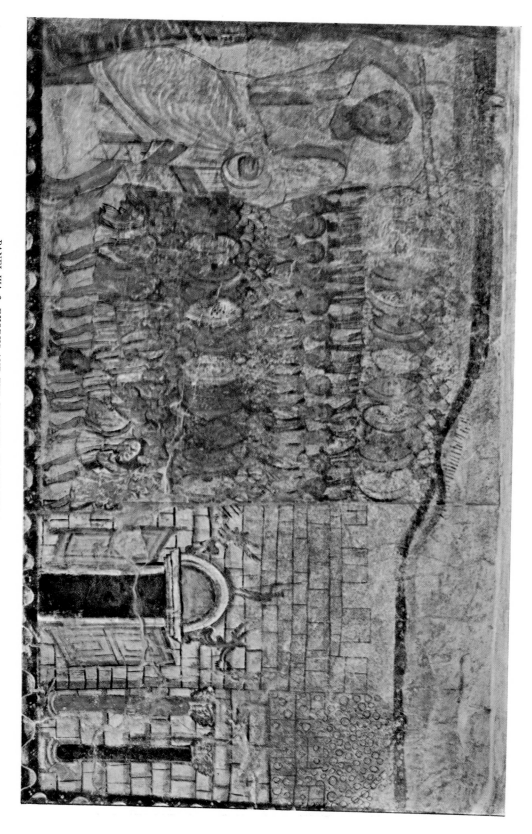

PANEL WA 3. EXODUS AND THE CROSSING OF THE RED SEA, SCENE I

PLATE LIII

PANEL WA 3. EXODUS AND THE CROSSING OF THE RED SEA, SCENE 2

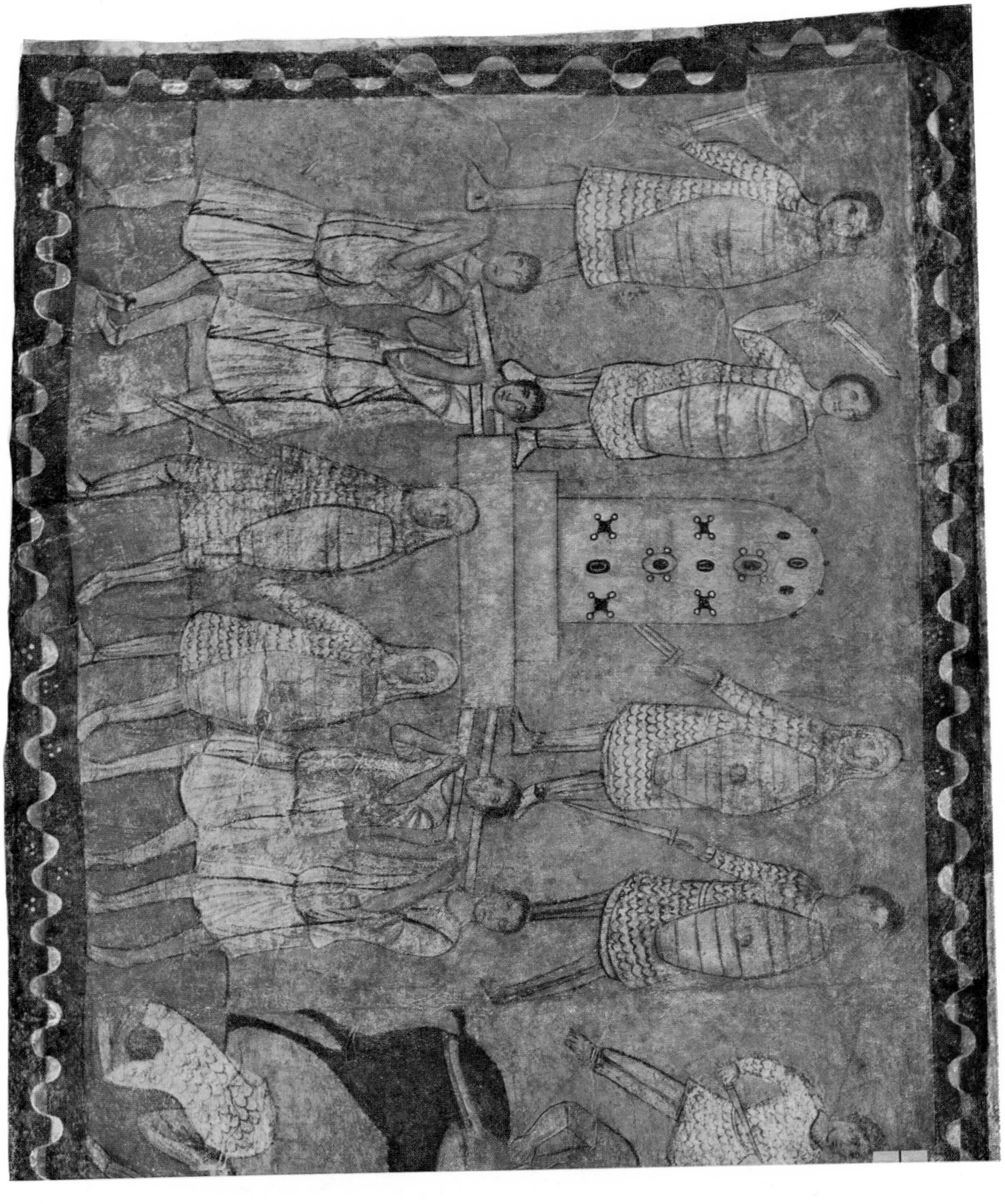

PLATE LIV

PANEL NB I. THE BATTLE OF EBEN-EZER, SCENE I

PLATE LV

PANEL NB I. THE BATTLE OF EBEN-EZER, SCENE 2

PANEL WB 4. THE ARK IN THE LAND OF THE PHILISTINES

PLATE LVII

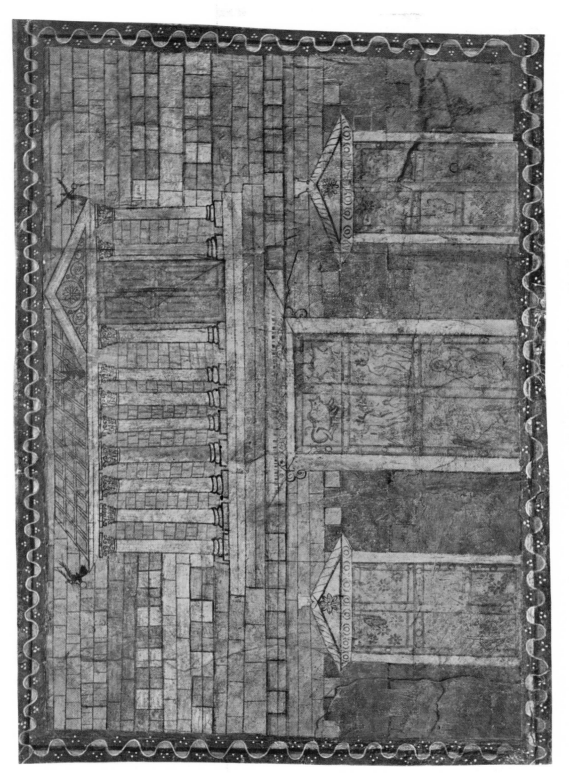

PANEL WB 3. JERUSALEM AND THE TEMPLE OF SOLOMON

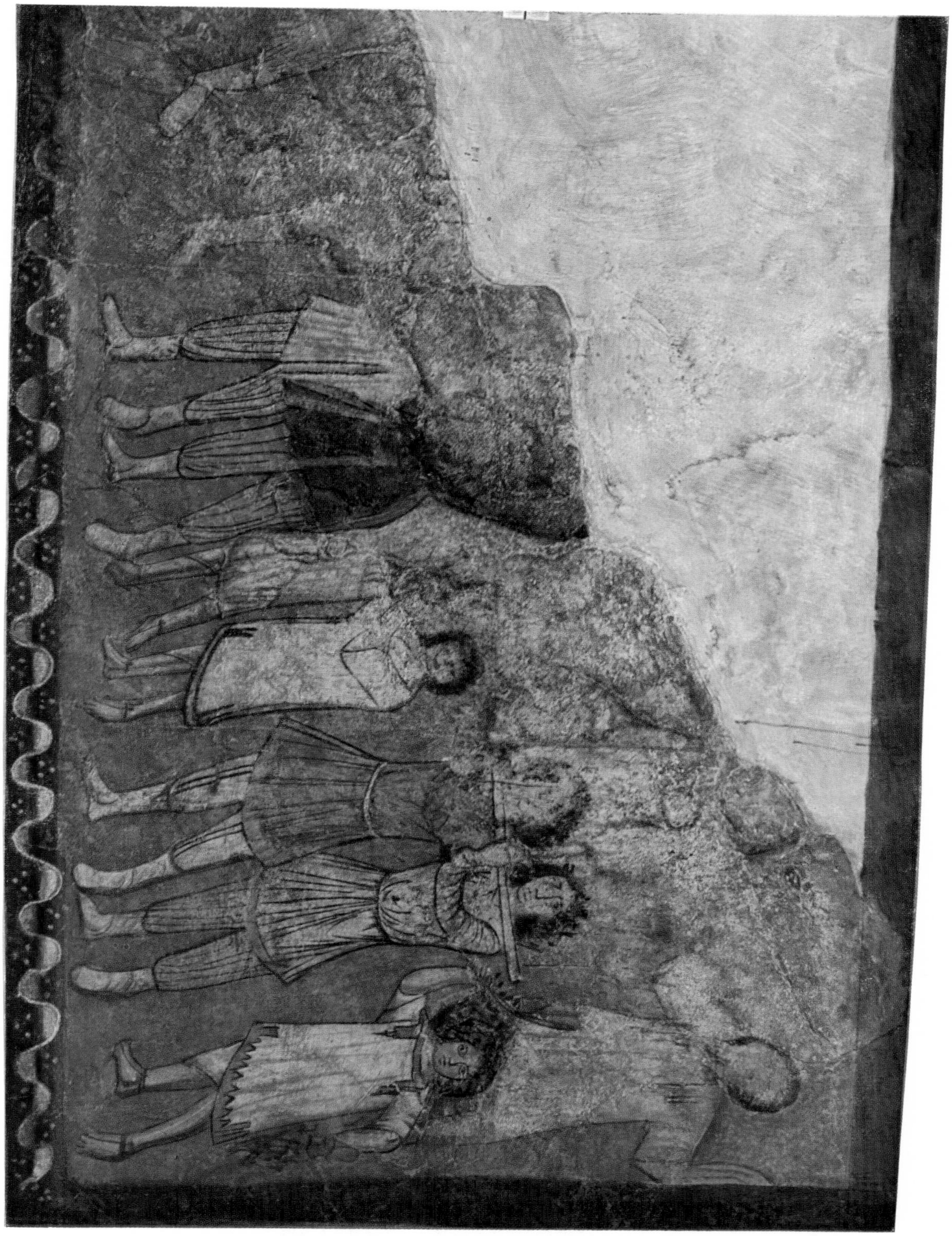

PLATE LVIII

PANEL SB I. THE DEDICATION OF THE TEMPLE

PLATE LIX

PANEL WB I. THE WILDERNESS ENCAMPMENT AND THE MIRACULOUS WELL OF BE'ER

PLATE LX

PANEL WB 2. THE CONSECRATION OF THE TABERNACLE AND ITS PRIESTS

PLATE LXI

PANEL SC 3. THE PROPHETS OF BAAL ON MOUNT CARMEL

PLATE LXII

PANEL SC 4. ELIJAH ON MOUNT CARMEL

PLATE LXIII

PANEL WC I. ELIJAH REVIVES THE WIDOW'S CHILD

PLATE LXIV

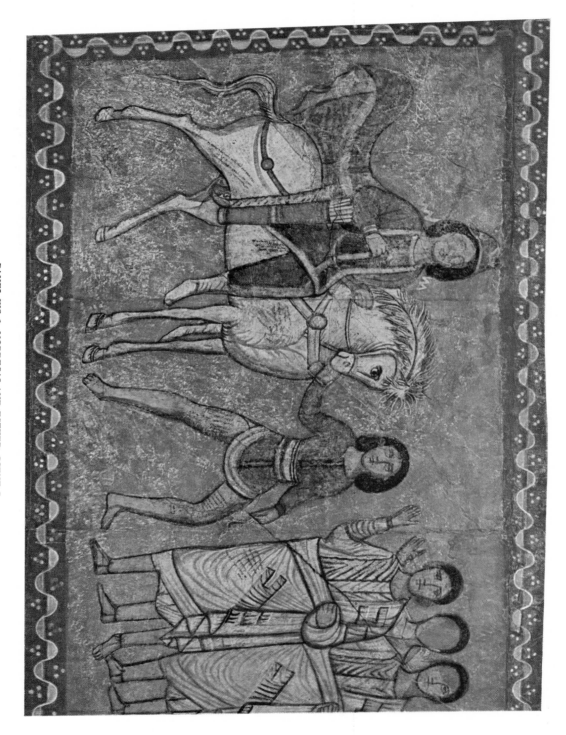

PANEL WC 2. MORDECAI AND ESTHER, SCENE I

PLATE LXV

PANEL WC 2. MORDECAI AND ESTHER, SCENE 2

PLATE LXVI

PANEL WC 3 · SAMUEL ANOINTS DAVID

PLATE LXVII

PANEL WC 4. PHARAOH AND THE INFANCY OF MOSES, SCENES 1-2

PLATE LXVIII

PANEL WC 4. PHARAOH AND THE INFANCY OF MOSES, SCENES 3–4

PLATE LXIX

PANEL NC I. EZEKIEL, THE DESTRUCTION AND RESTORATION OF NATIONAL LIFE, SECTION A

PLATE LXX

PANEL NC I. EZEKIEL, THE DESTRUCTION AND RESTORATION OF NATIONAL LIFE, SECTION B, SCENES 1–2

PLATE LXXI

PANEL NC I. EZEKIEL, THE DESTRUCTION AND RESTORATION OF NATIONAL LIFE, SECTION B, SCENES 3–4

PLATE LXXII

PANEL NC 1, EZEKIEL, THE DESTRUCTION AND RESTORATION OF NATIONAL LIFE, SECTION C

PLATE LXXIII

PANEL EC I. DAVID AND SAUL IN THE WILDERNESS OF ZIPH, SCENES 1–2

PLATE LXXIV

LOWER CENTER PANEL. THE BLESSINGS OF JACOB AND DAVID, PIOUS KING

PLATE LXXV

UPPER CENTER PANEL. DAVID, KING OVER ALL ISRAEL

PLATE LXXVI

WING PANEL I. MOSES AND THE BURNING BUSH

PLATE LXXVII

WING PANEL III. EZRA READS THE LAW

PLATE LXXVIII

WING PANEL IV. ABRAHAM RECEIVES THE PROMISE

DURA-EUROPOS

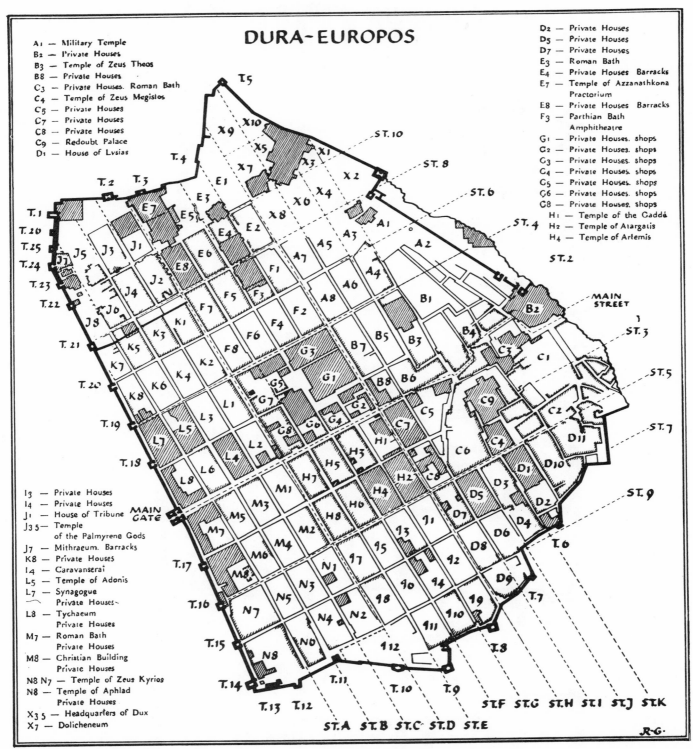

A1 — Military Temple
B2 — Private Houses
B3 — Temple of Zeus Theos
B8 — Private Houses
C3 — Private Houses. Roman Bath
C4 — Temple of Zeus Megistos
C5 — Private Houses
C7 — Private Houses
C8 — Private Houses
C9 — Redoubt Palace
D1 — House of Lysias

D2 — Private Houses
D5 — Private Houses
D7 — Private Houses
E3 — Roman Bath
E4 — Private Houses Barracks
E7 — Temple of Azzanathkona
        Praetorium
E8 — Private Houses Barracks
F3 — Parthian Bath
        Amphitheatre
G1 — Private Houses. shops
G2 — Private Houses. shops
G3 — Private Houses. shops
G4 — Private Houses. shops
G5 — Private Houses. shops
G6 — Private Houses. shops
G8 — Private Houses. shops
H1 — Temple of the Gaddé
H2 — Temple of Atargatis
H4 — Temple of Artemis

I3 — Private Houses
I4 — Private Houses
J1 — House of Tribune
J3 5 — Temple
        of the Palmyrene Gods
J7 — Mithraeum. Barracks
K8 — Private Houses
I4 — Caravanserai
L5 — Temple of Adonis
L7 — Synagogue
        Private Houses
L8 — Tychaeum
        Private Houses
M7 — Roman Bath
        Private Houses
M8 — Christian Building
        Private Houses
N8 N7 — Temple of Zeus Kyrios
N8 — Temple of Aphlad
        Private Houses
X3 5 — Headquarters of Dux
X7 — Dolicheneum

CITY PLAN OF DURA

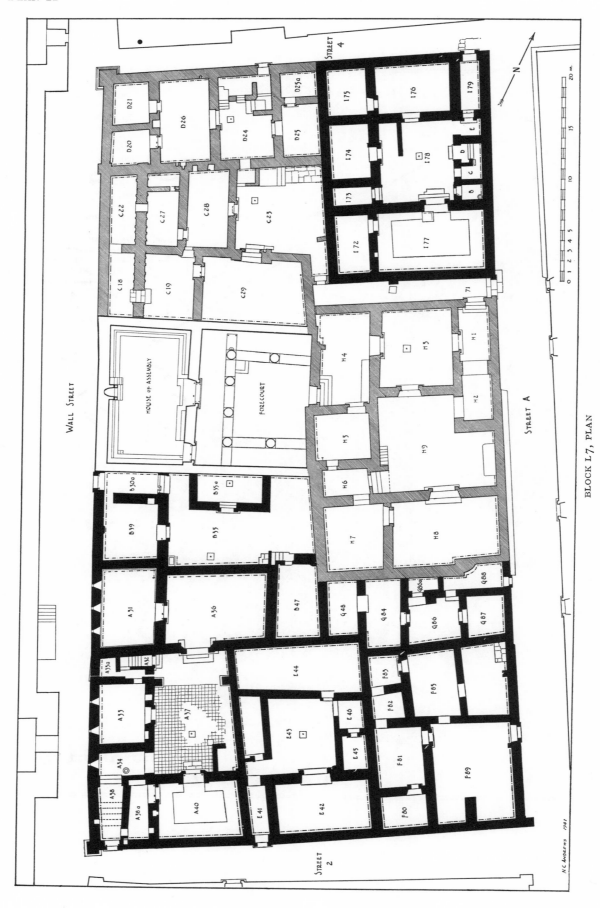

BLOCK L 7, PLAN

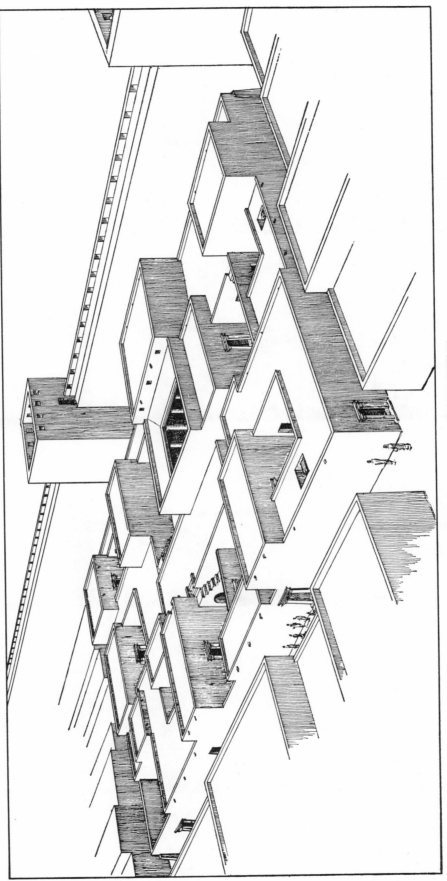

BLOCK L 7, ISOMETRIC RECONSTRUCTION

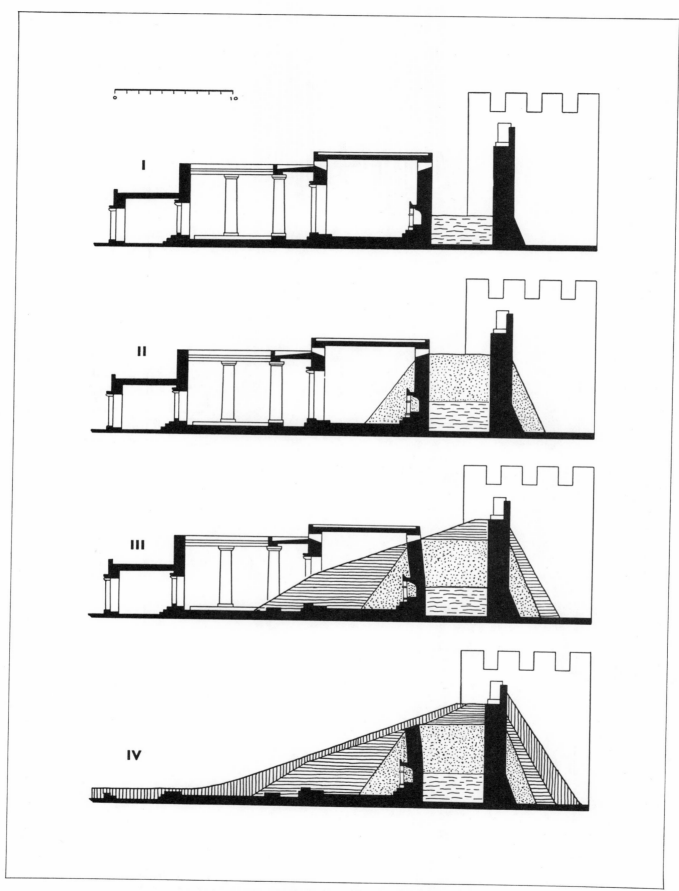

STAGES OF RAMP CONSTRUCTION IN VICINITY OF SYNAGOGUE

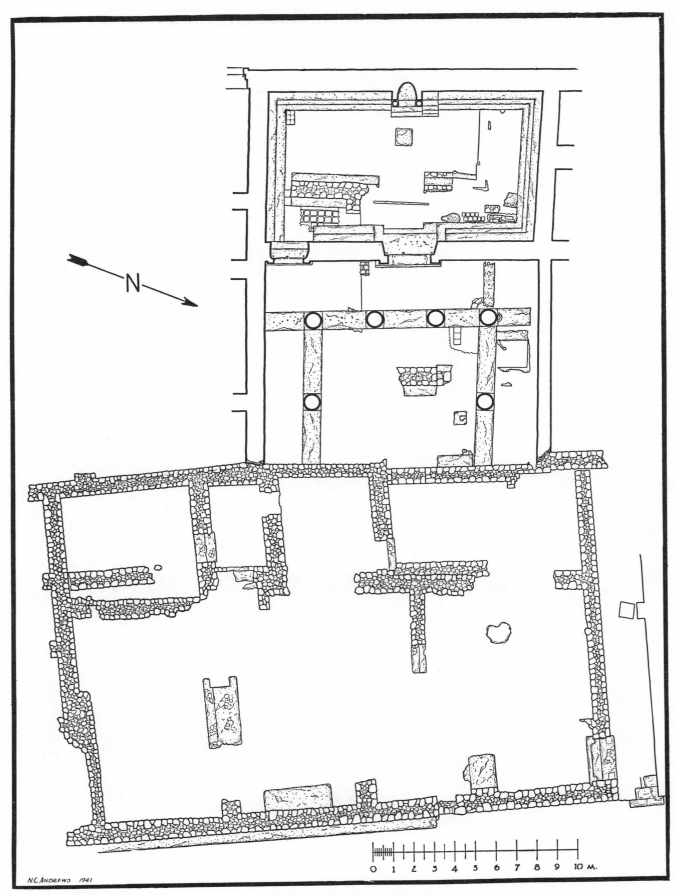

N

N.C. ANDREWS 1941

0 1 2 3 4 5 6 7 8 9 10 M.

HOUSE H AND SYNAGOGUE, FIELD PLAN

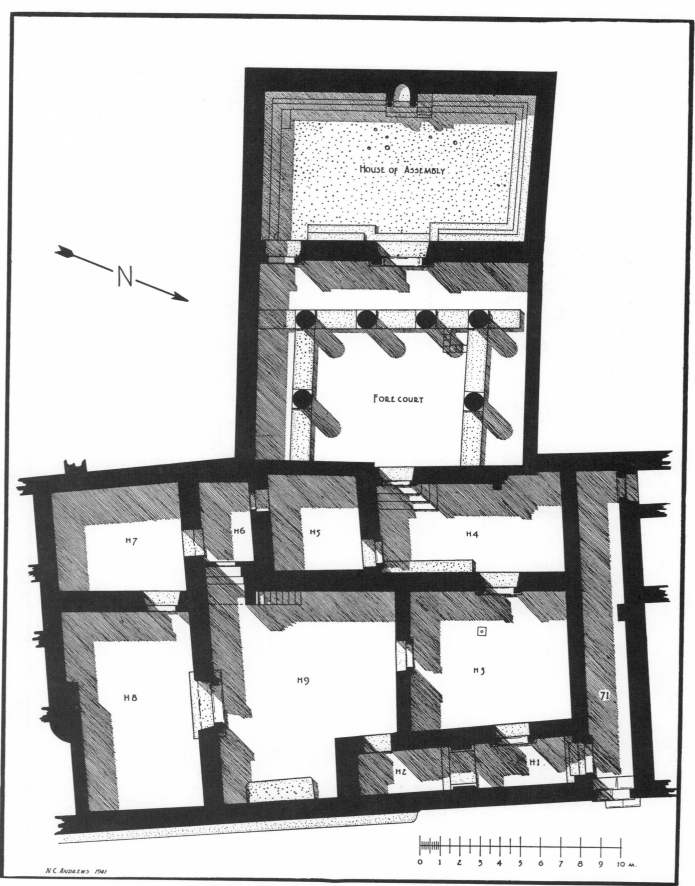

N

HOUSE OF ASSEMBLY

FORE COURT

H7   H6   H5   H4

H8   H9   H3   71

H2   H1

N.C. Andrews 1941

0 1 2 3 4 5 6 7 8 9 10 M.

HOUSE H AND SYNAGOGUE, RECONSTRUCTED PLAN

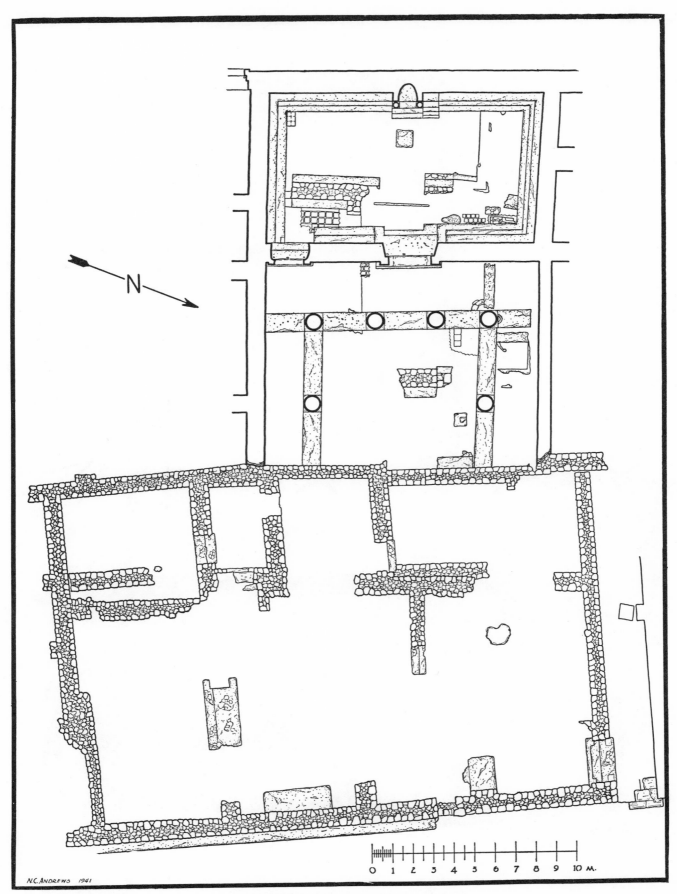

N.C. Andrews 1941

0 1 2 3 4 5 6 7 8 9 10 M.

HOUSE H AND SYNAGOGUE, FIELD PLAN

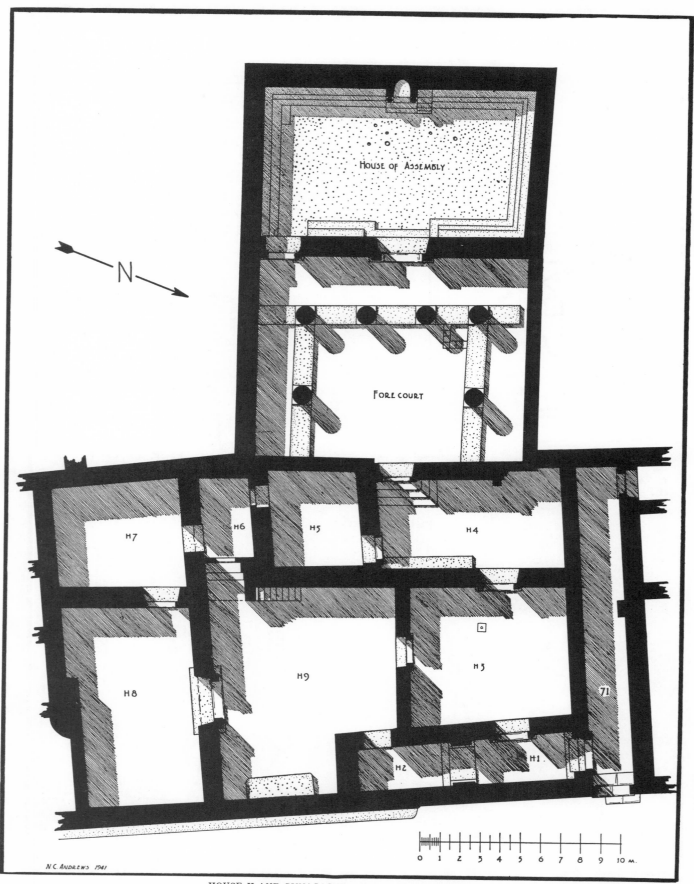

House of Assembly

Fore Court

H7 H6 H5 H4

H8 H9 H3

71

H2 H1

N

0 1 2 3 4 5 6 7 8 9 10 M.

N.C. ANDREWS 1941

HOUSE H AND SYNAGOGUE, RECONSTRUCTED PLAN

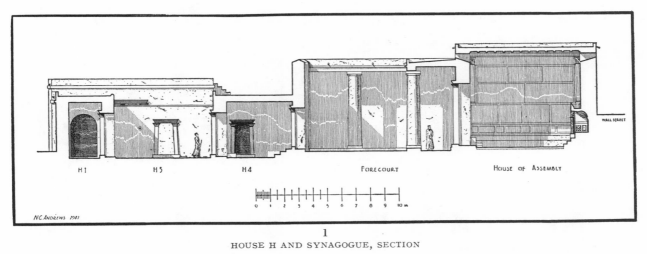

1

HOUSE H AND SYNAGOGUE, SECTION

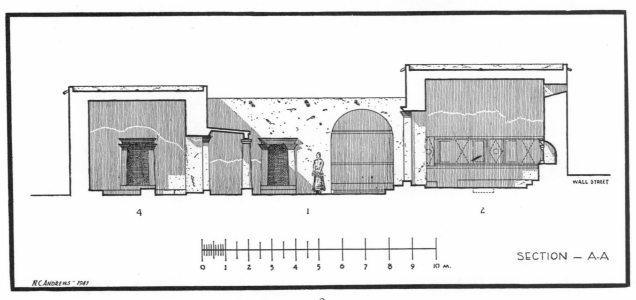

2

EARLIER BUILDING, SECTION

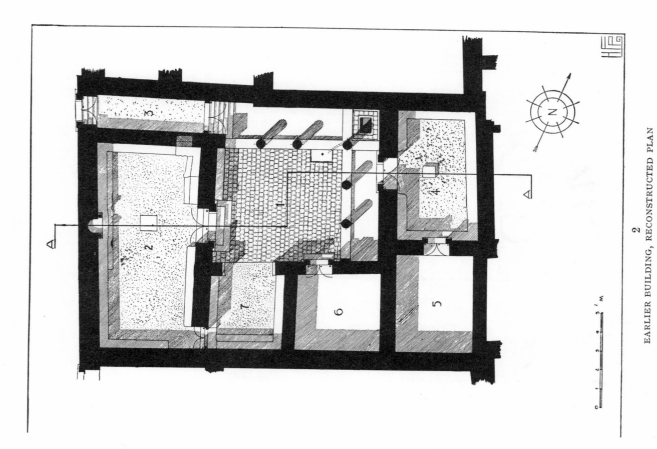

2

EARLIER BUILDING, RECONSTRUCTED PLAN

1

EARLIER BUILDING, FIELD PLAN

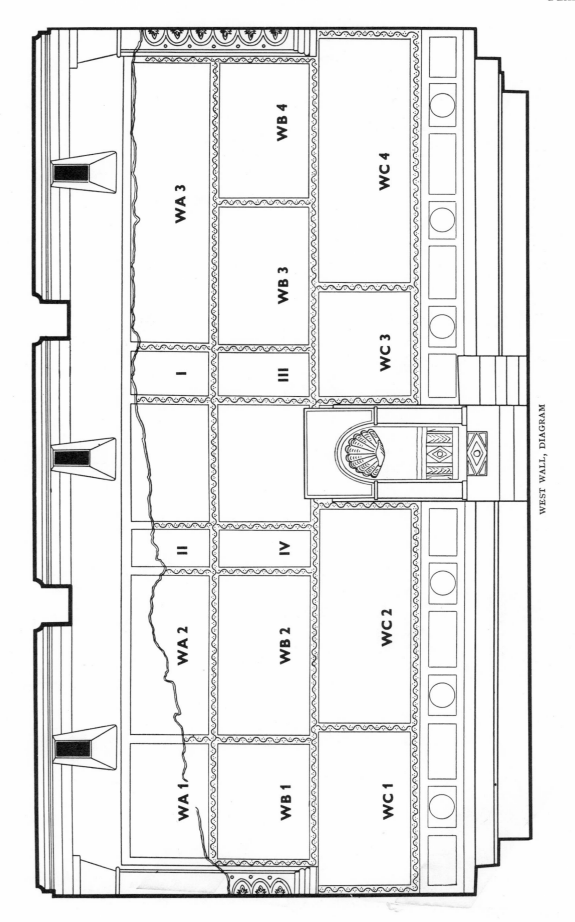

WEST WALL, DIAGRAM

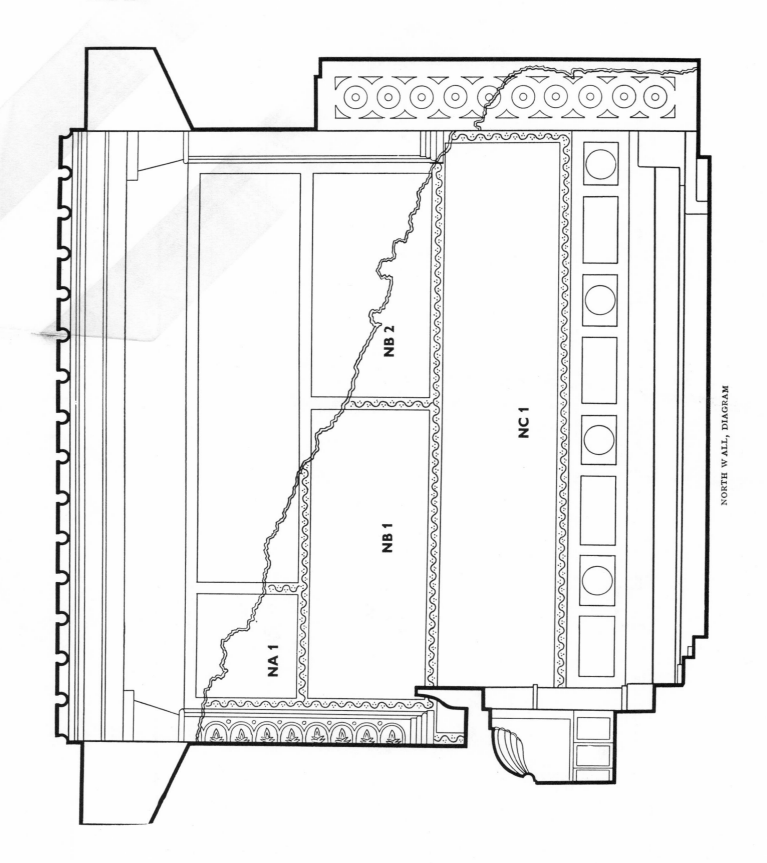

NA 1

NB 1

NB 2

NC 1

NORTH WALL, DIAGRAM

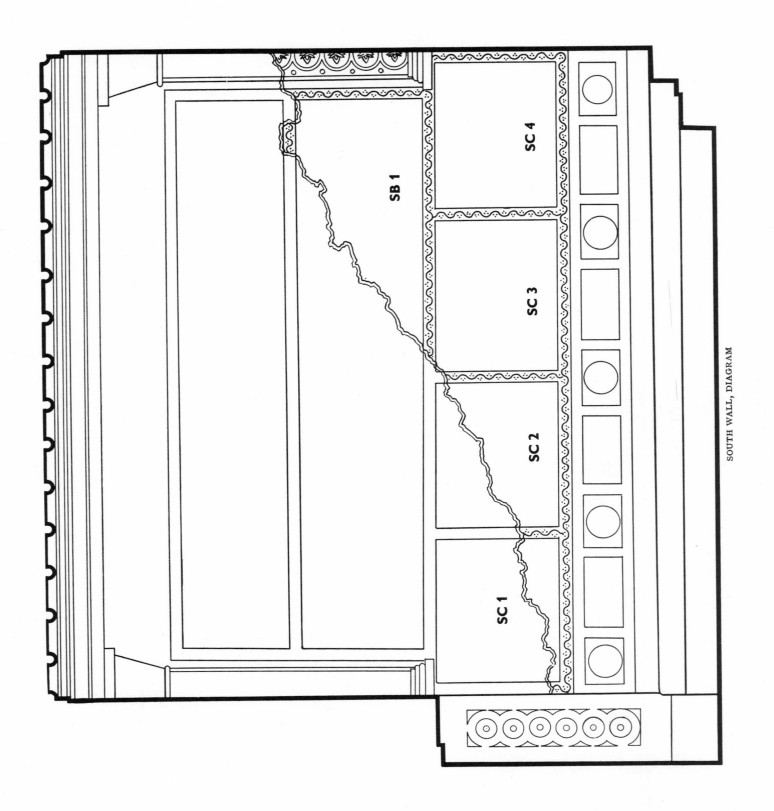

SOUTH WALL, DIAGRAM

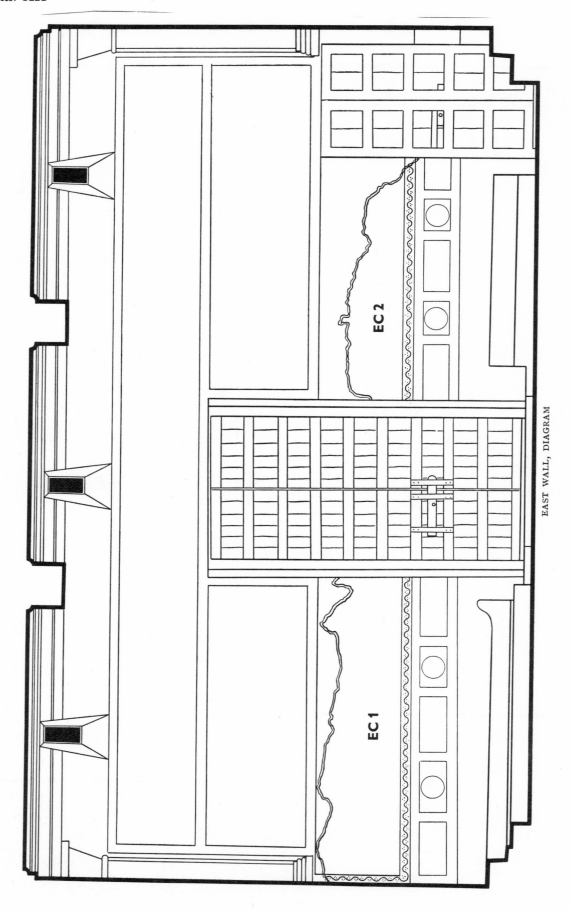

EC 2

EC 1

EAST WALL, DIAGRAM